Mander Portman Woodward

D1381885

UNIVERSITY DEGREE COURSE OFFERS

The essential guide to winning
your place at university

Brian Heap

43rd edition

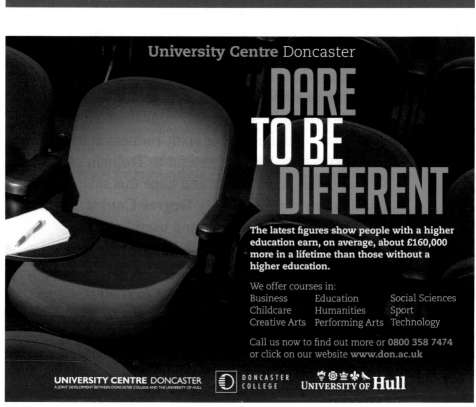

The credible alternative to university...

Make the grade

At CIFE we're not just about getting the right grades or getting you into the best university. We're about bringing out the best in you as an individual. That's why our 2-year A level courses have so much choice and flexibility built in. In fact it's what our association of highly accredited independent sixth form colleges is all about. Yes, we'll help you meet others' standards – but fulfil your own promise too.

To discover how CIFE can enable you to achieve your full potential, call **020 8767 8666** or visit **www.cife.org.uk**

The Council for Independent Education (CIFE), founded in 1972, is a national association representing 18 of the best independent sixth form colleges in the UK. Its colleges are spread widely over the country, each one offering individual features but all subject to high standards of accreditation. Details of each college can be found at www.cife.org.uk CIFE colleges offer:

A wide variety of courses and range of subjects

A major advantage of CIFE colleges over a school's sixth form lies in the wider range of choice of subjects and much greater flexibility of subject combinations. Most colleges allow you to pick virtually any combination of subjects and there are commonly over forty different AS and A level subjects to choose from. Different types and lengths of A level course are also available. If you want to join a college for the second year of A level, not only will you find many colleges which can provide the right A2 courses, but most will allow you to combine A2 courses with a new AS level or even a subject in which you cover both the AS and A2 during the year. So, apart from the variety of subjects, you will find standard two-year courses, final-year (ie second year) courses, one-year courses (covering AS and A2 modules) and retake courses (both one term and one-year). GCSE courses are also offered at all colleges. Intensive Easter Revision courses at both A level and GCSE are available at many CIFE colleges.

High quality teaching

CIFE colleges have experienced and enthusiastic teachers who are A level subject specialists. They are familiar with all the requirements of the various examination boards and are often examiners for the syllabuses they teach. They often have the advantage of being able to specialise in their subject at a particular level for a particular exam syllabus throughout their whole teaching timetable, unburdened by any lower school teaching requirements.

Small class sizes

All CIFE colleges offer small group teaching, with a maximum of 8 students per class in most colleges. The informal, relaxed nature of the small-group environment enables the teacher to establish quickly and maintain a very productive and beneficial working relationship with you, with close supervision of your work and plenty of individual attention, encouragement and advice.

Successful preparation for university entrance

Academic and pastoral support is a high priority for all CIFE colleges. Their academic advisors keep up-to-date on the latest requirements of the university admissions departments and will make sure that you receive plenty of support in completing your UCAS form as effectively as possible. Some colleges run very sophisticated and targeted programmes of support for students applying for the most challenging university courses, e.g. Medicine.

call **020 8767 8666** or visit **www.cife.org.uk**

Stand out from the crowd...
...with a vocational degree
from Liverpool John Moores University

LJMU provides vocational degrees which set graduates up for the **world of work**

Marketing **Creative Writing** Policing Studies Journalism Business Management Film Studies **Criminology** Spatial Design Accounting and Finance **Media Professional Studies English History** Architecture Sociology Business and Public Relations **Fashion** Drama **Law** Fine Art History of Art Business Studies **Graphic Design and Illustration** Media, Culture, Communication **Criminal Justice** Popular Music Studies **Business Communications Human Resource Management**

Faculty of **Arts, Professional and Social Studies -** find out more by visiting ljmu.ac.uk/aps call us on **+44 (0)151 231 5090** or email apsadmissions@ljmu.ac.uk

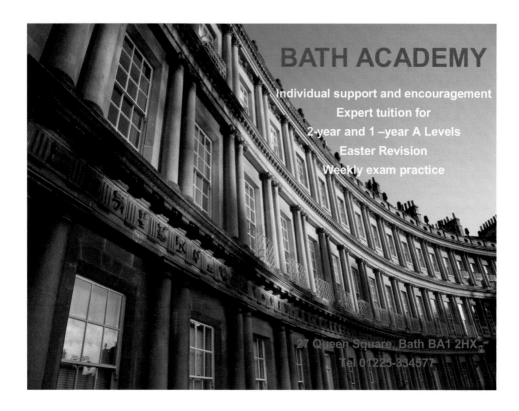

Bath Academy provides students with individual expert guidance and an outstanding bespoke academic education for entry to their chosen university.

Our students are successful because their courses of studies are individually designed - building upon their existing strengths - to meet their unique needs. With the support of their Personal Tutor they are sympathetically supported in their personal development, in making informed decisions about future careers and in learning to study at an advanced level.

Knowing students well leads to good teaching, better learning and a positive experience.

2011 A Level Results: 77% A*-B

A word from the Head...

The key to our success at Oxford Tutorial College is our individual approach to students, both as learners and personalities, and it is this aspect of the college that makes it such an enjoyable place to study and work. The emphasis on small group work and one-to-one tutorials enables a clear focus on individual needs and learning styles and a variation of pace and emphasis, which helps students to approach their work calmly and objectively. The one-to-one tutorial method that we employ also acts as an excellent introduction to university life, engendering maturity and self-confidence.

At OTC, students flourish within a less formal environment than they have been used to at a more traditional school, and they find their energies channeled fruitfully into academic and personal development.

A number of our students have come to us in order to re-take exams. Some students choose to re-take a whole year, whilst we may advise others to re-sit just one or two modules in order to boost their grade up a notch. Unlike most schools, at OTC we provide tuition and exams for every UK exam board, enabling us to select the exam boards that will suit a student best. The support provided by both subject tutors and other academic staff is thoughtful and creative and students are encouraged at every stage to take an active part in the learning process.

Our week long Easter Revision courses take place on a residential and non-residential basis. Examination-oriented lessons are taught in small groups and/or one-to-one tutorials by expert tutors. Study skills sessions and mock examination practice also form a significant part of the course.

Do get in touch if you would like to find out more about OTC and/or our Easter Revision courses.

**Joel Roderick MA (Oxon)
Principal, Oxford Tutorial College**

QUOTES

'*Degree Course Offers ... will keep aspirations realistic*'
www.newteachers.tes.co.uk, 2011

'*An extremely useful guide ...*'
Woodhouse Grove School, 2010

'*Look out for Brian Heap's excellent books on choosing higher education courses*'
Carre's Grammar School, 2010

'*Degree Course Offers by Brian Heap – not to be missed. Invaluable*'
Maidstone Grammar School, 2010

'*Degree Course Offers ... a really good resource*'
www.positive-parents.com, 2009

'*The guru of university choice*'
The Times, 2007

'*For those of you going through Clearing, an absolute must is the Degree Course Offers book. This guide operates subject by subject and gives you each university's requirements, standard offers and, most importantly, "course features"*'
The Independent, August 2007

'*Brian Heap, the guru of university admissions*'
The Independent, September 2007

'*I would like to take this opportunity to congratulate you in maintaining the quality and currency of the information in your guide. We are aware of its wide range and its reputation for impartiality*'
University Senior Assistant Registrar, 2007

'*Degree Course Offers is probably the UK's longest running and best known reference work on the subject*'
www.universityadvice.co.uk, 2005

'*This guide contains useful, practical information for all university applicants and those advising them. I heartily recommend it*'
Dr John Dunford, General Secretary, Association of School and College Leaders, 2005

'*An invaluable guide to helping students and their advisers find their way through the maze of degree courses currently on offer*'
Kath Wright, President, Association for Careers Education and Guidance, 2005

'*No one is better informed or more experienced than Brian Heap in mediating this range of information to university and college applicants*'
Careers Education and Guidance, October 2005

'*The course-listings bible*'
The Guardian, June 2005

'*After consulting this you won't be able to say "I didn't know!" For every school library*'
The Teacher, Nov 2003

'*A must buy ... one of the best single reference sources to degree course offers available*'
Career Guidance Today, July 2003

'*The most comprehensive guide is Degree Course Offers by Brian Heap*'
John Clare in The Daily Telegraph, April 2003

CONTENTS

Author's Acknowledgements	*xix*
About this book	*xx*

1 YOUR FIRST DECISIONS — 1

Higher Education or Not?	1
Section A: Choosing Your Course by Examination Subjects	1
Section B: Choosing Your Course by Career Interests	8
Course Types and Differences	13
Sandwich Courses and Professional Placements	13
Mature Applicants	15
Modular Courses and Credit Accumulation and Transfer Schemes (CATS)	15
Foundation Degrees and Foundation Courses	16
Next Steps	16
Taking a Gap Year	17

2 UNIVERSITY CHOICE AND FINANCE — 19

Choosing Your University or College	19
Action Points	19
Finance: What Will It Cost and What Help Is There?	20
Information Sources	22

3 UNIVERSITY COURSE PROFILES — 23

Universities and their Courses	23
Colleges and their Courses	40

4 UNIVERSITY ADMISSIONS — 41

Admissions Policies	41
Universities' Admissions Information	42

5 APPLICATIONS — 59

Entry Requirements	59
Applications for University and College Courses through UCAS	59
Applications for Music Courses at Conservatoires	61
Applications for Teacher Training Courses	61
The UCAS Application	61
Applications to the University of Cambridge	63
Applications to the University of Oxford	64
Applications to Irish Universities	64
Applications to Commonwealth Universities	65
Applications to American Universities	65
The Erasmus Programme	65

And Finally ... Before You Send in Your Application   65
What to Do on Results Day ... and After   69

6 ADMISSIONS TESTS, SELECTION OF APPLICANTS AND INTERVIEWS   71
Admissions Tests   71
Degree Subject Lists of Universities and Colleges using Tests and Assessments   73
Selection of Applicants   87
Interviews   87

7 HOW TO USE THE SUBJECT TABLES   89
Course Offers Information   89
Examples of Foundation Degrees in the Subject Field   93
Choosing Your Course   94
Admissions Information   94
After-Results Advice   95
Graduate Destinations and Employment   95
Other Degree Subjects for Consideration   95
Abbreviations Used in the Subject Tables   96

8 DEGREE COURSE OFFERS SUBJECT TABLES   109

9 INFORMATION FOR INTERNATIONAL STUDENTS   579
Applications and the Points-based Immigration System   579
Selection, Admission and Finance   579
University Information and Fees for Undergraduate International Students   580
British Overseas Territories Students   590

10 DIRECTORY OF UNIVERSITIES AND COLLEGES OFFERING HIGHER EDUCATION COURSES   591
Section 1: Universities   591
Section 2: University Colleges, Institutes, and Specialist Colleges of Agriculture and Horticulture, Art, Dance, Drama, Music, Osteopathy and Speech   601
Section 3: University Centres, Further Education and Other Colleges offering Higher Education Courses   605

APPENDICES
Appendix 1: UCAS 2013 Entry Tariff Points Tables   621
Appendix 2: International Qualifications   625
Appendix 3: Professional Associations   627
Appendix 4: Booklist and Useful Websites   635

Course Index   637
Index of Advertisers   733

AUTHOR'S ACKNOWLEDGEMENTS

This book is a team effort, in which I, my editor Beth Bishop and a supporting team at Trotman Publishing make every effort each year to check the contents for accuracy, including all offers from official sources, up to the deadline for publication in February. My team's effort throughout the months of preparation therefore deserves my gratitude and praise. In respect of the offers however and the range and abilities of candidates, the reader should recognise that offers are constantly changing and in most cases are shown as 'typical' or target offers.

In the ever-changing world of higher education, research must be on-going and each year many individuals are involved in providing additional up-to-date information. These include Caroline Russell at UCAS, Sarah Hannaford at the Cambridge Admissions Office, Clare Woodcock at the University of Oxford Public Relations Office and also my daughter Jane Heap (Head of Careers), Putney High School. In addition deserving of mention are the admissions staff at the many universities who return our annual requests for information and the many teachers and students who furnish me with information on their experiences. To all, I add my grateful thanks.

Finally, I should also add my appreciation to my wife Rita for her 'on the spot' administrative help (and patience!) through 43 years of publication.

Brian Heap BA DA (Manc) ATD
March 2012

ABOUT THIS BOOK

University Degree Course Offers for 43 years has been a first-stop reference for university and college applicants choosing their courses in higher education by providing information from official sources about how to choose courses and how admissions tutors select students.

For 2013/14 higher education applicants, this edition of *University Degree Course Offers* again aims to provide the latest possible information from universities to help equip them to obtain a degree course place in a fiercely competitive applications process. This level of competition will make it essential for every applicant to research carefully courses and institutions. Latest statistics show that over 604,000 applicants applied for university places for entry in 2011.

There are many students who restrict their applications to a small number of well-known universities. They must realise that in doing so they are very likely to receive rejections from all of them. Applicants must spread their choices across a wide range of institutions.

Many universities and colleges have a limited number of places and are setting their offers higher for places on their courses in 2013 and 2014. How do applicants decide on a strategy to find a place on a degree course? There are more than 1000 separate degree subjects and over 18,000 Joint and Combined Honours courses so how can applicants choose a course that is right for them, especially at a time of recession and employment difficulties? What can applicants do to find a course place and a university or college that is right for them?

University Degree Course Offers 2013 is intended to help applicants find their way through these problems by providing the latest possible information about university course offers from official sources, and by giving guidance and information about:

- **Degree courses** – what Honours level courses involve, the range and differences between them, and what applicants need to consider when choosing and deciding on subjects and courses
- **Universities and higher education colleges** – the range and differences between universities and colleges, and the questions applicants might ask when deciding where to study
- **Admissions information** for every university (listed in **Chapter 4**)
- **Target A/AS grade/UCAS points offers** (listed in points order in the Subject Tables in **Chapter 8**) for 2013 entry to Honours degree courses in universities and colleges, with additional Appendix data for applicants with IB, the Progression and Advanced Diplomas, the Extended Project, Scottish Highers, the Welsh Baccalaureate, the Irish Leaving Certificate and international qualifications
- **The UCAS applications process** – what to do, when to do it and how to prepare the personal statement in the UCAS application
- **Universities' and colleges' admissions policies** – how admissions tutors select students
- **Which universities, colleges and courses use admissions tests for entry**
- **Finance, fees and sources of help**
- **Graduate destinations data for each subject area**
- **Action after results day** – and what to do if your grades don't match your offer
- **Entry to UK universities and higher education colleges for international students**

University Degree Course Offers provides essential information for all students preparing to go into higher education in 2013, covering all stages of researching, planning, deciding and applying to courses and universities. To provide the latest possible information the book is compiled each year between October and March for publication in May and includes important data from the many universities and colleges responding to questionnaires each year.

Every effort is made to ensure the book is as up-to-date as possible. Nevertheless, the increased demand for places and cuts in the number of places available are expected to lead to offers changes during 2013/14, and after prospectuses have been published. Some institutions may also discontinue courses as a result of government cuts and the changes in tuition fees. It will be essential for applicants to check institutions' websites **frequently** to find out any changes in offers, course availability and requirements. If you have any queries, contact admissions staff without delay to find out the latest information as institutions, for many courses, will be looking for a very close, if not precise, match between their requirements and what you offer in your application, qualifications and grades.

University Degree Course Offers 2013 is your starting point for moving on into higher education and planning ahead. Used in conjunction with *Choosing Your Degree Course & University* (see **Appendix 4**) it will take you through all the stages in choosing the course and place of study which is right for you.

Brian Heap
May 2012

Every effort has been made to maintain absolute accuracy in providing course information and to ensure that the entire book is as up-to-date as possible. However, changes are constantly taking place in higher education so it is important for readers to check carefully with prospectuses and websites before submitting their applications.

BPP

UNIVERSITY
COLLEGE

YOUR FIRST DECISIONS

HIGHER EDUCATION OR NOT?

Why do you want to go on to higher education? If you are taking GCE Advanced (AL) and Advanced Subsidiary (AS) qualifications, the International Baccalaureate, Scottish Highers and Advanced Highers, the Welsh Baccalaureate, the Cambridge Pre-U or the new Advanced Diploma this is an important question to ask. In 2011 (Feb) there were 604,705 applicants, including 153,340 mature students (over 21 years old), for full-time first degree and diploma courses in the United Kingdom. However, higher education is just one of two options you have. Increasingly, with the shortage of university places, full-time employment is the other option and it's important to remember that higher education is not necessarily the best option for everyone, but it should not be rejected lightly. Higher education has the advantage however of opening many doors and giving you opportunities for work and leisure that otherwise you might not have. Also, very often and quite accidentally, it can lead into careers that you might not have considered before.

Choosing your AS/A-levels (or equivalent qualifications) is done on the basis of your best subjects and those which you find most interesting. However, leading universities (and, especially, those with popular and competitive courses) may seek a grouping of subjects with 'academic weight'. Usually at least two AS/A-level 'academic' subjects are preferred.

In some cases the following may not be regarded as strong academic subjects: accounting, art and design, business studies, communication studies, dance, design and technology, drama/theatre studies, film studies, health and social care, home economics, information and communication, leisure studies, media studies, music technology, performance studies, performing arts, photography, physical education, sports studies, technology, travel and tourism.

If you are taking two or more of these subjects at AS/A-level you should check with your preferred universities whether they will be accepted for your chosen course before you apply.

Most courses in higher education lead to a degree or a diploma and for either you will have to make a subject choice. This can be difficult because the universities alone offer over 1200 degree subjects and over 50,000 course combinations within the UCAS scheme. You have two main options:

A Choosing a course that is either similar to, or the same as, one (or more) of your examination subjects, or related to an interest outside the school curriculum, such as Anthropology, American Studies, Archaeology. See **Section A** below.

B Choosing a course in preparation for a future career, for example Medicine, Architecture, Engineering. See **Section B** below and also **Appendix 3**.

SECTION A

Choosing your course by examination subjects

Deciding your degree or diploma course on the basis of your A-level (or equivalent) subjects is a reasonably safe option since you are already familiar with the subjects themselves and what they involve. Inevitably, long-term career prospects will be of some concern, especially in a period of economic recession. However, it is important to remember that a degree in higher education gives you many skills, including, for example, those for critical thinking, assessment and research and, for many occupations, the degree subject is often not as important as the degree itself. If you are taking science subjects, they can lead naturally on to a range of scientific careers, although many scientists follow non-science careers such as law and accountancy. If you are taking arts or social science subjects, remember that specialist training for most non-scientific careers often starts once you have your degree.

When choosing your degree course by examination subjects it is important to consider the subjects you are taking at A-level (or equivalent) as universities may 'require' or 'prefer' certain subjects for entry to some courses. To make sure you have the right subjects, check the course subject requirements in university/college prospectuses and on their websites. Many universities, especially those giving high level offers, have increasingly detailed A-level requirements, so it is very important that you find out the latest information. This also applies to GCSE subjects and grade requirements. When choosing AS-level subjects, students sometimes prefer to select those with a similar subject base, for example four science subjects, or four arts, or four humanities subjects. However, some institutions welcome one, or even two, contrasting subjects, even for specialist courses such as Medicine, providing the required subjects are also offered.

Subjects do not stand on their own, in isolation. Each subject you are taking is one of a much larger family. Each has many similarities to subjects studied in degree and diploma courses that you might never have considered, so before you decide finally on taking a subject to degree level read through the list of A-level subjects below, each followed by examples of degree courses in the same subject field which will give you some idea of degree courses with similarities to the subjects you might be taking. (These lists are also useful if you have to consider alternative courses after the examination results are published!)

Accounting Accountancy, Accounting, Actuarial Mathematics, Banking and Finance, Business Studies (Finance), Economics, Finance Investment and Risk, Financial Mathematics, Financial Software Engineering, Management Sciences, Mathematics. See also **Section B**.

Ancient history Archaeology, Biblical Studies, Classical Greek, Classics and Classical Civilisation, Latin, Middle and Near Eastern Studies.

Arabic Arabic. See also **Languages** below.

Archaeology Ancient History, Anthropology, Archaeological Sciences, Archaeology, Bioarchaeology, Classical Civilisation, Conservation of Objects in Museums and Archaeology, Egyptology, Geology, History, Marine Archaeology, Viking Studies. See also **Section B**.

Art and design Art, Fine Art, Furniture Design, Graphic Design, Photography, Textile Design, Theatre Design, Three Dimensional Design, Typography and Graphic Communication. See also **Section B**.

Bengali Bengali. See also **Languages** below.

Biblical Hebrew Hebrew, Religious Studies, Theology.

Biology Agricultural Sciences, Animal Behaviour, Audiology, Bioinformatics, Biological Sciences, Biology, Biomedical Sciences, Biotechnology, Dental Hygiene, Ecology and Conservation, Environmental Sciences, Genetics, Human Embryology, Infection and Immunity, Life Sciences, Medicine, Microbiology, Molecular Sciences, Natural Sciences, Physiology, Plant Biology, Plant Science, Veterinary Science, Zoology. See also **Section B**.

Business Accounting, Banking, Business Management, Business Statistics, Computing, Economics, Entrepreneurship, Finance, Hospitality Management, Human Resource Management, Information Systems, Logistics, Management Sciences, Marketing, Mathematics, Publishing, Retail Management, Transport Management, Web Design and Development. See also **Section B**.

Chemistry Biochemistry, Cancer Biology, Chemical Engineering, Chemical Physics, Chemistry, Dentistry, Environmental Sciences, Fire Engineering, Forensic Sciences, Medicinal Chemistry, Medicine, Microbiology, Natural Sciences, Nutritional Biochemistry, Pharmacology, Pharmacy, Veterinary Science, Virology and Immunology. See also **Section B**.

Chinese Chinese. See also **Languages** below.

Classics and classical civilisation Ancient History, Archaeology, Classical Studies, Classics, Greek (Classical), Latin.

Communication studies Advertising, Communication Studies, Drama, Education, English Language, Information and Library Studies, Journalism, Languages, Linguistics, Media and Communications, Psychology, Public Relations, Publishing, Speech Sciences. See also **Section B**.

UNDERGRADUATE

LIVE
WORK

Undergraduates at Bath Spa University have
room to become who they want to be as well
as doing what they want to do.
Give yourself some space and start exploring
Bath Spa University.

For more information visit:
www.bathspa.ac.uk

BATH
SPACE TO DISCOVER
UNIVERSITY

Computing Artificial Intelligence, Business Information Systems, Computer Engineering, Computer Science, Computing, Cybernetics, E-Commerce, Electronic Engineering, Games Technology, Intelligent Product Design, Multimedia Systems Engineering, Network Management and Security, Robotics, Software Engineering. See also **Section B**.

Critical thinking (Check acceptability with universities and colleges: subject may not be included in offers.)

Dance Arts Management, Ballet Education, Choreography, Dance, Drama, Education, Music, Musical Theatre, Performance Management, Performing Arts, Sport and Exercise, Street Arts, Theatre and Performance, Theatre Arts, Writing Directing and Performance. See also **Section B**.

Design technology Food Technology, Manufacturing Engineering, Product Design, Sport Equipment Design, Systems and Control. See also **Section B**.

Drama and theatre studies Acting, Community Drama, Costume Production, Creative Writing, Dance, Drama, Education Studies, English Comedy: Writing and Performance, International Theatre, Music, Performing Arts, Scenic Arts, Scriptwriting, Set Design, Stage Management, Theatre Arts, Theatre Practice. See also **Section B**.

Dutch Dutch. See also **Languages** below.

Economics Accountancy, Banking, Business Administration, Business Economics, Business Studies, Development Studies, Economics, Estate Management, Finance, Management Science, Mathematics, Political Economy, Politics, Quantity Surveying, Sociology, Statistics.

Electronics Computing, Electronics, Engineering (Aeronautical, Aerospace, Communication, Computer, Software, Systems), Mechatronics, Medical Electronics, Multimedia Technology, Technology. See also **Section B**.

English language and literature Communication Studies, Comparative Literature, Creative Writing, Drama, Education, English Language, English Literature, Information and Library Studies/Management, Journalism, Linguistics, Media Writing, Philosophy, Publishing, Scottish Literature, Scriptwriting, Theatre Studies.

Environmental sciences Biological Sciences, Biology, Earth Sciences, Ecology, Environment and Planning, Environmental Management, Environmental Sciences, Forestry, Geography, Geology, Land Management, Marine Biology, Meteorology, Oceanography, Outdoor Education, Plant Sciences, Sustainable Development, Wastes Management, Water Science, Wildlife Biology, Wildlife Conservation, Zoology.

French French, International Business Studies, International Hospitality Management, Law with French Law. See also **Languages** below.

General studies (Check acceptability with universities and colleges: subject may not be included in offers.)

Geography Development Studies, Earth Sciences, Environmental Policy, Environmental Sciences, Estate Management, Forestry, Geographical Information Science, Geography, Geology, Land Economy, Meteorology, Oceanography, Surveying, Town and Country Planning, Urban Studies, Water Science.

Geology Earth Sciences, Geography, Geology, Geophysical Sciences, Geosciences, Meteorology, Mining Engineering, Natural Sciences, Oceanography, Palaeontology and Evolution, Planetary Sciences, Water and Environmental Management. See also **Section B**.

German German, International Business Studies, International Hospitality Management, Law with German Law. See also **Languages** below.

Government/Politics Development Studies, Economics, Global Politics, Government, History, Human Rights, Industrial Relations, International Politics, Law, Peace Studies, Politics, Public Administration, Social and Political Science, Social Policy, Sociology, Strategic Studies, War Studies.

Gujarati Gujarati. See also **Languages** below.

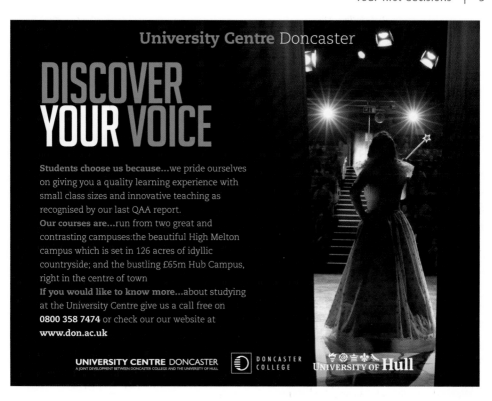

Health and social care Early Childhood Studies, Environmental Health, Health and Social Care, Health Promotion, Health Psychology, Health Sciences, Health Studies, Nursing, Nutrition, Public Health, Social Sciences, Social Work, Sport and Health, Working with Children and Young People, Youth and Community Work. See also **Section B**.

History African Studies, American Studies, Ancient History, Archaeology, Art History, Classical Civilisations, Classical Studies, Education, Egyptology, Fashion and Dress History, History, International Relations, Law, Literature, Medieval Studies, Museum and Heritage Studies, Philosophy, Politics, Russian Studies, Scandinavian Studies, Scottish History, Social and Economic History, Theology and Religious Studies, Victorian Studies.

Home economics Culinary Arts Management, Design and Technology Education, Food and Consumer Management, Food Science, Home Economics (Food Design and Technology), Hospitality Management, Nutrition.

Information and communication technology Business Information Systems, Communications Systems Design, Communications Technology, Digital Communications, Electrical and Electronic Engineering, Geographic Information Science, Information and Library Studies, Information Management, Information Sciences, Information Systems, Internet Engineering, Mobile Computing, Multimedia Computing, Telecommunications Engineering. See also **Section B**.

Italian Italian. See also **Languages** below.

Japanese Japanese. See also **Languages** below.

Languages Languages, Modern Languages, Translating and Interpreting. **NB** Apart from French and German – and Spanish for some universities – it is not usually necessary to have completed an A-level language course before studying the many languages (over 60) offered at degree level. Many universities provide opportunities to study a language in a wide range of degree courses. See also **the Erasmus programme** details in **Chapter 5**.

Law Criminal Justice, Criminology, European Business Law, Human Rights, International Business, International Relations, Law, Legal Studies, Police Sciences, Social Sciences, Sociology, Youth Justice. See also **Section B**.

Leisure studies Adventure Tourism Management, Countryside Recreation and Tourism, Equine Business Management, Events Management, Fitness and Health, Health and Leisure Studies, Hospitality and Leisure Management, Leisure Marketing, Outdoor Leadership, Personal Fitness Training, Sport and Leisure Management, Sport Leisure and Culture, Sports Education, Tourism Management, Tourism Marketing.

Mathematics Accountancy, Actuarial Mathematics, Aeronautical Engineering, Astrophysics, Business Management, Chemical Engineering, Civil Engineering, Computational Science, Computer Systems Engineering, Control Systems Engineering, Cybernetics, Economics, Engineering Science, Ergonomics, Financial Mathematics, Further and Additional Mathematics, Geophysics, Management Science, Materials Science and Technology, Mechanical Engineering, Meteorology, Naval Architecture, Physics, Quantity Surveying, Statistics, Systems Analysis, Telecommunications.

Media studies Advertising, Animation, Broadcasting, Communication Studies, Creative Writing, English, Film and Television Studies, Journalism, Mass Communication, Media courses, Media Culture and Society, Media Production, Media Technology, Multimedia, Photography, Publishing, Radio Production and Communication, Society Culture and Media, Translation Media and French/Spanish, Web and Broadcasting. See also **Section B**.

Modern Greek Greek. See also **Languages** above.

Modern Hebrew Hebrew. See also **Languages** above.

Music Audio and Music Production, Creative Music Technology, Education, Music, Music Broadcasting, Music Informatics, Music Management, Music Systems Engineering, Musical Theatre, Musician, Performance Arts, Popular and World Musics, Sonic Arts. See also **Section B**.

Persian Persian. See also **Languages** above.

Philosophy Classical Studies, Cultural Studies, Divinity, Educational Studies, Ethics, History of Ideas, History of Science, Law, Mathematics, Natural Sciences, Philosophy, Politics Philosophy and Economics, Psychology, Religious Studies, Social Sciences, Theology.

Physics Aeronautical Engineering, Architecture, Astronomy, Astrophysics, Automotive Engineering, Biomedical Engineering, Biophysics, Chemical Physics, Civil Engineering, Communications Engineering, Computer Science, Cybernetics, Education, Electrical/Electronic Engineering, Engineering Science, Ergonomics, Geophysics, Materials Science and Technology, Mechanical Engineering, Medical Physics, Meteorology, Nanotechnology, Naval Architecture, Oceanography, Optometry, Photonics, Planetary Science, Quantum Informatics, Radiography, Renewable Energy, Telecommunications Engineering.

Polish Polish. See also **Languages** above.

Portuguese Portuguese. See also **Languages** above.

Psychology Advertising, Animal Behaviour, Anthropology, Artificial Intelligence, Behavioural Science, Childhood Strudies, Cognitive Science, Counselling Studies, Criminology, Education, Human Resource Management, Marketing, Neuroscience, Nursing, Politics, Psychology, Social Sciences, Sociology, Speech and Language Therapy. See also **Section B**.

Punjabi Punjabi. See also **Languages** above.

Religious studies Abrahamic Religions (Christianity, Islam and Judaism), Anthropology, Archaeology, Biblical Studies, Christian Youth Work, Comparative Religion, Divinity, Education, Ethics, History of Art, International Relations, Islamic Studies, Jewish Studies, Philosophy, Psychology, Religious Studies, Social Policy, Theology.

Russian Russian. See also **Languages** above.

Sport and physical education Chiropractic, Coaching Science, Community Sport Development, Dance Studies, Exercise and Health, Exercise Science, Fitness Science, Football Studies, Golf Studies, Osteopathy,

Higher Education & Careers Advice

The range of options open to students can be quite bewildering.
Our Higher Education and Careers team can assist in a number of ways.

HIGHER EDUCATION ADVICE

Choosing the right course and subjects is vital, especially with the heightened competition for university places and the increase in tuition fees. For students who are not sure which A level subjects to choose, or who may want to look at alternative courses or career paths, good advice is essential. Gabbitas works with parents and students to help consider all the options.

We also use established on line questionnaires which generate detailed reports to assist with selecting both A level and university subject choices. There are many factors to consider when selecting a university, such as location, accommodation, facilities, atmosphere, drop-out rates, league tables etc. Gabbitas can support you in making these very important decisions.

We are experienced in helping with the university application process at every key stage, including the crucial personal statement and can also provide advice on postgraduate study options.

CAREERS ADVICE

We can help provide guidance through our in depth careers questionnaire. This is a simple and flexible on line tool that helps individuals of all ages to research potential career routes and course options, as well as revealing alternative paths they could take to move forward.

The questionnaire is based on 28 key indicators identified from analyzing the responses of over 80,000 individuals to careers and course based questions. This enables accurate suggestions to be made regarding career pathways and associated courses.

ADDITIONAL SERVICES

- **CV writing** - We can provide information on the various types of CV and how to target different job areas. We also help with preparing strong covering letters to support the CV.

- **Interview skills** - Making a good impression is very important. We can offer a practice interview with detailed feedback to help prepare.

- **International Students** - We offer support to help international students understand their options, smoothing entry to the UK education system.

- **Overseas Study** - We can support students thinking of studying abroad, in particular elsewhere in Europe or the USA.

If you would like to find out more about the above services please contact **Gabbitas** on the phone number below or e mail us at **he@gabbitas.co.uk**

Gabbitas Educational Consultants
Norfolk House, 30 Charles II Street
London SW1Y 4AE
Tel: 020 7734 0161 Fax: 020 7437 1764
www.gabbitas.co.uk

Gabbitas Education
CONSULTANTS SINCE 1873

The global experts in British independent education

Outdoor Pursuits, Physical Education, Physiotherapy, Sport and Exercise Science, Sport and Health, Sport Coaching, Sport Equipment Design, Sport Management, Sport Marketing, Teaching (Primary) (Secondary).

Statistics Actuarial Studies, Business Analysis, Business Studies, Informatics, Management Sciences, Statistics. See also Mathematics above and **Section B** Mathematics-related careers.

Travel and tourism See **Section B**.

Turkish Turkish. See also **Languages** above.

Urdu Urdu. See also **Languages** above.

SECTION B
Choosing your course by career interests
An alternative strategy for deciding on the subject of your degree or diploma course is to relate it to your career interests. However, even though you may have set your mind on a particular career, it is important to remember that sometimes there are others which are very similar to your planned career. The following lists give examples of career areas, each followed by examples of degree subjects in the subject field.

Accountancy Accountancy, Accounting, Actuarial Science, Banking, Business Studies, Economics, Finance and Business, Finance and Investment, Financial Services, Management Science, Real Estate Management, Risk Management.

Actuarial work Actuarial Mathematics, Actuarial Science, Actuarial Studies, Financial Mathematics, Risk Analysis and Insurance.

Agricultural careers Agri-Business, Agricultural Engineering, Agriculture, Animal Sciences, Aquaculture and Fishery Sciences, Conservation and Habitat Management, Countryside Management, Crop Science, Ecology, Environmental Science, Estate Management, Forestry, Horticulture, Landscape Management, Plant Sciences, Rural Resource Management, Soil Science, Wildlife Management.

Animal careers Agricultural Sciences, Animal Behaviour and Welfare, Biological Sciences, Bioveterinary Science, Equine Management/Science/Studies, Veterinary Nursing, Veterinary Practice Management, Veterinary Science, Zoology.

Archaeology Ancient History, Anthropology, Archaeology, Bioarchaeology, Classical Civilisation and Classics, Egyptology, Geography, History, History of Art and Architecture, Viking Studies.

Architecture Architectural Design, Architectural Technology, Architecture, Building, Building Conservation, City and Regional Planning, Civil Engineering, Conservation and Restoration, Construction Engineering and Management, Interior Architecture, Stained Glass Restoration and Conservation, Structural Engineering.

Art and Design careers Advertising, Animation, Architecture, Art, Design, Digital Media Design, Education (Art), Fashion and Textiles, Fine Art, Games Art and Design, Glassware, Graphic Design, Illustration, Industrial Design, Jewellery, Landscape Architecture, Photography, Stained Glass, Three Dimensional Design.

Astronomy Astronomy, Astrophysics, Mathematics, Natural Sciences, Planetary Geology, Physics, Quantum and Cosmological Physics, Space Science, Space Technology and Planetary Exploration.

Audiology Audiology, Education of the Deaf, Human Communication, Nursing, Speech and Language Therapy.

Banking/Insurance Accountancy, Actuarial Sciences, Banking, Business Studies, Economics, Financial Services, Insurance, Real Estate Management, Risk Management.

Biology-related careers Agricultural Sciences, Animal Sciences, Biochemistry, Biological Sciences, Biology, Biomedical Sciences, Biotechnology, Cell Biology, Ecology, Education, Environmental Biology, Environmental Sciences, Freshwater Science, Genetics, Immunology, Life Sciences, Marine Biology, Medical Biochemistry, Medicine, Microbiology, Molecular Biology, Natural Sciences, Oceanography, Pharmacy, Plant Science, Physiology, Wildlife Conservation, Zoology.

Book Publishing Advertising, Business Studies, Communications, Creative Writing, Illustration, Journalism, Media Communication, Photography, Printing, Publishing, Science Communication, Web and Multimedia.

Brewing and Distilling Biochemistry, Brewing and Distilling, Chemistry, Food Science and Technology, Viticulture and Oenology.

Broadcasting Audio Video and Digital Broadcast Engineering, Broadcast Documentary, Broadcast Media, Broadcast Technology and Production, Digital Media, Electronic Engineering (Broadcast Systems), Film and TV Broadcasting, Media and Communications Studies, Media Production, Multimedia, Music Broadcasting, Outside Broadcast Technology, Radio Journalism, Television Studio Production, TV Production, Video and Broadcasting.

Building Architecture, Building Conservation, Building Services Engineering, Building Studies, Building Surveying, Civil Engineering, Estate Management, General Practice Surveying, Land Surveying, Quantity Surveying.

Business Accountancy, Advertising, Banking, Business Administration, Business Analysis, Business Studies, Business Systems, E-Commerce, Economics, Estate Management, European Business, Hospitality Management, Housing Management, Human Resource Management, Industrial Relations, Insurance, Logistics, Management Sciences, Marketing, Property Development, Public Relations, Publishing, Supply Chain Management, Transport Management, Tourism.

Cartography Geographic Information Systems, Geographical Information Science, Geography, Land Surveying.

Catering Consumer Studies, Culinary Arts Management, Dietetics, Food Science, Hospitality Management, International and Hospitality Business Management, Nutrition.

Chemistry-related careers Agricultural Science, Biochemistry, Botany, Ceramics, Chemical Engineering, Chemistry, Colour Chemistry, Education, Environmental Sciences, Geochemistry, Materials Science and Technology, Medical Chemistry, Nanotechnology, Natural Sciences, Pharmacology, Pharmacy, Physiology, Technologies (for example Food, Plastics).

Computing Artificial Intelligence, Bioinformatics, Business Computing, Business Studies, Computer Engineering, Computer Games Development, Computer Science, Computers, Electronics and Communications, Digital Forensics and System Security, Electronic Engineering, Games Design, Information and Communication Technology, Internet Computing, Mathematics, Multimedia Computing, Physics, Software Systems, Telecommunications, Virtual Reality Design.

Construction Architectural Technology, Architecture, Building, Building Services Engineering, Civil Engineering, Construction Management, Fire Risk Engineering, Landscape Architecture, Quantity Surveying, Surveying, Town and Country Planning.

Dance Ballet Education, Choreography, Dance, Drama, Movement Studies, Performance/Performing Arts, Physical Education, Theatre Studies.

Dentistry Biochemistry, Dental Materials, Dental Technician, Dentistry, Equine Dentistry, Medicine, Nursing, Oral Health Sciences, Pharmacy.

Drama Dance, Drama, Education, Movement Studies, Musical Theatre, Scenic Arts, Teaching, Theatre Management.

Education Ballet Education, British Sign Language, Childhood Studies, Coach Education, Deaf Studies, Early Years Education, Education Studies, Education with QTS, Education without QTS, Music Education, Physical Education, Primary Education, Psychology, Secondary Education, Social Work, Special Educational Needs, Speech and Language Therapy, Sport and Exercise, Teaching, Technology for Teaching and Learning, Youth Studies.

Electronics Automotive Electronics, Avionics, Computer Systems, Computer Technology, Computing, Digital Electronics, Digital Media Technology, Electronic Design, Electronic Engineering, Electronics, Information Systems, Internet Engineering, Mechatronics, Medical Electronics, Motorsport Electronic Systems, Multimedia Computing, Software Development, Sound Engineering.

Engineering Engineering (including Aeronautical, Aerospace, Chemical, Civil, Computing, Control, Electrical, Electronics, Energy, Environmental, Food Process, Manufacturing, Mechanical, Motorsport, Nuclear, Product Design, Software, Telecommunications Electronics), Geology and Geotechnics, Horology, Mathematics, Physics.

Estate Management Architecture, Building, Civil Engineering, Economics, Estate Management, Forestry, Housing Studies, Landscape Architecture, Property Development, Real Estate Management, Town and Country Planning.

Food Science and Technology Biochemistry, Brewing and Distilling, Chemistry, Culinary Arts, Dietetics, Food and Consumer Studies, Food Safety Management, Food Science and Technology, Food Supply Chain Management, Fresh Produce Management, Hospitality and Food Management, Nutrition, Public Health Nutrition, Viticulture and Oenology.

Forestry Arboriculture, Biological Sciences, Countryside Management, Ecology, Environmental Science, Forestry, Horticulture, Plant Sciences, Rural Resource Management, Tropical Forestry, Urban Forestry.

Furniture Design Furniture Design, Furniture Production, History of Art and Design, Three Dimensional Design, Timber Technology.

Geology-related careers Chemistry, Earth Sciences, Engineering (Civil, Minerals), Environmental Sciences, Geochemistry, Geography, Geology, Land Surveying, Oceanography, Soil Science.

Graphic Design Advertising, Graphic Design, Photography, Printing, Web Design.

Health and Safety careers Biomedical Informatics, Biomedical Sciences, Community and Health Studies, Environmental Health, Exercise and Health Science, Fire Science Engineering, Health and Social Care, Health Management, Health Promotion, Health Psychology, Health Sciences, Holistic Therapy, Nursing, Occupational Safety and Health, Paramedic Science, Public Health, Public Services Management. (See also **Medical careers**.)

Horticulture Agriculture, Crop Science, Horticulture, Landscape Architecture, Plant Science, Soil Science.

Hospitality Management Business and Management, Culinary Arts Management, Events and Facilities Management, Food Science, Food Technology, Heritage Management, Hospitality Management, Human Resource Management, International Hospitality Management, Leisure Services Management, Licensed Retail Management, Spa Management, Travel and Tourism Management.

Housing Architecture, Estate Management, General Practice Surveying, Housing, Social Administration, Town and Country Planning.

Law Business Law, Commercial Law, Consumer Law, Criminal Justice, Criminology, European Law, Government and Politics, International History, Land Management, Law, Legal Studies, Politics, Sociology.

Leisure and Recreation Adventure Tourism, Airline and Airport Management, Business Travel and Tourism, Community Arts, Countryside Management, Dance, Drama, Event Management, Fitness Science, Hospitality Management, International Tourism Management, Leisure Management, Movement Studies, Music, Physical Education, Sport and Leisure Management, Sport Development, Sports Management, Theatre Studies, Travel and Tourism.

Library and Information Management Administration, Business Information Systems, Digital Media, Education Studies, Information and Communication Studies, Information and Library Studies, Information Management, Information Sciences and Technology, Management and Marketing, Media and Cultural Studies, Media Communications, Museum and Galleries Studies, Publishing.

Marketing Advertising, Business Studies, Consumer Science, E-Marketing, Health Promotion, International Business, Marketing, Psychology, Public Relations, Retail Management, Sports Development, Travel and Tourism.

Materials Science/Metallurgy Automotive Materials, Chemistry, Engineering, Glass Science and Technology, Materials Science and Technology, Mineral Surveying, Physics, Polymer Science, Sports Materials, Textile Science.

Mathematics-related careers Accountancy, Actuarial Science, Astronomy, Banking, Business Decision Mathematics, Business Studies, Computer Studies, Economics, Education, Engineering, Financial Mathematics, Mathematical Physics, Mathematics, Physics, Quantity Surveying, Statistics.

Media careers Advertising, Broadcasting, Communications, Computer Graphics, Creative Writing, Film/Video Production, Journalism, Media, Multimedia, Photography, Public Relations, Psychology, Visual Communication.

Medical careers Anatomy, Biochemistry, Biological Sciences, Biomedical Sciences, Chiropractic, Dentistry, Genetics, Human Physiology, Immunology, Medical Engineering, Medical Sciences/Medicine, Nursing, Occupational Therapy, Orthoptics, Osteopathy, Pathology and Microbiology, Pharmacology, Pharmacy, Physiotherapy, Radiography, Speech and Language Therapy, Sports Biomedicine, Virology.

Music Commercial Music, Creative Music Technology, Digital Music, Drama, Folk and Traditional Music, Music, Music Composition, Music Education, Music Industry Management, Music Performance, Music Production, Music Studies, Musical Theatre, Performance/Performing Arts, Popular Music, Sonic Arts, Sound and Multimedia Technology, Theatre Studies.

Nautical careers Marine Engineering, Marine Studies, Nautical Studies, Naval Architecture, Oceanography, Offshore Engineering, Ship Science.

Naval Architecture Boat Design, Marine Engineering, Marine Studies, Naval Architecture, Offshore Engineering, Ship Science, Yacht and Powercraft Design, Yacht Production.

Nursing Anatomy, Applied Biology, Biochemistry, Biological Sciences, Biology, Dentistry, Education, Environmental Health and Community Studies, Health Studies, Human Biology, Medicine, Midwifery, Nursing, Occupational Therapy, Orthoptics, Physiotherapy, Podiatry, Psychology, Radiography, Social Administration, Speech and Language Therapy, Veterinary Nursing. (See also **Medical careers**.)

Nutrition Dietetics, Food Science and Technology, Health Promotion, Human Nutrition, Nursing, Nutrition, Sport and Fitness.

Occupational Therapy Art, Nursing, Occupational Therapy, Orthoptics, Physiotherapy, Psychology, Social Sciences, Speech and Language Therapy.

Optometry Applied Physics, Optometry, Orthoptics, Physics.

Photography/Film/TV Animation, Communication Studies (some courses), Digital Video Design, Documentary Communications, Film and Media, Graphic Art, Media Studies, Moving Image, Multimedia, Photography.

Physics-related careers Applied Physics, Astronomy, Astrophysics, Avionics and Space Systems, Education, Electronics, Engineering (Civil, Electrical, Mechanical), Laser Physics, Mathematical Physics, Medical Instrumentation, Molecular Physics, Nanotechnology, Natural Sciences, Optometry, Physics, Planetary and Space Physics, Quantum and Cosmological Physics, Theoretical Physics.

Physiotherapy Chiropractic, Exercise Science, Nursing, Orthoptics, Osteopathy, Physical Education, Physiotherapy, Sport and Exercise, Sports Rehabilitation.

Production Technology Engineering (Manufacturing, Mechanical), Materials Science.

Property and Valuation Management Architecture, Building Surveying, Estate Agency, Property Investment and Finance, Property Management and Valuation, Quantity Surveying, Real Estate Management, Residential Property, Urban Land Economics.

Psychology Advertising, Animal Sciences, Anthropology, Applied Social Studies, Behavioural Science, Business, Cognitive Science, Criminology, Early Childhood Studies, Education, Human Resource Management, Human Sciences, Linguistics, Marketing, Neuroscience, Occupational Therapy, Psychology (Clinical, Developmental, Educational, Experimental, Forensic, Health, Occupational, Social, Sports), Psychosocial Sciences, Public Relations, Social Sciences, Sociology.

Public Administration Applied Social Studies, Business Studies, Public Administration, Public Policy Investment and Management, Public Services, Social Administration, Social Policy, Youth Studies.

Quantity Surveying Architecture, Building, Civil Engineering, Construction and Commercial Management, Environmental Construction Surveying, Quantity Surveying, Surveying (Building, Land, Quantity and Valuation), Surveying Technology.

Radiography Anatomy, Audiology, Biological Sciences, Clinical Photography, Diagnostic Imaging, Diagnostic Radiography, Digital Imaging, Imaging Science and Technology, Medical Imaging, Moving Image, Nursing, Orthoptics, Photography, Physics, Physiology, Physiotherapy, Radiography, Radiotherapy, Therapeutic Radiography.

Silversmithing/Jewellery Design Silversmithing and Jewellery, Silversmithing Goldsmithing and Jewellery, Silversmithing Metalwork and Jewellery, Three Dimensional Design.

Social Work Abuse Studies, Applied Social Science, Community Work, Counselling Studies, Early Childhood Studies, Education, Health and Social Care, Human Rights, Journalism, Law, Nursing, Playwork, Politics and Government, Psychology, Public Administration, Religious Studies, Social Administration, Social Policy, Social Work, Sociology, Town and Country Planning, Youth Studies.

Speech and Language Therapy Audiology, Education (Special Education), Linguistics, Nursing, Occupational Therapy, Psychology, Radiography, Speech and Language Therapy.

Sport and Physical Education Coaching Sciences, Exercise Sciences, Fitness Science, Health and Fitness Management, Leisure and Recreation Management, Physical Education, Sport and Recreational Studies, Sport Journalism, Sports Psychology, Sports Science, Sports Studies.

Statistics Business Studies, Economics, Informatics, Mathematics, Operational Research, Population Sciences, Statistics.

Surveying Building Surveying, General Practice Surveying, Property Development, Quantity Surveying, Real Estate Management.

Technology Audio Technology, Dental Technology, Design Technology, Food Science and Technology, Football Technology, Logistics Technology, Medical Technology, Music Studio Technology, Paper Science, Polymer Science, Product Design Technology, Sports Technology, Technology for Teaching and Learning, Timber Technology.

Textile Design Applied Art and Design, Art, Clothing Studies, Fashion Design, Interior Design, Textile Design (Embroidery, Constructive Textiles, Printed Textiles), Textile Management.

Theatre Design Drama, Interior Design, Leisure and Recreational Studies, Theatre Design, Theatre Management, Theatre Studies.

Three Dimensional Design Architecture, Industrial Design, Interior Design, Theatre Design, Three Dimensional Design.

Town and Regional Planning Architecture, Architecture and Planning, City and Regional Planning, Environmental Planning, Estate Management, Geography, Housing, Land Economy, Planning and Development, Population Sciences, Property Planning and Development, Spatial Planning, Statistics, Sustainable Development, Town and Regional Planning, Transport Management, Urban and Regional Planning.

Transport Air Transport Engineering, Air Transport Operations, Air Transport with Pilot Training, Business Studies, Civil and Transportation Engineering, Cruise Operations Management, Industrial Design Transport, Logistics, Planning with Transport, Supply Chain Management, Sustainable Transport Design, Town and Regional Planning, Urban Planning Design and Management.

Typography and Graphic Communication Design (Graphic and Typographic Design), Digital Graphics, Fine Art (Print and Digital Media), Graphic Communication and Typography, Graphic Design, Illustration, Illustration and Print, Printmaking, Publication Design, Publishing, Visual Communication.

Veterinary careers Agricultural Sciences, Agriculture, Anatomical Science, Animal Behaviour and Welfare, Animal Sciences, Bioveterinary Sciences, Equine Dentistry, Equine Science, Medicine, Pharmacology, Pharmacy, Veterinary Medicine, Veterinary Nursing, Veterinary Practice Management, Zoology.

COURSE TYPES AND DIFFERENCES

You will then need to decide on the type of course you want to follow. The way in which Honours degree courses are arranged differs between institutions. For example, a subject might be offered as a single subject course (a Single Honours degree), or as a two-subject course (a Joint Honours degree), or as one of two, three or four subjects (a Combined Honours degree) or a major–minor degree (75% and 25% of each subject respectively). The chapter **University Course Profiles** gives more information about the different types of courses and provides for each university a resumé of the ways their courses are structured and the range of courses they offer.

Courses in the same subject at different universities and colleges can have different subject requirements so it is important to check the acceptability of your GCE A/AS and GCSE subjects (or equivalent) for all your preferred courses. Specific GCE A/AS-levels, and in some cases, GCSE subjects, may be stipulated. (See also **Chapter 7** and **Appendix 1** for information on the International Baccalaureate, Scottish Highers/ Advanced Highers, the Welsh Baccalaureate, the Cambridge Pre-U Diploma, the Advanced Diploma, the Extended Project Qualification and the Irish Leaving Certificate, and **Appendix 2** for international qualifications.)

SANDWICH COURSES AND PROFESSIONAL PLACEMENTS

One variation on Single Honours courses is that of the sandwich course, in which students will spend part of their degree course on professional, industrial or commercial placements. Media coverage on student debt and the introduction of tuition fees (see **Chapter 2**) highlight the importance of sandwich courses. Many sandwich and placement courses are on offer, in which industrial, commercial and public sector placements take place, usually, in the third year of a four-year degree course. There is also a Work-Based Learning (WBL) programme, which Chester University established several years ago, with some other institutions following suit, in which students take a WBL module in the second year of their degree course. This involves a placement lasting a few weeks when students can have the opportunity to try out possible careers. Other universities and colleges may offer longer placements of periods of six months with different employers for students taking vocational courses.

However, the most structured arrangements are known as 'professional placements' which a number of universities offer and which are very advantageous to students (see the subject tables in **Chapter 8** and university/college websites and prospectuses). Although placements in some fields such as health, social care, and education may be unpaid, in most cases a salary is paid. Where a placement is unpaid the placement period is shorter – 30 weeks – to allow students time to undertake paid work. It is important to note that during the placement year students' tuition fees will be reduced by 50% except for those on one-year courses on the Erasmus programme (see **Chapter 5**) when no fees are paid but student loans will still apply.

The advantages of sandwich courses are quite considerable although students should be aware that in the present period of recession safeguards are necessary when selecting courses and universities. While students can arrange their own placement, with the approval of their Head of Department, it is more usual for university staff to make contacts with firms and to recommend students. With the present cutbacks, however, some firms may be less likely to take on students or to pay them during their placement. This is an important issue to raise with admissions tutors before applying and it is important also to find out how your studies would continue if placements are not possible. To help you to consider the advantages of sandwich courses, included below are views of some students, employers and university staff. They could well help you decide whether a four-year sandwich course is, for you, preferable to a three-year full-time degree.

Students report ...

'I was able to earn £15,000 during my year out and £4000 during my three-month vacation with the same firm.' (**Bath** Engineering)

'There's really no other better way to find out what you want to do for your future career than having tried it for a year.' (**Aston** Human Resources Management)

'It was a welcome break in formal university education: I met some great people including students from other universities.' (**Kingston** Biochemistry)

'Having experienced a year in a working environment, I am more confident and more employable than students without this experience.' (**Aston** Business Studies)

'At Sanolfi in Toulouse, I learned to think on my feet – no two days were the same.' (**Aston** European Studies)

'I have seen how an organisation works at first-hand, learned how academic skills may be applied in a working environment, become proficient in the use of various software, acquired new skills in interpersonal relationships and communications and used my period away to realign my career perspectives.' (**Aston** European Studies)

'I was working alongside graduate employees and the firm offered me a job when I graduated.' (**Bath** Mathematics)

Employers, too, gain from having students ...
'We meet a lot of enthusiastic potential recruits who bring new ideas into the firm, and we can offer them commercially sponsored help for their final year project.'

'The quality of this student has remained high throughout the year. He will do well for his next employer, whoever that may be. However, I sincerely hope that it will be with us.'

University staff advise ...
'We refer to sandwich courses as professional placements, not "work experience" which is a phrase we reserve for short non-professional experiences, for example summer or pre-university jobs. The opportunity is available to all students but their success in gaining a good placement depends on academic ability.' (**Bath**)

'Where a placement year is optional, those who opt for it are more likely to be awarded a First or an Upper Second compared to those who don't, not because they are given more marks for doing it, but because they always seem to have added context and motivation for their final year.' (**Aston**)

When choosing your sandwich course, check with the university (a) that the institution will guarantee a list of employers, (b) whether placement experience counts towards the final degree result, (c) that placements are paid and (d) that placements are validated by professional bodies. Finally, once you start on the course, remember that your first-year academic performance will be taken into account by potential employers. Now read on!

What do employers require when considering students?
Aston (Biol) Successful second year undergraduates; (Bus) Number of UCAS points, degree programme, any prior experience; (Eng) UCAS points scores and expected degree classification; (Mech Eng) Students interviewed and selected by the company according to student ability, what they are studying and specific needs of the job. **Bath** (Chem) 'Good students': Upper Second or above and non-international students (those without work visas). Students with strong vivisection views rejected; (Mech Elec Eng) Subject-based, eg electronics, aerospace, computing and electrical engineering; (Mech Eng) Good communication, IT and social skills; (Maths) Interest in positions of responsibility, teamwork, integrity, self-motivation, analytical ability, communication, recent work experience, knowledge of the company, desire to work for the company; GCSE maths/English A/B, AL 300 UCAS points minimum (excluding general studies), predicted 2.1; (Phys) Many organisations have cut-offs regarding students' first-year performance (eg must be heading for a 2.1 although some require better than this), some need students to be particularly good in some areas (eg lab work, computer programming), many require UK nationality with minimum residency condition. **Brunel** Requirements not usually specified except for IT jobs since they need technical skills. **Cardiff Met** (Clsrm Asst) Criminal Records Bureau (CRB) checks. **Kingston** (Bus Law) Theoretical knowledge and a stated interest in certain areas (eg finance, human resources, marketing, sales, IT), excellent communication skills, teamwork, ability to prioritise, time management and a professional attitude; (Sci) Grades are rarely mentioned: it's usually a specific module or course requirement undertaken by the students that they are looking for, as well as a good attitude, motivation, initiative: a good all-rounder. **Loughborough** (Civ Eng) Target specific courses.

What are the advantages of placements to the students?
Aston (Biol) Many take jobs with their placement employers (eg NHS), gaining valuable research and clinical experience; (Bus) Graduate job offers, sponsorship through the final year of the course, gym

membership, staff discounts; (Eng) Some students are fast-tracked into full-time employment and, in some cases, have been given higher starting salaries as a result of the placement with the company; (Mech Eng) Offers of full-time employment on graduation, bursaries for their final year of study, final year projects following placements, better class of degree. **Bath** (Chem) Sponsorships for final year project work, offers of full-time employment, PhD offers and work-to-study courses, industrial references, establishment of prizes; (Maths) Sponsorship in the second year, graduate employment, bonuses during placement, travel abroad during placement, sponsorship during final year; (Phys) Job offers on graduation, sponsored final year, improved study skills for final year, job market awareness, career decisions. **Brunel** Higher percentage of students get Firsts, many students get a job offer from the placement provider, higher salaries often paid to sandwich course students, some students get exemptions from professional exams, eg ACCA, ACA and IMechE. **Cardiff Met** (Clsrm Asst) Good experience in team work, classroom experience, coaching, mentoring: decisions made whether or not to follow a teaching career. **Kingston** (Bus Law) Sponsorships fewer these days but students return with more confidence and maturity and better able to complete their final year; 60% receive job offers on completion of a successful placement; (Sci) Full-time employment on graduation and occasionally part-time work in the final year; many students are encouraged to write their final year dissertation whilst on placement and benefit from the company's support, subject matter and validation. **Loughborough** (Civ Eng) Most students are sponsored by their firms and perform better in their final examinations; (Prod Des) Final year bursary for some students, offer of employment by the sponsor and a final year design project for the sponsor.

MATURE APPLICANTS

There are a great many mature students following first degree courses in UK universities and colleges. The following is a list of key points a group of mature students found useful in exploring and deciding on a university course.

- Check with your nearest university or college to find out about the courses they can offer, for example degrees, diplomas, full-time, part-time.
- Some institutions will require examination passes in some subjects, others may not.
- An age limit may apply for some vocational courses, for example Medicine, Dentistry and Teaching.
- If entry requirements are an obstacle, prospective students should approach their local colleges for information on Access or Open College courses. These courses are fast-growing in number and popularity, offering adults an alternative route into higher education other than A-levels. They are usually developed jointly by colleges of further education and the local higher education institution.
- Demands of the course – how much time will be required for study? What are the assignments and the deadlines to be met? How is your work assessed – unseen examinations, continuous assessment, practicals?
- The demands on finance – cost of the course – loan needed – loss of earnings – drop in income if changing to another career – travel requirements – accommodation – need to work part-time for income?
- The availability and suitability of the course – geographical location – competition for places – where it will lead – student support services, for example childcare, library.
- What benefits will you derive? Fulfilment, transferable skills, social contacts, sense of achievement, enjoyment, self-esteem, career enhancement?
- Why would employers want to recruit you? Ability to adapt to the work scene, realistic and balanced approach, mature attitude to work?
- Why would employers not want to recruit you? Salary expectations, inability to fit in with younger colleagues, limited mobility? However, some employers particularly welcome older graduates: Civil Service, local authorities, Health Service, religious, charitable and voluntary organisations, teaching, social/probation work, careers work, housing.

MODULAR COURSES AND CREDIT ACCUMULATION
AND TRANSFER SCHEMES (CATS)

Courses can also differ considerably not only in their content but in how they are organised. Many universities and colleges of higher education have modularised their courses which means you can choose modules of different subjects, and 'build' your course within specified 'pathways' with the help and approval of your course tutor. It also means that you are likely to be assessed after completing each module, rather than in your last year for all your previous years' learning. In almost every course the options and modules offered include some which reflect the research interests of individual members of staff. In some courses subsidiary subjects are available as minor courses alongside a Single Honours course. In an increasing number of courses these additional subjects include a European language, and the importance of this cannot be over-emphasised with the United Kingdom's membership of the European Union. Such links are also reinforced by way of the Erasmus Programme (see **Chapter 5**) which enables university students to apply for courses in Europe for periods of up to a year, some of the courses being taught in English. Many institutions have introduced credit accumulation and transfer schemes (CATS). These allow students to be awarded credits for modules or units of study they have successfully completed which are accumulated towards a certificate, diploma or degree. They can also put their completed modules towards higher education study in other universities or colleges. Students wanting to transfer their credits should talk to the admissions office of the university they want to enter as there may be additional special subjects or module requirements for the degree they want to study.

FOUNDATION DEGREES AND FOUNDATION COURSES

Foundation courses, not be confused with Foundation degrees, normally require two years' full-time study, or longer for part-time study. They are also often taught in local colleges and may be taken part-time to allow students to continue to work. In comparison a Foundation degree can lead into the second or final year of related Honours degree courses when offered by the university validating the Foundation degree. Two-year Higher National Diplomas will also qualify for entry into the second or final year of degree courses. These, too, are often offered at universities as well as colleges of further education and partnership colleges linked to universities.

Part-time degrees and lifelong learning or distance learning courses are also often available and details of these can be found on university websites and in prospectuses. Some universities publish separate prospectuses for part-time courses.

NEXT STEPS

When choosing your course remember that one course is not better than another – it is just different. The best course for you is the one which best suits you. To give some indication of the differences between courses, see **Chapter 3** and also *Choosing Your Degree Course & University*, the companion book to *Heap 2013: University Degree Course Offers* (see **Appendix 4**). After provisionally choosing your courses, read the prospectuses again carefully to be sure that you understand what is included in the three, four or more years of study. Each institution differs in its course content even though the course titles may be the same and courses differ in other ways, for example:

- methods of assessment (eg unseen examinations, continuous assessment, project work, dissertations)
- contact time with tutors
- how they are taught (for example, frequency and size of lectures, seminars)
- practicals; field work requirements
- library, computing, laboratory and studio facilities
- amount of free study time available.

These are useful points of comparison between courses in different institutions when you are on an open day visit or making final course choices. Other important factors to consider when comparing courses include the availability of opportunities for studying and working abroad during your course, professional body accreditation of courses leading to certain professional careers (see **Appendix 3**) and in the career destinations of their graduates.

Once you have chosen your course subject(s) and the type of course you want to follow, the next step is to find out about the universities and colleges offering courses in your subject area, how much a higher education course will cost you and what financial help is available. The next chapter, **University Choice and Finance** provides information to help you do this.

TAKING A GAP YEAR

Choosing your course is the first decision you need to make, the second is choosing your university and then, for an increasing number, the third is deciding whether or not to take a Gap Year. But there lies the problem. Because of the very large number of things to do and places to go, you'll find that you almost need a Gap Year to choose the right one (although a read through *Your Gap Year* by Susan Griffith (see **Appendix 4**) is a good place to start)!

Planning ahead is important but, in the end, bear in mind that you might be overtaken by events, not least in failing to get the grades you need for a place on the course or at the university you were counting on. This could mean repeating A-levels and re-applying, which in turn could mean waiting for interviews and offers and, possibly, deferring the start of your 'gap' until February or March.

Once you have decided to go, however, it's a question of whether you will go under your own steam or through a Gap Year agency. Unless you are streetwise, or preferably 'world wise', then an agency offers several advantages. Some agencies may cover a broad field of opportunities whilst others will focus on a specific region and activity, such as the African Conservation Experience, offering animal and plant conservation work in game and nature reserves in southern Africa.

When making the choice, some students will always prefer a 'do-it-yourself' arrangement. However, there are many advantages to going through specialist agencies. Not only can they offer a choice of destinations and opportunities but also they can provide a lot of essential and helpful advice before your departure on issues such as health precautions and insurance. Support is also available in the case of accidents or illnesses when a link can be established between the agency and parents.

Finally in order to enhance your next university or college application, applying for a job for the year could be an even better option than spending a year travelling. Not only will it provide you with some financial security but it will also introduce you to the world of work, which could be more challenging than the Inca Trail!

2

UNIVERSITY CHOICE AND FINANCE

CHOOSING YOUR UNIVERSITY OR COLLEGE
Location, reputation and Open Days

For many applicants the choice of university or college is probably the main priority, with location being a key factor. However, many students have little or no knowledge of regional geography and have no concept of where universities are located: one student thought that Bangor University (situated in North Wales) was located at Bognor on England's south coast!

Some institutions – probably those nearest home or those farthest away – will be rejected quickly. In addition to the region, location and immediate surroundings of a university or college, applicants have their own individual priorities – perhaps a hectic city life or, alternatively, a quiet life in the country! But university isn't all about studying, so it's not a bad idea to link your leisure interests with what the university or college can offer or with the opportunities available in the locality. Many applicants have theatrical, musical or artistic interests while others have sporting interests and achievements ranging from basketball, cricket and football to riding, rowing, sailing, mountaineering, and even fishing for England!

Some other decisions about your choice of university or college, however, could be made for the wrong reasons. Many students, for example, talk about 'reputation' or base their decisions on league tables. Reputations are fairly clear-cut in the case of some institutions. Oxford and Cambridge are both top world-class universities in which all courses have been established for many years and are supported by first class facilities. In other universities certain subjects are predominant, such as the social sciences at the London School of Economics, and the sciences and technologies at Imperial London.

Many other leading universities in the UK are also very strong in some subjects but not necessarily in all. This is why it is wrong to conclude that a 'university has a good reputation' – most universities are not necessarily good at everything! In seeking advice, you should also be a little wary of school staff who will usually always claim that their own university or college has a 'good reputation'. Teachers obviously can provide good advice on the courses and the general atmosphere of their own institution, but they are not in a good position to make comparisons with other universities.

The best way to find out about universities and colleges and the courses that interest you is to visit your preferred institutions. Open Days provide the opportunity to talk to staff and students although, with thousands of students wandering round campuses, it may be difficult to meet and talk to the right people. Also, many institutions hold Open Days during vacations when many students are away which means that you may only hear talks from the staff, and not have any opportunity to meet students. However, it is often possible to visit a university or college in your own time and simply 'walk in'. Alternatively, a letter to the Head of Department requesting a visit could enable you to get a closer look at the subject facilities. But failing this, you will be invited automatically to visit when you receive an offer and then you can meet the students in the department.

ACTION POINTS

Before deciding on your preferred universities and courses check out the following points:

Teaching staff

How do the students react to their tutors? Do staff have a flair and enthusiasm for their subject? Are they approachable? Do they mark your work regularly and is the feedback helpful, or are you left to get on with your own work with very little direction? What are the research interests of the staff?

Teaching styles

How will you be taught, for example, lectures, seminars, tutorials? Are lectures popular? If not, why not? How much online learning will you have? How much time will you be expected to work on your own? If there are field courses, how often are they arranged and are they compulsory? How much will they cost?

Facilities

Are the facilities of a high standard and easily available? Is the laboratory equipment 'state of the art' or just adequate? Are the libraries well-stocked with software packages, books and journals? What are the computing facilities? Is there plenty of space to study or do rooms and workspaces become overcrowded? Do students have to pay for any materials?

New students

Are there induction courses for new students? What student services and facilities are available? Is it possible to buy second-hand copies of set books?

Work placements

Are work placements an optional or compulsory part of the course? Who arranges them? Are the placements popular? Do they count towards your degree? Are work placements paid? How long are they?

Transferable skills

Transferable skills are now regarded as important by all future employers. Does the department provide training in communication skills, teamwork, time-management and information technology as part of the degree course?

Accommodation

How easy is it to find accommodation? Where are the halls of residence? Are they conveniently located for libraries and lecture theatres? Are they self-catering? Alternatively, what is the cost of meals in the university refectory? Which types of student accommodation are the most popular? What is the annual cost of accommodation? If there is more than one campus, is a shuttle-bus service provided?

Costs

Find out the costs of materials, accommodation and travel in addition to tuition fees (see below) and your own personal needs. What are the opportunities for earning money, on or off campus? Does the department or faculty have any rules about part-time employment?

FINANCE: WHAT WILL IT COST AND WHAT HELP IS THERE?

Tuition fees and other costs

Tuition fees are charged for degree courses in England, Wales and Northern Ireland. The level of tuition fees for courses has in the past been decided annually and has varied between institutions. However as a result of recent Government decisions a rise in the cost of tuition fees is planned to come into effect for students commencing courses in 2013. Maintenance grants and loans will still be available

Specific details of the charges to be made by individual universities for each course will be available on websites, but depending on the popularity of universities and certain courses the maximum charge will be £9000, although some institutions will charge a lower level of fees of up to £6000.

Students starting their courses in 2013 should check university and college websites, and websites listed in this section, for the latest information about fees.

You may also have additional charges, depending on your course of study. For example, studio fees for Art courses could reach £300 per year, while for other courses, such as Architecture, Science and Engineering, there could be charges for equipment. Additionally, there could also be charges for fieldwork trips, study abroad and vacation courses. To find out your likely yearly course costs, in addition to your tuition fees, check with your subject department.

Also, check your fee status if you are planning a sandwich course involving either unpaid or paid placements. You can receive a salary of up to £12,000 doing a one-year placement but if you earn more than this you'll need to check your fee status carefully with your finance officer and consult the relevant websites listed below.

Loans Students will not have to pay tuition fees before starting their courses or while they are studying. Depending on their household income, students can apply for a tuition fee grant or they will be able to take out a student loan to pay for their fees. Loan repayments are made only after graduation and currently when annual earnings are more than £21,000 per year.

University scholarships These are usually merit-based and are often competitive although some universities offer valuable scholarships to any new entrant who has achieved top grades at A-level. Scholarships vary considerably and are often subject-specific, offered through faculties or departments, so check the availability of any awards with the subject departmental head. Additionally, there are often music, choral and organ awards, and scholarships and bursaries for sporting achievement. Entry scholarships are offered by several universities which normally stipulate that the applicant must place the university as their first choice and achieve the specified high grades. Changes in bursaries and scholarships take place every year so it is important to check university and college websites.

University bursaries These are usually paid in cases of financial need: all universities charging course fees are obliged to offer some bursaries to students receiving maintenance grants. The term 'bursary' is usually used to denote an award to students requiring financial assistance or who are disadvantaged in various ways. Universities are committed to fair access to all students from lower income backgrounds and individual universities and colleges have bursaries, trust funds and sponsorships for those students receiving maintenance grants, although reports suggest that many such students fail to claim the money due to them. These non-repayable awards are linked to the size of the maintenance grant students receive and vary between universities.

Living costs

Most students spend their first year in university accommodation. This is usually the highest single cost in a typical weekly budget and the costs will vary considerably between universities. Rooms may be single or shared and include catering or self-catering arrangements. Outside university in the private sector additional costs are likely to include heating, electricity, hot water and water rates.

In addition, other living expenses will need to be considered. These include insurance, healthcare, food, books and stationery, photocopying, computing and telephone calls, clothes and toiletries, local travel, travel to and from university, entertainment, socialising and sport or leisure activities.

Help towards living costs

Maintenance grants These government grants are available but depend on the student's household income. They are paid on a sliding scale to students depending on the family income. These grants are not repayable. Loans to help towards living costs are also available, and details of these are found on the websites listed below. In addition, price reductions are often available for students at some shops, restaurants, cinemas, museums and galleries. Contact the University Student Union before or when you arrive to find out more about these arrangements.

Other financial support

Many major organisations also provide financial help to those in various categories. These include the Lawrence Atwell's Charity for refugee young people from low income backgrounds, the Prince's Trust for disadvantaged young people aged between 14 and 25, and grants of up to £2000 for the disabled from the Snowdon Award Scheme.

Similarly, many scholarships are also offered by professional, commercial and other organisations. These include the armed services and the engineering professional organisations, particularly those specialising in civil or mechanical engineering, and also the Institute of Materials, Minerals and Mining. There are also sponsorships in which the student joins a firm on leaving school, combining university study with work experience and with an almost guaranteed offer of full-time employment on graduation. And there is the alternative route of taking a sandwich course and being placed with a firm for a year on full pay, often up to £12,000 (see **Chapter 1**).

Some universities also offer additional bursaries to encourage applications from the locality. These may be available to students applying from partner schools or colleges and living in certain postcode areas, in some cases to the brothers and sisters of current students at the university, or to students who have been in care or are homeless. These awards are not repayable.

In addition, students on some health-related courses, for example Dental Hygiene, Nursing, Occupational Therapy, Physiotherapy, Radiography will be eligible for NHS student bursaries. Other bursaries are also payable for programmes funded through the General Social Care Council and also for shortage subjects for those on teacher training courses.

After starting the course, Access to Learning funds are available to help students in financial hardship or through emergency payments for unexpected financial crises. Hardship funds are also offered in very special cases, particularly to students with children or to single parents, mature students and, in particular, to students with disabilities who may also claim Disability Living Allowance (replaced by the Personal Independence Payment from April 2013). These payments are made in instalments or as a lump sum or as a short-term loan.

Useful websites   Students from England www.direct.gov.uk/en/EducationAndLearning/
                UniversityAndHigherEducation/studentfinance
            Students from Scotland www.saas.gov.uk/student_support
            Students from Wales www.studentfinancewales.co.uk
            Students from Northern Ireland www.studentfinanceni.co.uk

For comprehensive finance information see the useful websites above, *University Scholarships, Awards and Bursaries* and other sources listed in **Appendix 4**.

INFORMATION SOURCES

Prospectuses, websites and Open Days are key sources of the information you need to decide where to study and at the back of this book a directory of institutions is provided, with full contact details, for you to use in your research. Other sources of information include the books and websites listed in **Appendix 4**, the professional associations listed in **Appendix 3**, and the websites given in the subject tables in **Chapter 8**. It is important to take time to find out as much as you can about your preferred universities, colleges and courses, and to explore their similarities and differences. The following chapter **University Course Profiles** gives you information about the types of courses offered by each university and how they are organised. This is important information that you need to know when choosing your university or college because those factors affect, for example, the amount of choice you have in what you study, and the opportunities you have for sandwich placements (see **Chapter 1**). You therefore need to read **Chapter 3** to give you an insight into universities so that you can find the one that is right for you.

3

UNIVERSITY COURSE PROFILES

UNIVERSITIES AND THEIR COURSES

Choosing a degree subject is one step of the way to higher education (see **Chapter 1**), choosing a university or college is the next stage (see **Chapters 2** and **10**). However, in addition to such features as location, entry requirements, accommodation, students' facilities and the subjects offered, many universities differ in the way they organise and teach their courses. The course profiles which follow aim to identify the main course features of each of the universities and to provide some brief notes about the types of courses they offer and how they differ.

Although universities have their own distinct identities and course characteristics, they have many similarities. Apart from full-time and sandwich courses, one-year foundation courses are also offered in many subjects which can help the student to either convert or build on existing qualifications to enable them to start an Honours degree programme. All universities also offer one-year international foundation courses for overseas students to provide a preliminary introduction to courses and often to provide English language tuition.

Course profiles

Aberdeen Students applying for the MA degree in Arts and Social Sciences are admitted to a degree rather than a subject. Students select from a range of courses in the first year, leading up to the final choice of subject and Honours course in the fourth year. The BSc degree is also flexible but within the Science framework. Engineering students follow a common core course in Years 1 and 2, specialising in Year 3. There is less flexibility, however, in some vocational courses such as Accountancy, Law, Medicine and Dentistry. For some degree programmes, highly qualified applicants may be admitted to the second year of the course. Other courses cover Divinity and Theology, Education and Music.

Abertay Dundee Courses have a strong vocational bias and are offered in the Schools of Arts, Media and Computing, Creative Technologies, Business, Contemporary Sciences and Social and Health Sciences. Four-year courses are offered on a modular basis. Sandwich courses may be either thick (one-year placement) or thin (two six-month placements) and placements are usually at the end of the second and/or third years.

Aberystwyth The University offers Single, Joint and major/minor Honours courses on a modular basis. In Part 1 (Year 1) core topics related to the chosen subject are studied alongside optional subjects. This arrangement allows some flexibility for change when choosing final degree subjects in Part 2 (Years 2 and 3). Some students take a year in industry or commerce between Years 2 and 3. Courses include Accountancy, Agriculture, the Arts and Humanities, Business, Economics, Computer Science, Education, Law, Languages, Management and Marketing, Mathematics, the Sciences, Sport, Theatre and TV Studies, and Welsh and Celtic Studies.

Anglia Ruskin Courses are modular which enables students to choose from a range of subject topics in addition to the compulsory subject core modules. Single and Combined Honours courses are offered in the Faculties of Arts, Law and Social Sciences, Science and Technology, Health and Social Care, Education, and in the Business School. Many programmes have a strong vocational focus, with some opportunities to study abroad.

Arts London This University is Europe's largest institution offering courses in Art and Design, Communication and Performing Arts, focusing on creativity and practice in a large number of specialist fields.

Aston The University offers modular courses in Single Honours degrees (one subject), Joint Honours (two subjects, usually in related areas) and in Combined Honours and interdisciplinary studies in which programmes are organised across different subjects. Combined Honours courses may be weighted

50%–50%, and major/minor programmes weighted 67% for the major element and 33% for the minor. A distinctive feature of Aston is that most degrees allow students to spend the third year on a one-year sandwich placement; 70% of students follow sandwich courses or study-abroad programmes, leading to a high percentage of employed graduates. Courses are taught in the Schools of Engineering and Applied Science, Languages and Social Sciences, Life and Health Sciences and in the Aston Business School.

Bangor Modular courses are offered in Single and Joint Honours programmes. A broad and flexible programme is taken in Level 1 (Year 1) with the opportunity to study modules outside the chosen subject including a language. This is followed by greater specialisation in Levels 2 and 3. Courses include Agriculture and Forestry, Arts subjects, Business and Management, Computer Science and Electronics, Creative Studies, Education, Archaeology, History, Law, Health Studies, Languages, Music, Psychology, Biological Sciences, Chemistry, Ocean Sciences, Geography, Social Sciences, Sport and Religious Studies. Contrary to popular belief, two-thirds of the students come from outside Wales and all courses are taught in English.

Bath The academic year is divided into two semesters with Single and Combined Honours degrees composed of core units and optional units, allowing students some flexibility in shaping their courses with 10–12 units taken each year. A central feature of all programmes is the opportunity to take a sandwich course as part of the degree: this is usually taken as either one 12-month placement or two periods of six months. Courses are offered in the Faculties of Engineering and Design, Humanities and Social Sciences, Science, Sport and the School of Management.

Bath Spa Most courses – for Single awards, specialised awards and Combined awards – are part of a flexible modular scheme with students taking six modules each year. Some modules are compulsory but there is a good range of optional modules. The wide range of courses on offer include Biology, Business and Management, Creative Studies, Cultural Studies, Dance, Drama, Education, English Literature, Food Studies, Geography, Health Studies, History, Media Communications, Music, Psychology, Sociology and Study of Religions.

Bedfordshire The University offers BA and BSc undergraduate, Foundation and Extended degrees in Advertising, Marketing and Communications, Art and Design, Biosciences, Business, Computing, Journalism, Law, Media, Nursing, Psychology, Social Sciences, Sport and Leisure and Tourism. Most of the courses are vocational, some of which offer a placement year in industry or commerce.

Birmingham Courses cover Arts subjects (including Drama), Social Sciences, Business and Commerce, Education, Engineering, Law, Life and Environmental Sciences, Medicine and Dentistry and Health Sciences. Single subject and Joint Honours courses are offered. In Joint Honours courses the two chosen subjects may have common ground or can be very disparate, for example technology and a modern language. Some major/minor combinations are also possible. The modular system provides opportunities for students to study a subject outside their main degree.

Birmingham City Courses are offered through the Birmingham Institute of Art and Design, the Business School, the School of Computing, the School of Jewellery and the Faculties of the Built Environment, Education, Health and Community Care, Law, Humanities and Social Sciences and the Technology Innovation Centre. Many courses have a vocational focus and include sandwich placements. Music is offered through the Birmingham Conservatoire, a music college of international standing. There is also an extensive International Exchange Programme, with many courses abroad being taught in English.

Bolton Modular Single and Combined Honours courses are available, with many offering vocational or professional content and work experience elements. Courses include Art and Design, Built Environment, Business Studies, Computing and Electronics, Cultural and Creative Studies, Education, Engineering, Health and Social Studies, Product Design, Psychology and Sport, Leisure and Tourism. Teaching and learning take place through a mixture of lectures, practicals, seminars and small tutorial groups.

Bournemouth The University offers undergraduate degrees leading to BA, BSc and LLB. The programmes, which are mainly vocational and include sandwich placements, often carry professional recognition. The academic schools cover Arts and Humanities, Business and Management, Design, Food and Nutrition, Law, Media and Communications, Technology, Tourism, Sport and Hospitality.

Bradford Single, Joint and major/minor Honours degree courses are offered, many of which are vocational, leading to professional accreditation, and include sandwich placements in industry and commerce. Other courses offer work-shadowing placements. Language options are available to all students irrespective of their chosen degree course. Subjects are taught in the Schools of Computing, Informatics and Media, The School of Engineering Design and Technology, The School of Health Studies, The School of Life Sciences, The School of Management, The School of Social and International Studies and The School of Lifelong Education and Development.

Brighton BA, BSc and BEng courses are offered, 90% with industrial placements including some in Europe, the USA and Canada. Courses include Accounting, Art and Architecture, Business, Education and Sport, Health, Law, Information Sciences and Science and Engineering. Brighton and Sussex Medical School students are based at the Falmer campus for the first two years, with academic and clinical studies integrated from Year 1, and thereafter in the education centre at the Royal Sussex County Hospital in Brighton.

Bristol The University offers Single and Joint Honours programmes, mostly of three or four years and, except for Dentistry, Medicine and Veterinary Science, they are based on a modular structure. Students on Single Honours courses have open units allowing optional choices from a range of subjects. Lectures play an important part in teaching and are supported by tutorials and seminars which, in Arts and Social Sciences, tend to dominate the final year. Other subject areas offered in Sciences and Engineering (some courses include a year abroad), Arts, Social Sciences and Law.

Bristol UWE The University offers Single and Joint Honours courses organised on a modular basis which gives flexibility in the choice of options. Many courses include sandwich placements and, in addition, students have the opportunity to undertake a period of study in another EU country. The language centre is open to all students. Courses cover a full range of subjects in the Faculties of Media and Design, Applied Sciences, Built Environment, Computing, Education, Engineering and Mathematical Sciences, Health and Social Care, Humanities, Law, Languages and Social Sciences, the Bristol Business School and Hartpury College (offering Agricultural and Equine Business courses).

Brunel All courses are made up of self-contained modules enabling students, within their scheme of studies, to choose a broad range of topics or greater specialisation as they prefer. Some modern language modules may be taken, depending on the timetable of the chosen subjects. Almost all degree courses are available in a three-year full-time mode or in four-year thick or thin sandwich courses which combine academic work with industrial experience. Some exchange schemes also operate in Europe and the USA. Degree programmes are offered in the Schools of Arts (Drama, English, Media), Business, Engineering and Design, Health Sciences and Social Care, Information Systems, Law, Social Sciences and Sport and Education.

Buckingham The University is an educational charity with its main income provided by the students who pay full tuition fees. A unique feature is the two-year degree programme which starts in January although some courses start in September and may extend to 2¼ years, and some last three years. Courses are offered in Business, Humanities, Law, International Studies and Sciences.

Bucks New Courses are focused on vocational studies in a wide range of subjects in three main groups. These cover Creativity and Culture (Art, Design, Music and Media), Enterprise and Innovation (Business, Computing, Law, Human Sciences and Sport) and Society and Health (Health and Social Care and Nursing).

Cambridge The University offers undergraduate courses in Arts and Sciences and postgraduate degree programmes. Three-year degree courses (Triposes) provide a broad introduction to the subject followed by options at a later stage, and are divided into Part 1 (one or two years) and Part 2. In some Science and Engineering courses there is a fourth year (Part 3). In college-based teaching sessions (supervisions), essays are set for discussion to support university lectures, seminars and practicals.

Canterbury Christ Church A wide range of BA and BSc courses are on offer in addition to a wide choice of combined courses. Most of these courses are offered at the Canterbury campus and include Primary Education and Law, Arts and Social Science and Science subjects. Nursing and other Paramedical courses are also offered at the Medway campus at Chatham, Visual and Performing Arts are studied at Folkestone and Music and some Business courses are taken at the Broadstairs campus.

Cardiff All students taking the very flexible BA degree study three subjects in the first year and then follow a Single or Joint Honours course in their chosen subject(s). Similarly, BSc Econ courses offer the option to transfer to an alternative degree course at the end of Year 1, depending on the subjects originally chosen. Many degree schemes have a vocational and professional content with a period of attachment in industry, and there are well established links with universities abroad. Degrees schemes are offered by 26 Schools covering Architecture and Planning, Arts and Humanities subjects, Business, Computer Science, Earth, Ocean and Planetary Sciences, Engineering, Healthcare Studies, Law, Media Studies, Medicine, Dentistry and Nursing, Music, Optometry, Pharmacy, Psychology, Religious Studies, Sciences, Social Sciences and Welsh Studies.

Chester Single and Combined Honours courses are offered in a wide range of subjects on the Chester campus. Subjects offered include Art and Design, Drama and Theatre Studies, Business and Social Studies courses and Nutrition and Health Care. The Warrington campus offers well-established courses in Media (Radio, TV, Music) and Journalism in addition to Computer Science and Sports courses.

Chichester Degree subjects can be studied in major, joint or minor programmes. All undergraduate courses comprise a number of individual short course units/modules, taught and assessed separately. Each degree course consists of compulsory and optional modules enabling students to follow their own interests. BA courses are offered in a range of subjects covering Dance, Education, English, Fine Art, History, Media Studies, Music, Performing Arts, Sports Studies and Theology at Chichester, and Business, Education and Tourism at the Bognor Regis campus.

City The University offers a wide range of three-year and four-year programmes leading to degrees in Business and Management, Communication, Computing, Engineering and Mathematical Sciences, Health Sciences, Law, Nursing and Social Sciences. Some Schools and Departments provide a common first year, allowing students to make a final decision on their degree course at the end of the first year. Some sandwich courses are optional, others compulsory. Students in some subject areas may apply to study abroad.

Coventry Courses are offered in the Schools of Art and Design, Business, Environment and Society (including Law, Geography and Social Science), Engineering and Computing (including mathematical sciences) and Health and Life Sciences. Many courses are industry linked and offer sandwich placements in industry and commerce, with some opportunities to study abroad. Individual programmes of study are usually made up of compulsory modules, core options from a prescribed list and free choice modules.

Creative Arts Foundation and Honours degree courses are offered covering Art and Design, Architecture, Media and Communications.

Cumbria Courses cover Art, Design, Media and Performance, Arts, Humanities and Social Science, Business, IT and Law, Education, Health and Social Care, Natural Resources and Outdoor Studies and Sport.

De Montfort Courses cover Art and Design, Business and Management, Computing Sciences, Creative Technologies, Dance and Drama, Engineering, Health and Society, Humanities, Law, Life Sciences and Music. Single Honours programmes are offered together with sandwich courses and an extensive Joint Honours programme in which two subjects are chosen to be studied equally. Courses are modular, some assessed by coursework only, or by a combination of coursework and examination and a few by examination only. It is possible to change a selected module early in the year.

Derby Courses in Derby are offered across three subject areas – Arts, Design and Technology, Business and Education, Health and Sciences, whilst at the Buxton campus Foundation degrees and Higher National Diploma courses are offered as well as some BA and BSc degrees. There is also a comprehensive Joint Honours programme offering two subjects and Combined Honours courses with a choice of up to three subjects. Major/minor courses are also available.

Dundee Courses are offered in Accountancy, Architecture and Planning, Art and Design, Arts, Education, Engineering, Law, Medicine and Dentistry, Nursing, Sciences and Social Sciences. A flexible modular system is offered in which Arts and Social Science students have a choice of up to three or four subjects in Year 1 leading to greater specialisation as students progress through the next three years. A similar system applies to courses in Life Sciences and Physical Sciences. In Engineering a common core curriculum operates in Level 1 and in the first half of Level 2.

Durham Degree options include Single and Joint Honours courses to which subsidiary subjects can be added. There are named routes in Natural Sciences and courses in Combined Arts and Social Sciences in which students may design their own degree course by choosing several subjects from a wide range. Courses include the Arts, Business, Computer Science, Education, Engineering, Law, Medicine, Science and Social Science.

Edge Hill The University has three-year programmes including Business, English, Film, Geographical Sciences, History, Law, Media, Midwifery, Nursing, Performance Studies, Social and Psychological Sciences, Sport and Teacher Training.

Edinburgh Courses are offered in Humanities and the Social Sciences, Medicine and Veterinary Medicine and in Science and Engineering. Depending on the choice of degree, three or more subjects are taken in the first year followed by second level courses in at least two of these subjects in Year 2, thus allowing a range of subjects to be studied at degree level. There is a considerable choice of subjects although there may be restrictions in the case of high-demand subjects such as English, Economics and Psychology. General or Ordinary degrees take three years and Honours degrees take four years. Joint Honours degrees are also offered.

Edinburgh Napier Students choose between Single and Joint (two subject) degrees and customised degrees which can include a range of subjects. Courses are offered in Accounting, Economics and Financial Services, Business, Management, Languages and Law, Computing, Creative Industries, Engineering and the Built Environment, Life Sciences, Nursing, Social Sciences and Tourism and Hospitality.

Edinburgh Queen Margaret The five main areas at this new university (2007) cover Business and Enterprise, Health, Media and Social Sciences, Drama and the Creative Industries. All courses focus on vocational careers.

Essex Undergraduate departments are grouped in Schools of study covering Humanities and Comparative Studies, Social Sciences, Law and Sciences and Engineering. In Year 1 students take four or five courses including modules for their chosen degree. In Year 2 they may follow their chosen degree or choose another degree, including combined and joint courses. The four-year BA and some Law degrees include a year abroad and/or industrial placements. Degree schemes in Health, Business and the Performing Arts are also offered at the Southend campus.

Exeter The University has seven Schools of study: Business, Engineering, Maths and Physical Sciences, Humanities, Life and Environmental Sciences, Social Sciences and International Studies and Medicine. In some courses it is possible to study for up to a year in Europe, North America, Australia or New Zealand. Some subjects, including Mining Engineering, Geology and Law, can be taken at the Cornwall campus at Penryn.

Glamorgan Many of the courses are vocational and can be studied as Single or Joint Honours courses or major/minor degrees. Courses are offered in the fields of Art and Design, Built Environment, Business, Computing and Mathematics, Education, Engineering, English and Creative Writing, Geography and the Environment, Health Sciences, Life and Physical Sciences, Humanities and Social Sciences, Law, Policing and Crime, Media and Drama Studies and Sport.

Glasgow Applicants choose a Faculty and a degree from the Faculties of Arts, Education, Engineering, Law, Business and Social Sciences, Medicine, Science and Veterinary Medicine. Flexible arrangements allow students to build their own degree programme from all the courses on offer. Honours degrees normally take four years, with the decision for Honours taken at the end of Year 2 (not automatic). General degrees take three years except for those involving a foreign language. Creative, Cultural, Environmental, Health and Scottish Studies can also be taken at the Crichton campus in Dumfries.

University of Greenwich School of Science

Science is a voyage of discovery. You learn about the physical and biological world from experiments you design and carry out yourself. You will have many opportunities to undertake fascinating and inspirational work at our School of Science.

The School is diverse and vibrant, with nearly 2,000 students studying at our Medway Campus in Chatham Maritime, which benefits from continuous investment in facilities. The School offers programmes across a range of areas, from environmental science and geography, through to nutrition, sports science, biomedical science, pharmaceutical science and chemistry.

Teaching and learning

We employ the very latest learning and assessment techniques, provide pastoral care to ensure students achieve their goals, and deliver academic and professional programmes supported by research and scholarship. We have some of the most sophisticated instrumentation and most modern facilities in the UK, including a £1.5 million chemistry laboratory. Most of our programmes are accredited or recognised by relevant professional bodies, so you can have total confidence in the quality of our teaching programmes.

Employability

The earning potential for science graduates is excellent and we take our graduates' careers very seriously. During the course of your degree, we will help prepare you for the world of work. You can meet prospective employers and find out what they are looking for, take up placement opportunities and prepare for job applications.

Research

The School attracts multimillion-pound funding to support its research, and many of these activities have gained international praise and recognition. Recent research includes a potential treatment for multiple sclerosis, developed in association with King's College London.

To find out more, visit
www.gre.ac.uk/science

Glasgow Caledonian The University offers a wide range of vocational full-time and sandwich courses organised in the Schools of the Built and Natural Environment, Computing and Engineering, Health and Social Care, Law and Social Sciences, Life Sciences, Nursing, Midwifery and Community Health and the Caledonian Business School.

Gloucestershire Courses are made up of individual study units (modules). Some are compulsory for the chosen course but other modules can be chosen from other subjects. There are three main Faculties: Arts and Education, Business and Social Sciences and Environment and Leisure. Modular, Single and Joint Honours courses are offered, many with work placements and some with exchange schemes with institutions in the USA.

Glyndŵr This university in North Wales (Wrexham) offers a range of courses including Art and Design, Business, Computing and Communications Technology, Education and Community, Health, Social Sciences, Social Care and Sport and Exercise Sciences, Humanities and Science and Technology.

Greenwich Courses include Architecture and Construction, Business, Chemical and Life Sciences, Computing and Mathematical Sciences, Earth and Environmental Sciences, Education and Training, Engineering, Languages, Health and Social Care, Humanities and Social Sciences and Law. There is also a flexible and comprehensive Combined Honours degree programme offering two joint subjects of equal weight or, alternatively, major/minor combinations.

Heriot-Watt The year is divided into three 10-week terms with four modules taken each term. The six Schools cover the Built Environment, Engineering and Physical Sciences, Management and Languages, Mathematical and Computer Sciences, Textiles and Design and Life Sciences.

Hertfordshire Honours degree courses, including sandwich degrees, are offered including Art and Design, Astronomy and Astrophysics, Business, Computer Science, Education, Engineering, Humanities, Law, Life and Physical Sciences, Geography, Music, Sport, Nursing and Health subjects, Psychology, Social Studies and many courses are vocational. There is also an extensive Combined modular programme in which students choose three subjects in Year 1, followed by specialisation in Years 2 and 3.

Huddersfield The modular approach to study provides a flexible structure to all courses which are offered as full-time or sandwich options. All students also have the opportunity to study a modern language either as a minor option or by studying part-time through the Modern Languages Centre. Most courses are vocational and include such subjects as Accountancy and Business, Architecture, Art and Design, Computing, Education, Engineering, Geography and Environmental Sciences, Food Sciences, Hospitality and Tourism, Human and Health Sciences, Law, Marketing, Music and Sciences.

Hull All full-time courses are made up of core and optional modules with a free elective scheme which allows students to take one module each year outside their main subject. A 'Languages for All' programme is available for all students irrespective of their degree course subject. The wide range of subjects offered include Arts and Humanities, Business, Computing, Drama, Economics, Education, Engineering, Law, Medicine (offered at Hull York Medical School), Music, Nursing, Physical Sciences, Social Sciences and Sport. The Scarborough campus also offers a wide range of courses.

Imperial London The College offers world-class programmes in Science, Medicine, Engineering and Management. Joint Honours courses and degree courses abroad with a year abroad are also available. Science courses are offered primarily in one principal subject, but flexibility is provided by the possibility to transfer at the end of the first year and by the choice of optional subjects in the later years of the course. A Humanities programme is also open to all students with a wide range of options whilst the Tanaka Business School offers Management courses which form an integral part of undergraduate degrees.

Keele Flexibility is provided through either interdisciplinary Single Honours degrees, bringing together a number of topics in an integrated form, or Dual Honours degrees in which two principal subjects are studied to degree level to the same depth as a Single Honours course. In addition, all students take a first-year course in Complementary Studies and may also study a foreign language. Courses are offered in Arts subjects, Biosciences and Physical Sciences, Economics, Education, Law, Management Science, Media, Music and Social Sciences.

Kent Single Honours courses can include the option of taking up to 25% of the degree in another subject, or to change the focus of a degree at the end of the year. Two subjects are studied on a 50/50 basis in Joint Honours courses and there are also major/minor Honours degrees. Degrees include Accountancy and Business courses, Arts subjects, Biological and Physical Sciences, Computer Science, Drama and Theatre and Film Studies, Languages, Law, Music Technology, Pharmacy, Psychology, Religious Studies and Social Sciences.

Kingston Single and Joint Honours courses are offered within a modular structure, with the opportunity to take a language option in French, German, Italian, Japanese, Mandarin Chinese, Russian or Spanish. Several courses are available as a minor field, for example, Business, which adds an extra dimension to the chosen degree. Subjects are offered in Architecture, Art, Design and Music, Arts and Social Sciences, Business, Computing, Earth Sciences, Economics, Education, Engineering, Humanities, Law, Life Sciences, Mathematics, Health and Social Care Sciences, Media, Performance Studies, Pharmacy, Social Sciences and Surveying. Exchange schemes are offered with 72 universities in Europe and five in the USA.

Lancaster Each college has its own social activities and events. The degree programme is split into Part 1 (Year 1) and Part 2 (Years 2 and 3). Students study up to three subjects in Year 1 and then choose to major in one or a combination of subjects in Years 2 and 3. Single and Joint courses are offered in a wide range of subjects, for example, Business, Computer Science, Engineering, Finance, Languages, Mathematics, Medicine, Natural Sciences, Music, Politics and Psychology. There are study opportunities abroad in the USA and Canada, the Far East and Australasia.

Leeds A very wide range of courses are on offer in most subject areas (Leeds is a pioneer of Joint Honours degrees). In the first year, Joint Honours students normally divide their time equally between three subjects, with a wide choice of the third or elective subject in the first year. In many cases, students can transfer to a different course at the end of the first year and delay their final choice of degree. A wide range of subjects is offered in Arts and Humanities, Medicine and Dentistry, Theatre and Performance, Science and Engineering, Social Sciences and in the Business School.

Leeds Met Many of the degrees are vocational with links to industry and commerce. Courses are modular with core studies and optional modules. Degree programmes are offered in the Faculties of Arts and Society, Information and Technology, Health, Sport and Recreation, the Leslie Silver International Faculty and the Leeds Business School.

Leicester Single Honours courses are offered in all the main disciplines and are taken by 75% of students. The main subject of study may be supported by one or two supplementary subjects taken in the first, and sometimes the second, year. Joint Honours courses are also offered. A three-year Combined Studies degree is also available in which three subjects are studied, one taken for two years only. Apart from Medicine, all programmes have a common modular structure with compulsory modules and a wide choice of optional modules.

Lincoln There are Faculties of Art, Architecture and Design, Business and Law, Health, Life and Social Sciences, Media, Humanities and Technology. Single and Joint subject degrees are offered on a modular basis, with some subjects offering the chance to study abroad.

Liverpool The University offers degrees in the Faculties of Arts, Engineering, Medicine, Science, Social and Environmental Studies and Veterinary Science. Apart from courses with a clinical component, programmes are modular. In some cases they include placements in industry or in another country whilst a 'Languages for All' scheme offers European languages. A Combined Honours programme in Arts gives students the chance to choose three subjects in Year 1, reducing to two subjects in Years 2 and 3. A similar Combined Honours course in Social and Environmental Studies is also offered.

Liverpool Hope Single Honours courses leading to degrees of BA and BSc are offered and there is also a wide range of options by way of two combined subjects. Courses include Business, Computing, Dance, Drama, Education, English, Environmental Management, Film Studies, Fine Art and Design, Geography, Health, History, Human Biology, Law, Leisure, Marketing, Mathematics, Media, Music, Politics, Psychology, Sports Studies, Theology and Religious Studies and Tourism.

LJMU Courses are offered in the Faculties of Business, Law and Languages, Education, Community and Leisure, Health and Applied Social Sciences, Media, Arts and Social Science, Science and Technology and the Environment. The majority of courses provide the opportunity for work-based learning or for a year-long industrial placement.

London (Birk) Part-time evening courses are offered for mature students wishing to read for first and higher degrees. Courses are offered in the Faculties of Arts, Science, Social Science and Continuing Education.

London (Gold) Programmes include Art, Drama and Media, the Arts, Education and Social Sciences. Like most London University degrees, the majority of undergraduate degrees are made up of course units giving some flexibility. Twelve units are taken over three years.

London (Hey) Nine BA courses are offered in Philosophy and Theology and a Foundation degree in Pastoral Mission. Some part-time undergraduate courses available. The supportive and learning environment is enhanced by one-to-one tutorials for all students throughout their courses.

London (Inst in Paris) A Single Honours course in French Studies is offered to English-speaking applicants who study in France for the whole of their course. The course is taught almost entirely in French. Students graduate after their three year course with a University of London BA.

London (King's) The College offers more than 200 degree programmes in the Faculties of Arts and Humanities, Biomedical and Health Sciences, Law, Nursing and Midwifery, Physical Sciences, Social Science and Public Policy, and Medicine and Dentistry at the Guy's or King's Denmark Hill and St Thomas's campuses. The degree course structure varies with the subject chosen and consists of Single Honours (one subject), Joint Honours (two subjects), Combined Honours (a choice of over 60 programmes) and major/minor courses.

London (QM) The College offers courses in the Arts and Humanities, Biological and Physical Sciences, Business Management and Economics, Computer Science, Engineering, Languages, Materials Science, Mathematics, Medicine and Social Sciences. In most subjects, students choose compulsory and optional course units which allow for some flexibility in planning a course to suit individual interests.

London (RH) The College offers Single, Joint and major/minor Honours degrees in three Faculties: Arts, History and Social Sciences, and Science. Many courses offer the opportunity to study abroad and all students can compete for international exchanges.

London (RVC) Courses are offered in Veterinary Medicine and Bioveterinary Sciences; the latter does not qualify graduates to practise as veterinary surgeons. There is also a Veterinary Gateway course and a four-year Veterinary Nursing programme.

London (St George's) Courses are offered in Biomedical Informatics, Biomedical Science, Medicine, Physiotherapy and Diagnostic and Therapeutic Radiography.

London (Sch Pharm) The School offers the Master of Pharmacy degree. Except for hospital and extra-mural projects, all the teaching takes place on the Bloomsbury campus.

London (SOAS) Single subject degrees include compulsory and optional units, with two-thirds of the total units studied in the chosen subject and the remaining units or 'floaters' from a complementary course offered at SOAS or another college of the University. In addition, two-subject degrees give great flexibility in the choice of units, enabling students to personalise their degrees to match their interests.

London (UCL) Subjects are organised in Faculties: Arts and Humanities, Social and Historical Sciences (with a flexible course unit system), Fine Art (the Slade School), Law, Built Environment (the Bartlett), Engineering Sciences, Mathematical and Physical Sciences and Life Sciences. In addition, there is the School of Medicine. The School of Slavonic and East European Studies also offers degrees which focus on developing a high level of proficiency in speaking, writing and understanding the chosen language.

London LSE The School offers courses not only in Economics and Political Science but also in a wide range of other Social Science subjects taught in 19 Departments. Programmes are offered as Single Honours, Joint Honours or major/minor courses. All undergraduates study a compulsory course in

Year 1 called 'Understanding the causes of things' (LSE 100) which aims to actively challenge them to analyse questions of current public concern and to develop their critical skills.

London Met Single and Joint Honours courses are made up of compulsory and optional modules allowing students some flexibility to follow their particular interests. Courses are offered in Accountancy and Business, Art and Architecture, Arts, Humanities and Languages, Computing, Economics and Finance, Education, Health and Human Sciences and Law.

London NCH NCH offers degrees in BSc Economics, BA English, BA History, Law LLB or BA Philosophy. In addition to studying towards a University of London degree, all students study a contextual subject chosen from one of the other degree subjects alongside four core courses; Logic and Critical Thinking, Science Literacy, Applied Ethics and Professional Skills. To reflect this further study, students are awarded the Diploma of NCH. The College is supported by a stellar professoriate who lecture at the College at times throughout the year. Weekly teaching is by one, one hour, one to one tutorial, one small group tutorial and four participative lectures in the degree subject and seminars and lectures in the Diploma subjects. All students typically receive 12–13 contact hours a week. Scholarships are offered.

London South Bank Subject areas cover Arts and Human Sciences including Law and Psychology, Business, Computing and Information Management, Engineering, Science and the Built Environment and Health and Social Care. All courses have flexible modes of study and many vocational courses offer sandwich placements.

Loughborough Academic programmes cover Art and Design, Business, Chemistry, Computer Science, Economics, Engineering, Mathematics, Politics and International Relations, Humanities, Sciences, Social Science and Sport. Degree programmes combine compulsory and optional modules and some transfers between courses are possible. Additional language study is possible in French, German or Spanish (including beginners' courses) for students on most courses. Sandwich degree courses with a year's paid work experience in industry result in high graduate employment. World-class sporting facilities and an unrivalled reputation in sporting success attract applicants at junior international level and above.

Manchester The University offers Single and Joint Honours courses which are divided into course units, some of which are compulsory and others optional, and some are taken from a choice of subjects offered by other Schools and Faculties. A comprehensive Combined Studies degree enables students to choose course units from Arts, Humanities, Social Sciences and Sciences, and this provides the flexibility for students to alter the emphasis of their studies from year to year. Degree programmes are offered in the Faculties of Engineering and Physical Sciences, Humanities, Life Sciences and Medical and Human Sciences.

Manchester Met Degree programmes are offered in the Faculties of Art and Design, Community Studies and Education, Food, Clothing and Hospitality Management, Humanities, Law and Social Science, Science and Engineering and the Manchester Metropolitan Business School. A large number of courses involve industrial and commercial placements. It is also possible to take Combined Honours degrees selecting a combination of two or three subjects. Many programmes have a modular structure with compulsory and optional core modules.

Middlesex Single and Joint Honours courses are offered on a modular basis, most programmes having an optional work placement. Courses cover Art and Design, Arts subjects, Biological and Health Sciences, Business and Management, Computing and IT, Dance, Drama and Music, Social Sciences and Teaching and Education.

Newcastle Degree programmes are available in the Faculties of Arts, Biological Sciences, Business and Law, Engineering, Medical Sciences, Physical Sciences and Social Sciences. Single, Joint and Combined Honours programmes are offered, in some cases providing students with the opportunity either to defer their choice of final degree or to transfer to other subjects at a later stage. In the Combined Studies BA and BSc courses it is possible to combine the study of up to three different subjects.

Newport The University consists of seven Schools – Art and Design, Humanities, Business, Computing and Engineering, Social Studies, Education and the Centre for Community and Lifelong Learning. Courses include Single and Joint Honours and major/minor studies; they vary in structure but many are based on a modular system.

Northampton Courses are offered in seven schools: Applied Sciences (Computing, Mechanical and Electrical/Electronic Engineering), Business, Education, Health, Social Sciences, Arts (including Fine Art and Design) and Land-based subjects at Moulton College. Courses are offered as Single, Combined and Joint Honours programmes.

Northumbria A wide range of courses is offered with an emphasis on vocational studies, including Art and Design, Arts subjects, Built Environment, Business and Financial Management, Computing, Education and Sport, Engineering, Health and Social Care, Humanities, Languages, Law, Mathematics, Nursing and Midwifery, Psychology and Sciences. Single and Joint Honours courses are offered, and a Combined Honours course allows a choice of up to three subjects.

Nottingham Single and Joint Honours courses are available, with some sandwich courses. Programmes are modular with compulsory and optional modules, the latter giving some flexibility in the selection of topics from outside the chosen subject field. Degree programmes are offered in the Faculties of Arts, Business, Engineering, Law, Medicine and Health Sciences, Science and Social Sciences.

Nottingham Trent Degree programmes are offered in a range of subjects covering Animal, Rural and Environmental Sciences, Architecture, Arts and Humanities, Art and Design, Business, Education, Law, Sciences and Technology and Social Sciences. Many courses are vocational with industrial and commercial placements and some students are also able to spend a semester (half an academic year) studying at a partner university in Europe, the USA or Australia.

Open University Degree and diploma courses are offered in the following subject areas: Arts and Humanities, Business and Management, Childhood and Youth, Computing and ICT, Education, Engineering and Technology, Environmental Development and International Studies, Health and Social Care, Languages, Law, Mathematics and Statistics, Psychology, Science and Social Sciences. Students study at home and are sent learning materials by the OU, maintaining contact with their tutors by email, post and telephone.

Oxford Candidates apply to a college and for a Single or Joint Honours programme. Courses are offered with a core element plus a variety of options. Weekly contact with a college tutor assists students to tailor their courses to suit personal interests. Arts students are examined twice, once in the first year (Preliminary examinations) and at the end of the course (Final Honours School). Science students are similarly examined although in some subjects examinations also take place in the second year.

Oxford Brookes Single Honours courses are offered with modules chosen from a field of study or, alternatively, Combined Honours courses in which two subjects are chosen. These subjects may be in related or unrelated subjects. There is also a Combined Studies degree in which students 'build' their own degree by taking approved modules from a range of the subjects offered by the University.

Plymouth A broad portfolio of degree courses is available including Medicine at the Peninsula Schools of Medicine and Dentistry. Other courses cover Agriculture, Art and Design, Biological and Physical Sciences, Built Environment, Business and Financial Management, Computing, Drama, Education, Engineering, Health and Social Sciences, Humanities, Languages, Law, Marine Studies, Mathematics and Sport Studies. Single Honours courses are offered, with many vocational programmes offering work placements.

Portsmouth The University of Portsmouth is a leading modern university with a strong reputation for teaching and research. Many of the academics are international leaders in their fields and the students can learn from experts who are pushing forward the boundaries of knowledge. The University has excellent links with industry and a strong record of student employability. The University recruitment agency, Purple Door Careers and Recruitment, offers a wide range of careers resources, skills workshops, careers guidance, and employer events to support students and graduates in gaining graduate employment. Their experienced recruitment consultants work in collaboration with local and national businesses, charities, and organisations to source graduate opportunities and assist graduates at every step of the recruitment process. A new Dental Academy was opened in 2010. This is a collaborative partnership between the University of Portsmouth and King's College London Dental Institute; the Dental

Academy is the largest dental academic centre in the UK and is the first of its kind in the country offering integrated team-based training programmes for dentists and dental care professionals. The Faculties of Creative and Cultural Industries, Humanities and Social Sciences, Science, Technology and the Portsmouth Business School offer Single and Joint Honours courses. Sandwich programmes are also available in many subjects and there is also an opportunity for all students to learn a foreign language. Many courses are planned on a modular basis which allows students to defer specialisation until after their first year.

Queen's Belfast The academic year is divided into two semesters of 15 weeks each (12 teaching weeks and three examination weeks), with degree courses (pathways) normally taken over three years of full-time study. Six modules are taken each year (three in each semester) and, in theory, a degree can involve any combination of six Level 1 modules. Single, Joint and Combined Honours courses are offered and, in addition, major/minor combinations; some courses include sandwich placements. Courses cover Agriculture and Food Science, Education, Engineering, Humanities and Social Sciences, Management and Economics, Law and Medicine and Health Sciences.

Reading Faculties of Arts and Humanities and Economics and Social Sciences provide flexible arrangements for students. A teaching system operates in Year 1 in which students can take modules in their chosen subject and in two or three other subjects. At the end of the first year they may transfer from Single Honours to Joint Honours courses or change to another subject. Reading has close links with business and industry through collaborative research projects, the creation of spin-out companies and graduate placement schemes.

Richmond (Am Int Univ) The University runs British and American courses. American courses are accredited by the Middle States Commission on Higher Education, an agency recognised by the US Department of Education. Courses are also approved by the Open University and can lead to Open University Validated Awards.

Robert Gordon The University offers a wide range of vocational courses including Accountancy and Business, Architecture, Art and Design, Computer Science, Engineering, Law, Nursing, Occupational Therapy, Pharmacy, Physiotherapy, Radiography, Sciences, Social Sciences and Sports Science. Many courses offer work placements and there are some opportunities to study abroad in Europe, Canada and the USA.

Roehampton The University manages its academic programmes in eight Schools – Arts and Business, Social Sciences and Computing, Education Studies, English and Modern Languages, Humanities and Cultural Studies, Initial Teacher Education, Sports Science and Psychological and Therapeutic Studies. All programmes operate within a modular and semester-based structure.

St Andrews A very wide range of subjects is offered across the Faculties of Arts, Divinity, Medicine and Science. A flexible programme is offered in the first two years when students take several subjects. The decision of Honours degree subject is made at the end of Year 2 when students choose between Single or Joint Honours degrees for the next two years. A broadly-based General degree programme is also offered lasting three years. After two years of a General degree programme students may transfer onto a named Honours degree programme if they meet the requirements of the department(s).

Salford The University offers BA, BSc and BEng degrees with teaching methods depending on the degree (it is equally likely to accept students with BTECs and Access qualifications as well as those with A-levels). There is a wide range of professionally accredited programmes many involving work placements. All undergraduates may study a foreign language. Subjects include Accountancy and Business, Art and Design, Computer Science, Drama, Engineering, Humanities, Journalism, Leisure and Tourism, Languages, Music, Nursing, Physiotherapy, Psychology, Sciences, Social Sciences and Sport Science.

Sheffield The teaching year consists of two semesters (two periods of 15 weeks). Courses are fully modular, with the exceptions of Dentistry and Medicine. Students register for a named degree course which has a number of core modules, some optional modules chosen from a prescribed range of topics and some unrestricted modules chosen from any at the University. Programmes offered include Accounting and Business, Arts and Humanities, Computer Science, Engineering and Materials Science, Languages, Law, Nursing, Psychology, Sciences, Social Sciences and Town and Country Planning.

Sheffield Hallam A large number of vocational courses are offered in addition to those in Arts, Humanities and Social Sciences. The University is the largest provider of sandwich courses in the UK with most courses offering work placements, usually between the second and third years. Most students are able to study an additional language from French, German, Italian, Spanish and Japanese.

Southampton A wide range of courses is offered in the Faculties of Law, Arts and Social Sciences, Engineering, Science and Mathematics and Medicine, Health and Life Sciences. Programmes are generally for three years. All students have the chance to study a language as part of their degree and there are many opportunities for students to study abroad or on Erasmus-Socrates exchange programmes whether or not they are studying modern languages.

Southampton Solent Courses are offered in the Faculties of Technology, Media, Arts and Society and the Southampton Business School. Subjects cover Art and Design, Business and Finance including Accountancy, Marketing and Personnel, Computing, Construction, Engineering and Technology, the Environment, Human and Social Sciences and Law, Leisure, Sport and Tourism, Maritime Studies and Media, Film and Journalism.

Staffordshire The Stafford campus focuses on courses in Computing, Engineering, Technology and Health Studies whilst at Stoke programmes are offered in Art and Design, Law, Business, Humanities, Social Sciences and Science subjects. Single and Joint Honours are available, some of which are for four years and include a work placement year. Part-time courses are also offered.

Stirling A flexible system operates in which students can delay their final degree choice until midway through the course. The University year is divided into two 15-week semesters, from September to December and February to May with a reading/study block and exams at the end of each semester. Innovative February entry is possible to some degree programmes. There are 250 degree combinations with the opportunity to study a range of disciplines in the first two years. In addition to Single and Combined Honours degrees, there is a General degree which allows for greater breadth of choice. Subjects range across the Arts, Social Sciences and Sciences.

Strathclyde A credit-based modular system operates with a good degree of flexibility in course choices. The University offers many vocational courses in the Faculties of Engineering and Science and in the Strathclyde Business School. There are also degree programmes in Arts subjects, Education, Law and the Social Sciences.

Sunderland There are five Schools of study: Arts, Media and Culture, Business, Computer Science and Technology. Single, Joint Honours and sandwich courses are offered, with strong links with industry. A modular programme provides maximum flexibility in choosing appropriate subjects. Some placements are possible in Canada, USA, Australia, New Zealand, India and Europe. There is a large number of mature and local students.

Surrey Degree programmes are offered in the Arts, Biomedical and Molecular Sciences, Electronics and Physical Sciences, Engineering, Health and Medical Sciences, Human Sciences and Management. Some 80% of students spend a professional training year as part of their course and in some cases there are placements abroad. There is also a part-time BSc degree in Professional Development through work-based learning.

Sussex Teaching is structured around five Schools of study, the Brighton and Sussex Medical School and the Science and Technology Policy Research Unit. Courses cover a wide range of subjects in Humanities, Life Sciences, Science and Technology, Social Sciences and Cultural Studies. Students are registered in a School depending on the degree taken. The flexible structure allows students to interrupt their degree programme to take a year out.

Swansea Courses are offered in Arts and Social Sciences, Business, Economics and Law, Engineering, Languages, Medicine and Health Sciences and Science. Degree courses are modular with the opportunity to take some subjects outside the chosen degree course. Part-time degrees are available and study abroad arrangements are possible in several subject areas.

Swansea Met The University consists of three main faculties. The faculty of Applied Design and Engineering offers a broad spectrum of courses from Automotive Engineering to Multimedia. The Faculty of Art and Design established 150 years ago is a major centre for art and crafts in Wales. The Faculty of Humanities comprises Schools of Business, Education, Health Sciences, Humanities, the Performing Arts, Leisure, Tourism and Recreation.

Teesside Single and Combined Honours degrees are offered with the major subject occupying two thirds of the course and the minor option one third. There is a wide choice of vocational courses, many with sandwich arrangements in industry, commerce and the professions. Courses are offered in the Arts, Business, Engineering, Law, Media, Social Sciences and Sport with large Schools of Health and Social Care and Computing and Mathematics. There is a high mature student intake.

Trinity Saint David Courses are offered in the Humanities, Business and Management, Education, Art, Design, the Performing Arts, and the Social Sciences.

UCLan The University has five Faculties (Cultural, Legal, Social Studies, Health, Science). Subjects are taught in a series of modules which gives maximum flexibility in the final choice of degree course. Students may specialise or keep their options open with a choice of Single Honours, Joint or Combined Honours, or they can choose three subjects in Year 1 and reduce to two in the second and third years. Some sandwich courses are offered.

UEA There are 24 Schools of study spanning the Arts, Humanities, Biological Sciences, Business, Computing Sciences, Social Sciences, Health Professions, Mathematics, World Art Studies and Meteorology. Many Schools are interdisciplinary or multidisciplinary, allowing students to combine a specialist study with complementary subjects and optional units. Some courses include study abroad in Europe, North America and Australasia. There is also the University Language Programme offering all undergraduate students 'non-credit' language courses with a choice from nine modern languages and British Sign Language.

UEL The University offers Single Honours and Combined Honours programmes. Courses provide a flexibility of choice and are based on a modular structure with compulsory and optional course units. Courses include Architecture, Art and Design, Business, Computing, Engineering, Health Sciences, Humanities, Law, Media, Social Sciences, Sciences and Sport. A very large number of extended degrees are also available for applicants who do not have the normal university entrance requirements.

Ulster The Faculties of Arts, Business and Management, Engineering and Built Environment, Life and Health Sciences and Social Sciences offer a wide range of courses. There are various styles of learning supported by formal lectures and many courses include periods of work placement.

Warwick Courses are offered by Departments in the Faculty of Arts, Science and Social Studies, the Warwick Business School, the Warwick Institute of Education and the Warwick Medical School. Students may choose single subject degrees or combine several subjects in a joint degree. Options offered in each course provide flexibility in the choice of subjects although courses are not fully modularised. Many degrees offer the opportunity to study abroad and work placements on some science courses.

West London Bias towards vocational studies. Subjects offered cover Business, Management and Law, Tourism, Hospitality and Leisure, Music, Media and Creative Technologies and Health and Human Sciences. Credit-rated Single and Joint Honours courses are offered, many with year-long work placements between Years 2 and 3. There are some study-abroad arrangements in Europe, Canada and the USA and there is a large mature student intake.

West Scotland The University provides a distinctive educational experience through a range of vocationally related courses, supported by strong applied research and knowledge transfer activities. Courses are offered in the Business School and the School of Computing, Education, Engineering and Science, Health, Nursing and Midwifery, Media, Language and Music.

Westminster Courses include Architecture and the Built Environment, Biosciences, Business Management, Complementary Therapies, Computer Sciences, Electronics, English and Linguistics, Languages, Law, Media and Arts and Design and Psychology and Social Sciences. Undergraduate courses are modular and taught over two semesters. The University has a broad network of partnerships within the EU which enables students to include a period of study abroad as part of their degree.

Be a name...

A lifetime experience...

Great Courses... that develop your professional and personal skills

Small campuses in Carmarthen and Lampeter... with all you need in one place

Friendly atmosphere... where you won't be lost in a crowd

Scholarships available... to help you make ends meet

Fantastic location... with excellent facilities, and spectacular countryside and coastline

Excellent student life... with an active Students' Union that gets you involved in university life

A commitment to sustainability... within the curriculum and on the campus

Great Courses

The University offers a range of courses – from those aiming for specific vocations, for example Archaeology or Teaching, to programmes leading to a range of suitable employment opportunities e.g. English, Classics and History, which combine academic knowledge with a range of the transferable skills that employers seeks.

//Life's going well at the University. The lectures are good and the social activities are fun. I love living on the campus and having some independence.//

Ashley Joseph
BA Physical Education

Our campuses

Our campuses in Carmarthen and Lampeter are excellent places to live and study. Both sites are based around the original nineteenth century college buildings and comprise beautiful landscaped grounds with modern and well-equipped buildings. Each campus has accommodation, learning resources, a lively Students' Union, catering and sports facilities on site so that there is no need for a long daily commute, saving you both time and money.

PRIFYSGOL CYMRU
Y Drindod Dewi Sant

UNIVERSITY OF WALES
Trinity Saint David

not a number

A friendly atmosphere

Our campuses and location foster a close-knit and friendly atmosphere and you will get to know other students from other courses and year groups. The range of clubs and societies - sports and others - encourages this and means that there is plenty to do outside of lectures and your academic work.

Fantastic location

Our campuses and excellent links with the local community mean that students quickly settle in and make friends, both within the University and outside. Both our campuses are surrounded by green fields and there are a host of opportunities for outdoor recreation such as hill walking, mountain biking, canoeing, coasteering, and surfing as well as visits to sites of historical and cultural interest. The additional advantages of living in West Wales is that the cost of living is much lower than in many urban areas, which means that your student loan may go further, while crime rates are amongst some of the lowest in the UK, allowing you a greater sense of personal freedom.

Scholarships available

The University has a number of scholarships and bursaries available to provide extra financial support for students.

Excellent student life

The Students' Union works across both campuses to enhance your social, cultural and academic experience.

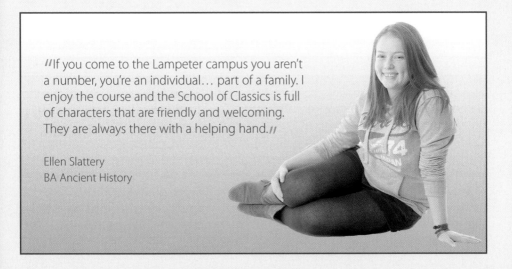

//If you come to the Lampeter campus you aren't a number, you're an individual... part of a family. I enjoy the course and the School of Classics is full of characters that are friendly and welcoming. They are always there with a helping hand.//

Ellen Slattery
BA Ancient History

Winchester Single and two-subject courses are offered consisting of either one subject, or two subjects studied equally (a Joint Honours degree) or a 75%–25% split by way of a main and subsidiary subject Honours degree. Courses are offered in American Studies, Archaeology, Business, Dance, Drama and Performance, Education, English and Creative Writing, Film Studies, History, Journalism and Media Studies, Psychology, Sport Science, Theology and Tourism.

Wolverhampton A large number of specialist and Joint Honours degrees are offered and many have work placements at home or abroad. Except for courses linked to specific professional requirements, programmes are modular providing flexibility of choice. Courses include Art and Design, Humanities, Business Studies, Computer Science, Education, Engineering, Environmental Studies, Health Studies, Law, Media, Nursing, Sciences and Social Studies.

Worcester The courses are grouped into six institutes: Health and Society, Humanities and Creative Arts, Science and the Environment, Sport and Exercise Science, the Worcester Business School and Education.

York Thirty departments and centres cover a range of subjects in the arts, social sciences, technology and medicine. The 'Languages for All' programme enables any student to take a course in any one of 14 languages, in addition to which there are several opportunities to build a period abroad into a degree course. Courses offered include Archaeology, Arts subjects, Computer Science, Economics, Education, Electronics, Health Sciences, Languages, Management, Medicine, Music, Psychology, Sciences and Social Sciences.

York St John The Faculties of Education and Theology, Business and Communication, Health and Life Sciences and Art offer a range of specialist degrees and Joint Honours courses are offered in Business, Management, Languages and Linguistics, Peace Studies, Health Studies, Counselling, Design, Education, Information Technology, Occupational Therapy, Physiotherapy, Psychology, Sport and Theology.

COLLEGES AND THEIR COURSES

In addition to the large numbers of universities offering degree courses, there are over 100 colleges admitting several thousands of students, each on full degree courses. These include University Colleges, University Centres, Colleges of Further and Higher Education and specialist colleges of Agriculture and Horticulture, Art, Drama and Music: see the directory of institutions at the back of the book (**Chapter 10**). Larger institutions will offer a range of Single subject, Joint and Combined Honours degree courses leading to BA, BSc and BEd degrees whilst the smaller colleges may only offer one or two degree programmes. A large number, however, also provide full- or part-time Foundation degrees which can lead to Honours degree courses. These colleges are listed in the subject tables. The next chapter **University Admissions** outlines how universities select applicants for their courses and it provides information for each university relating to key points of their admissions policies.

4

UNIVERSITY ADMISSIONS

ADMISSIONS POLICIES

Although the UCAS application process is standard for all undergraduate Honours degree courses (see **Chapter 5**) the admissions policies adopted by individual departments in universities and colleges often differ, depending on the popularity of the course and the quality of applicants. There are, however, common areas of agreement concerning applications, in particular the acceptance of the different qualifying examinations being offered. Apart from a diverse range of international qualifications, A-level grades, the International Baccalaureate (IB) and BTEC have been the common currency of selection linked with the UCAS Tariff points system for many years, although some very popular universities and courses do not make points offers, preferring to set their entry standards in the grades awarded in specific subjects.

Most universities are still making decisions on the timing and introduction of the new A* grades, although this year an A* grade has been stipulated in over 6000 offers. Most, if not all, institutions accept recent qualifications such as the Advanced Diplomas, the Extended Project Qualification and the Cambridge Pre-U Diploma although there may be some additional requirements depending on the degrees applied for when specified subjects may be required. A-levels in general studies and critical thinking are nearly always taken into account when selecting applicants although they rarely form part of an offer. Key Skills may also be noted by selectors and for some courses they could be worth up to 20 Tariff points. BTEC is also acceptable with two passes for some Foundation courses to full distinction for some competitive degree programmes. However, it should also be noted that a number of universities and degree courses also have general entry requirements which include GCSE grade C or above in English and mathematics.

Interview policies vary considerably and, in most cases, offers will simply be based on the information on the UCAS application with the personal statement being highly important for many courses. Candidates receiving offers will be invited to visit their universities. Interviews are usual for Medicine, Dentistry, Veterinary Science, Art, Social Work and for Teaching courses and inevitable for Dance, Drama and Music (see **Chapter 6**). Mature students (defined as those over 21 on entry) are often interviewed. Normal published offers may not apply to mature students. In all universities certain courses require Criminal Records Bureau (CRB) checks or medical examinations; students should check these requirements before applying for courses.

Deferred entry is acceptable in almost all cases although many universities ask that the intention to take a Gap Year be included on the application if firm arrangements have been made. It is worth noting, however, that there may well be fewer places available on a subsequent course for students wanting to defer.

Several universities have advised that if a student fails to achieve the grades required for an offer, they may still be awarded a place; however they may receive a changed offer for an alternative course. Many universities are also prepared to provide feedback on the results of unsuccessful applications.

In addition, all universities have a number of schemes in place to enable admissions tutors to identify and make offers to applicants who, for example, may have had their education affected by circumstances outside their control. A major initiative is Widening Participation in which various schemes can assist school and college students in getting into university. These programmes focus on specific groups of students and communities including:

- students from low participation areas
- low-performing schools and colleges or those without a strong history of progression to higher education
- students with disabilities

- people living in deprived geographical areas, including deprived rural areas
- students from black or ethnic minority backgrounds
- students from the lower socio-economic groups 4–8 including mature learners
- students requiring financial assistance or who are disadvantaged in various ways
- families with little or no experience of higher education
- students from homes with low household incomes
- students returning to study after a period of time spent away
- students from state schools.

Students who feel that they might qualify for Widening Participation programmes should find out from their school or college about the schemes offered by universities including their local university. In addition to the general information above, universities have emphasised certain aspects of their selection procedures and these are listed below. Even so, applicants are strongly advised to check prospectuses and websites for up-to-date information on admissions and, in particular, any entrance test to be taken (see also **Chapter 6**).

UNIVERSITIES' ADMISSIONS INFORMATION

The following information provides a selection of relevant aspects of universities' admissions policies and practice. Where institutions have provided the information, details of courses that were not available through Clearing in 2011 have been provided as well as details of the subjects attracting the highest number of applicants in the 2011 application cycle.

Information on alternative qualifications to A-levels such as the Cambridge Pre-U Diploma, the Advanced Diploma, BTEC qualifications, Key Skills and Access courses is not always published in prospectuses, it is usually available on universities' websites. While it can be assumed that applicants will be considered and accepted with these alternative qualifications, depending on the requirements for individual degree programmes, it is important to check with university admissions staff **before** you make your application that your qualifications will meet their requirements. Applicants whose first language is not English should refer to **Chapter 9** for details of the English Language entry requirements.

Applicants for places at popular universities of for popular courses cannot assume that they will receive an offer even if their predicted grades are the same or higher than a stated standard offer.

Aberdeen Selectors look for evidence of subject knowledge and understanding, commitment, motivation and responsibility, and the ability to cope with a university education.

Abertay Dundee Only applicants for courses in Nursing, Ethical Hacking and Computer Arts are interviewed. *Most popular subjects 2011* Nursing, Psychology, Sport and Exercise Science, Forensic Science, Criminological Studies, Food Nutrition and Health and Law.

Aberystwyth Offers are made centrally except for the following Departments: Psychology, Geography and Earth Sciences, Biological Sciences, Art, Welsh, Information Studies. Offers are made on the basis of academic criteria determined by the departments concerned. Personal statements and references are scrutinised by experienced staff in the central office and in departments. Following unprecedented recruitment of very well qualified students in 2011, they have reviewed and raised the entry requirements for most of their study schemes. The University states that it is important that applications are made by the initial closing date of 15 January. They cannot guarantee to consider late applications. The number of applicants considerably exceeds the number of places for Drama and Theatre Studies courses. Offers will be made on the basis of the application form and interviews are required for some subjects. Decisions are made within four weeks of receiving the application and all those receiving an offer will be invited to visit the University. Applicants are advised not to depend on Clearing as there is very limited flexibility in August. None of the other schemes interview candidates unless there are special reasons for doing so – eg the candidate has been away from study for a long time, is not offering standard qualifications, the candidate requests an interview. *Clearing 2011* No courses entered Clearing. *Most popular subjects 2011* Accounting and Finance, Biological Sciences, Business and Management, Computer Science, Creative Writing, Drama/Film/TV/Performance Studies, Economics, English, Geography, History, International Politics, Law, Marketing.

Anglia Ruskin The University interviews all shortlisted applicants for Art and Design, Education, Nursing, Social Work, and Midwifery. Some applicants are interviewed for Business. Maths and English testing is also used for some Education (ITT), Nursing, Midwifery and Social Work courses. Entry requirements may change for 2013 entry. Applicants should visit the website regularly to view any changes to entry requirements, and for further information regarding the courses and applications procedures. The University is happy to give advice and guidance about the admissions process.

Arts London In addition to formally qualified applicants, the University welcomes applications from candidates without formal qualifications who can demonstrate equivalent skills, knowledge and ability gained from work or life experience.

Aston There are no entrance tests in the selection process and offers are not normally made simply on the basis of UCAS points. Interviews are only used in special cases, for example, mature students, or those with non-standard entry qualifications. Most courses include a one-year placement as part of the degree; this is normally paid, and also has a reduced tuition fee and placement bursary. Aston is one of only four UK universities with more than 50% of students taking sandwich courses or year-abroad programmes. Applications from high-achieving students taking Applied A-levels are welcomed and all degree programmes will consider a single award Applied A-level in place of a third A-level subject. For all degree programmes, except those in the School of Health and Life Sciences, a relevant Applied A-level double award plus one relevant A-level will normally be accepted. BTEC awards are acceptable and a mix of BTEC and A-levels welcomed. High-achieving Level 3 Diploma students in relevant subjects will be considered. Key Skills will be taken into account but will not be included in offers; Access programmes are accepted.

Bangor Applications welcomed from students taking validated Access courses and 14–19 Diplomas in specified subjects. *Most popular subjects 2011* Nursing, Psychology.

Bath Some departments interview promising applicants; those not receiving an offer can obtain feedback on the reasons for their rejection. Students are encouraged to take the Extended Project and to provide details on their personal statement. Students taking the Advanced Diploma should check the requirements of individual degree courses. Applicants who are re-sitting A-levels will not be accepted on Economics and Business Management Courses.

Bath Spa All eligible candidates are interviewed for the following courses: Art and Design, Broadcast Media, Creative Media Practice, Music and Performing Arts, Publishing. All applicants will be invited to visit the University after receiving an offer. Gap Years are acceptable.

Birmingham Courses are academic and 75% of the personal statement should relate to the proposed course of study. General studies A-level is not accepted for most degree courses. Some subjects of the Advanced Diploma are acceptable for some courses, with an A-level as the ASL in all cases. The Extended Project will not be included in the University's offers but it welcomes applicants taking this qualification and it may make a difference to a borderline applicant. Some applicants are interviewed, for example for Medicine, Dentistry and for Social Work. The University uses LNAT (see **Chapter 6**) as its admissions test for Law applicants. Gap Years are acceptable and should be mentioned on the UCAS application or as soon as arrangements have been made. Decisions are devolved to departments for Chemistry, Computer Science, Dentistry, Drama, Education Programmes, Law, Medicine, Music, Nursing, Physics, Physiotherapy, Psychology and Social Work. *Clearing 2011* No courses entered Clearing. *Most popular subjects 2011* Accounting and Finance, Business Management, Medicine, Nursing, Psychology and Law.

Birmingham City Admissions are administered centrally through the Admissions Unit in the Academic Registry. Some applicants will be called to interview and others invited to the Department before an offer is made. If the required grades of an offer are not achieved it may still be possible to be accepted on to a course. Deferred entry is acceptable. *Most popular subjects 2011* Adult Nursing, Law, Midwifery, Music, Primary Education Psychology.

Bolton Applicants are advised to apply through UCAS as early as possible. The University welcomes the AL and AS general studies and also Key Skills at Level 3. If admissions staff consider that the course applied for is not suitable then an offer for an alternative course may be made.

Bournemouth The personal statement is regarded as an important aspect of the application process. Some subject areas may require applicants to attend for interview. Deferred entry is acceptable.

Bradford It is not anticipated that the A* grade will be used in any offers. Candidates will not be accepted on to any degree course purely on the basis of AS-level results (including the double award) although two AS-levels or an AS double award may be accepted instead of a non-essential A-level. Low offers may be made to applicants showing considerable promise in academic or in other areas. Offers are normally based on the UCAS Tariff. The University accepts a range of alternative qualifications and takes a very positive view on the value of the new Advanced Diploma. These qualifications will be considered on a course-by-course basis.

Brighton The University welcomes applications from students with qualifications and experience other than traditional A-levels. The Advanced Diploma, Access courses and BTEC are acceptable alternative qualifications. *Clearing 2011* No courses entered Clearing. *Most popular subject 2011* Medicine.

Brighton and Sussex (MS) The School welcomes candidates offering A*, or predicted to achieve A*, and will account for this level of achievement when the school shortlists for interview. The same policy applies to applicants offering the Extended Project.

Bristol A* grades may be included in the offers for some applicants depending on the application, the subject and the competition for places; if an A* grade is required this will be made clear in the relevant admissions statement and prospectus entry. Students choosing to take the Extended Project may receive two offers, one of which includes the Extended Project, for example, AAA, or AAB plus the Extended Project. Requirements for the Advanced Diploma are detailed in each prospectus entry. Up to two Applied A-levels may be considered with an A-level. Some admissions tutors may take unit grade information into account when making selection decisions. However, as usual, admissions tutors will make decisions within the context of the whole application, and will not disadvantage applicants who are unable to provide unit grade information. If unit grades are to be taken into account, this will be clearly specified in the relevant admissions statement. It is possible that some departments may also wish to specify unit grade achievement in the terms of offers. If so, this information will be published in the relevant prospectus entry and in the admissions statement. In addition, in some marginal cases unit grade information will continue to be used to inform decisions about applicants who have missed the terms of their offers at Confirmation. Deferred entry is acceptable but intention to defer should be indicated in the personal statement, giving information about your plans. However, in some cases the number of places available might be limited and higher offers may be made. An interview is required for an offer for Medicine, Dentistry, Veterinary Science, Drama, Engineering Design and Veterinary Nursing, but not all applicants are interviewed. LNAT (see **Chapter 6**) is used for admission to the Law programmes. Applicants who are re-sitting A-levels or who are re-applying will not be given offers for Medicine, Dentistry or Law. Advice to applicants can be found on www.bristol.ac.uk/study. All programmes at Bristol are extremely competitive with an average of over 10 applicants per place. *Clearing 2011* Bristol does not go into Clearing. *Most popular subjects 2011* English, Geography, History, Law, Mathematics, Medicine, Psychology, Veterinary Science.

Bristol UWE Typical offers are made for each degree programme although these offers may vary between applicants since selection is based on individual merit. Students applying for courses 'subject to approval' or 'subject to validation' will be kept informed of the latest developments. Many offers will be made in terms of Tariff points.

Brunel All applicants are interviewed for Design, Electrical Engineering, Social Work and Education courses. All offers for degree courses are for three A-levels and either one AS-level or the Extended Project. If an applicant has not been able to take a fourth subject at AS-level, or complete a Project, this should be indicated in the application; offers will then be made for three A-levels (or equivalent). For some courses, students who have re-sat A-levels and/or re-applied for the course will be given a higher offer then the standard entry requirements. The University accepts relevant Advanced Diplomas (see www.brunel.ac.uk).

Buckingham Candidates apply through UCAS in the normal way or directly with a paper application obtainable from the University. Applicants may be invited for interview.

Bucks New It may be possible to transfer to the University from another university under the credit accumulation and transfer scheme (CATS), and to gain exemptions from part of the course if the student has CATS credit points from their relevant previous study. Transfer from full-time to part-time study is possible. BTEC qualifications are acceptable. Admissions tests will be used for entry to Nursing and Social Work courses.

Cambridge Currently, the standard offer is A*AA but the subject in which the A* is to be achieved is unlikely to be specified. All Colleges modify offers to take account of individual circumstances, for example, lower offers may be made to students applying through the Cambridge Special Access Scheme – see the University's website. Self-discipline, motivation and commitment are required together with the ability to think critically and independently, plus passion or, at the very least, real enthusiasm for the chosen course. If examination predictions are good then the chance of admission may be better than one in five. Applicants are encouraged to take the Extended Project although it will not be a requirement of any offer. Although AS and AL critical thinking and general studies are acceptable as a fourth AS or A-level subject, neither is considered acceptable as a third A-level. For many courses admissions tests are used – and written work may be required – so it is very important to check the university website and prospectus well before completing the application to find out exactly what is needed for entry. See **Chapter 6**, and also www.cam.ac.uk/admissions/undergraduate/tests.

Canterbury Christ Church The personal statement and school references are regarded as highly important. Applicants for Teaching and Health-related courses must show evidence on their application of relevant experience. If they do not, they will be rejected without interview. Other subjects, including Geography, History and Music, also interview candidates. *Most popular subjects 2011* Child Nursing, Midwifery, Primary Education, Psychology.

Cardiff Applicants are required to take only three A-levels for degree courses. Deferred entry is acceptable. The 14–19 Diploma is an acceptable qualification for entry. Key Skills should be mentioned in an application but will not form part of an offer.

Chester Interviews and workshops are required for some courses to support applications. General studies at A-level is acceptable for entry to courses in addition to other A-levels.

Chichester Early application is advised for popular courses such as Dance, Physical Education, Primary Education and Teaching. Teaching applicants should have spent a minimum of two weeks observing/helping out in a state school within two years of applying. Significant experience is also required for applicants for Social Work courses. Applicants taking a Level 3 Diploma will be considered for entry to the relevant course. Dance, Music and Performing Arts applicants will be required to prepare a set piece in advance and to perform it in front of a group. Decisions on applications are normally made within two weeks, and, except for some courses where interviews are required (see **Chapter 6**) most decisions are made on the basis of the application form. Some applicants will be interviewed for Teacher Training, Physical Education, Social Work, Dance, Fine Art, Music, Musical Theatre, Drama, Performing Arts and Childhood Studies courses. Chichester uses more grade-based offers rather than UCAS Tariff points offers for entry. *Most popular subjects 2011* Primary Education, Sports Coaching and PE, History, Dance and Sport and Exercise Sciences.

City It is hoped that applicants will have taken four AS-level subjects in Year 13, one of which is a contrasting subject.

Coventry The University welcomes applications from those with significant work or life experience who do not necessarily meet the published academic requirements for the course. Applicants will be required to demonstrate evidence of motivation, potential and knowledge of the subject. Some candidates will be required to attend interviews depending on their course choice. Decisions are made centrally, with the exception of applications to courses funded by the NHS and the General Social Care Council where applications are handled by the Admissions Unit in the Faculty of Health and Life Sciences. Applications from international students (including EU) are handled by the International Office. The most popular programmes are those funded by the NHS, eg Paramedic Science, Social Work, Nursing, Occupational Therapy and Dietetics. The only courses interviewing candidates are Physiotherapy and Dietetics whilst literacy and numeracy tests are used for entry to Nursing, Occupational Therapy, Midwifery, Operating Department Practice and Paramedic Science.

Creative Arts Interviews and portfolios are required for all courses. There is no minimum age requirement for entry to undergraduate courses.

Cumbria Candidates without GCSE English, mathematics or science at grade C or above (which are required for some courses) take an equivalency test at the University. The new Diploma qualification is acceptable for some subjects and will be recognised as equivalent to 3.5 A-levels with a possible total Tariff score of 300 points. Key Skills at Level 3 may be allowed to contribute up to 20 UCAS Tariff points towards meeting the conditions of an offer.

De Montfort Selection criteria depend on the chosen course. Some courses require a personal interview and/or examination of portfolios.

Derby The Level 2 Diploma is regarded as equivalent to GCSEs and the Level 3 Diploma to A-levels. Students without formal qualifications can take an Access course or the Modular Foundation course to gain entry to degree programmes.

Dundee All applications are held until the January 15th deadline (except for Medicine and Dentistry: October 15th) before decisions are made. The published grades indicate the minimum which can be accepted at one sitting. The University considers applicants who are resitting although offers would be higher than the published grades. All offers are made through the Central Office or devolved to the Departments of Architecture, Community Learning and Development, Education, Dentistry, Medicine, Nursing or Social Work. *Clearing 2011* Subjects not entering Clearing in 2011 were Business, Computing, Dentistry, Engineering, Environment, Humanities, Law, Life Sciences, Mathematics, Medicine, Physics and Psychology.

Durham Since September 2010 a number of changes have been introduced to the Durham admissions policy.

(a) Successful applicants will be informed of the decision on their application before a college is allocated. See www.durham.ac.uk/undergraduate/apply/process

(b) Students applying for more than one type of course or institution may submit a substitute personal statement of the same length as the original personal statement on the UCAS form. See www.durham.ac.uk/undergraduate/apply/personalstatement

(c) Durham has reviewed their policy towards the A* grade at A-level. In brief an A* will be required for Mathematical Sciences but for no other programmes. See www.durham.ac.uk/undergraduate/apply/faqs/?/faqno=1985

(d) In addition the following factors are reviewed: A-level or equivalent grades, GCSE performance, the personal statement, the school/college reference, motivation for the chosen degree programme, independence of thought and working, skills derived from non-academic activities, eg sport, the arts, and voluntary and community work.

Admission decisions are made by Academic Departments. Durham University does not use interviews as a means of selection except in the following circumstances:

- where external bodies determine that interviewing is compulsory (applicants to Initial Teacher Training and Medicine)
- applicants to the Foundation Centre
- applicants who do not in their application show adequate evidence of recent and relevant knowledge or who have experienced a break in their study prior to application. This will be determined by academic departments on an individual basis having considered all the information provided in the application.

All candidates are interviewed for Medicine and Primary Education. The top five departments receiving most applications in 2011 (in actual numbers) were History, Business Accounting and Finance, English Studies, Modern Languages and Cultures and Economics. *Most popular subjects 2011* Economics, English Studies, History, Philosophy, PPE.

Edge Hill With the exception of courses in Journalism, Animation, Media (Film and TV), TV Production, Performing Arts, Social and Psychological Sciences, Teacher Training, Nursing and Midwifery, most decisions are made without an interview. Those applicants who receive offers are invited to visit the University. The new Advanced Diploma is accepted as equivalent to three A-levels.

Edinburgh Admission decisions are made by the University's five undergraduate admissions offices: The College of Humanities and Social Science, College of Science and Engineering, Medicine, Veterinary

Medicine, and Medical Sciences. Decisions on the majority of applications will be made after the UCAS deadline, once all applications have been received. All offers will be expressed in grades, not Tariff points. *Clearing 2011* No courses entered Clearing. *Most popular subjects 2011* Architecture, Biological Sciences, Business Studies, Economics, Education, Engineering, English Literature, History, Informatics, Law, Medicine, Veterinary Medicine.

Edinburgh Napier Offers are normally based on the UCAS Tariff system. The normal offers may not apply to candidates aged over 21, who should contact the admissions tutor for details. Interviews may be required for some courses.

Edinburgh Queen Margaret Applicants are interviewed for some courses including Physiotherapy and Speech Sciences.

Essex Candidates are required to have two full A-levels or equivalent - students re-sitting some subjects may get a higher offer. All departments accept general studies and critical thinking. Key Skills at Level 3 can be used as part of the points total providing they do not overlap with other qualifications (eg numeracy or A-level mathematics). Unit grades are not used as standard procedure. Additional aptitude tests are not used. Interviews may be required for some subjects. Admission decisions are made departmentally. *Clearing 2011* Biomedical Sciences, Biochemistry, Drama, Economics, English Language and Linguistics, Modern Languages and Politics did not enter Clearing. *Most popular subjects 2011* Acting, Accounting, Finance and Banking, Business Management and Nursing.

Exeter The University welcomes applications that offer a greater breadth of experience both academically and vocationally. Key indicators include predicted and achieved academic performance in Level 2 and 3 qualifications; candidates normally would be expected to take four AS-levels followed by three A-levels in Year 13. The personal statement should cover the reasons for your course choice and how the course relates to your current or previous studies and experience. It should also give evidence of your motivation to study at a higher level, details of work experience or positions of responsibility and what you have gained from these. The University supports the introduction of the new qualifications including the Advanced Diplomas, the Extended Project and the Cambridge Pre-U Diploma. Deferred applications are acceptable but the number of places for deferred applicants for popular courses can be limited and in some cases higher offers may be made. The subjects interviewing all candidates are Physics, Drama, Medical Imaging and Applied Psychology (Clinical). *Most popular subjects 2011* English, History and Economics.

Glamorgan Candidates applying for the Excellence Award must submit their applications by the 15 January deadline. Key Skills points can contribute to the overall Tariff point requirement. *Most popular subjects 2011* Nursing, Social Work, Fashion Design, Fashion Promotion, Police Sciences, Sports Science and Business Management.

Glasgow Normally all subjects apart from Dentistry, Education (for the BEd Primary programme), Medicine, Veterinary Medicine, Social Sciences and Law accept applications after the 15 January deadline, but this is not guaranteed and will depend on the pressure on places and the academic qualifications of the applicant. Offers are made from early to late March. The University does not interview applicants to all faculties, some exceptions being the Medical and Veterinary Sciences, Music, Education and Technological Education. Deferred entry is not guaranteed for all subjects (eg Dentistry, Veterinary Medicine and Primary Education): check with the University. Admissions organised centrally except for Medicine, Dentistry, Education, Veterinary Medicine and the School of Interdisciplinary Studies at the Dumfries campus.

Glasgow Caledonian Nursing and Health courses interview applicants. Applicants who are considering deferred entry should contact the admissions tutor before applying.

Gloucestershire Students failing to meet the UCAS Tariff requirements may be eligible for entry based on life or work experience following an interview. Entry with the Advanced Diploma, BTEC, NVQ Level 3 and Access to Higher Education qualifications is acceptable.

Glyndŵr Offers are made through the Central Office for courses in Sports, Business, Engineering, Communications and Technology, Humanities, Journalism and Media. Enquiries for other courses should be made to the Head of Department. Short-listed candidates are interviewed for Nursing, Social Work, Psychology, Criminal Justice, Education/Families and Childhood Studies. The general requirement for entry to most degree courses is 240–260 UCAS Tariff points and 120 UCAS Tariff points for foundation degrees. UCAS points may be counted from a wide variety of qualifications but offers are usually made based on points from GCE A-levels or equivalent. Applications are also welcomed from candidates who do not possess the standard qualifications but who can demonstrate their capacity to pursue the course successfully. Entrance can be based on past experience, skills, organisational capabilities and the potential to succeed. Portfolios are required for Art and Design courses and an audition is required for Theatre and Performance. *Clearing 2011* Nursing and Social Work did not enter Clearing. *Most popular subjects 2011* Nursing, Social Work.

Heriot-Watt In order to give candidates as much flexibility as possible, many will receive offers for both first and second year entry. Although one of these will be the main offer, candidates accepting this can easily change their main offer to the alternative year if they subsequently want to do so. Applicants are interviewed for some programmes.

Hertfordshire Applicants wanting to take a Gap Year should finalise their arrangements before asking for deferment and accepting a place. Once a place has been accepted for the following year it will not be possible to change their application for entry to the current year. They would need to withdraw their application and apply again through Clearing.

Hull All criteria for selection are set by the academic faculty. Offers for the more straightforward applications are made centrally, within those criteria, for five areas: Business School, Education (non-QTS), Biological Sciences, Psychology, and Sport, Health and Exercise Science. A mandatory interview process operates for shortlisted applicants for Nursing, Operating Department Practice, Midwifery, Teaching (QTS), Social Work. Music applicants are invited to a practical session as part of an open day. A new course in Chemical Engineering (subject to approval) is due to start in 2012 whilst Sport and Leisure Management and Design and Technology have been withdrawn. A wide range of qualifications are accepted for entry to degree courses. Applications are also welcomed from those who can demonstrate Level 3 work-based learning such as Advanced Apprenticeships and NVQ 3. Bridging study may be recommended by way of a foundation year. Most courses welcome applications for deferred entry although this should be stated on the application. Deferred entry is not available for Nursing courses. *Clearing 2011* Medicine, Nursing, Operating Department Practice, Primary Teaching, Sport Health and Exercise Science, Computer Science and Social Science (including Social Work) did not enter Clearing. *Most popular subjects 2011* Biological Sciences, Business School programmes, Nursing, Psychology, Social Sciences.

Imperial London Except for courses where three specific A-levels are required for admission, candidates with two A-levels and two AS-levels will normally be considered equally with other candidates offering three A-levels. The College considers candidates with the Advanced Engineering Diploma if they also have A–levels in specified subjects which meet the College's entry requirements. Applicants for entry to Year 2 of some courses can also be considered if they have completed the first year of a comparable degree at another institution with a high level of achievement, but they need to contact the relevant department before applying. A college admissions and appeals and complaints procedure is available to applicants dissatisfied with the way their application has been considered. Applicants should note the College's policy on dress, health and safety published on its website. An offer for an alternative course may be made to rejected applicants.

Keele Conditional offers are normally made in grades for Medicine, Pharmacy and Physiotherapy. For other subjects offers are usually made in Tariff points and include points for Key Skills at Level 3, stand-alone AS-levels and Advanced Extension Awards. The Advanced Diploma is accepted as equivalent to three A-levels and general studies is also accepted as a condition of an offer. Applicants are normally required to be currently undertaking some formal study before starting a course, but if this is not possible the University may make an offer for a Foundation course.

Kent The University accepts a wide range of qualifications. For mature students and those without the required qualifications Foundation course offers may be made. Applicants returning to study after a long break are advised to contact the admissions staff before making a UCAS application. Deferred entry is acceptable but should be mentioned on the application. The University regards the personal statement as important and recommends that applicants research their chosen courses thoroughly, and show an understanding of the curriculum.

Kingston Admissions staff look carefully at each applicant's academic record, references and personal statement. Some courses require interviews where selectors look for evidence of the applicant's intellectual capacity, course knowledge and enthusiasm. Punctuality and a smart appearance could be important.

Lancaster The University welcomes applications from students wishing to defer entry. General studies is acceptable for the majority of courses. Admissions tutors accept a range of qualifications for entry. Some candidates are interviewed before an offer is made, but most are invited to an informal post-offer Open Day which can involve an interview or discussion with an admissions tutor.

Leeds The University welcomes students who do not come straight from school or college or who wish to defer entry. It also welcomes the increased breadth of post-16 qualifications. Some courses do not accept AL general studies or critical thinking.

Leeds Met Most offers are made in UCAS Tariff points, and interviews are held before an offer is made for some courses. Deferred entry is acceptable although applicants should be aware that some courses may change slightly each year. Students without the required qualifications may provide a 'portfolio of achievement', giving, for example, information about their work experience and their reasons for applying for the course, and also providing references.

Leicester Most courses do not interview applicants although invitations to visit the University will follow any offers made. Most offers are made on the basis of three A-levels although in some cases two A-levels and two AS-levels may be accepted. The University welcomes the Extended Project which should be mentioned in the personal statement. The Advanced Diploma and the Cambridge Pre-U Diploma are also acceptable qualifications. Applications from suitably qualified students are also considered for second year entry. Contact the subject department for further information.

Lincoln On some courses, notably Art and Design and Architecture, an interview with a portfolio is sometimes required before an offer can be made. The University accepts a wide range of qualifications but students without the standard entry requirements may still be offered a place on the basis of prior experience and qualifications.

Liverpool Decisions on offers for most Schools/Departments are made centrally. The exceptions are in the Schools of Architecture, Medical Education, Music, Dentistry, Health Sciences and the Faculty of Veterinary Science. There are some programmes within the following Schools/Departments where the decisions are devolved to the School. These are programmes within the Department of Physics and some programmes run in conjuncture with Carmel College. Most departments will invite applicants to visit the University before or after an offer is made. Some Departments require interviews. Offers are normally based on three A-levels or equivalent (a wide range of qualifications is accepted). Some programmes will accept two A-levels and two AS-levels. Candidates should note that there are several new Law and Computer courses for 2013. *Clearing 2011* Management School, Medicine, Dentistry, Veterinary Science and Engineering.

Liverpool Hope Students who are invited for audition or interview are encouraged to bring their Records of Achievement.

LJMU Admissions decisions are made through the Faculty 'Hubs' (Science; Health and Applied Social Sciences; Technology and Environment; Arts, Professional and Social Studies). The personal statement is regarded as highly important and students are advised to include all relevant interests and work experience. The University welcomes a wide range of entry qualifications. If an applicant fails to receive an offer for their chosen course then an offer for an alternative course may be made. All candidates are interviewed for Drama, Primary Education, Pharmacy (including an admissions test), Nursing, Social Work. *Most popular subjects 2011* Drama, Nursing, Paramedic Practice, Pharmacy, Primary Education, Social Work.

London (Birk) Applications are made online. For details contact the Registry at www.bbk.ac.uk.

London (Gold) While offers are stipulated for courses, candidates are assessed individually and may receive an offer lower than the published grades. Some applicants are interviewed, in particular those for Art and Design degrees for which examples of current art and design work are required before interview. Applicants requiring deferred entry (which may or may not be acceptable depending on the course) should contact the admissions tutor before applying. International students applying for the BA in Design, or the MEng/BEng in Design and Innovation who are unable to attend for interview are asked to send photographs and explanations of their work.

London (Hey) When considering applications, Heythrop takes note of applicants' current and predicted performance at A-level, their ability to study at the relevant level, to take increasing responsibility for their own learning and their motivation to engage intellectually with issues in theology and philosophy.

London (King's) Applicants will normally have taken four AS-level subjects and pursued three of these at A-level. However, departments will also consider those who have taken five AS-levels and passed only two of these at A-level. Applicants may take all their examinations at the end of Year 13 without prejudice. Conditional offers may include the fourth AS-level, a high grade possibly compensating for a failure to obtain the right grade in one of the A-level subjects. AS and A-level general studies and critical thinking are not accepted although the grade achieved may be considered when the required grades of an offer have not been met. Deferred entry is acceptable.

London (QM) It is possible for students to join undergraduate degree programmes at the beginning of the second and sometimes the third year. Those wishing to transfer their degree studies from another UK higher education institution may be considered but should contact the subject department before applying.

London (RH) Applicants likely to meet the entry requirements may be called for interview or invited to an Open Day. International students may be asked to submit an example of academic work or other exercise although it would be preferable if they could visit the campus. Interviews are not intended to be nerve-wracking or daunting but rather a chance to assess the candidate's potential. In Music there may be an audition, in Drama a workshop session, and in Modern Languages some conversation in the appropriate language. Candidates who fail to meet the requirements of their offer may still be offered a place, particularly if they shone at interview.

London (RVC) Applications for deferred entry are considered but the offer conditions must be met in the same academic year as the application. Applicants holding offers from RVC who fall slightly below the grades required are always reconsidered and may be offered entry if places are available.

London (St George's) Interviews are required for most courses and admissions tests are required for some courses. Once admitted students are not allowed to change courses. Candidates will be interviewed for all courses in Medicine, Physiotherapy, Healthcare Science and Therapeutic and Diagnostic Radiography. *Most popular subjects 2011* Biomedical Science, Medicine 5 Yr, Medicine 4 Yr (Graduate Stream).

London (Sch Pharm) The School looks for students who are intellectually curious, willing to study hard, and who will thrive in a small, friendly environment where the emphasis is on team work and academic achievement. All students who are based in the UK and have educational qualifications which meet or are expected to meet the entry requirements are required to attend an interview before a final decision is taken on their application. Applicants whose UCAS personal statement is aimed at a subject other than pharmacy are recommended to write a supplementary personal statement which can be sent to the Registry once the UCAS application has been submitted. *Clearing 2011* The Master of Pharmacy course does not go into Clearing.

London (SOAS) Offers may be made without an interview and particular attention is paid to past and predicted academic performance. SOAS is happy to consider deferred entry which should be stated on the UCAS application.

London (UCL) UCL welcomes applications from students proposing to spend a pre-university year engaged in constructive activity in the UK or abroad. About 9% of UCL's undergraduates take a Gap Year. Those wanting to enter the second or third year of a degree programme should make early contact with the relevant subject department to obtain approval. Applications are assessed on the basis of the personal statement, the referee's report and the predicted academic performance. UCL is one of the few universities that interviews a significant proportion of its applicants. The programme for the day varies but will include a talk about the subject, a tour of the campus, a discussion with current students and the interview itself. Interviews vary, some being subject-based, others focusing on motivation and communication skills. Decisions on admission are final and there is normally no right of appeal.

London LSE While many other qualifications are considered in the selection of applicants, the vast majority of applicants are expected to have taken four AS-level subjects, followed by three at A-level. Applicants will not be penalised if they have not been able to take the normal number of AS and AL subjects but referees should advise on such circumstances. Applicants normally offer A-levels in LSE's preferred subjects which do not include AS/AL accounting, art and design, business studies, communication studies, design and technology, drama and theatre studies (for some departments), home economics, ICT, law, media studies, music technology, sports studies, travel and tourism. The A* grade may be used for 2013 entry – check with the individual departments. Competition is particularly high for the Accounting and Finance, Economics, Law, and Management courses. Predicted grades on the application will not guarantee an offer of a place. Applications are often held in a 'gathered field' (candidates are informed) and decisions made only when all on-time applications have been received. Some applicants will be asked to take an entrance examination (held in March each year), which lasts for three hours and consists of a précis of an English language text, essays on general discussion topics and tests of mathematical understanding. Sample papers are available from web pages from January to March. *Clearing 2011* It is unlikely that there will be any course vacancies when the A-level results are published.

London Met Applicants may be required to sit a test or to submit a portfolio of work.

London NCH Students must apply to NCH directly rather than through UCAS, and applications can be made any time before term starts. The application form is similar to the traditional UCAS form. NCH will consider your application individually, personally and on its merits. Decisions are quick – usually within 4–6 weeks. As well as personal details and academic records, applicants are required to supply a reference and piece of written work. An application to NCH can be made in addition to any application made to other universities through UCAS. All students that make it successfully past the application form stage are interviewed. As a general rule, all courses require three As at A level or 38 points (including core points) in the IB Diploma or AAABB in Scottish Higher. NCH accept deferred entries for those wishing to take a Gap Year.

London South Bank Applicants not achieving the grades required for their chosen course should contact the University which may still be able to make an offer of a place. All applicants are interviewed for Nursing, Allied Health Professions and Architecture courses.

Loughborough The University will not use admissions tests for entry in 2013. It does not differentiate between applicants taking A-levels for the first time or re-sitting subjects. The Advanced Diploma is acceptable for most undergraduate degrees (see below) although for some degrees applicants may be asked to achieve an A-level in an appropriate subject or relevant Additional Specialist Learning. In most cases offers are based on the application following an invitation to visit the University. Transfers between courses may be possible providing that the required entry requirements have been achieved. The following Advanced Diploma subjects are accepted for some courses:

Business, Administration and Finance Diploma Business and Management, Economics, History and International Relations, Information Science, Politics.

Construction Diploma Architectural Engineering, Commercial Management and Quantity Surveying, Geography.

Creative and Media Diploma Business and Management, Design and Technology, Drama, English, Ergonomics, History and International Relations, Information Science, Politics, Psychology, Social Sciences.

Engineering Diploma Chemistry, Computer Science, Design and Technology, all Engineering subjects, Mathematics.

Environmental and Land-Based Studies Diploma Architectural Engineering, Commercial Management and Quantity Surveying, Geography.

IT Diploma Architectural Engineering, Business and Management, Chemistry, Commercial Management and Quantity Surveying, Computer Science, Design and Technology, Drama, Economics, Electronic and Electrical Engineering, English, Ergonomics, Geography, History and International Relations, Information Science, Mathematics, Politics, Psychology, Social Sciences.

Manufacturing and Product Design Diploma Design and Technology, Manufacturing Engineering, Materials Engineering.

The University's admissions and associated policies are available on its website: www.lboro.ac.uk/admin/ar/admissions/sacop/index.htm. All applicants are interviewed prior to making an offer for courses in Aeronautical, Automotive, Manufacturing, Chemical, Civil and Building Engineering, Information Science, Design and Technology and Art and Design. *Most popular subjects 2011* Civil Engineering, Geography, Mechanical Engineering, Psychology, Sport and Exercise Science.

Manchester Strong examination results are the main factor in the admission of students to courses and the University accepts a wide range of qualifications. All decisions are made by the academic departments and their individual requirements. For example, some programmes may require you to have GCSE maths at grade C or above for entry, others may require a compulsory subject at A-level. Other factors that are considered are prior and predicted grades; evidence of knowledge and commitment in your personal statement; and teacher references. Some courses may also take into account performance at interview, aptitude tests and portfolios. Where places are limited they are offered to those eligible applicants who best meet the selection criteria and who, according to the admissions team, are most likely to benefit from their chosen course and to contribute both to their academic School and the wider University. *Clearing 2011* Adult Nursing and Mental Health Nursing. *Most popular subjects 2011* Business Studies, Dentistry, English Literature, Law LLB and Medicine.

Manchester Met Admissions staff look for personal statements showing evidence of the applicants' motivation and commitment to their chosen courses, work or voluntary experience relevant to any chosen career, and extra-curricular activities, achievements and interests which are relevant to the chosen courses.

Middlesex Some courses start in January (see www.mdx.uk/janstart).

Newcastle In general, offers will be made in grades to be achieved, not in Tariff points. A and AS-level critical thinking and in some cases general studies will be considered. The Advanced Diploma is welcomed although it may not be acceptable for some courses. Offers will also be made for the Cambridge Pre-U Diploma, together with other specified subjects.

Newport Applicants for courses in Art and Design, Teacher Training and Social Work are interviewed.

Northampton Achievement in Key Skills units counts towards the final UCAS Tariff points score.

Northumbria Interviews are compulsory for courses in Architecture, most courses in Art and Design and courses in Health and Teaching. There are no admissions tests.

Nottingham Although grade predictions may match the offers published for the course there is no guarantee that an offer can be made. There are three new courses for 2013 in Agriculture, two in Environmental Engineering and four in Chemical Engineering. There is also a new course in Medicine with a Foundation year. *Clearing 2011* The only courses that went into Clearing in 2011 were Contemporary Chinese Studies and German with Dutch. *Most popular subjects 2011* Medicine, Veterinary Medicine and Economics.

Nottingham Trent The UCAS personal statement is seen as a key part of the application process; the University website provides a guide on its possible content and preparation.

Open University There are no formal entry qualifications for admission to courses.

Oxford The University will use the A* grade when making some offers for 2012 entry. All A-levels except general studies are approved for admissions purposes but specific subject requirements must be met. If applicants have taken the Extended Project (EP), the University will not make it a condition for an offer but it does recognise its potential value to applicants for study at the University and encourages applicants to use their experience of the EP when writing their personal statements, especially if their EP topic is related to their chosen degree course. The Advanced Diploma in Engineering will be accepted for Engineering courses provided candidates obtain both an A-level in Physics and the new Level 3 Certificate in Mathematics for Engineering.

Oxford Brookes For all applications considerable emphasis is placed on the personal statement. Fine Art applicants wishing to take a Gap Year should contact the admissions tutor before applying.

Plymouth The University looks for evidence in the UCAS personal statement of your understanding of the course, good numeracy and literacy skills, motivation and commitment, work experience or placement or voluntary work, especially if it is relevant to your course, any sponsorships or placements you have applied for, and your possible plans for a Gap Year.

Portsmouth Decisions on offers are made by the following academic departments - Creative and Cultural Industries, Humanities, Portsmouth Business School, Science and Technology. For some courses applicants will be expected to attend an interview as part of the selection process (Art and Design, Architecture, Animation, Drama, Pharmacy, Health Science, Social work, Dentistry and Radiography). The University accepts the principle of credit transfer and wherever possible, recognition will be given to prior learning in order to facilitate admission with advanced standing. It also welcomes applications from those taking the Advanced Diploma: one A-level will be required in most cases. The Extended Project is not a requirement but may be taken into consideration. Admissions tests are used for Journalism. *Clearing 2011* Most courses did not enter Clearing. *Most popular subjects 2011* Architecture, Biomedical Sciences, Business Studies, Dentistry, History, Law, Paramedic Science, Pharmacy, Psychology, and NS Accounting with Finance.

Queen's Belfast Applications for admission to full-time undergraduate courses are made through UCAS except for courses in Midwifery and Nursing. These should be made direct to the University's School of Nursing and Midwifery (see www.qub.ac.uk). Interviews are essential for Medicine and Dentistry.

Reading Approximately two-thirds of decisions on applications to undergraduate study are made by the central Admissions Office and one-third of decisions are recommended to the Admissions Office by academic departments/schools. This is agreed on an annual basis according to the requirements of the School or Department. In all cases, the criteria on which successful applicants are admitted is agreed with the academic admissions tutor of the relevant School or Department, who also maintains oversight of decisions during the year and will be involved in decisions on specific cases. Candidates are interviewed for Art, Biological Sciences, Chemistry, Education, Film and Theatre, Food and Nutritional Sciences, Graphic Communication, Pharmacy and Psychology. Typical offers are presented in terms of A-level grades (or in a few cases UCAS Tariff points) but applications are welcomed from those presenting a wide range of qualifications. For some courses selection criteria will include interview, portfolio submission or attendance at a selection centre. *Most popular subjects 2011* Biological Sciences, Business Management, Economics, English Literature, Geography, History, Law, Mathematics, Pharmacy and Psychology.

Robert Gordon Interviews are held for some courses, for example Social Work.

Roehampton Applicants successfully achieving the new Level 3 Advanced Diplomas will be considered for entry onto degrees in closely related subjects. For entry to other subjects, each application will be judged taking the applicant's entire academic record into account and on its own merit.

St Andrews The University highlights the importance of the personal statement and the quality of this is likely to decide which applicants receive offers. It looks for well-organised, well-written statements which include information about the applicants, their interests, relevant work experience, any voluntary work, ideas about career choice and, importantly, their reasons for their choice of course. Admissions tutors prefer candidates to achieve their grades at the first sitting, and if they re-apply, to upgrade their academic attainment if that was the main reason for UCAS rejection. Apart from Medicine and Gateway to Physics no candidates are interviewed.

Salford The University is committed to Widening Participation but it does not make lower offers on the basis of educational or social disadvantage.

Sheffield The University considers qualifications already achieved (including GCSEs), predicted grades and personal statements as the most important parts of an application. Interviews are not a pre-requisite of admission; however, some departments do interview to further assess the motivation and personal qualities of applicants. Departments that interview include Medicine, Dentistry, Orthoptics and Human Communication Science (for Speech Science). The Applicant Information Desk (AiD) provides a first point of contact for people who have applied to the University. AiD can help with any questions applicants have about the process of applying to Sheffield and the current status of their application. More information, including contact details, can be found at: www.sheffield.ac.uk/aid. (See also **Medicine** admissions information in **Chapter 8**.) *Most popular subjects 2011* Medicine, Psychology, Law, Management and English.

Southampton The University looks for a well-considered personal statement, focusing on your reasons for choosing a particular course, the skills you would bring to it, information about any relevant work experience, your career ideas, your personal interests related to the course, and your thoughts about 'what makes you stand out in a crowd'.

Southampton Solent Admissions staff look for applicants' reasons for their course choice, and for evidence of their abilities and ambitions.

Staffordshire The University provides an online workbook for helping applicants to prepare their personal statements.

Stirling Admissions are administered through a central office. It is essential to include in the personal statement your reasons for choosing your specified course. The University also looks for evidence of your transferable skills, for example communication skills, teamwork, and how you acquired these, for example through work experience, voluntary work, academic studies, hobbies and general life experience. All candidates are interviewed for Nursing, Primary Education, Sports Studies, Physical Education and Professional Education (over 600 applying for 20 places). No admissions tests are used. *Clearing 2011* Only Primary Education went into Clearing in 2011. *Most popular subjects 2011* Sports Studies, Physical Education and Professional Education.

Strathclyde Formal interviews are required for some vocational courses; informal interviews are held by some Science and Engineering courses.

Sunderland The University holds informal interviews for certain courses, when applicants will be asked to present their portfolio, or to give an audition, or to talk about themselves and why they want to study for that particular course.

Surrey The University is willing to consider deferring an application for one year, providing it considers that this will benefit the applicant's studies. Contact the admissions staff if you are considering deferred entry.

Sussex Apart from Social Work and Medicine, interviews at Sussex are increasingly unusual, but some departments may ask for examples of written work or for an additional reference. Mature students submitting a strong application but without the relevant qualifications will probably be asked to attend an interview and submit an essay of up to 1500 words on their chosen subject.

Swansea Admissions test is required for Medicine. Selectors take into account the candidate's ability to contribute to the cultural, sporting and social life of the University.

Swansea Met For many courses an interview is an important part of the selection process.

Teesside Interviews are held for a wide range of courses, and successful applicants are given an individualised offer. Each course accepts a minimum of 20 UCAS Tariff points for Level 3 Key Skills.

Trinity Saint David The University guarantees to give equal consideration to all applicants irrespective of when their applications are received. Applicants who successfully complete the residential Wales Summer School at Lampeter, Aberystwyth or Carmarthen are offered a place on an appropriate course of study on completion of their current school or college course. All other candidates will be invited to an interview to discuss their course choice. Entry is based on individual merit.

UCLan The University looks for grades C/D plus Additional and Specialist Learning for applicants with the new Advanced Diplomas. Grades B/C will be required from students with the Progression Diploma.

UEA Offers are normally made in terms of three A-levels although applicants with two A-levels and AS-levels are welcome. Critical thinking and general studies A-levels are not accepted for most courses. Interviews are necessary for some courses. Deferred entry is acceptable.

UEL Candidates are advised to apply as soon as possible and results are normally announced within seven days. Some students may be called for interview and in some cases an essay or a portfolio may be required. The interviewers will be looking for evidence of a real interest in the chosen subject. Rejected applicants may receive an offer of a place on an Extended degree or another course.

Ulster Applicants seeking admission to any of the following courses should use the University's direct entry form: BSc courses in Community Nursing, Specialist Nursing Practice, Nursing Sciences, and Health Sciences.

Warwick The University welcomes the introduction of the A* grade and is monitoring developments. Students taking the Advanced Diploma will be considered if they are taking subjects closely aligned to the chosen degree courses, and they must also take appropriate additional specialised learning options: they are advised to contact the admissions team before making their application. Advice on the completion of the application is available on www.warwick.ac.uk/go/study. Feedback can be provided if requested for candidates whose application has been rejected. The University welcomes applications for deferred entry in most subjects except that for mathematics, applicants are recommended to maintain and sharpen their competence in the subject during their year out, and for English, in which there is intense competition.

West London The University accepts each of the new 14–19 Diplomas as qualification for entry on to all of its undergraduate courses, providing the UCAS Tariff points achieved by applicants match or exceed the UCAS Tariff points listed in the course entry requirements. The University welcomes applicants with the Extended Project, and offers an Extended Project module to students in Years 12 and 13 in the school holidays. It is also possible to transfer credits achieved at another university to a course at this university.

West Scotland Admissions are undertaken by central office for Engineering, Business, Social Sciences, Computing and Science courses only. Applications to Nursing and Midwifery courses are not made through UCAS but through the Centralised Applications to Nursing and Midwifery Training Clearing House (CATCH): contact the University for details. Interviews are held for applicants for Education, Social work, Computer Animation, Sports, Engineering (L9), Creative and Cultural Industries, Health, Nursing and Midwifery. These departments will make the decisions independently of the central office. *Clearing 2011* Social Work, Sports and Engineering did not enter Clearing. *Most popular subjects 2011* Sports, Social Sciences, Business, Health, Nursing and Midwifery.

Westminster Interviews are usually only required for Media, Art and Design and Complementary Therapy courses. The University accepts transfers into Years 1, 2 or 3 of a full-time degree programme if students have studied similar units to the chosen Westminster course, and have passed Year 1 and Year 2, each with 120 credits.

Winchester The following programmes require applicants to take a second subject at Level 1: Childhood, Youth and Community Studies; Education Studies; Education Studies (Early Childhood); Film Studies; Media Studies; Politics and Global Studies; Psychology; Theology and Religious Studies. Second subjects can be contrasting or complementary. Interviews are required for courses in Teaching, Performing Arts and Social Work. *Clearing 2011* No courses entered Clearing. *Most popular subjects 2011* Primary Teaching, Psychology, English and History.

Wolverhampton Admissions staff make decisions on the basis of the application, and may invite applicants for interview or audition. If an applicant cannot meet the entry requirements for the chosen course, the University may offer an alternative course, or give the applicant feedback about why it was unable to offer a place.

Worcester The University advises applicants to consider their personal statements carefully. It advises them to include their reasons for their choice of degree programme, their career plans, their outside interests and work experience, and any other information they consider relevant. Applicants who are not accepted are not necessarily rejected: they may receive a 'changed programme' offer which they need not accept if they prefer to enter Clearing.

York Decisions on offers are made in the following ways. Centralised decision making: Archaeology, Economics, Education, History, History of Art, Language and Linguistic Science, PEP, Philosophy, Politics, Psychology, Social Policy, Social and Political Sciences, Sociology. Semi-centralised decision making: Law, Mathematics, Physics. Devolved decision making in academic departments: Biology, Biochemistry, Chemistry, Computer Science, Electronics, English, Environment, HYMS, Music, Nursing and Midwifery, Social Work, Theatre Film and Television. *Clearing 2011* Departments with limited Clearing vacancies included Environment, Management, Physics and Nursing. *Most popular subjects 2011* Biology, English, History, Midwifery, Nursing, Psychology.

York St John Interviews are compulsory for the following courses: Primary Education, Occupational Therapy, Physiotherapy, Product Design, Fine Art and Counselling.

OXFORD
INTERNATIONAL
COLLEGE

A Level Study & Retake Courses

We offer a highly personal approach to education that sets us apart from most other educational establishments. Our students have access to Oxford's finest tutors to help them achieve their highest potential and to develop the self-confidence they need for successful learning. Our students benefit from individual subject tuition and a personal study plan.

- Full-time and part-time A level retakes
- Flexible A level booster courses
- One year full A level courses for new subjects
- Registered examination centre for all British exam boards
- Exam resit places for external candidates

Fast Track University Foundation Course

This one-year Foundation Programme combines rigorous academic study with a range of enrichment programmes that provide opportunities for students to develop wider skills that are increasingly valued by universities. Career pathways offered include business management, economics, engineering, art and design.

"My 100% score in my Chemistry practical exam was made possible by my excellent tutors and helped me realise my goal of studying Medicine at St. Andrews."

Outstanding Independent College

'Exceeds Expectations' in all categories
Independent School Inspectorate, Nov 2011

5 | APPLICATIONS

ENTRY REQUIREMENTS

Before applying to universities and colleges, be sure that you have the required subjects and qualifications for entry to your chosen course. Details of entry requirements are available direct from the universities and colleges. You will need to check:

(i) the general entry requirements for courses

(ii) any specific subject requirements to enter a particular course, for example, study of specified GCE A- and/or AS-levels, Scottish Highers/Advanced Highers, GCSEs, Scottish Standard Grades, or BTEC qualifications (for example, National Diploma, National Certificate). The course requirements are set out in prospectuses and on websites

(iii) any age, health, Criminal Records Bureau (CRB) clearance or other requirements for entry to particular courses and universities and colleges. For entry to some specific courses such as Medicine and Nursing, offers are made subject to health screening for hepatitis B, for example, and immunisation requirements. Owing to Government regulations, some universities will insist on a minimum age at entry of 18 years. Check university and college websites and prospectuses for these particular course requirements

(iv) admissions tests required by a number of universities for a range of subjects, including Dentistry, Law, Medicine and Veterinary Science/Medicine. Offers of places made by these universities are dependent on an applicant's performance in the relevant test. It is important to find out full details about universities' course requirements for possible admissions tests well before submitting the UCAS application and to make all the necessary arrangements for registering and taking any required admissions tests. See **Chapter 6** and check university/college and admissions tests websites for the latest information.

Potential applicants should ask the advice of teachers, careers advisers and university and college advisers before submitting their application.

APPLICATIONS FOR UNIVERSITY AND COLLEGE COURSES THROUGH UCAS

UCAS, the organisation responsible for managing applications to higher education courses in the UK, deals with applications for admission to full-time and sandwich first degrees, Foundation degrees, Diploma of Higher Education and Higher National Diploma courses and some full-time Higher National Certificate courses in nearly all universities (but not the Open University), university colleges, colleges and institutes of higher education, specialist colleges and some further education colleges.

The UCAS application process

Full details of application procedures and all course information can be found on the UCAS website. Other information is also available in the *UCAS Guide to Getting Into University and College* and other UCAS publications (available from www.ucasbooks.com or from UCAS Media, PO Box 130, Cheltenham GL52 3ZF, tel 01242 544610).

Applications are made online at www.ucas.com using **Apply**. This is a secure web-based application system, which has been designed for all applicants whether they are applying through a UCAS-registered centre, such as a school or college, or applying independently from anywhere in the world.

Applications can be sent to UCAS from mid-September. The first deadline is 15 October for applications to Oxford or Cambridge universities and applications for courses in Medicine, Dentistry and Veterinary Science/Medicine. The deadline for UK and EU applicants to apply for all other courses is 15 January, except for some Art and Design courses that have a 24 March deadline. You can still apply after these deadlines up to 30 June, but institutions may not be able to consider you.

On the UCAS application, you have up to five course choices unless you are applying for Dentistry, Medicine or Veterinary Science/Medicine. For these courses only four choices are permitted.

It is important to note that some universities (for example Cambridge) now require their applicants to complete a Supplementary Application Questionnaire after they have received your UCAS application. Check the websites of your listed universities for their latest application information.

Each university or college makes any offer through the UCAS system. UCAS does not make offers, or recruit on behalf of universities and colleges. It does not advise applicants on their choice of subject although it does publish material which applicants may find useful.

Applicants may receive an 'unconditional' offer in the case of those who already hold the required qualifications, or, for those awaiting examination results, a 'conditional' offer or a rejection. When all decisions have been received from universities or colleges, applicants may finally hold up to two offers: a firm choice (first) offer and an insurance offer. Applicants who have made five choices and have no offers or have declined any offers received can use **Extra**. Applicants are told when they become eligible for **Extra** and can apply online for one further course at a time using **Track** at www.ucas.com. **Extra** runs from 26 February until 3 July. Courses available in **Extra** will be highlighted on **Course Finder** at www.ucas.com. Applicants not placed through this system will be eligible to contact institutions with vacancies in **Clearing** from mid-July.

If you already have your qualifications and are not waiting for any exam results, your place can be confirmed at any time after you send in your application. However, for thousands of applicants confirmation starts on the day when the A-level examination results are released. **Clearing** vacancy lists are also published on A-level results day. Applicants meeting the conditions of their offers for their firm choice will receive confirmation from their university or college and may still be accepted even if their results are slightly lower than those stipulated in the original offer. If rejected by their firm choice university/college, applicants will have their places confirmed by their insurance choice institution providing they have obtained the right grades. Applicants who are unsuccessful with both their institutions will be eligible to go into **Clearing** in which they can select an appropriate course in the same or a different institution where places are available. Each year up to 40,000 applicants obtain places through **Clearing**, and over 5500 applicants found a place though **Extra** last year.

UCAS timetable

Mid-September 2012	UCAS begins accepting applications.
15 October	Deadline for UCAS to receive applications to Oxford University or the University of Cambridge, and applications to courses in Medicine, Dentistry or Veterinary Medicine/Science.
15 January 2013	Deadline for UCAS to receive applications from UK and EU applicants for all other courses, except for some Art and Design courses that have a 24 March deadline. Visit **Course Finder** at www.ucas.com to find out whether Art and Design courses have a 15 January or 24 March deadline.
16 January–30 June	Applications received by UCAS are forwarded to the institutions for consideration at their discretion. Applications received after 30 June are processed through **Clearing**.
26 February–3 July	Applicants who have made five choices and have no offers or who have declined any offers received can use **Extra** to apply for one further course at a time on **Track** at www.ucas.com. Institutions will show which courses have vacancies in **Extra** on the UCAS website. Details of the **Extra** service will be included in *Your UCAS Welcome Guide* sent to applicants.
24 March	Deadline for UCAS to receive applications for some Art and Design courses. Visit **Course Search** at www.ucas.com to find out whether Art and Design courses have a 15 January or 24 March deadline.
9 May	Applicants who have received all their decisions from universities and colleges by the end of March are asked to reply to their offers by this date.
7 June	Applicants receiving decisions from all their choices by 9 May must reply to their offers by this date.
30 June	Last date for receiving applications. Applications received after this date are entered directly into **Clearing**. In mid-July **Clearing** starts.

4 August	Scottish SQA results published.
16 August	GCE A-level and AS results published. **Clearing** vacancy information available. (See **What To Do on Results Day ... and After** below.)

PLEASE NOTE

- You are not required to reply to any university/college offers until you have received your last decision.
- Do not send a firm acceptance to more than one offer.
- Do not try to alter a firm acceptance.
- If you decide not to go to university or college this year you can go to **Track** to completely cancel your application. But don't forget, you will not be able to reapply until next year.
- Remember to tell the institutions and UCAS if you change your address, or change your examination board, subjects or arrangements.

Information on the special arrangements for applications for Law, Medicine and Dentistry can be found under separate headings in Chapter 6.

APPLICATIONS FOR MUSIC COURSES AT CONSERVATOIRES

The Conservatoires UK Admissions Service (CUKAS) handles applications for practical Music courses. Applications can be made simultaneously to a maximum of six of the conservatoires listed below and simultaneous applications can also be made to both UCAS and CUKAS. Full details of CUKAS are given on www.cukas.ac.uk. The conservatoires taking part in this online admissions system are:

- Birmingham Conservatoire www.conservatoire.uce.ac.uk
- Leeds College of Music www.lcm.ac.uk
- Royal College of Music www.rcm.ac.uk
- Royal Northern College of Music www.rncm.ac.uk
- Royal Conservatoire of Scotland www.rcs.ac.uk
- Royal Welsh College of Music and Drama www.rwcmd.ac.uk
- Trinity Laban Conservatoire of Music and Dance www.tcm.ac.uk

See also the **Music** table of interview requirements/tests in **Chapter 6**.

APPLICATIONS FOR TEACHER TRAINING COURSES

Applicants intending to start a course of initial teacher training in England leading to Qualified Teacher Status can find information on the Teaching Agency website www.education.gov.uk/get-into-teaching. See also www.gttr.ac.uk/students/beforeyouapply and www.tda.gov.uk for full details of applying for undergraduate (and postgraduate) training courses. Students in Wales and Northern Ireland should also check with this website; Scottish students should check www.gtcs.org.uk.

THE UCAS APPLICATION

Two important aspects of the UCAS application concern Sections 3 and 10. In Section 3 all your university/college choices (a maximum of five) are to be listed, but remember that you should not mix your subjects. For example, in popular subject areas such as English, History or Physiotherapy, it is safer to show total commitment by applying for all courses in the same subject and not to include second and/or third subject alternatives on the form. (See advice in separate tables in **Chapter 8** for **Medicine**, **Dentistry** and **Veterinary Science/Medicine**.)

A brief glance at the subject tables in **Chapter 8** will give you some idea of the popularity of various courses. In principle, institutions want the best applicants available so if there are large numbers of applicants the offers made will be higher. For Medicine and a number of other courses, offers in terms of A-level grades are now reaching AAA or A* grades, and often with additional AS-levels. Conversely, for the less popular subjects such as Chemistry or Manufacturing Engineering, the offers can be much lower – down to CCC.

Similarly, some institutions are more popular (not necessarily better) than others. Again, this popularity can be judged easily in the tables in **Chapter 8**: the higher the offer, the more popular the institution. Popular universities often are located in attractive towns or cities such as Bristol, Exeter, Warwick, Bath or York. Additionally, some institutions have established a good 'reputation' for various reasons, for example, Oxford, Cambridge and Durham. Conversely and unfortunately, some universities have confused applicants with unfamiliar names and no immediate identity as to their location, such as De Montfort and Brunel. More students would apply to these excellent institutions if they knew where they were situated! Because of the intense competition for places at the popular universities, applications to five of them could result in rejections from all of them! (If you are not good enough for one of them you won't be good enough for the other four!) Spread your choice of institutions.

When you have chosen your courses and your institutions, look again at the offers made and compare these with the grades projected by your teachers on your UCAS reference. It is most important to maximise your chances of a place by choosing institutions which might make you a range of offers. When all universities have considered your application you can hold only two offers (one firm and one insurance offer) and naturally it is preferable for one to be lower than the other in case you do not achieve the offer grades or equivalent points for your first choice of university or college.

The other section of the UCAS application that deserves careful thought is Section 10 (the personal statement). This seems simple enough but it is the only part of the application where you can put in a personal bid for a place! In short, you are asked to give relevant background information about yourself, your interests and your choice of course and career. Give yourself plenty of time to prepare Section 10 – if you have a Record of Achievement you could use it as a guide – as this part of your application could make all the difference to getting an offer or not.

Motivation to undertake your chosen course is very important. You can show this by giving details of any work experience and work shadowing you have done (and for History courses, for example, details of visits to places of historical interest). It is a good idea to begin your statement with such evidence and explain how your interest in your chosen subject has developed. In the subject tables in **Chapter 8** under **Advice to applicants and planning the UCAS personal statement**, advice is given on what you might include in Section 10. You should also include various activities in which you have been involved in the last three or four years. Get your parents and other members of the family to refresh your memory – it is easy to forget something quite important. You might consider planning out this section in a series of sub-sections – and if you have a lot to say, be brief. The sub-sections can include the following.

- **School activities** Are you a prefect, chairperson or treasurer of a society? Are you involved in supervisory duties of any kind? Are you in a school team? Which team? For how long? (Remember, team means any team: sports, chess, debating, even business.)
- **Intellectual activities** Have you attended any field or lecture courses in your main subjects? Where? When? Have you taken part in any school visits? Do you play in the school orchestra or have you taken part in a school drama production – on or off stage? Do you go to the theatre, art galleries or concerts?
- **Out-of-school activities** This category might cover many of the topics above, but it could also include any community or voluntary work you do, or Duke of Edinburgh's Awards, the Combined Cadet Force (CCF), sport, music and drama activities etc. The countries you have visited might also be mentioned – for example, any exchange visits with friends living abroad.
- **Work experience** Details of part-time, holiday or Saturday jobs could be included here, particularly if they have some connection with your chosen course. Some applicants plan ahead and arrange to visit firms and discuss career interests with various people who already work in their chosen field. For some courses such as Veterinary Science, work experience is essential, and it certainly helps for others, for example Medicine and Business courses.
- **Key Skills** These cover numeracy, communication and information technology (the basics) and also advanced skills involving teamwork, problem solving and improving your own learning. If you are not offering the Key Skills Certificate then evidence of your strengths in these areas may be mentioned in the school or college reference or you may include examples in your personal statement relating to your out-of-school activities.

Finally, plan your personal statement carefully. You may write short statements if you wish. It is not essential to write in prose except perhaps if you are applying for English or language courses in which case your statement will be judged grammatically! Take a copy to use as a trial and a copy of your complete application to keep by you for reference if you are called for interview. Almost certainly you will be questioned on what you have written.

Admissions tutors always stress the importance of the confidential report from your head teacher or form tutors. Most schools and colleges will make some effort to find out why you want to apply for a particular course, but if they do not ask, do not take it for granted that they will know! Consequently, although you have the opportunity to write about your interests on the form, it is still a good idea to tell your teachers about them. Also, if you have to work at home under difficult conditions or if you have any medical problem, your teachers must be told since these points should be mentioned on the report.

Deferred entry
Although application is usually made in the autumn of the year preceding the proposed year of entry, admissions tutors may be prepared to consider an application made two years before entry, so that the applicant can, perhaps, gain work experience or spend a period abroad. Policies on deferred entry may differ from department to department, so you should check with admissions tutors before applying. Simply remember that there is no guarantee that you will get the grades you need or a place at the university of your first choice at the first attempt! If not, you may need to repeat A-levels and try again. It may be better not to apply for deferred entry until you are certain in August of your grades and your place.

APPLICATIONS TO THE UNIVERSITY OF CAMBRIDGE
If you are a UK or EU applicant, you need to only complete the UCAS application. You will then receive an email from the University, confirming the arrival of your application and giving you the website address of their online Supplementary Application Questionnaire (SAQ) which you will then need to complete and return by the specified date. Check with the Admissions Office or on www.cam.ac.uk/admissions/undergraduate/apply for the latest information.

Your UCAS application listing Cambridge as one of your university choices must be sent to UCAS by 15 October. If you are applying for Medicine or Veterinary Medicine you must include your BMAT registration with your application. You can indicate your choice of college or make an Open application if you have no preference. Open applicants are allocated by a computer program to colleges that have had fewer applicants per place for your chosen subject.

The Cambridge Special Access Scheme (CSAS) is also available for applicants whose schooling has been disrupted or disadvantaged. You need to complete a CSAS application by 15 October but discuss this with your school/college higher education adviser and check with the UCAS website for more information. Interviews take place in Cambridge in the first three weeks of December, although some may be a little earlier. Many of the University's colleges use tests as part of the selection process for specific courses and written work also may be requested before interview. This practice, however, varies between colleges and subjects. See the University website and **Chapter 6** for information you need to know before completing and submitting your application.

In January applicants receive either an offer conditional upon certain grades in examinations to be taken the following summer, or a rejection. Alternatively, you may be placed in a pool for further consideration. About one in five applicants are pooled and one in four receive an offer. Decisions are made on the basis of academic record, reference, personal statement, submitted work/test results and interviews. The conditions set are grades to be obtained in examinations such as A-levels, Scottish Highers/Advanced Highers or the International Baccalaureate. Offers made by some Cambridge University colleges may also include Sixth Term Examination Papers (STEP) in mathematics (see **Chapter 6** under **Mathematics**). The STEPs are taken in June and copies of past papers and full details are available from www.admissionstests.cambridgeassessment.org.uk.

College policies
All colleges which admit undergraduates use the selection procedures described in **Chapter 6**. However, there will be some minor variations between the various colleges, within each college and also between

subjects. Further information about the policies of any particular college can be found in the Cambridge Undergraduate Prospectus and may also be obtained from the admissions tutor of the college concerned. No college operates a quota system for any subject except Medicine and Veterinary Medicine, for which there are strict quotas for the University from which places are allocated to each college.

Full details of the admissions procedures are contained in the current Cambridge Undergraduate Prospectus. Copies of the prospectus are available from Cambridge Admissions Office, Fitzwilliam House, 32 Trumpington Street, Cambridge CB2 1QY, or via the website www.cam.ac.uk/admissions.

APPLICATIONS TO THE UNIVERSITY OF OXFORD

Application procedures to Oxford are similar to all other universities except that candidates applying to Oxford must submit a UCAS application by 15 October 2012 for those applying for entry in October 2013 or for deferred entry in October 2014. Admissions are carried out on a college basis: candidates can name a college of preference and may be allocated second and third preference colleges, but if they do not have a specific college in mind, they can make an open application. This means that they will be allocated a college by the Admissions Office computer which takes account of their chosen course and the approximate number of applicants per place that each college has received that year.

For some subjects at some colleges at Oxford, applicants are required to sit aptitude or admissions tests (for example, the History Aptitude Test, the National Admissions Test for Law (LNAT) and the BioMedical Admissions Test (BMAT)) or to provide essays or a portfolio for interview. Specimen test questions are published on the website. See **Chapter 6** for more information and see www.ox.ac.uk/admissions/ undergraduatecourses/howtoapply for full details. All candidates are considered carefully on their individual merits. Tutors take into account a range of information from the candidate's application including details of their academic record and the reference in order to assess a candidate's suitability and potential for his or her proposed course. Candidates applying for some courses may be required to submit samples of marked school work by early November, and/or to take a short written test when they are in Oxford for interview (see **Chapter 6**). The majority of candidates applying to Oxford are invited for interview at the beginning of December and this is an integral part of the selection procedure. Candidates will be interviewed at their college of preference and also may be interviewed by other colleges. Colleges co-operate and pool candidates to ensure that the most able candidates are offered places. Successful candidates who have not completed their school-leaving examinations will be made conditional offers based on their forthcoming examinations such as A-levels, Scottish Highers, Advanced Highers, International Baccalaureate, European Baccalaureate and other European and international qualifications. Decisions are notified to candidates via UCAS by the end of January. Candidates are welcome to attend Open Days which are held at all of the colleges and a number of departments, usually during the summer term or in September.

Common Framework

The University and Colleges have agreed to a Common Framework for Colleges and Faculties (see www. admissions.ox.ac.uk/news/common_framework.shtml) which lays down key principles and procedures for undergraduate admissions. The Common Framework is designed to make admissions more transparent, improve methods of assessing candidates and ensure that selection is unaffected by the applicant's choice of college. Colleges will continue to have the final say over whom they admit but they will be guided by the central banding of candidates by faculties based on the whole range of information arising from the selection process. This information may include results from pre-interview tests, written work, school qualifications and/or predicted school-leaving grades, interviews and contextual information about a candidate's educational background.

Where a college wishes to offer a place to a candidate below the 'selection threshold', it will be required to explain the reasons to the relevant faculty with reference to the agreed admissions criteria.

APPLICATIONS TO IRISH UNIVERSITIES

All applications to universities in the Republic of Ireland are made through the Central Application Office, Tower House, Eglinton Street, Galway, Ireland; see www.cao.ie or telephone 091 509 800. The Central Application Office website gives full details of all 44 institutions and details of the application procedure. Applications are made by 1 February. Individual institutions publish details of their entry requirements for courses, but unlike applications through UCAS in the UK, no conditional offers are made. Applicants are judged purely on their academic ability except for the Royal College of Surgeons which also requires a school reference and a personal statement. The results are published in August when institutions make their offers and when successful students are required to accept or decline the offer.

APPLICATIONS TO COMMONWEALTH UNIVERSITIES
Details of universities in 38 commonwealth countries (all charge fees) are published on www.acu.ac.uk or for Australia (www.students.idp.com) and Canada (www.studyincanada.com).

APPLICATIONS TO AMERICAN UNIVERSITIES
There are over 2000 universities and colleges offering degree course programmes in the USA; some institutions are independent and others state-controlled. Unlike the UK, however, where UCAS control nearly all university and college applications, it is necessary to apply separately to all American universities. Most American universities will expect applicants to have A-levels or IB qualifications and in addition, usually require students to complete a School Assessment Test (SAT) covering mathematical and verbal reasoning abilities. In some cases applicants may be required to take SAT II tests which are based on specific subjects. Tests can be taken at centres in the UK: see www.collegeboard.com.

Unlike the usual specialised subject degrees at UK universities, 'Liberal Arts programmes' in the USA have considerable breadth and flexibility, although subjects requiring greater specialised knowledge such as Medicine and Law require further study at Medical or Law School.

Because of the complexities of an application to American universities, such as financial implications, visas etc, students should initially refer to www.fulbright.co.uk. It is also important to be able to identify the differences between and the quality of institutions and a valuable guide can be sourced through www.petersons.com (*General Guides to Colleges, Scholarships and Admissions*) or see *Barrons Guide*.

THE ERASMUS PROGRAMME
Many universities in the UK have formal agreements with partner institutions in Europe through the Erasmus Programme which enables UK university students to apply for courses in Europe for periods up to one year. Some of these courses are taught in English and students can receive help with accommodation and other expenses through the Erasmus Student Grant scheme.

The Erasmus Programme is for undergraduates in all subject areas who would like to study or do a work placement for three to 12 months as part of their degree course in one of 30 other European countries. Most universities offer it although it is not available with every course so students are advised to check with their chosen universities before making an application. Students do not pay any fees to the European university they visit and those who go for the full academic year (24 weeks) have their UK tuition fees waived.

AND FINALLY ... BEFORE YOU SEND IN YOUR APPLICATION
CHECK that you have passes at grade C or higher in the GCSE (or equivalent) subjects required for the course at the institutions to which you are applying. FAILURE TO HAVE THE RIGHT GCSE SUBJECTS OR THE RIGHT NUMBER OF GRADE C PASSES OR HIGHER IN GCSE WILL RESULT IN A REJECTION.

CHECK that you are taking (or have taken) the GCE A and AS-level (or equivalent) subjects required for the course at the institution to which you are applying. FAILURE TO BE TAKING OR HAVE TAKEN THE RIGHT A-levels WILL ALSO RESULT IN A REJECTION.

CHECK that the GCE A-levels and other qualifications you are taking will be accepted for the course for which you are applying. Some subjects and institutions do not stipulate any specific A-levels, only that you are required to offer two or three subjects at GCE A-level. In the view of some admissions tutors NOT ALL GCE A-levels CARRY THE SAME WEIGHT (see **Chapter 1**).

CHECK that you can meet the requirements for all relevant admissions/interview tests.

CHECK that you have made all the necessary arrangements for sitting any required admissions tests.

CHECK that you can meet any age, health and CRB requirements for entry to your listed courses.

Maastricht University

Leading in Learning

Maastricht University has already established itself as one of the world's best universities, with a reputation as an outstanding centre of teaching and research. Its prime location, outstanding reputation and highly competitive fees have attracted ever-increasing numbers of students from home and abroad. Numerous parallels can be drawn between the iconic universities at Cambridge and Maastricht; not only are they both housed in medieval riverside buildings - scattered liberally with bicycles - but also both are internationally recognised as leaders in their fields.

Innovator in education

The university has also established itself as an international leader in the innovative teaching methods of Problem-Based Learning (PBL). While some aspects of PBL are also starting to be adopted by other educational establishments, Maastricht University, as one of the first, remains a leader. PBL is a seven-step process for group learning; using small texts to stimulate discussion and work towards the establishment of learning objectives. It utilizes lectures and smaller group-based, problem-solving sessions to empower students. From the outset, students have to be active- all great skills for the workplace for the student upon graduation.

English as the language of choice

Almost all of its bachelor programmes at Maastricht University are offered in English - unparalleled in continental Europe. Its exceptional capabilities have already earned it numerous international accolades, including amongst others a prestigious Triple Crown accreditation for Economics and Business Administration. It is ranked 109 in the world by QS World University.

With its location in Maastricht, one of the oldest and most beautiful cities in The Netherlands, the university sits at the crossroads of different cultures and in the heart of Europe. Maastricht University is internationally oriented, outward looking and dynamic.

A student-orientated research university, Maastricht University has much to offer the ambitious motivated student in search of academic excellence.

To plan your visit to Maastricht University or to request a school visit please contact us at **info-uk@maastrichtuniversity.nl**

Visit us online at **www.maastrichtuniversity.nl**

Case Study

"*Since making the decision to come and study in Maastricht I can honestly say I haven't looked back. The standard of teaching has far exceeded my expectations and studying Cultural studies in such an international environment is fascinating.*

Within the small tutorial based learning system they have here you really get a chance to discuss and debate academic questions with your fellow students and the professors. Whilst the high expectations and regular assessments (exams every eight weeks from day one)is tough it also gives you a real sense of achievement.

For anyone who really wants a unique experience and an academic challenge that really makes you feel like you are getting a top University education I would strongly urge you to consider Maastricht."

Dani Older is 23 years old. In 2009 she decided to leave the UK and head to Europe to xperience something a little bit different...

Dani has found part time work alongside her studies within the University. She is employed to help UK students who are interested in joining her in Maastricht. If you want more information or are thinking about applying for Maastricht contact Dani with any questions on
Info-uk@maastrichtuniversity.nl

www.maastrichtuniversity.nl

WHAT TO DO ON RESULTS DAY ... AND AFTER

BE AT HOME! Do not arrange to be away when your results are published. If you do not achieve the grades you require, you will need to follow an alternative course of action and make decisions that could affect your life during the next few years. Do not expect others to make these decisions for you. If you achieve the grades or points which have been offered you will receive confirmation of a place, but this may take a few days to reach you. Once your place is confirmed contact the accommodation office at the university or college and inform them that you will need a place in a hall of residence or other accommodation.

If you achieve grades or points higher than your conditional firm (CF) choice you can reconsider where and what to study by registering with UCAS to use the **Adjustment in Track** process. This is available from A-level results day until 31 August and you have five days to register and secure an alternative course. You must check very carefully all the **Adjustment** information on the UCAS website (www.ucas. com) before changing your CF choice to make sure you are eligible and that a vacancy is available. There is no guarantee of a vacancy on a course you are aiming for, and it is very unlikely that competitive courses will have places. If you decide definitely to change courses advise the university or college immediately, but check with www.ucas.com and your school/college adviser for the latest information.

If your grades or points are higher than you expected and you are not holding any offers you can telephone or email the admissions tutor at the universities and colleges which rejected you and request that they might reconsider you.

If you just miss your offers then telephone or email the universities and colleges to see if they can still offer you a place. ALWAYS HAVE YOUR UCAS REFERENCE NUMBER AVAILABLE WHEN YOU CALL. Their decisions may take a few days. You should check the universities and colleges in your order of preference. Your first choice must reject you before you contact your second choice.

If you have not applied to any university or college earlier in the year then you can apply through the **Clearing** scheme which runs from the middle of July. Check the tables in **Chapter 8** to identify which institutions normally make offers matching your results, then telephone or email the institution to see if they have any vacancies before completing your **Clearing** form.

If you learn finally that you do not have a place you will receive automatically a **Clearing** form to enable you to re-apply. Before you complete this form follow the instructions above.

If an institution has vacancies they will ask you for your grades. If they can consider you they will ask you for your **Clearing** form. You can only be considered by one institution at a time.

If you have to re-apply for a place, check the vacancies on the UCAS website (www.ucas.com), in the national press and through your local careers office. If there are vacancies in your subject, check with the university or college that these vacancies have not been taken.

REMEMBER – There are many thousands of students just like you. Admissions tutors have a mammoth task checking how many students will be taking up their places since not all students whose grades match their offers finally decide to do so!

IF YOU HAVE AN OFFER AND THE RIGHT GRADES BUT ARE NOT ACCEPTING THAT OR AN ALTERNATIVE PLACE – TELL THE UNIVERSITY OR COLLEGE. Someone else is waiting for your place! If you are applying for a place through **Clearing** it may even be late September before you know you have a place so BE PATIENT AND STAY CALM!

Good luck!

6 | ADMISSIONS TESTS, SELECTION OF APPLICANTS AND INTERVIEWS

The selection of applicants by universities and colleges takes many forms. However, with rising numbers of applicants for places (especially in the popular subjects) and increasing numbers of students with high grades, greater importance is now attached not only to applicants' predicted A-level grades and GCSE attainments, but also to other aspects of their applications, especially the school reference and the personal statement and, for some courses and some institutions, performance at interview, and performance in admissions tests.

ADMISSIONS TESTS

Admissions tests are now increasingly used for undergraduate entry to specific courses and specific institutions. These include national subject-based tests such as LNAT, BMAT and UKCAT (see below) which are used for selecting applicants for entry to specified courses at particular institutions in subjects such as Law, Medicine, Dentistry and Veterinary Sciences. Admissions tests are also set by individual universities and colleges (or commercial organisations on their behalf) for entry, again, to particular courses in the individual institutions. Examples of these include the Thinking Skills Assessment (TSA) used by, for example, many Cambridge University colleges, and the Health Professions Aptitude Test (HPAT) used by Ulster University for entry to some health-related courses. Other examples include the subject-based admissions tests used by many universities and colleges for entry to particular courses in subjects such as Art, Dance, Construction, Design, Drama and other Performance-based courses, Education and Teacher Training, Economics, Engineering, Journalism, Languages, Music, Nursing and Social Work.

Admissions tests are usually taken before or at interview and, except for courses requiring auditions or portfolio inspections, they are generally timed, unseen, written, or online tests. They can be used on their own, or alongside other selection methods used by university and college admissions staff, including:

- questionnaires or tests to be completed by applicants prior to interview and/or offer
- examples of school work to be submitted prior to interview and/or offer
- written tests at interview
- mathematical tests at interview
- practical tests at interview
- a response to a passage at interview
- performance-based tests (for example, for Music, Dance, Drama).

Applicants should find out early from university prospectuses and websites whether admissions tests are required for entry to their preferred courses, and if so, what these will be, and the arrangements for taking them. This is important, especially for Oxford and Cambridge applicants as many of their courses and colleges also require submission of marked written work done in Years 12 or 13 at school or college.

Here is a list of commonly used admissions tests, and this is followed by degree subject lists showing subject-based and individual institutions' admissions tests.

English

English Literature Admissions Test (ELAT)
The ELAT is a pre-interview admissions test for applicants to English courses at the University of Oxford (see the ELAT pages on the Cambridge Assessment website www.admissionstests.cambridgeassessment. org.uk).

Health Professions
Health Professions Admissions Test (HPAT)
The HPAT is used by the University of Ulster for entry to Dietetics, Occupational Therapy, Physiotherapy, Podiatry, Radiography and Speech and Language Therapies.

History
History Aptitude Test (HAT)
The HAT is a two-hour test sat by all candidates applying for History courses at Oxford University (see *History* below). See www.history.ox.ac.uk.

Law
Cambridge Law Test
This is a new paper-based, one-hour, one-question test designed and used by most of the Cambridge University Colleges with Law applicants who are called for interview. No prior knowledge of law is required for the test. See www.law.cam.ac.uk/admissions/cambridge-law-test.php for full details.

National Admissions Test for Law (LNAT)
The LNAT is an on-screen test for applicants to specified undergraduate Law programmes at the **Birmingham**, **Bristol**, **Durham**, **Glasgow**, **Leeds**, **London (King's)**, **London (UCL)**, **Nottingham** and **Oxford** universities. (See *Law* below, and **Law** in the subject tables in **Chapter 8**.) Applicants need to check universities' websites and the LNAT website (www.lnat.ac.uk) for the UCAS codes for courses requiring applicants to sit the LNAT. (**NB** Cambridge does not now require Law applicants to take the LNAT but see above and the Cambridge entry under *Law* below.) Details of LNAT (which includes multiple-choice and essay questions), practice papers, registration dates, test dates, test centres and fees are all available on the LNAT website.

Mathematics
Sixth Term Examination Paper (STEP)
Applicants with offers for Mathematics courses at Cambridge and Warwick universities are usually required to take STEP. Bristol and Oxford Universities, and Imperial London also encourage applicants for their Mathematics courses to take STEP. For details, see the STEP pages on the Cambridge Assessment website (www.admissionstests.cambridgeassesssment.org.uk).

Medicine, Dentistry, Veterinary Science/Medicine, and related subjects
Most medical schools require applicants to sit the UK Clinical Aptitude Test (UKCAT) or the BioMedical Admissions Test (BMAT) or, for graduate entry, the Graduate Australian Medical Schools Admissions Test (GAMSAT) for specified Medicine courses. Applicants are advised to check the websites of all universities and medical schools offering Medicine for their latest admissions requirements, including admissions and aptitude tests, to check the UKCAT website www.ukcat.ac.uk or the BMAT pages on www.admissionstests.cambridgeassessment.org.uk (and for graduate entry www.gamsat.co.uk) for the latest information.

The BioMedical Admissions Test (BMAT)
This is a pen-and-paper admissions test taken by undergraduate applicants to specified Medicine, Veterinary Science/Medicine courses at Cambridge and Oxford universities, and at Imperial London, London (RVC) and London (UCL). Imperial London also requires BMAT for entry to Biomedical Science, and Pharmacology with Translational Medical Science; BMAT is also a requirement for entry to Biomedical Sciences at Oxford University. A list of the courses requiring BMAT is available on the BMAT pages of the Cambridge Assessment website (www.admissionstests.cambridgeassessment.org.uk) and also on university websites and in their prospectuses. It is important to note BMAT's early closing date for entries and also the test dates. The two-hour test consists of three sections:

- aptitude and skills
- scientific knowledge and application
- writing task.

Applicants sit the test only once and pay one entry fee no matter how many courses they apply for. However, if they re-apply to universities the following year they will need to re-take the BMAT and pay another fee. Past question papers are available (see website) and an official study guide *Preparing for the BMAT* is also available at www.pearsonschoolsandfecolleges.co.uk. Results of the BMAT are first sent to the universities, and then to the BMAT test centres. Candidates need to contact their test centres direct for their results. See **Dentistry**, **Medicine** and **Veterinary Science/Medicine** below and relevant subject tables in **Chapter 8**.

The UK Clinical Aptitude Test (UKCAT)

The UKCAT is a clinical aptitude test used by the majority of medical and dental schools in the selection of applicants for Medicine and Dentistry, alongside their existing selection processes, for undergraduate entry. The tests are not curriculum-based and do not have a science component. No revision is necessary; there is no textbook and no course of instruction. In the first instance, the UKCAT is a test of cognitive skills involving problem-solving and critical reasoning. With over 150 test centres, it is an on-screen test (not paper-based), and is marked electronically. Some bursaries are available to help towards the cost of the test. Further details (including the most recent list of universities requiring applicants to sit the UKCAT) are found on the website www.ukcat.ac.uk. See also the **Dentistry** and **Medicine** subject tables in **Chapter 8**, the entries for **Dentistry** and **Medicine** below, and **Chapter 5** for application details. See www.ukcat.ac.uk.

Modern and Medieval Languages

The Modern and Medieval Languages Test (MML)

This written test is used by the University of Cambridge for selecting applicants for entry to courses involving modern and medieval languages. See www.mml.cam.ac.uk/prospectus/undergrad/applying/test.html.

General Admissions Test

Thinking Skills Assessment (TSA)

The TSA is a 90-minute multiple choice test consisting of 50 questions which test applicants' critical thinking and problem-solving skills. It is used at or before interview by applicants for some courses at Cambridge University by some colleges, by University College London for applicants to European Social and Political Studies, and by Oxford University for entry to several courses (see below and see the TSA web pages on www.admissionstests.cambridgeassessment.org.uk).

LSE Entrance Exam

The LSE Entrance Exam is used for some applicants with non-standard backgrounds. The test is not subject or course specific and consists of English comprehension exercises, essay, questions and mathematical problems.

DEGREE SUBJECT LISTS OF UNIVERSITIES AND COLLEGES USING TESTS AND ASSESSMENTS

Many universities and colleges set their own tests for specific subjects so it is important to check the websites for your preferred institutions and courses for the latest information about their applications and selection processes. The following list provides a guide to the subjects and institutions requiring admissions tests and other forms of assessment.

Accountancy

Buckingham Written test for non-English-speaking applicants.
Lancaster (Acc, Audt Fin) Ernst & Young assessment.
Leeds (Acc Law) LNAT.

Anglo Saxon, Norse and Celtic

Cambridge *Interview only:* Fitzwilliam, Girton, Murray Edwards, St Edmund's, St John's; *Test at interview:* Hughes Hall, Lucy Cavendish, Wolfson; *School/college essays:* all other colleges offering the subject. Check www.cam.ac.uk/admissions/undergraduate/apply/tests.html.

Animal Management
Kirklees (Coll) Mature applicants screening test.

Anthropology
Cambridge See Archaeology.
Oxford See Archaeology.

Arabic
Oxford Language aptitude or translation test.
Salford (Arbc Engl Transl Interp – for native speakers of Arabic) Applicants may be required to sit Arabic or English language tests.

Archaeology
Bournemouth Test for mature applicants.
Cambridge (Arch Anth) *Interview only:* Jesus; College-set essay: Newnham, Peterhouse, St Catharine's; *Test at interview:* Clare, Emmanuel, Girton, Hughes Hall, King's, Lucy Cavendish, Robinson, St Edmunds; *Preparatory study/assignment before interview*: Churchill, Robinson, Trinity; *School/college essays:* Christ's, Churchill, Corpus Christi, Downing, Fitzwilliam, Gonville and Caius, Homerton, Magdalene, Murray Edwards, Pembroke, Queens', Robinson, St John's, Selwyn, Sidney Sussex, Trinity Hall. Check www.cam.ac.uk/admissions/undergraduate/apply/tests.html.
Oxford (Arch Anth) Two recent marked essays are required, preferably in different subjects, plus a statement of no more than 300 words setting out your understanding of the relations between archaeology and social, cultural and biological anthropology required before interview. No written test at interview. Check www.admissions.ox.ac.uk/tests.
Oxford (Class Arch Anc Hist) Two recent marked essays are required. No written test at interview. Check www.admissions.ox.ac.uk/tests.

Architecture
Bradford (Coll Univ Centre) Questionnaire and samples of work before interview. Literacy and numeracy test at interview.
Cambridge *Interview only:* Downing, Girton, King's, Queens', Robinson, Sidney Sussex, Trinity Hall; *Test at interview:* Jesus, Lucy Cavendish, Pembroke, Trinity; *Preparatory study/assignment at/ before interview*: Clare, Emmanuel, Fitzwilliam, Magdalene, Murray Edwards, St Edmund's, Selwyn, Wolfson; *Project*: Peterhouse; *School/college essays:* Churchill, Clare, Gonville and Caius, Newnham, St John's. **NB All colleges offering course require a portfolio of recent work at interview.** Check www.cam.ac.uk/admissions/undergraduate/apply/tests.html.
Cardiff (also Archit Eng) Samples of work to be sent before interview.
Dundee Samples of work required before interview.
Huddersfield Portfolio of work required.
Liverpool The interview will be based on the portfolio of work.
London Met Portfolio of work required.
London South Bank Samples of work to be sent before interview.
Nottingham Trent Examples of work are required.
Sheffield Art portfolio required for applicants without A-level art.
Westminster Samples of work required before interview.

Art and Design
Bournemouth (Comp Vis Animat) Maths, logic and life-drawing tests at interview, and portfolio of work required.
Bournemouth Arts (UC) Practical test.
Creative Arts Tests.
Oxford (Fn Art) No written work required. Portfolio to be submitted by mid-November. Drawing examination. Two drawings in pencil or pencil and ink from a number of possible subjects. Check www.admissions.ox.ac.uk/tests.
Oxford and Cherwell Valley (Coll) A drawing examination is taken by all candidates who are interviewed (two drawings in pencil or pen and ink).

Ravensbourne Verbal examination. (Animat) Written test.
Westminster (Fash Mrchnds Mgt) Interview and numeracy test.

Asian and Middle Eastern Studies
Cambridge *Interview only:* St Edmund's; *Test at interview:* Girton (depending on subject), Fitzwilliam, Hughes Hall, Lucy Cavendish, Magdalene (depending on subject), Murray Edwards (depending on subject), Robinson, Sidney Sussex (depending on subject), Trinity Hall (depending on subject); *Preparatory study at/before interview:* Robinson, St John's, Selwyn; *School/college essays:* Christ's, Churchill, Clare, Corpus Christie, Downing, Emmanuel, Fitzwilliam, Girton, Gonville and Caius, Homerton, Jesus, King's, Magdalene, Murray Edwards, Newnham, Pembroke, Peterhouse, Queens', St Catharine's, St John's, Trinity, Trinity Hall, Wolfson. Check www.cam.ac.uk/admissions/undergraduate/apply/tests.html.

Biochemistry
London South Bank Degree subject-based test at interview.

Biological Sciences
London South Bank Degree subject-based test at interview.
Nottingham Trent Essay.

Biomedical Sciences
Hull (Coll) Essay.
Imperial London BMAT.
Nottingham Trent Essay.
Oxford BMAT is required for entry into all colleges. Check www.medsci.ox.ac.uk/study/bms.
Portsmouth Test of motivation and knowledge of the subject, the degree and careers to which it leads.

Bioveterinary Science
London (RVC) BMAT is not required for entry but applicants wanting to be considered for Merit Scholarships will have to take BMAT.

Broadcast Technology
Birmingham City Mature students to take English and mathematics tests.
Ravensbourne Written test.

Building/Construction
Bradford (Coll Univ Centre) Questionnaire before interview, literacy and numeracy tests at interview.
London South Bank (Bld Serv Eng) Degree subject-based test and numeracy test at interview.

Business Courses
Arts London (CFash) School work to be submitted before interview. Degree subject-based test and numeracy test at interview.
Bolton Literacy and numeracy tests.
Bradford (Coll Univ Centre) Written test.
Buckingham English test for applicants without English as a first language.
Farnborough (CT) Written test.
Newcastle Some short-listed applicants will be given a variety of assessment tests at interview.
Nottingham Trent Short-listed applicants are invited to a day-long business style assessment.
Westminster (Fash Mrchnds Mgt) Interview and numeracy test.

Celtic
Oxford Language aptitude or translation test.

Chemistry
London South Bank Degree subject-based test.

Classical Studies
Birmingham Language aptitude test for students without a language at GCSE.

Classics (See also *Archaeology*)
Cambridge *Test at interview:* Clare, Corpus Christi, Fitzwilliam, Girton, Hughes Hall, Lucy Cavendish, Newnham, St Catharine's, St Edmund's, St John's, Wolfson; *Preparatory study at/before interview:* Downing, Emmanuel, Jesus, Magdelene, Murray Edwards, Newnham, Peterhouse, Sidney Sussex; *School/college essays:* Christ's, Churchill, Clare, Corpus Christi, Downing, Emmanuel, Fitzwilliam, Girton, Gonville and Caius, Homerton, Jesus, King's, Magdalene, Murray Edwards, Newnham, Pembroke, Peterhouse, Queen's, Robinson, St Catharine's, St Edmund's, St John's, Selwyn, Sidney Sussex, Trinity, Trinity Hall. Check www.cam.ac.uk/admissions/undergraduate/apply/tests.html.
Oxford Two recently marked essays required, normally in areas related to Classics. Written tests at interview. Check www.admissions.ox.ac.uk/tests.

Classics and English
Oxford The ELAT and the Classics test. Two pieces of written work, relevant to either Classics or English also required. Check www.admissions.ox.ac.uk/tests.

Classics and Modern Languages
Oxford Classics and Modern Languages tests; two Classics essays and two modern language essays also required, one in the chosen language. Check with www.admissions.ox.ac.uk/tests.

Classics and Oriental Studies
Oxford Classics test; also language aptitude test for applicants planning to study Arabic, Hebrew, Persian or Turkish as main language; two pieces written work also required, at least one on classical topic. Check www.admissions.ox.ac.uk/tests.

Communication Studies
Buckingham English test for non-native-English-speaking applicants.
Cardiff Short essay.

Computer Science
Abertay Dundee (Comp Arts) Portfolio of work required. Practical tests at interview.
Blackburn (Coll) Questionnaire and tests before interview.
Cambridge *Interview only:* Magdalene, Girton, St Catharine's, Sidney Sussex, Wolfson; *Test at interview:* Churchill, Downing, Homerton, Hughes Hall, Peterhouse, Trinity; *Thinking Skills Assessment at interview:* Christ's, Clare, Corpus Christi, Emmanuel, Fitzwilliam, Gonville and Caius, Jesus, King's, Lucy Cavendish, Murray Edwards, Newnham, Pembroke, Peterhouse, Queens', Robinson, St Edmund's, St John's, Selwyn, Trinity Hall; *Preparatory study at/before interview:* Clare, Gonville and Caius, King's, Robinson. **NB** STEP used for conditional offers. Check www.cam.ac.uk/admissions/undergraduate/apply/tests.html.
Cumbria Literacy test at interview.
LJMU Questionnaire before interview. Literacy test at interview.
London (Gold) Degree subject-based test.
London (QM) Mathematical test at interview.
Oxford Maths aptitude test. See also *Mathematics* below. Check www.admissions.ox.ac.uk/tests.
UCLan Test for Foundation course applicants.

Counselling
Hull (Coll) Written test.

Czech
Oxford Language aptitude or translation test.

Dance
Chichester (Perf Arts) Group practical test.
Liverpool (LIPA) See **Dance/Dance Studies** in **Chapter 8** (Interview advice and questions).

Dental Nursing
Portsmouth (Dntl Nurs; Dntl Hyg Dntl Thera) Interview.

Dentistry
London (King's) UKCAT
Manchester UKCAT and interview.

Dietetics
London Met Interview and essay.
Ulster Health Professions Admissions Test: www.hpat.org.uk and www.ulster.ac.uk before completing the UCAS application.

Drama
De Montfort Written papers and/or tests.
Liverpool (LIPA) (Perf Arts (Actg)) Applicants will be expected to perform one devised piece, one Shakespearean piece and a song and give a short review of a performance they have seen recently.
London (Central Sch SpDr) Written papers and/or tests.
London (RH) Written work required at interview. At interview the University looks for students who are mentally agile and versatile who enjoy reading as well as taking part in productions.
Royal Welsh (CMusDr) Written papers and/or tests.
UCLan Written papers and/or tests.

Economics
Buckingham English test for non-native-English-speaking applicants.
Cambridge *Interview only:* Clare, Girton, Selwyn; *Test at interview:* Corpus Christi, Downing (mathematical test), Gonville and Caius, Homerton, Hughes Hall, Lucy Cavendish, Pembroke, Robinson, Sidney Sussex, Wolfson; *Thinking Skills Assessment:* Fitzwilliam, Jesus, King's, Newnham, Peterhouse, Queens', St Edmund's, St John's; *Preparatory study at/before interview:* Christ's, Churchill, Emmanuel, Fitzwilliam, Jesus, King's, Magdalene, Murray Edwards, Newnham, St Catherine's, St John's; *College-set essay/work:* Peterhouse, St John's, Trinity Hall; *School/college essays:* Christ's, Churchill, Homerton, Magdalene, Newnham, Robinson. Check www.cam.ac.uk/ admissions/undergraduate/apply/tests.html.
Lancaster Workshop.
Oxford (Econ Mgt) Thinking Skills Assessment (Oxford University). Check www.admissions.ox.ac.uk/ tests, and also www.admissionstests.cambridgeassessment.org.uk.

Education Studies (See also *Teacher Training*)
Anglia Ruskin Numeracy tests.
Cambridge *Interview only:* Clare, Fitzwilliam, Girton, Jesus, Murray Edwards, St Edmund's, St John's, Selwyn; *Test at interview:* Churchill (depending on subject), Downing (depending on subject), Homerton (depending on subject), Hughes Hall, Lucy Cavendish, Magdalene (depending on subjects), Trinity Hall, Wolfson; *Preparatory study at/before interview:* Churchill, Emmanuel, Homerton, Magdalene, Robinson, Trinity Hall; *College-set essay:* Emmanuel; *School/college essays:* Christ's, Churchill, Downing, Gonville and Caius, Homerton, Magdalene, Queens', Trinity Hall. Check www.cam.ac.uk/admissions/undergraduate/apply/tests.html.
Cumbria (Science and Education) Literacy test.
Durham (Primary Teaching) Key Skills tests at interview.
Newman (UC) Basic numeracy and literacy tests.

Engineering
Birmingham City Mature students without GCSE English and/or mathematics are required to take a literacy and/or numeracy test. (Snd Eng Prod) Mature students to take English and mathematics tests.
Blackburn (Coll) Questionnaire and tests before interview.
Bristol (Eng Des) A-level-based test.
Cambridge *Interview only:* Corpus Christi, Girton, Murray Edwards, St Catharine's; *Test at interview:* Churchill, Downing (maths test), Fitzwilliam, Gonville and Caius, Hughes Hall, King's (problem-solving), Lucy Cavendish, Magdalene, Newnham, Peterhouse, Robinson, St John's (maths test), Trinity; *Thinking Skills Assessment:* Christ's, Clare, Emmanuel, Gonville and Caius, Homerton, Jesus,

King's, Lucy Cavendish, Newnham, Pembroke, Queens', St Edmund's, Selwyn, Sidney Sussex, Trinity Hall, Wolfson; *Preparatory study at/before interview:* Clare, St John's (and possible STEP requirement). Check www.cam.ac.uk/admissions/undergraduate/apply/tests.html.

Kingston (Aircrft Eng) Numeracy and basic physics test.

London South Bank (Bld Serv Eng; Civ Eng; Elec Eng; Mech Eng) Degree subject-based test and numeracy test at interview.

Southampton Literacy and numeracy tests for foundation course applicants.

Southampton Solent Mathematical test at interview.

Suffolk (Univ Campus) (Civ Eng, Elec Electron Eng, Mech Eng courses) Interviews.

English

Anglia Ruskin Samples of written work required.

Birmingham City Samples of work required.

Blackpool and Fylde (Coll) Samples of work before interview.

Bristol Samples of work required.

Buckingham English test for non-native-English-speaking applicants.

Cambridge *Test at interview:* Churchill, Clare, Corpus Christi, Downing, Emmanuel, Fitzwilliam, Girton, Homerton, Hughes Hall, Jesus, King's, Lucy Cavendish, Magdalene, Murray Edwards, Newnham, Pembroke, Peterhouse, Queens', Robinson, St Catharine's, St Edmund's, St John's, Selwyn, Sidney Sussex, Trinity, Trinity Hall, Wolfson; *Preparatory study at/before interview:* Christ's, Churchill, Clare, Corpus Christi, Emmanuel, Fitzwilliam, Jesus, Newnham, Robinson, Selwyn, Sidney Sussex; *School/college essays:* Christ's, Churchill, Clare, Corpus Christi, Emmanuel, Fitzwilliam, Girton, Homerton, Jesus, King's, Magdalene, Murray Edwards, Newnham, Peterhouse, Queens', Robinson, St Catharine's, St John's, Selwyn, Sidney Sussex, Trinity, Trinity Hall. Check www.cam.ac.uk/admissions/undergraduate/apply/tests.html.

Cardiff Short essay.

London (UCL) After interview applicants are asked to write a critical commentary on an unseen passage of prose or verse.

Newport (Crea Writ) Samples of creative writing before interview.

Oxford (Engl Lang Lit) ELAT and one recent marked essay. (Engl Modn Langs) Modern Language(s) test, one recent marked essay. Check www.admissions.ox.ac.uk/tests.

Portsmouth (Engl Crea Writ; Crea Writ Dr) All applicants will be required to submit a short piece of creative writing to the admissions office. This should be between 400 and 500 words long and should include the following words and use each one twice: shell, flicker, knit, coin, compose, lark, stream, root. All the words must be used and each word must be used in a different context and/or with a different meaning on each occasion. Language should be used imaginatively and accurately.

Southampton Examples of written work required from Access students.

Equine Science

Lincoln Applicants are required to show that they can ride to BHS Level 2 or equivalent.

European and Middle Eastern Languages (See also Modern and Medieval Languages)

Oxford Language aptitude test, modern language test, TSA. Check www.admissions.ox.ac.uk/tests.

European Studies

London (Gold) Informal conversation in the relevant language (French, German or Spanish).

Film Production

Birmingham City (Film Prod Tech) Mature students to take English and mathematics tests.

Film Studies

Bournemouth (Script) A 20-page screenplay required before interview.

Bournemouth Arts (UC) Portfolio. Practical test of short film stills.

Creative Arts Portfolio at interview.

LJMU Questionnaire and test before interview.

Newport Portfolio of work.

Roehampton Essays taken to interview and discussed.
Westminster Questionnaire to be completed and samples of work required before interview.

Geography
Cambridge *Interview only:* Christ's, Downing, St Edmund's, St John's; *Test at interview:* Hughes Hall,
   Lucy Cavendish, Murray Edwards, Wolfson; *Preparatory study at/before interview:* Churchill, Clare,
   Corpus Christi, Emmanuel, Fitzwilliam, Girton, Homerton, King's, Newnham, Robinson, St
   Catharine's, Selwyn; *School/college essays:* Churchill, Clare, Corpus Christi, Emmanuel, Fitzwilliam,
   Girton, Gonville and Caius, Homerton, Jesus, King's, Magdalene, Murray Edwards, Newnham,
   Queens', Robinson, Sidney Sussex, Trinity, Trinity Hall. Check www.cam.ac.uk/admissions/
   undergraduate/apply/tests.html.
Cardiff Test for some joint courses.
Oxford No test. Two pieces of Geography-based work to be submitted by mid-November. Check
   www.admissions.ox.ac.uk/tests.

German (See also Modern and Medieval Languages)
Aston Written test at interview.
LJMU Written test at interview.

History
Bangor Samples of work only required from mature applicants without conventional qualifications.
Buckingham English test for non-native-English-speaking applicants.
Cambridge *Test at interview:* Hughes Hall, Lucy Cavendish, Newnham, Pembroke, Peterhouse,
   Robinson, St Edmund's, St John's, Sidney Sussex, Wolfson; *Thinking Skills Assessment:* St John's;
   Preparatory study at/before interview: Christ's, Churchill, Clare, Corpus Christi, Downing,
   Emmanuel, Fitzwilliam, Girton, Homerton, Murray Edwards, Newnham, Pembroke, Queens',
   Robinson, St Catharine's, St John's, Selwyn, Sidney Sussex, Trinity; *School/college essays:* Christ's,
   Churchill, Clare, Corpus Christi, Downing, Emmanuel, Fitzwilliam, Girton, Gonville and Caius,
   Homerton, Jesus, King's, Magdalene, Murray Edwards, Newnham, Pembroke, Peterhouse, Queens',
   Robinson, St Catharine's, Selwyn, Sidney Sussex, Trinity, Trinity Hall, Wolfson. Check www.cam.
   ac.uk/admissions/undergraduate/apply/tests.html.
Liverpool Test for mature applicants.
LJMU Mature students not in education must submit an essay.
London (Gold) Samples of written work from non-standard applicants and from those without
   academic qualifications.
Oxford (Hist (Anc Modn)) (Hist Econ) History Aptitude Test. (Hist Modn Langs) History Aptitude Test
   and Modern Language Test. (Hist Pol) No test. Those called for interview send an essay by end of
   November. Check www.admissions.ox.ac.uk/tests.
Roehampton Essays taken to interview and discussed.

History of Art
Cambridge *Interview only:* Fitzwilliam, Robinson, Selwyn; *Test at interview:* Hughes Hall, Lucy
   Cavendish, St Edmund's, Wolfson; *School/college essays:* Christ's, Churchill, Clare, Corpus Christi,
   Downing, Emmanuel, Girton, Gonville and Caius, Homerton, Jesus, King's, Magdalene, Murray
   Edwards, Newnham, Pembroke, Peterhouse, Queens', St John's, Sidney Sussex, Trinity, Trinity Hall.
   Check www.cam.ac.uk.admissions/ undergraduate/apply/tests.html.
Oxford Two pieces required: (a) a marked essay from an A-level or equivalent course, and (b) a brief
   account of no more than 750 words responding to an item of art or design to which the
   applicant has had first-hand access with a photograph or photocopy of the item provided if
   possible. No written test at interview although the applicant may be presented with photographs
   or artefacts for discussion at interview. Submitted written work may also be discussed at
   interview. Check www.admissions.ox.ac.uk/tests.

Italian (see also Medieval and Modern Languages)
Cardiff Test for some joint courses.

Journalism (see also **Media Studies**)
Glamorgan Test and interview.
Kent Written test.
Nottingham Trent Written test.
Portsmouth Admissions test required.

Land Economy
Cambridge *Interview only:* Christ's, Downing, Girton, Gonville and Caius, Pembroke, Queens', St Catharine's, St John's, Selwyn, Sidney Sussex, Trinity Hall; *Test at interview:* Hughes Hall, Lucy Cavendish, Wolfson; *Thinking Skills Assessment:* Jesus, Lucy Cavendish, Newnham, Robinson, St Edmund's; *Preparatory study at/before interview:* Fitzwilliam (written test prior to interview), Jesus, Magdalene, Trinity; *School/college essays:* Clare, Fitzwilliam, Homerton, Magdalene, Murray Edwards, Newnham. Check www.cam.ac.uk/admissions/undergraduate/apply/tests.html.

Law
Birmingham LNAT.
Birmingham City Questionnaire to be completed and an IQ test.
Bolton Own diagnostic test used (logic and reasoning).
Bradford (Coll Univ Centre) Academic tests at interview for mature students.
Bristol Check with the Law Department for LNAT requirements.
Cambridge *Test at interview:* Churchill, Hughes Hall, St Edmund's, Wolfson; *Cambridge Law Test:* Christ's, Clare, Corpus Christi, Downing, Emmanuel, Fitzwilliam, Girton, Gonville and Caius, Homerton, Jesus, King's, Lucy Cavendish, Magdalene, Murray Edwards, Newnham, Pembroke, Peterhouse, Queens', Robinson, St Catharine's, St John's, Selwyn, Sidney Sussex, Trinity, Trinity Hall; *Preparatory study at/before interview*: Christ's, Corpus Christi, Emmanuel, Homerton, Jesus, King's, Magdalene, Newnham, Pembroke, Selwyn, Sidney Sussex, St John's, Trinity, Trinity Hall. *Separate tests at interview*: Hughes Hall, St Edmund's, Wolfson. *School/college essays:* Emmanuel, Magdalene, Wolfson. Check www.cam.ac.uk/admissions/undergraduate/apply/tests.html.
London (King's) LNAT.
Nottingham LNAT.
Oxford All applicants take the LNAT. (Law Law St Euro) LNAT plus, at interview, a short oral test in the modern language for students taking a joint language, except for those taking European Legal Studies. No other written work required except for Harris Manchester College. Check www. admissions.ox.ac.uk/tests.

Linguistics
Cambridge *Interview only:* Christ's, Homerton, King's, Robinson, Wolfson; *Test at interview:* Churchill, Fitzwilliam, Girton, Jesus, Magdelene, St Johns; *Preparatory study at/before interview:* Churchill, Robinson, Sidney Sussex, Trinity. *School/college essays:* Churchill, Clare, Corpus Christi, Downing, Emmanuel, Gonville and Caius, Murray Edwards, Newnham, Peterhouse, Selwyn, Sidney Sussex, St John's, Trinity, Trinity Hall; *Contact the College:* Hughes Hall, Lucy Cavendish, Pembroke, Queens', St Catharine's, St Edmund's. Check www.cam.ac.uk/admissions/undergraduate/apply/tests.html.

LSE Entrance Exam
London LSE The LSE Entrance Examination is used for some applicants with non-standard backgrounds. The test is not subject or course-specific and consists of English comprehension exercises, essay questions and mathematical problems.

Mathematics
Cambridge *Test at interview:* Christ's, Churchill, Corpus Christi, Downing, Girton, Homerton, Hughes Hall, King's, Lucy Cavendish, Magdalene, Murray Edwards, Robinson, St Edmunds, St John's, Trinity; *Maths STEP:* Christ's, Churchill, Clare, Corpus Christi, Downing, Emmanuel, Fitzwilliam, Girton, Gonville and Caius, Homerton, Jesus, King's, Lucy Cavendish, Magdalene, Murray Edwards, Newnham, Pembroke, Peterhouse, Queens', Robinson, St Catharine's, St John's, Selwyn, Sidney Sussex, Trinity, Trinity Hall; *Preparatory study at/before interview:* King's, Newnham. Check www. cam.ac.uk/admissions/undergraduate/apply/tests.html.
LJMU Literacy and numeracy tests.

Oxford (Maths; Maths Comp Sci; Maths Stats) Mathematics Aptitude Test. Overseas candidates unable to attend for interview may be required to submit written work; (Maths Phil) Mathematics Aptitude Test; two essays showing capacity for reasoned argument and clear writing, not expected to be on a philosophical subject. Check www.admissions.ox.ac.uk/interviews/tests.

Media Studies
Blackpool and Fylde (Coll) Samples of work before interview.
Bolton Samples of work at interview.
Bournemouth 250-word essay.
Bournemouth and Poole (Coll) Degree subject-based test at interview.
Brighton (Spo Jrnl) Test for those called to interview: contact admissions tutor.
City Spelling, punctuation, grammar, general knowledge tests and an essay assignment. Tests on current affairs and use of English.
Coventry Interview and portfolio.
Edinburgh Napier (Jrnl) Samples of work before interview.
Hull (Coll) Essay required before interview.
LJMU Questionnaire to be completed before interview. Degree subject-based test at interview.
London Met Mathematics and written English test.
Newport Portfolio of work.
Westminster Questionnaire to be completed before interview.

Media Technology
Glamorgan Portfolio and interview.

Medicine
Cambridge *BMAT required by:* Christ's, Churchill, Clare, Corpus Christi, Downing, Emmanuel, Fitzwilliam, Girton, Gonville and Caius, Jesus, King's, Lucy Cavendish, Magdalene, Murray Edwards, Newnham, Pembroke, Peterhouse, Queens', Robinson, St Catharine's, St Edmund's, St John's, Selwyn, Sidney Sussex, Trinity, Trinity Hall, Wolfson. Check www.cam.ac.uk/admissions/undergraduate/apply/tests.html.
Hull UKCAT.
Imperial London (Six-year course) BMAT.
London (King's) UKCAT.
London (UCL) (Six year course) BMAT.
Manchester UKCAT and interview.
Nottingham UKCAT.

Modern and Medieval Languages (See also *Asian and Middle Eastern Studies, Oriental Studies and separate languages*)
Bangor Offer may be lowered after interview.
Cambridge *Test at interview:* Christ's, Churchill, Clare, Corpus Christi, Downing, Emmanuel, Fitzwilliam, Girton, Gonville and Caius, Homerton, Hughes Hall, Jesus, King's, Lucy Cavendish, Magdalene, Murray Edwards, Newnham, Pembroke, Peterhouse, Queens', Robinson, St Catharine's, St Edmund's, St John's, Selwyn, Sidney Sussex, Trinity Hall, Wolfson; *Preparatory study at/before interview:* Churchill, Clare, Emmanuel, Homerton, Jesus, Magdalene, Murray Edwards, Newnham, Pembroke, Peterhouse, Queens', Robinson, St Edmund's, St John's, Selwyn, Trinity, Trinity Hall; *School/college essays:* Christ's, Churchill, Corpus Christi, Downing, Emmanuel, Gonville and Caius, Homerton, Jesus, King's, Magdalene, Murray Edwards, Newnham, Pembroke, Peterhouse, Queens', Robinson, St Catharine's, St Edmund's, St John's, Selwyn, Trinity, Trinity Hall. Check www.cam.ac.uk/admissions/undergraduate/apply/tests.html.
Liverpool The interview lasts approximately 20 minutes with part of it to be conducted in the language(s) to be studied. Occasionally the applicant may be asked to sit a short grammar test.
Oxford (Modn Langs) Modern Languages Test(s). Two marked essays for each language being studied. (Modn Lang Ling) Language Aptitude Test and Modern Language Test. (Euro Mid E Langs) Language Aptitude Test and Modern Language Test. Two recent marked essays, one in the European language. Check course requirements carefully on the University website and check test requirements on www.admissions.ox.ac.uk/tests.

Multimedia Journalism

Glasgow Caledonian At interview candidates will be asked to complete a test to assess current affairs knowledge and written English as well as complete a voice test in the digital radio studio.

Music

Bangor Candidates offered the option of an audition.

Birmingham City Some subject-based and practical tests.

Cambridge *Test at interview:* Clare, Downing, Fitzwilliam, Girton, Gonville and Caius, Homerton, Hughes Hall, Jesus, King's, Lucy Cavendish, Magdalene, Murray Edwards, Newnham, Pembroke, Peterhouse, Queens', Robinson, St Catharine's, St Edmunds, St John's (possible keyboard test), Selwyn, Trinity, Trinity Hall; *Preparatory study at/before interview:* Churchill, Clare, Emmanuel, Newnham, Robinson, St Edmund's, Sidney Sussex, Wolfson; *School/college essays:* Christ's, Churchill, Corpus Christi, Downing, Emmanuel, Fitzwilliam, Girton, Gonville and Caius, Homerton, Jesus, King's, Magdalene, Murray Edwards, Newnham, Pembroke, Peterhouse, Queens', Robinson, St Catharine's, St John's, Selwyn, Sidney Sussex, Trinity, Trinity Hall. Check www.cam.ac.uk/admissions/undergraduate/apply/tests.html.

Coventry Music theory exam and audition held alongside an interview.

Edinburgh Napier Audition and theory test.

Leeds (CMus) (Jazz; Pop Mus) In-house theory test to determine level of musical theory ability.

Liverpool Interview.

London (Gold) Degree subject-based test.

London (King's) Only borderline applicants are interviewed. Samples of written work may be requested.

London (RAcMus) (BMus) 50-minute written test; possible keyboard and aural skills test.

London Met Performance tests and essay.

Oxford One marked sample of harmony and/or counterpoint and two marked essays on any areas or aspects of music. Candidates may submit a portfolio of compositions (these are non-returnable). Performance tests at interview. Check www.admissions.ox.ac.uk/tests.

West London (Mus Tech) Students required to produce a portfolio of work. (Mus Perf) Students attend an audition: see www.uwl.ac.uk.

TABLE OF INTERVIEW REQUIREMENTS FOR MUSIC COURSES

Key　P = Performance　　A = Aural　　S = Sight-singing
　　　　K = Keyboard tests　H = Harmony and Counterpoint (Written)
　　　　E = Essay　　　　　X = Extracts for analysis or 'guessing the composer', dates etc.

Bangor* PAX (bring example)	**Lancaster** PAH
Bath Spa PHES	**Leeds** P
Birmingham HE	**Liverpool Hope** PKH
Birmingham City P	**London (Gold)** PX
Bristol PSKHEXA	**London (King's)** PASK
Cambridge* AHEX (bring example)	**London (RAcMus)** PKHX
Cardiff PX	**London (RCMus)** PS
Chichester P	**Oxford** PKXS
City P	**RConsvS** PSA
Colchester (Inst) PAKE	**Royal Welsh (CMus/Dr)** PE (submit example)
Derby PE	**Salford** PHS
Durham PKXA	**Sheffield** PEA
Edinburgh PHES	**Ulster** P
Glasgow PS	**Wolverhampton** PE
Huddersfield P	**York** PAKS

* Examples may include essays, harmony and counterpoint compositions. Performance tests/auditions are standard practice for Music courses in all universities and colleges.

Natural Sciences (Biological Sciences)

Cambridge *Interview only:* Churchill, Corpus Christi, Downing, Fitzwilliam, Girton, Jesus, King's, Newnham, Pembroke, St Catharine's, Selwyn; *Test at interview:* Homerton, Hughes Hall, Lucy Cavendish, Magdalene, Murray Edwards, Robinson, St Edmund's, St John's, Trinity; *Thinking Skills Assessment:* Clare, Emmanuel, Gonville and Caius, Peterhouse, Queens', St Edmund's, Trinity Hall, Wolfson; *Preparatory study at/before interview:* Emmanuel, Homerton, Magdalene, Robinson; *School/college essays:* Christ's (or project work), Peterhouse, Robinson. Check www.cam.ac.uk/admissions/undergraduate/apply/tests.html.

Natural Sciences (Physical Sciences)

Cambridge *Interview only:* Christ's, Churchill, Fitzwilliam, Girton, Jesus, Pembroke, St Catharine's, Selwyn; *Test at interview:* Corpus Christi, Downing (mathematical test), Homerton, Hughes Hall, Lucy Cavendish, Magdalene, Robinson, St John's, Trinity; *Thinking Skills Assessment:* Clare, Emmanuel, Gonville and Caius, King's, Murray Edwards, Newnham, Peterhouse, Queens', St Edmund's, Trinity Hall, Wolfson; *Preparatory study at/before interview:* Emmanuel (for Chemistry), Homerton; *School/college essays:* Murray Edwards. Check www.cam.ac.uk/admissions/undergraduate/apply/tests.html.

Nursing

Birmingham City Literacy and numeracy tests at interview.
Bolton Literacy test.
Bristol UWE Questionnaire/test before interview.
Bucks New Tests for BSc and DipHE Nursing.
City Written test.
Derby Literacy and numeracy tests at interview.
Dundee Literacy test.
Liverpool A group of candidates is given a task to undertake during which applicants are assessed for their ability to work in a team, maturity, communication skills and their level of involvement.
London South Bank (Nurs A, C, MH) Literacy and numeracy tests at interview.
Suffolk (Univ Campus) Interview and tests.
UEA Tests.
West London Numeracy and literacy tests.
Wolverhampton Tests.
York Literacy and numeracy tests.

Occupational Therapy

Bristol UWE Questionnaire/test before interview.
Ulster Health Professions Admissions Test: see www.hpat.org.uk and www.ulster.ac.uk before completing the UCAS application.

Optometry

Bradford (Coll Univ Centre) Literacy and numeracy tests.

Oriental Studies

Cambridge See Asian and Middle Eastern Studies.
Oxford Language Aptitude Test. Two essays, preferably of different kinds. Essays in a European language are acceptable. No prior knowledge of Oriental languages required. Occasional written tests. Check the University website and prospectuses and www.admissions.ox.ac.uk/tests.

Osteopathy

British Sch Ost All prospective students are required to attend an Interview and Evaluation Day where they are normally required to perform a range of aptitude tests, a written English test and a personal interview in order to determine their suitability for the course and the BSO.

Paramedic Science
Canterbury Christ Church Candidates must pass a fitness test at interview and are subject to a satisfactory health clearance and Criminal Records Bureau check before an offer can be made.
Coventry Fitness and literacy test.

Pharmacology/Pharmaceutical Sciences
Imperial London (Pharmacology and Translational Medical Sciences) BMAT.
Portsmouth Test of motivation, knowledge of the subject, of the degree course and the careers to which it leads.

Pharmacy
LJMU Literacy and numeracy tests.
Portsmouth (A-level students) Test of motivation and knowledge of Pharmacy as a profession. (Other applicants) Test of chemistry and biology, plus literacy and numeracy tests.

Philosophy
Cambridge *Test at interview:* Christ's, Churchill, Clare, Corpus Christi, Downing, Emmanuel, Fitzwilliam, Girton, Gonville and Caius, Homerton, Hughes Hall, Jesus, King's, Lucy Cavendish, Magdalene, Newnham, Pembroke, Peterhouse, Queens', Robinson, St Catharine's, St Edmund's, St John's, Selwyn, Sidney Sussex, Trinity, Trinity Hall, Wolfson; *School/college essays:* Churchill, Downing, Emmanuel, Homerton, Magdalene, Peterhouse, St Catharine's, Trinity. Check www.cam.ac.uk/admissions/undergraduate/apply/tests.html.
Leeds Written test at interview.
Liverpool Samples of written work may be requested in cases where there is a question of the applicant's ability to cope with the academic skills required of them.
London (UCL) Written test at interview.
Oxford (Phil Modn Langs) Philosophy and Modern Languages tests; two pieces of written work required. (Phil Theol) Philosophy test and two pieces of written work; (Phil Pol Econ (PPE)) Thinking Skills Assessment (Oxford University); no written work required. Check course pages on University website and www.admissions.ox.ac.uk/tests.
Warwick Written test at interview.

Physical Education
Chichester Physical test.
LJMU Literacy and numeracy tests and gym assessment.

Physics
Oxford Physics Aptitude test; no written work required. Check www.admissions.ox.ac.uk/tests.

Physics and Philosophy
Oxford Physics Aptitude test; two pieces of written work required.

Physiotherapy
Liverpool A group of candidates is given a task to undertake, during which they are assessed for their ability to work in a team, maturity, communication skills and their level of involvement.
Robert Gordon Practical testing varies from year to year.
UEA Tests.
Ulster Health Professions Admissions Test: see www.hpat.org.uk and www.ulster.ac.uk before completing the UCAS application.

Podiatry
Ulster Health Professions Admissions Test: see www.hpat.ac.uk and www.ulster.ac.uk before completing the UCAS application.

Politics
Buckingham English test for non-native-English-speaking applicants.
Cambridge *Test at interview:* Churchill, Jesus, Lucy Cavendish, Robinson, St John's, Sidney Sussex; *Thinking Skills Assessment:* Clare, Gonville and Caius, King's, Newnham, Queens', St John's;

Preparatory work at/before interview: Emmanuel, Magdalene, Murray Edwards, Newnham, Robinson, Sidney Sussex; *School/college essays:* Christ's, Churchill, Corpus Christi, Downing, Emmanuel, Fitzwilliam, Girton, Gonville and Caius, Homerton, Jesus, King's, Magdalene, Murray Edwards, Newnham, Pembroke, Robinson, St Edmund's, St John's, Selwyn, Sidney Sussex, Trinity, Trinity Hall (College-set essay), Wolfson. Check www.cam.ac.uk/admissions/undergraduate/apply/tests.html.

Kent Written test.

LJMU Mature students not in education must submit an essay.

London (Gold) Essays from current A/AS-level course to be submitted before interview.

Oxford See (Phil, Pol and Econ (PPE)) under Philosophy.

Popular Music

Glamorgan Audition.

Product Design

Dundee Portfolio and interview will determine the appropriate entry point for candidate (Level 1 or 2).

Psychology

Bangor Access course entry students may be asked to submit an essay.

Birmingham Written tests at interview.

LJMU Written tests at interview.

London (UCL) Questionnaire to be completed.

Oxford (Expmtl Psy) Thinking Skills Assessment test (Oxford University); no written work required. See www.admissions.ox.ac.uk/tests.

Roehampton Questionnaire before interview; test at interview.

Radiography

Liverpool (Diag Radiog Radiothera) A group of candidates is given a task to undertake, during which they are assessed for their ability to work in a team, maturity, communication skills and their level of involvement.

Ulster Health Professions Admissions Test: see www.hpat.org.uk and www.ulster.ac.uk before completing the UCAS application.

Retail Store Management

Hull (Coll) Literacy and numeracy tests.

Social Policy

London LSE Two essays to be submitted before interview.

Social Work

Anglia Ruskin Samples of written work required.

Bangor Written test at interview.

Birmingham Written test at interview.

Birmingham City Some tests are set at interview.

Bristol UWE Questionnaire before interview.

Brunel Written test at interview.

Bucks New Tests.

De Montfort Written test at interview.

Derby Literacy and numeracy tests at interview.

Dundee Literacy test.

Durham New (Coll) Written test at interview.

London (Gold) Written test at interview. Questions on social work practice and the applicant's experience of working in the social work/social care field.

London Met Pre-interview literacy test and if successful, an interview.

London South Bank Literacy and numeracy tests.

Manchester Met (Yth Commun Wk) Tests.

NEW (Coll) Test.
Newman (UC) (Yth Commun Wk) Written test.
Portsmouth Test.
Sheffield Literacy and numeracy tests.
Suffolk (Univ Campus) Interview and test.
UEA Test.
Wolverhampton Tests.

Sociology
Leeds Copy of written work requested.
London Met Where appropriate separate tests in comprehension and mathematical skills that will be used to help us reach a decision.

Speech Sciences
Manchester Met Two essays and a questionnaire.
Sheffield Listening test and problem-solving.
Ulster Health Professions Admissions Test: see www.hpat.org.uk and www.ulster.ac.uk before completing the UCAS application.

Sports Sciences/Studies
Nottingham Trent (Spo Hrs Mgt) Riding test.

Stage Management
Hull (Coll) Essay.

Teacher Training
Anglia Ruskin Literacy test at interview; maths test for some courses.
Bath Spa Written test at interview.
Bishop Grosseteste (UC) Literacy and numeracy tests are part of the selection critera at interview.
Brighton Written test at interview.
Bristol UWE Literacy and mathematical tests at interview.
Brunel Literacy, mathematical and practical tests depending on subject.
Canterbury Christ Church All candidates are interviewed in groups of 8-10 and assessments are made based on the results of a written English test and performance in the group interview.
Cardiff Met Literacy and numeracy test.
Chester Literacy and numeracy tests.
Chichester Written test at interview.
Cumbria Written test at interview.
De Montfort Written test at interview.
Dundee Literacy and numeracy tests.
Durham Key Skills test.
Gloucestershire Mathematical test at interview. Written test at interview.
LJMU Written test at interview. Mathematical and diagnostic tests on interview day.
London South Bank Literacy and numeracy tests.
Newman (UC) Basic literacy and numeracy tests for QTS and other courses.
Nottingham Trent Practical presentation. Written test at interview.
Plymouth Mathematical test at interview. Written test at interview.
Roehampton Written test at interview.
St Mary's Twickenham (UC) Literacy and mathematical tests at interview. Practical tests for PE.
Sheffield Hallam Interview with numeracy and literary tests.
Winchester Literacy test at interview.
Worcester Written test at interview.

Theology and Religious Studies
Cambridge *Test at interview:* Clare, Corpus Christi, Fitzwilliam, Hughes Hall, Lucy Cavendish, St Edmund's; *Preparatory work at/before interview:* Corpus Christi, Emmanuel, Girton, Jesus, Magdalene, Newnham, Selwyn; *School/college essays:* Christ's, Clare, Corpus Christi, Downing,

Emmanuel, Fitzwilliam, Girton, Gonville and Caius, Homerton, Jesus, King's, Magdalene, Murray Edwards, Newnham, Pembroke, Peterhouse, Queens', Robinson, St Catharine's, St John's, Selwyn, Sidney Sussex, Trinity, Trinity Hall, Wolfson. Check www.cam.ac.uk/admissions/undergraduate/apply/tests.html.

Oxford (Theol) No test; two pieces written work required. (Theol Orntl St) Oriental Studies Language Aptitude Test for candidates planning to study Islam or Judaism; two pieces written work required. Check www.admissions.ox.ac.uk/tests.

Veterinary Science/Medicine

Cambridge *BMAT:* Churchill, Clare, Downing, Emmanuel, Fitzwilliam, Girton, Gonville and Caius, Jesus, Lucy Cavendish, Magdalene, Murray Edwards, Newnham, Pembroke, Queens', Robinson, St Catharine's, St Edmund's, St John's, Selwyn, Sidney Sussex, Trinity Hall, Wolfson; *Preparatory work at/before interview:* Emmanuel, Robinson. Check www.cam.ac.uk/admissions/undergraduate/apply/tests.html.

Liverpool Candidates are asked to write an essay on a veterinary topic prior to interview.

London (RVC) BMAT (see www.admissionstests.cambridgeassessment.org.uk and www.rvc.ac.uk).

Myerscough (Coll) (Vet Nurs) Subject-based test at interview.

SELECTION OF APPLICANTS

University and college departmental admissions tutors are responsible for selecting candidates, basing their decisions on the policies of acceptable qualifications established by each institution and, where required, applicants' performance in admissions tests. There is little doubt that academic achievement, aptitude and promise are the most important factors although other subsidiary factors may be taken into consideration. The outline which follows provides information on the way in which candidates are selected for degree and diploma courses.

- Grades obtained by the applicant in GCE A-level and AS-level examinations and the range of subjects studied may be considered.

- Applicant's performance in aptitude and admissions tests, as required by universities and colleges.

- Academic record of the applicant throughout his or her school career, especially up to A-level and AS-levels, Highers, Advanced Highers or other qualifications and the choice of subjects. If you are taking general studies at A-level or AS-level confirm with the admissions tutor that this is acceptable.

- Time taken by the applicant to obtain good grades at GCSE/Standard Grade and A-level and AS-levels/Highers/Advanced Highers.

- Forecast or the examination results of the applicant at A-level and AS-level and head teacher's report.

- The applicant's intellectual development; evidence of ability and motivation to follow the chosen course.

- The applicant's range of interests, both in and out of school; aspects of character and personality.

- The vocational interests, knowledge and experience of the applicant particularly if they are choosing vocational courses.

INTERVIEWS

Fewer applicants are now interviewed than in the past but even if you are not called you should make an effort to visit your chosen universities and/or colleges before you accept any offer. Interviews may be arranged simply to give you a chance to see the institution and the department and to meet the staff and students. Alternatively, interviews may be an important part of the selection procedure for specific courses such as Law, Medicine and Teaching. If they are, you need to prepare yourself well. Most interviews last approximately 20–30 minutes and you may be interviewed by more than one person. For practical subjects such as Music and Drama almost certainly you will be asked to perform, and for artistic subjects, to take examples of your work. For some courses you may also have a written or other test at interview (see above).

How best can you prepare yourself?

Firstly, as one applicant advised, 'Go to the interview – at least you'll see the place.'

Secondly, on the question of dress, try to turn up looking smart (it may not matter, but it can't be wrong).

Two previous applicants were more specific: 'Dress smartly but sensibly so you are comfortable for travelling and walking round the campus.'

More general advice is also important

- 'Prepare well – interviewers are never impressed by applicants who only sit there with no willingness to take part.'
- 'Read up the prospectus and course details. Know how their course differs from any others you have applied for and be able to say why you prefer theirs.'
- 'They always ask if you have any questions to ask them: prepare some!' For example, How many students are admitted to the course each year? What are the job prospects for graduates? How easy is it to change from your chosen course to a related course?

Questions which you could ask might focus on the ways in which work is assessed, the content of the course, field work, work experience, teaching methods, accommodation and, especially for vocational courses, contacts with industry, commerce or the professions. However, don't ask questions which are already answered in the prospectus!

These are only a few suggestions and other questions may come to mind during the interview which, above all, should be a two-way flow of information. It is also important to keep a copy of your UCAS application (especially Section 10) for reference since your interview will probably start with a question about something you have written.

Usually interviewers will want to know why you have chosen the subject and why you have chosen their particular institution. They will want to see how motivated you are, how much care you have taken in choosing your subject, how much you know about your subject, what books you have read. If you have chosen a vocational course they will want to find out how much you know about the career it leads to, and whether you have visited any places of work or had any work experience. If your chosen subject is also an A-level subject you will be asked about your course and the aspects of the course you like the most.

Try to relax. For some people interviews can be an ordeal; most interviewers know this and will make allowances. The following extract from the Oxford prospectus will give you some idea of what admissions tutors look for.

- 'Interviews serve various purposes and no two groups of tutors will conduct them in the same way or give them exactly the same weight. Most tutors wish to discover whether a candidate has done more than absorb passively what he/she has been taught. They try to ascertain the nature and strength of candidates' intellectual interests and their capacity for independent development. They are also likely to ask about applicants' other interests outside their school curriculum. This is partly because between two candidates of equal academic merit, preference will be given to the one who has the livelier interests or activities, and partly because it is easier to learn about candidates when they talk about what interests them most.'
- 'Interviews are in no sense hostile interrogations. Those candidates who show themselves to be honest, thoughtful and unpretentious will be regarded more favourably than those who try to impress or take the view that it is safest to say as little as possible. We do not expect candidates to be invariably mature and judicious.'

In the tables in **Chapter 8** (**Selection interviews, Interview advice and questions** and **Reasons for rejection**) you will also find examples of questions which have been asked in recent years for which you might prepare, and non-academic reasons why applicants have been rejected! **Chapter 5**, Applications, provides a guide through the process of applying to your chosen universities and courses and highlights key points for your action.

The subject tables in the next chapter represent the core of the book, listing degree courses offered by all UK universities and colleges. These tables are designed to provide you with the information you need so that you can match your abilities and interests with your chosen degree subject, prepare your application and find out how applicants are selected for courses.

At the top of each table there is a brief overview of the subject area, together with a selection of websites for organisations that can provide relevant careers or course information. This is then followed by the subject tables themselves in which information is provided in sequence under the following headings.

Course offers information
- Subject requirements/preferences (GCSE/A-level/other requirements)
- NB Offers statement
- Your target offers and examples of courses provided by each institution
- Alternative offers

Examples of Foundation degrees in the subject field

Choosing your course
- Some course features
- Universities and colleges teaching quality
- Top universities and colleges (research)
- Examples of sandwich degree courses

Admissions information
- Number of applicants per place
- Advice to applicants and planning the UCAS personal statement
- Misconceptions about this course
- Selection interviews
- Interview advice and questions
- Reasons for rejection (non-academic)

After-results advice
- Offers to applicants repeating A-levels

Graduate destinations and employment
- Career note

Other degree subjects for consideration

When selecting a degree course it is important to try to judge the points score or grades that you are likely to achieve and compare them with the offers listed under **Your target offers and examples of courses provided by each institution**. However, even though you might be capable of achieving the indicated grades or UCAS Tariff points, it is important to note that these are likely to be the minimum grades or points required and that there is no guarantee that you will receive an offer: other factors in your application, such as the personal statement, references, and admissions test performance will be taken into consideration (see also **Chapters 4** and **6**).

University departments frequently adjust their offers, depending on the numbers of candidates applying, so you must not assume that the offers and policies published now will necessarily apply to courses starting in 2013 or thereafter. Even though offers may change during the 2012/13 application cycle, you can assume that the offers published in this book represent the typical academic levels at which you should aim.

Below are explanations of the information given under the headings in the subject tables. It is important that you read these carefully so that you understand how they can help you to choose and apply for courses that are right for you.

COURSE OFFERS INFORMATION
Subject requirements/preferences
Brief information is given on the GCSE and A-level requirements. Specific A-level subject requirements for individual institutions are listed separately. Other requirements are sometimes specified, where these

are relevant to the course subject area, for example, medical requirements for health-related courses and Criminal Records Bureau (CRB) clearance. Check prospectuses and websites of universities and colleges for course requirements.

Your target offers and examples of courses provided by each institution
Universities and colleges offering degree courses in the subject area are listed in descending order according to the number of UCAS Tariff points and/or A-level grades they are likely to require applicants to achieve. The UCAS Tariff points total is listed down the left-hand side of the page, and to the right appear all the institutions (in alphabetical order) likely to make offers in this Tariff point range. (Information on the UCAS Tariff is given in **Appendix 1** and guidance on how to calculate your offers is provided on the inside back cover of this book. Please also read the information in the **Important Note** box below.)

The courses included on the offers line are examples of the courses available in the subject field at that university or college. You will need to check prospectuses and websites for a complete list of the institution's single, joint, combined or major/minor degree courses available in the subject. For each institution listed, the following information may be given.

Name of institution
Note that the name of an institution's university college or campus may be given in brackets after the institution title, for example London (King's) or Kent (Medway Sch Pharm). Where the institution is not a university, further information about its status may also be given to indicate the type of college – for example (UC) to mean University College or (CAg) to mean College of Agriculture. This is to help readers to differentiate between the types of colleges and to help them identify any specialisation a college may have, for example art or agriculture. A full list of abbreviations used is given under the heading **INSTITUTION ABBREVIATIONS** later in this chapter.

Grades/points offer
After the institution's name, a line of offers information is given, showing a typical offer made by the institution for the courses indicated in brackets at the end of the line. **Offers, however, may vary between applicants and the published grades and/or points offers should be regarded as targets to aim for and not necessarily the actual grades or points required**. Offers may be reduced after the publication of A-level results, particularly if a university or college is left with spare places. However, individual course offers listed in the Tables in **Chapter 8** are abridged and should be used as a first source of reference and comparison only. It is not possible to publish all the variables relevant to each offer: applicants must check prospectuses and websites for full details of all offers and courses.

Depending on the details given by institutions, the offers may provide information as follows.

- **Grades** The specific grades, or average grades, required at GCE A-level or at A-level plus AS-level or, if specified, EPQ for the listed courses. (NB Graded offers may require specific grades for specific subjects.) A-level grades are always presented in capital letters; AS-levels and EPQ grades are shown in lower case – so the offer BBBc would indicate three grade Bs at A-level, plus an additional EPQ or AS-level at grade c. Where necessary, the abbreviation 'AL' is used to indicate A-level, 'AS' to indicate AS-level and EPQ to indicate that an Extended Project Qualification is part of the offer. Offers are usually shown in terms of three A-level grades although some institutions accept two grades with the same points total or, alternatively, two A-level grades accompanied by AS-level grades. Two AS-levels may generally be regarded as equivalent to one A-level, and one Double Award A-level as equivalent to two standard A-levels.

NB Unit grade and module information, now introduced into the admissions system, is most likely to be required by universities where a course is competitive, or where taking a specific unit is necessary or desirable for entry. Check with institutions' websites for their latest information.

- **UCAS Tariff points** A, AS-levels, International Baccalaureate (IB), Scottish Highers, the Advanced Diploma and a range of other qualifications have a unit value in the UCAS Tariff system (see **The UCAS Tariff Points Table** in **Appendix 1**). Where a range of Tariff points is shown, for example 220–180 points, offers are usually made within this points range for these specified courses. Note that, in some cases, an institution may require a points score which is higher than the specified grade offer given. This can be for a number of reasons – for example, you may not be offering the standard subjects that would have been stipulated in a grades offer. In such cases additional points may be added by way of AS-levels, Key Skills etc.

A Tariff point offer will not usually discriminate between the final year exam subjects being taken by the applicant unless otherwise stated, although certain GCSE subjects may be stipulated eg English or mathematics.

Admission tutors have the unenviable task of trying to assess the number of applicants who will apply for their courses against the number of places available and so judging the offers to be made. It is therefore important when reading the offers tables to be aware that variations occur each year. Lower offers or equivalents may be made to disadvantaged students, mature and international applicants.

The offers published in this edition therefore are based on expected admission policies operating from September to January 2012/13. They are targets to be achieved and in the case of popular courses at popular universities they should be regarded as minimum entry qualifications.

See **Chapter 4** for information from universities about their admissions policies including, for example, information about their expected use of A*, unit grades, the Advanced Diploma, the Extended Project and the Cambridge Pre-U in their offers for applicants. See **Appendix 1** for **The UCAS 2013 Entry Tariff Points** tables.

● **Admissions tests for Law, Medicine and Veterinary Science/Medicine** Where admissions tests form part of a university's offer for any of these subjects, this is indicated on the offers line in the subject tables for the relevant university. This is shown by '+LNAT' (for Law), '+BMAT' or '+UKCAT' (for Medicine), and '+BMAT' (for Veterinary Science/Medicine). For example, the offers lines could read as follows:

Edinburgh – AAAb +UKCAT (incl AL chem+1 from maths/phys/biol; AS biol min) (Medicine 5/6 yrs) (IB 37 pts HL 766)
London (King's) – AAAb +LNAT (Law) (IB 38 pts HL 555–554)
London (RVC) – AAA +BMAT (incl AL chem+biol+1 other) (Vet Med)

Entry and admissions tests will be required for 2013 by a number of institutions for a wide range of subjects: see **Chapter 6** and the subject tables in **Chapter 8** for more information and check university websites and prospectuses.

Course title(s)
After the offer, an abbreviated form of the course title(s) to which the offers information refers is provided, also in brackets. The abbreviations used (see **COURSE ABBREVIATIONS** at the end of this chapter) closely relate to the course titles shown in the institutions' prospectuses. When the course gives the opportunity to study abroad (for example, in Continental Europe, Australia, North America) the abbreviated name of the relevant country is shown after the abbreviated course title. For example:

Lancaster – AAB 340 pts (Env Sci (N Am/Aus); MChem Env Chem (St Abrd)) (IB 30 pts)

When experience in industry is provided as part of the course (not necessarily a sandwich course) this can be indicated on the offers line by including 'Ind' after the abbreviated course title. For example:

Bristol – ABB (Pharmacol; Pharmacol (Ind)) (IB 34 pts)

Sometimes the information in the offers line relates to more than one course (see **Plymouth** below). In such cases, each course title is separated with a semicolon.

Plymouth – 300 pts (MEng Civ Eng; Civ Cstl Eng)

When a number of joint courses exist in combination with a major subject, they may be presented using a list separated by slashes – for example '(Euro Mgt with Fr/Ger/Ital/Span)' indicates European Management with French or German or Italian or Spanish. Some titles may be followed by the word 'courses' – for example, (Geog courses):

St Andrews – AAB (Theol St; Bib St courses) (IB 30 pts)

This means that the information on the offers line refers not only to the Single Honours course in Theological Studies, but also to the range of Biblical Studies courses. For some institutions with extensive Combined Honours programmes, the information given on the offers line may specify (Comb Hons) or (Comb courses).

Courses awaiting validation are usually publicised in prospectuses and on websites. However, these are not included in the tables in **Chapter 8** since there is no guarantee that they will run. You should check with the university that a non-validated course will be available.

To help you understand the information provided under the **Your target offers and examples of courses provided by each institution** heading, the box below provides a few examples with their meaning explained underneath.

OFFERS LINES EXPLAINED

320 pts [University/College name] – BBCc **or** BBccc (Fr Ger)
For the joint course in French and German, the University requires grades of BBC (280 pts) at A-level plus AS-level grade c (40 pts) making a total of 320 points or, alternatively, BB (200 pts) at A-level plus AS-level grades ccc (120 pts), making the same total.

320 pts [University/College name] – 320 pts BBC +AS/EPQ c (Biomed Sci (Genet))
For the Biomedical Sciences course specialising in Genetics the University requires 320 pts, typically from 3 A-levels, together with either one AS-level or Extended Project Qualification (EPQ). The typical offer will be BBC at A-level plus c in either an AS-level or an EPQ.

220 pts [University/College name] – 220–280 pts (Geography)
For Geography, the University usually requires 220 UCAS Tariff points, but offers may range up to 280 UCAS Tariff points.

Alternative offers
In each of the subject tables, offers are shown in A-level grades or equivalent UCAS Tariff points, and in some cases as points offers of the International Baccalaureate Diploma (see above). However, applicants taking Scottish Highers/Advanced Highers, the Welsh Baccalaureate, Advanced Diploma, the IB Diploma, the Irish Leaving Certificate, the Advanced Diploma, the Extended Project and the Cambridge Pre-U should refer to **Appendix 1 UCAS 2013 Entry Tariff Points**. For more information, see www.ucas.com/students/ucas_Tariff/Tarifftables or contact the institution direct.

IB offers
A selection of IB points offers appears at the end of some university/subject entries. For comparison of entry requirements, applicants with IB qualifications should check the A-level offers required for their course and then refer to **Appendix 1** which gives the revised IB UCAS points Tariff for 2013 entry. The figures under this subheading indicate the number or range of International Baccalaureate (IB) Diploma points likely to be requested in an offer. A range of points indicates variations between Single and Joint Honours courses. Applicants should check with the universities for any requirements for points gained from specific Higher Level subjects. Applicants offering the IB should check with prospectuses and websites and, if in doubt, contact admissions tutors for the latest information on IB offers.

Scottish offers
Scottish Honours degrees normally take four years. However, students with very good qualifications may be admitted into the second year of courses (Advanced entry). In some cases it may even be possible to enter the third year.

This year we have not included the offers details for Advanced entry. Any student with sufficient A-levels or Advanced Highers considering this option should check with the university to which they are applying. The policies at some Scottish universities are listed below:

Aberdeen Advanced entry possible for many courses, but not for Education, Law or Medicine.

Abertay Dundee No advanced entry.

Dundee Advanced entry possible for many courses, but not Art, Education, Law or Medicine.

Edinburgh Only in very unusual cases is entry to the second year accepted.

Edinburgh Napier Advanced entry to Stages 2, 3 or 4 of a programme, particularly for those with an HNC/HND or those with (or expecting to obtain) good grades in Advanced Highers or A-levels.

Glasgow No advanced entry except in some cases for Engineering and Sciences, but not for Accountancy, Arts or Social Science courses.

Glasgow Caledonian No advanced entry.

Queen Margaret Advanced entry for some courses.

St Andrews Advanced entry for some courses.

Stirling Advanced entry for some courses.

Strathclyde Advanced entry for some courses.

West Scotland Advanced entry for some courses.

For others not on this list, please check individual university and college websites.

Student number controls

Universities and colleges have been given the freedom to expand their number of places for highly-qualified applicants – defined as those who hold the following grades at A level, or equivalent, qualifications:

- $A^*A^*A^*$
- A^*A^*A
- A^*AA
- AAA
- A^*AB
- A^*A^*C
- AAB
- A^*A^*D
- A^*AC
- A^*BB
- A^*A and an A at AS-level.

IMPORTANT NOTE ON THE COURSE OFFERS INFORMATION

The information provided in **Chapter 8** is presented as a first reference source as to the target levels required. Institutions may alter their standard offers in the light of the qualifications offered by applicants.

The offers they publish do not constitute a contract and are not binding on prospective students: changes may occur between the time of publication and the time of application in line with market and student demand.

The points levels shown on the left-hand side of the offers listings are for ease of reference for the reader: not all universities will be making offers using the UCAS Tariff points system and it cannot be assumed that they will accept a points equivalent to the grades they have stipulated. Check university and college prospectuses, and also their websites, for their latest information before submitting your application.

EXAMPLES OF FOUNDATION DEGREES IN THE SUBJECT FIELD

This section lists examples of universities and colleges offering Foundation degrees in the subject field. Foundation degrees are employment-related higher education qualifications bringing higher education and business closer together to meet the needs of employers. The degrees are at a lower level than Honours degrees and can be studied on a part-time basis or full-time over two years. Entry requirements for these courses vary, but many institutions request between 60 and 140 UCAS Tariff points.

CHOOSING YOUR COURSE

The information under this heading (to be read in conjunction with **Chapter 1**) covers factors that are important to consider in order to make an informed decision on which courses to apply for. The information is organised under the following subheadings.

Some course features

The purpose of this section is to alert you to the diversity of courses on offer and the importance of checking the content of your chosen course. It should be noted that many departments provide a common first year in the same subject, for example Biological Sciences, with a choice of specialisation in Year 2. (The courses listed have not been selected on the basis of academic reputation or course quality.)

Universities and colleges teaching quality

The Unistats website (http://unistats.direct.gov.uk) provides official information where available for different subjects and universities and colleges in the United Kingdom to help prospective students and their advisers make comparisons between them and so make informed choices about what and where to study. Information is updated annually and is available for each subject taught at each university and college (and for some further education colleges). The Quality Assurance Agency (www.qaa.ac.uk) reviews the quality and standards of all universities and colleges and official reports of their reviews are available on their website but it is important to note their dates of publication.

Top research universities and colleges (RAE 2008)

In December 2008 the latest research assessment exercise took place covering certain subject areas. The leading universities in the relevant subject areas are listed in the order of achievement. It should be noted that not all subjects were assessed.

Examples of sandwich degree courses

This section lists examples of institutions that offer sandwich placements for some of their courses in the subject field shown. The institutions listed offer placements of one-year duration and do not include language courses or work experience or other short-term placements. Check with the institutions too, since new courses may be introduced and others withdrawn depending on industrial or commercial arrangements. Further information on sandwich courses with specific information on the placements of students appears in **Chapter 1**.

NB During a period of recession, universities and colleges may have problems placing students on sandwich courses. Applicants applying for courses are therefore advised to check with admissions tutors that these courses will run, and that placements will be available.

ADMISSIONS INFORMATION

Under this heading, information gathered from the institutions has been provided. This will be useful when planning your application.

Number of applicants per place (approx)

These figures show the approximate number of applicants initially applying for each place before any offers are made. It should be noted that any given number of applicants represents candidates who have also applied for up to four other university and college courses. In some subject areas some universities have provided details of the actual breakdown of numbers of applicants under the following headings: UK, EU (non-UK), non-EU (overseas), mature (over 21).

Advice to applicants and planning the UCAS personal statement

This section offers guidelines on information that could be included in the personal statement section of your UCAS application. In most cases, applicants will be required to indicate why they wish to follow a particular course and, if possible, to provide positive evidence of their interest. See also **Chapters 5** and **6**.

Misconceptions about this course

Admissions tutors are given the opportunity in the research for this book to set the record straight by clarifying aspects of their course they feel are often misunderstood by students, and in some cases, advisers!

Selection interviews
Institutions that normally use the interview as part of their selection procedure are listed here. Those institutions adopting the interview procedure will usually interview only a small proportion of applicants. It is important to use this section in conjunction with **Chapters 4** and **6**.

Interview advice and questions
This section includes information from institutions on what candidates might expect in an interview to cover, and examples of the types of interview questions posed in recent years. Also refer to **Chapters 4** and **6**: these chapters provide information on tests and assessments which are used in selecting students.

Reasons for rejection (non-academic)
Academic ability and potential to suceed on the course are the major factors in the selection (or rejection) of applicants. Under this subheading, admissions tutors give other reasons for rejecting applicants.

AFTER-RESULTS ADVICE
Under this heading, information for helping you decide what to do after the examination results are published is provided (see also the section on **What to do on Results Day ... and After** in **Chapter 5**). Details refer to the main subject area unless otherwise stated in brackets.

Offers to applicants repeating A-levels
This section gives details of whether second-time offers made to applicants repeating their exams may be 'higher', 'possibly higher' or the 'same' as those made to first-time applicants. The information refers to Single Honours courses. It should be noted that circumstances may differ between candidates – some will be repeating the same subjects taken in the previous year, while others may be taking different subjects. Offers will also be dictated by the grades you achieved on your first sitting of the examinations. Remember, if you were rejected by all your universities and have achieved good grades, contact them by telephone on results day – they may be prepared to revise their decision. This applies particularly to medical schools.

GRADUATE DESTINATIONS AND EMPLOYMENT
The information under this heading has been provided by the Higher Education Statistics Agency (HESA) and is taken from their report *Destinations of Leavers from Higher Education 2009/10*. The report can be obtained from www.hesa.ac.uk.

Details are given of the total number of graduates surveyed whose destinations have been recorded – not the total number who graduated in that subject. Employment figures relate to those in full-time permanent paid employment after six months in a variety of occupations not necessarily related to their degree subject (part-time employment figures are not included). Figures are also given for those in voluntary, unpaid work. 'Further Study' includes research into a subject-related field, higher degrees, private study or, alternatively, career training involving work and further study. The 'Assumed unemployed' category refers to those students who were believed to be unemployed for various reasons (eg travelling, personal reasons) or those students still seeking permanent employment six months after graduating. The figures given do not equal the total number of graduates surveyed as we have chosen only to include the most relevant or interesting areas.

Career note
Short descriptions of the career destinations of graduates in the subject area are provided.

OTHER DEGREE SUBJECTS FOR CONSIDERATION
This heading includes some suggested alternative courses that have similarities to the courses listed in the subject table.

ABBREVIATIONS USED IN THE SUBJECT TABLES IN CHAPTER 8

INSTITUTION ABBREVIATIONS

The following abbreviations are used to indicate specific institutions or types of institution:

Ac	Academy
AI	Arts Institute
ALRA	Academy of Live and Recorded Arts
AMD	Academy of Music and Drama
Birk	Birkbeck (London University)
CA	College of Art(s)
CAD	College of Art and Design
CAFRE	College of Agriculture, Food and Rural Enterprise
CAg	College of Agriculture
CAgH	College of Agriculture and Horticulture
CAT	College of Advanced Technology or Arts and Technology
CComm	College of Communication
CDC	College of Design and Communication
CECOS	London College of IT and Management
CFash	College of Fashion
CHort	College of Horticulture
CmC	Community College
CMus	College of Music
CMusDr	College of Music and Drama
Coll	College
Consv	Conservatoire (Birmingham)
Court	Courtauld Institute (London University)
CT	College of Technology
CTA	College of Technology and Arts
Gold	Goldsmiths (London University)
Hey	Heythrop College (London University)
IA	Institute of Art(s)
IFHE	Institute of Further and Higher Education
Inst	Institute
King's	King's College (London University)
LIPA	Liverpool Institute of Performing Arts
LSE	London School of Economics and Political Science
Met	Metropolitan
MS	Medical School
NCH	New College of the Humanities
QM	Queen Mary (London University)
RAcMus	Royal Academy of Music
RCMus	Royal College of Music
Reg Coll	Regional College
Reg Fed	Regional Federation (Staffordshire)
RH	Royal Holloway (London University)
RNCM	Royal Northern College of Music
RVC	Royal Veterinary College (London University)
SA	School of Art
SAC	Scottish Agricultural College
SAD	School of Art and Design
Sch	School
Sch SpDr	School of Speech and Drama

SMO	Sabhal Mòr Ostaig		
SOAS	School of Oriental and African Studies (London University)		
UC	University College		
UCL	University College (London University)		
UCP	Marjon University College Plymouth St Mark and St John		
UHI	University of the Highlands and Islands		
Univ	University		

COURSE ABBREVIATIONS

The following abbreviations are used to indicate course titles:

Ab	Abrahamic	Anth	Anthropology
Abrd	Abroad	Antq	Antique(s)
Acc	Accountancy/Accounting	App(s)	Applied/Applicable/
Accs	Accessories		Applications
Acoust	Acoustics/Acoustical	Appr	Appropriate
Acpntr	Acupuncture	Apprsl	Appraisal
Acq	Acquisition	Aqua	Aquaculture/Aquatic
Act	Actuarial	Ar	Area(s)
Actg	Acting	Arbc	Arabic
Actn	Action	Arbor	Arboriculture
Actr	Actor	Arch	Archaeology
Actv	Active	Archit	Architecture
Actvt(s)	Activity/Activities	Archvl	Archival
Add	Additional	Aroma	Aromatherapy
Adlscn	Adolescence	Arst	Artist
Adlt	Adult	Artfcts	Artefacts
Admin	Administration/Administrative	Artif	Artificial
Adt	Audit	As	Asian
Adv	Advertising	Ass	Assessment
Advc	Advice	Assoc	Associated
Advnc	Advanced	Asst	Assistant
Advntr	Adventure	Assyr	Assyriology
Aero	Aeronautical/Aeronautics	Ast	Asset
Aerodyn	Aerodynamics	Astnaut	Astronautics/Astronautical
Aeromech	Aeromechanical	Astro	Astrophysics
Aerosp	Aerospace	Astron	Astronomy
Aeroth	Aerothermal	A-Sxn	Anglo-Saxon
Af	Africa(n)	Ated	Accelerated
Affrs	Affairs	Atel	Atelier
Age	Ageing	Atlan	Atlantic
Agncy	Agency	Atmos	Atmospheric
Agric	Agriculture/Agricultural	Attrctns	Attractions
Agrofor	Agroforestry	Auc	Auctioneering
Agron	Agronomy	Aud	Audio
Aircft	Aircraft	Audiol	Audiology
Airln	Airline	Audtech	Audiotechnology
Airpt	Airport	Aus	Australia(n)
Am	American	Austr	Australasia
Amen	Amenity	Auth	Author/Authoring/Authorship
Analys	Analysis	Auto	Automotive
Analyt	Analytical	Autom	Automated/Automation
Anat	Anatomy/Anatomical	Automat	Automatic
Anim	Animal	Autombl	Automobile
Animat	Animation	AV	Audio Video
Animatron	Animatronics	Avion	Avionics

Avn	Aviation	Cell	Cellular
Ay St	Ayurvedic Studies	Celt	Celtic
		Cent	Century
Bank	Banking	Ceram	Ceramics
Bch	Beach	Cert	Certificate
Bd	Based	Ch Mgt	Chain Management
Bdwk	Bodywork	Chc	Choice
Bhv	Behaviourial	Chch	Church
Bib	Biblical	Chem	Chemistry
Bio Ins	Bio Instrumentation	Cheml	Chemical
Bioarch	Bioarchaeology	Chin	Chinese
Bioch	Biochemistry/Biochemical	Chiro	Chiropractic
Biodiv	Biodiversity	Chld	Child/Children/Childhood
Bioelectron	Bioelectronics	Chn	Chain
Biogeog	Biogeography	Chng	Change
Biogeosci	Biogeoscience	Choreo	Choreography
Bioinform	Bioinformatics	Chr	Christian(ity)
Biokin	Biokinetics	Chtls	Chattels
Biol	Biological/Biology	Cits	Cities
Biom	Biometry	Civ	Civilisation/Civil
Biomed	Biomedical/Biomedicine	Class	Classical/Classics
Biomol	Biomolecular	Clim	Climate/Climatic
Biophys	Biophysics	Clin	Clinical
Bioproc	Bioprocess	Cllct	Collect/Collecting
Biorg	Bio-organic	Clnl	Colonial
Biotech	Biotechnology	Cloth	Clothing
Biovet	Bioveterinary	Clsrm	Classroom
Bkbnd	Bookbinding	Cmbt	Combat
Bld	Build/Building	Cmdy	Comedy
Blt	Built	Cmn	Common
Bngli	Bengali	Cmnd	Command
Br	British	Cmplrs	Compilers
Braz	Brazilian	Cmpn	Companion
Brew	Brewing	Cmpsn	Composition
Brit	British	Cmpste	Composite
Brnd	Brand/Branding	Cmwlth	Commonwealth
Broad	Broadcast	Cncr	Cancer
Bspk	Bespoke	Cnflct	Conflict
Bty	Beauty	Cnma	Cinema/Cinematics
Bulg	Bulgarian	Cnslg	Counselling
Burm	Burmese	Cnsltncy	Consultancy
Bus	Business	Cnt	Central
Buy	Buying	Cntnt	Content
Byz	Byzantine	Cntrms	Countermeasures
		Cntry	Country/Countryside
Callig	Calligraphy	Cntxt	Context
Can	Canada/Canadian	Cnty	Century
Cap	Capital	Coach	Coaching
Cardio	Cardiology	Cog	Cognitive
Carib	Caribbean	Col	Colour
Cart	Cartography	Coll	Collaborative
Cat	Catering	Comb	Combined
CATS	Credit Accumulation and Transfer Scheme	Combus	Combustion
		Comm(s)	Communication(s)
Cdtng	Conditioning	Commer	Commerce/Commercial

Commun	Community	Def	Defence
Comp	Computer/Computerised/	Defer	Deferred Choice
	Computing	Deg	Degree
Compar	Comparative	Demcr	Democratic
Complem	Complementary	Dept	Department
Comput	Computation/al	Des	Design(er)
Con	Context	Desr	Desirable
Concur	Concurrent	Dev	Development/Developmental
Cond	Conductive	Devsg	Devising
Condit	Conditioning	Df	Deaf
Cons	Conservation	Diag	Diagnostic
Constr	Construction	Diet	Diet/Dietetics/Dietitian
Consum	Consumer	Dif	Difficulties
Cont	Contour	Dig	Digital
Contemp	Contemporary	Dip Ing	Diplom Ingeneur
Contnl	Continental	Dir	Direct/Direction/Director/
Contr	Control		Directing
Conv	Conveyancing	Dis	Diseases
Corn	Cornish	Disab	Disability
Corp	Corporate/Corporation	Disas	Disaster
Cos	Cosmetic	Discip	Disciplinary
Cosmo	Cosmology	Diso	Disorders
Cr	Care	Disp	Dispensing
Crcs	Circus	Dist	Distributed/Distribution
Crdc	Cardiac	Distil	Distillation/Distilling
Crea	Creative/Creation	Div	Divinity
Crfts	Crafts/Craftsmanship	d/l	distance learning
Crim	Criminal	Dlvry	Delivery
Crimin	Criminological/Criminology	Dnstry	Dentistry
Crit	Criticism/Critical	Dntl	Dental
Crm	Crime	Doc	Document/Documentary
Cro	Croatian	Dom	Domestic/Domesticated
Crr	Career	Dr	Drama
Crs	Course	Drg	Drawing
Crsn	Corrosion	Drs	Dress
Cru	Cruise	Dscrt	Discrete
Crypt	Cryptography	Dscvry	Discovery
Cstl	Coastal	Dsply	Display
Cstm	Costume	Dtbs	Databases
Cstmd	Customised	Dth	Death
Ctln	Catalan	Dvc	Device
Ctlys	Catalysis	Dvnc	Deviance
Ctzn	Citizenship	Dynmcs	Dynamics
Culn	Culinary		
Cult	Culture/Cultural	Ecol	Ecology/Ecological
Cur	Curation	Ecomet	Econometrics
Cy	Cyber	e-Commer	E-Commerce
Cyber	Cybernetics/Cyberspace	Econ	Economics
Cybertron	Cybertronics	Econy	Economy/ies
Cym	Cymraeg	Ecosys	Ecosystem(s)
Cz	Czech	Ecotech	Ecotechnology
		Ecotour	Ecotourism
Dan	Danish	Ecotox	Ecotoxicology
Decn	Decision	Edit	Editorial
Decr	Decoration/Decorative	Educ	Education

Educr	Educare	**Expnc**	Experience
Efcts	Effects	**Expr**	Expressive
EFL	English as a Foreign	**Ext**	Extended
	Language	**Extr**	Exterior
Egypt	Egyptian/Egyptology	**Extrm**	Extreme
Elec	Electrical		
Elecacoust	Electroacoustics	**Fabs**	Fabric(s)
Electromech	Electromechanical	**Fac**	Faculty
Electron	Electronics	**Facil**	Facilities
ELT	English Language Teaching	**Fash**	Fashion
Ely	Early	**Fbr**	Fibre
Emb	Embryo	**Fctn**	Fiction
Embd	Embedded	**Fd**	Food
Embr	Embroidery	**Fdn**	Foundation
Emer	Emergency	**Filmm**	Filmmaking
Emp	Employment	**Fin**	Finance/Financial
Ener	Energy	**Finn**	Finnish
Eng	Engineering	**Fish**	Fisheries
Engl	English	**Fit**	Fitness
Engn	Engine	**Fl**	Fluid
Ent	Enterprise	**Fld**	Field
Enter	Entertainment	**Flex**	Flexible
Entre	Entrepreneur/Entrepreneurship	**Flor**	Floristry
Env	Environment/Environmental	**FMaths**	Further Mathematics
Eql	Equal	**Fmly**	Family
Eqn	Equine	**Fn**	Fine
Eqstrn	Equestrian	**Foot**	Footwear
Equip	Equipment	**For**	Foreign
Equit	Equitation	**Foren**	Forensic
Ergon	Ergonomics	**Foss**	Fossil(s)
Est	Estate	**Fr**	French
Eth	Ethics	**Frchd**	Franchised
Ethl	Ethical	**Frcst**	Forecasting
Eth-Leg	Ethico-Legal	**Frm**	Farm
Ethn	Ethnic	**Frmwk**	Framework
Ethnol	Ethnology	**Frshwtr**	Freshwater
Ethnomus	Ethnomusicology	**Frst**	Forest
EU	European Union	**Frsty**	Forestry
Euro	European	**Frtlty**	Fertility
EPQ	Extended Project Qualification	**Fst Trk**	Fast Track
Eval	Evaluation	**Fstvl**	Festival
Evnglstc	Evangelistic	**Ftbl**	Football
Evnt(s)	Event(s)	**Ftre**	Feature(s)
Evol	Evolution/Evolutionary	**Ftwr**	Footwear
Ex	Executing	**Furn**	Furniture
Excl	Excellence	**Fut**	Futures
Exer	Exercise		
Exhib	Exhibition	**Gael**	Gaelic
Exmp	Exempt(ing)	**Gam**	Gambling
Exp	Export	**Gdn**	Garden
Explor	Exploration	**Gdnc**	Guidance
Explsn	Explosion	**Gem**	Gemmology
Expltn	Exploitation	**Gen**	General
Expmtl	Experimental	**Genet**	Genetics

Geochem	Geochemistry		**Hort**	Horticulture
Geog	Geography		**Hosp**	Hospital
Geoinform	Geoinformatics		**Hous**	Housing
Geol	Geology		**HR**	Human Resources
Geophys	Geophysics		**Hrdrs**	Hairdressing
Geophysl	Geophysical		**Hrs**	Horse
Geopol	Geopolitics		**Hse**	House
Geosptl	Geospatial		**Hspty**	Hospitality
Geotech	Geotechnics		**Htl**	Hotel
Ger	German/Germany		**Hum**	Human(ities)
Gerc	Germanic		**Hung**	Hungarian
GIS	Geographical Information		**Hydrog**	Hydrography
	Systems		**Hydrol**	Hydrology
Gk	Greek		**Hyg**	Hygiene
Glf	Golf			
Glf Crs	Golf Course		**Iber**	Iberian
Gllry	Gallery/Galleries		**Ice**	Icelandic
Glob	Global/Globalisation		**ICT**	Information and
Gls	Glass			Communications Technology
Gmg	Gaming		**Id**	Ideas
Gmnt	Garment		**Idnty**	Identity
Gms	Games		**Illus**	Illustration
Gmtc	Geomatic		**Imag**	Image/Imaging/Imaginative
Gndr	Gender		**Immun**	Immunology/Immunity
Gnm	Genome/Genomics		**Impair**	Impairment
Gov	Government		**Incl**	Including
Govn	Governance		**Incln**	Inclusion
Graph	Graphic		**Inclsv**	Inclusive
Grgn	Georgian		**Ind**	Industrial/Industry
Grn	Green		**Indep St**	Independent Study
gs	General Studies		**Indsn**	Indonesian
Guj	Gujerati		**Inf**	Information
			Infec	Infectious/Infection
Hab	Habitat		**Infml**	Informal
Hack	Hacking		**Inform**	Informatics
Hard	Hardware		**Infra**	Infrastructure
Haz	Hazard		**Inftq**	Informatique
Heal	Healing		**Injry**	Injury
Heb	Hebrew		**Innov**	Innovation
Herb	Herbal		**Ins**	Insurance
Herit	Heritage		**Inst**	Institution(al)
Hisp	Hispanic		**Instln**	Installation
Hist	History/Historical		**Instr**	Instrument/Instrumentation
HL	IB Higher level		**Int**	International
Hlcst	Holocaust		**Intcult**	Intercultural
Hlnds	Highlands		**Integ**	Integrated/Integration
Hlth	Health		**Intel**	Intelligent/Intelligence
Hlthcr	Healthcare		**Inter**	Interior
HlthSC	Health and Social Care		**Interact**	Interaction/Interactive
Hm	Home		**Interd**	Interdisciplinary
Hol	Holistic		**Interp**	Interpretation
Hom	Homeopathic		**Intlctl**	Intellectual
Homin	Hominid		**Intnet**	Internet
Horol	Horology		**Intr**	Interest(s)

Intrmdl	Intermodal	**Lrng**	Learning
Inv	Investment	**Ls**	Loss
Invn	Innovation	**Lsr**	Laser
Invstg	Investigating/Investigation	**Ltg**	Lighting
Ir	Irish	**Ltr**	Later
Is	Issues	**Lv**	Live
Isl	Islands	**Lvstk**	Livestock
Islam	Islamic		
Isrl	Israel/Israeli	**Mach**	Machine(ry)
IT	Information Technology	**Mait**	Maitrise Internationale
Ital	Italian	**Mak**	Making
ITE	Initial Teacher Education	**Mand**	Mandarin
ITT	Initial Teacher Training	**Manuf**	Manufacturing
		Map	Map/Mapping
Jap	Japanese	**Mar**	Marine
Jew	Jewish	**Marit**	Maritime
Jewel	Jewellery	**Mark**	Market(ing)
Jrnl	Journalism	**Masch**	Maschinenbau
Jud	Judaism	**Mat**	Materials
Juris	Jurisprudence	**Mathem**	Mathematical
Just	Justice	**Maths**	Mathematics
		Mbl	Mobile
Knt	Knit/Knitted	**Mdl**	Modelling
Kntwr	Knitwear	**Measur**	Measurement
Knwl	Knowledge	**Mech**	Mechanical
Kor	Korean	**Mecha**	Mechatronics
KS	Key Stage	**Mechn**	Mechanisation
		Mechnsms	Mechanisms
Lab	Laboratory	**Med**	Medicine/cal
Lang(s)	Language(s)	**Medcnl**	Medicinal
Las	Laser	**Mediev**	Medieval
Lat	Latin	**Medit**	Mediterranean
Lcl	Local	**Metal**	Metallurgy/Metallurgical
LD	Learning Disabilities	**Meteor**	Meteorology/Meteorological
Ldrshp	Leadership	**Meth**	Method(s)
Lea	Leather	**Mgr**	Manager
Leg	Legal	**Mgrl**	Managerial
Legis	Legislative	**Mgt**	Management
Leis	Leisure	**Microbiol**	Microbiology/Microbiological
Lf	Life	**Microbl**	Microbial
Lfstl	Lifestyle	**Microcomp**	Microcomputer/Microcomputing
Lgc	Logic	**Microelec**	Microelectronics
Lib	Library	**Mid E**	Middle Eastern
Libshp	Librarianship	**Midwif**	Midwifery
Lic	Licensed	**Min**	Mining
Lic de Geog	Licence de Geographie	**Miner**	Minerals
Lic de Let	Licence de Lettres	**Mkup**	Make-up
Ling	Linguistics	**Mling**	Multilingual
Lit	Literature/Literary	**Mltry**	Military
Litcy	Literacy	**MML**	Master of Modern Languages
Lnd	Land(scape)	**Mnd**	Mind
Lndbd	Land-based	**Mndrn**	Mandarin
Lns	Lens	**Mnrts**	Minorities
Log	Logistics	**Mnstry**	Ministry
Lrn	Learn	**Mnswr**	Menswear

Mntl Hlth	Mental Health	Nursy	Nursery
Mntn	Mountain	Nutr	Nutrition(al)
Mntnce	Maintenance	Nvl	Naval
Mny	Money	NZ	New Zealand
Mod	Modular		
Modl	Modelling/Modelmaking	Objs	Objects
Modn	Modern	Obs	Observational
Modnty	Modernity	Occ	Occupational
Mol	Molecular	Ocean	Oceanography
Monit	Monitoring	Ocn	Ocean
Mov	Movement/Moving	Ocnc	Oceanic
Mrchnds	Merchandise	Oeno	Oenology
Mrchnt	Merchant	Ofce	Office
Mrl	Moral	Off	Offshore
Msg	Massage	Offrd	Off-road
Mslm	Muslim	Okl	Oklahoma
Mtl	Metal(s)	Onc	Oncology
Mtlsmth	Metalsmithing	Onln	Online
Mtn	Motion	Op(s)	Operation(s)
Mtr	Motor	Oph	Ophthamic
Mtrcycl	Motorcycle	Oprtg	Operating
Mtrg	Motoring	Opt	Optical
Mtrspo	Motorsports	Optim	Optimisation
Multid	Multidisciplinary	Optn/s	Optional/Options
Multim	Multimedia	Optoel	Optoelectronics
Mus	Music(ian)	Optom	Optometry
Muscskel	Musculoskeletal	OR	Operational Research
Musl	Musical	Ord	Ordinary
Musm	Museum	Org	Organisation
Mushp	Musicianship	Orgnc	Organic
		Orgnsms	Organisms
N	New	Orn	Ornithology
N Am	North America	Orntl	Oriental
Nano	Nanoscience	Orth	Orthoptics
Nanotech	Nanotechnology	Orthot	Orthotics
Nat	Nature/Natural	Oseas	Overseas
Natpth	Naturopathy	Ost	Osteopathy
Navig	Navigation	Out	Outdoor
Nds	Needs	Out Act	Outdoor Activity
Neg	Negotiated	Outsd	Outside
Net	Network	Ovrs	Overseas
Neuro	Neuroscience		
Neuropsy	Neuropsychology	P	Primary
News	Newspaper	P Cr	Primary Care
NGO	Non-Governmental	Pacif	Pacific
	Organisation(s)	Pack	Packaging
NI	Northern Ireland/Northern Irish	PActv	Physical Activity
NMedia	New Media	Pal	Palaeobiology
Nnl	National	Palae	Palaeoecology/Palaeontology
Norw	Norwegian	Palaeoenv	Palaeoenvironments
Npli	Nepali	Paramed	Paramedic(al)
Nrs	Norse	Parasit	Parasitology
Ntv	Native	Parl	Parliamentary
Nucl	Nuclear	Pat	Patent
Nurs	Nursing	Path	Pathology

Pathobiol	Pathobiological	**Ppl**	People
Pathogen	Pathogenesis	**Ppr**	Paper
Patt	Pattern	**Pptry**	Puppetry
Pblc	Public	**PR**	Public Relations
Pce	Peace	**Prac**	Practice/Practical
PE	Physical Education	**Practnr**	Practitioner
Per	Person/Personal	**Prchsng**	Purchasing
Perf	Performance	**Prcrmt**	Procurement
Perfum	Perfumery	**Prdcl**	Periodical
Pers	Personnel	**Precsn**	Precision
Persn	Persian	**Pref**	Preferable/Preferred
Petrol	Petroleum	**Prehist**	Prehistory
PGCE	Postgraduate Certificate in Education	**Prem**	Premises
		Proc	Process/Processing
Pharm	Pharmacy	**Prod**	Product/Production/Produce
Pharmacol	Pharmacology	**Prodg**	Producing
Pharml	Pharmaceutical	**Prof**	Professional/Professions
Phil	Philosophy	**Prog**	Programme/Programming
Philgy	Philology	**Proj**	Project
Phn	Phone	**Prom**	Promotion
Phon	Phonetics	**Prop**	Property/ies
Photo	Photography/Photographic	**Pros**	Prosthetics
Photojrnl	Photojournalism	**Prot**	Protection/Protected
PhotoM	Photomedia	**Prplsn**	Propulsion
Photon	Photonic(s)	**Prsts**	Pursuits
Phys	Physics	**Prt**	Print
Physio	Physiotherapy	**Prtcl**	Particle
Physiol	Physiology/Physiological	**Prtd**	Printed
Physl	Physical	**Prtg**	Printing/Printmaking
Pks	Parks	**Prvntn**	Prevention
Plan	Planning	**Pst**	Post
Planet	Planetary	**Pstcolnl**	Postcolonial
Plas	Plastics	**Pstrl**	Pastoral
Play	Playwork	**Psy**	Psychology
Plcg	Police/Policing	**Psybiol**	Psychobiology
Plcy	Policy	**Psyling**	Psycholinguistics
Plmt	Placement	**Psysoc**	Psychosocial
Plnt	Plant	**p/t**	part-time
Plntsmn	Plantsmanship	**Ptcl**	Particle
Plt	Pilot	**Pub**	Publishing
Pltry	Poultry	**Pvt**	Private
PMaths	Pure Mathematics	**Pwr**	Power
Pntg	Painting	**Pwrcft**	Powercraft
Pod	Podiatry/Podiatric		
Pol	Politics/Political	**Qntm**	Quantum
Polh	Polish	**Qry**	Quarry
Pollut	Pollution	**Qtrnry**	Quaternary
Poly	Polymer/Polymeric	**QTS**	Qualified Teacher Status
Pop	Popular	**Qual**	Quality
Popn	Population	**Qualif**	Qualification
Port	Portuguese	**Quant**	Quantity/Quantitative
PPE	Philosophy, Politics and Economics or Politics, Philosophy and Economics	**Rad**	Radio
		Radiog	Radiography
PPI	Private Pilot Instruction	**Radiothera**	Radiotherapy

Rbr	Rubber
Rce	Race
Rcycl	Recycling
Rdtn	Radiation
Realsn	Realisation
Rec	Recording
Reclam	Reclamation
Recr	Recreation
Reg	Regional
Regn	Regeneration
Rehab	Rehabilitation
Rel	Relations
Relgn	Religion
Relig	Religious
Reltd	Related
Rem Sens	Remote Sensing
Ren	Renaissance
Renew	Renewable
Rep	Representation
Reqd	Required
Res	Resources
Resid	Residential
Resoln	Resolution
Resp	Response
Restor	Restoration
Rev	Revenue
Rflxgy	Reflexology
Rgby	Rugby
Rgstrn	Registration
Rl	Real
Rlblty	Reliability
Rlwy	Railway
Rmnc	Romance
RN	Registered Nurse
Rnwl	Renewal
Robot	Robotics
Rom	Roman
Romn	Romanian
Rsch	Research
Rspnsb	Responsibility
Rsprty	Respiratory
Rsrt	Resort
Rstrnt	Restaurant
Rtl	Retail
Rts	Rights
Rur	Rural
Russ	Russian
Rvr	River
S	Secondary
Sansk	Sanskrit
S As	South Asian
Sat	Satellite
Sbstnce	Substance
Scand	Scandinavian

Schlstc	Scholastic
Schm	Scheme
Sci	Science/Scientific
Scnc	Scenic
Scngrph	Scenographic/Scenography
Scot	Scottish
Scr	Secure
Script	Scriptwriting
Scrn	Screen
Scrnwrit	Sreenwriting
Scrts	Securities
Scrty	Security
Sctr	Sector
Sculp	Sculpture/Sculpting
Sdlry	Saddlery
SE	South East
Sec	Secretarial
Semicond	Semiconductor
SEN	Special Educational Needs
Serb Cro	Serbo-Croat
Serv	Services
Set	Settings
Sfc	Surface
Sfty	Safety
Sgnl	Signal
Ship	Shipping
Simul	Simulation
Sit Lrng	Situated Learning
Sk	Skills
Slf	Self
Sln	Salon
Slov	Slovak/Slovene/Slavonic
Sls	Sales
Sml	Small
Smt	Smart
Smtc	Semitic
Snc	Sonic
Snd	Sound
Sndtrk	Soundtrack
Sndwch	Sandwich
Sng	Song
Soc	Social
Sociol	Sociology
SocioLeg	Socio-Legal
Socling	Sociolinguistics
Soft	Software
Sol	Solution(s)
Soty	Society
Sov	Soviet
Sp	Speech
Span	Spanish
Spat	Spatial
Spc	Space
SPD	Surface Pattern Design
Spec	Special/Specialisms/Specialist

Spec Efcts	Special Effects	Thera	Therapy
Sply	Supply	Tht	Thought
Spn	Spain	Tiss	Tissue
Spo	Sports	Tlrg	Tailoring
Spowr	Sportswear	Tm	Time
Sprtd	Supported	Tmbr	Timber
Sprtng	Supporting	Tnnl	Tunnel/Tunnelling
Sqntl	Sequential	Tns	Tennis
Srf	Surf/Surfing	Topog	Topographical
Srgy	Surgery	Tour	Tourism
SS	Solid-state	Tox	Toxicology
St	Studies	TQ	Teaching Qualification
St Reg	State Registration	Tr	Trade
Stats	Statistics	Tr Stands	Trading Standards
Std	Studio	Trad	Traditional
Stg	Stage	Trans	Transport(ation)
Stgs	Settings	Transat	Transatlantic
Stnds	Standards	Transl	Translation
STQ	Scottish Teaching Qualification	Transnl Med Sci	Translational Medical Science
Str	Stringed	Trav	Travel
Strat	Strategic/Strategy	Trfgrs	Turfgrass
Strg	Strength	Trg	Training
Strt	Street	Trnrs	Trainers
Struct	Structural/Structures	Trpcl	Tropical
Stt	State	Trpl	Triple
Stwdshp	Stewardship	Trstrl	Terrestrial
Surf	Surface	Tstmnt	Testament
Surv	Surveying	Ttl	Total
Sust	Sustainability/Sustainable	Turk	Turkish
Swed	Swedish	Twn	Town
Swli	Swahili	Typo	Typographical/Typography
Sxlty	Sexuality		
Sys	System(s)	Ukr	Ukrainian
Systmtc	Systematic	Un	Union
		Undwtr	Underwater
Tap	Tapestry	Unif	Unified
Tax Rev	Taxation and Revenue	Up	Upland
Tbtn	Tibetan	Urb	Urban
Tcnqs	Techniques	USA	United States of America
Teach	Teaching	Util	Utilities/Utilisation
Tech	Technology/Technician/		
	Technical	Val	Valuation
Technol	Technological	Vcl	Vocal
TEFL	Teaching English as a Foreign	Veh	Vehicle
	Language	Vet	Veterinary
Telecomm	Telecommunications	Vntr	Venture
Ter	Terrestial	Vib	Vibration
TESOL	Teaching English to Speakers of	Vict	Victorian
	Other Languages	Vid	Video
Testmt	Testament	Viet	Vietnamese
Tex	Textiles	Virol	Virology
Thea	Theatre	Vis	Visual/Visualisation
Theol	Theology	Vit	Viticulture
Theor	Theory/Theoretical	Vkg	Viking
Ther	Therapeutic	Vnu	Venue

Voc	Vocational	**Wrld**	World
Vol	Voluntary	**Wrlss**	Wireless
Vrtbrt	Vertebrate	**Wst**	Waste(s)
Vrtl Rlty	Virtual Reality	**Wstn**	Western
Vsn	Vision	**Wtr**	Water
Vstr	Visitor	**Wtrspo**	Watersports
		Wvn	Woven
Wdlnd	Woodland	**www**	World Wide Web
Welf	Welfare		
Wk	Work	**Ycht**	Yacht
Wkg	Working	**Ychtg**	Yachting
Wlbng	Well-being	**Yng**	Young
Wldlf	Wildlife	**Yrs**	Years
Wls	Wales	**Yth**	Youth
Wmnswr	Womenswear		
Wn	Wine	**Zool**	Zoology
Wrbl	Wearable		
Writ	Writing/Writer	**3D**	Three dimensional

ACCOUNTANCY/ACCOUNTING

(see also **Finance**)

Accountancy and Accounting degree courses include accounting, finance, economics, law, management, qualitative methods and information technology. Many, but not all, Accountancy and Accounting degrees give exemptions from the examinations of some or all of the accountancy professional bodies. Single Honours courses are more likely to give full exemptions, while Joint Honours courses are more likely to lead to partial exemptions. Students should check with universities and colleges which professional bodies offer exemptions for their courses before applying. Most courses are strongly vocational and many offer sandwich placements or opportunities to study Accountancy/Accounting with a second subject.

Useful websites www.acca.co.uk; www.cimaglobal.org.uk; www.cipfa.org.uk; www.tax.org.uk; www.icaew.com; www.bized.co.uk.

NB The points totals shown to the left of the institutions are for ease of reference only. It must not be assumed that Tariff points are always used by institutions or that they can be substituted for an offer in grades. The level of an offer is not necessarily indicative of the quality of a course.

COURSE OFFERS INFORMATION

Subject requirements/preferences GCSE English and mathematics required: popular universities may specify grades. **AL** mathematics or accounting required or preferred for some courses. Business studies accepted for some courses.

Your target offers and examples of courses provided by each institution

390 pts **Warwick** – AAAb–A*AA (Acc Fin) (IB 38 pts)
380 pts **Exeter** – A*AA–AAB (Maths Acc) (IB 38–34 pts)
360 pts **Bath** – AAA (Acc Fin) (IB 38 pts HL 5–6 maths)
　　　　　 Bristol – AAA–AAB incl maths (Acc Mgt) (IB 37–35 pts)
　　　　　 City – AAA 360 pts (Econ Acc) (IB 35 pts)
　　　　　 Edinburgh – AAA–BBB 300–360 pts (Bus St Acc) (IB 34–42 pts)
　　　　　 Exeter – AAA–ABB (Acc Ldrshp) (IB 36–34 pts)
　　　　　 Glasgow – AAA–A*AB (Acc Maths/App Maths/PMaths) (IB 36 pts)
　　　　　 ifs School of finance – 360 pts (Fin Analys Rk)
　　　　　 Lancaster – AAA–AAB (Acc) (IB 36 pts)
　　　　　 Leeds – AAA (Acc Fin) (IB 35 pts HL 17 pts)
　　　　　 London LSE – AAA (Acc Fin) (IB 38 pts HL 666)
　　　　　 Manchester – AAA–AAB (Acc) (IB 37–35 pts)
　　　　　 Newcastle – AAA–AAB 340–360 pts (Bus Acc Fin) (IB 34–38 pts)
　　　　　 Queen's Belfast – AAA (Acc Modn Lang (Fr/Ger/Span)) (IB 34 pts)
　　　　　 Southampton – AAA (Acc Econ) (IB 36 pts HL 18 pts)
340 pts **Aston** – AAB–AAA 340–360 pts (Acc Mgt) (IB 34 pts)
　　　　　 Birmingham – AAB (Acc Fin) (IB 34–36 pts)
　　　　　 Bradford – AAB (Acc Fin)
　　　　　 Bristol – AAA–AAB 340–360 pts (Acc Fin) (IB 35–37 pts)
　　　　　 Cardiff – AAB (Acc Euro Lang) (IB 35 pts)
　　　　　 Kent – AAB–ABB (Acc Fin courses) (IB 33 pts)
　　　　　 Lancaster – AAB (Acc Econ) (IB 34 pts)

Liverpool – AAB (Acc Fin) (IB 32 pts)
London (QM) – 340 pts (Maths Fin Acc) (IB 34 pts)
London (RH) – AAB (Mgt Acc) (IB 35 pts)
Loughborough – AAB (Acc Fin Mgt) (IB 36 pts HL 6 maths)
Manchester – AAB (Acc Fin) (IB 35–37 pts)
Newcastle – AAB (Acc Maths) (IB 34 pts)
Nottingham – AAB (Fin Acc Mgt) (IB 34 pts)
Reading – AAB (Acc Mgt) (IB 34 pts)
Strathclyde – AAB (Acc Fin)
Sheffield – AAB (Acc Fin Mgt Joint Hons) (IB 35 pts)
Southampton – AAB (Mgt Sci Acc) (IB 34 pts HL 17 pts)
Surrey – AAB (Acc Fin) (IB 36 pts)
Sussex – AAB (Acc Fin) (IB 35 pts)

320 pts **Bournemouth** – 320 pts (Acc Fin)
De Montfort – 320 pts (Acc courses)
Durham – ABB (Acc Fin) (IB 34 pts)
Essex – ABB 320 pts (Acc Fin) (IB 29 pts)
Keele – ABB (Acc Fin) (IB 28–30 pts)
Kent – 320 pts (Acc Mgt) (IB 33 pts)
Lancaster – ABB (Acc Fin Comp Sci) (IB 34 pts)
Northumbria – 320 pts (Acc) (IB 26 pts)
Nottingham – ABB (Acc Fin Contemp Chin) (IB 32 pts)
Strathclyde – AAB–ABB (Acc) (IB 32 pts)
Sheffield – ABB (Acc Fin Mgt) (IB 33 pts)
Swansea – ABB–BBB (Mgt Sci (Acc))
UEA – ABB–BBB (Econ Acc) (IB 32–31 pts)
York – ABB (Acc Bus Fin Mgt) (IB 34 pts)

300 pts **Aberystwyth** – 300 pts (Acc Fin) (IB 27 pts)
Bristol UWE – 300 pts (Acc Fin) (IB 24–28 pts)
Brunel – BBB (Fin Acc) (IB 32 pts)
Cardiff Met – 300 pts (Acc)
Edinburgh – AAA–BBB 300–360 pts (Acc Fin) (IB 34–42 pts)
Essex – 300 pts (Acc) (IB 29 pts)
Greenwich – 300 pts (Acc Fin)
Heriot-Watt – ABC–BBB (Acc Fin)
Huddersfield – 300 pts (Acc Fin)
***ifs** School of finance* – 300 pts (Bank Prac Mgt; Fin Acc Fin Serv)
Nottingham Trent – 300 pts (Acc Fin) (IB 25 pts)
Portsmouth – 300 pts (Acc Fin; Acc Bus; Acc)
Salford – 300 pts (Fin Acc) (IB 28 pts)
Sheffield Hallam – 300 pts (Acc Fin; Foren Acc)
UEA – BBB (Acc Fin) (IB 30 pts)

280 pts **Birmingham City** – (Acc; Acc Joint Hons)
Brighton – BBC (Acc Fin) (IB 30 pts)
Coventry – 280–300 pts (Acc Fin)
De Montfort – 280 pts (Acc Law) (IB 30 pts)
Derby – 280 pts (Acc Fin)
Edge Hill – 280 pts (Acc)
Glamorgan – 280 pts (Acc Fin; Foren Acc; Int Acc)
Hertfordshire – 280–300 pts (Acc Langs) (IB 28 pts)
Holborn (Coll) – 280 pts (Acc Fin)
Hull – 280 pts (Acc; Acc Log)
Lincoln – 280 pts (Acc Fin)
LJMU – 280 pts (Acc Fin) (IB 28 pts)
London South Bank – 280 pts (Acc Fin)

Manchester Met – 280 pts (Acc Fin) (IB 28 pts)
Oxford Brookes – BBC (Acc Fin) (IB 30 pts)
Stirling – BBC (Acc) (IB 32 pts)
UCLan – 280–300 pts (Acc)
Worcester – 280 pts (Acc; Bus Acc Econ)

260 pts **Bangor** – 260–300 pts (Acc Fin; Acc Bank; Acc Econ; Mgt Acc)
Bolton – 260 pts (Acc courses)
BPP (UC) – 260 pts (Prof Acc)
Buckingham – 260 pts (Comp Acc Fin)
Derby – 260–300 pts (Acc Joint Hons)
Dundee – BCC (Acc) (IB 30 pts)
Edinburgh Napier – BCC 260 pts (Acc Law)
Glasgow Caledonian – BCC (Acc) (IB 24 pts)
Gloucestershire – 260–300 pts (Acc Fin Mgt)
Liverpool Hope – 260–320 pts (Acc Joint Hons)
Northampton – 260–300 pts (Acc courses) (IB 24 pts)
Robert Gordon – BCC (Acc Fin) (IB 20 pts)
Staffordshire – BCC 260 pts (Acc Fin) (IB 26 pts)
UCLan – 260 pts (Acc Int Bus)
Winchester – 260–300 pts (Acc Fin) (IB 25 pts)

240 pts **Bradford (Coll Univ Centre)** – 240 pts (Acc Law)
Chester – 240–280 pts (Acc Fin)
Chichester – CCC (Acc Fin)
Farnborough (CT) – BCD (Mgt Acc)
Glyndŵr – 240 pts (Bus Acc)
London Met – 240 pts (Acc Fin; Acc Bank)
Newport – 240 pts (Acc Fin)
Plymouth – 240 pts (Acc Fin)
Teesside – 240 pts (Acc Fin) (IB 30 pts)
Ulster – 240–340 pts (Acc)
West Scotland – CCC (Acc)

230 pts **Edinburgh Napier** – 230 pts (Acc; Econ Acc)
220 pts **Leeds Met** – 220 pts (Acc Fin) (IB 24 pts)
Southampton Solent – 220 pts (Acc)

200 pts **Anglia Ruskin** – 240–200 pts (Acc Fin)
Bedfordshire – 200 pts (Acc)
Blackburn (Coll) – 200 pts (Bus Acc)
Bucks New – 200–240 pts (Acc Fin)
London (Birk) – 200 pts (Acc Mgt)
Middlesex – 200–300 pts (Acc Fin)
Peterborough (Univ Centre) – 200 pts (Acc Fin)
UEL – 200 pts (Acc Fin)
West London – 200 pts (Acc Fin)

180 pts **Bradford (Coll Univ Centre)** – 180 pts (Acc)
160 pts **Greenwich (Sch Mgt)** – 160 pts (Acc Fin)
Swansea Met – 160 pts (Acc)

120 pts **Grimsby (IFHE)** – 120pts (Bus Mgt Acc)
Holborn (Coll) – 120 pts (Acc)
Norwich City (Coll) – 120 pts (Bus Mgt (Fin Acc))

Alternative offers
See **Chapter 7** and **Appendix 1** for grades/UCAS Tariff points information for the International Baccalaureate, Scottish Highers/Advanced Highers, the Welsh Baccalaureate, the Irish Leaving Certificate, the Cambridge Pre-U Diploma, the Advanced Diploma and the Extended Project.

Check **Chapter 4** when choosing your university and **Chapter 7** on how to read the subject tables.

EXAMPLES OF FOUNDATION DEGREES IN THE SUBJECT FIELD

Aberdeen (Coll); Adam Smith (Coll); Anniesland (Coll); Ayr (Coll); Banff and Buchan (Coll); Blackburn (Coll); Blackpool and Fylde (Coll); Bournemouth; Cardiff Met; Cornwall (Coll); Croydon (Coll); Darlington (Coll); Doncaster (Coll Univ Centre); Glamorgan; Glyndŵr; Hertfordshire; Highbury Portsmouth (Coll); Kensington Bus (Coll); Lambeth (Coll); Langside (Coll); Leeds Met; London Met; London South Bank; Manchester (Coll); Northampton; Northbrook (Coll); Plymouth; Salford; Southampton Solent; Suffolk (Univ Campus); UCLan; West Cheshire (Coll); Westminster Kingsway (Coll); Wirral Met (Coll).

CHOOSING YOUR COURSE (SEE ALSO CH.1)
Some course features
Anglia Ruskin Course can be started in February.
Aston Third year spent in paid professional placement; experience can count towards professional recognition by major accounting bodies.
Exeter Courses can include a year of study or a combination of study and work placement in Europe or in North America, Japan or China.
Lancaster (Acc Adt Fin) The 60 students on this course spend up to 18 months on salaried placement with Ernst & Young; first year bursary paid to all students achieving A*, A, A in A-level examinations.
London LSE A broad course, focusing on both accounting and its applications in different management areas. Options in first year depend on students' level of mathematics.
Portsmouth Professional mentoring scheme, pairing Level 2 and 3 students with practising accountant.

Universities and colleges teaching quality See www.qaa.ac.uk; http://unistats.direct.gov.uk.

Top research universities and colleges (RAE 2008) (Accounting and Finance) Bangor; Essex; Exeter; Bristol; Glasgow; Stirling; Bristol UWE; Dundee; Huddersfield.

Examples of sandwich degree courses Aston; Bath; Birmingham City; Bournemouth; Bradford; Brighton; Bristol UWE; Brunel; Coventry; De Montfort; Derby; Glamorgan; Gloucestershire; Greenwich; Hertfordshire; Huddersfield; Lancaster; Leeds Met; Loughborough; Middlesex; Nottingham Trent; Plymouth; Portsmouth; Sheffield Hallam; Staffordshire; Swansea Met; Teesside; Ulster; West Scotland; Westminster; Wolverhampton; Worcester.

ADMISSIONS INFORMATION
Number of applicants per place (approx) Bath 13; Birmingham 12; Bristol 10; Dundee 5; Essex 7; Exeter 18; Glasgow 10; Heriot-Watt 7; Hull 8; Kent 10; Lancaster 20; Leeds 25; London LSE 17; Loughborough 12; Manchester 22; Oxford Brookes 9; Salford 8; Sheffield 40; Southampton 13; Staffordshire 3; Stirling 20; Strathclyde 10; UEA 17; Ulster 10; Warwick 14.

Advice to applicants and planning the UCAS personal statement Universities look for good numerical and communication skills, interest in the business and financial world, teamwork, problem-solving and computing experience. On the UCAS application you should be able to demonstrate your interest and understanding of accountancy and to give details of any work experience or work shadowing undertaken. Try to arrange meetings with accountants, or work shadowing or work experience in accountants' offices, commercial or industrial firms, town halls, banks or insurance companies and describe the work you have done. Obtain information from the main accountancy professional bodies (see **Appendix 3**). Refer to current affairs which have stimulated your interest from articles in the *Financial Times*, *The Economist* or the business and financial sections of the weekend press. **Bath** Gap year welcomed. Extra-curricular activities important and should be described on the personal statement. There should be no gaps in your chronological history. **Bristol** Deferred entry accepted. **Brunel** (Bus Mgt (Acc)) Extended Project qualification accepted in place of AS-level; AL critical thinking and general studies acceptable. **Lancaster** (Acc Adt Fin) Selected UCAS applicants complete supplementary application form and online test. They may then be invited to a selection workshop.

Misconceptions about this course Many students believe incorrectly that you need to be a brilliant mathematician. However, you do have to be numerate and enjoy numbers (see **Subject requirements/preferences**). Many underestimate the need for a high level of attention to detail.

Buckingham Some students think it's a maths course. **Salford** Some applicants believe the course is limited to financial knowledge when it also provides an all-round training in management skills.

Selection interviews Yes West London; **Some** Abertay Dundee, Aberystwyth, Anglia Ruskin, Buckingham, Cardiff, Cardiff Met, De Montfort, Dundee, Kent, Lincoln, LJMU, London LSE, Staffordshire, Stirling, Sunderland, Warwick, Wolverhampton; **No** Birmingham, Bristol, Essex, UEA.

Interview advice and questions Be prepared to answer questions about why you have chosen the course, the qualities needed to be an accountant, and why you think you have these qualities! You should also be able to discuss any work experience you have done and to describe the differences in the work of chartered, certified, public finance and management accountants. See also **Chapter 6**. **Buckingham** Students from a non-English-speaking background are asked to write an essay. If their maths results are weak they may be asked to do a simple arithmetic test. Mature students with no formal qualifications are usually interviewed and questioned about their work experience.

Reasons for rejection (non-academic) Poor English. Lack of interest in the subject because they realise they have chosen the wrong course! No clear motivation. Course details not researched. **London South Bank** Punctuality, neatness, enthusiasm and desire to come to London South Bank not evident.

AFTER-RESULTS ADVICE
Offers to applicants repeating A-levels Higher Brunel, Glasgow Caledonian, Hull, Manchester Met; **Possibly higher** Brighton, Leeds, Newcastle, Oxford Brookes, Sheffield Hallam, UCLan, UEA; **Same** Abertay Dundee, Aberystwyth, Anglia Ruskin, Bangor, Birmingham City, Bolton, Bradford, Buckingham, Cardiff, Cardiff Met, Chichester, De Montfort, Derby, Dundee, Durham, Edinburgh Napier, Glasgow, Heriot-Watt, Huddersfield, LJMU, Loughborough, Northumbria, Portsmouth, Salford, Staffordshire, Stirling, Swansea Met, UEL, West London, West Scotland, Wolverhampton.

Check **Chapter 4** when choosing your university and **Chapter 7** on how to read the subject tables.

GRADUATE DESTINATIONS AND EMPLOYMENT (2009/10 HESA)

Graduates surveyed 5965 **Employed** 2085 **In voluntary employment** 45 **In further study** 1275 **Assumed unemployed** 445

Career note Most Accountancy/Accounting graduates enter careers in finance.

OTHER DEGREE SUBJECTS FOR CONSIDERATION

Actuarial Studies; Banking; Business Studies; Economics; Financial Services; Insurance; International Securities and Investment Banking; Mathematics; Quantity Surveying; Statistics.

ACTUARIAL SCIENCE/STUDIES

Actuaries deal with the evaluation and management of financial risks, particularly those associated with insurance companies and pension funds. Although Actuarial Science/Studies degrees are vocational and give full or partial exemptions from some of the examinations of the Institute and Faculty of Actuaries, students are not necessarily committed to a career as an actuary on graduation. However, many graduates go on to be actuary trainees, leading to one of the highest-paid careers.

Useful websites www.actuaries.org.uk; www.soa.org; www.beanactuary.org.

NB The points totals shown to the left of the institutions are for ease of reference only. It must not be assumed that Tariff points are always used by institutions or that they can be substituted for an offer in grades. The level of an offer is not necessarily indicative of the quality of a course.

COURSE OFFERS INFORMATION

Subject requirements/preferences Most institutions require grades A or B in **GCSE** mathematics or **AL** mathematics at a specified required grade.

Your target offers and examples of courses provided by each institution

440 pts **Warwick** – A*AA–AAB (Maths OR Stats Econ (MORSE)) (IB 39 pts HL 6 maths)
420 pts **City** – A*AA (Act Sci) (IB 35 pts)
         Queen's Belfast – AAAa (Act Sci Rsk Mgt)
360 pts **Kent** – AAA incl maths (Act Sci) (IB 33 pts HL 6 maths)
         London LSE – AAA incl maths (Act Sci) (IB 38 pts HL 766)
         Manchester – A*AB–AAB 340–360 pts (Act Sci Maths) (IB 36 pts)
         Southampton – AAA incl maths (Econ Act Sci) (IB 36 pts HL 18 pts)
340 pts **Heriot-Watt** – AAB incl maths A (Act Sci)
         Keele – AAB (Act Sci)
         Leeds – AAB (Act Maths) (IB 34 pts HL 6 maths)
         UEA – AAB incl AL maths A (Act Sci (Yr Ind)) (IB 33 pts)
300 pts **City** – BBB (Act Sci 4 yrs incl Fdn)
         Kingston – 300 pts (Act Sci)
280 pts **Kingston** – 280 pts (Act Maths Stats) (IB 26–28 pts)

Alternative offers

See **Chapter 7** and **Appendix 1** for grades/UCAS Tariff points information for the International Baccalaureate, Scottish Highers/Advanced Highers, the Welsh Baccalaureate, the Irish Leaving Certificate, the Cambridge Pre-U Diploma, the Advanced Diploma and the Extended Project.

CHOOSING YOUR COURSE (SEE ALSO CH.1)

Some course features

Heriot-Watt Opportunities for industrial placements or year abroad. University has active Students' Actuarial Society.
Kent Core actuarial modules taught by qualified actuaries. Optional year in industry in Year 3.
London LSE The Actuarial Science degree and the BSc Business Mathematics and Statistics degree have the same first year. Transfer between the two courses possible in Year 2.

Queen's Belfast Nine-month placement in Year 3 in either an actuarial or risk management setting in mainland UK, Ireland, the US or mainland Europe.

Southampton Both courses offer some exemptions from the examinations of the Institute of Actuaries.

Universities and colleges teaching quality See www.qaa.ac.uk; http://unistats.direct.gov.uk.

Examples of sandwich degree courses Kent; Queen's Belfast; UEA.

ADMISSIONS INFORMATION

Number of applicants per place (approx) City 6; Heriot-Watt 5; Kent 6; London LSE 9; Southampton (Maths Act Sci) 9, (Econ Act Sci) 8; Swansea 9.

Advice to applicants and planning the UCAS personal statement Demonstrate your knowledge of this career and its training, and mention any contacts you have made with an actuary. (See **Appendix 3** for contact details of professional associations for further information.) Any work experience or shadowing in insurance companies should be mentioned, together with what you have learned about the problems facing actuaries. It is important to show motivation and sheer determination for training as an actuary which is long and tough (up to three or four years after graduation). Mathematical flair, an ability to communicate and an interest in business are paramount.

Misconceptions about this course There is a general lack of understanding of actuaries' career training and of the career itself.

Selection interviews Yes UEA; **Some** Heriot-Watt, Kent, Southampton, Swansea.

Interview advice and questions In view of the demanding nature of the training, it is important to have spent some time discussing this career with an actuary in practice. Questions, therefore, may focus on the roles of the actuary and the qualities you have to succeed. You should also be ready to field questions about your AL mathematics course and the aspects of it you most enjoy. See also **Chapter 6**. **Swansea** The interview does not determine who will be accepted or rejected, only the level of the offer made.

Reasons for rejection (non-academic) Kent Poor language skills.

AFTER-RESULTS ADVICE

Offers to applicants repeating A-levels Higher City; **Same** Heriot-Watt, Southampton.

GRADUATE DESTINATIONS AND EMPLOYMENT (2009/10 HESA)

See **Finance**.

Career note Graduates commonly enter careers in finance, many taking further examinations to qualify as actuaries.

OTHER DEGREE SUBJECTS FOR CONSIDERATION

Accountancy; Banking; Business Studies; Economics; Financial Risk Management; Financial Services; Insurance; Mathematics; Money, Banking and Finance; Statistics.

AFRICAN AND CARIBBEAN STUDIES

(see also **Languages**)

African Studies courses tend to be multi-disciplinary, covering several subject areas and can include anthropology, history, geography, sociology, social psychology and languages. Most courses focus on Africa and African languages (Amharic (Ethiopia), Hausa (Nigeria), Somali (Horn of Africa), Swahili (Somalia and Mozambique), Yoruba (Nigeria, Sierra Leone, Ghana and Senegal), and Zulu (South Africa)).

Useful websites www.britishmuseum.org; www.africanstudies.org; www.black-history-month.co.uk.

NB The points totals shown to the left of the institutions are for ease of reference only. It must not be assumed that Tariff points are always used by institutions or that they can be substituted for an offer in grades. The level of an offer is not necessarily indicative of the quality of a course.

COURSE OFFERS INFORMATION

Subject requirements/preferences GCSE Grade A–C in mathematics and English may be required. **AL** For language courses a language subject or demonstrated proficiency in a language is required.

Your target offers and examples of courses provided by each institution
340 pts London (SOAS) – AAB (Af Lang Cult) (IB 36 pts HL 666)
320 pts Birmingham – ABB–BBB 300–320 pts (Af St Joint Hons) (IB 32–34 pts)
300 pts Birmingham – BBB (Af St Dev) (IB 32 pts)
260 pts London Met – 260 pts (Carib St Int Tour Mgt) (IB 28 pts)

Alternative offers
See **Chapter 7** and **Appendix 1** for grades/UCAS Tariff points information for the International Baccalaureate, Scottish Highers/Advanced Highers, the Welsh Baccalaureate, the Irish Leaving Certificate, the Cambridge Pre-U Diploma, the Advanced Diploma and the Extended Project.

CHOOSING YOUR COURSE (SEE ALSO CH.1)

Some course features
Birmingham A broad multi-disciplinary degree, offering Single and Joint Honours courses.
London (SOAS) Six African languages taught at undergraduate level; students have some flexibility in constructing their own course of study.
London Met One-semester or one-year placement in the Caribbean, United States or Europe.

Universities and colleges teaching quality See www.qaa.ac.uk; http://unistats.direct.gov.uk.

Top research universities and colleges (RAE 2008) (Middle Eastern and African Studies) Cambridge; Oxford; Edinburgh; London (SOAS); Durham.

ADMISSIONS INFORMATION

Number of applicants per place (approx) Birmingham 5.

Advice to applicants and planning the UCAS personal statement Describe any visits you have made to African or Caribbean countries, and why you wish to study this subject. Embassies in London may be able to provide information about the history, geography, politics, economics and the culture of the countries in which you are interested. Keep up-to-date with political developments in African or Caribbean countries. Discuss any aspects which interest you.

Selection interviews No Birmingham.

Interview advice and questions Questions are likely on your choice of country or geographical region, your knowledge of it and your awareness of some of the political, economic and social problems that exist. See also **Chapter 6**.

AFTER-RESULTS ADVICE

Offers to applicants repeating A-levels Higher Information not available from institutions.

GRADUATE DESTINATIONS AND EMPLOYMENT (2009/10 HESA)

Graduates surveyed 40 **Employed** 20 **In voluntary employment** 0 **In further study** 5 **Assumed unemployed** 5

Career note The language skills and knowledge acquired in African Studies courses, particularly when combined with periods of study in Africa, are relevant to a wide range of careers.

OTHER DEGREE SUBJECTS FOR CONSIDERATION

Anthropology; Geography; History; Languages; Sociology.

AGRICULTURAL SCIENCES/AGRICULTURE

(see also **Animal Sciences, Food Science/Studies and Technology, Forestry, Horticulture, Landscape Architecture, Surveying, Zoology**)

Courses in Agriculture recognise that modern farming practice requires sound technical and scientific knowledge, together with appropriate management skills, and most courses focus to a greater or lesser extent on all these requirements. Your choice of course depends on your particular interest and aims: some courses will give greater priority than others to practical application. Most graduates enter the agriculture industry whilst others move into manufacturing, wholesale and retail work.

Useful websites www.defra.gov.uk; www.naturalengland.org.uk; www.ccw.gov.uk; www.rase.org.uk; www.scienceyear.com; www.iah.bbsrc.ac.uk; www.lantra.co.uk; www.nfuonline.com; www.nfyfc.org.uk; www.iagre.org; www.afuturein.com.

NB The points totals shown to the left of the institutions are for ease of reference only. It must not be assumed that Tariff points are always used by institutions or that they can be substituted for an offer in grades. The level of an offer is not necessarily indicative of the quality of a course.

COURSE OFFERS INFORMATION

Subject requirements/preferences GCSE English and mathematics usually required; chemistry sometimes required. Practical experience may be required. **AL** One or two maths/biological science subjects may be required or preferred. Geography may be accepted as a science subject. Similar requirements apply for Agricultural Business Management courses. (Crop Sci) Two science subjects may be required. (Cntry Mgt) Geography or biology preferred.

Your target offers and examples of courses provided by each institution

320 pts **Newcastle** – AAB–ABB 320–340 pts (Agri Bus Mgt) (IB 34 pts)

300 pts **CAFRE** – BBB incl chem/biol (Agric Tech)
Newcastle – ABB–BBB 300–320 pts (Cntry Mgt) (IB 30 pts)
Queen's Belfast – BBB (Lnd Use Env Mgt) (IB 30 pts)
Reading – 300 pts (Agric) (IB 29 pts HL 655)
Royal (CAg) – 300 pts (Rur Lnd Mgt)

280 pts **Newcastle** – BBB–BBC 280–300 pts (Frm Bus Mgt) (IB 28 pts)
Nottingham – BBC–BCC (Agric) (IB 28–26 pts)
Stirling – BBC (Cons Biol Mgt) (IB 32 pts)

260 pts **Bangor** – 260–320 pts (Agric Cons Env)
Harper Adams (UC) – 260–300 pts (Agric courses; Agric Mark)
Lincoln – 260 pts (Agric Env Mgt)
Nottingham – BBC–BCC 260–280 pts (Agric Lvstk Sci) (IB 28–26 pts)

240 pts **Aberystwyth** – 240 pts (Cntry Recr Tour) (IB 28 pts)
Royal (CAg) – 240 pts (Agric (Crop))
Sparsholt (Coll) – 240–280 pts (Aquacult Fish Mgt)
Writtle (Coll) – 240 pts (Agric courses)

220 pts **Askham Bryan (Coll)** – 220 pts (Agric Lnd Mgt)
Harper Adams (UC) – 220–260 pts (Agri-Bus)
Myerscough (Coll) – 220 pts (Agric)

200 pts **Royal (CAg)** – 240 pts (Agric (Cntry Mgt)) (IB 26–28 pts)

160 pts **Greenwich** – 160 pts (Sust Lnd Mgt) (IB 24 pts)
SAC (Scottish CAg) – CC (Agric Sci)

Alternative offers
See **Chapter 7** and **Appendix 1** for grades/UCAS Tariff points information for the International Baccalaureate, Scottish Highers/Advanced Highers, the Welsh Baccalaureate, the Irish Leaving Certificate, the Cambridge Pre-U Diploma, the Advanced Diploma and the Extended Project.

Check **Chapter 4** when choosing your university and **Chapter 7** on how to read the subject tables.

EXAMPLES OF FOUNDATION DEGREES IN THE SUBJECT FIELD

Aberystwyth; Askham Bryan (Coll); Bath; Bath City (Coll); Bath Spa; Berkshire (CAg); Bishop Burton (Coll); Bournemouth; Bridgend (Coll); Brighton; Bucks New; CAFRE; Cumbria; Duchy (Coll); Easton (Coll); Greenwich; Guildford (Coll); Hadlow (Coll); Harper Adams (UC); Hertfordshire; Kingston Maurward (Coll); Lincoln; Manchester (Coll); Moulton (Coll); Myerscough (Coll); Northampton; Northop (Coll); Nottingham Trent; Oatridge (Coll); Oxford Brookes; Plymouth; Reaseheath (Coll); Royal (CAg); South Staffordshire (Coll); Sparsholt (Coll); Suffolk (Univ Campus); Sunderland; UEA; Warwickshire (Coll); Wiltshire (Coll); Wolverhampton; Writtle (Coll).

CHOOSING YOUR COURSE (SEE ALSO CH.1)

Some course features

Other universities offer a very wide choice of courses including many specialisms associated with land use including Forest and Woodland Management (**Cumbria**, **Myerscough (Coll)**, **Worcester**), Garden Design (**Greenwich**), Wildlife Conservation (**Kent**, **Plymouth**).

Aberystwyth (Agric) Nine months of work experience in third year.
Bristol UWE (Cons Cntry Mgt) Range of optional modules allow students to develop interests in, for example, woodland management.
Greenwich (Int Agric) Worldwide focus on agriculture science and practice, business, trade, development and sustainability; placement opportunities in the UK, Europe and the US, with study tours in UK and Europe.
Harper Adams (UC) (Rur Ent Lnd Mgt) Course includes surveying, valuation, law, taxation, the rural economy (including woodlands and field sports management), business finance, and agriculture and the environment. Options include languages and property investment.
Newcastle Choice of degree deferred to third year.

Nottingham Trent Opportunities exist to spend a year in placement.
Reading Wide range of optional modules in every year includes subjects from other departments, for example languages, marketing and ecology.
Royal (CAg) (Int Eqn Agric Bus Mgt) Twenty-week work placement in second year; links with the Westphalian Riding School.

Universities and colleges teaching quality See www.qaa.ac.uk; http://unistats.direct.gov.uk.

Top research universities and colleges (RAE 2008) (Agriculture, Veterinary and Food Science) Warwick; Aberdeen; Nottingham; Leeds; Reading (Food Biosciences); London (RVC); Aberystwyth; Glasgow; Edinburgh; Stirling; Cambridge; Liverpool; Newcastle; Bristol UWE; Bangor.

Examples of sandwich degree courses Aberystwyth; Bangor; Harper Adams (UC); Nottingham Trent; Royal (CAg).

ADMISSIONS INFORMATION
Number of applicants per place (approx) Aberystwyth (Agric courses) 2–3; Bangor (Agric Cons Env) 4; Newcastle 6; Nottingham 4; Royal (CAg) (Agric) 2.

Advice to applicants and planning the UCAS personal statement First-hand farming experience is essential for most courses and obviously important for all. Check prospectuses and websites. Describe the work done. Details of experience of work with agricultural or food farms (production and laboratory work), garden centres, even with landscape architects, could be appropriate. Keep up-to-date with European agricultural and fishing policies and mention any interests you have in these areas. Read farming magazines and discuss any articles which have interested you. You may even have had first-hand experience of the serious problems facing farmers. Interest or experience in practical conservation work. Ability to work both independently or as a member of a team is important.

Selection interviews Some Bangor, Bishop Burton (Coll), Derby, Edinburgh, Harper Adams (UC), Queen's Belfast, Royal (CAg); **No** Reading.

Interview advice and questions You should be up-to-date with political and scientific issues concerning the farming community in general and how these problems might be resolved. You are likely to be questioned on your own farming background (if relevant) and your farming experience. Questions asked in the past have included: What special agricultural interests do you have? What types of farms have you worked on? What farming publications do you read and which agricultural shows have you visited? What is meant by the term 'sustainable development'? Are farmers custodians of the countryside? What are the potential sources of non-fossil-fuel electricity generation? See also **Chapter 6**. **Bangor** (Agric Cons Env) No tests at interview. **Derby** (Cntry Mgt) Discussion about fieldwork experience.

Reasons for rejection (non-academic) Insufficient motivation. Too immature. Unlikely to integrate well. Lack of practical experience with crops or animals.

AFTER-RESULTS ADVICE
Offers to applicants repeating A-levels Possibly higher Newcastle (Agric); **Same** Bangor (Agric Cons Env), Derby, Harper Adams (UC), Nottingham, Royal (CAg), Writtle (Coll).

GRADUATE DESTINATIONS AND EMPLOYMENT (2009/10 HESA)
Agriculture; graduates surveyed 1800 **Employed** 940 **In voluntary employment** 45 **In further study** 430 **Assumed unemployed** 90

Agricultural Science; graduates surveyed 10 **Employed** 5 **In voluntary employment** 0 **In further study** 0 **Assumed unemployed** 0

Career note The majority of graduates entered the agricultural industry whilst others moved into manufacturing, the wholesale and retail trades and property development.

Check **Chapter 4** when choosing your university and **Chapter 7** on how to read the subject tables.

OTHER DEGREE SUBJECTS FOR CONSIDERATION

Agroforestry; Animal Sciences; Biochemistry; Biological Sciences; Biology; Biotechnology; Chemistry; Conservation Management; Crop Science; Ecology (Biological Sciences); Environmental Sciences; Estate Management (Surveying); Food Science and Technology; Forestry; Horticulture; Land Surveying; Landscape Architecture; Plant Sciences; Veterinary Science; Zoology.

AMERICAN STUDIES

(see also Latin American Studies)

Courses normally cover American history, politics and literature, although there are opportunities to study specialist fields such as drama, film studies, history of art, linguistics, politics or sociology. In some universities a year, term or semester spent in the USA (or Canada) is compulsory or optional whilst at other institutions the course lasts three years without a placement abroad.

Useful websites www.historynet.com; www.americansc.org.uk; www.theasa.net.

NB The points totals shown to the left of the institutions are for ease of reference only. It must not be assumed that Tariff points are always used by institutions or that they can be substituted for an offer in grades. The level of an offer is not necessarily indicative of the quality of a course.

COURSE OFFERS INFORMATION

Subject requirements/preferences GCSE Specific grades in some subjects may be specified by some popular universities. AL English, a modern language, humanities or social science subjects preferred.

Your target offers and examples of courses provided by each institution

380 pts **Warwick** – AABc (Hist Lit Cult Am) (IB 36 pts)
360 pts **Sussex** – AAA–AAB (Law Am St 3/4 yrs) (IB 35–36 pts)
340 pts **Kent** – AAB (Engl Am Lit; Engl Am Postcol Lit)
        London (Gold) – AAB (Am Lit)
        Loughborough – AAB (Engl Am St) (IB 34 pts)
        Nottingham – AAB (Am Engl St) (IB 34 pts)
        Sussex – AAB (Am St courses) (IB 35 pts)
        UEA – AAB–ABB incl Engl (Am Lit Crea Writ) (IB 33–32 pts HL 5 Engl)
320 pts **Birmingham** – ABB (Engl Am St) (IB 36 pts)
        Essex – ABB 320 pts (Am (US) St courses) (IB 32 pts)
        Kent – ABB (Engl Am Lit Joint Hons)
        Leicester – ABB (Hist Am St)
        Manchester – ABB (Am St) (IB 33 pts)
300 pts **Hertfordshire** – 300 pts (Am St)
        Leicester – BBB (Am St) (IB 30 pts)
        Liverpool – BBB (Compar Am St) (IB 30 pts)
        Nottingham – ABC–BBB (Am Can Lit Hist Cult) (IB 30 pts)
        Swansea – BBB 300 pts (Int Rel Am St)
280 pts **Glamorgan** – BBC (Am St)
        Hull – 280–300 pts (Am St (Comb))
        Keele – 280–300 pts (Am St) (IB 28–32 pts)
260 pts **Derby** – 260 pts (Am St)
        Dundee – BCC (Am St) (IB 30 pts HL 555)
        Lincoln – 260 pts (Am St courses)
        Sunderland – 260 pts (Am St (Comb))
        Ulster – BCC (Am St courses)
        Winchester – 260–300 pts (Am St Ccourses)
240 pts **Canterbury Christ Church** – 240 pts (Am St)
        Manchester Met – 240–260 pts (Am Hist) (IB 28 pts)
        Portsmouth – 240–300 pts (Am St Hist) (IB 25 pts)

UCLan – 240–200 pts (Am St (Comb))
Ulster – 240 pts (Bus Am St) (IB 24 pts)
Winchester – 240–280 pts (Am St Media St; Am St Dr; Am St Engl)
220 pts York St John – 220–260 pts (Am St courses) (IB 24 pts)
200 pts UEL – 200 pts (Anth Ntv Am St)

Alternative offers
See **Chapter 7** and **Appendix 1** for grades/UCAS Tariff points information for the International Baccalaureate, Scottish Highers/Advanced Highers, the Welsh Baccalaureate, the Irish Leaving Certificate, the Cambridge Pre-U Diploma, the Advanced Diploma and the Extended Project.

CHOOSING YOUR COURSE (SEE ALSO CH.1)
Some course features
Canterbury Christ Church American Studies is available as Single Honours and Joint or Combined Honours courses. Opportunity to spend either a semester or a year in the US.
Kent (Am St courses) Students spending a third year at an American university do not pay American tuition fees – only travel and living costs.
Liverpool An inter-disciplinary course covering North America, Latin America and the Caribbean. Option to learn Spanish or Portuguese from scratch, or to combine study of AL French, Spanish or Portuguese to degree level.
Manchester (Am St) Course covers the history, literature, film, politics and popular culture of the United States. Opportunity to study in US university for one or two semesters.
Nottingham (Am St courses) Part-time (4–7 yrs) study is also available.
UEA Students on four-year programme spend third year at American, Australian or Canadian university and are eligible for local education authority financial support.
Ulster Programme combines study of American history, literature, film, politics, music and cultural studies in an area study of the US.

Universities and colleges teaching quality See www.qaa.ac.uk; http://unistats.direct.gov.uk.

Top research universities and colleges (RAE 2008) Sussex; Birmingham; UEA; Nottingham; London (King's).

ADMISSIONS INFORMATION
Number of applicants per place (approx) Birmingham 4; Dundee 5; Essex 6; Hull 15; Keele 7; Leicester 7; Manchester 6; Nottingham 12; Swansea 2; UEA 7; Warwick 14.

Advice to applicants and planning the UCAS personal statement Visits to America should be described, and any knowledge or interests you have of the history, politics, economics and the culture of the USA should be included on the UCAS application. The US Embassy in London may be a useful source of information. American magazines and newspapers are good reference sources and also give a good insight to life in the USA. Applicants should demonstrate an intelligent interest in both North American literature and history in their personal statement. State why you are interested in the subject and dedicate at least half of your personal statement to how and why your interest has developed - for example through extra-curricular reading, projects, films and academic study. **Manchester** Due to the detailed nature of entry requirements for American Studies courses, we are unable to include full details in the prospectus. For complete and up-to-date information on our entry requirements for these courses, please visit our website at www.manchester.ac.uk/ugcourses.

Misconceptions about this course Swansea Some candidates feel that American Studies is a soft option. While we study many topics which students find interesting, we are very much a humanities-based degree course incorporating more traditional subjects like history, literature and English. Our graduates also find that they are employable in the same jobs as those students taking other degrees.

Selection interviews Yes Dundee, Hull, Sussex, Winchester; **Some** Derby, Kent, Warwick; **No** Birmingham, Essex, UEA.

Interview advice and questions Courses often focus on history and literature so expect some questions on any American literature you have read and also on aspects of American history, arts and culture. You may also be questioned on visits you have made to America (or Canada) and your impressions. Current political issues might also be raised, so keep up-to-date with the political scene. See also **Chapter 6**. **Birmingham** Access course and mature students are interviewed and also those students with strong applications but whose achieved grades do not meet entrance requirements. **Derby** The purpose of the interview is to help applicants understand the interdisciplinary nature of the course. **Swansea** Our interviews are very informal, giving students the chance to ask questions about the course. **UEA** Admissions tutors want to see how up-to-date is the applicant's knowledge of American culture.

Reasons for rejection (non-academic) If personal reasons prevent year of study in America. **Birmingham** Lack of commitment to the course. **Swansea** Lack of knowledge covering literature, history and politics.

AFTER-RESULTS ADVICE
Offers to applicants repeating A-levels Higher Essex, Warwick, Winchester; **Possibly higher** Nottingham; **Same** Birmingham, Derby, Dundee, Hull, Swansea, UEA.

GRADUATE DESTINATIONS AND EMPLOYMENT (2009/10 HESA)
Graduates surveyed 710 **Employed** 310 **In voluntary employment** 15 **In further study** 135 **Assumed unemployed** 55

Career note All non-scientific careers are open to graduates. Start your career planning during your degree course and obtain work experience.

OTHER DEGREE SUBJECTS FOR CONSIDERATION
Business Studies; Cultural Studies; English Literature; Film Studies; Government; History; International History; International Relations; Latin-American Literature/Studies; Politics.

ANATOMICAL SCIENCE/ANATOMY
(including **Neuroscience**; see also **Biological Sciences, Physiology**)

Anatomy is the study of the structures of living creatures, from the sub-cellular level to the whole individual, and relates structure to function in the adult and during embryonic development.

Useful websites www.scienceyear.com; www.innerbody.com; www.instantanatomy.net.

NB The points totals shown to the left of the institutions are for ease of reference only. It must not be assumed that Tariff points are always used by institutions or that they can be substituted for an offer in grades. The level of an offer is not necessarily indicative of the quality of a course.

COURSE OFFERS INFORMATION
Subject requirements/preferences GCSE Mathematics usually required. **AL** One or two mathematics/science subjects usually required; biology and chemistry preferred.

Your target offers and examples of courses provided by each institution
380 pts **Cambridge** – A*AA (Nat Sci (Neuro)) (IB 40–42 pts)
    London (King's) – AABc (Neuro) (IB 36 pts HL 6 chem 6 biol 5)
360 pts **Edinburgh** – AAA-ABB 320–360 pts (Neuro) (IB 37–32 pts)
    Leeds – AAA-AAB (Neuro) (IB 35 pts)
    Liverpool – AAA-AAB incl biol A (Anat Hum Biol) (IB 33–36 pts)
    London (UCL) – AAA-AAB incl chem (Neuro) (IB 36–38 pts)
    Manchester – AAA-ABB 320–360 pts (Neuro) (IB 37–33 pts)
    Nottingham – AAA-AAB (Phys Nanosci)
340 pts **Bristol** – AAB-ABB 320–340 pts (Neuro) (IB 35 pts)

Cardiff – AAB–ABB (Biomed Sci (Anat)) (IB 34 pts)
Leicester – AAB (Neuro Psy)
Nottingham – AAB (Neuro) (IB 34 pts)
St Andrews – AAB (Neuro) (IB 35 pts)
Sussex – AAB–ABB (Med Neuro) (IB 34–36 pts)
320 pts **Glasgow** – ABB (Neuro) (IB 32 pts)
Manchester – AAA–ABB 320–360 pts (Anat Sci) (IB 37–33 pts)
300 pts **Aberdeen** – CCC–BBB 240–300 pts (Neuro Psy)
Dundee – BBB (Anat Sci) (IB 34 pts)
Keele – 300 pts (Neuro)
Westminster – BBB (Cog Neuro)
260 pts **UCLan** – 260–300 pts (Neuro)

Alternative offers
See **Chapter 7** and **Appendix 1** for grades/UCAS Tariff points information for the International Baccalaureate, Scottish Highers/Advanced Highers, the Welsh Baccalaureate, the Irish Leaving Certificate, the Cambridge Pre-U Diploma, the Advanced Diploma and the Extended Project.

CHOOSING YOUR COURSE (SEE ALSO CH.1)
Some course features
Cardiff A common Biosciences first year programme (with the chance to change degrees) with following years centred on human anatomy, with dissection.
Dundee Emphasis on human anatomy.
Glasgow Students may choose to extend programme to an MSci, which includes a one-year research placement.
Liverpool Practical degree involving dissection and module choices from Biomedical and Biological Sciences and Psychology.
Manchester Part of the Life Sciences programme, with a common first year and options to change between degree courses.

Universities and colleges teaching quality See www.qaa.ac.uk; http://unistats.direct.gov.uk.

Top research universities and colleges (RAE 2008) See **Biological Sciences**.

Examples of sandwich degree courses Bristol; Cardiff; Manchester.

ADMISSIONS INFORMATION
Number of applicants per place (approx) Bristol 10; Cardiff 8; Dundee 6; Liverpool 7.

Advice to applicants and planning the UCAS personal statement Give reasons for your interest in this subject (usually stemming from school work in biology). Discuss any articles in medical and other scientific journals which have attracted your attention and any new developments in medicine related to anatomical science.

Selection interviews **Yes** Liverpool (Offer subject to interview); **Some** Cardiff; **No** Bristol, Dundee.

Interview advice and questions Questions are likely on your particular interests in biology and anatomy, why you wish to study the subject and your future career intentions. See also **Chapter 6**.

Reasons for rejection (non-academic) **Liverpool** Unfocused applications with no evidence of basic knowledge of the course.

AFTER-RESULTS ADVICE
Offers to applicants repeating A-levels **Higher** Bristol, Dundee; **Possibly higher** Liverpool; **Same** Cardiff.

GRADUATE DESTINATIONS AND EMPLOYMENT (2009/10 HESA)
Including Pathology and Physiology; graduates surveyed 3805 **Employed** 2075 **In voluntary employment** 65 **In further study** 740 **Assumed unemployed** 255

Career note The subject leads to a range of careers in various laboratories, in government establishments, the NHS, pharmaceutical and food industries. It can also lead to postgraduate studies in physiotherapy, nursing, osteopathy and, in exceptional cases, in medicine, dentistry and veterinary science.

OTHER DEGREE SUBJECTS FOR CONSIDERATION

Biological Sciences; Biology; Genetics; Microbiology; Neuroscience; Osteopathy; Physiology; Physiotherapy.

ANIMAL SCIENCES

(see also **Agricultural Sciences/Agriculture, Biological Sciences, Biology, Physiology, Psychology, Veterinary Science/Medicine, Zoology**)

Animal Sciences is a broad-based subject involving both farm and companion animals. The range of specialisms is reflected in the table of courses below and can focus on animal nutrition and health, animal biology, behaviour, ecology and welfare. In addition, many courses specialise in equine science, studies and management. **NB** It is important to note that Bioveterinary Science graduates are not qualified to practise as vets (see **Veterinary Sciences/Medicine**).

Useful websites www.rspca.org.uk; www.iah.bbsrc.ac.uk; www.bhs.org.uk; www.wwf.org.uk; www.bsas.org.uk.

NB The points totals shown to the left of the institutions are for ease of reference only. It must not be assumed that Tariff points are always used by institutions or that they can be substituted for an offer in grades. The level of an offer is not necessarily indicative of the quality of a course.

COURSE OFFERS INFORMATION

Subject requirements/preferences GCSE Mathematics/science subjects required. Also check any weight limits on equitation modules. **AL** One or two science subjects required for scientific courses, biology and chemistry preferred.

Your target offers and examples of courses provided by each institution

340 pts **Exeter** – AAB–BBB 340–300 pts (Anim Bhv) (IB 34–30 pts)
320 pts **Bristol** – ABB (Anim Bhv Welf) (IB 34 pts HL 665)
300 pts **Glamorgan** – BBB (Int Wldlf Biol)
LJMU – 300–260 pts (Anim Bhv)
London (RVC) – BBB–BBC (Biovet Sci 4 yrs) (HL 555)
Newcastle – BBB (Anim Sci) (IB 32 pts)
Reading – 300 pts (Anim Sci) (IB 30 pts HL 655)
280 pts **Aberystwyth** – 280–320 pts (Anim Bhv) (IB 26 pts)
Bristol UWE – 280 pts incl biol (Biovet Sci) (IB 24 pts)
Gloucestershire – 280–300 pts (Anim Biol)
Manchester Met – 280 pts (Anim Bhv) (IB 27 HL biol)
Newcastle – BBB–BBC 280–300 pts (Anim Prod Sci) (IB 28 pts)
Nottingham – BBB–BBC 280–300 pts (Anim Sci) (IB 30–28 pts)
Oxford Brookes – BBC (Eqn Sci Thoroughbred Mgt) (IB 30 pts)
Plymouth – 280–320 pts (Anim Bhv Welf)
Stirling – BBC (Aqua) (IB 32 pts)
260 pts **Aberystwyth** – 260–320 pts (Anim Sci) (IB 28 pts)
Harper Adams (UC) – 260–300 pts (Biovet Sci)
Lincoln – 260 pts (Anim Mgt Welf) (IB 30 pts)
LJMU – 260–300 pts (Wldlf Cons) (IB 25 pts)
240 pts **Aberdeen** – CCC (Wldlf Mgt) (IB 28 pts)
Anglia Ruskin – 240 pts (Anim Bhv; Anim Bhv Welf)
Bristol UWE – 240 pts (Anim Sci; Anim Bhv Welf)

CAFRE – 240 pts (Eqn Mgt)
Canterbury Christ Church – 240 pts (Anim Sci)
Chester – 240–280 pts (Anim Bhv Welf; Anim Bhv)
Cumbria – 240 pts (Anim Cons Sci)
Glamorgan – 240–280 pts (Nat Hist)
Greenwich – 240 pts (Eqn Mgt; Anim Cons Biodiv)
Hadlow (Coll) – 240 pts (Anim Mgt; Eqn Mgt; Anim Cons Biodiv; App Bhv Sci Welf)
Nottingham Trent – 240 pts (Eqn Spo Sci; Anim Biol; Eqn Psy Spo Sci; Wldlf Cons)
Reaseheath (Coll) – 240 pts (Eqn Sci)
Royal (CAg) – 240 pts (Int Eqn Agric Bus Mgt; Agric (Lvstk); Eqn Mgt)
Sparsholt (Coll) – 240–280 pts (Eqn St; Anim Mgt; Eqn Sci)
Worcester – 240–280 pts (Anim Biol)
Writtle (Coll) – 240 pts (Anim Mgt) (IB 24 pts)
230 pts Edinburgh Napier – 230 pts (Anim Biol)
220 pts Askham Bryan (Coll) – 220 pts (Anim Mgt Sci)
Moulton (Coll) – 220 pts (App Anim St; App Eqn St)
Myerscough (Coll) – 220 pts (Anim Bhv Welf; Eqn Mgt (Physiol); Eqn Sci Mgt (Bhv Welf))
Warwickshire (Coll) – 220 pts (Eqn Hum Spo Sci; Eqn Bus Mgt; Eqn Sci; Equit Coach Spo Sci; Eqn St)
West Anglia (Coll) – 220 pts (Eqn St)
200 pts Bishop Burton (Coll) – 200 pts (Eqn Sci; App Anim Sci; App Anim Bhv Trg; Eqn Bus Mgt; Eqn Thera Rehab; Eqn Spo Coach; Eqn Spo Perf; Eqn St)
Northampton – 200–240 pts (App Anim St; Eqn St)
Salford – 200 pts (Wldlf Cons Zoo Biol)
Wolverhampton – 200–260 pts (Anim Mgt)
Writtle (Coll) – 200–360 pts (Eqn Spo Thera)

Check **Chapter 4** when choosing your university and **Chapter 7** on how to read the subject tables.

180 pts Writtle (Coll) – 180 pts (Eqn St)
160 pts SAC (Scottish CAg) – CC (App Anim Sci)
Warwickshire (Coll) – 160 pts (Anim Sci Hlth)

Alternative offers
See **Chapter 7** and **Appendix 1** for grades/UCAS Tariff points information for the International Baccalaureate, Scottish Highers/Advanced Highers, the Welsh Baccalaureate, the Irish Leaving Certificate, the Cambridge Pre-U Diploma, the Advanced Diploma and the Extended Project.

EXAMPLES OF FOUNDATION DEGREES IN THE SUBJECT FIELD
Aberystwyth; Abingdon and Witney (Coll); Askham Bryan (Coll); Berkshire (CAg); Bicton (Coll); Bishop Burton (Coll); Bournemouth; Bridgwater (Coll); Brighton; Brooksby Melton (Coll); Bucks New; CAFRE; Chester; Cornwall (Coll); Craven (Coll); Derby; Duchy (Coll); Easton (Coll); Greenwich; Guildford (Coll); Hadlow (Coll); Harper Adams (UC); Kingston Maurward (Coll); Leeds City (Coll); Lincoln; Moulton (Coll); Myerscough (Coll); Northampton; Nottingham Trent; Otley (Coll); Plymouth; Reaseheath (Coll); Shuttleworth (Coll); Solihull (Coll); Sparsholt (Coll); UEA; Warwickshire (Coll); Weston (Coll); Wiltshire (Coll); Worcester; Writtle (Coll).

CHOOSING YOUR COURSE (SEE ALSO CH.1)
Some course features
Aberdeen Field courses in land use and zoology compulsory. Opportunities for expeditions, volunteering work overseas and year-out placements. All students carry out work experience.
Bristol UWE (Anim Sci) A science-based programme focusing on anatomy, physiology, nutrition and welfare, and including, eg animal management, equine therapy, animal psychology with work experience.
Newcastle Range of Animal Science courses with a common first year followed by specialisation in, eg Companion Animal Studies or Livestock Technology.
Nottingham Trent The course covers the study of wild animal populations and captive animals, both domestic and exotic.
Oxford Brookes (Eqn Sci) Practical and vocational course with range of opportunities in second year to study in Europe or the US or Canada or Australia.
Writtle (Coll) (Anim Sci) Common first year with Animal Management degree focusing on development of practical husbandry in each of the three major animal groups (farm animals, horses and companion animals). Business skills also important.

Universities and colleges teaching quality See www.qaa.ac.uk; http://unistats.direct.gov.uk.

Top research universities and colleges (RAE 2008) See **Agricultural Sciences/Agriculture** and **Biological Sciences**.

Examples of sandwich degree courses Aberystwyth; Harper Adams (UC); Nottingham Trent; Royal (CAg); Warwickshire (Coll).

ADMISSIONS INFORMATION
Number of applicants per place (approx) Aberystwyth 6; Bristol 8; Harper Adams (UC) 5; Leeds 6; Newcastle (all courses) 9; Nottingham 6; Nottingham Trent (Eqn Spo Sci) 4; Reading 10; Royal (CAg) 4.

Advice to applicants and planning the UCAS personal statement Describe any work you have done with animals which generated your interest in this subject. Work experience in veterinary practices, on farms or with agricultural firms would be useful. Read agricultural/scientific journals for updates on animal nutrition or breeding. For Equine courses, details of practical experience with horses (eg BHS examinations, Pony Club tests) should be included. **London (RVC)** BMAT is not required for entry but applicants wanting to be considered for the Merit Scholarships will have to take BMAT.

Misconceptions about this course Students are not always aware that horse studies courses cover science, business management, nutrition, health and breeding. **Bishop Burton (Coll)** (Eqn Sci) Some students wrongly believe that riding skills and a science background are not required for this course which, in fact, is heavily focused on the scientific principles and practice of horse management.

Selection interviews Yes Bristol, Cumbria (usually), Lincoln, Newcastle, Nottingham (depends on application), Plymouth, Royal (CAg), SAC (Scottish CAg), Writtle (Coll); **Some** Anglia Ruskin, Bishop Burton (Coll), Bristol UWE, Harper Adams (UC), Stirling.

Interview advice and questions Questions are likely about your experience with animals and your reasons for wishing to follow this science-based subject. Other questions asked in recent years have included: What do your parents think about your choice of course? What are your views on battery hens and the rearing of veal calves? The causes of blue-tongue disease, foot and mouth disease and BSE may also feature. (Equine courses) Students should check the level of riding ability expected (eg BHS Level 2 or PC B-test level). Check the amount of riding, jumping and competition work on the course. (See also **Chapter 6**.) **Lincoln** (Eqn Spo Sci) Applicants required to show that they can ride to BHS Level 2. Experience with animals in general.

Reasons for rejection (non-academic) Uncertainty as to why applicants chose the course. Too immature. Unlikely to integrate well.

AFTER-RESULTS ADVICE
Offers to applicants repeating A-levels Possibly higher Nottingham; **Same** Anglia Ruskin, Bishop Burton (Coll), Bristol UWE, Chester, Harper Adams (UC), LJMU, Royal (CAg), Stirling.

GRADUATE DESTINATIONS AND EMPLOYMENT (2009/10 HESA)
Graduates surveyed 990 **Employed** 515 **In voluntary employment** 30 **In further study** 290 **Assumed unemployed** 70

Career note The majority of graduates obtained work with animals whilst others moved towards business and administration careers. This is a specialised subject area and undergraduates should start early to make contacts with organisations and gain work experience.

OTHER DEGREE SUBJECTS FOR CONSIDERATION
Agriculture; Biological Sciences; Biology; Food Science; Natural Sciences; Veterinary Science; Zoology.

ANTHROPOLOGY
(including **Social Anthropology**; see also **Archaeology, Sociology**)

Anthropology is the study of people's behaviour, beliefs and institutions and the diverse societies in which they live, and is concerned with the biological evolution of human beings. It also involves our relationships with other primates, the structure of communities and the effects of diet and disease on human groups. Alternatively, social or cultural anthropology covers aspects of social behaviour in respect of family, kinship, marriage, gender, religion, political structures, law, psychology and language.

Useful websites www.britishmuseum.org; www.therai.org.uk.

NB The points totals shown to the left of the institutions are for ease of reference only. It must not be assumed that Tariff points are always used by institutions or that they can be substituted for an offer in grades. The level of an offer is not necessarily indicative of the quality of a course.

COURSE OFFERS INFORMATION
Subject requirements/preferences GCSE English and mathematics usually required. A foreign language may be required. **AL** Biology and geography preferred for some biological anthropological courses. (Soc Anth) No specific subjects required.

Your target offers and examples of courses provided by each institution
380 pts Cambridge – A*AA (Arch Anth) (IB 40–42 pts)
360 pts Edinburgh – AAA–BBB 300–360 pts (Soc Anth) (IB 34–42 pts HL 555)
    London (SOAS) – AAA (Soc Anth) (IB 38 pts HL 766)
    London (UCL) – AAAe–AABe (Anth) (IB 38 pts)
    Oxford – AAA (Arch Anth) (IB 38–40 pts)
    St Andrews – AAA–AAB (Soc Anth courses) (IB 35–38 pts)

340 pts **Bristol** – AAB–BBB (Arch Anth Sci) (IB 35–32 pts HL 665–666)
        Durham – AAB (Anth Arch) (IB 36 pts)
        Exeter – AAB–BBB 340–300 pts (Arch Anth) (IB 34–30 pts)
        Kent – AAB (Anth) (IB 33 pts)
        London (UCL) – AAB (Arch Anth) (IB 36 pts)
        London LSE – AAB (Anth Law) (IB 37 pts HL 666)
        Manchester – AAB 340 pts (Pol Soc Anth) (IB 34 pts)
        St Andrews – AAB (Phil Soc Anth) (IB 35 pts)
        Southampton – AAB (App Soc Sci (Anth)) (IB 34 pts HL 17 pts)
        Sussex – AAB–ABB (Geog Anth) (IB 32–34 pts)
        UEA – AAB–BBB (Arch Anth Art Hist) (IB 33–31 pts)
320 pts **Birmingham** – ABB–BBB (Anth Joint Hons) (IB 32–34 pts)
        Kent – ABB (Arch Anth) (IB 33 pts)
        Liverpool – ABB (Evol Anth) (IB 33 pts)
        London (Gold) – ABB–BBB (Anth courses) (IB 32 pts HL 766)
        Manchester – ABB–BBB 300–320 pts (Arch Anth) (IB 34–31 pts)
300 pts **Aberdeen** – BBB (Anth) (IB 30 pts)
        Birmingham – ABB–BBB (Anth Pol Sci) (IB 32–34 pts)
        Bournemouth – BBB (Biol Anth)
        Brunel – BBB (Anth courses) (IB 32 pts)
        Dundee – BBB (Foren Anth) (IB 34 pts)
        Edinburgh – BBB–AAA (Persn Soc Anth) (IB 34–42 pts)
        Kent – BBB (Med Anth) (IB 33 pts)
        London (Gold) – BBB (Anth Media) (IB 32 pts)
        London Met – 300 pts (Anth) (IB 24 pts)
        Queen's Belfast – BBB (Soc Anth courses)
280 pts **Oxford Brookes** – BBC (Anth) (IB 31 pts)
        Roehampton – 280–340 pts (Anth; Biol Anth)
        UCLan – BBC (Foren Sci Anth)
260 pts **Hull** – 260–300 pts (Sociol Anth; Anth)
        LJMU – 260–300 pts (Foren Anth) (IB 24 pts)
200 pts **UEL** – 200 pts (Anth Ntv Am St; Anth (Comb))
180 pts **Trinity Saint David** – 180–200 pts (Anth)

Alternative offers
See **Chapter 7** and **Appendix 1** for grades/UCAS Tariff points information for the International Baccalaureate, Scottish Highers/Advanced Highers, the Welsh Baccalaureate, the Irish Leaving Certificate, the Cambridge Pre-U Diploma, the Advanced Diploma and the Extended Project.

CHOOSING YOUR COURSE (SEE ALSO CH.1)
Some course features
Birmingham A broad course taught in the Centre of West African Studies.
Durham A wide choice of social and biological anthropology courses including Joint and Combined Honours and a route via Natural Sciences.
Kent The course covers both biological and social aspects of anthropology.
Liverpool (Evol Anth) Unique course focusing on human evolution, evolutionary psychology and hominid palaeontology.
Sussex Opportunities for overseas placements.
UEL (Anth Ntv Am St) The degree includes one year in the University of New Mexico.

Universities and colleges teaching quality See www.qaa.ac.uk; http://unistats.direct.gov.uk.

Top research universities and colleges (RAE 2008) Cambridge; London (SOAS); London LSE; Roehampton; London (UCL); Sussex; Queen's Belfast; Aberdeen; London (Gold); Oxford; Edinburgh; St Andrews; Manchester.

Examples of sandwich degree courses Brunel; LJMU; Oxford Brookes.

ADMISSIONS INFORMATION

Number of applicants per place (approx) Bristol 5; Cambridge 2; Durham 14; Hull 11; Kent 6; LJMU 4; London (Gold) 7; London (SOAS) 10; London (UCL) 3; London LSE 9; Manchester 5; Oxford Brookes 8; Queen's Belfast 10; Southampton 6; Sussex 10.

Advice to applicants and planning the UCAS personal statement Visits to museums should be discussed, for example, museums of anthropology (London, Oxford, Cambridge). Describe any aspect of the subject which interests you (including books you have read) and how you have pursued this interest. Give details of any overseas travel. Give reasons for choosing course: since this is not a school subject, you will need to convince the selectors of your knowledge and interest. **Bristol** Deferred entry acceptable. **Oxford** See **Archaeology**.

Selection interviews Yes Cambridge, Dundee (Foren Anth), Hull, London (Gold) (mature students), London (UCL) (mature students), Oxford (88% (successsful applicants 29%)), Oxford Brookes, UEA; **Some** London LSE, Roehampton; **No** Bristol.

Interview advice and questions This is a broad subject and questions will tend to emerge as a result of your interests in aspects of anthropology or social anthropology and your comments on your personal statement. Past questions have included: What stresses are there among the nomads of the North African desert? What is a society? What is speech? If you dug up a stone axe what could you learn from it? What are the values created by a capitalist society? Discuss the role of women since the beginning of this century. **Cambridge** See **Chapter 6** and **Archaeology**. **Oxford** See **Chapter 6** and **Archaeology**.

Reasons for rejection (non-academic) Lack of commitment. Inability to deal with a more philosophical (less positivist) approach to knowledge.

AFTER-RESULTS ADVICE

Offers to applicants repeating A-levels Possibly higher Oxford Brookes; **Same** Cambridge, Durham, LJMU, London (UCL), Roehampton, UEA.

GRADUATE DESTINATIONS AND EMPLOYMENT (2009/10 HESA)

Graduates surveyed 735 **Employed** 375 **In voluntary employment** 40 **In further study** 205 **Assumed unemployed** 75

Career note All non-scientific careers are open to graduates. However, career planning should start early and efforts made to contact employers and gain work experience.

OTHER DEGREE SUBJECTS FOR CONSIDERATION

Archaeology; Egyptology; Heritage Studies; History; Human Sciences; Political Science; Psychology; Religious Studies; Social Science; Sociology.

ARABIC AND ANCIENT NEAR AND MIDDLE EASTERN STUDIES

(see also History (Ancient))

Arabic is one of the world's most widely used languages, spoken by more than 300 million people in 21 countries in the Middle East and countries right across north Africa. Links between Britain and Arabic-speaking countries have increased considerably in recent years and most of the larger UK organisations with offices in the Middle East have only a relatively small pool of Arabic-speaking graduates from which to recruit future employees each year. Islamic Studies focuses on a faith which has much in common with Christianity and Judaism, is the second largest religion in the world, extending from Africa to the East Indies, and is focused on the Middle East.

Useful websites www.cilt.org.uk; www.iol.org.uk; www.bbc.co.uk/languages; www.languageadvantage.com; www.languagematters.co.uk; www.reed.co.uk/multilingual; www.metimes.com; www.merip.org; www.memri.org; www.mei.edu.

Check **Chapter 4** when choosing your university and **Chapter 7** on how to read the subject tables.

NB The points totals shown to the left of the institutions are for ease of reference only. It must not be assumed that Tariff points are always used by institutions or that they can be substituted for an offer in grades. The level of an offer is not necessarily indicative of the quality of a course.

COURSE OFFERS INFORMATION

Subject requirements/preferences GCSE English, mathematics and a foreign language usually required. A high grade in Arabic may be required. **AL** A modern language is usually required or preferred.

Your target offers and examples of courses provided by each institution

380 pts **Cambridge** – A*AA 380 pts (As Mid E St (Persn)) (IB 40–42 pts HL 776–777)
         London (King's) – AABc (Turk Modn Gk St) (IB 36 pts)
360 pts **Oxford** – AAA (Arbc courses) (IB 38–40 pts)
         St Andrews – AAA (Arbc Econ) (IB 38 pts)
340 pts **Leeds** – AAB (Arbc Engl) (IB 35 pts HL 6 Engl)
         London (SOAS) – AAB (Heb Isrl St) (IB 36 pts HL 666)
         Manchester – AAB–BBB 300–340 pts (Modn Mid E Hist) (IB 31–36 pts)
         St Andrews – AAB (Arbc Mid E St) (IB 35 pts)
320 pts **Exeter** – ABB–BBB (Islam St) (IB 32–30 pts)
         Leeds – ABB (Arbc Class Lit)
         London (UCL) – ABBe (Heb Jew St) (IB 34 pts)
300 pts **Edinburgh** – BBB–AAA (Persn Soc Anth) (IB 34–42 pts)
         Exeter – BBB–ABB 300–320 pts (Arbc Persn) (IB 30–32 pts)
         Leeds – lower access offer ABC/BBB (Islam St) (IB 32 pts HL 15 pts)
         Trinity Saint David – individual offers made after interview 220–300 pts (Islam St)
280 pts **Westminster** – BBC (Contemp Arbc St)
260 pts **UCLan** – 260–300 pts (Arbc (Comb))
240 pts **Islamic Advanced St (Coll)** – 240 pts (Mslm Cult Civ)
200 pts **Middlesex** – 200-300 pts (Int Bus Arbc)
         Salford – 200 pts (Arbc/Engl Transl Interp)
         UCLan – 200–300 pts (Islam St (Comb))
140 pts **Islamic Advanced St (Coll)** – 140–220 pts (Islam St)

Alternative offers
See **Chapter 7** and **Appendix 1** for grades/UCAS Tariff points information for the International Baccalaureate, Scottish Highers/Advanced Highers, the Welsh Baccalaureate, the Irish Leaving Certificate, the Cambridge Pre-U Diploma, the Advanced Diploma and the Extended Project.

CHOOSING YOUR COURSE (SEE ALSO CH.1)

Some course features
Edinburgh (Arbc) Students usually spend part of their third year in an Arabic speaking country.
Exeter Single and Combined Honours Arabic courses provide a strong language base combined with study of the culture, literature and history. All four-year Arabic students spend their second year in, eg Morocco, Egypt, Damascus or Jordan.
Leeds (Mid E St) Course focuses on the culture, politics and economy of the region. No knowledge of the Arabic language is required; an Arabic option is available.
Liverpool (Egypt) Course covers the language, archaeology and history of Ancient Egypt, together with a study of Egyptian art, religion and society.
Salford The only undergraduate course offering Arabic/English translation and interpreting.

Universities and colleges teaching quality See www.qaa.ac.uk; http://unistats.direct.gov.uk.

Top research universities and colleges (RAE 2008) (Middle Eastern and African Studies) Cambridge; Oxford; Edinburgh; London (SOAS); Durham.

ADMISSIONS INFORMATION

Number of applicants per place (approx) Cambridge 3; Leeds 6; London (SOAS) 5; Salford 5.

Advice to applicants and planning the UCAS personal statement Describe any visits to, or your experience of living in, Arabic-speaking countries. Develop a knowledge of Middle Eastern cultures, history and politics and mention these topics on the UCAS application. Provide evidence of language-learning skills and experience. **Salford** Students whose first language is Arabic are normally expected to have passed their secondary school leaving certificate and to demonstrate an acceptable command of English. English-speaking and European applicants should also be able to speak Arabic.

Selection interviews Yes Cambridge, Exeter, Leeds, Oxford; **Some** Salford.

Interview advice and questions You will need to be able to justify your reasons for wanting to study Arabic or other languages and to discuss your interest in, and awareness of, cultural, social and political aspects of the Middle East. **Cambridge** See **Chapter 6** under **Modern and Medieval Languages**. **Oxford** See **Chapter 6** under **Modern and Medieval Languages**. **Salford** (Arbc Engl Transl Interp) Applicants may be required to sit Arabic language tests. See also **Chapter 6**.

AFTER-RESULTS ADVICE
Offers to applicants repeating A-levels Higher Leeds, St Andrews; **Same** Exeter, Salford.

GRADUATE DESTINATIONS AND EMPLOYMENT (2009/10 HESA)
Graduates surveyed 185 **Employed** 85 **In voluntary employment** 0 **In further study** 40 **Assumed unemployed** 20

Career note Most graduates entered business and administrative work, in some cases closely linked to their language studies.

OTHER DEGREE SUBJECTS FOR CONSIDERATION
Anthropology; Archaeology; Classical Studies; Hebrew; History; Persian; Politics; Turkish.

ARCHAEOLOGY
(see also **Anthropology, Classical Studies/Classical Civilisation, History (Ancient)**)

Courses in Archaeology differ between institutions but the majority focus on the archaeology of Europe, the Mediterranean and Middle Eastern countries and on the close examination of discoveries of pre-historic communities and ancient, medieval and post-medieval societies. Hands-on experience is involved in all courses as well as a close study of the history of the artefacts themselves and, in some courses, an appreciation of the application of science.

Useful websites www.britarch.ac.uk; www.english-heritage.org.uk; www.prehistoric.org.uk; www.britishmuseum.org; www.archaeologists.net.

NB The points totals shown to the left of the institutions are for ease of reference only. It must not be assumed that Tariff points are always used by institutions or that they can be substituted for an offer in grades. The level of an offer is not necessarily indicative of the quality of a course.

COURSE OFFERS INFORMATION
Subject requirements/preferences GCSE English and mathematics or science usually required for BSc courses. **AL** History, geography, English or a science subject may be preferred for some courses and two science subjects for Archaeological Science courses.

Your target offers and examples of courses provided by each institution
410 pts **London (King's)** – AAAb (Class Arch) (IB 38 pts)
380 pts **Cambridge** – A*AA (Arch Anth) (IB 40–42 pts)
360 pts **Durham** – AAA (Anc Hist Arch) (IB 37 pts)
　　　　 Edinburgh – AAA–BBB 300–360 pts (Arch Soc Anth) (IB 34–42 pts HL 555)
　　　　 London (UCL) – AABe–ABBe (Arch) (IB 34 pts)
　　　　 Oxford – AAA (Arch Anth) (IB 38–40 pts)
　　　　 Warwick – AABc (Anc Hist Class Arch) (IB 32–36 pts)

Check **Chapter 4** when choosing your university and **Chapter 7** on how to read the subject tables.

340 pts   **Bristol** – AAB–BBB (Arch Anth Sci) (IB 35–32 pts HL 665–666)
         Cardiff – AAB–BBB (Arch Joint Hons)
         Durham – AAB (Anth Arch) (IB 36 pts)
         Exeter – AAB–BBB 340–300 pts (Arch Anth) (IB 34–30 pts)
         Kent – AAB–ABB (Class Arch St) (IB 33 pts)
         London (UCL) – AAB (Arch Anth) (IB 36 pts)
         St Andrews – AAB (Mediev Hist Arch) (IB 35 pts)
         UEA – AAB–BBB (Arch Anth Art Hist) (IB 33–31 pts)
320 pts   **Birmingham** – ABB (Arch Anc Hist) (IB 34 pts)
         Exeter – ABB–BBB (Arch) (IB 32–30 pts)
         Glasgow – ABB (Arch Joint Hons) (IB 36 pts)
         Kent – ABB (Arch Anth) (IB 33 pts)
         Leicester – ABB (Hist Arch)
         Liverpool – ABB (Arch BA/BSc) (IB 33 pts)
         London (SOAS) – ABB (Hist Art Arch) (IB 34 pts HL 555)
         London (UCL) – ABB (Class Arch Class Civ; Eygpt Arch) (IB 34 pts)
         Manchester – ABB–BBB 300–320 pts (Arch Art Hist) (IB 33–32 pts)
         Newcastle – ABB–BBB 300–320 pts (Arch) (IB 30–35 pts)
         Nottingham – ABB–BBB 300–320 pts (Arch Art Hist) (IB 32–30 pts)
         Sheffield – ABB–BBC (Class Hist Arch) (IB 33–30 pts)
         Southampton – ABB–BBB (Arch) (IB 32–30 pts HL 16 pts)
         Sussex – ABB–BBB (Art Hist Arch) (IB 32–34 pts)
         York – AAB–ABB 320–340 pts (Hist Arch) (IB 34–35 pts)
300 pts   **Aberdeen** – BBB 300 pts (Scot Arch) (IB 28 pts)
         Bournemouth – 300 pts (Arch)
         Bristol – BBB–BCC (Arch) (IB 32–29 pts)
         Cardiff – BBB–BBC (Arch)
         Edinburgh – BBB–AAA (Class Arch Gk) (IB 34–42 pts)
         Hull – 300 pts (Arch)
         Leicester – BBB (Arch) (IB 32 pts)
         Queen's Belfast – BBB–BBCb (Arch Palae Geog)
         Sheffield – BBB (Arch Joint Hons) (IB 32 pts)
         Southampton – BBB incl geog (Arch Geog) (IB 30 pts HL 16 pts)
         Winchester – 260–300 pts (Relig St Arch)
280 pts   **Bradford** – 280 pts (Arch) (IB 28 pts)
         Cardiff – BBC (Conserv Obj Mus Arch)
         Reading – 280–360 pts (Arch courses) (IB 30 pts)
260 pts   **Bradford** – 260 pts (Geog Arch)
         Chester – 260–300 pts (Arch courses) (IB 24 pts)
         Hull – 260–320 pts (Geog Arch) (IB 28 pts)
         Reading – 260–300 pts (Chem Arch)
         Winchester – 260–300 pts (Arch Prac)
240 pts   **Bangor** – 240–280 pts (Welsh Hist Arch) (IB 28 pts)
         Portsmouth – 240–300 pts (Pal Evol)
         UCLan – 240 pts (Arch courses) (IB 26 pts)
         Winchester – 240–280 pts (Arch) (IB 24 pts)
         Worcester – 240–280 pts (Arch Herit St courses)
200 pts   **Trinity Saint David** – 200–260 pts (Arch) (IB 26 pts)
180 pts   **Trinity Saint David** – 180–260 pts (Arch (Prac/Env)) (IB 26 pts)
160 pts   **UHI** – CC–AA (Arch; Scot Hist Arch; Arch Env St)
120 pts   **Peterborough (Univ Centre)** – 120 pts (Arch Lnd Hist)
 80 pts   **London (Birk)** – p/t for under 21s (over 21s varies) (Arch)

Alternative offers
See **Chapter 7** and **Appendix 1** for grades/UCAS Tariff points information for the International Baccalaureate, Scottish Highers/Advanced Highers, the Welsh Baccalaureate, the Irish Leaving Certificate, the Cambridge Pre-U Diploma, the Advanced Diploma and the Extended Project.

EXAMPLES OF FOUNDATION DEGREES IN THE SUBJECT FIELD
Bournemouth; Cornwall (Coll).

CHOOSING YOUR COURSE (SEE ALSO CH.1)
Some course features
Bangor (Herit Arch Hist) Focus on historical and archaeological evidence and its use in the heritage industry.
Bournemouth (Fld Arch) Focuses on a practical training for a career in archaeology.
Glasgow (Arch) A study of Scottish archaeology and field projects in Britain, Europe and the Mediterranean.
Leicester (Arch) Option to study another subject outside Archaeology in Year 1.
London (SOAS) Wide range of Archaeology courses, many with languages and History of Art.
York Archaeology courses provide wide range of options and opportunity to spend a term in another discipline, for example History, Biology.

Universities and colleges teaching quality See www.qaa.ac.uk; http://unistats.direct.gov.uk.

Top research universities and colleges (RAE 2008) Durham; Reading; Oxford; Cambridge; Liverpool; London (UCL); Leicester; Southampton; Sheffield; York; Queen's Belfast; Exeter; Nottingham.

Examples of sandwich degree courses Bradford.

ADMISSIONS INFORMATION
Number of applicants per place (approx) Birmingham 5; Bradford 4; Bristol 7; Cambridge 2; Cardiff 6; Durham 6; Leicester 6; Liverpool 12; London (UCL) 5; Manchester (Anc Hist Arch) 15, (Arch) 4; Newcastle 14; Nottingham 11; Sheffield 5; Southampton 6; Trinity Saint David 2; York 3.

Advice to applicants and planning the UCAS personal statement First-hand experience of digs and other field work should be described. The Council for British Archaeology (see **Appendix 3**) can provide information on where digs are taking place. Describe any interests in fossils and any museum visits as well as details of visits to current archaeological sites. Your local university archaeological department or central library can also provide information on contacts in your local area (each county council employs an archaeological officer). Since this is not a school subject, the selectors will be looking for good reasons for your choice of subject. Gain practical field experience and discuss this in the personal statement. Show your serious commitment to archaeology through your out-of-school activities (fieldwork, museum experience) (see **Chapter 6**). (See also **Anthropology**.) **Bristol** Deferred entry accepted. **Cambridge** Most colleges require a school/college essay.

Misconceptions about this course Bristol We are not an élitist course: 75% of applicants and students come from state schools and non-traditional backgrounds. **Liverpool** (Egypt) Some students would have been better advised looking at courses in Archaeology or Ancient History and Archaeology which offer major pathways in the study of Ancient Egypt.

Selection interviews Yes Bangor, Bournemouth, Bradford, Cambridge, Durham, Glasgow, Liverpool, London (UCL), Newcastle, Oxford (Arch) 30%, (Class Arch Anc Hist) 23%, Southampton, Swansea, Trinity Saint David, UEA; **Some** Bristol, Cardiff, York; **No** Birmingham, Nottingham, Reading.

Interview advice and questions Questions will be asked about any experience you have had in visiting archaeological sites or taking part in digs. Past questions have included: How would you interpret archaeological evidence, for example a pile of flints, coins? What is stratification? How would you date archaeological remains? What recent archaeological discoveries have been made?

How did you become interested in archaeology? With which archaeological sites in the UK are you familiar? See also **Chapter 6**. **Birmingham** Questions may cover recent archaeological events. **Cambridge** (see **Chapter 6**). **Oxford** (see **Chapter 6**). Interviews involve artefacts, maps and other material to be interpreted. Successful entrants average 30.7%. **York** What are your views on the archaeology programmes on TV? What would you do with a spare weekend?

Reasons for rejection (non-academic) (Mature students) Inability to cope with essay-writing and exams. **Bournemouth** Health and fitness important for excavations. **Liverpool** (Egypt) Applicant misguided on choice of course – Egyptology used to fill a gap on the UCAS application.

AFTER-RESULTS ADVICE

Offers to applicants repeating A-levels **Same** Birmingham, Bradford, Cambridge, Chester, Durham, Leicester, Liverpool, London (UCL), Sheffield, Trinity Saint David, UEA, Winchester.

GRADUATE DESTINATIONS AND EMPLOYMENT (2009/10 HESA)

Graduates surveyed 1085 **Employed** 495 **In voluntary employment** 30 **In further study** 305 **Assumed unemployed** 120

Career note Vocational opportunities closely linked to this subject are limited. However, some graduates aim for positions in local authorities, libraries and museums. A number of organisations covering water boards, forestry, civil engineering and surveying also employ field archaeologists.

OTHER DEGREE SUBJECTS FOR CONSIDERATION

Ancient History; Anthropology; Classical Studies; Classics; Geology; Heritage Studies; History; History of Art and Architecture; Medieval History.

ARCHITECTURE

(including **Architectural Technology** and **Architectural Engineering**; see also **Art and Design (Product and Industrial Design)**, **Building and Construction**)

Courses in Architecture provide a broad education consisting of technological subjects covering structures, construction, materials and environmental studies. Project-based design work is an integral part of all courses and in addition, history and social studies will also be incorporated into degree programmes. After completing the first three years leading to a BA (Hons), students aiming for full professional status take a further two-year course leading to eg, the BArch, MArch degrees or Diploma and after a year in an architect's practice, the final professional examinations are taken.

Useful websites www.ciat.org.uk; www.architecture.com; www.rias.org.uk; www.archrecord. construction.com.

NB The points totals shown to the left of the institutions are for ease of reference only. It must not be assumed that Tariff points are always used by institutions or that they can be substituted for an offer in grades. The level of an offer is not necessarily indicative of the quality of a course.

COURSE OFFERS INFORMATION

Subject requirements/preferences GCSE English and mathematics, in some cases at certain grades, are required in all cases. A science subject may also be required. **AL** Mathematics and/or physics required or preferred for some courses. Art and design may be preferable to design and technology. Art is sometimes a requirement and many schools of architecture prefer it; a portfolio of art work is often requested and, in some cases, a drawing test will be set.

Your target offers and examples of courses provided by each institution

380 pts   **Bath** – A*AA (Civ Archit Eng) (IB 36 pts HL 6 maths)
          Cambridge – A*AA (Archit) (IB 40–42 pts)

360 pts   **Bath** – A*AA (Archit) (IB 36–38 pts HL 6 maths)
          Cardiff – AAA (Archit) (IB 35 pts)
          Edinburgh – AAA–ABB incl maths (Struct Eng Arch) (IB 37–32 pts)
          Liverpool – AAA (Archit) (IB 36 pts)
          Manchester – AAA (Archit) (IB 37 pts)
          Manchester Met – AAA (Archit) (IB 36 pts)
          Newcastle – AAA (Archit St) (IB 37 pts HL 6 art)
          Nottingham – AAA (Archit Env Des) (IB 36 pts)
          Sheffield – AAA (Archit) (IB 37 pts)
          Southampton – AAA (Civ Eng Archit) (IB 36 pts HL 18 pts)

340 pts   **Bristol UWE** – 340 pts (Archit Plan) (IB 24–32 pts)
          Glasgow – AAB (Civ Eng Archit MEng) (IB 34 pts)
          Kent – AAB (Archit) (IB 33 pts HL 15 pts)
          Leeds – AAB (Archit Eng)
          London (UCL) – ABBe (Archit) (IB 34 pts)
          Oxford Brookes – AAB (Inter Archit) (IB 32–34 pts)
          Westminster – 340 pts (Archit courses) (IB 28 pts)

320 pts   **Birmingham City** – 320 pts (Archit) (IB 31 pts)
          Brighton – offers may vary ABB (Archit) (IB 34pts)
          Bristol UWE – 320 pts (Archit Env Eng; Archit Tech Des)
          Glasgow – ABB (Civ Eng Archit BEng) (IB 32 pts)
          Glasgow (SA) – ABB (Archit)
          Kingston – 320 pts (Archit)
          Lincoln – 320 pts (Archit)
          Northumbria – ABB (Archit) (IB 27 pts)
          Nottingham Trent – 320 pts (Archit) (IB 28 pts)
          Plymouth – 320 pts (Archit) (IB 30 pts)
          Queen's Belfast – ABB–BBBb (Struct Eng Archit MEng)
          Strathclyde – ABB (Archit St) (IB 34 pts)
          Westminster – ABB 320 pts (Archit Eng) (IB 28 pts)

300 pts   **Archit Assoc Sch London** – BBB 300 pts (Archit)
          Brighton – BBB (Archit Tech) (IB 28 pts)
          Bristol UWE – 300–360 pts (Archit Plan)
          Cardiff Met – 300 pts (Archit Des Tech)
          Coventry – BBB 300 pts (Archit)
          Dundee – ABC–BBB (Archit) (IB 30 pts)
          Edinburgh – BBB–AAA (Soc Arch Hist) (IB 34–42 pts)
          Greenwich – 300 pts (Archit)
          Heriot-Watt – ABC–BBB (Archit Eng) (IB 29 pts)
          Huddersfield – 300 pts (Archit Tech) (IB 28–26 pts)
          Leeds Met – 300 pts (Archit) (IB 26 pts)
          LJMU – 300 pts (Archit) (IB 30 pts)
          London Met – 300 pts (Archit St) (IB 32 pts)
          Loughborough – 300 pts (Archit Eng) (IB 32 pts)
          Nottingham – BBB (Archit Env Eng) (IB 30 pts)
          Robert Gordon – BBB (Archit) (IB 30 pts)
          Sheffield Hallam – 300 pts (Archit Env Des)
          UCLan – 300 pts (Archit) (IB 32 pts)
          Ulster – 300 pts (Archit) (IB 25 pts)

280 pts   **Birmingham City** – 280 pts (Archit Tech)
          Bournemouth Arts (UC) – BBC (Archit)

Check **Chapter 4** when choosing your university and **Chapter 7** on how to read the subject tables.

City – 280 pts (Civ Eng Archit) (IB 38 pts)
De Montfort – 280 pts (Archit) (IB 30 pts)
Derby – 280 pts (Archit Tech Prac)
London Met – 280 pts (Archit) (IB 32 pts)
Northumbria – 280 pts (Archit Tech) (IB 24 pts)
Norwich (UCA) – BBC (Arch) (IB 25 pts)
Portsmouth – 280–320 pts (Archit) (IB 28 pts)
Salford – 280 pts (Archit Tech)
Sheffield Hallam – 280 pts (Archit Tech)
Westminster – 280 pts (Archit Tech)
260 pts **Creative Arts** – 260 pts (Archit) (IB 28 pts)
Derby – 260–300 pts (Archit Des Joint Hons)
LJMU – 260 pts (Archit Tech)
Nottingham Trent – 260 pts (Archit Tech) (IB 28 pts)
Plymouth – 260 pts (Archit Tech Env) (IB 26 pts)
Salford – 260 pts (Civ Archit Eng) (IB 35 pts)
UCLan – 260 pts (Archit Tech) (IB 26 pts)
UEL – 260 pts (Archit)
Ulster – 260 pts (Archit Tech Mgt) (IB 24 pts)
245 pts **Edinburgh Napier** – 245 pts (Archit Tech)
240 pts **Anglia Ruskin** – 240 pts (Archit) (IB 26 pts)
Bolton – 240 pts (Archit Tech) (IB 30 pts)
Coventry – CCC (Archit Des Tech)
Glyndŵr – 240 pts (Archit Des Tech)
Leeds Met – 240 pts (Archit Tech) (IB 27 pts)
Northampton – 240–280 pts (Archit Tech) (IB 24 pts)
Ravensbourne – AA–CC (Archit)
Robert Gordon – CCC 240 pts (Archit Tech) (IB 26 pts)
220 pts **Anglia Ruskin** – 220 pts (Archit Tech) (IB 26 pts)
200 pts **Hull (Coll)** – 200 pts (Archit Des)
London South Bank – 200 pts (Archit Tech)
Wolverhampton – 200 pts (Archit Des Tech; Inter Archit Prop Dev)
180 pts **Pembrokeshire (Coll)** – 180 pts (Archit Tech)
160 pts **London South Bank** – 160 pts (Archit) (IB 24 pts)
150 pts **West London** – 150 pts (Blt Env (Archit Tech))
120 pts **Southampton Solent** – 120 pts (Archit Tech)
 80 pts **Arts London** – 80 pts (Archit (Spc Objs))

Alternative offers
See **Chapter 7** and **Appendix 1** for grades/UCAS Tariff points information for the International Baccalaureate, Scottish Highers/Advanced Highers, the Welsh Baccalaureate, the Irish Leaving Certificate, the Cambridge Pre-U Diploma, the Advanced Diploma and the Extended Project.

EXAMPLES OF FOUNDATION DEGREES IN THE SUBJECT FIELD
Bolton; Bournemouth; Brighton; Derby; Huddersfield; Northumbria; Oldham (Coll); West London.

CHOOSING YOUR COURSE (SEE ALSO CH.1)
Some course features
Architecture is a broad subject combining the vocational with the academic. To practise as an architect it is important to check that your chosen courses follow the requirements of the Royal Institute of British Architects (see **Appendix 3**).

Bath Four-year full-time thin sandwich BSc degree with second and third-year placements, and opportunity for third-year Erasmus exchange at a European school of architecture.

Edinburgh Wide range of architecture-related courses delivered jointly by University and Edinburgh College of Art. Choice of three-year BA or four-year MA Architecture course, both with options to proceed to MArch degree which completes RIBA/ARB Part 2 qualification for architects.

Huddersfield (Archit (Int)) Course focuses on the built environment in the developing world, with extensive overseas field work.

Northumbria Technological and managerial skills are included in the Architecture course, which carries RIBA Part 1 exemption.

Oxford Brookes (Archit) Wide-ranging three-year full-time course, with teaching centred on the design studio, technology, practice and historical and theoretical approaches to architecture.

Westminster Modular course largely based on design project work and covers a study of architectural form and the physical, social and psychological needs of the user.

Universities and colleges teaching quality See www.qaa.ac.uk; http://unistats.direct.gov.uk.

Top research universities and colleges (RAE 2008) (Architecture and Built Environment) Cambridge; London (UCL); Sheffield; Liverpool; Loughborough; Bath; Reading; Edinburgh.

Examples of sandwich degree courses Bath; Bristol UWE; Glasgow (SA); London South Bank; Northumbria; Nottingham Trent; Sheffield Hallam; Ulster.

ADMISSIONS INFORMATION

Number of applicants per place (approx) Archit Assoc Sch London 2; Bath 13; Cambridge 8; Cardiff 12; Cardiff Met 2; Creative Arts 4; Dundee 6; Edinburgh 18; Glasgow 16; London (UCL) 16; London Met 13; Manchester Met 25; Newcastle 11; Nottingham 30; Oxford Brookes 15; Queen's Belfast 9; Robert Gordon 8; Sheffield 20; Southampton 10; Strathclyde 10.

Admissions tutors' advice London (UCL) Selection test and portfolio of work required.

Advice to applicants and planning the UCAS personal statement You should describe any visits to historical or modern architectural sites and give your opinions. Contact architects in your area and try to obtain work shadowing or work experience in their practices. Describe any such work you have done. Develop a portfolio of drawings and sketches of buildings and parts of buildings (you will probably need this for your interview). Show evidence of your reading on the history of architecture in Britain and modern architecture throughout the world. Discuss your preferences among the work of leading 20th century world architects (see **Chapter 5**). **Cambridge** Check college requirement for preparatory work.

Misconceptions about this course Some applicants believe that Architectural Technology is the same as Architecture. Some students confuse Architecture with Architectural Engineering.

Selection interviews The majority of universities and colleges interview or inspect portfolios for Architecture. **Yes** Archit Assoc Sch London, Birmingham City, Bradford, Brighton, Cambridge, Cardiff, Coventry, Derby, Dundee, Edinburgh, Huddersfield, Kingston, Liverpool, London (UCL), London South Bank, Newcastle, Portsmouth, Sheffield, UEL; **Some** Anglia Ruskin, Cardiff Met; **No** Nottingham.

Interview advice and questions Most Architecture departments will expect to see evidence of your ability to draw; portfolios are often requested at interview and, in some cases, drawing tests are set prior to the interview. You should have a real awareness of architecture with some knowledge of historical styles as well as examples of modern architecture. If you have gained some work experience then you will be asked to describe the work done in the architect's office and any site visits you have made. Questions in the past have included the following: What is the role of the architect in society? Is the London Eye an eyesore? Discuss one historic and one 20th century building you admire. Who is your favourite architect? What sort of buildings do you want to design? How do you make a place peaceful? How would you reduce crime through architecture? Do you like the

University buildings? Do you read any architectural journals? Which? What is the role of an architectural technologist? See also **Chapter 5**. **Archit Assoc Sch London** The interview assesses the student's potential and ability to benefit from the course. Every portfolio we see at interview will be different; sketches, models, photographs and paintings all help to build up a picture of the student's interests. Detailed portfolio guidelines are available on the website. **Cambridge** Candidates who have taken, or are going to take, A-level art should bring with them their portfolio of work (GCSE work is not required). All candidates, including those who are not taking A-level art, should bring photographs of any three dimensional material. Those not taught art should bring a sketch book (for us to assess drawing abilities) and analytical drawings of a new and old (pre-1900) building and a natural and human-made artefact. We are interested to see any graphic work in any medium that you would like to show us – please do not feel you should restrict your samples to only those with architectural reference. All evidence of sketching ability is helpful to us. (NB All colleges at Cambridge and other university Departments of Architecture will seek similar evidence.) **Sheffield** Art portfolio required for those without AL/GCSE art.

Reasons for rejection (non-academic) Weak evidence of creative skills. Folio of art work does not give sufficient evidence of design creativity. Insufficient evidence of interest in architecture. Unwillingness to try freehand sketching. **Archit Assoc Sch London** Poor standard of work in the portfolio.

AFTER-RESULTS ADVICE

Offers to applicants repeating A-levels Higher Huddersfield; **Possibly higher** Brighton, De Montfort, Glasgow, Newcastle; **Same** Archit Assoc Sch London, Bath, Birmingham City, Cambridge, Cardiff, Cardiff Met, Creative Arts, Derby, Dundee, Greenwich, Kingston, LJMU, London Met, London South Bank, Manchester Met, Nottingham, Nottingham Trent, Oxford Brookes, Queen's Belfast, Robert Gordon, Sheffield.

GRADUATE DESTINATIONS AND EMPLOYMENT (2009/10 HESA)

Graduates surveyed 4315 **Employed** 1965 **In voluntary employment** 70 **In further study** 705 **Assumed unemployed** 375

Career note Further study is needed to enter architecture as a profession. Opportunities exist in local government or private practice – areas include planning, housing, environmental and conservation fields. Architectural technicians support the work of architects and may be involved in project management, design presentations and submissions to planning authorities.

OTHER DEGREE SUBJECTS FOR CONSIDERATION

Architectural Engineering; Building; Building Surveying; Civil Engineering; Construction; Heritage Management; History of Art and Architecture; Housing; Interior Architecture; Interior Design; Landscape Architecture; Property Development; Quantity Surveying; Surveying; Town and Country Planning; Urban Studies.

ART and DESIGN (General)

Art and Design degree courses cover a wide range of subjects. These are grouped together in the following five tables:

Art and Design (Fashion and Textiles)
Art and Design (Fine Art)
Art and Design (Graphic Design)
Art and Design (Product and Industrial Design)
Art and Design (Three Dimensional Design).
(**History of Art** and **Photography** are listed in separate tables.)

COURSE OFFERS INFORMATION

Subject requirements/preferences Entry requirements for Art and Design courses vary between institutions and courses (check prospectuses and websites). Most courses require an Art and Design Foundation course. **AL** grades or points may be required plus five GCSE subjects at grades A–C, or a recognised equivalent. A portfolio of work demonstrating potential and visual awareness will also be required. (Des Tech) Design technology or a physical science may be required or preferred. (Crea Arts courses) Music/art/drama may be required.

CHOOSING YOUR COURSE (SEE ALSO CH. 1)

Top research universities and colleges (RAE 2008) Loughborough (Design Technology); Reading (Typographic/Graphic Communication); Lancaster; Newcastle; Westminster; London (UCL); Brighton; Bournemouth; Oxford; Cardiff (UWIC); Newport.

ADMISSIONS INFORMATION

Advice to applicants and planning the UCAS personal statement Admissions tutors look for a wide interest in aspects of art and design. Discuss the type of work and the range of media you have explored through your studies to date. Refer to visits to art galleries and museums and give your opinions of the styles of painting and sculpture, both historical and present-day. Mention art-related hobbies. Good drawing skills and sketchbook work, creative and analytical thinking will be needed. See also **Appendix 4**.

Interview advice and questions All courses require a portfolio inspection. Admissions tutors will want to see both breadth and depth in the applicant's work and evidence of strong self-motivation. They will also be interested to see any sketchbooks or notebooks. However, they do not wish to see similar work over and over again! A logical, ordered presentation helps considerably. Large work, especially three dimensional work, can be presented by way of photographs. Video or film work should be edited to a running time of no more than 15 minutes. Examples of written work may also be provided. Past questions have included: How often do you visit art galleries and exhibitions? Discuss the last exhibition you visited. What are the reactions of your parents to your choice of course and career? How do they link up with art? Do you feel that modern art has anything to contribute to society compared with earlier art? Is a brick a work of art? Show signs of life – no apathy! Be eager and enthusiastic. See also **Chapter 6**.

Reasons for rejection (non-academic) Lack of enthusiasm for design issues or to acquire design skills. Poorly presented practical work. Lack of interest or enthusiasm in contemporary visual arts. Lack of knowledge and experience of the art and design industry.

GRADUATE DESTINATIONS AND EMPLOYMENT (2009/10 HESA)

Graduates surveyed 18,730 **Employed** 9530 **In voluntary employment** 535 **In further study** 2740 **Assumed unemployed** 1700

Career note Many Art and Design courses are linked to specific career paths which are achieved through freelance consultancy work or studio work. Some enter teaching and many find other areas such as retail and management fields. Opportunities for fashion and graphic design specialists exceed those of the other areas of art and design. Opportunities in industrial and product design and 3D design are likely to be limited and dependent on the contacts that students establish during their degree courses. Only a very limited number of students committed to painting and sculpture can expect to succeed without seeking alternative employment.

OTHER DEGREE SUBJECTS FOR CONSIDERATION

Animation; Architecture; Art Gallery Management; Communication Studies; Computer Studies; Education; Film Studies; History of Art; Media Studies; Photography; see other **Art and Design** tables.

ART and DESIGN (Fashion and Textiles)

(including Surface Design)

Fashion Design courses involve drawing and design, research, pattern cutting and garment construction for clothing for men, women and children. Courses may also cover design for textiles, commercial production and marketing. Some institutions have particularly good contacts with industry and are able to arrange sponsorships for students.

Useful websites www.fashion.net; www.londonfashionweek.co.uk; www.texi.org; www.yourcreativefuture.org.uk.

NB The points totals shown to the left of the institutions are for ease of reference only. It must not be assumed that Tariff points are always used by institutions or that they can be substituted for an offer in grades. The level of an offer is not necessarily indicative of the quality of a course.

COURSE OFFERS INFORMATION

Subject requirements/preferences AL Textiles or textile science and technology may be required.

Your target offers and examples of courses provided by each institution

340 pts Manchester – AAB (Mat Sci Eng) (IB 37 pts)
320 pts Glasgow (SA) – ABB (Fash Des; Fash Tex)
Loughborough – 320 pts (Tex Innov Des) (IB 32 pts)
Manchester – ABB (Tex Tech (Bus Mgt)) (IB 34–33 pts)
Southampton – ABB (Fash Tex Des) (IB 32 pts HL 16 pts)
Southampton (Winchester SA) – ABB (Fash Mark) (IB 32 pts)
300 pts Edinburgh (CA) – BBB (Tex) (IB 34 pts)
Heriot-Watt – BBB (Fash Comm; Fash Wmnswr; Fash Mnswr; Fash Tech; Fash)
Huddersfield – 300 pts (Fash Des Tex)
Leeds – BBB–BBC (Tex Des) (IB 30 pts)
Northumbria – 300 pts (Fash Mark)
Nottingham Trent – 300 pts (Fash Mark Brnd; Fash Comm Prom)
280 pts Arts London (CFash) – 280 pts (Fash Mgt)
Birmingham City – 280 pts (Fash Des courses)
Bournemouth Arts (UC) – BBC (Mkup Media Perf)
Brighton – BBC (Fash Bus St) (IB 28 pts)
Glamorgan – 280 pts (Fash Des; Fash Prom; Cstm Constr Scrn Stg)
LJMU – 280–320 pts (Fash)
London (Central Sch SpDr) – BBC (Thea Prac Cstm Constr)
Manchester Met – 280 pts (Fash Des Tech) (IB 28 pts)
Northumbria – 280 pts (Fash)
Norwich (UCA) – BBC (Fash) (IB 25 pts)
Nottingham Trent – 280 pts (Decr Art)
Sheffield Hallam – 280–300 pts (Fash Des)
Westminster – BBC 280 pts (Fash Merch Mgt)
260 pts Bournemouth Arts (UC) – BCC (Fash St; Fash Des Tech; Tex)
De Montfort – 260 pts (Fash Cont Des; Rtl Buy (Fash) (Tex); Fash Des; Tex Des; Fash Fabs Accs)
Derby – 260 pts (Fash St)
Huddersfield – 260 pts (Fash Des Mark Prod; Fash Tex Buy; Fash Tex Mgt)
Robert Gordon – BCC (Fash Mgt) (IB 27 pts)
Sheffield Hallam – 260–280 pts (Prod Des Jewel Fash)
Southampton Solent – 260 pts (Writ Fash Cult)

240 pts **Arts London (CFash)** – 240 pts (Mkup Pros Perf; Tech Efcts Perf)
Bolton – 240 pts (Tex Sfc Des; Fash Prod Dev)
Cleveland (CAD) – 240 pts (Tex Sfc Des; Fash Ent)
Coventry – CCC (Fash; Fash Accs)
Creative Arts – 220–240 pts (Fash Jrnl)
Leeds (CAD) – 240 pts (Fash (Des Realsn); Fash (Conc Comm))
Lincoln – 240 pts (Fash St)
Newport – 240–260 pts (Fash Des)
Nottingham Trent – 240 pts (Fash Kntwr Des Knit Tex; Cstm Des Mak; Fash Accs Des)
Ravensbourne – AA–CC (Fash Lfstl Prod; Fash Prom)

220 pts **Bournemouth** – 220 pts (Fash Tex)
Bradford (Coll Univ Centre) – 220 pts (Contemp Surf Des Tex; Fash Des)
Falmouth (UC) – 220 pts (Fash Des; Fash Photo; Perf Spo; Tex Des)
Glasgow Caledonian – CCD (Fash Bus)
Northampton – 220–260 pts (Fash Mark; Fash; Fash (Ftwr Accs); Sfc Des Prntd Tex)

200 pts **Anglia Ruskin** – 200–240 pts (Fash Des)
Arts London (CFash) – p/t 200 pts (Fash Bus)
Creative Arts – 200 pts (Fash Atel; Tex Fash Inter; Fash Prom Imag; Contemp Jewel)
Doncaster (Coll Univ Centre) – 200 pts (Fash Tex Des)
Hereford (CA) – 200 pts (Tex Des; Jewel Des)
Plymouth (CA) – 200 pts (Contemp Cfts; Fash; Jewel Silver; Tex)
Portsmouth – 200–280 pts (Fash Tex Des Ent)
Staffordshire – 200 pts (Tex Sfc; Sfc Pattn Des)
Salford – 200 pts (Fash) (IB 26 pts)
Swansea Met – 200 pts (Sfc Pattn Des (Tex Fash); Sfc Pattn Des (Tex Inter); Sfc Pattn Des (Contemp App Art Prac))
UCLan – 200–240 pts (Dig Des Fash; E Fash Des; Fash Prom Styl; Fash Brnd Mgt)
UHI – BB–AA (Contemp Tex)
Wolverhampton – 200 pts (Fash Tex)

160 pts **Arts London (CFash)** – 160 pts (Fash Tex)
Cardiff Met – 160 pts (Fash Inter Art Tex)
Colchester (Inst) – 160 pts (Art Des (Fash Tex))
Leeds Met – 160 pts (Des (App Tex)) (IB 24 pts)
Robert Gordon – CC (Fash Des) (IB 24 pts)
Sir Gâr (Coll) – 160 pts (Ceram Jewel; Fash Appar Des Constr)
Southampton Solent – 160 pts (Fash Graph; Fash PR)
South Essex (Coll) – 160 pts (Fash Des)
UHI – CC–AA (Fn Art Tex)
Ulster – 160 pts (Tex Fash Des)
West London – 160 pts (Fash Tex)

120 pts **Basingstoke (CT)** – 120 pts (Tex Fash)
Blackpool and Fylde (Coll) – 120–360 pts (Fash Cstm Perf)
Northbrook (Coll) – 120 pts (Fash Des; Fash Media Prom; Tex Des)

100 pts **and below or other selection criteria (Foundation course, interview and portfolio inspection)**
Arts London; Arts London (CFash); Arts London (Chelsea CAD); Arts London (Wimb CA); Bath Spa; Birmingham City; Birmingham City (Coll); Brighton; Bristol UWE; Cardiff Met; Chesterfield (Coll); Coventry; Croydon (Coll) 80 pts (Fash Des Bus); Edinburgh (CA); Glamorgan; Havering (Coll); Hertfordshire; Kingston; Leeds Met; Leicester (Coll); Lincoln; LJMU; London Met; Loughborough; Manchester (Coll); Menai (Coll); Middlesex; NEW (Coll); Newcastle (Coll); Nottingham New (Coll); Pembrokeshire (Coll); Plymouth; Robert Gordon; Staffordshire Reg Fed (SURF); Somerset (CAT); Southampton (Winchester SA); UEL; Westminster; York (Coll); Yorkshire Coast (Coll).

Check **Chapter 4** when choosing your university and **Chapter 7** on how to read the subject tables.

Alternative offers
See **Chapter 7** and **Appendix 1** for grades/UCAS Tariff points information for the International Baccalaureate, Scottish Highers/Advanced Highers, the Welsh Baccalaureate, the Irish Leaving Certificate, the Cambridge Pre-U Diploma, the Advanced Diploma and the Extended Project.

EXAMPLES OF FOUNDATION DEGREES IN THE SUBJECT FIELD
Arts London (CFash); Barnfield (Coll); Bath City (Coll); Bath Spa; Bedfordshire; Blackburn (Coll); Bournemouth Arts (UC); Brighton; Bristol UWE; Chesterfield (Coll); Cleveland (CAD); Colchester (Inst); Cornwall (Coll); Creative Arts; Croydon (Coll); Derby; Exeter (Coll); Hereford (CT); Hertfordshire; Hull (Coll); Kent; Kirklees (Coll); Leeds Met; Leicester (Coll); Liverpool (CmC); London Met; Manchester (Coll); Mid-Cheshire (Coll); Newcastle (Coll); Newport; Nottingham New (Coll); Plymouth City (Coll); Sheffield (Coll); South Essex (Coll); Suffolk (Univ Campus); West Anglia (Coll).

CHOOSING YOUR COURSE (SEE ALSO CH.1)
Some course features
Universities and colleges offer a very wide range of specialist and individual subjects. In each case programmes will differ, often depending on the specialist interests of teaching staff. When considering specialist courses, eg Fashion Retail Management, Fashion Embroidery, Fashion Journalism, choose only named courses since a number of institutions claim to offer these subjects but only as a minor study.

Universities and colleges teaching quality See www.qaa.ac.uk; http://unistats.direct.gov.uk.

Top research universities and colleges (RAE 2008) See **Art and Design (General)**.

Examples of sandwich degree courses Huddersfield; Manchester Met; Northumbria; Southampton Solent; Westminster.

ADMISSIONS INFORMATION
Number of applicants per place (approx) Arts London 5; Arts London (CFash) (Fash Mgt) 20; Birmingham City (Tex Des) 4; Bournemouth Arts (UC) 6; Brighton 6; Bristol UWE 4; Creative Arts 8; De Montfort 5; Derby (Tex Des) 2; Essex 2; Heriot-Watt 6; Huddersfield 4; Kingston 5; Leeds (CAD) 4; LJMU 6; London (Gold) 5; Loughborough 5; Manchester Met 3; Middlesex 5; Northampton 4; Northumbria 8; Nottingham Trent 8, (Tex Des) 3; Southampton 4; Southampton (Winchester SA) 3; Staffordshire 3; UCLan 4; Wolverhampton 2.

Advice to applicants and planning the UCAS personal statement A well-written statement is sought, clearly stating an interest in fashion and how prior education and work experience relate to your application. You should describe any visits to exhibitions, and importantly, your views and opinions. Describe any work you have done ('making' and 'doing' skills, if any, for example, pattern cutting, sewing) or work observation in textile firms, fashion houses, even visits to costume departments in theatres can be useful. These contacts and visits should be described in detail, showing your knowledge of the types of fabrics and production processes. Give opinions on trends in haute couture, and show awareness of the work of others. Provide evidence of materials handling. Show good knowledge of the contemporary fashion scene. See also **Art and Design (Graphic Design)**.

Misconceptions about this course Some students expect the Fashion degree to include textiles. (Tex) Some applicants feel that it's necessary to have experience in textiles – this is not the case. The qualities sought in the portfolio are analytical drawing, good colour sense and a sensitivity to materials.

Selection interviews Most institutions interview and require a portfolio of work. You should be familiar with current fashion trends and the work of leading designers.

Check **Chapter 4** when choosing your university and **Chapter 7** on how to read the subject tables.

Interview advice and questions Questions mostly originate from student's portfolio. See also **Art and Design (General)** and **Chapter 6**. **Birmingham City** (Tex Des) What do you expect to achieve from a degree in Fashion? **Creative Arts** Describe in detail a specific item in your portfolio and why it was selected.

Reasons for rejection (non-academic) Portfolio work not up to standard. Not enough research. Not articulate at interview. Lack of sense of humour, and inflexibility. Narrow perspective. Lack of resourcefulness, self-motivation and organisation. Complacency, lack of verbal, written and self-presentation skills. Not enough experience in designing or making clothes. See also **Art and Design (General)**.

AFTER-RESULTS ADVICE
Offers to applicants repeating A-levels Same Birmingham City, Bournemouth Arts (UC), Creative Arts, Huddersfield, Manchester Met, Nottingham Trent, South Essex (Coll), Staffordshire.

GRADUATE DESTINATIONS AND EMPLOYMENT (2009/10 HESA)
See **Art and Design (General)**.

Career note See **Art and Design (General)**.

OTHER DEGREE SUBJECTS FOR CONSIDERATION
History of Art; Retail Management; Theatre Design.

ART and DESIGN (Fine Art)
(including **Printing**, **Printmaking** and **Sculpture**; see also **Art and Design (Graphic Design)**, **Photography**)

Fine Art courses can involve a range of activities such as painting, illustration and sculpture and often fine art media – electronic media, film, video, photography and print – although course options will vary between institutions. As in the case of most Art degrees, admission to courses usually requires a one-year Foundation Art course before applying.

Useful websites www.artcyclopedia.com; www.fine-art.com; www.nationalgallery.org.uk; www.britisharts.co.uk; www.tate.org.uk; www.yourcreativefuture.org.uk.

NB The points totals shown to the left of the institutions are for ease of reference only. It must not be assumed that Tariff points are always used by institutions or that they can be substituted for an offer in grades. The level of an offer is not necessarily indicative of the quality of a course.

COURSE OFFERS INFORMATION
Subject requirements/preferences See **Art and Design (General)**.

Your target offers and examples of courses provided by each institution
360 pts **Glasgow (SA)** – AAA–AAB (Fn Art (Sculp Env Art); Fn Art (Pntg/Prtg))
      Oxford – AAA (Fn Art) (IB 38–40 pts)
320 pts **Glasgow (SA)** – ABB (Fn Art (Photo)) (IB 30 pts)
      Kent – ABB–BBB (Fn Art) (IB 33 pts)
      Lancaster – ABB (Fn Art) (IB 32 pts)
      London (UCL) – ABB (Fn Art) (IB 34 pts)
      London (UCL/Slade SA) – BBBe (Fn Art) (IB 32 pts)
      Southampton – ABB (Fn Art) (IB 32 pts HL 16 pts)

300 pts **Cardiff Met** – 300 pts (Fn Art)
Edinburgh – AAA–BBB 300–360 pts (Fn Art) (IB 34–42 pts)
Edinburgh (CA) – BBB (Ptng) (IB 34 pts)
Leeds – BBB (Fn Art) (IB 32 pts)
Newcastle – ABB–BBB 300–320 pts (Fn Art) (IB 28–30 pts HL 555+)

280 pts **Aberystwyth** – 280 pts (Musm Gllry St) (IB 28 pts)
Birmingham City – 280 pts (Fn Art)
Bournemouth Arts (UC) – BBC (Fn Art)
Brighton – BBC (Fn Art Ptg; Fn Art Sculp; Crit Fn Art Prac)
Gloucestershire – 280 pts (Fn Art Pntg Drg; Fn Art Photo)
LJMU – 280–320 pts (Fn Art)
London (Central Sch SpDr) – BBC (Thea Prac Scnc Art)
Manchester Met – 280 pts (Fn Art) (IB 28 pts)
Norwich (UCA) – BBC (Fn Art) (IB 25 pts)
Oxford Brookes – BBC (Fn Art) (IB 31 pts)

260 pts **Gloucestershire** – 260 pts (Fn Art)
Liverpool Hope – 260 pts (Fn Art)
Newman (UC) – 260 pts (Art Des)
Northumbria – 260 pts (Fn Art)
Nottingham – BCC (Fn Art)
Sheffield Hallam – 260 pts (Crea Art Prac)

240 pts **Bath Spa** – 240–300 pts (Crea Arts)
Bolton – 240 pts (Fn Art)
Canterbury Christ Church – 240 pts (Fn App Arts)
Chester – 240–280 pts (Fn Art) (IB 26 pts)
Chichester – BCD 240 pts (Fn Art courses) (IB 28 pts)
Coventry – 240 pts (Fn Art)
Cumbria – 240 pts (Fn Art)
De Montfort – 240 pts (Fn Art)
Derby – 240 pts (Fn Art)
Hertfordshire – 240 pts (Fn Art)
Huddersfield – 240–300 pts (Fn Art)
Leeds (CAD) – 240 pts (Fn Art)
Leeds Met – 240 pts (Fn Art) (IB 24 pts)
Lincoln – 240 pts (Fn Art)
London Met – 240 pts (Fn Art)
Newport – 240–260 pts (Fn Art)
Nottingham Trent – 240 pts (Fn Art)
Plymouth – 240 pts (Fn Art Art Hist; Fn Art)
Staffordshire – 240 pts (Fn Art) (IB 28 pts)
York St John – 240 pts (Fn Art courses)

220 pts **Bradford (Coll Univ Centre)** – 220 pts (Fn Art)
Falmouth (UC) – 220 pts (Fn Art; Drng)
Northampton – 220 pts (Fn Art; Fn Art Pntg Drg)
Sunderland – 220 pts (Fn Art)
UCLan – 220 pts (Fn Art)
Worcester – 220–260 pts (Fn Art Prac)

205 pts **Reading** – 205 pts (Fn Art (Post Fdn))
200 pts **Anglia Ruskin** – 200–240 pts (Fn Art)
Blackburn (Coll) – 200 pts (Fn Art (Integ Media))
Bristol UWE – 200 pts (Fn Art)
Doncaster (Coll Univ Centre) – 200 pts (Fn Art Crft)

Check **Chapter 4** when choosing your university and **Chapter 7** on how to read the subject tables.

       Glamorgan – 200–240 pts (Art Prac)
       Glyndŵr – 200 pts (Fn Art)
       Hereford (CA) – 200 pts (Fn Art)
       Hull (Coll) – 200 pts (Contemp Fn Art Prac)
       Middlesex – 200–240 pts (Fn Art)
       Plymouth (CA) – 200 pts (Fn Art)
       Portsmouth – 200–280 pts (Fn Art)
       Southampton Solent – 200 pts (Fn Art)
       Suffolk (Univ Campus) – 200 pts (Fn Art; Fn Art Prac)
       Swansea Met – 200 pts (Fn Art (Comb Media); Fn Art (Pntg Drg))
180 pts **Dundee** – 180 pts (Fn Art)
       Stamford New (Coll) – 180 pts (Fn Art)
160 pts **Blackpool and Fylde (Coll)** – 160 pts (Fn Art Prof Prac)
       Colchester (Inst) – 160 pts (Art Des (Fn Art))
       Creative Arts – 160 pts (Fn Art courses)
       Grimsby (IFHE) – 160 pts (Fn App Arts)
       Kingston – 160 pts (Fn Art)
       Robert Gordon – 160–180 pts (Pntg; Prtg; Sculp)
       Sir Gâr (Coll) – 160 pts (Fn Art Sculp; Fn Art (Pntg Drtg Prtg); Fn Art (Contemp Prac))
       South Essex (Coll) – 160 pts (Fn Art)
       Swindon (Coll) – 160–200 pts (Fn Art)
       UHI – CC–AA (Fn Art Tex; Fn Art)
       Ulster – 160 pts (Fn App Arts)
       Yorkshire Coast (Coll) – 160 pts (Fn Art)
100 pts **and below or other selection criteria (Foundation course, interview and portfolio inspection)**
       Arts London; Arts London (Camberwell CA); Arts London (Chelsea CAD); Arts London (Wimb CA); Barking (Coll); Bath Spa; Bedfordshire; Brighton; Bristol UWE; Bucks New; Cardiff Met; Cornwall (Coll); Coventry; Creative Arts; Croydon (Coll); De Montfort; Edinburgh (CA); Glamorgan; Glyndŵr; Havering (Coll); Hopwood Hall (Coll); Kingston; Kirklees (Coll); Leeds Met; Liverpool (CmC); LJMU; London (Gold); Loughborough; Middlesex; NEW (Coll); Northbrook (Coll); North Warwickshire and Hinckley (Coll); Nottingham; Reading; Staffordshire Reg Fed (SURF); St Helens (Coll); Stourbridge (Coll); Salford; Sheffield (Coll); Solihull (Coll); Southgate (Coll); South Nottingham (Coll); Suffolk (Univ Campus); Trinity Saint David; Tyne Met (Coll); UCLan; UEL; Walsall (Coll); West London; Westminster; West Thames (Coll); Wirral Met (Coll).

Alternative offers
See **Chapter 7** and **Appendix 1** for grades/UCAS Tariff points information for the International Baccalaureate, Scottish Highers/Advanced Highers, the Welsh Baccalaureate, the Irish Leaving Certificate, the Cambridge Pre-U Diploma, the Advanced Diploma and the Extended Project.

EXAMPLES OF FOUNDATION DEGREES IN THE SUBJECT FIELD
All are practical workshop courses. Arts London; Bath Spa; Bedfordshire; Blackpool and Fylde (Coll); Brighton; Bristol UWE; Central Bedfordshire (Coll); Cornwall (Coll); Creative Arts; De Montfort; Exeter (Coll); Glyndŵr; Greenwich; Hereford (CA); Huddersfield; Leeds Met; Leicester (Coll); Liverpool (CmC); Llandrillo Cymru (Coll); Newcastle (Coll); Plymouth; Plymouth (CA); Sheffield (Coll); Somerset (CAT); Southgate (Coll); Suffolk (Univ Campus); Sunderland; Sunderland City (Coll); Tyne Met (Coll); West London.

CHOOSING YOUR COURSE (SEE ALSO CH.1)
Universities and colleges teaching quality See www.qaa.ac.uk; http://unistats.direct.gov.uk.

Top research universities and colleges (RAE 2008) See **Art and Design (General)**.

ADMISSIONS INFORMATION

Number of applicants per place (approx) Arts London (Chelsea CAD) 5; Arts London (Wimb CA) (Sculp) 3; Bath Spa 8; Birmingham City 6; Bournemouth Arts (UC) 6; Bristol UWE 3; Cardiff Met 3; Cleveland (CAD) 2; Creative Arts 2; Cumbria 4; De Montfort 5; Derby 3; Dundee 5; Gloucestershire 5; Hertfordshire 6; Hull (Scarborough) 2; Hull (Coll) 2; Kingston 9; Lincoln 4; LJMU 3; London (Gold) 10; London (UCL) 26; London Met 11; Loughborough 4; Manchester Met 4; Middlesex 3; Newcastle 30; Northampton 3; Northumbria 4; Norwich (UCA) 3; Nottingham Trent 5; Portsmouth 6; Robert Gordon 5; Sheffield Hallam 4; Solihull (Coll) 4; Southampton 3; Staffordshire 3; Sunderland 3; UCLan 4; UHI 2; Wirral Met (Coll) 3.

Advice to applicants and planning the UCAS personal statement Since this is a subject area that can be researched easily in art galleries, you should discuss not only your own style of work and your preferred subjects but also your opinions on various art forms, styles and periods. Keep up-to-date with public opinion on controversial issues. Give your reasons for wishing to pursue a course in Fine Art. Visits to galleries and related hobbies, for example reading, cinema, music, literature should be mentioned. Show the nature of your external involvement in art. **Oxford** No deferred applications are accepted for this course; successful applicants average 11.5%.

Misconceptions about this course That Fine Art is simply art and design. Sixth form applicants are often unaware of the importance of a Foundation Art course before starting a degree programme. **Bournemouth Arts (UC)** Applicants need to make the distinction between fine art and illustration.

Selection interviews Most institutions interview and require a portfolio of work. **Yes** Arts London (Chelsea CAD) (interviews with portfolios and essays), Oxford (Fn Art) 12%.

Interview advice and questions Questions asked on portfolio of work. Be prepared to answer questions on your stated opinions on your UCAS application and on current art trends and controversial topics reported in the press. Discussion covering the applicant's engagement with contemporary fine art practice. Visits to exhibitions, galleries etc. Ambitions for their own work. How do you perceive the world in a visual sense? Who is your favourite living artist and why? See also **Art and Design (General)** and **Chapter 6**. **UHI** Applicants are asked to produce a drawing in response to a set topic.

Reasons for rejection (non-academic) Lack of a fine art specialist portfolio. No intellectual grasp of the subject – only interested in techniques.

AFTER-RESULTS ADVICE

Offers to applicants repeating A-levels Same Anglia Ruskin, Arts London, Birmingham City, Cumbria, Manchester Met, Nottingham Trent, Staffordshire, Sunderland, UHI; **No** Oxford (No deferred entry).

GRADUATE DESTINATIONS AND EMPLOYMENT (2009/10 HESA)

Graduates surveyed 4115 **Employed** 2005 **In voluntary employment** 130 **In further study** 755 **Assumed unemployed** 440

Career note See **Art and Design (General)**.

OTHER DEGREE SUBJECTS FOR CONSIDERATION

Art Gallery Management; History of Art; see other **Art and Design** tables.

ART and DESIGN (Graphic Design)

(including **Advertising, Animation, Design, Graphic Communication, Illustration** and **Visual Communication**; see also **Art and Design (Fine Art), Film, Radio, Video and TV Studies**)

Graphic Design ranges from the design of websites, books, magazines and newspapers to packaging and advertisements. Visual communication uses symbols as teaching aids and also includes TV graphics. An Art Foundation course is usually taken before entry to degree courses. Graphic Design students are probably the most fortunate in terms of the range of career opportunities open to them on graduation. These include advertising, book and magazine illustration, film, interactive media design, typography, packaging, photography and work in publishing and television.

Useful websites www.graphicdesign.about.com; www.graphic-design.com; www.allgraphicdesign. com; www.yourcreativefuture.org.uk.

NB The points totals shown to the left of the institutions are for ease of reference only. It must not be assumed that Tariff points are always used by institutions or that they can be substituted for an offer in grades. The level of an offer is not necessarily indicative of the quality of a course.

COURSE OFFERS INFORMATION

Subject requirements/preferences See **Art and Design (General)**.

Your target offers and examples of courses provided by each institution

340 pts **Bournemouth** – 340 pts (Comp Animat Art)

320 pts **Kent** – ABB (Dig Art) (IB 33 pts)
Southampton – ABB (Graph Arts) (IB 32 pts HL 16 pts)

300 pts **Derby** – 300 pts (Comp Gms Modl Animat)
Edinburgh (CA) – BBB (Intermed Art) (IB 34 pts)
Huddersfield – 300 pts (Animat Mtn Graph)
Leeds – BBB (Graph Comm Des) (IB 32 pts)
Reading – 300–330 pts (Graph Comm)
Teesside – 300 pts (Graph Des)
Worcester – 220–300 pts (Graph Des)

280 pts **Birmingham City** – 280 pts (Animat)
Bournemouth Arts (UC) – BBC (Illus; Vis Comm)
Glamorgan – 280–300 pts (Animat)
Lincoln – 280 pts (Contemp Lns Media)
LJMU – 280–320 pts (Graph Des Illus)
Manchester Met – 280 pts (Crea Multim) (IB 28 pts)
Northumbria – 280 pts (Comp Animat; Graph Des)
Norwich (UCA) – BBC (Animat) (IB 25 pts)
Nottingham Trent – 280 pts (Graph Des)
Sheffield Hallam – 280–300 pts (Graph Des)
Suffolk (Univ Campus) – 280 pts (Graph Des; Graph Des (Graph Illus); Graph Des (Mtn Graph))

260 pts **Bournemouth Arts (UC)** – BCC (Animat Prod; Dig Media Prod)
Canterbury Christ Church – 260 pts (Film Animat)
Derby – 260 pts (Animat; Graph Des; Illus)
Gloucestershire – 260 pts (Adv; Graph Des)

240 pts **Anglia Ruskin** – 200–240 pts (Illus)
Bolton – 240 pts (Animat; Animat Illus)
Bradford (Coll Univ Centre) – 240 pts (Adv Cmpn Mgt)
Bristol UWE – 240 pts (Animat)
Chester – 240–280 pts (Graph Des) (IB 26 pts)
Coventry – 240 pts (Graph Des; Illus Graph)

Cumbria – 240 pts (Graph Des)
De Montfort – 240 pts (Animat Des; Animat)
Edinburgh Napier – 240 pts (Graph Des)
Hertfordshire – 240 pts (Graph Des Illus)
Huddersfield – 240 pts (Graph Des)
Kingston – 240 pts (Animat)
Leeds (CAD) – 240 pts (Graph Des; Art Des (Interd); Dig Film Gms Animat; Vis Comm)
Leeds Met – 240 pts (Graph Art Des) (IB 24 pts)
Lincoln – 240 pts (Animat)
London Met – 240 pts (Graph Des)
Newport – 240–280 pts (Graph Des; Adv Des)
Plymouth – 240 pts (Dig Art Tech; Animat)
Portsmouth – 240 pts (Comp Animat)
Ravensbourne – AA–CC (Animat) (IB 28 pts)
Staffordshire – 240 pts (Graph Des)
Salford – 240 pts (Graph Des)
Sheffield Hallam – 240 pts (Interact Media Animat)
UCLan – 240–300 pts (Animat)
Ulster – 240 pts (Dig Animat)
Wolverhampton – 240 pts (Graph Comm; Graph Comm Illus)

230 pts   **Greenwich** – 230 pts (Graph Dig Des)
220 pts   **Bradford (Coll Univ Centre)** – 220 pts (Graph Des Illus Dig Media)
Falmouth (UC) – 220 pts (Illus)
Middlesex – 220 pts (Graph Des; Illus)
Northampton – 220–260 pts (Graph Arts)
Sheffield Hallam – 220 pts (Comp-ad Des Tech)
Sunderland – 220 pts (Adv Des; Animat Des; Des Multim Graph)
Worcester – 220 pts (Animat)

200 pts   **Anglia Ruskin** – 200–240 pts (Illus Animat)
Blackburn (Coll) – 200 pts (Des (Graph Comm); Des (Illus Animat); Des (Mov Imag); Des (N Media))
Bucks New – 200–240 pts (Crea Adv; Graph Arts)
Creative Arts – 200 pts (Graph Des; Graph Comm)
Doncaster (Coll Univ Centre) – 200 pts (Graph Des)
Hereford (CA) – 200 pts (Graph Media Des; Illus)
Hull – 200–240 pts (Dig Arts; Des Dig Media)
Hull (Coll) – 200 pts (Animat)
Leeds Met – 200 pts (Animat) (IB 24 pts)
Middlesex – 200 pts (Animat)
Plymouth (CA) – 200 pts (Animat; Des Gms; Illus; Interd Art Des Media; Graph Des)
Portsmouth – 200–280 pts (Illus; Graph Des)
Robert Gordon – BB–CCC (Animat)
Salford – 200 pts (Des Dig Media; Des Fut)
Southampton Solent – 200 pts (Animat; Graph Des)
Swansea Met – 200 pts (Gen Illus)
West London – 200 pts (Adv; Dig Animat)
Westminster – BB (Graph Inf Des)
Wolverhampton – 200 pts (Animat)

180 pts   **Coventry** – 180–200 pts (Animat)
Dundee – 180 pts (Graph Des) (IB 24 pts)
Stamford New (Coll) – 180 pts (Graph Des)

160 pts   **Bedfordshire** – 160 pts (Adv Des)
Blackpool and Fylde (Coll) – 160 pts (Graph Des)
Colchester (Inst) – 160 pts (Art Des (Graph Media))

Check **Chapter 4** when choosing your university and **Chapter 7** on how to read the subject tables.

The Hull College Group is recognised nationally and internationally for it's centre of excellence as a specialist and creative centre for Higher Education, including the Hull School of Art and Design which this year celebrates its 150th anniversary and has close association with the Harrogate School of Arts. The range of programmes includes Foundation Degrees, BA (Hons) and Masters in Art and Design disciplines such as Architectural Design, Illustration, Graphic Design, Fashion, Media and Photography.

We continually update our facilities and environment and maintain the ethos of a specialist art and design school for our students to innovate and work in.

ART & DESIGN
at Hull & Harrogate College

OPEN DAYS

Thurs 26 Jan
Wed 29 Feb

Hull Campus:
01482 598744
hull-college.ac.uk/HE

Harrogate Campus:
01423 878211
harrogate.ac.uk/HE

Creative Arts – 160–200 pts (Arts Animat)
Leeds Met – 160 pts (Des (Play)) (IB 24 pts)
Robert Gordon – CC (Graph Des) (IB 24 pts)
Sir Gâr (Coll) – 160 pts (Art Des (Multid); Dig Illus; Graph Comm)
Swansea Met – 160 pts (Crea Comp Gms Des)
Swindon (Coll) – 160–200 pts (Graph Des; Illus)
UEL – 160 pts (Graph Des; Illus)
Ulster – 160 pts (Des Vis Comm)
Westminster – 160 pts (Illus; Animat)
West Scotland – CC (Comp Animat)
120 pts **Northbrook (Coll)** – 120 pts (Comm Des)
Stockport (Coll) – 120–240 pts (Des Vis Arts (Graph Des); Des Vis Arts (Illus))
100 pts **Bucks New** – 100–140 pts (Dig Animat)
100 pts **and below or other selection criteria (Foundation course, interview and portfolio inspection)**
Arts London; Arts London (Camberwell CA); Arts London (Chelsea CAD); Bath Spa; Bradford; Brighton; Bristol City (Coll); Bristol UWE; Bucks New; Cardiff Met; Coventry; Croydon (Coll); Edinburgh (CA); Gloucestershire (Coll); Greenwich; Grimsby (IFHE); Havering (Coll); Hertfordshire; Hopwood Hall (Coll); Kent; Kingston; Leeds Met; LJMU; Loughborough; Manchester (Coll); Mid-Cheshire (Coll); NEW (Coll); Northbrook (Coll); Rotherham (CAT); St Helens (Coll); Solihull (Coll); Somerset (CAT); Southampton (Winchester SA); South Nottingham (Coll); Southwark (Coll); Suffolk (Univ Campus); Tyne Met (Coll); West London; Westminster; West Thames (Coll); Wigan and Leigh (Coll); Wiltshire (Coll); Worcester; Yorkshire Coast (Coll).
South Essex (Coll) – contact admissions tutor (Graph Des)

For a quick reference offers calculator, fold out the inside back cover.

Alternative offers
See **Chapter 7** and **Appendix 1** for grades/UCAS Tariff points information for the International Baccalaureate, Scottish Highers/Advanced Highers, the Welsh Baccalaureate, the Irish Leaving Certificate, the Cambridge Pre-U Diploma, the Advanced Diploma and the Extended Project.

EXAMPLES OF FOUNDATION DEGREES IN THE SUBJECT FIELD

Arts London; Bath Spa; Bedfordshire; Bournemouth; Brighton; Bristol City (Coll); Bucks New; Cardiff Met; Chichester; Cleveland (CAD); Cornwall (Coll); Creative Arts; Cumbria; Durham New (Coll); Exeter (Coll); Greenwich; Hereford (CA); Hertfordshire; Kingston; Kirklees (Coll); Leeds (CAD); Leicester (Coll); Mid-Cheshire (Coll); Middlesex; Newcastle (Coll); Norwich (UCA); Plymouth (CA); Rotherham (CAT); St Helens (Coll); Sheffield (Coll); Somerset (CAT); Southwark (Coll); Staffordshire Reg Fed (SURF); Suffolk (Univ Campus).

CHOOSING YOUR COURSE (SEE ALSO CH.1)

Some course features
These courses offer a wide range of specialisms; check the course contents before selecting.

Universities and colleges teaching quality See www.qaa.ac.uk; http://unistats.direct.gov.uk.

Top research universities and colleges (RAE 2008) See **Art and Design (General)**.

Examples of sandwich degree courses Aberystwyth; Huddersfield; Kingston; Northumbria.

ADMISSIONS INFORMATION

Number of applicants per place (approx) Anglia Ruskin (Illus) 3; Arts London 4; Bath Spa 9; Blackburn (Coll) 2; Bournemouth Arts (UC) 6; Bristol UWE 4; Cardiff Met 5; Colchester (Inst) 3; Coventry 6; Creative Arts 5; Derby 5; Edinburgh Napier 7; Glamorgan 3; Hertfordshire 6; Kingston 8; Lincoln 5; LJMU 7; Loughborough 5; Manchester Met 8; Middlesex 3; Northampton 3; Northumbria 8; Norwich (UCA) 4; Nottingham Trent 6; Ravensbourne 9; Solihull (Coll) 3; South Essex (Coll) 2; Southampton 6; Staffordshire 3; Swansea Met 10; Teesside 5; UCLan 5; Wolverhampton 5.

Advice to applicants and planning the UCAS personal statement Discuss your special interest in this field and any commercial applications that have impressed you. Discuss the work you are enjoying at present and the range of media that you have explored. Show your interests in travel, architecture, the arts, literature, film, current affairs (see also **Appendix 3** for contact details of relevant professional associations). Awareness of the place of design in society.

Misconceptions about this course Bath Spa Some students think that they can start the course from A-levels, that a course in Illustration is simply 'doing small drawings' and that Graphic Design is a soft option with little academic work.

Selection interviews All institutions interview and require a portfolio of work.

Interview advice and questions Questions may be asked on recent trends in graphic design from the points of view of methods and designers and, particularly, art and the computer. Questions are usually asked on applicant's portfolio of work. See also **Art and Design (General)** and **Chapter 6**. **Nottingham Trent** Why Graphic Design? Why this course? Describe a piece of graphic design which has succeeded.

Reasons for rejection (non-academic) Not enough work in portfolio. Inability to think imaginatively. Lack of interest in the arts in general. Lack of drive. Tutor's statement indicating problems. Poorly constructed personal statement. Inability to talk about your work. Lack of knowledge about the chosen course. See also **Art and Design (General)**.

AFTER-RESULTS ADVICE

Offers to applicants repeating A-levels Same Bath Spa, Blackpool and Fylde (Coll), Bournemouth Arts (UC), Cardiff Met, Creative Arts, Lincoln, Manchester Met, Nottingham Trent, Salford, South Essex (Coll), Staffordshire.

GRADUATE DESTINATIONS AND EMPLOYMENT (2009/10 HESA)
See **Art and Design (General)**.

Career note See **Art and Design (General)**.

OTHER DEGREE SUBJECTS FOR CONSIDERATION
Art Gallery Management; Film and Video Production; History of Art; Multimedia Design, Photography and Digital Imaging. See also other **Art and Design** tables.

ART and DESIGN (Product and Industrial Design)

(including **Design Technology, Footwear Design, Furniture Design, Product Design, Theatre Design** and **Transport Design**; see also **Architecture, Art and Design (3D Design)**)

The field of industrial design is extensive and degree studies are usually preceded by an Art Foundation course. Product Design is one of the most common courses in which technological studies (involving materials and methods of production) are integrated with creative design in the production of a range of household and industrial products. Other courses on offer include Furniture Design, Interior, Theatre, Museum and Exhibition, Automotive and Transport Design. It should be noted that some Product Design courses have an engineering bias: see **Subject requirements/preferences** below. These are stimulating courses but graduate opportunities in this field are very limited. Good courses will have good industrial contacts for sandwich courses or shorter work placements – check with course leaders (or students) before applying.

Useful websites www.ergonomics.org.uk; www.yourcreativefuture.org.uk; www.productdesignforums. com; www.carbodydesign.com; www.shoe-design.com.

NB The points totals shown to the left of the institutions are for ease of reference only. It must not be assumed that Tariff points are always used by institutions or that they can be substituted for an offer in grades. The level of an offer is not necessarily indicative of the quality of a course.

COURSE OFFERS INFORMATION
Subject requirements/preferences AL Check Product Design, Industrial Design and Engineering Design course requirements since these will often require mathematics and/or physics.

Your target offers and examples of courses provided by each institution

340 pts **Glasgow** – AAB (Prod Des Eng MEng) (IB 34 pts)
Liverpool – AAB incl maths phys (Eng Prod Des MEng) (IB 35 pts HL 5 maths phys)
Queen's Belfast – AAB (Prod Des Dev MEng)
Strathclyde – AAB (Prod Des Eng MEng) (IB 36 pts)

320 pts **Brighton** – ABB (Spo Prod Des)
Glasgow – ABB (Prod Des Eng BEng) (IB 32 pts)
Glasgow (SA) – ABB (Prod Des; Des (Inter Des))
Leeds – ABB (Prod Des) (IB 34 pts HL 16 pts)
Nottingham – ABB (Prod Des Manuf MEng)
Nottingham Trent – 320 pts (Inter Arch Des)
Strathclyde – ABB (Prod Des Eng BEng) (IB 32 pts)
Sussex – ABB–BBB (Prod Des) (IB 32 pts)

300 pts **Aston** – BBB–ABB 300–320 pts (Trans Prod Des) (IB 32 pts)
Bournemouth – 300–320 pts (Ind Des)
Brighton – BBB 300 pts (Spo Prod Des (Yr Ind)) (IB 32 pts)
Brunel – BBB (Ind Des Tech) (IB 32 pts)
Brunel – BBB 300 pts (Prod Des) (IB 31 pts)
Cardiff Met – 300 pts (Prod Des)

Edinburgh (CA) – BBB (Prod Des) (IB 34 pts)
Huddersfield – 300 pts (Prod Des (3D Animat); Exhib Rtl Des; Prod Des (Child Prod Toys/ Sust Des); Prod Innov Des Dev)
Leeds – BBB (Des Tech Mgt) (IB 30 pts)
Liverpool – BBB incl maths phys (Eng Prod Des BEng) (IB 32 pts HL 5 maths phys)
Loughborough – 300 pts (Ind Des Tech) (IB 32 pts)
Queen's Belfast – BBB (Prod Des Dev BEng)

285 pts **Kingston** – 285 pts (Prod Des)
280 pts **Birmingham City** – 280 pts (Prod Des)
De Montfort – 280 pts (Prod Furn Des)
Derby – 280 pts (Prod Des)
Leeds Met – 280–300 pts (Inter Arch Des) (IB 26 pts)
London (Central Sch SpDr) – BBC (Thea Prac Stg Des; Thea Prac Prod Ltg; Thea Prac Prop Mak; Thea Prac Ltg Des)
London Met – 280 pts (Furn Prod Des)
Manchester Met – 280 pts (Prod Des Tech) (IB 28 pts)
Nottingham – BBC (Prod Des Manuf BEng) (IB 30–32 pts)
Nottingham Trent – 280 pts (Prod Des)
Teesside – 280 pts (Inter Archit; Prod Des; Inter Des)

260 pts **Bournemouth Arts (UC)** – BCC (Inter Arch Des)
De Montfort – 260 pts (Prod Des BA)
LJMU – 260 pts (Spat Des) (IB 28 pts)
Northampton – 260–280 pts (Prod Des)
Northumbria – 260 pts (Prod Des Tech)
Salford – 260 pts (Prod Des) (IB 26 pts)
Sheffield Hallam – 260–300 pts (Prod Des)
Ulster – 260 pts (Tech Des)

240 pts **Bristol UWE** – 240–300 pts (Crea Prod Des) (IB 24–28 pts)
Coventry – 240 pts (Ind Prod Des; Prod Des Spo; Prod Des Toy)
De Montfort – 240–260 pts (Furn Des)
Dundee – CCC (Prod Des)
Edinburgh Napier – CCC 240 pts (Prod Des Eng)
Glyndŵr – 240 pts (Mtrspo Des Mgt)
Hertfordshire – 240 pts (Prod Des; Ind Des)
Hull – 240 pts (Des Tech)
Leeds (CAD) – 240 pts (Inter Des)
Lincoln – 240 pts (Prod Des)
LJMU – Check with university 240 pts (Inter Des)
Nottingham Trent – 240 pts (Thea Des)
Plymouth – 240 pts (3D Des (Des Mkr/Furn Inter Des))
Ravensbourne – AA–CC (Inter Des Env Archit) (IB 28 pts)
Rose Bruford (Coll) – 240 pts (Ltg Des)
Staffordshire – 240 pts (Trans Des)
Sheffield Hallam – 240–260 pts (Furn Prod Des)
Swansea – 240–300 pts (Prod Des Eng BEng)
UCLan – 240–260 pts (Photo Fash Brnd Prom)
Wolverhampton – 240 pts (Inter Des; Prod Des)

220 pts **Falmouth (UC)** – 220 pts (Inter Des)
Hull – 220–260 pts (Med Prod Des)
Moulton (Coll) – 220 pts (Inter Des)
Northampton – 220–260 pts (Inter Des)
Swansea Met – 220 pts (Prod Des)

200 pts **Abertay Dundee** – CDD (Fd Prod Des)
Bangor – 200–220 pts (Prod Des)
Bradford – 200–240 pts (Prod Des)

Check **Chapter 4** when choosing your university and **Chapter 7** on how to read the subject tables.

Bucks New – 200–240 pts (Furn Des)
Creative Arts – 200 pts (Prod Des Sust Fut; Prod Des)
London South Bank – CDD 200 pts (Prod Des)
Plymouth (CA) – 200 pts (Sculp Mtl)
Portsmouth – 200 pts (Prod Des Modn Mat)
Sheffield Hallam – 200 pts (Des Tech)
Suffolk (Univ Campus) – 200 pts (Inter Des)
UEL – 200 pts (Prod Des; Prod Des Fut)
York St John – 200–220 pts (Prod Des courses)

180 pts **Dundee** – 180 pts (Jewel Metal Des)
Greenwich – 180 pts (Des Tech Educ)
Kingston – 180–220 pts (Des St)
Liverpool (LIPA) – 180 pts (Thea Perf Des)

160 pts **Leeds Met** – 160 pts (Des (Prod)) (IB 24 pts)
Robert Gordon – CC (Prod Des) (IB 24 pts)
Southampton Solent – 160 pts (Prod Des; Inter Des (Decr))
West Scotland – CC (Prod Des Dev)

120 pts **Southampton Solent** – 120 pts (Mech Des)

100 pts **and below or other selection criteria (Foundation course, interview and portfolio inspection)**
Arts London; Arts London (Chelsea CAD); Arts London (Wimb CA); Barking (Coll); Bath Spa; Bolton; Bournemouth Arts (UC); Brighton; Bucks New; Cardiff Met; De Montfort; Dundee; Easton (Coll); Edinburgh (CA); Forth Valley (Coll); Glasgow Caledonian; Glasgow Met (Coll); Heriot-Watt; Hertfordshire; Kingston; Kirklees (Coll); Lincoln; London South Bank; NEW (Coll); Royal Welsh (CMusDr); Shrewsbury (CAT); Southampton Solent; South Essex (Coll).

Alternative offers
See **Chapter 7** and **Appendix 1** for grades/UCAS Tariff points information for the International Baccalaureate, Scottish Highers/Advanced Highers, the Welsh Baccalaureate, the Irish Leaving Certificate, the Cambridge Pre-U Diploma, the Advanced Diploma and the Extended Project.

EXAMPLES OF FOUNDATION DEGREES IN THE SUBJECT FIELD
Arts London; Barking (Coll); Bath Spa; Bedfordshire; Bishop Burton (Coll); Blackburn (Coll); Bournemouth Arts (UC); Bristol City (Coll); Bristol UWE; Bucks New; Cornwall (Coll); Croydon (Coll); Greenwich; Kirklees (Coll); Leeds (CAD); Leicester (Coll); London Met; Plymouth (CA); Rose Bruford (Coll); Somerset (CAT); South Devon (Coll); Swansea Met; West London.

CHOOSING YOUR COURSE (SEE ALSO CH.1)
Some course features
Note that there is an engineering element in some Product Design courses, and several specifically lead to an Engineering degree. Many are accredited by the Institution of Engineering Designers (see **Appendix 3**).

Ulster Live projects undertaken in all three years of course. Furniture Design covers public, contract, domestic and street furniture.

Universities and colleges teaching quality See www.qaa.ac.uk; http://unistats.direct.gov.uk.

Top research universities and colleges (RAE 2008) See **Art and Design (General)**.

Examples of sandwich degree courses Aston; Bournemouth; Bradford; Brighton; Bristol UWE; Brunel; De Montfort; Huddersfield; Lincoln; LJMU; London South Bank; Manchester Met; Middlesex; Nottingham Trent; Portsmouth; Sheffield Hallam; Staffordshire; West Scotland.

ADMISSIONS INFORMATION
Number of applicants per place (approx) Arts London 2; Arts London (Chelsea CAD) 2; Arts London (Wimb CA) 2; Aston 6; Bath Spa 4; Birmingham City (Inter Des) 9; Bolton 1; Brunel 4; Cardiff Met 6;

Colchester (Inst) 4; Coventry 5; Creative Arts 4; De Montfort 5; Derby 2; Edinburgh Napier 6; Loughborough 9; Manchester Met 2; Middlesex (Inter Archit Des) 4; Northampton (Prod Des) 2; Northumbria 4; Nottingham Trent (Inter Archit Des) 7, (Prod Des) 5; Portsmouth 3; Ravensbourne (Inter Des) 4, (Prod Des) 7; Salford 6; Sheffield 4; Shrewsbury (CAT) 6; Staffordshire 3; Swansea Met 3; Teesside 3; UCLan 7.

Advice to applicants and planning the UCAS personal statement Your knowledge of design in all fields should be described, including any special interests you may have, for example in domestic, rail and road aspects of design, and visits to exhibitions, motor shows. **School/college reference** Tutors should make it clear that the applicant's knowledge, experience and attitude match the chosen course – not simply higher education in general. Admissions tutors look for knowledge of interior design and interior architecture, experience in 3D-design projects (which include problem-solving and sculptural demands), model-making experience in diverse materials, experience with 2D illustration and colour work, and knowledge of computer-aided design. Photography is also helpful, and also model-making and CAD/computer skills. See also **Art and Design (Graphic Design)**.

Misconceptions about this course Theatre Design is sometimes confused with Theatre Architecture or an academic course in Theatre Studies. **Birmingham City** (Inter Des) Some applicants believe that it is an interior decorating course (carpets and curtains). **Lincoln** (Musm Exhib Des) This is a design course, not a museum course. **Portsmouth** (Inter Des) Some students think that this is about interior decorating after Laurence Llewelyn-Bowen!

Selection interviews Most institutions will interview and require a portfolio of work. **Yes** Brunel, Cardiff Met, Dundee; **Some** Salford, Staffordshire.

Interview advice and questions Applicants' portfolios of art work form an important talking-point throughout the interview. Applicants should be able to discuss examples of current design and new developments in the field and answer questions on the aspects of industrial design which interest them. See also **Art and Design (General)** and **Chapter 6**. **Creative Arts** No tests. Discuss any visits to modern buildings and new developments, eg British Museum Great Court or the Louvre Pyramid.

Reasons for rejection (non-academic) Not hungry enough! Mature students without formal qualifications may not be able to demonstrate the necessary mathematical or engineering skills. Poor quality and organisation of portfolio. Lack of interest. Inappropriate dress. Lack of enthusiasm. Insufficient portfolio work (eg exercises instead of projects). Lack of historical knowledge of interior design. Weak oral communication. See also **Art and Design (General)**. **Creative Arts** Not enough 3D model-making. Poor sketching and drawing.

AFTER-RESULTS ADVICE
Offers to applicants repeating A-levels **Same** Birmingham City, Bournemouth, Creative Arts, Nottingham Trent, Salford, Staffordshire.

GRADUATE DESTINATIONS AND EMPLOYMENT (2009/10 HESA)
See **Art and Design (General)**.

Career note See **Art and Design (General)**.

OTHER DEGREE SUBJECTS FOR CONSIDERATION
Architectural Studies; Architecture; Art Gallery Management; Design (Manufacturing Systems); History of Art; Manufacturing Engineering; Multimedia and Communication Design and subjects in other **Art and Design** tables.

ART and DESIGN (3D Design)

(including **Ceramics, Design Crafts, Glassmaking, Jewellery, Metalwork, Silversmithing, Plastics** and **Woodwork**; see also **Art and Design (Product and Industrial Design)**)

This group of courses covers mainly three dimensional design work, focusing on creative design involving jewellery, silverware, ceramics, glass, wood and plastics. Some institutions offer broad three dimensional studies courses while others provide the opportunity to study very specialised subjects such as stained glass, gemology and horology. Students normally take an Art Foundation course before their degree level studies.

Useful websites www.ergonomics.org.uk; www.yourcreativefuture.org.uk; www.top3D.net; www.glassassociation.org.uk; www.bja.org.uk; www.cpaceramics.com.

NB The points totals shown to the left of the institutions are for ease of reference only. It must not be assumed that Tariff points are always used by institutions or that they can be substituted for an offer in grades. The level of an offer is not necessarily indicative of the quality of a course.

COURSE OFFERS INFORMATION

Subject requirements/preferences See **Art and Design (General)**.

Your target offers and examples of courses provided by each institution

360 pts **Glasgow (SA)** – ABB (Des (Silver Jewel))
300 pts **Edinburgh (CA)** – BBB (Sculp) (IB 34 pts)
280 pts **Birmingham City** – 280 pts (Jewel Silver)
       Manchester Met – 280 pts (3D Des) (IB 28 pts)
       Northumbria – 280 pts (3D Des)
260 pts **Bournemouth Arts (UC)** – BCC (Modl)
       Liverpool Hope – 260–300 pts (Des)
       Stranmillis (UC) – BCC (Tech Des Educ)
240 pts **Cleveland (CAD)** – 240 pts (Enter Des Crfts)
       Coventry – 240 pts (3D Des)
       Cumbria – 240 pts (Contemp Crft Des)
       De Montfort – 240–260 pts (Des Crafts)
       Glyndŵr – 240 pts (Des Decr Arts; App Arts)
       Hertfordshire – 240 pts (Contemp App Arts)
       Lincoln – 240 pts (Jewel Obj)
       London Met – 240 pts (Jewel Silver)
       Plymouth – 240 pts (3D Des; 3D Des (Des Mkr/Furn Inter Des))
       Staffordshire – 240–280 pts (Dig Film 3D Animat Tech)
       Sheffield Hallam – 240–260 pts (Mtl Jewel)
       Suffolk (Univ Campus) – 240 pts (Des)
220 pts **Falmouth (UC)** – 220 pts (3D Des)
       Sunderland – 220 pts (Glass Ceram)
200 pts **Bucks New** – 200–240 pts (3D Contemp Crfts Prods)
       Hereford (CA) – 200 pts (Contemp App Arts; Jewel Des; Arst Blksmthg)
       Plymouth (CA) – 200 pts (Ceram; Gls)
       Portsmouth – 200–280 pts (3D Des)
       Swansea Met – 200 pts (3D Comp Animat)
       Wolverhampton – 200 pts (App Arts)
160 pts **Colchester (Inst)** – 160 pts (Art Des (3D Des Crft))
       Creative Arts – 160–200 pts (App Arts)
       Robert Gordon – 160–180 pts (3D Des (Ceram/Gls/Jewel))
       Sir Gâr (Coll) – 160 pts (Fn Art Sculp)
       Swansea Met – 160 pts (Gls)

120 pts **Havering (Coll)** – 120 pts (3D Des)
100 pts **and below or other selection criteria (Foundation course, interview and portfolio inspection)**
Anglia Ruskin; Arts London; Arts London (Camberwell CA); Barking (Coll); Bath Spa; Bedfordshire; Brighton; Bucks New; Cornwall (Coll); Dundee; Edinburgh (CA); Greenwich; Hertfordshire; Lincoln; Loughborough; Manchester (Coll); Menai (Coll); Middlesex; NEW (Coll); Northampton; Northbrook (Coll); Northumbria; Nottingham New (Coll); Plymouth; Staffordshire Reg Fed (SURF); UCLan; UEL; York St John.
Bournemouth and Poole (Coll) – one year top-up degree; check with College (3D Comp Gen Img)

Alternative offers
See **Chapter 7** and **Appendix 1** for grades/UCAS Tariff points information for the International Baccalaureate, Scottish Highers/Advanced Highers, the Welsh Baccalaureate, the Irish Leaving Certificate, the Cambridge Pre-U Diploma, the Advanced Diploma and the Extended Project.

EXAMPLES OF FOUNDATION DEGREES IN THE SUBJECT FIELD
Barking (Coll); Bedfordshire; Bournemouth and Poole (Coll); Bournemouth Arts (UC); Brighton; Cleveland (CAD); Croydon (Coll); Cumbria; Hereford (CA); Hertfordshire; London Met; Manchester (Coll); Newcastle (Coll); Plymouth; Plymouth (CA); South Devon (Coll); South Essex (Coll); Truro (Coll); UEA; UEL; Writtle (Coll).

CHOOSING YOUR COURSE (SEE ALSO CH.1)
Some course features
Courses available specialise in ceramics, glassware, jewellery and silversmithing.

Manchester Met Three-year course offers a study exchange to Norway.
Plymouth Opportunity for European study exchange or work placement for 12 weeks in Year 2.
Staffordshire 3D Design courses cover Cermaics, Crafts and Jewellery.
Wolverhampton A combination of theory and practice is offered.

Universities and colleges teaching quality See www.qaa.ac.uk; http://unistats.direct.gov.uk.

Top research universities and colleges (RAE 2008) See **Art and Design (General)**.

ADMISSIONS INFORMATION
Number of applicants per place (approx) Arts London (Ceram) 2; Arts London (Camberwell CA) 2, (Ceram) 3, (Jewel) 2; Bath Spa 3; Birmingham City 4, (Jewel) 5; Brighton 3; Creative Arts 4; De Montfort 3; Dundee 5; Manchester Met 5; Middlesex (3D Des) 4, (Jewel) 4; Portsmouth 3; Ravensbourne Total of 110 first-choice applicants.

Advice to applicants and planning the UCAS personal statement Describe your art studies and your experience of different types of materials used. Discuss your special interest in your chosen field. Compare your work with that of professional artists and designers and describe your visits to museums, art galleries, exhibitions etc. Submit a portfolio of recent work to demonstrate drawing skills, visual awareness, creativity and innovation, showing examples of 3D work in photographic or model form. See also **Art and Design (Graphic Design)**.

Selection interviews All institutions will interview and require a portfolio of work. **Yes** Birmingham City.

Interview advice and questions Questions focus on the art work presented in the student's portfolio. See also **Art and Design (General)** and **Chapter 6**.

Reasons for rejection (non-academic) Lack of pride in their work. No ideas. See also **Art and Design (General)**.

AFTER-RESULTS ADVICE
Offers to applicants repeating A-levels Same Brighton, Creative Arts, Dundee, Manchester Met.

Check **Chapter 4** when choosing your university and **Chapter 7** on how to read the subject tables.

GRADUATE DESTINATIONS AND EMPLOYMENT (2009/10 HESA)
See **Art and Design (General)**.

Career note See **Art and Design (General)**.

OTHER DEGREE SUBJECTS FOR CONSIDERATION
Design Technology; see other **Art and Design** tables.

ASIA-PACIFIC STUDIES

(including **East** and **South Asian Studies**; see also **Chinese, Japanese, Languages**)

These courses focus on the study of the cultures and the languages of this region of the world, such as Korean, Sanskrit, Thai, Vietnamese. Work experience during undergraduate years will help students to focus their interests. Many courses have a language bias or are taught jointly with other subjects.

Useful websites www.dur.ac.uk/oriental.museum; www.bubl.ac.uk; www.asia-alliance.org; www.bacsuk.org.uk.

NB The points totals shown to the left of the institutions are for ease of reference only. It must not be assumed that Tariff points are always used by institutions or that they can be substituted for an offer in grades. The level of an offer is not necessarily indicative of the quality of a course.

COURSE OFFERS INFORMATION
Subject requirements/preferences GCSE A language subject grade A–C. **AL** A language or a second joint subject may be required.

Your target offers and examples of courses provided by each institution
380 pts **Cambridge** – A*AA (As Mid E St) (IB 40–42 pts HL 776–777)
360 pts **Oxford** – AAA (Jap) (IB 38–40 pts)
340 pts **London (SOAS)** – AAB (Viet Joint Hons 3/4 yrs) (IB 36 pts HL 666)
          Nottingham – AAB (Mgt As/Chin St) (IB 34 pts)
          Sheffield – AAB–ABB (Jap St) (IB 35–33 pts)
320 pts **Leeds** – ABB (As Pacif St Int Rel) (IB 32 pts HL 15 pts)
          Sheffield – ABB (Kor St Joint Hons) (IB 33 pts)
300 pts **Leeds** – BBB (As Pacif St) (IB 32 pts HL 15 pts)
200 pts **UCLan** – 200–240 pts (As Pacif St)

Alternative offers
See **Chapter 7** and **Appendix 1** for grades/UCAS Tariff points information for the International Baccalaureate, Scottish Highers/Advanced Highers, the Welsh Baccalaureate, the Irish Leaving Certificate, the Cambridge Pre-U Diploma, the Advanced Diploma and the Extended Project.

CHOOSING YOUR COURSE (SEE ALSO CH.1)
Some course features
Leeds (As Pacif St courses) Courses deal mainly with the region's politics, economics and culture. Single Honours, major and Joint courses available.
UCLan A sandwich course covering business, politics and Asian languages – Chinese and Japanese.

Universities and colleges teaching quality See www.qaa.ac.uk; http://unistats.direct.gov.uk.

Top research universities and colleges (RAE 2008) London (SOAS); Oxford; Cambridge; Leeds; Manchester; Sheffield.

Examples of sandwich degree courses UCLan.

ADMISSIONS INFORMATION

Number of applicants per place (approx) London (SOAS) 4, (Thai) 2, (Burm) 1.

Advice to applicants and planning the UCAS personal statement Connections with, and visits to, South and South East Asia should be mentioned. You should give some indication of what impressed you and your reasons for wishing to study these subjects. An awareness of the geography, culture and politics of the area also should be shown on the UCAS application. Show your skills in learning a foreign language (if choosing a language course), interest in current affairs of the region, experience of travel and self-discipline.

Selection interviews Yes Cambridge, Manchester, Oxford (Orntl St) 26%.

Interview advice and questions General questions are usually asked that relate to applicants' reasons for choosing degree courses in this subject area and to their background knowledge of the various cultures. See also **Chapter 6**.

AFTER-RESULTS ADVICE

Offers to applicants repeating A-levels No Information not available from institutions.

GRADUATE DESTINATIONS AND EMPLOYMENT (2009/10 HESA)

South Asian Studies; graduates surveyed 45 **Employed** 10 **In voluntary employment** 0 **In further study** 15 **Assumed unemployed** 5

Other Asian Studies; graduates surveyed 35 **Employed** 15 **In voluntary employment** 0 **In further study** 5 **Assumed unemployed** 5

Career note Graduates enter a wide range of careers covering business and administration, retail work, education, transport, finance, community and social services. Work experience during undergraduate years will help students to focus their interests. Graduates may have opportunities of using their languages in a range of occupations.

OTHER DEGREE SUBJECTS FOR CONSIDERATION

Anthropology; Development Studies; Far Eastern Languages; Geography; History; International Relations; Politics; Social Studies.

ASTRONOMY and ASTROPHYSICS

(including **Planetary Science** and **Space Science.**; see also **Geology/ Geological Sciences, Physics**)

All Astronomy-related degrees are built on a core of mathematics and physics which, in the first two years, is augmented by an introduction to the theory and practice of astronomy or astrophysics. Astronomy emphasises observational aspects of the science and includes a study of the planetary system whilst Astrophysics tends to pursue the subject from a more theoretical stand-point. Courses often combine Mathematics or Physics with Astronomy.

Useful websites www.ras.org.uk; www.scicentral.com; www.iop.org.

NB The points totals shown to the left of the institutions are for ease of reference only. It must not be assumed that Tariff points are always used by institutions or that they can be substituted for an offer in grades. The level of an offer is not necessarily indicative of the quality of a course.

COURSE OFFERS INFORMATION

Subject requirements/preferences GCSE English and a foreign language may be required by some universities; specified grades may be stipulated for some subjects. **AL** Mathematics and physics usually required.

Your target offers and examples of courses provided by each institution

380 pts **Cambridge** – A*AA (Nat Sci (Astro)) (IB 40–42 pts HL 776–777)
Durham – A*AA (Phys Astron) (IB 38 pts HL 6 maths phys)

360 pts **Birmingham** – AAA (Phys Prtcl Phys Cosmo) (IB 34–38 pts)
Edinburgh – AAA–ABB incl maths phys 320–360 pts (Astro) (IB 37–32 pts)
Exeter – AAA–ABB (Phys Astro) (IB 34–31 pts)
Lancaster – AAA 360 pts (Phys Prtcl Phys Cosmo MPhys) (IB 34–36 pts)
Leeds – AAA–AAB (Phys Astro MPhys 4 yrs) (IB 33 pts)
Leicester – AAA–AAB (Phys Planet Sci)
Liverpool – AAA–ABB (Astro MPhys) (IB 35 pts HL 6 maths phys)
LJMU – 360–320 pts (Astro MPhys)
London (UCL) – AAA–AAB (Astro) (IB 34–36 pts)
Nottingham – AAA–AAB (Phys Astron) (IB 34–36 pts HL 6 maths 65)
St Andrews – AAA (Astro) (IB 38 pts)
Southampton – AAA (Maths Astron) (IB 36 pts HL 18 pts)

340 pts **Cardiff** – AAB (Astro MPhys; Phys Astron MPhys)
Lancaster – AAB 340 pts (Phys Prtcl Phys Cosmo BSc) (IB 34–36 pts)
Leicester – AAB (Maths Astron) (IB 28–32 pts)
London (QM) – AAB incl maths phys (Astro MSci) (IB 34 pts HL 6 maths phys)
London (RH) – AAB (Astrophy) (IB 34 pts HL 6–7 maths phys)
Loughborough – AAB–ABB (Phys Cosmo) (IB 34 pts)
Queen's Belfast – AAB (Phys Astro MSci)
Southampton – AAB incl maths phys (Phys Astron) (IB 34 pts HL 17 pts)
Surrey – AAB (Psy Nucl Astro MPhys) (IB 36–34 pts)
Sussex – AAB–BBB incl phys maths (Astro) (IB 32–36 pts)

320 pts **Bath** – ABB (Electron Eng Spc Sci Tech BEng) (IB 34 pts HL 6 maths phys)
Cardiff – ABB (Astro BSc)
Glasgow – ABB (Astron) (IB 32 pts)
Kent – ABB (Phys Astro)
Liverpool – ABB–BBB (Phys Astron) (IB 33 pts HL 6 maths phys)
London (QM) – ABB incl maths phys (Astro BSc) (IB 32 pts HL 6 maths phys)
Manchester – ABB (Geol Planet Sci) (IB 33 pts)
Swansea – ABB (Phys Prtcl Phys Cosmo)
York – AAA–ABB 320–360 pts (Phys Astro) (IB 32–36 pts)

300 pts **Keele** – 300–320 pts (Astro)
LJMU – 300–340 pts (Phys Astron) (IB 24–28 pts)
London (Birk) – BBB (Planet Sci Astron)
Queen's Belfast – BBB (Phys Astro BSc)

280 pts **Aberystwyth** – 280 pts (Spc Sci Robot) (IB 27 pts)
Hertfordshire – 280 pts (Astro) (IB 24 pts)
Hull – 280–300 pts (Phys Astro)
UCLan – 280–320 pts (Astro)

260 pts **Nottingham Trent** – 260 pts (Phys Astro)

200 pts **Glamorgan** – 200–240 pts (Obs Astron)

Alternative offers

See **Chapter 7** and **Appendix 1** for grades/UCAS Tariff points information for the International Baccalaureate, Scottish Highers/Advanced Highers, the Welsh Baccalaureate, the Irish Leaving Certificate, the Cambridge Pre-U Diploma, the Advanced Diploma and the Extended Project.

CHOOSING YOUR COURSE (SEE ALSO CH.1)

Some course features

Aberystwyth New Astrophysics course designed for students with a general interest in astronomy; it includes core physics modules and broader modules in cosmology and galactic astronomy; progression possible to MPhys degree.

Glamorgan Course provides practical experience of observational astronomy and training in astrophysical techniques, with astronomy field schools in Poland, La Palma, Andalusia and other overseas locations.

Kent Course includes involvement in space missions and work on Hubble Telescope data and an exchange programme in Year 3 in the USA.

London (QM) Astronomy and Astrophysics programmes are similar and transfer is possible up to the final year.

Surrey (Spc Tech Planet Explor) Courses include hands-on spacecraft engineering, have a strong international focus with close ties with space industries and European Space Agency; opportunities for a professional training year. Surrey is the only university building complete satellites.

Universities and colleges teaching quality See www.qaa.ac.uk; http://unistats.direct.gov.uk.

Top research universities and colleges (RAE 2008) See **Physics**.

Examples of sandwich degree courses Hertfordshire; Kingston.

ADMISSIONS INFORMATION

Number of applicants per place (approx) Bristol 8; Cardiff 6; Durham 3; Hertfordshire 5; Leicester 12; London (QM) 6; London (RH) 6; London (UCL) 5; Newcastle 7; Southampton 6.

Advice to applicants and planning the UCAS personal statement Books and magazines you have read on astronomy and astrophysics are an obvious source of information. Describe your interests and why you have chosen this subject. Visits to observatories would also be important. **Bristol** Deferred entry accepted. **York** Advanced Diploma not generally accepted.

Misconceptions about this course Career opportunities are not as limited as some students think. These courses involve an extensive study of maths and physics, opening many opportunities for graduates such as geodesy, rocket and satellite studies and engineering specialisms.

Selection interviews Yes Bristol, Cambridge, London (UCL), Newcastle; **Some** Cardiff.

Interview advice and questions You will probably be questioned on your study of physics and the aspects of the subject you most enjoy. Questions in the past have included: Can you name a recent development in physics which will be important in the future? Describe a physics experiment, indicating any errors and exactly what it was intended to prove. Explain weightlessness. What is a black hole? What are the latest discoveries in space? See also **Chapter 6**. **Southampton** Entrance examination for year abroad courses.

AFTER-RESULTS ADVICE

Offers to applicants repeating A-levels Higher St Andrews; **Same** Cardiff, Durham, London (UCL), Newcastle; **No** Cambridge.

GRADUATE DESTINATIONS AND EMPLOYMENT (2009/10 HESA)

Graduates surveyed 275 **Employed** 85 **In voluntary employment** 0 **In further study** 80 **Assumed unemployed** 20

Career note The number of posts for professional astronomers is limited although some technological posts are occasionally offered in observatories. However, degree courses include extensive mathematics and physics so many graduates can look towards related fields including telecommunications and electronics.

OTHER DEGREE SUBJECTS FOR CONSIDERATION

Aeronautical/Aerospace Engineering; Computer Science; Earth Sciences; Geology; Geophysics; Mathematics; Meteorology; Mineral Sciences; Oceanography; Physics.

BIOCHEMISTRY

(see also **Biological Sciences, Chemistry, Food Science/Studies and Technology, Pharmacy and Pharmaceutical Sciences**)

Biochemistry is the study of life processes at molecular level. Most courses are extremely flexible and have common first years. Modules could include genetics, immunology, blood biochemistry, physiology and biotechnology. The option to choose other courses in the subject field features at many universities. Many courses allow for a placement in industry in the UK or in Europe or North America.

Useful websites www.biochemistry.org; www.scienceyear.com; www.bioworld.com; www.arjournals. annualreviews.org; see also **Biological Sciences** and **Biology**.

NB The points totals shown to the left of the institutions are for ease of reference only. It must not be assumed that Tariff points are always used by institutions or that they can be substituted for an offer in grades. The level of an offer is not necessarily indicative of the quality of a course.

COURSE OFFERS INFORMATION

Subject requirements/preferences GCSE English, mathematics and science usually required; leading universities often stipulate A–B grades. **AL** Chemistry required and biology usually preferred; one or two mathematics/science subjects required.

Your target offers and examples of courses provided by each institution

380 pts **Cambridge** – A*AA (Nat Sci (Biochem)) (IB 40–42 pts HL 766–777)
Oxford – A*AA (Bioch (Mol Cell)) (IB 39 pts)

360 pts **Edinburgh** – AAA–ABB 360–320 pts (Biochem) (IB 37–32 pts)
Imperial London – AAA (Bioch courses) (IB 38 pts HL 6 biol chem)
London (UCL) – AAA+AS–AAB+AS (Bioch) (IB 36–38 pts)
Manchester – AAA–ABB 320–360 pts (Med Bioch) (IB 37–33 pts)
Southampton – AAA–ABB 360–320 pts (Bioch) (IB 36–32 pts HL 18–16 pts)
York – AAA–ABB 320–360 pts (Chem Biol Medcnl Chem) (IB 32–34 pts)

340 pts **Bath** – AAB (Bioch Eng MEng) (IB 35 pts HL 6 chem)
Birmingham – AAB–ABB (Bioch) (IB 32–34 pts)
Bristol – AAB (Bioch Mol Biol Biotech) (IB 35 pts)
Cardiff – AAB–ABB incl chem (Biochem) (IB 34 pts)
Exeter – AAB–BBB (Bioch) (IB 34–30 pts)
Leeds – AAB–BBB (Med Bioch) (IB 36–32 pts HL 15–17 pts)
London (King's) – AAB (Bioch) (IB 36 pts HL 6 chem biol)
Newcastle – AAB (Bioch) (IB 32 pts HL 6 biol chem)
Nottingham – AAB–BBB 300–340 pts (Bioch Mol Med) (IB 34–30 pts)
St Andrews – AAB (Bioch) (IB 35 pts)
Sheffield – AAB (Med Bioch) (IB 35 pts)
Surrey – AAB (Bioch) (IB 35 pts)
Warwick – AAB (Cheml Biol) (IB 36 pts)
York – AAB–ABB (Bioch) (IB 35 pts)

320 pts **Bath** – ABB (Bioch) (IB 34 pts HL 6 chem)
Glasgow – ABB (Bioch) (IB 32 pts)
Lancaster – AAB–ABB (Bioch) (IB 32–34 pts)
Leicester – ABB (Med Bioch) (IB 32–34 pts)
Liverpool – ABB (Bioch (Yr Ind/Rsch)) (IB 33 pts)
London (RH) – ABB (Mol Biosci (Bioch)) (IB 34 pts)
Nottingham – ABB–BBB (Nutr Biochem) (IB 28–32 pts)
Reading – 320 pts (Bioch) (IB 30 pts)
Strathclyde – ABB (Bioch courses) (IB 28 pts)
Sussex – ABB incl biol chem (Biochem) (IB 34 pts)

Swansea – 320 pts (Genet Bioch)
UEA – ABB incl chem (Bioch (Yr Ind)) (IB 32 pts HL 555)
Warwick – AAB (Biomed Chem) (IB 36 pts)

300 pts Aberdeen – BBB (Bioch courses)
Aston – BBB–ABB 300–320 pts (Biol Chem) (IB 32 pts)
Brunel – BBB (Biomed Sci (Bioch)) (IB 32 pts HL 5 biol)
Heriot-Watt – BBB (Chem Bioch; Brew Distil)
Keele – 300–320 pts (Bioch courses) (IB 26–28 pts)
Kent – BBB (Bioch) (IB 31–33 pts HL 14–15 pts)
LJMU – 300–260 pts (Bioch)
London (QM) – 300 pts incl chem biol (Bioch) (IB 32 pts HL 5 chem biol)
London (RH) – 300– 320 pts (Bioch) (IB 34 pts)
Queen's Belfast – BBB/BBCd (Biochem) (IB 28 pts HL 555)
Swansea – ABB 300–320 pts (Bioch)

280 pts Dundee – 280 pts (Bioch) (IB 30 pts)
Essex – BBC–CCC (Bioch) (IB 30–26 pts)
Huddersfield – 280 pts (Bioch)
Manchester Met – 280 pts (Medcnl Biol Chem) (IB 27 pts)
Nottingham Trent – 280 pts incl biol (Bioch)
Portsmouth – 280–300 pts (Bioch Gnm Sci)

260 pts Aberystwyth – 260–320 pts (Bioch) (IB 26 pts)
Bradford – 260 pts (Med Bioch; Biomed Sci)
Hertfordshire – 260–240 pts (Bioch; Bioch (St Abrd))
Huddersfield – 260 pts (Med Bioch)
Sheffield Hallam – 260 pts incl biol+chem (Bioch)

240 pts LJMU – 240 pts (App Bioch)
London Met – 240 pts (Bioch)
Salford – 240 pts (Bioch St USA)

220 pts Westminster – CCD (Bioch) (IB 26 pts)

200 pts Kingston – 200–280 pts (Bioch; Med Bioch; Bioch Nutr)
London South Bank – 200 pts (Bioch)
Staffordshire – 200–260 pts (Bioch Microbiol) (IB 28 pts)
Salford – 200 pts (Bioch) (IB 34 pts)
UEL – 200 pts (Biochem)
Wolverhampton – 200–260 pts (Bioch)

Alternative offers
See **Chapter 7** and **Appendix 1** for grades/UCAS Tariff points information for the International Baccalaureate, Scottish Highers/Advanced Highers, the Welsh Baccalaureate, the Irish Leaving Certificate, the Cambridge Pre-U Diploma, the Advanced Diploma and the Extended Project.

EXAMPLES OF FOUNDATION DEGREES IN THE SUBJECT FIELD
Truro (Coll).

CHOOSING YOUR COURSE (SEE ALSO CH.1)
Some course features
Birmingham (Bioch) A range of Biochemistry programmes offers specialisation in several fields.
Bristol (Bioch) A choice to include a period of industrial placement is made in Year 1 from any one of the Biochemistry courses.
Imperial London Biochemistry and Biotechnology students follow a similar programme with specialisations in Year 3.
Lancaster (Bioch) Specialisation follows in Year 2.
Leeds A modular course within the School of Biological Sciences which gives great flexibility of choice. Specialisms at Level 3 include plant and medical options, and an original research project is undertaken in the final year.

Sussex (Bioch) Optional sandwich year.
UEA (Bioch) Options to study for a year in Australia, Europe or North America.
Wolverhampton (Bioch) Joint courses and an optional year's placement are offered.

Universities and colleges teaching quality See www.qaa.ac.uk; http://unistats.direct.gov.uk.

Top research universities and colleges (RAE 2008) See **Biological Sciences**.

Examples of sandwich degree courses Bath; Bristol; Brunel; Cardiff; Essex; Hertfordshire; Huddersfield; Kent; Kingston; Leeds; LJMU; London South Bank; Manchester; Nottingham Trent; Sheffield Hallam; Surrey; Sussex; UEL; West Scotland; Wolverhampton; York.

ADMISSIONS INFORMATION
Number of applicants per place (approx) Aberystwyth 5; Bath 7; Birmingham 5; Bradford 7; Bristol 10; Cardiff 6; Dundee 6; Durham 6; Edinburgh 8; Essex 5; Imperial London 6; Keele 7; Leeds 10; Leicester (Med Bioch) 5; London (RH) 8; London (UCL) 8; Newcastle 7; Nottingham 14; Salford 4; Southampton 8; Staffordshire 6; Strathclyde 7; Surrey 3; UEA 10; UEL 5; Warwick 6; York 6.

Advice to applicants and planning the UCAS personal statement It is important to show by reading scientific journals that you have interests in chemistry and biology beyond the exam syllabus. Focus on one or two aspects of biochemistry that interest you. Attend scientific lectures (often arranged by universities on Open Days), find some work experience if possible, and use these to show your understanding of what biochemistry is. Give evidence of your communication skills and time management. **Bristol** Deferred entry accepted. **Oxford** No written or work tests; successful entrants 42.7%. Further information may be obtained from the Institute of Biology and the Royal Society of Chemistry.

Misconceptions about this course **York** Students feel that being taught by two departments could be a problem but actually it increases their options.

Selection interviews **Yes** Birmingham (Clearing only), Bradford, Brunel, Cambridge, Essex, Keele (mature students only), Kingston, Leeds, London (RH), London (UCL), London South Bank, Oxford (38%), Portsmouth (mature students only), Surrey, UEL, Warwick; **Some** Aberystwyth (mature students only), Bath, Cardiff, LJMU, Salford, Sheffield, Staffordshire, UEA, Wolverhampton; **No** Dundee.

Interview advice and questions Questions will be asked on your study of chemistry and biology and any special interests. They will also probe your understanding of what a course in Biochemistry involves and the special features offered by the university. In the past questions have been asked covering Mendel, genetics, RNA and DNA. See also **Chapter 6**. **LJMU** Informal interviews. It would be useful to bring samples of coursework to the interview.

Reasons for rejection (non-academic) Borderline grades plus poor motivation. Failure to turn up for interviews or answer correspondence. Inability to discuss subject. Not compatible with A-level predictions or references. **Birmingham** Lack of total commitment to Biochemistry, for example intention to transfer to Medicine without completing the course.

AFTER-RESULTS ADVICE
Offers to applicants repeating A-levels **Higher** Leeds, Leicester, Nottingham, St Andrews, Strathclyde, Surrey, UEA, Warwick; **Possibly higher** Bath, Bristol, Brunel, Keele, Kent, Lancaster, Newcastle; **Same** Aberystwyth, Birmingham, Bradford, Cardiff, Dundee, Durham, Heriot-Watt, Hull, Liverpool, LJMU, London (RH), London (UCL), Salford, Sheffield, Staffordshire, Wolverhampton, York; **No** Cambridge.

GRADUATE DESTINATIONS AND EMPLOYMENT (2009/10 HESA)
Biophysics and Molecular Biology; graduates surveyed 2255 Employed 795 In voluntary employment 25 In further study 725 Assumed unemployed 180

Career note Biochemistry courses involve several specialities which offer a range of job opportunities. These include the application of biochemistry in industrial, medical and clinical areas with additional openings in pharmaceuticals and agricultural work, environmental science and in toxicology.

For a quick reference offers calculator, fold out the inside back cover.

OTHER DEGREE SUBJECTS FOR CONSIDERATION

Agricultural Sciences; Agriculture; Biological Sciences; Biology; Biotechnology; Botany; Brewing; Chemistry; Food Science; Genetics; Medical Sciences; Medicine; Microbiology; Neuroscience; Nursing; Nutrition; Pharmaceutical Sciences; Pharmacology; Pharmacy; Plant Science.

BIOLOGICAL SCIENCES

(including **Biomedical Science, Cosmetic Science, Forensic Science, Immunology** and **Virology**; see also **Anatomical Science/Anatomy, Animal Sciences, Biochemistry, Biology, Biotechnology, Environmental Sciences/Studies, Genetics, Medicine, Microbiology, Natural Sciences, Nursing and Midwifery, Pharmacology, Plant Sciences, Psychology, Zoology**)

Biological Science (in some universities referred to as Biosciences) is a fast-moving, rapidly expanding and wide subject area, ranging from, for example, conservation biology to molecular genetics. Boundaries between separate subjects are blurring and this is reflected in the content and variety of the courses offered. Many universities offer a common first year allowing final decisions to be made later in the course. Since most subjects are research-based, students undertake their own projects in the final year.

Useful websites http://bsi.immunology.org; www.ibms.org; www.scienceyear.com; www.scicentral. com; www.forensic.gov.uk; www.bbsrc.ac.uk; see also **Biochemistry** and **Biology**.

NB The points totals shown to the left of the institutions are for ease of reference only. It must not be assumed that Tariff points are always used by institutions or that they can be substituted for an offer in grades. The level of an offer is not necessarily indicative of the quality of a course.

COURSE OFFERS INFORMATION

Subject requirements/preferences

GCSE English, mathematics and science usually required. Grades AB often stipulated by popular universities. **AL** Chemistry required plus one or two other mathematics/science subjects, biology preferred. (Ecol) Biology and one other science subject may be required or preferred. (Neuro) Mathematics/science subjects with chemistry and/or biology required or preferred.

London (St George's) (Biol Inform) Computer science, mathematics and/or science advantageous.

Your target offers and examples of courses provided by each institution

410 pts **Imperial London** – AAAb (Biomed Sci) (IB 38 pts)

380 pts **Cambridge** – A*AA (Nat Sci (Neuro)) (IB 40–42 pts)

Edinburgh – A*AA (Biol Sci Physiol) (IB 38 pts)

London (UCL) – AAAe–AABe (Biomed Sci) (IB 36–38 pts)

Oxford – A*AA (Biol Sci) (IB 38–40 pts)

360 pts **Edinburgh** – AAA–ABB incl chem maths (Medcnl Biol Chem) (IB 37–32 pts HL 5 chem)

London (UCL) – AAA–AAB incl biol (Bioproc N Med (Sci Eng)) (IB 36–38 pts)

Manchester – AAA–ABB 320–360 pts (Biomed Sci) (IB 37–33 pts)

Southampton – AAA–ABB 360–320 pts (Biomed Sci) (IB 36–32 pts HL 18–16 pts)

UEA – AAA–AAB (Biol Sci (St Abrd)) (IB 33–34 pts)

340 pts **Birmingham** – AAB–ABB (Biol Sci (Biotech/Env Biol/Genet)) (IB 32–34 pts)

Bristol – AAB–ABB incl biol (Palae Evol) (IB 35–33 pts)

Cardiff – AAB–ABB (Biomed Sci (Anat)) (IB 34 pts)

Cardiff – AAB–ABB (Mol Biol; Biomed Sci; Ecol)

Durham – AAB (Biomed Sci) (IB 36 pts)

Edinburgh – AAA–ABB 340–360 pts (Biol Sci Pharmacol) (IB 37–32 pts)

Exeter – AAB–BBB (Hum Biosci) (IB 34–30 pts)

Kent – AAB (Biol Anth) (IB 33 pts)

Lancaster – AAB (Biol Sci (St Abrd)) (IB 34 pts)
Leeds – AAB–BBB (Biol Sci) (IB 32 pts)
London (King's) – AAB incl chem/biol (Anat Dev Hum Biol) (IB 36 pts HL 6 chem biol)
London (QM) – AAB incl biol chem (Biomed Sci) (IB 34 pts)
Newcastle – AAB (Biomed Sci) (IB 32 pts)
Nottingham – AAB (Neuro Biochem) (IB 34 pts)
St Andrews – AAB (Neuro) (IB 35 pts)
Sheffield – AAB incl chem sci (Biomed Sci) (IB 35 pts)
Surrey – AAB (Biomed Sci) (IB 35 pts)
Sussex – AAB–ABB (Neuro) (IB 34–36 pts)
Warwick – AAB (Biol Sci) (IB 36 pts)

320 pts **Aberdeen** – ABB (Biol Sci)
Aston – ABB 320 pts (Biol Sci) (IB 33 pts)
Birmingham – ABB (Med Sci) (IB 32–34 pts)
Bristol – ABB incl chem (Cell Mol Med) (IB 35 pts)
Dundee – ABB (Biol Sci)
Edinburgh – AAA–ABB 320–360 pts (Biol Sci Genet) (IB 37–32 pts)
Glamorgan – ABB (Immun; Med Sci)
Glasgow – ABB (Anim Sci) (IB 32 pts)
Lancaster – ABB (Biol Sci) (IB 30 pts)
Leeds – ABB–BBB (Med Sci) (IB 32 pts)
Leicester – ABB (Biol Sci (Microbiol)) (IB 32 pts HL 66)
Liverpool – ABB (Biol Med Sci) (IB 33 pts HL 6/5 biol chem)
London (RH) – ABB (Biomed Sci) (IB 34 pts)
Manchester – AAA–ABB 320–360 pts (Biomed Sci (Yr Ind)) (IB 37–33 pts)
Queen's Belfast – ABB/BBBb (Biomed Sci)
Reading – 320 pts (Biomed Sci) (IB 30–32 pts)
Strathclyde – ABB (Foren Biol) (IB 26 pts)
Swansea – ABB (Biol Sci Joint Hons) (IB 32–34 pts)
UEA – ABB incl chem (Biol Medcnl Chem) (IB 32 pts HL 6 chem)

300 pts **Bournemouth** – 300 pts (Biol Sci; Foren Sci)
Bradford – optional transfer for some students to Medicine at Leeds 300 pts (Clin Sci)
Bristol UWE – 300 pts (Biol Sci; Biomed; Foren Sci)
Brunel – BBB (Biomed Sci (Foren)) (IB 32 pts HL 5 biol)
Dundee – BBB (Foren Anth) (IB 34 pts)
Edinburgh – BBB (Med Sci) (IB 36 pts)
Essex – 300–260 pts incl BB–CC with biol (Biol Sci) (IB 32–28 pts)
Greenwich – 300 pts (Biomed Sci)
Heriot-Watt – BBB (Brew Distil; Biol Sci)
Keele – 300 pts incl BC (Biomed Sci)
Kent – BBB (Biomed Sci) (IB 33 pts HL 5 biol)
Lancaster – ABB–BBB (Biol Sci Biomed) (IB 30 pts)
Leicester – BBB (Chem Foren Sci)
LJMU – 300–260 pts (Biomed Sci) (IB 25 pts)
London (St George's) – BBB (Biomed Sci) (IB 28 pts)
London Met – 300 pts (Biomed Sci)
Manchester Met – 300 pts (Foren Sci/Psy) (IB 30 pts)
Nottingham Trent – 300 pts (Biomed Sci)
Queen's Belfast – BBB–BBC (Biol Sci)
Strathclyde – 300 pts (Biomed Sci) (IB 26 pts)
Westminster – BBB (Cog Neuro)

280 pts **Aberystwyth** – 280–320 pts (Biol Sci) (IB 26 pts)
Anglia Ruskin – 280 pts (Foren Sci)
Bangor – 280–320 pts (Biomed Sci)
Brighton – BBC 280 pts (Biomed St) (IB 30 pts)

De Montfort – 280 pts (Cos Sci)
Derby – 280 pts (Foren Sci Crimin; Foren Sci)
Essex – 280 pts (Biomed Sci) (IB 28–26 pts)
Glamorgan – 280 pts (Foren Sci)
Manchester Met – 280 pts (Biomed Sci) (IB 27 pts HL biol)
Northumbria – 280 pts (Foren Sci; Chem Biomed Sci)
Oxford Brookes – BBC (Biol Sci) (IB 30 pts)
Plymouth – 280–320 pts (Biol Sci) (IB 26 pts)
Portsmouth – 280–300 pts (Foren Biol)
Stirling – BBC (Cell Biol) (IB 32 pts)
Strathclyde – BBC (Biol Sci) (IB 26 pts)
Teesside – 280 pts (Biol Sci; Foren Sci)
Ulster – 280 pts (Biomed Sci)

260 pts Bradford – 260 pts (Biomed Sci; Foren Sci; Foren Med Sci)
Cardiff Met – 260 pts (Biomed Sci)
De Montfort – 260 pts (Med Sci)
Dundee – BCC (Biomed Sci) (IB 30 pts)
Glasgow Caledonian – BCC (Biomed Sci)
Greenwich – 260 pts (Biol Sci; Foren Sci; Foren Sci Crim)
Hertfordshire – 260 pts (Biol Sci; Biomed Sci)
Huddersfield – 260 pts (Foren Analyt Sci; Med Bioch)
Hull – 260–300 pts (Biomed Sci; Foren Sci Crimin)
Keele – 260–300 pts (Foren Sci) (IB 26–28 pts)
LJMU – 260–300 pts (Foren Sci)
Nottingham Trent – 260 pts (Foren Biol; Foren Sci (Physl); Foren Sci)
Staffordshire – 260 pts (Foren Biol) (IB 28 pts)
Sheffield Hallam – 260 pts (Biomed Sci)
Sunderland – 260 pts (Biomed Sci)
UCLan – 260–300 pts (Neuro)

245 pts Abertay Dundee – CCC 245 pts (Biomed Sci)

240 pts Aberdeen – CCC 240 pts (Immun) (IB 28 pts)
Anglia Ruskin – 240 pts (Biomed Sci)
Canterbury Christ Church – 240 pts (Biosci; Foren Sci)
Chester – 240–280 pts (Wldlf Cons Ecol) (IB 26 pts)
Coventry – 240 pts (Biomed Sci; Biol Foren Sci)
De Montfort – 240–260 pts (Biomed Sci) (IB 28 pts)
Hertfordshire – 240 ots (Biol (Yr Abrd))
Lincoln – 240 pts (Foren Sci; Biomed Sci)
London Met – 240 pts (Biol Sci)
Nescot – CCC (App Biol Sci)
Nottingham Trent – 240 pts incl biol (Biol Sci)
Robert Gordon – CCC (Foren Sci)
Roehampton – 240–300 pts (Hum Sci; Biomed Sci)
UCLan – 240–260 pts (Biomed Sci; Biol Sci; Foren Sci)
West Scotland – CCC (App Biosci; App Biosci Psy; App Biosci Zool; Biomed Sci; Foren Sci)
Wolverhampton – 240 pts (Biomed Sci)

230 pts Edinburgh Napier – 230 pts (Biomed Sci; Biol Sci; Foren Biol)

220 pts Abertay Dundee – CCD (Foren Sci)
Glamorgan – 220–260 pts (Comb Sci)
Moulton (Coll) – 220 pts (App Cons Biol)
Westminster – CCD min (Biomed Sci) (IB 26 pts)

200 pts Bedfordshire – 200 pts (Biol Sci)
Chester – 200–240 pts (Foren Biol) (IB 24 pts)
Kingston – 200–280 pts (Biomed Sci)
Middlesex – 200–300 pts (Biomed Sci; Biol Sci)

Check **Chapter 4** when choosing your university and **Chapter 7** on how to read the subject tables.

Salford – 200 pts (Biomed Sci) (IB 24 pts)
UEL – 200 pts (Biomed Sci; Foren Sci)
Wolverhampton – 200 pts (Foren Sci; Foren Mol Biol)
180 pts **Kingston** – 180–280 pts (Foren Sci)
Leeds Met – 180 pts (Biomed Sci courses) (IB 24 pts HL 5 biol)
160 pts **Abertay Dundee** – CC (Foren Psychobiol)
London South Bank – 160 pts (Foren Sci)
Robert Gordon – CC (App Biomed Sci) (IB 24 pts)
SAC (Scottish CAg) – CC (App Biosci)
100 pts **UEL** – 100 pts (Extd Hlth Biosci)
80 pts **London (Birk)** – p/t for under 21s (over 21 varies) (Biol Sci Biomed)
Oxford Brookes – BBC (Hum Biosci (Comb))

Alternative offers
See **Chapter 7** and **Appendix 1** for grades/UCAS Tariff points information for the International Baccalaureate, Scottish Highers/Advanced Highers, the Welsh Baccalaureate, the Irish Leaving Certificate, the Cambridge Pre-U Diploma, the Advanced Diploma and the Extended Project.

EXAMPLES OF FOUNDATION DEGREES IN THE SUBJECT FIELD
Aston; Brighton; Bristol UWE; Cornwall (Coll); Glyndŵr; Hertfordshire; Hull (Coll); Kent; London (QM); Myerscough (Coll); Nescot; Nottingham Trent; Petroc; Plymouth; Plymouth City (Coll); Preston (Coll); Riverside Halton (Coll); Sheffield (Coll); Staffordshire; Truro (Coll); West London; Weymouth (Coll); Wigan and Leigh (Coll); Worcester; Writtle (Coll); York (Coll).

CHOOSING YOUR COURSE (SEE ALSO CH.1)
Some course features
Brighton (Biol Sci) A sandwich placement in Year 3 is optional. Specialist fields include animal sciences, ecology, forestry and countryside management.
Bristol (Immun) One of eight Cellular and Molecular Medicine courses, with flexibility to transfer between programmes as students' scientific interests develop. All have option for a year in industry.
Lancaster (Biol Sci) Opportunity to mix and match subjects such as genetics, biomedicine, land environment and ecology.
Leeds (Biol Sci) Students may transfer to any other course in the Faculty in Year 2.
Leicester The Biological Sciences programme offers specialist options in biochemistry, genetics, microbiology, physiology with pharmacology or zoology. All courses have a common first year with specialist decisions made in year 2.
Liverpool (Biol Sci) A broad programme, with option in first two years to specialise by transferring to any one of a range of courses in the subject field, eg Ecology, Genetics, Molecular Biology.
Warwick (Biol Sci) Specialisations in biochemistry, cell biology, biological sciences, environmental biology, microbiology and virology.
Westminster (Biol Sci) Students plan their programme with tutors through the course, combining core subjects (eg cell science, physiology) with option modules from a wide range of bioscience modules.

Universities and colleges teaching quality See www.qaa.ac.uk; http://unistats.direct.gov.uk.

Top research universities and colleges (RAE 2008) Oxford (Biochemistry); Manchester; Sheffield; Dundee; Bristol (Biochemistry); London (RH); York; Imperial London; London (King's); Leeds; Cambridge; Edinburgh.

Examples of sandwich degree courses See **Biology**.

ADMISSIONS INFORMATION
Number of applicants per place (approx) Aston (Biomed Sci) 8; Bristol 8, (Neuro) 10; Cardiff 8; Durham 11; Edinburgh 8; Essex 8; Lancaster (Biol Sci) 12; Leeds (Med Sci) 25; Leicester 10; London

(King's) 7; London (QM) 8; London (St George's) 15; Newcastle 14; Nottingham 11; Southampton 8; Stirling 7; UEA (Biol Sci) 15; York 9.

Advice to applicants and planning the UCAS personal statement Read scientific journals and try to extend your knowledge beyond the A-level syllabus. Discuss your special interests, for example, ecology, microbiology, genetics or zoology (read up thoroughly on your interests since questions could be asked at interview). Voluntary attendance on courses, work experience, voluntary work, holiday jobs. Demonstrate good oral and written communication skills and be competent at handling numerical data. Interest in the law for Forensic Science courses.

Misconceptions about this course Anglia Ruskin (Foren Sci) Students are not aware that modules in management and quality assurance are taken as part of the course. **Birmingham** We offer a range of degree labels each with different UCAS codes, for example Biol Sci Genet, Biol Sci Microbiol: all have the same first year and students can freely transfer between them. It is not necessary to apply for more than one except Biol Sci Euro. (Med Sci) Applicants often use this course as an insurance for a vocational course (usually Medicine). If they are unsuccessful for their first choice, they occasionally find it difficult to commit themselves to Medical Sciences and do not perform as well as their academic performance would predict. **Cardiff** Some students mistakenly believe that they can transfer to Medicine. **De Montfort** (Foren Sci) Students are often unaware of how much of the work is analytical biology and chemistry: they think they spend their time visiting crime scenes. **London (St George's)** It is not possible to transfer to Medicine after the first year of the Biomedical Science course. Students may be able to transfer to Year 3 of the Medical course on completion of the BSc degree. **Swansea** (Med Sci Hum) Some applicants think the course is a form of medical training – it isn't, but it is relevant to anyone planning graduate entry for courses in Medicine or paramedical careers. (Biol Sci deferred entry) Some applicants think that this is a degree in its own right. In fact, after the first year, students have to choose one of the other degrees offered by the School of Biological Sciences. This course allows students an extra year in which to consider their final specialisation.

Selection interviews Yes Bangor, Bristol UWE, Durham, Essex, Greenwich, Hull, London (RH), London (St George's), London (UCL), London South Bank, Manchester, Newcastle, Nottingham Trent, Oxford (Biol Sci) 38%, Oxford Brookes, Reading, Stirling, Strathclyde, Sunderland, Surrey (Biomed Sci), Sussex, Swansea (Med Sci Hum), Warwick; **Some** Anglia Ruskin, Aston, Bristol, Cardiff, Cardiff Met, De Montfort, Derby, Kent, LJMU, Roehampton, Salford, Sheffield, Sheffield Hallam, Staffordshire, UEA, Wolverhampton, York; **No** Birmingham, Dundee, Nottingham.

Interview advice and questions You are likely to be asked about your main interests in biology and your choice of specialisation in the field of biological sciences or, for example, about the role of the botanist, specialist microbiologist in industry, your understanding of biotechnology or genetic engineering. Questions likely to be asked on field courses attended. If you have a field course workbook, take it to interview. See also **Chapter 6. London (St George's)** (Biomed Sci) What career path do you envisage for yourself with this degree? **Oxford** No written or work tests. Interviews are rigorous but sympathetic; successful entrants average 38.8%. Applicants are expected to demonstrate their ability to understand whatever facts they have encountered and to discuss a particular aspect of biology in which they are interested. What problems does a fish face under water? Are humans still evolving?

Reasons for rejection (non-academic) Oxford He appeared to have so much in his head that he tended to express his ideas in too much of a rush. He needs to slow down a bit and take more time to select points that are really pertinent to the questions.

AFTER-RESULTS ADVICE
Offers to applicants repeating A-levels Higher Bristol, Bristol UWE, Glasgow Caledonian, Hull, London (St George's), Newcastle, St Andrews, Sheffield; **Possibly higher** Aston, Essex, Lancaster, Manchester Met; **Same** Abertay Dundee, Aberystwyth, Anglia Ruskin, Birmingham, Birmingham City, Bolton, Cardiff, Cardiff Met, Chester, Chichester, De Montfort, Derby, Durham, Edinburgh Napier, Exeter, Glasgow, Harper Adams (UC), Heriot-Watt, Huddersfield, Kingston, Leeds, Lincoln, Liverpool Hope,

LJMU, London (RH), Oxford Brookes, Plymouth, Portsmouth, Robert Gordon, Roehampton, Salford, Sheffield Hallam, Stirling, UEA, UEL, West London, West Scotland, Wolverhampton, Worcester, York; **No** Cambridge.

GRADUATE DESTINATIONS AND EMPLOYMENT (2009/10 HESA)
See also **Biology**

Forensic Science and Archaeology graduates surveyed 2135 **Employed** 1160 **In voluntary employment** 35 **In further study** 410 **Assumed unemployed** 190

Career note Degrees in biological science subjects often lead graduates into medical, pharmaceutical, veterinary, food and environmental work, research and education, in both the public and private sectors (see also **Biology**). Sandwich courses are offered at a number of institutions enabling students to gain paid experience in industry and commerce, often resulting in permanent employment on graduation. In recent years there has been a considerable increase in the number of Biomedical Science courses designed for students interested in taking a hands-on approach to studying the biology of disease. However, students should be warned that the ever-popular Forensic Science courses may not always pave the way to jobs in this highly specialised field.

OTHER DEGREE SUBJECTS FOR CONSIDERATION
Biochemistry; Biology; Biotechnology; Botany; Chemistry; Consumer Sciences; Ecology; Environmental Health; Environmental Science; Genetics; Genomics; Immunology; Microbiology; Pharmaceutical Sciences; Pharmacology; Pharmacy; Physiology; Plant Sciences; Psychology; Sport and Exercise Science; Toxicology; Virology; Zoology.

BIOLOGY
(see also **Animal Sciences, Biological Sciences, Biotechnology, Environmental Sciences/Studies, Microbiology, Plant Sciences, Zoology**)

The science of biology is a broad and rapidly developing subject that increasingly affects our lives. Biologists address the challenges faced by human populations such as disease, conservation and food production, and the continuing advances in such areas as genetics and molecular biology that have applications in medicine and agriculture.

Useful websites www.societyofbiology.org; www.scienceyear.com; www.bbsrc.ac.uk; see also **Biochemistry**.

NB The points totals shown to the left of the institutions are for ease of reference only. It must not be assumed that Tariff points are always used by institutions or that they can be substituted for an offer in grades. The level of an offer is not necessarily indicative of the quality of a course.

COURSE OFFERS INFORMATION
Subject requirements/preferences **GCSE** Mathematics and English stipulated in some cases. **AL** Biology and chemistry important, other science subjects may be accepted. Two and sometimes three mathematics/science subjects required including biology.

Your target offers and examples of courses provided by each institution
380 pts **Bristol** – A*AA–AAB (Biol) (IB 38–35 pts)
360 pts **Edinburgh** – AAA–ABB 320–360 pts (Repro Bio) (IB 37–32 pts)
      Imperial London – AAA (Biol Microbiol) (IB 38 pts)
      Manchester – AAA–ABB 320–360 pts (Mol Biol) (IB 37–33 pts)
      St Andrews – AAA–AAB (Biol courses) (IB 35–38 pts)
      Sheffield – AAA–AAB (Biol Cons Biodiv) (IB 37–35 pts)
      Southampton – AAA (Maths Biol) (HL 18 pts)

340 pts **Bath** – AAB (Biol) (IB 36 pts)
        Birmingham – AAB–ABB (Hum Biol) (IB 32–34 pts)
        Cardiff – AAB–ABB (Biol)
        Durham – AAB (Biol) (IB 36 pts)
        Exeter – AAB–BBB (Evol Biol) (IB 34–29 pts)
        Leeds – AAB–BBB (Biol) (IB 34–32 pts)
        Newcastle – AAB–ABB 320–340 pts (Biol (Ecol Env Biol)) (IB 32 pts)
        Nottingham – AAB–ABB 320–340 pts (Biol) (IB 34–32 pts)
        Reading – AAB–ABBb (Psy Biol)
        Sheffield – AAB incl biol sci (Biol BSc) (IB 35 pts)
        Warwick – AAB (Env Biol) (IB 36 pts)
        York – AAB–ABB (Mol Cell Biol) (IB 32 pts)

320 pts **Aston** – ABB 320 pts (Hum Biol) (IB 33 pts)
        Bath – ABB (Mol Cell Biol) (IB 34 pts)
        Birmingham – ABB–ABB 320-340 pts (Biol Sci (Env Biol/Plnt Biol)) (IB 32–34 pts)
        Glasgow – ABB (Infec Biol) (IB 32 pts)
        Lancaster – ABB 320 pts (Biol courses) (IB 32 pts)
        Leeds – ABB–BBB (Biol Mgt) (IB 34–32 pts)
        Liverpool – ABB (Biol (Yr Ind/Rsch)) (IB 33 pts HL 6 biol)
        London (RH) – ABB (Mol Biol) (IB 34 pts)
        Newcastle – AAB–ABB 320–340 pts (Mar Biol) (IB 32 pts HL 6 biol)
        Nottingham – ABB–BCC 260–320 pts (App Biol) (IB 32–26 pts)
        Plymouth – 320–360 pts (Mar Biol courses) (IB 28 pts)
        Queen's Belfast – ABB/BBBb (Hum Biol)
        Strathclyde – ABB (Foren Biol) (IB 26 pts)
        Sussex – ABB (Biol) (IB 34 pts)
        Swansea – ABB (Biol) (IB 33 pts)
        UEA – ABB incl biol (Biol Sci Comm) (IB 32 pts)
        York – ABB (Biol) (IB 32 pts)

300 pts **Aberdeen** – BBB (Mar Biol; Biol; Cons Biol)
        Bristol UWE – 300 pts (Hum Biol) (IB 32 pts)
        Dundee – BBB (Mol Biol) (IB 32 pts)
        Essex – 300–340 pts (Spo Sci Biol) (IB 30–28 pts)
        Essex – 300–320 pts (Maths Biol) (IB 29–32 pts)
        Glamorgan – BBB (Int Wldlf Biol)
        Greenwich – 300 pts (App Biomed Sci)
        Heriot-Watt – BBB (Brew Distil; App Mar Biol)
        Keele – incl BC (Hum Biol) (IB 26–28 pts)
        Kent – BBB (Biol courses) (IB 33 pts HL 5 biol)
        LJMU – 300–260 pts (Biol) (IB 25 pts)
        London (QM) – BBB incl biol (Biol) (IB 30–32 pts HL 5 biol)
        Loughborough – BBB–ABB 300 pts (Hum Biol) (IB 32–34 pts)
        Northumbria – 300 pts (Biomed Sci)
        Nottingham – ABC/BBB–BCC (Env Biol) (IB 34–26 pts)
        Queen's Belfast – BBB (Mol Biol)

280 pts **Aberystwyth** – 280–320 pts (Plnt Biol) (IB 26 pts)
        Bangor – 280–320 pts (App Mar Biol)
        Dundee – BBC (Mathem Biol) (IB 32 pts)
        Gloucestershire – 280 pts (Biol)
        Hertfordshire – 280 pts (Hum Bio)
        Huddersfield – 280 pts (Med Biol; Hum Bio)
        Hull – 280–300 pts (Biol; Hum Biol)
        Lincoln – 280 pts (Biol)
        Manchester Met – 280 pts (Hum Biol) (IB 28 pts)

Check **Chapter 4** when choosing your university and **Chapter 7** on how to read the subject tables.

Northumbria – 280 pts (Biol Foren Biol)
Oxford Brookes – BBC (Hum Biol) (IB 30 pts)
Plymouth – 280 pts (Hum Biosci) (IB 26 pts)
Portsmouth – 280–300 pts (Biol; Mar Biol; Foren Biol)
Stirling – BBC (Biol) (IB 32 pts)
Teesside – 280 pts (Foren Biol)

260 pts   **Bangor** – 260–320 pts (Mar Biol Zool) (IB 28 pts)
Bradford – 260 pts (Med Cell Biol)
Brighton – BCC–CCC (Hum Biol Educ; Biol)
Derby – 260–300 pts (Biol)
Glamorgan – BCC 260 pts (Biol; Hum Biol; Foren Biol)
Glasgow Caledonian – BCC (Hum Biol Sociol Psy) (IB 24 pts)
Liverpool Hope – 260–320 pts (Biol)
Northampton – 260–280 pts (Biol)
Nottingham Trent – 260 pts (Zoo Biol) (IB 26 pts)
Portsmouth – 260 pts (Biomed Sci)
Staffordshire – 260 pts (Hum Biol) (IB 28 pts)
Sheffield Hallam – 260 pts (Hum Biol; Biol)
Ulster – 260 pts (Biol) (IB 28 pts)
Wolverhampton – 260–320 pts (Hum Biol)

240 pts   **Anglia Ruskin** – 240 pts (Biol courses)
Bangor – 240 pts (Mar Biol Ocean) (IB 28 pts)
Bolton – 240 pts (Biol)
Canterbury Christ Church – 240 pts (Env Biol) (IB 24 pts)
Chester – 240–280 pts (Biol courses) (IB 24 pts)
Cumbria – 240 pts (Cons Biol)
De Montfort – 240–260 pts (Foren Sci) (IB 24 pts)
Edge Hill – 240 pts (Biol)
Huddersfield – 240 pts (Biol (Mol Cell))
Hull – 240–280 pts (Cstl Mar Biol)
Lincoln – 240 pts (Cons Biol)
Manchester Met – 280–300 pts (Biol Joint Hons) (IB 28 pts)
Northampton – 240–280 pts (App Cons Biol) (IB 24 pts)
Nottingham Trent – 240 pts (Anim Biol)
Worcester – 240–280 pts (Biol) (IB 25 pts)

230 pts   **Edinburgh Napier** – 230 pts (Mar Frshwtr Biol; Anim Biol)
220 pts   **Bath Spa** – 220–260 pts (Biol courses)
Westminster – CCD (Mol Biol Genet) (IB 28 pts)
200 pts   **Chester** – 200–240 pts (Foren Biol) (IB 24 pts)
Glyndŵr – 200 pts (Foren Sci; Foren Sci Crim Just)
London South Bank – 200 pts (App Sci)
Staffordshire – 200–260 pts (Biol) (IB 28 pts)
Salford – 200 pts (Biol courses)
UEL – 200 pts (App Biol; Hum Biol)
West London – 200 pts (Foren Sci)
Wolverhampton – 200 pts (Genet Mol Biol; App Microbiol)
180 pts   **Glasgow Caledonian** – DDD (Foren Invstg; Cell Mol Biol)
Kingston – 180–280 pts (Biol; Foren Biol; Hum Biol; Cell Mol Biol)
160 pts   **Edinburgh Queen Margaret** – 160 pts (Hum Biol) (IB 26 pts)
140 pts   **West Scotland** – CD (Biol courses)
120 pts   **Huddersfield** – 120 pts (Sci Fdn)
80 pts   **London (Birk)** – p/t for under 21s (over 21s varies) (Mol Biol)

Alternative offers
See **Chapter 7** and **Appendix 1** for grades/UCAS Tariff points information for the International Baccalaureate, Scottish Highers/Advanced Highers, the Welsh Baccalaureate, the Irish Leaving Certificate, the Cambridge Pre-U Diploma, the Advanced Diploma and the Extended Project.

EXAMPLES OF FOUNDATION DEGREES IN THE SUBJECT FIELD
Anglia Ruskin; Bedfordshire; Blackpool and Fylde (Coll); Bournemouth; Cornwall (Coll); Harlow (Coll); Nottingham Trent; Truro (Coll).

OTHER HIGHER EDUCATION COURSES IN THIS FIELD
See **Biological Sciences**.

CHOOSING YOUR COURSE (SEE ALSO CH.1)
Some course features
Bangor (Biol) Some students take a 3–6-month exchange programme in Europe or the USA.
Cardiff Applied Biology and Biology courses have a common first year with the option to change at the end of Year 1.
Gloucestershire A hands-on Biology course with an emphasis on laboratory projects and field work. A short placement is included.
Leeds (Biol) An optional year in industry is offered.
London (UCL) The course provides a broad and flexible Biology programme and also acts as an entry route for those who decide to transfer to more specialised degrees including Cellular and Molecular Biology, Environmental Biology and the Biology of Fertility and Embryo Development.
Nottingham (Biol) A comprehensive modern treatment of microbial, plant, animal and human biology.
Swansea (Biol) A deferred choice course enables students to choose their final degree subjects in Year 2.

Universities and colleges teaching quality See www.qaa.ac.uk; http://unistats.direct.gov.uk.

Top research universities and colleges (RAE 2008) See **Biological Sciences**.

Examples of sandwich degree courses Aston; Bath; Bradford; Bristol; Bristol UWE; Cardiff; Coventry; De Montfort; Edinburgh Napier; Glamorgan; Harper Adams (UC); Hertfordshire; Huddersfield; Kent; Kingston; Leeds; LJMU; London South Bank; Loughborough; Manchester; Manchester Met; Middlesex; Northumbria; Nottingham Trent; Plymouth; Reading; Sheffield Hallam; Surrey; Teesside; UEL; Ulster; York.

ADMISSIONS INFORMATION
Number of applicants per place (approx) Aberdeen 8; Aberystwyth 5; Aston 6; Bath 7; Birmingham 3; Bradford 7; Bristol 9; Cardiff 8; Dundee 6; Durham 11; Exeter 6; Hull 4; Imperial London 4; Kent 10; Leeds 6; Leicester 15; London (RH) 5; Newcastle (Mar Biol) 15; Nottingham 9; Oxford Brookes 13; Salford 3; Southampton (Mar Biol Ocean) 6, (Biol) 7; Stirling 15; Sussex 4; Swansea (Mar Biol) 8, (Biol) 4; York 5.

Advice to applicants and planning the UCAS personal statement See **Biochemistry** and **Biological Sciences**. **York** Advanced Diploma not generally accepted.

Misconceptions about this course **Sussex** Many students think that a Biology degree limits you to being a professional scientist which is not the case. **York** Some fail to realise that chemistry beyond GCSE is essential. Mature students often lack the confidence to consider the course.

Selection interviews **Yes** Bangor, Bath, Birmingham, Bradford (informal, after offer), Cambridge, Durham, Essex, Hertfordshire, Imperial London, Kent, Kingston, London (RH), London (UCL), London South Bank, SAC (Scottish CAg), Sheffield Hallam, Southampton, Staffordshire, Surrey, Swansea, UEA, Writtle (Coll); **Some** Anglia Ruskin, Aston, Bath Spa, Derby, LJMU, Roehampton, Salford, Sheffield, Stirling, Wolverhampton, York; **No** Dundee, Nottingham.

Check **Chapter 4** when choosing your university and **Chapter 7** on how to read the subject tables.

Interview advice and questions Questions are likely to focus on your studies in biology, on any work experience or any special interests you may have in biology outside school. In the past, questions have included: Is the computer like a brain and, if so, could it ever be taught to think? What do you think the role of the environmental biologist will be in the next 40–50 years? Have you any strong views on vivisection? You have a micro-organism in the blood: you want to make a culture. What conditions should be borne in mind? What is a pacemaker? What problems will a giraffe experience? How does water enter a flowering plant? Compare an egg and a potato. Discuss a family tree of human genotypes. Discuss fish farming in Britain today. See also **Chapter 6**. **LJMU** Informal interview. It is useful to bring samples of coursework to the interview. **York** Why Biology? How do you see your future?

Reasons for rejection (non-academic) **Bath Spa** Poor mathematical and scientific knowledge.

AFTER-RESULTS ADVICE
Offers to applicants repeating A-levels **Higher** Cardiff, St Andrews, Strathclyde, UEL; **Possibly higher** Aston, Bath, Bradford, Durham, Leeds, London (RH), Nottingham, Portsmouth; **Same** Aberystwyth, Anglia Ruskin, Bangor, Bedfordshire, Brunel, Chester, Derby, Dundee, Edinburgh Napier, Heriot-Watt, Hull, LJMU, London (UCL), London South Bank, Loughborough, Manchester Met, Newcastle, Oxford Brookes, Plymouth, Roehampton, Salford, Sheffield, Southampton, Staffordshire, Stirling, Teesside, Ulster, Wolverhampton, York.

GRADUATE DESTINATIONS AND EMPLOYMENT (2009/10 HESA)
Graduates surveyed 5210 **Employed** 2060 **In voluntary employment** 125 **In further study** 1435 **Assumed unemployed** 445

Career note Some graduates go into research, but many will go into laboratory work in hospitals, food laboratories, agriculture, the environment and pharmaceuticals. Others go into teaching, management and other professional and technical areas.

OTHER DEGREE SUBJECTS FOR CONSIDERATION
Anatomy; Biochemistry; Biological Sciences; Biotechnology; Chemistry; Dentistry; Ecology; Environmental Health; Environmental Science/Studies; Food Science; Genomics; Health Studies; Medicine; Midwifery; Nursing; Nutrition; Optometry; Orthoptics; Pharmaceutical Sciences; Pharmacology; Pharmacy; Physiology; Physiotherapy; Plant Sciences; Radiography; Speech and Language Therapy; Zoology.

BIOTECHNOLOGY
(see also **Biological Sciences, Biology, Engineering (Medical), Microbiology, Technologies**)

Biotechnology is a multidisciplinary subject which can include chemistry, biological sciences, microbiology, genetics and chemical engineering. Medical engineering involves the design, installation, maintenance and provision of technical support for diagnostic, therapeutic and other clinical equipment used by doctors, nurses and other clinical healthcare workers.

Useful websites www.bbsrc.ac.uk; www.scienceyear.com; www.abcinformation.org.

NB The points totals shown to the left of the institutions are for ease of reference only. It must not be assumed that Tariff points are always used by institutions or that they can be substituted for an offer in grades. The level of an offer is not necessarily indicative of the quality of a course.

COURSE OFFERS INFORMATION
Subject requirements/preferences **GCSE** Mathematics and science subjects required. **AL** Courses vary but one, two or three subjects from chemistry, biology, physics and mathematics may be required.

Your target offers and examples of courses provided by each institution

360 pts **Imperial London** – AAA (Biomat Tiss Eng) (IB 36 pts HL 6 phys maths)
London (UCL) – AAA+AS–AAB+AS incl chem (Biotech) (IB 36–38 pts)
Manchester – AAA–ABB 320–360 pts (Biotech) (IB 37–33 pts)

340 pts **Bristol** – AAB (Geol Biol) (IB 33 pts)
Cardiff – AAB–ABB 340–320 pts (Biotech)
Newcastle – AAB (Bioproc Eng) (IB 36 pts HL 5 chem maths)
Surrey – AAB (Biotech) (IB 35 pts)
York – AAB (Biotech Microbiol) (IB 35 pts)

320 pts **Aberdeen** – ABB (Biotech) (IB 30 pts)
Edinburgh – AAA–ABB 320–360 pts (Biotech) (IB 37–32 pts)
Liverpool – ABB (Microbl Biotech) (IB 33 pts)
Newcastle – ABB (Biotech Ind Expnc) (IB 32 pts)
Nottingham – ABB–BCC 260–320 pts (Biotech) (IB 32–26 pts)
Strathclyde – ABB (Pros Orthot) (IB 34 pts)

300 pts **Northumbria** – 300 pts (Biotech) (IB 28 pts)
Nottingham – BBB 300 pts (Biomed Mat Sci) (IB 30 pts)

280 pts **Salford** – 280 pts (Pros Orthot) (IB 24 pts)

260 pts **Bradford** – 260 pts (App Biotech)
Bristol UWE – 260–320 pts (Biotech)
Greenwich – 260 pts (Biotech)

240 pts **Hertfordshire** – 240 pts (Biotech)
London Met – 240 pts (Biotech)

230 pts **Edinburgh Napier** – 230 pts (Microbiol Biotech)

220 pts **Westminster** – CCD (Biotech) (IB 26 pts)

200 pts **UEL** – 200 pts (Med Biotech)

160 pts **Wolverhampton** – 160–220 pts (Biotech) (IB 24 pts)

Alternative offers

See **Chapter 7** and **Appendix 1** for grades/UCAS Tariff points information for the International Baccalaureate, Scottish Highers/Advanced Highers, the Welsh Baccalaureate, the Irish Leaving Certificate, the Cambridge Pre-U Diploma, the Advanced Diploma and the Extended Project.

EXAMPLES OF FOUNDATION DEGREES IN THE SUBJECT FIELD
Edinburgh Napier.

CHOOSING YOUR COURSE (SEE ALSO CH.1)
Some course features

Leeds (Med Eng) The course combines engineering science, biological science and medicine. It has study abroad and work placement opportunities and strong links with industry.
Manchester (Biotech) A common first year covering several life science subjects provides the opportunity to change at a later stage.
Newcastle Twelve degrees covering the biomedical and biomolecular sciences have a common first year allowing the flexibility to make a final choice at the end of Stage 1.
Northumbria (Biotech) Main focus of course is on molecular biotechnology, including molecular biology, immunology and bioinformatics.
Wolverhampton (Biotech) Specialisation in gene manipulation, plant or microbial biotechnology.

Universities and colleges teaching quality See www.qaa.ac.uk; http://unistats.direct.gov.uk.

Examples of sandwich degree courses Bristol; Cardiff; Manchester; Northumbria; Sussex.

ADMISSIONS INFORMATION
Number of applicants per place (approx) Birmingham 6; Bristol 9; Cardiff 4; Imperial London 4; Leeds 7; London (UCL) 4; Strathclyde 4.

Advice to applicants and planning the UCAS personal statement See **Biological Sciences**, **Biochemistry** and **Appendix 3**.

Check **Chapter 4** when choosing your university and **Chapter 7** on how to read the subject tables.

Selection interviews **Yes** Bradford, Imperial London, Leeds, Strathclyde, Surrey; **Some** Cardiff, Wolverhampton; **No** Dundee.

Interview advice and questions See **Biology**, **Biological Sciences** and **Chapter 6**.

AFTER-RESULTS ADVICE

Offers to applicants repeating A-levels **Possibly higher** Nottingham; **Same** Cardiff, Leeds, LJMU, Wolverhampton.

GRADUATE DESTINATIONS AND EMPLOYMENT (2009/10 HESA)

Biotechnology; graduates surveyed 90 **Employed** 40 **In voluntary employment** 0 **In further study** 15 **Assumed unemployed** 10

Medical Technology; graduates surveyed 1610 **Employed** 1295 **In voluntary employment** 5 **In further study** 150 **Assumed unemployed** 50

Career note Biotechnology, biomedical and biochemical engineering opportunities exist in medical, agricultural, food science and pharmaceutical laboratories. Some Bioengineering graduates apply for graduate medical courses and obtain both engineering and medical qualifications.

OTHER DEGREE SUBJECTS FOR CONSIDERATION

Agriculture; Biochemistry; Biological Sciences; Biomedicine; Chemistry; Food Technology; Genetics; Materials Science and Technology; Microbiology; Molecular Biology; Pharmacology.

BUILDING and CONSTRUCTION

(including **Building Design, Building Services Engineering, Building Surveying, Construction, Fire Risk Engineering** and **Fire Safety Management**; see also **Architecture, Engineering (Civil), Housing, Surveying**)

The building and construction industry covers a wide range of activities and is closely allied to civil, municipal and structural engineering and quantity surveying. One branch of the industry covers building services engineering, a career which involves specialised areas such as heating, acoustics, lighting, refrigeration and air conditioning. Many Building, Construction, Building Surveying and Building Services Engineering courses include industrial placements and are accredited by professional bodies such as the Chartered Institute of Building, the Royal Institution of Chartered Surveyors and the Engineering Council.

Useful websites www.ciob.org.uk; www.cibse.org; www.cskills.org.

NB The points totals shown to the left of the institutions are for ease of reference only. It must not be assumed that Tariff points are always used by institutions or that they can be substituted for an offer in grades. The level of an offer is not necessarily indicative of the quality of a course.

COURSE OFFERS INFORMATION

Subject requirements/preferences **GCSE** English, mathematics and science usually required. **AL** Physics, mathematics or a technical subject may be required for some courses.

Your target offers and examples of courses provided by each institution
340 pts **Bristol UWE** – 340 pts (Bld Surv) (IB 24–28 pts)
          Leeds – AAB (Civ Eng Constr Mgt) (IB 36 pts HL 17 pts)
320 pts **LJMU** – 320 pts (Bld Serv Eng MEng)
          London (UCL) – ABBe (Proj Mgt Constr) (IB 32 pts)
300 pts **Brighton** – BBB (Constr Mgt) (IB 28 pts)
          Brunel – BBB (Mech Eng Bld Serv BEng) (IB 32 pts)
          Kingston – 300 pts (Quant Surv Cnsltncy) (IB 32 pts)

Loughborough – 300 pts (Commer Mgt Quant Surv) (IB 32 pts)
Newcastle – AAB–BBB 300–340 pts (Surv Map Sci) (IB 32 pts)
Reading – 300–320 pts (Constr Mgt)
Ulster – 300 pts (Constr Eng Mgt) (IB 25–32 pts)

285 pts **Glasgow Caledonian** – 285 pts (Bld Surv; Constr Mgt)

280 pts **Aston** – 280–300 pts (Constr Proj Mgt) (IB 29 pts)
Bristol UWE – 280 pts (Constr Mgt)
Derby – 280 pts (Constr Mgt) (IB 26 pts)
Heriot-Watt – BBC (Constr Proj Mgt) (IB 31 pts)
London (Central Sch SpDr) – BBC (Thea Prac Scnc Constr)
Loughborough – 280 pts (Constr Eng Mgt) (IB 30 pts)
Northumbria – 280 pts (Bld Surv) (IB 25 pts)
Nottingham – BBC (Sust Blt Env) (IB 28 pts)
Nottingham Trent – 280 pts (Bld Surv)
Oxford Brookes – BBC–BCC 260–280 pts (Cnstr Proj Mgt) (IB 30–31 pts)
Salford – 280 pts (Constr Mgt; Constr Proj Mgt; Bld Surv)
Sheffield Hallam – BBC 280 pts (Bld Surv)
Westminster – BBC (Constr Mgt) (IB 26 pts)

270 pts **Anglia Ruskin** – 270 pts (Bld Surv)
LJMU – 270 pts (Bld Serv Eng BEng) (IB 25 pts)

260 pts **Glamorgan** – BCC (Proj Mgt (Constr))
LJMU – 260 pts (Constr Mgt)
Oxford Brookes – BBC–BCC 260–280 pts (Constr Mgt) (IB 30–31 pts)
Plymouth – 260 pts (Bld Surv Env) (IB 27 pts)
Ulster – 260 pts (Bld Eng Mat) (IB 32 pts)

245 pts **Edinburgh Napier** – 245 pts (Bld Surv)

240 pts **Anglia Ruskin** – 240 pts (Constr Mgt)
Bolton – 240 pts (Constr; Bld Surv)
Coventry – 240 pts (Bld Surv; Constr Mgt)
Edinburgh Napier – CCC 240 pts (Constr Proj Mgt)
Glamorgan – 240–280 pts (Bld Serv Eng)
Glyndŵr – 240 pts (Bld St (Constr/Mntnce Mgt))
Greenwich – 240 pts (Constr Surv Mgt) (IB 24 pts)
Hull (Coll) – 240 pts (Constr Mgt)
Leeds Met – 240 pts (Bld Surv) (IB 27 pts)
Newport – 240 pts (Bld St)
Northumbria – 240–280 pts (Bld Proj Mgt) (IB 25 pts)
Nottingham Trent – 240 pts (Constr Mgt) (IB 24 pts)
Plymouth – 240 pts (Constr Mgt Env) (IB 26 pts)
Sheffield Hallam – 240 pts (Constr Proj Mgt)
UCLan – 240–260 pts (Bld Serv Sust Eng) (IB 24 pts)
Wolverhampton – CCC (Bld Surv) (IB 26 pts)

230 pts **CEM** – d/l 230 pts (Bld Surv; Bld Serv Quant Surv)

220 pts **London South Bank** – 220 pts (Prop Mgt (Bld Surv)) (IB 24 pts)

200 pts **Huddersfield** – 200 pts (Constr Proj Mgt)
Portsmouth – 200–260 pts (Constr Eng Mgt) (IB 24 pts)
UCLan – 200 pts (Fire Sfty Risk Mgt)

180 pts **Glasgow Caledonian** – 180 pts (Bld Serv Eng)
Greenwich – 180 pts (Des Constr Mgt) (IB 24 pts)
Plymouth – 180 pts (Env Constr Surv) (IB 24 pts)

160 pts **Glasgow Caledonian** – CC (Bld Surv Eng)
Kingston – 160 pts (Constr Mgt) (IB 32 pts)
Swansea Met – 160 pts (Proj Constr Mgt) (IB 24 pts)
Wolverhampton – 160–220 pts (Constr Mgt) (IB 24 pts)

150 pts **West London** – 150 pts (Blt Env (Quant Surv); Blt Env (Archit Tech))

Check **Chapter 4** when choosing your university and **Chapter 7** on how to read the subject tables.

120 pts **Colchester (Inst)** – 120 pts (Constr Mgt (Commer Mgt); Constr Mgt (Site Mgt))
Southampton Solent – 120 pts (Constr Mgt)
100 pts **and below**
CEM – d/l (Constr Mgt)

Alternative offers
See **Chapter 7** and **Appendix 1** for grades/UCAS Tariff points information for the International Baccalaureate, Scottish Highers/Advanced Highers, the Welsh Baccalaureate, the Irish Leaving Certificate, the Cambridge Pre-U Diploma, the Advanced Diploma and the Extended Project.

EXAMPLES OF FOUNDATION DEGREES IN THE SUBJECT FIELD
Bedfordshire; Blackburn (Coll); Bolton; Bournemouth; Bradford; Brighton; Colchester (Inst); Cornwall (Coll); Cumbria; Derby; Ealing, Hammersmith and West London (Coll); Glamorgan; Glyndŵr; Greenwich; Huddersfield; Kent; Kingston; Northampton; Northumbria; Suffolk (Univ Campus); Swansea Met; UCLan; UEL; West London; West Nottinghamshire (Coll); Westminster City (Coll); Weymouth (Coll); Wolverhampton.

CHOOSING YOUR COURSE (SEE ALSO CH.1)
Some course features
Aston Construction and Construction Project Management courses have a common first year; sandwich course has good industrial contacts.
Heriot-Watt (Constr Proj Mgt) Three options are offered in Project Management, Surveying or Building Services.
Loughborough (Constr Eng Mgt) Course sponsored by industry. Two six-month placements of industrial training.
Northumbria The Foundation degree route enables entry to Architectural Technology, Building Services Engineering or Surveying, Construction Management, Estate Management or Quantity Surveying.
Plymouth The course is accredited by the Chartered Institute of Building and focuses on the environmental and sustainability performance of buildings.
Reading Students taking Construction Management, Quantity Surveying and Building Surveying follow the same course for two years, choosing the specialism in Year 3.

Universities and colleges teaching quality See www.qaa.ac.uk; http://unistats.direct.gov.uk.

Top research universities and colleges (RAE 2008) See **Architecture**.

Examples of sandwich degree courses Aston; Bristol UWE; Glasgow Caledonian; Kingston; Leeds Met; London South Bank; Loughborough; Northumbria; Nottingham Trent; Sheffield Hallam; Ulster; Wolverhampton.

ADMISSIONS INFORMATION
Number of applicants per place (approx) Bristol UWE (Constr Mgt) 5; Edinburgh Napier 8; Glamorgan 3; Glasgow Caledonian 6; Heriot-Watt 6; Kingston 4; London (UCL) 4; Loughborough 4; Northumbria 6; Salford (Bld Surv) 6; Strathclyde 5.

Advice to applicants and planning the UCAS personal statement Details of work experience with any levels of responsibility should be included. Make contact with any building organisation to arrange a meeting with staff to discuss careers in building. Give evidence of your ability to work in a team and give details of any personal achievements in technological areas and work experience. Building also covers civil engineering, surveying, quantity surveying etc and these areas should also be explored.

Misconceptions about this course **Loughborough** Some students fail to realise that the degree includes law, finance, economics and management plus constructional technology.

Selection interviews **Yes** Brunel, Derby, Glamorgan, Glasgow Caledonian, Greenwich, Kingston, LJMU, London South Bank, Loughborough, Plymouth, Robert Gordon, Sheffield Hallam, Staffordshire, Westminster; **Some** Anglia Ruskin, Birmingham City, Brighton, Salford; **No** Nottingham, Reading.

Interview advice and questions Work experience in the building and civil engineering industries is important and you could be expected to describe any building project you have visited and any problems experienced in its construction. A knowledge of the range of activities to be found on a building site will be expected, for example the work of quantity and land surveyors and of the various building trades. See also **Chapter 6**. **Loughborough** The applicant should show an understanding of the role of the quantity surveyor.

Reasons for rejection (non-academic) Inability to communicate. Lack of motivation. Indecisiveness about reasons for choosing the course. **Loughborough** Applicant more suited to hands-on rather than an academic course.

AFTER-RESULTS ADVICE
Offers to applicants repeating A-levels Higher LJMU, Strathclyde; **Possibly higher** Bristol UWE; **Same** Birmingham City, Bolton, Brighton, Coventry, Heriot-Watt, Huddersfield, Kingston, London (UCL), Loughborough, Northumbria, Robert Gordon, Swansea Met.

GRADUATE DESTINATIONS AND EMPLOYMENT (2009/10 HESA)
Building; graduates surveyed 7885 **Employed** 3565 **In voluntary employment** 35 **In further study** 1255 **Assumed unemployed** 385

Career note There is a wide range of opportunities within the building and construction industry for building technologists and managers. This subject area also overlaps into surveying, quantity surveying, civil engineering, architecture and planning and graduates from all these subjects commonly work together as members of construction teams.

OTHER DEGREE SUBJECTS FOR CONSIDERATION
Architectural Technology; Architecture; Civil Engineering; Property Planning and Development; Quantity Surveying; Surveying.

BUSINESS AND MANAGEMENT COURSES

(see also **Business and Management Courses (International and European), Business and Management Courses (Specialised), Economics, Hospitality and Hotel Management, Human Resource Management, Leisure and Recreation Management/Studies, Marketing, Retail Management, Tourism and Travel)**

Business degrees attract more applicants than any other degree subject, with a further rise in the past year for places on a wide range of programmes. Financial studies form part of most courses, in addition to sales, marketing, human resources management and general management. Since this is a vocational subject, some work experience in the field is generally required prior to application. Many courses offer industrial placements, in some cases in the USA, Australia and New Zealand and, for those students with an A-level in a language (and in some cases a good GCSE), placements in Europe are possible.

Useful websites www.civilservice.gov.uk/jobs/faststream; www.bized.co.uk; www.icsa.org.uk; www.oft.gov.uk; www.adassoc.org.uk; www.cipr.co.uk; www.ismm.co.uk; www.export.org.uk; www.ipsos-mori.com; www.capitaresourcing.co.uk; www.tax.org.uk; www.hmrc.gov.uk; www.camfoundation.com; www.shell-livewire.org; www.iconsulting.org.uk; www.managers.org.uk; www.cipd.co.uk; www.inprad.org; www.managementhelp.com.

NB The points totals shown to the left of the institutions are for ease of reference only. It must not be assumed that Tariff points are always used by institutions or that they can be substituted for an offer in grades. The level of an offer is not necessarily indicative of the quality of a course.

COURSE OFFERS INFORMATION
Subject requirements/preferences GCSE Mathematics and English often at grade A or B required. **AL** Mathematics required for some courses. In some cases grades A, B or C may be required.

Check **Chapter 4** when choosing your university and **Chapter 7** on how to read the subject tables.

Your target offers and examples of courses provided by each institution

410 pts **London (King's)** – AAAb (Bus Mgt) (IB 38 pts HL 666)

400 pts **Warwick** – AAAc (Law Bus St) (IB 36 pts)

380 pts **Durham** – A*AA (Bus Econ) (IB 38 pts)
Exeter – A*AA–AAB (Maths Mgt) (IB 38–34 pts)
Warwick – A*AA–AAAb (Mgt) (IB 38 pts)

360 pts **Bath** – AAA (Bus Admin) (IB 38 pts)
Birmingham – AAA (Mat Sci Eng Bus Mgt MEng) (IB 36–38 pts)
Bristol – AAA–AAB incl maths (Acc Mgt) (IB 37–35 pts)
Cambridge – (Mgt St) (IB 38–42 pts)
City – AAA (Mgt) (IB 35 pts)
Edinburgh – AAA–ABB incl maths (Soft Eng Mgt) (IB 37–32 pts)
Exeter – AAA–AAB (Mgt Ldrshp) (IB 36–34 pts)
Lancaster – AAA (Mgt courses) (IB 36 pts)
Leeds – AAA (Mgt) (IB 35 pts HL 17 pts)
London LSE – AAA incl maths (Bus Maths Stats) (IB 38 pts HL 7 maths 66)
Nottingham – AAA–BBB 300–360 pts (Elec Electron Eng Mgt St) (IB 36 pts)
St Andrews – AAA (Mgt Sci) (IB 38 pts)
Southampton – AAA incl AS maths (Econ Mgt Sci) (IB 36 pts HL 18 pts)
Sussex – AAA–AAB (Law Bus)
Warwick – AAA (Phys Bus St) (IB 36 pts)
York – AAA–ABB 320–360 pts (Phys Bus Mgt) (IB 36–32 pts)

340 pts **Aston** – AAB–ABB 320–340 pts (Pol Bus courses)
Bath – AAB (Chem Mgt) (IB 34–36 pts HL 6 chem)
Birmingham – AAB (Bus Mgt courses) (IB 36–38 pts)
Bournemouth – 340 pts (Bus St)
Bristol – AAA–AAB 340–360 pts (Mgt) (IB 37–35)
Cardiff – AAB (Bus Mgt (Mark); Bus Mgt; Fin Mgt)
City – AAB (Bus St) (IB 35 pts)
Huddersfield – 340 pts (Bus Law)
Kent – AAB–ABB (Bus Admin courses) (IB 33 pts HL 15 pts)
Leicester – AAB (Mgt St courses)
Liverpool – AAB (Bus St Ind) (IB 35 pts)
London (QM) – AAB (Bus Mgt) (IB 34 pts)
London (RH) – AAB (Mgt Acc) (IB 35 pts)
London LSE – AAB (Mgt Sci) (IB 37 pts HL 766)
Loughborough – AAB (Maths Mgt) (IB 36 pts)
Manchester – AAB (Comp Sci Bus Mgt) (IB 35 pts)
Newcastle – AAB (Fin Bus Econ) (IB 34 pts)
Nottingham – AAB (Mgt St) (IB 34 pts)
Nottingham Trent – AAB (Bus Mgt)
St Andrews – AAB–AAA (Mgt Span) (IB 38 pts)
Sheffield – AAB (Bus Mgt Joint Hons) (IB 35 pts)
Southampton – AAB (Mgt Sci Acc) (IB 34 pts HL 17 pts)
Surrey – AAA–AAB 340–360 pts (Bus Econ) (IB 36–35 pts)
Sussex – AAB (Bus Hum Res Mgt) (IB 35 pts)
Warwick – AAB (Comp Bus St) (IB 36 pts)
York – AAB (Mgt) (IB 34 pts)

320 pts **Birmingham** – ABB (Comp Sys Eng Bus Mgt) (IB 32–34 pts)
Cardiff – ABB (Bus Inf Sys)
Durham – ABB (Acc Mgt) (IB 34 pts)
Essex – 320 pts (Bus Mgt) (IB 32 pts)
Glasgow – ABB (Bus Mgt Joint Hons) (IB 36 pts)
Kent – 320 pts (Acc Mgt) (IB 33 pts)
Lancaster – ABB (Ops Mgt) (IB 32 pts)

Liverpool – ABB (Maths Bus St) (IB 33 pts HL 6 maths)
Loughborough – ABB–AAC (Geog) (IB 34 pts)
Northumbria – ABB 320 pts (Bus St; Bus Mgt)
Nottingham – ABB (Bus Econy Contemp Chin) (IB 32 pts)
Queen's Belfast – ABB/BBBb (Bus Mgt)
Reading – AAB (Bus Mgt) (IB 33 pts)
Strathclyde – ABB (Econ Mgt; Electron Elec Eng Bus St; Bus; Bus Ent courses; Bus Ent Mgt)
Sheffield – ABB (Sociol Bus Mgt) (IB 33 pts)
Sussex – ABB (Comp Bus Mgt) (IB 34 pts)
Swansea – ABB–BBB (Bus Mgt; Bus Mgt Fin)
UEA – ABB (Bus Mgt) (IB 30–32 pts)

300 pts **Aberdeen** – BBB (Mgt St) (IB 30 pts)
Bradford – 300 pts (Bus Mgt St)
Bristol UWE – 300 pts (Mgt) (IB 26–32 pts)
Brunel – BBB (Bus Mgt (Acc/Mark)) (IB 32 pts)
Buckingham – 300 pts (Law Mgt St)
Cardiff Met – 300 pts (Bus Mgt St HR Mgt; Bus Mgt Fin; Bus Mgt St Law; Bus Mgt St courses)
Coventry – 300 pts (Law Bus)
Edinburgh – BBB–AAA (Bus St) (IB 34–42 pts)
Huddersfield – 300 pts (Bus Mgt Fin)
Leicester – BBB (Comp Mgt)
Liverpool – BBB incl maths phys (Mech Eng Bus BEng) (IB 32 pts HL 5 maths phys)
London (QM) – 300 pts (Bus Comp) (IB 32 pts)
Northumbria – 300 pts (Fr Bus; Bus Econ)
Nottingham Trent – 300–320 pts (Mgt Joint Hons)
Oxford Brookes – BBB (Bus Mgt) (IB 31 pts)
Plymouth – 300 pts (Law Bus)
Salford – 300 pts (Bus St HR Mgt)
Sheffield Hallam – 300–260 pts (Bus courses)
Swansea – BBB (Bus Mgt Econ) (IB 30–32 pts)
UEA – BBB (Cr-Cult Comm Bus Mgt) (IB 31 pts)
Westminster – BBB 300 pts (Bus St courses) (IB 28 pts)
Winchester – 260–300 pts (Relig St Bus Mgt)

280 pts **Aberystwyth** – 280 pts (Bus Mgt) (IB 27 pts)
Birmingham City – 280 pts (Bus courses) (IB 32 pts)
Brighton – BBC 280 pts (Bus Mgt courses) (IB 30 pts)
Bristol UWE – 280 pts (Spo Bus Mgt)
Derby – 280 pts (Bus St) (IB 26 pts)
Edge Hill – 280 pts (Bus Mgt St; Bus Mgt (Acc/HR Mgt/Int Bus/Mark); Chin Bus St; Bus Mgt HR Mgt; Bus Mgt (Leis Tour))
Gloucestershire – 280–300 pts (Bus Mgt)
Greenwich – 280 pts (Bus Mgt; PR)
Hull – 280 pts (Bus Fin Mgt) (IB 28 pts)
Keele – flexible offers 280–340 pts incl BB/AB (Bus Mgt) (IB 28–32 pts)
Kingston – 280–320 pts (Bus Sys Mgt; Bus Mgt; Bus St; Bus Ops Mgt)
Leeds Trinity (UC) – 280 pts (Bus; Bus Mgt; Bus Mark)
LJMU – 280 pts (Bus Mgt) (IB 28 pts)
Loughborough – 280 pts (Air Trans Mgt)
Manchester Met – 280 pts (Bus) (IB 28 pts)
Northumbria – 280 pts (Bus Mark) (IB 25 pts)
Nottingham Trent – 280 pts (Bus Ed Dev; Ely Yrs Bus Educ)
Portsmouth – 280 pts (Bus Admin; Bus St; Fin Bus)
Stirling – BBC (Mgt Sci) (IB 32 pts)
Stranmillis (UC) – BBC (Bus Ent Educ)

Salford – 280 pts (Bus St Mark Mgt)
Suffolk (Univ Campus) – 280 pts (Bus Mgt) (IB 24 pts)
Worcester – 280 pts (Bus Acc Econ)

260 pts **Bangor** – 260–300 pts (Mgt Acc; Bus St courses; Admin Mgt)
Bolton – 260 pts (Bus Mgt; Bus Mgt Lang; Bus Mgt (Mark); Bus Inf Sys)
BPP (UC) – 260 pts (Bus St; Bus St Fin)
Coventry – 260–280 pts (Bus Mgt) (IB 24 pts)
Derby – 260–300 pts (Bus Mgt)
Dundee – BCC (Bus Mgt) (IB 30 pts)
Glamorgan – 260 pts (Bus Mgt; Bus Ent)
Greenwich – 260 pts (Bus Prchsg Sply Chn Mgt; Bus Law; Bus Entre Innov)
Heriot-Watt – BCC (Bus Mgt Ind Expnc)
Hertfordshire – 260–300 pts (Bus St; Mgt)
Lincoln – 260 pts (Bus Mgt; Bus St; Mgt)
Liverpool Hope – 260 pts (Bus Mgt)
LJMU – 260 pts (Bus Comm) (IB 28 pts)
Plymouth – 260 pts (Marit Bus courses) (IB 26 pts)
Portsmouth – 260–280 pts (Bus Ent Dev)
Sheffield Hallam – 260–320 pts (Bus Inf Sys)
Sunderland – 260 pts (Bus HR Mgt; Bus Mark Mgt; Bus Ent Mgt; Bus Fin Mgt; Bus Mgt)
UCLan – 260–300 pts (Bus Mgt Chin) (IB 28 pts)
Ulster – 260 pts (Bus Joint Hons; Bus St courses)
Westminster – BCC (Bus Mgt (Mark)) (IB 28 pts)
Winchester – 260–300 pts (Bus Mgt Fin Econ; Psy Bus Mgt; Bus Mgt HR Mgt; Bus Mgt Mark)

245 pts **Edinburgh Napier** – 245 pts (Bus Inf Sys)
240 pts **Bath Spa** – 240–280 pts (Bus Mgt HR Mgt; Bus Mgt (Mark))
Bradford (Coll Univ Centre) – 240 pts (Bus St)
Bristol UWE – 240–300 pts (Bus St HR Mgt)
Buckingham – 240 pts (Bus Mgt courses; Bus Ent)
Canterbury Christ Church – 240 pts (Bus St; Bus Mgt)
Chester – 240–280 pts (Bus) (IB 26 pts)
Chichester – CCC (Bus St) (IB 26 pts)
City – 240 pts (Air Trans Mgt) (IB 31 pts)
Coventry – 240–260 pts (Span Bus)
Cumbria – 240 pts (App Bus Mgt)
De Montfort – 240–280 pts (Bus courses (13)) (IB 24–28 pts)
Farnborough (CT) – BCD (Mgt Acc)
Glasgow Caledonian – CCC (Bus St) (IB 24 pts)
Gloucestershire – 240–280 pts (Evnts Mgt)
Greenwich (Sch Mgt) – 240 pts (Law Mgt)
Hull – 240–300 pts (Chem Bus)
Leeds Met – 240 pts (Bus Inf Tech; Rtl Leis Mgt)
London Met – 240–300 pts (Bus courses; Mgt)
Manchester Met – 240–280 pts (Bus Admin Joint Hons) (IB 28 pts)
Middlesex – 240–280 pts (Bus Mark)
Newport – 240 pts (Bus St) (IB 24 pts)
Northampton – 240–280 pts (Bus Entre) (IB 24 pts)
Robert Gordon – CCC (Mgt) (IB 26 pts)
Roehampton – 240–280 pts (Bus Mgt)
Royal (CAg) – 240 pts (Bus Mgt)
Southampton Solent – 240 pts (Bus Mgt)
Teesside – 240 pts (Bus Mgt; Bus Law)
UCLan – 240–280 pts (Bus St courses (38)) (IB 24 pts)
West Scotland – CCC (Bus)
Winchester – 240–280 pts (Bus Mgt courses) (IB 24 pts)

Check **Chapter 4** when choosing your university and **Chapter 7** on how to read the subject tables.

Writtle (Coll) – 240 pts (Hort Bus Mgt)
230 pts **Edinburgh Napier** – 230 pts (Bus St; Bus Mgt HR)
220 pts **Bath Spa** – 220–260 pts (Bus Mgt courses)
Harper Adams (UC) – 220–260 pts (Agri-Bus)
Leeds Met – 220 pts (Int Bus) (IB 24 pts)
London South Bank – 220 pts (Bus Inf Sys)
Northampton – 220–260 pts (Bus St) (IB 24 pts)
Oldham (Coll Univ Centre) – 220–300 pts (Bus Mgt)
St Mary's Twickenham (UC) – 220 pts (Bus Law) (IB 28 pts)
Sunderland – 220–360 pts (App Mgt)
Wolverhampton – 220 pts (Bus Mgt)
York St John – 220–260 pts (Bus Mgt Ger; Bus Mgt courses)
200 pts **Anglia Ruskin** – 240-200 pts (Bus Econ)
Bedfordshire – 200 pts (Bus Mgt) (IB 24 pts)
Blackburn (Coll) – 200 pts (Bus HR Mgt; Bus St)
Bucks New – 200–240 pts (Bus; Int Ftbl Bus Mgt)
Doncaster (Coll Univ Centre) – 200 pts (Bus Mgt)
Edinburgh Queen Margaret – 200 pts (PR)
Glamorgan – 200–260 pts (Bus Span)
Glyndŵr – 200 pts (Bus Mgt)
Greenwich – 200 pts (Bus Admin)
London (Birk) – 200 pts (Mgt)
London Met – 200–280 pts (Bus Law courses)
Middlesex – 200–300 pts (Bus Mgt)
Peterborough (Univ Centre) – 200 pts (Bus Mgt)
Swansea Met – 200 pts (Bus IT)
UEL – 200 pts (Bus Mgt) (IB 24 pts)
West London – 200 pts (Bus St; Bus St Fin; Bus St HR Mgt; Mark Bus)
Writtle (Coll) – 200–360 pts (Bus Mgt) (IB 28 pts)
York St John – 200–240 pts (Bus IT; Bus St HR Mgt)
180 pts **Abertay Dundee** – DDD (Bus) (IB 24 pts)
Bradford – 180–220 pts (Psy Mgt)
Greenwich – 180 pts (Est Mgt)
Newman (UC) – 180–260 pts (Mgt St)
Stamford New (Coll) – 180 pts (Bus)
160 pts **Bradford (Coll Univ Centre)** – 2 A2 GCEs (not gs) 160 pts (Bus Admin)
Greenwich – 160 pts (Eng Bus Mgt)
Greenwich (Sch Mgt) – 160 pts (Bus Mgt IT; Bus Mgt; Mgt HR Mgt; Comp Sci Bus Inform)
London South Bank – 160 pts (Mgt Comb courses) (IB 24 pts)
SAC (Scottish CAg) – CC (Rur Bus Mgt)
South Essex (Coll) – 160 pts (Bus St)
Swansea Met – 160 pts (Mgt Ldrshp; Bus; Bus Fin)
UHI – CC–AA (Bus Mgt)
140 pts **Trinity Saint David** – 140–360 pts (Bus IT)
120 pts **Bradford (Coll Univ Centre)** – 120 pts (Bus Comp Sol)
Colchester (Inst) – 120 pts (Mgt)
Croydon (Coll) – 120 pts (Bus Fin; Bus Mgt; Bus Mark)
Grimsby (IFHE) – 120–240 pts (Bus courses)
Holborn (Coll) – 120 pts (Bus Mgt)
Llandrillo Cymru (Coll) – 120 pts (Mgt Bus) (IB 24 pts)
Northbrook (Coll) – 120 pts (Bus Admin)
Norwich City (Coll) – 120 pts (Bus Mgt (Fin Acc))
West Anglia (Coll) – 120 pts (Bus Mgt)
80 pts **Croydon (Coll)** – 80 pts (Fash Des Bus)
Kensington Bus (Coll) – 80 pts (Bus St)

40 pts Sir Gâr (Coll) – (Bus Mgt)

> **Open University** – contact +44 (0)845 300 6090 **or** www.openuniversity.co.uk/you (Bus St)

Alternative offers
See **Chapter 7** and **Appendix 1** for grades/UCAS Tariff points information for the International Baccalaureate, Scottish Highers/Advanced Highers, the Welsh Baccalaureate, the Irish Leaving Certificate, the Cambridge Pre-U Diploma, the Advanced Diploma and the Extended Project.

EXAMPLES OF FOUNDATION DEGREES IN THE SUBJECT FIELD
Askham Bryan (Coll); Bedfordshire; Bexley (Coll); Birmingham (UC); Blackburn (Coll); Blackpool and Fylde (Coll); Bolton; Bournemouth; Bournemouth and Poole (Coll); Bradford; Brighton; Bristol City (Coll); Bristol UWE; Colchester (Inst); Cornwall (Coll); Croydon (Coll); De Montfort; Doncaster (Coll Univ Centre); Duchy (Coll); Durham New (Coll); Ealing, Hammersmith and West London (Coll); Edge Hill; Farnborough (CT); Glamorgan; Gloucestershire; Glyndŵr; Greenwich; Grimsby (IFHE); Harper Adams (UC); Hertfordshire; K (Coll); Kirklees (Coll); Knowsley (CmC); Lakes (Coll); Leeds Met; LJMU; London South Bank; Manchester (Coll); Mid-Cheshire (Coll); Middlesex; NEW (Coll); Newcastle (Coll); North Lindsey (Coll); Northampton; Northbrook (Coll); Nottingham New (Coll); Plymouth; Riverside Halton (Coll); Royal (CAg); St Helens (Coll); Sheffield (Coll); Sheffield Hallam; Somerset (CAT); South Devon (Coll); South Essex (Coll); Southampton Solent; Suffolk (Univ Campus); UCLan; UEL; Wakefield (Coll); Warwickshire (Coll); Westminster Kingsway (Coll); Writtle (Coll); York (Coll).

CHOOSING YOUR COURSE (SEE ALSO CH.1)
Some course features
Bath (Bus Admin) A popular and highly respected sandwich course with placements in the UK and abroad.
Brunel (Bus Mgt) Three-year or four-year sandwich courses allowing for specialisation in management, accounting, business systems or marketing.

Check **Chapter 4** when choosing your university and **Chapter 7** on how to read the subject tables.

De Montfort (Bus Mgt Ent) Course focuses on entrepreneurship and business practice, researching and developing new business opportunities and ideas, with an optional paid placement year.

London LSE (Mgt) Course has compulsory modules in economics, psychology, accounting and finance and marketing. (Mgt Sci) Course focuses on quantitative analysis, decision making and economic and social issues. Operational research and statistics are taken in Years 2 and 3.

Nottingham (Mgt St) Core modules include organisation studies, entrepreneurship, accounting, business computing, business, business ethics, human resource management and economics. French, German, Spanish or Chinese Studies can be selected as major/minor combinations.

Oxford Brookes (Bus Mgt) Course aimed at students not wanting to specialise in any particular area of business or are undecided. At the end of the first year, students can opt for one of the named Business degrees.

Southampton (Mgt Sci) Courses allow for specialisation in mathematical or non-mathematical aspects of management including accounting and finance, languages, entrepreneurship and music.

Winchester (Bus Mgt) Optional pathway to BA in Business Management with Public Service Management. Modules include quality management and customer care, local government, public administration and European culture and institutions.

Universities and colleges teaching quality See www.qaa.ac.uk; http://unistats.direct.gov.uk.

Top research universities and colleges (RAE 2008) (Business and Management Studies) Imperial London; Cambridge; Cardiff; Bath; London (King's); London LSE; Oxford; Lancaster; Warwick; Manchester; Strathclyde; Leeds; Nottingham; Aston; Loughborough; Sheffield.

Examples of sandwich degree courses Abertay Dundee; Aston; Bath; Birmingham (UC); Birmingham City; Bournemouth; Bradford; Brighton; Bristol UWE; Brunel; City; Coventry; De Montfort; Glasgow Caledonian; Gloucestershire; Greenwich; Harper Adams (UC); Hertfordshire; Huddersfield; Hull; Kingston; LJMU; Loughborough; Manchester Met; Newcastle; Nottingham Trent; Oxford Brookes; Plymouth; Portsmouth; Royal (CAg); Sheffield Hallam; Staffordshire; Surrey; Swansea Met; Teesside; UCLan; Ulster; Warwickshire (Coll); West Scotland; Westminster; Wolverhampton.

ADMISSIONS INFORMATION

Number of applicants per place (approx) Abertay Dundee (Bus St) 4; Aberystwyth 3; Anglia Ruskin 5; Aston (Bus Mgt) 12, (Mgt) 5; Bangor 4; Bath (Bus Admin) 7; Birmingham 28; Birmingham (UC) 5; Blackpool and Fylde (Coll) 2; Bolton 3; Bournemouth 30; Bradford 12; Bristol 28; Brunel 12; Canterbury Christ Church 20; Cardiff 8; City (Bus St) 17, (Mgt Sys) 6; Colchester (Inst) 2; De Montfort (Bus Mgt) 5; Edge Hill 4; Glasgow Caledonian 18; Heriot-Watt 5; Hertfordshire 10; Huddersfield 5; Hull (Bus St) 19, (Mgt) 10; Hull (Coll) 3; Kent 30; Kingston 50; Leeds 27, (Mgt St) 16; Leeds Trinity (UC) 3; Llandrillo Cymru (Coll) 2; London (King's) 25, (Mgt Sci) 12; London (RH) 9; London LSE 18; London Met 10; London South Bank 4; Loughborough 5; Manchester Met (Bus St) 26; Middlesex 12; Newcastle 27, (Bus Mgt) 40; Northumbria 10; Oxford Brookes 40; Plymouth 4; Portsmouth 10, (Bus Admin) 7, (Bus St) 6; Regents Bus Sch London 25; Robert Gordon 5; Salford (Bus St) 9, (Mgt Sci) 2; Southampton Solent 13; Strathclyde 12; Sunderland 20; Surrey (Bus Mgt) 6; Swansea Met 7; Teesside (Bus St) 4; UCLan 15; Warwick 22; West London 4; West Scotland 5; Westminster 12; Winchester 4; Wolverhampton 7; York 6; York St John 3.

Advice to applicants and planning the UCAS personal statement There are many different kinds of businesses and any work experience is almost essential for these courses. This should be described in detail: for example, size of firm, turnover, managerial problems, sales and marketing aspects, customers' attitudes. Any special interests in business management should also be included, for example, personnel work, purchasing, marketing. Give details of travel or work experience abroad and, for international courses, language expertise and examples of leadership and organising skills. Reference can be made to any particular business topics you have studied in the *Financial Times*, *The Economist* and the business sections in the weekend press. Applicants need to be sociable, ambitious, team players. Say why you are interested in the course, identify your academic strengths, your personal strengths and interests. Check information on the websites of the Chartered Institute of Public Relations, the Chartered Institute of Marketing and the Chartered Institute of Personnel and Development. See **Appendix 3**; see also **Accountancy/Accounting**.

The Faculty of Business and Science incorporates the Harrogate International Business School, which offers a range of tailor made programmes to fit employer requirements as well as recognised professional qualifications to individuals and employers.

With a wide range of experienced tutors who have vital links within the various industry sectors, we offer BA (Hons) and Foundation Degrees in Business Management, Logistics, IT and Network Management to Professional Graduate Certificates in Education and Professional Management options.

BUSINESS
at Hull & Harrogate College

OPEN DAYS

Tues 10th Jan
Thurs 8th March
Sat 16th June

Hull Campus:
01482 598744
hull-college.ac.uk/HE

Harrogate Campus:
01423 878211
harrogate.ac.uk/HE

Misconceptions about this course Aberystwyth Students are unaware that the course addresses practical aspects of business. **Salford** (Mgt Sci) Students should appreciate that the courses are fairly mathematical. **York** A previous study of management, IT or languages at A-level is necessary.

Selection interviews Yes Birmingham City, Bradford, Coventry, Doncaster (Coll Univ Centre), Durham, Edge Hill, Euro Bus Sch London, Glamorgan, Glasgow Caledonian, Hull, Kent (mature and Access students), London Met, Middlesex, Northumbria, Nottingham Trent, Plymouth, Robert Gordon, Roehampton, Sheffield Hallam, Sir Gâr (Coll), Strathclyde, Swansea, Teesside, Trinity Saint David, West London, West Thames (Coll), York; **Some** Abertay Dundee, Aberystwyth, Anglia Ruskin, Bath, Bath Spa, Blackpool and Fylde (Coll), Brighton, Buckingham, Cardiff Met, City, De Montfort, Derby (Int Bus), Greenwich, Kent, Leeds, Lincoln, LJMU, Manchester Met, Salford, South Kent (Coll), Southampton, Staffordshire, Stirling, Sunderland, UEA, Warwick, Winchester, Wolverhampton; **No** Birmingham, Chichester, Dundee, Nottingham, West Scotland.

Interview advice and questions Any work experience you describe on the UCAS application probably will be the focus of questions which could include topics covering marketing, selling, store organisation and management and customer problems. Personal qualities are naturally important in a career in business, so be ready for such questions as: What qualities do you have which are suitable and important for this course? Describe your strengths and weaknesses. Why should we give you a place on this course? Is advertising fair? What qualities does a person in business require to be successful? What makes a good manager? What is a cash-flow system? What problems can it cause? How could supermarkets improve customer relations? See also **Chapter 6**. **Buckingham** Why Business? How do you see yourself in five years' time? Have you had any work experience? If so, discuss. **Wolverhampton** Mature students with no qualifications will be asked about their work experience.

Reasons for rejection (non-academic) Hadn't read the prospectus. Lack of communication skills. Limited commercial interest. Weak on numeracy and problem-solving. Lack of interview preparation

Check **Chapter 4** when choosing your university and **Chapter 7** on how to read the subject tables.

(no questions). Lack of outside interests. Inability to cope with a year abroad. The candidate brought his parent who answered all the questions. See also **Marketing**. **Aberystwyth** Would have trouble fitting into the unique environment of Aberystwyth. Casual approach to learning. **Bournemouth** The Business Studies course is very popular. **Surrey** Hesitation about the period abroad.

AFTER-RESULTS ADVICE

Offers to applicants repeating A-levels **Higher** Bradford, Bristol UWE, Brunel, Greenwich, Hertfordshire, Kingston, Lancaster, Liverpool, Manchester Met, St Andrews, Sheffield, Strathclyde, Teesside; **Same** Abertay Dundee, Aberystwyth, Anglia Ruskin, Aston, Bath, Bath Spa, Birmingham City, Bolton, Bournemouth, Brighton, Brunel, Buckingham, Cardiff, Cardiff Met, Chester, Chichester, De Montfort, Derby, Durham, Glasgow, Gloucestershire, Harper Adams (UC), Huddersfield, Hull, Kent, Leeds, Lincoln, Liverpool Hope, LJMU, Loughborough, Newman (UC), Northumbria, Oxford Brookes, Portsmouth, Robert Gordon, Roehampton, Royal (CAg), Salford, Sheffield Hallam, Staffordshire, Stirling, Suffolk (Univ Campus), Sunderland, Surrey, Trinity Saint David, UEA, UEL, Ulster, West London, West Scotland, Winchester, Wolverhampton, Worcester, York, York St John.

GRADUATE DESTINATIONS AND EMPLOYMENT (2009/10 HESA)

Business Studies; graduates surveyed 18990 **Employed** 9965 **In voluntary employment** 145 **In further study** 3025 **Assumed unemployed** 1270

Management Sciences; graduates surveyed 9990 **Employed** 6420 **In voluntary employment** 100 **In further study** 2090 **Assumed unemployed** 630

Career note The majority of graduates enter trainee management roles in business-related and administrative careers, many specialising in some of the areas listed in **Other degree subjects for consideration** below. The main graduate destinations are in finance, property development, wholesale, retail and manufacturing.

OTHER DEGREE SUBJECTS FOR CONSIDERATION

Accountancy; Banking; Business Information Technology; E-Business; Economics; Estate Management; Finance; Hospitality Management; Housing Management; Human Resource Management; Insurance; Leisure Management; Logistics; Marketing; Public Administration; Retail Management; Sports Management; Surveying.

BUSINESS AND MANAGEMENT COURSES (INTERNATIONAL AND EUROPEAN)

(including **Business** and **Management Courses with Languages**; see also **Business and Management Courses, Business and Management Courses (Specialised), Hospitality and Hotel Management, Human Resource Management, Leisure and Recreation Management/Studies, Marketing, Retail Management, Tourism and Travel**)

Similar to Business and Management Courses, this subject area focuses on business but with more of an international theme. Studying or taking part in an industrial placement abroad is another higlight of this subject area.

Useful websites See **Business and Management Courses**.

NB The points totals shown to the left of the institutions are for ease of reference only. It must not be assumed that Tariff points are always used by institutions or that they can be substituted for an offer in grades. The level of an offer is not necessarily indicative of the quality of a course.

COURSE OFFERS INFORMATION

Subject requirements/preferences **GCSE** Mathematics and English often at grade A or B required. **AL** A language will be stipulated for most courses in this subject area. In some cases grades A, B or C may be required.

Your target offers and examples of courses provided by each institution

390 pts **Warwick** – A*AA–AAAb (Int Mgt) (IB 38 pts)

360 pts **Lancaster** – AAA (Bus St (St Abrd))

Leeds – AAA (Int Bus)

London (UCL) – AABe–ABBe (Econ Bus E Euro St) (IB 34–36 pts)

Sheffield – AAA (Int Bus Mgt (Yr Abrd)) (IB 37 pts)

340 pts **Aston** – AAB (Int Bus Fr/Ger/Span) (IB 34 pts)

Bath – AAB (Int Bus Ger) (IB 34–36 pts)

Birmingham – AAB (Int Bus) (IB 36–38 pts)

Bournemouth – 340 pts (Int Bus)

Cardiff – AAB (Bus Mgt Euro Lang) (IB 35 pts)

Liverpool – AAB (Int Bus) (IB 35 pts)

London (RH) – AAB (Mgt Int Bus) (IB 35 pts)

London (SOAS) – AAB (Int Mgt) (IB 36 pts HL 666)

Loughborough – AAB 340 pts (Int Bus) (IB 36 pts)

Manchester – AAB (Int Mgt Am Bus St) (IB 35 pts)

Newcastle – AAB (Int Bus Mgt) (IB 34 pts)

Nottingham – AAB (Mgt As/Chin St) (IB 34 pts)

Reading – AAB (Int Mgt Bus Admin Fr/Ger/Ital) (HL 666)

Southampton – AAB–ABB (Mgt Sci Fr/Ger/Span)

Surrey – AAB (Bus Mgt Fr/Ger/Span) (IB 36 pts)

320 pts **Bath** – ABB (Int Mgt Ger) (IB 36 pts)

Bradford – 320 pts (Int Bus Mgt)

Essex – 320 pts (Bus Mgt Modn Lang) (IB 28–29 pts)

Kent – ABB (Int Bus) (IB 33 pts)

Queen's Belfast – ABB/BBBb (Int Bus Fr/Ger) (IB 32 pts)

Roehampton – 320 pts (Int Bus) (IB 26 pts)

Swansea – ABB–BBB (Int Bus; Int Mgt Sci (St Abrd); Int Mgt Sci (Lang); Int Bus Mgt (St Abrd))

300 pts **Bristol UWE** – 300 pts (Int Bus St Span; Int Bus St)

Brunel – BBB (Int Bus) (IB 32 pts)

Cardiff Met – 300 pts (Int Bus Mgt) (IB 24 pts)

Coventry – BBB (Int Bus Mgt) (IB 28 pts)

Dundee – BBB–BCC (Int Bus Ger)

Edinburgh – AAA–BBB 300–360 pts (Bus St Fr/Ger/Span; Int Bus)

Heriot-Watt – BBB (Int Bus Mgt Fr/Ger/Span)

Huddersfield – 300 pts (Int Bus)

Keele – 300–360 pts (Int Bus)

Liverpool – BBB (Bus St Modn Lang) (IB 30 pts HL 6 lang)

London (QM) – 300–340 pts (Russ Bus Mgt) (IB 32 pts)

Northumbria – 300 pts (Int Bus Mgt) (IB 25 pts)

Nottingham Trent – 300 pts (Int Bus Joint Hons) (IB 24 pts)

Oxford Brookes – BBB (Int Bus Fin Econ) (IB 31 pts)

Sheffield Hallam – 300 pts (Int Bus St; Int Bus St Lang)

Westminster – BBB 300 pts (Int Bus) (IB 28 pts)

280 pts **Brighton** – BBC 280 pts (Int Bus)

De Montfort – 280 pts (Int Bus Glob) (IB 24 pts)

Derby – 280 pts (Int Spa Mgt) (IB 26 pts)

Edge Hill – 280 pts (Int Bus) (IB 24 pts)

Greenwich – 280 pts (Int Bus)

Hertfordshire – 280 pts (Int Mgt)

Hull – 280 pts (Bus Econ (Int))

Kingston – 280–320 pts (Int Bus Fr/Span) (IB 25 pts)

Manchester Met – 280 pts (Int Bus) (IB 28 pts)

Portsmouth – 280 pts (Euro Bus (UK Ger); Int Bus St; Euro Bus courses)

Check **Chapter 4** when choosing your university and **Chapter 7** on how to read the subject tables.

Staffordshire – BBC–BB (Int Bus Mgt) (IB 24 pts)
Stirling – BBC (Int Mgt St Euro Lang Socty) (IB 32 pts)
Salford – BBC (Bus Mgt (Int)) (IB 28 pts)
Sheffield Hallam – 280 pts (Int Htl Mgt; Tour Mgt (Int); Tour Hspty Bus Mgt (Int))

260 pts **Anglia Ruskin** – 260–300 pts (Int Bus)
Dundee – BCC (Int Bus) (IB 34 pts)
Gloucestershire – 260–300 pts (Int Bus St)
Hertfordshire – 260 pts (Int Bus; Bus Mand Chin/Euro Langs)
Lincoln – 260 pts (Euro Bus; Int Bus)
UCLan – 260 pts (Acc Int Bus)

240 pts **Chester** – 240–280 pts (Int Bus) (IB 26 pts)
Euro Bus Sch London – 240–300 pts (Int Bus HR Mgt 2 Langs)
Glasgow Caledonian – CCC (Int Bus) (IB 24 pts)
Hull – 240 pts (Int Bus)
London Met – 240 pts (Int Bus Mgt) (IB 28 pts)
Plymouth – 240 pts (Int Bus) (IB 24 pts)
Regents Bus Sch London – CCC 240 pts (Glob Bus Des Mgt) (IB 32 pts)
Robert Gordon – CCC (Int Bus Mgt)
Salford – 240–260 pts (Bus St Int Bus Mgt) (IB 28 pts)
Southampton Solent – 240 pts (Int Bus Mgt)
Teesside – 240 pts (Int Mgt)
UCLan – 240–280 pts (Int Bus) (IB 28 pts)
Ulster – 240 pts (Bus Am St) (IB 24 pts)

230 pts **Edinburgh Napier** – 230 pts (Bus Mgt Ger)

220 pts **Leeds Met** – 220 pts (Langs Int Bus) (IB 24 pts)
Wolverhampton – 220–240 pts (Int Bus Mgt; Bus Fr)

200 pts **Abertay Dundee** – 200 pts (Int Econ Mgt)
Anglia Ruskin – 240–200 pts (Int Bus Strat) (IB 24 pts)
Bedfordshire – 200 pts (Int Bus St)
Bucks New – 200–240 pts (Int Mgt)
Hull (Coll) – 200 pts (Int Bus)
Middlesex – 200-300 pts (Int Bus Arbc)
Plymouth – 200–240 pts (Marit Bus Fr/Ger/Span) (IB 24 pts)
UEL – 200 pts (Int Bus) (IB 24 pts)

160 pts **Euro Bus Sch London** – CC (Int Bus Span)

Open University – contact +44 (0)845 300 6090 **or** www.openuniversity.co.uk/you (Bus St Fr/Span)

Alternative offers

See **Chapter 7** and **Appendix 1** for grades/UCAS Tariff points information for the International Baccalaureate, Scottish Highers/Advanced Highers, the Welsh Baccalaureate, the Irish Leaving Certificate, the Cambridge Pre-U Diploma, the Advanced Diploma and the Extended Project.

EXAMPLES OF FOUNDATION DEGREES IN THE SUBJECT FIELD

Askham Bryan (Coll); Bedfordshire; Bexley (Coll); Birmingham (UC); Blackburn (Coll); Blackpool and Fylde (Coll); Bolton; Bournemouth; Bradford; Brighton; Bristol City (Coll); Bristol UWE; Colchester (Inst); Cornwall (Coll); Croydon (Coll); De Montfort; Doncaster (Coll Univ Centre); Duchy (Coll); Durham New (Coll); Ealing, Hammersmith and West London (Coll); Edge Hill; Farnborough (CT); Glamorgan; Gloucestershire; Glyndŵr; Greenwich; Grimsby (IFHE); Harper Adams (UC); Hertfordshire; K (Coll); Kirklees (Coll); Knowsley (CmC); Lakes (Coll); Leeds Met; LJMU; London South Bank; Manchester (Coll); Mid-Cheshire (Coll); Middlesex; NEW (Coll); Newcastle (Coll); North Lindsey (Coll); Northampton; Northbrook (Coll); Nottingham New (Coll); Plymouth; Riverside Halton (Coll); Royal (CAg); St Helens (Coll); Sheffield (Coll); Sheffield Hallam; Somerset (CAT); South Devon (Coll); South Essex (Coll); Southampton Solent; Suffolk (Univ Campus); UCLan; UEL; Wakefield (Coll); Warwickshire (Coll); Westminster Kingsway (Coll); Writtle (Coll); York (Coll).

CHOOSING YOUR COURSE (SEE ALSO CH.1)

Some course features

De Montfort (Bus Mgt Ent) Course focuses on entrepreneurship and business practice, researching and developing new business opportunities and ideas, with an optional paid placement year.

Oxford Brookes (Bus Mgt) Course aimed at students not wanting to specialise in any particular area of business or are undecided. At the end of the first year, students can opt for one of the named Business degrees.

Universities and colleges teaching quality See www.qaa.ac.uk; http://unistats.direct.gov.uk.

Top research universities and colleges (RAE 2008) (Business and Management Studies) Imperial London; Cambridge; Cardiff; Bath; London (King's); London LSE; Oxford; Lancaster; Warwick; Manchester; Strathclyde; Leeds; Nottingham; Aston; Loughborough; Sheffield.

Examples of sandwich degree courses Aston; Bath; Bournemouth; Brighton; Brunel; De Montfort; Greenwich; Hertfordshire; Kingston; Leeds Met; Manchester Met; Middlesex; Northumbria; Nottingham Trent; Oxford Brookes; Plymouth; Portsmouth; Sheffield Hallam; Staffordshire; Teesside.

ADMISSIONS INFORMATION

Number of applicants per place (approx) Abertay Dundee (Bus St) 4; Aberystwyth 3; Anglia Ruskin 5; Aston (Int Bus) 6, (Int Bus Econ) 8; Bangor 4; Bath (Int Mgt Lang) 14; Birmingham 28; Birmingham (UC) 5; Blackpool and Fylde (Coll) 2; Bolton 3; Bradford 12; Bristol 28; Brunel 12; Canterbury Christ Church 20; Cardiff 8; Colchester (Inst) 2; Derby (Int Bus) 4; Edge Hill 4; Glasgow Caledonian 18; Heriot-Watt 5; Hertfordshire 10; Huddersfield 5; Hull (Scarborough) 3; Hull (Coll) 3; Kent 30; Kingston 50; Leeds 27; Leeds Trinity (UC) 3; LJMU (Int Bus) 16; Llandrillo Cymru (Coll) 2; London (King's) 25; London (RH) 9; London Met 10; London South Bank 4; Loughborough 5; Manchester Met (Int Bus) 8; Middlesex 12; Newcastle 27, (Int Bus Mgt) 25; Northumbria 10; Oxford Brookes 40; Plymouth 4; Portsmouth 10, (Int Bus) 5; Regents Bus Sch London 25; Robert Gordon 5; Sheffield Hallam (Int Bus) 6; Southampton Solent 13; Strathclyde 12, (Int Bus Modn Lang) 6; Sunderland 20; Swansea Met 7; UCLan 15; Warwick 22; West London 4; West Scotland 5; Westminster 12; Winchester 4; Wolverhampton 7; York 6; York St John 3.

Advice to applicants and planning the UCAS personal statement See **Business and Management Courses**.

Misconceptions about this course **Aston** (Int Bus Fr) Not two separate disciplines – the two subjects are integrated involving the study of language in a business and management context.

Selection interviews **Yes** Birmingham City, Bradford, Coventry, Doncaster (Coll Univ Centre), Durham, Edge Hill, Euro Bus Sch London, Glamorgan, Glasgow Caledonian, Hull, Kent (mature and Access students), London Met, Middlesex, Northumbria, Nottingham Trent, Plymouth, Robert Gordon, Roehampton, Sheffield Hallam, Sir Gâr (Coll), Strathclyde, Swansea, Teesside, Trinity Saint David, West London, West Thames (Coll), York; **Some** Abertay Dundee, Aberystwyth, Anglia Ruskin, Bath, Bath Spa, Blackpool and Fylde (Coll), Brighton, Buckingham, Cardiff Met, Chichester, City, De Montfort, Derby (Int Bus), Greenwich, Kent, Leeds, Lincoln, LJMU, Manchester Met, Salford, South Kent (Coll), Staffordshire, Stirling, Sunderland, UEA, Warwick, Winchester, Wolverhampton; **No** Birmingham.

Interview advice and questions See **Business and Management Courses**. **Wolverhampton** Mature students with no qualifications will be asked about their work experience.

Reasons for rejection (non-academic) See **Business and Management Courses**. **Bournemouth** The Business Studies course is very popular. **Surrey** Hesitation about the period abroad.

AFTER-RESULTS ADVICE

Offers to applicants repeating A-levels **Higher** Bradford, Bristol UWE, Brunel, Greenwich, Hertfordshire, Kingston, Lancaster, Liverpool, Manchester Met, St Andrews, Sheffield, Strathclyde, Teesside; **Same** Aberystwyth, Anglia Ruskin, Aston, Bath, Birmingham City, Bournemouth, Brighton, Buckingham, Cardiff, Cardiff Met, Chester, Chichester, De Montfort, Derby, Durham, Gloucestershire, Huddersfield, Hull, Kent, Leeds, Lincoln, Liverpool Hope, LJMU, Loughborough, Northumbria, Oxford

Brookes, Robert Gordon, Roehampton, Royal (CAg), Salford, Sheffield Hallam, Staffordshire, Stirling, Suffolk (Univ Campus), Sunderland, Surrey, UEA, Ulster, West London, Winchester, Wolverhampton, Worcester, York, York St John.

GRADUATE DESTINATIONS AND EMPLOYMENT (2009/10 HESA)
See **Business and Management Courses**.

Career note See **Business and Management Courses**.

OTHER DEGREE SUBJECTS FOR CONSIDERATION
Accountancy; Banking; Business Information Technology; E-Business; Economics; Estate Management; Finance; Hospitality Management; Housing Management; Human Resource Management; Insurance; Leisure Management; Logistics; Marketing; Public Administration; Retail Management; Sports Management; Surveying.

BUSINESS AND MANAGEMENT COURSES (SPECIALISED)

(including **Advertising, E-Commerce, Entrepreneurship, Operations Management, Public Relations** and **Publishing**; see also **Business and Management Courses, Business and Management Courses (International and European), Hospitality and Hotel Management, Human Resource Management, Leisure and Recreation Management/Studies, Marketing, Retail Management, Tourism and Travel**)

This subject contains courses that are business and management related but which allow students to focus on business within a particular area such as agriculture, media, extreme sports or creative events to give a few examples.

Useful websites See **Business and Management Courses**.

NB The points totals shown to the left of the institutions are for ease of reference only. It must not be assumed that Tariff points are always used by institutions or that they can be substituted for an offer in grades. The level of an offer is not necessarily indicative of the quality of a course.

COURSE OFFERS INFORMATION
Subject requirements/preferences **GCSE** Mathematics and English often at grade A or B required. **AL** Mathematics required for some courses. In some cases grades A, B or C may be required. (Publishing) English required for some courses.

Your target offers and examples of courses provided by each institution
360 pts **London (UCL)** – AAA–ABB incl chem (Chem Mgt Sci) (IB 32–36 pts)
Ulster – AAA (Comm Adv Mark)
340 pts **Lancaster** – AAB 340 pts (Adv Mark) (IB 34 pts)
Southampton – AAB (Mgt Entre) (IB 34 pts HL 17 pts)
320 pts **Bournemouth** – 320 pts (PR)
Lancaster – ABB (Ops Mgt) (IB 32 pts)
Loughborough – 320 pts (Inf Mgt Bus St) (IB 34 pts)
Newcastle – AAB–ABB 320–340 pts (Agri Bus Mgt) (IB 34 pts)
Northumbria – 320 pts (Adv Mgt)
UEA – ABB (Bus Inf Sys) (IB 32 pts)
300 pts **Aston** – BBB 300 pts (Tech Ent Mgt) (IB 32 pts)
Bournemouth – 300 pts (Des Bus Mgt)
Huddersfield – 300 pts (PR)
Royal (CAg) – 300 pts (Rur Lnd Mgt)
Sheffield Hallam – 300 pts (Evnts Mgt Art Enter; Evnts Mgt Tour Destin; Int Evnts Mgt Tour Destin)

280 pts **Arts London (CFash)** – 280 pts (Fash Mgt)
Coventry – BBC 280 pts (Disas Mgt Emer Plan)
De Montfort – 280 pts (Mark Mgt; Adv)
Derby – 280 pts (Mark Brnd Mgt; Tour Mgt)
Harper Adams (UC) – 280 pts (Agric Frm Bus Mgt)
Huddersfield – 280 pts (Adv Mark Comm; Adv Media)
London (Central Sch SpDr) – BBC (Thea Prac Stg Mgt; Thea Prac Tech Prod Mgt)
Loughborough – 280 pts (Air Trans Mgt)
Manchester Met – 280 pts (Bus Ent Mark) (IB 29 pts)
Nottingham Trent – 280 pts (Fash Mgt)
Oxford Brookes – BBC (Pub Media) (IB 30 pts)
Sheffield Hallam – 280 pts (Hspty Bus Mgt; Tour Mgt (Int))
Worcester – 280 pts (Mark Adv PR)
260 pts **Aberdeen** – BCC–CCC (Entre)
Birmingham City – 260–280 pts (Bus Adv) (IB 30–32 pts)
Bolton – 260 pts (Bus Mgt (Sply Chn Mgt))
Bournemouth Arts (UC) – BCC (Arts Evnt Mgt)
Coventry – 260–280 pts (Disas Mgt; Disas Reconstr Dev; Adv Bus; Adv Media)
Derby – 260–280 pts (Cntry Mgt)
Edinburgh Queen Margaret – 260 pts (PR Media)
Huddersfield – 260 pts (Air Trans Log Mgt; Trans Mgt)
Leeds Met – 260 pts (PR) (IB 26 pts)
Lincoln – 260 pts (Adv courses)
LJMU – 260 pts (Mgt Trans Log; Marit Bus Mgt)
Portsmouth – 260–300 pts (Bus Ent Sys)
Sheffield Hallam – 260 pts (PR)
Sunderland – 260 pts (Spo Mgt; Tour Mgt; Evnts Mgt; PR (Comb))
UCLan – 260–300 pts (PR)
Winchester – 260–300 pts (Arts Mgt Dr; Arts Mgt Choreo Dance)
240 pts **Arts London (CFash)** – 240 pts (Fash PR)
Bradford (Coll Univ Centre) – 240 pts (Adv Cmpn Mgt)
City – CCC 240 pts (Air Trans Ops) (IB 26 pts)
Edinburgh Napier – 240 pts (Comm Adv PR)
Leeds Met – 240 pts (Spo Evnt Mgt) (IB 24 pts)
Liverpool (LIPA) – 240 pts (Mus Thea Enter Mgt)
London Met – 240 pts (Adv Mark Comm; Arts Mgt Evnts Mgt; Arts Mgt Thea St; Arts Mgt joint courses)
London South Bank – 240 pts (Arts Mgt)
Northampton – 240–280 pts (Bus Entre) (IB 24 pts)
Plymouth – 240 pts (Cru Mgt)
Robert Gordon – CCC (Comm PR) (IB 26 pts)
Royal (CAg) – 240 pts (Int Eqn Agric Bus Mgt; Agric (Frm Mechn Mgt))
Sheffield Hallam – 240 pts (IT Mgt)
Southampton Solent – 240 pts (Evnts Mgt; Fd Mgt Prom)
Sparsholt (Coll) – 240–280 pts (Aquacult Fish Mgt)
UCLan – 240 pts (Adv) (IB 28 pts)
UCP Marjon – 240 pts (Int Spo Evnt Mgt)
Winchester – 240–280 pts (Arts Mgt) (IB 24 pts)
230 pts **CEM** – d/l 230 pts (Est Mgt)
Edinburgh Napier – 230 pts (Econ Mgt)
220 pts **Edge Hill** – 220–260 pts (PR)
Edinburgh Queen Margaret – 220 pts (PR Mark)
Falmouth (UC) – 220 pts (Crea Evnts Mgt)
Northampton – 220–260 pts (Adv courses)
Staffordshire – 220 pts (Adv Brnd Mgt)

Southampton Solent – 220–240 pts (Cru Ind Mgt)
Warwickshire (Coll) – 220 pts (Eqn Bus Mgt)
200 pts **Arts London (CFash)** – p/t 200 pts (Fash Bus)
Birmingham (UC) – 200 pts (Fd Media Comm Mgt)
Bishop Burton (Coll) – 200 pts (Eqn Bus Mgt)
Bucks New – 200–240 pts (Bus Adv Mgt; PR Mark Comm; Airln Mgt; Airpt Mgt)
Coventry – 200 pts (Bus Inf Tech) (IB 24 pts)
Middlesex – 200–280 pts (Adv PR Media)
Salford – 200 pts incl art C (Adv Des)
UCLan – 200 pts (Fire Sfty Risk Mgt)
UEL – 200 pts (Adv)
West London – 200 pts (Culn Art Mgt; Adv; PR)
180 pts **London Met** – 180 pts (Avn Aerosp Mgt)
West London – 180 pts (Airln Airpt Mgt)
160 pts **Bedfordshire** – 160–240 pts (PR; Adv Mark Comm)
Greenwich (Sch Mgt) – 160 pts (Bus Mgt (Trav Tour); Oil Gas Mgt)
Southampton Solent – 160 pts (Bus Inf Sys; Fash Mgt Mark)
Swansea Met – 160 pts (Int Trav Tour Mgt; Tour Mgt; Spo Mgt; Evnt Mgt)
UHI – CC–AA (Glf Mgt)
West Scotland – CC (Eng Mgt)
Wolverhampton – 160–220 pts (PR courses)
120 pts **Colchester (Inst)** – 120 pts (Constr Mgt (Site Mgt))
Swansea Met – 120–160 pts (Mtrspo Mgt)
80 pts **and below**
Arts London – 80 pts (PR)
CEM – d/l (Constr Mgt; Prop Mgt)
UHI – D–A (Mus Bus)

Open University – contact +44 (0)845 300 6090 **or** www.openuniversity.co.uk/you (Bus Law)

Alternative offers
See **Chapter 7** and **Appendix 1** for grades/UCAS Tariff points information for the International Baccalaureate, Scottish Highers/Advanced Highers, the Welsh Baccalaureate, the Irish Leaving Certificate, the Cambridge Pre-U Diploma, the Advanced Diploma and the Extended Project.

EXAMPLES OF FOUNDATION DEGREES IN THE SUBJECT FIELD
Askham Bryan (Coll); Bedfordshire; Bexley (Coll); Birmingham (UC); Blackburn (Coll); Blackpool and Fylde (Coll); Bolton; Bournemouth; Bradford; Brighton; Bristol City (Coll); Bristol UWE; Colchester (Inst); Cornwall (Coll); Croydon (Coll); De Montfort; Doncaster (Coll Univ Centre); Duchy (Coll); Durham New (Coll); Ealing, Hammersmith and West London (Coll); Edge Hill; Farnborough (CT); Glamorgan; Gloucestershire; Glyndŵr; Greenwich; Grimsby (IFHE); Harper Adams (UC); Hertfordshire; K (Coll); Kirklees (Coll); Knowsley (CmC); Lakes (Coll); Leeds Met; LJMU; London South Bank; Manchester (Coll); Mid-Cheshire (Coll); Middlesex; NEW (Coll); Newcastle (Coll); North Lindsey (Coll); Northampton; Northbrook (Coll); Nottingham New (Coll); Plymouth; Riverside Halton (Coll); Royal (CAg); St Helens (Coll); Sheffield (Coll); Sheffield Hallam; Somerset (CAT); South Devon (Coll); South Essex (Coll); Southampton Solent; Suffolk (Univ Campus); UCLan; UEL; Wakefield (Coll); Warwickshire (Coll); Westminster Kingsway (Coll); Writtle (Coll); York (Coll).

CHOOSING YOUR COURSE (SEE ALSO CH.1)
Some course features
De Montfort (Bus Mgt Ent) Course focuses on entrepreneurship and business practice, researching and developing new business opportunities and ideas, with an optional paid placement year.
Oxford Brookes (Bus Mgt) Course aimed at students not wanting to specialise in any particular area of business or are undecided. At the end of the first year, students can opt for one of the named Business degrees.
Southampton (Mgt Sci) Courses allow for specialisation in mathematical or non-mathematical aspects of management including accounting and finance, languages, entrepreneurship and music.

Check **Chapter 4** when choosing your university and **Chapter 7** on how to read the subject tables.

Winchester (Bus Mgt) Optional pathway to BA in Business Management with Public Service Management. Modules include quality management and customer care, local government, public administration and European culture and institutions.

Universities and colleges teaching quality See www.qaa.ac.uk; http://unistats.direct.gov.uk.

Top research universities and colleges (RAE 2008) (Business and Management Studies) Imperial London; Cambridge; Cardiff; Bath; London (King's); London LSE; Oxford; Lancaster; Warwick; Manchester; Strathclyde; Leeds; Nottingham; Aston; Loughborough; Sheffield.

Examples of sandwich degree courses Abertay Dundee; Aberystwyth; Aston; Bath; Birmingham (UC); Birmingham City; Bournemouth; Bradford; Brighton; Bristol UWE; Brunel; City; Coventry; De Montfort; Edinburgh Napier; Glamorgan; Glasgow Caledonian; Gloucestershire; Greenwich; Harper Adams (UC); Hertfordshire; Huddersfield; Hull; Kingston; Lancaster; Leeds Met; Lincoln; LJMU; London (QM); Loughborough; Manchester; Manchester Met; Middlesex; Newcastle; Northumbria; Nottingham Trent; Oxford Brookes; Plymouth; Portsmouth; Reading; Royal (CAg); Sheffield Hallam; Southampton Solent; Staffordshire; Surrey; Swansea Met; Teesside; UCLan; Ulster; Warwickshire (Coll); West Scotland; Westminster; Wolverhampton.

ADMISSIONS INFORMATION

Number of applicants per place (approx) Abertay Dundee (Bus St) 4; Aberystwyth 3; Anglia Ruskin 5; Aston (Bus Mgt) 12, (Int Bus) 6, (Mgt) 5, (Int Bus Econ) 8; Bangor 4; Bath (Bus Admin) 7, (Int Mgt Lang) 14; Birmingham 28; Birmingham (UC) 5; Blackpool and Fylde (Coll) 2; Bolton 3; Bournemouth (PR) 10; Bradford 12; Bristol 28; Brunel 12; Canterbury Christ Church 20; Cardiff 8; Colchester (Inst) 2; Edge Hill 4; Edinburgh Napier (Pub) 7; Glasgow Caledonian 18; Heriot-Watt 5; Hertfordshire 10; Huddersfield 5; Hull (Coll) 3; Kent 30; Kingston 50; Leeds 27; Leeds Trinity (UC) 3; Llandrillo Cymru (Coll) 2; London (King's) 25; London (RH) 9; London Met 10; London South Bank 4; Loughborough 5; Middlesex 12; Newcastle 27; Northumbria 10; Oxford Brookes 40; Plymouth 4; Portsmouth 10; Regents Bus Sch London 25; Robert Gordon 5; Southampton Solent 13; Strathclyde 12; Sunderland 20; Swansea Met 7; UCLan 15; Warwick 22; West London 4; West Scotland 5; Westminster 12; Winchester 4; Wolverhampton 7; York 6; York St John 3.

Advice to applicants and planning the UCAS personal statement There are many different kinds of businesses and any work experience is almost essential for these courses. This should be described in detail: for example, size of firm, turnover, managerial problems, sales and marketing aspects, customers' attitudes. Any special interests in business management should also be included, for example, personnel work, purchasing, marketing. Give details of travel or work experience abroad and, for international courses, language expertise and examples of leadership and organising skills. Reference can be made to any particular business topics you have studied in the *Financial Times*, *The Economist* and the business sections in the weekend press. Applicants need to be sociable, ambitious, team players. Say why you are interested in the course, identify your academic strengths, your personal strengths and interests. Check information on the websites of the Chartered Institute of Public Relations, the Chartered Institute of Marketing and the Chartered Institute of Personnel and Development. See also **Appendix 3** and **Accountancy/Accounting**.

Misconceptions about this course Loughborough (Pub Engl) That this is a course in Journalism: it is not!

Selection interviews Yes Birmingham City, Bradford, Coventry, Doncaster (Coll Univ Centre), Durham, Edge Hill, Euro Bus Sch London, Glamorgan, Glasgow Caledonian, Hull, Kent (mature and Access students), London Met, Middlesex, Northumbria, Nottingham Trent, Plymouth, Robert Gordon, Roehampton, Sheffield Hallam, Sir Gâr (Coll), Strathclyde, Swansea, Teesside, Trinity Saint David, West London, West Thames (Coll), York; **Some** Abertay Dundee, Aberystwyth, Anglia Ruskin, Bath, Bath Spa, Blackpool and Fylde (Coll), Brighton, Buckingham, Cardiff Met, Chichester, City, De Montfort, Derby (Int Bus), Greenwich, Kent, Leeds, Lincoln, LJMU, Manchester Met, Salford, Staffordshire, Stirling, Sunderland, UEA, Warwick, Winchester, Wolverhampton; **No** Birmingham.

Interview advice and questions See **Business and Management Courses**. **Loughborough** (Pub Engl) No tests at interview. We seek students with an interest in information issues within society.

Reasons for rejection (non-academic) See **Business and Management Courses**. **Bournemouth** The Business Studies course is very popular.

AFTER-RESULTS ADVICE

Offers to applicants repeating A-levels **Higher** Bradford, Bristol UWE, Brunel, Greenwich, Hertfordshire, Kingston, Lancaster, Liverpool, Manchester Met, Sheffield, Strathclyde, Teesside; **Same** Aberystwyth, Anglia Ruskin, Aston, Bath, Birmingham City, Bournemouth, Brighton, Buckingham, Cardiff, Cardiff Met, Chester, Chichester, De Montfort, Derby, Durham, Gloucestershire, Huddersfield, Hull, Kent, Leeds, Lincoln, Liverpool Hope, LJMU, Loughborough, Northumbria, Oxford Brookes, Robert Gordon, Roehampton, Royal (CAg), Salford, Sheffield Hallam, Staffordshire, Stirling, Suffolk (Univ Campus), Sunderland, Surrey, UEA, Ulster, West London, Winchester, Wolverhampton, Worcester, York, York St John.

GRADUATE DESTINATIONS AND EMPLOYMENT (2009/10 HESA)

See **Business and Management Courses**.

Career note See **Business and Management Courses**.

OTHER DEGREE SUBJECTS FOR CONSIDERATION

Accountancy; Banking; Business Information Technology; E-Business; Economics; Estate Management; Finance; Hospitality Management; Housing Management; Human Resource Management; Insurance; Leisure Management; Logistics; Marketing; Public Administration; Retail Management; Sports Management; Surveying.

CELTIC, IRISH, SCOTTISH AND WELSH STUDIES

(including **Cornish Studies** and **Gaelic Studies**)

Irish, Scottish, Gaelic, Welsh, Breton, Manx, Cornish, Gaulish and Celtiberian languages are all included in this subject area. Courses may also include the history and civilisation of the Celtic peoples.

Useful websites www.byig-wlb.org.uk; http://new.wales.gov.uk; www.bbc.co.uk/wales; www.daltai. com; www.eisteddfod.org.uk; www.digitalmedievalist.com; www.gaelic-scotland.co.uk.

NB The points totals shown to the left of the institutions are for ease of reference only. It must not be assumed that Tariff points are always used by institutions or that they can be substituted for an offer in grades. The level of an offer is not necessarily indicative of the quality of a course.

COURSE OFFERS INFORMATION

Subject requirements/preferences **GCSE** A foreign language or Welsh may be required. **AL** Welsh may be required for some courses.

Your target offers and examples of courses provided by each institution
380 pts **Cambridge** – A*AA (A-Sxn Nrs Celt) (IB 40–42 pts)
360 pts **Oxford** – AAA (Celt courses) (IB 38–40 pts)
           St Andrews – AAA (Geog Scot Hist) (IB 36 pts)
340 pts **Cardiff** – AAB incl maths (Maths Welsh) (IB 33 pts HL 6 maths)
           St Andrews – AAA–AAB 340–360 pts (Scot Hist courses) (IB 35–38 pts)
           Strathclyde – AAB (Scots Law LLB)
320 pts **Cardiff** – ABB (Welsh)
           Glasgow – ABB (Gael Joint Hons) (IB 36 pts)
           Liverpool – ABB (Ir St Joint Hons) (IB 33 pts)
           Ulster – ABB (Law Ir) (IB 26 pts)
300 pts **Aberdeen** – BBB (Celt Civ; Celt St; Gael St; Engl Scot Lit; Celt Civ Engl)
           Aberystwyth – 300 pts (Hist Welsh Hist) (IB 29 pts)
           Cardiff – BBB–BBC (Welsh Joint Hons)
           Edinburgh – AAA–BBB 300–360 pts (Engl Scot Lit) (IB 34–42 pts)

Check **Chapter 4** when choosing your university and **Chapter 7** on how to read the subject tables.

          Queen's Belfast – BBB/BBCb (Irish Celt St)
          Swansea – BBB (Welsh courses)
280 pts **Stirling** – BBC (Scot Hist) (IB 32 pts)
          Ulster – BBC (Mus Ir)
260 pts **Aberystwyth** – 260 pts (Welsh courses) (IB 24 pts)
          Cardiff Met – 260 pts (Educ St Welsh)
          Glamorgan – 260 pts (Welsh Educ)
          Ulster – BCC 260 pts (Irish Hist courses)
240 pts **Bangor** – also available in Welsh 240–260 pts (Welsh Hist)
          St Mary's Twickenham (UC) – 240 pts (Ir St) (IB 28 pts)
          Ulster – BCD (Ir courses)
220 pts **Ulster** – 220 pts (Dance Ir) (IB 24 pts)
200 pts **Glamorgan** – 200–240 pts (Welsh)
160 pts **UHI** – CC–AA (Scot Hist; Gael Dev; Scot Hist Arch; Scot Cult St; Gael Trad Mus; Gael Media St)
 80 pts **UHI** – CC–AA (Gael Lang Cult)

Alternative offers
See **Chapter 7** and **Appendix 1** for grades/UCAS Tariff points information for the International Baccalaureate, Scottish Highers/Advanced Highers, the Welsh Baccalaureate, the Irish Leaving Certificate, the Cambridge Pre-U Diploma, the Advanced Diploma and the Extended Project.

CHOOSING YOUR COURSE (SEE ALSO CH.1)
Some course features
Aberystwyth There are beginners' courses for those with no previous knowledge of Welsh or Celtic languages. (Welsh Celt Langs) One or more Celtic languages, together with Welsh, are studied, with a semester spent in Brittany or Ireland.
Bangor (Welsh Hist Arch) The course focuses on the development of Wales over the centuries, the changing nature of society and settlements, and the historical context of contemporary Wales.
Edinburgh In addition to studying the cultures of Ireland and Wales, Scottish Gaelic is offered on the course in Celtic Studies.
Queen's Belfast (Ir Celt) The course focuses on modern Irish language and literature and contemporary Irish culture and society, but also provides a study of Old and Middle Irish, Scottish Gaelic, Welsh and Cornish. Students spend at least six weeks in the Gaeltacht.
UHI The only degree in Scotland delivered entirely through Gaelic.

Universities and colleges teaching quality See www.qaa.ac.uk; http://unistats.direct.gov.uk.

Top research universities and colleges (RAE 2008) (Celtic studies) Cambridge; Ulster; Aberystwyth; Swansea; Cardiff; Glasgow; Bangor; Edinburgh.

ADMISSIONS INFORMATION
Number of applicants per place (approx) Aberystwyth 6; Bangor 8; Cambridge 2; Cardiff 2; Exeter 5; St Mary's Twickenham (UC) 3; Swansea 7.

Advice to applicants and planning the UCAS personal statement Interests in this field largely develop through literature, museum visits or archaeology which should be fully described in the UCAS application.

Selection interviews Yes Aberystwyth; **No** St Mary's Twickenham (UC).

Interview advice and questions Past questions have included: Why do you want to study this subject? What specific areas of Celtic culture interest you? What do you expect to gain by studying unusual subjects? See **Chapter 6**.

AFTER-RESULTS ADVICE
Offers to applicants repeating A-levels Higher Glasgow (AAA); **Same** Aberystwyth, Bangor, Cardiff, Swansea.

GRADUATE DESTINATIONS AND EMPLOYMENT (2009/10 HESA)

Celtic Studies; graduates surveyed 310 **Employed** 135 **In voluntary employment** 0 **In further study** 100 **Assumed unemployed** 10

Career note See **Combined Courses** and **Languages.**

OTHER DEGREE SUBJECTS FOR CONSIDERATION

Anthropology; Archaeology; History.

CHEMISTRY

(see also **Biochemistry, Engineering (Chemical), Pharmacy and Pharmaceutical Sciences**)

There is a shortage of applicants for this subject despite the fact that it is the basis of a wide range of careers in the manufacturing industries. These focus on such areas as pharmaceuticals, medicine, veterinary science and health, agriculture, petroleum, cosmetics, plastics, the food industry, colour chemistry and aspects of the environment such as pollution and recycling.

Useful websites www.rsc.org; www.chem.ox.ac.uk/vrchemistry.

NB The points totals shown to the left of the institutions are for ease of reference only. It must not be assumed that Tariff points are always used by institutions or that they can be substituted for an offer in grades. The level of an offer is not necessarily indicative of the quality of a course.

COURSE OFFERS INFORMATION

Subject requirements/preferences GCSE English, mathematics/science subjects usually required. A/B grades often stipulated by popular universities. **AL** Two science subjects including chemistry required.

Your target offers and examples of courses provided by each institution

380 pts **Bristol** – A*AA–ABB (Chem) (IB 38–35 pts HL 665)
Cambridge – A*AA (Nat Sci (Chem)) (IB 40–42 pts HL 766–777)
Durham – A*AA (Chem) (38 pts)
London (King's) – AABc (Chem Biomed) (IB 36 pts HL 6 chem maths)
Oxford – A*AA (Chem) (IB 38–40 pts)
360 pts **Edinburgh** – AAA–ABB incl chem maths (Medcnl Biol Chem) (IB 37–32 pts HL 5 chem)
Imperial London – AAA (Chem Mol Phys) (IB 38 pts HL 7 chem 6 maths)
London (UCL) – AAA–AAB incl maths+chem+phys (Cheml Phys) (IB 34–36 pts HL 6 maths phys)
St Andrews – AAA–AAB incl chem (Chem courses) (IB 35–38 pts)
Southampton – AAA–ABB 360–320 pts (Chem Medcnl Sci) (IB 34 pts HL 18 pts)
York – AAA–ABB 320–360 pts (Chem Res Env) (IB 32–34 pts)
340 pts **Bath** – AaB (Chem Educ) (IB 34–36 pts HL 6 chem)
Cardiff – AAB–ABB (Chem MChem)
Edinburgh – AAA–ABB 340–360 pts (Cheml Phys) (IB 37–32 pts)
Leicester – AAB–BBB (Chem)
Nottingham – AAB–ABB 320–340 pts (Chem) (IB 36–34 pts)
St Andrews – AAB (Chem Medcnl Chem) (IB 35 pts)
Sheffield – AAB incl chem (Chem (Yr Abrd)) (IB 35 pts)
Surrey – AAB (Chem) (IB 35 pts)
Sussex – AAB–ABB (Chem) (IB 34–36 pts)
UEA – AAB incl chem (Foren Invest Chem MChem) (IB 33 pts HL 6 chem)
Warwick – AAB (Chem Medcnl Chem) (IB 36 pts)
320 pts **Aberdeen** – ABB–BBB (Chem; Biomed Mat Chem; Chem Off Ind; Env Chem; Medcnl Chem)
Birmingham – ABB–BBB 300–320 pts (Chem Pharmacol)
Cardiff – ABB–BBB (Chem BSc)

Studying Chemistry?
Join RSC ChemNet today

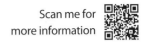

Latest chemistry news, information and support

RSC ChemNet membership offers a wide range of services and support for chemistry students

Join RSC ChemNet, the Royal Society of Chemistry network for 16-18 year olds studying chemistry, and benefit from online access to the latest advances in chemistry and the support of the RSC community. Members also have the opportunity to explore chemistry in the real world by attending local and national RSC ChemNet events.

- **e-magazines**
  Access *Chemistry World* and *The Mole* online, for cutting-edge research, news analysis, and webinars

- **Online resources**
  Ask experts about tricky topics, view tutorials and see other students' FAQs on ChemNet ReAct

- **Visits to universities and industry**
  Experience what life is like as a student and see where chemistry can lead in the future

- **Online Chemistry Network**
  Join discussion groups, explore blogs and connect with other RSC ChemNet members

- **Specialist university information**
  Attend 'Meet the Universities' event and take part online to get assistance with making university choices

- **Careers advice**
  Access advice on scientific careers through the RSC's online careers fair, ChemCareers

www.rsc.org/chemnet

Edinburgh – AAA–ABB incl chem maths 320–360 pts (Chem Mat Chem) (IB 37–32 pts)
Glasgow – ABB (Chem Medcnl Chem) (IB 32 pts)
Leeds – ABB (Chem courses) (IB 32 pts)
Liverpool – ABB (Chem) (IB 33 pts HL 6 chem 5 sci)
Manchester – ABB (Chem Medcnl Chem) (IB 33 pts)
Newcastle – ABB–BBB 300–320 pts (Chem BSc) (IB 32 pts HL 6 chem)
Nottingham – ABB–BBB 300–320 pts (Bioch Biol Chem) (IB 32–30 pts)
Reading – ABB–BBB (Chem courses MChem)
Sheffield – ABB (Chem) (IB 33 pts)
UEA – ABB incl chem (Chem) (IB 32 pts)
Warwick – AAB (Biomed Chem) (IB 36 pts)

300 pts **Aston** – BBB–ABB 300–320 pts (Chem courses)
Birmingham – ABB–BBB 300–320 pts (Chem Modn Lang)
Bradford – 300 pts (Chem) (IB 28 pts)
Bristol UWE – 300 pts (Foren Chem) (IB 27 pts)
Dundee – BBB (Biol Chem Drug Dscvry) (IB 30 pts)
Heriot-Watt – BBB 300 pts (Chem Mat)
Kent – BBB (Foren Chem) (IB 33 pts)
Leicester – BBB (Chem Foren Sci)
London (QM) – 300 pts incl chem (Chem) (IB 32 pts HL 5 chem)
Loughborough – 300–320 pts (Chem MChem) (IB 32–34 pts)
Northumbria – 300 pts (App Chem) (IB 26 pts)
Plymouth – 300–280 pts (Analyt Chem) (IB 28 pts)
UEA – BBB incl chem (Env Chem) (IB 31 pts)

280 pts **Brighton** – BBC 280 pts (Pharml Cheml Sci) (IB 30 pts)
Hull – 280–300 pts (Chem)
Keele – 280–300 pts (Chem) (IB 26–28 pts)
London (QM) – 280 pts (Pharml Chem) (IB 28 pts)
Manchester Met – 280 pts (Medcnl Biol Chem) (IB 27 pts)
Northumbria – 280 pts (Pharml Chem) (IB 25 pts)
Nottingham Trent – 280 pts (Chem MChem)
Queen's Belfast – BBC/BCCb (Chem; Medcnl Chem; Chem Foren Analys; Chem Euro)
Strathclyde – BBC (Foren Chem) (IB 28 pts)
Teesside – 280 pts (Chem)
UCLan – 280 pts (Foren Chem)

260 pts **Greenwich** – 260 pts (Chem)
LJMU – 260 pts (App Cheml Pharml Sci) (IB 25 pts)
Nottingham Trent – 260 pts (Chem BSc)
Reading – 260–300 pts (Chem BSc; Chem Arch; Chem Educ)
Sheffield Hallam – 260 pts (Chem)
UCLan – 260 pts (Chem)

240 pts **Bangor** – 240–300 pts (Chem; Chem Biomol Sci; Mar Chem)
Huddersfield – 240 pts (Chem courses)
Hull – 240–300 pts (Chem Bus)
London Met – 240 pts (Chem)
West Scotland – CCC (Chem)

220 pts **Glamorgan** – 220–260 pts (Foren Chem)
200 pts **Kingston** – 200–280 pts (Chem; App Chem)
80 pts **London (Birk)** – p/t for under 21s (over 21s varies) (Chem)

Open University – contact +44 (0)845 300 6090 **or** www.openuniversity.co.uk/you (Nat Sci)

Alternative offers

See **Chapter 7** and **Appendix 1** for grades/UCAS Tariff points information for the International Baccalaureate, Scottish Highers/Advanced Highers, the Welsh Baccalaureate, the Irish Leaving Certificate, the Cambridge Pre-U Diploma, the Advanced Diploma and the Extended Project.

EXAMPLES OF FOUNDATION DEGREES IN THE SUBJECT FIELD
London Met.

CHOOSING YOUR COURSE (SEE ALSO CH.1)
Some course features
Birmingham Single Honours or major/minor courses which link chemistry with business, environmental science, pharmacology or psychology.
Durham Chemistry is offered as a Single or Joint Honours course or as part of the Natural Sciences programme.
Leeds Industrial bursary scheme for students.
London (UCL) MSc and BSc courses are common in the first two years after which a choice can be made. MSc courses provide greater depth and are aimed at those wishing to follow a scientific career.
Loughborough Strong links with industry for sandwich courses.
Manchester A range of course options including placements in industry, Europe and North America.
Warwick MSc and BSc courses are common in the first two years after which a choice can be made. MSc courses provide greater depth and are aimed at those wishing to follow a scientific career.
York Sponsorships and sandwich courses available.

Universities and colleges teaching quality See www.qaa.ac.uk; http://unistats.direct.gov.uk.

Top research universities and colleges (RAE 2008) Cambridge; Nottingham; Oxford; Edinburgh; St Andrews; Bristol; Imperial London; Leeds; Warwick; York; Liverpool; Manchester; Sheffield.

Examples of sandwich degree courses Aston; Bangor; Bath; Cardiff; Dundee; Glamorgan; Kingston; LJMU; Loughborough; Manchester; Manchester Met; Northumbria; Nottingham Trent; Queen's Belfast; St Andrews; Surrey; Teesside; West Scotland; York.

ADMISSIONS INFORMATION
Number of applicants per place (approx) Bangor (Mar Chem) 3, (Chem) 6; Bath 7; Bradford (Chem Pharml Foren Sci) 10; Bristol 5; Durham 6; Edinburgh 5; Heriot-Watt 6; Hull 7; Imperial London 3; Kingston 4; Leeds 3; Leicester 9; London (QM) 3; London (UCL) 5; Newcastle 5; Nottingham (Chem Mol Phys) 4, (Chem) 8; Oxford (success rate 63%); Southampton 7; Surrey 3; York 5.

Advice to applicants and planning the UCAS personal statement Extend your knowledge beyond your exam studies by reading scientific journals and keeping abreast of scientific developments in the news. Discuss any visits to chemical firms and laboratories, for example, pharmaceutical, food science, rubber and plastic, paper, photographic, environmental health. **Bristol** Deferred entry accepted.

Misconceptions about this course Many students do not fully appreciate the strengths of a Chemistry degree for any career despite the fact that graduates regularly go into a diverse range of careers. **Durham** Students fail to realise that they require mathematics and that physics is useful.

Selection interviews Yes Bangor, Bath, Bristol, Cambridge, Coventry, Durham, Greenwich, Huddersfield, Hull, Imperial London, Keele (mature students only), Kingston, London (UCL), London Met, Loughborough, Newcastle, Northumbria, Nottingham, Nottingham Trent, Oxford (success rate 39%), Reading, Sheffield, Surrey, Warwick, York; **Some** Aston, Cardiff, Dundee, LJMU, Plymouth, UEA; **No** Bristol UWE, Southampton.

Interview advice and questions Be prepared for questions on your chemistry syllabus and aspects that you enjoy the most. In the past a variety of questions have been asked, for example: Why is carbon a special element? Discuss the nature of forces between atoms with varying intermolecular distances. Describe recent practicals. What is acid rain? What other types of pollution are caused by the human race? What is an enzyme? What are the general properties of benzene? Why might sciences be less popular among girls at school? What can a mass spectrometer be used for? What would you do if a river turned bright blue and you were asked how to test a sample? What would be the difference between metal and non-metal pollution? See also **Chapter 6**. **Bath** Why Chemistry?

What gives you your edge?

"Finding out what I'm made of"

BSc/MChem programmes in:

- Chemistry
- Chemistry with Forensic Investigation
- Medicinal Chemistry

For more information please visit
www.surrey.ac.uk/heapchem
or scan the QR code.

University of Surrey
Guildford
Surrey
GU2 7XH
UK

T: 0800 980 3200 / +44 (0)1483 681 681
E: ug-enquiries@surrey.ac.uk

What will you discover?

At the University of Surrey, we've got just the right chemistry of world-leading, world-changing research and exciting teaching programmes.

You could learn from the experts in our state-of-the-art teaching laboratories, with facilities including a new inductively coupled plasma mass spectrometer (ICP-MS) and Nuclear Magnetic Resonance (NMR) spectrometer.

Many students take our four-year MChem programme, with its strong emphasis on modern, practical chemistry allied to core theory and a salaried Professional Training Placement during your third year.

If you prefer, we also offer a traditional BSc (Honours) degree. This programme gives you a thorough grounding in chemistry, together with training in communication skills, teamwork and leadership abilities.

To hear why our students love Surrey's Chemistry, scan the QR code or visit **www.surrey.ac.uk/heap13** for a video.

Discuss the practical work you are doing. **Oxford** No written or work tests. Evidence required of motivation and further potential and a capacity to analyse and use information to form opinions and a willingness to discuss them. **York** Discuss your favourite areas of chemistry, some of your extra-curricular activities, your preferred learning styles – for example, small tutorials of four or fewer, lectures.

Reasons for rejection (non-academic) Didn't attend interview. Rude and unco-operative. Arrived under influence of drink. Poor attitude and poor commitment to chemistry. Incomplete, inappropriate, illegible, illiterate personal statements. **Southampton** Applicants called for interview are not normally rejected.

AFTER-RESULTS ADVICE
Offers to applicants repeating A-levels Higher Bangor, Dundee, Hull, Leeds, Northumbria, Nottingham, St Andrews, Warwick; **Possibly higher** Coventry, Edinburgh, Newcastle; **Same** Aston, Bath, Bristol (no offer if first-time grades are low), Cardiff, Durham, Greenwich, Heriot-Watt, Huddersfield, Keele, Kingston, LJMU, London (UCL), London Met, Loughborough, Plymouth, Sheffield, Surrey, UEA; **No** Cambridge.

GRADUATE DESTINATIONS AND EMPLOYMENT (2009/10 HESA)
Graduates surveyed 4015 **Employed** 1400 **In voluntary employment** 20 **In further study** 1125 **Assumed unemployed** 275

Career note A large number of chemistry graduates choose to go on to further study as well as into scientific careers in research, analysis or development. Significant numbers also follow careers in a wide range of areas in management, teaching and retail work.

OTHER DEGREE SUBJECTS FOR CONSIDERATION
Agriculture; Biochemistry; Biological Sciences; Biomedical Science; Chemical Engineering; Environmental Science; Forensic Science; Genetics; Materials Science; Medicine; Microbiology; Oceanography; Pharmacology; Pharmacy.

CHINESE

(including **Korean**; see also **Asia-Pacific Studies, Languages**)

Oriental languages are not necessarily difficult languages but they differ considerably in their writing systems which present their own problems for the new student. Even so, Chinese is not a language to be chosen for its novelty and students should have a strong interest in China and its people.

Useful websites www.cilt.org.uk; www.iol.org.uk; www.bbc.co.uk/languages; www.china.org.cn/english; www.languageadvantage.com; www.languagematters.co.uk; www.reed.co.uk/multilingual; www.chineseculture.about.com.

NB The points totals shown to the left of the institutions are for ease of reference only. It must not be assumed that Tariff points are always used by institutions or that they can be substituted for an offer in grades. The level of an offer is not necessarily indicative of the quality of a course.

COURSE OFFERS INFORMATION
Subject requirements/preferences GCSE A language is required. **AL** A modern language is usually required.

Your target offers and examples of courses provided by each institution
380 pts **Cambridge** – A*AA (As Mid E St (Chin St)) (IB 40–42 pts HL 776–777)
        Nottingham – A*AA–AAA 360–380 pts (Econ Chin St) (IB 38–36 pts)
360 pts **Manchester** – AAA (Russ Chin MML) (IB 37 pts)
        Oxford – AAA (Chin) (IB 38–42 pts)
340 pts **Durham** – AAB (Chin St) (IB 36 pts)

London (SOAS) – AAB (Kor Joint Hons) (IB 36 pts HL 666)
Manchester – AAB–BBB 300–340 pts (Chin courses) (IB 31–36 pts)
Nottingham – AAB (Span Contemp Chin St) (IB 34 pts)

320 pts Leeds – ABB (Chin Joint Hons) (IB 34 pts)
Newcastle – AAB–ABB 320–340 pts (Ling Chin/Jap) (IB 32 pts HL 5 Engl)
Nottingham – ABB (Glob Is Contemp Chin St) (IB 32 pts)
Salford – ABB–BBB 320–300 pts (Law Chin)
Sheffield – ABB (Chin St courses) (IB 33 pts)

300 pts Edinburgh – AAA–BBB 300–360 pts (Econ Chin) (IB 34 pts HL 555)
Manchester – AAB–BBB 300–340 pts (Russ Chin BA) (IB 31–36 pts)

280 pts Edge Hill – 280 pts (Engl Chin St) (IB 24 pts)
Westminster – BBC–CCC (Chin Engl Lang)

260 pts Bolton – 260 pts (Bus Mgt Lang)
Nottingham Trent – 260 pts (Chin (Mand) Joint Hons) (IB 24 pts)
UCLan – 260–300 pts (Chin courses) (IB 28 pts)
Westminster – BCC (Chin courses)

240 pts Middlesex – 240–280 pts (Trad Chin Acu)
Trinity Saint David – 240 pts (Chin St courses)

Alternative offers
See **Chapter 7** and **Appendix 1** for grades/UCAS Tariff points information for the International Baccalaureate, Scottish Highers/Advanced Highers, the Welsh Baccalaureate, the Irish Leaving Certificate, the Cambridge Pre-U Diploma, the Advanced Diploma and the Extended Project.

CHOOSING YOUR COURSE (SEE ALSO CH.1)

Some course features
Edinburgh (Chin) This is an intensive language course in Mandarin Chinese and Modern Standard (colloquial) Chinese. Year 3 is spent in China.
Leeds (Chin Int Rel) Year 2 spent in China taking language courses at a university in Beijing, Tianjin or Taipei. Students expected to reach a high standard of language ability.
London (SOAS) (Chin (Modn Class)) Course designed to give broad understanding of Chinese culture, past and present, through its language, history and literature. In Years 3 and 4 students can choose to specialise in either modern or classical China.
Manchester (Chin St) Course covers both language (Mandarin) and culture, society, economics, politics and international relations.
Newcastle (Chin/Jap Cult St) Course provides language tuition in either language.
Sheffield (Mus Chin St) Dual Honours course allows students to design their own Music programme, specialising in composition, dissertation or performance. Chinese Studies involves intensive language learning (from scratch or with some prior knowledge). Year 2 at Nanjing University, and modules in Chinese business, literature, history and the environment.
Trinity Saint David (Chin St) A broad course covering the language, culture, politics, economics, philosophy and religions of China. There is the opportunity to study in China.

Universities and colleges teaching quality See www.qaa.ac.uk; http://unistats.direct.gov.uk.

Top research universities and colleges (RAE 2008) (Asian Studies) London (SOAS); Oxford; Cambridge; Leeds; Manchester; Nottingham; Westminster.

Examples of sandwich degree courses Westminster.

ADMISSIONS INFORMATION

Number of applicants per place (approx) Leeds 5; London (SOAS) 8; Westminster 18.

Advice to applicants and planning the UCAS personal statement It will be necessary to demonstrate a knowledge of China, its culture, political and economic background. Visits to the Far East should be mentioned, with reference to any features which have influenced your choice of degree course.

Selection interviews Yes Cambridge, Leeds, London (SOAS), Oxford.

Interview advice and questions You will be expected to convince the admissions tutor why you want to study the language. Your knowledge of Chinese culture, politics and society in general, and of Far Eastern problems, could also be tested. See also **Chapter 6**.

Reasons for rejection (non-academic) Oxford His language background seemed a little weak and his written work not as strong as that of other applicants. At interview he showed himself to be a dedicated hard-working young man but lacking in the imagination, flexibility and the intellectual liveliness needed to succeed on the course.

AFTER-RESULTS ADVICE
Offers to applicants repeating A-levels Higher Leeds; **No** Cambridge.

GRADUATE DESTINATIONS AND EMPLOYMENT (2009/10 HESA)
Graduates surveyed 210 **Employed** 70 **In voluntary employment** 5 **In further study** 40 **Assumed unemployed** 15

Career note China is a country with a high economic growth rate and there are good opportunities for graduates, an increasing number being recruited by firms based in East Asia. Other opportunities exist in diplomacy, aid work and tourism throughout China, Taiwan and Mongolia as well as most non-scientific career areas in the UK. See also **Languages**.

OTHER DEGREE SUBJECTS FOR CONSIDERATION
Traditional Chinese Medicine; other Oriental languages.

CLASSICAL STUDIES/CLASSICAL CIVILISATION
(see also **Archaeology, Classics, Greek, History (Ancient), Latin**)

Classical Studies and Classical Civilisation courses cover the literature, history, philosophy and archaeology of Ancient Greece and Rome. A knowledge of Latin or Greek is not necessary for many courses, but check subject requirements carefully.

Useful websites www.britishmuseum.org; see also **History** and **History (Ancient)**.

NB The points totals shown to the left of the institutions are for ease of reference only. It must not be assumed that Tariff points are always used by institutions or that they can be substituted for an offer in grades. The level of an offer is not necessarily indicative of the quality of a course.

COURSE OFFERS INFORMATION
Subject requirements/preferences GCSE English and a foreign language often required. **AL** A modern language is required for joint language courses. Relevant subjects include classical civilisation, English literature, archaeology, Latin, Greek.

Your target offers and examples of courses provided by each institution
410 pts **London (King's)** – AAAb (Class St Engl) (IB 38 pts HL 666)
360 pts **Bristol** – AAA–AAB (Engl Class St) (IB 37–35 pts)
       Exeter – AAA–AAB (Class St) (IB 36 pts)
       Warwick – AABc (Class Civ) (IB 36 pts)
340 pts **Bristol** – AAB (Class St) (IB 35 pts HL 666)
       Exeter – AAB–ABB (Class St Modn Lang) (IB 34–32 pts)
       Kent – AAB–ABB (Class Arch St) (IB 33 pts)
       Leeds – AAB–ABB (Class Civ; Rom Civ Russ Civ; Gk Civ courses)
       Nottingham – AAB (Class Civ Phil) (IB 34 pts)
       St Andrews – AAB (Art Hist Class St) (IB 35 pts)
       Warwick – AAB (Class Civ (St Euro)) (IB 36 pts)

320 pts **Birmingham** – ABB 320 pts (Class Lit Civ) (IB 34 pts)
Liverpool – ABB (Class St Modn Lang) (IB 33 pts)
London (RH) – ABB (Class St Ital) (IB 34 pts)
London (UCL) – ABB (Class Arch Class Civ) (IB 34 pts)
Manchester – ABB–BBB 300–320 pts (Class St) (IB 34–31 pts)
Newcastle – AAB–ABB 320–340 pts (Class St) (IB 32 pts)
Nottingham – ABB–AAC (Arch Class Civ) (IB 32 pts)
Reading – 320–340 pts (Class St) (IB 30 pts)
Sheffield – ABB–BBC (Class Hist Arch) (IB 33–30 pts)
Swansea – ABB (Class Civ; Class Civ Lat)
300 pts **Edinburgh** – AAA–BBB 300–360 pts (Class St) (IB 34–42 pts)
Reading – 300–340 pts (Class Mediev St) (IB 30 pts)
Roehampton – 300 pts (Class Civ)
180 pts **Trinity Saint David** – 180–240 pts (Class St courses)
80 pts **London (Birk)** – p/t for under 21s (over 21s varies) (Class St)

Alternative offers
See **Chapter 7** and **Appendix 1** for grades/UCAS Tariff points information for the International Baccalaureate, Scottish Highers/Advanced Highers, the Welsh Baccalaureate, the Irish Leaving Certificate, the Cambridge Pre-U Diploma, the Advanced Diploma and the Extended Project.

CHOOSING YOUR COURSE (SEE ALSO CH.1)

Some course features
Birmingham (Class Lit Civ) Broad course covering literature, history, drama, politics, philosophy, art, religion and science.
Durham Three courses (Classical Past, Ancient History and Classics) have a common first year.
London (King's) (Class St) One language option module (Greek or Latin) to be taken in Year 1.
London (RH) (Class St) Option courses in Year 1 include Greek law, Roman Egypt, the built environment and women in classical antiquity.
Manchester (Class St) Greek or Latin options available including beginners' courses.

Universities and colleges teaching quality See www.qaa.ac.uk; http://unistats.direct.gov.uk.

Top research universities and colleges (RAE 2008) See **Classics**.

ADMISSIONS INFORMATION

Number of applicants per place (approx) Birmingham 3; Bristol 9; Durham (Class Past) 10; Exeter 3; Leeds 7; London (RH) 4; Manchester (Class St) 4; Newcastle 8; Nottingham 6; Reading 10; Swansea 5; Trinity Saint David 2; Warwick 23.

Advice to applicants and planning the UCAS personal statement Discuss any A-level work and what has attracted you to this subject. Describe visits to classical sites or museums and what impressed you.

Misconceptions about this course Birmingham (Class Lit Civ) A study of classics at school is not necessary although while many people catch the classics bug by doing classical civilisation at A-level, others come to classics through reading the myths or seeing the plays and being fascinated by them. For others the inter-disciplinary nature of the subject attracts them – literature, drama, history, politics and philosophy. **Exeter** (Class St) This is not a language degree. There is no requirement for either A-level Latin or Greek.

Selection interviews Yes Durham, Kent, London (RH), Newcastle, Nottingham, Trinity Saint David; **Some** Bristol, Warwick; **No** Birmingham.

Interview advice and questions In the past questions have included: What special interests do you have in Classical Studies/Classics? Have you visited Greece, Rome or any other classical sites or museums and what were your impressions? These are the types of questions to expect, along with those to explore your knowledge of the culture, theatre and architecture of the period. See also **Chapter 6**. **Birmingham** (Class Lit Civ) The programme includes some language study and, if applicants do not have a GCSE in a foreign language, we ask them to do a short language aptitude test. Interview questions are likely to focus on your reading interests (not necessarily classical texts!) and your own reflections on them. We are interested in your ability to think for yourself and we want to be sure that you are someone who will enjoy three years of reading and talking about books. **Swansea** Reasons for choosing the subject and how the student hopes to benefit from the course.

Reasons for rejection (non-academic) Birmingham Lukewarm interest in the subject. Lack of clear idea why they wanted to do this degree.

AFTER-RESULTS ADVICE
Offers to applicants repeating A-levels Higher Nottingham, St Andrews, Warwick; **Same** Birmingham, Bristol, Durham, Exeter, Leeds, London (RH), Newcastle.

GRADUATE DESTINATIONS AND EMPLOYMENT (2009/10 HESA)
Classical Studies; graduates surveyed 1185 **Employed** 395 **In voluntary employment** 45 **In further study** 345 **Assumed unemployed** 90

Career note As with other non-vocational subjects, graduates enter a wide range of careers. In a small number of cases this may be subject-related with work in museums and art galleries. However, much will depend on how the student's interests develop during the undergraduate years and career planning should start early.

OTHER DEGREE SUBJECTS FOR CONSIDERATION
Archaeology; Ancient History; Classics; Greek; History; History of Art; Latin; Philosophy.

CLASSICS
(see also Classical Studies/Classical Civilisation, Greek, Latin)

Classics courses focus on a study of Greek and Latin but may also include topics related to ancient history, art and architecture, drama and philosophy. These subjects are also frequently offered in joint courses.

Useful websites www.classicspage.com; www.classics.ac.uk; www.cambridgescp.com; www.bbc.co.uk/history/ancient/greeks; www.bbc.co.uk/history/ancient/romans.

NB The points totals shown to the left of the institutions are for ease of reference only. It must not be assumed that Tariff points are always used by institutions or that they can be substituted for an offer in grades. The level of an offer is not necessarily indicative of the quality of a course.

COURSE OFFERS INFORMATION
Subject requirements/preferences GCSE English and a foreign language usually required. Grades A*/A/B may be stipulated. **AL** Check courses for Latin/Greek requirements.

Your target offers and examples of courses provided by each institution
410 pts **London (King's)** – AAAb (Class) (IB 38 pts HL 666)
380 pts **Cambridge** – A*AA (Educ Class) (IB 40–42 pts)
360 pts **Bristol** – AAA–AAB (Class) (IB 37–35 pts)
Durham – AAA (Class Past) (IB 37 pts)
Edinburgh – AAA–BBB (Class Ling) (IB 42–34 pts)
Exeter – AAA–AAB (Classics) (IB 36–34 pts HL 6 Lat/Gk)
London (UCL) – AABe (Class) (IB 34 pts)
Oxford – AAA (Class Modn Langs) (IB 38–40 pts)
Warwick – AABc (Class) (IB 36 pts)
340 pts **Leeds** – ABB–BBB 340–300 pts (Class Lit courses)
London (UCL) – AAB (Class (Yr Abrd)) (IB 34 pts)

Nottingham – AAB (Class) (IB 34 pts)
St Andrews – AAB (Class Lat) (IB 35 pts)
320 pts Birmingham – ABB 320 pts (Class Lit Civ) (IB 34 pts)
Leeds – ABB (Class)
Liverpool – ABB (Class) (IB 33 pts)
London (RH) – ABB (Class) (IB 34 pts)
Manchester – ABB–BBB 300–320 pts (Class Anc Hist) (IB 34–31 pts)
Newcastle – AAB–ABB 320–340 pts (Class) (IB 32 pts)
Reading – 320–340 pts (Classics) (IB 32–34 pts)
Swansea – ABB (Class)
300 pts Edinburgh – AAA–BBB 300–360 pts (Class Engl Lang) (IB 34–42 pts)
200 pts Trinity Saint David – 200 pts (Class)
80 pts London (Birk) – p/t for under 21s (over 21s varies) (Class)

Alternative offers
See **Chapter 7** and **Appendix 1** for grades/UCAS Tariff points information for the International Baccalaureate, Scottish Highers/Advanced Highers, the Welsh Baccalaureate, the Irish Leaving Certificate, the Cambridge Pre-U Diploma, the Advanced Diploma and the Extended Project.

CHOOSING YOUR COURSE (SEE ALSO CH.1)
Some course features
Bristol (Class) Greek and Latin languages are studied for the first two years plus option topics from literature, art, philosophy, political, social and cultural history.
Cambridge (Class Gk Lat) Latin or Greek A-levels not required for the four-year course.
Liverpool (Class) 50% of the course consists of language study (Greek or Latin) including beginners' level. The remainder is a study of literature, art, history and archaeology.
Newcastle (Class) A concentration on the study of Greek and Latin languages and literature.
Oxford Course II (Latin or Greek) requires no formal qualifications.
St Andrews (Class) A wide range of related subjects is offered as part of the Single Honours course and a wide choice of complementary courses from other departments.

Universities and colleges teaching quality See www.qaa.ac.uk; http://unistats.direct.gov.uk.

Top research universities and colleges (RAE 2008) (Including Classics, Ancient History, Byzantine and Modern Greek Studies) Cambridge; Oxford; London (UCL); London (King's); Durham; Warwick; Exeter; Manchester; Bristol; St Andrews.

ADMISSIONS INFORMATION
Number of applicants per place (approx) Bristol 14; Cambridge 2; Durham (Class) 8, (Class Past) 10; Leeds 4; London (King's) 6; London (RH) 6; Manchester (Class) 10, (Class Anc Hist) 8; Newcastle 14; Nottingham 6; Oxford 2; Swansea 6; Trinity Saint David 5.

Advice to applicants and planning the UCAS personal statement Describe any visits made to classical sites or museums, or literature which you have read and enjoyed. Discuss any significant aspects which impressed you. Classics is an interdisciplinary subject and universities are looking for people who are versatile, imaginative and independently minded, so all types of extra-curricular activities (drama, music, philosophy, creative arts, politics, other languages and cultures) will be relevant. See also **Classical Studies/Classical Civilisation**.

Misconceptions about this course While Classics can appear irrelevant and élitist, universities aim to assist students to leave with a range of transferable skills that are of importance to employers.

Selection interviews **Yes** Bristol (Mature Students), Cambridge, London (RH), London (UCL), Newcastle, Oxford (Class) 45%, (Class Eng) 20%, (Class Mod Lang) 33%, Swansea; **Some** Warwick; **No** Dundee, Durham, Leeds, Nottingham, Reading, St Andrews.

Interview advice and questions What do you think it means to study Classics? Do you think Classics is still a vital and central cultural discipline? What made you apply to study Classics at this university?

Check **Chapter 4** when choosing your university and **Chapter 7** on how to read the subject tables.

There are often detailed questions on the texts which the students have read, to find out how reflective they are in their reading. See also **Classical Studies/Classical Civilisation** and **Chapter 6**. **Cambridge** What would happen if the Classics department burned down? Do you think feminism is dead? Emma has become a different person since she took up yoga. Therefore she is not responsible for anything she did before she took up yoga. Discuss. **Oxford** Written tests to demonstrate ability in linguistics, competence in translation. Use of dictionaries not permitted. Classics and English applicants take the English Admissions Test.

Reasons for rejection (non-academic) Did not demonstrate a clear sense of why they wanted to study Classics rather than anything else.

AFTER-RESULTS ADVICE
Offers to applicants repeating A-levels Higher Leeds, Nottingham, St Andrews; **Same** Cambridge, Durham, Newcastle, Swansea.

GRADUATE DESTINATIONS AND EMPLOYMENT (2009/10 HESA)
See **Classical Studies/Classical Civilisation**.

Career note See **Classical Studies/Classical Civilisation**.

OTHER DEGREE SUBJECTS FOR CONSIDERATION
See **Classical Studies/Classical Civilisation**.

COMBINED COURSES

Many different subjects are offered in combined or modular arrangements. These courses are particularly useful for those applicants who have difficulty in deciding on one specialist subject to follow, allowing students to mix and match according to their interests and often enabling them to embark on new subjects.

Useful websites www.artscouncil.org.uk; www.scottisharts.org.uk; www.arts.org.uk; www.artsprofessional.co.uk; www.culturalstudies.net.

NB The points totals shown to the left of the institutions are for ease of reference only. It must not be assumed that Tariff points are always used by institutions or that they can be substituted for an offer in grades. The level of an offer is not necessarily indicative of the quality of a course.

COURSE OFFERS INFORMATION
Subject requirements/preferences GCSE English, mathematics or science and foreign language may be required by some universities. **AL** Some joint courses may require a specified subject.

Your target offers and examples of courses provided by each institution
430 pts **London (King's)** – A*AAb (Librl Arts) (IB 39 HL 666)
380 pts **Durham** – offers listed are average offers; specific offers will vary depending on the popularity of the subjects in combination A*AA (Comb Soc Sci) (IB 38 pts)
　　　　Exeter – A*AA–AAB (Flex Comb Hons) (IB 38–34 pts)
360 pts **Edinburgh** – AAA–BBB 300–360 pts (Span) (IB 34–42 pts)
　　　　Lancaster – AAA 360 pts (Nat Sci) (IB 36 pts)
　　　　Liverpool – AAA (Law Joint Hons) (IB 36 pts)
　　　　London (UCL) – AAA (Arts Sci) (IB 38 pts)
　　　　St Andrews – AAA–BBB (General Arts Sci) (IB 32 pts)
　　　　Sheffield – AAA–ABB (Hist Joint Hons) (IB 37–33 pts HL 6 hist)
340 pts **Cardiff** – AAB (Anc Hist Joint Hons)
　　　　Cardiff – AAB–BBB (Arch Joint Hons)
　　　　Durham – AAB (Mus) (IB 36 pts)
　　　　Heriot-Watt – AAB 340 pts (Act Sci Comb St)
　　　　Liverpool – AAB–BBB (Hisp St Joint Hons) (IB 32 pts)

London (QM) – AAB (Econ Joint Hons) (IB 36 pts HL 5 maths)
Sheffield – AAB (Bioch Joint Hons) (IB 35 pts)
UEA – AAB–ABB incl Engl (Engl Lit Joint Hons)
320 pts Heriot-Watt – ABB (Comb St)
Liverpool – ABB (Ir St Joint Hons) (IB 33 pts)
Sheffield – ABB (Mus Joint Hons) (IB 33 pts)
UEA – ABB (Int Rel Joint Hons) (IB 32 pts)
300 pts Aston – 300–320 pts (Comb Hons)
Cardiff – BBB–BBC (Welsh Joint Hons)
Oxford Brookes – BBB (Jap St (Comb))
280 pts Bath Spa – 220–280 pts (Dance Comb Hons) (IB 24 pts)
Birmingham City – 280 pts (Comb St)
Essex – 280 pts (Hum)
Manchester Met – 280 pts (Chem Foren Sci) (IB 29 pts)
Oxford Brookes – BBC–ABB (Phil (Comb))
260 pts Hertfordshire – 260 pts (Comb courses)
Nottingham – BCC 260 pts (Hum)
UCLan – 260–300 pts (Comb Hons) (IB 28 pts)
Winchester – 260–280 pts (Arts Mgt Perf Arts)
240 pts Aberdeen – CCC (Arts Soc Sci) (IB 28 pts)
Dundee – CCC 240 pts (Art Phil Contemp Prac) (IB 29 pts)
Manchester Met – 240–280 pts (Comb Hons)
220 pts Bath Spa – 220–300 pts (Psy Comb Hons)
Bradford – 220 pts (Comb St)
Glamorgan – 220–260 pts (Comb St)
200 pts Hertfordshire – 200–240 pts (Joint Hons Prog)
160 pts Glamorgan – 160-200 pts (Comb St Dr)
120 pts Wirral Met (Coll) – DD 120 pts (Cult St (Comb))
80 pts London (Birk) – p/t for under 21s (over 21s varies) (Hum Engl/Fr/Ger; Hum Hisp St; Hum Hist Art; Hum Hist; Hum Media St; Hum Phil)
Newham (CFE) – 80 pts (Comb St)

Open University – contact +44 (0)845 300 6090 or www.openuniversity.co.uk/you (Hum Engl/Fr/Ger/Span)

The offers listed below are average offers. Specific offers will vary depending on the relative popularity of each subject. Check with the admissions tutor of your selected institution.

Alternative offers
See Chapter 7 and Appendix 1 for grades/UCAS Tariff points information for the International Baccalaureate, Scottish Highers/Advanced Highers, the Welsh Baccalaureate, the Irish Leaving Certificate, the Cambridge Pre-U Diploma, the Advanced Diploma and the Extended Project.

EXAMPLES OF FOUNDATION DEGREES IN THE SUBJECT FIELD
Bedfordshire; Canterbury Christ Church; Colchester (Inst); Norwich (UCA); Suffolk (Univ Campus); Truro (Coll).

CHOOSING YOUR COURSE (SEE ALSO CH.1)
Some course features
Birmingham (Nat Sci) The course covers biochemistry, biology, chemistry, computer science and earth science, mathematics and physics.
Cardiff In the BA degree scheme three subjects are studied in Year 1, followed in Years 2 and 3 by a study of one or two of these subjects.
Kent (Cult St) A study of popular culture, the arts and everyday life in the context of the social sciences and humanities.
Leeds (Cult St) Course focuses on languages of texts, images, bodies, technologies, spaces and power, the possibilities for radical changes and the constraints and failures of modernity.

Check Chapter 4 when choosing your university and Chapter 7 on how to read the subject tables.

Manchester Met (Cult St Comb Hons) Opportunity for exchange study visit to USA in second year.
Nottingham (Cult Sociol) Course based on aspects of philosophy, sociology, history, linguistics and politics.
UEL (Cult St) Exploration of social and political issues and the media.

Universities and colleges teaching quality See www.qaa.ac.uk; http://unistats.direct.gov.uk.

Top research universities and colleges (RAE 2008) (Cultural Studies) See **Communication Studies/ Communication**.

ADMISSIONS INFORMATION

Number of applicants per place (approx) Birmingham 9; Dundee (average) 13; Durham (Comb Arts) 7; Heriot-Watt 3; Leeds 15; Liverpool 6; Newcastle 7; Strathclyde 9.

Advice to applicants and planning the UCAS personal statement Refer to chosen subject tables. **Bath Spa** (Crea Arts) Looks for personal statements which clarify relevant work done outside the school syllabus (eg creative writing). **De Montfort** Give information about practical experience and a personal interest in one or more areas of the arts. Show a mature attitude on arts/culture and be an original thinker. **Liverpool** (Comb Hons) We look for evidence of a broad interest across a range of subjects.

Misconceptions about this course Bath Spa (Crea Arts) Some applicants wish to specialise in one subject not realising it is a Joint Honours course. **Liverpool** (Comb Hons) Some students deterred because they believe that the course is too general. This is not so. The degree certificate shows the names of the two subjects taken to Honours degree level.

Selection interviews Yes Aberdeen, Bath Spa, Bristol UWE, De Montfort, Dundee, Durham, London Met, Manchester Met, Roehampton, St Mary's Twickenham (UC), Worcester; **Some** Bath Spa (Comb courses incl Drama), Bournemouth Arts (UC), Liverpool.

Interview advice and questions Questions will focus on your chosen subjects. See under separate subject tables. See also **Chapter 6**. **De Montfort** What do you understand to be the role of the Arts Council of England? What recent arts events have you seen/enjoyed?

Reasons for rejection (non-academic) Lack of clarity of personal goals.

AFTER-RESULTS ADVICE

Offers to applicants repeating A-levels Higher Glamorgan, St Andrews; **Possibly higher** Bristol UWE, Leeds, Newcastle, Roehampton, St Mary's Twickenham (UC); **Same** Bath Spa, Birmingham, De Montfort, Derby, Durham, Greenwich, Leicester, Liverpool, London Met, Manchester Met, Worcester.

GRADUATE DESTINATIONS AND EMPLOYMENT (2009/10 HESA)

Career note Graduates enter a wide range of careers covering business and administration, retail work, education, transport, finance, community and social services. Work experience during undergraduate years will help students to focus their interests.

OTHER DEGREE SUBJECTS FOR CONSIDERATION

See **Social Sciences/Studies**.

COMMUNICATION STUDIES/COMMUNICATION

(including **Advertising, Communications, Information Studies, Public Relations** and **Telecommunications**; see also **Computer Courses, Engineering (Communications), Film, Radio, Video and TV Studies, Media Studies, Speech Pathology/Sciences/therapy**)

Some courses combine academic and vocational studies, whilst others may be wholly academic or strictly vocational. The subject thus covers a very wide range of approaches concerning communication which should be carefully researched before applying. Graduates have developed a range of transferable skills in their courses which open up opportunities in several areas. There are obvious links with openings in the media, public relations and advertising.

Useful websites www.camfoundation.com; www.coi.gov.uk; www.aejmc.org.

NB The points totals shown to the left of the institutions are for ease of reference only. It must not be assumed that Tariff points are always used by institutions or that they can be substituted for an offer in grades. The level of an offer is not necessarily indicative of the quality of a course.

COURSE OFFERS INFORMATION
Subject requirements/preferences GCSE English and mathematics grade A–C may be required. **AL** No specific subjects required.

Your target offers and examples of courses provided by each institution

380 pts **City** – A*AA–AAB+c 380 pts (Hum Comm) (IB 32 pts)
London (King's) – AABc (Engl Lang Comm) (IB 36 pts HL 6 Engl)

360 pts **Edinburgh** – AAA–ABB incl maths (Electron Elec Eng (Comms)) (IB 37–32 pts)
Ulster – AAA (Comm Adv Mark)

340 pts **City** – AAB 340 pts (Media St Sociol)
Liverpool – AAB–BBB (Comm St Joint Hons) (IB 36 pts HL 7 Engl)
London (Gold) – AAB–ABB (Media Comm) (IB 34 pts)
Manchester – AAB–BBB 300–340 pts (Lang Litcy Comm) (IB 31–36 pts)
Newcastle – AAB (Media Comm Cult St) (IB 32 pts)

320 pts **Bournemouth** – 320 pts (Comm Media) (IB 32 pts)
Cardiff – ABB (Engl Lang Comm) (IB 32 pts)
Leeds – ABB (Comms) (IB 33 pts)
Leicester – ABB 320 pts (Comms Media Soty) (IB 30 pts)
Liverpool – ABB (Pol Comm St) (IB 33 pts)
Loughborough – ABB (Comm Media St) (IB 34 pts)
Nottingham – ABB (Span Int Media Comms St) (IB 32 pts)
Swansea – ABB–BBB (Lang Comm)
UEA – ABB incl biol (Biol Sci Comm) (IB 32 pts)

300 pts **Bristol UWE** – 300 pts (Mark Comm)
Leeds – BBB (Graph Comm Des) (IB 32 pts)
Liverpool – BBB (Comm St Ital) (IB 30 pts)
Northumbria – 300 pts (Fash Comm) (IB 25 pts)
Sheffield – BBB (Hum Comm Sci) (IB 32 pts)
Sheffield Hallam – 300 pts (Mark Comm Adv)
UEA – BBB (Cr-Cult Comm Bus Mgt) (IB 31 pts)

280 pts **Birmingham City** – 280 pts (Media Comm courses)
Brunel – BBC (Comm Media St) (IB 30 pts)
Glamorgan – 280–320 pts (Media Comm)
Glasgow Caledonian – BBC 280 pts (Media Comm) (IB 24 pts)
Gloucestershire – 280–300 pts (Media Comm Cult)
Greenwich – 280 pts (Media Comm) (IB 24 pts)
Hertfordshire – 280–260 pts (Comm courses)
London Met – 280 pts (Comms) (IB 28 pts)
Manchester Met – 280–240 pts (Dig Media Comm) (IB 28 pts)
Oxford Brookes – BBC (Engl Lang Comm) (IB 30 pts)

260 pts **Keele** – 260–320 pts (Media Comm Cult)
Leeds Met – 260 pts (Media Comm Cult) (IB 24 pts)
Lincoln – 260 pts (Comms)
Liverpool Hope – 260–300 pts (Media Comm)
LJMU – 260 pts (Bus Comm) (IB 28 pts)
Newman (UC) – 260 pts (Media Comm)
Nottingham Trent – 260 pts (Comm Soty)
Sheffield Hallam – 260 pts (PR Media)

Sunderland – 260 pts (Mass Comm)
UCLan – 260–300 pts (Comm St Pop Cult) (IB 28 pts)
Ulster – 260 pts (Ling Comm) (IB 24 pts)
240 pts **Bolton** – 240 pts (Intnet Comm Tech)
Buckingham – 240 pts (Mark Media Comm) (IB 26 pts)
Canterbury Christ Church – 240 pts (Media Comm)
Coventry – 240–280 pts (Comm Cult Media) (IB 27 pts)
De Montfort – 240–260 pts (Media Comm)
Edinburgh Napier – 240 pts (Comm Adv PR)
Manchester Met – 240 pts (Inf Comm) (IB 28 pts)
Robert Gordon – CCC (Comm PR) (IB 26 pts)
Southampton Solent – 240 pts (Media Comms)
Westminster – CCC 240 pts (Comp Net Comm)
220 pts **Bath Spa** – 220–280 pts (Media Comms) (IB 24 pts)
Kingston – 220–360 pts (Engl Lang Comm)
Sunderland – 220 pts (Graph Comm)
200 pts **Middlesex** – 200–300 pts (Comp Net Comm)
200 pts **Bedfordshire** – 200 pts (Media Prac (Mass Comm))
Blackburn (Coll) – 200 pts (Dig Comm Sys)
Buckingham – 200 pts (Comm Media Jrnl courses) (IB 24 pts)
Glyndŵr – 200 pts (Media Comms)
Middlesex – 200–300 pts (Jrnl Comms)
Newman (UC) – 200–240 pts (Psy Media Comm) (IB 24 pts)
UEL – 200 pts (Comm St) (IB 24 pts)
180 pts **Aberystwyth** – 180 pts (Inf Lib St)
Bangor – 180–200 pts (Inf Comm Tech)
160 pts **Wolverhampton** – 160–220 pts (Media Comm St)

Alternative offers
See **Chapter 7** and **Appendix 1** for grades/UCAS Tariff points information for the International Baccalaureate, Scottish Highers/Advanced Highers, the Welsh Baccalaureate, the Irish Leaving Certificate, the Cambridge Pre-U Diploma, the Advanced Diploma and the Extended Project.

EXAMPLES OF FOUNDATION DEGREES IN THE SUBJECT FIELD
See also **Film, Radio, Video and TV Studies** and **Media Studies**. Blackpool and Fylde (Coll); Oxford Brookes; Ravensbourne; Truro (Coll).

CHOOSING YOUR COURSE (SEE ALSO CH.1)
Some course features
Middlesex (Jrnl Comms) A communications course with a strong media focus.
Ulster Course includes one-to-one communication, language and communication, communication within and between social groups, mass communication and communication research. Course emphasis on students' own communication skills and inter-personal effectiveness.

Universities and colleges teaching quality See www.qaa.ac.uk; http://unistats.direct.gov.uk.

Top research universities and colleges (RAE 2008) (Communication, Cultural and Media Studies) Westminster; UEA; London (Gold); Cardiff; UEL; London (RH); Sussex; Nottingham Trent; Ulster; Lincoln; Sunderland; Stirling.

Examples of sandwich degree courses Birmingham City; Bournemouth; Leeds Met; Nottingham Trent; UCLan; Ulster.

ADMISSIONS INFORMATION
Number of applicants per place (approx) Brunel 9; Cardiff 6; Leicester 9; Manchester 5.

Advice to applicants and planning the UCAS personal statement Applicants should be able to give details of any work experience/work shadowing/discussions they have had in the media including, for example, in newspaper offices, advertising agencies, local radio stations or film companies (see also **Media Studies**). **Huddersfield** Critical awareness. Willingness to develop a range of communication skills including new technologies. **London (Gold)** Interest in a study in depth of media theory plus some experience in media practice. **Manchester Met** Motivation more important than grades.

Selection interviews Yes Brunel, Buckingham, Coventry, Glamorgan, Glasgow Caledonian, Leicester, Middlesex, Southampton Solent, Ulster; **Some** Anglia Ruskin, Cardiff, Chester, Huddersfield (rarely), London (Gold) (mature students), Sheffield Hallam (mature students).

Interview advice and questions Courses differ in this subject and, depending on your choice, the questions will focus on the type of course, either biased towards the media, or towards human communication by way of language, psychology, sociology or linguistics. See also separate subject tables and **Chapter 6**.

Reasons for rejection (non-academic) Unlikely to work well in groups. Poor writing. Misguided application, for example more practical work wanted. Poor motivation. Inability to give reasons for choosing the course. More practice needed in academic writing skills. Wrong course choice, wanted more practical work.

AFTER-RESULTS ADVICE
Offers to applicants repeating A-levels Possibly higher Coventry; **Same** Brunel, Cardiff, Chester, Huddersfield, Loughborough, Nottingham Trent, Robert Gordon, Sheffield Hallam.

GRADUATE DESTINATIONS AND EMPLOYMENT (2009/10 HESA)
See **Business and Management Courses (Specialised)**, **Marketing** and **Media Studies**.

Career note Graduates have developed a range of transferable skills in their courses which open up opportunities in several areas. There are obvious links with openings in the media, public relations and advertising.

OTHER DEGREE SUBJECTS FOR CONSIDERATION
Advertising; Art and Design; Cultural Studies; Digital Communications; English; Film, Radio, Video and TV Studies; Information Studies; Journalism; Languages; Linguistics; Marketing; Media Studies; Psychology; Public Relations; Speech Sciences.

COMMUNITY STUDIES/DEVELOPMENT

(see also **Health Sciences/Studies, Nursing and Midwifery, Social and Public Policy and Administration, Social Work**)

These courses cover aspects of community social issues, for example housing, food, health, the elderly, welfare rights and counselling and features of community development such as education, arts, sport and leisure. Work experience is very important. Most courses will lead to professional qualifications.

Useful websites www.csv.org.uk; www.infed.org/community.

NB The points totals shown to the left of the institutions are for ease of reference only. It must not be assumed that Tariff points are always used by institutions or that they can be substituted for an offer in grades. The level of an offer is not necessarily indicative of the quality of a course.

COURSE OFFERS INFORMATION
Subject requirements/preferences GCSE English and mathematics grade A–C may be required at some institutions. **AL** No specific subjects required. **Other** Minimum age 19 plus youth work experience for some courses. Health and CRB checks required for some courses.

Check **Chapter 4** when choosing your university and **Chapter 7** on how to read the subject tables.

Your target offers and examples of courses provided by each institution

320 pts **Manchester** – ABB–BBB 300–320 pts (App Commun Yth Wk St)
Sussex – ABB–BBB (Wkg Chld Yng Ppl) (IB 34–32 pts)

280 pts **Gloucestershire** – 280–300 pts (Yth Commun Wk Theol)
Huddersfield – 280 pts (Yth Commun Wk)
Hull – 280 pts (Commun Yth Wk St)
London Met – 280 pts (Commun Sctr Mgt)
Manchester Met – 280 pts (Yth Commun Wk) (IB 28 pts)

260 pts **Newman (UC)** – 260 pts (Yth Commun Wk)
Sunderland – 260 pts (Commun Yth St; Commun Mus; Commun Pblc Hlth)
Winchester – 260–300 pts (Chld Yth Commun St)

240 pts **Birmingham City** – 240–280 pts (Commun App Thea) (IB 25 pts)
Bolton – 240 pts (Commun Hlth Wlbng; Commun St)
Bournemouth – 240 pts (Commun Dev)
Dundee – AB–CCC (Commun Learn Dev)
Newport – 240 pts (Yth Commun Wk)
Sheffield Hallam – 240 pts (Spo Commun Dev)
West Scotland – CCC (Commun Lrng)

220 pts **Bishop Grosseteste (UC)** – 220 pts (Dr Commun)
Coventry – 220 pts (App Commun Soc St)
Gloucestershire – 220 pts (Hlth Commun Soc Cr)

200 pts **Cardiff Met** – 200 pts (Yth Commun Educ)
Leeds Met – 200 pts (Yth Wrk Commun Dev) (IB 24 pts)
UCLan – 200 pts (Commun Ldrshp)
UEL – 200 pts (Commun Serv Ent; Yth Commun Wk)
Ulster – 200 pts (Commun Yth Wk)

180 pts **Bedfordshire** – 180–220 pts (Disab St)
Bolton – 180 pts (App Commun St)
Sheffield Hallam – 180 pts (Yth Commun Wk)
UCP Marjon – 180 pts (Commun Soc; Commun Dev; Yth Commun Wk)

160 pts **De Montfort** – 160 pts (Yth Commun Dev)
London (Gold) – CC (App Soc Sci Commun Dev Yth Wk)

140 pts **Trinity Saint David** – individual offers made after interview (Yth Commun Wk)

100 pts **Newport** – 100–120 pts (Commun Hlth Wlbng)

 80 pts **Cumbria** – 80 pts (Yth Commun Wk)
London (Birk) – p/t for under 21s (over 21s varies) (Comm St)
Bradford (Coll Univ Centre) – (Yth Commun Dev)

Alternative offers
See **Chapter 7** and **Appendix 1** for grades/UCAS Tariff points information for the International Baccalaureate, Scottish Highers/Advanced Highers, the Welsh Baccalaureate, the Irish Leaving Certificate, the Cambridge Pre-U Diploma, the Advanced Diploma and the Extended Project.

EXAMPLES OF FOUNDATION DEGREES IN THE SUBJECT FIELD
Bradford; Cornwall (Coll); De Montfort; Derby; Durham New (Coll); Glyndŵr; Grimsby (IFHE); Kent; Leeds Met; Lincoln; Llandrillo Cymru (Coll); Newcastle (Coll); Newport; Northampton; Northumberland (Coll); Norwich (UCA); Sheffield Hallam; Somerset (CAT); South Devon (Coll); Staffordshire Reg Fed (SURF); Truro (Coll); Walsall (Coll); Warwickshire (Coll); Wirral Met (Coll); Wolverhampton; Worcester; York (Coll).

CHOOSING YOUR COURSE (SEE ALSO CH.1)
Some course features
Bolton A wide range of specialist modules and work experience in Years 2 and 3.
Derby A vocational course leading to careers in community and youth work.

Edinburgh Course focuses on adult education, community work, community arts and youth work and people's participation in all aspects of community life. Practice placement blocks in Years 2 and 3, and concurrent practice placements in Year 4.

Newport An initial qualifying course leading to a recognised youth work programme.

Universities and colleges teaching quality See www.qaa.ac.uk; http://unistats.direct.gov.uk.

ADMISSIONS INFORMATION

Number of applicants per place (approx) LJMU 2; Manchester Met 8; UCP Marjon 7.

Advice to applicants and planning the UCAS personal statement You should describe work you have done with people (elderly or young), particularly in a caring capacity, such as social work, or with the elderly or young children in schools, nursing, hospital work, youth work, community or charity work. You should also describe any problems arising and how staff dealt with them. **UCP Marjon** Strong multi-cultural policy. English as a Foreign Language teaching offered.

Selection interviews **Yes** Bradford, Derby, Huddersfield (in groups), Manchester Met, Strathclyde; **Some** LJMU.

Interview advice and questions This subject has a vocational emphasis and work experience, or even full-time work in the field, will be expected. Community work varies considerably so, depending on your experiences, you could be asked about the extent of your work and how you would solve the problems which occur. See also **Chapter 6. Derby** Take us through your experience of youth and community work. What are the problems facing young people today?

Reasons for rejection (non-academic) Insufficient experience. Lack of understanding of community and youth work. Uncertain career aspirations. Incompatibility with values, methods and aims of the course. No work experience.

AFTER-RESULTS ADVICE

Offers to applicants repeating A-levels **Same** LJMU, UCP Marjon.

GRADUATE DESTINATIONS AND EMPLOYMENT (2009/10 HESA)

See **Social Work**.

Career note Social and welfare areas of employment provide openings for those wanting to specialise in their chosen field of social work. Other opportunities will also exist in educational administration, leisure and outdoor activities.

OTHER DEGREE SUBJECTS FOR CONSIDERATION

Communication Studies; Education; Health and Social Care; Nursing; Politics; Psychology; Social Policy and Administration; Social Work; Sociology; Youth Studies.

COMPUTER COURSES

(including **Artificial Intelligence, Computing, Computer Networks, Computer Science, Games Technology** and **Web Management**; see also **Communication Studies/Communication, Information Management and Librarianship, Media Studies, Technologies**)

Computer courses are popular and provide graduates with good career prospects. Courses vary in content and in the specialisations offered which may include software engineering, programming languages, artificial intelligence, data processing and graphics. Many universities offer sandwich placements in industry and commerce.

Useful websites www.bcs.org; www.intellectuk.org; www.e-skills.com; www.iap.org.uk.

NB The points totals shown to the left of the institutions are for ease of reference only. It must not be assumed that Tariff points are always used by institutions or that they can be substituted for an offer in grades. The level of an offer is not necessarily indicative of the quality of a course.

COURSE OFFERS INFORMATION

Subject requirements/preferences GCSE Mathematics usually required. A*/A/B grades may be stipulated for some subjects. **AL** Mathematics, a science subject or computer science required for some courses.

Cambridge (Churchill, Magdalene) STEP used as part of the offer; (Gonville and Caius) AEA mathematics required (see **Chapter 6**).

Your target offers and examples of courses provided by each institution

410 pts **London (King's)** – AAAc (Comp Sci Robot) (IB 38 pts)
400 pts **Imperial London** – A*A*A (Maths Mathem Comp) (IB 39 pts HL 7 maths)
380 pts **Bristol** – A*AA–AAA (Comp Sci Electron) (IB 38–37 pts HL 665)
        Cambridge – A*AA (Comp Sci) (IB 40–42 pts HL 766–777)
        Exeter – A*AA–AAB (Comp Sci Maths) (IB 38–34 pts HL 6 maths)
        Imperial London – A*mathsAA (Comp (Comp Biol Med)) (IB 39 pts HL maths)
        London (King's) – AABc (Comp Sci) (IB 36 pts)
        Oxford – A*AA (Comp Sci) (IB 39 pts)
        Southampton – A*AA incl maths (Comp Sci Soft Eng) (IB 38 pts HL 19 pts)
360 pts **Bath** – AAA (Comp Sci) (IB 36 pts HL 6 maths)
        Edinburgh – AAA–ABB incl maths (Inform) (IB 37–32 pts HL maths)
        Leeds – AAA–AAB (Comp Sci Maths) (IB 34 pts HL 6 maths)
        London (UCL) – AAA incl maths/fmaths (Mathem Comp) (IB 38 pts)
        Nottingham – AAA–A*AB (Maths Comp Sci) (IB 36–34 pts HL 6 maths)
        St Andrews – AAA (Comp Sci Psy) (IB 36 pts)
        Southampton – AAA (Maths Comp Sci) (IB 36 pts HL 18 pts)
        Surrey – AAA (Dig Med Eng MEng) (IB 36 pts)
        Sussex – AAA–AAB incl maths (Maths Comp Sci) (IB 35–36 pts)
        Warwick – AAA (Comp Mgt Sci) (IB 38 pts)
340 pts **Aston** – AAB–AAA 340–360 pts (Bus Comp IT) (IB 35 pts)
        Birmingham – AAB (Comp Sci) (IB 34–36 pts)
        Durham – AAB (Comp Sci) (IB 36 pts)
        Exeter – AAB–ABB (Electron Eng Comp Sci MEng) (IB 34–32 pts)
        Kent – AAB (Comp Sci) (IB 33 pts)
        Lancaster – ABB (Comp Sci courses) (IB 32 pts)
        Leeds – AAB incl maths (Artif Intel) (IB 36 pts)
        Liverpool – AAB (Comp Sci) (IB 33 pts HL 5 maths)
        London (QM) – 340 pts (Comp Sci MSc) (IB 34 pts)
        London (RH) – 300–340 pts (Comp Sci) (IB 30 pts)
        Loughborough – AAB–AAA (Comp Sci MSci) (IB 34 pts HL 5 maths)
        Manchester – AAB (Comp Sci Bus Mgt) (IB 35 pts)
        Newcastle – AAB (Comp Sci (Net Sys Intnet Tech)) (IB 35 pts)
        Queen's Belfast – AAB (Maths Comp Sci MSci)
        Sheffield – AAB incl maths (Ent Comp IT Mgt Bus) (IB 35 pts HL 6 maths)
        Surrey – AAB (Dig Med Eng BEng) (IB 35 pts)
        UEA – AAB (Comp Sci MComp) (IB 33 pts)
        Warwick – AAB (Comp Bus St) (IB 36 pts)
        York – AAB (Comp Sci courses) (IB 35 pts)
320 pts **Aston** – BBB–ABB 320–300 pts (Comp Bus) (IB 32 pts)
        Birmingham – ABB (Comp Sys Eng Bus Mgt) (IB 32–34 pts)
        Bristol UWE – 320 pts (Comp courses; Comp Sci Gms Tech)
        Cardiff – ABB (Comp Maths) (IB 33 pts)
        City – 320–280 pts (Inf Sys) (IB 28 pts)
        Derby – 320 pts (Comp Gms Prog)
        Exeter – ABB–BBB 320–300 pts (Electron Eng Comp Sci BEng) (IB 32–30 pts)
        Glasgow – ABB (Comp Sci courses) (IB 32 pts)
        Kent – ABB (Web Comp) (IB 33 pts)

Lancaster – ABB (Acc Fin Comp Sci) (IB 34 pts)
Leicester – ABB (Comp Sci)
Loughborough – ABB–AAB (Comp Sci BSc) (IB 32 pts HL 5 maths)
Newcastle – AAB–ABB 320–340 pts (Comp Sci (Bioinform)) (IB 30 pts)
Nottingham – ABB (Comp Sci Artif Intel) (IB 32 pts)
Reading – 320 pts (Cyber) (IB 33 pts)
Sussex – ABB (Gms Multim Env) (IB 34 pts)
Swansea – ABB 320–280 pts (Comp Sci)
UEA – ABB (Comp Bus) (IB 32 pts)

300 pts **Aberdeen** – BBB (Comp Sci)
Bournemouth – 300 pts (Web Des)
Brunel – contact admissions office (Maths Comp)
Derby – 300 pts (Comp Gms Modl Animat; Maths Comp Sci)
Essex – 300 pts (Comp Gms) (IB 29 pts)
Glamorgan – BBB 300 pts (Comp Gms Dev)
Heriot-Watt – BBB (Comp Sci)
Keele – 300 pts incl BC (Comp Sci) (IB 26–28 pts)
Kingston – 300 pts (Inf Sys)
Leicester – BBB (Comp; Comp Mgt)
London (Gold) – BBB (Crea Comp; Comp Sci; Interact Des)
London (QM) – 300 pts (Comp ICT Bus Mgt) (IB 32 pts)
Loughborough – BBB (Inf Mgt Web Dev) (IB 32 pts HL 5 maths)
Plymouth – BBB (Comp Sci; Comp Inf Scrty; Comp Net; Comp Gms Dev)
Reading – 300–340 pts (Comp Sci courses)
Strathclyde – ABC (Comp Sci) (IB 28 pts)
Teesside – 300 pts (Comp Gms Prog)
Ulster – 300 pts (Comp Sci; Comp Sci (Embd Comp/Intel Sys/Mbl Comp/Robot); Comp Gms Des; Comp Sci Maths)

280 pts **Aberystwyth** – 280 pts (Comp Sci Artif Intel) (IB 24 pts)
Brighton – BBC 280 pts (Web Des) (IB 28 pts)
Bristol UWE – 280–300 pts (Gms Tech)
Brunel – BBC (Comp Sci (Artif Intel)) (IB 30 pts)
Cardiff Met – 280 pts (Web Des)
City – 280–320 pts (Comp Sci Gms Tech) (IB 28 pts)
Derby – 280 pts (IT; Comp Sci; Comp Foren Inv; Net Scrty)
Hertfordshire – 280 pts (Comp Maths)
Huddersfield – 280 pts (Comp Sci; Comp; Gms Tech)
Kingston – 280 pts (Comp Sci; Web Dev)
Lincoln – 280 pts (Comp Sci; Gms Dev)
LJMU – 280 pts (Comp Aid Des; Comp Tech)
Loughborough – BBC–ABB 280–320 pts (Comp Sci Artif Intel BSc) (IB 30 pts)
Manchester Met – 280 pts (Web Mob App Dev) (IB 28 pts)
Northumbria – 280 pts (Comp Sci; Comp Gms Des Prod; Web Dev; Ethl Hack Comp Scrty)
Norwich (UCA) – BBC (Gms Art Des) (IB 25 pts)
Nottingham Trent – 280 pts (Comp Sci courses; Comp Sys (Foren/Net))
Oxford Brookes – BBC (Comp Gms Animat) (IB 30 pts)
Stirling – BBC (Bus Comp) (IB 32 pts)
Salford – 280 pts (Gms Tech)
Teesside – 280 pts (Crea Dig Media; ICT)

260 pts **Bolton** – 240–260 pts (Comp Gms Des)
Buckingham – 260 pts (Comp courses)
Coventry – BCC (Comp Gms Tech)
De Montfort – 260 pts (Comp courses; Gms Tech)
Glamorgan – 260–300 pts (Comp Sci)
Greenwich – 260 pts (Maths Comp)

Check **Chapter 4** when choosing your university and **Chapter 7** on how to read the subject tables.

Hull – 260–280 pts (Comp Sci; Comp Gms; Web Des Dev)
Liverpool Hope – 260 pts (Comp)
LJMU – 260 pts (Comp Gms Tech) (IB 24 pts)
Northampton – 260–280 pts (Comp courses)
Portsmouth – 260–300 pts (Gms Tech; Comp Sci; Comp; Web Tech)
Sheffield Hallam – 260 pts (Comp Sci; Comp Scrty Foren; Gms Des)
Sunderland – 260 pts (Comp Sci; Net Comp; Bus Comp; Comp Foren; Comp; ICT)

240 pts **Aberdeen** – CCC (Artif Intel)
Abertay Dundee – CCC (Comp Arts; Comp Gms Tech; Web Des)
Bangor – 240–280 pts (Comp Sci; Comp Sci Bus)
Bradford – 240–260 pts (Comp Sci Gms; Web Des Tech; Comp courses)
Canterbury Christ Church – 240 pts (Web Des)
Chester – 240–280 pts (Comp Sci) (IB 26 pts)
Cumbria – 240 pts (App Bus Comp)
Edge Hill – 240 pts (Comp courses)
Gloucestershire – 240–280 pts (Comp; Comp Gms)
Glyndŵr – 240 pts (Comp Net Mgt Scrty)
Hertfordshire – 240 pts (IT; Web Des; Comp Sci)
Leeds Met – 240 pts (Bus Inf Tech; Comp Foren Scrty; Comp; Comp Foren)
LJMU – 240 pts (IT Multim Comp)
Manchester Met – 240 pts (Web Dev) (IB 28 pts)
Newport – 240–260 pts (Comp Gms Des)
Nottingham Trent – 240 pts (Comp St; Inf Sys)
Ravensbourne – AA–CC (Web Media) (IB 28 pts)
Staffordshire – 240 pts (Comp Sci; Dig Foren)
Sheffield Hallam – 240 pts (Net Mgt Des; Web Sys Des)
UCLan – 240–280 pts (Gms Des; Web Multim; Comp)
UEA – CCC (App Comp Sci incl Fdn Yr) (IB 28 pts)
UEL – 240 pts (Comp Net)
Westminster – AA–CCC (Comp Sci) (IB 28 pts)
Worcester – 240 pts (Comp Gms Des Dev; Comp)

230 pts **Edinburgh Napier** – (Comp; Web Tech)
220 pts **Dundee** – CCD (Comp Sci) (IB 28 pts HL 554)
Falmouth (UC) – 220 pts (Crea Comp) (IB 26 pts)
London Met – 220 pts (Comp courses; Comp Gms Prog)
London South Bank – 220 pts (Comp courses)
Sheffield Hallam – 220 pts (Comp-ad Des Tech)
West Scotland – CCD (Comp Gms Tech)

200 pts **Anglia Ruskin** – 200 pts (Comp Sci; Comp Gmg)
Bedfordshire – 200 pts (Comp Sci; Comp Net; Gms Dev; Comp Maths)
Birmingham City – 200–280 pts (Web Des; Comp Net Scrty; Comp Sci; Gms Tech)
Bucks New – 200–240 pts (Comp courses; Gms Dev)
Hull (Coll) – 200 pts (Gms Des; Web Des)
Leeds Met – 200 pts (Gms Des) (IB 24 pts)
Middlesex – 200–280 pts (Comp Gms; Comp Sci; Comp Net; Comp Comm Net)
Robert Gordon – BB–CCC (Comp Sci)
Staffordshire – 200–240 pts (Comp Gms Des)
Sheffield Hallam – 200 pts (App Comp)
Suffolk (Univ Campus) – 200 pts (Comp Gms)
Swansea Met – 200 pts (Comp Gms Dev; Bus IT; Comp Inf Sys; Comp Net)
UEL – 200 pts (Comp; Gms Des)
West Anglia (Coll) – 200 pts (Comp Sci)
West London – 200 pts (Comp Inf Sys; Net Mbl Comp; Comp Sci; Inf Sys Bus)
York St John – 200–240 pts (Bus IT)

180 pts **Greenwich** – 180 pts (Comp Net; Comp Net Server Admin)
Plymouth – 180 pts (Mech Eng Comp Aid Des) (IB 24 pts)
Sir Gâr (Coll) – 180 pts (Intnet Comp)
160 pts **Farnborough (CT)** – 160 pts (Comp; Comp Gmg; Comp Netwrkg)
Glasgow Caledonian – CC (Comp Gms)
Greenwich (Sch Mgt) – 160 pts (HR Mgt Inform Sys; Comp Sci; Comp Sci Bus Inform; Bus Mgt IT)
Peterborough (Univ Centre) – 160 pts (Comp Inf Sys)
Southampton Solent – 160 pts (Gms Dev; Web Des; Comp Net Mgt)
South Essex (Coll) – 160 pts (Comp Gms Des)
Swansea Met – 160 pts (Web Dev; Crea Comp Gms Des)
West Scotland – CC (Comp Gms Dev; Comp Net; Comp; Comp/Muiltm Mbl Dev; Web Dev; IT)
Wolverhampton – 160–220 pts (IT Scrty; Comp Sci (Gms Dev))
140 pts **Trinity Saint David** – 140–360 pts (Bus IT; Comp)
120 pts **Bradford (Coll Univ Centre)** – 120 pts (Bus Comp Sol; Soft Apps Dev)
Colchester (Inst) – 120 pts (Comp Sol (Intnet); Comp Sol (Net))
Grimsby (IFHE) – 120 pts (Gms Des)
80 pts **UHI** – C–A (Comp)

Open University – contact +44 (0)845 300 6090 **or** www.openuniversity.co.uk/you (Comp IT; Comp Bus/Des/Maths/Psy/Stats; ICT)

Alternative offers
See **Chapter 7** and **Appendix 1** for grades/UCAS Tariff points information for the International Baccalaureate, Scottish Highers/Advanced Highers, the Welsh Baccalaureate, the Irish Leaving Certificate, the Cambridge Pre-U Diploma, the Advanced Diploma and the Extended Project.

Check **Chapter 4** when choosing your university and **Chapter 7** on how to read the subject tables.

EXAMPLES OF FOUNDATION DEGREES IN THE SUBJECT FIELD

Chesterfield (Coll); Colchester (Inst); Cornwall (Coll); Croydon (Coll); Cumbria; Doncaster (Coll Univ Centre); Durham New (Coll); Ealing, Hammersmith and West London (Coll); East Berkshire (Coll); Edge Hill; Kent; Kingston; Kirklees (Coll); Lakes (Coll); Leeds (CAD); Llandrillo Cymru (Coll); London Met; Manchester (Coll); Mid-Cheshire (Coll); NEW (Coll); Newcastle (Coll); Newport; Northbrook (Coll); Nottingham New (Coll); Ravensbourne; Riverside Halton (Coll); St Helens (Coll); Sheffield (Coll); Shrewsbury (CAT); Somerset (CAT); South Devon (Coll); South Essex (Coll); Southampton Solent; Staffordshire Reg Fed (SURF); Stockport (Coll); Stockton Riverside (Coll); Stoke on Trent (Coll); Suffolk (Univ Campus); Truro (Coll); Tyne Met (Coll); Warrington (Coll); West Cheshire (Coll); Westminster Kingsway (Coll); Wigan and Leigh (Coll); Wiltshire (Coll); York (Coll).

CHOOSING YOUR COURSE (SEE ALSO CH.1)

Some course features

Abertay Dundee (Ethl Hack Cntrms) An unusual course, designed in collaboration with computer security companies and is accredited by the British Computer Society.

Brighton The Computing programme offers a wide range of different degrees with the final choice being made at the end of the first semester.

Reading A course is offered in Computer Science and Cybernetics involving applications with human activities and systems.

Salford A broad course with the option to spend a year in industry between the second and final year.

Southampton All computer courses are accredited by the British Computer Society.

Warwick Students can apply for a place in the Erasmus programme or similar programme for study in an overseas university or salaried employment in industry.

Universities and colleges teaching quality See www.qaa.ac.uk; http://unistats.direct.gov.uk.

Top research universities and colleges (RAE 2008) (Computer Science and Informatics) Cambridge; Imperial London; Southampton; Edinburgh; Oxford; London (UCL); Manchester; Nottingham; Glasgow; Liverpool; Lancaster; Leeds.

Examples of sandwich degree courses Aberystwyth; Aston; Bath; Birmingham City; Bournemouth; Bradford; Brighton; Bristol UWE; Brunel; Cardiff; Cardiff Met; City; Coventry; De Montfort; Derby; Edinburgh Napier; Glamorgan; Glasgow Caledonian; Gloucestershire; Greenwich; Hertfordshire; Huddersfield; Kent; Kingston; Leeds Met; Lincoln; LJMU; London South Bank; Loughborough; Manchester; Manchester Met; Northumbria; Nottingham Trent; Oxford Brookes; Plymouth; Portsmouth; Queen's Belfast; Reading; Salford; Sheffield Hallam; Southampton Solent; Staffordshire; Surrey; Teesside; UEL; Ulster; West Scotland; Westminster; Wolverhampton; Worcester; York.

ADMISSIONS INFORMATION

Number of applicants per place (approx) Abertay Dundee 2; Aberystwyth 8; Aston (Bus Comp IT) 12; Bath 9; Birmingham 7; Bournemouth 8; Bradford 13; Bristol 8; Bristol UWE 4; Brunel 10; Buckingham 6; Cambridge 3; Cardiff 5; City 10; Coventry 10; Derby 3; Dundee 6; Durham 10; Edinburgh 4; Essex 2; Exeter 10; Glasgow Caledonian 8; Glyndŵr 3; Heriot-Watt 6; Hull (Comp Sci) 6; Imperial London 6; Kent 8; Kingston 10; Lancaster 5; Leeds 10; Leicester 13; Lincoln 5; LJMU 3; London (King's) 20; London (QM) 6; London (RH) 5; Loughborough (CT) 2; Manchester Met 10, (Bus IT) 8; Newcastle 7; Northumbria 4; Nottingham 8; Nottingham Trent 4; Oxford Brookes 18; Plymouth 12; Portsmouth 6; Robert Gordon 3; Roehampton 3; Sheffield Hallam 5; Southampton 10; Staffordshire 4; Stirling 6; Strathclyde 16; Surrey 9; Swansea 5; Teesside 4; UEA (Maths Comp) 7; Warwick 11; York 9.

Advice to applicants and planning the UCAS personal statement Your computer and programming interests in and outside school or college should be described. It is also useful to give details of any visits, work experience and work shadowing relating to industrial or commercial organisations and their computer systems. (See **Appendix 3**.) Give details of your interests in, and knowledge of computer hardware, software and multimedia packages. Contact the Chartered Institute for IT for information. **Bristol** Deferred entry accepted.

Misconceptions about this course That anyone who plays computer games or uses a word processor can do a degree in Computer Studies. Some think Computing degrees are just about programming; in reality, programming is only one, albeit essential, part of computing. **Aston** (Bus Comp IT) 60% business, 40% computing and IT; compulsory placement year in industry. **City** (Bus Comp Sys) Some applicants think that it is a Business degree: it is a Computing degree focused on computing in business. **London (QM)** There are many misconceptions – among students, teachers and careers advisers – about what computer science entails. The main one is to confuse it with what schools call information and communication technology which is about the use of computer applications. Computer science is all about software – ie programming – and will generally only cover a limited study of hardware.

Selection interviews Yes Abertay Dundee, Bath, Blackburn (Coll), Bradford, Bristol UWE, Brunel, Buckingham, Cambridge, Cardiff, City, Coventry, Cumbria, Durham, Edinburgh, Edinburgh Napier, Glamorgan, Hertfordshire, Hull, Kingston, Liverpool Hope, London (Gold), London (QM), London (UCL), London South Bank, Loughborough, Newcastle, Newport, Northampton, Northbrook (Coll), Nottingham Trent, Oxford (Comp Sci) 19%, Plymouth, Portsmouth, Sheffield Hallam, Southampton, Surrey, West London, Wigan and Leigh (Coll), York; **Some** Aberystwyth, Anglia Ruskin, Birmingham City, Blackpool and Fylde (Coll), Brighton, Chichester, Exeter, Imperial London, LJMU, London Met, Manchester Met, Salford, Staffordshire, Sunderland, UEA, Warwick (5–10%); **No** Dundee, Nottingham, West Scotland.

Interview advice and questions While A-level computer studies is not usually required, you will be questioned on your use of computers and aspects of the subject which interest you. How do you organise your homework/social life? What are your strengths and weaknesses? Do you have any idea of the type of career you would like? See also **Chapter 6**. **Cambridge** Why is the pole-vaulting world record about 6.5m and why can't it be broken? **City** The aim of the interview is to obtain a full picture of the applicant's background, life experiences etc, before making an offer. **York** No tests. Questions for discussion at the whiteboard are usually mathematical or are about fundamental computer science such as sorting.

Reasons for rejection (non-academic) Little practical interest in computers/electronics. Inability to work as part of a small team. Mismatch between referee's description and performance at interview. Unsatisfactory English. Can't communicate. Inability to convince interviewer of the candidate's worth. Incoherent, unmotivated, arrogant and without any evidence of good reason. **London (QM)** Misunderstanding of what computer science involves as an academic subject – especially in personal statements where some suggest that they are interested in a course with business and administrative skills. Lack of sufficient mathematics. Computer science is a mathematical subject and we cannot accept applicants who are unable to demonstrate good mathematical skills. **Southampton** Lack of motivation; incoherence; carelessness.

AFTER-RESULTS ADVICE
Offers to applicants repeating A-levels Higher Brighton, De Montfort, Greenwich, Kingston, St Andrews, Surrey, Sussex, Warwick; **Possibly higher** Bath, Bristol UWE, Edinburgh, Lancaster, Leeds, Newcastle, Oxford Brookes, Portsmouth, Sheffield, Teesside; **Same** Abertay Dundee, Aberystwyth, Anglia Ruskin, Aston, Blackpool and Fylde (Coll), Brunel, Buckingham, Cambridge, Cardiff, Cardiff Met, Chichester, City, Derby, Dundee, Durham, Exeter, Farnborough (CT), Huddersfield, Hull, Kent, Lincoln, Liverpool, Liverpool Hope, LJMU, London (RH), London (UCL), London South Bank, Loughborough, Manchester Met, Newman (UC), Northumbria, Nottingham Trent, Robert Gordon, Salford, Sheffield Hallam, Staffordshire, Suffolk (Univ Campus), Sunderland, UEA, UEL, Ulster, West London, Wolverhampton, Worcester, York.

GRADUATE DESTINATIONS AND EMPLOYMENT (2009/10 HESA)
Computer Science; graduates surveyed 13355 **Employed** 5060 **In voluntary employment** 85 **In further study** 1790 **Assumed unemployed** 1165

Information Systems; graduates surveyed 3980 **Employed** 1760 **In voluntary employment** 30 **In further study** 685 **Assumed unemployed** 345

Check **Chapter 4** when choosing your university and **Chapter 7** on how to read the subject tables.

Artificial Intelligence graduates surveyed 125 **Employed** 55 **In voluntary employment** 0 **In further study** 25 **Assumed unemployed** 10

Career note A high proportion of graduates go to work in the IT sector with some degrees leading towards particular fields (usually indicated by the course title). Significant areas include software design and engineering, web and internet-based fields, programming, systems analysis and administration.

OTHER DEGREE SUBJECTS FOR CONSIDERATION

Business Studies; Communications Engineering; Computer Engineering; Electrical and Electronic Engineering; Geographical Information Systems; Information Studies; Mathematics; Physics; Software Engineering.

CONSUMER STUDIES/SCIENCES

(including **Consumer Product Design** and **Trading Standards**; see also **Food Science/Studies and Technology, Hospitality and Hotel Management**)

Consumer Studies courses involve topics such as food and nutrition, shelter, clothing, community studies and consumer behaviour and marketing. Trading Standards courses focus on consumer law, contract law, food law, weights and measures, criminal investigation, fraud, counterfeit, and fair trading. Accredited by the Trading Standards Institute, they can lead to careers as trading standards officers.

Useful websites www.which.co.uk; www.tradingstandards.gov.uk.

NB The points totals shown to the left of the institutions are for ease of reference only. It must not be assumed that Tariff points are always used by institutions or that they can be substituted for an offer in grades. The level of an offer is not necessarily indicative of the quality of a course.

COURSE OFFERS INFORMATION

Subject requirements/preferences **GCSE** Mathematics and English usually required. **AL** No specific subjects required.

Your target offers and examples of courses provided by each institution

300 pts **Reading** – 300 pts (Consum Bhv Mark) (HL 655)
260 pts **Reading** – 260 pts (Consum Electron) (HL 555)
240 pts **Edinburgh Napier** – CCC 240–230 pts (Mark Mgt Consum St)
 Glasgow Caledonian – CCC (Psy (Consum St))
 Ulster – CCC 240 pts (Consum St)
220 pts **Harper Adams (UC)** – 220–260 pts (Consum St)
200 pts **Abertay Dundee** – CDD (Fd Consum Sci)
 Birmingham (UC) – 200 pts (Fd Consum Mgt) (IB 24 pts)

Alternative offers
See **Chapter 7** and **Appendix 1** for grades/UCAS Tariff points information for the International Baccalaureate, Scottish Highers/Advanced Highers, the Welsh Baccalaureate, the Irish Leaving Certificate, the Cambridge Pre-U Diploma, the Advanced Diploma and the Extended Project.

EXAMPLES OF FOUNDATION DEGREES IN THE SUBJECT FIELD

Leeds Met.

CHOOSING YOUR COURSE (SEE ALSO CH.1)

Some course features
Coventry (Consum Prod Des) The four-year course covers the field of industrial design related to household products with an emphasis on styling and ergonomics. Towards the end of Year 3 students may apply for an industrial placement.

Manchester Met (Consum Mark) Course covers communications, brand design, consumer behaviour, retailing and buying. The course is validated by the Chartered Institute of Marketing.
Reading (Consum Bhv Mark) Course focuses on marketing, psychology, economics and research methods, with a wide range of optional modules from across the University including management, languages, politics and sociology.

Universities and colleges teaching quality See www.qaa.ac.uk; http://unistats.direct.gov.uk.

Examples of sandwich degree courses Birmingham (UC); Cardiff Met; Harper Adams (UC); Manchester Met; Teesside.

ADMISSIONS INFORMATION
Number of applicants per place (approx) Birmingham (UC) 2; Cardiff Met 5; Edinburgh Queen Margaret 3; London Met 5; Manchester Met 4.

Advice to applicants and planning the UCAS personal statement Relevant work experience or work shadowing in, for example, business organisations, restaurants, cafes, or the school meals service, would be appropriate. (See also **Hospitality and Hotel Management** and **Dietetics**.)

Selection interviews Yes Teesside; **Some** Manchester Met.

Interview advice and questions Questions will stem from your special interests in this subject and in the past have included: What interests you in consumer behaviour? What are the advantages and disadvantages? What is ergonomics? What do you understand by the term sustainable consumption? What world or national news has annoyed, pleased or upset you? What relevance do textiles and dress have to home economics? How would you react in a room full of fools? See also **Chapter 6**.
Edinburgh Queen Margaret Very informal interviews covering work experience and career aspirations.

AFTER-RESULTS ADVICE
Offers to applicants repeating A-levels Same Edinburgh Queen Margaret, Manchester Met, Ulster.

GRADUATE DESTINATIONS AND EMPLOYMENT (2009/10 HESA)
Career note The various specialisms involved in these courses allow graduates to look for openings in several other career areas, for example, food quality assurance, consumer education and advice. Many graduates enter business administration and careers in particularly retailing, evaluating new products and liaising with the public.

OTHER DEGREE SUBJECTS FOR CONSIDERATION
Biological Sciences; Business Studies; Dietetics; Environmental Health; Food Science; Health Studies; Hospitality Management; Marketing; Nutrition; Psychology; Retail Management.

DANCE/DANCE STUDIES
(see also **Drama**)

Every aspect of dance can be studied in the various courses on offer as well as the theoretical, educational, historical and social aspects of the subject.

Useful websites www.arts.org.uk; www.cdet.org.uk; www.ballet.co.uk; www.ndta.org.uk.

NB The points totals shown to the left of the institutions are for ease of reference only. It must not be assumed that Tariff points are always used by institutions or that they can be substituted for an offer in grades. The level of an offer is not necessarily indicative of the quality of a course.

COURSE OFFERS INFORMATION
Subject requirements/preferences GCSE English usually required. Practical dance experience essential.
AL No specific subjects required. **Other** CRB checks required for some courses: check websites.

Check **Chapter 4** when choosing your university and **Chapter 7** on how to read the subject tables.

Your target offers and examples of courses provided by each institution

320 pts **Surrey** – ABB (Danc Cult)

Winchester – 280–320 pts (Choreo Dance) (IB 25 pts)

300 pts **Kingston** – BBB 300–360 pts (Dance)

Leeds – BBB (Dance) (IB 32 pts)

Middlesex – 200–300 pts (Dance) (IB 24 pts)

UCLan – 260–300 pts (Dance Perf Teach)

280 pts **Bath Spa** – 220–280 pts (Dance Comb Hons) (IB 24 pts)

Brighton – Fdn Dip required (check) BBC (Perf Vis Arts (Dance))

Chichester – BBC 280–300 pts (Dance) (IB 28 pts)

Cumbria – 280 pts (Perf Art)

Edge Hill – offer may be altered based on audition 280 pts (Dance Dr) (IB 24 pts)

LJMU – 280 pts (Dance Prac)

London (RAc Dance) – 280 pts (Ballet Educ)

Manchester Met – 280 pts (Dance) (IB 28 pts)

Middlesex – 280 pts (Dance St) (IB 24 pts)

Northampton – 260–280 pts (Dance Joint Hons) (IB 24 pts)

Roehampton – 280–340 pts (Dance St) (IB 25 pts)

Suffolk (Univ Campus) – 280 pts (Dance)

Teesside – 280 pts (Dance) (IB 24 pts)

Ulster – BBC (Mus Dance)

260 pts **Chester** – 260–300 pts (Dance) (IB 28 pts)

De Montfort – 260 pts (Dance) (IB 24 pts)

Derby – 260–300 pts (Dance Mov St Joint Hons) (IB 26 pts)

Lincoln – 260–280 pts (Dance; Dance Dr)

Liverpool Hope – 260–280 pts (Dance) (IB 25 pts)

Ulster – 260 pts (Dr Dance)

Winchester – 260–300 pts (Arts Mgt Choreo Dance)

240 pts **Bath Spa** – 240–280 pts (Dance) (IB 24 pts)

Bedfordshire – 240 pts (Dance Prof Pr)

Birmingham City – 240 pts (Commun App Dance Thea)

Canterbury Christ Church – 240 pts (Perf Arts (Dance))

Cardiff Met – 240 pts (Dance) (IB 24 pts)

Coventry – 240 pts (Dance Thea Prof Prac) (IB 27 pts)

Hull – 240 pts (Thea Perf)

Leeds Met – 240 pts (Dance) (IB 24 pts)

York St John – 200–240 pts (Dance) (IB 24 pts)

220 pts **Falmouth (UC)** – 220 pts (Choreo) (IB 24 pts)

Northampton – 220–260 pts (Dance) (IB 24 pts)

Plymouth – 220 pts (Dance Thea) (IB 24 pts)

Sunderland – 220 pts (Dance)

Ulster – CCD 220 pts (Dance Mus) (IB 24 pts)

200 pts **Bucks New** – 200–240 pts (Dance Perf) (IB 24 pts)

Doncaster (Coll Univ Centre) – (Dance Prac)

UEL – 200 pts (Prof Dance Musl Thea) (IB 24 pts)

West London – 200 pts (Dance)

180 pts **Liverpool (LIPA)** – 180 pts (Dance)

160 pts **Greenwich** – 160 pts (Dance Thea Perf)

London (RAc Dance) – d/l 160 pts (Dance Edu)

Wolverhampton – 160 pts (Dance)

80 pts **and below**

Grimsby (IFHE) – 80 pts (Perf (Dance))

Northern (Sch Contemp Dance) – check with School 80 pts (Contemp Dance)

RConsvS – 80 pts (Modn Ballet)

Trinity Laban Consv – (Dance Thea)

UHI – C–A (Class Bal Dance Perf)

For a quick reference offers calculator, fold out the inside back cover.

Hull School of Performance Arts was established in 1989 and is now respected throughout the region and nationally as a leading provider of Performance Arts training. We currently offer Foundation Degrees and BA (Hons) Degrees in Dance, Musical Theatre, Broadcast Media, Stage Management and Technical Theatre, Acting, Music Performance and Music Production.

DANCE
at Hull College

HC UK

OPEN DAYS

Thurs 26 Jan
Wed 29 Feb
Sat 31 March

Hull Campus: 01482 598744
hull-college.ac.uk/HE

Alternative offers
See **Chapter 7** and **Appendix 1** for grades/UCAS Tariff points information for the International Baccalaureate, Scottish Highers/Advanced Highers, the Welsh Baccalaureate, the Irish Leaving Certificate, the Cambridge Pre-U Diploma, the Advanced Diploma and the Extended Project.

EXAMPLES OF FOUNDATION DEGREES IN THE SUBJECT FIELD
Bournemouth; Bristol City (Coll); Farnborough (CT); Hull (Coll); Leeds City (Coll); Manchester (Coll); Newcastle (Coll); Northbrook (Coll); Nottingham New (Coll); Truro (Coll).

CHOOSING YOUR COURSE (SEE ALSO CH.1)
Some course features
Edge Hill (Dance) Topics covered include dance analysis, applied dance, dance production and dance techniques.
Kingston (Dance) Two themes – technique and expression and a study of British dance in modern muticultural Britain.
Surrey (Dance Cult) Focus on dance of the 20th and 21st centuries, on dance techniques (including ballet, kathak, contemporary, and African people's dance), together with choreography and dance policy and practice.

Universities and colleges teaching quality See www.qaa.ac.uk; http://unistats.direct.gov.uk.

Top research universities and colleges (RAE 2008) See **Drama**.

ADMISSIONS INFORMATION
Number of applicants per place (approx) Chichester 6; De Montfort (Dance) 13, (Perf Arts) 9; Derby 12; Liverpool (LIPA) 24; LJMU 3; Middlesex 12; Northern (Sch Contemp Dance) 6; Roehampton 17; Surrey 5; Trinity Laban Consv 5; York St John 3.

Check **Chapter 4** when choosing your university and **Chapter 7** on how to read the subject tables.

Advice to applicants and planning the UCAS personal statement Full details should be given of examinations taken and practical experience in contemporary dance or ballet. Refer to your visits to the theatre and your impressions. You should list the dance projects in which you have worked, productions in which you have performed and the roles. State any formal dance training you have had and the grades achieved. Applicants need to have dedication, versatility, inventiveness and individuality, practical experience of dance, theoretical ability and language competency. **Bath Spa** Dance experience outside education should be mentioned.

Misconceptions about this course That Performing Arts is only an acting course: it also includes music.

Selection interviews Yes Birmingham City; **No** Dundee.

Interview advice and questions Nearly all institutions will require auditions or interviews or attendance at a workshop. The following scheme required by **Liverpool (LIPA)** may act as a guide:

1 Write a short essay (500 words) on your own views and experience of dance.
   (i) You should take into account the following.
   (ii) Your history and how you have developed physically and intellectually in your run-up to applying to LIPA.
   (iii) Your main influences and what inspires you.
   (iv) What you want to gain from training as a dancer.
   (v) Your ideas on health and nutrition as a dancer, taking into account gender and physicality.
2 All candidates must prepare **two** practical audition pieces.
   (i) Whatever you like, in whatever style you wish, as long as the piece does not exceed two minutes (please note: panel will stop anyone exceeding this time-limit). There will be no pianist at this part of the session, so if you're using music please bring it with you. This devised piece should be created by you and this means that you should feel comfortable with it and that it expresses something personal about you. You should wear your regular practice clothes for your presentation.
   (ii) You are asked to sing a musical theatre solo as part of the audition and will be accompanied by a pianist. An accompanist is provided, but you must provide the sheet music for your song, fully written out for piano accompaniment and in the key you wish to sing (the accompanist will **not** transpose at sight). **Important** Do NOT choreograph your song. You should expect to sit on a high stool or stand when singing for the audition.
3 Additionally, all candidates will participate in a class given on the day of audition.
   (i) Please ensure that you are dressed appropriately for class with clothing you are comfortable in but allows your movement to be seen. In preparing the practical elements of the audition, please remember that audition panels are not looking for a polished performance. The panel will be looking for candidates' ability to make a genuine emotional and physical connection with the material that they are presenting which shows clear intent and focus.

Remember that it is in your best interest to prepare thoroughly. Nerves inevitably play a part in any audition and can undermine even the best-prepared candidate. Your best defence is to feel confident in your preparation. See also **Chapter 6**. **Chichester** Applicants will be asked to prepare a set-piece in advance and to perform the piece in front of a group. **De Montfort** (Perf Arts) Practical workshops in dance and theatre plus a written paper. **Salford** (Perf Arts) Audition and interview. **Surrey** Applicants invited to spend a day at the university for interview and a practical class to assess dance skills. An audition fee may be charged. **Wolverhampton** Audition in the form of a dance class.

Reasons for rejection (non-academic) Applicants more suitable for an acting or dance school course than a degree course. No experience of dance on the UCAS application. Limited dance skills. **Surrey** Inadequate dance background. Had not seen/read about/done any dance.

AFTER-RESULTS ADVICE
Offers to applicants repeating A-levels Same Chester, Chichester, De Montfort (Perf Arts), LJMU, Salford, Surrey, Trinity Laban Consv, Winchester, Wolverhampton, York St John.

GRADUATE DESTINATIONS AND EMPLOYMENT (2009/10 HESA)
Graduates surveyed 865 **Employed** 530 **In voluntary employment** 10 **In further study** 210
Assumed unemployed 45

Career note Teaching is the most popular career destination for the majority of graduates. Other opportunities exist as dance animators working in education or in the community to encourage activity and participation in dance. There is a limited number of openings for dance or movement therapists who work with the emotionally disturbed, the elderly or physically disadvantaged.

OTHER DEGREE SUBJECTS FOR CONSIDERATION
Arts Management; Drama; Education (Primary); Music; Performance Studies; Physical Education; Sport and Exercise Science.

DENTISTRY

(including **Dental Technology, Dental Hygiene, Equine Dental Science** and **Oral Health Science**)

Dentistry involves the treatment and prevention of a wide range of mouth diseases from tooth decay and gum disease to mouth cancer. Courses in Dentistry/Dental Surgery cover the basic medical sciences, human disease, clinical studies and clinical dentistry. The amount of patient contact will vary between institutions but will be considerable in all Dental Schools. Intercalated courses in other science subjects are offered on most courses. The great majority of Dental Technology graduates gain employment in this career with job opportunities excellent in both the UK and Europe. There are openings in the NHS, commercial dental laboratories and the armed services.

Useful websites www.bda.org; www.bsdht.org.uk; www.dla.org.uk.

NB The points totals shown to the left of the institutions are for ease of reference only. It must not be assumed that Tariff points are always used by institutions or that they can be substituted for an offer in grades. The level of an offer is not necessarily indicative of the quality of a course.

COURSE OFFERS INFORMATION
Subject requirements/preferences GCSE English, mathematics and science subjects required in most cases for Dentistry courses. A*/A/B grades stipulated in certain subjects by many dental schools. **AL** Chemistry plus biology or a science subject usually required for Dentistry: see offers lines below. (Dntl Tech, Oral Hlth Sci) Science subject required or preferred. **Other** Many dental schools use admissions tests (eg UKCAT: see **Chapter 6**). Evidence of non-infectivity or hepatitis-B immunisation required and all new dental students screened for hepatitis-C. CRB check at enhanced level is also required.

Your target offers and examples of courses provided by each institution

420 pts London (King's) – contact Health Schools Admissions for further information AAAa–BBBc 340–420 pts (Dnstry) (IB 38 pts HL 666)
Queen's Belfast – AAAa incl AL/AS chem A +1 from biol/maths/phys (Dnstry) (IB 37 pts HL 666)

400 pts Birmingham – AAAa/b (Dntl Srgy) (IB 36 pts)

390 pts London (QM) – AAAb incl 2ALs chem/biol/sci subj **or** chem/biol bb (Dnstry) (IB 36 pts HL 665)

360 pts Bristol – AAA incl chem + other lab-based sci (Dnstry) (IB 37 pts HL 666)
Dundee – AAA incl biol +2 subj chem/phys/maths (Dnstry) (IB 37 pts)
Leeds – AAA incl AL chem biol (Dntl Srgy) (IB 35 pts HL 6 chem biol)
Liverpool – AAA incl chem/biol +1 subj not gen st **or** crit thinking (Dntl Srgy) (IB 36 pts HL 6 chem biol)
Manchester – AAA (Dnstry) (IB 34 pts)
Newcastle – AAA (incl chem and biol) (Dnstry) (IB 35 pts HL 6 chem biol)
Sheffield – AAA (Dntl Srgy) (IB 37 pts HL 6 chem biol)

340 pts **Cardiff** – AAA incl chem/biol+2 sci subj (Dnstry 5 yrs) (IB 34 pts HL 5 chem)
Glasgow – AAB incl chem+phys/maths/biol, min AS bbb (Dnstry) (IB 36 pts)

320 pts **Birmingham** – ABB (Dntl Hyg Thera) (IB 32–34 pts)
Manchester – ABB incl 2 arts+sci subj (Dnstry Pre-Dntl entry) (IB 33 pts)

300 pts **Cardiff** – BBB (Dntl Ther Hyg)
Edinburgh – BBB incl biol (Oral Hlth Sci) (IB 32 pts)
Liverpool – BBB (Dntl Hyg Dntl Thera) (IB 30 pts)
London (QM) – BBB (Dntl Mat BEng) (IB 26–28 pts)
Portsmouth – 300 pts (Dntl Hyg Dntl Thera)

280 pts **Bristol UWE** – 280 pts (Eqn Dntl Sci)
Manchester Met – 280 pts (Dntl Tech) (IB 28 pts)

260 pts **Dundee** – BCC (Oral Hlth Sci) (IB 30 pts)

240 pts **Teesside** – 240 pts (Dntl Hyg Dntl Thera)

200 pts **Cardiff Met** – 200 pts incl CD one in sci subj (Dntl Tech)
UHI – BB–AA (Oral Hlth Sci)

Alternative offers
See **Chapter 7** and **Appendix 1** for grades/UCAS Tariff points information for the International Baccalaureate, Scottish Highers/Advanced Highers, the Welsh Baccalaureate, the Irish Leaving Certificate, the Cambridge Pre-U Diploma, the Advanced Diploma and the Extended Project.

EXAMPLES OF FOUNDATION DEGREES IN THE SUBJECT FIELD
London (QM) (Dntl Hyg); Bedfordshire (Dntl Nurs; Dntl Prac Mgt); De Montfort (Dntl Tech); Essex (Oral Hlth Sci); Northampton (Dntl Nurs).

CHOOSIN i YOUR COURSE (SEE ALSO CH.1)
Some cour e features
Birmingham Basic sciences are covered in Years 1 and 2, and clinical studies in Years 3, 4 and 5.
Bristol This is a six-year course, academically able students are encouraged to intercalate.
Cardiff Clinical teaching starts at an early stage.
Leeds Focus on clinical dentistry from the outset.
Liverpool Clinical skills introduced from Year 2.
London (King's) Main components cover the basic sciences, diagnosis and treatment of oral and dental conditions and clinical dentistry. These are vertically integrated with a larger component of basic sciences at the beginning and a larger clinical component at the end.
London (QM) Clinical skills introduced from Year 2.
Manchester Clinical skills introduced from Year 2.
Newcastle Basic sciences are covered in Years 1 and 2, and clinical studies in Years 3, 4 and 5.
Queen's Belfast Basic sciences are covered in Years 1 and 2, and clinical studies in Years 3, 4 and 5.
Sheffield Main components cover the basic sciences, diagnosis and treatment of oral and dental conditions and clinical dentistry. These are vertically integrated with a larger component of basic sciences at the beginning and a larger clinical component at the end.

Universities and colleges teaching quality See www.qaa.ac.uk; http://unistats.direct.gov.uk.

Top research universities and colleges (RAE 2008) Manchester; London (QM); London (King's); Sheffield; Bristol; Cardiff; Leeds; Newcastle; London (UCL).

ADMISSIONS INFORMATION
Number of applicants per place (approx) Birmingham 10, (Dntl Hyg Thera) 17, International applicants 129 (no quota); Bristol 9 (Pre-Dntl 22; Dnstry); Cardiff 14; Cardiff Met (Dntl Tech) 1; Dundee 8, (Pre-Dntl) 5; Edinburgh (Oral Hlth Sci) 10 places every 2nd yr; Glasgow 7; Leeds 11.5; Liverpool 15; London (King's) 128 places (offers to 1 in 5 applicants); London (QM) 18, (300 interviewed and 200 offers made); Manchester 11, (Pre-Dntl) 21, (Oral Hlth Sci) 18, (Dnstry) 10; Manchester Met 16; Newcastle 12; Portsmouth 2; Queen's Belfast 5; Sheffield 16 (interviews not held for non-EU students: 3 accepted each year).

Numbers of applicants (**a** UK **b** EU (non-UK) **c** non-EU **d** mature) Bristol **a**633 **b**633 **c**83 **d**148; Glasgow **a**437 **b**45 **c**70 **d**79; Leeds **a**877 **b**42 **c**97 **d**158; Liverpool **a**704 **b**46 **c**73 **d**143; London (King's) **a**137 **b**137 **c**25; Manchester **a**1290 **b**81 **c**152 **d**331.

Advice to applicants and planning the UCAS personal statement UCAS applications listing four choices only should be submitted by 15 October. Applicants may add one alternative (non-Dentistry) course. However, if they receive an offer for this courses and are rejected for Dentistry, they will not be considered for Dentistry courses in Clearing if they perform better than expected in the examinations. On your UCAS application show evidence of your manual dexterity, work experience and awareness of problems experienced by dentists. Details should be provided of discussions with dentists and work shadowing in dental surgeries. Employment (paid or voluntary) in any field, preferably dealing with people in an environment widely removed from your home or school, could be described. Discuss any specialised fields of dentistry in which you might be interested. **Bristol** Applications are not segregated by type of educational institution. Candidates are assessed on general presentation. At least 20 days of work experience is expected, if possible in different fields of dentistry. Re-sit candidates only considered if they failed to get the grades by a small margin and they had originally placed Bristol as their first firm choice. **Cardiff** Applicants must be able to demonstrate (a) evidence of, and potential for, high academic achievement, (b) an understanding of the demands of dental training and practice, (c) a caring and committed attitude towards people, (d) a willingness to accept resonsibility, (e) an ability to communicate effectively, (f) evidence of broad social, cultural or sporting interests. **Glasgow** Applicants invited to submit portfolio as evidence of their suitability. This will be assessed against the BDS Person Specification available from the Dental School. Candidates who do not submit a portfolio are not invited to selection interview. **London (King's)** School activities desirable, for example, general reading, debating, theological interests. Community activities very desirable. General activities desirable, for example, sport, first-aid, handiwork (which can be shown at interview to demonstrate manual dexterity). Work shadowing and paid or voluntary work very desirable (check website). **Manchester** Resit offers normally only made to students who firmly accepted an offer the previous year. Resit offers AAA. Applicants are required to have observed a general dental practitioner at work before applying; a minimum of two weeks is expected. **Newcastle** Applications from students with disabilities welcomed.

Misconceptions about this course Cardiff Met (Dntl Tech) Some think that the course allows them to practise as a dentist. Some think the degree is entirely practical.

Selection interviews (Dnstry) Most dental schools will interview candidates. **Yes** Birmingham (400–450 applicants and only 50% of applicants get through the initial sort), Bristol, Cardiff, Dundee, Glasgow, Leeds, Liverpool, London (King's), London (QM), London (St George's), Newcastle, Portsmouth, Sheffield; **Some** Cardiff Met.

Interview advice and questions Dental work experience or work shadowing is essential (check with university websites) and, as a result, questions will be asked on your reactions to the work and your understanding of the different types of treatment that a dentist can offer. In the past questions at interview have included: What is conservative dentistry? What does integrity mean? Do you think the first-year syllabus is a good one? What qualities are required by a dentist? What are prosthetics, periodontics, orthodontics? What causes tooth decay? Questions asked on the disadvantages of being a dentist, the future of dentistry and how you could show that you are manually dexterous. Other questions on personal attributes and spare time activities. What are the careers within the profession open to dentists? Questions on the future of dentistry (preventative and cosmetic dentistry), the problems facing dentists, the skills needed and the advantages and disadvantages of fluoride in water. How do you relax? How do you cope with stress? See also **Chapter 6**. **Bristol** All candidates called for interview must attend in order to be considered for a place; 200 are selected for interview for the five-year course and 15 for the six-year course. Offers are made to 180 and six respectively. An essay is set on a dental subject and will be assessed for spontaneity, written content and clear thought processes. Candidates at interview are assessed on general presentation, response to questions, knowledge of dentistry, evidence of teamwork, leadership, general interests, manual dexterity and good eyesight (a practical test is taken). Examples of practical work, for example, art work, needlework etc may be taken to interview as evidence of manual dexterity. **Leeds** The interview assesses personality, verbal and communication skills and knowledge of dentistry. **London (King's)** 220 applicants are interviewed of whom 180 will receive offers. All applicants receiving offers will have been interviewed. Applicants complete a questionnaire prior to interview and the interviews last about 20 minutes. Applicants may take to interview any examples of practical work, for example, art, woodwork, needlework etc as evidence of manual dexterity.

Reasons for rejection (non-academic) Lack of evidence of a firm commitment to dentistry. Lack of breadth of interests. Lack of motivation for a health care profession. Unprofessional attitude. Poor manual dexterity. Poor communication skills. Poor English. Lack of evidence of ability to work in groups. Not for the faint-hearted! More interested in running a business and making money than in caring for people. **Cardiff Met** (Dntl Tech) Target numbers need to be precise so the course fills at a late stage.

Mature students The following universities/dental schools offer shortened (usually four years) courses in Dentistry/Dental Surgery for graduates with at least 2.1 degrees in specified subjects. GCE A-level subjects and grades are also specified. Check with universities: Aberdeen, Central Lancashire, Liverpool, London (King's), (QM), Plymouth.

AFTER-RESULTS ADVICE
Offers to applicants repeating A-levels Higher Bristol (AAA), Cardiff (preference given to students who previously applied), Dundee, Leeds (very few), Manchester (AAA – only to previous applicants who firmly accepted offer of a place); **Same** Cardiff Met (Dntl Tech), Queen's Belfast.

GRADUATE DESTINATIONS AND EMPLOYMENT (2009/10 HESA)
Clinical Dentistry; graduates surveyed 1305 **Employed** 950 **In voluntary employment** 0 **In further study** 85 **Assumed unemployed** 5

Career note The great majority of Dental Technology graduates gain employment in this career with job opportunities excellent in both the UK and Europe. There are openings in the NHS, commercial dental laboratories and the armed services.

OTHER DEGREE SUBJECTS FOR CONSIDERATION
Anatomy; Biochemistry; Biological Sciences; Biomedical Materials Science; Chemistry; Medical Sciences; Medicine; Nursing; Optometry; Pharmacy; Physiology; Physiotherapy; Radiography; Speech Therapy/Sciences; Veterinary Medicine/Science.

DEVELOPMENT STUDIES

(see also **International Relations, Politics, Town and Country Planning**)

Development Studies courses are multi-disciplinary and cover a range of subjects including economics, geography, sociology, social anthropology, politics, natural resources, with special reference to countries overseas.

Useful websites www.devstud.org.uk; www.dfid.gov.uk; www.ids.ac.uk; see also **Politics**.

NB The points totals shown to the left of the institutions are for ease of reference only. It must not be assumed that Tariff points are always used by institutions or that they can be substituted for an offer in grades. The level of an offer is not necessarily indicative of the quality of a course.

COURSE OFFERS INFORMATION
Subject requirements/preferences GCSE Mathematics, English and a foreign language may be required. **AL** Science or social science subjects may be required or preferred for some courses.

Check **Chapter 4** when choosing your university and **Chapter 7** on how to read the subject tables.

Your target offers and examples of courses provided by each institution

340 pts Essex – AAB–ABB (Int Dev)
Manchester – AAB (Dev St Pol) (IB 35 pts)
Sussex – AAB (Int Dev) (IB 35 pts)
UEA – AAB (Int Dev) (IB 31 pts)

320 pts Birmingham – ABB (Plan Econ) (IB 32–34 pts)
Leeds – ABB 320 pts (Int Dev courses) (IB 34 pts HL 16 pts)
Manchester – AAB (Dev St Sociol) (IB 35 pts)
Sussex – ABB–BBB (Sociol Int Dev) (IB 32 pts)

300 pts Birmingham – BBB (Af St Dev) (IB 32 pts)
UEA – BBB 300 pts (Int Dev Soc Anth Pol) (IB 31 pts)

280 pts Bradford – 280 pts (Dev Pce St) (IB 30 pts)
Westminster – BBC (Dev St Int Rel)

260 pts Derby – 260–300pts (Thrd Wrld Dev)
Dundee – BCC (Spat Econ Dev)
Northampton – 260–280 pts (Int Dev courses)

240 pts London Met – 240 pts (Int Dev; Int Dev Int Rel)

220 pts Leeds Met – 220 pts (Glob Dev Pce St; Glob Dev Int Rel)
Ulster – 220–240 pts (Geog Int Dev)

200 pts Portsmouth – 200–280 pts (Int Dev St)
Sheffield Hallam – 200 pts (Blt Env)
UEL – 200 pts (Int Dev Third Wrld NGO Mgt)

160 pts UHI – CC–AA (Gael Dev; Sust Rur Dev)

80 pts London (Birk) – p/t for under 21s (over 21s varies) (Dev St)

Alternative offers

See **Chapter 7** and **Appendix 1** for grades/UCAS Tariff points information for the International Baccalaureate, Scottish Highers/Advanced Highers, the Welsh Baccalaureate, the Irish Leaving Certificate, the Cambridge Pre-U Diploma, the Advanced Diploma and the Extended Project.

CHOOSING YOUR COURSE (SEE ALSO CH.1)

Some course features

Bradford Development Studies is offered with Economics or Peace Studies.
Derby (Int Rel Glob Dev) Course explores environmental, geographical, political, social, cultural and economic aspects of international relations and global development. Visits to key development organisations.
Leeds This is an interdisciplinary degree course with opportunity to study a language alongside. There are opportunities to spend a year abroad.
Manchester (Dev St) Students start to specialise in Year 2, choosing options from 10 study areas; in Year 3 they take a single or a joint specialisation with another area of study, for example, politics, economics.
Sussex International Development is also offered with French, Spanish or Italian, Geography, Economics, Anthropology, International Relations and Sociology.

Universities and colleges teaching quality See www.qaa.ac.uk; http://unistats.direct.gov.uk.

Top research universities and colleges (RAE 2008) Oxford; Manchester; UEA; Bath; London (SOAS); Birmingham.

ADMISSIONS INFORMATION

Number of applicants per place (approx) Bradford 6; Leeds 8; UEA 8.

Admissions tutors' advice Discuss aspects of development studies which interest you, for example in relation to geography, economics, politics. Interests in Third World countries should be mentioned. Knowledge of current events.

Advice to applicants and planning the UCAS personal statement Some students think that Development Studies has something to do with property, with plants or with childhood. It is none of these and is about international processes of change, development, progress and crisis.

Interview advice and questions Since this is a multi-disciplinary subject, questions will vary considerably. Initially they will stem from your interests and the information given on your UCAS application and your reasons for choosing the course. In the past, questions at interview have included: Define a Third World country. What help does the United Nations provide in the Third World? Could it do too much? What problems does the United Nations face in its work throughout the world? Why Development Studies? What will you do in your Gap Year, and what do you want to achieve? See also **Chapter 6**.

AFTER-RESULTS ADVICE
Offers to applicants repeating A-levels **Same** UEA.

GRADUATE DESTINATIONS AND EMPLOYMENT (2009/10 HESA)
Career note The range of specialisms offered on these courses will encourage graduates to make contact with and seek opportunities in a wide range of organisations, not necessarily limited to the Third World and government agencies.

OTHER DEGREE SUBJECTS FOR CONSIDERATION
Economics; Environmental Science/Studies; Geography; Government; International Relations; Politics; Sociology; Sustainable Development.

DIETETICS
(see also **Food Science/Studies and Technology, Nutrition**)

In addition to the scientific aspects of dietetics covering biochemistry, human physiology, food and clinical medicine, students are also introduced to health promotion, psychology, counselling and management skills. (See **Appendix 3**.)

Useful websites www.nutrition.org; www.bda.uk.com; www.dietetics.co.uk.

NB The points totals shown to the left of the institutions are for ease of reference only. It must not be assumed that Tariff points are always used by institutions or that they can be substituted for an offer in grades. The level of an offer is not necessarily indicative of the quality of a course.

COURSE OFFERS INFORMATION
Subject requirements/preferences **GCSE** English, mathematics and science usually required. **AL** Biology and/or chemistry may be required. **Other** Health and CRB checks required and possible immunisation against hepatitis-B for practice placements.

Your target offers and examples of courses provided by each institution

380 pts	**London (King's)** – AABc (Nutr Diet) (IB 36 pts HL chem biol)	
340 pts	**Nottingham** – AAB–ABB (Nutr (Diet) MNutr) (IB 32–34 pts)	
320 pts	**Surrey** – ABB–BBB 320–300 pts (Nutr Diet) (IB 34–32 pts)	
300 pts	**Leeds Met** – BBB incl chem (Diet) (IB 26 pts HL 5 chem)	
	London Met – 300 pts (Diet Nutr) (IB 28 pts)	
	Plymouth – 300 pts (Diet) (IB 31 pts)	
	Ulster – 300 pts (Diet)	
280 pts	**Chester** – 280–300 pts (Nutr Diet) (IB 28 pts)	
	Hertfordshire – 280 pts incl chem B biol C (Diet)	
260 pts	**Cardiff Met** – 260 pts (Hum Nutr Diet)	
	Coventry – BCC 260 pts (Diet)	
	Glasgow Caledonian – BB–BCC (Hum Nutr Diet)	
240 pts	**Bath Spa** – 240–280 pts (Diet Hlth)	
	Robert Gordon – CCC 240 pts (Nutr Diet) (IB 28 pts)	
200 pts	**Edinburgh Queen Margaret** – 200 pts (Diet)	

Alternative offers
See **Chapter 7** and **Appendix 1** for grades/UCAS Tariff points information for the International Baccalaureate, Scottish Highers/Advanced Highers, the Welsh Baccalaureate, the Irish Leaving Certificate, the Cambridge Pre-U Diploma, the Advanced Diploma and the Extended Project.

CHOOSING YOUR COURSE (SEE ALSO CH.1)
Some course features
Bath Spa (Diet Hlth) Course focuses on the impact of diet, nutrition and lifestyle on health. It is not a Dietetics course and is aimed at students without a science background.
Hertfordshire Three-year course leading to registration with the Health Professions Council to practise as a dietitian.
London (King's) Clinical placements in Years 2, 3 and 4.
Nottingham This is a four-year Master of Nutrition course which includes three integreated clinical placements.
Plymouth Supervised clinical practice in Year 2.
Surrey A professional training year is included.

Universities and colleges teaching quality See www.qaa.ac.uk; http://unistats.direct.gov.uk.

Examples of sandwich degree courses Cardiff Met; Glasgow Caledonian; Leeds Met; Surrey; Ulster.

ADMISSIONS INFORMATION
Number of applicants per place (approx) Edinburgh Queen Margaret 5; Glasgow Caledonian 11; Nottingham 7; Surrey 1.

Advice to applicants and planning the UCAS personal statement Discuss the work with a hospital dietitian and describe fully work experience gained in hospital dietetics departments or with the schools meals services, and the problems of working in these fields. Admissions tutors expect applicants to have at least visited a dietetics department, and to be outgoing with good oral and written communication skills. Contact the British Dietetic Association (see **Appendix 3**). **Bath Spa** £1000 scholarships available.

Selection interviews **Yes** Coventry.

Interview advice and questions Your knowledge of a career in dietetics will be fully explored and questions will be asked on your work experience and how you reacted to it. See also **Chapter 6**.

AFTER-RESULTS ADVICE
Offers to applicants repeating A-levels **Possibly higher** Glasgow Caledonian.

GRADUATE DESTINATIONS AND EMPLOYMENT (2009/10 HESA)
See **Nutrition**.

Career note Dietitians are professionally trained to advise on diets and aspects of nutrition and many degree courses combine both subjects. They may work in the NHS as hospital dietitians collaborating with medical staff on the balance of foods for patients, or in local health authorities working with GPs, or in health centres or clinics dealing with infant welfare and ante-natal problems. In addition, dietitians advise consumer groups in the food industry and government and may be involved in research. Courses can lead to professional registration: check with admissions tutors.

OTHER DEGREE SUBJECTS FOR CONSIDERATION
Biological Sciences; Biochemistry; Biology; Consumer Studies; Food Science; Health Studies; Hospitality Management; Human Nutrition; Nursing; Nutrition.

DRAMA

(including **Performing Arts/Studies**, **Theatre Arts**, **Theatre Studies** and **Theatre Design**; see also Dance/Dance Studies)

Drama courses are popular, with twice as many women as men applying each year. Lack of confidence in securing appropriate work at the end of the course, however, tends to encourage many applicants to bid for joint courses although these are usually far more competitive since there are fewer places available. Most schools of acting and drama provide a strong vocational bias whilst university drama departments offer a broader field of studies combining theory and practice. The choice of course will depend on personal preferences, either practical or theoretical, or a combination of both.

Useful websites www.equity.org.uk; www.abtt.org.uk; www.thestage.co.uk; www.uktw.co.uk; www.ukperformingarts.co.uk; www.arts.org.uk; www.stagecoach.co.uk.

NB The points totals shown to the left of the institutions are for ease of reference only. It must not be assumed that Tariff points are always used by institutions or that they can be substituted for an offer in grades. The level of an offer is not necessarily indicative of the quality of a course.

COURSE OFFERS INFORMATION

Subject requirements/preferences **GCSE** English usually required. **AL** English, drama, theatre studies may be required or preferred. (Thea Arts) English, theatre studies or drama may be required for some courses. **Other** CRB clearance required for some courses: check websites.

Your target offers and examples of courses provided by each institution
390 pts **Warwick** – AABb (Engl Thea St) (IB 36 pts)
380 pts **Cambridge** – A*AA (Educ Engl Dr) (IB 40–42 pts)
360 pts **Bristol** – AAA–AAB (Dr Engl) (IB 37–35 pts)
       Exeter – AAA–ABB (Dr) (IB 36–32 pts)
       London (QM) – 360 pts (Dr) (IB 32 pts)
       Manchester – AAB (Mus Dr) (IB 36–35 pts)
340 pts **Birmingham** – AAB–ABB 320–340 pts (Dr Thea Art) (IB 34–36 pts)
       Bristol – AAB incl modn lang (Dr Modn Lang 4 yrs) (IB 35 pts)
       Kent – AAB–ABB (Vis Perf Arts) (IB 33 pts)
       Lancaster – ABB (Thea St) (IB 32 pts)
       London (RH) – AAB–ABB (Dr Phil)
       Loughborough – AAb (Engl Dr) (IB 34 pts)
       Manchester – AAB (Dr Engl/Scrn St/Mus) (IB 35 pts)
       Sheffield – AAB (Thea Perf) (IB 35 pts)
       Surrey – AAB (Thea St) (IB 35–34 pts)
       Sussex – AAB–ABB (Dr St Span) (IB 34–36 pts)
       UEA – AAB (Script Perf) (IB 33 pts)
320 pts **Birmingham** – ABB (Span Thea St) (IB 32 pts)
       Glasgow – ABB (Thea St) (IB 36 pts)
       Kent – 320–300 pts (Dr courses) (IB 33–31 pts)
300 pts **Aberystwyth** – 300–320 pts (Perf St Joint Hons) (IB 30 pts)
       Bristol UWE – 300–340 pts (Dr courses)
       Edinburgh Queen Margaret – 300 pts (Dr Perf)
       Essex – 300 pts (Dr Lit) (IB 32 pts)
       Glamorgan – 300–360 pts (Perf Media)
       Huddersfield – 300–280 pts (Mus Dr)
       Hull – BBB 300 pts (Dr Engl; Dr Thea Prac)
       Kingston – 300–360 pts (Dr)
       London (Central Sch SpDr) – BBB (Dr App Thea Educ)
       London (Gold) – ABB (Dr Thea Arts)
       London (QM) – 300–320 pts (Fr/Ger/Russ Dr) (IB 32 pts)

MOUNTVIEW
ACADEMY OF THEATRE ARTS

Ralph Richardson Memorial Studio
Kingfisher Place, Clarendon Road,
Wood Green, London N22 6XF

Tel: 020 8881 2201
Fax: 020 8829 0034

enquiries@mountview.org.uk
www.mountview.org.uk

CDS MEMBER

Mountview is committed to equal opportuniti

Undergraduate &
Postgraduate Courses

Plus an exciting programme of
Part-time and Summer Courses

Musical Theatre

Acting

Production

Northumbria – 300 pts (Dr; Perf)
Queen's Belfast – BBB/BBCb (Dr courses)
Reading – 300–340 pts (Thea)
Roehampton – 300 pts (Dr Thea Perf St)
Salford – 300 pts (Perf Actg)

280 pts **Bangor** – 280–300 pts (Engl Thea St) (IB 28 pts)
Birmingham City – 280 pts (Engl Dr)
Bournemouth Arts (UC) – BBC (Actg)
Brighton – Fdn Dip required BBC (Perf Vis Arts (Thea))
Chichester – BBC 280–320 pts (Perf Arts (Thea Perf)) (IB 28 pts)
Cumbria – 280 pts (Musl Thea Perf courses; Dr Perf; Perf Art)
Edge Hill – 280 pts (Dr; Mus Snd Dr)
Glamorgan – BBC (Thea Dr)
Huddersfield – 280 pts (Dr; Dr Engl)
Lincoln – 280 pts (Dr; Dr Hist)
London (Central Sch SpDr) – BBC (Thea Prac Thea Snd; Thea Prac Cstm Constr; Thea Prac
    Stg Des; Thea Prac Perf Arts; Thea Prac Prod Ltg; Thea Prac Pptry; Thea Prac Prop Mak;
    Thea Prac Scnc Art; Thea Prac Scnc Constr; Thea Prac Stg Mgt; Thea Prac Tech Prod Mgt;
    Thea Prac Ltg Des)
Manchester Met – 280 pts (Actg) (IB 28 pts)
Oxford Brookes – BBC (Dr (Comb)) (IB 29 pts)
Teesside – 280 pts (Perf Lv Rec Media)
Worcester – 280–300 pts (Dr; Dr Perf)

260 pts **Brunel** – BCC (Thea courses)
Cardiff Met – 260 pts (Engl Dr)
Chester – 260-300 pts (Dr Thea St courses) (IB 28 pts)
De Montfort – 260 pts (Dr St) (IB 28 pts)
Derby – 260 pts (Thea Arts) (IB 26 pts)
Lincoln – 260–280 pts (Dance Dr)
Liverpool Hope – 260–280 pts (Crea Perf Arts) (IB 25 pts)
LJMU – 260 pts (Dr) (IB 28 pts)
Newman (UC) – 260 pts (Dr courses)
Newport – 260 pts (App Dr)
Northampton – 260 pts (Dr courses; Actg)
Plymouth – 260 pts (Thea Perf)
St Mary's Twickenham (UC) – 260 pts (Dr App Thea) (IB 28 pts)
Salford – 260 pts (Engl Dr Perf)
Sunderland – 260 pts (Engl Dr)
UCLan – 260–300 pts (Contemp Thea Perf; Actg)
Ulster – 260 pts (Dr; Dr Ir; Dr Dance; Dr Psy; Dr Mark)
Winchester – 260–300 pts (Arts Mgt Dr; Strt Arts; Dr Perf; Dr)

240 pts **Bath Spa** – 240–300 pts (Dr St) (IB 24 pts)
Birmingham City – 240–280 pts (Stg Mgt) (IB 25 pts)
Canterbury Christ Church – 240 pts (Perf Arts (Dr)) (IB 24 pts)
Coventry – 240 pts (Thea Prof Prac)
Greenwich – 240 pts (Dr)
London Met – 240 pts (Arts Mgt Thea St)
London South Bank – 240 pts (Engl Dr Perf; Dr Perf St; Thea Prac Crea Prodg)
Middlesex – 240 pts (Thea Arts (Perf))
Portsmouth – 240–300 pts (Engl Dr; Dr Perf; Crea Perf Arts)
Rose Bruford (Coll) – 240–280 pts (Am Thea Arts; Euro Thea Arts)
Staffordshire – 240–200 pts (Thea St Tech Stg Prod)
Sheffield Hallam – 240 pts (Perf Stg Scrn)
Southampton Solent – 240 pts (Perf; Pop Mus Perf)
Winchester – 240–280 pts (Am St Dr) (IB 24 pts)

Check **Chapter 4** when choosing your university and **Chapter 7** on how to read the subject tables.

MOUNTVIEW
ACADEMY OF THEATRE ARTS
LONDON

TRAIN FOR THE DRAMATIC ARTS

"The education and training offered by Mountview is second to none and the quality and confidence of the graduates always impresses me." – John Caird

Mountview Academy of Theatre Arts is one of the UK's leading drama schools with a worldwide reputation for excellence in education and training.

Mountview is situated in Wood Green, in the Borough of Haringey, North London, home of the famous Alexandra Palace, and is well placed for easy access to West End theatres, fringe theatres and London nightlife. Mountview boasts an extensive and respected alumni who have worked in all media, including Oscar-winning actress Melissa Leo, the much loved Amanda Holden, Award-winning West End stars Connie Fisher and Leanne Jones, as well as acclaimed actors Eddie Marsan, Douglas Henshall, Don Gilet, Brendan Coyle, Glynis Barber and Nick Moran.

The Academy offers extensive and stimulating training for those interested in pursuing a Performance, Directing or Technical Theatre career. The courses are structured to give students a thorough grounding in all aspects of their chosen field. Students are trained to a high level to develop a range of skills which will enable them to bring thought, energy and commitment to their professional work, giving them the tools to succeed in a competitive industry.

Students work, not only with Mountview's experienced teaching staff but also with current theatre practitioners - directors, set designers, lighting and sound designers, choreographers, musical directors, actors and stage management. As well as keeping students in touch with current professional practice, this provides valuable contacts on completion of the course. Additionally, students explore and develop the necessary skills to promote themselves professionally.

Mountview also has a strong commitment to training in television with its specialised requirements and students are given opportunities to work with the Academy's professional television staff. Acting students also study radio technique. After completing their chosen course, many students have gone on to enjoy highly successful careers in theatre and related media.

Additionally, Mountview's Community Outreach and Professional Development Department offers a rich and diverse programme of courses for adults, young people and children, attracting students from local, national and international communities.

The course programme offers high quality part-time training at all levels with courses for beginners and those who want to learn new skills, students who are revisiting prior training, or for a practicing professional who wishes to develop further.

Mountview is committed to equal opportunities and widening participation. It works to create significant opportunities for people of all ages and backgrounds to develop and enrich their life through the practice of theatre and dramatic arts.

For further information please visit our website:

www.mountview.org.uk

Check **Chapter 4** when choosing your university and **Chapter 7** on how to read the subject tables.

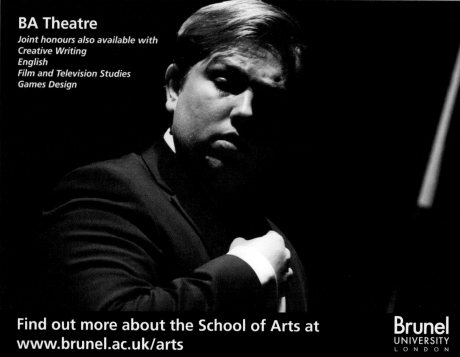

Bristol Old Vic Theatre School

An Affiliate of the Conservatoire for Dance & Drama

WORLD CLASS TRAINING - MADE IN BRISTOL

www.oldvic.ac.uk

220 pts **Anglia Ruskin** – 220–260 pts (Dr; Dr Engl Lit)
Bishop Grosseteste (UC) – 220 pts (Dr Commun; App Dr Mus; App Dr Vis Art)
Falmouth (UC) – 220 pts (Mus Thea; Thea)
Sunderland – 220 pts (Perf Arts)
Ulster – 220 pts (Dance Dr) (IB 24 pts)
200 pts **Bucks New** – 200–240 pts (Perf Arts)
Cumbria – 200 pts (Dr)
Doncaster (Coll Univ Centre) – (Contemp Perf Prac)
Glyndŵr – 200 pts (Thea TV Perf)
Greenwich – 200 pts (Actg)
Leeds Met – 200 pts (Art Evnt Perf)
Staffordshire – 200–240 pts (Dr Perf Thea Arts)
Salford – 200 pts (Vis Arts)
UEL – 200 pts (Thea St)
Wolverhampton – 200 pts (Dr courses; Dr Film St)
York St John – 200–240 pts (Thea)
180 pts **Liverpool (LIPA)** – 180 pts (Commun Dr; Thea Perf Des; Thea Perf Tech; Actg)
Manchester (Coll) – 180 pts (Actg Media)
Swansea Met – 180 pts (Dr Educ St; Cnslg Dr; Dr Psy; Perf Arts)
160 pts **Bedfordshire** – 160 pts (Thea Prof Prac)
Colchester (Inst) – 160 pts (Musl Thea; Crea Perf)
Glamorgan – 160-200 pts (Comb St Dr)
Grimsby (IFHE) – interview+audition 160 pts (Perf (Dr))
London (Central Sch SpDr) – CC (Act Mus Thea; Actg Coll Thea; Actg)
Rose Bruford (Coll) – 160 pts (Actg)
Trinity Saint David – individual offers made after audition 160–360 pts (Actg)
West London – 160 pts (Actg)

Check **Chapter 4** when choosing your university and **Chapter 7** on how to read the subject tables.

Bristol Old Vic Theatre School

An Affiliate of the Conservatoire for Dance & Drama

The Bristol Old Vic Theatre School provides the premier, conservatoire level drama training in the South West of England. For over sixty years the School has enjoyed a national and international reputation for excellence. Students are selected solely on the basis of talent.

All training courses are designed to provide students with the necessary skills and experience to sustain professional careers in their chosen area of work. Students are taught in a 'producing-house' environment, working to industry standards. All staff have considerable professional backgrounds in their area of specialism. There is an outstanding employment record from all courses, with many past students becoming movers and shakers in their field.

The Courses

3 year Professional Acting BA (Hons)

Broad and comprehensive training and preparation for professional performance in theatre, radio, television and film.

2 year Professional Acting (FdA)

Specially modified to provide as much as is possible in a reduced time. Less opportunity for "performance-under-tuition" and less time to experiment.

1 year Professional Acting for International students (MA)

An intensive three-term (33 weeks) training in the core-skills, techniques and approaches to acting on stage.

3 year Professional Stage Management BA

Provides a broad-based training, combining theatre production skills with television and radio drama experience.

2 Year Professional Stage Management (FdA)

Long established training in theatre production skills offers a fast track course for more mature students.

1 year Theatre Production Management (PG Dip)

A one year course for only two students who will have previous training in a practical theatre discipline and/or have worked professionally in a stage management or technical theatre department.

1 year Theatre Arts Management (PG Dip)

A one year course for two students who will normally have previous training in a practical theatre discipline and/or professional experience in a theatre environment.

2 year Costume (FdA & BA Hons top up)

An intensive vocational and highly practical course for four students per year covering all aspects of costume work.

1 year Scenic Art (PG Dip)

Entirely practical, intensive, three-term course. Students will have a high level of painting and drawing skills.

4 term Theatre Design (MA)

The only course of its kind in the U.K. which is set in a Theatre School and integrated with a producing company, training designers in a realistic environment, working closely with directors, actors and technicians.

4 term Drama Directing (MA)

A four term course for up to four students with the career aim of directing drama. Students come from a very wide range of backgrounds but must have previous directing experience.

To apply go to: www.oldvic.ac.uk

140 pts **Birmingham City** – 140 pts (Actg; Actg (Musl Thea))
120 pts **Blackpool and Fylde (Coll)** – 120–360 pts (Actg; Musl Thea)
Royal Welsh (CMusDr) – 120–200 pts (Actg; Stg Mgt; Thea Des)
100 pts **Guildhall (Sch Mus Dr)** – 100 pts (Actg; Stg Mgt Tech Thea)
100 pts **Arts London** – (Perf Des Prac)
Colchester (Inst) – (Tech Thea)
LAMDA – (Prof Actg; Stg Mgt Tech Thea)
London (RADA) – interview (Tech Thea Stg Mgt)
 80 pts **and below**
ALRA – some theatre schools and drama departments do not select on the basis of
academic qualifications (Actg)
Arts Educ Sch – entry by audition; contact admissions tutor (Actg Film TV; Musl Thea)
Bristol Old Vic (Thea Sch) – interview (Prof Stg Mgt)
Croydon (Coll) – 80–100 pts (Des Crft Stg Scrn)
Essex – EE 80 pts (Actg; Actg Contemp Thea)
GSA Conservatoire – audition (Actg; Musl Thea)
London (Birk) – p/t for under 21s (over 21s varies) (Thea Dr St)
London Mountview (Ac Thea Arts) – audition (Perf Musl Thea; Actg; Tech Thea)
RConsvS – min b 80 pts (Contemp Perf Prac; Actg; Tech Prod Arts)
Trinity Laban Consv – (Dance Thea)

Alternative offers
See **Chapter 7** and **Appendix 1** for grades/UCAS Tariff points information for the International
Baccalaureate, Scottish Highers/Advanced Highers, the Welsh Baccalaureate, the Irish Leaving
Certificate, the Cambridge Pre-U Diploma, the Advanced Diploma and the Extended Project.

EXAMPLES OF FOUNDATION DEGREES IN THE SUBJECT FIELD
Blackpool and Fylde (Coll); Bournemouth; Bournemouth and Poole (Coll); Bournemouth Arts (UC);
Bradford; Bristol City (Coll); Chichester; Colchester (Inst); Cornwall (Coll); Craven (Coll); Exeter (Coll);
Farnborough (CT); Hereford (CA); Hertfordshire; Hull (Coll); Kirklees (Coll); Leeds City (Coll); NEW (Coll);
Newcastle (Coll); Northbrook (Coll); Norwich City (Coll); Nottingham New (Coll); Rose Bruford (Coll);
Rotherham (CAT); St Helens (Coll); Sheffield (Coll); South Devon (Coll); South Essex (Coll); Staffordshire
Reg Fed (SURF); Suffolk (Univ Campus); Sunderland; Truro (Coll); Wigan and Leigh (Coll).

CHOOSING YOUR COURSE (SEE ALSO CH.1)
Some course features
Anglia Ruskin (Dr) The course content depends on the options chosen, for example dramatic
performance, technical theatre, drama in theory and practice, directing and TV drama.
Bedfordshire (Perf Arts) Focus on dance and theatre.
Brunel (Dr) A strong practical emphasis.
De Montfort (Perf Arts) A highly practical programme covering acting, directing, dance, film, arts
management and community education.
Edge Hill (Dr) Options in directing, design, writing, educational or community drama.
Lincoln (Dr) A balanced course covering acting, directing, history and technical aspects.
Liverpool Hope (Crea Perf Arts) There are two main strands – artistic and vocational. The course
covers drama, music, dance, visual art, writing and work-related skills.
London (RH) (Int Thea) Practical and theoretical studies, with study in Australia. Year's study abroad
also possible in other programmes.
Loughborough (Dr) Throughout the course, theoretical studies support the practical aspects with
historical and analytical elements of European and American Theatre.
Newport (Perf Arts) Performance for film, radio, TV, theatre and drama.

Universities and colleges teaching quality See www.qaa.ac.uk; http://unistats.direct.gov.uk.

Top research universities and colleges (RAE 2008) (Drama, Dance and Performing Arts) Warwick
(Film and TV Studies); Roehampton (Dance); London (QM); St Andrews; Manchester; Bristol; Glasgow;
Exeter; London (RH).

Check **Chapter 4** when choosing your university and **Chapter 7** on how to read the subject tables.

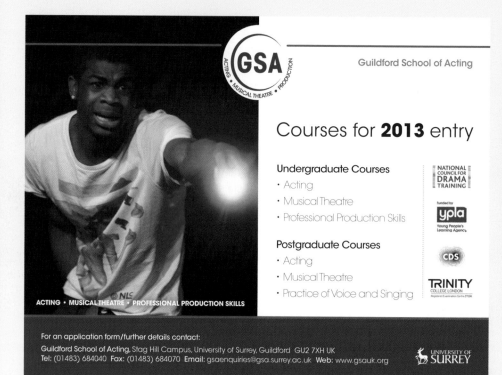

Guildford School of Acting

Courses for **2013** entry

Undergraduate Courses

· Acting
· Musical Theatre
· Professional Production Skills

Postgraduate Courses

· Acting
· Musical Theatre
· Practice of Voice and Singing

ACTING · MUSICAL THEATRE · PROFESSIONAL PRODUCTION SKILLS

For an application form/further details contact:
Guildford School of Acting, Stag Hill Campus, University of Surrey, Guildford GU2 7XH UK
Tel: (01483) 684040 Fax: (01483) 684070 Email: gsaenquiries@gsa.surrey.ac.uk Web: www.gsauk.org

UNIVERSITY OF SURREY

ADMISSIONS INFORMATION

Number of applicants per place (approx) Aberystwyth 10; Arts London (Actg) 32, (Dir) 10;
Birmingham 15; Bishop Grosseteste (UC) 4; Bristol 19; Brunel 9; Chester 14; Cumbria 4; De Montfort
(Perf Arts) 5; Edge Hill 8; Edinburgh Queen Margaret 4; Essex 15; Exeter 20; Glamorgan 6;
Huddersfield 5; Hull 16, (Scarborough) 2; Hull (Coll) 2; Kent 24; Lancaster 18; Leeds 10; Liverpool
(LIPA) (Perf Arts (Actg)) 48; LJMU 10; London (Central Sch SpDr) (Thea Prac) 5; London (Gold) 28;
London (RH) 10; London Met 20; London Mountview (Ac Thea Arts) (Musl Thea) 8; Loughborough 6;
Manchester (Dr) 6, (Dr Engl Lit) 8; Manchester (Coll) 10; Manchester Met 48; Middlesex 26;
Northampton 3; Northumbria 25; Nottingham Trent 4; Reading 17; Roehampton 6; Royal Welsh
(CMusDr) (Actg) 50, (Stg Mgt) 10; UEA 13; Warwick 18; Winchester (Dr) 6; Worcester 4; York 4; York
St John 9.

Advice to applicants and planning the UCAS personal statement List the plays in which you have
performed and specify the characters played. Indicate any experience in other areas of theatre,
especially directing or writing. Add any information on projects you have initiated or developed or
worked on in theatre craft, such as set design, costume design, lighting design, prop-making, scene
painting. List any community arts projects such as work with youth clubs, hospital radio, amateur
dramatics, music/drama workshops and voluntary work within the arts. Show your strengths in dance
and theatre, and your commitment to drama in all its aspects. See **Chapter 6**. **Bristol** Deferred entry
accepted. **London (Central Sch SpDr)** (Dr App Thea Educ) We look for an interest in theatre and
performance in different social and cultural settings, for example, community, schools, prisons. We also
look for an enquiring mind, practical drama skills, flexibility and focus. **Manchester** Due to the detailed
nature of entry requirements for Drama courses, the University is unable to include full details in the
prospectus. For complete and up-to-date information on the entry requirements for these courses,
please visit the website at www.manchester.ac.uk/ugcourses. **Warwick** Gap year only acceptable in
exceptional circumstances. **York** (Writ Dir Perf) Strong analytical ability plus experience in a related
field, eg stage management/design, drama, writing are important factors.

Guys and Dolls
Photo Mark Dean

GUILDFORD SCHOOL OF ACTING

GSA has built an international reputation for excellence in training for actors and technicians in all areas of theatre and the recorded media.

Situated in brand new building where it is part of the School of Arts at the University of Surrey, GSA offers the very best vocational training in Acting, Musical Theatre and Professional Production Skills with courses ranging from National Diplomas and Foundation Degrees through to Post Graduate qualifications in Acting, Musical Theatre and Practice of Voice and Singing. We currently offer both funded places as well as private ones.

The opening of the Ivy Arts centre in 2011 has ensured new state of the art facilities for Professional Production Skills training and a versatile theatre space for productions. An excellent film and TV department and access to a number of other local theatres and a very special creative community make GSA a top choice amongst candidates wishing to train for the performing arts industry.

GSA also offers the only full-time Foundation Course in Musical Theatre at an accredited drama school. In addition GSA offers a Part-time evening course for students who intend to complete their A Levels prior to applying for full-time training. These new courses complement GSA's existing Saturday School and well subscribed Summer Schools.

GSA also offers a full syllabus for Musical Theatre Singing Examinations ranging from Grades 1 – 8 through to Diploma, Licentiate and Fellowship level.

Current high profile graduates include Tom Chambers, Brenda Blethyn OBE, Celia Imrie, Michael Ball, Bill Nighy, Chloe Hart, Chris Geere, Ellie Paskell, Claire Cooper, Rob Kazinsky, Ian Kelsey and Justin Fletcher MBE.

Virtually every West End show features performers who trained at GSA. Current students have performed at the Olivier Awards ceremony, the opening of G-Live, Guildford, The Festival of Remembrance at The Royal Albert Hall and numerous other prestigious events.

www.gsauk.org

Misconceptions about this course That a Theatre Studies course is a training for the stage: it is not. **Arts London** Provides a long-established classical conservatoire-type training for actors, and not Theatre Studies or Performance Arts courses, contrary to the views of some students. It is no longer a private school and home and EU students pay the standard degree fee. **De Montfort** (Perf Arts) Students are unaware that the course involves music. **Kent** This is not like an acting school. **Staffordshire** We stress to applicants that this is not a drama school course. **Winchester** This is not an Acting course although practical work is involved. **York St John** This is not a course for intending actors.

Selection interviews Most institutions, usually with auditions which are likely to involve solo and group tests. **Some** Anglia Ruskin, Bristol, Bucks New, Chester, St Mary's Twickenham (UC); **No** Dundee.

Interview advice and questions See also **Chapter 6**. **Arts London** (Actg) Two three-minute speeches or scenes, one of which must be from the classical repertoire. (Dir) Interview and practical workshop which may involve directing actors. **Bristol** Assesses each case on its merits, paying attention to candidate's educational and cultural opportunities. Particularly interested in applicants who have already shown some evidence of commitment in their approach to drama in practical work, theatre-going, film viewing or reading. One fifth of applicants are called for interview and take part in practical sessions. They may present any art work, photography or similar material. (London Board Practical Music not acceptable for Drama/Music unless offered with theoretical music + one other A-level.) **Brunel** All applicants to whom an offer may be made will be auditioned, involving a practical workshop, voice, movement improvisation and a short prepared speech. Offers unlikely to be made to those with less than a grade B in drama or theatre studies. **Chichester** Applicants will be asked to prepare a set-piece in advance and to perform it before a group. **De Montfort** (Perf Arts) What do you hope to gain on a three-year course in Performing Arts? Interviews involve practical workshops in drama and theatre and a written paper. **Hull** Interviews two groups of 18 for whole day which presents a mini-version of the course, with entire staff and number of current students present. Offers then made to about half. Selection process is all-important. More applicants for the Joint Honours courses with English, Theology, American Studies or Modern Language, who have a conventional half-hour interview. Drama/English is the most popular combination and the offer includes a B in English. **Kent** No Single Honours candidate accepted without interview. Emphasis equally on academic and practical abilities. Questions asked to probe the applicant's creative and analytical grasp of theatre. **Lancaster** (Thea St) Candidates invited for interview and should be prepared to take part in a workshop with other candidates. We are just as interested in backstage people as actors and now have an arts administration option. **Loughborough** Candidates judged as individuals. Applicants with unconventional subject combinations and mature students considered. Final selection based on interview and audition. Applicants ought to show experience of practical drama, preferably beyond school plays. **Royal Welsh (CMusDr)** (Actg) audition; (Stg Mgt) interview; (Thea Des) interview and portfolio presentation. All applicants are charged an audition/interview fee. **UEA** Looks for candidates with a sound balance of academic and practical skills. Applicants will be expected to analyse performance and to understand what is entailed in the production of a drama. **Warwick** Interview is important to assess academic potential and particularly commitment to, and suitability for, teaching; offers therefore variable.

Reasons for rejection (non-academic) Poor ambition. Wrong expectations of the course. Several students clearly want a drama school acting training rather than a degree course. Not enough background reading. **Arts London** Insufficient clarity about career aims. **De Montfort** (Perf Arts) Candidate more suitable for a drama or dance school than for a degree course. No genuine engagement with the subject. Evidence of poor attendance at school.

AFTER-RESULTS ADVICE

Offers to applicants repeating A-levels Higher Bristol, Glasgow (AAA), Hull, Warwick; **Possibly higher** London (RH); **Same** Brunel, Chichester, De Montfort (Perf Arts), GSA Conservatoire, Huddersfield, Kent, Leeds (further audition required), Liverpool Hope, LJMU, Loughborough, Manchester (Coll), Newman (UC), Nottingham Trent, Roehampton, Royal Welsh (CMusDr), St Mary's Twickenham (UC), Staffordshire, Sunderland, UEA, Winchester, York St John.

GRADUATE DESTINATIONS AND EMPLOYMENT (2009/10 HESA)
Graduates surveyed 5960 **Employed** 3295 **In voluntary employment** 115 **In further study** 925 **Assumed unemployed** 440

Career note Some graduates develop careers in performance, writing, directing and producing as well as wider roles within the theatre. Others go on to careers such as teaching, media management and retail where their creativity and communication skills are valued.

OTHER DEGREE SUBJECTS FOR CONSIDERATION
Art and Design (Costume Design, Stage Design); Arts Management; Dance; Education (Primary); English; Performance Studies.

ECONOMICS

(see also **Business and Management Courses, Mathematics, Statistics**)

Economics is about how society makes good use of the limited resources available. Degree courses cover all aspects of finance, taxation and monetary union between countries, aiming to equip the student to analyse economic problems in a systematic way and thus acquire an understanding of how economic systems work. Economics involves mathematics and statistics, and applicants without economics at A or AS-level should be prepared for this.

Useful websites www.bized.co.uk; www.iea.org.uk; www.res.org.uk; www.economist.com; www.neweconomics.org; see also **Finance**.

NB The points totals shown to the left of the institutions are for ease of reference only. It must not be assumed that Tariff points are always used by institutions or that they can be substituted for an offer in grades. The level of an offer is not necessarily indicative of the quality of a course.

COURSE OFFERS INFORMATION
Subject requirements/preferences GCSE English, mathematics and occasionally a foreign language required. A*/A/B may be stipulated by some universities. **AL** Mathematics, economics or business studies may be required or preferred. Business studies may be preferred if economics is not offered. Applicants should note that many courses will accept students without economics (check prospectuses and websites).

Your target offers and examples of courses provided by each institution
440 pts **Warwick** – A*AAa (Econ Pol Int St) (IB 38 pts)
430 pts **Warwick** – A*AAb–AAAb (PPE) (IB 38 pts)
380 pts **Bath** – A*AA (Econ Int Dev) (IB 38 pts)
    Bristol – A*AA–ABB (Econ courses) (IB 38–35 pts)
    Cambridge – A*AA (Lnd Econ) (IB 40–42 pts HL 766–777)
    Durham – A*AA (Econ) (IB 38 pts)
    Exeter – A*AA–AAB 380–340 pts (Econ Pol) (IB 38–34 pts)
    London (UCL) – A*AA–AAA incl maths (Econ Stats) (IB 38–39 pts)
    London LSE – A*(maths)AA (Econ) (IB 38 pts HL 766)
    Nottingham – A*AA–AAA 360–380 pts (Econ Fr/Ger/Russ) (IB 38–36 pts)
    Oxford – A*AA (Mat Econ Mgt) (IB 40 pts)
    Warwick – A*AA–AAA (Econ Econ Hist) (IB 38 pts)
360 pts **Birmingham** – AAA (Econ Russ St) (IB 36–38 pts)
    Bristol – AAA–AAB 340–360 pts (Phil Econ) (IB 37–35 HL 666)
    City – AAA 360 pts (Fin Econ) (IB 35 pts)
    Durham – AAA (Econ Pol) (IB 37 pts)
    Edinburgh – AAA–BBB (Econ Hist Bus St) (IB 42–34 pts)
    Lancaster – AAA 360 pts (Econ (St Abrd)) (IB 36 pts)
    Leeds – AAA (Econ) (IB 35 pts HL 17 pts)

London (RH) – AAA–ABB 360–320 pts (Econ Pol Int Rel) (IB 32–35 pts)
London (SOAS) – AAA (Dev Econ) (IB 38 pts HL 766)
London (UCL) – AABe–ABBe (Econ Bus E Euro St) (IB 34–36 pts)
London LSE – AAA (Gov Econ) (IB 38 pts HL 766)
London NCH – AAA–AAB 340–360 pts (Econ) (IB 37–38 pts HL 77)
Oxford – AAA (Hist Econ) (IB 38–40 pts)
St Andrews – AAA (Bib St Econ) (IB 38 pts)
Southampton – AAA incl maths (Econ Act Sci) (IB 36 pts HL 18 pts)
Sussex – AAA–AAB incl maths (Maths Econ) (IB 35–36 pts HL 6 maths)
York – AAA (Phil Pol Econ) (IB 36 pts)

340 pts Aston – AAB–AAA 340–360 pts (Econ Mgt) (IB 35 pts HL 665)
Birmingham – AAA–AAB 340–360 pts (Pol Econ) (IB 34–38 pts)
Cardiff – AAB (Bus Econ; Econ; Bus Econ Euro Lang)
Exeter – A*AA–AAB (Bus Econ Euro St) (IB 38–34 pts)
Lancaster – AAB (Phil Pol Econ) (IB 34 pts)
Leicester – AAB incl maths (Maths Econ)
Liverpool – AAB (Bus Econ) (IB 35 pts)
London (QM) – AAB (Econ Fin Mgt) (IB 36 pts HL 5 maths)
London LSE – AAB (Env Plcy Econ) (IB 37 pts HL 666)
Loughborough – AAB (Econ) (IB 34 pts)
Manchester – AAB (Int Bus Fin Econ) (IB 35 pts)
Newcastle – AAB (Econ Maths) (IB 34 pts)
Nottingham – AAB (Ind Econ Ins) (IB 34 pts)
Queen's Belfast – AAB/ABBa (PPE)
Sheffield – AAB (Econ) (IB 35 pts)
Southampton – AAB incl AS maths (Econ Phil) (IB 34 pts HL 17 pts)
Surrey – AAA–AAB 340–360 pts (Econ) (IB 36–35 pts)
Sussex – AAB (Econ Pol) (IB 35 pts)
Swansea – AAB (PPE)
UEA – AAB (Econ Econ Psy) (IB 34–33 pts)
York – AAB (Econ/Maths) (IB 36 pts HL 666)

320 pts Birmingham (UC) – ABB (Geog Econ) (IB 32–34 pts)
Bournemouth – 320 pts (Econ Fin; Econ)
Edinburgh – ABB–ABC (Econ Stats) (IB 34–42 pts)
Essex – 320 pts (Econ; Fin Econ; Int Econ; Mgt Econ; Econ Langs; Econ Fr)
Glasgow – ABB (Econ Joint Hons) (IB 36 pts)
Hull – 320–340 pts (PPE) (IB 34 pts)
Kent – ABB (Econ Comp) (IB 34 pts H16 pts)
Leeds – ABB (As Pacif St Econ) (IB 32 pts HL 15 pts)
Leicester – ABB (Pol Econ)
Liverpool – ABB (Econ Maths) (IB 33 pts HL 6 maths)
London LSE – ABB (Soc Plcy Econ) (IB 37 pts)
Newcastle – AAB–ABB 320–340 pts (Pol Econ) (IB 34–36 pts)
Queen's Belfast – ABB/BBBb (Econ courses)
Reading – 320 pts (Geog Econ (Reg Sci)) (IB 34–31 pts)
Strathclyde – ABB (Econ; Econ Maths Stats; Econ Psy; Econ Mgt)
Swansea – ABB (Geog Econ)
UEA – ABB (Maths Econ) (IB 32 pts HL 6 maths)

300 pts Aberdeen – BBB (Econ) (IB 28 pts)
Aberystwyth – 300 pts (Econ Mark) (IB 27 pts)
Bristol UWE – 300 pts (Econ) (IB 24–28 pts)
Buckingham – 300 pts (Law Econ)
Cardiff Met – 300 pts (Econ; Int Econ Fin)
Coventry – BBB (Econ; Bus Econ; Int Econ Tr)
Edinburgh – AAA–BBB 300–360 pts (Econ Chin) (IB 34 pts HL 555)

Essex – 300–320 pts (Econ Pol) (IB 32–36 pts)
Heriot-Watt – ABC–BBB (Econ)
Keele – 300 pts (Econ) (IB 28–30 pts)
London (QM) – 300–340 pts (Glob Chn Env Econ Dev) (IB 32 pts)
Northumbria – 300 pts (Bus Econ)
Nottingham Trent – 300 pts (Econ; Bus Econ; Econ Fin Bank)
Reading – 300 pts (Fd Mark Bus Econ)
Sheffield Hallam – 300 pts (Bus Econ)
Swansea – BBB (Bus Mgt Econ) (IB 30–32 pts)
UEA – BBB (Bus Fin Econ) (IB 32 pts)
Westminster – BBB (Bus Econ) (IB 28 pts)

280 pts **Birmingham City** – 280 pts (Econ courses)
Brighton – BBC 280 pts (Econ Fin)
Bristol UWE – 280–340 pts (Bus St Econ) (IB 24–28 pts)
Brunel – BBC (Econ Bus Fin) (IB 32–33 pts)
Coventry – BBC (Fin Econ)
De Montfort – 280 pts (Econ Fin)
Greenwich – 280 pts (Econ Bank; Econ; Int St Econ)
Hull – 280 pts (Econ; Bus Econ (Int); Econ Log; Bus Econ; Econ (Int))
Manchester Met – 280 pts (Bus Econ) (IB 28 pts)
Oxford Brookes – BBC (Econ Fin Int Bus) (IB 29 pts)
Portsmouth – 280–320 pts (Econ Fin Bank; Econ; Bus Econ; App Econ)
Stirling – BBC (Econ) (IB 32 pts)
Worcester – 280 pts (Bus Acc Econ; Bus Econ Adv; Bus Econ PR)

260 pts **Bangor** – 260–300 pts (Econ Joint Hons) (IB 28 pts)
Dundee – BCC (Spat Econ Dev)
Greenwich – 260 pts (Bus Econ)
Hertfordshire – 260 pts (Econ; Bus Econ)
Kingston – 260 pts (Econ) (IB 24 pts)
Northampton – 260–280 pts (Econ courses)
Oxford Brookes – BCC (Econ Pol Int Rel) (IB 29 pts)
Staffordshire – BCC–BB 260 pts (Acc Econ; Econ Phil)
Ulster – 260 pts (Soc Plcy Econ)
Winchester – 260–300 pts (Bus Mgt Fin Econ)

240 pts **Bradford** – 240–280 pts (Econ; Fin Econ; Econ Mark; Econ Psy; Int Econ)
Leeds Met – 240 pts (Econ Bus) (IB 24 pts)
London Met – 240 pts (Econ; Econ St; Fin Econ; Int Econ)
Manchester Met – 240–280 pts (Econ) (IB 28 pts)
Newport – 240 pts (Econ Law; Bus Econ)
Plymouth – 240 pts (Econ courses; Bus Econ courses; Fin Econ; Bus Econ Mark)
UCLan – 240–280 pts (Econ courses)
Ulster – 240 pts (Econ; Econ Mark)

230 pts **Edinburgh Napier** – 230 pts (Econ Acc; Econ Mgt)

200 pts **Abertay Dundee** – 200 pts (Int Econ Mgt)
Anglia Ruskin – 240–200 pts (Bus Econ)
Middlesex – 200–280 pts (Bus Econ)
UEL – 200 pts (Bus Econ) (IB 24 pts)

160 pts **Greenwich (Sch Mgt)** – 160 pts (Econ)

80 pts **London (Birk)** – p/t for under 21s (over 21 varies) (Fin Econ)

Open University – contact +44 (0)845 300 6090 **or** www.openuniversity.co.uk/you (Econ Mathem Sci; PPE; Soc Sci Econ)

Alternative offers

See **Chapter 7** and **Appendix 1** for grades/UCAS Tariff points information for the International Baccalaureate, Scottish Highers/Advanced Highers, the Welsh Baccalaureate, the Irish Leaving Certificate, the Cambridge Pre-U Diploma, the Advanced Diploma and the Extended Project.

Check **Chapter 4** when choosing your university and **Chapter 7** on how to read the subject tables.

CHOOSING YOUR COURSE (SEE ALSO CH.1)
Some course features
Aberystwyth A modular Economics course is offered consisting of core subjects and electives in a complementary subject, for example computing, accountancy, marketing, human resource management or smalll business management. A course in Business Economics is also offered.
Brunel Three courses are offered in Economics, Economics and Business Finance and Business Economics. All students take the same core modules at Level 1 before specialising in Years 2 and 3.
De Montfort Courses are offered in Economics with Finance or Government each with a one year placement in industry or commerce.
Durham Single and Joint Honours Economics students follow the same first-year course in economics. This allows flexibility in the choice of combined degree at the end of the first year, leading on to courses in Economics, Business Economics or Economics with French or Politics. There is also a course in PPE and a Combined Honours programme in Social Sciences.
Heriot-Watt Six Economics courses are offered, including options in Business, Law, Management, Finance and Accountancy. There are opportunities to study abroad.
Hertfordshire Optional year in industry.
Kent The Economics course has a strong European flavour and a European course enables students to spend a year in France or Spain.
London (RH) The Economics course deals with all aspects of the subject including financial and industrial economics, and analytical political economy. Ten courses are also offered with economics as a major subject and there is a separate degree in Financial and Business Economics.
London (SOAS) Single or Joint Economics courses are offered with a focus on Africa and Asia and their languages. Units are offered on developing countries, Japan, China and the Middle East. There are also courses in Development Economics and Financial and Management Studies.
London LSE Ten courses are offered with Economics as a major subject.
Portsmouth The Economics degree is an extremely flexible course that allows students to move between various Economics schemes in the Business School. These include Business Economics (which can also be studied with law), Applied Economics and Economics, each course offers an optional work placement.
York A modular Economics course with a wide range of options including some which can be taken from other departments.

Universities and colleges teaching quality See www.qaa.ac.uk; http://unistats.direct.gov.uk.

Top research universities and colleges (RAE 2008) (Economics and Econometrics) London LSE; London (UCL); Essex; Oxford; Warwick; Bristol; Nottingham; London (QM); Cambridge; Manchester; Glasgow; London (RH); Southampton.

Examples of sandwich degree courses Aston; Bath; Birmingham City; Bournemouth; Brighton; Bristol UWE; Brunel; Coventry; De Montfort; Essex; Greenwich; Hertfordshire; Kingston; Leeds Met; Loughborough; Newcastle; Nottingham Trent; Oxford Brookes; Plymouth; Portsmouth; Salford; Sheffield Hallam; Staffordshire; Surrey; Ulster; Westminster; Worcester.

ADMISSIONS INFORMATION
Number of applicants per place (approx) Aberystwyth 3; Anglia Ruskin 10; Aston 8; Bangor 4; Bath 9; Birmingham 10; Birmingham City 16; Bradford 5; Bristol 41; Brunel 12; Buckingham 4; Cambridge 6; Cardiff 8; City 18, (Econ Acc) 12; Coventry 10; Dundee 5; Durham (Econ) 10; Essex 6; Exeter 12; Greenwich 8; Heriot-Watt 4; Hull 15; Kent 11; Kingston 9; Lancaster 14; Leeds 16; Leicester 10; Liverpool 4; LJMU 8; London (UCL) 12; London LSE (Econ) 15, (Econ Econ Hist) 8, (Ecomet Mathem Econ) 20; Loughborough 15; Manchester (Econ) 8, (Econ Fin) 22, (Econ Pol) 27, (Econ Sociol) 27; Manchester Met 5; Middlesex 8; Newcastle 11, (Econ Bus Mgt) 27; Northampton 8; Northumbria 16; Nottingham (Econ Chin) 8; Nottingham Trent 2; Oxford Brookes 51; Plymouth 4; Portsmouth 6; Queen's Belfast 10; St Andrews 5; Salford 6; Sheffield 10; Southampton 8; Staffordshire 4; Stirling 6; Surrey 5; Swansea 7; UCLan 5; UEA 15; Warwick 16; West Scotland 7; York 4.

Numbers of applicants (a UK **b** EU (non-UK) **c** non-EU **d** mature) Aston **a**300 **b**30 **c**50 **d**20; Leeds **b**5 **c**70 **d**33.

Advice to applicants and planning the UCAS personal statement Visits, work experience and work shadowing in banks, insurance companies, accountants' offices etc should be described. Keep up-to-date with economic issues by reading *The Economist* and the *Financial Times* and find other sources of information. Describe any particular aspects of economics which interest you – and why. Make it clear on the statement that you know what economics is and why you want to study it. Give evidence of your interest in economics and your reasons for choosing the course and provide information about your sport/extra-curricular activities and positions of responsibility.

Misconceptions about this course Bradford That the Economics course is very mathematical and that students will not get a good job, eg management. **Kent** That the Economics course is mathematical, has a high failure rate and has poorer job prospects than Business Studies courses. **London (UCL)** Some think the Economics course is a Business course.

Selection interviews Yes Birmingham, Bristol, Bristol UWE, Brunel, Cambridge, Coventry, Edinburgh, Essex, Keele, London (RH), London (UCL), Manchester Met, Middlesex, Nottingham, Nottingham Trent, Oxford (Econ Mgt) 9%, Reading, Southampton (Acc Econ) (interviews influence level of offer), Surrey, UEA, UEL; **Some** Aberystwyth, Anglia Ruskin, Bangor, Buckingham, Dundee, Kent, Leeds, London LSE, London Met (mature students), Loughborough, Staffordshire, Swansea.

Interview advice and questions If you have studied economics at A-level or in other examinations, expect to be questioned on aspects of the subject. This is a subject which is constantly in the news, so keep abreast of developments and be prepared to be asked questions such as: What is happening to sterling at present? What is happening to the dollar? How relevant is economics today? What are your views on the Government's economic policy? Do you think that the family is declining as an institution? Discuss Keynesian economics. Is the power of the Prime Minister increasing? What is a recession? How would you get the world out of recession? What causes a recession? See also **Chapter 6. Cambridge** What is the point of using NHS money to keep old people alive? **Oxford** (Econ Mgt) 'I was asked questions on a newspaper article I had been given to read 45 minutes beforehand, followed by a few maths problems and an economics question.' Explain why teachers might be changing jobs to become plumbers. (Econ Mgt) What is the difference between the buying and selling of slaves and the buying and selling of football players? Should a Wal-Mart store be opened in the middle of Oxford?

Reasons for rejection (non-academic) Lack of knowledge about the course offered and the subject matter; lack of care in preparing personal statement; poor written English; the revelation on the statement that they want a course different from that for which they have applied! **Aberystwyth** Would have trouble fitting into the unique environment at Aberystwyth.

AFTER-RESULTS ADVICE
Offers to applicants repeating A-levels Higher Birmingham City, City, Essex, Leeds, Newcastle, Northumbria, Nottingham, Queen's Belfast, St Andrews, UEA, Warwick, York; **Possibly higher** Bradford, Brunel, Durham, Lancaster, Oxford Brookes; **Same** Aberystwyth, Anglia Ruskin, Bangor, Bath, Buckingham, Cambridge, Cardiff, Coventry, Dundee, Edinburgh Napier, Heriot-Watt, Hull, Kingston, Liverpool, LJMU, London (RH), London Met, Loughborough, Nottingham Trent, Salford, Sheffield, Staffordshire, Surrey, Swansea, UEL, Ulster.

GRADUATE DESTINATIONS AND EMPLOYMENT (2009/10 HESA)
Graduates surveyed 6565 **Employed** 2310 **In voluntary employment** 75 **In further study** 1160 **Assumed unemployed** 400

Career note Most graduates work within areas of business and finance, and in a range of jobs including management and administration posts across both public and private sectors.

OTHER DEGREE SUBJECTS FOR CONSIDERATION
Accountancy; Actuarial Studies; Administration; Banking; Business Studies; Development Studies; Estate Management; Financial Services; Government; Politics; Management Sciences/Studies; Property Development; Quantity Surveying; Social Sciences; Sociology; Statistics.

Check **Chapter 4** when choosing your university and **Chapter 7** on how to read the subject tables.

EDUCATION STUDIES

(see also **Physical Education, Social Sciences/Studies, Teacher Training**)

There are two types of degree course in Education – those which cover the history, philosophy and theory of education but which are not necessarily teacher training courses, and those which prepare the student for a career in the teaching profession. This subject table contains courses that are related to the study of education. For teacher training please see **Teacher Training**. Interview panels look for candidates with confidence in their own ability, a lively personality, patience and optimism. Experience of working with children is important. Students planning to follow a degree with a Postgraduate Certificate in Education (PGCE) are advised that problems may arise if their first degree subject is not a National Curriculum subject.

Two-year BEd courses are also offered for holders of HND or equivalent qualifications (minimum age in some cases 23–25) in the following subject areas: Business Studies (S); Chemistry (S); Design and Technology (S); English (P); French (S); General Primary; German (S); Language Studies (P); Mathematics (S); Music (S); Physics (S); Science (S); Spanish (S); Welsh (S).

Useful websites www.tda.gov.uk; www.gtcs.org.uk; www.gttr.ac.uk; http://educationcymru.org; www.education.gov.uk.

NB The points totals shown to the left of the institutions are for ease of reference only. It must not be assumed that Tariff points are always used by institutions or that they can be substituted for an offer in grades. The level of an offer is not necessarily indicative of the quality of a course.

COURSE OFFERS INFORMATION

Subject requirements/preferences GCSE English, mathematics and a science subject for those born after 1 September 1979. **AL** One A-level is usually required in the main subject of choice plus one or two other subjects. **Other** CRB Enhanced Level clearance and health checks required.

Your target offers and examples of courses provided by each institution

380 pts **Cambridge** – A*AA (Educ Relig St) (IB 40–42 pts)
340 pts **Bath** – AAB (Coach Educ Spo Dev) (IB 35 pts)
   Durham – AAB (Educ St (Biol Sci/Engl St/Geog/Hist/Phil/Psy/Sociol/Theol)) (IB 36 pts)
   Huddersfield – 340 pts (Educ P BA QTS)
   Lancaster – AAB (Psy Educ) (IB 34 pts)
   Stranmillis (UC) – AAB (P Educ)
   Southampton – AAB (Educ St Psy) (IB 34 pts HL 17 pts)
320 pts **Bath** – ABB (Chld Yth Educ St) (IB 35 pts)
   Birmingham – ABB (Chld Cult Educ) (IB 32–34 pts)
   Bristol – ABB (Chld St) (IB 33 pts HL 665)
   Bristol UWE – 320 pts (Educ: P ITE) (IB 32 pts)
   Cardiff – ABB (Educ) (IB 32–34 pts)
   Durham – ABB (P Educ) (IB 34 pts)
   Liverpool – ABB (Maths Educ) (IB 33 pts HL 6 maths)
   Manchester – ABB–BBB 300–320 pts (Lrn Disab St) (IB 31–35 pts)
   Roehampton – 320 pts (Educ St)
   Southampton – ABB (Educ St) (IB 32 pts HL 16 pts)
300 pts **Aberdeen** – BBB (Pol Educ; Educ P; Educ S; Educ P Psy)
   Aberystwyth – 300 pts (Educ Stats) (IB 28 pts)
   Birmingham City – 300 pts (Educ Pr QTS)
   Brighton – BBB (P Educ) (IB 32 pts)
   Cardiff – BBB (Educ Sociol; Educ Welsh)
   Derby – 300 pts (Educ)
   Edge Hill – 300 pts (Ely Chld St)
   Glasgow – BBB (Technol Educ) (IB 32 pts)
   Keele – 300 pts (Educ St) (IB 28–30 pts)

Leeds – BBB (Chld St) (IB 30 pts)
Newman (UC) – 300 pts (P Educ)
Roehampton – 300–360 pts (P Educ BA/BSc QTS; P Educ (Maths); P Educ (Mus))
Sheffield – BBB (Educ Cult Chld) (IB 32 pts)
UEA – BBB (Educ St) (IB 31pts)
Warwick – BBB (Chld Educ Soc) (IB 34 pts)
York – BBB (Educ St) (IB 31–30 pts)

280 pts **Aberystwyth** – 280 pts (Educ Joint Hons) (IB 28 pts)
Brighton – BBC–BBB (Educ) (IB 28 pts)
Bristol UWE – 280 pts (Educ St)
Cardiff Met – 280 pts (Educ St Psy)
De Montfort – 280 pts (Educ St) (IB 24 pts)
Derby – 280 pts (Maths Educ)
Glamorgan – BBC 280 pts (Sociol Educ)
Gloucestershire – 280–300 pts (Spo Educ; Educ P)
Huddersfield – 280 pts (Relgn Educ)
LJMU – 280–300 pts (Educ St (P))
London (Gold) – BBC (Educ Cult Soty) (IB 28 pts)
Manchester Met – 280 pts (Chld Yth St) (IB 28 pts)
Newman (UC) – 280–300 pts (P Educ Arts QTS)
Northampton – 280–300 pts (Educ St courses; Ely Chld St; Chld Yth)
Northumbria – 280 pts (Educ P) (IB 24 pts)
Nottingham Trent – 280 pts (Bus Ed Dev; Ely Yrs Educl Dev; Ely Yrs Spec Inclsv Educ; Ely Yrs Bus Educ; Ely Yrs Psy Educ; Psy Spec Incl Educ; Spec Incl Educ Educl Dev)
Oxford Brookes – BBC (Educ Studies) (IB 30 pts)
Suffolk (Univ Campus) – 280 pts (Ely Chld St)
Worcester – 280 pts (Educ St; Educ courses)

260 pts **Brighton** – BCC–CCC (Hum Biol Educ)
Brunel – BBC (S PE BSc)
Canterbury Christ Church – 260 pts (Educ Pr)
Cardiff Met – 260 pts (Educ St Welsh)
Derby – 260 pts (Ely Chld St)
Glamorgan – 260 pts (Welsh Educ)
Hull – 260 pts (Educ P; Educ courses)
Leeds Met – 260 pts (P Educ) (IB 24 pts)
Liverpool Hope – 260 pts (Chld St; Educ St; Disab St; Inclsv Educ)
LJMU – 260 pts (Educ St Ely Yrs; Ely Chld St; Out Educ; Educ St Spec Inclsv Nds)
London Met – 260 pts (Educ P; Educ St)
Nottingham Trent – 260 pts (Chld St)
Reading – 260–300 pts (Chem Educ)
Sheffield Hallam – 260 pts (Educ St Psy Cnslg)
Sunderland – 260 pts (Educ; Chld St)
UCLan – 260–300 pts (Educ courses)
Winchester – 260–300 pts (Educ St courses; Ely Chld St; Fr P Teach; Educ P; P Educ Geog)
York St John – 260 pts (Educ P)

240 pts **Aberystwyth** – 240 pts (Chld St) (IB 28 pts)
Anglia Ruskin – 240 pts (P Educ Modn Lang)
Canterbury Christ Church – 240 pts (Chld St; Educ St)
Chester – 240–280 pts (Ely Chld St) (IB 26 pts)
Chichester – CCC (Ely Chld St) (IB 28 pts)
Edge Hill – 240–280 pts (P/S Educ courses)
Gloucestershire – 240–300 pts (Ely Chld St; Educ St courses)
Glyndŵr – 240 pts (Educ St)
Greenwich – 240 pts (Chld St)
Hertfordshire – 240–300 pts (Educ St; Educ P BEd QTS)

Check **Chapter 4** when choosing your university and **Chapter 7** on how to read the subject tables.

Leeds Trinity (UC) – 240 pts (Ely Yrs Educ St)
Newport – 240–260 pts (Crea Ther Educ)
Plymouth – 240 pts (Ely Chld St; P Mus BEd; Educ St)
Portsmouth – 240–300 pts (Ely Chld St)
Staffordshire – 240 pts (Ely Chld St)
Stirling – CCD–BCC (Educ (P); Educ (S))
St Mary's Twickenham (UC) – 240 pts (P Educ) (IB 28 pts)
Sheffield Hallam – 240 pts (Educ Disab St; Educ St; Engl Educ St)
Trinity Saint David – 240–360 pts (P Educ)
Ulster – 240–260 pts (Educ courses)
Winchester – 240–280 pts (Maths P Educ)

220 pts **Bangor** – 220–240 pts (Chld St)
Bath Spa – 220–280 pts (Educ St courses; Ely Yrs Educ courses; Int Educ)
Bishop Grosseteste (UC) – 220 pts (Educ St courses; Spec Educl Nds Incln courses)
Newport – 220 pts (Ely Yrs; Educ St; Educ P)
St Mary's Twickenham (UC) – 220 pts (Educ Soc Sci) (IB 28 pts)
Teesside – 220 pts (Ely Chld St; Chld Yth St)

200 pts **Anglia Ruskin** – 200 pts (Educ St)
Birmingham (UC) – 200–220 pts (Ely Chld St)
Blackburn (Coll) – 200 pts (Educ St)
Canterbury Christ Church – 200 pts (P Educ Modn Lang)
Cardiff Met – 200 pts (Yth Commun Educ)
Leeds Met – 200 pts (Chld St) (IB 24 pts)
Middlesex – 200–300 pts (Educ St courses; Ely Chld St; Educ Relig St)
UCLan – 200 pts (Df St courses) (IB 28 pts)
UEL – 200 pts (Educ Commun Dev; Educ St; Ely Chld St; SEN)
Wolverhampton – 200–260 pts (Educ P; Cond Educ)

180 pts **Bedfordshire** – 180–220 pts (Ely Yrs Educ; Educ St)
Bradford (Coll Univ Centre) – 180 pts (P Educ BA QTS; Educ St)
Chichester – 180–220 pts (Advntr Educ)
Reading – 180 pts (Educ St (P) Art)
Swansea Met – 180 pts (Educ St Psy; Educ St; Cnslg Educ St; Dr Educ St)
Trinity Saint David – 180–360 pts (Ely Yrs Educ)
UCP Marjon – 180 pts (Educ St courses; Spec Educ Nds)

160 pts **South Essex (Coll)** – 160 pts (Ely Yrs Educ)
UHI – CC–AA (Educ P)

140 pts **Queen's Belfast** – concurrent option available at St Mary's **or** Stranmillis; check with admissions tutor (Educ)

120 pts **Stockport (Coll)** – 120 pts (Ely Chld St)

Open University – contact +44 (0)845 300 6090 **or** www.openuniversity.co.uk/you (Chld Yth St; Ely Yrs)

EXAMPLES OF FOUNDATION DEGREES IN THE SUBJECT FIELD

Bath City (Coll); Blackburn (Coll); Blackpool and Fylde (Coll); Bournemouth and Poole (Coll); Bradford; Bristol City (Coll); Bucks New; Cornwall (Coll); Doncaster (Coll Univ Centre); Duchy (Coll); Exeter (Coll); Farnborough (CT); Grimsby (IFHE); Guildford (Coll); Havering (Coll); Hopwood Hall (Coll); Kirklees (Coll); Lakes (Coll); Leeds City (Coll); Loughborough (Coll); Manchester (Coll); Mid-Cheshire (Coll); Northbrook (Coll); Norwich City (Coll); Peterborough (Univ Centre); Petroc; Plymouth City (Coll); Riverside Halton (Coll); St Mary's Twickenham (UC); Sheffield (Coll); South Cheshire (Coll); South Devon (Coll); Southgate (Coll); Stratford-upon-Avon (Coll); Truro (Coll); Wakefield (Coll); Warrington (Coll); West Anglia (Coll); Wigan and Leigh (Coll); Wirral Met (Coll).

CHOOSING YOUR COURSE (SEE ALSO CH.1)
Some course features
Bristol (Chld St) This new course is provided in the Department of Social Policy and Social Work. It focuses on children, their communities and on the political and economic environment. A study of children, social policy and psychology (not a teacher training course).
Canterbury Christ Church Single, Joint and combined courses are offered in Early Childhood Studies. Primary Teaching courses leading to Qualified Teacher Status, degree in Education Studies and courses in Physical Education and Maths Education at Secondary Level.
Chichester Courses in Education include Adventure Education, Childhood Studies including health, child development and special needs.
Glyndŵr Courses focus on childhood care and education by way of degrees in Early Childhood Studies, Education Studies and Play and Playwork.
Leeds There is a course in Childhood Studies covering education, sociology and psychology.
Plymouth General Primary courses are offered in Art and Design, Early Childhood Studies, English, ICT, Mathematics, Music, Physical Education and Science. There is also a course in Steiner Waldorf Education. Some work experience abroad is possible in the state of New York, Finland and Denmark.
UEA The Educational Studies degree offers a flexible pathway enabling students to tailor their degree to their own interests. It involves a balance between theory and practical experience and a study of the whole field of education in the UK and abroad including modules in teaching, learning and assessment.

Universities and colleges teaching quality See www.qaa.ac.uk; http://unistats.direct.gov.uk.

Top research universities and colleges (RAE 2008) London (Inst Ed); Oxford; Cambridge; London (King's); Bristol; Leeds; Exeter; Manchester Met; Warwick; York; Durham; Sussex; Stirling.

ADMISSIONS INFORMATION
Number of applicants per place (approx) Aberystwyth 6; Anglia Ruskin 1; Bangor 5; Bath 17; Bath Spa 5; Birmingham 8; Bishop Grosseteste (UC) 12; Bristol (Chld St) 6; Bristol UWE 20; Brunel (PE) 5; Cambridge 2.5; Canterbury Christ Church 15; Cardiff (Educ) 8; Cardiff Met 3; Chester 25; Chichester 12; Cumbria 5; Derby 13; Dundee 5; Durham 8; Edge Hill 17; Edinburgh (P) 3; Gloucestershire 20; Glyndŵr 15; Greenwich 3; Hull 7; Hull (Coll) 4; Kingston 9; Leeds 4; Liverpool Hope 5; LJMU 3; London (Gold) 5, (Des Tech) 4; Manchester 3; Manchester Met 23, (Maths) 4; Middlesex 7; Newman (UC) (S Engl) 3, (Theol) 3, (Ely Yrs) 5, (Biol) 7, (Geog) 3, (PE) 6, (Sci) 1; Northampton 7; Northumbria 8; Nottingham Trent 11; Oxford Brookes 6; Plymouth 14; Roehampton 6; St Mary's Twickenham (UC) 19; Sheffield Hallam 7, (PE) 60; Strathclyde 7; Swansea Met 10; Trinity Saint David 10; UCLan 5; UCP Marjon 5; West Scotland 7; Winchester 4; Wolverhampton 4; Worcester 21, (Engl) 51; York 3.

Advice to applicants and planning the UCAS personal statement **Chichester** Applicants should have spent a minimum of two weeks observing/helping out in a state school.

Misconceptions about this course That Childhood Studies is a childcare, child health or teaching course: it is not. That Educational Studies leads to a teaching qualification – it does not. **Bath Spa** (Educ St) Applicants should note that this is not a teacher training course – it leads on to PGCE teacher training (this applies to other Education Studies courses). **Newman (UC)** That the Theology course only concentrates on the Christian/Catholic religions – all major religions are covered. **UHI** Candidates are unaware that online methods form a significant part of the course delivery.

Selection interviews Check all institutions. It is a requirement that all candidates for teacher training are interviewed. **Yes** Birmingham City, Bishop Grosseteste (UC), Brighton, Bristol UWE, Brunel, Cambridge, Cardiff Met, Chichester, Derby, Durham, Glyndŵr, Kingston, LJMU, London (Gold), Manchester Met (group interviews), Newman (UC), Nottingham, Nottingham Trent, Oxford Brookes, Plymouth, Reading, Stirling, Stockport (Coll), West Scotland, Worcester, York St John; **Some** Anglia Ruskin, Bangor, Cardiff, Dundee, Lincoln, Roehampton, UCP Marjon, Winchester, York; **No** UEA.

Interview advice and questions **Cambridge** The stage is a platform for opinions or just entertainment? **Derby** Applicants are asked about an aspect of education. **LJMU** Discussion regarding any experience the applicant has had with children. **Worcester** Interviewees are asked to write a statement concerning their impressions of the interview.

Reasons for rejection (non-academic) Unable to meet the requirements of written standard English. Ungrammatical personal statements. Lack of research about teaching at primary or secondary levels. Lack of experience in schools. Insufficient experience of working with people; tendency to be racist.

AFTER-RESULTS ADVICE
Offers to applicants repeating A-levels Higher Oxford Brookes, Warwick; **Possibly higher** Cumbria; **Same** Anglia Ruskin, Bangor, Bishop Grosseteste (UC), Brighton, Brunel, Cambridge, Canterbury Christ Church, Cardiff, Chester, Chichester, De Montfort, Derby, Dundee, Durham, Lincoln, Liverpool Hope, LJMU, London (Gold), Manchester Met, Newman (UC), Northumbria, Nottingham Trent, Roehampton, St Mary's Twickenham (UC), Stirling, Sunderland, UCP Marjon, UEA, UHI, Winchester, Wolverhampton, Worcester, York, York St John; **No** Kingston.

GRADUATE DESTINATIONS AND EMPLOYMENT (2009/10 HESA)
Academic Studies in Education; graduates surveyed 10,090 **Employed** 7150 **In voluntary employment** 85 **In further study** 4260 **Assumed unemployed** 355

Career note Education Studies degrees prepare graduates for careers in educational administration although many will move into more general areas of business or into aspects of work with Social Services. If courses in Education include Qualified Teacher Status (QTS), graduates can enter the teaching profession. Prospects are generally good. Courses in Childhood Studies could lead to work in health or childcare-related posts, in social work or administration.

OTHER DEGREE SUBJECTS FOR CONSIDERATION
Psychology; Social Policy; Social Sciences; Social Work.

ENGINEERING/ENGINEERING SCIENCES
(including **General Engineering, Integrated Engineering, Engineering Design** and **Product Design**; see also **Engineering (Manufacturing), Technologies, Transport Management and Planning**)

Many of the Engineering courses listed below enable students to delay their decision of their final engineering specialism. Mathematics and physics provide the basis of all Engineering courses although several universities and colleges now provide one-year Foundation courses for applicants without science A-levels. Many institutions offer sandwich courses and firms also offer sponsorships. In prospectuses it will be noted that some courses are subject to approval. The problem which can arise is that the examinations taken on these courses may not be accepted by the professional body overseeing that particular branch of engineering and examinations set by these professional bodies (see **Appendix 3**) will have to be retaken in order that graduates can obtain Chartered Engineer status.

Useful websites www.ukrc4setwomen.org.uk; www.ergonomics.org.uk; www.scicentral.com; www.engc.org.uk; www.noisemakers.org.uk; www.etrust.org.uk; www.enginuity.org.uk; www.engc.org.uk/ukspec.

ENGINEERING COUNCIL UK (ECUK) STATEMENT
Recent developments in the engineering profession and the regulations that govern registration as a professional engineer (UK-SPEC) mean that MEng and Bachelors degrees are the typical academic routes to becoming registered.

Chartered Engineers (CEng) develop solutions to engineering problems, using new or existing technologies, through innovation, creativity and change. They might develop and apply new technologies, promote advanced designs and design methods, introduce new and more efficient production techniques, marketing and construction concepts, and pioneer new engineering services and management methods.

Incorporated Engineers (IEng) act as exponents of today's technology through creativity and innovation. They maintain and manage applications of current and developing technology, and may be involved in engineering design, development, manufacture, construction and operation. Both Chartered and Incorporated Engineers are variously engaged in technical and commercial leadership and possess effective interpersonal skills.

You should confirm with universities whether their courses are accredited for CEng or IEng by relevant professional engineering institutions. To become a Chartered or Incorporated Engineer, you will have to demonstrate competence and commitment appropriate to the registration category. On top of your academic knowledge, you will also need to demonstrate your professional development and experience. Most of this will come after you graduate but placements in industry during your degree course are also available. Both Chartered and Incorporated Engineers usually progress to become team leaders or to take other key management roles. For full information check www.engc. org.uk/ukspec.

NB The points totals shown to the left of the institutions are for ease of reference only. It must not be assumed that Tariff points are always used by institutions or that they can be substituted for an offer in grades. The level of an offer is not necessarily indicative of the quality of a course.

COURSE OFFERS INFORMATION

Subject requirements/preferences GCSE English, mathematics and a science subject required. **AL** Mathematics and/or physics, engineering or another science usually required. Design technology may be acceptable or in some cases required.

Cambridge (Churchill, Peterhouse) STEP may be used as part of conditional offer; (Trinity) if student does not have AL further mathematics, AEA mathematics is required.
Oxford AL mathematics mechanics modules is recommended, further mathematics is helpful.

Your target offers and examples of courses provided by each institution
400 pts London (King's) – AAAc (Robot Intel Sys) (IB 38 pts HL 666 incl maths/phys)
380 pts Cambridge – A*AA (Eng) (IB 40–42 pts)
    London (UCL) – A*AA–AAB (Eng Bus Fin MEng) (IB 38–39 pts)
    Oxford – A*AA (Eng Econ Mgt) (IB 38–40 pts)
360 pts Bristol – A*AB–AAA incl maths (Eng Maths)
    Durham – AAA (Gen Eng MEng) (IB 37 pts)
    Edinburgh – AAA–ABB 320–360 pts (Eng) (IB 37–32 pts)
    Nottingham – AAA (Des Eng MEng) (IB 36–34 pts)
    Sheffield – AAA incl maths sci (Archit Eng Des) (IB 37 pts HL 6 maths sci)
    Southampton – AAA incl maths (Env Eng) (IB 36 pts HL 18 pts)
    Swansea – AAA–AAB (Prod Des Eng MEng)
340 pts Durham – AAB (Gen Eng BEng) (IB 36 pts)
    Exeter – AAB–ABB (Eng MEng) (IB 34–32 pts)
    Lancaster – AAA–AAB 340 pts (Eng (St Abrd) MEng) (IB 34 pts)
    Leicester – AAB–ABB (Eng MEng)
    Liverpool – AAB incl maths phys (Eng MEng) (IB 35 pts)
    Loughborough – AAB (Prod Des Eng MEng) (IB 34 pts)
    Newcastle – AAB (Sust Eng MEng) (IB 36 pts)
    Nottingham – AAB (Des Eng BEng) (IB 32–30 pts)
    Queen's Belfast – AAB (Prod Des Dev MEng)
    Strathclyde – AAB (Mech Eng Aero BEng; Prod Des Eng MEng) (IB 36 pts)
    Warwick – AAB (Auto Eng) (IB 36 pts)
320 pts Birmingham – ABB (Mat Sci Ener Eng) (IB 32 pts)
    Cardiff – ABB (Integ Eng MEng)
    Exeter – ABB–BBB (Eng Mgt BEng) (IB 32–30 pts)
    Glasgow – ABB (Prod Des Eng BEng) (IB 32 pts)
    Lancaster – ABB (Eng BEng) (IB 32 pts)
    Loughborough – ABB (Eng Mgt) (IB 33 pts HL 665)
    Strathclyde – ABB (Prod Des Innov) (IB 34 pts)
    Westminster – ABB 320 pts (Archit Eng) (IB 28 pts)

Check **Chapter 4** when choosing your university and **Chapter 7** on how to read the subject tables.

300 pts **Aberdeen** – BBB (Eng) (IB 30 pts)
Aston – BBB–ABB 280–320 pts (Des Eng BEng) (IB 32 pts)
Bournemouth – 300 pts (Des Eng; Prod Des)
Brunel – BBB (Prod Des Eng) (IB 30 pts)
Cardiff – BBB 300 pts (Integ Eng BEng) (IB 28 pts)
Cardiff Met – 300 pts (Prod Des)
Heriot-Watt – BBB (Eng)
Leeds – BBB (Des Tech Mgt) (IB 30 pts)
Leicester – BBB–BBC (Eng BEng)
Liverpool – BBB incl maths phys (Eng Prod Des BEng) (IB 32 pts HL 5 maths phys)
Loughborough – 300 pts (Archit Eng) (IB 32 pts)
Newcastle – AAB–BBB 300–340 pts (Off Eng BEng) (IB 32–34 pts)
Nottingham – BBB (Archit Env Eng) (IB 30 pts)
Queen's Belfast – BBB (Prod Des Dev BEng)
Strathclyde – BBB (Eng MEng)
Ulster – 300 pts (Eng MEng)
280 pts **De Montfort** – 280 pts (Prod Des BSc)
LJMU – 280 pts (Prod Innov Dev)
London (QM) – 280–340 pts (Eng Sci) (IB 30–32 pts)
Manchester Met – 280 pts (Eng) (IB 28 pts)
Salford – 280 pts (Pros Orthot) (IB 24 pts)
260 pts **Birmingham** – AAA–BCC 260–360 pts (Eng incl Fdn Yr) (IB 25–36 pts)
Northumbria – 260 pts (Prod Des Tech)
Salford – 260 pts (Prod Des) (IB 26 pts)
Sunderland – 260 pts (Renew Ener Eng)
Ulster – 260–300 pts (Eng Mgt)
240 pts **Bradford** – 240 pts (Prod Ind Des) (IB 26 pts)
De Montfort – 240 pts (Eng Des)
Edinburgh Napier – CCC 240 pts (Prod Des Eng)
Hull – 240–260 pts (Prod Innov)
Leeds Met – 240 pts (Env Des Eng) (IB 24 pts)
Northampton – 240–280 pts (Eng)
Plymouth – BCC 240–260 pts (Robot)
Robert Gordon – CCC (Eng) (IB 24 pts)
Swansea – 240–300 pts (Prod Des Eng BEng)
220 pts **Hull** – 220–260 pts (Med Prod Des)
London South Bank – 220 pts (Eng Prod Des)
Sheffield Hallam – 220 pts (Foren Eng)
200 pts **Bradford** – 200–240 pts (Eng Mgt)
Bristol UWE – 200–240 pts (Eng BSc)
Glamorgan – 200–240 pts (Eng Tech Mgt)
UCLan – 200–260 pts (Eng Bus Ent)
UEL – 200 pts (Prod Des)
Wolverhampton – 200–260 pts (Eng Des Mgt)
160 pts **Greenwich** – 160 pts (Eng Bus Mgt)
Southampton Solent – 160 pts (Prod Des)
West Scotland – CC (Eng Mgt)
120 pts **Southampton Solent** – 120–180 pts (Eng Bus)
60 pts **UHI** – D–A (Ener Eng)

Open University – contact +44 (0)845 300 6090 **or** www.openuniversity.co.uk/you (Eng BEng)

Alternative offers
See **Chapter 7** and **Appendix 1** for grades/UCAS Tariff points information for the International Baccalaureate, Scottish Highers/Advanced Highers, the Welsh Baccalaureate, the Irish Leaving Certificate, the Cambridge Pre-U Diploma, the Advanced Diploma and the Extended Project.

EXAMPLES OF FOUNDATION DEGREES IN THE SUBJECT FIELD

Blackburn (Coll); Bolton; Bristol City (Coll); Greenwich; Harper Adams (UC); Hull (Coll); London Met; Manchester (Coll); Mid-Cheshire (Coll); Middlesex; Newcastle (Coll); Newman (UC); Newport; Northumbria; Oxford Brookes; Sheffield Hallam; Somerset (CAT); Suffolk (Univ Campus); Tyne Met (Coll); Warwickshire (Coll); West Thames (Coll).

CHOOSING YOUR COURSE (SEE ALSO CH.1)

Some course features

Bath All Engineering courses share the first two years, with the choice of specialisation made in Year 3.

Bristol Nine specialisations follow a study of core subjects.

Cardiff The first year is common to all nine Engineering programmes.

Durham All Engineering courses share the first two years, with the choice of specialisation made in Year 3.

Lancaster All students follow a common first year followed by a choice from six Engineering specialisations.

London (QM) (MEng/BEng Des Innov) The course is run jointly by the Engineering Departments at London (QM) and the Department of Design at London (Goldsmiths). It consists of core studio practice (at QM), design context study (at Goldsmiths) and design engineering (at QM). Applications are to London (QM), via UCAS.

Warwick All Engineering courses share the first two years, with the choice of specialisation made in Year 3.

Universities and colleges teaching quality See www.qaa.ac.uk; http://unistats.direct.gov.uk.

Top research universities and colleges (RAE 2008) (General, Mineral and Mining Engineering) Cambridge; Oxford; Nottingham; Leeds; Imperial London; Swansea; Manchester; Surrey; Warwick.

Check **Chapter 4** when choosing your university and **Chapter 7** on how to read the subject tables.

Examples of sandwich degree courses Aston; Bath; Bradford; Bristol UWE; Brunel; Cardiff; Coventry; Leicester; London South Bank; Loughborough; Manchester Met; Ulster; Wolverhampton.

ADMISSIONS INFORMATION

Number of applicants per place (approx) Aberdeen 6; Aston 8; Bath 15; Birmingham 6; Bournemouth 5; Bristol (Eng Des) 3, (Eng Maths) 5; Brunel (Ind Des Eng) 10; Cambridge 4; Cardiff 5; City 3; Coventry 6; Durham 9; Edinburgh 5; Exeter 6; Hull 6; Lancaster 15; Leicester 10; London (UCL) 5; Loughborough 9; Manchester Met 2; Northampton 3; Robert Gordon 2; Salford (Pros Orthot) 3; Sheffield Hallam 6; Strathclyde 5; Warwick 10.

Advice to applicants and planning the UCAS personal statement Details of careers in the various engineering specialisms should be obtained from the relevant engineering institutions (see **Appendix 3**). This will enable you to describe your interests in various aspects of engineering. Contact engineers to discuss their work with them. Try to arrange a visit to an engineering firm relevant to your choice of specialism.

Selection interviews Yes Bristol, Brunel, Cambridge, Coventry, Durham, Lancaster, Leicester, London (QM), London (UCL), Loughborough, Manchester Met, Oxford, Oxford Brookes (English test for overseas students), Robert Gordon, Salford, Sheffield Hallam, Strathclyde, West Scotland; **Some** Cardiff; **No** Dundee.

Interview advice and questions Since mathematics and physics are important subjects, it is probable that you will be questioned on the applications of these subjects to, for example, the transmission of electricity, nuclear power, aeronautics, mechanics etc. Past questions have included: Explain the theory of an arch; what is its function? What is the connection between distance and velocity and acceleration and velocity? How does a car ignition work? See also separate **Engineering** tables and **Chapter 6**. **Nottingham Trent** What is Integrated Engineering?

Reasons for rejection (non-academic) Made no contribution whatsoever to the project discussions during the UCAS interview. Forged reference! Poor work ethic. Lack of motivation towards the subject area. Better suited to an alternative Engineering course. Failure to attend interview. Poor interview preparation. **Salford** (Pros Orthot) Lack of sympathy with people with disabilities.

AFTER-RESULTS ADVICE

Offers to applicants repeating A-levels Higher Loughborough, Warwick; **Possibly higher** Coventry, Edinburgh, Lancaster, Manchester Met, Robert Gordon, Sheffield Hallam; **Same** Birmingham City, Brunel (good reasons needed for repeating), Cambridge, Cardiff, Derby, Durham, Edinburgh Napier, Exeter, Heriot-Watt, Hull, Liverpool, London (UCL), Nottingham Trent.

GRADUATE DESTINATIONS AND EMPLOYMENT (2009/10 HESA)

Graduates surveyed 2685 **Employed** 1320 **In voluntary employment** 10 **In further study** 415 **Assumed unemployed** 125

Career note A high proportion of Engineering graduates go into industry as engineers, technicians, IT specialists or managers, irrespective of their engineering speciality. However, the transferable skills gained during their courses are also valued by employers in other sectors.

OTHER DEGREE SUBJECTS FOR CONSIDERATION

Computer Science; Materials Science; Mathematics; Physics; Technology; all branches of Engineering (see also following **Engineering** tables).

ENGINEERING (ACOUSTICS and SOUND)

(including **Audio Engineering** and **Sound Technology**; see also **Engineering (Electrical and Electronic)**, **Film, Radio, Video and TV Studies**, **Media Studies**, **Music**)

Apart from the scientific aspect of sound, these courses also involve the measurement of sound, hearing, environmental health and legal aspects of sound and vibration. Acoustics topics are also included in some Music and Media Technology courses.

Useful websites www.ioa.org.uk; www.engc.org.uk; www.enginuity.org.uk.

NB The points totals shown to the left of the institutions are for ease of reference only. It must not be assumed that Tariff points are always used by institutions or that they can be substituted for an offer in grades. The level of an offer is not necessarily indicative of the quality of a course.

COURSE OFFERS INFORMATION

Subject requirements/preferences AL Mathematics and physics usually required; music is also required for some courses. See also **Engineering/Engineering Sciences**.

Your target offers and examples of courses provided by each institution
380 pts **Surrey** – A*AA–AAA (Mus Snd Rec (Tonmeister))
360 pts **Glasgow** – AAA (AV Eng MEng Faster Route)
        Surrey – AAA (Dig Med Eng MEng) (IB 36 pts)
340 pts **Glamorgan** – ABB (Snd Tech)
        Glasgow – AAB (AV Eng MEng) (IB 34 pts)
        Surrey – AAB (Dig Med Eng BEng) (IB 35 pts)
        York – AAB–ABB (Mus Tech Sys MEng)
320 pts **Glasgow** – ABB (AV Eng BEng) (IB 32 pts)
        Southampton – ABB–BBB (Acoust Eng) (IB 32–30 pts HL 16 pts)
300 pts **Birmingham City** – 300 pts (Snd Multim Tech; Snd Eng Prod)
        London (QM) – BBB (Aud Sys Eng) (IB 28 pts)
        Salford – 300 pts (Phys Acoust MPhys)
        Southampton – BBB incl maths phys mus (Acoust Mus) (IB 30 pts)
280 pts **Liverpool (LIPA)** – 280 pts (Snd Tech)
        LJMU – 280 pts (Aud Mus Prod)
        London (Central Sch SpDr) – BBC (Thea Prac Thea Snd)
        Oxford Brookes – BBC (Mus; Snd Tech Dig Mus)
        Salford – 280 pts (Dig Broad Tech; Acoust; Aud Tech)
260 pts **Bolton** – 260 pts (Snd Eng Des)
        Brunel – BCC (Gms Des Snc Arts) (IB 29 pts)
        De Montfort – 260 pts (Aud Rec Tech)
        Portsmouth – 260–300 pts (Comp Dig Snd)
240 pts **Glyndŵr** – 240 pts (Std Rec Perf Tech)
        Huddersfield – 240 pts (Snd Rec; Electron Mus Tech)
        London Met – 240 pts (Mus Tech (Aud Sys/Snd Media))
        Ravensbourne – AA–CC (Broad Inf Tech; Broad Tech; Outsd Broad Tech)
220 pts **Hertfordshire** – 220 pts (Snd Des Tech)
200 pts **Rose Bruford (Coll)** – check with admissions tutor 200 pts (Perf Snd)
        West London – 200 pts (App Snd Eng)
160 pts **Southampton Solent** – 160 pts (Aud Tech; Snd Eng)
120 pts **Bournemouth** – 120 pts (Mus Snd Tech)
        Southampton Solent – 120–160 pts (Liv Std Snd; Mus Std Tech)
100 pts **Glyndŵr** – 100 pts (Snd/Broad Eng)
 80 pts **Arts London** – 80 pts (Snd Arts Res)
 60 pts **UHI** – D–A (Aud Eng)

Alternative offers
See **Chapter 7** and **Appendix 1** for grades/UCAS Tariff points information for the International Baccalaureate, Scottish Highers/Advanced Highers, the Welsh Baccalaureate, the Irish Leaving Certificate, the Cambridge Pre-U Diploma, the Advanced Diploma and the Extended Project.

EXAMPLES OF FOUNDATION DEGREES IN THE SUBJECT FIELD
St Helens (Coll).

CHOOSING YOUR COURSE (SEE ALSO CH.1)

Some course features

Salford (Acoust) Course includes electronics, computing, maths and specialist acoustic topics, for example musical acoustics, psychoacoustics and acoustics of performance spaces.

Southampton (Acoust Eng) The course involves engineering design to minimise noise and vibration, ocean acoustics and sonar and sound reproduction and musical instrument acoustics. There are 10-week industrial placements. The Acoustics and Music degree allows students to weight their studies in favour of either subject 75/25 or 25/75.

Surrey (Mus Snd Rec (Tonmeister)) This well-established course comprises three areas of study: the technical aspects of audio, practical experience of recording, and music theory and practice.

Universities and colleges teaching quality See www.qaa.ac.uk; http://unistats.direct.gov.uk.

Examples of sandwich degree courses Birmingham City; De Montfort; Glamorgan; Huddersfield; Portsmouth; Surrey; York.

ADMISSIONS INFORMATION

Number of applicants per place (approx) Anglia Ruskin 5; Salford 4; Southampton 4.

Advice to applicants and planning the UCAS personal statement See **Engineering/Engineering Sciences**. See also **Appendix 3**.

Misconceptions about this course Anglia Ruskin Failure to appreciate the emphasis that the course gives to science and technology.

Selection interviews Yes Salford, Southampton; **Some** Anglia Ruskin.

Interview advice and questions What interests you about acoustics engineering? What career do you have in mind on graduating? See also **Chapter 6**.

Reasons for rejection (non-academic) See **Engineering/Engineering Sciences**.

AFTER-RESULTS ADVICE

Offers to applicants repeating A-levels Same Anglia Ruskin, Salford.

GRADUATE DESTINATIONS AND EMPLOYMENT (2009/10 HESA)

See **Engineering/Engineering Sciences**.

Career note Specialist topics on these courses will enable graduates to make decisions as to their future career destinations.

OTHER DEGREE SUBJECTS FOR CONSIDERATION

Audiology; Broadcast Engineering; Communications Engineering; Computer Engineering; Computer Science; Media Technology; Music; Radio and TV; Technology; Telecommunications Engineering and Electronic Engineering.

ENGINEERING (AERONAUTICAL and AEROSPACE)

(see also Engineering (Electrical and Electronic))

Courses cover the manufacture of military and civil aircraft, theories of mechanics, thermodynamics, electronics, computing and engine design. Avionics courses include flight and energy control systems, airborne computing, navigation, optical and TV displays, airborne communications, and radar systems for navigation and power.

Useful websites www.raes.org.uk; www.engc.org.uk; www.enginuity.org.uk.

NB The points totals shown to the left of the institutions are for ease of reference only. It must not be assumed that Tariff points are always used by institutions or that they can be substituted for an offer in grades. The level of an offer is not necessarily indicative of the quality of a course.

Engineering Council statement *See* **Engineering/Engineering Sciences**.

COURSE OFFERS INFORMATION

Subject requirements/preferences See **Engineering/Engineering Sciences**.

Your target offers and examples of courses provided by each institution

380 pts **Bath** – A*AA (Aerosp Eng) (IB 36 pts HL 6 maths phys)

Bristol – A*AA–AAB (Aero Eng (St Abrd)) (IB 36 pts)

Cambridge – A*AA (Aerosp Aeroth Eng) (IB 40–42 pts)

Imperial London – A*A*A incl phys maths (Aero Eng St Abrd) (IB 40 pts)

360 pts **City** – AAA–AAB 360 pts (Aero Eng) (IB 32 pts)

Durham – AAA (Aero) (IB 37 pts)

Glasgow – AAA (Aero Eng MEng)

Imperial London – AAA incl phys maths (Aerosp Mat) (IB 37 pts)

London (QM) – AAA incl maths sci (Aerosp Eng MEng) (IB 34 pts)

Loughborough – AAA (Aero Eng MEng) (IB 36 pts)

Manchester – AAA (Aerosp Eng Mgt) (IB 37 pts)

Strathclyde – AAA (Mech Eng Aero MEng) (IB 36 pts)

Sheffield – AAA incl maths phys (Aerosp Eng (PPI) MEng) (IB 37 pts HL 6 maths phys)

Southampton – AAA incl maths phys (Aero Astnaut) (IB 36 pts HL 18 pts)

Surrey – AAA (Aerosp Eng MEng) (IB 36 pts)

340 pts **Brunel** – AAB (Avn Eng MEng) (IB 32 pts)

City – AAB 340 pts (Air Trans Ops Mgt)

Glasgow – AAB (Aerosp Sys MEng) (IB 34 pts)

Leeds – AAB (Aero Aerosp Eng) (MEng IB 36 pts HL 17 pts)

Leicester – AAB–ABB (Aerosp Eng MEng)

Liverpool – AAB incl maths phys (Aerosp Eng MEng) (IB 34 pts)

Manchester – AAB (Aerosp Eng BEng) (IB 35 pts)

Strathclyde – AAB (Aero Mech Eng BEng; Mech Eng Aero BEng)

Sheffield – AAB incl maths phys (Aerosp Mat MEng) (IB 35 pts HL 6 maths phys)

Surrey – AAB (Aerosp Eng BEng) (IB 34 pts)

York – AAB–ABB (Avion MEng) (IB 34 pts)

320 pts **Glasgow** – ABB (Aerosp Sys BEng) (IB 32 pts)

Hertfordshire – 320 pts (Aerosp Sys Eng MEng) (IB 30 pts)

Liverpool – ABB (Avion Sys MEng) (IB 33 pts HL 5 maths phys/elect)

Loughborough – ABB–AAA (Aero Eng) (IB 34 pts)

Queen's Belfast – ABB–BBB (Aerosp Eng MEng)

300 pts **Brighton** – BBB (Aero Eng)

Bristol UWE – 300 pts (Aerosp Sys Eng; Aerosp Des Eng; Aerosp Manuf Eng)

Brunel – BBB (Avn Eng Plt St BEng) (IB 32 pts)

Glamorgan – 300 pts (Aero Eng)

Kingston – 300 pts (Aerosp Eng Astnaut Spc Tech) (IB 30 pts)

Leicester – BBB–BBC (Aerosp Eng BEng)

Liverpool – BBB incl maths phys (Aerosp Eng Plt St) (IB 32 pts)

London (QM) – BBB incl maths sci (Aerosp Eng BEng) (IB 28 pts)

Salford – 300 pts (Aero Eng MEng)

Sheffield – ABC/BBB (Aerosp Mat BEng) (IB 32 pts)

Sheffield Hallam – 300 pts incl maths (Aero Eng MEng; Avion MEng)

Swansea – ABB–BBB 300–320 pts (Aerosp Eng)

Teesside – 300–340 pts (Aerosp Eng MEng)

York – BBB–BBC (Avion BEng) (IB 31 pts)

280 pts **Queen's Belfast** – BBB–BBC (Aero Eng BEng)

Teesside – 280–320 pts (Aerosp Eng BEng)

260 pts **Coventry** – 260 pts (Aerosp Sys Eng)

Hertfordshire – 260 pts (Aerosp Eng BEng; Aerosp Sys Eng Plt St BEng; Aerosp Sys Eng BEng)

Check **Chapter 4** when choosing your university and **Chapter 7** on how to read the subject tables.

Salford – 260 pts (Aero Eng BEng; Aircft Eng Plt St)
Swansea – 260–300 pts (Aerosp Eng Prplsn BEng)

240 pts **Glyndŵr** – 240 pts (Aero Mech Eng; Aero Electron Eng)
Hertfordshire – 240 pts (Aerosp Tech Mgt; Aerosp Tech Plt St: Multim Tech)
Sheffield Hallam – 240 pts (Aerosp Eng BEng; Aerosp Tech; Avion BEng)
220 pts **Glamorgan** – 220–260 pts (Aircrft Mntnc Eng)
200 pts **Coventry** – 200 pts (Aerosp Tech; Avn Mgt)
Sheffield Hallam – 200 pts incl AL maths (Aero Eng)
180 pts **London Met** – 180 pts (Avn Aerosp Mgt)
160 pts **Kingston** – 160 pts (Aerosp Eng BSc)
 60 pts **UHI** – D–A (Aircrft Eng)

Alternative offers

See **Chapter 7** and **Appendix 1** for grades/UCAS Tariff points information for the International Baccalaureate, Scottish Highers/Advanced Highers, the Welsh Baccalaureate, the Irish Leaving Certificate, the Cambridge Pre-U Diploma, the Advanced Diploma and the Extended Project.

EXAMPLES OF FOUNDATION DEGREES IN THE SUBJECT FIELD

Bristol City (Coll); Bristol UWE; Farnborough (CT); Glyndŵr; Hertfordshire; Kingston; London Met; Sheffield Hallam.

CHOOSING YOUR COURSE (SEE ALSO CH.1)

Some course features

Bath All courses have sandwich placements.
Brunel Pilot Studies available with Aviation Engineering.
Durham A common course for Years 1 and 2 and then two years specialising in the chosen discipline.
Hertfordshire Pilot Studies available with Aerospace Systems Engineering.
Imperial London Fourth year students may take the European option spending four months research in universities in the UK or abroad.
Liverpool Pilot Studies available in some Aeronautical or Aerospace Engineering courses.
Loughborough The first two years are common for all BEng and MEng students allowing the former to transfer to the MEng course at the end of the second year.
Manchester A year out in industry or in Europe are options.
Sheffield Pilot Studies available in some Aeronautical or Aerospace Engineering courses.
Swansea Aerospace Engineering can be taken as an BEng or MEng or with a year in industry.
York All Electronics courses have a common first year with specialisation following in Avionics in Year 2 or allowing students to transfer to one of eight Electronics courses.

Universities and colleges teaching quality See www.qaa.ac.uk; http://unistats.direct.gov.uk.

Top research universities and colleges (RAE 2008) See **Engineering (Mechanical)**.

Examples of sandwich degree courses Bath; Brighton; Bristol UWE; Brunel; City; Coventry; Glamorgan; Hertfordshire; Kingston; Liverpool; London (QM); Loughborough; Sheffield Hallam; Surrey; York.

ADMISSIONS INFORMATION

Number of applicants per place (approx) Bath 13, (MEng) 18; Bristol 7; Bristol UWE 4; City 17; Coventry 7; Farnborough (CT) 7; Glyndŵr 5; Hertfordshire 17; Kingston 9; London (QM) 8; Loughborough 10; Queen's Belfast 6; Salford 6; Southampton 10; York 3 av.

Advice to applicants and planning the UCAS personal statement Interest in engineering and aerospace. Work experience in engineering. Flying experience. Personal attainments. Relevant hobbies. Membership of Air Training Corps. See also **Engineering/Engineering Sciences** and **Appendix 3**. **Bristol** Deferred entry accepted. **Imperial London** Deferred entry acceptable.

Misconceptions about this course That Aeronautical Engineering is not a highly analytical subject: it is.

Selection interviews **Yes** Bristol, Cambridge, Farnborough (CT), Hertfordshire, Imperial London, Kingston, London (QM), Loughborough, Salford, Southampton.

Interview advice and questions Why Aeronautical Engineering? Questions about different types of aircraft and flight principles of helicopters. Range of interests in engineering. See also **Chapter 6**.

Reasons for rejection (non-academic) See **Engineering/Engineering Sciences**.

AFTER-RESULTS ADVICE
Offers to applicants repeating A-levels **Higher** Bristol, Queen's Belfast; **Possibly higher** Hertfordshire; **Same** Bath, City, Farnborough (CT), Kingston, Liverpool, Loughborough, Salford, Southampton, York; **No** Cambridge.

GRADUATE DESTINATIONS AND EMPLOYMENT (2009/10 HESA)
Aerospace Engineering; graduates surveyed 1835 **Employed** 670 **In voluntary employment** 5 **In further study** 325 **Assumed unemployed** 95

Career note Specialist areas of study on these courses will open up possible career directions. See also **Engineering/Engineering Sciences**.

OTHER DEGREE SUBJECTS FOR CONSIDERATION
Astronomy; Astrophysics; Computer Science; Electronics and Systems Engineering; Materials Science; Mathematics; Naval Architecture; Physics.

ENGINEERING (CHEMICAL)

(including **Fire Engineering, Fire Safety** and **Nuclear Engineering**; see also **Chemistry**)

Courses involve chemistry, microbiology, physics and mathematics. Management, economics, process dynamics, process design and safety are introduced in Years 2 and 3.

Useful websites www.icheme.org; www.engc.org.uk; www.enginuity.org.uk; www.whynotchemeng. com.

NB The points totals shown to the left of the institutions are for ease of reference only. It must not be assumed that Tariff points are always used by institutions or that they can be substituted for an offer in grades. The level of an offer is not necessarily indicative of the quality of a course.

Engineering Council statement See **Engineering/Engineering Sciences**.

COURSE OFFERS INFORMATION
Subject requirements/preferences **AL** Mathematics and chemistry required. See also **Engineering/ Engineering Sciences**.

Your target offers and examples of courses provided by each institution
380 pts **Cambridge** – A*AA (Cheml Eng) (IB 40–42 pts HL 766–777)
Imperial London – A*mathsAA (Cheml Eng) (IB 39 pts HL 6 maths chem phys)
Oxford – A*AA (Cheml Eng) (IB 38–40 pts)
360 pts **Birmingham** – AAA (Cheml Eng MEng) (IB 36–38 pts)
Edinburgh – AAA–ABB 320–360 pts (Cheml Eng Mgt) (IB 37–32 pts)
London (UCL) – AAA–AAB incl maths (Cheml Bioch Eng) (IB 36–38 pts)
Manchester – AAA (Chem Eng) (IB 37 pts)
Nottingham – AAA (Civ Env Eng MEng) (IB 36 pts)
340 pts **Aston** – AAB–AAA 340–360 pts (Cheml Eng MEng) (IB 34 pts)
Bath – AAB (Bioch Eng MEng) (IB 35 pts HL 6 chem)
Birmingham – AAB (Nucl Eng) (IB 34–36 pts)
Lancaster – AAB (Nucl Eng) (IB 34 pts)
Leeds – AAB (Cheml Eng) (IB 36 pts HL 17 pts)

shape the future...

Engineering your future –
Why chemical is the way to go...
By Matt Stalker

Chemical engineers are considered to be the problem-solvers of the science and engineering community. Whether it's working out how to make industrial processes more environmentally friendly or deciding which fuels are best suited to Formula One racing cars, chemical engineers have usually got the answers.

If you're reading this, you're probably already thinking about studying chemical engineering at university.

It's a career path that offers variety, travel and outstanding earning potential – 2011 chemical engineering graduates got an average starting salary of £28,000/y, the third highest in the UK. Chemical engineering is all about changing raw materials into useful, everyday products in a safe and cost effective way. For example, did you know that petrol, plastics and synthetic fibres such as polyester and nylon, all come from oil? Chemical engineers understand how to alter the chemical, biochemical or physical state of a substance, to create everything from face creams to fuels. Whynotchemeng.com is a website that's full of information about chemical engineering. Whether you're trying to better understand what chemical engineers do on a day-to-day basis, which companies employ chemical engineers, or which universities offer chemical engineering degree courses, whynotchemeng can help.

Since the campaign's launch, volunteers have visited hundreds of schools and colleges throughout the UK and played a key role in the staggering rise in number of students choosing to study chemical engineering at UK universities. Last year, a record intake of over 1800 students chose to start studying the subject at university.

Companies such as BP, Shell, Sellafield, Tate and Lyle, Foster Wheeler and Davy Process Technology all employ chemical engineering graduates in a wide range of roles.

Because the skills of a chemical engineer are so transferable, international travel is a very real possibility for chemical engineers.

Sheida Khajavi studied chemical engineering at Delft University in the Netherlands, and now works as an oil markets analyst for Shell: "Chemical engineering is a really exciting subject and there are many different aspects to it. It's not just about the sciences, you need to be analytical too and there is lots of variety within the profession. Just about everything we see and touch throughout our lives has at some point, been touched by chemical engineering", she explained.

Al Sacco is another chemical engineer and he's got further than most...much further. Al spent time working for NASA and has been into space, spending three weeks doing research into Earth's orbit!

"When people ask how far chemical engineering has taken me, I can tell them that it's taken me into space – it doesn't get much further than that!" said Al.

Whilst a chemical engineering degree isn't certain to take you as far as Al, it's a door-opening degree that equips graduates with an outstanding grasp of project management, design and how industrial processes operate. So maybe it's time to think...whynotchemeng?

Links

www.whynotchemeng.com
www.icheme.org
www.facebook.com/whynotchemeng
www.twitter.com/whynotchemeng

London (UCL) – AAB–ABB (Bioch Eng BEng) (IB 34–36 pts)
Loughborough – 340 pts (Cheml Eng Mgt (5 yrs sandwich)) (IB 36 pts HL maths, phys chem)
Manchester – AAB (Petrol Eng) (IB 35 pts)
Newcastle – AAB (Bioproc Eng) (IB 36 pts HL 5 chem maths)
Nottingham – AAB–ABB 320–340 pts (Cheml Eng Env Eng) (IB 34–32 pts)
Strathclyde – AAB (Cheml Eng MEng) (IB 34 pts)
Sheffield – AAB (Cheml Eng) (IB 35 pts)
Surrey – AAB (Cheml Eng MEng) (IB 35 pts)
Swansea – AAB (Cheml Eng MEng)

320 pts Edinburgh – AAA–ABB incl maths 320–360 pts (Struct Fire Sfty Eng) (IB 37–32 pts)
Heriot-Watt – ABB (Cheml Eng Comb St)
Liverpool – AAB–BBB (Phys Nucl Sci) (IB 33 pts HL 6 maths phys)
Loughborough – 320 pts (Cheml Eng BEng) (IB 34 pts)
Newcastle – AAB–ABB 320–340 pts (Cheml Eng BEng) (IB 34 pts HL 5 chem maths)
Queen's Belfast – ABB/BBBb (Cheml Eng MEng)
Strathclyde – ABB–AAC (App Chem Cheml Eng) (IB 34 pts)
Sheffield – ABB (Cheml Proc Eng) (IB 33 pts)
Surrey – ABB (Cheml Eng BEng) (IB 34 pts)

300 pts Aberdeen – BBB 300 pts (Cheml Eng)
Aston – BBB–ABB 300–320 pts (Cheml Eng BEng)
Heriot-Watt – BBB (Brew Distil)
Strathclyde – BBB (Cheml Eng BEng) (IB 31 pts)

280 pts Queen's Belfast – BBC (Cheml Eng BEng)
Teesside – 280–300 pts (Cheml Eng MEng)
West Scotland – BBC (Cheml Eng)

260 pts Bradford – 260 pts (Cheml Eng)
240 pts Huddersfield – 240 pts (Chem Cheml Eng)
London South Bank – 240 pts (Cheml Proc Eng) (IB 24 pts)
Newport – 240 pts (Fire Sfty Eng)
Portsmouth – 240–280 pts (Petrol Eng)
200 pts UCLan – 200 pts (Fire Sfty Risk Mgt)

Alternative offers
See **Chapter 7** and **Appendix 1** for grades/UCAS Tariff points information for the International Baccalaureate, Scottish Highers/Advanced Highers, the Welsh Baccalaureate, the Irish Leaving Certificate, the Cambridge Pre-U Diploma, the Advanced Diploma and the Extended Project.

CHOOSING YOUR COURSE (SEE ALSO CH.1)
Some course features
Aberdeen Close contacts with the oil and gas industries.
Birmingham One third of the course with Business Management is devoted to management subjects.
Heriot-Watt Direct entry to Year 2 depending on A-level results. Courses have a common structure up to Year 3 allowing for a change in specialisation.
London (UCL) The MEng course leads directly to Chartered Engineer status. Students taking the BEng course will need to complete a period of further training to achieve this.
Newcastle Stages 1 and 2 are common for all nine courses in the department.
Nottingham Environmental Engineering can be combined with Chemical Engineering.

Universities and colleges teaching quality See www.qaa.ac.uk; http://unistats.direct.gov.uk.

Top research universities and colleges (RAE 2008) Cambridge; Imperial London; Manchester; London (UCL); Birmingham; Sheffield; Newcastle; Bath.

Examples of sandwich degree courses Aston; Bath; Bradford; Huddersfield; London South Bank; Loughborough; Queen's Belfast; Surrey; Teesside.

Check **Chapter 4** when choosing your university and **Chapter 7** on how to read the subject tables.

ADMISSIONS INFORMATION

Number of applicants per place (approx) Aston 4; Bath 9; Birmingham 8; Heriot-Watt 8; Huddersfield 7; Imperial London 4, (MEng) 4; Leeds 9; London (UCL) 8; Loughborough 7; Newcastle (MEng/BEng) 6; Nottingham 6; Sheffield 14; Strathclyde 6; Surrey 5; Swansea 3.

Misconceptions about this course Surrey That chemical engineering is chemistry on a large scale: physics is as applicable as chemistry.

Selection interviews Yes Bath, Cambridge, Imperial London, Leeds, London (UCL), London South Bank, Loughborough, Newcastle, Oxford, Surrey, Sussex, Teesside; **No** Nottingham.

Interview advice and questions Past questions have included the following: How would you justify the processing of radioactive waste to people living in the neighbourhood? What is public health engineering? What is biochemical engineering? What could be the sources of fuel and energy in the year 2020? Discuss some industrial applications of chemistry. Regular incidents occur in which chemical spillage and other problems affect the environment. Be prepared to discuss these social issues. See also **Chapter 6**. **Imperial London** Interviews can be conducted in South East Asia if necessary.

Reasons for rejection (non-academic) See **Engineering/Engineering Sciences**.

AFTER-RESULTS ADVICE

Offers to applicants repeating A-levels Higher Swansea; **Possibly higher** Bath, Leeds, London South Bank, Queen's Belfast; **Same** Aston, Birmingham, Cambridge, Loughborough, Newcastle, Nottingham, Sheffield, Surrey, Teesside.

GRADUATE DESTINATIONS AND EMPLOYMENT (2009/10 HESA)

Chemical, Process and Energy Engineering; graduates surveyed 1150 **Employed** 460 **In voluntary employment** 5 **In further study** 185 **Assumed unemployed** 90

Career note Chemical engineering is involved in many aspects of industry and scientific development. In addition to the oil and chemical-based industries, graduates enter a wide range of careers including the design and construction of chemical process plants, food production, pollution control, environmental protection, energy conservation, waste recovery and recycling, medical science, health and safety, and alternative energy sources.

OTHER DEGREE SUBJECTS FOR CONSIDERATION

Biochemistry; Biotechnology; Chemistry; Colour Chemistry; Cosmetic Science; Environmental Science; Food Science and Technology; Materials Science; Mathematics; Nuclear Engineering; Physics.

ENGINEERING (CIVIL)

(including **Architectural, Coastal, Disaster Management, Environmental, Offshore, Structural** and **Transportation Engineering**; see also **Building and Construction, Environmental Sciences/ Studies**)

Civil engineering is concerned with the science and art of large-scale projects. This involves the planning, design, construction, maintenance and environmental assessment of roads, railways, bridges, airports, tunnels, docks, offshore structures, dams, high rise buildings and other major works. Specialist courses may also involve water, drainage, irrigation schemes and waste engineering, traffic and coastal engineering.

Useful websites www.ice.org.uk; www.engc.org.uk; www.enginuity.org.uk.

NB The points totals shown to the left of the institutions are for ease of reference only. It must not be assumed that Tariff points are always used by institutions or that they can be substituted for an offer in grades. The level of an offer is not necessarily indicative of the quality of a course.

Engineering Council statement *See* **Engineering/Engineering Sciences**.

COURSE OFFERS INFORMATION

Subject requirements/preferences See **Engineering/Engineering Sciences**.

Your target offers and examples of courses provided by each institution

400 pts **Imperial London** – A*mathsA*A (Civ Eng) (IB 39 pts HL 7 maths 6 phys)

380 pts **Bath** – A*AA (Civ Eng) (IB 36 pts HL 6 maths)
Bristol – A*AA–AAA (Civ Eng) (IB 38–37 pts HL 666)
Cambridge – A*AA (Eng (P II Civ Eng)) (IB 40–42 pts)
London (UCL) – A*AA–AAA (Civ Eng) (IB 38–39 pts)
Oxford – A*AA (Civ Eng) (IB 38–40 pts)

360 pts **Birmingham** – AAA–AAB 340–360 pts (Civ Ener Eng) (IB 34–38 pts)
Durham – AAA (Civ Eng) (IB 37 pts)
Edinburgh – AAA–ABB incl maths (Struct Eng Arch) (IB 37–32 pts)
Manchester – AAA (Civ Eng) (IB 37 pts)
Newcastle – AAA (Civ Struct Eng MEng) (IB 37 pts HL 5 maths)
Nottingham – AAA (Civ Eng MEng) (IB 36 pts)
Strathclyde – AAA (Civ Eng MEng/BEng)
Sheffield – AAA incl maths sci (Struct Eng Archit) (IB 37 pts HL 6 maths sci)
Southampton – AAA (Civ Eng Archit) (IB 36 pts HL 18 pts)
Swansea – AAA–AAB incl maths (Civ Eng MEng) (IB 34 pts)

340 pts **Brunel** – AAB (Mech Eng Bld Serv MEng) (IB 35 pts)
Cardiff – AAB incl maths (Archit Eng) (IB 30 pts)
City – AAB 340 pts (Civ Eng) (IB 30 pts)
Glasgow – AAB (Civ Eng Archit MEng) (IB 34 pts)
Leeds – AAB (Civ Eng Constr Mgt) (IB 36 pts HL 17 pts)
Liverpool – AAB incl maths (Civ Eng MEng) (IB 35 pts HL 5 maths)
Newcastle – AAB (Off Eng MEng) (IB 37 pts HL 5 maths phys)
Queen's Belfast – AAB (Civ Eng MEng)
Surrey – AAB–ABB (Civ Eng MEng/BEng)
Swansea – AAB–ABB incl maths (Civ Eng BEng) (IB 32 pts)
Warwick – AAB (Civ Eng) (IB 36 pts)

320 pts **Brighton** – ABB (Civ Eng MEng) (IB 28 pts)
Bristol UWE – 320 pts (Archit Env Eng)
Brunel – ABB (Civ Eng Sust MEng) (IB 32 pts)
Exeter – ABB–BBB 320–300 pts (Civ Eng BEng) (IB 32–30 pts)
Glasgow – ABB (Civ Eng Archit BEng) (IB 32 pts)
LJMU – 320 pts (Bld Serv Eng MEng; Civ Eng MEng)
Loughborough – AAB–ABB 320–340 pts (Civ Eng) (IB 34–36 pts)
Newcastle – AAB–ABB 320–340 pts (Civ Eng BEng) (IB 34 pts)
Nottingham – ABB (Civ Env Eng BEng) (IB 32 pts)
Queen's Belfast – ABB–BBBb (Struct Eng Archit MEng)
Strathclyde – ABB–BBB (Archit Eng) (IB 32 pts HL 5 maths 5 phys)

300 pts **Aberdeen** – BBB (Civ Env Eng) (IB 24 pts)
Anglia Ruskin – 300 pts (Civ Eng MEng)
Bradford – 240–300 pts (Civ Struct Eng) (IB 28–32 pts)
Brighton – BBB (Civ Env Eng) (IB 32 pts)
Edinburgh Napier – BBB 300 pts (Civ Trans Eng MEng)
Glamorgan – BBB (Civ Eng BEng)
Heriot-Watt – BBB–ABC (Civ Eng Struct Eng BEng) (IB 35 pts)
Liverpool – BBB incl maths (Civ Eng BEng) (IB 32 pts HL 5 maths)
Portsmouth – 300–360 pts (Civ Eng MEng)
Queen's Belfast – BBB (Civ Eng BEng)
Teesside – 300 pts (Civ Eng MEng)

280 pts **Bristol UWE** – 280 pts (Civ Eng) (IB 24–28 pts)
Brunel – BBC (Civ Eng Sust BEng) (IB 30 pts)

Check **Chapter 4** when choosing your university and **Chapter 7** on how to read the subject tables.

City – 280–320 pts (Civ Eng Surv) (IB 30–32 pts)
Derby – 280 pts (Civ Infra Eng)
Edinburgh Napier – BBC 280 pts (Civ Eng MEng)
Kingston – 280 pts (Civ Eng)
London (QM) – 280–340 pts (Sust Ener Eng)
Teesside – 280 pts (Civ Eng Disas Mgt; Civ Eng BEng) (IB 30 pts)

270 pts **Glasgow Caledonian** – 270 pts (Env Civ Eng)
LJMU – 270 pts (Civ Eng BEng; Bld Serv Eng BEng)
Portsmouth – 270–300 pts (Civ Eng BEng)
Ulster – 270 pts (Civ Eng) (IB 24 pts)

260 pts **Coventry** – 260–320 pts (Civ Eng; Civ Struct Eng; Civ Eng Mgt)
Edinburgh Napier – 260 pts (Civ Trans Eng BEng)
Heriot-Watt – BCC–ABC (Civ Eng BEng) (IB 35 pts)
LJMU – 260 pts (Bld Serv Eng Proj Mgt)
Nottingham Trent – 260 pts (Civ Eng BEng) (IB 28 pts)
Plymouth – 260 pts (Civ Cstl Eng BEng/BSc)
Salford – 260 pts (Civ Archit Eng) (IB 35 pts)

240 pts **Bolton** – 240 pts (Civ Eng)
Coventry – 240 pts (Bld Serv Eng) (IB 27 pts)
Dundee – CCC (Civ Eng)
Edinburgh Napier – CCC 240 pts (Civ Eng BEng)
Glamorgan – 240 pts (Civ Eng BSc)
Greenwich – 240 pts (Civ Eng Wtr Env Mgt; Civ Eng Proj Mgt)
Newport – 240 pts (Civ Constr Eng)
UEL – 240 pts (Civ Eng) (IB 26 pts)

225 pts **Anglia Ruskin** – 225 pts (Civ Eng BEng)

220 pts **Derby** – 220 pts (Civ Eng)
Edinburgh Napier – 220 pts (Civ Tmbr Eng)

200 pts **Abertay Dundee** – CDD 200 pts (Civ Eng) (IB 26 pts)
Anglia Ruskin – 200 pts (Civ Eng BSc) (IB 26 pts)
Glamorgan – 200–300 pts (Civ Eng Int St)
Leeds Met – 200 pts (Civ Eng) (IB 24 pts)
London South Bank – 200–240 pts (Civ Eng) (IB 24 pts)
UEL – 200 pts (Civ Eng Surv)
West London – 200 pts (Civ Env Eng)

180 pts **Greenwich** – 180 pts (Civ Eng)
Plymouth – 180–260 pts (Civ Eng BEng/BSc)
Salford – 180 pts (Civ Eng BSc)

160 pts **Swansea Met** – 160 pts (Civ Eng Env Mgt)
West Scotland – CC–DD (Civ Eng)
Wolverhampton – 160–220 pts (Civ Eng BEng)

Alternative offers

See **Chapter 7** and **Appendix 1** for grades/UCAS Tariff points information for the International Baccalaureate, Scottish Highers/Advanced Highers, the Welsh Baccalaureate, the Irish Leaving Certificate, the Cambridge Pre-U Diploma, the Advanced Diploma and the Extended Project.

EXAMPLES OF FOUNDATION DEGREES IN THE SUBJECT FIELD

Bedfordshire; Blackburn (Coll); Bolton; Bristol UWE; Derby; Glamorgan; Kent; Kingston; Northampton; Nottingham Trent; Somerset (CAT); Suffolk (Univ Campus); Swansea Met.

CHOOSING YOUR COURSE (SEE ALSO CH.1)

Some course features

Cardiff The first and second year is common to all nine Engineering programmes.
Durham A common course for Years 1 and 2 and then two years specialising in the chosen discipline.
Exeter A multidisciplinary first year before specialising in Year 2.

LJMU Projects include highways, railways, airports, flood control and sports stadia.
Portsmouth The course leads to a professional qualification in civil engineering.
Southampton Options to take a year in industry or Europe.

Universities and colleges teaching quality See www.qaa.ac.uk; http://unistats.direct.gov.uk.

Top research universities and colleges (RAE 2008) Imperial London; Swansea; Cardiff; Nottingham; Newcastle; Southampton; Sheffield; Bristol; Dundee.

Examples of sandwich degree courses Bath; Bradford; Brighton; Bristol UWE; Cardiff; City; Coventry; Glamorgan; Kingston; LJMU; London South Bank; Loughborough; Nottingham Trent; Portsmouth; Queen's Belfast; Salford; Surrey; Teesside; UEL; Ulster; West Scotland; Wolverhampton.

ADMISSIONS INFORMATION

Number of applicants per place (approx) Abertay Dundee 8; Bath 13; Birmingham 6; Bradford (BEng) 5; Bristol 10; Brunel 4; Cardiff 5; City 11; Coventry 10, (Civ Eng) 11; Dundee 5; Durham 8; Edinburgh Napier 4; Glamorgan 6; Glasgow Caledonian 4; Greenwich 11; Heriot-Watt 7; Imperial London 4; Kingston 8; Leeds 10; LJMU 16; London (UCL) 5; London South Bank 5; Loughborough 6; Newcastle 11, (Off Eng) 9; Nottingham 6; Nottingham Trent 11; Plymouth 3; Portsmouth 3; Queen's Belfast 6; Salford 5; Sheffield 7; Southampton 8; Strathclyde 4; Surrey 5; Swansea 3; Teesside 6; West Scotland 4; Wolverhampton 3.

Advice to applicants and planning the UCAS personal statement See **Engineering/Engineering Sciences**. Also read the magazine *The New Civil Engineer* and discuss articles which interest you on your application. **Bristol** Deferred entry accepted.

Selection interviews Yes Bath, Brighton, Bristol, Brunel, Cambridge, Coventry, Durham, Edinburgh Napier, Glamorgan, Greenwich, Heriot-Watt, Imperial London, Kingston, Leeds, London (UCL), London South Bank, Loughborough, Newcastle, Oxford, Queen's Belfast, Southampton, Surrey, Sussex, Warwick; **Some** Abertay Dundee, Anglia Ruskin, Cardiff, Dundee, Nottingham Trent, Salford; **No** Nottingham.

Interview advice and questions Past questions have included: Why have you chosen Civil Engineering? Have you contacted the Institution of Civil Engineers/Institution of Structural Engineers? How would you define the difference between the work of a civil engineer and the work of an architect? What would happen to a concrete beam if a load were applied? Where would it break and how could it be strengthened? The favourite question: Why do you want to be a civil engineer? What would you do if you were asked to build a concrete boat? Do you know any civil engineers? What problems were faced in building the Channel Tunnel? See also **Chapter 6**. **Cambridge** Why did they make mill chimneys so tall?

Reasons for rejection (non-academic) Lack of vitality. Lack of interest in buildings, the built environment or in civil engineering. Poor communication skills. See also **Engineering/Engineering Sciences**.

AFTER-RESULTS ADVICE

Offers to applicants repeating A-levels Higher Kingston, LJMU, Nottingham, Queen's Belfast, Teesside, UEL, Warwick; **Possibly higher** Portsmouth, Southampton; **Same** Abertay Dundee, Bath, Birmingham, Bradford, Brighton, Bristol, Cardiff, City, Coventry, Dundee, Durham, Greenwich, Heriot-Watt, Leeds, London (UCL), London South Bank, Loughborough, Newcastle, Nottingham Trent, Salford, Sheffield, Wolverhampton; **No** Cambridge.

GRADUATE DESTINATIONS AND EMPLOYMENT (2009/10 HESA)

Civil Engineering; graduates surveyed 4990 **Employed** 2175 **In voluntary employment** 25 **In further study** 740 **Assumed unemployed** 320

Career note The many aspects of this subject will provide career directions for graduates with many openings with local authorities and commercial organisations.

OTHER DEGREE SUBJECTS FOR CONSIDERATION

Architecture; Building; Surveying; Town and Country Planning.

Check **Chapter 4** when choosing your university and **Chapter 7** on how to read the subject tables.

ENGINEERING (COMMUNICATIONS)

(including Mobile Communications; see also Communication Studies/Communication, Engineering (Electrical and Electronic))

Communications Engineering impacts on many aspects of the engineering and business world. Courses overlap considerably with Electronic, Computer, Digital, Media and Internet Engineering and provide graduates with expertise in such fields as telecommunications, mobile communications and microwave engineering, optoelectronics, radio engineering and internet technology. Sandwich courses and sponsorships are offered by several universities.

Useful websites See **Computer Courses** and **Engineering (Electrical and Electronic)**.

NB The points totals shown to the left of the institutions are for ease of reference only. It must not be assumed that Tariff points are always used by institutions or that they can be substituted for an offer in grades. The level of an offer is not necessarily indicative of the quality of a course.

Engineering Council statement *See* **Engineering/Engineering Sciences**.

COURSE OFFERS INFORMATION

Subject requirements/preferences See **Engineering/Engineering Sciences**.

Your target offers and examples of courses provided by each institution
380 pts **London (UCL)** – AAA+AS–ABB+AS (Electron Eng Comms Eng) (IB 34–38 pts)
360 pts **Bristol** – A*AB–AAA (Electron Comm Eng) (IB 35 pts)
     Durham – AAA (Comm Eng) (IB 37 pts)
     Nottingham – AAA–BBB 320–360 pts (Electron Comms Eng) (IB 36 pts)
     Southampton – AAA incl maths phys (Electron Eng Wrlss Comms) (IB 36 pts HL 18 pts)
     Surrey – AAA–AAB (Electron Sat Eng MEng) (IB 34–32 pts)
     Swansea – AAA–AAB (Telecomm Eng MEng)
340 pts **Bath** – AAB (Electron Comm Eng MEng) (IB 36 pts HL 6 maths phys)
     Birmingham – AAA–AAB (Electron Elec Eng) (IB 32–36 pts)
     City – AAB 340 pts (Multim Intnet Sys Eng) (IB 30 pts)
     Leeds – AAB (Electron Comm Eng) (IB 36pts HL 17 pts)
     Leicester – AAB–ABB (Comms Electron Eng MEng)
     London (QM) – 340 pts (Elect Eng Telecomm MEng) (IB 34 pts)
     Newcastle – AAB–ABB 320-340 pts (Electron Comm MEng) (IB 32 pts HL 5 maths phys)
     Sheffield – AAB incl maths (Electron Comms Eng MEng) (IB 35 pts)
     Surrey – 340 pts (Telecomm Sys) (IB 34–32 pts)
     York – AAB–ABB (Electron Comm Eng MEng)
320 pts **Bath** – ABB (Electron Comm Eng BEng) (IB 34 pts)
     Brunel – ABB 320–370 pts (Electron Comm Eng) (IB 33 pts HL 6 maths)
     Cardiff – ABB (Electron Comm Eng MEng)
     Kent – ABB (Electron Comm Eng MEng) (IB 33 pts)
     Lancaster – ABB–BBB (Comm Sys Electron) (IB 32 pts)
     London (QM) – 320 pts (Elect Eng Telecomm BEng)
     Newcastle – AAB–ABB 320-340 pts (Electron Comm BEng) (IB 32 pts HL 5 maths phys)
     Sheffield – ABB incl maths (Electron Comms Eng BEng) (IB 33 pts)
300 pts **Aberdeen** – BBB (Electron Eng Comm)
     Birmingham City – 300 pts (Telecomm Net Eng)
     Bournemouth – 300 pts (Intnet Comm Tech)
     Bradford – BBB 300 pts (Electron Telecomm Intnet Eng MEng) (IB 28–32 pts)
     Cardiff – BBB (Electron Comm Eng BEng)
     Essex – BBB 300 pts (ICT) (IB 29 pts)
     Leicester – BBB–BBC (Comms Electron Eng BEng) (IB 32 pts)
     Liverpool – BBB (Electron Comm Eng BEng) (IB 30 pts HL 5 maths phys/elec)
     Portsmouth – 300–360 pts (Comm Sys MEng)

Swansea – BBB 300 pts (Telecomm Eng BEng)
York – BBB–BBC (Electron Comm BEng) (IB 32 pts)
280 pts **Brunel** – BBC (Comm Net Eng BEng) (IB 30 pts)
Glamorgan – BBC (Mbl Telecomm)
Manchester Met – 280 pts (Comp Comm Eng) (IB 28 pts)
260 pts **Brunel** – BCC 260 pts (Elec Electron Eng (Comm))
De Montfort – 260 pts (Electron Eng (Telecomm) (Broad Sys); Electron Eng Comm)
Greenwich – 260 pts (Comm Sys Soft Eng; Wrlss Mob Comm Sys Eng; Telecomm Sys Eng)
Hertfordshire – 260–320 pts (Dig Comm Electron)
Huddersfield – 260 pts (Electron Comm Eng)
Portsmouth – 260–300 pts (Comm Sys BEng)
240 pts **Bradford** – 240 pts (Electron Telecomm Intnet Eng BEng) (IB 26 pts)
London South Bank – 240 pts (Telecomm Comp Net Eng)
Newport – 240 pts (Electron Eng)
UCLan – 240 pts (Dig Comm) (IB 26 pts)
220 pts **UEL** – 220 pts (Elec Electron Eng (Comm))
200 pts **Kingston** – 200–280 pts (Comm Sys)
160 pts **Wolverhampton** – 160–220 pts (Electron Comm Eng)
100 pts **Bedfordshire** – 100 pts (Telecomm Net Eng)

Alternative offers
See **Chapter 7** and **Appendix 1** for grades/UCAS Tariff points information for the International Baccalaureate, Scottish Highers/Advanced Highers, the Welsh Baccalaureate, the Irish Leaving Certificate, the Cambridge Pre-U Diploma, the Advanced Diploma and the Extended Project.

EXAMPLES OF FOUNDATION DEGREES IN THE SUBJECT FIELD
Plymouth.

CHOOSING YOUR COURSE (SEE ALSO CH.1)
Some course features
Durham A common course for Years 1 and 2 and then two years specialising in the chosen discipline.
Leicester Communications and Electronic Engineering combined. Options to study for a year in industry or in Europe.
London (QM) There are a range of degree programmes offered in the Department of Electronic Engineering, and there is some flexibility and overlap.
Portsmouth A Foundation Year can lead to a number of Engineering and Technological degree courses.

Universities and colleges teaching quality See www.qaa.ac.uk; http://unistats.direct.gov.uk.

Examples of sandwich degree courses Aston; Bath; Brighton and Hove City (Coll); Brunel; Glamorgan; Glasgow Caledonian; Hertfordshire; Kingston; London Met; Manchester Met; Northumbria; UCLan; Westminster.

ADMISSIONS INFORMATION
Number of applicants per place (approx) Birmingham 10; Bradford 9; Bristol 2; Coventry 7; Hull 8; London Met 5; London South Bank 3; Northumbria 7; Plymouth 4; York 8 av.

Advice to applicants and planning the UCAS personal statement See **Engineering (Electrical and Electronic)** and **Appendix 3**.

Selection interviews Yes Bradford, Bristol, Hertfordshire, Kent, London Met, London South Bank, Sunderland.

Interview advice and questions See **Engineering (Electrical and Electronic)**.

Reasons for rejection (non-academic) See **Engineering (Electrical and Electronic)**.

Check **Chapter 4** when choosing your university and **Chapter 7** on how to read the subject tables.

AFTER-RESULTS ADVICE

Offers to applicants repeating A-levels **Same** Loughborough.

GRADUATE DESTINATIONS AND EMPLOYMENT (2009/10 HESA)

See **Engineering (Electrical and Electronic)** and **Engineering/Engineering Sciences**.

Career note Many commercial organisations offer opportunities in the specialist areas described at the top of this table. Work placements and sandwich courses have, in the past, resulted in over 60% of graduates gaining employment with their firms.

OTHER DEGREE SUBJECTS FOR CONSIDERATION

Computer Science; Engineering (Computer, Control, Electrical, Electronic, Systems); Physics.

ENGINEERING (COMPUTER, CONTROL, SOFTWARE and SYSTEMS)

The design and application of modern computer systems is fundamental to a wide range of disciplines which also include electronic, software and computer-aided engineering. Most courses give priority to reinforcing the essential transferable skills' consisting of management techniques, leadership skills, literacy, presentation skills, business skills and time management. At many universities Computer Engineering is offered as part of a range of Electronics degree programmes when the first and even the second year courses are common to all students, who choose to specialise later. A year in industry is a common feature of many of these courses.

Useful websites See **Computer Courses** and **Engineering/Engineering Sciences**.

NB The points totals shown to the left of the institutions are for ease of reference only. It must not be assumed that Tariff points are always used by institutions or that they can be substituted for an offer in grades. The level of an offer is not necessarily indicative of the quality of a course.

Engineering Council statement See **Engineering/Engineering Sciences**.

COURSE OFFERS INFORMATION

Subject requirements/preferences See **Engineering/Engineering Sciences**.

Your target offers and examples of courses provided by each institution

380 pts **Cambridge** – Yrs 3 and 4 specialisation via Engineering Tripos A*AA (Eng (Inf Comp Eng)) (IB 40–42 pts)

Imperial London – A*mathsAA (Comp (Soft Eng)) (IB 39 pts HL maths)

Oxford – A*AA (Inf Eng) (IB 38–40 pts)

Southampton – A*AA incl maths (Comp Sci Soft Eng) (IB 38 pts HL 19 pts)

360 pts **Edinburgh** – AAA–ABB incl maths (Soft Eng Mgt) (IB 37–32 pts)

Southampton – AAA–AAB (Comp Sci Artif Intel) (IB 34 pts)

Warwick – AAA (Comp Sys) (IB 38 pts)

340 pts **Aberystwyth** – 340 pts (Soft Eng MEng) (IB 28 pts)

Bath – AAB (Comp Sys Eng MEng) (IB 36 pts HL 6 maths phys)

City – AAB 340 pts (Comp Sys Eng) (IB 28 pts)

Glasgow – AAB (Microcomp Sys Eng MEng) (IB 34 pts)

Leeds – AAB (Electron Comm Eng) (IB 36pts HL 17 pts)

Leicester – AAB–ABB (Soft Electron Eng MEng)

Liverpool – AAB (Soft Dev) (IB 33 pts HL 5 maths)

London (QM) – 340 pts (Comp Eng MEng) (IB 34 pts)

Loughborough – AAB (Sys Eng MEng) (IB 34 pts)

Manchester – AAB (Comp Sys Eng) (IB 35 pts)

Strathclyde – AAB (Comp Electron Sys MEng)

Sheffield – AAB incl maths (Sys Cntrl Eng (Eng Mgt) MEng) (IB 35 pts)
Sussex – AAB–BBB incl maths (Comp Eng) (IB 32–35 pts HL 5/6 maths)
Warwick – AAB (Sys Eng) (IB 36 pts)
York – AAB–ABB (Comp Sci Embd Sys)

320 pts **Bath** – ABB (Comp Sys Eng BEng) (IB 34 pts HL 6 maths phys)
Birmingham – ABB (Comp Sys Eng Bus Mgt) (IB 32–34 pts)
Brunel – ABB+AS 320–370 pts (Sys Comp Eng MEng) (IB 33 pts)
Cardiff – ABB (Comp Sys Eng BSc; Soft Eng)
Edinburgh – AAA–ABB incl maths 320–360 pts (Electron Comp Sci) (IB 37–32 pts)
Glasgow – ABB (Electron Soft Eng) (IB 32 pts)
Kent – ABB (Comp Sys Eng MEng) (IB 33 pts)
Lancaster – ABB (Soft Eng) (IB 32 pts)
Liverpool – ABB (Comp Sci Electron Eng MEng) (IB 33 pts HL 5 maths phys elec)
Newcastle – AAB–ABB 320–340 pts (Electron Comp Eng) (IB 32 pts HL 5 maths phys)
Nottingham – ABB (Soft Eng) (IB 32 pts HL 5 maths)
Reading – 320 pts (Comp Sci Cyber MEng; Cyber)
Strathclyde – ABB (Comp Electron Sys BEng)
Sheffield – ABB (Comp Sys Eng BEng) (IB 33 pts)
UEA – ABB (Comp Sys Eng (Yr Ind)) (IB 32 pts)

300 pts **Aberdeen** – BBB (Electron Comp Eng) (IB 30 pts)
Bangor – 300–320 pts (Comp Sys Eng MEng)
Bournemouth – 300 pts (Soft Eng Mgt; Soft Eng; Soft Prod Des)
Bradford – BBB 300 pts (Electron Telecomm Intnet Eng MEng) (IB 28–32 pts)
Brunel – BBB (Gms Des Engl) (IB 32 pts)
Cardiff – BBB (Comp Sys Eng BEng) (IB 30–32 pts)
Essex – 300 pts (Comp Net) (IB 29 pts)
Heriot-Watt – BBB (Comp Electron)
Kent – BBB (Comp Sys Eng BEng) (IB 33 pts)
Kingston – 300 pts (Soft Eng)
Leicester – BBB–BBC (Soft Electron Eng BEng)
Liverpool – BBB (Comp Sci Electron Eng BEng) (IB 30 pts HL 5 maths phys elec)
London (QM) – 300 pts (Comp Eng BEng) (IB 28 pts)
Loughborough – BBB (Sys Eng BEng) (IB 32 pts)
Plymouth – 300 pts (Comp Sys Net)
Portsmouth – 300–360 pts (Comp Eng MEng) (IB 30 pts)
Reading – 300–340 pts (Comp Eng BSc) (IB 30 pts)
Strathclyde – ABC (Soft Eng BEng) (IB 32 pts)
Westminster – BBB (Comp Sys Eng MEng) (IB 32 pts))

280 pts **Aberystwyth** – 280 pts (Spc Sci Robot) (IB 27 pts)
Brunel – BBC (Comp Sys Eng BEng) (IB 29 pts)
Glamorgan – BBC 280 pts (Comp Sys Eng)
LJMU – 280–240 pts (Comp Eng)
Manchester Met – 280 pts (Soft Eng) (IB 28 pts)
Northumbria – 280 pts (Comp Net Tech)
Nottingham Trent – 280 pts (Soft Eng; Comp Sys Eng)
Oxford Brookes – BBC (Soft Eng) (IB 29 pts)
Stirling – BBC (Soft Eng) (IB 32 pts)
Teesside – 280–300 pts (Instr Contr Eng MEng)
UCLan – 280 pts (Comp Aid Eng MEng)
Westminster – BBC (Comp Sys Eng BEng) (IB 30 pts)

260 pts **Brunel** – 260–300 pts (Intnet Eng) (IB 30 pts)
Greenwich – 260 pts (Comm Sys Soft Eng)
Huddersfield – 260 pts (Comp Sys Eng) (IB 26 pts)
Hull – 260–380 pts (Comp Sys Eng)
LJMU – 260 pts (Soft Eng) (IB 24 pts)

Check **Chapter 4** when choosing your university and **Chapter 7** on how to read the subject tables.

Northampton – 260–280 pts (Comp (Comp Sys Eng))
Portsmouth – 260–300 pts (Comp Eng BSc)
Sunderland – 260 pts (Gms Soft Dev)
Teesside – 260–280 pts (Soft Dev)
240 pts **Bangor** – 240–260 pts (Comp Sys Eng BEng)
Bolton – 240 pts (Comp Aid Eng)
Bradford – 240 pts (Soft Eng)
Bristol UWE – CCC (Soft Eng) (IB 24–28 pts)
Coventry – 240 pts (Soft Eng)
Greenwich – 240 pts (Soft Eng; Comp Sys Soft Eng BSc)
Huddersfield – 240 pts (Comp Cntrl Sys) (IB 26 pts)
Newport – 240 pts (Robot Intel Sys Eng)
Sheffield Hallam – 240–300 pts (Gms Soft Dev; Soft Eng)
UCLan – 240–280 pts (Comp Aid Eng BEng)
230 pts **Edinburgh Napier** – 230 pts (Embd Comp Sys)
220 pts **London Met** – 220 pts (Comp Sys Eng)
Robert Gordon – 220–240 pts (Comp Net Mgt Des)
200 pts **Bedfordshire** – 200 pts (Comp Sys Eng)
Coventry – 200 pts (Comp Hard Soft Eng; Sys Eng; Vrtl Eng)
Heriot-Watt – CDD (Comp Electron BEng)
Hertfordshire – 200–240 pts (Comp Sci (Soft Eng))
Swansea Met – 200 pts (Comp Sys Eng)
UEL – 200 pts (Soft Eng)
170 pts **Glasgow Caledonian** – CD/DDE 170 pts (Comp Eng; Comp Aid Mech Eng)
London South Bank – 170 pts (Comp Sys Net)
160 pts **Bedfordshire** – 160 pts (Comp Sci Soft Eng)
Farnborough (CT) – 160 pts (Soft Eng)
Southampton Solent – 160 pts (Comp Sys Net)
South Essex (Coll) – 160 pts (Net Tech)
Wolverhampton – 160–220 pts (Comp Sci (Soft Eng; Comp Sys Eng)
120 pts **London South Bank** – 120 pts (Comp Aid Eng)
Swansea Met – 120 pts (Soft Eng)

Alternative offers
See **Chapter 7** and **Appendix 1** for grades/UCAS Tariff points information for the International Baccalaureate, Scottish Highers/Advanced Highers, the Welsh Baccalaureate, the Irish Leaving Certificate, the Cambridge Pre-U Diploma, the Advanced Diploma and the Extended Project.

EXAMPLES OF FOUNDATION DEGREES IN THE SUBJECT FIELD
Bedfordshire; Bournemouth; Manchester (Coll); Swansea Met.

CHOOSING YOUR COURSE (SEE ALSO CH.1)
Some course features
Bristol UWE (Comp Sys Integ) A practical course covering all aspects of computer systems, but also focuses on networks, CPU architecture and embedded systems development.
Cardiff The first year is common to all nine Engineering programmes.
Durham (MEng courses) A common course for Years 1 and 2 and then two years specialising in one of four streams, with a major design project (from design to manufacture) in Year 3.
Heriot-Watt The Software Engineering course involves a study of computer science in the first three years followed in Year 4 and 5 by specialist studies in software technology.
London (QM) The MEng programme covers all the material of the BEng programme with more time spent on professional development and advanced studies.
Plymouth Four final year pathways from which to choose your specialisation.

Universities and colleges teaching quality See www.qaa.ac.uk; http://unistats.direct.gov.uk.

Top research universities and colleges (RAE 2008) See **Computer Courses**.

Examples of sandwich degree courses Aberystwyth; Aston; Bath; Bournemouth; Bradford; Bristol UWE; Brunel; Cardiff; Cardiff Met; City; De Montfort; Glamorgan; Glasgow Caledonian; Greenwich; Hertfordshire; Huddersfield; Kent; Kingston; Lincoln; London South Bank; Loughborough; Manchester; Manchester Met; Middlesex; Newcastle; Northumbria; Nottingham Trent; Plymouth; Reading; Sheffield Hallam; Staffordshire; Ulster; Westminster.

ADMISSIONS INFORMATION

Number of applicants per place (approx) Birmingham 10; Birmingham City 6; Bournemouth 3; Bristol 4; Bristol UWE 12; Cardiff 6; Coventry 2; Durham 6; Edinburgh 3; Huddersfield 2; Imperial London 5; Kent 5; Lancaster 12; LJMU 2; London South Bank 3; Loughborough 17; Sheffield 10; Sheffield Hallam 8; Southampton 4; Staffordshire 5; Stirling 7; Strathclyde 7; Surrey (MEng, BEng) 3; Swansea Met 4; Teesside 3; UCLan 12; UEA 4; Westminster 5; York 3 av.

Advice to applicants and planning the UCAS personal statement See **Computer Courses**, **Engineering (Electrical and Electronic)** and **Appendix 4**.

Selection interviews **Yes** Bath, Bradford, Cardiff, Durham, Glamorgan, Hertfordshire, Huddersfield, Kent, LJMU, London South Bank, Nottingham Trent, Sheffield Hallam, Swansea Met, UEA, Westminster, York; **Some** Exeter, Loughborough, Manchester; **No** Reading.

Interview advice and questions See **Computer Courses**, **Engineering (Electrical and Electronic)** and **Chapter 6**.

Reasons for rejection (non-academic) Lack of understanding that the course involves engineering. See also **Computer Courses** and **Engineering (Electrical and Electronic)**.

AFTER-RESULTS ADVICE

Offers to applicants repeating A-levels **Higher** Bristol, Strathclyde, Warwick, York; **Possibly higher** City, Huddersfield, Sheffield; **Same** Bath, Birmingham, Coventry, Exeter, Lancaster, LJMU, London South Bank, Loughborough, Salford, Teesside, UEA, Ulster; **No** Cambridge.

GRADUATE DESTINATIONS AND EMPLOYMENT (2009/10 HESA)

Software Engineering; graduates surveyed 1405 **Employed** 530 **In voluntary employment** 5 **In further study** 125 **Assumed unemployed** 140

Career note Career opportunities extend right across the whole field of electronics, telecommunications, control and systems engineering.

OTHER DEGREE SUBJECTS FOR CONSIDERATION

Computer Science; Computing; Engineering (Aeronautical, Aerospace, Communications, Electrical and Electronic); Mathematics; Media (Systems/Engineering/Technology); Physics.

ENGINEERING (ELECTRICAL and ELECTRONIC)

(see also **Engineering (Acoustics and Sound)**, **Engineering (Aeronautical and Aerospace)**, **Engineering (Communications)**, **Technologies**)

Electrical and Electronic Engineering courses provide a sound foundation for those looking for a career in electricity generation and transmission, communications or control systems, including robotics. All courses cater for students wanting a general or specialist Engineering education and options should be considered when choosing degree courses. These could include optoelectronics and optical communication systems, microwave systems, radio frequency engineering and circuit technology. Many courses have common first years, allowing transfer in Year 2. Most universities and colleges have good industrial contacts and can arrange industrial placements, in some cases abroad.

Check **Chapter 4** when choosing your university and **Chapter 7** on how to read the subject tables.

Useful websites www.theiet.org; www.engc.org.uk; www.enginuity.org.uk.

NB The points totals shown to the left of the institutions are for ease of reference only. It must not be assumed that Tariff points are always used by institutions or that they can be substituted for an offer in grades. The level of an offer is not necessarily indicative of the quality of a course.

Engineering Council statement *See* **Engineering/Engineering Sciences**.

COURSE OFFERS INFORMATION

Subject requirements/preferences See **Engineering/Engineering Sciences.**

Your target offers and examples of courses provided by each institution

380 pts **Cambridge** – A*AA (Eng (Elec Inf Sci/Elec Electron Eng)) (IB 40–42 pts)
Imperial London – A*mathsAphysA (Elec Electron Eng) (IB 38 pts HL 6 maths 6 phys)
London (UCL) – AAA+AS–ABB+AS (Electron Eng Nanotech) (IB 34–38 pts)
Oxford – A*AA (Elec Eng) (IB 38–40 pts)
370 pts **Brunel** – ABB +AS 370 pts (Elec Eng Renew Ener Sys) (IB 33 pts)
360 pts **Bristol** – A*AB–AAA (Elec Electron Eng) (IB 37 pts)
Durham – AAA (Electron Eng) (IB 37 pts)
Edinburgh – AAA–ABB incl maths (Electron Bioelectron) (IB 37–32 pts)
Leeds – AAA (Electron Nanotech)
Nottingham – AAA–BBB 300–360 pts (Electron Comp Eng) (IB 36 pts)
Southampton – AAA incl maths phys (Electron Eng Pwr Sys) (IB 36 pts HL 18 pts)
Surrey – AAA–AAB (Electron Sat Eng MEng) (IB 34–32 pts)
340 pts **Aston** – AAB–AAA 340–360 pts (Elec Electron Eng) (IB 34 pts)
Bath – AAB (Elec Pwr Eng MEng) (IB 36 pts HL 6 maths phys)
Birmingham – AAA–AAB (Electron Elec Eng) (IB 32–36 pts)
City – AAB 340 pts (Elec Electron Eng) (IB 30 pts)
Edinburgh – AAA–ABB 340–360 pts (Elec Eng Renew Ener) (IB 37–32 pts)
Exeter – AAB–ABB (Electron Eng Comp Sci MEng) (IB 34–32 pts)
Glasgow – AAB (Elec Electron Eng MEng) (IB 34 pts)
Lancaster – AAB–ABB 340–320 pts (Mecha Eng) (IB 34–32 pts)
Leeds – AAB (Electron Comm Eng) (IB 36pts HL 17 pts)
Leicester – AAB–ABB (Comms Electron Eng MEng)
London (QM) – 340 pts (Electron Eng MEng courses) (IB 34 pts)
Loughborough – AAB (Electron Comp Sys Eng MEng) (IB 34 pts)
Manchester – AAB (Mecha Eng) (IB 35 pts)
Newcastle – AAB-ABB 320-340 pts (Electron Comm MEng) (IB 32 pts HL 5 maths phys)
Strathclyde – AAB–BBB (Elec Electron Eng) (IB 36 pts)
Sheffield – AAB incl maths (Electron Eng MEng) (IB 35 pts)
Southampton – AAB incl maths phys (Electromech Eng) (IB 34 pts HL 17 pts)
Surrey – AAB 340 pts (Electron Comp Eng BEng) (IB 35 pts)
Sussex – AAB–BBB incl maths (Electron Eng) (IB 32–35 pts HL 5/6 maths)
Warwick – AAB (Electron Eng) (IB 36 pts)
York – AAB–ABB (Electron Eng MEng; Electron Eng Nanotech MEng; Electron Comm Eng MEng)
320 pts **Bath** – ABB (Electron Comm Eng BEng) (IB 34 pts)
Birmingham – ABB (Elec Ener Eng) (IB 32–34 pts)
Brunel – ABB + AS 320–370 pts (Sys Comp Eng MEng) (IB 33 pts)
Cardiff – ABB (Electron Comm Eng MEng; Elect Electron Eng MEng)
Exeter – ABB–BBB 320–300 pts (Electron Eng Comp Sci BEng) (IB 32–30 pts)
Glasgow – ABB (Elec Electron Eng BEng) (IB 32 pts)
Kent – ABB (Electron Comm Eng MEng) (IB 33 pts)
Lancaster – ABB (Electron Elec Eng BEng) (IB 30 pts)
Liverpool – ABB (Electron MEng) (IB 33 pts HL 5 maths phys/elec)
Newcastle – AAB–ABB 320–340 pts (Electron Comp Eng) (IB 32 pts HL 5 maths phys)

Queen's Belfast – ABB (Elec Electron Eng MEng) (IB 31–32 pts)
Strathclyde – ABB (Electron Elec Eng Bus St) (IB 32 pts)
Sheffield – ABB incl maths (Electron Comms Eng BEng) (IB 33 pts)

300 pts **Aberdeen** – BBB 300 pts (Elec Electron Eng) (IB 30 pts)
Aston – BBB–ABB 300–320 pts (Electromech Eng) (IB 32 pts)
Bangor – 300–320 pts (Electron Eng MEng)
Birmingham City – 300 pts (Electron Elec Eng)
Brighton – BBB (Elec Electron Eng) (IB 28 pts)
Bristol UWE – 300pts (Elec Electron Eng) (IB 28–30 pts)
Cardiff – BBB (Electron Comm Eng BEng)
Dundee – BBB (Electron Eng Mgt MEng) (IB 32 pts)
Essex – 300 pts (Comp Electron) (IB 32 pts)
Kent – BBB (Electron Comm Eng BEng) (IB 33 pts)
Leicester – BBB–BBC (Comms Electron Eng BEng) (IB 32 pts)
Liverpool – BBB (Electron BEng) (IB 30 pts HL 5 maths phys/elec)
London (QM) – 300 pts (Elec Electron Eng) (IB 32 pts)
Loughborough – BBB 300 pts (Electron Comp Sys Eng BEng) (IB 32 pts)
Nottingham – AAA–BBB 300–360 pts (Elec Electron Eng) (IB 36 pts)
Plymouth – 300 pts (Elec Electron Eng MEng) (IB 26 pts)
Portsmouth – 300 pts (Electron Elec Eng MEng)
Reading – 300 pts (Electron Eng courses MEng) (IB 29–32 pts)
Sheffield Hallam – 300 pts (Elec Electron Eng MEng)
Swansea – BBB 300 pts (Nanoelectron BEng)
Westminster – BBB (Electron Eng MEng) (IB 32 pts)
York – BBB–BBC (Electron Eng Nanotech BEng) (IB 32 pts)

280 pts **Bangor** – (Mus Tech Electron)
Brunel – BBC 280 pts (Electron Elec Eng courses BEng) (IB 30 pts)
Derby – 280 pts (Elec Electron Eng)
Glamorgan – 280–320 pts (Elec Electron Eng; Electron Eng; Ltg Des Tech)
Heriot-Watt – BBC 280 pts (Elec Electron Eng courses)
Hull – 280–320 pts (Electron Eng MEng)
Leicester – BBB–BBC (Elec Electron Eng BEng) (IB 30 pts)
LJMU – 280 pts (Elec Electron Eng MEng)
London (QM) – 280 pts (Electron Eng BEng courses) (IB 28 pts)
Northumbria – 280 pts (Elec Electron Eng)
Queen's Belfast – BBB–BBC (Electron Eng courses) (IB 29–30 pts)
Teesside – 280–300 pts (Elec Electron Eng MEng)
Westminster – BBC (BEng Electron Eng)

260 pts **Bangor** – 240–260 pts (Electron Eng BEng)
Coventry – BCC 260 pts (Elec Electron Eng)
De Montfort – 260 pts (Electron Eng (Telecomm) (Broad Sys))
Greenwich – 260–280 pts (Electron Eng)
Hertfordshire – 260 pts (Elec Electron Eng)
Huddersfield – 260 pts (Electron Eng MEng)
LJMU – 260 pts (Elec Electron Eng BEng)
Plymouth – 260 pts (Elec Electron Eng BEng)
Portsmouth – 260–300 pts (Elect Electron Eng BEng)
Reading – 260 pts (Electron Eng Cyber BEng; Electron Eng)
Robert Gordon – BCC (Electron Elec Eng MEng)
Sunderland – 260 pts (Electron Elec Eng)
Swansea – BCC 260 pts (Elec Eng)
Ulster – 260 pts (Electron Comp Sys; Electron Eng BEng)

240 pts **Bradford** – 240 pts (Elec Electron Eng; Med Eng)
De Montfort – 240 pts (Electron Eng)
Dundee – 240 pts (Electron Eng Phys BEng) (IB 28 pts)

Edinburgh Napier – CCC 240 pts (Elec Eng; Electron Elec Eng)
Glyndŵr – 240 pts (Elec Electron Eng; Aero Electron Eng)
Greenwich – 240 pts (Elec Eng)
Huddersfield – 240 pts (Electron Des; Electron Mus Tech; Electron Eng BEng)
Hull – 240–260 pts (Electron Eng BEng)
London South Bank – 240 pts (Elec Electron Eng)
Manchester Met – 240-280 pts (Elec Electron Eng) (IB 28 pts)
Newport – 240 pts (Elec Eng; Electron Eng)
Staffordshire – 240 pts (Elec Eng; Electron Eng)
Sheffield Hallam – 240 pts (Elec Electron Eng BEng)
UCLan – 240–280 pts (Electron Eng)
220 pts **Robert Gordon** – 220–240 pts (Electron Elec Eng BEng) (IB 26 pts)
Sheffield Hallam – 220 pts (Electron Eng)
UEL – 220 pts (Elec Electron Eng (Comm); Elec Electron Eng BEng; Elec Electron Eng (Contr/Pwr/Comms))
200 pts **Blackburn (Coll)** – 200 pts (Elec/Electron Eng)
Coventry – 200 pts (Electron Eng)
London Met – Check with admissions 200 pts (Electron Comm Eng)
West London – 200 pts (Elec Electron Eng; Electron Eng)
180 pts **Glasgow Caledonian** – BC 180 pts (Elec Pwr Eng)
Robert Gordon – BC (Elec Pwr Eng)
120 pts **Southampton Solent** – 120 pts (Electron Eng)
60 pts **UHI** – D–A (Elec Mech Eng; Elec Electron Eng)

Alternative offers

See **Chapter 7** and **Appendix 1** for grades/UCAS Tariff points information for the International Baccalaureate, Scottish Highers/Advanced Highers, the Welsh Baccalaureate, the Irish Leaving Certificate, the Cambridge Pre-U Diploma, the Advanced Diploma and the Extended Project.

EXAMPLES OF FOUNDATION DEGREES IN THE SUBJECT FIELD

Bedfordshire; Bolton; Bournemouth; Bournemouth and Poole (Coll); Brighton; De Montfort; Exeter (Coll); Farnborough (CT); Glamorgan; Greenwich; Havering (Coll); Hertfordshire; Leeds Met; London South Bank; Manchester (Coll); Newcastle (Coll); Northbrook (Coll); Plymouth; Ravensbourne; St Helens (Coll); South Cheshire (Coll); Southampton Solent; Swansea Met; Walsall (Coll); West London; York (Coll).

CHOOSING YOUR COURSE (SEE ALSO CH.1)

Some course features

Bath After a common two-year introduction covering electronics, communications, electrical engineering, mathematics and design, students specialise in Years 3 and 4, choosing from a range of optional and core modules. Individual and group project and design work and placement opportunities are key features of these modular courses.

Exeter A multidisciplinary first year before specialising in Year 2.

Leicester Options to study for a year in industry, in Europe or the USA.

London (QM) The MEng and BEng courses include modules on telecoms, programming, digital systems, multimedia systems, wireless networks and video and image processing.

London (UCL) (Electron Eng Nanotech) Course has solid foundation of traditional electronics and specialisation in Years 3 and 4 in fast-developing field of nanotechnology (a research specialisation at UCL).

Loughborough There is a common first year for all students in the Department, followed by a choice of five degrees.

Manchester (Electron Sys Eng) Course focuses on embedded computer systems, for example in engine management systems, MP3 players and mobile phones, with emphasis on system design.

Universities and colleges teaching quality See www.qaa.ac.uk; http://unistats.direct.gov.uk.

Top research universities and colleges (RAE 2008) Leeds; Surrey; Bangor; Manchester; Imperial London; Sheffield (Automatic Control and Systems Engineering); Southampton; London (UCL); Glasgow; Bath.

Examples of sandwich degree courses Aston; Bath; Birmingham City; Bradford; Brighton; Bristol UWE; Brunel; Cardiff; City; Coventry; De Montfort; Glamorgan; Glasgow Caledonian; Hertfordshire; Huddersfield; Leicester; LJMU; London Met; London South Bank; Loughborough; Manchester Met; Northumbria; Plymouth; Portsmouth; Queen's Belfast; Sheffield Hallam; Staffordshire; Sunderland; Surrey; Teesside; UCLan; UEL; Ulster; Westminster; York.

ADMISSIONS INFORMATION

Number of applicants per place (approx) Aston 6; Bath 8; Birmingham 18; Birmingham City 11; Bolton 3; Bournemouth 3; Bradford (Elec Electron Eng) 8; Bristol 5; Bristol UWE 8; Cardiff 7; City 10; Coventry 8; De Montfort 1; Derby 8; Dundee 5; Edinburgh Napier 8; Glamorgan 2; Glasgow Caledonian 5; Greenwich 10; Heriot-Watt 6; Hertfordshire 7; Huddersfield 5; Hull 8; Kent 5; Kingston 8; Lancaster 7; Leeds 15; Leicester 15; Lincoln 8; LJMU 2; London (UCL) 9; London South Bank 5; Manchester Met 5; Newcastle 9; Northumbria 7; Nottingham 8; Plymouth 22; Portsmouth 4; Robert Gordon 3; Salford 5; Sheffield 15; Sheffield Hallam 2; Southampton 8; Staffordshire 7; Strathclyde 7; Sunderland 6; Surrey (BEng) 6, (MEng) 3; Swansea 3; Teesside 4; UCLan 4; Warwick 8; Westminster 5; York 5.

Advice to applicants and planning the UCAS personal statement Enthusiasm for the subject, for example career ambitions, hobbies, work experience, attendance at appropriate events, competitions etc. Evidence of good ability in mathematics and also a scientific mind. Applicants should show that they can think creatively and have the motivation to succeed on a demanding course. See also **Engineering/Engineering Sciences** and **Appendix 4**. **Bristol** Deferred entry accepted.

Selection interviews Yes Aston, Bangor (Electron Eng only), Bath, Bournemouth, Bradford, Bristol, Bristol UWE, Brunel, Cambridge, De Montfort, Derby, Durham, Essex, Heriot-Watt, Hertfordshire, Huddersfield, Hull, Imperial London, Kingston, Lancaster, Liverpool, London (UCL), London South Bank, Newcastle, Nottingham, Oxford, Plymouth, Portsmouth, Queen's Belfast, Southampton, Strathclyde, Sunderland, Surrey, UCLan, West London, Westminster, York; **Some** Anglia Ruskin, Brighton, Cardiff, Dundee, Kent, Leicester, LJMU, Loughborough, Salford, Staffordshire.

Interview advice and questions Past questions have included: How does a combustion engine work? How does a trumpet work? What type of position do you hope to reach in five to 10 years' time? Could you sack an employee? What was your last physics practical? What did you learn from it? What are the methods of transmitting information from a moving object to a stationary observer? Wire bending exercise – you are provided with an accurate diagram of a shape that could be produced by bending a length of wire in a particular way. You are supplied with a pair of pliers and the exact length of wire required and you are given 10 minutes to reproduce as accurately as possible the shape drawn. A three-minute talk had to be given on one of six subjects (topics given several weeks before the interview); for example, 'The best is the enemy of the good'. Is there a lesson here for British industry? 'I was asked to take my physics file and discuss some of my conclusions in certain experiments.' Explain power transmission through the National Grid. How would you explain power transmission to a friend who hasn't done physics? See also **Chapter 6**. **York** Questions based on a mathematical problem.

Reasons for rejection (non-academic) Poor English. Inability to communicate. Frightened of technology or mathematics. Poor motivation and work ethic. Better suited to a less specialised engineering/science course. Some foreign applicants do not have adequate English. See also **Engineering/Engineering Sciences**. **Surrey** Can't speak English (it has happened!).

AFTER-RESULTS ADVICE

Offers to applicants repeating A-levels Higher Brighton, Greenwich, Huddersfield, Kingston, Newcastle, Queen's Belfast, Strathclyde, UCLan, Warwick; **Possibly higher** Aston, City, De Montfort, Derby, Glasgow, Hertfordshire, London Met, Portsmouth, Sheffield; **Same** Anglia Ruskin, Bangor, Bath, Birmingham, Bolton, Bradford, Cardiff, Coventry, Dundee, Durham, Hull, Kent, Leeds, Liverpool, LJMU,

London South Bank, Loughborough, Northumbria, Nottingham (usually), Nottingham Trent, Robert Gordon, Salford, Southampton, Staffordshire, Surrey, West London, Wolverhampton, York; **No** Cambridge.

GRADUATE DESTINATIONS AND EMPLOYMENT (2009/10 HESA)
Graduates surveyed 5055 **Employed** 1980 **In voluntary employment** 15 **In further study** 795 **Assumed unemployed** 345

Career note Electrical and Electronic Engineering is divided into two main fields – heavy current (electrical machinery, distribution systems, generating stations) and light current (computers, control engineering, telecommunications). Opportunities exist with many commercial organisations.

OTHER DEGREE SUBJECTS FOR CONSIDERATION
Computer Science; Engineering (Aeronautical, Communications, Computer, Control); Mathematics; Physics.

ENGINEERING (MANUFACTURING)

(see also **Engineering/Engineering Sciences**)

Manufacturing engineering is sometimes referred to as production engineering. It is a branch of the subject concerned with management aspects of engineering such as industrial organisation, purchasing, and the planning and control of operations. Manufacturing Engineering courses are therefore geared to providing the student with a broad-based portfolio of knowledge in both the technical and business areas.

Useful websites www.engc.org.uk; www.imeche.org; www.enginuity.org.uk.

NB The points totals shown to the left of the institutions are for ease of reference only. It must not be assumed that Tariff points are always used by institutions or that they can be substituted for an offer in grades. The level of an offer is not necessarily indicative of the quality of a course.

Engineering Council statement *See* **Engineering/Engineering Sciences**.

COURSE OFFERS INFORMATION
Subject requirements/preferences See **Engineering/Engineering Sciences**.

Your target offers and examples of courses provided by each institution

380 pts	**Bath** – A*AA (Mech Manuf Eng Mgt) (IB 36 pts HL 6 maths phys)
	Cambridge – A*AA (Eng (Manuf Eng)) (IB 40–42 pts)
360 pts	**Durham** – AAA (Des Ops Eng) (IB 37 pts)
	Loughborough – AAA (Innov Manuf Eng) (IB 34 pts)
	Newcastle – AAA (Mech Des Manuf Eng MEng) (IB 37 pts)
	Nottingham – AAA (Manuf Eng Mgt MEng) (IB 36–34 pts)
340 pts	**Glasgow** – AAB (Prod Des Eng MEng) (IB 34 pts)
	Liverpool – AAB incl maths phys (Mech Eng Bus MEng) (IB 35 pts HL 5 maths phys)
	Newcastle – AAB (Mech Des Manuf Eng BEng) (IB 34 pts)
	Strathclyde – AAB (Prod Des Eng MEng) (IB 36 pts)
	Warwick – AAB (Manuf Mech Eng) (IB 36 pts)
320 pts	**Nottingham** – AAB (Manuf Eng Mgt BEng) (IB 32–30 pts)
	Strathclyde – ABB (Prod Des Eng BEng) (IB 32 pts)
300 pts	**Aston** – BBB–ABB 280–320 pts (Ind Prod Des) (IB 32 pts)
	Bristol UWE – 300 pts (Aerosp Manuf Eng)
	Loughborough – BBB (Manuf Eng) (IB 32 pts)
280 pts	**Birmingham City** – 280 pts (Mgt Manuf Sys) (IB 28 pts)
	LJMU – 280 pts (Auto Prod Dev)

Nottingham – BBC (Prod Des Manuf BEng) (IB 30–32 pts)
Queen's Belfast – BBC–BCC (Manuf Eng BEng) (IB 29–30 pts)
240 pts **Bradford** – 240 pts (Prod Ind Des) (IB 26 pts)
Edinburgh Napier – CCC 240 pts (Prod Des Eng)
Glamorgan – 240 pts (Mech Manuf Eng)
Greenwich – 240 pts (Manuf Sys Eng)
Newport – 240 pts (Mech Manuf Eng)
220 pts **Sheffield Hallam** – 220 pts (Manuf Eng)
200 pts **Plymouth** – 200 pts (Mech Des Manuf) (IB 24 pts)
Portsmouth – 200–240 pts (Manuf Eng)
180 pts **Southampton Solent** – 180 pts (Manuf Mech Eng)

Alternative offers
See **Chapter 7** and **Appendix 1** for grades/UCAS Tariff points information for the International Baccalaureate, Scottish Highers/Advanced Highers, the Welsh Baccalaureate, the Irish Leaving Certificate, the Cambridge Pre-U Diploma, the Advanced Diploma and the Extended Project.

EXAMPLES OF FOUNDATION DEGREES IN THE SUBJECT FIELD
Blackpool and Fylde (Coll); Brighton; Bristol City (Coll); Exeter (Coll); Havering (Coll); Myerscough (Coll); Somerset (CAT); Sunderland; Swansea Met; York (Coll).

CHOOSING YOUR COURSE (SEE ALSO CH.1)
Some course features
Greenwich The degree programme in Manufacturing Systems Engineering shares the first two years with Mechanical Engineering, opening doors to a wide range of engineering technologies, eg aeronautical, automotive and process engineering.
Loughborough Courses include an industrial placement year leading to both a degree and a Diploma in Industrial Studies.
Newcastle Mechanical or Manufacturing Engineering is an option which is chosen after the first two years.
Nottingham (Manuf Eng Mgt) Management and business modules support studies in engineering science and design.

Universities and colleges teaching quality See www.qaa.ac.uk; http://unistats.direct.gov.uk.

Top research universities and colleges (RAE 2008) See **Engineering (Mechanical)**.

Examples of sandwich degree courses Aston; Bath; Brunel; London South Bank; Loughborough; Queen's Belfast; Staffordshire; Ulster.

ADMISSIONS INFORMATION
Number of applicants per place (approx) Aston 6; Bath 18; Huddersfield 1; Loughborough 6; Nottingham 5; Strathclyde 8; Warwick 8.

Advice to applicants and planning the UCAS personal statement Work experience or work shadowing in industry should be mentioned. See **Engineering/Engineering Sciences** and **Appendix 4**.

Selection interviews Yes Cambridge, Loughborough, Nottingham, Strathclyde.

Interview advice and questions Past questions include: What is the function of an engineer? Describe something interesting you have recently done in your A-levels. What do you know about careers in manufacturing engineering? Discuss the role of women engineers in industry. Why is a disc brake better than a drum brake? Would you be prepared to make people redundant to improve the efficiency of a production line? See also **Chapter 6**.

Reasons for rejection (non-academic) Mature students failing to attend interview are rejected. One applicant produced a forged reference and was immediately rejected. See also **Engineering/ Engineering Sciences**.

AFTER-RESULTS ADVICE
Offers to applicants repeating A-levels Higher Strathclyde; **Same** Cambridge, Huddersfield, Loughborough, Nottingham.

GRADUATE DESTINATIONS AND EMPLOYMENT (2009/10 HESA)
Production and Manufacturing Engineering; graduates surveyed 1275 **Employed** 555 **In voluntary employment** 10 **In further study** 140 **Assumed unemployed** 85

Career note Graduates with experience in both technical and business skills have the flexibility to enter careers in technology or business management.

OTHER DEGREE SUBJECTS FOR CONSIDERATION
Business Studies; Computer Science; Engineering (Electrical, Mechanical); Physics; Technology.

ENGINEERING (MECHANICAL)

(including **Agricultural Engineering**, **Automotive Engineering** and **Motorsport Engineering**)

Mechanical Engineering is one of the most wide-ranging engineering disciplines. All courses involve the design, installation and maintenance of equipment used in industry. Several universities include a range of Engineering courses with a common first year allowing students to specialise from Year 2. Agricultural Engineering involves all aspects of off-road vehicle design and maintenance of other machinery used in agriculture.

Useful websites www.imeche.org; www.engc.org.uk; www.iagre.org.

NB The points totals shown to the left of the institutions are for ease of reference only. It must not be assumed that Tariff points are always used by institutions or that they can be substituted for an offer in grades. The level of an offer is not necessarily indicative of the quality of a course.

Engineering Council statement *See* **Engineering/Engineering Sciences**.

COURSE OFFERS INFORMATION
Subject requirements/preferences (Prod Des courses) Design technology or art may be required or preferred. See also **Engineering/Engineering Sciences**.

Your target offers and examples of courses provided by each institution

380 pts **Bath** – A*AA (Mech Eng) (IB 35–37 pts HL 6 maths phys)
Bristol – A*AA–AAB (Mech Eng) (IB 38–35 pts)
Cambridge – A*AA (Eng (Mech Eng)) (IB 40–42 pts)
Imperial London – A*mathsAA (Mech Eng) (IB 40 pts HL 6 maths phys)
Loughborough – A*AA (Mech Eng MEng) (IB 34 pts)
Oxford – A*AA (Mech Eng) (IB 38–40 pts)

360 pts **Bath** – AAA (Integ Mech Elec Eng) (IB 35–37 pts HL 6 maths phys)
Birmingham – AAA (Mech Eng MEng) (IB 36–38 pts)
Durham – AAA (Mech Eng MEng) (IB 37 pts)
Edinburgh – AAA–ABB incl maths (Elec Mech Eng) (IB 37–32)
London (QM) – AAA (Mech Eng MEng) (IB 34 pts)
London (UCL) – AAA–AAB incl maths+phys (Mech Eng MEng) (IB 36–38 pts)
Loughborough – AAA (Auto Eng MEng) (IB 36 pts)
Manchester – AAA (Mech Eng MEng) (IB 37 pts)
Newcastle – AAA (Mech Low Carbon Trans Eng) (IB 37 pts)
Nottingham – AAA (Mech Eng MEng) (IB 36–34 pts)
Strathclyde – AAA (Mech Eng Fin Mgt MEng) (IB 36 pts)
Sheffield – AAA incl maths sci (Mech Eng Fr/Ger/Ital) (IB 37 pts HL 6 maths sci)
Southampton – AAA incl maths phys (Mech Eng (Advnc Mat)) (IB 36 pts HL 18 pts)

Surrey – AAA 360 pts (Mech Eng MEng) (IB 34 pts)

Swansea – AAA–AAB (Mech Eng MEng; Med Eng MEng)

340 pts **Aston** – AAB–AAA 340–360 pts (Mech Eng MEng) (IB 34 pts)

Birmingham – AAB (Mech Eng incl Fdn Yr) (IB 34–36 pts)

Brunel – AAB 340 pts (Mech Eng Aero MEng) (IB 35 pts)

Cardiff – AAB (Mech Eng MEng) (IB 32–34 pts)

City – 340–360 pts (Mech Eng) (IB 32 pts)

Durham – AAB (Mech Eng BEng)

Exeter – AAB–BBB (Min Eng) (IB 30–34 pts)

Glasgow – AAB (Mech Des Eng MEng) (IB 34 pts)

Lancaster – AAB (Eng (Mech) MEng) (IB 34 pts)

Leeds – AAB (Mecha Robot Mech Eng) (IB 36 pts HL 17 pts)

Liverpool – AAB incl maths phys (Mech Mat Eng MEng) (IB 35 pts)

London (UCL) – AAB–ABB incl maths+phys (Mech Eng BEng) (IB 34–36 pts)

Manchester – AAB (Mecha Eng) (IB 35 pts)

Newcastle – AAB (Mech Eng BEng) (IB 34 pts HL 5 maths phys)

Nottingham – AAB (Mech Eng BEng) (IB 32–30 pts)

Queen's Belfast – AAB (Mech Manuf Eng MEng) (IB 31–32 pts)

Strathclyde – AAB (Mech Eng BEng) (IB 32 pts)

Sheffield – AAB incl maths sci (Mech Eng BEng) (IB 35 pts HL 6 maths sci)

Surrey – AAB (Mech Eng BEng) (IB 27 pts)

Sussex – AAB–ABB incl maths (Mech Eng) (IB 34–35 pts HL 5/6 maths)

Warwick – AAB (Manuf Mech Eng) (IB 36 pts)

320 pts **Bristol UWE** – 320 pts (Mech Eng) (IB 28–30 pts)

Cardiff – ABB (Mech Eng BEng) (IB 30–32 pts HL 5)

City – 320 pts (Auto Mtrspo Eng MEng) (IB 30 pts)

Exeter – ABB–BBB (Mech Eng BEng) (IB 32–29 pts)

Glasgow – ABB (Mech Eng Aero BEng) (IB 32 pts)

Glasgow (SA) – Check with Ad Tutor ABB (Prod Des Eng)

Hertfordshire – 320 pts (Auto Eng Mtrspo MEng) (IB 30 pts)

Lancaster – ABB (Eng (Mech) BEng) (IB 32 pts)

Leicester – AAB–ABB (Mech Eng MEng) (IB 32 pts)

Liverpool – ABB (Mecha Robot Sys MEng) (IB 35 pts HL 5 maths phys elec)

Loughborough – ABB (Auto Eng BEng) (IB 32 pts)

Manchester – AAB (Mech Eng BEng) (IB 35 pts)

Oxford Brookes – ABB (Mech Eng; Auto Eng MEng; Mtrspo Eng MEng)

Swansea – ABB–BBB (Mech Eng BEng)

300 pts **Aberdeen** – BBB (Mech Eng Euro St) (IB 30–28 pts)

Aston – BBB–ABB 320 pts (Mech Eng BEng) (IB 32 pts)

Birmingham City – 300 pts (Auto Eng) (IB 28 pts)

Bradford – 300 pts (Mech Eng MEng) (IB 28–32 pts)

Brighton – BBB (Auto Eng) (IB 30 pts)

Brunel – BBB (Mech Eng BEng) (IB 32 pts)

Harper Adams (UC) – 300 pts (Agric Eng) (IB 30 pts)

Heriot-Watt – BBB (Mech Eng Ener Eng; Mech Eng)

Huddersfield – 300 pts (Mech Eng MEng)

Liverpool – BBB incl maths phys (Mech Eng Bus BEng) (IB 32 pts HL 5 maths phys)

London (QM) – 300 pts (Des Innov BEng) (IB 28 pts)

Loughborough – BBB 280–300 pts (Des Ergon)

Northumbria – 300 pts (Mech Eng)

Plymouth – 300 pts (Mech Eng MEng) (IB 30 pts)

Portsmouth – 300–360 pts (Mech Eng MEng) (IB 30 pts)

Queen's Belfast – BBB (Mech Eng BEng) (IB 31–32 pts)

Salford – 300 pts (Mech Eng MEng) (IB 32 pts)

Sheffield Hallam – 300 pts (Mech Eng MEng)

Check **Chapter 4** when choosing your university and **Chapter 7** on how to read the subject tables.

280 pts **Bristol UWE** – 280–300 pts (Mtrspo Eng) (IB 28–30 pts)
City – BBC 280 pts (Auto Mtrspo Eng BEng) (IB 28 pts)
Coventry – BBC 280 pts (Mtrspo courses; Mech Eng)
Derby – 280 pts (Mtrcycl Eng; Mtrspo Eng; Mech Eng)
Dundee – BBC 280 pts (Mech Eng)
Edinburgh Napier – BBC 280 pts (Mech Eng MEng)
Heriot-Watt – BBC (Auto Eng)
Hull – 280–320 pts (Mech Med Eng MEng)
Leicester – BBB–BBC (Mech Eng BEng) (IB 30 pts)
LJMU – 280 pts (Mech Mar Eng MEng; Mech Eng MEng; Auto Eng MEng)
London (QM) – 280 pts (Mech Eng BEng) (IB 28 pts)
Manchester Met – 280 pts (Mech Des Tech) (IB 28 pts)
Oxford Brookes – BBC (Mtrspo Eng BEng; Auto Eng BEng)
Robert Gordon – BBC (Mech Elec Eng MEng) (IB 28 pts)
Teesside – 280 pts (Mech Eng BEng)
UCLan – 240–280 pts (Mtrspo Eng)

260 pts **Birmingham City** – 260–280 pts (Mtrspo Tech) (IB 28 pts)
Brighton – BCC–BBD (Mech Eng) (IB 30 pts)
Greenwich – 260–280 pts (Mech Eng)
Hertfordshire – 260 pts (Auto Eng BEng; Mech Eng; Auto Eng Mtrspo BEng)
Hull – 260–320 pts (Mech Eng)
Lincoln – 260–300 pts (Mech Eng)
LJMU – 260 pts (Auto Eng BEng; Mech Mar Eng BEng; Mech Eng BEng)
Plymouth – BCC 260 pts (Mech Eng Cmpsts) (IB 24–25 pts)
Robert Gordon – BCC (Mech Off Eng; Mech Eng BEng; Mech Elec Eng BEng)
Salford – 260 pts (Mech Eng BEng) (IB 30 pts)
Sunderland – 260 pts (Mech Eng) (IB 32 pts)

240 pts **Bolton** – 240 pts (Auto Eng; Mech Eng)
Bradford – 240–300 pts (Mech Auto Eng) (IB 28–32 pts)
De Montfort – 240 pts (Mech Eng; Mecha)
Edinburgh Napier – CCC 240 pts (Mech Eng BEng)
Glamorgan – 240 pts (Mech Manuf Eng)
Glyndŵr – 240 pts (Aero Mech Eng; Mtrspo Des Mgt)
Harper Adams (UC) – 240 pts (Offrd Veh Des)
Huddersfield – 240 pts (Mech Eng BEng) (IB 26 pts)
Kingston – 240 pts (Mech Eng)
London South Bank – 240 pts (Mech Eng; Mecha)
Newport – 240 pts (Mech Manuf Eng)
Portsmouth – 240–280 pts (Mech Eng BEng) (IB 28 pts)
Staffordshire – 240 pts (Mtrspo Tech; Mech Eng)
Sheffield Hallam – 240 pts (Auto Des Tech)
Swansea Met – 240–200 pts (Mtrcycl Eng)

220 pts **Glasgow Caledonian** – AB 220 pts (Mech Electron Sys Eng)
Plymouth – 220 pts (Mar Spo Tech)
Sheffield Hallam – 220 pts incl maths (Mech Eng; Auto Eng)
Sunderland – 220 pts (Auto Eng) (IB 32 pts)
Ulster – CC 220 pts (Mech Eng BEng)

200 pts **Blackburn (Coll)** – 200 pts (Mech Eng; Mecha)
Glamorgan – 200–240 pts (Mecha Eng)
Plymouth – 200 pts (Mech Des Manuf) (IB 24 pts)
Portsmouth – 200–240 pts (Mech Manuf Eng) (IB 24 pts)
Staffordshire – 200–240 pts (Mecha)
Swansea Met – 200 pts (Mtrspo Eng)
Ulster – BB 200 pts (Mech Eng MEng)

180 pts **Plymouth** – 180 pts (Mech Eng Comp Aid Des) (IB 24 pts)
Southampton Solent – 180 pts (Manuf Mech Eng)
160 pts **Harper Adams (UC)** – 160–180 pts (Agric Eng Mark Mgt) (IB 24 pts)
Kingston – 160 pts (Mtrcycl Eng; Mtrspo Eng)
West Scotland – CC (Mtrspo Des Eng; Mech Eng)
Wolverhampton – 160–200 pts (Mech Eng)
150 pts **Anglia Ruskin** – 150 pts (Mech Eng)
60 pts **UHI** – D–A (Elec Mech Eng)

Alternative offers
See **Chapter 7** and **Appendix 1** for grades/UCAS Tariff points information for the International Baccalaureate, Scottish Highers/Advanced Highers, the Welsh Baccalaureate, the Irish Leaving Certificate, the Cambridge Pre-U Diploma, the Advanced Diploma and the Extended Project.

EXAMPLES OF FOUNDATION DEGREES IN THE SUBJECT FIELD
Bath; Blackburn (Coll); Blackpool and Fylde (Coll); Brighton; Bristol City (Coll); Bristol UWE; Derby; Exeter (Coll); Glyndŵr; Greenwich; Harper Adams (UC); (Agricultural Engineering) Havering (Coll); Kingston; Loughborough (Coll); Myerscough (Coll); Oxford Brookes; Plymouth; Queen's Belfast; Sheffield Hallam; Somerset (CAT); South Cheshire (Coll); Staffordshire; Sunderland; Swansea Met; Warwickshire (Coll).

CHOOSING YOUR COURSE (SEE ALSO CH.1)
Some course features
Brunel (Mech Eng) Course combines fundamental elements of mechanical engineering and design with study in associated disciplines including computing, electronics, environment and energy systems. All courses emphasise importance of industrial and commercial insight and awareness.
Cardiff The first year is common to all Engineering programmes. Core subjects include mathematics, dynamics, properties of materials, electrical engineering, electronics and business management.
Durham A common course for Years 1 and 2 and then two years specialising in the chosen discipline.
Exeter A multidisciplinary first year before specialising in Year 2. Emphasis on design skills practice and development.
Leicester Options to study for a year in industry, in Europe or the USA.
Lincoln The Mechanical Engineering programme has options in Power and Energy or Control Systems.
Newcastle Ten Mechanical Engineering options with common first and second years for all students.
Salford (MEng Mech Eng) Programme has broad engineering themes and the option to spend a year in industry.
Strathclyde Four and Five year degrees offered in Mechanical Engineering.
Surrey Mechanical, medical and aerospace programmes have a common first year allowing for a final choice of degree in Year 2.

Universities and colleges teaching quality See www.qaa.ac.uk; http://unistats.direct.gov.uk.

Top research universities and colleges (RAE 2008) (Mechanical, Aeronautical and Manufacturing Engineering) Imperial London; Sheffield; Bristol (Aerospace Engineering); Greenwich; Nottingham; Leeds; Loughborough; Birmingham; Cardiff.

Examples of sandwich degree courses Aston; Bath; Birmingham City; Bradford; Brighton; Bristol UWE; Brunel; Cardiff; City; Coventry; De Montfort; Glamorgan; Glasgow Caledonian; Harper Adams (UC); Hertfordshire; Huddersfield; Kingston; Leicester; LJMU; London South Bank; Loughborough; Manchester Met; Northumbria; Oxford Brookes; Plymouth; Portsmouth; Queen's Belfast; Sheffield Hallam; Staffordshire; Sunderland; Surrey; Teesside; UCLan; Ulster.

ADMISSIONS INFORMATION
Number of applicants per place (approx) Abertay Dundee 4; Aston 8; Bath (MEng) 13; Birmingham 6; Bradford 4; Brighton 10; Bristol 8; Bristol UWE 17; Brunel 12; Cardiff 8; City 13; Coventry 8; Dundee 5; Durham 8; Glamorgan 6; Glyndŵr 4; Heriot-Watt 9; Hertfordshire 10; Huddersfield 1; Hull 11;

Check **Chapter 4** when choosing your university and **Chapter 7** on how to read the subject tables.

Kingston 8; Lancaster 8; Leeds 15; Leicester 11; Liverpool 6; LJMU (Mech Eng) 2; London (QM) 6; London South Bank 4; Loughborough 8, (Mech Eng) 12, (Auto Eng) 7; Manchester Met 6, (Mech Eng) 6; Newcastle 10; Northumbria 4; Nottingham 8; Plymouth 6; Portsmouth 6; Sheffield 10; Southampton 8; Staffordshire 6; Strathclyde 6; Surrey 9; Teesside 7; Warwick 8; Westminster 11.

Advice to applicants and planning the UCAS personal statement Work experience; hands-on skills. An interest in solving mathematical problems related to physical concepts. Enjoyment in designing mechanical devices or components. Interest in engines, structures, dynamics or fluid flow and efficient use of materials or energy. Apply to the Year in Industry Scheme (www.etrust.org.uk) for placement. Scholarships are available to supplement the scheme. See **Engineering/Engineering Sciences** and **Appendix 4**.

Misconceptions about this course Loughborough Although organised by the Wolfson School of Manufacturing and Mechanical Engineering, the degree does not include manufacturing.

Selection interviews Yes Aston, Birmingham, Bolton, Bradford, Brighton, Bristol, Brunel, Cambridge, Cardiff, Durham, Harper Adams (UC), Hertfordshire, Huddersfield, Imperial London, Kingston, Lancaster, Leeds, Leicester, LJMU, London (QM), London South Bank, Loughborough (Auto Eng), Manchester Met, Newcastle, Nottingham, Oxford, Queen's Belfast, Sheffield, Sheffield Hallam, Strathclyde, Sunderland, Surrey, Sussex; **Some** Blackpool and Fylde (Coll), Dundee, Liverpool, Staffordshire.

Interview advice and questions Past questions include: What mechanical objects have you examined and/or tried to repair? How do you see yourself in five years' time? What do you imagine you would be doing (production, management or design engineering)? What engineering interests do you have? What qualities are required to become a successful mechanical engineer? Do you like sixth form work? Describe the working of parts on an engineering drawing. How does a fridge work? What is design in the context of mechanical engineering? What has been your greatest achievement to date? What are your career plans? See also **Engineering/Engineering Sciences** and **Chapter 6**. **Hertfordshire** All interviewees receive a conditional offer. Provide an example of working as part of a team, meeting a deadline, working on your own.

Reasons for rejection (non-academic) See **Engineering/Engineering Sciences**.

AFTER-RESULTS ADVICE
Offers to applicants repeating A-levels Higher Brighton, Dundee, Kingston, Newcastle, Queen's Belfast, Swansea, Warwick; **Possibly higher** City, Huddersfield; **Same** Aston, Bath, Bradford, Bristol, Brunel, Coventry, Derby, Durham, Edinburgh Napier, Harper Adams (UC), Heriot-Watt, Leeds (usually), Lincoln, Liverpool, LJMU, London South Bank, Loughborough, Manchester Met, Northumbria, Nottingham, Nottingham Trent, Oxford Brookes, Sheffield, Sheffield Hallam, Southampton, Staffordshire, Sunderland, Surrey, Teesside, UEL, Wolverhampton; **No** Cambridge.

GRADUATE DESTINATIONS AND EMPLOYMENT (2009/10 HESA)
Graduates surveyed 5460 **Employed** 2075 **In voluntary employment** 25 **In further study** 750 **Assumed unemployed** 270

Career note Mechanical Engineering graduates have a wide choice of career options. Apart from design and development of plant and machinery, they are also likely to be involved in production processes and working at various levels of management. Mechanical engineers share interests such as structures and stress analysis with civil and aeronautical engineers, and electronics and computing with electrical and software engineers.

OTHER DEGREE SUBJECTS FOR CONSIDERATION
Engineering (Aeronautical/Aerospace, Building, Computer (Control, Software and Systems), Electrical/ Electronic, Manufacturing, Marine); Materials Science; Mathematics; Physics; Product Design; Technologies.

ENGINEERING (MEDICAL)

(including **Clinical Engineering**, **Medical Electronics** and **Instrumentation**, **Mechanical** and **Medical Engineering**, **Medical Physics**, **Medical Product Design**, **Product Design for Medical Devices** and **Rehabilitation Engineering**; see also **Biotechnology**)

Biomedical Engineering lies at the interface between engineering, mathematics, physics, chemistry, biology and clinical practice. This makes it a branch of engineering that has the most direct effect on human health. It is a rapidly expanding inter-disciplinary field that applies engineering principles and technology to medical and biological problems. Biomedical engineers work in fields as diverse as neuro-technology, fluid mechanics of the blood and respiratory systems, bone and joint biomechanics, biosensors, medical imaging, synthetic biology and biomaterials. These can lead to novel devices such as joint replacements and heart valves, new surgical instruments, rehabilitation protocols and even prosthetic limbs.

NB The points totals shown to the left of the institutions are for ease of reference only. It must not be assumed that Tariff points are always used by institutions or that they can be substituted for an offer in grades. The level of an offer is not necessarily indicative of the quality of a course.

COURSE OFFERS INFORMATION

Subject requirements/preferences GCSE Mathematics and science subjects, chemistry and/or biology an advantage but not essential. Design and technology for Product Design courses.

Your target offers and examples of courses provided by each institution

380 pts **Oxford** – A*AA (Biomed Eng) (IB 38-40 pts)

360 pts **Imperial London** – AAA (Biomat Tiss Eng) (IB 36 pts HL 6 phys maths)
London (King's) – AAA incl maths phys (Biomed Eng) (IB 38 pts HL 6 maths phys)
London (QM) – AAA (Med Eng MEng) (IB 34 pts)
London (UCL) – AAA–ABB (Med Phys) (IB 34–36 pts)
Manchester – AAA–ABB 320–360 pts (Biomed Sci) (IB 37–33 pts)

340 pts **Cardiff** – AAB (Med Eng MEng) (IB 32–34 pts)
City – AAB 340 pts (Biomed Eng) (IB 30 pts)
Glasgow – AAB (Biomed Eng MEng) (IB 34 pts)
London (King's) – AABc (Phys Med Apps) (IB 36 pts)
Sheffield – AAB (Bioeng MEng) (IB 35 pts)
Swansea – ABB–BBB (Med Eng BEng) (IB 32 pts)

320 pts **Cardiff** – ABB (Med Eng BEng) (IB 30–32 pts HL 5 maths)
Glasgow – ABB (Biomed Eng BEng) (IB 32 pts)
Reading – 320 pts (Biomed Eng)

300 pts **London (QM)** – BBB (Med Eng BEng) (IB 28 pts)
Queen's Belfast – BBB (Phys Med Apps BSc; Phys Med App MSci)
Sheffield – BBB incl maths (Bioeng BEng) (IB 32 pts)
Surrey – BBB 300 pts (Med Eng BEng) (IB 30–32 pts)

Alternative offers
See **Chapter 7** and **Appendix 1** for grades/UCAS Tariff points information for the International Baccalaureate, Scottish Highers/Advanced Highers, the Welsh Baccalaureate, the Irish Leaving Certificate, the Cambridge Pre-U Diploma, the Advanced Diploma and the Extended Project.

CHOOSING YOUR COURSE (SEE ALSO CH.1)

Some course features
Cardiff A long-standing Medical Engineering course blending engineering knowledge with biomechanical applications. Lectures delivered by research-active biomechanists, clinicians and industrialists.
London (UCL) (Medical Physics) Graduates have an Institute of Physics accredited degree with a range of careers open to students not committed to a career in medical physics. Those taking this subject usually train to be an NHS medical physicist, seek a position in industry or take a higher degree.

Check **Chapter 4** when choosing your university and **Chapter 7** on how to read the subject tables.

Swansea BEng and MEng courses are offered with the fourth year of the MEng course covering advanced studies. Courses are accredited by the Institute of Mechanical Engineers.

Universities and colleges teaching quality See www.qaa.ac.uk; http://unistats.direct.gov.uk.

Examples of sandwich degree courses Cardiff (One year paid employment. MEng students have the opportunity to spend a year in a European University); Swansea.

ADMISSIONS INFORMATION
Number of applicants per place (approx) Cardiff 4; London (UCL) 6; Swansea 5.

Advice to applicants and planning the UCAS personal statement Cardiff An appreciation of the typical careers available within medical engineering and an interest in engineering and anatomy would be preferable. **London (UCL)** Evidence of interest in medical physics/physics eg visits to hospitals or internships.

Selection interviews Yes Cardiff (all applicants), London (UCL); **Some** Swansea (Not usually except for applicants not fitting their usual academic profile).
Interview advice and questions London (UCL) Searching questions at interview. Test may be included.

AFTER-RESULTS ADVICE
Offers to applicants repeating A-levels Same Cardiff, Liverpool, London (UCL), Swansea.

GRADUATE DESTINATIONS AND EMPLOYMENT (2009/10 HESA)
See **Biotechnology**.

Career note High rate of graduate employment. *Money* magazine ranks Biomedical Engineering number 1 for job growth prospects for the next 10 years.

ENGLISH

(including **Creative Writing**; see also **Languages, Linguistics, Literature**)

English courses continue to be extremely popular and competitive. They are an extension of school studies in literature and language and may cover topics ranging from Anglo-Saxon literature to writing in the present day. Most courses, however, will focus on certain areas such as the Medieval or Renaissance periods of literature or on English language studies. Admissions tutors will expect students to have read widely outside their A-level syllabus.

Useful websites www.bl.uk; www.lrb.co.uk; www.literature.org; www.bibliomania.com; www.online-literature.com.

NB The points totals shown to the left of the institutions are for ease of reference only. It must not be assumed that Tariff points are always used by institutions or that they can be substituted for an offer in grades. The level of an offer is not necessarily indicative of the quality of a course.

COURSE OFFERS INFORMATION
Subject requirements/preferences GCSE English Language and English Literature required and a foreign language may be preferred. Grades may be stipulated. **AL** English with specific grades usually stipulated. Modern languages required for joint courses with languages.

Your target offers and examples of courses provided by each institution
410 pts **London (King's)** – AAAb (Engl Film St) (IB 38 pts HL 666 incl Engl)
380 pts **Cambridge** – A*AA (Educ Engl) (IB 40–42 pts)
      Durham – A*AA (Engl Lit) (IB 38 pts)
      Exeter – A*AA–AAB 380–340 pts (Engl) (IB 38–34 pts)
      London (King's) – AABc (Engl Lang Comm) (IB 36 pts HL 6 Engl)
      Warwick – AABc (Engl Lat Lit) (IB 36 pts)

360 pts **Bristol** – AAA (Engl Phil) (IB 37 pts HL 6 Engl)
Edinburgh – AAA–BBB (Ling Engl Lang) (IB 42–34 pts)
Exeter – AAA–AAB 360–340 pts (Class St Engl) (IB 36–34 pts)
Lancaster – AAA–AAB 340–360 pts (Engl Lang Lit) (IB 34–36 pts)
London (QM) – 360 pts (Engl) (IB 32 pts)
London (UCL) – AAA (Engl) (IB 38 pts)
London NCH – AAA–AAB 340–360 pts (Engl) (IB 37–38 pts HL 77)
Nottingham – AAA–AAB 340–360 pts (Engl St) (IB 34–36 pts)
Oxford – AAA (Class Engl) (IB 38–40 pts)
St Andrews – AAA (Engl courses) (IB 36–38 pts)
Sheffield – AAA (Engl Lit) (IB 37 pts)
Sussex – AAA–AAB (Engl Lang) (IB 35–36 pts)
UEA – AAA incl Engl (Engl Lit) (IB 34 pts HL 6 Engl)
Warwick – AAA (Engl Lit Crea Writ) (IB 38 pts)
York – AAA–AAB (Engl courses) (IB 36 pts)

340 pts **Birmingham** – AAB (Engl) (IB 36 pts)
Bristol UWE – 340 pts (Engl Jrnl)
Cardiff – AAB (Engl Lang Engl Lit)
Essex – AAB (Engl Fr Law) (IB 36 pts)
Kent – AAB (Engl Am Postcol Lit) (IB 33 pts)
Lancaster – AAA–AAB 340–360 pts (Engl Lang Crea Writ) (IB 34–36 pts)
Leeds – AAA–AAB (Engl) (IB 36 pts HL 6 Engl)
Leicester – AAB–ABB (Engl courses)
Liverpool – AAB (Engl) (IB 35 pts HL 6 Engl)
London (Gold) – AAB (Engl Crea Writ)
London (QM) – 340 pts (Engl Lit Ling) (IB 32 pts)
London (RH) – AAB–ABB (Engl Dr) (IB 35 pts)
Loughborough – AAb (Engl Dr) (IB 34 pts)
Newcastle – AAB (Engl Lang) (IB 33 pts)
Nottingham – AAB (Engl St Hist) (IB 34 pts)
Sheffield – AAB–ABB (Engl Joint Hons) (IB 35–33 pts)
Southampton – AAB (Film Engl) (IB 34 pts HL 17 pts)
Surrey – AAB (Engl Lit Crea Writ) (IB 35 pts)
UEA – AAB–ABB incl Engl (Engl Lit Joint Hons)
Warwick – AAB (Engl Ger Lit) (IB 36 pts)

320 pts **Aston** – ABB–AAB 320–340 pts (Psy Engl Lang) (IB 33 pts)
Birmingham – ABB (Engl Lang) (IB 36 pts)
Bournemouth – 320 pts (Engl)
Cardiff – ABB (Engl Lang)
Essex – ABB 320 pts (Lit Myth) (IB 29 pts)
Glasgow – ABB (Engl Lang) (IB 36 pts)
Kent – ABB (Engl Am Lit Joint Hons)
Leeds – ABB (Engl Gk Civ) (IB 33 pts)
London (Birk) – ABB (Engl)
Manchester – AAA–ABB 320–360 pts (Engl Lang courses) (IB 33–37 pts)
Nottingham – ABB (Engl St Russ) (IB 32 pts)
Oxford Brookes – ABB (Engl) (IB 34 pts)
Queen's Belfast – ABB/BBBb (Engl courses)
Strathclyde – ABB (Engl courses) (IB 34 pts)
Sheffield – ABB (Engl Lang Sociol) (IB 33 pts)
Sussex – ABB–BBB (ELT) (IB 32–34 pts)
Swansea – ABB–BBB (Engl Lit Lang St)

300 pts **Aberdeen** – BBB (Celt Civ Engl) (IB 30 pts)
Aberystwyth – 300 pts (Engl Lit) (IB 28 pts)
Brighton – BBB 300 pts (Engl Lit) (IB 28–30 pts)

Check **Chapter 4** when choosing your university and **Chapter 7** on how to read the subject tables.

Brunel – BBB (Gms Des Engl) (IB 32 pts)
Edinburgh – AAA–BBB 300–360 pts (Engl Scot Lit) (IB 34–42 pts)
Essex – ABB–BBB 300 pts (Engl Lang Lit) (IB 29 pts)
Gloucestershire – 280–300 pts (Crea Writ)
Hertfordshire – 300 pts (Engl Lit)
Huddersfield – 300 pts (Engl St; Engl Lang; Engl Lit)
Hull – BBB 300 pts (Dr Engl)
Keele – 300–320 pts (Engl) (IB 30–32 pts)
Kent – BBB (Engl Lit) (IB 33–35 pts)
Lincoln – 300 pts (Engl Psy)
London (Gold) – BBB–ABB (Engl)
Loughborough – 300 pts (Pub Engl) (IB 32 pts)
Northumbria – 300 pts (Engl Lit; Engl Lang Lit; Engl Lit Crea Writ)
Reading – 300–360 pts (Engl Lang courses) (IB 31–32 pts)
Roehampton – 300 pts (Engl Lit; Crea Writ; Engl Lang Ling)
Sheffield Hallam – 300 pts (Engl Lit)

280 pts **Bangor** – 280–300 pts (Engl courses; Engl Thea St; Engl Lang Lit)
Birmingham City – 280 pts (Engl Lit courses)
Brunel – BBC (Crea Writ) (IB 30 pts)
Coventry – BBC 280 pts (Engl; Engl Jrnl St)
Edge Hill – 280 pts (Engl Med)
Glamorgan – BBC 280 pts (Engl Lit; Crea Prof Writ; Engl Lang)
Glyndŵr – 280–300 pts (Engl; Engl Crea Writ)
Huddersfield – 280 pts (Dr Engl)
Hull – 280–320 pts (Engl)
Lincoln – 280 pts (Engl; Engl Pol)
LJMU – 280 pts (Crea Writ Flm St) (IB 29 pts)
Manchester Met – 280 pts (Crea Writ) (IB 28 pts)
Nottingham Trent – 280 pts (Engl Crea Writ)
Oxford Brookes – BBC (Engl Lang Comm) (IB 30 pts)
Stirling – BBC (Engl St) (IB 32 pts)
Suffolk (Univ Campus) – 280 pts (Engl)
Teesside – 280 pts (Engl St; Engl St Crea Writ)
Westminster – BBC (Engl Lang) (IB 30 pts)
Winchester – 280–320 pts (Crea Writ courses) (IB 24–26 pts)

260 pts **Anglia Ruskin** – 220–260 pts (Writ Film St)
Bangor – 260–300 pts (Mus Crea Writ)
Bath Spa – 260–300 pts (Engl Lit courses; Crea Writ)
Cardiff Met – 260 pts (Educ St Engl; Engl Contemp Media; Engl Dr; Engl Crea Writ)
Chester – 260–300 pts (Engl Lang) (IB 28 pts)
Chichester – BCC (Engl Crea Writ) (IB 30 pts)
De Montfort – 260 pts (Engl; Engl Lang; Crea Writ)
Derby – 260–300 pts (Prof Writ Joint Hons)
Dundee – BCC (Engl)
Leeds Met – 260 pts (Engl Lit) (IB 24 pts)
Liverpool Hope – 260–320 pts (Engl Lang)
LJMU – 260 pts (Hist Engl; Crea Writ; Engl)
London Met – 260 pts (Crea Writ; Engl Lit; Engl Lit Film TV St)
Newman (UC) – 260 pts (Engl)
Newport – 260 pts (Engl; Engl Hist)
Northampton – 260–280 pts (Engl courses; Crea Writ courses)
Nottingham – BCC (Crea Prof Writ)
Plymouth – 260 pts (Crea Writ; Engl courses)
Salford – 260–240 pts (Engl Lit Engl Lang) (IB 31 pts)
Sheffield Hallam – 260 pts (Engl Hist)

BA English

Joint honours also available with
Theatre
Creative Writing
Film and Television Studies
Games Design

BA Creative Writing

Joint honours also available with
Theatre
English
Games Design

Find out more about the School of Arts at
www.brunel.ac.uk/arts

Brunel
UNIVERSITY
L O N D O N

Sunderland – 260 pts (Engl; Engl Crea Writ; Engl Dr; Engl Lang Ling; Engl Film; Engl Lang Lit; Script (Film TV Rad))
Ulster – BCC 260 pts (Engl courses)
Winchester – 260–300 pts (Engl Lit courses) (IB 24–26 pts)

240 pts **Bangor** – 240–300 pts (Engl Lang courses)
Bath Spa – 240–280 pts (Engl Lit Pub)
Bolton – 240 pts (Crea Writ) (IB 24 pts)
Buckingham – CCC–BCC 240–260 pts (Engl St courses) (IB 27 pts)
Canterbury Christ Church – 240 pts (Engl; Engl Lang Comm)
Chester – 240–280 pts (Crea Writ) (IB 26 pts)
Cumbria – 240 pts (Engl Crea Writ; Engl)
Greenwich – 240 pts (Crea Writ; Eng Lang ELT)
Leeds Trinity (UC) – 240 pts (Engl; Engl Writ; Eng Film St; Engl Hist; Engl Media)
London South Bank – 240 pts (Engl Dr Perf; Engl Crea Writ)
Portsmouth – 240–300 pts (Engl Dr; Engl Lang courses; Crea Writ; Engl Hist)
Staffordshire – 240 pts (Engl Lit) (IB 28 pts)
St Mary's Twickenham (UC) – 240 pts (Crea Writ) (IB 28 pts)
Sheffield Hallam – 240 pts incl Engl (Film Engl)
Southampton Solent – 240 pts (Engl Film; Jrnl Engl Media; Engl)
UCLan – 240–260 pts (Engl Lang St; Engl Lit)
Winchester – 240–280 pts (Am St Engl) (IB 24 pts)
Worcester – 240–260 pts (Engl Lang courses; Engl Lit St courses)

220 pts **Anglia Ruskin** – 220–260 pts (Engl Lang Engl Lang Teach)
Bishop Grosseteste (UC) – 220 pts (Engl Lit courses)
Edinburgh Napier – 220 pts (Engl Film)
Falmouth (UC) – 220pts (Engl)

Check **Chapter 4** when choosing your university and **Chapter 7** on how to read the subject tables.

Kingston – 220–360 pts (Engl Lang Comm; Crea Writ)
UCP Marjon – 220 pts (Engl Lit; Crea Writ; Ling Engl Lang)
200 pts **Anglia Ruskin** – 200 pts (Engl)
Blackburn (Coll) – 200 pts (Engl Lang Lit St; Engl Lang)
Blackpool and Fylde (Coll) – 200 pts (Engl Lang Lit Writ)
Bucks New – 200–240 pts (Crea Writ; Script)
Doncaster (Coll Univ Centre) – 200 pts (Engl)
Glamorgan – 200–260 pts (Engl Span)
Middlesex – 200–300 pts (Engl Lit courses; Engl Lang Lit; Crea Writ Engl Lit; Crea Writ)
Peterborough (Univ Centre) – 200 pts (Engl)
Trinity Saint David – 200–300 pts (Engl Lit courses)
UEL – 200 pts (Engl Lang; Engl Lit; Crea Prof Writ)
York St John – 200–260 pts (Engl Lit courses)
180 pts **Bedfordshire** – 180–220 pts (Engl courses; Crea Writ)
Bradford – 180–220 pts (Engl; Crea Writ)
Leeds Met – 180 pts (Engl Hist) (IB 24 pts)
Reading – 180 pts (Educ St (P) Engl) (IB 24 pts)
160 pts **Norwich City (Coll)** – 160 pts (Engl Psy Soc; Engl Cult St)
UHI – CC–AA (Lit)
Wolverhampton – 160–220 pts (Engl courses; Crea Prof Writ courses)
120 pts **Arts London** – 120 pts (Mag Pub)
Grimsby (IFHE) – 120–240 pts (Engl St)
Trinity Saint David – 120–360 pts (Engl)
West Anglia (Coll) – 120 pts (Hist Engl Lit)
80 pts **Newham (CFE)** – check with College 80 pts (Engl)

Alternative offers
See **Chapter 7** and **Appendix 1** for grades/UCAS Tariff points information for the International Baccalaureate, Scottish Highers/Advanced Highers, the Welsh Baccalaureate, the Irish Leaving Certificate, the Cambridge Pre-U Diploma, the Advanced Diploma and the Extended Project.

EXAMPLES OF FOUNDATION DEGREES IN THE SUBJECT FIELD
Greenwich; Plymouth.

CHOOSING YOUR COURSE (SEE ALSO CH.1)
Some course features
Cardiff Met English can be taken with Creative Writing, Drama or Contemporary Media.
Durham English Literature is a wide-ranging course focusing on poetry, drama and the novel in Year 1 with modules on selected themes. Years 2 and 3 enable students to follow their special interest. Joint courses are offered with History and Philosophy and the subject can be studied in combined honours in Arts.
Liverpool English Language and Literature can be studied from its origins in the Anglo-Saxon period to the modern period, covering all the major literary and linguistic developments. Optional courses are available in the second and third years. There are also seven joint courses with English including Communication Studies, languages, History and Philosophy.
Manchester Nineteen courses are offered involving English Language and Literature. The courses focus on language and the entire range of English literature. A large number of joint courses are offered with Drama, Languages, Philosophy and Linguistics. (High research rating).
Middlesex Thirteen English courses are offered covering English language, English Literature and Creative Writing. A Teaching English as a Foreign Language course is also available.
Nottingham The English Studies course covers the entire range of English literature from its beginnings to the 20th century and also medieval and modern English language. English Studies can also be taken with, for example, Latin, Philosophy, Theology and Hispanic Studies. There is also a unique course in Viking Studies covering language, literature, history and archaeology.

UEA The School of English Literature and Creative Writing offers a wide range of courses including American and English Literature, English Literature and Drama. There are also courses in English Literature with Creative Writing, English and Comparative Literature, and Literature and joint courses with History, Drama, American Literature, Politics, Film, Philsophy and Art History. Degree courses in Linguistics are also offered.

Universities and colleges teaching quality See www.qaa.ac.uk; http://unistats.direct.gov.uk.

Top research universities and colleges (RAE 2008) (English Language and Literature) York; London (QM); Edinburgh; Manchester; Exeter; Oxford; Nottingham; Cambridge; De Montfort; Leeds; Warwick; Glasgow; St Andrews; Queen's Belfast; Liverpool; Newcastle.

Examples of sandwich degree courses Brighton; UEL.

ADMISSIONS INFORMATION
Number of applicants per place (approx) Bangor 5; Bath Spa 8; Birmingham 7, (Engl Educ) 4; Birmingham City 9; Blackpool and Fylde (Coll) 2; Bristol 18, 14; Bristol UWE 4; Brunel 10; Buckingham 2; Cambridge (A-Sxn Nrs Celt) 2, (Engl) 4.9; Cardiff (Engl Lit) 6; Chester 20; Chichester 4; Cumbria 24; De Montfort 7; Derby 6; Dundee 6; Durham 20; Edge Hill 4; Exeter 13; Glamorgan 8; Gloucestershire 35; Glyndŵr 2; Hertfordshire 6; Huddersfield 5; Hull 14; Hull (Coll) 1; Kingston 6; Lancaster 12; Leeds 10; Leeds Trinity (UC) 7; Leicester 6; Liverpool (Engl Comm St) 7; London (Gold) 9; London (King's) (Engl Film) 15; London (QM) 9; London (RH) 9; London (UCL) 13; London South Bank 5; Loughborough 40; Manchester (Engl Lit) 11, (Engl Lang) 7; Manchester Met 7; Middlesex 8; Newman (UC) 3; Northampton 3; Nottingham 22; Nottingham Trent 21; Oxford (success rate 25%), (Magdalen) 15; Oxford Brookes 15; Portsmouth 8; Reading 11; Roehampton 5; Salford 12; Sheffield 12; Sheffield Hallam 4; Southampton 4; Stirling 9; Sunderland 10; Swansea Met 4; Teesside 5; Trinity Saint David 4; UCLan 10; UEA (Engl Lit Dr) 22, (Engl Lit Crea Writ) 17, (Engl St) 12; Warwick 15, (Engl Thea) 26; Winchester 3; York 8; York St John 3.

Advice to applicants and planning the UCAS personal statement Applicants should read outside their subject. Details of any writing you have done (for example poetry, short stories) should be provided. Theatre visits and play readings are also important. Keep up-to-date by reading literary and theatre reviews in the national newspapers (keep a scrapbook of reviews for reference). Evidence is needed of a good writing style. Favourite authors, spare-time reading. Ability to write lucidly, accurately and succinctly. Evidence of literary enthusiasm. General interest in communications – verbal, visual, media. **Bristol** Deferred entry accepted in some cases. Late applications may not be accepted. **Manchester** Due to the detailed nature of entry requirements for English Literature and American Studies courses, we are unable to include full details in the prospectus. For complete and up-to-date information on our entry requirements for these courses, please visit our website at www.manchester.ac.uk/ugcourses.

Misconceptions about this course Birmingham City The study of English language means descriptive linguistics – the course won't necessarily enable students to speak or write better English. **Buckingham** Native speakers of English often do not realise that the EFL degree courses are restricted to non-native speakers of English. **Liverpool** (Engl Comm St) The course is not a training in journalism, although some students go on to work in the press, radio or TV. **UEA** (Engl Lit Crea Writ) This is not simply a creative writing course: English literature is the predominant element.

Selection interviews Yes Bangor (mature students), Birmingham, Brunel, Cambridge, Canterbury Christ Church, Chichester, Essex, Exeter, Gloucestershire, Huddersfield, Hull, Hull (Coll), Kingston, Lancaster, Leeds Trinity (UC), London (Gold), London (RH), London South Bank, Middlesex, Newcastle, Newport, Nottingham, Oxford (Engl) 27%, (Engl Econ Mgt) 11%, (Engl Lang Lit) 21%, (Engl Mod Lang) 16%, Portsmouth, Reading, Roehampton, Trinity Saint David, UEA, Warwick; **Some** Bangor, Bath Spa, Birmingham City, Blackburn (Coll), Blackpool and Fylde (Coll), Bristol, Cardiff Met, Chester, De Montfort, Derby, Dundee, Leeds, Liverpool (Engl Comm St), London (King's), London Met, Loughborough, Salford, Southampton, Swansea Met, Truro (Coll), Wolverhampton.

Interview advice and questions Questions will almost certainly be asked on set A-level texts and any essays which have been submitted prior to the interview. You will also be expected to have read outside your A-level subjects and to answer questions about your favourite authors, poets, dramatists etc. Questions in the past have included: Do you think that class discussion plays an important part in your English course? What is the value of studying a text in depth rather than just reading it for pleasure? What is the difference between satire and comedy? Are books written by women different from those written by men? Why would you go to see a production of *Hamlet*? What are your views on the choice of novels for this year's Booker Prize? Short verbal tests and a précis may be set. See also **Chapter 6**. **Buckingham** It is useful to know if there is any particular reason why students want a particular programme; for example, for the TEFL degree is a member of the family a teacher? **Cambridge** We look for interviewees who respond positively to ideas, can think on their feet, engage intelligently with critical issues and sustain an argument. If they don't evince any of these we reject them. What books are bad for you? **Leeds** Interview questions based on information supplied in the personal statement. One third of the applicants are interviewed. Academic ability; current reading interests. **Liverpool** (Engl Comm St) General questions only. Reading interests, general interests, career ambitions. **London (King's)** Interview questions are based on the information in the personal statement. Applicants are asked to prepare a short literary text which will be discussed at interview. **London (UCL)** The interview will focus on an ability to discuss literature in terms of language, plot, characters and genre. Following the interview applicants will be asked to write a critical commentary on an example of unseen prose or verse. **Oxford** Is there a difference between innocence and naivety? If you could make up a word, what would it be? Why? Do you think *Hamlet* is a bit long? No? Well I do. Is the Bible a fictional work? Was Shakespeare a rebel? **Roehampton** Samples of work taken to interview and discussed. **UEA** (Engl Lit Dr) How do you reconcile yourself to an academic interest in literature on the one hand and the belief in practical performance on the other? Interviews are accompanied by auditions. **Warwick** We may ask students to sight-read or to analyse a text. **York** Written essays are required to be submitted at interview.

Reasons for rejection (non-academic) Some are well-informed about English literature – others are not. Inability to respond to questions about their current studies. Lack of enthusiasm for the challenge of studying familiar subjects from a different perspective. Must be able to benefit from the course. Little interest in how people communicate with each other. They don't know a single thing about our course. **Bangor** We reject those who decline interviews. **Bristol** Not enough places to make offers to all those whose qualifications deserve one. **Cambridge** See **Interview advice and questions**. **Leeds** Unsuitable predictions. **Liverpool** (Engl Comm St) Student more suited to a practical course. Ungrammatical personal statement. **Oxford** (1) The essay she submitted was poorly written, careless and reductive and, in general, lacking in attention to the subject. She should be encouraged to write less and think more about what she is saying. She seems to put down the first thing that comes into her head. (2) We had the feeling that he rather tended to dismiss texts which did not satisfy the requirements of his personal canon and that he therefore might not be happy pursuing a course requiring the study of texts from all periods. (3) In her essay on Bronte she took a phrase from Arnold which was metaphorical (to do with hunger) and applied it literally, writing at length about the diet of the characters. **Reading** None. If they have reached the interview we have already eliminated all other factors. **Sheffield Hallam** Apparent lack of eagerness to tackle all three strands of the course (literature, language and creative writing). **Southampton** Insufficient or patchy academic achievement. Applicants coming from non-standard academic backgrounds are assessed in terms of their individual situations. **UEA** (Engl Am Lit) Personal statement unconvincing in its commitment to American literature. (Other courses) Poor examples of work submitted.

AFTER-RESULTS ADVICE
Offers to applicants repeating A-levels Higher Sheffield Hallam, Southampton (varies), Warwick; **Possibly higher** Lancaster, Newcastle, Oxford Brookes; **Same** Bangor, Birmingham City, Blackpool and Fylde (Coll), Bristol, Cambridge, Cardiff, Cardiff Met, Chester, Chichester, Cumbria, De Montfort, Derby, Dundee, Durham, Edge Hill, Hull, Leeds, Leeds Trinity (UC), Liverpool, Liverpool Hope, London (Gold), London (RH), Loughborough, Manchester Met, Newman (UC), Newport, Nottingham, Nottingham Trent, Portsmouth, Reading, Roehampton, St Mary's Twickenham (UC), Salford, Sheffield, Staffordshire, Stirling, Suffolk (Univ Campus), Trinity Saint David, UEA, Ulster, Winchester, Wolverhampton, York, York St John.

For a quick reference offers calculator, fold out the inside back cover.

GRADUATE DESTINATIONS AND EMPLOYMENT (2009/10 HESA)
English Studies; graduates surveyed 11,585 **Employed** 5450 **In voluntary employment** 295 **In further study** 2930 **Assumed unemployed** 830

Career note English graduates work in the media, management, public and social services, business, administration and IT, sales retail, the cultural industries and the teaching profession. Those who have undertaken courses in creative writing could aim for careers in advertising, public relations, journalism or publishing.

OTHER DEGREE SUBJECTS FOR CONSIDERATION
Communication Studies; Drama; Language courses; Linguistics; Literature; Media Studies.

ENVIRONMENTAL SCIENCES/STUDIES

(including **Conservation, Ecology, Environmental Health, Environmental Management** and **Meteorology**; see also **Biological Sciences, Biology, Engineering (Civil), Geography, Geology/ Geological Sciences, Health Sciences/Studies, Marine/Maritime Studies, Town and Country Planning**)

Environmental Science/Studies courses need to be considered with care as, depending on their content and specialisms, they lead to very different careers. Environmental Health courses usually focus on the training of environmental health officers whilst Environmental Studies or Science degrees cover a range of subjects with options which may include biology, geography, geology, oceanography, chemistry, legal, social and political issues.

Useful websites www.cieh.org; www.ends.co.uk; www.enn.com; www.iagre.org.uk; www.defra.gov. uk; www.socenv.org.uk; www.ies-uk.org.uk; www.noc.soton.ac.uk.

NB The points totals shown to the left of the institutions are for ease of reference only. It must not be assumed that Tariff points are always used by institutions or that they can be substituted for an offer in grades. The level of an offer is not necessarily indicative of the quality of a course.

COURSE OFFERS INFORMATION
Subject requirements/preferences GCSE English, mathematics and a science (often chemistry or biology) usually required. **AL** One or two science subjects are usually stipulated; mathematics may be required. (Meteor) Mathematics, physics and another science may be required sometimes with specified grades, eg **Reading** mathematics and physics grade B.

Your target offers and examples of courses provided by each institution
380 pts **London (UCL)** – A*AA–AAA incl maths (Env Eng) (IB 38–39 pts)
360 pts **Edinburgh** – AAA–ABB (Env Geosci) (IB 37–32 pts)
       Glasgow – AAA (Earth Sci Faster Route) (IB 38 pts HL 665)
       Imperial London – AAA 360 pts (Env Geosci) (IB 38 pts)
       London (UCL) – AAA–AAB incl geog (Env Geog) (IB 36–38 pts)
       Nottingham – AAA (Archit Env Des) (IB 36 pts)
       Sheffield – AAA incl biol sci (Ecol MBiolSci) (IB 37 pts)
       UEA – AAA–AAB (Env Geophys) (IB 34–33 pts)
       York – AAA–ABB 320–360 pts (Chem Res Env) (IB 32–34 pts)
340 pts **Bristol** – AAB–ABB 320–340 pts (Env Geosci) (IB 35–33 pts)
       Bristol UWE – 340 pts (Geog Env Mgt) (IB 28 pts)
       Cardiff – AAB–ABB (Ecol) (IB 34 pts)
       Durham – AAB (Env Geosci) (IB 36 pts)
       Edinburgh – AAA–AAB 340–360 pts (Ecol) (IB 32–37 pts)
       Exeter – AAB–BBB (Renew Ener) (IB 34–32 pts)
       Lancaster – AAB–ABB 340–320 pts (Earth Env Sci (St Abrd)) (IB 32–34 pts)
       Leicester – AAB–ABB (App Env Geol)

Check **Chapter 4** when choosing your university and **Chapter 7** on how to read the subject tables.

London (QM) – 340 pts (Env Geog) (IB 32 pts)
London LSE – AAB (Env Plcy Econ) (IB 37 pts HL 666)
Newcastle – AAB (Env Sci) (IB 30 pts)
Nottingham – AAB–ABB 320–340 pts (Env Eng) (IB 34–32 pts)
St Andrews – AAB (Ecol Cons) (IB 35 pts)
Sheffield – AAB (Env Sci MEnvSci) (IB 35 pts)
Southampton – AAB–ABB 340–320 pts (Env Sci) (IB 34–32 pts HL 17–16 pts)
Warwick – AAB (Env Biol) (IB 36 pts)
York – AAB (Ecol) (IB 35 pts)

320 pts **Birmingham** – ABB (Pal Palaeoenv) (IB 32–34 pts)
Cardiff – ABB (Env Geosci) (IB 30–32 pts)
Edinburgh – AAA–ABB 320–360 pts (Ecol Env Sci) (IB 37–32 pts)
Glasgow – ABB (Earth Sci) (IB 32 pts)
Kent – ABB (Env St) (IB 33 pts)
Lancaster – ABB (Ecol) (IB 32 pts)
Leeds – ABB (Env Sci) (IB 34 pts)
Liverpool – ABB (Ecol Env) (IB 33 pts HL 6 biol)
London (Birk) – ABB (Env Mgt)
London (RH) – AAB–BBB (Ecol Env) (IB 34 pts)
Manchester – ABB (Env Res Geol) (IB 33 pts)
Nottingham – ABB–BBC 280–320 pts (Env Sci) (IB 32–38 pts)
Plymouth – ABB 320–360 pts (Mar Biol Cstl Ecol) (IB 24 pts)
Reading – 320 pts (Env Sci) (IB 31 pts)
Strathclyde – ABB (Env Hlth)
Sheffield – ABB (Env Sci BSc) (IB 33 pts)
Sussex – ABB (Ecol Cons) (IB 32 pts)
UEA – ABB (Clim Sci BSc) (IB 32 pts HL 555)
York – ABB (Env Econ Env Mgt) (IB 34 pts)

300 pts **Bournemouth** – 300 pts (Ecol Wldlf Cons) (IB 31 pts)
Brighton – BBB (Env Media St) (IB 32 pts)
Bristol UWE – 300 pts (Cons Biol) (IB 24–28 pts)
Glasgow – Dumfries Campus BBB (Env Stwdshp) (IB 30 pts)
Huddersfield – 300 pts (Bus St Env Mgt)
Keele – 300 pts (Env Sust)
Liverpool – BBB (Env Plan) (IB 31 pts)
London (QM) – 300–340 pts (Glob Chn Env Econ Dev) (IB 32 pts)
London (RH) – BBB 300–320 pts (Env Cons) (IB 32 pts HL 6)
Manchester – BBB (Env Mgt) (IB 33 pts)
Northumbria – 300 pts (Geog Env Mgt) (IB 28 pts)
Nottingham – ABC/BBB–BCC (Env Biol) (IB 34–26 pts)
Queen's Belfast – BBB (Env Biol) (IB 30 pts)
Reading – 300 pts (Meteor Clim)
UEA – BBB incl chem (Env Chem) (IB 31 pts)

285 pts **Glasgow Caledonian** – 285 pts (Env Mgt Plan)
280 pts **Aberystwyth** – 280 pts (Env Sci) (IB 28 pts)
Bangor – 280–320 pts (Env Sci Ecol) (IB 28 pts)
Brighton – 280 pts (Ecol Biogeog)
Coventry – 280–300 pts (Clim Chng Sust)
Essex – BBB–BBC 280–300 pts (Ecol) (IB 26–28 pts)
Hertfordshire – 280 pts (Env St)
Keele – 300 pts (App Env Sci courses)
Lincoln – 280 pts (Cons Restor)
Manchester Met – 280 pts (Ecol Cons (St Abrd)) (IB 28 pts)
Northumbria – 280 pts (Env Mgt; Hlth Cotemp Soc)

For a quick reference offers calculator, fold out the inside back cover.

Nottingham – BBB–BBC 280–300 pts (Agric Env Sci) (IB 28–26 pts)
Oxford Brookes – BBC (Env Sci) (IB 30 pts)
Plymouth – 280 pts (Env Biol) (IB 26 pts)
Portsmouth – 280 pts (Env Geog)
Staffordshire – 280 pts (Env Sust) (IB 24 pts)
Stirling – BBC (Env Sci Out Educ) (IB 32 pts)
Sheffield – BBC (Lnd Archit Ecol) (IB 30 pts)
Ulster – 280 pts (Env Hlth) (IB 32 pts)

260 pts **Bangor** – 260–320 pts (Agric Cons Env; App Ter Mar Ecol)
Bradford – 260 pts (Env Sci)
Derby – 260–280 pts (Cntry Mgt)
Dundee – BCC (Env Sci; Env Sci Geog; Int Bus Env Sust; Renew Ener)
Greenwich – 260 pts (Env Sci)
Hertfordshire – 260 pts (Env Mgt) (IB 24–26 pts)
Lincoln – 260 pts (Agric Env Mgt)
Liverpool Hope – 260–320 pts (Env Sci)
LJMU – 260 pts (Env Hlth) (IB 24 pts)
Northampton – 260–280 pts (Env Sci courses) (IB 24 pts)
Plymouth – 260 pts (Archit Tech Env) (IB 26 pts)
Sheffield Hallam – 260 pts (Env Sci; Env Cons)
Teesside – 260–280 pts (Env Hlth)

240 pts **Aberdeen** – CCC 240 pts (Ecol Env Sci) (IB 28 pts)
Canterbury Christ Church – CCC 240 pts (Ecol Cons)
Chester – 240–280 pts (Nat Haz Mgt) (IB 26 pts)
Cumbria – 240 pts (Sust Ener Tech)
Edge Hill – 240 pts (Env Sci)
Glyndŵr – 240 pts (Env Sci)
Greenwich – 240 pts (Civ Eng Wtr Env Mgt)
Kingston – 240–280 pts (Env Mgt; Env Sci)
Leeds Met – 240 pts (Env Des Eng) (IB 24 pts)
Lincoln – 240 pts (Cons Biol)
Northampton – 240–280 pts (App Cons Biol) (IB 24 pts)
Nottingham Trent – 240 pts (Env Sci)
Portsmouth – 240–300 pts (Mar Env Sci; Env Sci)
Sparsholt (Coll) – 240–280 pts (Cons Wldlf Mgt)
Worcester – 240–280 pts (Cons Ecol; Env Sci)

220 pts **Bangor** – 220–260 pts (Mar Env St) (IB 28 pts)
Bath Spa – 220–280 pts (Env Sci)
Cardiff Met – 220–240 pts (Env Hlth)
Nottingham Trent – 220 pts (Env Cons)
Ulster – 220 pts (Env Sci courses) (IB 24 pts)

200 pts **Bishop Burton (Coll)** – 200 pts (Env Cons)
Glyndŵr – 200 pts (Sust Dev)
Middlesex – 200–280 pts (Env Pblc Hlth)
Salford – 200–240 pts (Env Geog) (IB 24 pts)
UCLan – 200–240 pts (Env Mgt; Env Haz Sci Plcy Mgt)
Wolverhampton – 200 pts (Env Hlth)

180 pts **Plymouth** – 180 pts (Env Constr Surv) (IB 24 pts)
Southampton Solent – 180 pts (Geog Env St)

160 pts **Leeds Met** – 160–200 pts (Pblc Hlth (Env Hlth)) (IB 28 pts)
Swansea Met – 160–340 pts (Env Cons)
UHI – CC–AA (Env Sci; Nat Env Sci; Arch Env St; Env Sust St)

120 pts **Bournemouth** – 120 pts (Mar Ecol Cons)

Open University – contact +44 (0)845 300 6090 **or** www.openuniversity.co.uk/you (Env St)

Check **Chapter 4** when choosing your university and **Chapter 7** on how to read the subject tables.

Alternative offers
See **Chapter 7** and **Appendix 1** for grades/UCAS Tariff points information for the International Baccalaureate, Scottish Highers/Advanced Highers, the Welsh Baccalaureate, the Irish Leaving Certificate, the Cambridge Pre-U Diploma, the Advanced Diploma and the Extended Project.

EXAMPLES OF FOUNDATION DEGREES IN THE SUBJECT FIELD
Askham Bryan (Coll); Bournemouth; Cumbria; Glyndŵr; Leeds City (Coll); Manchester (Coll); Nottingham Trent; Suffolk (Univ Campus); Writtle (Coll).

CHOOSING YOUR COURSE (SEE ALSO CH.1)
Some course features
Birmingham Specialisation in four pathways (applied ecology, water in the environment, atmospheric processes and earth surface processes) follows a broad first year Environmental Science course. There are also courses in Environmental Management and Environmental Geoscience.
Brighton The Environmental Sciences course involves a study of the human and physical environment, ecology, energy and pollution. There are also degrees in Environmental Hazards, covering geography, health, pollution and human hazards, and Earth and Ocean Science, Environmental Biology and Ecology and Biogeography.
Kingston Pathways in Environmental Science include ecology, conservation and resource management. Options include languages, business and human geography. Enviromental Studies is offered with a range of subjects including Business Management. There are also degree courses in Natural History, Sustainable Development, Environmental Hazards and Disaster Management.
Liverpool Hope Environmental Sciences is offered as part of a combined honours (BA/BSc) programme. Popular combinations incude Geography, Sport Studies and Sport Development.
Manchester The Environmental Science degree programme enables students to specialise in their particular fields of interest within biology, earth sciences, chemistry or biology. Entrance scholarships available.
Newcastle The Environmental Science course covers management, ecology, tropical environments and biological conservation. Courses are also offered in Countryside Management and Rural Studies.

Universities and colleges teaching quality See www.qaa.ac.uk; http://unistats.direct.gov.uk.

Top research universities and colleges (RAE 2008) (Geography and Environmental Studies) Bristol; Cambridge; Durham; Oxford; London (QM); Leeds; London (King's); London (UCL); London LSE; Sheffield; London (RH); Aberystwyth; London (Birk); Reading; UEA; Manchester; Southampton.

(Earth Systems and Environmental Sciences) Cambridge; Oxford; London (UCL); Bristol; London (RH).
Examples of sandwich degree courses Bangor; Bradford; Bristol UWE; Cardiff; Cardiff Met; Coventry; Glasgow Caledonian; Hertfordshire; Huddersfield; Kingston; LJMU; Manchester Met; Nottingham Trent; Reading; Salford; Teesside; Ulster; West Scotland.

ADMISSIONS INFORMATION
Number of applicants per place (approx) Abertay Dundee 5; Aberystwyth 3; Bangor 3; Bath Spa 2; Birmingham 5; Bournemouth 4; Bradford 3; Bristol 7; Bristol UWE 1; Cardiff Met 4; Coventry 9; De Montfort 9; Dundee 6; Durham 5; Edinburgh 1; Essex 3; Glamorgan 1; Glasgow Caledonian 1; Gloucestershire 11; Glyndŵr 3; Greenwich 2; Harper Adams (UC) 5; Hertfordshire 5; Hull 8; Kingston 3; Lancaster 11; Leeds (Env Sci Ener) 2; LJMU 5; London (King's) 5; London (RH) 8; London LSE 7; Manchester Met (Env Sci) 5; Northampton 4; Northumbria 8; Nottingham 6; Nottingham Trent 3; Oxford Brookes 13; Plymouth 8; Portsmouth 5; Roehampton 3; Salford 8; Sheffield Hallam 8; Southampton 5; Stirling 10; Strathclyde 1; Trinity Saint David 3; UEA 7; Ulster 16; Wolverhampton 2; Worcester 7; York 4.

Advice to applicants and planning the UCAS personal statement 'We want doers, not just thinkers' is one comment from an admissions tutor. Describe any field courses which you have attended; make an effort to visit one of the National Parks. Discuss these visits and identify any particular aspects which impressed you. Outline travel interests. Give details of work as a conservation volunteer and other outside-school activities. Strong communication skills, people-oriented work experience. Watch your spelling and grammar! What sparked your interest in Environmental Science? Discuss your field trips. (Env Hlth courses) A basic knowledge of environmental health as opposed to environmental sciences. Work experience in an environmental health department is looked upon very favourably. **Lancaster** Two A-level subjects required from biology, chemistry, computing, environmental science, geography or geology.

Misconceptions about this course Bangor Students should note that only simple mathematical skills are required for this course. **Leeds** (Ener Env Sci) Note that the course is closer to environmental technology than to environmental science. **Southampton** This is not just a course for environmentalists, for example links with BP, IBM etc. **Wolverhampton** This is a course in Environmental Science, not Environmental Studies: there is a difference. **York** (Env Econ Env Mgt) Some students worry that the economics part of the course will be too difficult, which is not the case.

Selection interviews Yes Bradford, Bristol UWE, Cambridge, Coventry, Durham, Glamorgan, Gloucestershire, Greenwich, Harper Adams (UC) (advisory), Hertfordshire, Kingston, Manchester Met, Newcastle, Newport, Nottingham, Nottingham Trent, Oxford Brookes, Sheffield Hallam, Strathclyde, Sussex, Trinity Saint David; **Some** Anglia Ruskin, Bangor, Bath Spa, Birmingham, Cardiff Met, Derby, London (King's), Plymouth, Salford, Southampton, Staffordshire, UEA, York; **No** Dundee.

Interview advice and questions Environmental issues are constantly in the news, so keep abreast of developments. You could be asked to discuss any particular environmental problems in the area in which you live and to justify your stance on any environmental issues on which you have strong opinions. See also **Chapter 6**. **Bath Spa** Questions on school work, current affairs and field courses. **UEA** Can you display an informed interest in any aspect of environmental science?

Reasons for rejection (non-academic) Inability to be aware of the needs of others.

AFTER-RESULTS ADVICE
Offers to applicants repeating A-levels Higher Greenwich, Lancaster, London (King's), Nottingham, Nottingham Trent, Strathclyde; **Possibly higher** Aberystwyth, Bradford, Northumbria; **Same** Bangor, Birmingham, Brighton, Cardiff Met, Derby, Dundee, Leeds, LJMU, Manchester Met, Plymouth, SAC (Scottish CAg), Salford, Southampton, UEA, Ulster, Wolverhampton.

GRADUATE DESTINATIONS AND EMPLOYMENT (2009/10 HESA)
See **Biological Sciences**.

Career note Some graduates find work with government departments, local authorities, statutory and voluntary bodies in areas like land management and pollution control. Others go into a range of non-scientific careers.

OTHER DEGREE SUBJECTS FOR CONSIDERATION
Biological Sciences; Biology; Chemistry; Earth Sciences; Environmental Engineering; Geography; Geology; Meteorology; Ocean Sciences/Oceanography; Town and Country Planning.

EUROPEAN STUDIES
(see also **French, German, International Relations, Languages, Russian and East European Studies**)

European Studies is a popular subject and in many cases offers the language student an opportunity to study modern languages within the context of a European country (covering economics, politics, legal, social and cultural aspects). In these courses there is usually a strong emphasis on the written and spoken word. It is important to note, also, that many courses in other subjects offer the opportunity to study in Europe.

Useful websites www.europa.eu; www.eaces.net; www.britishcouncil.org/erasmus; see also Languages.

NB The points totals shown to the left of the institutions are for ease of reference only. It must not be assumed that Tariff points are always used by institutions or that they can be substituted for an offer in grades. The level of an offer is not necessarily indicative of the quality of a course.

COURSE OFFERS INFORMATION

Subject requirements/preferences GCSE English and a foreign language for all courses and possibly mathematics. Grades may be stipulated. **AL** A modern language usually required.

Your target offers and examples of courses provided by each institution

380 pts **Birmingham** – A*AA 380 pts (Nat Sci Euro) (IB 36–38 pts)
 Durham – A*AA (Maths (Euro St)) (IB 38 pts)
 London (King's) – AABc (Euro St (Fr/Ger/Span)) (IB 36 pts)
 London (UCL) – A*AA (Euro Soc Pol St) (IB 39 pts)

360 pts **Birmingham** – AAA–ABB 320–360 pts (Euro Pol Soty Econ) (IB 34–36 pts)
 Exeter – AAA–AAB (Law (Euro)) (IB 36–34 pts)
 Southampton – AAA (Aero Astnaut (Euro St)) (IB 36 pts HL 18 pts)

340 pts **Cardiff** – AAB (Euro Pol Int Rel)
 Exeter – A*AA–AAB (Bus Econ Euro St) (IB 38–34 pts)
 Kent – AAB (Psy St Euro) (IB 33 pts)
 London (UCL) – AAB (Pol E Euro St) (IB 34–36 pts)
 Newcastle – AAB–ABB (Gov EU St) (IB 34–36 pts)
 Southampton – AAB (Langs Contemp Euro St) (IB 34 pts HL 17 pts)
 Warwick – AAB (Compar Ital Euro St) (IB 36 pts)

320 pts **Birmingham** – ABB (Modn Langs Euro St) (IB 32 pts)
 Glasgow – ABB (Cnt E Euro St) (IB 36 pts)
 Kent – ABB (Euro Hist (St Abrd)) (IB 33 pts)
 Leicester – ABB (Euro St) (IB 28–30 pts)
 London (RH) – ABB–BBB (Euro St Fr/Ger/Ital/Span)
 London (UCL) – ABB (E Euro St) (IB 34 pts)
 Manchester – AAB–ABB 320–340 pts (Euro St Modn Lang) (IB 33–36 pts)
 Nottingham – ABB (Euro Pol) (IB 32 pts)
 Reading – 320–340 pts (Engl Lit Euro Lit Cult)
 Swansea – ABB (Geog Euro St)

300 pts **Aberdeen** – BBB (Euro St) (IB 28 pts)
 Dundee – BBB–CCC 300–240 pts (Euro St) (IB 29 pts)
 Essex – ABB–BBB 300 pts (Euro St Lang) (IB 27 pts)

280 pts **London (QM)** – 280 pts (Euro St) (IB 32 pts)
 Queen's Belfast – BBC/BCCb (Chem Euro)
 Stirling – BBC (Int Mgt St Euro Lang Socty) (IB 32 pts)

260 pts **Nottingham Trent** – 260 pts (Euro St Joint Hons)
 Portsmouth – 260–300 pts (Law Euro St)

240 pts **Ulster** – 240 pts (Euro St courses) (IB 24 pts)

200 pts **Portsmouth** – 200–280 pts (Euro St courses)

 Open University – contact +44 (0)845 300 6090 **or** www.openuniversity.co.uk/you (Euro St)

Alternative offers

See **Chapter 7** and **Appendix 1** for grades/UCAS Tariff points information for the International Baccalaureate, Scottish Highers/Advanced Highers, the Welsh Baccalaureate, the Irish Leaving Certificate, the Cambridge Pre-U Diploma, the Advanced Diploma and the Extended Project.

CHOOSING YOUR COURSE (SEE ALSO CH.1)

Some course features

Aberystwyth The four-year BA course in European Studies combines a European language (French, German or Spanish) with a study of European economic, political and legal institutions. There are also separate degree courses in European Languages, European History and European Politics.

Aston The European Studies programme is a Joint or Combined Honours course offering a choice between French or German and topics covering the history and development of the European Union, European law, current affairs and international relations. European Studies is also offered with Business Administration, Public Policy and Management, and Sociology. There is a one year placement year following Year 2.

Essex European Studies is offered with a range of subjects including French, German, Italian, Spanish, and Politics and Economics. Beginners courses are possible and it is possible to transfer between courses. Previous language skills are not a necessity as the year abroad is taught in English.

Hertfordshire The European Studies programme offers courses with 12 other subjects such as Business, Health Studies, Biology, Geography, Law, Sports Studies and Tourism.

London (UCL) European Social and Political Studies is a four-year degree that combines the study of one or two European languages (from Dutch, French, German, Italian, Russian, Scandinavian languages and Spanish) with a chosen humanities or social science specialisation including Anthropology, Economics, Geography, History, Law, Philosophy or Politics. The third year is spent abroad. Degree courses are also offered in East European Studies with Bulgarian, Czech, Slovak, Finnish, Hungarian, Polish, Romanian, Serbian, and Ukrainian.

Portsmouth European Studies is a three-year course covering European history, culture and a specialist knowledge of EU policy of a particular European country. Language study is optional. European Studies can be taken with International Relations, Law or languages.

Southampton The Contemporary Europe degree comprises a study of the history and politics of Europe and European Union institutions, with options in economics, history, law or politics. Two European languages are studied from French, German or Spanish. Portuguese is offered as a minor language. Scholarships available.

Sussex There is a degree in International Relations and Contemporary European Studies. The latter can be taken as part of a joint degree or as a minor subject.

UEA In the School of International and European Studies a foundation (first) year leads to a wide range of options.

Universities and colleges teaching quality See www.qaa.ac.uk; http://unistats.direct.gov.uk.

Top research universities and colleges (RAE 2008) Southampton; Sussex; Birmingham; Portsmouth; Cardiff; Bath; Liverpool; Aberystwyth.

ADMISSIONS INFORMATION

Number of applicants per place (approx) Aberystwyth 10; Aston 5; Cardiff 5; Dundee 6; Durham 2; Hull 6; Kent 11; Lancaster 9; Leicester 15; London (King's) 7; London (UCL) 2; London South Bank 6; Loughborough 4; Northumbria 7; Nottingham 6; Nottingham Trent 12; Portsmouth 5; UEA 11.

Advice to applicants and planning the UCAS personal statement Try to identify an interest you have in the country relevant to your studies. Visits to that country should be described. Read the national newspapers and magazines and keep up to date with political and economic developments. Show your interest in the culture and civilisation of Europe as a whole, through, for example, European travel. Show your motivation for choosing the course and give details of your personal achievements and any future career plans, showing your international awareness and perspective.

Selection interviews Yes Durham, Hull, London (Gold), London Met, London South Bank, Stirling, Sussex, UEA; **Some** Cardiff, Dundee, Kent (not usually), LJMU, Loughborough, Portsmouth; **No** Essex, Reading.

Interview advice and questions Whilst your interest in studying a language may be the main reason for applying for this subject, the politics, economics and culture of European countries are constantly in the news. You should keep up-to-date with any such topics concerning your chosen country and be prepared for questions. A language test may occupy part of the interview. See also **Chapter 6**. **Loughborough** No tests. Interview designed to inform students about the course.

Reasons for rejection (non-academic) Poor powers of expression. Lack of ideas on any issues. Lack of enthusiasm.

Check **Chapter 4** when choosing your university and **Chapter 7** on how to read the subject tables.

AFTER-RESULTS ADVICE

Offers to applicants repeating A-levels Higher Aberystwyth, UEA; **Same** Aston, Cardiff, Dundee, LJMU, London South Bank, Loughborough.

GRADUATE DESTINATIONS AND EMPLOYMENT (2009/10 HESA)

Graduates surveyed 290 **Employed** 110 **In voluntary employment** 15 **In further study** 80 **Assumed unemployed** 10

Career note See **Languages**.

OTHER DEGREE SUBJECTS FOR CONSIDERATION

Business and Management; History; International Relations; Politics; Language courses.

FILM, RADIO, VIDEO and TV STUDIES

(see also Art and Design (Graphic Design), Communication Studies/Communication, Engineering (Acoustics and Sound), Media Studies, Photography)

A wide range of courses in this field are on offer although applicants should be aware that many courses cover theoretical or historical aspects of the subject. Students wishing to follow courses with practical applications must check with the institution beforehand to determine how much time in the course is spent on actual film-making or video production.

Useful websites www.bfi.org.uk; www.film.com; www.allmovie.com; www.bksts.com; www.imdb. com; www.fwfr.com; www.bafta.org; www.movingimage.us; www.britfilms.com; www.filmsite.org; www.festival-cannes.com/en; www.bbc.co.uk/jobs; http://rogerebert.suntimes.com; www. radiostudiesnetwork.org.uk.

NB The points totals shown to the left of the institutions are for ease of reference only. It must not be assumed that Tariff points are always used by institutions or that they can be substituted for an offer in grades. The level of an offer is not necessarily indicative of the quality of a course.

COURSE OFFERS INFORMATION

Subject requirements/preferences GCSE English usually required. Courses vary, check prospectuses. **AL** English may be stipulated for some courses.

Your target offers and examples of courses provided by each institution
410 pts London (King's) – AAAb (Engl Film St) (IB 38 pts HL 666 incl Engl)
400 pts London (King's) – AAAc (Compar Lit Film St) (IB 38 pts HL 6 Engl)
390 pts Warwick – AABb (Film Lit) (IB 36 pts)
380 pts London (King's) – AABc (Film St) (IB 36 pts HL 6 Engl)
360 pts Newcastle – AAA (Film St Comb Hons)
    St Andrews – AAA–AAB (Film St courses) (IB 35–38 pts)
340 pts Exeter – AAB–ABB (Film St courses)
    Kent – AAB (Film St) (IB 33 pts)
    Lancaster – AAB (Film St Engl Lit) (IB 34 pts)
    St Andrews – AAB (Anc Hist Film St) (IB 35 pts)
    Southampton – AAB (Film St) (IB 34 pts HL 17 pts)
    Sussex – AAB–ABB (Film St) (IB 34 pts)
    UEA – AAB–BBB (Film Am St/Engl St/TV St) (IB 31–33 pts)
320 pts Birmingham – ABB (Modn Lang Film St) (IB 32 pts)
    Bristol UWE – 320–340 pts (Film St Engl/Media/Scr Writ)
    Essex – 300–320 pts (Phil Film) (IB 29 pts)
    Glasgow – ABB (Film TV St Joint Hons) (IB 36 pts)
    Kent – ABB (Film St courses) (IB 33 pts)
    Lancaster – ABB (Film St) (IB 32 pts)

Leeds – ABB–AAB (Span Wrld Cnma) (IB 34 pts HL 16 pts)
London (QM) – 320–340 pts (Film St) (IB 32 pts)
London (RH) – ABB–ABbb (Film TV St)
Nottingham – ABB (Film TV St Fr) (IB 32 pts)
Surrey – ABB 320 pts (Film St Crea Writ)
UEA – ABB–BBB (Phil Film St) (IB 32–31 pts)
Westminster – ABB (Film TV Prod) (IB 30 pts)
York – ABB (Film TV Prod) (IB 31 pts)

300 pts Aberdeen – BBB (Film Vis Cult) (IB 28 pts)
Aberystwyth – 300–320 pts (Film TV St) (IB 30 pts)
Birmingham City – 300 pts (TV Tech Prod)
Brunel – contact admissions office BBB (Engl Film TV St) (IB 32 pts)
Edinburgh (CA) – BBB (Film TV) (IB 34 pts)
Essex – ABB–BBB 320–300 pts (Film St) (IB 34–32 pts)
Glamorgan – BBB 300 pts (Film Vid; Film St)
Hertfordshire – 280–300 pts (Film TV (Fctn/Doc/Enter); Engl Lang Comm Film)
Keele – 300–320 pts (Film St)
Leeds – BBB (TV Prod) (IB 32 pts)
Leicester – BBB (Film St Vis Art)
Liverpool – BBB (Film St (Euro) Modn Lang) (IB 30–35 pts)
Northumbria – 300 pts (Film TV St)
Nottingham – BBB (Film TV St Ger) (IB 30 pts)
Queen's Belfast – BBB/BBCb (Film St courses)
Reading – 300–340 pts (Engl Lit Film Thea Arts; Film Thea; Film)
Roehampton – 300 pts (Film)
Teesside – 300 pts (Fn Art)

280 pts Brighton – BBC (Film Script St) (IB 28 pts)
Derby – 280 pts (Media Prod)
Edge Hill – 280 pts (Film TV Prod; Media Film TV; Film St)
Gloucestershire – 280–300 pts (Film St; Dig Film Prod; Film St Media Writ)
Greenwich – 280 pts (Film St; Film TV Prod; Dig Film Prod)
Leeds Trinity (UC) – 280 pts (Film St; Film TV St; TV)
Lincoln – 280 pts (Film TV; Film TV Jrnl Joint Hons)
LJMU – 280 pts (Crea Writ Flm St) (IB 29 pts)
Manchester Met – 280 pts (St Film) (IB 28 pts)
Norwich (UCA) – BBC (Film Mov Imag Prod) (IB 25 pts)
Oxford Brookes – BBC (Film St) (IB 30 pts)
Reading – 280–300 pts (Art Film Thea)
Stirling – BBC (Glob Cin Cult) (IB 32 pts)
Salford – (Film St)
Sheffield Hallam – 280 pts (Film Media Prod)
Suffolk (Univ Campus) – 280 pts (Film)
Teesside – 280 pts (TV Film Prod)

260 pts Anglia Ruskin – 220–260 pts (Writ Film St)
Bangor – 260–300 pts (Film St courses; Mus Film St)
Bournemouth Arts (UC) – BCC (Film Prod; Animat Prod)
Brunel – BCC (Film TV St) (IB 29 pts)
Canterbury Christ Church – 260 pts (Film Rad TV St courses)
Chester – 260–300 pts (TV Prod) (IB 28 pts)
De Montfort – 260 pts (Aud Rec Tech)
Derby – 260 pts (Film Vid Prod)
Dundee – BCC (Engl Film St)
Edinburgh Queen Margaret – 260 pts (Film Media)
Hull – 260–300 pts (Sociol Film St)
London Met – 260 pts (Film St; Engl Lit Film TV St)

Check **Chapter 4** when choosing your university and **Chapter 7** on how to read the subject tables.

Newport – 240–260 pts (Film Vid)
Northampton – 260–280 pts (Film TV St courses)
Nottingham Trent – 260 pts (Film TV Joint Hons)
Sunderland – 260 pts (Film Media; Dig Film Prod; Engl Film; Media Prod (Vid N Media); Script (Film TV Rad); Media Prod (TV Rad))
UCLan – 260 pts (Film TV Scrnwrit; Film Prod; Film Media)
Ulster – BCC (Film St courses)
Winchester – 260–300 pts (Film St courses)

240 pts **Arts London (CFash)** – 240 pts (Tech Efcts Perf)
Bournemouth – 240 pts (Film Prod Cnma)
Bradford – 240 pts (TV Prod; Film St)
Chester – 240–280 pts (Film St) (IB 26 pts)
Cumbria – 240 pts (Film TV Prod)
De Montfort – 240 pts (Rad Prod; Film St Photo Vid)
Derby – 240 pts (Film TV St; Film St)
Huddersfield – 240 pts (Dig Film Vis Efcts Prod; Film Animat Mus Enter)
Kingston – 240 pts (Film St)
Leeds Met – 240 pts (Film Mov Imag Prod) (IB 24 pts)
Leeds Trinity (UC) – 240 pts (Eng Film St)
London South Bank – 240 pts (Film St; Dig Film Vid)
Newport – 240-260 pts (Doc Film TV)
Nottingham Trent – 240 pts (Des Film TV; Dig Media Tech; Dig Media Tech)
Portsmouth – 240–300 pts (Film St courses)
Ravensbourne – AA–CC (Dig Film Prod) (IB 28 pts)
Staffordshire – 240 pts (Media (Film) Prod; Film TV Rad St)
St Mary's Twickenham (UC) – 240 pts (Film Pop Cult) (IB 28 pts)
Sheffield Hallam – 240 pts (Film Scrnwrit)
Southampton Solent – 240 pts (Film TV St; Film; Engl Film; Scrnwrit; TV Vid Prod; TV Std Prod)
West Scotland – CCC (Film Scrnwrit)
Worcester – 240–300 pts (Film St Scrn Writ)

220 pts **Anglia Ruskin** – 220–260 pts (Film St)
Bath Spa – 220–280 pts (Film Scrn St courses)
Bishop Grosseteste (UC) – 220 pts (Vis Art Hist)
Edinburgh Napier – 220 pts (Engl Film)
Falmouth (UC) – 220 pts (Film)
Sunderland – 220 pts (Photo Vid Dig Imag)
Wolverhampton – 160–220 pts (Film St courses)
Worcester – 220–260 pts (Dig Film Prod)
York St John – 220–260 pts (Film TV Prod)

200 pts **Anglia Ruskin** – 200–240 pts (Film TV Prod)
Bedfordshire – 200 pts (TV Prod)
Bucks New – 200–240 pts (Film TV Prod)
Creative Arts – 200 pts (Film Prod) (IB 30 pts)
Doncaster (Coll Univ Centre) – 200 pts (Mov Imag Prod)
Hull – 200 pts (TV Film Des)
Hull (Coll) – 200 pts (TV Film Des)
Middlesex – 200–300 pts (Film St; Film Media Cult St)
Plymouth (CA) – 200 pts (Film)
Salford – 200 pts (Vis Arts)
Swansea Met – 200 pts (Vid Art; Doc Vid; Vid)
UEL – 200 pts (Film St; Film Vid (Theor Prac))
West London – 200 pts (Film)
Wolverhampton – 200 pts (Dr Film St)

180 pts **West Scotland** – BC–CC (Broad Prod)

BA Film and Television Studies
Joint honours also available with
Theatre
English
Games Design

BA Games Design
Joint honours also available with
Theatre
English
Creative Writing
Sonic Arts
Film and Television Studies

Find out more about the School of Arts at
www.brunel.ac.uk/arts

Brunel
UNIVERSITY
L O N D O N

160 pts Colchester (Inst) – 160 pts (Film Mus Sndtrk Prod)
 80 pts Arts London – 80 pts (Film TV)
       RConsvS – 80 pts (Dig Film TV)

Alternative offers
See **Chapter 7** and **Appendix 1** for grades/UCAS Tariff points information for the International Baccalaureate, Scottish Highers/Advanced Highers, the Welsh Baccalaureate, the Irish Leaving Certificate, the Cambridge Pre-U Diploma, the Advanced Diploma and the Extended Project.

EXAMPLES OF FOUNDATION DEGREES IN THE SUBJECT FIELD
Accrington and Rossendale (Coll); Barking (Coll); Bournemouth and Poole (Coll); Bradford (Coll Univ Centre); Brooksby Melton (Coll); Cleveland (CAD); Colchester (Inst); Cornwall (Coll); Croydon (Coll); East Surrey (Coll); Exeter (Coll); Farnborough (CT); Grimsby (IFHE); Manchester (Coll); Nescot; SAE Institute; Solihull (Coll); Truro (Coll); Warwickshire (Coll).

CHOOSING YOUR COURSE (SEE ALSO CH.1)
Some course features
Bradford Film Studies is a largely theoretical course. 20% of the time is spent on practical work.
Bucks New The Film and TV Production course covers camera work, lighting, sound and editing. A creative production-based course is also offered in Digital Film Art. There is also a scriptwriting course.
Essex Film Studies is a broad course focusing on the social and historical aspects of the media. It is offered as a joint programme with Creative Writing, History of Art, Literature or History and American Studies, and a year abroad is available.
Hertfordshire These degrees are offered in Film and Television specialising in Fiction Documentary or Entertainment. There are also degrees in Screen Cultures with Media. There is also a course in Special Effects.

Check **Chapter 4** when choosing your university and **Chapter 7** on how to read the subject tables.

Manchester Theoretical and academic courses are offered in Film Studies which can be combined with Media and Cultural Studies, Creative Writing or Video. There are also courses in TV Journalism and Production.

Manchester Met Practical work is the main focus of the Studies in Film programme whilst the Film and Media Studies course is a predominantly critical and textual academic study.

Oxford Brookes Studies can be taken as a Single Honours course or combined with one of nine other subjects including Japanese language, Marketing or Music.

Portsmouth (Film St) The course allows students to combine their interests in reading, writing and the use of language.

Reading The Film, Theatre and Television course integrates practical work, a critical study of film and theatre and the historical and social significance of television.

Southampton Solent (Film Vid Tech) Practical production units in film and digital video-making alongside academic study.

UEA Emphasis on the history and theory of film with practical units offered in Years 2 and 3. Study abroad available in Europe, USA and Australia.

York (Film TV Prod) This new BSc course combines practical production work with theoretical and historical understanding, involving students in a wide range of technical roles.

Universities and colleges teaching quality See www.qaa.ac.uk; http://unistats.direct.gov.uk.

Top research universities and colleges (RAE 2008) See **Drama**.

Examples of sandwich degree courses Aberystwyth; Birmingham City; Bristol UWE; Hertfordshire; Kingston; Leeds Met; Portsmouth; Southampton Solent; Staffordshire; Surrey; Teesside; Wolverhampton.

ADMISSIONS INFORMATION

Number of applicants per place (approx) Bournemouth 30; Bournemouth Arts (UC) 9; Brunel 10; Canterbury Christ Church 50; Cardiff 11; Kent 30; Leicester 9; Leicester (Coll) 5; LJMU 17; London Met 7; Portsmouth 20; Sheffield Hallam 60; Southampton 5; Southampton Solent 7; Staffordshire 31; Stirling 12; UCLan 5; UEA (Film Engl St) 7, (Film Am St) 5; Warwick 18; Westminster 41; York 4; York St John 6.

Advice to applicants and planning the UCAS personal statement **Bournemouth Arts (UC)** Any experience in film-making (beyond home videos) should be described in detail. Knowledge and preferences of types of films and the work of some producers should be included on the UCAS application. Read film magazines and other appropriate literature to keep informed of developments. Show genuine interest in a range of film genres and be knowledgeable about favourite films, directors and give details of work experience or film projects undertaken. You should also be able to discuss the ways in which films relate to broader cultural phenomena, social, literary, historical. See also **Appendix 3**.

Newport We require a portfolio showing how your ideas have developed.

Misconceptions about this course That an A-level film or media studies is required; it is not. That it's Film so it's easy! That the course is all practical work. Some applicants believe that these are Media courses. Some applicants believe that Film and TV Studies is a training for production work. **Bournemouth Arts (UC)** (Animat Prod) This is not a Film Studies course but a course based on traditional animation with supported computer image processing. **De Montfort** Some believe that this is a course in practical film-making: it is not, it is for analysts and historians. **Winchester** That graduation automatically leads to a job in broadcasting!

Selection interviews Most institutions will interview some applicants in this subject. **Yes** Birmingham City, Bournemouth, Bournemouth Arts (UC), Brunel, Canterbury Christ Church, Chichester, LJMU, Newport, Reading, York, York St John; **Some** Southampton, Staffordshire, Wolverhampton; **No** Essex, Nottingham, UEA.

Interview advice and questions Questions will focus on your chosen field. In the case of films be prepared to answer questions not only on your favourite films but on the work of one or two directors you admire and early Hollywood examples. See also **Chapter 6**. **Bournemouth** (TV Script Film) Successful applicants will be required to submit a 20-page screenplay. A good applicant will have the ability to discuss media issues in depth, to have total commitment to TV and video production and will have attempted to make programmes. **Bournemouth Arts (UC)** Written piece prior to interview. Questions at interview relevant to the portfolio/reel. **Staffordshire** We assess essay-writing skills.

Reasons for rejection (non-academic) Not enough drive or ambition. No creative or original ideas. Preference for production work rather than practical work. Inability to articulate the thought process behind the work in the applicant's portfolio. Insufficient knowledge of media affairs. Lack of knowledge of film history. Wrong course choice, wanted more practical work.

AFTER-RESULTS ADVICE
Offers to applicants repeating A-levels **Higher** Bournemouth Arts (UC), Glasgow, Manchester Met; **Same** De Montfort, Liverpool Hope, St Mary's Twickenham (UC), Staffordshire, Stirling, UEA, Winchester, Wolverhampton, York St John.

GRADUATE DESTINATIONS AND EMPLOYMENT (2009/10 HESA)
See **Media Studies**.

Career note Although this is a popular subject field, job opportunities in film, TV and radio are limited. Successful graduates frequently have gained work experience with companies during their undergraduate years. The transferable skills (verbal communication etc) will open up other career opportunities.

OTHER DEGREE SUBJECTS FOR CONSIDERATION
Animation; Communication Studies; Creative Writing; Media Studies; Photography.

FINANCE

(including **Banking**, **Financial Services** and **Insurance**; see also **Accountancy/Accounting**)

Financial Services courses provide a comprehensive view of the world of finance and normally cover banking, insurance, investment, building societies, international finance, accounting and economics. Major banks offer sponsorships for some of the specialised Banking courses.

Useful websites www.cii.co.uk; www.secinst.co.uk; www.financialadvice.co.uk; www.efinancialnews. com; www.worldbank.org; www.ifslearning.ac.uk; www.ft.com.

NB The points totals shown to the left of the institutions are for ease of reference only. It must not be assumed that Tariff points are always used by institutions or that they can be substituted for an offer in grades. The level of an offer is not necessarily indicative of the quality of a course.

COURSE OFFERS INFORMATION
Subject requirements/preferences **GCSE** Most institutions will require English and mathematics grade C minimum. **AL** Mathematics may be required or preferred.

Your target offers and examples of courses provided by each institution
390 pts **Warwick** – AAAb-A*AA (Acc Fin) (IB 38 pts)
380 pts **Bristol** – A*AA-ABB (Econ courses) (IB 38–35 pts)
     Exeter – A*AA-AAB (Maths Fin) (IB 38–34 pts)
     London (UCL) – A*AA-AAB (Eng Bus Fin MEng) (IB 38–39 pts)
360 pts **Aston** – AAB-AAA 340–360 pts (Fin) (IB 35 pts)
     Bath – AAA (Acc Fin) (IB 38 pts HL 5–6 maths)
     Birmingham – AAA (Port Mny Bank Fin) (IB 36–38 pts)
     City – AAA 360 pts (Maths Fin) (IB 32 pts)
     Exeter – AAA-AAB (Acc Fin) (IB 36–34 pts)

Glasgow – AAA–A*AB (Fin Stats) (IB 36 pts)
Leeds – AAA (Int Bus Fin) (IB 35 pts HL 17 pts)
London (RH) – AAA–AAB (Fin Bus Econ) (IB 32 pts)
London LSE – AAA (Stats Fin) (IB 38 pts HL 17 pts)
Manchester – A*AB–AAB 340–360 pts (Maths Fin Maths) (IB 36 pts)
Nottingham – AAA–A*AB (Fin Maths) (IB 36 pts)
Reading – 340–360 pts (Fin Inv Bank)
St Andrews – AAA (Fin Econ) (IB 38 pts)
Strathclyde – AAA (Mech Eng Fin Mgt MEng) (IB 36 pts)
Southampton – AAA incl maths (Econ Fin) (IB 36 pts HL 18 pts)

340 pts **Birmingham** – AAB (Acc Fin) (IB 34–36 pts)
Bradford – AAB (Acc Fin)
Bristol – AAA–AAB 340–360 pts (Acc Fin) (IB 35–37 pts)
Cardiff – AAB (Fin Mgt)
ifs School of Finance – 340 pts (Fin Analys Rk)
Kent – AAB–ABB (Acc Fin courses) (IB 33 pts)
Lancaster – AAB 340 pts (Fin Mgt St) (IB 34 pts)
Leeds – AAB (Maths Fin) (IB 35 pts HL 17 pts)
Leicester – AAB (Fin Econ) (IB 32 pts)
Liverpool – AAB (e-Fin) (IB 33 pts HL 5 maths)
London (QM) – 340 pts (Maths Fin Acc) (IB 34 pts)
Loughborough – AAB (Bank Fin Mgt) (IB 36 pts HL 6 maths)
Manchester – AAB (Acc Fin) (IB 35–37 pts)
Newcastle – AAB (Fin Maths) (IB 34–36 pts)
Nottingham – AAB (Fin Acc Mgt) (IB 34 pts)
Reading – 340–360 pts (Invest Fin Bank)
Strathclyde – AAB (Acc Fin)
Sheffield – AAB (Acc Fin Mgt Joint Hons) (IB 35 pts)
Southampton – AAB 340 pts (Acc Fin) (IB 34 pts HL 17 pts)
Surrey – 340–360 pts (Fin Maths)
Sussex – AAB (Fin Bus) (IB 35 pts)
York – AAB (Econ Ecomet Fin) (IB 36 pts HL 666)

320 pts **Bournemouth** – 320 pts (Fin Bus; Econ Fin)
Bradford – 320 pts (Fin Plan)
Durham – ABB (Acc Fin) (IB 34 pts)
Essex – ABB 320 pts (Acc Fin) (IB 29 pts)
Keele – ABB (Acc Fin) (IB 28–30 pts)
Kent – ABB (Fin Econ) (IB 33 pts)
Lancaster – ABB (Acc Fin Comp Sci) (IB 34 pts)
Liverpool – ABB (Maths Fin) (IB 33 pts HL 6 maths)
London (QM) – 320 pts (Maths Stats Fin Econ) (IB 34 pts HL 6 maths)
Nottingham – ABB (Acc Fin Contemp Chin) (IB 32 pts)
Queen's Belfast – ABB/BBBb (Fin) (IB 32 pts)
Strathclyde – ABB (Fin courses) (IB 34 pts)
Sheffield – ABB (Acc Fin Mgt) (IB 33 pts)
Swansea – ABB–BBB (Bus Mgt Fin) (IB 33 pts)
York – ABB (Acc Bus Fin Mgt) (IB 34 pts)

300 pts **Aberdeen** – BBB (Fin) (IB 28 pts)
Aberystwyth – 300 pts (Acc Fin) (IB 27 pts)
Brighton – BBB (Fin Inv) (IB 32 pts HL 16 pts)
Bristol UWE – 300 pts (Bus St Acc Fin) (IB 24–28 pts)
Brunel – BBB (Fin Acc) (IB 32 pts)
Buckingham – 300 pts (Law Bus Fin)
Cardiff Met – 300 pts (Bus Mgt Fin; Int Econ Fin)
Edinburgh – AAA–BBB 300–360 pts (Econ Fin) (IB 34 pts)

Glamorgan – BBB (Fin Maths)
Greenwich – 300 pts (Acc Fin)
Heriot-Watt – ABC–BBB (Bus Fin; Acc Fin)
Huddersfield – 300 pts (Bus Fin Serv; Acc Fin)
ifs School of Finance – 300 pts (Bank Prac Mgt; Fin Acc Fin Serv)
Lincoln – 300 pts (Law Fin)
Northumbria – 300 pts (Fin Inv Mgt)
Nottingham Trent – 300 pts (Econ Fin Bank; Acc Fin)
Plymouth – 300 pts (Maths Fin)
Portsmouth – 300 pts (Acc Fin; Fin)
Salford – 300 pts (Bus Fin Mgt)
Sheffield Hallam – 300 pts (Acc Fin; Bus Fin; Int Fin)
UEA – BBB (Acc Fin) (IB 30 pts)

280 pts **Birmingham City** – 280 pts (Acc Fin; Bus Fin)
Brighton – BBC (Maths Fin) (IB 28 pts)
Brunel – BBC (Econ Bus Fin) (IB 32–33 pts)
Coventry – 280–300 pts (Acc Fin)
De Montfort – 280 pts (Econ Fin; Fin; Fin Mgt)
Derby – 280 pts (Acc Fin)
Glamorgan – 280 pts (Acc Fin)
Gloucestershire – 280 pts (Bus Fin Mgt)
Greenwich – 280 pts (Econ Bank)
Holborn (Coll) – 280 pts (Acc Fin)
Hull – 280 pts (Fin Mgt)
Keele – 280–340 pts incl BB/AB (Fin) (IB 28–30 pts)
Lincoln – 280 pts (Acc Fin; Bus Fin)
LJMU – 280 pts (Acc Fin) (IB 28 pts)
London South Bank – 280 pts (Acc Fin)
Manchester Met – 280 pts (Fin Serv Plan Mgt) (IB 28 pts)
Nottingham Trent – 280 pts (Fin Maths)
Oxford Brookes – BBC (Econ Fin Int Bus) (IB 29 pts)
Portsmouth – 280–320 pts (Econ Fin Bank)
Stirling – BBC (Fin) (IB 32 pts)
Suffolk (Univ Campus) – 280 pts (Bus Mgt Fin)
Westminster – BBC (Fin Mgt)

260 pts **Bangor** – 260–300 pts (Acc Fin; Bank Fin; Mgt Bank Fin)
BPP (UC) – check with admissions tutor (Bank Fin)
Buckingham – 260 pts (Comp Acc Fin)
Dundee – BCC (Fin) (IB 30 pts)
Gloucestershire – 260–300 pts (Acc Fin Mgt)
Greenwich – 260 pts (Bus Fin; Fin Maths)
Hertfordshire – 260 pts (Fin)
Northampton – 260–280 pts (Fin Serv Mgt)
Portsmouth – 260–280 pts (Int Fin Tr)
Robert Gordon – BCC (Acc Fin) (IB 20 pts)
Staffordshire – BCC 260 pts (Acc Fin) (IB 26 pts)
Sunderland – 260 pts (Bus Fin Mgt)
UCLan – 260–280 pts (Acc Fin St)
Winchester – 260–300 pts (Bus Mgt Fin Econ)

240 pts **Bradford (Coll Univ Centre)** – 240 pts (Fin Serv)
Canterbury Christ Church – 240 pts (Bus Fin)
Chester – 240–280 pts (Acc Fin)
Chichester – CCC (Acc Fin)
Edinburgh Napier – 240 pts (Fin Serv)
Euro Bus Sch London – 240 pts (Int Bus Fin Lang)

ifs *School of Finance*
Incorporated by Royal Charter

Professional degrees for careers in banking and finance

BSc (Hons) in Banking Practice and Management
UCAS Code N310

BSc (Hons) in Finance and Accounting for Financial Services
UCAS Code NN34

BSc (Hons) in Financial Analysis and Risk*
Available from September 2013

With its dedicated focus on banking and finance and over 130 years experience of educating financial services professionals, the *ifs* *School of Finance* offers you a learning experience of the highest quality designed to give you the knowledge, skills and insight that you need for a successful career.

Studying with the *ifs* not only gives you a recognised and respected honours degree on a par with any other, but also a professional qualification recognised by financial services employers the world over.

Our degrees have been designed with three core objectives in mind:

- providing the essential academic knowledge needed for a successful career in financial services
- developing the skills and understanding necessary to put this knowledge into practice in a fast-paced commercial environment
- enhancing employability prospects through access to industry professionals and employers via the *ifs*' extensive alumni network and industry contacts

*Subject to validation

enquiries@ifslearning.ac.uk   01227 829499

The *ifs* *School of Finance* is a not-for-profit professional body and registered charity, incorporated by Royal Charter.

Glasgow Caledonian – CCC (Fin Inv Risk)
Hertfordshire – 240 pts (Fin Maths)
London Met – 240 pts (Acc Fin; Bank; Bank Fin; Fin; Fin Serv; Fin Econ)
Newport – 240 pts (Acc Fin)
Plymouth – 240 pts (Int Fin; Fin Econ; Acc Fin)
Regents Bus Sch London – CCC (Glob Fin Mgt)
Teesside – 240 pts (Acc Fin) (IB 30 pts)
Ulster – 240 pts (Bank Fin)

220 pts **Leeds Met** – 220 pts (Acc Fin) (IB 24 pts)

200 pts **Bedfordshire** – 200 pts (Int Fin; Bus St (Fin))
Bucks New – 200–240 pts (Ftbl Bus Fin; Bus Fin; Acc Fin)
Kingston – check with admissions tutor 200 pts (Bank Fin)
Middlesex – 200–300 pts (Acc Fin)
Peterborough (Univ Centre) – 200 pts (Acc Fin)
UEL – 200 pts (Fin Mny Bank; Acc Fin)
West London – 200 pts (Acc Fin; Bus St Fin)
York St John – 200–240 pts (Bus Mgt (Fin))

180 pts **Abertay Dundee** – DDD (Fin Bus)

160 pts **Greenwich (Sch Mgt)** – 160 pts (Acc Fin)
Swansea Met – 160 pts (Bus Fin)

120 pts **Croydon (Coll)** – 120 pts (Bus Fin)

Alternative offers

See **Chapter 7** and **Appendix 1** for grades/UCAS Tariff points information for the International Baccalaureate, Scottish Highers/Advanced Highers, the Welsh Baccalaureate, the Irish Leaving Certificate, the Cambridge Pre-U Diploma, the Advanced Diploma and the Extended Project.

EXAMPLES OF FOUNDATION DEGREES IN THE SUBJECT FIELD

Blackburn (Coll); Chichester (Coll); Cornwall (Coll); Croydon (Coll); Dudley (Coll); Hertfordshire; Hopwood Hall (Coll); Loughborough (Coll); Manchester (Coll); Newcastle (Coll); Nottingham New (Coll); Truro (Coll); UCP Marjon.

CHOOSING YOUR COURSE (SEE ALSO CH.1)

Some course features

Brighton (Fin Invest) The course in Finance and Investment shares a common first year with the Economics and Finance degree, making transfers possible.

Durham A course in Business Finance covering economics, management, marketing and international money. It shares a first year with Accountancy and Business degrees with options to transfer at the end of the year.

Reading Courses are offered in Finance and Investment Banking or Property Investment. Internships can be arranged during summer vactations.

Surrey The course in Financial Mathematics is designed to match the needs of industry and can be taken to include a Professional Training year adding considerably to employment prospects.

Universities and colleges teaching quality See www.qaa.ac.uk; http://unistats.direct.gov.uk.

Top research universities and colleges (RAE 2008) See **Accountancy/Accounting**.

Examples of sandwich degree courses Abertay Dundee; Bath; Bournemouth; Brighton; Bristol UWE; Brunel; City; Coventry; De Montfort; Glamorgan; Gloucestershire; Hertfordshire; Huddersfield; Kingston; Lancaster; Leeds Met; Loughborough; Manchester Met; Middlesex; Nottingham Trent; Plymouth; Portsmouth; Sheffield Hallam; Surrey; Swansea Met; Teesside; Westminster; Wolverhampton; Worcester.

ADMISSIONS INFORMATION

Number of applicants per place (approx) Aberystwyth 4; Bangor 10; Birmingham 3; Birmingham City 13; Bristol UWE 4; Buckingham 4; Cardiff 10; City 10; Dundee 5; Durham 4; Glamorgan 3;

Loughborough 35; Manchester 22; Middlesex 3; Northampton 3; Portsmouth 4; Sheffield Hallam 4; UCLan 6.

Advice to applicants and planning the UCAS personal statement Visits to banks or insurance companies should be described, giving details of any work experience or work shadowing done in various departments. Discuss any particular aspects of finance etc which interest you. See also **Appendix 4**.

Misconceptions about this course Many applicants believe that they can only enter careers in banking and finance when they graduate. In fact, business and industry provide wide-ranging opportunities.

Selection interviews Yes Buckingham (pref), Huddersfield; **Some** Dundee, Staffordshire, Stirling; **No** City.

Interview advice and questions Banking involves both high street and merchant banks, so a knowledge of banking activities in general will be expected. In the past mergers have been discussed and also the role of the Bank of England in the economy. The work of the accountant may be discussed. See also **Chapter 6**.

Reasons for rejection (non-academic) Lack of interest. Poor English. Lacking in motivation and determination to complete the course.

AFTER-RESULTS ADVICE
Offers to applicants repeating A-levels Higher Glasgow; **Possibly higher** Bangor; **Same** Birmingham, Birmingham City, Bradford, Cardiff, City, Dundee, Edinburgh Napier, London Met, Loughborough, Northumbria, Stirling.

GRADUATE DESTINATIONS AND EMPLOYMENT (2009/10 HESA)
Graduates surveyed 2805 **Employed** 1220 **In voluntary employment** 15 **In further study** 575 **Assumed unemployed** 245

Career note Most graduates enter financial careers. Further study is required to qualify as an accountant and to obtain other professional qualifications, eg Institute of Banking.

OTHER DEGREE SUBJECTS FOR CONSIDERATION
Accountancy; Actuarial Studies; Business Studies; Economics.

FOOD SCIENCE/STUDIES and TECHNOLOGY
(see also **Agricultural Sciences/Agriculture, Biochemistry, Consumer Studies/Sciences, Dietetics, Hospitality and Hotel Management, Nutrition**)

Biochemistry, microbiology, dietetics, human nutrition, food processing and technology are components of Food Science courses as well as being degree courses in their own right (and appropriate alternative courses). The study depends for its understanding on a secure foundation of several pure sciences – chemistry and two subjects from physics, mathematics, biology, botany or zoology. Only students offering subjects from these fields are likely to be considered. Food Technology covers the engineering aspects of food processing and management. A number of bursaries are offered by the food industry. Check with admissions tutors. See also **Appendix 3**.

Useful websites www.scienceyear.com; www.sofht.co.uk; www.ifst.org; www.defra.gov.uk; www. iagre.org.

NB The points totals shown to the left of the institutions are for ease of reference only. It must not be assumed that Tariff points are always used by institutions or that they can be substituted for an offer in grades. The level of an offer is not necessarily indicative of the quality of a course.

Check **Chapter 4** when choosing your university and **Chapter 7** on how to read the subject tables.

COURSE OFFERS INFORMATION

Subject requirements/preferences **GCSE** English, mathematics and a science. **AL** One or two mathematics/science subjects; chemistry may be required.

Your target offers and examples of courses provided by each institution

340 pts **Newcastle** – AAB (Fd Mark Nutr) (IB 32–35 pts)
Surrey – AAB (Fd Sci Microbiol) (IB 35 pts)

320 pts **Nottingham** – ABB–BBC (Nutr Fd Sci) (IB 28–32 pts)

300 pts **Heriot-Watt** – BBB (Biol Sci (Fd Sci))
Leeds – BBB (Fd Sci courses) (IB 32 pts HL 15 pts)
Nottingham – ABB–BBB 300–320 pts (Fd Microbiol) (IB 32–30 pts)
Queen's Belfast – BBB (Fd Qual Sfty Nutr) (IB 32 pts)
Reading – 300 pts (Fd Tech) (HL 655)

280 pts **Brighton** – BBC (Vit Oeno) (IB 30 pts)
Hertfordshire – 280–300 pts (Acc Fin) (IB 28 pts)
Leeds Trinity (UC) – 280 pts (Nutr Fd)
Manchester Met – 280 pts (Fd Tech) (IB 28 pts)
Northumbria – 280–300 pts (Fd Sci Nutr) (IB 28 pts)
Nottingham – ABB–BBC 280–320 pts (Fd Sci) (IB 32–28 pts)
Sheffield Hallam – 280 pts (Fd Mark Mgt)

260 pts **Derby** – 260–280 pts (Culn Art)
Glasgow Caledonian – BCC (Fd Biosci)
LJMU – 260 pts (Home Econ (Fd Des Tech))
Teesside – 260–280 pts (Fd Nutr Hlth Sci)

240 pts **Coventry** – CCC 240 pts (Fd Sci Nutr)
Huddersfield – 240 pts (Fd Nutr Hlth)
Reaseheath (Coll) – 240 pts (Fd Tech)
Royal (CAg) – 240 pts (Fd Prod Sply Mgt)
Ulster – 240 pts (Fd Nutr)

220 pts **Abertay Dundee** – 220–240 pts (Fd Sci Tech)
Bath Spa – 220–280 pts (Fd Nutr) (IB 24 pts)
Harper Adams (UC) – 220–260 pts (Consum St)

200 pts **Abertay Dundee** – CDD (Fd Consum Sci; Fd Nutr Hlth; Fd Prod Des)
Birmingham (UC) – 200 pts (Fd Consum Mgt) (IB 24 pts)
CAFRE – 200 pts (Fd Mgt Mark; Fd Des Nutr)
Cardiff Met – 200 pts (Fd Sci Tech)
London South Bank – CDD 200 pts (Fd Nutr)

180 pts **Harper Adams (UC)** – 180–240 pts (Agri-Fd Mark Bus St)

160 pts **SAC (Scottish CAg)** – CC (Fd Sci; Rur Bus Mgt (Fd))

Alternative offers

See **Chapter 7** and **Appendix 1** for grades/UCAS Tariff points information for the International Baccalaureate, Scottish Highers/Advanced Highers, the Welsh Baccalaureate, the Irish Leaving Certificate, the Cambridge Pre-U Diploma, the Advanced Diploma and the Extended Project.

EXAMPLES OF FOUNDATION DEGREES IN THE SUBJECT FIELD

Bridgwater (Coll); Brighton; Duchy (Coll); Grimsby (IFHE); Leeds City (Coll); Loughborough (Coll); Middlesex; Neath Port Talbot (Coll); Nottingham New (Coll); Oxford Brookes; Plymouth; Warwickshire (Coll); Worcester.

CHOOSING YOUR COURSE (SEE ALSO CH.1)

Some course features

Coventry The Food Science and Nutrition course deals with food analysis, food safety and human nutrition. There is also a four year Dietetics course in which they seek 'strong interpersonal skills, adaptability and flexibility'.

Harper Adams (UC) Food, Nutrition and Well-being, Food Supply Chain Management and Food and Consumer Studies are offered with a placement year in industry. There is also a more business centred degree in Agri-Food Marketing with Business Studies.

LJMU The Home Economics course qualifies graduates to work in the consumer and services industries and also to teach (Food Design and Technology).

Reading (Fd Tech) The course focuses on food products manufacture, food engineering and food materials, chemicals and microbiology (with Bioprocessing).

Universities and colleges teaching quality See www.qaa.ac.uk; http://unistats.direct.gov.uk.

Top research universities and colleges (RAE 2008) See **Agricultural Sciences/Agriculture** and **Nutrition**.

Examples of sandwich degree courses Birmingham (UC) 1; Cardiff Met 4.

ADMISSIONS INFORMATION

Number of applicants per place (approx) Bath Spa 4; Cardiff Met 1; Dundee 3; Huddersfield 4; Leeds 5; LJMU 2; London Met 5; London South Bank 3; Manchester Met 3; Newcastle 13; Nottingham 7; Oxford Brookes 20; Queen's Belfast 10; Robert Gordon 4; Sheffield Hallam 4; Surrey 17.

Advice to applicants and planning the UCAS personal statement Visits, work experience or work shadowing in any food manufacturing firm, or visits to laboratories, should be described on your UCAS application. Keep up-to-date with developments by reading journals relating to the industry.

Misconceptions about this course Some applicants confuse food technology with catering or hospitality management. Applicants under-estimate the job prospects. **Leeds** (Fd Sci) Food Science is not food technology, catering or cooking. It aims to understand why food materials behave in the way they do, in order to improve the nutritive value, safety and quality of the food we eat.

Selection interviews Yes London South Bank, Nottingham (depends on application), Queen's Belfast, Reading, Surrey; **Some** Abertay Dundee, Bath Spa, Leeds (applicants with non-standard qualifications), LJMU, Manchester Met, Salford; **No** Dundee.

Interview advice and questions Food science and technology is a specialised field and admissions tutors will want to know your reasons for choosing the subject. You will be questioned on any experience you have had in the food industry. More general questions may cover the reasons for the trends in the popularity of certain types of food, the value of junk food and whether scientific interference with food is justifiable. See also **Chapter 6**. **Leeds** Questions asked to ensure that the student understands, and can cope with, the science content of the course.

Reasons for rejection (non-academic) Too immature. Unlikely to integrate well. Lack of vocational commitment.

AFTER-RESULTS ADVICE

Offers to applicants repeating A-levels Higher Heriot-Watt, Leeds; **Possibly higher** Nottingham; **Same** Abertay Dundee, LJMU, Manchester Met, Queen's Belfast, Salford, Sheffield Hallam, Surrey, Wolverhampton.

GRADUATE DESTINATIONS AND EMPLOYMENT (2009/10 HESA)

Food and Beverage Studies; graduates surveyed 555 **Employed** 310 **In voluntary employment** 0 **In further study** 125 **Assumed unemployed** 50

Career note Employment levels for food graduates are high mainly in manufacturing and retailing and increasingly with large companies.

OTHER DEGREE SUBJECTS FOR CONSIDERATION

Biochemistry; Biological Sciences; Biology; Biotechnology; Chemistry; Consumer Studies; Crop Science; Dietetics; Health Studies; Hospitality Management; Nutrition; Plant Science.

Check **Chapter 4** when choosing your university and **Chapter 7** on how to read the subject tables.

FORESTRY

(see also Agricultural Sciences/Agriculture)

Forestry is concerned with the establishment and management of woodlands and forests for timber production, environmental, conservation and amenity purposes.

Useful websites www.iagre.org.uk; www.forestry.gov.uk; www.rfs.org.uk; www.charteredforesters.org; www.iwsc.org.uk; www.british-trees.com; www.woodland-trust.org.uk.

NB The points totals shown to the left of the institutions are for ease of reference only. It must not be assumed that Tariff points are always used by institutions or that they can be substituted for an offer in grades. The level of an offer is not necessarily indicative of the quality of a course.

COURSE OFFERS INFORMATION

Subject requirements/preferences GCSE English, mathematics or science usually required. Check prospectuses. **AL** Two science subjects are usually stipulated which can include mathematics, geography or geology.

Your target offers and examples of courses provided by each institution
260 pts Bangor – 260–320 pts (Cons Frst Ecosys)
240 pts Aberdeen – 240 pts (Frsty; Frst Sci)
    Cumbria – 240 pts (Frsty Wdlnd Mgt; Frsty Wdlnd Cons)
 60 pts UHI – D–A (Sust Frst Mgt)

Alternative offers
See **Chapter 7** and **Appendix 1** for grades/UCAS Tariff points information for the International Baccalaureate, Scottish Highers/Advanced Highers, the Welsh Baccalaureate, the Irish Leaving Certificate, the Cambridge Pre-U Diploma, the Advanced Diploma and the Extended Project.

EXAMPLES OF FOUNDATION DEGREES IN THE SUBJECT FIELD
Brighton; Sparsholt (Coll).

CHOOSING YOUR COURSE (SEE ALSO CH.1)
Some course features
Bangor Students on the four-year Conservation and Forest Ecosystems course spend 7–12 months of practical work with a forestry organisation.
UHI This applied fieldwork-based course focuses on the practical aspects of either forest or arboricultural conservation and management. It provides a technical management qualification and includes wood technology, woodland ecology and conservation, environmental economics, environmental change and capital project planning.

Universities and colleges teaching quality See www.qaa.ac.uk; http://unistats.direct.gov.uk.

Examples of sandwich degree courses Bangor; Cumbria.

ADMISSIONS INFORMATION
Number of applicants per place (approx) Bangor 2; Edinburgh 9.

Advice to applicants and planning the UCAS personal statement Contact the Forestry Commission and the Woodland Trust and try to arrange visits to forestry centres, local community woodlands and forests and to the Woodland Trust's sites. Discuss the work with forest officers and learn about future plans for specific forest areas and describe any visits made. Mention any experience of forestry or wood processing industries (for example, visits to forests and mills, work experience in relevant organisations).

Misconceptions about this course Bangor That the course provides practical training in forestry (for example, in the use of chainsaws and pesticides) or wood processing. It does not: it is intended to educate future managers, for example; not to train forestry or mill workers.

Selection interviews Most institutions.

Interview advice and questions Work experience or field courses attended are likely to be discussed and questions asked such as: What is arboriculture? On a desert island how would you get food from wood? How do you see forestry developing in the next hundred years? What aspects of forestry are the most important? See also **Chapter 6**. **Bangor** Why are you interested in forestry?

AFTER-RESULTS ADVICE
Offers to applicants repeating A-levels **Same** Bangor.

GRADUATE DESTINATIONS AND EMPLOYMENT (2009/10 HESA)
Graduates surveyed 200 **Employed** 100 **In voluntary employment** 0 **In further study** 40 **Assumed unemployed** 20

Career note Opportunities exist with the Forestry Commission as supervisors, managers and in some cases, scientists. Other employers include private landowners (especially in Scotland), co-operative forest societies, local authorities and commercial firms.

OTHER DEGREE SUBJECTS FOR CONSIDERATION
Agriculture; Biological Sciences; Countryside Management; Crop Science; Ecology; Environmental Sciences; Woodland and Wildlife Management.

FRENCH
(see also European Studies, Languages)

Applicants should select courses according to the emphasis which they prefer. Courses could focus on literature or language (or both), or on the written and spoken word, as in the case of interpreting and translating courses, or on the broader study of French culture, political and social aspects found on European Studies courses.

Useful websites http://europa.eu; www.visavis.org; www.bbc.co.uk/languages; http://languageadvantage.com; www.languagematters.co.uk; www.iol.org.uk; www.reed.co.uk/multilingual; www.cilt.org.uk; www.lemonde.Fr; www.institut-francais.org.uk; www.academie-francaise.Fr; www.institut-de-france.Fr; www.sfs.ac.uk; http://fs.oxfordjournals.org.

NB The points totals shown to the left of the institutions are for ease of reference only. It must not be assumed that Tariff points are always used by institutions or that they can be substituted for an offer in grades. The level of an offer is not necessarily indicative of the quality of a course.

COURSE OFFERS INFORMATION
Subject requirements/preferences **GCSE** French, mathematics (for Business courses), grade levels may be stipulated. **AL** French is usually required at a specific grade and in some cases a second language may be stipulated.

Your target offers and examples of courses provided by each institution
380 pts **Cambridge** – A*AA (Modn Mediev Lang (Fr)) (IB 40–42 pts HL 766–777)
    London (King's) – AABc (Fr/Ger/Hisp St Phil) (IB 36 pts)
    Nottingham – A*AA–AAA 360–380 pts (Econ Fr/Ger/Russ) (IB 38–36 pts)
360 pts **Bristol** – AAA–A*AB (Phil Modn Lang) (IB 37–35 pts HL 666)
    Exeter – AAA–ABB 360–340 pts (Hist Joint Hons) (IB 36–31 pts)
    Leicester – AAA (Law Fr Law Lang)
    London (RH) – AAA–AAB (Econ Fr/Ger/Ital/Span) (IB 33–35 pts)
    London (UCL) – AAA+AS–AAB+AS incl Fr (Fr) (IB 34–36 pts)
    Nottingham – AAA (Law Fr Fr Law/Ger Ger Law/Span Span Law) (IB 38 pts HL 7)
    Oxford – AAA (Fr courses) (IB 38–40 pts)

Southampton – AAA–ABB (Ocean Fr) (IB 36–32 pts HL 18–16 pts)
Sussex – AAA–AAB (Law Fr/Ital/Span (Yr Abrd)) (IB 35–36 pts)
Warwick – AAA (Engl Fr) (IB 38 pts)
York – AAA (Fr Hist)

340 pts **Bath** – AAB (Int Bus Fr) (IB 34–36 pts)
Bristol – AAB–BBC (Fr Modn Lang) (IB 33–30 pts)
Essex – AAB (Engl Fr Law) (IB 36 pts)
Exeter – AAB–ABB (Fr courses) (IB 34–32 pts)
London (RH) – AAB (Mgt Fr/Ger/Ital/Span) (IB 35 pts)
Manchester – AAB–ABB 320–340 pts (Fr courses) (IB 33–36 pts)
Nottingham – AAB (Mgt St Fr/Ger/Span) (IB 34 pts)
St Andrews – AAA–AAB (Fr courses) (IB 35–38 pts)
Sheffield – AAB (Law Ger/Fr/Span) (IB 35 pts)
Southampton – AAB (Pol Fr/Ger) (IB 34 pts HL 17 pts)
Surrey – AAB (Engl Lit Fr/Span) (IB 35 pts)
UEA – AAB–ABB (Transl Med Fr/Span 3 yrs) (IB 32–33 pts)
Warwick – AAB (Fr Joint Hons) (IB 36 pts)

330 pts **Bath** – ABB (Modn Langs Euro St (Fr and Span/Ital/Russ/Ger)) (IB 34 pts HL 6 Fr)
320 pts **Aston** – ABB–BBB 300–320 pts (Fr courses) (IB 33–34 pts)
Birmingham – ABB (Fr St) (IB 32 pts)
Cardiff – ABB (Fr)
Essex – 320 pts (Econ Fr) (IB 34 pts)
Glasgow – ABB (Fr Joint Hons) (IB 36 pts)
Hertfordshire – 320 pts (Law Fr)
Kent – ABB (Fr) (IB 33 pts)
Lancaster – ABB (Fr St courses) (IB 32 pts)
Leeds – ABB–AAB (Fr/Ger Stats)
Leicester – ABB (Fr Joint Hons)
Liverpool – ABB–BBB (Fr Joint Hons) (IB 33–30 pts)
London (Inst in Paris) – ABB (Fr St)
London (QM) – 320–340 pts (Fr courses) (IB 32 pts HL 6 Fr)
London (RH) – ABB (Fr Lat) (IB 34 pts)
Newcastle – AAB–ABB 320–340 pts (Ling Fr) (IB 32 pts)
Nottingham – ABB (Class Civ Fr/Ger) (IB 32 pts)
Strathclyde – ABB (Fr courses)
Surrey – ABB–BBB (Fr courses)
Sussex – ABB–BBB (Fr courses) (IB 32–34 pts)
UEA – ABB–BBB (Int Dev St Fr/Span/Jap) (IB 32–31 pts)
York – ABB (Fr courses except under **360 pts**) (IB 32 pts)

300 pts **Aberdeen** – BBB (Fr) (IB 28 pts)
Buckingham – 300 pts (Law Fr) (IB 30 pts)
Coventry – 300 pts (Law Fr/Span)
Dundee – BBB–BCC (Law Fr/Ger/Span)
Edinburgh – AAA–BBB 300–360 pts (Bus St Fr/Ger/Span)
Essex – 300 pts (Fr St Modn Langs) (IB 30 pts)
Heriot-Watt – BBB (App Langs Transl (Fr/Ger))
Hull – 300 pts (Hist Fr/Ger/Ital/Span)
Leeds – ABC–BBB (Fr courses) (IB 34 pts HL 6 Fr)
Liverpool – BBB (Fr) (IB 30 pts HL 6 Fr)
Northumbria – 300 pts (Fr Bus; Int Bus Mgt Fr)
Queen's Belfast – BBB/BBCb (Fr courses)
Reading – 300–320 pts (Fr courses) (IB 28 pts)
Salford – 300 pts (Modn Lang Transl Interp St (Fr/Ger/Ital/Port/Span))
Sheffield – BBB incl Fr (Fr St) (IB 32 pts)
Swansea – ABB–BBB 300 pts (Fr)

For a quick reference offers calculator, fold out the inside back cover.

Westminster – ABC (Law Fr) (IB 30 pts)
280 pts **Aberystwyth** – 280 pts (Fr) (IB 28 pts)
Bristol – ABB–BBC (Fr) (IB 33–30 pts)
Hull – 280–300 pts (Fr Joint Hons)
Oxford Brookes – BBC (Fr St (Comb)) (IB 30 pts)
Plymouth – 280 pts (Fr courses)
Stirling – BBC (Fr) (IB 32 pts)
260 pts **Greenwich** – 260 pts (Fr)
Hull – 260–300 pts (Fr)
Manchester Met – 260 pts (Lang (Fr/Ger/Ital/Span) Ling) (IB 28 pts)
Northampton – 260–280 pts (Fr courses)
Nottingham Trent – 260 pts (Fr Joint Hons) (IB 24 pts)
Sunderland – 260 pts (Fr courses)
UCLan – 260–300 pts (Fr (Comb))
Westminster – BCC (Fr courses) (IB 28 pts)
Winchester – 260–300 pts (Fr P Teach)
240 pts **Bangor** – 240–260 pts (Fr courses)
Canterbury Christ Church – 240 pts (Fr) (IB 24 pts)
Chester – 240–280 pts (Fr) (IB 26 pts)
Coventry – BCC 240–260 pts (Fr courses)
Ulster – 240 pts (Fr courses)
220 pts **Kingston** – 220–360 pts (Fr courses)
Leeds Met – 220 pts (Fr courses) (IB 24 pts)
Wolverhampton – 220–240 pts (Bus Fr)
200 pts **Portsmouth** – 200–280 pts (Fr St)
80 pts **London (Birk)** – p/t for under 21s (over 21s varies) (Fr Ger; Fr Span; Fr Mgt; Fr St)

Alternative offers
See **Chapter 7** and **Appendix 1** for grades/UCAS Tariff points information for the International Baccalaureate, Scottish Highers/Advanced Highers, the Welsh Baccalaureate, the Irish Leaving Certificate, the Cambridge Pre-U Diploma, the Advanced Diploma and the Extended Project.

CHOOSING YOUR COURSE (SEE ALSO CH.1)

Some course features
Bangor A three-language Honours course is offered with languages chosen from French, German, Italian or Spanish. This is an exclusively practical language course, two semesters being spent at universities appropriate to the languages chosen.
Bath (Euro St Modn Langs) French is studied with a second, equally weighted, language. The course has a contemporary focus and a wide range of options.
Cardiff (Fr) The course has a vocational emphasis, and the opportunity to sit the Paris Chamber of Commerce examination and to gain a French language qualification recognised in France. The year abroad offers the opportunity to work as a teaching assistant in a French school.
Chester French can be studied as a Single Honours degree or as part of a Combined Honours programme.
Heriot-Watt (Langs (Interp Transl) (App Langs Transl)) Both degrees enable two main foreign languages to be studied to the same level throughout the course: the second language can be studied either from beginners' or post-beginners' level.
Leeds A large department offering a range of single, combined and major/minor courses.
Salford (Modn Langs Transl Interp St) Three languages are chosen from French, German, Italian, Portuguese, Spanish, and English as a Foreign Language. Modern languages are also available with TESOL (Teaching English to Speakers of Other Languages).

Universities and colleges teaching quality See www.qaa.ac.uk; http://unistats.direct.gov.uk.

Top research universities and colleges (RAE 2008) Oxford; London (King's); Warwick; Cambridge; Aberdeen; St Andrews; Sheffield; Nottingham; Kent; Leeds; Exeter; London (UCL).

Check **Chapter 4** when choosing your university and **Chapter 7** on how to read the subject tables.

ADMISSIONS INFORMATION

Number of applicants per place (approx) Aston 6; Bangor 4; Bath (Euro St Modn Langs) 6; Birmingham 5; Bradford 3; Bristol 7; Cardiff 6; Durham 8; Exeter 8; Huddersfield 3; Hull 12; Kent 10; Kingston 4; Lancaster 7; Leeds (Joint Hons) 8; Leicester (Fr Ital) 5; Liverpool 5; LJMU 8; London (Inst in Paris) 9; London (King's) 9; London (RH) 5; London (UCL) 8; Manchester Met 13; Middlesex 6; Newcastle 17; Northampton 3; Nottingham 16; Oxford Brookes 8; Portsmouth 20; Roehampton 5; UCLan 5; Warwick 7; York 8.

Advice to applicants and planning the UCAS personal statement Visits to France (including exchange visits) should be described, with reference to any particular cultural or geographical features of the region visited. Providing information about your contacts with French friends and experience in speaking the language are also important. Express your willingness to work/live/travel abroad and show your interests in French life and culture. Read French newspapers and magazines and keep up-to-date with news stories etc. **Bristol** Deferred entry accepted in some cases. Late applications may not be accepted.

Misconceptions about this course Leeds See **Languages. Swansea** Some applicants are not aware of the range of subjects which can be combined with French in our flexible modular system. They sometimes do not know that linguistics and area studies options are also available as well as literature options in French.

Selection interviews Yes Bangor, Birmingham, Cambridge, Canterbury Christ Church, Durham, Essex, Exeter, Heriot-Watt, Huddersfield, Hull, Kingston, Lancaster, Liverpool, LJMU, London (RH), London (UCL), Oxford, Portsmouth, Surrey, Sussex, UEA (after offer), Warwick; **Some** Brighton, Leeds; **No** Nottingham, Reading.

Interview advice and questions Questions will almost certainly be asked on your A-level texts, in addition to your reading outside the syllabus – books, magazines, newspapers etc. Part of the interview may be conducted in French and written tests may be involved. See also **Chapter 6. Leeds** See **Languages**.

Reasons for rejection (non-academic) Unstable personality. Known alcoholism. Poor motivation. Candidate unenthusiastic, unmotivated, ill-informed about the nature of the course (had not read the prospectus). Not keen to spend a year abroad.

AFTER-RESULTS ADVICE

Offers to applicants repeating A-levels Higher Aberystwyth, Bristol (Fr), Glasgow, Leeds, Oxford Brookes, Warwick; **Possibly higher** Aston (Fr; Fr Ger); **Same** Aston, Bradford, Brighton, Bristol (Phil Fr; Fr Lat), Chester, Durham, Lancaster, Liverpool, London (RH), Newcastle, Nottingham (Fr Ger; Fr Lat), Sheffield, Surrey, Sussex, UEA, Ulster; **No** Cambridge.

GRADUATE DESTINATIONS AND EMPLOYMENT (2009/10 HESA)

Graduates surveyed 1735 **Employed** 810 **In voluntary employment** 35 **In further study** 395 **Assumed unemployed** 85

Career note See **Languages**.

OTHER DEGREE SUBJECTS FOR CONSIDERATION

European Studies; International Business Studies; Literature; other language tables.

GENETICS

(see also **Biological Sciences, Microbiology**)

Over the years genetics, the science of heredity, has developed into a detailed and wide-ranging science. It involves, on the one hand, population genetics, and on the other, molecular interactions. Studies may therefore cover microbial, plant, animal and human genetics.

Useful websites www.genetics.org; www.nature.com/genetics; www.genetics.org.uk; see also **Biological Sciences**.

NB The points totals shown to the left of the institutions are for ease of reference only. It must not be assumed that Tariff points are always used by institutions or that they can be substituted for an offer in grades. The level of an offer is not necessarily indicative of the quality of a course.

COURSE OFFERS INFORMATION

Subject requirements/preferences GCSE English, mathematics and science subjects. **AL** Chemistry and/or biology are usually required or preferred.

Your target offers and examples of courses provided by each institution

380 pts **Cambridge** – A*AA (Nat Sci (Genet)) (IB 40–42 pts)
 London (King's) – AABc (Pharmacol Mol Genet) (IB 36 pts HL 6 chem biol)

360 pts **Edinburgh** – AAA–ABB (Genet) (IB 37–32 pts)
 Manchester – AAA–ABB 320–360 pts (Genet Modn Lang) (IB 37–33 pts)

340 pts **Cardiff** – AAB–ABB (Genet) (IB 34 pts)
 Newcastle – AAB (Biomed Genet) (IB 32 pts)
 Nottingham – AAB–ABB 320–340 pts (Hum Genet) (IB 34–32 pts)
 Sheffield – AAB (Genet Microbiol) (IB 35 pts)

320 pts **Birmingham** – AAB–ABB 320–340 pts (Biol Sci (Genet)) (IB 32–34 pts)
 Edinburgh – AAA–ABB 320–360 pts (Biol Sci Genet) (IB 37–32 pts)
 Glasgow – ABB (Genet) (IB 32 pts)
 Leicester – ABB (Biol Sci (Genet)) (IB 32 pts)
 Liverpool – ABB (Genet (Yr Ind)) (IB 33 pts HL 6 biol)
 Nottingham – AAB–ABB 320–340 pts (Genet) (IB 34–32 pts)
 Surrey – ABB–BBB (Microbl Genet) (IB 32–28 pts)
 Swansea – 320 pts (Med Genet; Genet Bioch)
 UEA – ABB–BBB (Mol Biol Genet) (IB 32–31 pts)
 York – AAB–ABB (Genet) (IB 32 pts)

300 pts **Brunel** – BBB (Biomed Sci (Genet)) (IB 32 pts HL 5 biol)
 Dundee – BBB (Mol Genet) (IB 30 pts)
 Essex – BBB–BBC 280–300 pts (Genet) (IB 30 pts)
 Leeds – AAB–BBB (Genet) (IB 34–32 pts HL 15–16 pts)
 London (QM) – 300 pts (Med Genet) (IB 28 pts)
 Queen's Belfast – BBB/BBCb (Genet) (IB 28 pts)

280 pts **Aberystwyth** – 280–320 pts (Genet Bioch) (IB 26 pts)
 Huddersfield – 280 pts (Med Genet)

240 pts **Aberdeen** – 240 pts (Genet; Genet (Immun); Genet Psy)
 Hertfordshire – 240 pts (Mol Biol Genet)

220 pts **Westminster** – CCD (Mol Biol Genet) (IB 28 pts)

200 pts **Wolverhampton** – 200 pts (Genet Mol Biol)

Alternative offers

See **Chapter 7** and **Appendix 1** for grades/UCAS Tariff points information for the International Baccalaureate, Scottish Highers/Advanced Highers, the Welsh Baccalaureate, the Irish Leaving Certificate, the Cambridge Pre-U Diploma, the Advanced Diploma and the Extended Project.

CHOOSING YOUR COURSE (SEE ALSO CH.1)

Some course features

Brunel Genetics is offered as part of the Biomedical Sciences programme.

Liverpool Modules are offered in genetic engineering, human and medical genetics. The year in industry/research enables students to work in the UK, Europe or the USA, and a field course in Uganda is offered.

London (UCL) After a common first year for all Biological Sciences students, Genetics and Human Genetics are two of the degree specialisms offered for the following years of the BSc and MSci courses. The Genetics programme focuses on genomic, evolutionary and population genetics, while

cytology, pre-natal diagnosis and genetic counselling are options in the Human Genetics programme.
Manchester Transfer possible between most life sciences degree programmes at the end of the first year; students can also opt on, or off, sandwich placement year, and a foundation year is also available. A programme is offered in Genetics with a Modern Language.
Nottingham Human Genetics is offered as a three- or four-year programme.
York Genetics is available as a specialist degree programme in the Biology degree programme, with an opportunity to spend a year abroad or in industry.

Universities and colleges teaching quality See www.qaa.ac.uk; http://unistats.direct.gov.uk.

Top research universities and colleges (RAE 2008) See **Biological Sciences**.

Examples of sandwich degree courses See also **Biological Sciences**. Brunel; Cardiff; Huddersfield.

ADMISSIONS INFORMATION
Number of applicants per place (approx) Cardiff 8; Dundee 5; Leeds 7; Leicester (all Biol Sci courses) 10;Newcastle 8; Nottingham 6; Swansea 7; Wolverhampton 4; York 9.

Advice to applicants and planning the UCAS personal statement See **Biological Sciences**.

Misconceptions about this course York Some fail to realise that chemistry (beyond GCSE) is essential to an understanding of genetics.

Selection interviews Yes Cambridge, Liverpool, Swansea; **Some** Anglia Ruskin, Cardiff, Wolverhampton, York; **No** Dundee.

Interview advice and questions Likely questions will focus on your A-level science subjects, particularly biology, why you wish to study genetics, and on careers in genetics. See also **Chapter 6**.

AFTER-RESULTS ADVICE
Offers to applicants repeating A-levels Higher Aberystwyth, Leeds, Newcastle, Nottingham, Swansea; **Same** Anglia Ruskin, Cardiff, Dundee, London (UCL), Wolverhampton, York; **No** Cambridge.

GRADUATE DESTINATIONS AND EMPLOYMENT (2009/10 HESA)
Graduates surveyed 415 **Employed** 140 **In voluntary employment** 10 **In further study** 185 **Assumed unemployed** 40

Career note See **Biological Sciences**.

OTHER DEGREE SUBJECTS FOR CONSIDERATION
Biochemistry; Biological Sciences; Biology; Biotechnology; Human Sciences; Immunology; Life Sciences; Medical Biochemistry; Medical Biology; Medicine; Microbiology; Molecular Biology; Natural Sciences; Physiology; Plant Sciences.

GEOGRAPHY

(including **Meteorology**; see also **Environmental Sciences/Studies**)

Students following BA and BSc Geography courses often choose options from the same range of modules, but the choice of degree will depend on the arts or science subjects taken at A-level (or equivalent). The content and focus of courses will vary between universities and could emphasise the human, physical, economic or social aspects of the subject.

Useful websites www.metoffice.gov.uk; www.ccw.gov.uk; www.rgs.org; www.ordnancesurvey.co.uk; www.geographical.co.uk; www.nationalgeographic.com; www.cartography.org.uk; www.naturalengland.org.uk; www.geography.org.uk; www.thepowerofgeography.co.uk; www.spatial-literacy.org; www.gis.com.

NB The points totals shown to the left of the institutions are for ease of reference only. It must not be assumed that Tariff points are always used by institutions or that they can be substituted for an offer in grades. The level of an offer is not necessarily indicative of the quality of a course.

COURSE OFFERS INFORMATION
Subject requirements/preferences GCSE Geography usually required. Mathematics/sciences often required for BSc courses. **AL** Geography is usually required for most courses. Mathematics/science subjects required for BSc courses. (Meteor) Mathematics, physics and another science may be required sometimes with specified grades, eg **Reading** mathematics and physics grade B.

Your target offers and examples of courses provided by each institution

380 pts **Cambridge** – A*AA (Geog) (IB 40–42 pts)
Durham – A*AA (Geog) (IB 38 pts)
London (King's) – AABc (Geog) (IB 36 pts HL 5 geog 66)
London (UCL) – AAA–AAB incl geog (Geog) (IB 36–38 pts)

360 pts **Bristol** – AAA–AAB (Geog) (IB 37–35 pts)
Cardiff – AAA (Geog (Hum))
Edinburgh – AAA–ABB incl maths phys (Phys Meteor) (IB 37–32 pts)
Exeter – AAA–BBB (Geog Joint Hons) (IB 36–30 pts)
Leeds – AAA (Meteor; Meteor Clim Sci (Int))
London (UCL) – AAA–AAB incl geog+maths (Econ Geog) (IB 34–38 pts)
Manchester – AAA (Geog Int St) (IB 37 pts)
Oxford – AAA (Geog) (IB 38–40 pts)
St Andrews – AAA (Geog Scot Hist) (IB 36 pts)
UEA – AAA (Meteor Ocean MSci) (IB 34 pts HL 666 maths)

340 pts **Birmingham** – AAB (Geog) (IB 34–36 pts)
Bristol UWE – 340 pts (Geog Env Mgt) (IB 28 pts)
Exeter – AAA–ABB (Geog) (IB 36–32 pts)
Hull – 340–360 pts (Geog)
Lancaster – AAB (Phys Geog) (IB 34 pts)
Leeds – AAA–AAB (Geog) (IB 34 pts HL 16 pts)
Liverpool – AAB (Geog BA/BSc) (IB 35 pts)
London (QM) – 340 pts (Hum Geog) (IB 32 pts)
London (SOAS) – AAB (Geog Joint Hons) (IB 36 pts HL 666)
London LSE – AAB (Geog Econ) (IB 37 pts)
Loughborough – AAB–ABB (Hist Geog) (IB 32–34 pts)
Manchester – AAB (Geog) (IB 36–35 pts)
Nottingham – AAA–AAB 300–340 pts (Geog) (IB 34–36 pts)
St Andrews – AAB (Geog Lang) (IB 32–36 pts)
Sheffield – AAB–ABB (Geog) (IB 33–35 pts)
Southampton – AAB incl geog (Popn Geog) (IB 34 pts HL 17 pts)
Sussex – AAB–ABB (Geog Dev St) (IB 32–34 pts)

320 pts **Birmingham** – ABB (Geol Geog) (IB 32–34 pts)
Birmingham (UC) – ABB (Geog) (IB 32–34 pts)
Cardiff – ABB (Mar Geog) (IB 30–32 pts)
Edinburgh – AAA–ABB 320–360 pts (Geog) (IB 37–32 pts)
Glasgow – ABB (Geog) (IB 32 pts)
Lancaster – ABB (Earth Sci Geog) (IB 32 pts)
Leicester – ABB (Geog Geol)
Liverpool – ABB (Ocns Clim Physl Geog) (IB 33 pts)
London (Birk) – ABB (Geog)
London (QM) – 320–340 pts (Cits Econy Soc Chng) (IB 32 pts)
London (RH) – ABB 320 pts (Geog Pol Int Rel) (IB 37 pts HL 666)
Loughborough – ABB–AAC (Geog) (IB 34 pts)
Manchester – ABB (Geog Geol) (IB 33 pts)
Newcastle – ABB–BBB 300–320 pts (Physl Geog) (IB 32 pts HL geog 6)
Nottingham – AAB–ABB 320–340 pts (Geog Chin St) (IB 32–34 pts)
Oxford Brookes – ABB (Geog (Comb)) (IB 29 pts)
Reading – 320 pts (Hum Physl Geog) (IB 34–31 pts)
Roehampton – 320 pts (P Educ (Geog))

Check **Chapter 4** when choosing your university and **Chapter 7** on how to read the subject tables.

Strathclyde – 320 pts (Geog)
Sheffield – ABB (Geog Plan) (IB 33 pts)
Swansea – ABB (Geog; Geog Econ; Geog Geoinform; Geog Euro St)
York – ABB (Env Geog)

300 pts **Aberystwyth** – 300 pts (Geog) (IB 28 pts)
Bournemouth – 300 pts (App Geog) (IB 28–30 pts)
Brighton – Offers may vary BBB (Geog Geol) (IB 30 pts)
Keele – 300 pts (Hum Geog) (IB 26–28 pts)
London (QM) – 300–340 pts (Russ Geog) (IB 32 pts)
Newcastle – AAB–BBB 300–320 pts (GIS) (IB 32 pts)
Northumbria – 300 pts (Geog Env Mgt) (IB 28 pts)
Queen's Belfast – BBB (Geog (St Abrd))
Reading – 300 pts (Meteor Clim)
Sheffield Hallam – 300 pts (Geog)
Southampton – BBB incl geog (Arch Geog) (IB 30 pts HL 16 pts)

280 pts **Bangor** – 280–320 pts (Cstl Geog) (IB 28 pts)
Brighton – 280 pts (Ecol Biogeog)
Bristol UWE – 280–300 pts (Geog) (IB 26–32 pts)
Coventry – BBC 280 pts (Disas Mgt Emer Plan)
Derby – 280 pts (Geog)
Gloucestershire – 280–300 pts (Geog courses)
Hull – 280 pts (Geog Spo Sci; Physl Geog; Hum Geog)
Manchester Met – 280 pts (Physl Geog) (IB 28 pts)
Newcastle – ABB–BBC 280–320 pts (Twn Plan) (IB 28 pts)
Northumbria – 280 pts (Geog) (IB 28 pts)
Plymouth – 280pts (Physl Geog Geol)
Portsmouth – 280 pts (Geog BA/BSc; Hum Geog; Physl Geog; Env Geog)
Queen's Belfast – BBB/BBCb (Geog)
Stirling – BBC (Geog) (IB 32 pts)
Sheffield Hallam – 280 pts incl geog (Geog Plan; Hum Geog)
Worcester – 280–300 pts (Geog; Hum Geog; Geog courses)

260 pts **Bangor** – 260–320 pts (Geog) (IB 28 pts)
Bradford – 260 pts (Geog; Env Sci; Physl Env Geog; Geog Arch)
Chester – 260–300 pts (Geog) (IB 28 pts)
Coventry – 260–280 pts (Disas Reconstr Mgt; Disas Mgt)
Dundee – BCC (Geog Plan) (IB 29 pts)
Hertfordshire – 260–280 pts (Hum Geog; Geog)
Hull – 260–320 pts (Geog Arch) (IB 28 pts)
Liverpool Hope – 260–320 pts (Geog)
LJMU – 260–300 pts (Geog) (IB 25 pts)
Northampton – 260–280 pts (Physl Geog; Geog)
Nottingham Trent – 260 pts (Geog (Physl))
Staffordshire – 260 pts (Geog Mntn Ldrshp) (IB 28 pts)
Winchester – 260–300 pts (P Educ Geog)

240 pts **Aberdeen** – 240 pts (Geog (Arts/Sci); GIS)
Bath Spa – 240–280 pts (Geog)
Canterbury Christ Church – 240–260 pts (Geog)
Edge Hill – 240 pts (Geog; Hum Geog; Physl Geog; Physl Geog Geol)
Glamorgan – CCC (Geog; Hum Geog; Physl Geog)
Kingston – 240 pts (Geog Inf Sys)
Leeds Met – 240 pts (Hum Geog Plan) (IB 24 pts)
Nottingham Trent – 240 pts (Geog) (IB 24 pts)

220 pts **Greenwich** – 220 pts (Geog)
St Mary's Twickenham (UC) – 220 pts (Geog) (IB 28 pts)
Ulster – 220–240 pts (Geog Int Dev)

200 pts **Salford** – 200–240 pts (Env Geog) (IB 24 pts)
UCLan – 200–240 pts (Geog)
180 pts **Southampton Solent** – 180 pts (Geog Env St; Geog Mar St)

Open University – contact +44 (0)845 300 6090 **or** www.openuniversity.co.uk/you (Soc Sci Geog)

Alternative offers
See **Chapter 7** and **Appendix 1** for grades/UCAS Tariff points information for the International Baccalaureate, Scottish Highers/Advanced Highers, the Welsh Baccalaureate, the Irish Leaving Certificate, the Cambridge Pre-U Diploma, the Advanced Diploma and the Extended Project.

EXAMPLES OF FOUNDATION DEGREES IN THE SUBJECT FIELD
Bournemouth.

CHOOSING YOUR COURSE (SEE ALSO CH.1)
Some course features
Lancaster The Geography degree schemes are flexible so students can specialise in human geography, physical geography, or geography, or study an outside related subject, in the second and third years. There are study abroad opportunities in Canada, North America, New Zealand and Australia, and an option to teach geography in a local school.
Newcastle Geography can be taken in the BA Combined Studies degree with three other subjects in Stage 1 and two in Stage 2.
Reading A leading university for the study of meteorology with opportunities for placement at the University of Oklahoma, equally renowned for this subject.
St Mary's Twickenham (UC) A flexible modular scheme allowing a choice of specialisms.
UEA (MSci Meteor Ocean) A new (2010) four-year course integrates a study of the Earth's oceans and atmosphere, their interactions and external influences on them and is run jointly by the Schools of Environmental Sciences and Mathematics, together with the School of Computing Sciences.

Universities and colleges teaching quality See www.qaa.ac.uk; http://unistats.direct.gov.uk.

Top research universities and colleges (RAE 2008) See **Environmental Science/Studies**.

Examples of sandwich degree courses Cardiff; Coventry; Hertfordshire; Kingston; Loughborough; Manchester Met; Nottingham Trent; Plymouth; Ulster.

ADMISSIONS INFORMATION
Number of applicants per place (approx) Aberystwyth 3; Birmingham 6; Bristol 15; Bristol UWE 10; Cambridge 3; Cardiff 5; Chester 10; Coventry 12; Derby 4; Dundee 5; Durham 8; Edge Hill 8; Edinburgh 8; Exeter 10; Glamorgan 5; Gloucestershire 40; Greenwich 2; Hull 10; Kent 15; Kingston 7; Lancaster 13; Leeds 12; Leicester 5; Liverpool 3; LJMU 6; London (King's) 5; London (QM) 5; London (RH) 7; London (SOAS) 5; London LSE 8; Loughborough 6, (Geog Spo Sci) 20; Newcastle 14; Newman (UC) 2; Northampton 4; Northumbria 16; Nottingham 7; Portsmouth (Geog) 5; St Mary's Twickenham (UC) 4; Salford 3; Sheffield (BA) 13, (BSc) 10; Southampton (Geog) 7; Staffordshire 10; Strathclyde 8; Swansea 5; UCLan 3; UEA (Meteor Ocean) 7; Wolverhampton 2; Worcester 5.

Advice to applicants and planning the UCAS personal statement Visits to, and field courses in, any specific geographical region should be fully described. Study your own locality in detail and get in touch with the area planning office to learn about any future developments. Read geographical magazines and describe any special interests you have – and why. Awareness of world issues and travel experience. **Bristol** Deferred entry accepted.

Misconceptions about this course Birmingham Some students think that the BA and BSc Geography courses are very different: in fact they do not differ from one another. All course options are available for both degrees. **Liverpool** Some applicants assume that a BSc course restricts them to physical geography modules. This is not so since human geography modules can be taken. Some students later specialise in human geography. **UEA** (Meteor Ocean) Some applicants don't realise that the course is a very mathematical and physics-based subject.

Check **Chapter 4** when choosing your university and **Chapter 7** on how to read the subject tables.

Selection interviews Yes Bristol UWE, Cambridge, Canterbury Christ Church, Coventry, Durham (essential for overseas applicants), Edge Hill, Greenwich, Kingston, London (King's), London (QM), London (RH), London (SOAS), London (UCL), Manchester Met, Northumbria, Oxford (Geog) 27%, UCLan, UEA; **Some** Bath Spa, Bristol, Cardiff, Dundee, Liverpool, Loughborough, Newcastle, Salford, Southampton, Staffordshire; **No** Birmingham, Nottingham, Reading.

Interview advice and questions Geography is a very broad subject and applicants can expect to be questioned on their syllabus and those aspects which they find of special interest. Some questions in the past have included: What fieldwork have you done? What are your views on ecology? What changes in the landscape have you noticed on the way to the interview? Explain in simple meteorological terms today's weather. Why are earthquakes almost unknown in Britain? What is the value of practical work in geography to primary school children? (BEd course) What do you enjoy about geography and why? Are there any articles of geographical importance in the news at present? Discuss the current economic situation in Britain and give your views. Questions on the Third World, on world ocean currents and drainage and economic factors world-wide. Expect to comment on local geography and on geographical photographs and diagrams. See also **Chapter 6**. **Cambridge** What do you think about those who regard global warming as nonsense? Are Fair-Trade bananas really fair? Imagine you are hosting the BBC radio show on New Year's day, what message would you send to listeners? **Liverpool** Looks for why students have chosen Geography and the aspects of the subject they enjoy. **Oxford** Is nature natural? **Southampton** Applicants selected on academic ability only.

Reasons for rejection (non-academic) Lack of awareness of the content of the course. Failure to attend interview. Poor general knowledge. Lack of geographical awareness. **Hull** (BSc) Usually insufficient science background. **Liverpool** Personal statement gave no reason for choosing Geography.

AFTER-RESULTS ADVICE

Offers to applicants repeating A-levels Higher Bournemouth, Glasgow, Hull, Kingston, Nottingham, St Andrews, Sussex (Geog Lang); **Possibly higher** Edinburgh; **Same** Aberystwyth, Birmingham, Bradford, Brighton, Bristol, Cardiff, Chester, Coventry, Derby, Dundee, Durham, Edge Hill, Lancaster, Leeds (applicants consider which A-levels to resit for the BSc course), Liverpool, Liverpool Hope, LJMU, London (RH), London (SOAS), Loughborough, Manchester Met, Newcastle, Newman (UC), Newport, Northumbria, Oxford Brookes, St Mary's Twickenham (UC), Salford, Southampton, Staffordshire, UEA, Ulster, Wolverhampton; **No** Cambridge.

GRADUATE DESTINATIONS AND EMPLOYMENT (2009/10 HESA)

Human and Social Geography; graduates surveyed 3185 **Employed** 1320 **In voluntary employment** 75 **In further study** 675 **Assumed unemployed** 205

Physical Geographical Studies; graduates surveyed 4285 **Employed** 1730 **In voluntary employment** 95 **In further study** 860 **Assumed unemployed** 260

Career note Geography graduates enter a wide range of occupations, many in business and administrative careers. Depending on specialisations, areas could include agriculture, forestry, hydrology, transport, market research and retail. Teaching is also a popular option.

OTHER DEGREE SUBJECTS FOR CONSIDERATION

Agriculture; Anthropology; Civil Engineering; Countryside Management; Development Studies; Environmental Engineering/Science/Studies; Forestry; Geology; Geomatic Engineering; Surveying; Town Planning; Urban Land Economics; Urban Studies.

GEOLOGY/GEOLOGICAL SCIENCES

(including **Earth Sciences**, **Geophysics** and **Geoscience**; see also **Astronomy and Astrophysics**, **Environmental Sciences/Studies**)

Topics in Geology courses include the physical and chemical constitution of the earth, exploration geophysics, oil and marine geology (oceanography) and seismic interpretation. Earth Sciences cover geology, environmental science, physical geography and can also include business studies and language modules. No previous knowledge of geology is required for most courses.

Useful websites www.geolsoc.org.uk; www.bgs.ac.uk; www.noc.soton.ac.uk; www.scicentral.com; www.cardiff.ac.ukearth/degreeprogrammes/index/html.

NB The points totals shown to the left of the institutions are for ease of reference only. It must not be assumed that Tariff points are always used by institutions or that they can be substituted for an offer in grades. The level of an offer is not necessarily indicative of the quality of a course.

COURSE OFFERS INFORMATION

Subject requirements/preferences GCSE English, mathematics and a science required. **AL** One or two mathematics/science subjects usually required. Geography may be accepted as a science subject.

Your target offers and examples of courses provided by each institution

380 pts **Cambridge** – A*AA (Nat Sci (Earth Sci)) (IB 40–42 pts)
London (UCL) – AAAe–ABBe (Geol) (IB 34–38 pts)
Oxford – A*AA–AAA (Earth Sci) (IB 38–40 pts)

360 pts **Cardiff** – AAA (Explor Res Geol (Int); Geol (Int))
Edinburgh – AAA–ABB 320–360 pts (Geol) (IB 37–32 pts)
Glasgow – AAA (Earth Sci Faster Route) (IB 38 pts HL 665)
Imperial London – AAA 360 pts (Petrol Geosci) (IB 35 pts)
Leeds – AAA (Geol Sci (Int)) (IB 36 pts HL 18 pts)
London (UCL) – AAA–ABB (Env Geosci) (IB 36–38 pts)
St Andrews – AAA–AAB (Geosci courses) (IB 35–38 pts)
Southampton – AAA–ABB (Geophys) (IB 36–32 pts HL 18–16 pts)
UEA – AAA–AAB (Clim Sci MSci) (IB 34–33 pts HL 666)

340 pts **Bristol** – AAB (Geol Biol) (IB 33 pts)
Cardiff – AAB (Geol MESci)
Durham – AAB (Geophys Geol) (IB 36 pts)
Exeter – AAB–BBB 340–300 pts (Eng Geol Geotech) (IB 34–30 pts)
Lancaster – AAB–ABB 340–320 pts (Earth Env Sci (St Abrd)) (IB 32–34 pts)
Leicester – AAB (Geol Palae; Geol MGeol)
Liverpool – AAB (Geol Physl Geog MESci) (IB 35 pts)
Manchester – AAB (Earth Sci) (IB 35 pts)
St Andrews – AAB (Env Geosci) (IB 35 pts)
Southampton – AAB incl geog (Geog Geol) (IB 34 pts HL 17 pts)
UEA – AAB (Geophys Sci (Yr Abrd)) (IB 33 pts)

320 pts **Birmingham** – ABB (Geol Geog) (IB 32–34 pts)
Bristol – AAB–ABB 320–340 pts (Geol) (IB 36 pts)
Cardiff – ABB (Geol BSc)
Glasgow – ABB (Arch Joint Hons) (IB 36 pts)
Leeds – ABB (Geol Sci) (IB 34 pts)
Leicester – ABB (Geol BSc; Geog Geol)
Liverpool – ABB (Geol Physl Geog BSc) (IB 33 pts)
London (RH) – ABB (Geoscience)
Manchester – ABB (Geog Geol) (IB 33 pts)
Swansea – ABB (Physl Earth Sci)
UEA – ABB (Clim Sci (Yr Ind)) (IB 32 pts)

300 pts **Birmingham** – BBB (Geol) (IB 28–34 pts)
Brighton – BBB 300 pts (Earth Ocn Sci) (IB 28 pts)
Keele – 300 pts (Geol) (IB 26–30 pts)
London (Birk) – BBB (Geol)
London (RH) – BBB (Geol) (IB 38 pts HL 66)

280 pts **Aberystwyth** – 280–300 pts (Env Earth Sci) (IB 28 pts)
Bangor – 280–320 pts (Geol Ocean) (IB 28 pts)
Brighton – BBC 280 pts (Geol) (IB 28 pts)
Plymouth – 280pts (Geol Ocn Sci; Physl Geog Geol)

260 pts **Derby** – 260–300 pts (Geol)
Plymouth – 260 pts (App Geol)

240 pts **Aberdeen** – 240 pts (Geol) (IB 32 pts)
Edge Hill – 240 pts (Physl Geog Geol)
Kingston – 240–280 pts (Earth Sys Sci; App Geol; Geol; App Env Geol)
Portsmouth – 240–300 pts (Eng Geol Geotech; Earth Sci; Geol; Geol Haz; Pal Evol)

200 pts **Glamorgan** – 200–260 pts (Geol)

Open University – contact +44 (0)845 300 6090 **or** www.openuniversity.co.uk/you (Geol St)

Alternative offers

See **Chapter 7** and **Appendix 1** for grades/UCAS Tariff points information for the International Baccalaureate, Scottish Highers/Advanced Highers, the Welsh Baccalaureate, the Irish Leaving Certificate, the Cambridge Pre-U Diploma, the Advanced Diploma and the Extended Project.

CHOOSING YOUR COURSE (SEE ALSO CH.1)
Some course features

Cardiff (Explor Res Geol) Course provides a grounding in applied geology and the evaluation and exploration of the Earth's natural resources. During the second summer, an industrial placement is offered with an exploration company in the UK or overseas. Option to spend Year 3 in the USA or Australia on the MESci courses.

Exeter Camborne School of Mines is a leader in the field of Engineering Geology and Geotechnics and Mining Engineering. £2000 scholarships are offered on the basis of academic excellence, together with some sponsorships.

Leeds Geological and Geophysical Sciences can be studied with placements in Europe or worldwide or with industrial placement. From 2012 there will be no additional charges for fieldwork programmes.

UEA A strong department of Environmental Sciences incorporating courses in Geophysical Sciences with opportunities to study abroad and in industry. A new range of integrated Masters degrees were introduced in 2010, including an MSci in Climate Science.

Universities and colleges teaching quality See www.qaa.ac.uk; http://unistats.direct.gov.uk.

Top research universities and colleges (RAE 2008) See **Environmental Science/Studies**.

Examples of sandwich degree courses Cardiff; Glamorgan; Kingston; West Scotland.

ADMISSIONS INFORMATION
Number of applicants per place (approx) Aberystwyth 5; Bangor 4; Birmingham 4; Bristol 7; Cardiff 6; Derby 4; Durham 4; Edinburgh 5; Exeter 5; Imperial London 5; Kingston 19, (Earth Sys Sci) 3; Leeds 8; Leicester 5; Liverpool 5; London (RH) 5; London (UCL) 3; Oxford 1.2; Plymouth 7; Portsmouth (Eng Geol Geotech) 2, (Goel) 2; Southampton 5; UEA 7.

Advice to applicants and planning the UCAS personal statement Visits to any outstanding geological sites and field courses you have attended should be described in detail. Apart from geological formations, you should also be aware of how geology has affected humankind in specific areas in the architecture of the region and artefacts used. Evidence of social skills could be given.
Bristol Only accepting a limited number of deferred applicants in fairness to next year's applicants. Apply early.

Misconceptions about this course London (UCL) Environmental geoscience is sometimes mistaken for environmental science; they are two different subjects. **UEA** Many applicants fail to realise that environmental earth science extends beyond geology to the links between the solid earth and its behaviour and society in general.

Selection interviews Yes Cambridge, Durham, Edinburgh, Kingston, Liverpool, London (RH), Oxford (Geol) 46%, Southampton, Sunderland; **Some** Aberystwyth (mature students only), Derby; **No** Birmingham, UEA.

Interview advice and questions Some knowledge of the subject will be expected and applicants could be questioned on specimens of rocks and their origins. Past interviews have included questions on the field courses attended, and the geophysical methods of exploration in the detection of metals. How would you determine the age of this rock (sample shown)? Can you integrate a decay curve function and would it help you to determine the age of rocks? How many planes of crystallisation could this rock have? What causes a volcano? What is your local geology? See also **Chapter 6**. **Oxford (Earth Sci)** Candidates may be asked to comment on specimens of a geological nature, based on previous knowledge of the subject.

Reasons for rejection (non-academic) Exeter Outright rejection uncommon but some applicants advised to apply for other programmes.

AFTER-RESULTS ADVICE
Offers to applicants repeating A-levels Higher Bristol, St Andrews; **Possibly higher** Cardiff, Portsmouth; **Same** Aberystwyth, Derby, Durham, Leeds, London (RH), Plymouth, Southampton, UEA; **No** Cambridge.

GRADUATE DESTINATIONS AND EMPLOYMENT (2009/10 HESA)
Graduates surveyed 1855 **Employed** 705 **In voluntary employment** 25 **In further study** 415 **Assumed unemployed** 135

Career note Areas of employment include mining and quarrying, the oil and gas industry, prospecting and processing.

OTHER DEGREE SUBJECTS FOR CONSIDERATION
Archaeology; Civil and Mining Engineering; Environmental Science; Geography; Meteorology; Oceanography; Physics.

GERMAN
(see also European Studies, Languages)

Language, literature, practical language skills or a broader study of Germany and its culture (European Studies) are alternative study approaches. See also **Appendix 3** under Languages.

Useful websites www.cilt.org.uk; www.goethe.de; www.bbc.co.uk/languages; www.iol.org.uk; http://languageadvantage.com; www.languagematters.co.uk; www.reed.co.uk/multilingual; www.deutsch-online.com; www.faz.net; www.sueddeutsche.de; http://europa.eu; www.gslg.org.uk; www.amgs.org.uk; www.wigs.ac.uk.

NB The points totals shown to the left of the institutions are for ease of reference only. It must not be assumed that Tariff points are always used by institutions or that they can be substituted for an offer in grades. The level of an offer is not necessarily indicative of the quality of a course.

COURSE OFFERS INFORMATION
Subject requirements/preferences GCSE English and German are required. **AL** German required usually at a specified grade.

Your target offers and examples of courses provided by each institution

380 pts **Cambridge** – A*AA (Modn Mediev Lang (Ger)) (IB 40–42 pts)
London (King's) – AABc (Ger) (IB 36 pts)
Nottingham – A*AA–AAA 360–380 pts (Econ Fr/Ger/Russ) (IB 38–36 pts)

360 pts **Birmingham** – A*AB–AAA (Law Ger) (IB 36 pts)
Bristol – AAA incl Ger (Law Ger) (IB 37 pts)
London (RH) – AAA–AAB (Econ Fr/Ger/Ital/Span) (IB 33–35 pts)
Nottingham – AAA (Law Fr Fr Law/Ger Ger Law/Span Span Law) (IB 38 pts HL 7)
Oxford – AAA (Ger courses) (IB 38–40 pts)
St Andrews – AAA–AAB (Ger courses) (IB 35–38 pts)
Southampton – AAA (Maths Fr/Ger/Span) (IB 36 pts HL 18 pts)

340 pts **Bath** – AAB (Int Bus Ger) (IB 34–36 pts)
Exeter – AAB–ABB (Ger Arbc) (IB 29 pts)
Lancaster – AAB 340 pts (Ger St courses) (IB 34 pts)
London (RH) – AAB (Mgt Fr/Ger/Ital/Span) (IB 35 pts)
London (UCL) – AAB–ABB incl Ger (Ger) (IB 34–36 pts)
Manchester – AAB–BBB 300–340 pts (Ger St) (IB 31–36 pts)
Nottingham – AAB (Mgt St Fr/Ger/Span) (IB 34 pts)
Sheffield – AAB–BBB (Ger St Joint Hons) (IB 35–32 pts)
Southampton – AAB (Film Fr/Ger/Span) (IB 34 pts HL 17 pts)
Warwick – AAB (Ger St) (IB 36 pts)

320 pts **Aston** – ABB–BBB 300–320 pts (Ger courses) (IB 33–34 pts)
Bath – ABB (Modn Langs Euro St (Ger and Fr/Ital/Russ/Span))
Bristol – ABB–BBC (Ger Modn Lang) (IB 33–30 pts)
Glasgow – ABB (Ger Joint Hons) (IB 36 pts)
Kent – 340 pts (Ger Joint Hons) (IB 33 pts)
Leeds – ABB–AAB (Fr/Ger Stats)
London (QM) – 320 pts (Ger Compar Lit) (IB 34 pts)
Nottingham – ABB–BBB incl Ger (Ger) (IB 32 pts HL 6 lang)
London (RH) – ABB–BBB incl Ger (Ger) (IB 32 pts HL 6 lang)
Nottingham – ABB (Class Civ Fr/Ger) (IB 32 pts)
Surrey – ABB–BBB (Ger courses) (IB 32 pts)
York – ABB (Ger courses) (IB 32 pts)

300 pts **Aberdeen** – BBB (Ger) (IB 28 pts)
Birmingham – BBB (Ger St courses) (IB 30 pts)
Cardiff – BBB (Ger)
Dundee – BBB–BCC (Law Fr/Ger/Span; Int Bus Ger; Phil Ger)
Edinburgh – AAA–BBB 300–360 pts (Bus St Fr/Ger/Span)
Essex – 300–320 pts (Ger St Modn Lang) (IB 30 pts)
Heriot-Watt – BBB (App Lang Ger; Langs (Interp Transl) (Fr/Ger) (Ger/Span))
Leeds – ABC–BBB (Ger courses)
Liverpool – BBB (Ger Joint Hons) (IB 30 pts)
London (QM) – 300–340 pts (Ger courses) (IB 32–36 pts)
Nottingham – ABC/BBB incl Ger (Ger) (Ib 30 pts HL 5 Ger)
Reading – 300–320 pts (Ger courses) (IB 28 pts)
Salford – 300 pts (Modn Lang Transl Interp St (Fr/Ger/Ital/Port/Span))
Sheffield – BBB incl Ger (Ger St) (IB 32 pts)
Sussex – ABB–BBB (Ger courses)
Swansea – BBB (Ger courses)
Westminster – BBB 300 pts (Int Bus Ger) (IB 28 pts)

280 pts **Aberystwyth** – 280 pts (Ger) (IB 28 pts)
Bristol – ABB–BBC 280–320 pts (Ger courses) (IB 33–30 pts)
Hull – 280–300 pts (Ger)
Northumbria – 280–300 pts (Ger Bus) (IB 26 pts)
Westminster – BBC (Int Rel Ger)

260 pts **Dundee** – BCC (Ger)
Hertfordshire – 260–300 pts (German)

        Hull – 260–300 pts (Ger Transl St) (IB 28 pts)
        Manchester Met – 260 pts (Lang (Fr/Ger/Ital/Span) Ling) (IB 28 pts)
        Nottingham Trent – 260 pts (Ger Joint Hons) (IB 24 pts)
        Sunderland – 260 pts (Ger (Comb))
        UCLan – 260–300 pts (Ger Bus Ger; Ger (Comb))
        Westminster – BCC (Ger courses)
240 pts **Bangor** – 240–260 pts (Ger courses)
        Chester – 240–280 pts (Ger courses) (IB 26 pts)
        Ulster – 240 pts (Ger courses; Bus St Fr/Ger/Span)
230 pts **Edinburgh Napier** – 230 pts (Bus Mgt Ger)
220 pts **Leeds Met** – 220 pts (Ger Int Rel; Ger Mark; Ger Tour Mgt)
        York St John – 220–260 pts (Bus Mgt Ger)
200 pts **Portsmouth** – 200–280 pts (Ger St)
 80 pts **London (Birk)** – p/t for under 21s (over 21s varies) (Fr Ger)

Alternative offers
See **Chapter 7** and **Appendix 1** for grades/UCAS Tariff points information for the International Baccalaureate, Scottish Highers/Advanced Highers, the Welsh Baccalaureate, the Irish Leaving Certificate, the Cambridge Pre-U Diploma, the Advanced Diploma and the Extended Project.

CHOOSING YOUR COURSE (SEE ALSO CH.1)
Some course features
Bangor German is offered with two other languages from Dutch, French, Italian and Spanish.
Durham (Modn Lang) Students take core language module each year and options from a range of modules, including film, history, literature, translation, interpreting and cultural studies.
Heriot-Watt The course focuses on practical language skills, linguistics and translation studies, communication studies and European studies.
Salford The only university to offer a course combining media, a language and business studies.
UEA German can be taken as part of the Law course with European Legal Systems.

Universities and colleges teaching quality See www.qaa.ac.uk; http://unistats.direct.gov.uk.

Top research universities and colleges (RAE 2008) (German, Dutch and Scandinavian languages) Oxford; Cambridge; London (King's); Leeds; London (UCL); Durham; London (RH); St Andrews; Manchester; Birmingham.

ADMISSIONS INFORMATION
Number of applicants per place (approx) Aston 4; Bangor 6; Birmingham 6; Bradford 6; Bristol 7; Cardiff 6; Durham 4; Exeter 4; Heriot-Watt 10; Hull 12; Kent 10; Lancaster 7; Leeds (Joint Hons) 8; Leicester 4; London (King's) 5; London (QM) 6; London (RH) 5; London (UCL) 4; Newcastle 6; Nottingham 5; Portsmouth 5; Salford 5; Staffordshire 5; Stirling 6; Surrey 2; Swansea 4; UCLan 2; UEA 4; Warwick (Ger Bus St) 16, (Ger) 8; York 6.

Advice to applicants and planning the UCAS personal statement Describe visits to Germany or a German-speaking country and the particular cultural and geographical features of the region. Contacts with friends in Germany and language experience should also be mentioned, and if you are bilingual, say so. Read German newspapers and magazines and keep up-to-date with national news.

Misconceptions about this course **Leeds** See **Languages**. **Swansea** Some students are afraid of the year abroad, which is actually one of the most enjoyable parts of the course.

Selection interviews **Yes** Bangor, Birmingham (short conversation in German), Bradford, Cambridge, Durham, Exeter, Heriot-Watt, Hull, Liverpool, London (RH), London (UCL), Newcastle, Oxford, Sheffield, Southampton, Surrey (always), UEA; **Some** Cardiff, Leeds, Portsmouth, Swansea; **No** Nottingham.

Interview advice and questions Questions asked on A-level syllabus. Part of the interview may be in German. What foreign newspapers and/or magazines do you read? Questions on German current affairs, particularly politics and reunification problems, books read outside the course, etc. See also **Chapter 6**. **Leeds** See **Languages**.

Reasons for rejection (non-academic) Unstable personality. Poor motivation. Insufficient commitment. Unrealistic expectations. Not interested in spending a year abroad.

AFTER-RESULTS ADVICE

Offers to applicants repeating A-levels Higher Birmingham, Glasgow, Leeds, Warwick; **Same** Aston, Cardiff, Chester, Durham, London (RH), Newcastle (not always), Nottingham, Salford, Surrey, Swansea, UEA, Ulster, York; **No** Cambridge.

GRADUATE DESTINATIONS AND EMPLOYMENT (2009/10 HESA)

Graduates surveyed 695 **Employed** 295 **In voluntary employment** 15 **In further study** 155 **Assumed unemployed** 35

Career note See **Languages**.

OTHER DEGREE SUBJECTS FOR CONSIDERATION

East European Studies; European Studies; International Business Studies.

GREEK

(see also Classical Studies/Classical Civilisation, Classics, Languages, Latin)

Courses are offered in Ancient and Modern Greek, covering the language and literature from ancient times to the present day. Classics and Classical Studies courses (see separate tables) also focus on Greek language and literature, and many provide the opportunity to learn Greek (and/or Latin) from scratch.

Useful websites www.greek-language.com; www.arwhead.com/Greeks; www.greekmyth.org; www.fhw.gr; www.culture.gr; www.greeklanguage.gr.

NB The points totals shown to the left of the institutions are for ease of reference only. It must not be assumed that Tariff points are always used by institutions or that they can be substituted for an offer in grades. The level of an offer is not necessarily indicative of the quality of a course.

COURSE OFFERS INFORMATION

Subject requirements/preferences GCSE English and a foreign language required. Greek required by some universities. **AL** Latin, Greek or a foreign language may be specified by some universities.

Your target offers and examples of courses provided by each institution
410 pts **London (King's)** – AAAb (Gk Engl) (IB 38 pts HL 666 incl Engl)
380 pts **Cambridge** – A*AA (Modn Mediev Lang (Class Gk)) (IB 40–42 pts)
  London (King's) – AABc (Turk Modn Gk St) (IB 36 pts)
360 pts **London (UCL)** – AABe (Lat Gk) (IB 36 pts)
  Oxford – AAA (Modn Gk) (IB 38–40 pts)
340 pts **Exeter** – AAB–ABB (Gk Arbc St) (IB 34–31 pts)
  Leeds – AAB (Gk) (IB 33 pts)
  London (UCL) – AAB incl Gk (Gk Lat) (IB 36 pts)
  Nottingham – AAB (Gk (Anc)) (IB 34 pts)
  St Andrews – AAB–AAA (Gk courses) (IB 35–38 pts)
320 pts **Glasgow** – ABB (Gk Joint Hons) (IB 36 pts)
  Leeds – ABB (Engl Gk Civ) (IB 33 pts)
  London (RH) – ABB 320 pts (Gk)
  Manchester – ABB–BBB 300–320 pts (Gk) (IB 34–31 pts)
  Swansea – ABB–BBB 320–300 pts (Gk courses) (IB 32–33 pts)
300 pts **Edinburgh** – BBB–AAA (Class Arch Gk) (IB 34–42 pts)
  Leeds – BBB (Gk Civ Phil) (IB 32 pts)
200 pts **Trinity Saint David** – 200–300 pts (Gk courses)

Alternative offers
See **Chapter 7** and **Appendix 1** for grades/UCAS Tariff points information for the International Baccalaureate, Scottish Highers/Advanced Highers, the Welsh Baccalaureate, the Irish Leaving Certificate, the Cambridge Pre-U Diploma, the Advanced Diploma and the Extended Project.

CHOOSING YOUR COURSE (SEE ALSO CH.1)
Some course features
Durham Classics courses have a common first year which allows the student to begin or continue a study of Greek.
Edinburgh (Gk St) The course covers archaeology, art, literature of Greek civilisation, with an intensive Greek course in the first term for beginners.
London (King's) The Modern Greek with English course focuses on studying the classical world through reading ancient texts in the original Greek. A-level Greek is required for entry.
Nottingham (Gk (Anc)) The course combines Greek language learning throughout (no prior knowledge required) with a study of Greek literature, history, society and culture. Intensive language study is provided so at each level of the course students can read texts in the original Greek.

Universities and colleges teaching quality See www.qaa.ac.uk; http://unistats.direct.gov.uk.

Top research universities and colleges (RAE 2008) See **Classics**.

ADMISSIONS INFORMATION
Number of applicants per place (approx) Leeds 2; London (King's) 3.

Advice to applicants and planning the UCAS personal statement See **Classical Studies/Classical Civilisation**.

Selection interviews Yes Cambridge, London (RH).

Interview advice and questions Questions asked on A-level syllabus: Why do you want to study Greek? What aspects of this course interest you? (Questions will develop from answers.) See also **Chapter 6**.

Reasons for rejection (non-academic) Poor language ability.

AFTER-RESULTS ADVICE
Offers to applicants repeating A-levels Higher St Andrews; **Same** Leeds; **No** Cambridge.

GRADUATE DESTINATIONS AND EMPLOYMENT (2009/10 HESA)
Classical Greek; graduates surveyed 20 **Employed** 10 **In voluntary employment** 0 **In further study** 10 **Assumed unemployed** 0

Career note See **Languages**.

OTHER DEGREE SUBJECTS FOR CONSIDERATION
Ancient History; Classical Studies; Classics; European Studies; Philosophy.

HEALTH SCIENCES/STUDIES

(including **Audiology, Chiropractic, Orthoptics, Osteopathy** and **Paramedic Science;** see also Community Studies/Development, Environmental Sciences/Studies, Nursing and Midwifery, Pharmacology, Pharmacy and Pharmaceutical Sciences, Physiotherapy, Radiography, Social Sciences/Studies, Speech Pathology/Sciences/therapy)

Health Sciences/Studies is a broad subject-field which offers courses covering both practical applications concerning health and well-being (some of which border on nursing) and also the administrative activities involved in the promotion of health in the community. Also included are some specialised careers which include Chiropractic, involving the healing process by way of manipulation, mainly in the spinal region, and Osteopathy in which joints and tissues are manipulated to correct abnormalities. Audiology is concerned with the treatment and diagnosis of hearing and balance

Check **Chapter 4** when choosing your university and **Chapter 7** on how to read the subject tables.

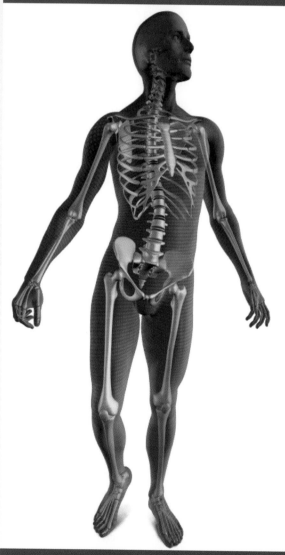

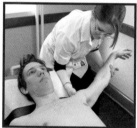

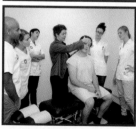

ANGLO-EUROPEAN COLLEGE OF CHIROPRACTIC

Become a top-earning healthcare professional with a BSc-MSc in Chiropractic!

Why study Chiropractic at the AECC?

Chiropractic is a highly rewarding healthcare profession, with earnings equivalent to Medical Doctors and Dentists.

Chiropractors enjoy excellent job satisfaction, based on the ability to diagnose and treat painful musculoskeletal issues, improve mobility and quality of life.

Being your own boss allows you to choose your own working hours, holidays and where you live.

The AECC is one of the world's leading providers of chiropractic education in a dynamic, state-of-the-art, hands-on, multidisciplinary environment.

Our faculty are among the most respected globally, based on their research and clinical expertise, offering our students a wealth of practical experience and support.

We benefit from a fantastic location in Bournemouth with superb recreational opportunities ranging from hills to forest, to coast, with our award winning seven mile beach!

Bournemouth is one of the most vibrant, cosmopolitan, and diverse communities in Britain, with excellent travel links to the city of London and international destinations.

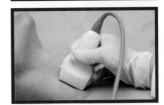

Get in touch!

Call **01202 436200**

Email **admissions@aecc.ac.uk**

or visit **www.aecc.ac.uk**

disorders while Prosthetics involves the provision and fitting of artificial limbs and Orthotics is concerned with making and fitting braces, splints and special footwear to ease pain and to assist movement.

Useful websites www.rsph.org.uk; www.bmj.com; www.reflexology.org; www.baap.org.uk; www.chiropractic-uk.co.uk; www.osteopathy.org.uk; www.who.int; www.csp.org.uk; www.scienceyear.com; www.intute.ac.uk.

NB The points totals shown to the left of the institutions are for ease of reference only. It must not be assumed that Tariff points are always used by institutions or that they can be substituted for an offer in grades. The level of an offer is not necessarily indicative of the quality of a course.

COURSE OFFERS INFORMATION

Subject requirements/preferences GCSE English, mathematics and a science important or essential for some courses. **AL** Mathematics, chemistry or biology may be required for some courses. **Other** Health checks and CRB clearance required for many courses.

Your target offers and examples of courses provided by each institution

340 pts **Exeter** – AAB–ABB (Clin Sci) (IB 32–34 pts)
Southampton – AAB (Audiol; Hlthcr Sci) (IB 34 pts HL 17 pts)

320 pts **Glamorgan** – 320 pts (Chiropractic)
Glasgow – ABB (Spo Med) (IB 32 pts)
Manchester – ABB–BBB (Audiol) (IB 33–30 pts)
Plymouth – 280–320 pts (Hlth Sci Physiol)
Roehampton – 320 pts (Nutr Hlth)
Strathclyde – ABB (Pros Orthot) (IB 34 pts)
Southampton – ABB (Hlthcr Sci (Cardio/Respir Slp Sci)) (IB 32 pts HL 16 pts)

300 pts **Bradford** – optional transfer for some students to Medicine at Leeds 300 pts (Clin Sci)
Bristol UWE – (Hlth Sci Physiol)
Brunel – BBB (Biomed Sci (Hum Hlth)) (IB 32 pts HL 5 Biol)
Durham – BBB (Hlth Hum Sci) (IB 32 pts)
Essex – 300–280 pts (Hlth St Sociol) (IB 32–30 pts)
Glasgow – BBB (Hlth Soc St) (IB 30 pts)
London (St George's) – BBB (Hlthcr Sci (Physiol Sci))
Manchester – BBB (Oral Hlth Sci) (IB 30 pts)
Nottingham Trent – 300 pts (Hlthcr Sci)
Oxford Brookes – BBB (Ost)
Sheffield – BBB (Orth) (IB 32 pts)
Surrey – ABB–BBB incl AL sci 300–320 pts (Paramed Sci)
Swansea – BBB (Audiol)

280 pts **Anglo-Euro (Coll Chiro)** – BBC (Chiro)

Brit Coll Ost Med – BBC (incl biol, chem) 280 pts (MOst)

British Sch Ost – BBC (incl biol + 1 other sci) 280 pts (Ost)

Essex – 280–300 pts (Hlth St) (IB 32–30 pts)

Glamorgan – 280 pts (Hlth Soc Cr)

Hertfordshire – check with admissions tutor 280–300 pts (Paramed Sci)

Kent – BBC (Hlth Soc Cr) (IB 33 pts)

London Met – (Hlth Soc Plcy)

Manchester Met – 280 pts (Acu) (IB 30 pts)

Northumbria – 280 pts (Hlth Cotemp Soc)

Plymouth – 280–300 pts (Pblc Hlth Nutr)

Portsmouth – BBC (Hlthcr Sci)

Salford – 280 pts (Pros Orthot) (IB 24 pts)

Sheffield Hallam – 280 pts (Pblc Hlth Nutr)

Swansea – 280 pts (Hlth Soc Cr; Med Sci)

Worcester – 280 pts (Hlth Psy)

260 pts **Anglo-Euro (Coll Chiro)** – 260 pts incl biol/chem (Exer Hlth (Hlth Rehab))

Brunel – BCC (Occ Thera) (IB 29 pts)

Derby – 260 pts (Hlth Soc Cr)

Dundee – BCC (Oral Hlth Sci) (IB 30 pts)

Edge Hill – BCC 260 pts (Nutr Hlth)

Edinburgh Queen Margaret – 260 pts (Hlth Psy)

European Sch Ost – BCC 260 pts (Ost)

Hull – BCC (Glob Hlth Hum Rlf)

Lincoln – 260 pts (Hlth Soc Cr)

Liverpool – BCC (Orth) (IB 28 pts HL 5 biol)

Liverpool Hope – 260 pts (Hlth Nutr Fit)

LJMU – 260 pts (Hlth Soc Cr Fmly Indiv Comm)

Northampton – 260–280 pts (Hlth St courses; Hum Biosci)

Nottingham – BCC (Hlthcr Sci) (IB 26 pts)

Nottingham Trent – 260 pts (Exer Nutr Hlth)

Sheffield – BCC (Hlth Hum Sci) (IB 29 pts)

Sunderland – 260 pts (Commun Pblc Hlth; Hlth Soc Cr; Hlthcr Sci (Physiol Sci/Lf Sci/Audiol))

Teesside – 260–280 pts (Fd Nutr Hlth Sci)

UCLan – 260–300 pts (Hlth St courses)

Ulster – 260 pts (Hlth Soc Cr Plcy)

240 pts **Arts London (CFash)** – 240 pts (Cos Sci)

Bangor – 240–260 pts (Hlth Soc Cr)

Bath Spa – 240–280 pts (Diet Hlth)

Birmingham City – 240 pts (Hlth Wlbng)

Bolton – 240 pts (Commun Hlth Wlbng)

Cardiff Met – 240 pts (Hlth Soc Cr)

Chester – 240–280 pts (Hlth Soc Cr)

Coventry – CCC 240 pts (Exer Nutr Hlth)

Glyndŵr – 240 pts (Complem Med Prac; Chin Med)

Huddersfield – 240 pts (Nutr Pblc Hlth)

Hull – 240 pts (Glob Hlth Hum Rts)

Leeds Met – Check with admissions tutor 240 pts (Ost) (IB 24 pts)

Middlesex – 240–280 pts (Trad Chin Acu)

Nescot – 240 pts (Ost Med)

Nottingham Trent – 240 pts (Hlth Soc Cr)

Southampton Solent – 240 pts (Hlth Psy)

Suffolk (Univ Campus) – 240 pts (Hlth Wlbng)

UCP Marjon – 240 pts (Hlth Exer Physl Actvt)

West Scotland – CCC (Env Hlth)

Check **Chapter 4** when choosing your university and **Chapter 7** on how to read the subject tables.

220 pts **Anglo-Euro (Coll Chiro)** – 220 pts (Comm Hlth Rehab)
Bath Spa – 220–280 pts (Hlth St courses)
Glamorgan – 220–260 pts (Actvty Commun Hlth) (IB 28 pts)
Gloucestershire – 220 pts (Hlth Commun Soc Cr)
Kingston – 220–280 pts (Exer Nutr Hlth)
St Mary's Twickenham (UC) – 220 pts (Hlth Exer Physl Actvts) (IB 28 pts)
Southampton Solent – 220 pts (Hlth Exer Physl Actvt; Hlth Prom Fit)
Westminster – CCD (Hlth Sci (Herb Med)) (IB 26 pts)

200 pts **Canterbury Christ Church** – 200–240 pts (Hlth St)
Greenwich – 200 pts (Hlth Wlbng)
Leeds Met – 200 pts (Pbl Hlth (Nutr)) (IB 24 pts HL 5 biol)
Middlesex – 200–300 pts (Complem Hlth Sci)
Plymouth – 200 pts (Hlth Soc Cr St)
Roehampton – 200–260 pts (Hlth Hum Sci)
Salford – 200 pts (Exer Physl Actvt Hlth) (IB 24 pts)
UCLan – 200 pts (Sex Hlth St)
UEL – 200 pts (Fit Hlth; Hlth Prom; Hlth St)
UHI – BB–AA (Oral Hlth Sci)
West London – 200 pts (Hlth St)

180 pts **Bedfordshire** – 180–220 pts (Disab St)
Greenwich – 180 pts (Pblc Hlth)
Trinity Saint David – 180–360 pts (Hlth Exer; Hlth Nutr Lfstl)

160 pts **Accrington and Rossendale (Coll)** – 160 pts (Hlth App Soc St)
Anglia Ruskin – 160 pts (Pblc Hlth)
Cumbria – 160 pts (Complem Thera)
Roehampton – 160–200 pts (Hlth Soc Cr)
Stockport (Coll) – 160 pts (Hlth Soc Cr)
UHI – CC–AA (Hlth St)
Wolverhampton – 160–220 pts (Hlth St Soc Cr; Hlth St; Df St)

140 pts **Bradford (Coll Univ Centre)** – 140 pts (Hlth Soc Welf)

120 pts **Cumbria** – 120 pts (Hlth Cr Prac)

100 pts **Newport** – 100–120 pts (Commun Hlth Wlbng)
Brighton – individual offers may vary (Acu St; Ost)

Brit Coll Ost Med – contact admissions tutor (Dip Ost; Dip Natpth)
Open University – contact +44 (0)845 300 6090 **or** www.openuniversity.co.uk/you (Hlth Soc Cr)
Staffordshire – contact University (Hlth St)

Alternative offers

See **Chapter 7** and **Appendix 1** for grades/UCAS Tariff points information for the International Baccalaureate, Scottish Highers/Advanced Highers, the Welsh Baccalaureate, the Irish Leaving Certificate, the Cambridge Pre-U Diploma, the Advanced Diploma and the Extended Project.

EXAMPLES OF FOUNDATION DEGREES IN THE SUBJECT FIELD

See also **Social and Public Policy and Administration.** Blackburn (Coll); Blackpool and Fylde (Coll); Bolton; Brighton; Bucks New; Croydon (Coll); Cumbria; Duchy (Coll); Durham New (Coll); Exeter (Coll); Grimsby (IFHE); Havering (Coll); Hopwood Hall (Coll); Lakes (Coll); Llandrillo Cymru (Coll); Manchester (Coll); Neath Port Talbot (Coll); Newport; North Lindsey (Coll); Norwich City (Coll); Oxford Brookes; Petroc; St Helens (Coll); Somerset (CAT); Stockport (Coll); Truro (Coll); Wakefield (Coll); Walsall (Coll); West Cheshire (Coll); Worcester (CT).

CHOOSING YOUR COURSE (SEE ALSO CH.1)

Some course features

Aberdeen The Health Sciences programme is based in the Medical School and combines courses on social, life and medical sciences. In the third year students are attached to a health or social care agency in the community.

British College of Osteopathic Medicine
a world leader in osteopathic education

The British College of Osteopathic Medicine (BCOM) is internationally regarded as one of the world's best specialist osteopathic education institutions. Founded in London in 1936 by the famous naturopathic osteopath, Stanley Lief, the College has become a world leader in osteopathic education and research.

Based in Hampstead opposite Finchley Road underground, BCOM's friendly campus has the most full-time academic staff in any UK osteopathic college and was the first institution in the UK to offer an osteopathic honours degree and to achieve a landmark "approval without conditions" QAA led RQ recognition from the General Osteopathic Council. BCOM has been running its much-praised four year undergraduate Masters in Osteopathy (M.Ost) since 2008.

Excellent Facilities
BCOM offers the most advanced osteopathic-research facilities in Europe, being the only specialist college to provide cutting-edge on-site human-performance and hydrotherapy laboratory facilities. Founder of the International Conference on Advances in Osteopathic Research (ICAOR), BCOM fosters a strong research environment that enables advances to be disseminated more generally, with the best student research being presented at leading international conferences. It also works to instil a research ethos into BCOM graduates, increasing the clinical knowledge base and providing Continuing Professional Development.

BCOM's Holistic Osteopathic Approach
BCOM is particularly regarded for its uniquely holistic or naturopathic approach to osteopathic care and works hard at promoting the philosophy, science and clinical application of holistic osteopathy and naturopathy within the UK and throughout the international community. BCOM's undergraduate and postgraduate students are an integral part of its teaching and research clinics.

A Degree and a Career

BCOM's graduates have proceeded to embark on rewarding careers within the osteopathic profession on completion of their Undergraduate Masters Degrees at the College.

New graduate Byung-ho Kim is the first Korean osteopath to be trained in the UK. Known as Kim to colleagues and friends, he now practices osteopathy at a busy clinic in Seoul, South Korea, working with US chiropractors. Kim views his experience at BCOM as a great turning point in his life and was given support throughout his degree by staff and fellow students. Kim said of his experience studying at BCOM: "During my degree I found that osteopathy is not just a branch of medicine, osteopathy is a principle of medicine and a connection between general medicine and alternative or complementary medicine. BCOM has been extraordinary for me as a foreign student because of the family-like atmosphere."

Stephania Humphrey is a practicing Osteopath and Naturopath. After Graduating from BCOM in 2010, Stephania set up in a GP practice in West London. Practicing on her own proved to be a challenge, but was an excellent learning curve where she gained invaluable business experience. Stephania then became an associate at a practice in South London, where she now works, as well as running her own private practice.

Stephania's experience at BCOM was an extremely positive one and she was made to feel very welcome and supported, finding the course to be both intense and rewarding. Of her time at BCOM, Stephania said: "The course helped me immensely with my career and I absolutely love being an osteopath and being part of this profession, and without BCOM I would not have been able to do what I enjoy most every day. There is no other degree like the one at BCOM, it is fun and rewarding, and the years fly by, so enjoy it all whilst you are there! You meet people you will know and be friends with for life, and generally the people drawn to work in this profession tend to all be very caring and respectful individuals. There is a strong osteopathic community which we are all proud of."

Contact Details

British College of Osteopathic Medicine
Lief House, 120-122 Finchley Road
London NW3 5HR
Tel: +44 (0)20 7435 6464
Email: admissions @bcom.ac.uk
www.bcom.ac.uk

What gives you your edge?

"Caring for the future"

The University of Surrey is a leading provider of Health and Social Care programmes. We offer the following undergraduate courses:

BSc Adult Nursing

BSc Mental Health Nursing

BSc Child Nursing

BSc Midwifery

BSc Paramedic Practice

Diploma of Higher Education Operating Department Practice

For more information please visit **www.surrey.ac.uk/heapcare** or scan the QR code.

**University of Surrey
Guildford
Surrey
GU2 7XH
UK**

T: 0800 980 3200 / +44 (0)1483 681 681
E: ug-enquiries@surrey.ac.uk

Duke of Kent building, School of Health & Social Care, University of Surrey

Bath Spa Health Studies is a part of the Combined Honours programme. In addition to health subjects the course focuses on social, cultural, economic and environmental factors.
Brunel Degrees are offered in Occupational Therapy and Physiotherapy. Both courses place an emphasis on preparing students for working life by promoting autonomy and clinical practice.
Essex Courses cover Health Studies and Social Psychology or Sociology relevant to health and communication skills.

Universities and colleges teaching quality See www.qaa.ac.uk; http://unistats.direct.gov.uk.

Top research universities and colleges (RAE 2008) (Allied Health Professions and Studies)
London (UCL); Lancaster; Surrey; Bristol UWE; Hull; Cardiff; Swansea; Glasgow; Strathclyde; Queen's Belfast.

ADMISSIONS INFORMATION
Number of applicants per place (approx) Anglo-Euro (Coll Chiro) 1; Bangor 2; Bath Spa 1; Bournemouth 4; Bristol (Audiol) 5, (Df St) 2; Brit Coll Ost Med 5; Brunel 2; Chester 6; Chichester 5; Cumbria 4; European Sch Ost 3; LJMU 10; London Met 7; Manchester 18; Manchester Met 10; Middlesex 4; Northampton 3; Portsmouth 12; Roehampton 10; Salford 8; Southampton 4; Swansea 1; UCLan 6; Worcester 3.

Admissions tutors' advice You should describe any work with people you have done, particularly in a caring capacity, for example, working with the elderly, nursing, hospital work. Show why you wish to study this subject. You should give evidence of your ability to communicate and to work in a group. Evidence needed of applicants' understanding of the NHS and health care systems. Osteopathy applicants should provide clear evidence of why they want to work as an osteopath: work shadowing in an osteopath's practice is important and should be described. Give details of any work using your hands.

Misconceptions about this course There is a mistaken belief that Health Science courses include nursing. **Bangor** (Hlth Soc Cr) This is an administration course, not a nursing course. **Brit Coll Ost Med** Some students think that we offer an orthodox course in medicine. **European Sch Ost** Some applicants think we teach in French: we do not although we do have a franchise with a French school based in St Etienne and a high percentage of international students. All lectures are in English. Applicants should note that cranial osteopathy – one of our specialisms – is only one aspect of the programme.

Selection interviews Yes Birmingham, Bristol, Chichester, Coventry, European Sch Ost, Glamorgan, London (St George's), Middlesex, Nottingham Trent, Portsmouth, Southampton, UCLan, West Scotland, Worcester; **Some** Abertay Dundee, Bath Spa, Canterbury Christ Church, Cardiff Met (Complem Thera), Derby, Huddersfield (mature students), LJMU, Salford, Swansea; **No** Dundee.

Interview advice and questions Courses vary considerably and you are likely to be questioned on your reasons for choosing the course at that university or college. If you have studied biology then questions are possible on the A-level syllabus and you could also be asked to discuss any work experience you have had. (Osteopathy) What personal qualities would you need to be a good osteopath? What have you done that you would feel demonstrates a sense of responsibility? What would you do if you were not able to secure a place on an Osteopathy course this year? See also **Chapter 6. LJMU** Interviews are informal. It would be useful for you to bring samples of coursework to the interview.

Reasons for rejection (non-academic) Some students are mistakenly looking for a professional qualification in, for example, occupational therapy, nursing. **Coventry** Inadequate mathematics.

AFTER-RESULTS ADVICE
Offers to applicants repeating A-levels Same Abertay Dundee, Aston, Bangor, Brighton, Chester, Derby, European Sch Ost, Huddersfield, Lincoln, LJMU, Nottingham Trent (Hlth Env), Roehampton, Salford, Surrey, Swansea.

For a quick reference offers calculator, fold out the inside back cover.

GRADUATE DESTINATIONS AND EMPLOYMENT (2009/10 HESA)

See also **Biotechnology**, **Dentistry**, **Medicine**, **Nursing and Midwifery**, **Nutrition** and **Optometry**.

Complementary Medicine; graduates surveyed 1165 **Employed** 715 **In voluntary employment** 5 **In further study** 215 **Assumed unemployed** 50

Aural and Oral Sciences; graduates surveyed 820 **Employed** 670 **In voluntary employment** 25 **In further study** 60 **Assumed unemployed** 65

Career note Graduates enter a very broad variety of careers depending on their specialism. Opportunities exist in the public sector, for example, management and administrative positions with health and local authorities and in health promotion.

OTHER DEGREE SUBJECTS FOR CONSIDERATION

Audiology; Biological Sciences; Biology; Community Studies; Consumer Studies; Dentistry; Dietetics; Medicine; Environmental Health; Nursing; Nutrition; Occupational Therapy; Optometry; Physiotherapy; Psychology; Podiatry; Radiography; Speech Therapy; Sport Science.

HISTORY

(including **Heritage Management** and **Medieval Studies**; see also **History (Ancient)**, **History (Economic and Social)**, **History of Art**)

Degrees in History cover a very broad field with many courses focusing on British and European history. However, specialised History degrees are available which cover other regions of the world and, in addition, all courses will offer a wide range of modules.

Useful websites www.english-heritage.org.uk; www.historytoday.com; www.genealogyarchives.com; www.historynet.com; www.archives.org.uk; www.royalhistoricalsociety.org; www.nationalarchives.gov. uk; www.historesearch.com.

NB The points totals shown to the left of the institutions are for ease of reference only. It must not be assumed that Tariff points are always used by institutions or that they can be substituted for an offer in grades. The level of an offer is not necessarily indicative of the quality of a course.

COURSE OFFERS INFORMATION

Subject requirements/preferences **GCSE** English and a foreign language may be required or preferred. **AL** History usually required at a specified grade. (Mediev St) History or English literature required for some courses. (Vkg St) English or history.

Your target offers and examples of courses provided by each institution

430 pts **London (King's)** – A*AAb (Hist) (IB 39 pts HL 666 incl hist)

400 pts **London (UCL)** – A*AA+AS–AAA+AS (Hist (St Abrd)) (IB 38–39 pts)
Warwick – AAAc (Hist Joint Hons) (IB 38 pts)

380 pts **Cambridge** – A*AA (Hist) (IB 40–42 pts)
Durham – A*AA (Engl Lit Hist) (IB 38 pts)
Exeter – A*AA–AAB (Hist) (IB 38–34 pts)
London (King's) – A*AA (War St Hist) (IB 39 pts)
Warwick – AABc (Hist Lit Cult Am) (IB 36 pts)

360 pts **Birmingham** – AAA–ABB 320–360 pts (Hist Joint Hons) (IB 34–38 pts)
Bristol – AAA–AAB (Hist) (IB 37–35 pts)
Durham – AAA (Modn Euro Langs Hist) (IB 37 pts)
Edinburgh – AAA–BBB (Econ Hist Bus St) (IB 42–34 pts)
Exeter – 360–340 pts (Hist Int Rel (St Abrd)) (IB 36–31 pts)
Leeds – AAA (Hist) (IB 35–37 pts)
Liverpool – AAA (Hist) (IB 33 pts HL 6 hist)
London (QM) – AAA 340 pts (Hist) (IB 32 pts)

Check **Chapter 4** when choosing your university and **Chapter 7** on how to read the subject tables.

London LSE – AAA (Hist) (IB 38 pts HL 766)
London NCH – AAA–AAB 340–360 pts (Hist) (IB 37–38 pts HL 77)
Manchester – AAA–AAB 340–360 pts (Hist) (IB 37 pts)
Newcastle – AAA–AAB 340–360 pts (Pol Hist) (IB 37 pts)
Nottingham – AAA (Hist) (IB 36 pts)
Oxford – AAA (Hist) (IB 38–40 pts)
St Andrews – AAA–AAB (Modn Hist courses) (IB 35–36 pts)
Sheffield – AAA incl hist (Int Hist Int Pol) (IB 37 pts HL 6 hist)
York – AAA–AAB (Engl Hist) (IB 36 pts)

340 pts **Cardiff** – AAB incl hist (Hist; Modn Hist Pol)
Kent – AAB (War St) (IB 33 pts)
Lancaster – AAB 340 pts (Hist) (IB 34 pts)
Leicester – AAB (Hist) (IB 34 pts)
London (Gold) – AAB (Hist)
London (QM) – AAB 340 pts (Hist Compar Lit) (IB 32 pts)
London (RH) – AAB (Hist) (IB 36 pts)
London (SOAS) – AAB (Hist) (IB 30–32 pts)
London (UCL) – AAB–ABB incl hist (Scand St Hist) (IB 34–36 pts)
Loughborough – AAB 340 pts (Hist) (IB 32–34 pts)
Manchester – AAB–ABB (Pol Modn Hist) (IB 35–34 pts)
Newcastle – AAA–AAB 340–360 pts (Hist) (IB 37–35 pts HL 6 hist)
Nottingham – AAB (Am St Hist) (IB 34 pts)
St Andrews – AAB (Mediev Hist Arch) (IB 35 pts)
Southampton – AAB incl hist (Modn Hist Pol) (IB 34 pts HL 17 pts)
Sussex – AAB (Hist) (IB 35 pts)
UEA – AAB–ABB (Am St Engl Hist) (IB 33–32 pts)

320 pts **Birmingham** – ABB (Hist) (IB 36 pts)
Bristol UWE – 320 pts (Hist) (IB 28–30 pts)
Essex – ABB 320 pts (Hist) (IB 32 pts)
Glasgow – ABB (Hist) (IB 36 pts)
Hertfordshire – 320 pts (Hist)
Hull – 320 pts (Hist)
Kent – ABB (Euro Hist (St Abrd)) (IB 33 pts)
Lancaster – ABB (Hist Mus) (IB 32 pts)
Leeds – ABB–BBB (Biol Hist Phil Sci) (IB 34–32 pts)
Leicester – ABB (Hist Am St; Hist Arch; Contemp Hist; Hist courses)
Liverpool – ABB (Hist Joint Hons) (IB 33 pts HL 6 hist lang)
London (Birk) – ABB (Hist)
London (Gold) – ABB–BBB (Hist Sociol)
London (UCL) – ABBc (Hist Jew St) (IB 34 pts)
Northumbria – 320 pts (Engl Lit Hist) (IB 26 pts)
Nottingham – ABB (Arch Hist) (IB 32 pts)
Queen's Belfast – ABB/BBBb (Hist)
Reading – 320–340 pts (Hist) (IB 32 pts HL 666)
Strathclyde – ABB (Hist) (IB 34 pts)
Southampton – ABB (Arch Hist) (IB 32 pts HL 16 pts)
Swansea – ABB–BBB (Euro Hist; Mediev St courses)

300 pts **Aberdeen** – BBB 300 pts (Hist)
Aberystwyth – 300–320 pts (Hist Media) (IB 30 pts)
Bristol UWE – 300 pts (Hist Sociol) (IB 28 pts)
Edinburgh – BBB–AAA (Scot Hist) (IB 34–42 pts)
Essex – 300–320 pts (Modn Hist) (IB 32 pts)
Gloucestershire – 280–300 pts (Hist)
Huddersfield – 300 pts (Pol Contemp Hist)
Hull – 300 pts (Hist Fr/Ger/Ital/Span; Hist Hist Art)

Keele – 300–320 pts (Hist) (IB 28–30 pts)
Kent – BBB (Hist Joint Hons)
Northumbria – 300 pts (Hist Pol) (IB 26 pts)
Nottingham – ABC–BBB (Am Can Lit Hist Cult) (IB 30 pts)
Roehampton – 300 pts (Hist) (IB 26 pts)
Swansea – ABB–BBB 300 pts (Hist)

280 pts **Bristol UWE** – 280–320 pts (Hist courses) (IB 28–30 pts)
Chichester – BBC–BCC 260–280 pts (Hist) (IB 28 pts)
Edge Hill – 280 pts (Hist Sociol)
Glamorgan – BBC 280 pts (Hist)
Hull – 280–300 pts (Marit Hist)
Lincoln – 280 pts (Dr Hist; Hist; Hist Pol)
Manchester Met – 280 pts (Hist Joint Hons) (IB 29 pts)
Nottingham Trent – 280 pts (Hist)
Oxford Brookes – BBC (Hist Art) (IB 30 pts)
Reading – 280–300 pts (Hist Art Hist)
Stirling – BBC (Hist) (IB 32 pts)
Suffolk (Univ Campus) – 280 pts (Hist)
Teesside – 280 pts (Hist) (IB 24 pts)
Westminster – BBC 280 pts (Engl Lit Hist) (IB 28 pts)

260 pts **Brighton** – BCC 260 pts (Cult Hist Lit)
Brunel – BCC 260 pts (Hist) (IB 31 pts)
Cardiff Met – 260 pts (Educ St Modn Hist)
Chester – 260–300 pts (History) (IB 28 pts)
Coventry – BCC 260 pts (Hist courses; Pol Hist)
De Montfort – 260 pts (Hist) (IB 24 pts)
Derby – 260 pts (Hist)
Dundee – BCC (Scot Hist St) (IB 29 pts HL 15 pts)
Greenwich – 260 pts (Hist)
Lincoln – 260 pts (Crimin Hist)
Liverpool Hope – 260–320 pts (Hist)
LJMU – 260 pts (Hist; Hist Engl)
Newman (UC) – 260 pts (Hist) (IB 24 pts)
Newport – 260 pts (Hist; Engl Hist)
Northampton – 260–280 pts (Hist courses) (IB 24 pts)
Nottingham Trent – 260 pts (Pol Hist)
Plymouth – 260 pts (Hist courses) (IB 27 pts)
Sheffield Hallam – 260 pts (Hist; Engl Hist)
Sunderland – 260 pts (Hist courses)
Ulster – BCC 260 pts (Irish Hist courses; Hist courses)
Westminster – BCC (Modn Hist) (IB 28 pts)
Winchester – 260–300 pts (Hist Mediev Wrld) (IB 24 pts)

240 pts **Aberystwyth** – 240 pts (Hist Archvl St) (IB 24 pts)
Bangor – 240–280 pts (Welsh Hist Arch) (IB 28 pts)
Bolton – 240 pts (Contemp Hist)
Bradford – 240 pts (Modn Euro Hist)
Brighton – CCC 240 pts (Engl Lit Commun Hist) (IB 30 pts)
Buckingham – 240-260 pts (Engl Lit Hist) (IB 27 pts)
Canterbury Christ Church – 240 pts (Hist; Hist Arch)
Glyndŵr – 240 pts (Hist)
Leeds Met – 240 pts (Hist) (IB 24 pts)
Leeds Trinity (UC) – 240 pts (Hist; Engl Hist)
Manchester Met – 240–260 pts (Pol Hist) (IB 28 pts)
Portsmouth – 240–300 pts (Engl Hist) (IB 25 pts)
Staffordshire – 240 pts (Modn Hist)

Check **Chapter 4** when choosing your university and **Chapter 7** on how to read the subject tables.

St Mary's Twickenham (UC) – 240 pts (Hist) (IB 28 pts)
Salford – 240 pts (Contemp Mltry Int Hist) (IB 27 pts)
UCLan – 240 pts (Modn Wrld Hist; Hist)

220 pts **Anglia Ruskin** – 220–260 pts (Hist; Hist Engl)
Bath Spa – 220–280 pts (Hist) (IB 24 pts)
Bishop Grosseteste (UC) – 220 pts (Vis Art Hist)
Kingston – 220 pts (Hist Joint Hons) (IB 30 pts)
Worcester – 220–260 pts (Hist courses) (IB 24 pts)
York St John – 220–260 pts (Hist courses) (IB 24 pts)

200 pts **Blackburn (Coll)** – 200 pts (Hist)
Trinity Saint David – individual offers made after interview 200–300 pts (Hist courses; Mediev St)
UEL – 200 pts (Hist)

180 pts **Leeds Met** – 180 pts (Engl Hist) (IB 24 pts)
160 pts **UHI** – CC–AA (Scot Hist Arch; Scot Hist; Hist Pol)
Wolverhampton – 160–220 pts (Hist; War St)
120 pts **West Anglia (Coll)** – 120 pts (Hist Engl Lit; Sociol Hist)
80 pts **London (Birk)** – p/t for under 21s (over 21s varies) (Hum Hist)

Alternative offers
See **Chapter 7** and **Appendix 1** for grades/UCAS Tariff points information for the International Baccalaureate, Scottish Highers/Advanced Highers, the Welsh Baccalaureate, the Irish Leaving Certificate, the Cambridge Pre-U Diploma, the Advanced Diploma and the Extended Project.

EXAMPLES OF FOUNDATION DEGREES IN THE SUBJECT FIELD
Blackpool and Fylde (Coll); Harper Adams (UC); Petroc; Truro (Coll).

CHOOSING YOUR COURSE (SEE ALSO CH.1)
Some course features
Kent History can be taken with an optional deferred subject. The Single Honours programme provides the opportunity of a work placement in a museum, a cathedral workshop or a year abroad in Europe.
Leicester A very large department offering specialisms in a wide range of subjects. The subject is also part of the Combined Studies programme with a choice of 17 subjects including Politics, Ancient History, Archaeology and International Relations.
Manchester The History programme enables students to study course units across the whole range of history topics including the history of science. There are opportunities to spend part of the course studying abroad.
Ulster In addition to the Single Honours course, History is offered as a joint course (two subjects) or under the Combined Arts programme when students choose three subjects in Year 1 continuing with a study of two subjects or one major and one minor subject.

Universities and colleges teaching quality See www.qaa.ac.uk; http://unistats.direct.gov.uk.

Top research universities and colleges (RAE 2008) Imperial London; Essex; Kent; Liverpool; Oxford; Warwick; Cambridge; London (UCL); London (Birk); Southampton; Hertfordshire; London LSE; Sheffield.

ADMISSIONS INFORMATION
Number of applicants per place (approx) Aberystwyth 6; Anglia Ruskin 4; Bangor 6; Bath Spa 6; Birmingham 8, (E Medit Hist) 3, (War St) 4; Bournemouth (Herit Cons) 3; Bristol 13; Bristol UWE 6; Brunel 6; Buckingham 10; Cambridge 3; Cardiff 7; Chichester 4; Cumbria 5; De Montfort 10; Dundee 6; Durham 15; Edge Hill 8; Exeter 9; Gloucestershire 26; Glyndŵr 2; Huddersfield 4; Hull 5; Kent 12; Kingston 6; Lancaster 11; Leeds 12; Leeds Trinity (UC) 14; Leicester 7; Liverpool 6; London (Gold) 6; London (King's) 10; London (QM) 5; London (RH) 9; London (UCL) 13; London LSE 19; London Met 2; Manchester 5; Manchester Met 8; Middlesex 10; Newcastle 13; Newman (UC) 2; Northampton 4; Nottingham 20; Oxford Brookes 25; Portsmouth 5; Roehampton 3; St Mary's Twickenham (UC) 5;

Sheffield Hallam 21; Southampton 5; Staffordshire 8; Stirling 2; Teesside 4; Trinity Saint David 6; UCLan 5; UEA 8; Warwick 17; York 7; York St John 3.

Advice to applicants and planning the UCAS personal statement Show your passion for the past! Visits to places of interest should be mentioned, together with any particular features which impressed you. Read historical books and magazines outside your A-level syllabus. Mention these and describe any special areas of study which interest you. (Check that these areas are covered in the courses for which you are applying!) **Bristol** Only accepting a limited number of deferred applicants in fairness to next year's applicants. Apply early. **Manchester** Due to the detailed nature of entry requirements for History courses, we are unable to include full details in the prospectus. For complete and up-to-date information on our entry requirements for these courses, please visit our website at www.manchester.ac.uk/ugcourses.

Misconceptions about this course Students sometimes under-estimate the amount of reading required. **Lincoln** Some students expect the subject to be assessed only by exams and essays. It is not – we use a wide range of assessment methods. **LJMU** Some applicants think that they have to study ancient and medieval history as well as modern; we actually only cover post-1750 history. **Stirling** Some applicants think that we only teach British history. We also cover European, American, African and Environmental History.

Selection interviews Yes Bangor, Birmingham, Bishop Grosseteste (UC), Brighton, Bristol, Brunel, Cambridge, Canterbury Christ Church, Chichester, Edge Hill, Hertfordshire, Hull, Lancaster, Leeds Trinity (UC), Lincoln (Cons Restor), London (King's), London (QM), London (RH), London (UCL), London Met, London South Bank, Middlesex, Oxford (Hist) 29% (Hist Mod Lang) 18%, Oxford Brookes, Portsmouth, Roehampton, Sussex, Warwick; **Some** Anglia Ruskin, Bath Spa, Buckingham, Cardiff, De Montfort, Exeter, Huddersfield, Kent, Lincoln, Liverpool, London LSE (rarely), Salford, Sheffield Hallam, Southampton, Staffordshire, Trinity Saint David, Winchester, Wolverhampton, York; **No** Dundee, Essex, Reading, UEA.

Interview advice and questions Questions are almost certain to be asked on those aspects of the history A-level syllabus which interest you. Examples of questions in previous years have included: Why did imperialism happen? If a Martian arrived on Earth what aspect of life would you show him/her to sum up today's society? Has the role of class been exaggerated by Marxist historians? What is the difference between power and authority and between patriotism and nationalism? Did Elizabeth I have a foreign policy? What is the relevance of history in modern society? Who are your favourite monarchs? How could you justify your study of history to the taxpayer? See also **Chapter 6**. **Cambridge** How would you compare Henry VIII to Stalin? In the 1920s did the invention of the Henry Ford car lead to a national sub-culture or was it just an aspect of one? Is there such a thing as 'race'? Should historians be allowed to read sci-fi novels? **Cumbria** Questions about interest in research, analysis, argument, information gathering, future plans after study, motivation. **De Montfort** Why History? Why is history important? **Oxford** Questions on submitted work and the capacity to think independently. What are the origins of your name? Why are you sitting in this chair? **Sheffield** Written work may be required. **Swansea** We ask applicants to explain something – a hobby, an historical problem or a novel. The subject is less important than a coherent and enthusiastic explanation.

Reasons for rejection (non-academic) Personal statements which read like job applications, focusing extensively on personal skills and saying nothing about the applicant's passion for history. Poor use of personal statement combined with predicted grades. Little commitment and enthusiasm. No clear reason for choice of course. Little understanding of history. Absence or narrowness of intellectual pursuits. Deception or concealment on the UCAS application. Knowledge of 19th century history (chosen subject) did not have any depth. Unwillingness to learn. Narrow approach to subject. Failure to submit requested information. **Birmingham** Commitment insufficient to sustain interest over three years. **London (King's)** Inability to think analytically and comparatively. **London (UCL)** The vast majority of applications are of a very high standard, many applicants being predicted AAA grades. We view each application as a complete picture, taking into account personal statement, reference and performance at any interview as well as actual and predicted academic performance.

Check **Chapter 4** when choosing your university and **Chapter 7** on how to read the subject tables.

There is no single rule by which applicants are selected and therefore no single reason why they are rejected. **Nottingham** No discrimination against Oxbridge applicants.

AFTER-RESULTS ADVICE

Offers to applicants repeating A-levels **Higher** Exeter, Glasgow, Huddersfield, Leeds, Liverpool, St Andrews, Trinity Saint David, Warwick; **Possibly higher** Aberystwyth, Birmingham, Cambridge, Portsmouth; **Same** Anglia Ruskin, Bangor, Bristol, Buckingham, Cardiff, Chester, Chichester, De Montfort, Dundee, Durham, Edge Hill, Hull, Kent, Lancaster, Lincoln, Liverpool Hope, LJMU, London (QM), London (RH), London (SOAS), Newcastle, Newman (UC), Newport, Nottingham Trent, Oxford Brookes, Roehampton, St Mary's Twickenham (UC), Staffordshire, Stirling, Suffolk (Univ Campus), UEA, Winchester, Wolverhampton, York, York St John.

GRADUATE DESTINATIONS AND EMPLOYMENT (2009/10 HESA)

Graduates surveyed 10,670 **Employed** 3890 **In voluntary employment** 265 **In further study** 2275 **Assumed unemployed** 650

Career note Graduates enter a broad spectrum of careers. Whilst a small number seek positions with museums and galleries, most will enter careers in management, public and social services and retail as well as the teaching profession.

OTHER DEGREE SUBJECTS FOR CONSIDERATION

Ancient History; Anthropology; Archaeology; Economic and Social History; Government; History of Art; International Relations; Medieval History; Politics.

HISTORY (ANCIENT)

(see also **Arabic and Ancient Near and Middle Eastern Studies, Archaeology, Classical Studies/ Classical Civilisation, History**)

Ancient History covers the Greek and Roman world, the social, religious, political and economic changes taking place in the Byzantine period and the medieval era which followed.

Useful websites www.royalhistoricalsociety.org; www.guardians.net; www.arwhead.com/Greeks; www.ancientworlds.net; www.bbc.co.uk/history/ancient; www.historesearch.com/ancient.

NB The points totals shown to the left of the institutions are for ease of reference only. It must not be assumed that Tariff points are always used by institutions or that they can be substituted for an offer in grades. The level of an offer is not necessarily indicative of the quality of a course.

COURSE OFFERS INFORMATION

Subject requirements/preferences **GCSE** A foreign language or classical language may be required. **AL** History or classical civilisation may be preferred subjects.

Your target offers and examples of courses provided by each institution
410 pts **London (King's)** – AAAb (Anc Hist) (IB 38 pts)
400 pts **London (UCL)** – A*AAe–AAAe (Anc Hist) (IB 38–39 pts)
380 pts **London (UCL)** – A*AA–AAA (Anc Hist Egypt) (IB 38–39 pts)
360 pts **Durham** – AAA (Anc Hist Arch) (IB 37 pts)
        Oxford – AAA (Anc Modn Hist) (IB 38–40 pts)
        St Andrews – AAA (Anc Hist Maths) (IB 36 pts)
        Warwick – AABc (Anc Hist Class Arch) (IB 32–36 pts)
340 pts **Bristol** – AAB (Anc Hist) (IB 35 pts)
        Cardiff – AAB incl hist/anc hist (Anc Mediev Hist)
        Exeter – AAB–AAA 340–360 pts (Anc Hist) (IB 36–34 pts)
        London (RH) – AAB–ABB (Anc Hist Phil)
        London (UCL) – AAB (Anc Wrld) (IB 36 pts)

Nottingham – AAB (Anc Hist Lat) (IB 34 pts)
St Andrews – AAB 340 pts (Anc Hist) (IB 35 pts)
320 pts **Birmingham** – ABB (Anc Hist) (IB 34 pts)
Cardiff – ABB (Anc Hist)
Leicester – ABB 320 pts (Anc Hist Hist)
Liverpool – ABB (Anc Hist Arch) (IB 33 pts)
London (RH) – ABB (Anc Hist) (IB 34 pts)
Manchester – ABB–BBB 300–320 pts (Anc Hist) (IB 34–31 pts)
Newcastle – AAB–ABB 320–340 pts (Anc Hist) (IB 32 pts)
Nottingham – AAB (Anc Hist) (IB 34 pts)
Swansea – ABB–BBB (Egypt Anc Hist; Anc Mediev Hist)
300 pts **Edinburgh** – BBB–AAA (Anc Medit Civ) (IB 34–42 pts)
Leicester – BBB (Anc Hist Arch) (IB 30 pts)
Swansea – ABB–BBB 300 pts (Anc Hist)
180 pts **Trinity Saint David** – Individual offers made after interview 180–200 pts (Anc Hist)

Alternative offers
See **Chapter 7** and **Appendix 1** for grades/UCAS Tariff points information for the International Baccalaureate, Scottish Highers/Advanced Highers, the Welsh Baccalaureate, the Irish Leaving Certificate, the Cambridge Pre-U Diploma, the Advanced Diploma and the Extended Project.

CHOOSING YOUR COURSE (SEE ALSO CH.1)

Some course features
Birmingham (Anc Hist) Course focuses on social history and the lives, work, trade and leisure of everyday people from around 1000BC to AD1500.
Cardiff (Anc Hist) Archaeological modules can be studied as well as language modules in Greek or Latin at beginners and advanced levels.
Leicester (Anc Hist Arch) The course centres on Ancient Greece and Rome, with particular reference to the interpretation of classical texts and material remains. There is an optional module in classical and post-classical Latin.
Swansea Egyptian language study is essential for Egyptology students but optional for the Ancient History and Egyptology course. Students use the resources of the Egypt Centre, with over 3000 Egyptian antiquities.

Universities and colleges teaching quality See www.qaa.ac.uk; http://unistats.direct.gov.uk.

Top research universities and colleges (RAE 2008) See **Classics**.

ADMISSIONS INFORMATION

Number of applicants per place (approx) Birmingham 7; Bristol 12; Cardiff 4; Durham 12; Leicester 32; London (RH) 3; Manchester 6; Newcastle 10; Nottingham 10; Oxford 2.

Advice to applicants and planning the UCAS personal statement Any information about experience of excavation or museum work should be given. Visits to Greece and Italy to study archaeological sites should be described. Show your interest in, for example, Ancient Egypt developed through, for example reading, television and the Internet. Be aware of the work of the career archaeologist, for example, sites and measurement officers, field officers and field researchers (often specialists in pottery, glass, metalwork). See also **History**.

Misconceptions about this course **Liverpool** (Egypt) Some students would have been better advised looking at V400 Archaeology or VV16 Ancient History and Archaeology, both of which offer major pathways in the study of Ancient Egypt.

Selection interviews **Yes** Durham, Leeds, London (RH), Oxford (Anc Hist) 21%; **Some** Cardiff, Newcastle; **No** Birmingham, Dundee.

Interview advice and questions See **History**.

Reasons for rejection (non-academic) **Liverpool** (Egypt) Egyptology used to fill a gap on the UCAS application. Applicant misguided in choice of subject.

AFTER-RESULTS ADVICE

Offers to applicants repeating A-levels Same Birmingham, Cardiff, Durham, Newcastle.

GRADUATE DESTINATIONS AND EMPLOYMENT (2009/10 HESA)
See **History**.

Career note See **History**.

OTHER DEGREE SUBJECTS FOR CONSIDERATION
Anthropology; Archaeology; Classical Studies; Classics; Greek; History of Art; Latin.

HISTORY (ECONOMIC and SOCIAL)
(see also **History**)

Economic and Social History is a study of societies and economies and explores the changes that have taken place in the past and the causes and consequences of those changes. The study can cover Britain, Europe and other major powers.

Useful websites www.royalhistoricalsociety.org; www.ehs.org.uk; see also **Economics** and **History**.

NB The points totals shown to the left of the institutions are for ease of reference only. It must not be assumed that Tariff points are always used by institutions or that they can be substituted for an offer in grades. The level of an offer is not necessarily indicative of the quality of a course.

COURSE OFFERS INFORMATION

Subject requirements/preferences GCSE Mathematics usually required and a language may be preferred. **AL** History preferred.

Your target offers and examples of courses provided by each institution

380 pts Warwick – A*AA-AAA (Econ Econ Hist) (IB 38 pts)

360 pts Edinburgh – AAA-BBB (Pol Econ Soc Hist) (IB 34–42 pts)

340 pts Kent – AAB (War St) (IB 33 pts)
       Lancaster – AAB (Soc Hist) (IB 34 pts)
       London LSE – AAB (Econ Hist) (IB 37 pts HL 666)
       York – AAB (Econ/Econ Hist) (IB 36 pts HL 666)

320 pts Birmingham – ABB (Econ Soc Hist) (IB 34 pts)
       Essex – ABB (Soc Cult Hist) (IB 32 pts)
       Glasgow – ABB (Econ Soc Hist) (IB 36 pts)
       Kent – ABB (Hist Sci Phil) (IB 33 pts)
       Liverpool – ABB (Hist (Soc Econ)) (IB 33 pts)

300 pts Aberystwyth – 300 pts (Econ Soc Hist) (IB 27 pts)
       Edinburgh – AAA-BBB 300–360 pts (Econ Hist) (IB 34 pts)

240 pts Manchester Met – 240–260 pts (Soc Hist) (IB 28 pts)

Alternative offers

See **Chapter 7** and **Appendix 1** for grades/UCAS Tariff points information for the International Baccalaureate, Scottish Highers/Advanced Highers, the Welsh Baccalaureate, the Irish Leaving Certificate, the Cambridge Pre-U Diploma, the Advanced Diploma and the Extended Project.

CHOOSING YOUR COURSE (SEE ALSO CH.1)
Some course features

Birmingham The course in History and Social Science offers a study of two social sciences from economics, sociology, politics and psychology.

Manchester The subject features in three degree courses within the overall Economic and Social Studies programme of 28 degree courses. All students follow a general and broad course in Year 1 specialising in their chosen field in Years 2 and 3.

Warwick (Econ Econ Hist) The course combines economic analysis with an historical understanding of economic development and policies, the causes of economic flutuations and unemployment, the conditions for exchange rate flexibility and European integration.

Universities and colleges teaching quality See www.qaa.ac.uk; http://unistats.direct.gov.uk.

ADMISSIONS INFORMATION
Number of applicants per place (approx) Birmingham 3; Liverpool 3; London LSE (Econ Hist) 3, (Econ Hist Econ) 5; York 8.

Advice to applicants and planning the UCAS personal statement See **History**.

Selection interviews Yes Aberystwyth, Birmingham, Liverpool, Warwick (rarely); **No** Dundee.

Interview advice and questions See **History**.

AFTER-RESULTS ADVICE
Offers to applicants repeating A-levels Higher Warwick, York; **Possibly higher** Liverpool.

GRADUATE DESTINATIONS AND EMPLOYMENT (2009/10 HESA)
See **History**.

Career note See **History**.

OTHER DEGREE SUBJECTS FOR CONSIDERATION
Economics; Government; History; Politics; Social Policy and Administration; Sociology.

HISTORY OF ART
(see also **History**)

History of Art (and Design) courses differ slightly between universities although most will focus on the history and appreciation of European art and architecture from the 14th to 20th centuries. Some courses also cover the Egyptian, Greek and Roman periods and at London (SOAS), Asian, African and European Art. The history of all aspects of design and film can also be studied in some courses. There has been an increase in the popularity of these courses in recent years.

Useful websites www.artchive.com; www.artcyclopedia.com; www.artguide.org; www.artefact.co.uk; www.fine-art.com; www.nationalgallery.org.uk; www.britisharts.co.uk; www.tate.org.uk.

NB The points totals shown to the left of the institutions are for ease of reference only. It must not be assumed that Tariff points are always used by institutions or that they can be substituted for an offer in grades. The level of an offer is not necessarily indicative of the quality of a course.

COURSE OFFERS INFORMATION
Subject requirements/preferences GCSE English required and a foreign language usually preferred. **AL** History is preferred for some courses.

Your target offers and examples of courses provided by each institution
380 pts **Cambridge** – A*AA (Hist Art) (IB 40–42 pts)
360 pts **Bristol** – AAA–AAB (Hist Art Modn Lang) (IB 37–35 pts)
            Newcastle – AAA (Hist Art Comb Hons) (IB 34 pts)
            Oxford – AAA (Hist Art) (IB 38–40 pts)
            St Andrews – AAA (Art Hist Psy) (IB 36 pts)
            Warwick – AABc (Hist Art) (IB 36 pts)
            York – AAA–AAB (Engl Hist Art) (IB 36 pts)
340 pts **Kent** – AAB–BBB (Hist Phil Art) (IB 33 pts)
            London (Court) – AAB 340 pts (Hist Art) (IB 30 pts)
            London (UCL) – AABe (Hist Art) (IB 34)

St Andrews – AAB (Art Hist Mediev Hist) (IB 35 pts)
UEA – AAB–BBB (Arch Anth Art Hist) (IB 33–31 pts)
York – AAB (Hist Hist Art) (IB 32–34 pts)
320 pts **Birmingham** – ABB (Hist Art) (IB 34 pts)
Essex – 320–300 pts (Lit Hist Art) (IB 34–32 pts)
Glasgow – ABB (Hist Art) (IB 36 pts)
Leeds – ABB (Hist Art) (IB 32 pts)
London (Gold) – ABB (Hist Art)
London (SOAS) – ABB (Hist Art (As Af Euro)) (IB 34 pts HL 555)
Manchester – ABB–BBB 300–320 pts (Arch Art Hist) (IB 33–32 pts)
Nottingham – ABB–AAC (Class Civ Art Hist; Art Hist)
Sussex – ABB (Art Hist Cult St) (IB 32–34 pts)
York – ABB (Hist Art) (IB 32–34 pts)
300 pts **Aberdeen** – BBB (Pol Hist Art)
Edinburgh – AAA–BBB 300–360 pts (Hist Art) (IB 34–42 pts HL 555)
Essex – ABB–BBB 300–320 pts (Hist Art) (IB 34–32 pts)
Hull – 300 pts (Hist Hist Art)
Leeds – ABB–BBB (Hist Art Musm St) (IB 32 pts)
Leicester – BBB (Hist Art)
280 pts **Aberystwyth** – 280 pts (Musm Gllry St) (IB 28 pts)
Brighton – BBC (Hist Decr Arts Crfts) (IB 28 pts)
Lincoln – 280 pts (Cons Restor)
Manchester Met – 280 pts (Contemp Art Hist) (IB 28 pts)
Oxford Brookes – BBC (Hist Art) (IB 30 pts)
Reading – 280–300 pts (Hist Art Hist)
260 pts **LJMU** – 260 pts (Hist Art) (IB 28 pts)
240 pts **Kingston** – 240 pts (Hist Art Des Film) (IB 30 pts)
Plymouth – 240 pts (Art Hist; Fn Art Art Hist)
200 pts **UCLan** – interview 200–250 pts (Contemp Vis Arts (Hist Theor))
80 pts **London (Birk)** – p/t for under 21s (over 21s varies) (Hum Hist Art)

Alternative offers
See **Chapter 7** and **Appendix 1** for grades/UCAS Tariff points information for the International Baccalaureate, Scottish Highers/Advanced Highers, the Welsh Baccalaureate, the Irish Leaving Certificate, the Cambridge Pre-U Diploma, the Advanced Diploma and the Extended Project.

CHOOSING YOUR COURSE (SEE ALSO CH.1)
Some course features
Aberystwyth (Art Hist) The course combines the study of art history and visual culture. In the second and third years students choose from a wide range of core and optional modules, including history of graphic art, history of photography, contemporary art and Renaissance art.
Kent (Hist Phil Art) The course has streams in art history, contemporary arts, philosophy of art or photographic studies.
Leeds (Hist Art Musm St) An unusual course focusing on art history, fine art and museum and gallery collections and country houses, with opportunities for related work experience.
Leicester (Hist Art) A wide range of supplementary subjects (including languages) can be studied including practical art which explores artistic techniques and problems.
Manchester (Hist Art) A study of art history, visual culture, architecture and theory from antiquity to the present day. The course focuses mainly on European art but there are opportunities to study non-Western cultures.
Manchester Met (Cont Art His) The course involves a work placement in the second year.

Universities and colleges teaching quality See www.qaa.ac.uk; http://unistats.direct.gov.uk.

Top research universities and colleges (RAE 2008) (History of Art, Architecture and Design)
Glasgow; London (Court); UEA; Sussex; Manchester; York; Birmingham; London (UCL); Essex; Nottingham; London (Birk); Warwick.

ADMISSIONS INFORMATION

Number of applicants per place (approx) Aberystwyth 9; Birmingham 14; Brighton 8; Bristol 8; Cambridge 4; Essex 5; Kent 3; Kingston 4; Leeds 29; Leicester 6; London (Gold) 10; London (SOAS) 4; Manchester 3; Manchester Met 10; Nottingham 10; UEA 7; York 4.

Advice to applicants and planning the UCAS personal statement Applicants for History of Art courses should have made extensive visits to art galleries, particularly in London, and should be familiar with the main European schools of painting. Evidence of lively interest required. Discuss your preferences and say why you prefer certain types of work or particular artists. You should also describe any visits to museums and any special interests in furniture, pottery or other artefacts. See also **Appendix 4**. **Bristol** Deferred entry may be considered. **London (Court)** A-levels in history, history of art, English, and modern European languages are the most relevant, however other subjects are considered. Art offered as an A-level should include a history of art paper.

Misconceptions about this course Kent The History of Art is not a practical course in fine arts. **York** Students do not need a background in art or art history. It is not a course with a studio element in it.

Selection interviews Yes Brighton, Cambridge, Essex, London (Court), London (UCL), Manchester Met, Oxford (Hist Art) 16%; **Some** Bristol, Buckingham, Kent, Warwick; **No** Birmingham, Dundee, Nottingham, UEA.

Interview advice and questions Some universities set slide tests on painting and sculpture. Those applicants who have not taken history of art at A-level will be questioned on their reasons for choosing the subject, their visits to art galleries and museums and their reactions to the art work which has impressed them. See **Chapter 6**. **Kent** Do they visit art galleries? Have they studied art history previously? What do they expect to get out of the degree? Sometimes they are given images to compare and discuss.

Reasons for rejection (non-academic) Poorly presented practical work. Students who do not express any interest or enthusiasm in contemporary visual arts are rejected.

AFTER-RESULTS ADVICE

Offers to applicants repeating A-levels Possibly higher St Andrews; **Same** Aberystwyth, Kent, Leeds, UEA, Warwick, York; **No** Cambridge.

GRADUATE DESTINATIONS AND EMPLOYMENT (2009/10 HESA)

Career note Work in galleries, museums and collections will be the objective of many graduates, who should try to establish contacts by way of work placements and experience during their undergraduate years. The personal skills acquired during their studies, however, open up many opportunities in other careers.

OTHER DEGREE SUBJECTS FOR CONSIDERATION

Art; Archaeology; Architecture; Classical Studies; Photography.

HORTICULTURE

(including **Garden Design**; see also **Agricultural Sciences/Agriculture, Landscape Architecture, Plant Sciences**)

Horticulture is a broad subject area covering amenity or landscape horticulture, production horticulture and retail horticulture.

Useful websites www.iagre.org; www.rhs.org.uk; www.horticulture.org.uk.

NB The points totals shown to the left of the institutions are for ease of reference only. It must not be assumed that Tariff points are always used by institutions or that they can be substituted for an offer in grades. The level of an offer is not necessarily indicative of the quality of a course.

Check **Chapter 4** when choosing your university and **Chapter 7** on how to read the subject tables.

COURSE OFFERS INFORMATION

Subject requirements/preferences GCSE Mathematics sometimes required. **AL** A science subject may be required or preferred for some courses.

Your target offers and examples of courses provided by each institution
240 pts **Greenwich** – 240 pts (Hort; Medcnl Hort)
      Hadlow (Coll) – 240 pts (Gdn Des; Hort)
      Writtle (Coll) – 240 pts (Hort (Plntsmn/Tree Mgt/Glob Crop Prot); Hort Bus Mgt)
180 pts **Worcester** – 180 pts (Hort)
160 pts **SAC (Scottish CAg)** – CC (Hort Plntsmn; Hort)
      Warwickshire (Coll) – 160 pts (Hort)

Alternative offers
See **Chapter 7** and **Appendix 1** for grades/UCAS Tariff points information for the International Baccalaureate, Scottish Highers/Advanced Highers, the Welsh Baccalaureate, the Irish Leaving Certificate, the Cambridge Pre-U Diploma, the Advanced Diploma and the Extended Project.

EXAMPLES OF FOUNDATION DEGREES IN THE SUBJECT FIELD

Askham Bryan (Coll); CAFRE; Duchy (Coll); Glyndŵr; Harper Adams (UC); Moulton (Coll); Myerscough (Coll); Nottingham Trent; Plymouth; Warwickshire (Coll).

CHOOSING YOUR COURSE (SEE ALSO CH.1)

Some course features
SAC (Scottish CAg) (Hort Plntsmn) The course combines a study of the diversity of plants and their cultivation, with practical horticultural skills, and is delivered in partnership with the Royal Botanic Garden, Edinburgh.
Worcester (Hort) Course based at Pershore College and enables students to gain practical experience in the horticultural industry in the UK at the end of the first and second years.
Writtle (Coll) The College, the largest provider of horticultural education in the country, encourages students to take a sandwich placement during their course, in the UK or overseas. Twelve-month practical training placements are available with the Royal Horticultural Society.

Universities and colleges teaching quality See www.qaa.ac.uk; http://unistats.direct.gov.uk.

Examples of sandwich degree courses Writtle (Coll).

ADMISSIONS INFORMATION

Number of applicants per place (approx) Greenwich 4; SAC (Scottish CAg) 1; Writtle (Coll) 3.

Advice to applicants and planning the UCAS personal statement Practical experience is important and visits to botanical gardens (the Royal Botanic Gardens, Kew or Edinburgh and the Royal Horticultural Society gardens at Wisley) could be described. Contact your local authority offices for details of work in parks and gardens departments. See also **Appendix 3**.

Misconceptions about this course Greenwich (Commer Hort) Students are unaware of the scope of this degree. The course covers commercial horticulture – plants, plant products, ornamentals, bedding plants, hardy trees and shrubs, salads, vegetables, fruit and organic crops from production to marketing.

Selection interviews Yes Greenwich, SAC (Scottish CAg), Worcester.

Interview advice and questions Past questions have included: How did you become interested in horticulture? How do you think this course will benefit you? Could you work in all weathers? What career are you aiming for? Are you interested in gardening? Describe your garden. What plants do you grow? How do you prune rose trees and fruit trees? Are there any EU policies at present affecting the horticulture industry? Topics relating to the importance of science and horticulture. See also **Chapter 6**.

AFTER-RESULTS ADVICE
Offers to applicants repeating A-levels **Same** Greenwich, SAC (Scottish CAg).

GRADUATE DESTINATIONS AND EMPLOYMENT (2009/10 HESA)
See **Agricultural Sciences/Agriculture**.

Career note Graduates seeking employment in horticulture will look towards commercial organisations for the majority of openings. These will include positions as growers and managers with fewer vacancies for scientists involved in research and development and advisory services.

OTHER DEGREE SUBJECTS FOR CONSIDERATION
Agriculture; Biology; Crop Science; Ecology; Forestry; Landscape Architecture; Plant Sciences.

HOSPITALITY and HOTEL MANAGEMENT

(including **Events Management**; see also **Business and Management Courses, Business and Management Courses (International and European), Business and Management Courses (Specialised), Consumer Studies/Sciences, Food Science/Studies and Technology, Leisure and Recreation Management/Studies, Tourism and Travel**)

Courses cover the full range of skills required for those working in the industry. Specific studies include management, food and beverage supplies, equipment design, public relations and marketing. Depending on the course, other topics may include events management, tourism and the international trade.

Useful websites www.baha.org.uk; www.cordonbleu.net; www.instituteofhospitality.org; www.people1st.co.uk.

NB The points totals shown to the left of the institutions are for ease of reference only. It must not be assumed that Tariff points are always used by institutions or that they can be substituted for an offer in grades. The level of an offer is not necessarily indicative of the quality of a course.

COURSE OFFERS INFORMATION
Subject requirements/preferences **GCSE** English and mathematics usually required together with a foreign language for International Management courses. **AL** No specified subjects.

Your target offers and examples of courses provided by each institution
320 pts **Bournemouth** – 320 pts (Evnt Mgt)
     Strathclyde – ABB (Hspty Tour Mgt)
     Surrey – ABB (Int Hspty Mgt) (IB 34 pts)
300 pts **Sheffield Hallam** – 300 pts (Evnt Mngt)
280 pts **Bournemouth** – 280 pts (Hspty Mgt)
     Brighton – BBC 280 pts (Int Hspty Mgt) (IB 28 pts)
     Cardiff Met – 280 pts (Int Tour Hspty Mgt)
     Derby – 280 pts (Hspty Mgt)
     Gloucestershire – 280–300 pts (Evnt Mgt Hspty Mgt) (IB 26–30 pts)
     Manchester Met – 280 pts (Int Hspty Mgt) (IB 28 pts)
     Oxford Brookes – BBC (Int Hspty Mgt) (IB 29 pts)
     Plymouth – 280 pts (Evnt Mgt)
     Salford – BBC 280 pts (Hspty Mgt) (IB 26 pts)
     Suffolk (Univ Campus) – 280 pts (Evnt Mgt)
260 pts **Coventry** – BCC (Evnt Mgt)
     De Montfort – 260 pts (Arts Fstvl Mgt)
     Derby – 260–280 pts (Evnt Mgt)
     Glamorgan – BCC (Evnt Mgt)

Greenwich – 260 pts (Evnt Mgt)
Hertfordshire – 260 pts (Evnt Mgt)
Huddersfield – 260 pts (Evnt Mgt)
LJMU – 260 pts (Evnt Mgt)
Northampton – 260–300 pts (Evnt Mgt Joint Hons)
Sunderland – 260 pts (Int Tour Hspty Mgt; Evnts Mgt)
Winchester – 260–300 pts (Evnt Mgt)

240 pts **Canterbury Christ Church** – 240 pts (Evnt Mgt)
Cardiff Met – 240–280 pts (Hspty Mgt courses; Evnts Mgt)
Chester – 240–280 pts (Evnts Mgt) (IB 26 pts)
Chichester – CCC (Evnt Mgt) (IB 28 pts)
Gloucestershire – 240–280 pts (Hspty Mgt)
Leeds Met – 240 pts (Hspty Ldrshp Mgt) (IB 24 pts)
London Met – 240 pts (Evnts Mgt Mark)
Plymouth – 240 pts (Cru Mgt)
Robert Gordon – CCC 240 pts (Int Hspty Mgt) (IB 24 pts)
Southampton Solent – 240 pts (Evnts Mgt)
UCLan – 240–280 pts (Evnt Mgt)
Ulster – 240 pts (Leis Evnts Mgt)
West Scotland – CCC (Evnt Mgt)
Writtle (Coll) – 240 pts (Evnt Mgt)

230 pts **Edinburgh Napier** – 230–240 pts (Hspty Mark Mgt)

220 pts **De Montfort** – 220 pts (Hspty Mgt)
Huddersfield – 220 pts (Hspty Mgt)
Lincoln – 220 pts (Evnt Mgt)
London Met – 220–240 pts (Evnts Mgt PR; Int Hspty Mgt)
Northampton – 220–260 pts (Evnt Mgt)
Plymouth – 220 pts (Int Hspty Mgt; Hspty Mgt)
Portsmouth – 220 pts (Hspty Mgt; Hspty Mgt Tour)

200 pts **Bedfordshire** – 200 pts (Evnt Mgt)
Birmingham (UC) – 200–220 pts (Hspty Bus Mgt; Hspty Fd Mgt; Spa Mgt)
Bucks New – 200–240 pts (Evnt Fstvl Mgt; Corp Evnts Conf Mgt)
Edinburgh Queen Margaret – 200 pts (Hspty Tour Mgt; Int Hspty Mgt; Evnts Mgt)
Staffordshire – BB–BBC (Evnt Mgt)
UEL – 200 pts (Evnt Mgt)
West London – 200 pts (Evnts Mgt) (IB 28 pts)
Wolverhampton – 200 pts (Int Hspty Mgt; Evnts Mgt)

140 pts **Blackpool and Fylde (Coll)** – 140 pts (Hspty Mgt)

120 pts **Colchester (Inst)** – 120 pts (Mgt Hspty)
Llandrillo Cymru (Coll) – 120 pts (Hspty Mgt)

60 pts **UHI** – D–A (Tour Hosp Prac)

Alternative offers

See **Chapter 7** and **Appendix 1** for grades/UCAS Tariff points information for the International Baccalaureate, Scottish Highers/Advanced Highers, the Welsh Baccalaureate, the Irish Leaving Certificate, the Cambridge Pre-U Diploma, the Advanced Diploma and the Extended Project.

EXAMPLES OF FOUNDATION DEGREES IN THE SUBJECT FIELD

Askham Bryan (Coll); Bedford (Coll); Bishop Burton (Coll); Blackburn (Coll); Bolton; Bradford (Coll Univ Centre); Chichester (Coll); Cornwall (Coll); Craven (Coll); Ealing, Hammersmith and West London (Coll); Farnborough (CT); Glasgow Caledonian; Greenwich; Grimsby (IFHE); Guildford (Coll); Highbury Portsmouth (Coll); Liverpool (CmC); Loughborough (Coll); Middlesex; Neath Port Talbot (Coll); NEW (Coll); Newcastle (Coll); North Lindsey (Coll); Northumbria; Norwich City (Coll); Nottingham New (Coll); South Cheshire (Coll); South Devon (Coll); Stratford-upon-Avon (Coll); UHI; West Cheshire (Coll); West Scotland; Westminster Kingsway (Coll); Worcester.

CHOOSING YOUR COURSE (SEE ALSO CH.1)
Some course features
Edinburgh Napier (Fstvl Evnts Mgt courses) Students learn how to plan, design, market, operate and develop events and how they can be used to help local economies. There are opportunities to study a European language and to study abroad.
Manchester Met The wide range of courses includes options in International Hospitality Management and Events Management.
Oxford Brookes (Int Hspty Mgt) A Single Honours course with a paid placement year and opportunities to study abroad. There is an emphasis on professional and personal development.
Surrey Opportunities for professional training places with leading UK and overseas companies.

Universities and colleges teaching quality See www.qaa.ac.uk; http://unistats.direct.gov.uk.

Examples of sandwich degree courses Birmingham (UC); Bournemouth; Brighton; Cardiff Met; Derby; Gloucestershire; Huddersfield; Leeds Met; Manchester Met; Oxford Brookes; Portsmouth; Sheffield Hallam; Sunderland; Surrey; UCLan; Ulster; Wolverhampton.

ADMISSIONS INFORMATION
Number of applicants per place (approx) Bournemouth 9; Cardiff Met 12; Edinburgh Napier 17; London Met 10; Manchester Met (Hspty Mgt) 12, (Hspty Mgt Tour) 20; Middlesex 4; Oxford Brookes 9; Portsmouth 10; Robert Gordon 3; Strathclyde 8; Surrey 12; UCLan 8.

Advice to applicants and planning the UCAS personal statement Experience in dealing with members of the public is an important element in this work which, coupled with work experience in cafés, restaurants or hotels, should be described fully. All applicants are strongly recommended to obtain practical experience in catering or hotel work. Admissions tutors are likely to look for experience in industry and for people who are ambitious, sociable and team players.

Misconceptions about this course **Cardiff Met** (Hspty Mgt) The course is not about cooking! We are looking to create managers, not chefs.

Selection interviews **Yes** Cardiff Met; **Some** Manchester Met, Portsmouth, Robert Gordon, Surrey; **No** Bucks New, Salford.

Interview advice and questions Past questions have included: What books do you read? What do you know about hotel work and management? What work experience have you had? What kind of job do you have in mind when you have qualified? How did you become interested in this course? Do you eat in restaurants? What types of restaurants? Discuss examples of good and bad restaurant organisation. What qualities do you have which make you suitable for management? See also **Chapter 6**.

Reasons for rejection (non-academic) Lack of suitable work experience or practical training. Inability to communicate. Lack of awareness of workload, for example shift working, weekend work. **Cardiff Met** Students looking specifically for licensed trade courses or a cookery course. **Oxford Brookes** Lack of commitment to the hotel and restaurant industry.

AFTER-RESULTS ADVICE
Offers to applicants repeating A-levels **Higher** Bournemouth, Huddersfield, Oxford Brookes, Surrey; **Same** Brighton, Cardiff Met, Manchester Met, Salford, Strathclyde, Suffolk (Univ Campus), Ulster, West London, Wolverhampton.

GRADUATE DESTINATIONS AND EMPLOYMENT (2009/10 HESA)
Including Leisure, Tourism and Transport; graduates surveyed 5475 **Employed** 2810 **In voluntary employment** 40 **In further study** 985 **Assumed unemployed** 350

Career note These business-focused hospitality programmes open up a wide range of employment and career opportunities in both hospitality and other business sectors. The demand for employees has been high in recent years. Events Management is currently a growth area with graduates working in sports and the arts, tourist attractions, hospitality, business and industry.

OTHER DEGREE SUBJECTS FOR CONSIDERATION
Business; Consumer Studies; Dietetics; Food Science; Health Studies; Leisure and Recreation Management; Management; Tourism and Travel.

HOUSING

(see also Building and Construction, Surveying, Town and Country Planning)

These courses prepare students for careers in housing management although topics covered will also be relevant to other careers in business and administration. Modules will be taken in housing, law, finance, planning policy, public administration and construction.

Useful websites www.housingcorp.gov.uk; www.communities.gov.uk/housing; www.rtpi.org.uk; www. freeindex.co.uk/categories/property/construction/Property_Development.

NB The points totals shown to the left of the institutions are for ease of reference only. It must not be assumed that Tariff points are always used by institutions or that they can be substituted for an offer in grades. The level of an offer is not necessarily indicative of the quality of a course.

COURSE OFFERS INFORMATION

Subject requirements/preferences GCSE English and mathematics required. **AL** No specified subjects.

Your target offers and examples of courses provided by each institution
240 pts **London South Bank** – 240 pts (Hous St; Sust Commun)
      Ulster – 240 pts (Hous Mgt)
200 pts **Middlesex** – 200–300 pts (Hous St)
140 pts **Cardiff Met** – 140 pts (Hous (Supptd Hous/Hous Plcy Prac))

Alternative offers
See **Chapter 7** and **Appendix 1** for grades/UCAS Tariff points information for the International Baccalaureate, Scottish Highers/Advanced Highers, the Welsh Baccalaureate, the Irish Leaving Certificate, the Cambridge Pre-U Diploma, the Advanced Diploma and the Extended Project.

EXAMPLES OF FOUNDATION DEGREES IN THE SUBJECT FIELD
Blackburn (Coll); St Helens (Coll); Truro (Coll).

CHOOSING YOUR COURSE (SEE ALSO CH.1)
Some course features
Cardiff Met (Hous (Supptd Hous)) The course involves social, emotional and/or lifestyle support for a variety of client needs, for example, learning disabilities, mental health, vulnerable people.
London South Bank (Hous St) The course focuses on the policy, management and economic aspects of housing, and on housing in the European context.
Ulster (Hous Mgt) The course, involving research, practical placements and links with practitioners, focuses on how housing management affects individuals in society, on the built environment, housing needs and the development and implementation of housing policy. The course links to others in the built environment, including Environmental Health, Construction Engineering and Management.

Universities and colleges teaching quality See www.qaa.ac.uk; http://unistats.direct.gov.uk.

ADMISSIONS INFORMATION
Number of applicants per place (approx) Cardiff Met 1.

Advice to applicants and planning the UCAS personal statement An interest in people, housing problems, social affairs and the built environment is important for this course. Contacts with local housing managers (through local authority offices or housing associations) are important. Describe any such contacts and your knowledge of the housing types and needs in your area. The planning department in your local council office will be able to provide information on the various types of developments taking place in your locality and how housing needs have changed during the past 50 years.

Misconceptions about this course Applicants do not appreciate that the course is very close to social work/community work and is most suitable for those wishing to work with people.

Selection interviews Some Cardiff Met.

Interview advice and questions Since the subject is not studied at school, questions are likely to be asked on reasons for choosing this degree. Other past questions include: What is a housing association? Why were housing associations formed? In which parts of the country would you expect private housing to be expensive and, by comparison, cheap? What is the cause of this? Have estates of multi-storey flats fulfilled their original purpose? If not, why not? What causes a slum? What is an almshouse? See also **Chapter 6**.

Reasons for rejection (non-academic) Lack of awareness of current social policy issues.

AFTER-RESULTS ADVICE
Offers to applicants repeating A-levels Same Cardiff Met, London South Bank.

GRADUATE DESTINATIONS AND EMPLOYMENT (2009/10 HESA)
See **Building and Construction**.

Career note Graduates aiming for openings in housing will be employed mainly as managers with local authorities; others will be employed by non-profit-making housing associations and trusts and also by property companies owning blocks of flats.

OTHER DEGREE SUBJECTS FOR CONSIDERATION
Architecture; Building; Business Studies; Community Studies; Environmental Planning; Estate Management; Property Development; Social Policy and Administration; Social Studies; Surveying; Town Planning; Urban Regeneration.

HUMAN RESOURCE MANAGEMENT

(see also **Business and Management Courses, Business and Management Courses (International and European), Business and Management Courses (Specialised)**)

This is one of the many branches of the world of business and has developed from the role of the personnel manager. HR managers may be involved with the induction and training of staff, disciplinary and grievance procedures, redundancies and equal opportunities issues. In large organisations some HR staff may specialise in one or more of these areas. Work experience dealing with the public should be stressed in the UCAS personal statement.

Useful websites www.hrmguide.co.uk; www.humanresourcemanagement.co.uk.

NB The points totals shown to the left of the institutions are for ease of reference only. It must not be assumed that Tariff points are always used by institutions or that they can be substituted for an offer in grades. The level of an offer is not necessarily indicative of the quality of a course.

COURSE OFFERS INFORMATION
Subject requirements/preferences GCSE English and mathematics at C or above. **AL** No subjects specified.

Your target offers and examples of courses provided by each institution
360 pts Aston – AAB–AAA 340–360 pts (HR Mgt) (IB 35 pts)
        Leeds – AAA (HR Mgt) (IB 33 pts HL 16 pts)

340 pts **Bournemouth** – 340 pts (Bus St (HR Mgt))
Cardiff – AAB (Bus Mgt (HR))
London (RH) – AAB (Mgt HR) (IB 35 pts)
Sussex – AAB (Bus Hum Res Mgt) (IB 35 pts)

320 pts **Bradford** – 320 pts (HR Mgt)
Essex – 320 pts (Mark HR Mgt)
Lancaster – ABB (Mgt Org (HR Mgt)) (IB 32 pts)
Strathclyde – ABB 320 pts (HR Mgt) (IB 32 pts)
Ulster – ABB (Law HR Mgt) (IB 26 pts)

300 pts **Cardiff Met** – 300 pts (Bus Mgt St HR Mgt)
Hertfordshire – 300 pts (Bus HR; HR Mand)
Huddersfield – 300 pts (Bus HR Mgt)
Salford – 300 pts (Bus St HR Mgt)

280 pts **Birmingham City** – 280 pts (PR HR Mgt) (IB 28 pts)
De Montfort – 280 pts (HR Mgt)
Edge Hill – 280 pts (Bus Mgt HR Mgt)
Greenwich – 280 pts (HR Mgt)
Keele – 280–340 pts (HR Mgt) (IB 28–30 pts)
Kingston – 280 pts (HR Mgt) (IB 31 pts)
Manchester Met – 280 pts (HR Mgt) (IB 28 pts)
Northumbria – BBC 280 pts (HR Mgt) (IB 28 pts)
Portsmouth – 280 pts (HR Mgt; HR Mgt Psy)
Stirling – BBC (HR Mgt) (IB 32 pts)
Suffolk (Univ Campus) – 280 pts (Bus HR Mgt)
Ulster – 280 pts (Adv HR Mgt; HR Mgt Mark)
Worcester – 280 pts (HR Mgt courses)

260 pts **Birmingham City** – 260–280 pts (Bus Law HR Mgt) (IB 28 pts)
Coventry – BCC 260 pts (HR Mgt)
Derby – 260–300 pts (HR Mgt)
Glamorgan – 260 pts (HR Mgt)
Gloucestershire – 260–300 pts (Bus Mgt (HR Mgt))
LJMU – 260 pts (HR Mgt) (IB 28 pts)
Northampton – 260–280 pts (HR Mgt courses)
Robert Gordon – BCC 260 pts (Mgt HR Mgt)
Sunderland – 260 pts (Bus HR Mgt; HR Mgt)
Westminster – BCC 260 pts (Bus HR Mgt) (IB 28 pts)
Winchester – 260–300 pts (Bus Mgt HR Mgt)

240 pts **Bath Spa** – 240–280 pts (Bus Mgt HR Mgt)
Bradford (Coll Univ Centre) – 240 pts (HR Mgt)
Bristol UWE – 240–300 pts (Bus St HR Mgt)
Canterbury Christ Church – 240 pts (HR Mgt Bus; HR Mgt Mark)
Chichester – CCC (HR Mgt)
Euro Bus Sch London – 240–300 pts (Int Bus HR Mgt 2 Langs)
London Met – 240 pts (HR Mgt)
Newport – 240 pts (Bus (HR Mgt))
Roehampton – 240–280 pts (Bus Mgt (HR Mgt))
UCLan – 240–280 pts (HR Mgt (Comb)) (IB 28 pts)
West Scotland – CCC (HR Mgt)

230 pts **Edinburgh Napier** – 230 pts (Bus Mgt HR)
220 pts **Leeds Met** – 220 pts (Bus HR Mgt) (IB 24 pts)
200 pts **Anglia Ruskin** – 240–200 pts (HR Mgt)
Bedfordshire – 200 pts (HR Mgt)
Bucks New – 200–240 pts (HR Mgt; Bus HR Mgt)
Middlesex – 200–300 pts (Bus HR Mgt; Psy HR Mgt)
Staffordshire – BB–BBC (HR Mgt)

UEL – 200 pts (HR Mgt)
West London – 200 pts (Bus St HR Mgt)
Wolverhampton – 200–240 pts (HR Mgt)
York St John – 200–240 pts (Bus St HR Mgt)
180 pts **Abertay Dundee** – DDD (HR Mgt)
160 pts **Greenwich (Sch Mgt)** – 160 pts (HR Mgt Inform Sys; Mgt HR Mgt)
Swansea Met – 160 pts (HR Mgt)
120 pts **Grimsby (IFHE)** – 120 pts (Bus HR)
Norwich City (Coll) – 120 pts (Bus Mgt (HR Mgt))

Alternative offers
See **Chapter 7** and **Appendix 1** for grades/UCAS Tariff points information for the International Baccalaureate, Scottish Highers/Advanced Highers, the Welsh Baccalaureate, the Irish Leaving Certificate, the Cambridge Pre-U Diploma, the Advanced Diploma and the Extended Project.

EXAMPLES OF FOUNDATION DEGREES IN THE SUBJECT FIELD
Worcester (CT).

CHOOSING YOUR COURSE (SEE ALSO CH.1)
Some course features
Cardiff Human Resources is an option within the Business programme which offers several specialist routes. The course provides the flexibility for students to transfer between degree programmes in the first year.
Lancaster (Mgt Org (HR Mgt)) The course focuses on social scientific concepts and an analysis of HR techniques, including recruitment, motivation, development and strategic planning. Students can opt to spend third year in industry.
London LSE (HR Mgt Emp Rel) This is a three-year full-time course with options from the first year which include economics, statistics, sociology, psychology, government, anthropology, information technology and language.
Portsmouth Optional industrial placement year between Year 2 and the final year.

Universities and colleges teaching quality See www.qaa.ac.uk; http://unistats.direct.gov.uk.

Examples of sandwich degree courses Aston; Bath; Birmingham City; Bradford; Bristol UWE; Coventry; De Montfort; Gloucestershire; Hertfordshire; Leeds Met; Northumbria; Plymouth; Portsmouth; Sheffield Hallam; Staffordshire; Swansea Met; Ulster; West Scotland; Westminster; Wolverhampton; Worcester.

ADMISSIONS INFORMATION
Number of applicants per place (approx) Anglia Ruskin 10; Aston 10; London LSE 16 (see also **Business and Management Courses**).

Advice to applicants and planning the UCAS personal statement See under **Business and Management Courses**.

Selection interviews **Yes** De Montfort; **Some** Anglia Ruskin (See **Business and Management Courses**).

Interview advice and questions See under **Business and Management Courses**.

Reasons for rejection (non-academic) See under **Business and Management Courses**.

AFTER-RESULTS ADVICE
Offers to applicants repeating A-levels **Higher** Anglia Ruskin.

GRADUATE DESTINATIONS AND EMPLOYMENT (2009/10 HESA)
Graduates surveyed 1185 **Employed** 1945 **In voluntary employment** 20 **In further study** 250 **Assumed unemployed** 105

Career note See under **Business and Management Courses**.

OTHER DEGREE SUBJECTS FOR CONSIDERATION

Business Studies; Information Systems; Management Studies/Sciences; Marketing; Psychology; Retail Management; Sociology; Sports Management.

HUMAN SCIENCES/HUMAN BIOSCIENCES

Human Sciences is a multi-disciplinary study relating to biological and social sciences and focuses on social and cultural behaviour. Topics range from genetics and evolution to health, disease, social behaviour and industrial societies.

Useful websites www.scienceyear.com; www.becominghuman.org; see also **Biology** and **Geography**.

NB The points totals shown to the left of the institutions are for ease of reference only. It must not be assumed that Tariff points are always used by institutions or that they can be substituted for an offer in grades. The level of an offer is not necessarily indicative of the quality of a course.

COURSE OFFERS INFORMATION

Subject requirements/preferences GCSE Science essential and mathematics usually required. **AL** Chemistry/biology usually required or preferred for some courses.

Your target offers and examples of courses provided by each institution

360 pts **London (UCL)** – AAA–AAB (Hum Sci) (IB 36 pts)
       Oxford – AAA (Hum Sci) (IB 38–40 pts)
340 pts **Exeter** – AAB–BBB (Hum Biosci) (IB 34 pts)
       London (King's) – ABB+AS (Hum Sci) (IB 34 pts)
       Sussex – AAB–ABB (Hum Sci) (IB 34–36 pts)
300 pts **Sheffield** – BBB (Hum Comm Sci) (IB 32 pts)
280 pts **Durham** – check with admissions tutor BBC (Hlth Hum Sci) (IB 30 pts)
       Loughborough – 280–300 pts (Ergonomics) (IB 30–32 pts)
       Plymouth – 280–320 pts (Hum Biosci) (IB 26 pts)
260 pts **Northumbria** – 260 pts (Hum Biosci) (IB 24 pts)
       Sheffield – BCC (Hlth Hum Sci) (IB 29 pts)
240 pts **Bolton** – 240 pts (Hum Sci courses)
       Coventry – 240 pts (Hum Biosci)
       Roehampton – 240–300 pts (Biol Sci)
220 pts **Northampton** – 220–260 pts (Hum Biosci courses)
200 pts **Roehampton** – 200–260 pts (Hlth Hum Sci)
       West London – 200 pts (Hum Sci pre-Med Yr 1: optional transfer to Med at London (UCL))
         (IB 30 pts)
180 pts **Bradford** – 180–220 pts (Interd Hum St)
       Glasgow Caledonian – BCC (Hum Biosci)

Alternative offers

See **Chapter 7** and **Appendix 1** for grades/UCAS Tariff points information for the International Baccalaureate, Scottish Highers/Advanced Highers, the Welsh Baccalaureate, the Irish Leaving Certificate, the Cambridge Pre-U Diploma, the Advanced Diploma and the Extended Project.

CHOOSING YOUR COURSE (SEE ALSO CH. 1)

Some course features

Bradford (Interd Hum St) The course covers philosophy, psychology and sociology.
Exeter The subject is taught equally between the Schools of Biosciences and Sport and Health Sciences and has a strong scientific element.
London (UCL) (Hum Sci) The course combines biological and social studies and covers such topics as anatomy, physiology, genetics, anthropology, geography and psychology.

Loughborough (Ergon) The course deals with human reactions to technical and social environments, and includes anatomy, physiology, bio-mechanics, human psychology, the principles of design and organisational behaviour.

Oxford (Hum Sci) The degree focuses on the biological, social and cultural aspects of human life. A-level or AS-level biology or mathematics may be helpful but are not a requirement.

Sussex (Hum Sci) The core of the degree is made up of anthropology, biology, psychology, linguistics and philosophy.

ADMISSIONS INFORMATION

Number of applicants per place (approx) Bradford 7; Oxford 4–5.

Advice to applicants and planning the UCAS personal statement See **Biology** and **Anthropology**. See also **Appendix 4**.

Selection interviews Yes London (UCL), Oxford (Hum Sci) 31%.

Interview advice and questions Past questions have included: What do you expect to get out of a degree in Human Sciences? Why are you interested in this subject? What problems do you think you will be able to tackle after completing the course? Why did you drop PE as an A-level given that it's relevant to Human Sciences? How do you explain altruism, given that we are surely programmed by our genes to be selfish? How far is human behaviour determined by genes? What do you think are the key differences between animals and human beings? See **Chapter 6**. **Oxford** Are there too many people in the world?

AFTER-RESULTS ADVICE

Offers to applicants repeating A-levels Information not available from institutions.

GRADUATE DESTINATIONS AND EMPLOYMENT (2007/8 HESA)

Career note As a result of the multi-disciplinary nature of these courses, graduates could focus on openings linked to their special interests or look in general at the scientific and health sectors. Health administration and social services work and laboratory-based careers are some of the more common career destinations of graduates.

OTHER DEGREE SUBJECTS FOR CONSIDERATION

Anthropology; Biology; Community Studies; Environmental Sciences; Life Sciences; Psychology; Sociology.

INFORMATION MANAGEMENT and LIBRARIANSHIP

(including **Business Information Systems, Information Technology** and **Library Studies**; see also **Computer Courses, Media Studies**)

Information Management and Library Studies covers the very wide field of information. Its organisation, retrieval, indexing, computer and media technology, classification and cataloguing are all included in these courses.

Useful websites www.aslib.co.uk; www.ukoln.ac.uk; www.cilip.org.uk; www.bl.uk.

NB The points totals shown to the left of the institutions are for ease of reference only. It must not be assumed that Tariff points are always used by institutions or that they can be substituted for an offer in grades. The level of an offer is not necessarily indicative of the quality of a course.

COURSE OFFERS INFORMATION

Subject requirements/preferences GCSE English, mathematics and occasionally a foreign language. **AL** No specified subjects.

Your target offers and examples of courses provided by each institution

340 pts **Leeds** – AAB 340 pts (IT)
London (UCL) – AAB 340 pts (Inf Mgt Bus) (IB 36 pts)
Manchester – AAB (IT Mgt Bus) (IB 35 pts)
Sheffield – AAB (IT Mgt) (IB 35 pts)
Southampton – AAB (IT Org) (IB 34 pts HL 17 pts)

320 pts **Exeter** – AAA-ABB (IT Mgt Bus) (IB 34–29 pts HL 6 maths)
Loughborough – AAB-ABB (IT Mgt Bus) (IB 34 pts)
Roehampton – 320 pts (Inf Mgt)

300 pts **Aberystwyth** – 240–300 pts (Inf Lib St Engl Lit)
Bournemouth – 300 pts (IT Mgt)
Glamorgan – 300 pts (ICT)
Heriot-Watt – BBB (Inf Sys courses)
Hertfordshire – 300 pts (Inf Sys)
Kent – BBB (IT courses) (IB 33 pts)
Kingston – 300 pts (Inf Sys)
Reading – 300–340 pts (IT; App IT; Bus IT)
Sheffield – BBB (Inform) (IB 32 pts)

280 pts **Birmingham City** – 280 pts (ICT)
Brighton – BBC (Musm Herit St) (IB 28 pts)
Lincoln – 280 pts (Des Exhib Musm)
Northumbria – 280 pts (Inf Lib Mgt) (IB 24 pts)
Oxford Brookes – BBC (IT Mgt Bus)
Plymouth – 280 pts (IT Mgt)
Stirling – BBC (Inf Sys) (IB 32 pts)

260 pts **De Montfort** – 260 pts (ICT)
Liverpool Hope – 260–320 pts (IT)
LJMU – 260 pts (Inf Sys)
Newport – 260 pts (Inf Scrty)
Portsmouth – 260 pts (Bus Inf Sys)

245 pts **Edinburgh Napier** – 245 pts (Bus Inf Sys)

240 pts **Aberystwyth** – 240 pts (Hist Archvl St) (IB 24 pts)
Cardiff Met – 240 pts (Bus Inf Sys)
Chester – 240–280 pts (Inf Sys Mgt) (IB 26 pts)
Chichester – CCC (IT Mgt Bus) (IB 28 pts)
Edge Hill – 240 pts (IT Mgt Bus)
Gloucestershire – 240 pts (Bus Inf Sys)
Greenwich – 240 pts (ICT; IT Scrty)
Huddersfield – 240 pts (ICT)
Kingston – 240 pts (Musm Gllry St)
Manchester Met – 240 pts (Inf Comm) (IB 28 pts)
Nottingham Trent – 240 pts (ICT; Inf Sys)
Westminster – CCC (Bus Inf Sys)

200 pts **Anglia Ruskin** – 200 pts (Bus Inf Sys)
Bedfordshire – 200 pts (Inf Sys)
Middlesex – 200–300 pts (Bus Inf Sys)
UEL – 200 pts (Inf Scrty Sys; ICT Int Dev)

160 pts **Southampton Solent** – 160 pts (ICT; Bus Inf Sys)
Wolverhampton – 160 pts (Inf Sys)

140 pts **Blackpool and Fylde (Coll)** – 140–360 pts (IT)

Alternative offers
See **Chapter 7** and **Appendix 1** for grades/UCAS Tariff points information for the International Baccalaureate, Scottish Highers/Advanced Highers, the Welsh Baccalaureate, the Irish Leaving Certificate, the Cambridge Pre-U Diploma, the Advanced Diploma and the Extended Project.

For a quick reference offers calculator, fold out the inside back cover.

EXAMPLES OF FOUNDATION DEGREES IN THE SUBJECT FIELD

Abertay Dundee; Coventry; Glyndŵr; Hopwood Hall (Coll); Leeds Met; Liverpool (CmC); Llandrillo Cymru (Coll); Northbrook (Coll); Nottingham New (Coll); Sir Gâr (Coll); Solihull (Coll); Teesside; Truro (Coll); UHI.

CHOOSING YOUR COURSE (SEE ALSO CH.1)

Some course features

Aberystwyth This leading department offers courses in Information and Library Studies by way of 10 specialist joint subjects. There is also a unique course in Historical and Archival Studies in addition to courses in Museum and Gallery Studies.

Bradford Information and Communication Technology Management can be taken as a 3 year full time course or 4 year sandwich course. The course is multidisciplinary and places emphasis on IT topics and business management issues.

Brighton The Museum Heritage course offers students an overview of the histories of art and design as well as engaging them in the ever changing world of museums and galleries. It is offered full- and part-time.

Manchester Met Information and Communications is a modular course, and offers the basic core subjects covering management, information systems, retrieval and information technology. Special studies in Year 3 provide flexibility to cover areas of special interest to students. These include working in academic, business and commercial communities. Students are required to undertake placements.

Universities and colleges teaching quality See www.qaa.ac.uk; http://unistats.direct.gov.uk.

Top research universities and colleges (RAE 2008) Sheffield; London (King's); London (UCL); Wolverhampton; City; Robert Gordon; Glasgow; Brunel; Loughborough; Edinburgh Napier.

Examples of sandwich degree courses Bristol UWE; Loughborough; Northumbria; Nottingham Trent; Plymouth; Staffordshire.

ADMISSIONS INFORMATION

Number of applicants per place (approx) Aberystwyth 4; London (UCL) 7; Loughborough 5; Manchester Met 4; Sheffield 30; Southampton 5.

Advice to applicants and planning the UCAS personal statement Work experience or work shadowing in local libraries is important but remember that reference libraries provide a different field of work. Visit university libraries and major reference libraries and discuss the work with librarians. Describe your experiences in the personal statement.

Misconceptions about this course Read the prospectus carefully. The course details can be confusing. Some courses have a bias towards the organisation and retrieval of information, others towards information systems technology.

Selection interviews Yes London (UCL), Loughborough, Southampton.

Interview advice and questions Past questions include: What is it about librarianship that interests you? Why do you think you are suited to be a librarian? What does the job entail? What is the role of the library in school? What is the role of the public library? What new developments are taking place in libraries? Which books do you read? How often do you use a library? What is the Dewey number for the history section in the library? (Applicant studying A-level history.) See also **Chapter 6**.

AFTER-RESULTS ADVICE

Offers to applicants repeating A-levels Higher Loughborough; **Same** Sheffield.

GRADUATE DESTINATIONS AND EMPLOYMENT (2009/10 HESA)

Career note Graduates in this subject area and in communications enter a wide range of public and private sector jobs where the need to process information as well as to make it easily accessible and user-friendly, is very high. Areas of work could include web content, design and internet management and library management.

Check **Chapter 4** when choosing your university and **Chapter 7** on how to read the subject tables.

OTHER DEGREE SUBJECTS FOR CONSIDERATION

Business Information Systems; Communication Studies; Computer Science; Geographic Information Systems; Media Studies.

INTERNATIONAL RELATIONS

(including **International Development, Peace Studies** and **War Studies**; see also **Development Studies, European Studies, Politics**)

A strong interest in international affairs is a prerequisite for these courses which often allow students to focus on a specific area such as African, Asian, West European politics.

Useful websites www.sipri.org; www.un.org; www.un.int; www.irc-online.org; see also **Politics**.

NB The points totals shown to the left of the institutions are for ease of reference only. It must not be assumed that Tariff points are always used by institutions or that they can be substituted for an offer in grades. The level of an offer is not necessarily indicative of the quality of a course.

COURSE OFFERS INFORMATION

Subject requirements/preferences GCSE English; a foreign language usually required. **AL** No specified subjects. (War St) History may be required.

Your target offers and examples of courses provided by each institution

440 pts **Warwick** – A*AAa (Econ Pol Int St) (IB 38 pts)
380 pts **Bath** – A*AA (Econ Int Dev) (IB 38 pts)
　　　　 London (King's) – A*AA (War St) (IB 39 pts)
　　　　 Nottingham – A*AA–AAA (Econ Int Econ) (IB 38–36 pts)
360 pts **Bath** – AAA (Pol Int Rel) (IB 38 pts)
　　　　 Durham – AAA (Int Rel) (37 pts)
　　　　 Edinburgh – AAA–BBB (Int Rel Law) (IB 42–34 pts)
　　　　 Exeter – AAA–AAB (Int Rel) (IB 36–34 pts)
　　　　 London (QM) – AAA 360 pts (Int Rel) (IB 32 pts)
　　　　 London (RH) – AAA–ABB 360–320 pts (Econ Pol Int Rel) (IB 32–35 pts)
　　　　 London LSE – AAA 360 pts (Int Rel) (IB 37 pts HL 666)
　　　　 Nottingham – AAA (Int Rel) (IB 36 pts)
　　　　 St Andrews – AAA (Int Rel courses) (IB 38 pts)
　　　　 Sheffield – AAA incl hist (Int Hist Int Pol) (IB 37 pts HL 6 hist)
　　　　 Sussex – AAA–AAB (Law Int Rel) (IB 35–36 pts)
340 pts **Aston** – AAB–ABB 340–320 pts (Pol Int Rel) (IB 34–35 pts)
　　　　 Birmingham – AAB (Int St Pol Sci) (IB 34–36 pts)
　　　　 Cardiff – AAB (Euro Pol Int Rel)
　　　　 Essex – AAB–ABB (Pol Int Rel; Int Rel)
　　　　 Exeter – AAB–ABB (Int Rel Modn Lang) (IB 32–29 pts)
　　　　 Lancaster – AAb (Pol Int Rel) (IB 34 pts)
　　　　 Leeds – AAB (Int Rel) (IB 34 pts HL 16 pts)
　　　　 London (Birk) – AAB (Glob Pol Int Rel)
　　　　 London (Gold) – AAB (Int St) (IB 28 pts)
　　　　 London (King's) – AAB (Pol Int Econ) (IB 36 pts HL 665)
　　　　 London (RH) – AAB 340 pts (Int Rel Pol) (IB 32–35 pts)
　　　　 Loughborough – AAB–ABB (Hist Int Rel) (IB 32–34 pts)
　　　　 Manchester – AAB (Pol Int Rel) (IB 35 pts)
　　　　 Sheffield – AAB (Inter Pol Scrty St) (IB 35 pts)
　　　　 Southampton – AAB 340 pts (Int Rel) (IB 34 pts HL 17 pts)
　　　　 Surrey – AAB (Law Int St) (IB 35 pts)
　　　　 Sussex – AAB (Int Bus) (IB 35 pts)
　　　　 York – AAB (Pol Int Rel) (IB 36 pts)

320 pts **Aston** – AAB–ABB 340–320 pts (Int Rel Bus) (IB 33 pts)
Birmingham – ABB (War St) (IB 34 pts)
Hull – 320 pts (Pol Int Rel) (IB 34–36 pts)
Kent – ABB (Int Rel Fr/Ger/Ital) (IB 33 pts)
Leeds – ABB (As Pacif St Int Rel) (IB 32 pts HL 15 pts)
Leicester – ABB (Int Rel Hist; Int Rel)
London (RH) – ABB–BBB (Mling St Int Rel) (IB 32 pts)
London Met – 320 pts (Law Int Rel)
Loughborough – ABC–ABB (Int Rel) (IB 32–34 pts)
UEA – ABB–BBB (Int Dev St Fr/Span/Jap) (IB 32–31 pts)
300 pts **Aberdeen** – BBB (Int Rel)
Aberystwyth – 300 pts (Int Pol Strat St) (IB 28 pts)
Bristol UWE – 300 pts (Int Rel courses) (IB 26–32 pts)
Brunel – BBB (Int Pol) (IB 32 pts)
Edinburgh – AAA–BBB 300–360 pts (Int Rel) (IB 34 pts)
Keele – 300–320 pts (Int Rel) (IB 28–30 pts)
Nottingham Trent – 300 pts (Int Law)
Plymouth – 300 pts (Int Rel Law)
Queen's Belfast – BBB/BBCb (Int Pol Cnflct St)
Reading – 300–320 pts (Pol Int Rel; War Pce Int Rel)
Sheffield Hallam – 300 pts (Int Evnts Mgt Tour Destin; Int Fin)
Swansea – BBB 300 pts (Int Rel; Int Rel Welsh; Int Rel Am St; War Soty)
Westminster – BBB (Int Rel courses) (IB 28 pts)
280 pts **Aberystwyth** – 280–300 pts (Int Pol) (IB 28 pts)
Bradford – 280 pts (Int Rel Scrty St) (IB 30 pts)
Brighton – individual offers may vary BBC (Hum: War Cnflct Modnty) (IB 28 pts)
Manchester Met – 280 pts (Int Pol Lang (Fr/Ger/Ital/Span)) (IB 28 pts)
Nottingham Trent – 280 pts (Int Rel Joint Hons)
Oxford Brookes – BBC (Int Rel Pol) (IB 31 pts)
Stirling – BBC (Pol (Int Pol)) (IB 32 pts)
Salford – 280 pts (Int Rel Pol) (IB 31 pts)
Westminster – BBC (Dev St Int Rel; Int Rel Ger)
260 pts **De Montfort** – 260 pts (Int Rel; Int Rel Pol)
Derby – 260–300pts (Thrd Wrld Dev)
Dundee – BCC (Int Rel Pol)
Liverpool Hope – 260–320 pts (Int Rel)
Nottingham Trent – 260 pts (Glob St Joint Hons)
Oxford Brookes – BCC (Econ Pol Int Rel) (IB 29 pts)
Portsmouth – 260–300 pts (Law Int Rel)
Winchester – 260–300 pts (Pol Glob St)
240 pts **Buckingham** – 240 pts (Int St)
Canterbury Christ Church – 240 pts (Pol Int Rel; Int Rel)
Chester – 240–280 pts (Int Dev St) (IB 26 pts)
Coventry – 240–260 pts (Span Int Rel)
Leeds Met – 240 pts (Int Rel Pce St) (IB 24 pts)
Lincoln – 240 pts (Int Rel)
London Met – 240 pts (Int Dev Int Rel; Int Rel)
London South Bank – 240 pts (Int Pol)
Plymouth – 240 pts (Int Rel Pol; Int Rel courses)
Portsmouth – 240–300 pts (Int Rel) (IB 24–25 pts)
Salford – 240 pts (Jrnl War St) (IB 31 pts)
Westminster – CCC–BCC (Int Rel) (IB 28 pts)
220 pts **Leeds Met** – 220 pts (Ger Int Rel; Glob Dev Int Rel)
200 pts **Lincoln** – 200–260 pts (Int Rel Pol)
Middlesex – 200–300 pts (Int Pol)
Wolverhampton – 200 pts (War St courses)

Check **Chapter 4** when choosing your university and **Chapter 7** on how to read the subject tables.

160 pts **Wolverhampton** – 160–220 pts (War St Phil)

Open University – contact +44 (0)845 300 6090 **or** www.openuniversity.co.uk/you (Int St)

Alternative offers

See **Chapter 7** and **Appendix 1** for grades/UCAS Tariff points information for the International Baccalaureate, Scottish Highers/Advanced Highers, the Welsh Baccalaureate, the Irish Leaving Certificate, the Cambridge Pre-U Diploma, the Advanced Diploma and the Extended Project.

CHOOSING YOUR COURSE (SEE ALSO CH.1)

Some course features

Cardiff There is also a joint degree in Politics and International Relations with Turin University.
London (King's) A unique range of courses in War Studies includes topics in strategy, security and intelligence.
London LSE The subject can be taken as a Single Honours degree or jointly with History. High percentage of international students.
UEL (Int Dev: Thrd Wrld NGO Mgt) An interdisciplinary course, this draws on economics, politics, sociology, history and cultural studies to focus on the role of NGOs, their functions and relationships. Students are encouraged to travel to Africa, Asia, Central and Latin America; there is also a final-year work placement scheme.

Universities and colleges teaching quality See www.qaa.ac.uk; http://unistats.direct.gov.uk.

Top research universities and colleges (RAE 2008) See **Politics**.

Examples of sandwich degree courses Aston; Plymouth; Portsmouth.

ADMISSIONS INFORMATION

Number of applicants per place (approx) Aberystwyth 6; Birmingham 10; De Montfort 6; Derby 3; Exeter 8; Leeds 13; London (King's) 6; London LSE (Int Rel) 21; Nottingham 5; Portsmouth 2; Reading 5; Southampton (Int Rel) 6.

Advice to applicants and planning the UCAS personal statement Describe any special interests you have in the affairs of any particular country. Contact embassies for information on cultural, economic and political developments. Follow international events through newspapers and magazines. Give details of any voluntary work you have done. **London (King's)** Substantial experience required in some area of direct relevance to War Studies. **St Andrews** Give reasons for choice of course and evidence of your interest.

Misconceptions about this course Some students think that this degree will give direct entry into the Diplomatic Service.

Selection interviews Yes London (King's), London Met, Nottingham Trent; **Some** De Montfort, Kent, Wolverhampton; **No** Birmingham, Nottingham, UEA.

Interview advice and questions Applicants are likely to be questioned on current international events and crises between countries. See also **Chapter 6**. **Nottingham Trent** Be prepared to be challenged on your existing views!

AFTER-RESULTS ADVICE

Offers to applicants repeating A-levels Same Chester, De Montfort, Exeter, Lincoln, Wolverhampton.

GRADUATE DESTINATIONS AND EMPLOYMENT (2009/10 HESA)

See **Politics**.

Career note See **Politics**.

OTHER DEGREE SUBJECTS FOR CONSIDERATION

Development Studies; Economics; European Studies; Government; Politics.

ITALIAN

(see also **Languages**)

The language and literature of Italy will feature strongly on most Italian courses. The majority of applicants have no knowledge of Italian. They will need to give convincing reasons for their interest and to show that they have the ability to assimilate language quickly. See also **Appendix 3** under Languages.

Useful websites http://europa.eu; www.italia.gov.it; www.bbc.co.uk/languages; http://languageadvantage.com; www.sis.ac.uk; www.italianstudies.org; www.languagematters.co.uk; www.reed.co.uk/multilingual; see also **Languages**.

NB The points totals shown to the left of the institutions are for ease of reference only. It must not be assumed that Tariff points are always used by institutions or that they can be substituted for an offer in grades. The level of an offer is not necessarily indicative of the quality of a course.

COURSE OFFERS INFORMATION

Subject requirements/preferences GCSE English and a foreign language required. **AL** Italian may be required for some courses.

Your target offers and examples of courses provided by each institution

380 pts **Cambridge** – A*AA (Modn Mediev Lang (Ital)) (IB 40–42 pts)

360 pts **London (RH)** – AAA–AAB (Econ Fr/Ger/Ital/Span) (IB 33–35 pts)
Manchester – AAB–BBB 300–340 pts (Ital courses) (IB 31–36 pts)
Oxford – AAA 360 pts (Ital) (IB 38–40 pts)
Sussex – AAA–AAB (Law Fr/Ital/Span (Yr Abrd)) (IB 35–36 pts)

340 pts **Bristol** – AAB–BBB (Ital Modn Lang) (IB 33–30 pts)
Cardiff – AAB–BBB (Ital)
Exeter – AAB–ABB (Ital) (IB 29 pts)
London (RH) – AAB–ABB (Dr Fr/Ger/Ital) (IB 35 pts)
London (UCL) – AAB (Ital) (IB 36 pts)
Manchester – AAB–BBB 300–340 pts (Ital St) (IB 36–31 pts)
St Andrews – AAB–AAA (Ital courses) (IB 36 pts)
Warwick – AAB (Ger St Ital) (IB 36 pts)

320 pts **Birmingham** – ABB (Ital St Joint Hons) (IB 32 pts)
Glasgow – ABB (Ital Joint Hons) (IB 36 pts)
Leicester – ABB (Ital Joint Hons) (IB 30 pts)
London (RH) – ABB–BBB (Euro St Fr/Ger/Ital/Span)
Strathclyde – ABB (Ital courses)
Sussex – ABB–BBB (Ital courses)
Warwick – ABB (Ital Joint Hons) (IB 32–34 pts)

300 pts **Cardiff** – BBB (Relig St Span/Ital)
Edinburgh – AAA–BBB 300–360 pts (Ital) (IB 34–42 pts)
Essex – BBB (Ital St Modn Lang) (IB 32 pts)
Hull – 300 pts (Hist Fr/Ger/Ital/Span)
Kent – BBB (Ital Joint Hons) (IB 33–35 pts)
Leeds – ABC–BBB (Ital Joint Hons) (IB 34 pts HL 16 pts)
Liverpool – BBB (Comm St Ital) (IB 30 pts)
Salford – 300 pts (Modn Lang Transl Interp St (Fr/Ger/Ital/Port/Span))
Swansea – BBB (Ital courses)

280 pts **Bangor** – 280 pts (Law Ital) (IB 28 pts)
Hull – 280–300 pts (Ital St; Ital Mgt; Ital Transl St; Ital Mark)
Reading – 280–300 pts (Ital)
Salford – 280–300 pts (Modn Lang St (Ital))

260 pts **Greenwich** – 260 pts (Ital) (IB 24 pts)
Hertfordshire – 260–300 pts (Ital)

Check **Chapter 4** when choosing your university and **Chapter 7** on how to read the subject tables.

Manchester Met – 260 pts (Lang (Fr/Ger/Ital/Span) Ling) (IB 28 pts)
Nottingham Trent – 260 pts (Ital Joint Hons)
240 pts **Bangor** – 240–300 pts (Ital Joint Hons) (IB 26–28 pts)
Euro Bus Sch London – 240–300 pts (Int Bus Ital)

Alternative offers

See **Chapter 7** and **Appendix 1** for grades/UCAS Tariff points information for the International Baccalaureate, Scottish Highers/Advanced Highers, the Welsh Baccalaureate, the Irish Leaving Certificate, the Cambridge Pre-U Diploma, the Advanced Diploma and the Extended Project.

CHOOSING YOUR COURSE (SEE ALSO CH.1)

Some course features

Bangor Italian can be studied with two other languages or with Law, Journalism or Media Studies.
Bath Italian is taken with a second European language as part of the European Studies course.
Hull In addition to modern language combinations, Italian can be studied with a choice from 17 other subjects.
Reading The History with Italian degree involves a year abroad.

Universities and colleges teaching quality See www.qaa.ac.uk; http://unistats.direct.gov.uk.

Top research universities and colleges (RAE 2008) Cambridge; Leeds; Warwick; Reading; Oxford; Bristol; Manchester; Birmingham; London (UCL); Exeter.

ADMISSIONS INFORMATION

Number of applicants per place (approx) Birmingham 5; Bristol 8; Cardiff 3; Hull 8; Lancaster 8; Leeds 3; London (RH) 4.

Advice to applicants and planning the UCAS personal statement Describe any visits to Italy and experience of speaking the language. Interests in Italian art, literature, culture, society and architecture could also be mentioned. Read Italian newspapers and magazines and give details if you have a bilingual background. Give evidence of your interest and your reasons for choosing the course. See also **Appendix 3** under Languages.

Misconceptions about this course **Leeds** See **Languages**.

Selection interviews **Yes** Birmingham (majority receive offers), London (RH), Oxford; **Some** Cambridge; **No** Reading.

Interview advice and questions Past questions include: Why do you want to learn Italian? What foreign newspapers or magazines do you read (particularly if the applicant has taken A-level Italian)? Have you visited Italy? What do you know of the Italian people, culture, art? See also **Chapter 6**. **Leeds** See **Languages**.

AFTER-RESULTS ADVICE

Offers to applicants repeating A-levels **Higher** Birmingham, Glasgow, Warwick; **Same** Cardiff, Hull, Leeds.

GRADUATE DESTINATIONS AND EMPLOYMENT (2009/10 HESA)

Graduates surveyed 300 **Employed** 130 **In voluntary employment** 10 **In further study** 60 **Assumed unemployed** 20

Career note See **Languages**.

OTHER DEGREE SUBJECTS FOR CONSIDERATION

European Studies; International Business Studies; other languages.

JAPANESE
(see also Asia-Pacific Studies, Languages)

A strong interest in Japan and its culture is expected of applicants. A number of four-year joint courses are now offered, all of which include a period of study in Japan. Potential employers are showing an interest in Japanese. Students report that 'it is not a soft option'. They are expected to be firmly committed to a Japanese degree (for example, by listing only Japanese on the UCAS application), to have an interest in using their degree in employment and to be prepared for a lot of hard work. See **Appendix 3** under Languages.

Useful websites www.cilt.org.uk; www.iol.org.uk; www.bbc.co.uk/languages; http://languageadvantage.com; www.languagematters.co.uk; www.reed.co.uk/multilingual; www.japanese-online.com; www.japaneselifestyle.com.au; www.thejapanesepage.com; www.japanesestudies.org.uk.

NB The points totals shown to the left of the institutions are for ease of reference only. It must not be assumed that Tariff points are always used by institutions or that they can be substituted for an offer in grades. The level of an offer is not necessarily indicative of the quality of a course.

COURSE OFFERS INFORMATION
Subject requirements/preferences GCSE A foreign language usually required. **AL** Modern language required for some courses.

Your target offers and examples of courses provided by each institution
380 pts **Cambridge** – A*AA (As Mid E St (Jap)) (IB 40–42 pts HL 776–777)
360 pts **Manchester** – AAA (Russ Jap MML) (IB 37 pts)
　　　　　Oxford – AAA (Jap) (IB 38–40 pts)
340 pts **Manchester** – AAB–ABB 320–340 pts (Jap St) (IB 33–36 pts)
　　　　　Sheffield – AAB–ABB (Jap St) (IB 35–33 pts)
320 pts **Cardiff** – ABB (Bus St Jap) (IB 32 pts)
　　　　　Leeds – AAB–ABB 320–340 pts (Jap courses) (IB 34 pts HL 16 pts)
　　　　　Manchester – AAB–ABB 320–340 pts (Jap Scrn St) (IB 33–36 pts)
　　　　　Newcastle – AAB–ABB 320–340 pts (Chin/Jap Cult St) (IB 32 pts)
　　　　　Sheffield – ABB (Jap St Joint Hons) (IB 33 pts)
　　　　　UEA – ABB–BBB (Int Dev St Fr/Span/Jap) (IB 32–31 pts)
300 pts **Edinburgh** – AAA–BBB 300–360 pts (Jap) (IB 34–42 pts)
　　　　　Oxford Brookes – BBB (Jap St; Jap St (Comb))
260 pts **UCLan** – 260–300 pts (Jap (Comb)) (IB 26 pts)

Alternative offers
See **Chapter 7** and **Appendix 1** for grades/UCAS Tariff points information for the International Baccalaureate, Scottish Highers/Advanced Highers, the Welsh Baccalaureate, the Irish Leaving Certificate, the Cambridge Pre-U Diploma, the Advanced Diploma and the Extended Project.

CHOOSING YOUR COURSE (SEE ALSO CH.1)
Some course features
Cardiff Courses are offered with Business or a choice of four European languages.
Manchester (Jap Scrn St) The course combines Japanese language and culture with core course units in understanding film, its history and pre-history, and its development across other media including television, DVD and the internet. The third year is spent abroad.
Newcastle (Jap Cult St) Course covers language, sociology, anthropology and Modern East and South East Asian History.
Sheffield Japanese can be studied in combination with 13 other subjects including Chinese, Korean and Business Management.

Universities and colleges teaching quality See www.qaa.ac.uk; http://unistats.direct.gov.uk.

Examples of sandwich degree courses Oxford Brookes.

Check **Chapter 4** when choosing your university and **Chapter 7** on how to read the subject tables.

ADMISSIONS INFORMATION

Number of applicants per place (approx) Cardiff 8; London (SOAS) 9; Sheffield 10.

Advice to applicants and planning the UCAS personal statement Discuss your interest in Japan and your reasons for wishing to study the language. Know Japan, its culture and background history. Discuss any visits you have made or contacts with Japanese nationals. See also **Appendix 3** under Languages. **Leeds** See **Languages**.

Selection interviews Yes Cambridge, Oxford, Southampton; **Some** Leeds.

Interview advice and questions Japanese is an extremely demanding subject and applicants are most likely to be questioned on their reasons for choosing this degree. They will be expected also to have some knowledge of Japanese culture, history and current affairs. See also **Chapter 6**.

Reasons for rejection (non-academic) Insufficient evidence of genuine motivation.

AFTER-RESULTS ADVICE

Offers to applicants repeating A-levels No Cambridge.

GRADUATE DESTINATIONS AND EMPLOYMENT (2009/10 HESA)

Graduates surveyed 150 **Employed** 55 **In voluntary employment** 0 **In further study** 25 **Assumed unemployed** 20

Career note See **Languages**.

OTHER DEGREE SUBJECTS FOR CONSIDERATION

Asia-Pacific Studies; International Business Studies; Oriental Languages; South East Asia Studies.

LANDSCAPE ARCHITECTURE

(including **Garden Design** and **Landscape Design** and **Management**; see also **Agricultural Sciences/Agriculture, Horticulture**)

Landscape architecture is a specialised branch of architecture for which an ability in art and design is sought and for some of these courses a portfolio of art work may be required. Courses focus on the design of the environment and surrounding buildings. Landscape architecture should not be confused with the work of a garden centre.

Useful websites www.landscape.co.uk; www.laprofession.org.

NB The points totals shown to the left of the institutions are for ease of reference only. It must not be assumed that Tariff points are always used by institutions or that they can be substituted for an offer in grades. The level of an offer is not necessarily indicative of the quality of a course.

COURSE OFFERS INFORMATION

Subject requirements/preferences GCSE English, geography, art and design, mathematics and at least one science usually required. **AL** Preferred subjects for some courses include biology, geography, environmental science. A portfolio may also be required.

Sheffield Art and design or design technology at A-level required.

Your target offers and examples of courses provided by each institution
360 pts **Sheffield** – AAA (Archit Lnd) (IB 37 pts)
300 pts **Edinburgh (CA)** – BBB 300 pts (Lnd Archit) (IB 34 pts)
280 pts **Birmingham City** – 280 pts (Land Archit) (IB 26 pts)
Gloucestershire – 280–300 pts (Lnd Archit)
Greenwich – 280 pts (Lnd Archit)
Kingston – 280 pts (Lnd Archit) (IB 28 pts)
Leeds Met – 280–300 pts (Lnd Archit) (IB 26 pts)

Manchester Met – 280–300 pts (Lnd Archit) (IB 28 pts)
Sheffield – BBC (Lnd Archit Ecol) (IB 30 pts)
240 pts **Greenwich** – 240 pts (Gdn Des)
Hadlow (Coll) – 240 pts (Lnd Mgt; Gdn Des)
Leeds Met – 240–280 pts (Gdn Art Des) (IB 26 pts)
200 pts **Writtle (Coll)** – 200 pts (Lnd Gdn Des; Gdn Des Restor Mgt; Lnd Archit)

Alternative offers
See **Chapter 7** and **Appendix 1** for grades/UCAS Tariff points information for the International Baccalaureate, Scottish Highers/Advanced Highers, the Welsh Baccalaureate, the Irish Leaving Certificate, the Cambridge Pre-U Diploma, the Advanced Diploma and the Extended Project.

EXAMPLES OF FOUNDATION DEGREES IN THE SUBJECT FIELD
Brighton; Brooksby Melton (Coll); Guildford (Coll); Harper Adams (UC); Kingston; Moulton (Coll); SAC (Scottish CAg); Sparsholt (Coll); Suffolk (Univ Campus).

CHOOSING YOUR COURSE (SEE ALSO CH.1)
Some course features
Birmingham City (Land Archit) The course is accredited by the Landscape Institute and combines a strong study of design with a focus on environmental and cultural issues and technical skills.
Gloucestershire Students have access to dedicated landscape studios as part of this vocational course studied at Francis Close Hall.
Manchester Met The three-year BA course can be followed by an MA in Landscape Architecture for those wanting to enter the profession of landscape architecture. The course focuses on the design of outdoor space and includes a European study tour and offers study opportunities in European universities.
Sheffield A multidisciplinary course providing a comprehensive training in landscape architecture with a specialism in either planning or ecology. The Ecology pathway focuses on habitat restoration, urban regeneration and green technologies, while the Planning pathway centres on the political, social and economic facors of urban and rural environments.

Universities and colleges teaching quality See www.qaa.ac.uk; http://unistats.direct.gov.uk.

Examples of sandwich degree courses Writtle (Coll).

ADMISSIONS INFORMATION
Number of applicants per place (approx) Edinburgh (CA) 7; Gloucestershire 9; Greenwich 3; Kingston 4; Manchester Met 9; Writtle (Coll) 5.

Advice to applicants and planning the UCAS personal statement Knowledge of the work of landscape architects is important. Arrange a visit to a landscape architect's office and try to organise some work experience. Read up on historical landscape design and visit country house estates with examples of outstanding designs. Describe these visits in detail and your preferences. Membership of the National Trust could be useful. See also **Appendix 3**.

Selection interviews Yes Birmingham City, Gloucestershire, Greenwich, Manchester Met, Sheffield, Writtle (Coll).

Interview advice and questions Applicants will be expected to have had some work experience and are likely to be questioned on their knowledge of landscape architectural work and the subject. Historical examples of good landscaping could also be asked for. See also **Chapter 6**.

Reasons for rejection (non-academic) Lack of historical knowledge and awareness of current developments. Poor portfolio.

AFTER-RESULTS ADVICE
Offers to applicants repeating A-levels Same Birmingham City, Edinburgh (CA), Greenwich, Manchester Met.

GRADUATE DESTINATIONS AND EMPLOYMENT (2009/10 HESA)

Landscape Design; graduates surveyed 465 **Employed** 230 **In voluntary employment** 15 **In further study** 120 **Assumed unemployed** 45

Career note Opportunities at present in landscape architecture are good. Openings exist in local government or private practice and may cover planning, housing, and conservation.

OTHER DEGREE SUBJECTS FOR CONSIDERATION

Architecture; Art and Design; Environmental Planning; Forestry; Horticulture.

LANGUAGES

(including **Dutch, Hebrew, Modern Languages** and **Translation Studies; see separate language tables;** see also **African and Caribbean Studies, Asia-Pacific Studies, Chinese, English, European Studies, French, German, Greek, Italian, Japanese, Latin, Linguistics, Russian and East European Studies, Scandinavian Studies, Spanish**)

Modern Language courses usually offer three main options: a single subject degree commonly based on literature and language, a European Studies course, or two-language subjects which can often include languages different from those available at school (such as Scandinavian Studies, Russian and the languages of Eastern Europe, the Middle and Far East).

Useful websites www.iol.org.uk; www.iti.org.uk; http://europa.eu; www.cilt.org.uk; www.bbc.co.uk/languages; http://languageadvantage.com; www.omniglot.com; www.languagematters.co.uk; www.reed.co.uk/multilingual.

NB The points totals shown to the left of the institutions are for ease of reference only. It must not be assumed that Tariff points are always used by institutions or that they can be substituted for an offer in grades. The level of an offer is not necessarily indicative of the quality of a course.

COURSE OFFERS INFORMATION

Subject requirements/preferences GCSE English and a modern language required. In some cases grades A and/or B may be stipulated. **AL** A modern foreign language required usually with a specified grade.

Your target offers and examples of courses provided by each institution

400 pts **London (UCL)** – A*AA+AS–AAA+AS (Hist Euro Lang) (IB 38–39 pts)
380 pts **Cambridge** – (Part II subject, taken after Part I in another, usually language-related, subject) A*AA (Modn Mediev Lang (Ling)) (IB 40–42 pts)
London (King's) – AABc (Port Braz St) (IB 36 pts HL 6 hist)
London (UCL) – A*AA–AAA (Psy Lang Sci) (IB 38–39 pts)
360 pts **Birmingham** – AAA (Port Mny Bank Fin) (IB 36–38 pts)
Bristol – AAA–AAB (Pol Modn Lang) (IB 37–35 pts)
Durham – AAA (Modn Euro Langs Hist) (IB 37 pts)
Imperial London – AAA (Chem Fr/Ger/Span Sci) (IB 38 pts HL 7 chem 6 maths)
London (UCL) – AAA–ABB incl chem (Chem Euro Lang) (IB 32–36 pts)
Manchester – AAA–AAB 320–360 pts (Cell Biol Modn Lang) (IB 37–33 pts)
Nottingham – AAA–AAB (Phys Euro Lang)
Oxford – AAA (Euro Mid E Langs (Cz/Russ)) (IB 38–40 pts)
St Andrews – AAA–AAB (Modn Lang courses) (IB 35–38 pts)
Sheffield – AAA incl maths sci (Mech Eng Fr/Ger/Ital) (IB 37 pts HL 6 maths sci)
340 pts **Birmingham** – AAB (Int Bus Lang) (IB 36–38 pts)
Bristol – AAB–BBB incl mus (Mus Modn Lang) (IB 35–32 pts)
Cardiff – AAB (Acc Euro Lang) (IB 35 pts)
Durham – AAB (Modn Langs) (IB 36 pts)

Exeter – AAB–ABB (Class St Modn Lang) (IB 34–32 pts)
Kent – AAB (Engl Fr Law/Ger Law/Ita Law/Span Law) (IB 33 pts)
London (RH) – AAB–ABB (Langs Phil)
London (SOAS) – AAB (Persn Joint Hons) (IB 36 pts HL 666)
Manchester – AAB–BBB 300–340 pts (Modn Lang Bus Mgt courses) (IB 31–36 pts)
St Andrews – AAB (Geog Lang) (IB 32–36 pts)
Sheffield – AAB (Mat Sci Eng (Modn Lang)) (IB 35 pts)
Southampton – AAB (Modn Lang) (IB 34 pts HL 17 pts)
Surrey – AAB (Bus Mgt Fr/Ger/Span) (IB 36 pts)
Sussex – AAB–ABB (Phil Langs) (IB 34–36 pts)
York – AAB–ABB (Modn Lang Ling) (IB 34 pts)

330 pts **Bath** – ABB (Modn Langs Euro St (Fr and Span/Ital/Russ/Ger)) (IB 34 pts HL 6 Fr)
320 pts **Bath** – ABB (Modn Langs Euro St (Span and Fr/Ger/Ital/Russ)) (IB 34 pts HL 6 Span)
Birmingham – ABB (Port Joint Hons) (IB 32 pts)
Bristol – ABB–BBC (Russ Modn Lang) (IB 33–30 pts)
Essex – 320 pts (Econ Langs)
Kent – ABB (Engl Am Lit Joint Hons; Int Rel Fr/Ger/Ital)
Lancaster – ABB (Euro Lang Film St) (IB 32 pts)
Leeds – ABB (Pol Port/Russ/Span) (IB 34 pts)
Leicester – ABB (Modn Lang St) (IB 28–30 pts)
Liverpool – ABB (Class St Modn Lang) (IB 33 pts)
London (RH) – ABB 320 pts (Mus Fr/Ger/Ital/Span) (IB 35 pts HL 6 mus)
London (SOAS) – ABB (Tbtn Joint Hons) (IB 34 pts HL 555)
London (UCL) – ABB (Dutch) (IB 34 pts)
Manchester – AAB–ABB 320–340 pts (Euro St Modn Lang) (IB 33–36 pts)
Newcastle – AAB–ABB 320–340 pts (Modn Langs Bus St) (IB 32 pts HL 6 Fr/Ger/Span)
Nottingham – ABB–BBB (Mod Lang St)
Sheffield – ABB (Modn Langs) (IB 33 pts HL 6 lang)
Sussex – ABB–BBB (Art Hist Lang) (IB 32–34 pts)
Swansea – ABB–BBB (Lang courses; Lang Comm)
UEA – ABB–BBB (Modn Langs 4 yrs dbl Hons) (IB 32–31 pts)

300 pts **Aberdeen** – BBB (Langs Lit Scot) (IB 30 pts)
Aberystwyth – 300 pts (Euro St Fr/Ger/Span) (IB 28 pts)
Aston – 300–320 pts (Modn Langs courses) (IB 31–33 pts)
Bath – AAA–BBB 300–360 pts (Modn Lang) (IB 34 pts HL 6 lang)
Birmingham – ABB–BBB 300–320 pts (Chem Modn Lang)
Bristol UWE – 300 pts (Engl Lang Ling) (IB 26–32 pts)
Edinburgh – BBB–AAA (Port) (IB 34–42 pts)
Essex – 300 pts (Fr St Modn Langs) (IB 30 pts)
Heriot-Watt – BBB 300 pts (App Langs Transl; Langs (Interp Transl))
Hertfordshire – 300 pts (HR Mand)
Hull – BBB 300 pts (Lang)
Liverpool – BBB (Film St (Euro) Modn Lang) (IB 30–35 pts)
London (QM) – 300–320 pts (Fr/Ger/Russ Dr) (IB 32 pts)
Roehampton – 300 pts (Modn Lang)
Strathclyde – BBB (Modn Langs)
Salford – 300 pts (Modn Lang courses; Modn Lang Transl Interp St (Fr/Ger/Ital/Port/Span))

280 pts **Aberystwyth** – 280 pts (Rmnc Langs) (IB 28 pts)
Brighton – BBC (Engl Lang Ling) (IB 28 pts)
Bristol – ABB–BBC (Fr) (IB 33–30 pts)
Chester – 280 pts (Modn Langs)
Essex – 280 pts (Modn Lang) (IB 30 pts)
Hertfordshire – 280–300 pts (Acc Langs) (IB 28 pts)
Manchester Met – 280 pts (Int Pol Lang (Fr/Ger/Ital/Span)) (IB 28 pts)
Plymouth – 280 pts (Geog Lang)

Check **Chapter 4** when choosing your university and **Chapter 7** on how to read the subject tables.

Stirling – BBC (Mod Lang) (IB 32 pts)
Salford – 280–300 pts (Modn Lang St (Ital))
Sheffield Hallam – 280 pts (Mark Lang; Tour Lang; Lang TESOL)
Ulster – 280 pts incl BC (Lang Ling courses)
Westminster – BBC (Engl Lang Ling) (IB 30 pts)

260 pts **Bolton** – 260 pts (Bus Mgt Lang)
Hull – 260–280 pts (Modn Lang St Fr/Ger/Ital/Span)
London Met – 260 pts (Transl)
Manchester Met – 260 pts (Lang (Fr/Ger/Ital/Span) Ling) (IB 28 pts)
Nottingham Trent – 260 pts (Ger Joint Hons) (IB 24 pts)
Westminster – BCC–BBB (Transl St (Span)) (IB 28 pts)

240 pts **Anglia Ruskin** – 240 pts (P Educ Modn Lang)
Bangor – 240–260 pts (Lang Fr/Ger/Ital/Span Joint Hons)
Coventry – BCC 240–260 pts (Fr courses)
Euro Bus Sch London – 240 pts (Int Bus Fin Lang)
Greenwich – 240 pts (Eng Lang ELT)
London Met – 240 pts (App Transl)
Plymouth – 240 pts (Modn Langs) (IB 24 pts)
Portsmouth – 240–300 pts (App Langs)
UCLan – 240 pts (Modn Langs)
Ulster – CCC 240 pts (Int Trav Tour St Langs)

230 pts **Edinburgh Napier** – 230 pts (Lang Joint courses)

220 pts **Leeds Met** – 220 pts (Lang St) (IB 24 pts)
York St John – 220–260 pts (Modn Lang)

200 pts **Canterbury Christ Church** – 200 pts (P Educ Modn Lang)
Middlesex – 200–240 pts (Transl; Int Bus Langs)
Plymouth – 200–240 pts (Marit Bus Fr/Ger/Span) (IB 24 pts)

160 pts **Wolverhampton** – 160–220 pts (Interp (Brit Sign Lang/Engl))

80 pts **London (Birk)** – p/t for under 21s (over 21s varies) (Hum Engl/Fr/Ger)

Open University – contact +44 (0)845 300 6090 **or** www.openuniversity.co.uk/you (Modn Lang St)

Alternative offers

See **Chapter 7** and **Appendix 1** for grades/UCAS Tariff points information for the International Baccalaureate, Scottish Highers/Advanced Highers, the Welsh Baccalaureate, the Irish Leaving Certificate, the Cambridge Pre-U Diploma, the Advanced Diploma and the Extended Project.

CHOOSING YOUR COURSE (SEE ALSO CH.1)

Some course features
See also separate language tables.

Coventry Modern Language programmes offer French and Spanish (not ab initio). There are optional placements of one year.
Durham The modern languages offered are French, German, Russian and Spanish, Arabic, Italian, Russian and Hispanic Studies with the option to study up to three. All courses involve a year spent abroad.
Edinburgh Language courses are offered in Arabic, Celtic, Chinese, French, German, Italian, Japanese, Persian, Russian, Scandinavian Studies (Danish, Swedish, Norwegian) and Hispanic Studies. There is also an Islamic Studies and Middle Eastern Studies course.
Glasgow French, German, Greek, Italian, Latin, Russian, Hispanic Studies, Spanish, and Slavonic Studies are offered. There are also courses in Gaelic and Celtic.
Surrey Language courses focus on contemporary language in business, culture and society and cover French, German, Russian and Spanish.

Universities and colleges teaching quality See www.qaa.ac.uk; http://unistats.direct.gov.uk.

Top research universities and colleges (RAE 2008) See separate language tables.

ADMISSIONS INFORMATION

Number of applicants per place (approx) Aston 4; Bangor 5; Bath 6; Birmingham 5; Brighton 4; Bristol 15; Bristol UWE 4; Cambridge 3; Cardiff 6; Durham 6; Heriot-Watt 5; Huddersfield 12; Lancaster 10; Leeds (Joint Hons) 8; Leicester 6; Liverpool 5; Newcastle 22; Northumbria 4; Roehampton 3; Salford 6; Swansea 4; UEA 15; Wolverhampton 10; York 4.

Advice to applicants and planning the UCAS personal statement Discuss any literature studied outside your course work. Students applying for courses in which they have no previous knowledge (for example, Italian, Portuguese, Modern Greek, Czech, Russian) would be expected to have done a considerable amount of language work on their own in their chosen language before starting the course.

Misconceptions about this course Leeds (Joint Hons) Some applicants think that studying languages means studying masses of literature – wrong. At Leeds, generally speaking, it's up to you; you study as much or as little literature as you choose. Residence abroad does not inevitably mean a university course (except where you are taking a language from scratch). Paid employment is usually another option.

Selection interviews Yes Aston, Cambridge, Coventry, Durham, Heriot-Watt, Hertfordshire, Huddersfield, Liverpool (Open Day invitation), London (RH), Oxford (Mod Lang) 32%, (Mod Lang Ling) 27%, Roehampton; **Some** Brighton, Bristol UWE, Leeds, Salford, Swansea; **No** Dundee, UEA.

Interview advice and questions See also **Chapter 6**. **Bangor** All applicants invited for interview after offer when a lower offer may be made. **Cambridge** Think of a painting of a tree. Is the tree real? **Leeds** (Joint Hons) Give an example of something outside your studies that you have achieved over the past year. **London (RH)** Conversation in the appropriate language.

Reasons for rejection (non-academic) Lack of commitment to spend a year abroad. Poor references. Poor standard of English. No reasons for why the course has been selected. Poor communication skills. Incomplete applications, for example missing qualifications and reference.

AFTER-RESULTS ADVICE

Offers to applicants repeating A-levels Higher Bristol UWE; **Possibly higher** Aston; **Same** Bangor (usually), Birmingham, Bristol, Durham, Leeds, Liverpool, Newcastle, Nottingham Trent, Salford, Stirling, UEA, Wolverhampton, York; **No** Cambridge.

GRADUATE DESTINATIONS AND EMPLOYMENT (2009/10 HESA)

See separate language tables.

Career note The only career-related fields for language students are teaching, which attracts some graduates, and the demanding work of interpreting and translating, to which only a small number aspire. The majority will be attracted to work in management and administration, financial services and a host of other occupations which may include the social services, law and property development.

OTHER DEGREE SUBJECTS FOR CONSIDERATION

Communication Studies; Linguistics; Modern Languages Education/Teaching.

LATIN

(see also **Classical Studies/Classical Civilisation, Classics, Greek, Languages**)

Latin courses provide a study of the language, art, religion and history of the Roman world. This table should be read in conjunction with the **Classical Studies/Classical Civilisation** and **Classics** tables.

Useful websites www.thelatinlibrary.com; www.la.wikipedia.org; www.arlt.co.uk.

NB The points totals shown to the left of the institutions are for ease of reference only. It must not be assumed that Tariff points are always used by institutions or that they can be substituted for an offer in grades. The level of an offer is not necessarily indicative of the quality of a course.

Check **Chapter 4** when choosing your university and **Chapter 7** on how to read the subject tables.

COURSE OFFERS INFORMATION

Subject requirements/preferences GCSE English, a foreign language and Latin may be stipulated. **AL** Check courses for Latin requirement.

Your target offers and examples of courses provided by each institution
380 pts **Cambridge** – A*AA (Class Gk Lat) (IB 40–42 pts)
         Warwick – AABc (Engl Lat Lit) (IB 36 pts)
360 pts **London (UCL)** – AABe (Lat Gk) (IB 36 pts)
340 pts **Leeds** – AAB 340 pts (Lat)
         London (UCL) – AAB incl Gk (Gk Lat) (IB 36 pts)
         Nottingham – AAB (Engl St Lat) (IB 34 pts)
         St Andrews – AAB (Class Lat) (IB 35 pts)
320 pts **Glasgow** – ABB (Latin) (IB 36 pts)
         London (RH) – ABB (Lat) (IB 34 pts)
         Swansea – ABB (Class Civ Lat)
300 pts **Edinburgh** – AAA–BBB 300–360 pts (Anc Hist Lat) (IB 34 pts)
         Manchester – ABB–BBB 300–320 pts (Lat) (IB 34–31 pts)
200 pts **Trinity Saint David** – 200–300 pts (Lat) (IB 24 pts)

Alternative offers
See **Chapter 7** and **Appendix 1** for grades/UCAS Tariff points information for the International Baccalaureate, Scottish Highers/Advanced Highers, the Welsh Baccalaureate, the Irish Leaving Certificate, the Cambridge Pre-U Diploma, the Advanced Diploma and the Extended Project.

CHOOSING YOUR COURSE (SEE ALSO CH.1)

Some course features
Edinburgh An intensive Latin course is offered to beginners.
Exeter (Lat) The Combined Honours course focuses on the language and society of Rome, with modules in literature, history and culture, and translation from set books from and into Latin.
Leeds Joint Honours Latin students focus on Latin language and literature, and do intensive beginners' Latin course. There may be opportunities for study abroad.
St Andrews Latin is available as a Single Honours degree or in a wide range of Joint Honours courses. The Single Honours course combines Latin language study (beginners' and post A-level/ Highers) with an in-depth reading and understanding of Latin classics and other texts.
Swansea Latin is offered as a Joint Honours course with History, Medieval Studies, Classical Civilisation or Modern Languages.
Trinity Saint David Latin is offered at beginners', intermediate and advanced levels.

Universities and colleges teaching quality See www.qaa.ac.uk; http://unistats.direct.gov.uk.

Top research universities and colleges (RAE 2008) See **Classics**.

ADMISSIONS INFORMATION

Number of applicants per place (approx) Leeds 2; Manchester 5; Nottingham 6; Trinity Saint David 6.

Advice to applicants and planning the UCAS personal statement See **Classical Studies/Classical Civilisation** and **Classics**.

Selection interviews Yes Cambridge, Exeter, London (RH), London (UCL), Nottingham, Oxford, Trinity Saint David.

Interview advice and questions See **Classical Studies/Classical Civilisation** and **Classics**.

AFTER-RESULTS ADVICE

Offers to applicants repeating A-levels Higher Leeds, St Andrews, Warwick.

GRADUATE DESTINATIONS AND EMPLOYMENT (2009/10 HESA)

Graduates surveyed 35 **Employed** 20 **In voluntary employment** 0 **In further study** 20 **Assumed unemployed** 0

Career note Graduates enter a broad range of careers within management, the media, commerce and tourism as well as social and public services. Some graduates choose to work abroad and teaching is a popular option.

OTHER DEGREE SUBJECTS FOR CONSIDERATION

Ancient History; Archaeology; Classical Studies; Classics.

LATIN AMERICAN STUDIES

(including **Hispanic Studies**; see also **American Studies, Spanish**)

Latin American courses provide a study of Spanish and of Latin American republics, covering both historical and present-day conditions and problems. Normally a year is spent in Latin America.

Useful websites www.iol.org.uk; www.bbc.co.uk/languages; http://languageadvantage.com; www.languagematters.co.uk; www.reed.co.uk/multilingual; www.cilt.org.uk; www.latinworld.com; www.wola.org; www.latinamericalinks.com; www.latinamericanassoc.org; see also **Languages** and **Spanish**.

NB The points totals shown to the left of the institutions are for ease of reference only. It must not be assumed that Tariff points are always used by institutions or that they can be substituted for an offer in grades. The level of an offer is not necessarily indicative of the quality of a course.

COURSE OFFERS INFORMATION

Subject requirements/preferences GCSE Aberdeen: English, mathematics or science and a foreign language. English and a foreign language required by most universities. **AL** Spanish may be required for some courses.

Your target offers and examples of courses provided by each institution

380 pts London (King's) – AABc (Port Braz St) (IB 36 pts HL 6 hist)
London (UCL) – AAAe-AABe (Lat Am St) (IB 34-36 pts)
Nottingham – A*AA-AAA 360-380 pts (Econ Hisp St) (IB 38-36 pts)

340 pts Bristol – AAB-BBC (Hisp St) (IB 35-30 pts)
Liverpool – AAB-BBB (Hisp St Joint Hons) (IB 32 pts)
Manchester – AAB-ABB (Span Port Lat Am St) (IB 33-36 pts)
Newcastle – AAB-ABB 320-340 pts (Span Port Lat Am St) (IB 32 pts HL 6 Span)
Nottingham – AAB (Am St Lat Am St) (IB 34 pts)
Sheffield – AAB-BBB (Hisp St Joint Hons) (IB 35-32 pts)
Southampton – AAB (Pol Span/Port Lat Am St) (IB 34 pts HL 17 pts)

320 pts Birmingham – ABB (Hisp St) (IB 32 pts)
Glasgow – ABB (Hisp St) (IB 36 pts)
Kent – ABB (Hisp St) (IB 33 pts)
Leeds – ABB-AAB (Hisp Lat Am St) (IB 34 pts HL 16 pts)
London (QM) – 320-340 pts (Hisp St courses) (IB 32 pts)
Nottingham – ABB (Hisp St) (IB 32 pts)
Southampton – AAB-ABB 320-340 pts (Span Lat Am St) (IB 32 pts)

300 pts Aberdeen – BBB (Hisp St (Lat Am/Spn)) (IB 30 pts)
Essex – ABB-BBB 300 pts (Lat Am St)
Liverpool – BBB (Hisp St) (IB 30 pts)
Manchester – AAB-BBB 300-340 pts (Lat Am St Scrn St) (IB 31-36 pts)
Sheffield – BBB (Hisp St) (IB 32 pts)

280 pts Stirling – BBC (Span Lat Am St) (IB 32 pts)
260 pts Hull – 260-300 pts (Hisp St Relgn)
London Met – 260 pts (Span Lat Am St; Lat Am St)
200 pts Portsmouth – 200-280 pts (Span Lat Am St)

Check **Chapter 4** when choosing your university and **Chapter 7** on how to read the subject tables.

Alternative offers
See **Chapter 7** and **Appendix 1** for grades/UCAS Tariff points information for the International Baccalaureate, Scottish Highers/Advanced Highers, the Welsh Baccalaureate, the Irish Leaving Certificate, the Cambridge Pre-U Diploma, the Advanced Diploma and the Extended Project.

CHOOSING YOUR COURSE (SEE ALSO CH.1)
Some course features
Birmingham (Hisp St) The first two years of the course focus on Spanish language skills and Hispanic literature and culture. The third year is spent in Spain or Latin America while the fourth year centres on students' individual programme interests, for example advanced translation skills or cultural studies.
Liverpool (Hisp St) Three Iberian Romance languages (Catalan, Portuguese or Galician) are studied in addition to the main degree of Spanish. The degree programme also focuses on Spanish, Portuguese, Galician and Latin American culture.
London (UCL) (Hisp St) Course combines a study of Spanish language with courses in film history and literature. (Lat Am St) The course focuses on a study of Spanish and Portuguese and the literature and history of Spain, Portugal and Latin America.
Portsmouth (Span Lat Am Dev St) Students study the language and culture of contemporary Latin American societies, taking Spanish throughout the course. Half the placement year is in Spain and the other half at a partner institution in Latin America.

Universities and colleges teaching quality See www.qaa.ac.uk; http://unistats.direct.gov.uk.

Top research universities and colleges (RAE 2008) See **Spanish**.

ADMISSIONS INFORMATION
Number of applicants per place (approx) Essex 3; Liverpool 3; Newcastle 25; Nottingham 7; Portsmouth 5.

Advice to applicants and planning the UCAS personal statement Visits and contacts with Spain and Latin American countries should be described. An awareness of the economic, historical and political scene of these countries is also important. Information may be obtained from respective embassies.

Selection interviews Yes Newcastle; **Some** Portsmouth.

Interview advice and questions Past questions include: Why are you interested in studying Latin American Studies? What countries related to the degree course have you visited? What career are you planning when you finish your degree? Applicants taking Spanish are likely to be asked questions on their syllabus and should also be familiar with some Spanish newspapers and magazines. See also **Chapter 6**.

AFTER-RESULTS ADVICE
Offers to applicants repeating A-levels Higher Essex; **Same** Newcastle, Portsmouth.

GRADUATE DESTINATIONS AND EMPLOYMENT (2009/10 HESA)
See **American Studies**.

Career note See **Languages**.

OTHER DEGREE SUBJECTS FOR CONSIDERATION
American Studies; Portuguese; Spanish.

LAW

(including **Criminology**; see also **Social Sciences/Studies**)

Law courses are usually divided into two parts. Part I occupies the first year and introduces the student to criminal and constitutional law and the legal process. Thereafter many different specialised topics can be studied in the second and third years. The course content is very similar for most courses. Applicants are advised to check with universities for their current policies concerning their use of the National Admissions Test for Law (LNAT). See **Subject requirements/preferences** below and also **Chapter 6**.

Useful websites www.barcouncil.org.uk; www.ilex.org.uk; www.lawcareers.net; www.lawsociety.org. uk; www.cps.gov.uk; www.hmcourts-service.gov.uk; www.lawscot.org.uk; www.lawsoc-ni.org; www. rollonfriday.com; www.lnat.ac.uk.

NB The points totals shown to the left of the institutions are for ease of reference only. It must not be assumed that Tariff points are always used by institutions or that they can be substituted for an offer in grades. The level of an offer is not necessarily indicative of the quality of a course.

COURSE OFFERS INFORMATION

Subject requirements/preferences GCSE Many universities will expect high grades. **AL** Arts, humanities, social sciences and sciences plus languages for courses combined with a foreign language. **All universities** Applicants offering art and music A-levels should check whether these subjects are acceptable.

Manchester Requirements are often higher than normal – minimum of five A-grades at GCSE.

Your target offers and examples of courses provided by each institution
440 pts **London (King's)** – A*AAa (Law) (IB 39 pts)
400 pts **Warwick** – AAAc (Law (St Abrd)) (IB 38 pts)
380 pts **Cambridge** – A*AA (Law) (IB 40–42 pts)
City – A*AA (Law) (IB 35 pts)
Durham – A*AA (Law) (IB 38 pts)
London (QM) – A*AA (Law) (IB 36 pts HL 666)
London (UCL) – AAA+AS (Law Fr Law/Ger Law/Hisp Law/Ital Law) (IB 38 pts)
London LSE – A*AA (Law) (IB 38 pts HL 766/666)
Warwick – AABc (Law Sociol) (IB 36 pts)
360 pts **Birmingham** – AAA–A*AB (Law Bus St) (IB 36 pts)
Bristol – AAA (Law Fr) (IB 37 pts HL 666)
Cardiff – AAA (Law) (IB 36 pts)
Edinburgh – AAA–BBB (Int Rel Law) (IB 42–34 pts)
Exeter – AAA–AAB (Law (Euro)) (IB 36–34 pts)
Lancaster – AAA 360 pts (Law) (IB 36 pts HL 17–18 pts)
Leeds – AAA (Law Mgt) (IB 38 pts HL 18 pts)
Leicester – AAA (Law; Law Fr Law Lang; Maîtrise Engl Fr Law)
Liverpool – AAA (Law Joint Hons) (IB 36 pts)
London (SOAS) – AAA (Law (Comb)) (IB 38 pts HL 766)
London NCH – AAA–AAB 340–360 pts (Law) (IB 37–38 pts HL 77)
Manchester – AAA (Law Crimin) (IB 37 pts)
Newcastle – AAA (Law) (IB 34 pts)
Nottingham – AAA (Law Fr Fr Law/Ger Ger Law/Span Span Law) (IB 38 pts HL 7)
Oxford – AAA (Law Euro Law) (IB 39 pts)
Queen's Belfast – AAA/AABa (Law Pol) (IB 34 pts HL 666)
Sheffield – AAA (Law (Euro Int)) (IB 37 pts HL 666)
Southampton – AAA (Law (Int Leg St)) (IB 36 pts HL 18 pts)
Sussex – AAA–AAB (Law Fr/Ital/Span (Yr Abrd)) (IB 35–36 pts)
UEA – AAA (Law Am Law) (IB 35 pts)

Check **Chapter 4** when choosing your university and **Chapter 7** on how to read the subject tables.

Warwick – AAA (Euro Law) (IB 38 pts)
York – AAA (Law) (IB 36 pts)
340 pts **Aberystwyth** – 340 pts (Euro Law)
Aston – AAB 340 pts (Law Mgt) (IB 34 pts)
Bournemouth – 340 pts (Law; Law Tax; Bus Law; Enter Law)
Brunel – AAB (Law) (IB 35 pts)
Durham – AAB (Crimin) (IB 36 pts)
Essex – AAB (Engl Fr Law) (IB 36 pts)
Glasgow – AAB (Law Joint Hons) (IB 36 pts)
Huddersfield – 340 pts (Bus Law; Law)
Keele – 340–360 pts (Law)
Kent – AAB (Law Joint Hons) (IB 36 pts)
Lancaster – AAB 340 pts (Law Crimin) (IB 34 pts)
London (Birk) – interview + reasoning test (p/t Accelerated Law) AAB (Law)
London (QM) – 340 pts (Law Pol) (IB 32 pts)
London LSE – AAB (Anth Law) (IB 37 pts HL 666)
Manchester – AAB (Law Pol) (IB 35 pts)
Reading – AAB (Law; Law Leg St Euro)
Strathclyde – AAB (Scots Law LLB)
Sheffield – AAB (Law Ger/Fr/Span) (IB 35 pts)
Surrey – AAB (Law) (IB 35 pts)
Swansea – AAB 340 pts (Law Bus) (IB 34 pts)
UEA – AAB (Law) (IB 33 pts)
320 pts **De Montfort** – 320 pts (Law)
Derby – 320 pts (Law LLB; Law Crimin)
Dundee – ABB (Law (Scot Engl))
Durham – ABB (Sociol Law)
Essex – ABB–BBB 300–320 pts (Phil Law) (IB 29 pts)
Greenwich – 320 pts (Law LLB) (IB 24 pts)
Hertfordshire – 320 pts (Law Fr; Law)
Hull – 320 pts (Law Phil) (IB 30 pts)
Keele – 320 pts (Law Joint Hons)
Kingston – 320 pts (Law; Law Crimin)
London Met – 320 pts (Law Int Dev LLB; Law Int Rel)
Manchester Met – ABB 320 pts (Law) (IB 30 pts)
Northumbria – ABB 320 pts (Law (Exmp)) (IB 32 pts)
Oxford Brookes – ABB (Law) (IB 33 pts)
Portsmouth – 320 pts (Law; Law Crimin)
Staffordshire – 320 pts (Law LLB)
Stirling – ABB (Law LLB) (IB 36 pts)
Salford – 320 pts (Law) (IB 31 pts)
UEA – ABB (Law Fr Law Lang) (IB 32 pts)
Ulster – ABB (Law Mark) (IB 26 pts)
Westminster – ABB (Law) (IB 32 pts)
300 pts **Aberdeen** – BBB (Law) (IB 34 pts)
BPP (UC) – 300 pts (Bus Law LLB (Hons); Law LLB)
Bradford – 300 pts (Law; Bus St Law)
Bristol UWE – 300–340 pts (Law; Law (Euro Int))
Buckingham – 300 pts (Law Fr) (IB 30 pts)
Cardiff Met – 300 pts (Bus Mgt St Law)
Coventry – 300 pts (Law; Law Bus; Law Fr/Span)
De Montfort – 300 pts (Law Hum Rts Soc Just)
Dundee – BBB–BCC (Law Fr/Ger/Span)
Edinburgh – AAA–BBB 300–360 pts (Law courses) (IB 34–42 pts)
Glamorgan – 300–340 pts (Law; Crim Law; Commer Law)

'I've been a solicitor for four years, and the skills I learned at the College are still helping me to move up the career ladder.'

A focused law degree for focused individuals

Book your law degree open day now
college-of-law.co.uk/degree14
0800 289 997

Muna Jallow
Solicitor, Gregory Rowcliffe Milners
Legal Practice Course 2005/2006,
London Bloomsbury

a focused law degree for focused individuals

A new undergraduate law degree

From September 2012 The College of Law is offering students a professional two-year law degree for undergraduates. The LL.B has the sole aim that you will learn the law in a professional and realistic context: how the law affects clients, and how lawyers think about and use the law to represent their clients' interests. It's more than "learning the law", it's learning **how** to **be** a lawyer, and enjoying the most relevant and rounded education to prepare you for a professional career in law.

The College's law degree will be academically challenging, and set in a real-world context from the start, so you can best understand how the law applies to individuals and businesses.

About The College of Law

The College of Law is acknowledged as the UK's leading professional law school. With many years of experience and unrivalled contacts within the legal profession, no other law school can match The College of Law for its reputation and commitment to preparing future lawyers for the fast-moving world of modern law.

More than 7,500 students take the postgraduate courses each year – the Graduate Diploma in Law for non-law graduates, the Legal Practice Course for aspiring solicitors and the Bar Professional Training Course for prospective barristers. This is because The College's unique mix of face-to-face teaching in small group workshops which reflect working in legal practice, along with market leading online learning, deliver better results. All of The College's tutors are qualified lawyers who can pass on their experience of working in practice. This unique combination ensures that you will get the best possible preparation for a career in law.

The College of Law develops self-reliant, confident future lawyers for the modern world of law. The Bachelor of Laws (LL.B) degree is the first step.

The College's specialist law careers service

Employability is at the heart of everything The College of Law does. The College understands that in the new era of higher university tuition fees, you want to be assured that you have the best possible chance of securing a job in your chosen profession. The College has the best team of specialist legal careers advisors in the business, offering personalised, face-to-face guidance on the recruitment process and how to succeed. It's no surprise that 84%* of students who pass the Legal Practice Course have training contracts or other legal work within the first few months of graduation.

based on known records of students successfully completing their studies in 2010

Seriously well connected

The legal services sector is one of the fastest growing and most dynamic parts of the economy, offering a wide range of careers whether as solicitors or barristers, in-house legal advisors, business managers or legal service entrepreneurs.

The College of Law has exclusive training arrangements with 30 major law firms, including three of the world's largest, work with 94 of the top 100 UK law firms and have thriving relationships with hundreds of regional firms. Internationally The College of Law has connections with a growing list of world class organisations including the International Bar Association, the British Council, Northwestern University School of Law in Chicago, Renmin University of China Law School and IE Law School in Spain.

> 'The College of Law is putting together an exciting LL.B which puts legal practice at the heart of the law degree. We welcome the focus on the practical aspects of law, which follows Allen & Overy's own approach to clients and client service. We would consider a potential trainee with a College of Law LL.B just as we consider LL.B students from other universities.'
>
> *Richard Hough Graduate Recruitment Partner, Allen & Overy*

A choice of locations

The College of Law has centres across the country (London, Bristol, Guildford, Birmingham, Chester, Manchester and York) offering you the widest choice of location of any law school. Initially you can choose to study your law degree in London, Birmingham or Chester, but whichever centre you choose you can be sure of the same high standards of tuition, support and facilities. Find out about each of the centres, and watch a short video, on our website: **college-of-law.co.uk/degree14**

Accommodation

The College of Law have reserved accommodation for our students with some of the UK's leading student accommodation providers, who pride themselves in ensuring you have a safe, comfortable place to live while you're studying with us.

We guarantee an offer of accommodation to all first year LL.B students who have made us their firm choice by 31 March.

The Future Lawyers Network

The College's Future Lawyers Network is a unique free-to-join resource for aspiring modern lawyers over the age of 16. You will get access to useful information on a career in law and what you need to do to succeed. **college-of-law.co.uk/futurelawyers**

Check **Chapter 4** when choosing your university and **Chapter 7** on how to read the subject tables.

Glasgow Caledonian – BBB (Law)
Heriot-Watt – ABC–BBB 300 pts (Bus Law) (IB 29 pts)
Lincoln – 300 pts (Law; Law Fin; Law Bus)
LJMU – 300 pts (Law Crim Just) (IB 29 pts)
London (Birk) – BBB (Crimin Crim Just)
Nottingham Trent – 300 pts (Int Law)
Plymouth – 300 pts (Law; Law Bus; Int Rel Law)
Salford – 300 pts (Law Crimin) (IB 29 pts)
Sheffield Hallam – 300 pts (Law; Law Crimin; Law Maîtrise Fr; Bus Law)
UCLan – BBB (Law)
West London – 300 pts (Commer Law; Law)
Westminster – ABC (Law Fr) (IB 30 pts)

280 pts **Bangor** – 280 pts (Law courses) (IB 28 pts)
Birmingham City – 280 pts (Law Bus Law) (IB 26 pts)
Bradford – BBC 280 pts (Pol Law)
Brighton – BBC 280 pts (Law Bus) (IB 30 pts)
Cumbria – 280 pts (Law)
De Montfort – 280 pts (Acc Law) (IB 30 pts)
Edge Hill – 280 pts (Crimin Crim Just; Law; Law Crimin; Law Mgt)
Gloucestershire – 280–300 pts (Law)
Nottingham Trent – 280 pts (Law Crimin; Law Psy)
Robert Gordon – BBC (Law) (IB 28 pts HL 5 Engl)
Staffordshire – 200-280 pts (Plcg Crim Invstg)
Stirling – BBC (Law BA) (IB 32 pts)
Sunderland – 280 pts (Law LLB)

260 pts **Abertay Dundee** – BCC (Law)
Birmingham City – 260 pts (Sociol Crimin)
Bolton – 260 pts (Law; Law (Comb))
Canterbury Christ Church – 260–200 pts (Law) (IB 24 pts)
Chester – 260–300 pts (Law Jrnl/Crimin) (IB 28 pts)
Coventry – BCC 260 pts (Sociol Crimin)
De Montfort – 260 pts (App Crimin; App Crimin Foren Sci)
Derby – 260–300 pts (Law Joint Hons)
Edinburgh Napier – 260 pts (Law LLB)
Greenwich – 260 pts (Bus Law)
Hertfordshire – 260 pts (Law Joint Hons)
Leeds Met – 260 pts (Law) (IB 28 pts)
Liverpool Hope – 260 pts (Law Comb Hons)
London South Bank – 260 pts (Law LLB)
Northampton – 260–280 pts (Law courses) (IB 24 pts)
Portsmouth – 260–300 pts (Law Euro St; Law Int Rel; Law Bus)
Sunderland – 260 pts (Law (Comb))
Teesside – 260 pts (Law)
Winchester – 260–300 pts (Law; Law (Comb))

245 pts **Glasgow Caledonian** – CCC 245 pts (Soc Sci (Crimin))
240 pts **Anglia Ruskin** – 240–280 pts (Law)
Bradford (Coll Univ Centre) – 240 pts (Law Soc Welf; Mark Law; Acc Law)
Bucks New – 240–280 pts (Law; Bus Law; Crimin)
Canterbury Christ Church – 240 pts (Leg St)
Chester – 240–280 pts (Law (Comb)) (IB 26 pts)
Greenwich (Sch Mgt) – 240 pts (Law Mgt; Law LLB)
Newport – 240 pts (Econ Law)
Plymouth – 240 pts (Marit Bus Marit Law)
St Mary's Twickenham (UC) – 240 pts (Law) (IB 28 pts)
Teesside – 240 pts (Bus Law)

UEL – 240 pts (Law)
West Scotland – CCC (Law)
230 pts **Edinburgh Napier** – 230 pts (Crimin)
220 pts **Blackburn (Coll)** – 220 pts (Law) (IB 26 pts)
St Mary's Twickenham (UC) – 220 pts (Bus Law) (IB 28 pts)
Southampton Solent – 220 pts (Law; Commer Law)
200 pts **Bedfordshire** – 200 pts (Law) (IB 24 pts)
Bucks New – 200–280 pts (Crimin Psy)
Cumbria – 200 pts (Crimin Law)
Glamorgan – 200–260 pts (Law Span)
London Met – 200–280 pts (Bus Law courses)
Middlesex – 200–300 pts (Law)
180 pts **Greenwich** – 180 pts (Phil Law)
Holborn (Coll) – 180 pts (Law)
160 pts **Wolverhampton** – 160–240 pts (Law; Law Phil)
120 pts **Croydon (Coll)** – 120 pts (Law)

Open University – contact +44 (0)845 300 6090 **or** www.openuniversity.co.uk/you (Law)

Alternative offers
See **Chapter 7** and **Appendix 1** for grades/UCAS Tariff points information for the International Baccalaureate, Scottish Highers/Advanced Highers, the Welsh Baccalaureate, the Irish Leaving Certificate, the Cambridge Pre-U Diploma, the Advanced Diploma and the Extended Project.

EXAMPLES OF FOUNDATION DEGREES IN THE SUBJECT FIELD
Bournemouth; Truro (Coll).

CHOOSING YOUR COURSE (SEE ALSO CH.1)
Some course features
Anglia Ruskin An integrated LLB degree is available for students seeking to qualify as a solicitor and aims to combine the academic and practical aspects of law to prepare students to enter a legal career.
Aston The Law with Management programme is a qualifying Law degree focusing on business skills.
Bournemouth All Law degrees have a common first year, with specialisation options made at the end. A minimum of 40 weeks is spent in industry.
Chester Core subjects are offered to fulfil the requirements for a Qualifying Law Degree, covering contract, land, European Community, constitutional and administrative law, crime and tort. Students studying combined law can apply for partial exemption.
Dundee English Law and Scots Law are both offered.
Edinburgh Over 12 joint courses with Law are offered including accountancy, business studies and languages.
Exeter (Law (Euro)) The fourth year is spent either at Rennes following a French Maîtrise en Droit programme or at Saabrucken following the German Magister programme. Graduates obtain a dual qualification, are exempt from the academic stages of UK professional training and are ready for the aptitude test to practise as a lawyer in France or Germany.
Huddersfield There is a Law (Exempting) course enabling students to qualify as a solicitor by incorporating the legal practice course in Years 3 and 4 (subject to an appropriate training contract). Degree courses are also offered in Law and Accountancy and Business.
Kent The Law course is designed to enable students to gain the necessary exemptions from the Law Society examinations. Other Law courses include English and French/German/Spanish/Italian Law. There is a law clinic enabling students to practise law under the supervision of solicitors.
London (King's) English Law can be studied with American, French, German or Australian Law. Transfers to these programmes take place only after completion of the first year.
London (UCL) Law can be studied with another legal system with a year spent at a host university in Australia or Singapore.

Check **Chapter 4** when choosing your university and **Chapter 7** on how to read the subject tables.

The City Law School
CITY UNIVERSITY LONDON

World-class legal educatic
in the heart of Londc

Are you a future law leader?

As one of London's major law school our **LLB** will give you the essential legal and academic skills that you need to be successful in law.

> **Explore** the core law subjects as well as a broad range of specialist subjects

> **Satisfy** the entry requirements of the Professional Stage of legal training (LPC or BPTC)

> **Enhance** your legal skills in mooting, legal research and debating

> **Benefit** from studying abroad in France, Australia, Poland, Moscow, or Spain

> **Improve** your job prospects at one of the top 10 universities in the UK for graduate employment

FOR MORE INFORMATION
+44 (0)20 7040 3309
www.city.ac.uk/law
law@city.ac.uk

When contacting us please quote the following reference: DC 0112

www.city.ac.uk/law

The City Law School
CITY UNIVERSITY LONDON

World-class legal education
in the heart of London

Are you a future law leader?

'Studying at City has broadened my horizons and allowed me to see where I want to be in the next 10 years."

Josh Olomo
LLB (Hons) 2008-2011

" I chose to come to The City Law School as it's conveniently placed amongst most of London's chambers and major law firms. I'm originally from a small town, so moving into London was a big deal for me. City life is different... but with time I've gotten use to it and I now love being a Londoner.

Right from the first day, studying the LLB at City has been challenging and invigorating experience keeping you on the edge of your seat. The teaching is second to none as we're taught by brilliant academics whose work is mentioned and cited in appeal cases in the House of Lords. The lecturers are also extremely supportive and help is always there when you need it.

Studying at City has broadened my horizons and allowed me to see where I want to be in the next 10 years."

The City Law School is one of London's major law schools and offers an impressive range of fully-accredited legal courses. Our LLB gives you the essential skills and knowledge to succeed in law. As one of the top 10 UK universities in terms of graduate employability, you will leave The City Law School confident in your abilities and equipped with the skills demanded by today's employers.

FOR MORE INFORMATION

☎ +44 (0)20 7040 3309
🖱 www.city.ac.uk/law
@ law@city.ac.uk

When contacting us please quote the following reference: DC 0112

St Mary's
University College
Twickenham
London

We offer Single Honours LLB Law and Joint Honours Business Law degree programmes as well as a host of other degree opportunities. From Management Studies to English and Sport to Sociology, St Mary's offers degrees for your future career.

For our full offer visit our website: www.smuc.ac.uk tel: 020 8240 2314

Universities and colleges teaching quality See www.qaa.ac.uk; http://unistats.direct.gov.uk.

Top research universities and colleges (RAE 2008) London LSE; London (UCL); Oxford; Durham; Nottingham; Kent; Cambridge; Cardiff; Queen's Belfast; Edinburgh; London (QM); Reading; Strathclyde; Ulster; Birmingham.

Examples of sandwich degree courses Aston (compulsory); Bournemouth; Brunel; Huddersfield; Nottingham Trent; Surrey; Teesside; Westminster.

ADMISSIONS INFORMATION

Number of applicants per place (approx) Abertay Dundee 3; Aberystwyth 8; Anglia Ruskin 10; Aston 10; Bangor 3; Birmingham 4; Birmingham City 20; Bournemouth 9; Bradford 2; Bristol 9; Bristol UWE 27; Brunel 2; Buckingham 3; Cambridge 7; Cardiff 12; City 23; Coventry 15; De Montfort 6; Derby 7; Dundee 6; Durham 14; Edinburgh 5; Edinburgh Napier 7; Essex 26; Exeter 15; Glamorgan 3; Glasgow 8; Glasgow Caledonian 10; Huddersfield 10; Hull 15; Kent 11; Kingston 25; Lancaster 8; Leeds 15; Leicester 9; Liverpool 10; LJMU 10; London (King's) 14; London (QM) 17; London (SOAS) 8; London (UCL) 21; London LSE 14; London Met 13; London South Bank 4; Manchester 8; Manchester Met 21; Middlesex 25; Newcastle 13; Northampton 4; Northumbria 12; Nottingham 9; Nottingham Trent 15; Oxford Brookes 18; Plymouth 14; Robert Gordon 4; Sheffield 16; Sheffield Hallam 6; Southampton 7; Southampton Solent 5; Staffordshire 16; Strathclyde (Law) 10; Sussex 10; Teesside 3; UCLan 36; UEA 14; UEL 13; Warwick 20; West London 18; Westminster 29; Wolverhampton 12; York 8.

Advice to applicants and planning the UCAS personal statement Visit the law courts and take notes on cases heard. Follow leading legal arguments in the press. Read the law sections in the *Independent*, *The Times* and the *Guardian*. Discuss the career with lawyers and, if possible, obtain work shadowing in lawyers' offices. Describe these visits and experiences and indicate any special areas of law which interest you. (Read *Learning the Law* by Glanville Williams.) Commitment is

WHAT'S THE NEXT BIG THING IN LAW? IT COULD BE YOU.

BPP UNDERGRADUATE DEGREES GET YOU CAREER READY FOR POTENTIAL EMPLOYERS.

Get ready for the next big thing in law with a BPP LLB. As a leading provider of legal education and training – with thousands of students and professionals choosing to study with us every year – BPP Law School has built an international reputation for excellence. With unique pro bono opportunities, highly experienced tutors, links with law firms and an extensive range of resources for ongoing professional development, we will equip you with real-world knowledge to make you the outstanding candidate. And our specialised career services team work with you to realise your ambition. Think big. Think BPP undergraduate degree.

BPP offers degrees in Birmingham, Bristol, Leeds, London, Manchester and Swindon.

bpp.com/ug
0203 131 0720

BPP
UNIVERSITY
COLLEGE

YOUR AMBITION REALISED

essential to the study of law as an academic discipline, not necessarily with a view to taking it up as a career.

When writing to admissions tutors, especially by email, take care to present yourself well: text language is not acceptable. You should use communication as an opportunity to demonstrate your skill in the use of English. Spelling mistakes, punctuation errors and bad grammar suggest that you will struggle to develop the expected writing ability (see **Misconceptions about this course**) and may lead to your application being rejected. When writing to an admissions tutor do not demand an answer immediately or by return or urgently. If your query is reasonable the tutor will respond without such urging. Adding these demands is bad manners and suggests that you are doing everything at the last minute and increases your chances of a rejection.

The criteria for admission are: motivation and capacity for sustained and intense work; the ability to analyse and solve problems using logical and critical approaches; the ability to draw fine distinctions, to separate the relevant from the irrelevant; the capacity for accurate and critical observation, for sustained and cogent argument; creativity and flexibility of thought and lateral thinking; competence in English; the ability to express ideas clearly and effectively, a willingness to listen and to be able to give considered responses. **Bristol** Deferred entry is limited.

Misconceptions about this course Aberystwyth Some applicants believe that all Law graduates enter the legal profession – this is incorrect. **Birmingham** Students tend to believe that success in the law centres on the ability to learn information. Whilst some information does necessarily have to be learnt, the most important skills involve (a) developing an ability to select the most relevant pieces of information and (b) developing the ability to write tightly argued, persuasively reasoned essays on the basis of such information. **Bristol** Many applicants think that most of our applicants have been privately educated: the reverse is true. **Derby** Many applicants do not realise the amount of work involved to get a good degree classification.

Selection interviews Approximately four well-qualified candidates apply for every place on undergraduate Law courses in the UK and the National Admissions Test for Law (LNAT) is used by a number of universities (see **Your target offers and examples of courses provided by each institution** and **Chapter 6**). **Yes** Aberystwyth, Anglia Ruskin, Bristol, Bristol UWE, Buckingham, Cambridge, Canterbury Christ Church, Coventry, Durham, Edinburgh Napier, Essex, Exeter, Glasgow, Lancaster, Liverpool, LJMU, London (King's), London (UCL), London South Bank, Northumbria, Oxford (Course 1) 18%, (Course 2) 10%, Queen's Belfast, Southampton Solent, Surrey, Teesside, UCLan, UEL, York; **Some** Bangor, Cardiff (Law Lang), Derby, Huddersfield, Kent (mature/Access students), Nottingham Trent (mature students), Oxford Brookes (mature students), Sheffield Hallam, Southampton (mature students), Staffordshire, Sunderland, Warwick; **No** Birmingham, Dundee, Nottingham, Reading, Sussex, UEA.

Interview advice and questions Law is a highly competitive subject and applicants will be expected to have a basic awareness of aspects of law and to have gained some work experience, on which they are likely to be questioned. It is almost certain that a legal question will be asked at interview and applicants will be tested on their responses. Questions in the past have included: What interests you in the study of law? What would you do to overcome the problem of prison overcrowding if you were (a) a judge, (b) a prosecutor, (c) the Prime Minister? What legal cases have you read about recently? What is jurisprudence? What are the causes of violence in society? A friend bought a bun which, unknown to him, contained a stone. He gave it to you to eat and you broke a tooth. Could you sue anyone? Have you visited any law courts? What cases did you see? A person arrives in England unable to speak the language. He lights a cigarette in a restaurant where smoking is not allowed. Can he be charged and convicted? What should be done in the case of an elderly person who steals a bar of soap? What, in your opinion, would be the two basic laws in Utopia? Describe, without using your hands, how you would do the butterfly stroke. What would happen if there were no law? Should we legalise euthanasia? If you could change any law, what would it be? How would you implement the changes? If a person tries to kill someone using black magic, are they guilty of attempted murder? If a jury uses a ouija board to reach a decision, is it wrong? If so, why? Jane attends a university interview. As she enters the building she sees a diamond brooch on the floor. She hands it to the interviewer who hands it to the police. The brooch is never claimed. Who is entitled to it? Jane? The interviewer? The police? The University authorities? The Crown? Mr Grabbit who owns the building?

For joint courses: what academic skills are needed to succeed? Why have you applied for a joint degree? Where does honesty fit into law? See also **Chapter 5**. **Cambridge** Logic questions. If I returned to the waiting room and my jacket had been taken and I then took another one, got home and actually discovered it was mine, had I committed a crime? If the interviewer pulled out a gun and aimed it at me, but missed as he had a bad arm, had he committed a crime? If the interviewer pulled out a gun and aimed it at me, thinking it was loaded but, in fact, it was full of blanks and fired it at me with the intention to kill, had he committed a crime? Which of the three preceding situations are similar and which is the odd one out? If a law is immoral, is it still a law and must people abide by it? For example, when Hitler legalised the systematic killing of Jews, was it still law? **Oxford** Should the use of mobile phones be banned on public transport? Is wearing school uniform a breach of human rights? If you could go back in time to any period of time, when would it be and why? Would you trade your scarf for my bike, even if you have no idea what state it's in or if I even have one? Is someone guilty of an offence if they did not set out to commit a crime but ended up doing so? Does a girl who joins the Scouts have a political agenda?

Reasons for rejection (non-academic) 'Dreams' about being a lawyer! Poorly informed about the subject. Badly drafted application. Under estimated work load. Poor communication skills. **Manchester Met** Some were rejected because they were obviously more suited to Psychology.

AFTER-RESULTS ADVICE
Offers to applicants repeating A-levels **Higher** Aberystwyth, Bristol UWE, Coventry, Dundee, Essex, Glamorgan, Glasgow, Hull, Leeds, London Met, Manchester Met, Newcastle, Nottingham, Oxford Brookes, Queen's Belfast, Sheffield, Sheffield Hallam, Strathclyde, Warwick; **Possibly higher** Liverpool; **Same** Anglia Ruskin, Bangor, Birmingham, Bradford, Brighton, Bristol, Brunel, Cardiff, De Montfort, Derby, Durham, Huddersfield, Kingston, Lincoln, Liverpool Hope, LJMU, Northumbria, Nottingham Trent, Staffordshire, Stirling, Sunderland, Surrey, UEA, Wolverhampton; **No** Cambridge.

GRADUATE DESTINATIONS AND EMPLOYMENT (2009/10 HESA)
Graduates surveyed 16680 **Employed** 7155 **In voluntary employment** 290 **In further study** 5965 **Assumed unemployed** 990

Career note Many graduates seek to practise in the legal profession after further training. However, a Law degree provides a good starting point for many other careers in industry, commerce and the public services. The study of consumer protection can lead to specialisation and qualification as a trading standards officer.

OTHER DEGREE SUBJECTS FOR CONSIDERATION
Criminology; Economics; Government; History; International Relations; Politics; Social Policy and Administration; Sociology.

LEISURE and RECREATION MANAGEMENT/STUDIES

(see also **Business and Management Courses, Business and Management Courses (International and European), Business and Management Courses (Specialised), Hospitality and Hotel Management, Sports Sciences/Studies, Tourism and Travel**)

The courses cover various aspects of leisure and recreation. Specialist options include recreation management, tourism and countryside management, all of which are offered as individual degree courses in their own right. There is also an obvious link with Sports Studies, Physical Education and Tourism and Travel courses. See also **Appendix 3**.

Useful websites www.ispal.org.uk; www.bized.co.uk; www.leisuremanagement.co.uk; www.baha.org. uk; www.leisureopportunities.co.uk; www.recmanagement.com; www.uksport.gov.uk; www. london2012.com.

NB The points totals shown to the left of the institutions are for ease of reference only. It must not be assumed that Tariff points are always used by institutions or that they can be substituted for an offer in grades. The level of an offer is not necessarily indicative of the quality of a course.

COURSE OFFERS INFORMATION

Subject requirements/preferences GCSE Normally English and mathematics grades A–C. **AL** No specified subjects. **Other** CRB clearance and health checks required for some courses.

Your target offers and examples of courses provided by each institution

300 pts **Bournemouth** – 300 pts (Leis Mark) (IB 30 pts)
Brighton – BBB (Spo Leis Mgt) (IB 30 pts)
Sheffield Hallam – 300 pts (Evnts Leis Mgt; Evnts Mgt Art Enter)

280 pts **Edge Hill** – 280 pts (Bus Mgt (Leis Tour))
Gloucestershire – 280 pts (Leis Spo Mgt)
Manchester Met – 280 pts (Out St) (IB 28 pts)
Nottingham Trent – 280 pts (Spo Leis)
Stirling – BBC (Env Sci Out Educ) (IB 32 pts)
Salford – 280–300 pts (Leis Tour Mgt) (IB 26 pts)
Suffolk (Univ Campus) – 280 pts (Leis Mgt)

260 pts **Cumbria** – 260 pts (Out St; Out Ldrshp; Out St (Env))
Derby – 260–280 pts (Out Recr)
Stranmillis (UC) – BCC (Hlth Leis St)

240 pts **Aberystwyth** – 240 pts (Cntry Recr Tour) (IB 28 pts)
Bolton – 240 pts (Spo Leis Mgt) (IB 20 pts)
Canterbury Christ Church – 240 pts (Tour Leis St) (IB 24 pts)
Cumbria – 240 pts (Advntr Media)
Hull – 240 pts (Spo Leis Mgt)
Leeds Met – 240 pts (Rtl Leis Mgt) (IB 24 pts)
Northampton – 240–260 pts (Leis Lfstl Mgt)
UCLan – 240–280 pts (Out Ldrshp)
Ulster – 240 pts (Leis Evnts Mgt)
Worcester – 240 pts (Out Advntr Ldrshp Mgt)

220 pts **Harper Adams (UC)** – 220–240 pts (Recr Env)
Leeds Met – 220 pts (Enter Mgt) (IB 24 pts)
Southampton Solent – 220 pts (Out Advntr Mgt; Wtrspo St Mgt)

200 pts **Bucks New** – 200–240 pts (Spo Mgt) (IB 20 pts)
180 pts **Glamorgan** – 180–240 pts (Spo Mgt)
160 pts **SAC (Scottish CAg)** – CC (Spo Recr Mgt)
UHI – CC–AA 160 pts (Advntr Tour Mgt)

Alternative offers

See **Chapter 7** and **Appendix 1** for grades/UCAS Tariff points information for the International Baccalaureate, Scottish Highers/Advanced Highers, the Welsh Baccalaureate, the Irish Leaving Certificate, the Cambridge Pre-U Diploma, the Advanced Diploma and the Extended Project.

EXAMPLES OF FOUNDATION DEGREES IN THE SUBJECT FIELD

See also **Tourism and Travel**. Bath Spa; Birmingham (UC); Bournemouth; Cornwall (Coll); Derby; Duchy (Coll); Edge Hill; Hertfordshire; Liverpool (CmC); Loughborough (Coll); Norwich City (Coll); Nottingham New (Coll); Pembrokeshire (Coll); Plymouth; Teesside; Truro (Coll); Warwickshire (Coll); West London.

CHOOSING YOUR COURSE (SEE ALSO CH.1)

Some course features

Birmingham (UC) The Adventure Tourism Management course involves studies in commercial and risk management, options include modern languages, sports international and nature tourism.
Brighton (Spo Leis Mgt) The course has options in sport psychology, performance and marketing.

Cumbria (Out St; Out Ldrshp) The courses involve climbing, canoeing, sailing and mountaineering and are based in the centre of the Lake District.

Harper Adams (UC) Leisure and Tourism Management is available and covers a range of key subjects including tourism policy, strategy and destination management. Options are available in Outdoor Adventure Design and Visitor Management.

Trinity Saint David A broad course in Outdoor Education is available which includes work placement.

UCP Marjon Single and combined courses can be taken with Outdoor Adventure.

Universities and colleges teaching quality See www.qaa.ac.uk; http://unistats.direct.gov.uk.

Top research universities and colleges (RAE 2008) See **Sports Sciences/Studies**.

Examples of sandwich degree courses Bournemouth; Gloucestershire; Ulster.

ADMISSIONS INFORMATION

Number of applicants per place (approx) Brighton 10; Cardiff Met 3; Gloucestershire 7; Hull 3; LJMU 3; SAC (Scottish CAg) 4.

Advice to applicants and planning the UCAS personal statement Work experience, visits to leisure centres and national parks and any interests you have in particular aspects of leisure should be described, for example, art galleries, museums, countryside management, sport. An involvement in sports and leisure as a participant or employee is an advantage.

Misconceptions about this course The level of business studies in leisure management courses is higher than many students expect.

Selection interviews Some Creative Arts, LJMU, Salford.

Interview advice and questions In addition to sporting or other related interests, applicants will be expected to have had some work experience and can expect to be asked to discuss their interests. What do you hope to gain by going to university? See also **Chapter 6**.

Reasons for rejection (non-academic) Poor communication or presentation skills. Relatively poor sporting background or knowledge.

AFTER-RESULTS ADVICE

Offers to applicants repeating A-levels Same Cardiff Met, LJMU, Salford.

GRADUATE DESTINATIONS AND EMPLOYMENT (2009/10 HESA)

See **Hospitality and Event Management**.

Career note Career opportunities exist in public and private sectors within leisure facilities, health clubs, the arts, leisure promotion, marketing and events management. Some graduates work in sports development and outdoor activities.

OTHER DEGREE SUBJECTS FOR CONSIDERATION

Business Studies; Events Management; Hospitality Management; Sports Studies; Tourism.

LINGUISTICS

(see also **English, Languages**)

Linguistics covers the study of language structure and function, and also includes areas such as children's language, slang, language handicap, advertising language, language styles and the learning of foreign languages.

Useful websites www.iol.org.uk; www.cal.org; http://web.mit.edu/linguistics; www.applij.oxfordjournals.org; www.lsadc.org; www.sil.org; www.baal.org.uk.

Check **Chapter 4** when choosing your university and **Chapter 7** on how to read the subject tables.

NB The points totals shown to the left of the institutions are for ease of reference only. It must not be assumed that Tariff points are always used by institutions or that they can be substituted for an offer in grades. The level of an offer is not necessarily indicative of the quality of a course.

COURSE OFFERS INFORMATION

Subject requirements/preferences GCSE English required and a foreign language preferred. **AL** English may be required or preferred for some courses.

Your target offers and examples of courses provided by each institution

380 pts Cambridge – (Part II subject, taken after Part I in another, usually language-related, subject) A*AA (Modn Mediev Lang (Ling)) (IB 40–42 pts)
London (UCL) – AAAe–ABBe (Ling) (IB 34–38 pts)

360 pts Edinburgh – AAA–BBB (Ling Soc Anth) (IB 34–42 pts HL 555)
Oxford – AAA (Modn Lang Ling) (IB 38–40 pts)
York – AAA (Phil Ling) (IB 34 pts)

340 pts Lancaster – AAA–AAB 340–360 pts (Socioling) (IB 34–36 pts)
Leeds – AAB (Ling Joint Hons) (IB 34 pts HL 16 pts)
London (QM) – 340 pts (Engl Lang Ling) (IB 32 pts)
London (SOAS) – AAB (Ling) (IB 36 pts HL 666)
Manchester – AAB–BBB 300–340 pts (Lang Litcy Comm) (IB 31–36 pts)
Sheffield – AAB (Engl Lang Ling) (IB 35 pts)
Southampton – AAB (Lang Soc) (IB 34 pts HL 17 pts)
York – AAB–ABB (Ling)

320 pts Kent – ABB (Engl Lang Ling) (IB 33 pts)
London (QM) – 320 pts (Ger Ling) (IB 34 pts)
Newcastle – AAB–ABB 320–340 pts (Modn Lang Ling) (IB 32 pts HL 6 Fr/Ger/Span)
Queen's Belfast – ABB/BBCb (Ling Joint Hons)
Sheffield – ABB (Ling Joint Hons) (IB 33 pts)

300 pts Aberdeen – BBB (Lang Ling) (IB 30 pts)
Bristol UWE – 300 pts (Engl Lang Ling) (IB 26–32 pts)
Edinburgh – AAA–BBB 300–360 pts (Ling) (IB 34–42 pts HL 555)
Essex – BBB 300 pts (Ling) (IB 32 pts)
Roehampton – 300 pts (Engl Lang Ling)

280 pts Brighton – BBC (Engl Lang Ling) (IB 28 pts)
Ulster – 280 pts incl BC (Lang Ling courses)
Westminster – BBC (Engl Lang Ling) (IB 30 pts)

260 pts Bangor – 260–320 pts (Ling Engl Lang; Ling Engl Lit)
Bristol UWE – 260–300 pts (Ely Chld St Ling) (IB 26–32 pts)
Manchester Met – 260 pts (Lang (Fr/Ger/Ital/Span) Ling) (IB 28 pts)
Nottingham Trent – 260 pts (Ling Joint Hons)
Sunderland – 260 pts (Engl Lang Ling)
UCLan – 260–300 pts (Engl Lang Ling)
Ulster – 260 pts (Ling Comm) (IB 24 pts)

240 pts Bangor – 240–280 pts (Ling) (IB 28 pts)

220 pts Anglia Ruskin – 220–260 pts (Eng Lang Ling)
Salford – 220–300 pts (Ling courses)
UCP Marjon – 220 pts (Ling Engl Lang)

200 pts UEL – 200 pts (Media (App Ling))

160 pts Wolverhampton – 160–220 pts (Ling courses)

80 pts London (Birk) – p/t no A-level reqs for under 21s (over 21s varies) (Ling Lang)

Alternative offers

See **Chapter 7** and **Appendix 1** for grades/UCAS Tariff points information for the International Baccalaureate, Scottish Highers/Advanced Highers, the Welsh Baccalaureate, the Irish Leaving Certificate, the Cambridge Pre-U Diploma, the Advanced Diploma and the Extended Project.

For a quick reference offers calculator, fold out the inside back cover.

CHOOSING YOUR COURSE (SEE ALSO CH.1)
Some course features
Edinburgh The University is regarded as a world leader in the study of linguistics. Opportunity to take an MA in Linguistics or as the lead subject combined with a second subject.
Lancaster (Ling (N Am)) The course focuses on the sound, grammar and meaning systems of different languages, and has a wide range of options. Study in a North American institution may be possible.
Leeds Linguistics and Phonetics can be taken as a single subject with opportunities to take electives from outside the subject area.
London (QM) (Compar Lit Ling) Students divide their time between the two subjects, the former making connections with literature and film, music, the visual arts and popular culture.

Universities and colleges teaching quality See www.qaa.ac.uk; http://unistats.direct.gov.uk.

Top research universities and colleges (RAE 2008) London (QM); Edinburgh; York; Essex; Sheffield; Wolverhampton; London (UCL); Manchester; Lancaster; UCLan; Cambridge; Bristol UWE.

ADMISSIONS INFORMATION
Number of applicants per place (approx) Bangor 3; Essex 1; Lancaster 12; Leeds 12; UEL 3; York 11.

Advice to applicants and planning the UCAS personal statement Give details of your interests in language and how it works, and about your knowledge of languages and their similarities and differences.

Selection interviews Yes Brighton, Cambridge, Essex, Lancaster, Newcastle, Reading, UEL; **Some** Salford, Sheffield.

Interview advice and questions Past questions include: Why do you want to study linguistics? What does the subject involve? What do you intend to do at the end of your degree course? What answer do you give to your parents or friends when they ask why you want to study the subject? How and why does language vary according to sex, age, social background and regional origins? See also **Chapter 6**.

Reasons for rejection (non-academic) Lack of knowledge of linguistics. Hesitation about the period to be spent abroad.

AFTER-RESULTS ADVICE
Offers to applicants repeating A-levels Higher Essex; **Same** Brighton, Leeds, Newcastle, Salford, York.

GRADUATE DESTINATIONS AND EMPLOYMENT (2009/10 HESA)
Graduates surveyed 730 **Employed** 435 **In voluntary employment** 20 **In further study** 180 **Assumed unemployed** 65

Career note Students enter a wide range of careers, with information management and editorial work in publishing offering some interesting and useful outlets.

OTHER DEGREE SUBJECTS FOR CONSIDERATION
Cognitive Science; Communication Studies; Education Studies; English; Psychology; Speech Sciences.

LITERATURE
(see also **English**)

This is a very broad subject introducing many aspects of the study of literature and aesthetics. Courses will vary in content. Degree courses in English and foreign languages will also include a study of literature.

Useful websites www.lrb.co.uk; www.literature.org; www.bibliomania.com; www.bl.uk; www.acla.org; http://icla.byu.edu.

NB The points totals shown to the left of the institutions are for ease of reference only. It must not be assumed that Tariff points are always used by institutions or that they can be substituted for an offer in grades. The level of an offer is not necessarily indicative of the quality of a course.

COURSE OFFERS INFORMATION

Subject requirements/preferences GCSE English and a foreign language usually required. **AL** English may be required or preferred for some courses.

Ulster (Ir Lang Lit) Applicants need at least grade B (or equivalent) in A-level Irish.

Your target offers and examples of courses provided by each institution

400 pts **London (King's)** – AAAc (Compar Lit Film St) (IB 38 pts HL 6 Engl)

390 pts **Warwick** – AABb (Film Lit) (IB 36 pts)

380 pts **Durham** – A*AA (Engl Lit Phil) (IB 38 pts)
Warwick – AABc (Engl Lat Lit) (IB 36 pts)

360 pts **Lancaster** – AAA–AAB 340–360 pts (Engl Lang Lit) (IB 34–36 pts)
Manchester – AAA–AAB 340–360 pts (Engl Lit courses) (IB 37–35 pts)
Newcastle – AAA 360 pts (Lit Comb Hons)
Nottingham – AAA–AAB 340–360 pts (Engl Lang Lit) (IB 36–34 pts)
Oxford – AAA (Engl Lang Lit) (IB 38–40 pts)
Sheffield – AAA (Engl Lit) (IB 37 pts)
Sussex – AAA–AAB (Engl Lang Lit) (IB 35–36 pts)
UEA – AAA incl Engl (Engl Lit) (IB 34 pts HL 6 Engl)
Warwick – AAA (Engl Lit Crea Writ) (IB 38 pts)

340 pts **Cardiff** – AAB (Engl Lang Engl Lit; Jrnl Media Engl Lit)
Kent – AAB (Engl Am Lit; Engl Am Postcol Lit)
Lancaster – AAB (Film St Engl Lit) (IB 34 pts)
Leeds – ABB–BBB 340–300 pts (Class Lit courses)
London (Gold) – AAB (Am Lit)
London (QM) – 340 pts (Engl Lit Ling) (IB 32 pts)
Newcastle – AAB (Engl Lang Lit) (IB 33 pts)
Reading – 340–360 pts (Engl Lit courses) (IB 31–32 pts)
Surrey – AAB (Engl Lit Crea Writ) (IB 35 pts)
UEA – AAB–ABB incl Engl (Am Engl Lit) (IB 32–33 pts HL 5 Engl)
Warwick – AAB (Engl Ger Lit) (IB 36 pts)

320 pts **Birmingham** – ABB (Engl Lang Lit Educ) (IB 32–34 pts)
Essex – ABB 320 pts (Lit Myth) (IB 29 pts)
Glasgow – ABB (Engl Lit) (IB 36 pts)
Hull – ABB 320 pts (Law Lit)
Kent – ABB (Engl Am Lit Joint Hons; Compar Lit St courses; Compar Lit)
Kingston – 320 pts (Jrnl Engl Lit)
London (QM) – 320 pts (Ger Compar Lit) (IB 34 pts)
London (RH) – ABB–BBB (Compar Lit Cult) (IB 32 pts)
Northumbria – 320 pts (Engl Lit Hist) (IB 26 pts)
Reading – 320–340 pts (Engl Lit Euro Lit Cult)
Swansea – ABB–BBB (Engl Lit Lang St)

300 pts **Aberdeen** – BBB (Lit Wrld Cntxt)
Aberystwyth – 300 pts (Engl Wld Lit) (IB 28 pts)
Brighton – BBB 300 pts (Engl Lit) (IB 28–30 pts)
Edinburgh – AAA–BBB 300–360 pts (Engl Lit) (IB 34–42 pts)
Essex – ABB–BBB 300 pts (Engl Lang Lit) (IB 29 pts)
Gloucestershire – 280–300 pts (Engl Lit)
Hertfordshire – 300 pts (Engl Lit)
Huddersfield – 300 pts (Engl Lit; Engl Lit Crea Writ)
Kent – BBB (Engl Lit) (IB 33–35 pts)
Northumbria – 300 pts (Engl Lit; Engl Lang Lit; Engl Lit Crea Writ)

Nottingham – ABC–BBB (Am Can Lit Hist Cult) (IB 30 pts)
Reading – 300–340 pts (Engl Lit Film Thea Arts)
Roehampton – 300 pts (Engl Lit)
Sheffield Hallam – 300 pts (Engl Lit)
York – BBB (Lang Lit Educ) (IB 31–30 pts)

280 pts **Bangor** – 280–300 pts (Engl Lang Lit)
Birmingham City – 280 pts (Engl Lit courses)
Brighton – 280 pts (Media Engl Lit) (IB 30 pts)
Edge Hill – 280 pts (Engl Lit)
Glamorgan – BBC 280 pts (Engl Lit)
Gloucestershire – 280–300 pts (Engl Lit Sociol)
Westminster – BBC 280 pts (Engl Lit Hist) (IB 28 pts)

260 pts **Aberystwyth** – 260 pts (Psy Engl Lit) (IB 28 pts)
Anglia Ruskin – 220–260 pts (Phil Engl Lit)
Bangor – 260–320 pts (Ling Engl Lit) (IB 28 pts)
Bath Spa – 260–300 pts (Engl Lit courses)
Brighton – BCC 260 pts (Cult Hist Lit)
Buckingham – 260 pts (Engl Lit courses)
Leeds Met – 260 pts (Engl Lit) (IB 24 pts)
Liverpool Hope – 260–300 pts (Engl Lit)
London Met – 260 pts (Engl Lit; Engl Lit Film TV St)
Salford – 260–240 pts (Engl Lit Engl Lang) (IB 31 pts)
Sunderland – 260 pts (Engl Lang Lit)
Winchester – 260–300 pts (Engl Lit courses) (IB 24–26 pts)

240 pts **Bath Spa** – 240–280 pts (Engl Lit Pub)
Brighton – CCC 240 pts (Engl Lit Commun Hist) (IB 30 pts)
Buckingham – 240-260 pts (Engl Lit Hist) (IB 27 pts)
Greenwich – 240 pts (Engl Lit)
Hull – 240 pts (Engl Lit Cult)
Portsmouth – 240–300 pts (Engl Lit courses)
Staffordshire – 240 pts (Engl Lit) (IB 28 pts)
UCLan – 240–260 pts (Engl Lit)
Ulster – 240 pts (Ir Lang Lit)
Worcester – 240–260 pts (Engl Lit St courses)

220 pts **Anglia Ruskin** – 220–260 pts (Dr Engl Lit)
Bishop Grosseteste (UC) – 220 pts (Engl Lit courses)
Kingston – 220–360 pts (Engl Lit)
UCP Marjon – 220 pts (Engl Lit)

200 pts **York St John** – 200–260 pts (Engl Lit courses)
200 pts **Blackburn (Coll)** – 200 pts (Engl Lit)
Blackpool and Fylde (Coll) – 200 pts (Engl Lang Lit Writ)
Middlesex – 200–300 pts (Crea Writ Engl Lit; Engl Lit courses; Engl Lang Lit)
Trinity Saint David – 200–300 pts (Engl Lit courses)
UEL – 200 pts (Engl Lit; Med Ind Lit)
York St John – 200–260 pts (Engl Lit Crea Writ)

160 pts **Glamorgan** – 160-220 pts (Comb Hons Lit)
UHI – CC–AA (Lit)

120 pts **West Anglia (Coll)** – 120 pts (Hist Engl Lit; Sociol Engl Lit)

Alternative offers

See **Chapter 7** and **Appendix 1** for grades/UCAS Tariff points information for the International Baccalaureate, Scottish Highers/Advanced Highers, the Welsh Baccalaureate, the Irish Leaving Certificate, the Cambridge Pre-U Diploma, the Advanced Diploma and the Extended Project.

EXAMPLES OF FOUNDATION DEGREES IN THE SUBJECT FIELD

Bath Spa; Truro (Coll); Winchester.

Check **Chapter 4** when choosing your university and **Chapter 7** on how to read the subject tables.

CHOOSING YOUR COURSE (SEE ALSO CH.1)

Some course features
Glasgow (Scot Lit) Course covers poetry, drama, fiction and prose of Scotland in English and Scots from the 14th century to the present day.
London (Gold) (Engl Compar Lit) There is an option to specialise in the literature of other countries, for example America, Europe, the Caribbean.
Reading (Engl Lit Euro Lit Cult) The course explores the inter-relationship between the literatures and cultures of different European countries to gain a comparative perspective on English literature, culture and history. All works are in translation for those without foreign language skills.
Ulster (Ir Lang Lit) Course focuses on an in-depth study of the literary and historical traditions of Gaelic Ireland from the Early Modern period (1200–1650) to the present day and gaining a high level of competence in written and spoken Irish.

Universities and colleges teaching quality See www.qaa.ac.uk; http://unistats.direct.gov.uk.

Top research universities and colleges (RAE 2008) See **English**.

ADMISSIONS INFORMATION

Number of applicants per place (approx) Essex 4; UEA 12.

Advice to applicants and planning the UCAS personal statement See **English**. **Kent** Interest in literatures other than English.

Misconceptions about this course **Kent** Some students think that a foreign language is required – it is not.

Selection interviews **Yes** Trinity Saint David; **No** Dundee.

Interview advice and questions See **English**. See also **Chapter 6**. **Kent** Which book would you take on a desert island, and why? What is the point of doing a Literature degree in the 21st century?

Reasons for rejection (non-academic) **Kent** Perceived inability to think on their feet.

GRADUATE DESTINATIONS AND EMPLOYMENT (2009/10 HESA)
See **English**.

Career note Students enter a wide range of careers, with information management and editorial work in publishing offering some interesting and useful outlets. See also **English**, **Linguistics** and **Celtic, Irish, Scottish and Welsh Studies**.

MARINE/MARITIME STUDIES

(including **Marine Engineering** and **Oceanography**; see also **Environmental Sciences/Studies, Naval Architecture**)

Marine and Maritime Studies can involve a range of subjects such as marine business, technology, navigation, nautical studies, underwater rescue and transport.

Useful websites www.bized.co.uk; www.british-shipping.org; www.uk-sail.org.uk; www.rya.org.uk; www.royalnavy.mod.uk; www.sstg.org; www.noc.soton.ac.uk; www.nautinst.org; www.mcsuk.org; www.nmm.ac.uk; www.imo.org; www.mcga.gov.uk.

NB The points totals shown to the left of the institutions are for ease of reference only. It must not be assumed that Tariff points are always used by institutions or that they can be substituted for an offer in grades. The level of an offer is not necessarily indicative of the quality of a course.

COURSE OFFERS INFORMATION

Subject requirements/preferences GCSE Mathematics and science are required for several courses. **AL** Science or mathematics will be required or preferred for some courses.

Your target offers and examples of courses provided by each institution

360 pts **Cardiff** – AAA (Mar Geosci (Int))
Southampton – AAA–ABB (Geol Mar Biol) (IB 36–32 pts HL 18–16 pts)
UEA – AAA (Meteor Ocean MSci) (IB 34 pts HL 666 maths)

340 pts **Cardiff** – AAB (Mar Geosci)
Newcastle – AAB (Sml Crft Tech MEng) (IB 37 pts)
St Andrews – AAB 340 pts (Mar Biol) (IB 35 pts)
Strathclyde – AAB (Nvl Archit Ocn Eng MEng) (IB 36 pts)
Southampton – AAB incl geog (Ocean Physl Geog) (IB 34 pts HL 17 pts)

320 pts **Cardiff** – ABB (Mar Geog) (IB 30–32 pts)
Glasgow – ABB (Mar Frshwtr Biol) (IB 32 pts)
Liverpool – ABB (Mar Biol) (IB 33 pts HL 6 biol sci)
Newcastle – AAB–ABB 320–340 pts (Mar Biol) (IB 32 pts HL 6 biol)
Plymouth – ABB 320–360 pts (Mar Biol Cstl Ecol) (IB 24 pts)
Strathclyde – ABB (Nvl Archit Ocn Eng BEng) (IB 32 pts)
UEA – AAA–ABB 320–360 pts (Ship Sci)

300 pts **Aberdeen** – BBB (Mar Biol)
Brighton – BBB 300 pts (Earth Ocn Sci) (IB 28 pts)
Essex – BBB–BBC (Mar Bio) (IB 32–28 pts)
Heriot-Watt – BBB (App Mar Biol)
Newcastle – AAB-BBB 300-340 pts (Sml Crft Tech BEng) (IB 32-34 pts)
Plymouth – BBB 300–360 pts (Mar Biol Ocen) (IB 24 pts)
Queen's Belfast – BBB/BBCb (Mar Biol)

280 pts **Aberystwyth** – 280–320 pts (Mar Frshwtr Biol) (IB 26 pts)
Bangor – 280–320 pts (App Mar Biol; Mar Vert Zool)
Hull – 280–300 pts (Mar Frshwtr Biol; Marit Hist)
Portsmouth – 280–300 pts (Mar Biol)
Stirling – BBC (Mar Biol) (IB 32 pts)

260 pts **Bangor** – 260–320 pts (App Ter Mar Ecol) (IB 28 pts)
LJMU – 260 pts (Marit St; Marit Bus Mgt; Port Marit Mgt)
Plymouth – BCC 260 pts (Mar Tech Mech Eng) (IB 27 pts)
UHI – BCC (Mar Sci)

240 pts **Aberdeen** – 240 pts (Mar Coast Res Mgt Mar Biol)
Anglia Ruskin – 240 pts (Mar Biol Cons)
Bangor – 240–300 pts (Mar Chem)
Hull – 240–280 pts (Cstl Mar Biol)
Plymouth – 240 pts (Cru Mgt)
Portsmouth – 240–300 pts (Mar Env Sci)

230 pts **Edinburgh Napier** – 230 pts (Mar Frshwtr Biol)

220 pts **Bangor** – 220–260 pts (Mar Env St) (IB 28 pts)
Falmouth (UC) – 220 pts (Mar Nat Hist Photo)
Plymouth – 220 pts (Mar Spo Tech)
Southampton Solent – 220 pts (Wtrspo St Mgt)
Ulster – 220 pts (Mar Sci) (IB 24 pts)

200 pts **Plymouth** – 200 pts (Mar Cmpstes Tech; Surf Sci Tech; App Mar Spo Sci; Mar St (Navig/Ocn Ychtg/Merchnt Ship))

180 pts **Greenwich** – 180 pts (Mar Eng Tech)
Southampton Solent – 180 pts (Ycht Prod Surv; Ycht Pwrcft Des)

120 pts **Bournemouth** – 120 pts (Mar Ecol Cons)
Plymouth – 120–180 pts (Mar Eng)
Southampton Solent – 120 pts (Ship Port Mgt)

Alternative offers
See **Chapter 7** and **Appendix 1** for grades/UCAS Tariff points information for the International Baccalaureate, Scottish Highers/Advanced Highers, the Welsh Baccalaureate, the Irish Leaving Certificate, the Cambridge Pre-U Diploma, the Advanced Diploma and the Extended Project.

Check **Chapter 4** when choosing your university and **Chapter 7** on how to read the subject tables.

EXAMPLES OF FOUNDATION DEGREES IN THE SUBJECT FIELD
Blackpool and Fylde (Coll); Bournemouth; Cornwall (Coll); Plymouth; Southampton Solent.

CHOOSING YOUR COURSE (SEE ALSO CH.1)
Some course features
Bangor A large department covering marine sciences, coastal geography and ocean sciences.
LJMU (Marit St) A broad-based programme for students with a general interest in ships and sea, with a wide range of optional maritime subjects (for example, maritime and port operations, navigation and meteorology, international trade and finance). Students can build their own degree course as their interests develop, based on core modules such as port and cargo operations, management of people and goods, management science and law. The course can be studied with a year in work placement.
Plymouth (App Mar Spo Sci) A unique course involving the study of human performance, equipment use and design, the nature of the marine environment and practical work. An optional professional diving module is available in the second year.
Southampton Solent Unique courses in Yacht and Powercraft Design and Yacht Production and Surveying.

Universities and colleges teaching quality See www.qaa.ac.uk; http://unistats.direct.gov.uk.

Examples of sandwich degree courses Blackpool and Fylde (Coll); Bournemouth; Cornwall (Coll); Plymouth.

ADMISSIONS INFORMATION
Number of applicants per place (approx) Glasgow 2; LJMU (Marit St) 3; Southampton 6; Southampton Solent (Ocean) 6, (Ocn Chem) 6.

Advice to applicants and planning the UCAS personal statement This is a specialised field and, in many cases, applicants will have experience of marine activities. Describe these experiences, for example, sailing, snorkelling, fishing. See also **Appendix 3**.

Selection interviews **Yes** Southampton, UHI; **No** Dundee.

Interview advice and questions Most applicants will have been stimulated by their studies in science or will have strong interests or connections with marine activities. They are likely to be questioned on their reasons for choosing the course. See also **Chapter 6**.

AFTER-RESULTS ADVICE
Offers to applicants repeating A-levels **Same** Bangor, LJMU, Plymouth, UHI.

GRADUATE DESTINATIONS AND EMPLOYMENT (2009/10 HESA)
Maritime Technology; graduates surveyed 280 **Employed** 140 **In voluntary employment** 0 **In further study** 35 **Assumed unemployed** 10

Career note This subject area covers a wide range of vocational courses, each offering graduates an equally wide choice of career openings in either purely scientific or very practical areas.

OTHER DEGREE SUBJECTS FOR CONSIDERATION
Biology; Civil Engineering; Environmental Studies/Sciences; Geography; Marine Engineering; Marine Transport; Naval Architecture; Oceanography.

MARKETING

(including **Public Relations**; see also **Business and Management Courses, Business and Management Courses (International and European), Business and Management Courses (Specialised), Retail Management)**

Marketing courses are very popular and applications should include evidence of work experience or work shadowing. Marketing is a subject also covered in most Business Studies courses and in specialist (and equally relevant) courses such as Leisure Marketing and Food Marketing, for which lower offers are often made. Most courses offer the same subject content.

Useful websites www.adassoc.org.uk; www.cim.co.uk; www.camfoundation.com; www.ipa.co.uk; www.ipsos-mori.com; www.marketingstudies.net; www.marketingtoday.com.

NB The points totals shown to the left of the institutions are for ease of reference only. It must not be assumed that Tariff points are always used by institutions or that they can be substituted for an offer in grades. The level of an offer is not necessarily indicative of the quality of a course.

COURSE OFFERS INFORMATION

Subject requirements/preferences GCSE English and mathematics. **AL** No specified subjects required.

Your target offers and examples of courses provided by each institution

360 pts Exeter – AAA–AAB (Mgt Mark) (IB 36–33 pts)
Lancaster – AAA 360 pts (Mark Mgt (St Abrd)) (IB 36 pts)
Leeds – AAA 360 pts (Mgt Mark) (IB 35 pts HL 17 pts)
Ulster – AAA (Comm Adv Mark)

340 pts Aston – AAB–AAA 340–360 pts (Mark) (IB 35 pts HL 665)
Bournemouth – 340 pts (Bus St (Mark))
Cardiff – AAB (Bus Mgt (Mark))
Lancaster – AAB 340 pts (Adv Mark) (IB 34 pts)
Liverpool – AAB (Mark) (IB 35 pts)
London (RH) – AAB (Mgt Mark) (IB 35 pts)
Loughborough – AAB (Rtl Mark Mgt) (IB 36 pts)
Manchester – AAB 340 pts (Mgt Mark Fash Tex) (IB 36–35 pts)
Newcastle – AAB 340 pts (Mark Mgt) (IB 34 pts)
Southampton – AAB (Mark) (IB 34 pts HL 17 pts)
Sussex – AAB (Mark Mgt) (IB 35 pts)

320 pts Bournemouth – 320 pts (Adv Mark Comm; Mark; PR)
Bradford – 320 pts (Mark) (IB 24 pts)
Durham – ABB 320 pts (Mark) (IB 34 pts)
Essex – 320 pts (Mark HR Mgt; Mark Innov; Mark Fin; Mark)
Lancaster – ABB 320 pts (Mark Des) (IB 32 pts)
Northumbria – ABB 320 pts (Mark Mgt)
Reading – 320 pts (Bus Stats Mark) (IB 36 pts)
Roehampton – 320 pts (Mark; Mark Multim)
Strathclyde – ABB (Mark courses)
Southampton – ABB (Fash Mark) (IB 32 pts HL 16 pts)
Southampton (Winchester SA) – ABB (Fash Mark) (IB 32 pts)
Swansea – ABB–BBB (Bus Mgt (Mark))
Ulster – ABB (Law Mark) (IB 26 pts)

300 pts Aberystwyth – 300 pts (Econ Mark) (IB 27 pts)
Bournemouth – 300 pts (Leis Mark) (IB 30 pts)
Bristol UWE – 300 pts (Mark Comm)
Cardiff Met – 300 pts (Mark Mgt)
Essex – ABB–BBB 300 pts (Mgt Mark) (IB 34 pts)
Heriot-Watt – ABC (Bus Mgt Mark)

Hertfordshire – 300 pts (Mark)
Huddersfield – 300 pts (Mark Brnd Mgt; Mark; Mark PR)
Kent – BBB (Bus Admin (Mark)) (IB 33 pts)
Kingston – 300 pts (Art Mark)
Lincoln – 300 pts (Psy Mark)
Northumbria – 300 pts (Fash Mark)
Nottingham Trent – 300 pts (Fash Comm Prom; Fash Mark Brnd; Mark Des Comm)
Oxford Brookes – BBB (Bus Mark Mgt) (IB 31 pts)
Reading – 300 pts (Consum Bhv Mark) (HL 655)
Royal (CAg) – 300 pts (Prop Agncy Mgt)
Sheffield Hallam – 300 pts (Mark; Mark Comm Adv; Mark Rtl)

280 pts **Aberystwyth** – 280 pts (Mark courses) (IB 27 pts)
Brighton – BBC (Bus Mgt Mark; Rtl Mark)
Buckingham – 280 pts (Mark Psy) (IB 26 pts)
Coventry – BBC 280 pts (Mark; Adv Mark)
De Montfort – 280 pts (Mark Mgt; Adv; Mark; Int Mark Bus)
Derby – 280 pts (Mark Adv; Mark Brnd Mgt)
Edge Hill – 280 pts (Mark)
Hertfordshire – 280 pts (Mark)
Huddersfield – 280 pts (Adv Mark Comm; Spo Mark PR; Spo Prom Mark)
Hull – 280–300 pts (Ital Mark)
Keele – 280–340 pts (Mark)
Kingston – 280 pts (Mark Mgt) (IB 31 pts)
Leeds Trinity (UC) – 280 pts (Media Mark)
Manchester Met – 280 pts (Mark Comb Hons) (IB 28 pts)
Northumbria – 280 pts (Bus Mark) (IB 25 pts)
Portsmouth – 280–300 pts (Mark; Mark Psy)
Stirling – BBC (Rtl Mark) (IB 32 pts)
Salford – 280 pts (Bus St Mark Mgt)
Sheffield Hallam – 280 pts (Mark Lang)
Suffolk (Univ Campus) – 280 pts (Bus Mgt Mark)
Ulster – 280 pts (Adv HR Mgt; HR Mgt Mark; Mark)
Worcester – 280 pts (Adv; Bus Mark; Mark Adv PR; Bus Econ Adv; Bus Mgt Mark; Mark)

260 pts **Bangor** – 260–300 pts (Mark)
Birmingham City – 260–280 pts (Mark Adv PR) (IB 24 pts)
Bolton – 260 pts (Bus Mgt (Mark)) (IB 24 pts)
Brighton – BCC (Trav Tour Mark) (IB 28 pts)
Coventry – BCC 260 pts (Spo Mark)
Derby – 260–300 pts (Mark) (IB 26 pts)
Dundee – BCC (Bus Econ Mark) (IB 30 pts)
Glamorgan – BCC 260 pts (Mark) (IB 24 pts)
Gloucestershire – 260 pts (Adv)
Greenwich – 260 pts (Adv Mark Comm; Mark)
Harper Adams (UC) – 260–300 pts (Agric Mark)
Leeds Met – 260 pts (PR Mark) (IB 26 pts)
Lincoln – 260–280 pts (Adv Mark; Mark; Mark PR)
Liverpool Hope – 260–320 pts (Mark) (IB 25 pts)
LJMU – 260 pts (Bus PR)
Northampton – 260–280 pts (Adv)
Plymouth – 260 pts (Mark) (IB 26 pts)
Robert Gordon – 260 pts (Mgt Mark)
Sunderland – 260 pts (Bus Mark Mgt)
Ulster – 260 pts (Dr Mark; Ling Adv)
Westminster – BCC (Mark Comms) (IB 28 pts)
Winchester – 260–300 pts (Bus Mgt Mark)

240 pts **Bath Spa** – 240–280 pts (Bus Mgt (Mark))
Bradford – 240–280 pts (Econ Mark)
Bradford (Coll Univ Centre) – 240 pts (Mark Sls)
Buckingham – 240–300 pts (Span Mark)
Canterbury Christ Church – CCC (Mark)
Chester – 240–280 pts (Adv; Mark PR)
Chichester – CCC (Mark) (IB 28 pts)
Edinburgh Napier – CCC 240–230 pts (Mark Mgt Consum St)
Euro Bus Sch London – 240 pts (Int Bus Mark Lang)
Farnborough (CT) – 240 pts (Psy Mark)
Glasgow Caledonian – CCC–CCD (Mark)
Gloucestershire – 240–300 pts (Mark Mgt Brnd; Mark Adv Comms; PR)
Glyndŵr – 240 pts (Bus Mark)
Leeds (CAD) – 240 pts (Crea Adv)
Leeds Met – 240 pts (Spo Mark) (IB 24 pts)
Lincoln – 240 pts (Tour Mark)
London Met – 240 pts (Fash Mark; PR; Evnts Mgt Mark)
Newport – 240 pts (Mark) (IB 24 pts)
Plymouth – 240 pts (Bus Econ Mark) (IB 24 pts)
Ravensbourne – AA–CC (Fash Prom) (IB 28 pts)
Regents Bus Sch London – CCC (Glob Mark Mgt) (IB 32 pts)
Southampton Solent – 220–240 pts (PR Comm)
Teesside – 240 pts (Mark Adv) (IB 24–28 pts)
UCLan – 240–280 pts (Adv Mark Comm) (IB 28 pts)
Ulster – 240 pts (Adv courses; Econ Mark)
West Scotland – CCC (Mark)
Wolverhampton – CCC (Mark Mgt; PR)

230 pts **Edinburgh Napier** – 230 pts (Mark Mgt; Mark Dig Media)

220 pts **Creative Arts** – 220–260 pts (Fash Mgt Mark) (IB 24 pts)
Falmouth (UC) – 220 pts (Adv)
Harper Adams (UC) – 220 pts (Bus Mgt Mark)
Leeds Met – 220 pts (Ger Mark)
Lincoln – 220–280 pts (Spo Mark)
London South Bank – 220 pts (Mark Comb courses)
Northampton – 220–260 pts (Fash Mark; Spo Mark)
Southampton Solent – 220–240 pts (Mark; Mark Adv Mgt; Mark Evnt Mgt)
Sunderland – 220 pts (Adv Des; Fash Prod Prom)

200 pts **Anglia Ruskin** – 240–200 pts (Mark)
Bedfordshire – 200 pts (Mark; Mark Media Prac)
Birmingham (UC) – 200 pts (Mark Mgt; Mark Evnts Mgt)
Bucks New – 200–240 pts (PR Mark Comm; Mark; Bus Mark Mgt)
Creative Arts – 200 pts (Adv Brnd Comm)
Edinburgh Queen Margaret – 200 pts (Mark Mgt)
Middlesex – 200–280 pts (Mark; Adv PR Media)
Peterborough (Univ Centre) – 200 pts (Mark)
Staffordshire – BB–BCC (Mark Mgt)
Swansea Met – 200 pts (Des Adv)
UEL – 200 pts (Adv; Mark)
West London – 200 pts (Mark Bus)
York St John – 200–240 pts (Mark Mgt)

180 pts **Abertay Dundee** – DDD (Mark Bus)
Harper Adams (UC) – 180–240 pts (Agri-Fd Mark Bus St)
Northampton – 180–220 pts (Crea Des Mark)

160 pts **Bedfordshire** – 160–240 pts (PR; Adv Mark Comm)
Swansea Met – 160 pts (Mark Mgt)

Check **Chapter 4** when choosing your university and **Chapter 7** on how to read the subject tables.

120 pts **Croydon (Coll)** – 120 pts (Bus Mark)
Grimsby (IFHE) – 120 pts (Mark)

Alternative offers
See **Chapter 7** and **Appendix 1** for grades/UCAS Tariff points information for the International Baccalaureate, Scottish Highers/Advanced Highers, the Welsh Baccalaureate, the Irish Leaving Certificate, the Cambridge Pre-U Diploma, the Advanced Diploma and the Extended Project.

EXAMPLES OF FOUNDATION DEGREES IN THE SUBJECT FIELD
Arts London; Bedfordshire; Birmingham (UC); Bournemouth; Cornwall (Coll); Glyndŵr; Harper Adams (UC); Hertfordshire; Hull (Coll); Manchester (Coll); Middlesex; Northbrook (Coll); Nottingham New (Coll); Petroc; Plymouth; South Devon (Coll); Stevenson Edinburgh (Coll); Truro (Coll); Warwickshire (Coll); West London; Worcester (CT); York (Coll).

CHOOSING YOUR COURSE (SEE ALSO CH.1)
Some course features
Bournemouth The course covers advertising communications, media and marketing methods. The Marketing Communications course involves a 40-week placement.
Brunel Marketing is offered as a pathway in the Business and Management programme and can be taken as a three-year full-time or four-year sandwich course.
Lancaster (Mark Mgt) There is a one-year work placement between the second and third years.
Loughborough (Rtl Mark Mgt) The third year is spent on a salaried business placement as a trainee manager in a UK retail or marketing organisation.
Manchester Met A full-time or sandwich course, the latter with placements in the UK and abroad. Special features include a study of the fashion business, fashion products and the world-wide fashion industry.
Northumbria The course integrates fashion design with the fashion business and marketing.
Oxford Brookes (Mark Mgt) The course gives students an understanding of international marketing.
Portsmouth (Mark) The course is recognised by the Chartered Institute of Marketing. The four-year sandwich course involves a paid marketing placement.
Westminster Students are expected to find employment for a period during the course, ideally abroad. Work placement officers have contacts with institutions overseas.

Universities and colleges teaching quality See www.qaa.ac.uk; http://unistats.direct.gov.uk.

Examples of sandwich degree courses Abertay Dundee; Aston; Birmingham City; Bournemouth; Bradford; Brighton; Bristol UWE; Brunel; De Montfort; Gloucestershire; Greenwich; Harper Adams (UC); Hertfordshire; Huddersfield; Lancaster; Leeds Met; LJMU; Manchester Met; Newcastle; Northumbria; Nottingham Trent; Plymouth; Portsmouth; Sheffield Hallam; Staffordshire; Swansea Met; UCLan; Ulster; Westminster; Wolverhampton; Worcester.

ADMISSIONS INFORMATION
Number of applicants per place (approx) Abertay Dundee 6; Aberystwyth 3; Anglia Ruskin 5; Aston 9; Birmingham City 4; Bournemouth 10; Brunel 10; De Montfort 3; Derby 5; Glasgow Caledonian 15; Harper Adams (UC) 3; Huddersfield 7; Lancaster 28; Lincoln 3; London Met 10; Northampton 4; Northumbria 8; Nottingham Trent 2; Plymouth 12; Portsmouth 4; Staffordshire 6; Stirling 10; Teesside 3; UCLan 13.

Advice to applicants and planning the UCAS personal statement See **Business and Management Courses** and **Appendix 4**.

Selection interviews **Yes** Harper Adams (UC) (advisory), Manchester Met, Middlesex, Northbrook (Coll), Writtle (Coll); **Some** Abertay Dundee, Aberystwyth, Anglia Ruskin, Aston, Buckingham, De Montfort, Edinburgh Queen Margaret, Staffordshire.

Interview advice and questions Past questions include: What is marketing? Why do you want to take a Marketing degree? Is sales pressure justified? How would you feel if you had to market a product which you considered to be inferior? See also **Chapter 6**. **Buckingham** What job do you see yourself doing in five years' time?

Reasons for rejection (non-academic) Little thought of reasons for deciding on a Marketing degree. Weak on numeracy and problem-solving. Limited commercial awareness. Poor inter-personal skills. Lack of leadership potential. No interest in widening their horizons, either geographically or intellectually. 'We look at appearance, motivation and the applicant's ability to ask questions.' Not hungry enough. Limited understanding of the career. No clear reasons for wishing to do the course.

AFTER-RESULTS ADVICE
Offers to applicants repeating A-levels **Same** Abertay Dundee, Aberystwyth, Anglia Ruskin, Aston, Buckingham, De Montfort, Edinburgh Queen Margaret, Lincoln, Manchester Met, Staffordshire.

GRADUATE DESTINATIONS AND EMPLOYMENT (2009/10 HESA)
Graduates surveyed 3915 **Employed** 2225 **In voluntary employment** 40 **In further study** 360 **Assumed unemployed** 320

Career note See **Business and Management Courses**.

OTHER DEGREE SUBJECTS FOR CONSIDERATION
Advertising; Art and Design; Business courses; Communications; Graphic Design; Psychology; Public Relations.

MATERIALS SCIENCE/METALLURGY

Materials Science is a broad subject which mainly covers physics, chemistry and engineering at one and the same time! From its origins in metallurgy, materials science has now moved into the processing, structure and properties of materials – ceramics, polymers, composites and electrical materials. Materials science and metallurgy are perhaps the most misunderstood of all careers and applications for degree courses are low with very reasonable offers. Valuable bursaries and scholarships are offered by the Institute of Materials, Minerals and Mining (check with Institute – see **Appendix 3**). Polymer Science is a branch of materials science and is often studied in conjunction with Chemistry and covers such topics as polymer properties and processing relating to industrial applications with, for example, plastics, paints, adhesives. Other courses under this heading include Fashion and Leather Technology.

Useful websites www.scienceyear.com; www.eef.org.uk/uksteel; www.iom3.org; www.noisemakers. org.uk; www.imm.org.

NB The points totals shown to the left of the institutions are for ease of reference only. It must not be assumed that Tariff points are always used by institutions or that they can be substituted for an offer in grades. The level of an offer is not necessarily indicative of the quality of a course.

COURSE OFFERS INFORMATION
Subject requirements/preferences **GCSE** (Eng/Sci courses) Science/mathematics subjects. **AL** Mathematics, physics and/or chemistry required for most courses. (Poly Sci) Mathematics and/or physics usually required; design technology encouraged.

Your target offers and examples of courses provided by each institution
380 pts **Cambridge** – A*AA (Nat Sci (Mat Sci)) (IB 40–42 pts)
Oxford – A*AA (Mat Sci) (IB 40 pts)
360 pts **Birmingham** – AAA (Mat Sci Eng Bus Mgt MEng) (IB 36–38 pts)
Imperial London – AAA–AAB 340–360 pts (Mat Nucl Eng) (IB 35–37 pts)
London (QM) – AAA (Med Mater Sci MEng)
Strathclyde – AAA 360 pts (Mech Eng Mat Eng) (IB 36 pts)
Southampton – AAA incl maths phys (Mech Eng (Advnc Mat)) (IB 36 pts HL 18 pts)
340 pts **Birmingham** – AAB (Metal) (IB 35–36 pts)
Exeter – AAB–BBB (Min Eng) (IB 30–34 pts)
Leeds – AAB (Cheml Miner Eng) (IB 36 pts HL 17 pts)

Liverpool – AAB incl maths phys (Mech Mat Eng MEng) (IB 35 pts)
Loughborough – 340 pts (Des Eng Mat MEng) (IB 34–36 pts)
Manchester – AAB (Mat Sci Eng) (IB 37 pts)
St Andrews – AAB (Mat Sci) (IB 35 pts)
Strathclyde – AAB (Mech Eng Mat Eng BEng) (IB 32 pts)
Sheffield – AAB incl maths phys (Aerosp Mat MEng) (IB 35 pts HL 6 maths phys)
Sheffield – AAB (Mat Sci Nucl Eng) (IB 35 pts)
Southampton – AAB (Ship Sci (Advncd Mat)) (IB 34 pts HL 17 pts)

320 pts **Aberdeen** – ABB–BBB (Biomed Mat Chem)
Birmingham – ABB (Spo Sci Mat Sci) (IB 32–34 pts)
Edinburgh – AAA–ABB incl chem maths 320–360 pts (Chem Mat Chem) (IB 37–32 pts)
Exeter – ABB–BBB (Mat Eng BEng) (IB 32–29 pts)
Swansea – ABB (Mat Sci Eng MEng)

300 pts **Aberdeen** – BBB (Mech Eng Mat) (IB 30–28 pts)
Birmingham – BBB (Metal Mat Eng) (IB 32 pts)
Heriot-Watt – BBB (Fash Tech)
Liverpool – BBB incl maths phys (Mech Mat Eng BEng) (IB 32 pts)
London (QM) – BBB (Med Mat Sci BEng) (IB 28 pts)
Loughborough – 300 pts (Auto Mat BEng) (IB 30–32 pts)
Nottingham – BBB 300 pts (Biomed Mat Sci) (IB 30 pts)
Sheffield – ABC/BBB (Aerosp Mat BEng) (IB 32 pts)
Swansea – BBB 300 pts (Spo Mat)

260 pts **Swansea** – 260 pts (Mat Sci Eng BEng)
Ulster – 260 pts (Bld Mat)

240 pts **Edinburgh Napier** – CCC 240 pts (Poly Eng)

220 pts **Sheffield Hallam** – 220 pts incl maths+chem (Mat Eng)

200 pts **Plymouth** – 200 pts (Mar Cmpstes Tech)

120 pts **Plymouth** – 120–180 pts (Mar Eng)

Alternative offers
See **Chapter 7** and **Appendix 1** for grades/UCAS Tariff points information for the International Baccalaureate, Scottish Highers/Advanced Highers, the Welsh Baccalaureate, the Irish Leaving Certificate, the Cambridge Pre-U Diploma, the Advanced Diploma and the Extended Project.

EXAMPLES OF FOUNDATION DEGREES IN THE SUBJECT FIELD
Blackburn (Coll); Bradford; Loughborough; Manchester Met.

OTHER HIGHER EDUCATION COURSES IN THIS FIELD
Birmingham (Nucl Sci/Eng, Spo Mat Sci); Imperial London (Aerosp Mat, Biomat); Manchester (Biomed Mat Sci).

CHOOSING YOUR COURSE (SEE ALSO CH.1)
Some course features
Birmingham Courses are offered in Mechanical and Materials Science, Metallurgy/Materials Engineering, Materials Science and Technology. There is also a course in Sports Science and Materials Technology.
Imperial London The Department offers three-year BEng courses in Materials Science and Engineering, Materials with Management, and Materials with a year abroad, and four-year courses in Aerospace Materials, and Materials Science and Engineering. Students are encouraged to gain practical experience during two summer vacations; some are spent abroad. There are also opportunities for industrial sponsorship. A course in Biomaterials and Tissue Engineering is also offered.
London (QM) The course in Materials Science and Engineering provides a bridge between pure and applied sciences and covers polymers, biomaterials, metals and ceramics. There are also courses in Biomedical, Aerospace, Dental and Environmental Materials Science.

London Met Three-year degree courses are offered in Polymer Engineering and in Polymer Science.
Loughborough The Materials Engineering programme allows students to develop either Materials Engineering or Business Management options in the final year. There is an optional third year in Europe or in industry. There are also courses in Automotive Materials. Scholarships available.
Manchester The Materials Science and Engineering programme focuses on engineering aspects whilst the Biomedical Materials Science programme can be taken with or without industrial experience. The Biomedical Materials Science course covers cell structure, anatomy, tissue interaction and drug release systems. There are also courses in Textile Sciences and Technology. Entrance scholarships.
Northampton (Mat Tech (Lea)) This course is unique. The University is the UK's leading provider of leather technology courses, and is the only one to have a tannery.
Sheffield In this Materials Science and Engineering course modules exist in biomaterials, mathematics and material chemistry. Admission can also be by way of Physical Sciences since final degree course decisions between Materials Science or Physics or Chemistry can be delayed. Various Engineering courses are also available.

Universities and colleges teaching quality See www.qaa.ac.uk; http://unistats.direct.gov.uk.

Top research universities and colleges (RAE 2008) (Metallurgy and Materials) Cambridge; Liverpool; Kent; Oxford; Manchester; Birmingham; Sheffield; Imperial London; Swansea; London (QM).

Examples of sandwich degree courses Loughborough; Plymouth.

ADMISSIONS INFORMATION

Number of applicants per place (approx) Birmingham 8; Imperial London 3; Liverpool 3; Manchester Met 7; Nottingham 7; Southampton 8; Swansea 4.

Advice to applicants and planning the UCAS personal statement Read scientific and engineering journals and describe any special interests you have. Try to visit chemical or technological installations (rubber, plastics, glass etc) and describe your visits.

Misconceptions about this course Students are generally unaware of what this subject involves or the opportunities within the industry.

Selection interviews Yes Birmingham, Imperial London, Nottingham, Oxford (Mat Sci) 44%; (Mat Sci Econ Mgt) 44%; **Some** Leeds.

Interview advice and questions Questions are likely to be based on A/AS-level science subjects. Recent examples include: Why did you choose Materials Science? How would you make each part of this table lamp (on the interviewer's desk)? Identify this piece of material. How was it manufactured? How has it been treated? (Questions related to metal and polymer samples.) What would you consider the major growth area in materials science? See also **Chapter 6**. **Birmingham** We try to gauge understanding; for example, an applicant would be unlikely to be questioned on specific facts, but might be asked what they have understood from a piece of coursework at school. **Oxford** Tutors look for an ability to apply logical reasoning to problems in physical science and an enthusiasm for thinking about new concepts in science and engineering.

AFTER-RESULTS ADVICE

Offers to applicants repeating A-levels Higher Swansea; **Same** Birmingham, Leeds (CAD), Liverpool, Manchester Met; **No** Cambridge.

GRADUATE DESTINATIONS AND EMPLOYMENT (2009/10 HESA)

Metallurgy; graduates surveyed 40 **Employed** 30 **In voluntary employment** 0 **In further study** 5 **Assumed unemployed** 0

Polymer and Textiles; graduates surveyed 465 **Employed** 325 **In voluntary employment** 10 **In further study** 50 **Assumed unemployed** 30

Materials Science; graduates surveyed 85 **Employed** 40 **In voluntary employment** 0 **In further study** 20 **Assumed unemployed** 10

Check **Chapter 4** when choosing your university and **Chapter 7** on how to read the subject tables.

Career note Materials scientists are involved in a wide range of specialisms in which openings are likely in a range of industries. These include manufacturing processes in which the work is closely linked with that of mechanical, chemical, production and design engineers.

OTHER DEGREE SUBJECTS FOR CONSIDERATION

Aerospace Engineering; Biotechnology; Chemistry; Dentistry; Engineering Sciences; Mathematics; Mechanical Engineering; Medical Engineering; Plastics Technology; Physics; Product Design and Materials; Prosthetics and Orthotics; Sports Technology.

MATHEMATICS

(including **Mathematical Sciences/Studies**; see also **Economics, Statistics**)

Mathematics at degree level is an extension of A-level mathematics, covering pure and applied mathematics, statistics, computing, mathematical analysis and mathematical applications. Mathematics is of increasing importance and is used in the simplest of design procedures and not only in applications in the physical sciences and engineering. It also plays a key role in management, economics, medicine and the social and behavioural sciences.

Useful websites www.ima.org.uk; www.gchq.gov.uk/codebreaking; www.orsoc.org.uk; www.scienceyear.com; www.m-a.org.uk; www.mathscareers.org.uk; www.imo.maths.ca; www.bmoc.maths.org; www.maths.org; www.ukmt.org.uk.

NB The points totals shown to the left of the institutions are for ease of reference only. It must not be assumed that Tariff points are always used by institutions or that they can be substituted for an offer in grades. The level of an offer is not necessarily indicative of the quality of a course.

COURSE OFFERS INFORMATION

Subject requirements/preferences GCSE English often required and mathematics is obviously essential at a high grade for leading universities. AS further mathematics may be required. GCSE **AL** Mathematics, in several cases with a specified grade, required for all courses. **Other** Maths AEA or STEP papers may be required by some universities (eg **Imperial**, **Warwick**). See also **Chapter 5**. NB The level of an offer may depend on whether an applicant is taking A/AS further maths; check websites.

Imperial London 5 A/A* grades at GCSE.

Your target offers and examples of courses provided by each institution

440 pts	**Warwick** – A*AA–AAB (Maths OR Stats Econ (MORSE)) (IB 39 pts HL 6 maths)
400 pts	**Imperial London** – A*A*A (Maths Mathem Comp) (IB 39 pts HL 7 maths)
	London (King's) – AAAc incl AL fmaths (A*AAa incl AS fmaths) (Maths Mgt Fin) (IB 38 pts HL 6 maths)
	London (UCL) – A*AA+AS incl maths/fmaths (Maths) (IB 36–38 pts HL 766)
	Oxford – A*A*A (Maths Stats) (IB 39 pts)
380 pts	**Bath** – A*AA–A*AB (Maths Stats) (IB 36 pts HL 6 maths)
	Bristol – A*AA–AAA 360–380 pts (Maths Phil) (IB 38–37 pts HL 666)
	Cambridge – A*AA (Educ Maths) (IB 40–42 pts HL 766–777)
	Durham – A*AA (Maths) (IB 38 pts)
	Exeter – A*AA–AAB (Maths Mgt) (IB 38–34 pts)
	London (King's) – A*AAa–AAAc (Maths Phys) (IB 38 pts HL 6 maths)
	London LSE – A*(maths)AA (Maths Econ) (IB 38 pts HL 766)
	Manchester – A*AA (Maths Phys) (IB 38 pts)
	Warwick – A*AA (Discr Maths) (IB 38 pts)
360 pts	**Bath** – AAA (Maths Phys) (IB 36 pts HL 6 maths)
	Birmingham – AAA (Mathem Econ Stats) (IB 36–38 pts)
	Bristol – A*AB–AAA incl maths (Eng Maths)

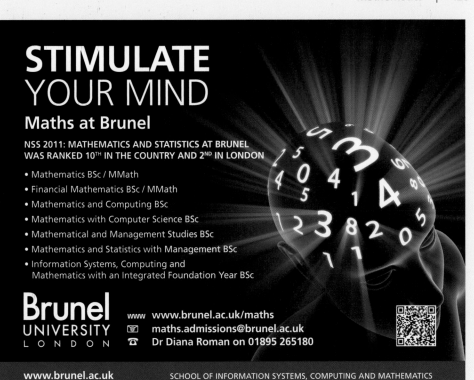
Cardiff – AAA incl maths (Maths MMaths) (IB 35 pts)
City – AAA 360 pts (Mathem Sci Stats) (IB 32 pts)
Glasgow – AAA–A*AB (Acc Maths/App Maths/PMaths) (IB 36 pts)
Lancaster – AAA (Theor Phys Maths) (IB 36 pts)
Leeds – AAA–AAB (Maths) (IB 34 pts HL 6 maths)
London (QM) – 360 pts (Maths Stats MSci) (IB 34 pts HL 6 maths)
London (RH) – AAA–AAB (Econ Maths) (IB 33–35 pts)
London (UCL) – AAA–ABB (Chem Maths) (IB 32–36 pts)
London LSE – AAA incl maths (Bus Maths Stats) (IB 38 pts HL 7 maths 66)
Loughborough – AAA–AAB (Maths Spo Sci) (IB 36 pts)
Manchester – A*AB–AAB (Maths Stats) (IB 36 pts)
Nottingham – AAA–A*AB (Maths Eng) (IB 37–36 pts HL 6 maths)
St Andrews – AAA (Maths Langs; Arbc Maths)
Sheffield – AAA incl maths (Maths MMaths) (IB 37 pts HL 6 maths)
Southampton – AAA (Maths Mus) (IB 36 pts HL 18 pts)
Surrey – AAA–AAB 360–340 pts (Maths courses) (IB 34–36 pts)
Sussex – AAA–AAB incl maths (Maths Comp Sci) (IB 35–36 pts)
Swansea – AAA (Maths MMaths)
York – AAA–AAB (Maths Stats)
340 pts **Aberystwyth** – 340 pts (Maths MMaths) (IB 31 pts)
Birmingham – AAB (Maths Bus Mgt) (IB 34–38 pts HL 6 maths)
Brunel – AAB incl AL maths/fmaths A (Fin Maths MMaths) (IB 33 pts)
Cardiff – AAB incl maths (Maths Welsh) (IB 33 pts HL 6 maths)
Lancaster – AAB (Maths Stats) (IB 34 pts HL 6 maths)
Leeds – AAB (Act Maths) (IB 34 pts HL 6 maths)

Leicester – AAB (Maths Mgt) (IB 28–32 pts)
London (RH) – AAB (Maths Psy)
Loughborough – AAB (Bank Fin Mgt) (IB 36 pts HL 6 maths)
Manchester – A*AB–AAB 340–360 pts (Maths Phil) (IB 36 pts)
Newcastle – AAB (Maths Biol) (IB 34–36 pts HL 6 maths)
Queen's Belfast – AAB/ABBa (App Maths Phys MSci)
St Andrews – AAB–AAA (Maths Span) (IB 38 pts)
Strathclyde – AAB–ABB (Maths courses)
Sheffield – AAB (Maths Joint Hons) (IB 35 pts HL 6 maths)
Southampton – AAB (Phil Maths) (IB 34 pts HL 17 pts)
Surrey – AAB 340 pts (Maths Stats) (IB 30–32 pts)
Swansea – AAB (Maths BSc)
UEA – AAB (Maths MMath) (IB 33 pts)
York – AAB (Econ/Maths) (IB 36 pts HL 666)

320 pts **Aberystwyth** – 320 pts (PMaths Stats) (IB 27 pts)
Aston – AAB–ABB 320–340 pts (Maths Joint Hons) (IB 31–33 pts)
Bristol UWE – 320 pts (Maths) (IB 24–28 pts)
Brunel – ABB incl AL maths/fmaths A (Maths MMaths) (IB 33 pts HL 6 maths)
Edinburgh – AAA–ABB 320–360 pts (Mathem Phys; Maths Stats) (IB 37–32 pts)
Glasgow – ABB (Maths/App Maths/PMaths) (IB 32 pts)
Keele – 320 pts (Maths)
Kent – ABB (Maths) (IB 33 pts)
Liverpool – ABB (Maths Fin) (IB 33 pts HL 6 maths)
London (QM) – 320 pts (Maths BSc) (IB 34 pts HL 6 maths)
London (RH) – ABB (Maths Stats) (IB 33 pts HL 6 maths)
Loughborough – AAB–ABB (Phys Maths) (IB 34 pts)
Northumbria – 320 pts (Maths) (IB 30 pts)
Queen's Belfast – ABB (Maths BSc; Maths Stats OR BSc; Maths (St Abrd))
Reading – 320–340 pts (Maths; Maths App Stats; Maths Meteor; Maths Stats Comput Maths)
Strathclyde – ABB (Econ Maths Stats)
UEA – ABB (Maths Comp) (IB 32 pts HL 6 maths)
York – ABB (Maths)

300 pts **Aberdeen** – BBB 300 pts (App Maths; Maths)
Brunel – BBB (Maths Stats Mgt; Maths)
Derby – 300 pts (Maths Comp Sci)
Edinburgh – BBB–AAA (Maths BSc) (IB 32 pts)
Essex – 300–320 pts (Maths Hum) (IB 29–32 pts)
Glamorgan – BBB (Fin Maths)
Heriot-Watt – BBB (Maths Joint courses; App Maths; Mathem Sci)
Plymouth – 300 pts (Maths Fin)
Queen's Belfast – ABC (Comput Maths BSc)
Roehampton – 300–360 pts (P Educ (Maths))
Ulster – 300 pts (Comp Sci Maths)

280 pts **Brighton** – BBC (Maths) (IB 28 pts)
Derby – 280 pts (Maths; Maths Educ)
Dundee – BBC (Mathem Biol) (IB 32 pts)
Glamorgan – 280–320 pts (Maths)
Hertfordshire – 280 pts (Comp Maths)
Kingston – 280 pts (Act Maths Stats) (IB 26–28 pts)
Manchester Met – 280 pts (Maths) (IB 28 pts)
Northampton – 280–320 pts (P Ed Maths)
Nottingham Trent – 280 pts (Spo Sci Maths; Maths)
Oxford Brookes – BBC 280 pts (Maths) (IB 30 pts)
Sheffield Hallam – 280 pts (Maths)
Staffordshire – 220–280 pts (Maths App Stats) (IB 26 pts)

Stirling – BBC (Maths App) (IB 32 pts)
UCLan – 280 pts (Maths)
260 pts **Bolton** – 260 pts (Maths)
Coventry – 260 pts (Maths courses)
Dundee – BCC 260 pts (Maths)
Greenwich – 260 pts (Fin Maths; Maths Comp; Maths)
Kingston – 260–280 pts (Maths) (IB 26–28 pts)
Liverpool Hope – 260–320 pts (Maths)
LJMU – 260 pts (Maths) (IB 24 pts)
Portsmouth – 260–300 pts (Maths Stats; Maths Fin Mgt)
Stranmillis (UC) – BCC (Maths Sci Educ)
240 pts **Bradford** – 240 pts (Comput Maths)
Canterbury Christ Church – 240 pts (Maths Educ QTS)
Chester – 240–280 pts (Maths) (IB 26 pts)
Hertfordshire – 240 pts (Maths; Fin Maths)
Winchester – 240–280 pts (Maths P Educ)
220 pts **Bishop Grosseteste (UC)** – 220 pts (Spo Maths)
200 pts **Bedfordshire** – 200 pts (Comp Maths)
London Met – 200 pts (Maths; Mathem Sci)
160 pts **UEL** – check with admissions tutor 160 pts (Maths)
Wolverhampton – 160–220 pts (Mathem Sci; Maths)
80 pts **London (Birk)** – p/t for under 21s (over 21s varies) (Maths Stats)

Open University – contact +44 (0)845 300 6090 **or** www.openuniversity.co.uk/you (Maths)

Alternative offers
See **Chapter 7** and **Appendix 1** for grades/UCAS Tariff points information for the International Baccalaureate, Scottish Highers/Advanced Highers, the Welsh Baccalaureate, the Irish Leaving Certificate, the Cambridge Pre-U Diploma, the Advanced Diploma and the Extended Project.

CHOOSING YOUR COURSE (SEE ALSO CH.1)
Some course features
Aston There is an emphasis on Applied Mathematics relevant to business, industry and computing in addition to combinations with Economics and Languages. There are sandwich placement opportunities allowing students to spend the third year gaining experience in paid work.
Bradford There is a course in Computational Mathematics with a Foundation year in Informatics for applicants with non-standard qualifications.
Coventry Courses focus on the applications of mathematics in engineering, finance, computing, business and statistics.
Exeter Most first-year modules are common to all Single Honours courses. Transfers to other courses are possible from Year 2. There is a wide range of degrees including combinations with Management, languages, Physics and Finance and Accounting.
Imperial London Twelve courses are offered with considerable flexibility to transfer between courses and between BSc and MSci options including Applied Maths, Statistics, Computer Science and a year in Europe.
Lancaster The Mathematics degree course is for those students wanting to specialise in pure mathematics whilst having the option to include some statistics or another subject.
Leicester BA, BSc and MMaths courses are offered in Mathematics, Financial Mathematics, Mathematics with Economics and Mathematics with Management. The MMath Mathematics degree comes is an opportunity to study abroad.
London (QM) A wide range of joint courses are available offering specialisms in accounting, business, computing and finance.
London (UCL) A range of courses, including Economics, Statistical Science and Theoretical Physics, is offered with Mathematics and some sponsorships are possible. Small group tutorials and computer-assisted learning are important features of this course. There are a range of options in Years 3 and 4. There are several Statistics degree courses.

Plymouth Five Mathematics courses are offered including combinations with Statistics, Education, Computing and Finance. Applied Statistics can also be taken with Management Science.

Universities and colleges teaching quality See www.qaa.ac.uk; http://unistats.direct.gov.uk.

Top research universities and colleges (RAE 2008) (Pure Maths) Imperial London; Warwick; Oxford; Cambridge; Bristol; Edinburgh; Heriot-Watt; Bath; Aberdeen; London (King's); Manchester; London (UCL); Durham; UEA; Sheffield; London (QM).

(Applied Maths) Cambridge; Oxford; Bristol; St Andrews; Bath; Portsmouth; Warwick; Manchester; Imperial London; Durham; Southampton; Nottingham; Surrey.

Examples of sandwich degree courses Aston; Bath; Bradford; Brighton; Bristol UWE; Brunel; Cardiff; Coventry; Glamorgan; Greenwich; Hertfordshire; Kingston; LJMU; Loughborough; Northumbria; Portsmouth; Staffordshire; Surrey; York.

ADMISSIONS INFORMATION

Number of applicants per place (approx) Aberystwyth 8, (App Maths) 5; Anglia Ruskin 6; Aston 8; Bangor 4; Bath 6; Birmingham 4; Bristol UWE 7; Brunel 5; Cambridge 4; Cardiff 5; City 6; Coventry 8; Cumbria 9; Derby 4; Dundee 5; Durham 5; Edinburgh 4; Exeter 6; Glamorgan 3; Greenwich 2; Heriot-Watt 5; Hertfordshire 9; Kent 8; Lancaster 12; Leeds (Maths) 5, (Maths Fin) 4; Leicester 14; Liverpool 5; London (Gold) 5; London (King's) 8; London (QM) 5; London (RH) 8; London (UCL) 8; London LSE (Maths) 11, (Bus Maths Stats) 10; London Met 3; Manchester Met 3; Middlesex 5; Newcastle 7; Northumbria 7; Nottingham Trent 7; Oxford Brookes 21; Plymouth 8; Portsmouth 7; Sheffield 5; Sheffield Hallam 3; Southampton 9–10; Strathclyde 6; Surrey 7; UCLan 7; UEA 5; UEL 2; Warwick 6; York 6.

Advice to applicants and planning the UCAS personal statement Any interests you have in careers requiring mathematical ability could be mentioned – for example, engineering, computers (hardware and software) and business applications. Show determination, love of mathematics and an appreciation of the rigour of the course. Give details of your skills, work experience, positions of responsibility. A variety of non-academic interests to complement the applicant's academic abilities preferred. For non-UK students fluency in oral and written English required. **Manchester** Unit grades may form part of an offer. **Warwick** Offers for courses in Statistics (MORSE, Mathematics and Statistics) include achievement requirements in STEP and other requirements. Check university websites for latest information.

Misconceptions about this course London (QM) Some believe that a study of mechanics is compulsory – it is not. **Surrey** Maths is not just about calculations: it focuses on reasoning, logic and applications. **York** Further maths is not required.

Selection interviews Yes Aberystwyth, Bath, Bishop Grosseteste (UC), Bristol UWE, Brunel, Cambridge, Cardiff, City, Coventry, Durham, Essex, Exeter, Glamorgan, Heriot-Watt, Imperial London, Kent, Kingston, Lancaster, Leeds, Liverpool, LJMU, London (Gold), London (King's), London (RH), London Met, Manchester Met, Newcastle, Northampton, Northumbria, Nottingham, Oxford (Maths) 20%, (Maths Comp Sci) 31%, (Maths Phil) 25%, (Maths Stats) 17%, Salford, Sheffield, Southampton, Sussex, UCLan, UEL, Warwick, York; **Some** Brighton, Bristol, Greenwich, London (UCL), London LSE (rarely), Loughborough, UEA; **No** Birmingham, Dundee, Reading.

Interview advice and questions Questions are likely to be asked arising from the information you have given in your UCAS application and about your interests in the subject. Questions in recent years have included: How many ways are there of incorrectly setting up the back row of a chess board? A ladder on a rough floor leans against a smooth wall. Describe the forces acting on the ladder and give the maximum possible angle of inclination possible. There are three particles connected by a string; the middle one is made to move – describe the subsequent motion of the particles. What mathematics books have you read outside your syllabus? Why does a ball bounce? Discuss the work of any renowned mathematician. Balance a pencil on your index fingers and then try to move both towards the centre of the pencil. Explain what is happening in terms of forces and friction. See also **Chapter 6**. **Cambridge** If you could spend half an hour with any mathematician past or present, who would it be?

Oxford (Maths Phil) What makes you think I'm having thoughts? What was the most beautiful proof in A-level mathematics? I am an oil baron in the desert and I need to deliver oil to four different towns which happen to lie in a straight line. In order to deliver the correct amount to each town I must visit each town in turn, returning to my warehouse in between each visit. Where would I position my warehouse in order to drive the shortest possible distance? Roads are no problem since I have a friend who will build me as many roads as I like for free. **Southampton** Personal statements generate discussion points. Our interviews are informal chats and so technical probing is kept low key.

Reasons for rejection (non-academic) Usually academic reasons only. Lack of motivation. We were somewhat uneasy about how much mathematics he will remember after a Gap Year running a theatre in South Africa. **Birmingham** A poorly-written and poorly-organised personal statement.

AFTER-RESULTS ADVICE

Offers to applicants repeating A-levels Higher Brighton, Coventry, Essex, Glasgow, London Met, Salford, Strathclyde, Surrey, Swansea, Warwick; **Possibly higher** Cambridge (Hom), Durham, Lancaster, Leeds, Newcastle, Sheffield; **Same** Aberystwyth, Aston, Bath, Birmingham, Bristol, Brunel, Chester, Liverpool, Liverpool Hope, London (RH), Loughborough (usually), Manchester Met, Nottingham, Nottingham Trent, Oxford Brookes, Sheffield Hallam, Southampton, Stirling, UEA, Ulster, Wolverhampton, York; **No** Cambridge.

GRADUATE DESTINATIONS AND EMPLOYMENT (2009/10 HESA)

Graduates surveyed 6850 **Employed** 2070 **In voluntary employment** 75 **In further study** 1720 **Assumed unemployed** 440

Career note Graduates enter a range of careers. Whilst business, finance and retail areas are popular options, mathematicians also have important roles in the manufacturing industries. Mathematics offers the pleasure of problem-solving, the satisfaction of a rigorous argument and the most widely employable non-vocational degree subject. A student's view: 'Maths trains you to work in the abstract, to think creatively and to come up with concrete conclusions.' These transferable skills are much sought-after by employers. Employment prospects are excellent, with high salaries.

OTHER DEGREE SUBJECTS FOR CONSIDERATION

Accountancy; Actuarial Studies; Astronomy; Astrophysics; Computer Science; Economics; Engineering Sciences; Operational Research; Physics; Statistics.

MEDIA STUDIES

(including **Broadcasting** and **Journalism**; see also **Communication Studies/Communication, Computer Courses, Engineering (Acoustics and Sound), Film, Radio, Video and TV Studies, Information Management and Librarianship, Photography**)

Intending Media applicants need to check course details carefully since this subject area can involve graphic design, illustration and other art courses as well as the media in the fields of TV, radio and journalism. Courses in Journalism include block and day release, evening/weekend magazine journalism, and photo-journalism. Full details can be obtained by referring to www.nctj.com/courses.

Useful websites www.bbc.co.uk/jobs; www.newspapersoc.org.uk; www.ppa.co.uk; http://careers. thomsonreuters.com; www.arts.org.uk; www.nctj.com; www.ipa.co.uk; www.camfoundation.com; www.mediastudies.com.

NB The points totals shown to the left of the institutions are for ease of reference only. It must not be assumed that Tariff points are always used by institutions or that they can be substituted for an offer in grades. The level of an offer is not necessarily indicative of the quality of a course.

COURSE OFFERS INFORMATION

Subject requirements/preferences GCSE English and mathematics often required. **AL** No specified subjects required.

Your target offers and examples of courses provided by each institution

340 pts **Bristol UWE** – 340 pts (Engl Jrnl)
Cardiff – AAB (Jrnl Media Engl Lit)
City – AAB 340 pts (Media St Sociol)
London (Gold) – AAB–ABB (Media Comm) (IB 34 pts)
Newcastle – AAB (Media Comm Cult St) (IB 32 pts)
Roehampton – 340 pts (Media Cult; Jrnl)
Strathclyde – AAB (Jrnl Crea Writ)
Sheffield – AAB (Jrnl St Joint Hons) (IB 35 pts)
Surrey – AAB (Aud Media Eng BEng) (IB 35 pts)
UEA – AAB–ABB (Media St) (IB 33–32 pts)

320 pts **Bournemouth** – 320 pts (Multim Jrnl; Multim Bus Entre)
Bristol UWE – 320–340 pts (Film St Engl/Media/Scr Writ)
Cardiff – ABB (Jrnl Media Sociol)
City – ABB 320 pts (Jrnl Psy)
Glasgow – ABB 320 pts (Arts Media Inform) (IB 36 pts)
Kent – ABB (Jrnl News Ind) (IB 33 pts HL 15 pts)
Kingston – 320 pts (Jrnl Engl Lit)
Lancaster – ABB 320 pts (Media Cult St) (IB 32 pts)
Leeds – ABB (Broad Jrnl)
Leicester – ABB 320 pts (Comms Media Soty) (IB 30 pts)
Liverpool – ABB (Comm Media Pop Mus) (IB 33 pts)
London (RH) – ABB–ABbb (Media Arts) (IB 34 pts)
Loughborough – ABB (Comm Media St) (IB 34 pts)
Nottingham – ABB (Int Media Comm St) (IB 32 pts)
Surrey – ABB (Media St; Social Cult Media) (IB 34 pts)
Sussex – ABB (Media St courses) (IB 34 pts)
UCLan – ABB 320 pts (Jrnl)
UEA – ABB–BBB (Transl Media Fr/Span/Jap 4 yrs) (IB 32–31 pts)

300 pts **Aberystwyth** – 300–320 pts (Hist Media) (IB 30 pts)
Brighton – BBB (Env Media St) (IB 32 pts)
Brunel – BBB 300 pts (Jrnl (NCTJ accredited)) (IB 32 pts)
Essex – 300–320 pts (Media Cult Soc)
Glamorgan – 300–360 pts (Perf Media)
Hertfordshire – 300 pts (Jrnl Media Cult; Scrn Cult Media Prac)
Huddersfield – 300 pts (Pol Media)
Kingston – 300–320 pts (Jrnl)
Leicester – BBB (Media Sociol)
Lincoln – 300 pts (Media Prod)
Loughborough – 300 pts (Pub Engl) (IB 32 pts)
Northumbria – 300 pts (Jrnl; Jrnl Engl Lit; Media Jrnl)
Nottingham Trent – 300 pts (Broad Jrnl)
Staffordshire – 300–260 pts (Jrnl)
Swansea – 300 pts (PR Media; Media St courses)
UCLan – 300 pts (Media Prod Tech)
Westminster – BBB (Jrnl) (IB 30 pts)

280 pts **Birmingham City** – 280 pts (Media (Mus)) (IB 30 pts)
Brighton – 280 pts (Media Engl Lit) (IB 30 pts)
Bristol UWE – 280–320 pts (Crimin Jrnl; Jrnl; Media Cult St)
Brunel – BBC (Comm Media St) (IB 30 pts)
Derby – 280 pts (Media Prod; Media Prod)
Edge Hill – 280 pts (Engl Med)
Glamorgan – 280–320 pts (Media Comm; Jrnl; Media Prod)
Glasgow Caledonian – BBC 280 pts (Jrnl; Media Comm)
Gloucestershire – 280–300 pts (Media Comm Cult; Multim Web Des; Jrnl)

For a quick reference offers calculator, fold out the inside back cover.

Greenwich – 280 pts (Media Comm) (IB 24 pts)
Huddersfield – 280 pts (Jrnl; Spo Jrnl) (IB 28 pts)
Hull – 280–300 pts (Media Cult Soty) (IB 28 pts)
Leeds Met – 280 pts (Jrnl) (IB 28 pts)
Leeds Trinity (UC) – 280 pts (Jrnl; Media)
Lincoln – 280 pts (Film TV Jrnl Joint Hons; Jrnl)
LJMU – 280 pts (Broad Media Prod; Jrnl; Media Prof St)
London Met – 280 pts (Media St)
Manchester Met – 280 pts (Dig Media Mark) (IB 28 pts)
Nottingham Trent – 280 pts (Media) (IB 24 pts)
Oxford Brookes – BBC (Comm Media Cult) (IB 30 pts)
Plymouth – 280 pts (Geog Media Arts)
Stirling – BBC (Euro Film Media) (IB 32 pts)
Salford – 280 pts (Jrnl courses)
Sheffield Hallam – 280 pts (Media; Jrnl)
Suffolk (Univ Campus) – 280 pts (Film Media) (IB 24 pts)
Teesside – 280 pts (Multim Jrnl Prof Prac)
Worcester – 280–300 pts (Jrnl)
260 pts **Bangor** – 260–300 pts (Media St courses)
Brunel – 260–300 pts (Sociol Media St) (IB 31–32 pts)
Cardiff Met – 260 pts (Engl Contemp Media)
Chester – 260–300 pts (Spo Jrnl) (IB 28 pts)
Chichester – BCC (Media St) (IB 28 pts)
Coventry – BCC (Jrnl Media; Media Prod)
Derby – 260 pts (Jrnl; Media St)
Edge Hill – 260–280 pts (Media Joint Hons)
Edinburgh Queen Margaret – 260 pts (Media; PR Media)

Check **Chapter 4** when choosing your university and **Chapter 7** on how to read the subject tables.

Keele – 260–300 pts (Media Comm)

Leeds Met – 260 pts (Media Comm Cult) (IB 24 pts)

Liverpool Hope – 260–300 pts (Media Comm)

LJMU – 260 pts (Media Cult Comm) (IB 28 pts)

Newman (UC) – 260 pts (Media Comm)

Nottingham Trent – 260 pts (Media Joint Hons) (IB 24 pts)

Plymouth – 260 pts (Media Arts) (IB 28 pts)

Sunderland – 260 pts (Mag Jrnl; Broad Jrnl; Fash Jrnl; Int Jrnl; Media Prod (Vid N Media); Media St (Comb); Media Cult Comm; News Jrnl; Spo Jrnl; Media Prod (TV Rad); Jrnl)

UCLan – 240–260 pts (Engl Lang Jrnl)

Ulster – BCC (Media St courses; Jrnl courses)

Winchester – 260–300 pts (Jrnl Psy; Media St Psy)

240 pts   **Arts London (CFash)** – 240 pts (Fash Journ (Prt/Broad))

Bolton – 240 pts (Film Media St)

Bradford – 240 pts (Media St courses)

Brighton – CCC 240 pts (Med St Sociol/Educ)

Canterbury Christ Church – 240 pts (Media Comm)

Chester – 240–280 pts (Media St) (IB 26 pts)

Coventry – 240–280 pts (Comm Cult Media) (IB 27 pts)

Creative Arts – 220–240 pts (Fash Jrnl)

Cumbria – 240 pts (Jrnl)

De Montfort – 240 pts (Graph Des Interact Media)

Edinburgh Napier – 240 pts (Jrnl)

Glyndŵr – 240 pts (Broad Jrnl Media Comms; Broad Jrnl Scrn St)

Kingston – 240–360 pts (Media Cult St; Media Tech)

Leeds Trinity (UC) – 240 pts (Engl Media)

London South Bank – 240 pts (Media Cult St; Mgt Media St; Prnt Onln Jrnl)

Northampton – 240–280 pts (Media St courses; Media Prod)

Portsmouth – 240–300 pts (Jrnl)

Ravensbourne – AA–CC (Edit Pst Prod) (IB 28 pts)

Robert Gordon – CCC (Jrnl; Media)

St Mary's Twickenham (UC) – 240 pts (Media Arts) (IB 28 pts)

Salford – 240 pts (Jrnl War St) (IB 31 pts)

Sheffield Hallam – 240 pts (Interact Media Animat)

Southampton Solent – 240 pts (Media; Cult Prod; Jrnl; Media Comms; Spo Jrnl; Jrnl Engl Media)

UCLan – 240–260 pts (Photo Jrnl)

West Scotland – CCC (Jrnl; Spo Jrnl)

Winchester – 240–300 pts (Jrnl) (IB 26–28 pts)

Wolverhampton – CCC (PR)

Worcester – 240–300 pts (Media Cult St)

220 pts   **Anglia Ruskin** – 220–260 pts (Media courses)

Bath Spa – 220–280 pts (Media Comms) (IB 24 pts)

Creative Arts – 220–240 pts (Spo Jrnl) (IB 24–30 pts)

Falmouth (UC) – 220 pts (Jrnl; Dig Media)

Kingston – 220–360 pts (Pol Jrnl)

UCP Marjon – 220 pts (Media St; Media Prod; Spo Media; Jrnl; Media Wrtg)

York St John – 220–260 pts (Media courses)

200 pts   **Bedfordshire** – 200 pts (Media Prod courses; Jrnl)

Buckingham – 200 pts (Comm Media Jrnl courses) (IB 24 pts)

Creative Arts – 200 pts (Arts Media) (IB 24–30 pts)

Hull (Coll) – 200 pts (Interact Media)

Leeds Met – 200 pts (Photo Journ) (IB 24 pts)

London Met – 200–240 pts (Mass Comms)

Middlesex – 200–300 pts (Jrnl Comms; Pub Jrnl Media)

For a quick reference offers calculator, fold out the inside back cover.

Newman (UC) – 200–240 pts (Psy Media Comm) (IB 24 pts)
Plymouth (CA) – 200 pts (Interd Art Des Media)
Portsmouth – 200–280 pts (Dig Media)
Salford – 200 pts (Des Dig Media)
Swansea Met – 200 pts (Multim; Interact Dig Media)
UEL – 200 pts (Media Crea Ind; Media St; Jrnl; Spo Jrnl)
West London – 200 pts (Broad; Media St; Mus Media)

180 pts **Farnborough (CT)** – 180–200 pts (Media Prod; Media Prod Mus)
Grimsby (IFHE) – 180 pts (Jrnl)
Manchester (Coll) – 180 pts (Actg Media)
Trinity Saint David – individual offers made after interview 180–300 pts (Media St courses)

160 pts **Abertay Dundee** – CC (Media Cult Soty)
Arts London – 160 pts (Jrnl; Media Cult St)
Arts London (CFash) – p/t 160 pts (Fash Media)
Peterborough (Univ Centre) – 160 pts (Media St)
South Essex (Coll) – 160 pts (Crea Writ Media)
UEL – 160 pts (Media Tech)
UHI – CC–AA (Gael Media St)
Wolverhampton – 160–220 pts (Media Cult St; Media Comm St; Broad Jrnl)

120 pts **Arts London** – 120 pts (Mag Pub)
Peterborough (Univ Centre) – 120 pts (Jrnl)
Wirral Met (Coll) – DD (Media St)

80 pts **London (Birk)** – p/t for under 21s (over 21s varies) (Hum Media St)

Alternative offers
See **Chapter 7** and **Appendix 1** for grades/UCAS Tariff points information for the International Baccalaureate, Scottish Highers/Advanced Highers, the Welsh Baccalaureate, the Irish Leaving Certificate, the Cambridge Pre-U Diploma, the Advanced Diploma and the Extended Project.

EXAMPLES OF FOUNDATION DEGREES IN THE SUBJECT FIELD

Bath; Bath Spa; Bedfordshire; Birmingham (UC); Blackpool and Fylde (Coll); Bolton; Bournemouth; Brighton; Bristol City (Coll); Bristol UWE; Bucks New; Cornwall (Coll); De Montfort; East Riding (Coll); Essex; Exeter (Coll); Falmouth (UC); Glyndŵr; Greenwich; Hertfordshire; Highbury Portsmouth (Coll); Hopwood Hall (Coll); Hull (Coll); Leeds Met; Liverpool (CmC); Llandrillo Cymru (Coll); Manchester (Coll); Neath Port Talbot (Coll); NEW (Coll); Newcastle (Coll); Northbrook (Coll); Norwich City (Coll); Nottingham New (Coll); Plymouth (CA); Sheffield (Coll); Somerset (CAT); South Cheshire (Coll); South Devon (Coll); South Essex (Coll); South Nottingham (Coll); South Tyneside (Coll); Stockport (Coll); Strathclyde; Suffolk (Univ Campus); Teesside; Truro (Coll); UCLan; Wigan and Leigh (Coll); York (Coll).

CHOOSING YOUR COURSE (SEE ALSO CH.1)

Some course features
Bangor The BA in Creative Studies enables students to pursue a variety of related subject areas including creative writing, film studies, theatre studies, media and journalism or to combine modules from these programmes. These subjects are also offered as separate degrees.
Bath Spa The Creative Media Practice course offers a choice of two options from interaction design, digital photography, music technology, media production for TV and radio, PR and marketing for publishing and scriptwriting for TV and radio. There is also a degree in Media Communication.
Birmingham The Modern Languages and European Studies BA focuses on culture, society and communication in Europe with some modules in media, culture and communication. The course involves the study of a modern language.
Birmingham City Media and Communication courses have specialisms in journalism, media photography, web and new media public relations, radio production and television and music industries. There is also a separate course in Television Technology and Production with a sandwich placement and Multimedia Technology.
Bradford The Media Studies course offers options in several subjects including web, computer games, 3D, animation, film and TV. Courses cover technical, social and cultural aspects.

Brunel A course is offered in Communications and Media Studies with the course focusing on the social aspects of the media and new communications and information technologies. A substantial amount of the course involves practical work. A rigorous and demanding course in Journalism is also offered.
Coventry A course in Media and Communications offers modules in film, television, photography, journalism, public relations and video. There are also courses in Media Production and Journalism.
Creative Arts Courses are offered in Journalism focusing on fashion, music and sport.

Universities and colleges teaching quality See www.qaa.ac.uk; http://unistats.direct.gov.uk.

Top research universities and colleges (RAE 2008) See **Communication Studies/Communication**.

Examples of sandwich degree courses Bournemouth; Bradford; Brighton; Brunel; De Montfort; Gloucestershire; Greenwich; Hertfordshire; Huddersfield; Kingston; Leeds Met; LJMU; Staffordshire; Surrey; Ulster; Worcester.

ADMISSIONS INFORMATION

Number of applicants per place (approx) Birmingham 10; Bournemouth (Interact Media Prod) 24, (Multim Jrnl) 30; Bradford 13; Bristol UWE 20; Canterbury Christ Church 23; Cardiff 11; Cardiff Met 3; Chichester 6; City 50; Creative Arts 3; Cumbria 4; De Montfort 11; Falmouth (UC) 4; Gloucestershire 25; Greenwich 12; Lincoln 4; London (Gold) 13; London (RH) 11; London South Bank 11; Newport 12; Northampton 4; Northumbria 14; Nottingham Trent 5; Plymouth City (Coll) 33; Portsmouth 5; Sheffield Hallam 56; South Essex (Coll) 10; Southampton Solent (Jrnl) 20, (Media Tech) 6; Strathclyde (Jrnl) 20; Swansea Met 5; Teesside 33; UCLan 33; UEL 27; West Scotland 6; Westminster 44; Winchester 7.

Advice to applicants and planning the UCAS personal statement Work experience or work shadowing is important. Contact local newspaper offices to meet journalists and to discuss their work. Contact local radio stations and advertising agencies, read newspapers (all types) and be able to describe the different approaches of newspapers. Watch TV coverage of news stories and the way in which the interviewer deals with politicians or members of the public. Give your opinions on the various forms of media. School magazine and/or any published work should be mentioned. A balance of academic and practical skills preferred. Creativity, problem-solving, cultural awareness, communication skills and commitment required. (International students: Fluency in written and spoken English required.) See also **Communication Studies/Communication**.

Misconceptions about this course Birmingham City That Media courses are soft options: they are not! **Cardiff Met** Some applicants believe that the course will automatically lead to a job in the media: it won't. This depends on the student developing other employment skills and experience. **Cumbria** This is not a Media Studies course: it is a highly practical media production course. **Lincoln** (Media Prod) BTEC applicants may think that this is a technology-based course.

Selection interviews Yes Anglia Ruskin, Birmingham City, Bournemouth, Brunel, Creative Arts, Glamorgan, Huddersfield, LJMU, London (Gold), London (RH), London South Bank, Portsmouth, Sheffield Hallam, Solihull (Coll), South Essex (Coll), Staffordshire, Swansea Met, UCP Marjon, UEA, West London (group interview), York; **Some** Abertay Dundee, Bath Spa, Cardiff, Cardiff Met, City, Nottingham Trent, Salford, Sunderland, Wolverhampton; **No** Chichester, Nottingham.

Interview advice and questions Past questions include: Which newspapers do you read? Discuss the main differences between the national daily newspapers. Which radio programmes do you listen to each day? Which television programmes do you watch? Should the BBC broadcast advertisements? What do you think are the reasons for the popularity of *EastEnders*? Film or video work, if required, should be edited to a running time of 15 minutes unless otherwise stated. See also **Chapter 6**.
Cardiff Met What is your favourite area in respect of popular culture? Are you considering taking up the work placement module? If so where would you plan to go? **Cumbria** Role of journalism in society. What is today's main news story? Who is Rupert Murdoch? **Lincoln** Give a written or verbal critique of a media product.

Reasons for rejection (non-academic) No clear commitment (to Broadcast Journalism) plus no evidence of experience (now proving to be essential). Mistaken expectations of the nature of the course. Can't write and doesn't work well in groups. Too specific and narrow areas of media interest, for example, video or scriptwriting. Lack of knowledge of current affairs. **Cardiff Met** Lack of experience in the field. Application arrived too late. **City** Inadequate English language.

AFTER-RESULTS ADVICE
Offers to applicants repeating A-levels Same Abertay Dundee, Birmingham City, Cardiff, Cardiff Met, Chester, Chichester, City, De Montfort, Huddersfield, Lincoln, Loughborough, Manchester Met, Nottingham Trent, St Mary's Twickenham (UC), Salford, South Essex (Coll), Staffordshire, Sunderland, Winchester, Wolverhampton.

GRADUATE DESTINATIONS AND EMPLOYMENT (2009/10 HESA)
Graduates surveyed 7165 **Employed** 3295 **In voluntary employment** 140 **In further study** 815 **Assumed unemployed** 720

Career note See **Film, Radio, Video and TV Studies**.

OTHER DEGREE SUBJECTS FOR CONSIDERATION
Advertising; Communication; English; Film, Radio, Video and TV Studies; Journalism; Photography; Public Relations.

MEDICINE

(including **Medical Sciences**; see also **Biological Sciences, Human Sciences/Human Biosciences**)

Medicine is a highly popular choice of degree subject and career. All courses listed below include the same areas of study and training and all lead to a qualification and career in medicine.

Medical schools aim to produce doctors who are clinically competent, who are able to see patients as people and have a holistic and ethical approach (including the ability to understand and manage each patient's case in a family and social context as well as in hospital), who treat patients and colleagues with respect, dignity and sensitivity, are skilled at teamwork and are prepared for continual learning. These aims in several ways reflect the qualities which selectors seek when interviewing applicants. In all cases, close attention will be paid to the confidential report on the UCAS application to judge the applicant's personality, communication skills, academic potential and commitment to a medical career. Methods of teaching may vary slightly, depending on the medical school. To achieve these aims, some medical schools adopt the system of self-directed learning (SDL) in which objectives are set to assess students' progress, and problem-based learning (PBL) which helps students to develop critical thinking and clinical problem-solving skills.

Whilst there is a core curriculum of knowledge, the first three years integrate scientific and clinical experience, and there are fewer formal lectures than before, with more group and individual work. For outstanding students without science A-levels, some pre-medical courses are available. Thereafter for all, a period of pre-clinical studies leads on to clinical studies. Most medical schools also offer an extra year of study, usually in the middle of the medical degree, to enable students to research a scientific subject leading to an 'intercalated' BSc degree. Additionally, elective periods abroad in the final year can sometimes be taken.

Home and EU-funded students applying for entry to Medicine are required by many universities to sit either the UKCAT or BMAT tests before applying. See **Your target offers and examples of courses provided by each institution** below, **Chapter 5** and **Chapter 6** for further information.

Applicants for places in Medicine may select only **four** universities or medical schools.

Useful websites www.scicentral.com; www.ipem.ac.uk; www.bmj.com; www.admissionstests. cambridgeassessment.org.uk; www.gmc-uk.org; www.nhscareers.nhs.uk.

NB The points totals shown to the left of the institutions are for ease of reference only. It must not be assumed that Tariff points are always used by institutions or that they can be substituted for an offer in grades. The level of an offer is not necessarily indicative of the quality of a course.

COURSE OFFERS INFORMATION

Subject requirements/preferences GCSE In all cases a good spread of science and non-science subjects will be expected at high grades.

Aberdeen English, mathematics, biology, physics or dual award science. Combinations of AB grades, especially in sciences.

Birmingham Seven GCSEs at A* including chemistry, English language and mathematics normally at grade A. Dual science award grade A acceptable as an alternative to physics and biology.

Brighton and Sussex (MS) Mathematics and English at grade B, biology and chemistry.

Bristol Five A/A* grades to include mathematics, English and two sciences.

Cambridge Mathematics, physics, chemistry or dual science award.

Cardiff English or Welsh at grade B, mathematics at grade B or above, grades AA in dual science or AAA in three sciences.

Dundee Chemistry and biology or human biology essential.

Durham See **Newcastle**.

Edinburgh English, mathematics, biology, chemistry or dual science award at grade B or higher.

Glasgow English, chemistry, biology (preferred), mathematics and physics.

Hull York (MS) Six subjects at grades A*–C: English and mathematics at grade B or higher plus chemistry and biology.

Imperial London Chemistry, biology, physics (or dual science award) plus mathematics and English. At least three subjects are required at grade A, and two subjects at grade B.

Keele Chemistry, physics, biology (dual science award acceptable, grades BB minimum), English language and mathematics at grade B minimum. A broad spread of subjects is expected with a minimum of four at grade A.

Lancaster See **Liverpool**.

Leeds Six subjects at grade B minimum including English, mathematics, chemistry and biology or dual science award.

Leicester English language and sciences (including chemistry) or dual science award.

Liverpool Nine subjects at grades A–C, including dual science (or biology, chemistry and physics), English language and mathematics at grade B minimum.

London (King's) Grade B (minimum) in chemistry, biology and physics (or dual science award), English and mathematics.

London (QM) Six subjects at AB minimum grades including English, mathematics and science subjects.

London (St George's) Six subjects at AB minimum grades including English, mathematics and science subjects.

London (UCL) English and mathematics at grade B minimum.

Manchester Seven subjects with five at grades A/A*. Chemistry, biology and physics required at either AS or GCSE grade C minimum, with English and mathematics at grade B minimum.

Newcastle At least five subjects with grades AAAAB to include English, mathematics and either biology, chemistry, physics or dual science award.

Nottingham Six subjects at grade A/A* to include biology, chemistry and physics or dual science award. (Grade A AS physics can compensate for a B at GCSE.)

Oxford Chemistry, mathematics, biology and physics or dual science award acceptable.

Queen's Belfast Chemistry, biology, mathematics and either physics or dual science award.

St Andrews Chemistry, biology, mathematics and physics. If mathematics and biology are not offered at A2 then each must have been passed at grade B or higher. English is required at grade B or higher.

Check **Chapter 4** when choosing your university and **Chapter 7** on how to read the subject tables.

Sheffield At least six subjects at grade A. English, mathematics, chemistry and a science required.

Southampton Seven subjects at grade B or above including English, mathematics and dual science award or equivalent. (Widening Access course BM6) Five GCSEs at grade C including English, mathematics and dual science award or equivalent. (Students join the five-year programme on completion of Year Zero.)

UEA Six GCSE subjects at grade A including science, mathematics and English.

AL See **Your target offers and examples of courses provided by each institution** below. Candidates applying for A104 courses at **Bristol**, **Cardiff**, **Dundee**, **East Anglia**, **Edinburgh**, **London (King's)**, **Manchester**, **Sheffield** and **Southampton** are not accepted if they are offering more than one laboratory-based subject (check with university). **Cambridge (Emmanuel)** AEA in one science subject when only two are taken may be required. **London (UCL)** Mathematics and further mathematics will not both be counted towards three AL subjects. **Other requirements:** See **Health Requirements** below; CRB clearance is also required.

NB Home and EU-funded students applying for entry to Medicine are required by many universities to sit either the UKCAT or BMAT tests before applying. See Your target offers and examples of courses provided by each institution below, Chapter 6 and Chapter 5 for further information.

Your target offers and examples of courses provided by each institution

420 pts **Queen's Belfast** – AAAa incl AL chem+sci/maths subj; AS biol b min (Med 5 yrs) (IB 37 pts HL 666)

410 pts **Edinburgh** – AAAb incl AL chem +1 from maths/phys/biol; AS biol min (Med 5/6 yrs) (IB 37 pts HL 766)

Hull York (MS) – AAAb incl chem biol (Med) (IB 36 pts HL 665)

Imperial London – AAAb incl AL biol/chem+sci/maths (Med) (HL 655)

Lancaster – application through Liverpool University. See **Admissions tutor's advice** below AAAb incl AL/AS chem+biol 410 pts (Med Srgy) (IB 36 pts)

Liverpool – AAAb incl chem biol 410 pts (Med 6 yrs) (IB 36 pts HL 676)

London (King's) – AAAb (Med 5 yrs) (IB 38 pts HL 666 incl chem biol)

London (QM) – AAAb incl AS chem/biol b +1 of these to A2 +1 other sci (Med 5 yrs) (IB 36 pts HL 665)

London (St George's) – AAAb–BBCb incl chem+biol (Med 5 yrs) (HL 665)

UEA – AAAb–AABb incl AL biol A (Med 5 yrs) (IB 34 pts HL 666)

380 pts **Birmingham** – A*AA–AAA incl AL chem +1 from biol/maths/phys; AS biol b if not offered at AL: hum biol acceptable 360–380 pts (Med 5 yrs) (IB 36 pts)

Cambridge – A*AA incl AL biol/chem/maths/phys; chem reqd at least at AS; some colleges may require 3 sci ALs (Med 6 yrs) (IB 40–42 pts)

Exeter – A*AA–AAA (Med) (IB 38–36 pts)

London (UCL) – contact admissions tutor AAAe incl chem+biol (Med 6 yrs)

Oxford – A*AA incl chem +1 from biol/phys/maths (Med 6 yrs) (IB 39 pts)

Plymouth – A*AA–AAA (Med 5 yrs) (IB 36 pts)

360 pts **Aberdeen** – AAA chem +1 from biol/maths/phys +1 other 360 pts (Med 5 yrs) (IB 36 pts HL 666)

Brighton and Sussex (MS) – A*AB–AAA (incl AS biol/chem) +AL 360 pts (Med 5 yrs) (IB 37 pts HL 17 pts)

Bristol – AAA–A*AB (Med 5 yrs) (IB 37 pts)

Cardiff – AAA 360 pts (Med 6 yrs Fdn course)

Dundee – AAA incl chem + any sci + any subj at grade A (Med 5 yrs) (IB 37 pts HL 766)

Durham – offered through a partnership between Newcastle and Durham Universities (only phase I of II available at Durham) AAA incl AL chem/biol +pref 1 non-sci at AL/AS (Med 5 yrs) (IB 37 pts HL 6 chem)

Glasgow – AAA incl AL chem +1 from maths/phys/bio, 4AS in yr 12 (Med 5 yrs) (IB 36 pts)

Leeds – AAA incl chem biol (Med 5 yrs) (IB 36 pts HL 6 chem)

Leicester – AAA 3AL **or** 340–400 pts (incl 4AS in yr 12 incl A chem, biol at AL/AS) (Med 5 yrs) (IB 36 pts HL 6 chem biol)

London (UCL) – AAA–AAB incl biol (Bioproc N Med (Sci Eng)) (IB 36–38 pts)

Manchester – AAA incl AL chem +1 from biol/hum biol/phys/maths +1 other subj (Med 5 yrs) (IB 37 pts)

Newcastle – offered through a partnership between Newcastle and Durham Universities AAA incl AL chem/biol +pref 1 non-sci at AL/AS (Med Srgy 5 yrs) (IB 38 pts HL 6 chem)

Nottingham – AAA incl chem biol (Med 5 yrs) (IB 36 pts)

St Andrews – AAA incl chem+biol/maths/phys 360 pts (Med 5/6 yrs) (IB 37 pts HL 766)

Sheffield – AAA incl chem+sci (Med) (IB 37 pts)

Southampton – AAA incl chem (Med 5 yrs) (IB 36 pts HL 18 pts)

340 pts **Bristol** – AAB incl chem (Cncr Biol Immun) (IB 35 pts HL 665)

Keele – AAB incl AL chem+biol +1 from maths/phys (Medicine) (IB 34 pts)

Manchester – AAB 340 pts (Med 6 yrs) (IB 35 pts)

Surrey – AAB (Medcnl Chem) (IB 35 pts)

320 pts **Bristol** – ABB incl chem (Cell Mol Med) (IB 35 pts)

300 pts **Bradford** – 300 pts (Clin Sci Med)

UEA – BBB (Med Fdn course) (IB 31 pts)

280 pts **London (King's)** – AAA–BBC 280–360 pts (Med Ext Prog 6 yrs) (IB 32 pts)

Manchester Met – 280 pts (Medcnl Biol Chem) (IB 27 pts)

260 pts **Bradford** – 260 pts (Med Cell Biol)

Portsmouth – 260 pts (Biomed Sci)

Sheffield Hallam – 260 pts incl biol/chem (Foren Sci)

240 pts **Nottingham** – CCC 240 pts (Med Fdn Yr)

220 pts **London (St George's)** – check with admissions tutor 220 pts (Fdn Med)

West London – CCD (incl C min chem) (Hum Sci (Pre-Med option))

Westminster – CCD (Hum Med Sci)

Medicine Foundation courses These are designed for students who have demonstrated high academic potential but who have taken non-science subjects or a combination including no more than one of biology, chemistry and physics.

Alternative offers
See **Chapter 7** and **Appendix 1** for grades/UCAS Tariff points information for the International Baccalaureate, Scottish Highers/Advanced Highers, the Welsh Baccalaureate, the Irish Leaving Certificate, the Cambridge Pre-U Diploma, the Advanced Diploma and the Extended Project.

CHOOSING YOUR COURSE (SEE ALSO CH.1)
Some course features
NB See **Chapter 6** for details of admissions tests to be taken **before** application.

Aberdeen Phase 1 covers the fundamentals of medical sciences followed in Phase 2 by the principles of clinical medicine. Clinical Teaching and Patient contact from Year 1. An intercalated BSc Medical Sciences degree is offered with placements across the Highlands and Islands.

Bradford (Clin Sci (Med)) Successful completion of the first year in Clinical Sciences will allow 20 students to progress to Year 2 at the Leeds Medical School, subject to grades achieved and the interview.

Brighton Brighton and Sussex Medical School students are members of both universities. The course offers an integrated programme of academic and clinical experience with students working with patients from the first term. From Year 3, students are based at the Royal Sussex County Hospital in Brighton. Experience of Medical Practice in different medical settings in the UK or abroad takes place in Year 4.

Keele The five year course has five themes, which run through the course: (a) scientific basis of medicine, (b) clinical communication, (c) individual communication and population health, (d) quality and efficiency in healthcare and (e) ethics, personal and professional development. There is also a Health Foundation year.

London (St George's) The MBBS has been designed to enhance the integration between scientific and clinical disciplines and to develop self-directed learning skills.

Check **Chapter 4** when choosing your university and **Chapter 7** on how to read the subject tables.

Newcastle Phase 1 (two years) of the medical course is taken either at Newcastle or Stockton. Students come into contact with patients at the start of their course, being attached to a GP and accompanying them on some of their rounds. Clinical applications are emphasised throughout the course alongside basic sciences. Students not taking science subjects may apply for the pre-medical course. See also **Durham**.

Oxford The course in Medicine lasts six years. The pre-clinical course lasts three years. This is followed by the clinical course, which is based in the John Radcliffe Hospital. A significant part of this course is examined by continuous assessment.

St Andrews Medical Sciences is a three-year degree course and leads to the ordinary degree of BSc in three years or to an honours degree in four years. Studies cover molecular biochemistry, human anatomy and human physiology. Half of graduates progress to a clinical place at Manchester University Medical School to follow the three-year clinical course, the remainder have a place at one of the four medical schools in Scotland, almost a third at Edinburgh.

Universities and colleges teaching quality See www.qaa.ac.uk; http://unistats.direct.gov.uk.

Top research universities and colleges (RAE 2008) (Pre-clinical and Human Biological Sciences) Oxford; London (UCL); Manchester; London (QM); London (King's); Bristol; Liverpool; Sussex. (Hospital-based Clinical subjects) Edinburgh; Cambridge; London (UCL); Oxford; Imperial London; London (King's); Birmingham; London (QM); Aberdeen; Manchester; Newcastle; Southampton; Bristol.

ADMISSIONS INFORMATION

Number of applicants per place (approx) Bristol (Med) 14, (Pre-Med) 30; Peninsula (MS) 11.

Numbers of applicants (a UK b EU (non-UK) c non-EU d mature) Aberdeen **a**1513 for 162 places **b**1513 for 162 places **c**270 for 13 places (preference given to applicants from countries unable to provide a medical training); Birmingham **a**5 **b**25, Grad entry 12; Brighton and Sussex (MS) **a**10 **c**10; Cambridge **a**5; Cardiff **a**20 (6 yr course) **c**22 (preference given to applicants from countries not providing medical training); Dundee **a**7, (Pre-Med yr) 11; Edinburgh **a**11 (international applicants not normally called for interview); Glasgow **a**6 **c**20; Hull York (MS) **a**130 **b**130 **c**10; Imperial London **a**7 **c**25; Leeds **a**2156 **b**97 **c**352 **d**488; Leicester **a**10; Liverpool **a**8; London (King's) **a**311 **b**311 **c**25; London (QM) **a**8 **c**20; London (St George's) **a**3200 **b**250 **c**260 **d**1950; Manchester **a**7 **c**10; Newcastle **a**10, (Pre-Med yr) 27 **c**14; Nottingham **a**9 **c**15; Oxford **a**26% success rate **c**10; Queen's Belfast **a**4 **c**(a small number of places are allocated); St Andrews **a**8; Sheffield **a**17 (av 30 applicants per place for 6 yr courses); UEA **a**7; London (UCL) **c**24.

Admissions tutors' advice Policies adopted by all medical schools are very similar. However, a brief outline of the information provided by admissions tutors is given below. Further information should be obtained direct from institutions. Applicants wishing to contact medical schools should do so either by letter or by telephone and not by email.

Aberdeen Applicants must take the UKCAT in the year of application. This also applies to those students seeking deferred entry and those who are reapplying. In the past, students with scores between 513 and 776 have been called for interview. Applicants to show a knowledge of the core qualities required by doctors and evidence of teamwork and non-academic pursuits. Overseas applicants may be interviewed abroad. Interviews last about 15 minutes. Most offers made in March. Points equivalent results not accepted. Re-sits not normally accepted. International students English language entry requirement (or equivalent): IELTS 7.0. Minimum age on entry 17 years 5 months. Clinical teaching and patient contact in Year 2.

Birmingham Non-academic interests and extra-curricular activities noted in addition to academic factors. General studies not accepted. Interviews last about 15 minutes with three interviewers: a GP, a surgeon and a student. Approximately 1000 called for interview; 10% take a year off which does not jeopardise the chances of an offer but candidates must be available for interview. Re-sit candidates who failed by a small margin are only considered in exceptional circumstances. Transfers of undergraduates from other medical schools not considered. International applicants must show a good standard of written and spoken English.

Check **Chapter 4** when choosing your university and **Chapter 7** on how to read the subject tables.

Brighton and Sussex (MS) An average UKCAT score is considered an advantage, a lower score is not regarded as a disadvantage. General studies not accepted. No offers made without an interview. Interviews last about 15 minutes with three selectors. Students are members of both universities. Years 3–5 take place in the Medical Education Centre at the Royal Sussex Hospital in Brighton. Clinical experience from Year 1.

Bristol No places are offered without an interview. The top 10% of applicants are called for an interview lasting 15 minutes; the remainder grouped into three categories: 'high reserve', 'hold' and 'unsuccessful' – some from the first two categories will be interviewed. Full details of the interview process are offered on the Bristol website. The Widening Participation panel considers appropriate candidates, an additional 50 of whom will be interviewed. Criteria for selection: realistic and academic interest in medicine, commitment to helping others, wide range of interests, contribution to school/college activities, personal achievements. Interview criteria: reasons for wanting to study Medicine, awareness of current developments, communication skills, self-confidence, enthusiasm and determination to study, ability to cope with stress, awareness of the content of the course and career. General studies and critical thinking not acceptable. Subject content overlap (eg Biology/PE/Sports Science) not allowed. Deferred entry welcomed (except for A101 (Graduate Entry)) but applicants must be available for interview. Points equivalent results not accepted. International students English language requirement (or equivalent): IELTS 7.5.

Cambridge Most applicants for Medicine at Cambridge have at least three science/mathematics A-levels and some Colleges require this or ask for particular A-level subject(s).) Normally two interviews, of 20 minutes each. Films of interviews on www.cam.ac.uk/interviews/. Gap Year acceptable but for positive reasons. Clinical studies from Year 4; 50% of students continue at the Cambridge Clinical School (Addenbrooke's Hospital).

Cardiff Great emphasis placed on evidence of a caring nature and exposure to hospital/health environments. Applicant's comment: 'Two interviewers and a 15-minute interview. Mainly questions on "Why Medicine?" Very helpful students'. Points-equivalent results not accepted. Clinical studies from Year 1.

Dundee Preference given to candidates who achieve the right grades at the first sitting. A system of mini interviews has been introduced which enable students separate opportunities to sell themselves. Deferred entry acceptable. Clinical attachments in Year 4.

Durham (See also **Newcastle**) The medical course is offered in partnership with Newcastle University. Study is at Queen's Campus, Stockton. Preference given to applicants with relevant work experience in caring environment, hospital, voluntary capacity or through previous employment. Particular interest in recruiting local students, either school leavers or mature students. Interviews at Stockton with two selectors; may include a written personal qualities assessment test (PQA). Graduate applicants with a 2.2 degree are not accepted even if they possess a Masters degree or a PhD. Applicants from non-EU countries must apply to Newcastle where there is a quota of places for overseas students. Clinical contact begins in Year 1.

Edinburgh All examination grades must be achieved at the first sitting; only in extenuating circumstances will re-sits be considered. Equal weighting given to academic and non-academic criteria. Non-academic criteria score based on personal qualities and skills, evidence of career exploration prior to application, breadth and level of non-academic achievements and interests. Work experience and work shadowing viewed positively but the admissions panel recognise that not all applicants have equal opportunities to gain such experience. Most school-leaving applicants are not interviewed. Graduate and mature applicants may be interviewed; 202 places available, one in seven receive an offer. International applicants not normally called for interview. Clinical experience from Year 1.

Glasgow General studies is not accepted as a third A-level. Formal work experience is desirable. An interest in caring for others is expected which can be demonstrated through voluntary or paid work in a community setting. Applicants may be assessed against some or all of the following criteria: Commitment to Medicine, Understanding of the core qualities of a Doctor, Team Work/Other interests and Knowledge of the Glasgow Curriculum.

Hull York (MS) Students apply to HYMS not to either the University of Hull or York. Students allocated places at Hull or York by ballot for Years 1 and 2. Non-EU applicants English language (or equivalent requirement) IELTS 7.5 with at least 7 in each component. Transfers from other medical schools not accepted. Disabilities listed on UCAS application do not affect the assessment of the application; 550 called for interview, 300 offered places. Interviews of 20 minutes with two people. Article to be read beforehand, with a question to follow. Formally structured interviews exploring academic ability, motivation, understanding of healthcare issues, communication skills, conscientiousness, empathy, tolerance and maturity. Questions are drawn from a bank of possible topics (sample questions available online prior to interview). A-level re-sits not usually accepted. Feedback to unsuccessful candidates after February. Clinical placements from Year 1.

Imperial London Fifteen-minute interviews with panel of four or five selectors. Not aimed at being an intimidating experience – an evaluation of motivation, capacity to deal with stress, evidence of working as a leader and team member, ability to multitask, likely contribution to university life, communication skills and maturity. Admissions tutor's comment: 'We look for resourceful men and women with wide interests and accomplishments, a practical concern for others and for those who will make a contribution to the life of the school and hospital.' Results within two weeks. Re-sit candidates must have applied to Imperial School of Medicine previously, have achieved at least CCC and have predictions of AAA in the winter re-sit examinations and have extenuating circumstances to explain previous failure in the referee's statement. Candidates may also write directly to the School. Clinical contact in Year 1.

Keele Keele is no longer in partnership with the Manchester Medical School. All applications are now submitted to Keele. There are 130 places available, 10 for international students. There are three entry routes for Medicine: there is a Health Foundation Year (A104) for home and international applicants without the science A-levels required for the five-year course (chemistry or biology and one subject from chemistry, biology, mathematics or physics) and with grades of AAB not including chemistry beyond GCSE) although A-level biology is acceptable with non-science A-levels. Four GCSEs are also required at grades A/A* including English and mathematics at grade C or above. Successful completion of this course gives automatic entry to Year 1 of the five-year Medicine degree; 10 places are available on the graduate entry course for home/EU applicants who enter directly into Module 2 of the five-year course. Graduates must offer a 2.1 honours degree or better in a biomedically-related science for entry to this course although applicants with other backgrounds can be successful with appropriate prior study and preparation for GAMSAT. Resit candidates must achieve AAA. English requirement for international applicants is IELTS 7.0.

Lancaster The University delivers the curriculum of the Medical School of Liverpool University, with the academic base at Lancaster University and clinical placements in Lancashire and Cumbria. To apply, use Liverpool University's UCAS code and see www.liv.ac.uk/sme for course and application information.

Leeds Admissions tutors' comment: 'Consider your motivation carefully – we do!' Good verbal, non-verbal and presentational skills required. Candidates should: (i) be able to report on some direct experience of what a career in medicine is about; (ii) show evidence of social activities on a regular basis (eg, part-time employment, organised community experiences); (iii) show evidence of positions of responsibility and interests outside medical and school activities. Gap years encouraged but candidates must be available for interview, 20% of all applicants interviewed. Points equivalent results not accepted. International students English language requirement (or equivalent): IELTS 7.5. Re-applications accepted from students who have achieved the right grades. Re-sits only considered in exceptional circumstances and with good supporting evidence; offer AAA. Transfers from other medical schools not encouraged. Clinical practice begins in Year 4.

Leicester Interview lasts 20 minutes with two selectors (one doctor and one final-year medical student; both have had interview training). Interview not an academic test. Selectors each score independently on motivation, communication skills and suitability for a career in medicine. Gap years acceptable. Re-sits considered only in exceptional circumstances; offer AAA. Transfers from other medical schools not accepted. Clinical work commences in Year 1.

Liverpool In addition to the 268 Home/EU places that are available on the A100 Liverpool medical programme, 50 medical places are currently offered at Lancaster University. Students follow the

Liverpool curriculum and graduate with a Liverpool degree. Applications are made to Liverpool University (Code L41, course code A105). Evidence of healthcare insight and awareness is necessary. Applicants wishing to take a Gap Year may be considered but applicants must be available for interview. The Liverpool A100 medical programme has usually 24 places available for international students. No international places are available on the Lancaster A105 programme. Under-qualified international students may be able to apply to Liverpool International College prior to placing an application for the Liverpool A100 medical programme. Applicants must meet minimum academic criteria and applications for the medical programme are placed via UCAS in the normal manner. For international students certain minimum language requirements for the course may exist (IELTS of no less than 7.0 in each component).

London (King's) Personal statement a significant factor in selection. Emphasis placed on appreciation of academic, physical and emotional demands of the course, commitment, evidence of working in a caring environment, communication skills and interaction with the general public. Approximately 30% of applicants are called for interview. Clinical contact in Year 1.

London (QM) Personal statement a significant factor in selection. 'You are expected to write your own, with an honest reflection of your strengths and interests and you will be closely questioned on this statement at interview. We don't want people who are simply good at science. High grades are no guarantee of a place.' For interview, applicants are ranked by their UKCAT score – no predetermined scores. Interview of 15–20 minutes. Re-sits only considered in exceptional cases; offer AAAb. Clinical experience from Year 1.

London (St George's) Applicants must be taking A-level chemistry and biology (or one to A-level and the other to AS-level). You will be required to complete your A-levels within two years of study and the standard offer is AAA and a b in a distinct AS-level. Applicants must have an average grade of A across their top 8 GCSEs including English language, maths and double award or the single sciences. Applicants are also required to take the UKCAT test in the year of application. Applicants who meet our A-level and GCSE requirements and achieve our required overall and section scores in UKCAT will be offered an interview. All offers are made post-interview. Applicants are expected to have relevant work experience which is assessed at interview. The English language requirement for international students is IELTS 7.0 with no section less than 6.5. Deferred entry welcome. Medicine (six years, including Foundation year) is for mature non-graduate students only. Medicine (four years, Graduate stream) is for graduates with a 2.2 Hons degree in any discipline. Graduates are not eligible for the five year Medicine programme. UKAT selection and overall scores for entry will be introduced for the five year Medicine programme for 2012 onwards.

London (UCL) Three selectors interview applicants, each interview lasting 15–20 minutes; 30% of applicants interviewed. Qualities sought include motivation, awareness of scientific and medical issues, ability to express and defend opinions, maturity and individual strengths. Deferred entry for good reason is acceptable. Repeat applications only considered if candidate has previously received and held a firm offer from Royal Free or University College Medical School. Minimum age of entry 18 years. Transfers from other medical schools not accepted. International students may take the University Preparation Certificate for Science and Engineering (UPCSE) which is the minimum entry requirement for entry to Medicine. Clinical attachments start in Year 3.

Manchester Minimum age of entry 17 years; 341 places. Interviews with three selectors last about 15 minutes. Mitigating circumstances regarding the health or disposition of the candidate should appear on the referee's report. If you feel unwell before the interview inform the admissions tutor and the interview will be re-scheduled; pleas of infirmity cannot be accepted after the interview! Candidates should be aware of the advantages and disadvantages of problem-based learning and opinions may be asked. Ethical questions may be raised. Decisions will be made by the end of March. Re-sit offers only made to applicants who received an offer after interview the previous year and who marginally failed to achieve the required grades; increasingly such offers are only made in the light of extenuating circumstances. Second-time applicants should include their previous UCAS number on their statement. Clinical attachments from Year 3.

Newcastle (See also **Durham**) 225 places at Newcastle; 102 places at Durham. Applicants' comments (Durham): 'Two interviewers and a 25 minute interview. Very relaxed interview. Stockton campus

A Career in Medicine

Duff Miller College has been specialising in preparing students for entry to Medical and Dental schools for the past fifty years. Our preparation for these competitive fields includes a range of work experience, guest speakers, mock interviews, coupled with the highest standards of academic achievement.

We offer one and two year A Level courses as well as a confidence building short retake programme for those who just missed the grade first time. We also offer specialist Easter programmes tailored for those applying for Medicine and Dentistry.

Specialist training courses include: BMAT training, UKCAT training and medical school interview training.

Duff MILLER
Established 1952

45 Medical/Dental Placements (2010-2011)

020 7225 0577

59 QUEEN'S GATE, KENSINGTON, LONDON SW7 5JP

www.duffmiller.com   email: enqs@duffmiller.com

Check **Chapter 4** when choosing your university and **Chapter 7** on how to read the subject tables.

small. Good community spirit but some way from Durham'; (Newcastle): 'I had an interview with two selectors who had a gentle, helpful manner. I didn't feel under pressure but felt stretched'. Retakes not considered except in special circumstances. Deferred entry accepted. Consideration given to candidates who have overcome significant disadvantages (eg caring for parents with ill health). Clinical experience from Year 3.

Nottingham Critical thinking and general studies not acceptable. Candidates requesting deferred entry are expected to undertake a constructive year. No offers are made without an interview. Candidates receive preliminary online questionnaire to be completed. Interviews are 15 minutes with two selectors. Re-sit applicants who have previously applied will be reconsidered but only in extenuating circumstances. Deferred entry acceptable. International students English language requirement (or equivalent): IELTS 7.5 (with no less than 7.0 in each element). No transfers accepted from other medical schools. Clinical experience from Year 1. Applicant's comments: 'I had one interview. There were two interviewers: the first asked me questions based on my personal statement, the second asked no scientific questions, focusing on the problems of the NHS and asking how I would deal with certain problems. He finally asked me to convince him why he should offer me a place.'

Oxford Critical thinking and general studies are not acceptable. Biology is recommended at AS-level. 425 applicants called for interview on the basis of academic performance, test score and information on the application form. Ratio of interviewees to places approximately 2.5 to 1. No student admitted without an interview. All colleges use a common set of selection criteria. Candidate's comment (Lincoln College): 'Two interviewers and two interviews. Questions covered my hobbies and social life, and scientific topics to test my logical train of thought. A great university, but it's not the be-all and end-all if you don't get in.' Clinical experience commences in Year 4.

Queen's Belfast Majority of applicants are school-leavers; 95% from Northern Ireland. When considering applicants' GCSE performance, the best nine subjects will be scored on the basis of 4 points for an A* and 3 points for an A. Points will also be given or deducted on each UKCAT paper. Offers for resitting applicants will be restricted. These applicants will have been expected to have missed their offer by one grade. A proportion of candidates will be called for interview. Interviews last about 15 minutes. A small number of places are allocated to non-EU applicants. Number of places restricted for re-sit applicants who have narrowly missed an offer at Queen's. Clinical experience from Year 1.

St Andrews Medical Science students take full three-year programme leading to BSc (Hons), followed by clinical studies at Manchester Medical School or one of their partner Medical Schools in Scotland. Interviews last about 20 minutes with two or three selectors. Special attention given to international students and those who achieve qualifications at more than one sitting. As far as possible the interview panel will reflect the gender and ethnic distribution of candidates for interview.

Sheffield Applications processed between October and end of March. Candidates may send additional information concerning extenuating circumstances or health problems via the University's Disrupted Studies form which can be found at: www.shef.ac.uk/undergraduate/apply/applying/disrupted. Interviews last 20 minutes with up to three selectors. A2 resits are not accepted. Gap Year acceptable; medicine-related work very helpful. Clinical experience from Year 1. For more information, please see: www.shef.ac.uk/medicine/prospective_ug.

Southampton Only mature, non-graduate applicants are selected for interview. All applicants should show in their UCAS personal statement and reference that they are (i) self-motivated and have initiative, (ii) literate and articulate, (iii) able to interact successfully with others, (iv) that they have learnt from their experiences with people in health and social care settings. Deferred entry accepted. Candidates who wish to change their year of entry should submit requests before mid-March. Patient contact from Year 1.

UEA Criteria include academic requirements, capacity to cope with self-directed learning, teamwork, responsibility, motivation. Interview regarded as the acid test; seven stations are used for the interviews, candidates visit each station for one question with six minutes at each station. Two scenario questions (see www.med.uea.ac.uk/mbbs/mbbs application). English entry requirement IELTS 7.5. Clinical experience from Year 1.

Warwick Graduate entry only to Medicine.

Advice to applicants and planning the UCAS personal statement (See also **Admissions tutors'**
advice) Nearly all universities now require either the UKCAT or BMAT entry tests to be taken before
applying for Medicine. Check websites (www.ukcat.ac.uk; www.bmat.org.uk) for details of test dates
and test centres and with universities for their requirements. It is essential that you check for the
latest information before applying and that you give yourself plenty of time to make arrangements
for sitting these tests (see also **Chapter 6**).

Admissions tutors look for certain personal qualities (see **Admissions tutors' advice**) and these will
emerge in your personal statement, at the interview and on your school or college reference. There
should be evidence of scientific interest, commitment, enthusiasm, determination, stability, self-
motivation, ability to organise your own work, interest in the welfare of others, communication skills,
modesty (arrogance and over-confidence could lead to rejection!), breadth of interest, leadership
skills, stamina, good physical and mental health.

Some kind of first-hand experience in a medical setting is almost obligatory for those applying for
Medicine (see also under **Admissions tutors' advice**). Depending on your personal contacts in the
medical profession, this could include observing operations (for example, orthopaedic surgery),
working in hospitals and discussing the career with your GP. Remember that your friends and
relatives may have medical conditions that they would be willing to discuss with you – and all this
will contribute to your knowledge and show that you are informed and interested. Read medical and
scientific magazines and keep up-to-date with important current issues – AIDS, swine 'flu, assisted
dying, abortion. Community work, clubs, societies, school and social activities should be mentioned.
Show that you have an understanding of the role of health professionals in society and the social
factors that influence health and disease. And finally, a comment from one admissions tutor 'Don't
rush around doing things just for your CV. If you are a boring student, be an incredibly well-read
boring student! You can play netball, rugby, hockey, make beautiful music and paint with your feet,
but if you fail to get the grades you'll be rejected.'

Bristol Deferred places are limited. Late applications may not be accepted.

Misconceptions about this course Liverpool Some applicants think that three science subjects at
A-level are required to study Medicine – wrong! **London (St George's)** That you should be white,
middle class and male: 60% of medical students are now female and 53% of our students are not
white.

Selection interviews Yes Dundee, Oxford (13%); **No** Birmingham, Edinburgh.

Interview advice and questions Questions will vary between applicants, depending on their UCAS
statements and their A/AS-level subjects. Questions are likely to relate to A-level specific subjects,
general medicine topics and unconnected topics (see also **Admissions tutors' advice**). The following
questions will provide a guide to the range of topics covered in past interviews. Outline the structure
of DNA. What is meant by homeostasis? Is a virus a living organism? What has been the most
important advance in biology in the last 50 years? What interests you about (i) science, (ii) biology,
(iii) chemistry? Why did you choose the particular AS/A-level subjects you are doing? Why do you
want to study Medicine/become a doctor? Do you expect people to be grateful? Why do you want to
study here? Why should we take you? What do you do to relax? What do you do when you have
three or four things to do, and they are all equally urgent? How do you balance work and all the
outside activities you do? Do you agree with the concept of Foundation hospitals? What do you think
about polyclinics? Do you think NHS doctors and staff should be able to take private patients? If you
were in charge of finances for a large health authority, what would be your priorities for funding? If
you had to decide between saving the life of a young child and that of an old person, what would
you do? Would you treat lung cancer patients who refuse to give up smoking? What do you
understand by 'gene therapy'? Can you give any examples? In your opinion what is the most serious
cause for concern for the health of the UK? What do you want to do with your medical degree? What
do you think the human genome project can offer medicine? Should we pay for donor organs? Where
do you see yourself in 15 years' time? What was the last non-technical book you read? What is your
favourite piece of classical music? List your top five novels. What is your favourite play? What

Check **Chapter 4** when choosing your university and **Chapter 7** on how to read the subject tables.

politician do you admire the most? Who made the most valuable contribution to the 20th century? Why do you think research is important? Why is teamwork important? What do you think about the NHS's problems? Do you think that sport is important? What did you gain from doing work experience in a nursing home? What were the standards like? How does the medical profession deal with social issues? What societies will you join at university? How could you compare your hobby of rowing to medicine? Do you agree that it is difficult to balance the demands of being a doctor with those of starting a family? In doing a medical course, what would you find the most emotionally challenging aspect? How would you cope with emotional strain? What do you think about going to war with Iraq? Who should have priority for receiving drugs in a flu epidemic/ pandemic? How would you deal with the death of a patient? What are stem cells? Why are they controversial? How is cloning done? What constitutes a human being? Describe an egg. How can you measure intelligence? How do we combat genetic diseases? How are genes actually implanted? What do you want to talk about? If you were a cardiothoracic surgeon, would you perform a heart by-pass operation on a smoker? What are the negative aspects of becoming a doctor? At some interviews essays may be set, eg (i) 'A scientific education is a good basis for a medical degree: discuss'; (ii) 'Only drugs that are safe and effective should be prescribed to patients: discuss'. Occasionally applicants at interview may be given scenarios to discuss (see **UEA** under **Admissions tutors' advice**). See also **Chapter 6**. **Oxford** Tell me about drowning. What do you think of assisted suicide? Would you give a 60-year-old woman IVF treatment? When are people dead?

Reasons for rejection (non-academic) Insufficient vocation demonstrated. No steps taken to gain practical experience relevant to medicine. Doubts as to the ability to cope with the stress of a medical career. Not enough awareness about the career. Lack of knowledge about the course. Applicant appears dull and lacking in enthusiasm and motivation. Lacking a caring, committed attitude towards people. No evidence of broad social, cultural or sporting interests or of teamwork. Poor or lack of communication skills. Arrogance. Over-confident at interview. Unrealistic expectations about being a doctor.

Age at entry Applicants must be 17 years old on 30 September of the year of entry. However, some medical schools stipulate 17 years 6 months, and a small number stipulate 18 years. Those considering entry at 17 would probably be advised to take a Gap Year. **London (St George's)** (Med with Fdn Yr) minimum age of applicants is 21.

Health requirements Medical schools require all students to have their immunity status for hepatitis B, tuberculosis and rubella checked on entry. Offers are usually made subject to satisfactory health screening for hepatitis B. In line with advice from the General Medical Council, students will not be admitted to courses who are found to be e-antigen positive when screened within the first week of the course. Candidates accepting offers should assure themselves of their immunity status.

Mature students Medical schools usually accept a small number of mature students each year. However, several, if not the majority, reject applicants over 30 years of age. Some medical schools accept non-graduates although A-level passes at high grades are usually stipulated. The majority of applicants accepted are likely to be graduates with a first or 2.1 degree. **Birmingham** Maximum age at entry is 30 years. **Bristol** Maximum age at entry is 30 years. **Leeds** Maximum age at entry is 30 years. Applicants should hold the required A-level grades or a high class science degree; 15–20 places. **Southampton** 36 places available, maximum age 40; Applicants with nursing qualifications should hold two grade B A-levels including chemistry. Mature students taking Access courses must achieve 70% in A2 chemistry.

Advice to graduate applicants Graduate applicants are considered by all medical schools. At some medical schools the Graduate Australian Medical Schools Admission Test (GAMSAT) and the Medical Schools Admissions Test (MSAT) are now being used to assess the aptitude of prospective applicants. Applicants at some institutions are selected on the basis of three criteria: (i) an Honours degree at 2.2 or above; (ii) the GAMSAT score; (iii) performance at interview. All applicants must be EU students. **London (St George's)** Some students think that science graduates are the only ones to do well in GAMSAT: 40% of those on the course do not have a science degree or A-levels; however, work experience is essential.

GRADUATE DESTINATIONS AND EMPLOYMENT (2009/10 HESA)
Clinical Medicine; graduates surveyed 7835 **Employed** 6190 **In voluntary employment** 20 **In further study** 475 **Assumed unemployed** 55

Career note Applicants should also bear in mind that while most doctors do work in the NHS, either in hospital services or in general practice, not a few graduates choose to work in other fields such as public health, pharmacology, the environment, occupational medicine with industrial organisations, the armed services and opportunities abroad.

OTHER DEGREE SUBJECTS FOR CONSIDERATION
Biomedical/Medical Materials Science; Biology; Biotechnology; Clinical Sciences; Dentistry; Dietetics; Genetics; Health Sciences; Immunology; Medical Biochemistry; Medical Engineering; Medical Microbiology; Medical Physics; Medical Product Design; Medical Sciences; Medicinal Chemistry; Midwifery; Nursing; Nutrition; Occupational Therapy; Optometry; Osteopathy; Pharmacology; Pharmacy; Physiology; Physiotherapy; Psychology; Radiography; Speech Sciences; Sports Medicine; Veterinary Medicine; Virology – and Law! (The work of doctors and lawyers is similar: both are required to identify the relevant information – clinical symptoms or legal issues!)

MICROBIOLOGY

(see also **Biological Sciences, Biology, Biotechnology, Genetics**)

Microbiology is a branch of biological science specialising in the study of micro-organisms: bacteria, viruses and fungi. The subject covers the relationship between these organisms and disease and industrial applications such as food and drug production, waste-water treatment and future biochemical uses.

Useful websites www.scienceyear.com; www.sgm.ac.uk; www.nature.com/micro; www.microbes.info; www.asm.org; www.microbiol.org; see also **Biochemistry**, **Biological Sciences** and **Biology**.

NB The points totals shown to the left of the institutions are for ease of reference only. It must not be assumed that Tariff points are always used by institutions or that they can be substituted for an offer in grades. The level of an offer is not necessarily indicative of the quality of a course.

COURSE OFFERS INFORMATION
Subject requirements/preferences GCSE English and mathematics and science subjects. **AL** One or two mathematics/science subjects including chemistry and/or biology, required or preferred; grades sometimes specified.

Your target offers and examples of courses provided by each institution

360 pts **Edinburgh** – AAA–ABB 320–360 (Mol Biol) (IB 37–32 pts)
Imperial London – AAA 360 pts (Microbiol) (IB 38 pts HL 6 biol)
340 pts **Birmingham** – AAB–ABB 320–340 pts (Biol Sci (Microbiol)) (IB 32–34 pts)
Bristol – AAB (Med Microbiol) (IB 35 pts HL 666)
Cardiff – AAB–ABB (Microbiol) (IB 34 pts HL 5 biol chem)
Newcastle – AAB (Biomed Sci Med Microbiol) (IB 32 pts)
Nottingham – AAB–ABB (Microbiol) (IB 34–32 pts)
Sheffield – AAB (Med Microbiol) (IB 35 pts)
Surrey – AAB (Microbiol) (IB 35 pts)
Warwick – AAB (Med Microbiol Virol) (IB 36 pts)
York – AAB (Biotech Microbiol) (IB 35 pts)
320 pts **Aston** – ABB 320 pts (Infec Immun) (IB 33 pts)
Bristol – ABB incl chem (Cell Mol Med) (IB 35 pts)
Glasgow – ABB (Microbiol) (IB 32 pts)
Leeds – ABB–BBB 320–300 pts (Microbiol Virol) (IB 34–32 pts HL 16–15 pts)
Leicester – ABB (Biol Sci (Microbiol)) (IB 32 pts HL 66)

Liverpool – ABB (Microbl Biotech) (IB 33 pts)
Manchester – AAA–ABB 320–360 pts (Microbiol Modn Langs) (IB 37–33 pts)
Strathclyde – ABB 320 pts (Immun Microbiol)
Surrey – ABB–BBB (Microbl Genet) (IB 32–28 pts)
UEA – ABB incl biol (Microbiol) (IB 32 pts HL 555)

300 pts **Dundee** – BBB (Microbiol) (IB 34 pts)
Heriot-Watt – BBB (Biol Sci (Microbiol))
Queen's Belfast – BBB/BBCb (Microbiol) (IB 28 pts HL 555)
Reading – 300 pts (Microbio)

280 pts **Aberystwyth** – 280–320 pts (Microbiol Zool) (IB 27 pts)
Manchester Met – 280 pts (Microbiol Mol Biol) (IB 27 pts)
Nottingham Trent – 280 pts (Microbiol)
Stirling – BBC (Cell Biol) (IB 32 pts)

260 pts **Bradford** – 260 pts (Med Microbiol)
Glasgow Caledonian – BCC 260 pts (Microbiol)

240 pts **Aberdeen** – 240 pts (Microbiol)
Hertfordshire – 240 pts (Mol Biol Genet)
Huddersfield – 240 pts (Biol (Mol Cell))

230 pts **Edinburgh Napier** – 230 pts (Microbiol Biotech)

220 pts **Westminster** – CCD (Microbiol)

200 pts **London South Bank** – 200 pts (Biosci (Microbiol))
Staffordshire – 200–260 pts (Bioch Microbiol) (IB 28 pts)
UEL – 200 pts (Med Microbiol)
Wolverhampton – 200 pts (App Microbiol)

180 pts **Glasgow Caledonian** – DDD (Cell Mol Biol)

Alternative offers

See **Chapter 7** and **Appendix 1** for grades/UCAS Tariff points information for the International Baccalaureate, Scottish Highers/Advanced Highers, the Welsh Baccalaureate, the Irish Leaving Certificate, the Cambridge Pre-U Diploma, the Advanced Diploma and the Extended Project.

EXAMPLES OF FOUNDATION DEGREES IN THE SUBJECT FIELD

Petroc; St Helens (Coll); South Devon (Coll); Truro (Coll).

CHOOSING YOUR COURSE (SEE ALSO CH.1)

Some course features

Aston (Infec Immun) Course is included in the Biology programmes and offers a placement year in industry.
Cardiff Modules offered in medical microbiology, genetic manipulation, ecology and microbial physiology and biochemistry.
Manchester Met Units cover medical microbiology, molecular biology, genetics biodiversity and micro-organisms. A 12 month placement is offered in Year 3.
Nottingham Special topics in virology, molecular biology, and food and environmental microbiology.

Universities and colleges teaching quality See www.qaa.ac.uk; http://unistats.direct.gov.uk.

Top research universities and colleges (RAE 2008) See **Biological Sciences**.

Examples of sandwich degree courses See also **Biochemistry** and **Biological Sciences**. Aston; Bristol; Cardiff; De Montfort; Leeds; London South Bank; Manchester; Nottingham Trent.

ADMISSIONS INFORMATION

Number of applicants per place (approx) Aberystwyth 5; Bradford 6; Bristol 5; Cardiff 4; Dundee 5; Leeds 7; Liverpool 3; Nottingham 7; Strathclyde 10; Surrey 4; Swansea 5; Wolverhampton 4.

Advice to applicants and planning the UCAS personal statement Relevant experience, particularly for mature students. See **Biological Sciences**.

Selection interviews Yes Bristol, London South Bank, Nottingham (depends on application), Surrey, Swansea; **Some** Aberystwyth (mature applicants only), Cardiff, Leeds, Wolverhampton; **No** Dundee.

Interview advice and questions Examples of past questions include: Is money spent on the arts a waste? How much does the country spend on research and on the armed forces? Discuss reproduction in bacteria. What do you particularly like about your study of biology? What would you like to do after your degree? Do you have any strong views on vivisection? Discuss the differences between the courses you have applied for. What important advances have been made in the biological field recently? How would you describe microbiology? Do you know anything about the diseases caused by micro-organisms? What symptoms would be caused by which particular organisms? See also **Chapter 6**.

AFTER-RESULTS ADVICE
Offers to applicants repeating A-levels Higher Bristol, Strathclyde, Swansea, Warwick; **Possibly higher** Nottingham, UEA; **Same** Aberystwyth, Anglia Ruskin, Bradford, Cardiff, Leeds, Liverpool, Wolverhampton.

GRADUATE DESTINATIONS AND EMPLOYMENT (2009/10 HESA)
Graduates surveyed 600 **Employed** 295 **In voluntary employment** 15 **In further study** 185 **Assumed unemployed** 35

Career note See **Biology**.

OTHER DEGREE SUBJECTS FOR CONSIDERATION
Animal Sciences; Biochemistry; Biological Sciences; Biology; Biotechnology; Genetics; Medical Sciences; Medicine; Molecular Biology; Pharmacology; Physiology.

MUSIC
(including **Music Technology**; see also **Engineering (Acoustics and Sound), Technologies**)

Theory and practice are combined to a greater or lesser extent in most university Music courses and from which about 50% or more of graduates will go on to non-music careers. However, courses are also offered by conservatoires and schools of music where the majority of applicants are aiming to become professional musicians. For these courses the ability to perform on an instrument is more important than academic ability and offers are therefore likely to be lower. See also **Appendix 1**. Some applications are made through the Conservatoires Admissions Service (CUKAS): see **Chapter 6** for details.

Useful websites www.arts.org.uk; www.communitymusic.org; www.ism.org; www.bpi-med.co.uk; www.roh.org.uk; www.nyo.org.uk; www.bbc.co.uk/youngmusican; www.cukas.ac.uk.

NB The points totals shown to the left of the institutions are for ease of reference only. It must not be assumed that Tariff points are always used by institutions or that they can be substituted for an offer in grades. The level of an offer is not necessarily indicative of the quality of a course.

COURSE OFFERS INFORMATION
Subject requirements/preferences GCSE A foreign language and mathematics may be required. A good range of As and Bs for popular universities. **AL** Music plus an instrumental grade usually required.

Your target offers and examples of courses provided by each institution
420 pts **London (King's)** – A*AAc-AAAc 400–420 pts (Ger Mus) (IB 39 pts HL 6 mus)
380 pts **Cambridge** – A*AA (Mus) (IB 40–42 pts HL 766–777)
          Imperial London – A*mathsAA (Phys St Musl Perf) (IB 38 pts. HL 666)
          London (King's) – A*AA-AAA 360–380 pts (Mus) (IB 39–38 pts HL 6 mus)
          Surrey – A*AA-AAA (Mus Snd Rec (Tonmeister))
360 pts **Edinburgh** – AAA-ABB (Phys Mus) (IB 37–32 pts)
          London (RH) – AAA-ABB (Phys Mus) (IB 36 pts)
          Manchester – AAB (Mus Dr) (IB 36–35 pts)

Oxford – AAA (Music) (IB 38–40 pts)
Southampton – AAA (Maths Mus) (IB 36 pts HL 18 pts)
340 pts **Birmingham** – AAA–AAB 340–360 pts (Mus) (IB 36–38 pts)
Bristol – AAB–BBB incl mus (Mus Modn Lang) (IB 35–32 pts)
Cardiff – AAB–BBB (Mus) (IB 33 pts)
Durham – AAB (Mus) (IB 36 pts)
Glasgow – ABB (Mus BMus) (IB 34 pts)
Lancaster – AAB 340 pts (Engl Lit Mus) (IB 34 pts)
London (RH) – AAB–ABB (Mus Phil)
Manchester – AAB (Mus) (IB 36–35 pts)
Newcastle – AAB (Mus BA) (IB 33 pts)
Nottingham – AAB–ABB (Music) (IB 34 pts)
Southampton – AAB (Engl Mus) (IB 34 pts HL 17 pts)
320 pts **City** – ABB–BBC (Mus)
Edinburgh – AAA–ABB 320–360 pts (Maths Mus) (IB 37–32 pts)
Glasgow – ABB (Mus MA) (IB 36 pts)
Kent – ABB–BBB (Pop Mus) (IB 33 pts)
Lancaster – applications are individually considered BBB (Mus)
Leeds – ABB (Mus (Perf)) (IB 33 pts HL 6 mus)
Liverpool – ABB 320 pts (Mus/Pop Mus) (IB 33 pts)
London (Gold) – ABB (Mus Cmpsn) (IB 32 pts)
London (RH) – ABB–BBB (Span Mus) (IB 32 pts)
Nottingham – ABB (Mus Phil) (IB 32 pts)
Sheffield – ABB incl mus (Theol Mus) (IB 33 pts)
Southampton – ABB incl mus (Mus) (IB 32 pts HL 16 pts)
Surrey – 320 pts (Crea Mus Tech) (IB 32 pts)
Sussex – ABB (Mus) (IB 34 pts)
York – ABB (Mus) (IB 34 pts HL 6 mus)
300 pts **Aberdeen** – BBB 300 pts (Mus)
Bournemouth – 300 pts (Mus Aud Tech)
Brunel – contact admissions office (Film TV St Mus)
Edinburgh – BBB 300 pts (Mus) (IB 34 pts HL 555)
Glamorgan – BBB (Pop Mus; Pop Mus Tech)
Huddersfield – 300–280 pts (Mus Dr; Mus Tech; Mus; Mus Jrnl)
Liverpool (LIPA) – 300 pts (Mus)
London (SOAS) – BBB (Mus Joint Hons) (IB 32 pts HL 554)
Newcastle – BBB (Folk Trad Mus) (IB 32 pts)
Oxford Brookes – BBB 300 pts (Mus Psy)
Queen's Belfast – BBB/BBCb (Mus Tech Snc Art) (IB 29 pts HL 655)
Roehampton – 300–360 pts (P Educ (Mus))
Southampton – BBB incl maths phys mus (Acoust Mus) (IB 30 pts)
UEA – BBB (Mus Tech) (IB 30 pts)
280 pts **Bangor** – (Mus Tech Electron)
Birmingham City – 280 pts (Media (Mus)) (IB 30 pts)
Brighton – BBC (Dig Mus Snd Arts)
Bristol UWE – 280–300 pts (Crea Mus Tech)
Cumbria – 280 pts (Musl Thea Perf courses)
Derby – 280 pts (Mus Tech Prod; Pop Mus Mus Tech)
Edge Hill – 280 pts (Media Mus Snd; Mus Snd Dr)
Gloucestershire – 280–300 pts (Pop Mus; Mus Media Mgt)
Hull – 280–300 pts (Mus) (IB 28 pts)
Liverpool (LIPA) – 280 pts (Snd Tech)
Manchester Met – 280 pts (Pop Mus) (IB 28 pts)
Oxford Brookes – BBC (Mus; Snd Tech Dig Mus)
Salford – 280 pts (Mus) (IB 30 pts)

Teesside – 280 pts (Mus Tech)

Ulster – BBC (Mus; Mus Dance; Mus Ir; Mus Psy)

260 pts **Bangor** – 260–300 pts (Mus Crea Writ; Mus Film St)

Bolton – 260 pts (Mus Crea Ind Bus)

Brunel – BCC (Snc Arts) (IB 29 pts)

Chester – 260–300 pts (Pop Mus Perf) (IB 28 pts)

De Montfort – 260 pts (Mus Tech Innov; Mus; Mus Tech Perf)

Derby – 260–300 pts (Pop Mus Prod Joint Hons)

Hertfordshire – 260 pts (Mus Cmpsn Tech; Mus Tech)

Keele – 260–320 pts (Mus; Mus Tech)

Liverpool Hope – 260–320 pts (Mus)

LJMU – 260 pts (Pop Mus St) (IB 28 pts)

Northampton – 260–280 pts (Pop Mus courses)

Strathclyde – BCC (App Mus)

Sunderland – 260 pts (Commun Mus)

UCLan – 260–300 pts (Mus Prac; Mus Prod; Mus Prod Arts; Mus)

240 pts **Bath Spa** – 240–300 pts (Mus) (IB 24 pts)

Canterbury Christ Church – 240 pts (Mus)

Chester – 240–280 pts (Commer Mus Prod)

Coventry – 240 pts (Mus Perf Prof Prac; Mus Cmpsn Prof Prac; Mus Tech)

Edinburgh Napier – 240 pts (Pop Mus)

Glyndŵr – 240 pts (Mus Tech)

Hull – 240 pts (Crea Mus Tech)

Kingston – 240–280 pts (Mus; Mus Tech)

Leeds (CMus) – 240 pts (Mus (Comb); Mus (Jazz); Mus (Pop Mus); Mus (Class Mus); Mus (Prod))

Leeds Met – 240 pts (Music Tech Prod) (IB 24 pts)

Newport – 240-260 pts (Crea Mus)

Plymouth – 240 pts (P Mus BEd)

Portsmouth – 240–300 pts (Mus Snd Tech)

Ravensbourne – AA–CC (Mus Prod Media) (IB 28 pts)

RConsvS – offered jointly with University of Glasgow 240 pts (Mus BEd)

Staffordshire – 240–280 pts (Crea Mus Tech; Mus Tech)

Southampton Solent – 240 pts (Mus Prom; Pop Mus Perf)

West Scotland – CCC (Commer Mus)

220 pts **Anglia Ruskin** – 220 pts (Aud Mus Tech)

Bath Spa – 220–280 pts (Crea Mus Tech)

Bishop Grosseteste (UC) – 220 pts (App Dr Mus)

Chichester – CCD 180–220 pts (Mus) (IB 26 pts)

Creative Arts – 220–240 pts (Mus Jrnl) (IB 24–30 pts)

Falmouth (UC) – 220 pts (Crea Mus Tech)

Plymouth – 200 pts (Mus)

Sunderland – 220 pts (Jazz Pop Commer Mus)

Ulster – CCD 220 pts (Dance Mus) (IB 24 pts)

York St John – 220–260 pts (Mus courses)

200 pts **Bedfordshire** – 200 pts (Mus Tech) (IB 24 pts)

Bucks New – 200–240 pts (Aud Mus Prod; Mus Arts Mgt; Mus Mgt Arst Dev)

Doncaster (Coll Univ Centre) – 200 pts (Crea Mus Tech)

Leeds Met – 200 pts (Perf) (IB 24 pts)

London Met – 200–240 pts (Musl Instr)

Middlesex – 200–300 pts (Jazz; Mus Perf; Mus Cmpsn; Mus Arts Mgt)

RCMus – CEcc (Mus)

Swansea Met – 200–300 pts (Mus Tech)

UCP Marjon – 200 pts (Live Mus)

UEL – 200 pts (Mus Cult (Theor Prod))

Check **Chapter 4** when choosing your university and **Chapter 7** on how to read the subject tables.

West London – 200 pts (Mus Media)
Wolverhampton – 200 pts (Mus; Mus Pop Mus; Mus Tech)
180 pts Farnborough (CT) – 180–200 pts (Media Prod Mus)
Reading – 180 pts (Ed St (P) Mus)
160 pts Colchester (Inst) – 160 pts (Mus; Musl Thea; Film Mus Sndtrk Prod; Pop Mus)
Grimsby (IFHE) – 160 pts (Crea Mus)
London (Central Sch SpDr) – CC (Act Mus Thea)
Rose Bruford (Coll) – 160–280 pts (Actr Mushp)
Southampton Solent – 160 pts (Aud Tech)
Truro (Coll) – 160 pts (Contemp Wrld Jazz)
UHI – CC–AA (Gael Trad Mus)
Westminster – CC (Commer Mus) (IB 24 pts)
West Scotland – CC (Mus Tech)
150 pts West London – 150 pts (Pop Mus Perf)
100 pts and below
Birmingham City – 80 pts (Jazz; Mus)
Guildhall (Sch Mus Dr) – contact the School (Mus)
Havering (Coll) – contact the College (Contemp Mus Tech)
London (RAcMus) – contact the Academy EE (Mus BMus)
RConsvS – 100 pts (Mus; Scot Mus BA; Mus Thea)
RNCM – 80 pts (Mus)
Royal Welsh (CMusDr) – contact College and apply direct (Pop Mus; Perf Prod)
Trinity Laban Consv – check with admissions tutor (Perf BMus; Perf St MMus)
UHI – D–A (Pop Mus)

Alternative offers

See **Chapter 7** and **Appendix 1** for grades/UCAS Tariff points information for the International Baccalaureate, Scottish Highers/Advanced Highers, the Welsh Baccalaureate, the Irish Leaving Certificate, the Cambridge Pre-U Diploma, the Advanced Diploma and the Extended Project.

EXAMPLES OF FOUNDATION DEGREES IN THE SUBJECT FIELD

Accrington and Rossendale (Coll); Anglia Ruskin; Bath Spa; Bedfordshire; Bournemouth; Brighton; Bucks New; Canterbury Christ Church; Chichester; Colchester (Inst); De Montfort; Glamorgan; Gloucestershire; Hull (Coll); Kent; Leeds (CMus); Liverpool (CmC); Loughborough (Coll); Mid-Cheshire (Coll); Neath Port Talbot (Coll); St Helens (Coll); South Devon (Coll); Staffordshire; Suffolk (Univ Campus); Sunderland City (Coll); Sussex; Truro (Coll); UCLan; UEL; Westminster; Wolverhampton; Worcester (CT).

CHOOSING YOUR COURSE (SEE ALSO CH.1)

Some course features

Bournemouth The Music and Audio Technology course focuses on the application of hardware and software technologies to create music. There is a 40 week placement in Year 3.
Brighton The course in Music and Visual Art utilises the visual art/music interface with close links between dance, theatre and music. There is also a Digital Music and Sound Arts degree in which music is studied relating to computers and electronic instruments, and a course in Music Production.
Chichester The Music degree has three strands – Performance and Direction, Composing, Arranging and Improvising and Style and Genre. There are also courses in Musical Theatre, Performing Arts, Commercial Music.
Edinburgh Music is a three-year or four-year honours course. In each year the curriculum is broadly divided between composition, history and practical studies. Options are introduced in the third year and include electronic music but also cover music technology and acoustics. There is also a BMus course in Music Technology.
Greenwich A HND degree in Music Technology is offered to school leavers with relevant qualifications. There is a Creative Production and Technology top-up course for students who have completed a HND in Music and who intend to pursue careers in the music industry.

Hertfordshire Courses are offered in Music Composition and Technology, Sound Design Technology and Music and Entertainment Industry Management, which has three pathways in studio production, entertainment industry and the classical music industry. There is also a course in Songwriting and Music Production.

Liverpool Hope Music can be studied as a single course or with a large number of combined courses in which students can specialise in popular or classical music. A BA (QTS) is also offered.

LJMU A very broad course in Popular Music Studies includes modules such as Popular Music Genres, Digital Music Production and Cultural Themes and Aesthetics. There is also a course in Audio and Music Production.

Teesside Music Technology allows students to perform and engineer live performances, set up an internet radio station and to create dub music, sound effects and foley to video and media. Students use the same technology used in the industry and have the chance to undertake exams in the hardware.

UCP Marjon The course in Live Music provides a programme of study focusing on performance technology and media work.

Universities and colleges teaching quality See www.qaa.ac.uk; http://unistats.direct.gov.uk.

Top research universities and colleges (RAE 2008) London (RH); Birmingham; Manchester; Southampton; Cambridge; London (King's); Sheffield; Oxford; York; Newcastle; Nottingham.

Examples of sandwich degree courses Birmingham City; Bournemouth; Bristol UWE; Gloucestershire; Staffordshire; Surrey; Teesside.

ADMISSIONS INFORMATION

Number of applicants per place (approx) Aberystwyth 5; Anglia Ruskin 5; Bangor 4; Bath Spa 8; Birmingham 8; Bristol 12; Brunel 7; Cambridge 3, (Hom) 4; Cardiff 6; Chichester 4; City 7; Colchester (Inst) 4; Cumbria 7; Durham 5; Edinburgh 11; Edinburgh Napier 3; Glasgow 4; Huddersfield 2; Hull 21; Kingston 18; Lancaster 8; Leeds 18; Liverpool 9; Liverpool (LIPA) 12; London (Gold) 7; London (King's) 10; London (RAcMus) 7; London (RH) 7; London (SOAS) 4; London Met 10; Middlesex 23; Newcastle 24; Northampton 3; Northumbria 12; Nottingham 7; Oxford Brookes 12; Queen's Belfast 6; RCMus 10; RConsvS 6; RNCM 8; Roehampton 4; Rose Bruford (Coll) 15; Salford 5; Southampton 5; Strathclyde 15; Surrey 6, (Tonmeister) 12; Trinity Laban Consv 4; UEA 12; Ulster 8; Worcester 8; York 8; York St John 2.

Advice to applicants and planning the UCAS personal statement In addition to your ability and expertise with your chosen musical instrument(s), it is also important to know your composers and to take a critical interest in various kinds of music. Reference should be made to these, visits to concerts listed and any special interests indicated in types of musical activity, for example, opera, ballet. Work with orchestras, choirs and other musical groups should also be included and full details given of any competitions entered and awards obtained. See **Chapter 5** for details of applications for Music courses at conservatoires. **Guildhall (Sch Mus Dr)** International applicants sending extra documentation from overseas must make sure that for Customs purposes they indicate that they will pay any import tax charged. **London (Gold)** We encourage students to bring examples of their written and creative work. **Royal Welsh (CMusDr)** Evidence of performance-related experience, eg youth orchestras, solo work, prizes, scholarships etc. Our course is a conservatoire course as opposed to a more academic university course. We offer a very high standard of performance tuition balanced with academic theory modules. **Surrey** (Snd Rec (Tonmeister)) Demonstration of motivation towards professional sound recording.

Misconceptions about this course **Cardiff** Some mistakenly think that the BMus scheme is either performance-based or something inferior to the principal music-based degree. **Salford** (Pop Mus Rec) This is not a specialised music technology degree: it is a music degree with specialisation in music technology and production. Specialisation can be significant in Year 3. BTEC Popular Music students must be prepared for the rigours of an academic degree. Some students expect the course to make them famous! **Surrey** Some believe that the Music course is exclusively performance-based (the course includes substantial academic and compositional elements).

Selection interviews Most institutions, plus audition to include a performance of a prepared piece (or pieces) on main instrument. **Yes** Birmingham City, Doncaster (Coll Univ Centre), Guildhall (Sch Mus

Check **Chapter 4** when choosing your university and **Chapter 7** on how to read the subject tables.

Dr) (Interviews mostly held at the School but also at Newcastle and in the USA.), Oxford (Music) 38%; **Some** Anglia Ruskin, Bath Spa, Bucks New, Cardiff, Coventry (Proforma used prior to interview – some students rejected at this stage), Liverpool (LIPA), Staffordshire (Mus Tech), Surrey; **No** Dundee.

Interview advice and questions See also **Chapter 5** under Music.

Anglia Ruskin In addition to A-levels, Grade 7 is required(with a good pass, first study) plus Grade 5 minimum keyboard standard. AS-level points are not counted towards the Tariff required for this subject. A demo CD may be required.

Bangor Offer depends on proven ability in historical or compositional fields plus acceptable performance standard. Options include music therapy, recording techniques, jazz.

Bath Spa Some candidates interviewed. Required to perform and sight-read on main instrument, and given aural and critical listening tests. Discussion of previous performing, composing and academic experience. (Fdn Commer Mus) All applicants must submit a self-composed audio prior to interview. (Mus Tech) Applicants will be required to submit an audio portfolio demonstrating technical and creative skills.

Bristol (Mus Fr/Ger/Ital) No in-depth interviews; candidates invited to Open Days. **Cambridge** (St Catharine's) At interview candidates may have to undergo some simple keyboard or aural tests (such as harmonisation of an unseen melody or memorisation of a rhythm). More importantly, they will have to comment on some unseen musical extracts from a stylistic and analytical point of view. Candidates are asked to submit some examples of work before the interview, from the fields of harmony and counterpoint, history and analysis; they are also encouraged to send any other material such as compositions, programme notes or an independent essay on a subject of interest to the candidate. (Taking the STEP examination is not a requirement for admission.) Above all this, though, the main prerequisite for reading Music at St Catharine's is an academic interest in the subject itself.

Canterbury Christ Church Associated Board examinations in two instruments (or one instrument and voice); keyboard competence essential, particularly for the BEd course.

Colchester (Inst) Great stress laid on candidate's ability to communicate love of the subject.

Cumbria Admission by live performance or as a demo. QTS applicants interviewed for teaching suitability. See also **Chapter 6**.

Durham Grade 6 piano (Associated Board), a foreign language (GCSE grade A–C), and A-level music grade B required.

Edinburgh Napier Most candidates are called for interview, although very well qualified candidates may be offered a place without interview. All are asked to submit samples of their work. Associated Board Grade 7 on piano is usually expected.

Huddersfield Have an open and inquisitive outlook with regard to all aspects of music from performing to composing, musicology to listening. Candidates auditioned on their principal instrument or voice. They will be asked about playing technique, interpretation and interests.

Hull (Coll) Good instrumental grades can improve chances of an offer and of confirmation in August. Students are not normally required to attend an audition/interview. Decisions will be made according to the information supplied on the UCAS application. Successful applicants will be invited to attend a departmental Open Day. We welcome applications from mature students and those with unconventional qualifications: in such cases an interview may be required.

Kingston Associated Board Grade 8 on main instrument is required, with at least Grade 4 on a keyboard instrument (where this is not the main instrument). Audition and interview may be required. Candidates with non-standard qualifications are interviewed and asked to bring samples of written work.

Lancaster Grade 8 Associated Board required on an instrument or voice and some keyboard proficiency (Grade 6) usually expected. We do not accept candidates without interview. For the Music degree, instrumental or vocal skills equivalent to Grade 8 required. For Music Technology, applicants should hold music theory Grade 5 or be able to demonstrate the ability to read a score. Applicants wishing to take practical studies will need instrumental or vocal skills equivalent to Grade 8.

BA Music

BA Sonic Arts
Joint honours also available with Games Design

BMus Musical Performance

BMus Musical Composition

Find out more about the School of Arts at www.brunel.ac.uk/arts

Brunel UNIVERSITY LONDON

Leeds Intending students should follow an academic rather than practical-oriented A-level course. The University is experimenting with abandoning the formal interview in favour of small group Open Days for those holding offers made on the UCAS information, to focus on a practical exchange of information relevant to the applicant's decision to accept or reject the offer. Grade 8 Associated Board on an instrument is a normal expectation.

Leeds (CMus) There will be an audition and an essay on music theory.

Liverpool (LIPA) In addition to performing in orchestras etc, give details of any compositions you have completed (the number and styles). Instrumentalists (including vocalists) should describe any performance/gig experience together with any musical instrument grades achieved. (Mus) Candidates should prepare two pieces of contrasting music to play on their chosen instrument. Candidates who have put song-writing/composition as either first or second choice should have a CD or minidisc of their work to play to the panel. (Snd Tech) Applicants must prepare a critical review of a sound recording of their choice which highlights the technical and production values that they think are the most important. Examples of recorded work they have undertaken should also be available at interview eg on CD or DAT. (Mus Perf Arts) Applicants should have A-levels (or equivalent) and have completed Grade 5 Music Theory before the course commences.

London (Gold) The interview will include an aural discussion of music and the personal interests of the applicant.

London (RAcMus) All candidates are called for audition, and those who are successful are called for a further interview; places are offered later, subject to the minimum GCSE requirements being achieved. (BMus) Applicants sit a 50-minute written paper, and may also be tested on keyboard and aural performance.

London (RH) Candidates are tested with an aural test, a harmony/counterpoint test, a conceptual essay, and a viva at which they are asked questions and asked to perform. On the basis of the

Check **Chapter 4** when choosing your university and **Chapter 7** on how to read the subject tables.

results in these tests we make offers. There is a tradition of caring for each individual and we strive to give each applicant a fair hearing. Musicality, a good intellect and real enthusiasm are the qualities we look for.

London (SOAS) Candidates are judged on individual merits. Applicants are expected to have substantial practical experience of musical performance, but not necessarily Western music.

Newcastle We expect a reasonable background knowledge of musical history, basic harmony and counterpoint and keyboard skills of approximately Grade 8 standard; if the main instrument is not piano or organ – Grade 5. While practical skills are important, academic ability is the primary requisite. Practical Music or Music Technology accepted in place of Music.

Nottingham A high standard of aural ability is expected. Interviewees take two short written papers, intellectual enquiry and attainment are looked for, together with a good range of knowledge and sense of enterprise. Only borderline/mature students are interviewed, successful applicants are invited to an Open Day.

Nottingham Trent Music students require Grade 6 on two instruments. Candidates submit a marked sample of harmony and/or counterpoint and two marked essays on any areas or aspects of music. Candidates may also submit a portfolio of compositions if they wish, but it is not possible to return any copies. Candidates will take the following tests at interview: (i) A one-hour harmony or counterpoint written test (candidates will not have access to a piano); there is no composition option; (ii) A 40-minute aural test in three parts: dictation of a Bach chorale (bass given)/melodic dictation, and identification of errors heard in a two-part piece; (iii) Performance of a prepared piece on the candidate's principal instrument or voice (organists, percussionists and candidates requiring an accompanist should inform the Faculty in advance of the interview period); (iv) Keyboard skills in three parts: score reading of a string quartet; keyboard harmony; and sight-reading (sight-reading examples will take into account candidates' keyboard proficiency).

RCMus All UK and Eire candidates are required to attend for audition in person but tapes are acceptable from overseas applicants. It must be stressed, however, that personal audition is preferable and those students offered places on the basis of a tape audition may be required to take a confirmatory audition on arrival. Candidates are required to perform on the principal study instrument as well as undertaking sight-reading, aural tests and paperwork. There is also an interview. Potential scholars sometimes proceed to a second audition, usually on the same day. The academic requirement for the BMus (RCM) course is two A-levels at pass grades. Acceptance is ultimately based on the quality of performance at audition, performing experience and perceived potential as a performer. As a guide, applicants should be of at least Grade 8 distinction standard.

RNCM All applicants are called for audition. Successful applicants proceed to an academic interview which will include aural tests and questions on music theory and history. Student comment: 'A 45-minute interview with a panel of three. Focus was on portfolio of compositions sent in advance. Prior to interview was asked to harmonise a short passage and study an orchestral excerpt followed up at interview. Aural test waived.'

Royal Welsh (CMusDr) All UK and Eire applicants are called to audition in person; overseas candidates may audition by tape. Candidates are required to perform on their sight-reading ability. Candidates who are successful in the audition proceed to interview in which there will be a short aural test. Candidates for the BA (Music) course are required to bring recent examples of harmony, counterpoint and essays.

Surrey (Music) Applicants may expect to be questioned in the interview about their musical experience, enthusiasm and any particular compositions they have studied. They will also be asked to perform on their first instrument. (Snd Rec (Tonmeister)) Applicants can expect to be questioned about their recording interests and motivation and show an ability to relate A-level scientific knowledge to simple recording equipment. They may be asked to perform on their first instrument.

Trinity Laban Consv Applicants for the BMus degree must attend an audition and show that they have attained a certain level of competence in their principal and second studies, musical subjects and in musical theory. Grade 8 practical and theory can count as one A-level, but not if the second

A-level is in music. Overseas applicants may submit a tape recording in the first instance when a place may be offered for one year. Thereafter they will have to undergo a further test. They must also show evidence of good aural perception in musical techniques and musical analysis.

UEA Only unusual and mature candidates are interviewed. Applicants are expected to perform music with insight and show genuine intellectual curiosity about music and its cultural background. At interview candidates will be asked to perform on their principal instrument. Those who play orchestral instruments or sing will also be expected to play simple music on the piano. At interview we look for applicants with proficiency in instrumental or vocal performance (preferably at Grade 8 standard or above), range of experience of music of many types and an intelligent attitude towards discussion.

Wolverhampton The audition will involve playing/singing a piece of own-choice music (up to five minutes – no longer). Accompanists may be brought along or the department may be able to provide one if requested in advance. Candidates will be requested to produce a short piece of written work. It would be helpful to see any music certificates and a Record of Achievement if available, together with examples of recent work in music (an essay, harmony, composition etc).

Reasons for rejection (non-academic) Usually academic (auditions, practical, aural/written test). Dull, unenthusiastic students, ignorant about their subject, showing lack of motivation and imagination. **Cambridge** Her harmony was marred by elementary technical errors and her compositions lacked formal and stylistic focus. **London (King's)** Apparent lack of interest, performance not good enough, lack of music history knowledge. Foreign students: language skills inadequate. **Royal Welsh (CMusDr)** Performing/technical ability not of the required standard.

AFTER-RESULTS ADVICE
Offers to applicants repeating A-levels Higher Aberystwyth, Leeds; **Same** Anglia Ruskin, Bath Spa, Bristol, Cardiff, City, Colchester (Inst), De Montfort, Durham, Guildhall (Sch Mus Dr), Huddersfield, Hull, Kingston, Leeds (CMus), London (RAcMus), London (RH), Nottingham, Rose Bruford (Coll), Royal Welsh (CMusDr), Salford, Staffordshire, Surrey, UEA, York, York St John.

GRADUATE DESTINATIONS AND EMPLOYMENT (2009/10 HESA)
Graduates surveyed 6895 **Employed** 2665 **In voluntary employment** 110 **In further study** 1715 **Assumed unemployed** 410

Career note Some graduates go into performance-based careers, many enter the teaching profession and others go into a wide range of careers requiring graduate skills.

OTHER DEGREE SUBJECTS FOR CONSIDERATION
Acoustics; Drama; Musical Theatre; Performance Arts.

NATURAL SCIENCES
(see also Biological Sciences)

Natural Sciences degrees allow the student to obtain a broad view of the origins and potential of science in general, and then to focus on one specialist area of scientific study.

Useful websites www.scienceyear.com; www.scicentral.com; www.nature.com; see also **Biology**, **Chemistry** and **Physics**.

NB The points totals shown to the left of the institutions are for ease of reference only. It must not be assumed that Tariff points are always used by institutions or that they can be substituted for an offer in grades. The level of an offer is not necessarily indicative of the quality of a course.

COURSE OFFERS INFORMATION
Subject requirements/preferences GCSE Strong results, particularly in the sciences. **AL** Science subjects required.

Cambridge (Emmanuel) One AEA science may be required when only two sciences taken; (Peterhouse) STEP may be used as part of conditional offer.

Your target offers and examples of courses provided by each institution

380 pts **Bath** – A*AA (Nat Sci (St Abrd)) (IB 38 pts HL 666)
Birmingham – A*AA (Nat Sci) (IB 36–38 pts)
Cambridge – A*AA (Nat Sci (Chem)) (IB 40–42 pts HL 766–777)
Durham – A*AA 380 pts (Nat Sci) (IB 38 pts)
London (UCL) – AAAe (Nat Sci) (IB 34–38 pts HL 766–777)

360 pts **Dundee** – AAA (Nat Sci) (34 pts)
Lancaster – AAA 360 pts (Nat Sci) (IB 36 pts)
Leeds – AAA (Nat Sci) (IB 34 pts)
Nottingham – AAA–AAB (Nat Sci) (IB 34–36 pts)
Southampton – AAA–AAB (Nat Sci) (IB 36–32 pts HL 18–16 pts)
UEA – AAA (Nat Sci Ind/Abrd) (IB 34 pts HL 66)

340 pts **Leicester** – AAB (Interd Sci MSci) (IB 30 pts)

300 pts **Leicester** – BBB (Interd Sci BSc) (28 pts)

160 pts **UHI** – CC–AA (Nat Env Sci)

Open University – contact +44 (0)845 300 6090 **or** www.openuniversity.co.uk/you (Nat Sci)

Alternative offers

See **Chapter 7** and **Appendix 1** for grades/UCAS Tariff points information for the International Baccalaureate, Scottish Highers/Advanced Highers, the Welsh Baccalaureate, the Irish Leaving Certificate, the Cambridge Pre-U Diploma, the Advanced Diploma and the Extended Project.

CHOOSING YOUR COURSE (SEE ALSO CH.1)

Some course features

Bath A flexible range of courses, with opportunity to transfer between the three- and four-year degree programmes and the new undergraduate Masters degree. Students can also apply for transfer to a Single Honours programme in Biology, Chemistry or Physics.

Cambridge (Nat Sci) Courses focus on the biological and physical sciences with a wide range of final year specialist subjects from which to choose, including Astrophysics, Chemistry, Geological Sciences, History and Philosophy of Science, Materials Science, Physics or Systems Biology.

Durham (Nat Sci) A very flexible degree programme, with specialisation in a range of subjects, ranging from Anthropology and Astronomy to Earth Sciences, Mathematics, Psychology and Statistics. Students take modules from the Faculties of Arts, Humanities and Social Sciences.

Lancaster (Nat Sci) Two or three science subjects can be studied throughout the course.

Universities and colleges teaching quality See www.qaa.ac.uk; http://unistats.direct.gov.uk.

Top research universities and colleges (RAE 2008) See separate science tables.

Examples of sandwich degree courses Bath; Nottingham Trent; Surrey.

ADMISSIONS INFORMATION

Number of applicants per place (approx) Bath 7; Birmingham 10; Cambridge 3; Durham 5; Nottingham 7.

Advice to applicants and planning the UCAS personal statement See **Biology, Chemistry, Physics** and **Appendix 3**.

Selection interviews **Yes** Bath, Cambridge, Southampton; **No** Birmingham, Dundee, UEA.

Interview advice and questions See also **Chapter 6**. **Cambridge** Questions depend on subject choices and studies at A-level and past questions have included the following: Discuss the setting up of a chemical engineering plant and the probabilities of failure of various components. Questions on the basic principles of physical chemistry, protein structure and functions and physiology. Questions on biological specimens. Comment on the theory of evolution and the story of the Creation in Genesis. What are your weaknesses? Questions on electro-micrographs. What do you talk about with your friends? How would you benefit from a university education? What scientific magazines do you read? Questions on atoms, types of bonding and structures. What are the problems of being tall? What are the differences between metals and non-metals? Why does graphite conduct? Questions on quantum physics and wave mechanics. How could you contribute to life here? What do you see yourself doing in five years' time? Was the Second World War justified? If it is common public belief that today's problems, for example industrial pollution, are caused by scientists, why do you wish to become one? Questions on the gyroscopic motion of cycle wheels, the forces on a cycle in motion and the design of mountain bikes. What do you consider will be the most startling scientific development in the future? What do you estimate is the mass of air in this room? If a carrot can grow from one carrot cell, why not a human?

AFTER-RESULTS ADVICE
Offers to applicants repeating A-levels **No** Cambridge.

GRADUATE DESTINATIONS AND EMPLOYMENT (2009/10 HESA)
See **Biology**, **Chemistry**, **Mathematics** and **Physics**.

Career note These courses offer a range of science and in some cases non-scientific subjects, providing students with the flexibility to develop particular interests as they progress through the course.

OTHER DEGREE SUBJECTS FOR CONSIDERATION
Anatomy; Anthropology; Archaeology; Astrophysics; Biochemistry; Biological Sciences; Biology; Chemistry; Earth Sciences; Ecology; Genetics; Geography; Geology; History and Philosophy of Science; Neuroscience; Pharmacology; Physics; Plant Sciences; Psychology; Zoology.

NAVAL ARCHITECTURE

(including **Marine Engineering** and **Ship Science**; see also **Marine/Maritime Studies**)

Professional naval architects or marine engineers are responsible for the design, construction and repair of cruise liners, yachts, submarines, container ships and oil tankers. Ship Science focuses on, for example, vehicles and structures that use the oceans for transport, recreation and energy generation. Courses cover marine structures, transport and operations, design, propulsion and mathematics. Ship design has many similarities to the design of aircraft.

Useful websites www.rina.org.uk; www.na-me.ac.uk; www.naval-architecture.co.uk.

NB The points totals shown to the left of the institutions are for ease of reference only. It must not be assumed that Tariff points are always used by institutions or that they can be substituted for an offer in grades. The level of an offer is not necessarily indicative of the quality of a course.

COURSE OFFERS INFORMATION
Subject requirements/preferences **GCSE** Grades A–C in mathematics and physics are normally required. **AL** Mathematics and physics usually required.

Your target offers and examples of courses provided by each institution
340 pts **Newcastle** – AAB (Nvl Archit MEng) (IB 37 pts HL 5 maths phys)
       Strathclyde – AAB (Nvl Archit MEng) (IB 36 pts)
       Southampton – AAB (Ship Sci (Advncd Mat)) (IB 34 pts HL 17 pts)
320 pts **Newcastle** – AAB-BBB 300–340 pts (Mar Eng BEng) (IB 32–34 pts HL 5 maths phys)
       Strathclyde – ABB (Nvl Archit Sml Crft Eng BEng) (IB 32 pts)
300 pts **Newcastle** – AAB-BBB 300–340 pts (Sml Crft Tech BEng) (IB 32–34 pts)
280 pts **LJMU** – 280 pts (Mech Mar Eng MEng)
260 pts **LJMU** – 260 pts (Mech Mar Eng BEng; Naut Sci)
200 pts **Plymouth** – 200 pts (Mar St (Ocn Ycht))
180 pts **Southampton Solent** – 180 pts (Ycht Prod Surv; Ycht Pwrcft Des)

Check **Chapter 4** when choosing your university and **Chapter 7** on how to read the subject tables.

Alternative offers
See **Chapter 7** and **Appendix 1** for grades/UCAS Tariff points information for the International Baccalaureate, Scottish Highers/Advanced Highers, the Welsh Baccalaureate, the Irish Leaving Certificate, the Cambridge Pre-U Diploma, the Advanced Diploma and the Extended Project.

EXAMPLES OF FOUNDATION DEGREES IN THE SUBJECT FIELD
Blackpool and Fylde (Coll); Cornwall (Coll); LJMU; Plymouth City (Coll); South Devon (Coll); Southampton Solent.

CHOOSING YOUR COURSE (SEE ALSO CH.1)
Some course features
Newcastle (Mar Tech; Off Eng; Sml Crft Tech; Nvl Archit) All MEng and BEng courses take a common Stage 1 first year and then follow their specialised degree programmes. Transfer is possible between MEng courses and to the Marine Technology BEng degree.
Southampton Solent (Ycht Pwrcrft Des) The course is fully accredited by the Royal Institution of Naval Architects. A foundation year is available.
Strathclyde (Nvl Archit) A broad-based engineering course covering engineering science, flotation and stability, ship and offshore structures design. Topics also include resistance and propulsion, ship structural analysis, marine engineering systems, business and management. Some opportunities for sponsorship and work experience.

Universities and colleges teaching quality See www.qaa.ac.uk; http://unistats.direct.gov.uk.

Top research universities and colleges (RAE 2008) (Naval Architecture and Marine Engineering) Glasgow; Strathclyde.

ADMISSIONS INFORMATION
Number of applicants per place (approx) Newcastle 9; Southampton 4.

Advice to applicants and planning the UCAS personal statement Special interests in this subject area should be described fully. Visits to shipyards and awareness of ship design from the *Mary Rose* in Portsmouth to modern speedboats should be fully explained and the problems noted. See also **Engineering/Engineering Sciences**, **Marine/Maritime Studies** and **Appendix 3**.

Selection interviews Yes Newcastle, Southampton.

Interview advice and questions Because of the highly vocational nature of this subject, applicants will naturally be expected to discuss any work experience and to justify their reasons for choosing the course. See also **Chapter 6**.

AFTER-RESULTS ADVICE
Offers to applicants repeating A-levels Higher Newcastle.

GRADUATE DESTINATIONS AND EMPLOYMENT (2009/10 HESA)
Graduates surveyed 110 **Employed** 50 **In voluntary employment** 0 **In further study** 10 **Assumed unemployed** 5

Career note A small proportion of naval architects work in the shipbuilding and repair industry, others are involved in the construction of oil rigs or may work for ship-owning companies. There are also a number of firms of marine consultants employing naval architects as managers or consultants.

OTHER DEGREE SUBJECTS FOR CONSIDERATION
Aeronautical Engineering; Civil Engineering; Electrical/Electronic Engineering; Geography; Marine Biology; Marine Engineering; Marine/Maritime Studies; Marine Technology; Mechanical Engineering; Oceanography; Physics; Shipping Operations; Transport Management.

NURSING and MIDWIFERY

(including Paramedic Science; see also Biological Sciences, Community Studies/Development, Health Sciences/Studies)

Nursing and Midwifery courses are designed to equip students with the scientific and caring skills demanded by medical science in the 21st century. Courses follow a similar pattern with an introductory programme of study covering clinical skills, nursing practice and the behavioural and social sciences. Thereafter, specialisation starts in adult, child or mental health nursing, or with patients with learning disabilities. Throughout the three-year course students gain extensive clinical experience in hospital wards, clinics, accident and emergency and high-dependency settings. UCAS handles applications for Nursing degree and diploma courses.

Useful websites www.scicentral.com; www.nhscareers.nhs.uk; www.nursingtimes.net; see also **Health Sciences/Studies** and **Medicine**.

NB The points totals shown to the left of the institutions are for ease of reference only. It must not be assumed that Tariff points are always used by institutions or that they can be substituted for an offer in grades. The level of an offer is not necessarily indicative of the quality of a course.

COURSE OFFERS INFORMATION

Subject requirements/preferences GCSE English and a science subject. Mathematics required at several universities. **AL** Science subjects required for some courses. **Other** requirements All applicants holding firm offers will require an occupational health check and Criminal Records Bureau (CRB) clearance and are required to provide documentary evidence that they have not been infected with hepatitis-B. (Paramed Sci) Full clean manual UK driving licence with at least a provisional C1 category.

Your target offers and examples of courses provided by each institution
Abbreviations used in this table A – Adult; C – Child; LD – Learning Disability; MH – Mental Health
340 pts London (King's) – BBBc (Nurs A/C/MH) (IB 32 pts HL 5 sci)
      Southampton – AAB (Midwif) (IB 34 pts HL 17 pts)
320 pts Bournemouth – 320 pts (Midwif)
      Nottingham – ABB (Nurs Sci MNursSci) (IB 27 pts)
      Surrey – ABB–BBB incl AL sci (Midwif; Nurs St)
300 pts Birmingham – BBB (Nurs A/MH) (IB 30–34 pts)
      Bristol UWE – 300 pts (Midwif)
      Cardiff – BBB (Midwif) (IB 28 pts)
      Cumbria – 300 pts (Midwif)
      Edinburgh – AAA–BBB 300–360 pts (Nurs St) (IB 34–42 pts HL 555)
      Glasgow – BBB (Nurs A/C/LD/MH)
      Leeds – BBB (Nurs A/C/LD/MH; Midwif)
      Liverpool – BBB 300 pts (Nurs) (IB 30 pts)
      LJMU – 300 pts (Midwif) (IB 26 pts)
      Manchester – BBB 300 pts (Midwif) (IB 31 pts)
      Sheffield Hallam – 300 pts (Midwif)
      Southampton – BBB–ABB 300–320 pts (Nurs A/C/MH) (IB 30 pts HL 16 pts)
      Surrey – ABB–BBB incl AL sci 300–320 pts (Paramed Sci)
      Swansea – BBB 300 pts (Midwif)
280 pts Bournemouth – 280 pts (Nurs A/C/LD/MH)
      Bradford – 280 pts (Midwif St)
      Brighton – BBC 280 pts (Nurs A/C/MH)
      Hertfordshire – check with admissions tutor 280–300 pts (Paramed Sci)
      Manchester – BBC (Nurs A/C/MH) (IB 30 pts)
      Manchester Met – 280 pts (Nurs A) (IB 29 pts)
      Northumbria – 280 pts (Midwif St)

Check **Chapter 4** when choosing your university and **Chapter 7** on how to read the subject tables.

Health
Sciences

UNIVERSITY OF
Southampton

The University of Southampton offers you more than just a degree. We're training the next generation of health professionals in a supportive and friendly environment.

Health Sciences is nationally regarded as a pioneering centre of excellence for developing innovative Health Science roles. We enable practitioners to combine clinically focused research with developing advanced clinical skills, as part of the modernisation of health care professional careers and the drive to deliver patient-focused translational research.

Our vision is to create a world-class environment of learning and discovery. Improving health outcomes and transforming health care drives our ambitions locally, nationally and globally. Practitioners who train at Southampton are well-placed to become expert clinicians and leaders across health and social care.

Our academic staff work together in multidisciplinary research groups tackling challenging issues such as cancer, palliative and end of life care, rehabilitation and the organisation of care.

www.southampton.ac.uk/healthsciences

Oxford Brookes – BBC (Midwif; Nurs Chld)
Suffolk (Univ Campus) – 280 pts (Midwif; Nurs A/C/MH)
Swansea – BBC–BBB 290 pts (Nurs A/C/MH)
UEA – 280 pts (Midwif)
Ulster – 280 pts (Nurs A/MH)
York – BBB–BBC 280–300 pts (Nurs Prac A/C/LD/MH) (IB 28 pts)

260 pts **Birmingham City** – 260 pts (Nurs A/C/LD/MH)
Brighton – offers may vary BCC 260 pts (Paramed Sci) (IB 28 pts)
Coventry – 260 pts (Midwif)
Edge Hill – BCC 260 pts (Nurs A/C/MH/LD; Midwif)
Huddersfield – BCC 260 pts (Midwif St)
Kingston – BCC (Midwif)
LJMU – 260 pts (Mntl Hlth Nurs) (IB 24 pts)
Northumbria – 260 pts (Nurs A/C/LD/MH) (IB 24 pts)
Nottingham – BCC (Nurs A/C/LD/MH) (IB 28 pts)
Queen's Belfast – BC/CCD (with relevant subj) **or** BB/CCC (without relevant subj) (Nurs A/C/LD/MH)
Salford – 260–280 pts (Midwif)
Teesside – 260–380 pts (Midwif)

240 pts **Anglia Ruskin** – 240 pts (Midwif)
Bangor – CCC 240 pts (Midwif)
Bedfordshire – 240 pts (Midwif)
Birmingham City – CCC 240 pts (Midwif)
Bradford – 240 pts (Nurs A/MH)
Brighton – CCC (Midwif) (IB 28 pts)
Bristol UWE – 240 pts (Nurs A/C/MH/LD) (IB 24 pts)
Bucks New – 200–240 pts (Nurs A/C/MH)
Canterbury Christ Church – CCC 240 pts (Midwif)
Chester – 240–280 pts (Midwif) (IB 26 pts)
Coventry – CCC 240 pts (Nurs A/C/LD/MH) (IB 27–28 pts)
Cumbria – 220–240 pts (Nurs A/MH/LD)
De Montfort – CCC 240 pts (Nurs A/C; Midwif)
Derby – 240 pts (Nursing A/MH)
Glamorgan – 240–280 pts (Midwif)
Hertfordshire – 240 pts (Nurs)
Kingston – 240 pts (Nurs (RN))
Leeds Met – 240 pts (Nurs A/MH)
Lincoln – CCC 240 pts (Nurs A)
Oxford Brookes – CCC (Nurs A/MH)
Plymouth – CCC 240 pts (Paramed Practnr)
Queen's Belfast – BCC/CCD (with relevant subj)/BB/CCC (without relevant subj) (Midwif)
Robert Gordon – CCC–BC (Nurs A/C/MH)
Staffordshire – CCC 240 pts (Nurs Prac A/C/MH; Midwif Prac)
Salford – 240 pts (Prof St Nurs Soc Wk) (IB 26 pts)
Sheffield Hallam – 240 pts (Nurs St A/C/MH)
Teesside – 240 pts (Nurs St A/C/LD/MH)
UCLan – 240 pts (Midwif)
Worcester – 240 pts (Midwif)

220 pts **Bedfordshire** – 220 pts (Nurs A/C/LD/MH)
Edinburgh Queen Margaret – 220 pts (Nurs)
Northampton – 220–260 pts (Midwif)
Salford – 220 pts (Nurs A/C/MH) (IB 26 pts)
UCLan – 220 pts (Nurs Pre Reg)

200 pts **Coventry** – 200 pts (Paramed Sci)
Glyndŵr – 200 pts (Nurs)

Check **Chapter 4** when choosing your university and **Chapter 7** on how to read the subject tables.

        Hull – 200 pts (Nurs A/C/MH/LD)
        Northampton – 200–220 pts (Nurs A/C/MH/LD)
        Plymouth – 200–240 pts (Midwif; Nurs A/C/MH)
        UCLan – 200 pts (Nurs A/C/MH)
        West London – 200 pts (Midwif)
        Wolverhampton – 200 pts (Nurs A/C/MH)
180 pts **Edinburgh Napier** – 180 pts (Nurs A/C/MH/LD; Midwif)
        Greenwich – 180–200 pts (Nurs A/C/LD/MH; Midwif)
160 pts **Abertay Dundee** – CC (Nurs MH)
        Anglia Ruskin – 160 pts (Nurs A/C/LD/MH)
        Bristol UWE – Check with admissions tutor 160 pts (Paramed Prac)
        Dundee – check with admissions tutor CC–DD (Midwif)
        Glasgow Caledonian – CC 160 pts (Nurs A/LD/MH; Nurs St; Midwif)
        Keele – 160–200 pts (Nurs A/C/MH/LD)
        London South Bank – CC (MH Nurs Soc Wk)
        Robert Gordon – check with admissions tutor CC (Midwif)
        West London – 160–200 pts (Nurs A/C/MH/LD)
        Worcester – CC (Nurs A/C/MH)
140 pts **West Scotland** – CD 140 pts (Nurs A/C/MH)
120 pts **West Scotland** – CD 120 pts (Midwif)

        Open University – contact +44 (0)845 300 6090 **or** www.openuniversity.co.uk/you (Nurs Prac)

Alternative offers

See **Chapter 7** and **Appendix 1** for grades/UCAS Tariff points information for the International Baccalaureate, Scottish Highers/Advanced Highers, the Welsh Baccalaureate, the Irish Leaving Certificate, the Cambridge Pre-U Diploma, the Advanced Diploma and the Extended Project.

CHOOSING YOUR COURSE (SEE ALSO CH.1)

Some course features

Anglia Ruskin There is a common element of Nursing for all specialised areas that cover nursing fields in child, adult and mental health. There is also an International Nursing Studies course and a BSc Midwifery degree course.

Bedfordshire Obstetrics, midwifery, the midwife practitioner, women's health, ethics and law are all covered in the Nursing degree. Specialisation is offered in adult, children's and mental health nursing. A Midwifery course is also provided.

Hertfordshire (Paramed Sci) The course runs over four extended academic years and leads to qualifying and registering as a professional paramedic. Theoretical studies are interspersed with clinical practice placements. The third year is a sandwich/practice year when students are paid employees of the London Ambulance Service NHS Trust.

Liverpool The Adult Nursing degree is a three-year course leading to the degree (BNurs), with modules covering physiology, pathophysiology, behavioural sciences, communication skills, clinical skills and curative, rehabilitative and palliative care.

Swansea Nursing students in Wales are paid by a bursary from the NHS Wales Bursary Scheme. It is not means tested. The courses covers adult, child and mental health nursing, prior to which a common foundation course is offered. There is also a Midwifery degree.

Universities and colleges teaching quality See www.qaa.ac.uk; http://unistats.direct.gov.uk.

Top research universities and colleges (RAE 2008) Manchester; Southampton; Ulster; York; City; Hertfordshire; Leeds; Nottingham; Stirling.

ADMISSIONS INFORMATION

Number of applicants per place (approx) Abertay Dundee 10; Anglia Ruskin 10; Bangor 10; Birmingham 8; Birmingham City 15; Bournemouth 9; Brighton 3; Bristol UWE 27; Cardiff 12, (non-EU) 6; City (Nurs MH) 4, (Nurs C) 8, (Midwif) 5; Cumbria 8; De Montfort 10; Edinburgh Queen Margaret 3;

Glasgow Caledonian 12; Glyndŵr 4; Huddersfield (Midwif St) 10; Hull 10; Leeds (Midwif) 12; LJMU (Nurs) 5; London (King's) 4; London South Bank 16; Middlesex 10; Northampton 17; Northumbria 16; Nottingham 3; Salford 10, (Midwif) 11; Sheffield Hallam 8; Southampton (Nurs) 15, (Midwif) 25; Staffordshire (Midwif Prac) 10; Surrey 10; Swansea 10; UCLan (Midwif) 14; York (Nurs) 8, (Midwif Prac) 2.

Advice to applicants and planning the UCAS personal statement Experience of care work – for example in hospitals, old people's homes, children's homes – is important. Describe what you have done and what you have learned. Read nursing journals in order to be aware of new developments in the treatment of illnesses. Note, in particular, the various needs of patients and the problems they experience. Try to compare different nursing approaches with, for example, children, people with learning disabilities, old people and terminally ill people. If you under-performed at GCSE, give reasons. If you have had work experience or a part-time job, describe how your skills have developed, for example responsibility, communication, team-building, organisational skills. How do you spend your spare time? Explain how your interests help with stress and pressure. See also **Appendix 3**. Admission is subject to eligibility for an NHS bursary. Contact NHS Student Grants Unit, tel 01253 655655.

Misconceptions about this course That Nursing programmes are not demanding. Midwives and nurses don't do shift work and are not involved in travelling! **City** Midwives are only involved at the birth stage and not at the ante-natal and post-natal stages, or in education and support.

Selection interviews Most institutions **Yes** Abertay Dundee, Anglia Ruskin, Bangor, Birmingham, Birmingham (UC), Birmingham City, Bournemouth (Midwif), Brighton, Cardiff, City, Dundee, Dundee, Essex, Glyndŵr, Hertfordshire, Hull, LJMU, Nottingham, Sheffield Hallam, Stirling, Surrey, Swansea, UEA, West Scotland, Wolverhampton, York; **Some** Bucks New, Salford.

Interview advice and questions Past questions have included: Why do you want to be a nurse? What experience have you had in nursing? What do you think of the nurses' pay situation? Should nurses go on strike? What are your views on abortion? What branch of nursing most interests you? How would you communicate with someone who can't speak English? What is the nurse's role in the community? How should a nurse react in an emergency? How would you cope with telling a patient's relative that the patient was dying? Admissions tutors look for communication skills, team interaction and the applicant's understanding of health/society-related subjects. See also **Chapter 6**. **London South Bank** What do you understand by equal opportunities? **Swansea** What is your perception of the role of the nurse? What qualities do you have that would be good for nursing?

Reasons for rejection (non-academic) Insufficient awareness of the roles and responsibilities of a midwife or nurse. Lack of motivation. Poor communication skills. Lack of awareness of nursing developments through the media. (Detailed knowledge of the NHS or nursing practice not usually required.) Failed medical. Unsatisfactory health record. Not fulfilling the hepatitis B requirements or police check requirements. Poor preparation for the interview. Too shy. Only wants nursing as a means to something else, for example commission in the armed forces. Too many choices on the UCAS application, for example Midwifery, Physiotherapy, Occupational Therapy. No care experience. Some applicants have difficulty with maths – multiplication and division – used in calculating dosage for medicines. **Birmingham** No work experience. **De Montfort** No insight as to nursing as a career or the various branches of nursing. **Swansea** Poor communication skills.

AFTER-RESULTS ADVICE
Offers to applicants repeating A-levels Higher Bristol UWE, Cardiff, Hull, LJMU (Midwif); **Same** De Montfort, Edinburgh Queen Margaret, Huddersfield, LJMU, London South Bank, Salford, Staffordshire, Stirling, Suffolk (Univ Campus), Surrey, Swansea, Wolverhampton.

GRADUATE DESTINATIONS AND EMPLOYMENT (2009/10 HESA)
Graduates surveyed 19,890 **Employed** 17365 **In voluntary employment** 10 **In further study** 2175 **Assumed unemployed** 445

Career note The majority of graduates aim to enter the nursing profession.

Check **Chapter 4** when choosing your university and **Chapter 7** on how to read the subject tables.

OTHER DEGREE SUBJECTS FOR CONSIDERATION

Audiology; Biological Sciences; Biology; Community Studies; Dietetics; Education; Health Studies; Medicine; Nutrition; Occupational Therapy; Optometry; Pharmacology; Pharmacy; Physiotherapy; Podiatry; Psychology; Radiography; Social Policy and Administration; Social Work; Sociology; Speech Therapy; Veterinary Nursing.

NUTRITION

(see also Dietetics, Food Science/Studies and Technology)

Nutrition attracts a great deal of attention in society and whilst controversy, claim and counter-claim seem to focus daily on the merits and otherwise of food, it is, nevertheless, a scientific study in itself. Courses involve topics relating to diet, health, nutrition and food policy and are designed to prepare students to enter careers as specialists in nutrition and dietetics.

Useful websites www.nutrition.org.uk; www.nutritionsociety.org; see also under **Dietetics**.

NB The points totals shown to the left of the institutions are for ease of reference only. It must not be assumed that Tariff points are always used by institutions or that they can be substituted for an offer in grades. The level of an offer is not necessarily indicative of the quality of a course.

COURSE OFFERS INFORMATION

Subject requirements/preferences GCSE Mathematics and science usually required. **AL** Science subjects required for most courses, biology and/or chemistry preferred.

Your target offers and examples of courses provided by each institution

380 pts London (King's) – AABc (Nutr Diet) (IB 36 pts HL chem biol)

360 pts London (King's) – ABBc (Nutr) (IB 34 pts)

340 pts Newcastle – AAB (Fd Mark Nutr) (IB 32–35 pts)
Nottingham – AAB–ABB (Nutr (Diet) MNutr) (IB 32–34 pts)
Surrey – AAB (Nutr) (IB 35 pts)

320 pts Glasgow – ABB (Physiol Spo Sci Nutr) (IB 32 pts)
Leeds – ABB (Fd St Nutr) (IB 32 pts)
Liverpool Hope – 260–320 pts (Hlth Nutr Joint Hons) (IB 28 pts)
Newcastle – AAB–ABB 320–340 pts (Fd Hum Nutr) (IB 32–35 pts)
Nottingham – ABB–BBC (Nutr Fd Sci) (IB 28–32 pts)
Roehampton – 320 pts (Nutr Hlth)
Surrey – ABB–BBB 320–300 pts (Nutr Diet) (IB 34–32 pts)

300 pts Leeds Met – BBB incl chem (Diet) (IB 26 pts HL 5 chem)
London Met – 300 pts (Diet Nutr) (IB 28 pts)
Queen's Belfast – BBB (Fd Qual Sfty Nutr) (IB 32 pts)
Reading – BBB 300 pts (Nutri Fd Sci)
UCLan – 260–300 pts (Hum Nutr; Nutr Exer Sci)

280 pts Bournemouth – 280 pts (Nutr) (28 pts)
Chester – 280–300 pts (Nutr Diet) (IB 28 pts)
Leeds Trinity (UC) – 280 pts (Spo Hlth Exer Nutr; Nutr Fd)
Manchester Met – 280 pts (Hum Nutr) (IB 28 pts)
Northumbria – 280–300 pts (Fd Sci Nutr; Spo Exer Nutr) (IB 28 pts)
Oxford Brookes – BBC (Nutr) (IB 30 pts)
Plymouth – 280–300 pts (Exer Nutr Hlth; Pblc Hlth Nutr)
Sheffield Hallam – 280 pts (Pblc Hlth Nutr; Nutr Hlth Lfstl)
Suffolk (Univ Campus) – 280 pts (Nutr Hum Hlth)
Worcester – 240–280 pts (Hum Nutr)

260 pts Cardiff Met – 260 pts (Hum Nutr Diet)
Edge Hill – BCC 260 pts (Nutr Hlth)

Glamorgan – 220–260 pts (Nutr) (IB 28 pts)
Glasgow Caledonian – BB–BCC (Hum Nutr Diet)
Harper Adams (UC) – 220–260 pts (Fd Nutr Wlbng)
Hertfordshire – 260 pts (Nutr)
Liverpool Hope – 260 pts (Nutr Hlth Prom) (IB 25 pts)
LJMU – 260 pts (Fd Nutr)
Nottingham Trent – 260 pts (Exer Nutr Hlth)
Teesside – 260–280 pts (Fd Nutr Hlth Sci)
Ulster – 260 pts (Hum Nutr)

240 pts **Bath Spa** – 240–280 pts (Hum Nutr)
Birmingham City – 240 pts (Nutr Sci)
Cardiff Met – 240 pts (Spo Biomed Nutr)
Chester – 240–280 pts (Hum Nutr) (IB 26 pts)
Coventry – CCC 240 pts (Exer Nutr Hlth; Fd Sci Nutr)
Huddersfield – 240 pts (Nutr Pblc Hlth; Fd Nutr Hlth)
Lincoln – 240 pts (Hum Nutr)
London Met – 240 pts (Hum Nutr) (IB 28 pts)
Newport – 240 pts (Nutr)
Robert Gordon – CCC 240 pts (Nutr Diet) (IB 28 pts)
Ulster – 240 pts (Fd Nutr)

220 pts **Bath Spa** – 220–280 pts (Fd Nutr) (IB 24 pts)
Glamorgan – 220–260 pts (Nutr Physl Actvt Commun Hlth) (IB 28 pts)
Greenwich – 220–240 pts (Hum Nutr)
St Mary's Twickenham (UC) – 220 pts (Nutr) (IB 28 pts)
Westminster – CCD (Nutr Exer Sci) (IB 26 pts)

200 pts **Abertay Dundee** – CDD (Fd Nutr Hlth)
CAFRE – 200 pts (Fd Des Nutr)
Kingston – 200–280 pts (Nutr Spo Sci; Nutr; Hum Biol Nutr; Bioch Nutr)
Leeds Met – 200 pts (Pbl Hlth (Nutr)) (IB 24 pts HL 5 biol)
London South Bank – CDD 200 pts (Fd Nutr)

180 pts **Abertay Dundee** – 180 pts (Spo Exer Nutr) (IB 26 pts)
Trinity Saint David – 180–360 pts (Hlth Nutr Lfstl)

160 pts **Edinburgh Queen Margaret** – 160 pts (Nutr)
Robert Gordon – CC (Nutr)

140 pts **Bradford (Coll Univ Centre)** – 140 pts (Diet Nutr Hlth)

Alternative offers
See **Chapter 7** and **Appendix 1** for grades/UCAS Tariff points information for the International Baccalaureate, Scottish Highers/Advanced Highers, the Welsh Baccalaureate, the Irish Leaving Certificate, the Cambridge Pre-U Diploma, the Advanced Diploma and the Extended Project.

EXAMPLES OF FOUNDATION DEGREES IN THE SUBJECT FIELD
CAFRE; Truro (Coll).

CHOOSING YOUR COURSE (SEE ALSO CH.1)
Some course features
London (King's) The BSc course is a modular programme with specialised options including diet, disease, obesity, antioxidants and cancer. There is a four year Nutrition and Dietetics course with clinical placements in Year 2, 3 and 4, leading to qualification as a dietician.
Newcastle (Fd Hum Nutr) Stages 1 and 2 focus on biology and biological chemistry, with an emphasis on nutrition and food science. After a work placement, Stage 3 covers nutrition, health and disease, biotechnology in the food industry, plants as food, and sport and exercise nutrition.
Reading (Nutr Fd Sci) Course is normally four years with a placement year in Year 3.
Sheffield Hallam (Pblc Hlth Nutr) Course includes business elements covering human resources and project management.

Universities and colleges teaching quality See www.qaa.ac.uk; http://unistats.direct.gov.uk.

Top research universities and colleges (RAE 2008) (Nutritional Sciences) See also **Agricultural Sciences/Agriculture**. London (King's).

Examples of sandwich degree courses Cardiff Met; Coventry; Glasgow Caledonian; Harper Adams (UC); Huddersfield; Kingston; Leeds Met; Lincoln; Manchester Met; Newcastle; Northumbria; Queen's Belfast; Reading; Sheffield Hallam; Surrey; Teesside; Ulster.

ADMISSIONS INFORMATION

Number of applicants per place (approx) Cardiff Met 5; Glasgow Caledonian 8; LJMU 10; London (King's) 6; London Met 9; London South Bank 5; Newcastle 5; Nottingham 7; Robert Gordon 4; Surrey 5.

Advice to applicants and planning the UCAS personal statement Information on relevant experience, reasons for wanting to do the degree and careers sought would be useful. See also **Dietetics**. **Surrey** Overseas students not eligible for Nutrition and Dietetics course.

Misconceptions about this course Some applicants do not realise that this is a science course.

Selection interviews Yes London Met, London South Bank, Nottingham (depends on application), Robert Gordon, Surrey; **Some** LJMU, Roehampton.

Interview advice and questions Past questions have focused on scientific A-level subjects studied and aspects of subjects enjoyed by the applicants. Questions then arise from answers. Extensive knowledge expected of nutrition as a career and candidates should have talked to people involved in this type of work, for example dietitians. They will also be expected to discuss wider problems such as food supplies in developing countries and nutritional problems resulting from famine. See also **Chapter 6**. **LJMU** Interviews are informal. It would be useful for you to bring samples of coursework to the interview.

AFTER-RESULTS ADVICE

Offers to applicants repeating A-levels Possibly higher Nottingham; **Same** LJMU, Manchester Met, Roehampton, St Mary's Twickenham (UC), Surrey.

GRADUATE DESTINATIONS AND EMPLOYMENT (2009/10 HESA)

Graduates surveyed 995 **Employed** 740 **In voluntary employment** 15 **In further study** 165 **Assumed unemployed** 70

Career note Nutritionists work in retail, health promotion and sport whilst others specialise in dietetics.

OTHER DEGREE SUBJECTS FOR CONSIDERATION

Biological Sciences; Biology; Consumer Studies; Dietetics; Food Sciences; Health Studies/Sciences.

OCCUPATIONAL THERAPY

Contrary to common belief, occupational therapy is not an art career although art and craftwork may be involved as a therapeutic exercise. Occupational therapists assess the physical, mental and social needs of ill or disabled people and help them regain lost skills and manage their lives to the best of their circumstances. Most courses include anatomy, physiology, physical rehabilitation, psychology, sociology, mental health and ethics. Selectors look for maturity, initiative, enterprise, tact, sound judgement and organising ability.

Useful websites www.cot.co.uk; www.otdirect.co.uk.

NB The points totals shown to the left of the institutions are for ease of reference only. It must not be assumed that Tariff points are always used by institutions or that they can be substituted for an offer in grades. The level of an offer is not necessarily indicative of the quality of a course.

COURSE OFFERS INFORMATION

Subject requirements/preferences GCSE English, mathematics and science grade A–C. **AL** A social science or science subjects required or preferred for most courses. **Other** All applicants need to pass an occupational health check and obtain Criminal Records Bureau (CRB) clearance.

Your target offers and examples of courses provided by each institution

340 pts **Bristol UWE** – 340 pts (Occ Thera) (IB 32 pts)
   Southampton – AAB (Occ Thera) (IB 34 pts HL 17 pts)
320 pts **Cardiff** – ABB (Occ Thera) (IB 27 pts)
300 pts **Bournemouth** – 300 pts (Occ Thera) (IB 28 pts)
   Plymouth – 300 pts (Occ Thera) (IB 27 pts)
   Ulster – BBB (Occ Thera) (IB 25 pts)
280 pts **Bradford** – 280 pts (Occ Thera) (IB 24 pts)
   Derby – 280 pts (Occ Thera) (IB 26 pts)
   Huddersfield – 280 pts (Occ Thera)
   Manchester Met – 280 pts (Acu) (IB 30 pts)
   Northampton – 260–280 pts (Occ Thera) (IB 24 pts)
   Northumbria – 280 pts (Occ Thera)
   Oxford Brookes – BBC (Occ Thera) (IB 30 pts)
   UEA – BBC (Occ Thera) (IB 30 pts HL 655)
260 pts **Brunel** – BCC (Occ Thera) (IB 29 pts)
   Coventry – 260 pts (Occ Thera)
   Cumbria – 260 pts (Occ Thera)
   Derby – 260–280 pts (Spo Msg Exer Thera Joint Hons)
   Edinburgh Queen Margaret – 260 pts (Occ Thera)
   Liverpool – BCC (Occ Thera) (IB 28 pts)
   Robert Gordon – 240–260 pts (Occ Thera) (IB 26 pts)
   Sheffield Hallam – 260 pts (Occ Thera)
   York St John – 260 pts (Occ Thera) (IB 24 pts)
240 pts **Canterbury Christ Church** – 240 pts (Occ Thera)
   Salford – 240 pts (Occ Thera)
   Teesside – 240–280 pts (Occ Thera)
220 pts **London South Bank** – 220 pts (Occ Thera) (IB 24 pts)
160 pts **Glasgow Caledonian** – CC (Occ Thera)

   Brighton – p/t, individual offers may vary, NHS bursaries are available for all courses (Occ Thera)

Alternative offers

See **Chapter 7** and **Appendix 1** for grades/UCAS Tariff points information for the International Baccalaureate, Scottish Highers/Advanced Highers, the Welsh Baccalaureate, the Irish Leaving Certificate, the Cambridge Pre-U Diploma, the Advanced Diploma and the Extended Project.

CHOOSING YOUR COURSE (SEE ALSO CH.1)

Some course features
See also **Health Sciences/Studies**.

Brunel (Occ Thera) Course can be taken for three years full time or four years part-time.
Liverpool (Occ Thera) Six placements take place throughout the course. 1000 hours required in practice settings for professional registration.
UEA (Occ Thera) Practice placements in hospitals and the community. Advanced units in Year 3 include Context of Practice, Placement and Professional Development.

Universities and colleges teaching quality See www.qaa.ac.uk; http://unistats.direct.gov.uk.

ADMISSIONS INFORMATION

Number of applicants per place (approx) Canterbury Christ Church 5; Cardiff 10; Coventry 15; Cumbria 20; Derby 5; Edinburgh Queen Margaret 7; Northampton 4; Northumbria 4; Oxford Brookes 12; Robert Gordon 6; Salford 5; Sheffield Hallam 7; Southampton 7; UEA 5; Ulster 13; York St John 5.

Health
Sciences

UNIVERSITY OF
Southampton

"I came to Southampton because it is one of the most respected Universities for health sciences. With my degree, I hope to work with injured soldiers in developing world countries. The University offers so many extra-curricular opportunities, there is simply not enough hours in the day. I love the fitness classes at the Jubilee Sports Centre and have kept my first aid certificate up-to-date with the Royal Yachting Association (RYA). I am also on the committee for the University Symphonic Wind Orchestra and play the flute. The library is one of the main attractions of this uni – it is huge. I often go there to work on essays with my friends because there are no distractions and you have all the books you could need."

Lydia Pavia | Occupational Therapy

www.southampton.ac.uk/healthsciences

Advice to applicants and planning the UCAS personal statement Contact your local hospital and discuss this career with the occupational therapists. Try to obtain work shadowing experience and make notes of your observations. Describe any such visits in full (see also **Reasons for rejection (non-academic)**). Applicants are expected to have visited two occupational therapy departments, one in a physical or social services setting, one in the mental health field. Good interpersonal skills. Breadth and nature of health-related work experience is important. Also skills, interests (for example, sports, design). Applicants should have a high standard of communication skills and experience of working with people with disabilities. See also **Appendix 3**. **York St John** Contact with the profession essential; very competitive course.

Selection interviews Most institutions. **Yes** Canterbury Christ Church, UEA.

Interview advice and questions Since this a vocational course, work experience is nearly always essential and applicants are likely to be questioned on the types of work involved and the career. Some universities may use admissions tests: check websites and see **Chapter 6**.

Reasons for rejection (non-academic) Poor communication skills. Lack of knowledge of occupational therapy. Little evidence of working with people. Uncertain about their future career. Lack of maturity. Indecision regarding the profession. **Salford** Failure to function well in groups and inability to perform practical tasks.

AFTER-RESULTS ADVICE
Offers to applicants repeating A-levels Same Derby, Salford, York St John.

GRADUATE DESTINATIONS AND EMPLOYMENT (2009/10 HESA)
Graduates surveyed 1165 **Employed** 715 **In voluntary employment** 5 **In further study** 215 **Assumed unemployed** 50

For a quick reference offers calculator, fold out the inside back cover.

Career note Occupational therapists (who work mostly in hospital departments) are involved in the rehabilitation of those who have required medical treatment and involve the young, aged and, for example, people with learning difficulties.

OTHER DEGREE SUBJECTS FOR CONSIDERATION

Audiology; Community Studies; Dietetics; Education; Health Studies/Sciences; Nursing; Nutrition; Physiotherapy; Podiatry; Psychology; Radiography; Social Policy and Administration; Social Work; Sociology; Speech Sciences.

OPTOMETRY (OPHTHALMIC OPTICS)

(including **Ophthalmic Dispensing** and **Orthoptics**)

Optometry courses (which are increasingly popular) lead to qualification as an optometrist (previously known as an ophthalmic optician). They provide training in detecting defects and diseases in the eye and in prescribing treatment with, for example, spectacles, contact lenses and other appliances to correct or improve vision. Orthoptics includes the study of general anatomy, physiology and normal child development and leads to a career as an orthoptist. This involves the investigation, diagnosis and treatment of binocular vision and other eye conditions. The main components of degree courses include the study of the eye, the use of diagnostic and measuring equipment and treatment of eye abnormalities. See also **Appendix 3**.

Useful websites www.optical.org; www.orthoptics.org.uk.

NB The points totals shown to the left of the institutions are for ease of reference only. It must not be assumed that Tariff points are always used by institutions or that they can be substituted for an offer in grades. The level of an offer is not necessarily indicative of the quality of a course.

COURSE OFFERS INFORMATION

Subject requirements/preferences **GCSE** Good grades in English and science subjects usually required. **AL** Science subjects required for all Optometry courses. Mathematics usually acceptable.

Your target offers and examples of courses provided by each institution

380 pts **City** – AABc (Optom) (IB 33 pts)
360 pts **Aston** – AAA (Optom) (IB 34–35 pts)
 Cardiff – AAA (Optom) (IB 34 pts)
340 pts **Bradford** – AAB 340 pts (Optom) (IB 33 pts)
 Glasgow Caledonian – AAB (Optometry)
 Manchester – AAB (Optom) (IB 35 pts)
 Plymouth – 340 pts (Optom)
 Ulster – AAB 340 pts (Optom) (IB 37 pts)
320 pts **Anglia Ruskin** – ABB (Optom) (IB 33 pts HL 6 chem biol maths)
300 pts **Sheffield** – BBB (Orth) (IB 32 pts)
260 pts **Liverpool** – BCC (Orth) (IB 28 pts HL 5 biol)
200 pts **Anglia Ruskin** – 200 pts (Oph Disp)
180 pts **City** – 180 pts (Oph Disp)
160 pts **Bradford (Coll Univ Centre)** – 160–180 pts (Oph Disp Mgt)
 Glasgow Caledonian – CC (Oph Disp)

Alternative offers
See **Chapter 7** and **Appendix 1** for grades/UCAS Tariff points information for the International Baccalaureate, Scottish Highers/Advanced Highers, the Welsh Baccalaureate, the Irish Leaving Certificate, the Cambridge Pre-U Diploma, the Advanced Diploma and the Extended Project.

EXAMPLES OF FOUNDATION DEGREES IN THE SUBJECT FIELD

Anglia Ruskin.

CHOOSING YOUR COURSE (SEE ALSO CH.1)
Some course features
Aston The course offers an integration of teaching and professional practice and a hospital placement scheme.
Bradford Placements take place after graduation during the pre-registration year.
Cardiff This is a three-year course after which graduates undertake a one-year pre-registration course.
City Extensive patient contact takes place in Year 3.

Universities and colleges teaching quality See www.qaa.ac.uk; http://unistats.direct.gov.uk.

Top research universities and colleges (RAE 2008) Aston (Optom); City (Biomed Vsn Sci); Cardiff (Optom Vsn Sci).

ADMISSIONS INFORMATION
Number of applicants per place (approx) Anglia Ruskin 12; Aston 7; Bradford 6; Cardiff 13; City 11; Glasgow Caledonian 9.

Numbers of applicants (a UK **b** EU (non-UK) **c** non-EU **d** mature) Anglia Ruskin **a**431 **b**431; Aston **a**700 **b**50 **c**70 **d**10; Bradford **a**600 **b**600 **c**90; Glasgow Caledonian **a**548 **c**23.

Advice to applicants and planning the UCAS personal statement For Optometry courses contact with optometrists is essential, either work shadowing or gaining some work experience. Make notes of your experiences and the work done and report fully on the UCAS application on why the career interests you.

Selection interviews Yes Bradford, City, Glasgow Caledonian; **Some** Anglia Ruskin, Aston, Cardiff.

Interview advice and questions Optometry is a competitive subject requiring applicants to have had some work experience on which they will be questioned. See also **Chapter 6**. **Anglia Ruskin** Why will you make a good optometrist? Describe the job.

AFTER-RESULTS ADVICE
Offers to applicants repeating A-levels Higher City; **Possibly higher** Aston; **Same** Anglia Ruskin, Cardiff.

GRADUATE DESTINATIONS AND EMPLOYMENT (2009/10 HESA)
Graduates surveyed 1050 **Employed** 580 **In voluntary employment** 0 **In further study** 265 **Assumed unemployed** 20

Career note The great majority of graduates enter private practice either in small businesses or in larger organisations (which have been on the increase in recent years). A small number work in eye hospitals. Orthoptists tend to work in public health and education dealing with children and the elderly.

OTHER DEGREE SUBJECTS FOR CONSIDERATION
Health Studies; Nursing; Occupational Therapy; Physics; Physiotherapy; Radiography; Speech Studies.

PHARMACOLOGY

(including **Toxicology**; see also **Biological Sciences, Health Sciences/Studies**)

Pharmacology is the study of drugs and medicines and courses focus on physiology, biochemistry, toxicology, immunology, microbiology and chemotherapy. Pharmacologists are not qualified to work as pharmacists. Toxicology involves the study of the adverse effects of chemicals on living systems. See also **Appendix 3** under **Pharmacology**.

Useful websites www.thebts.org; www.scienceyear.com; www.pharmacology.com.

NB The points totals shown to the left of the institutions are for ease of reference only. It must not be assumed that Tariff points are always used by institutions or that they can be substituted for an offer in grades. The level of an offer is not necessarily indicative of the quality of a course.

COURSE OFFERS INFORMATION

Subject requirements/preferences GCSE English, science and mathematics. **AL** Chemistry and/or biology required for most courses.

Your target offers and examples of courses provided by each institution

380 pts **Cambridge** – A*AA (Nat Sci (Pharmacol)) (IB 40–42 pts HL 766–777)
London (King's) – AABc (Pharmacol) (IB 36 pts HL 6 chem 6 biol)

360 pts **Edinburgh** – AAA–ABB (Pharmacol) (IB 37–32 pts)
Leeds – AAA–BBB (Pharmacol) (IB 36–32 pts HL 17–15 pts)
London (UCL) – AAAe–AABe (Pharmacol) (IB 36–38 pts)
Manchester – AAA–AAB 340–360 pts (Pharmacol (Yr Ind)) (IB 37–33 pts)
Southampton – AAA–ABB (Pharmacol) (IB 36–32 pts HL 18–16 pts)

340 pts **Bath** – AAB (Pharmacol) (IB 34 pts HL 666)
Cardiff – AAB–ABB (Med Pharmacol) (IB 34 pts)
Edinburgh – AAA–ABB 340–360 pts (Biol Sci Pharmacol) (IB 37–32 pts)
Newcastle – AAB (Pharmacol) (IB 32 pts HL 5 chem biol)
Nottingham – AAB (Neuro Pharmacol) (IB 34 pts)

320 pts **Birmingham** – ABB–BBB 300–320 pts (Chem Pharmacol)
Bristol – AAB–ABB 320–340 pts (Pharmacol (Yr Ind)) (IB 35 pts HL 666 incl 2 sci)
Glasgow – ABB (Pharmacol) (IB 32 pts)
Leicester – ABB (Biol Sci (Physiol Pharmacol)) (IB 32–34 pts)
Liverpool – ABB (Pharmacol) (IB 32 pts HL 6 chem sci)
Strathclyde – ABB (Pharmacol)

300 pts **Dundee** – BBB (Pharmacol) (IB 30 pts)

280 pts **Nottingham Trent** – 280 pts (Pharmacol)
Strathclyde – BBC–BCC (Immun Pharmacol) (IB 28 pts)

260 pts **Bradford** – 260 pts (Biomed Sci (Pharmacol)) (IB 28 pts)
Dundee – BCC (Pharmacol Physiol Sci) (IB 28 pts)
Glasgow Caledonian – BCC (Pharmacol)
Hertfordshire – 260 pts (Pharmacol; Pharmacol (Yr Abrd))
Portsmouth – BCC 260 pts (Pharmacol)

240 pts **Aberdeen** – CCC (Pharmacol) (IB 28 pts)
Coventry – 240 pts (Med Pharmacol Sci)
London Met – 240 pts (Pharmacol)
UCLan – 240–260 pts (Physiol Pharmacol)

220 pts **Westminster** – CCD/CC (Herb Med)

200 pts **Kingston** – 200–280 pts (Pharmacol; Pharmacol Bus)
UEL – 200 pts (Pharmacol) (IB 24 pts)
Wolverhampton – 200 pts (Pharmacol)

165 pts **Edinburgh Queen Margaret** – 165 pts (App Pharmacol)

Alternative offers

See **Chapter 7** and **Appendix 1** for grades/UCAS Tariff points information for the International Baccalaureate, Scottish Highers/Advanced Highers, the Welsh Baccalaureate, the Irish Leaving Certificate, the Cambridge Pre-U Diploma, the Advanced Diploma and the Extended Project.

CHOOSING YOUR COURSE (SEE ALSO CH.1)

Some course features
Coventry The course in Medical and Pharmacological Sciences focuses on a study of pharmacology and physiology and applications in medicine. It can be taken with a year in professional placement.
Kingston There is an optional sandwich year in full-time employment.

London (King's) A Single Honours degree is offered in Pharmacology. In the first two years the focus is on physiology, biochemistry and pharmacology. In the third year, specialist topics include toxicology, immunology and environmental pharmacology. See also **Biological Sciences**.

Newcastle (Drug Dev) This new course focuses on science and engineering, covering chemistry, genetics, biology and pharmacology as well as bioprocessing for the large-scale manufacture of biopharmaceuticals.

Portsmouth The Pharmacology course has a common first year with Biomedical Science. This is a three year full-time course and includes a study of physiology and chemistry to support studies in pharmacology. Overall the course has a biochemical focus towards modern pharmacology with an emphasis on pharmacology in all three years.

Southampton The Pharmacology degree is based on both physiology and biochemistry and looks at the design of drugs and their biological effects. A one year placement is possible.

Universities and colleges teaching quality See www.qaa.ac.uk; http://unistats.direct.gov.uk.

Examples of sandwich degree courses (Including Pharmaceutical Sciences, Pharmacology and Pharmacy) Arts London; Bath (Pharmacol); Bradford (Pharm); Bristol (Pharmacol); Coventry (Pharm Sci); De Montfort (Pharml Cos Sci); Hertfordshire (Pharml Sci); Huddersfield (Pharml Sci); Kingston (Pharml Sci, Pharmacol); Manchester (Pharmacol); Manchester Met (Physiol Pharmacol St); Nottingham Trent (Pharmacol); Sheffield Hallam (Pharml Sci); Southampton (Pharmacol); UEL (Pharmacol).

ADMISSIONS INFORMATION

Number of applicants per place (approx) Bath 6; Birmingham 6; Bradford 20; Bristol 8; Cardiff 8; Dundee 5; Hertfordshire 10; Leeds 7; Liverpool 5; London (King's) 6; Portsmouth 4; Southampton 8; Strathclyde 10; UEL 4; Wolverhampton 4.

Advice to applicants and planning the UCAS personal statement Contact with the pharmaceutical industry is important in order to be aware of the range of work undertaken. Read pharmaceutical journals (although note that Pharmacology and Pharmacy courses lead to different careers). See also **Pharmacy and Pharmaceutical Sciences**. **Bath** Interests outside A-level studies. Important to produce evidence that there is more to the student than A-level ability. **Bristol** Be aware that a Pharmacology degree is mainly biological rather than chemical although both subjects are important.

Misconceptions about this course Mistaken belief that Pharmacology and Pharmaceutical Sciences is the same as Pharmacy and that a Pharmacology degree will lead to work as a pharmacist.

Selection interviews Yes Bath, Birmingham (don't be anxious – this is an opportunity for you to see us!), Cambridge, Newcastle; **Some** Cardiff, Dundee, Portsmouth.

Interview advice and questions Past questions include: Why do you want to do Pharmacology? Why not Pharmacy? Why not Chemistry? How are pharmacologists employed in industry? What are the issues raised by anti-vivisectionists on animal experimentation? Questions relating to the A-level syllabus in chemistry and biology. See also **Chapter 6**.

Reasons for rejection (non-academic) Confusion between Pharmacology, Pharmacy and Pharmaceutical Sciences. One university rejected two applicants because they had no motivation or understanding of the course (one had A-levels at AAB!). Insurance against rejection for Medicine. Lack of knowledge about pharmacology as a subject.

AFTER-RESULTS ADVICE

Offers to applicants repeating A-levels Higher Bristol, Glasgow, Leeds; **Same** Bath, Bradford, Cardiff, Dundee, Portsmouth.

GRADUATE DESTINATIONS AND EMPLOYMENT (2009/10 HESA)

Including Toxicology and Pharmacy; graduates surveyed 3655 **Employed** 2105 **In voluntary employment** 10 **In further study** 835 **Assumed unemployed** 100

Career note The majority of pharmacologists work with the large pharmaceutical companies involved in research and development. A small number are employed by the NHS in medical research and clinical trials. Some will eventually diversify and become involved in marketing, sales and advertising.

OTHER DEGREE SUBJECTS FOR CONSIDERATION

Biochemistry; Biological Sciences; Biology; Biotechnology; Chemistry; Life Sciences; Medical Biochemistry; Medicinal Chemistry; Microbiology; Natural Sciences; Pharmaceutical Sciences; Pharmacy; Physiology; Toxicology.

PHARMACY and PHARMACEUTICAL SCIENCES

(including **Herbal Medicine**; see also **Biochemistry, Chemistry, Health Sciences/Studies**)

Pharmacy is the science of medicines, involving research into chemical structures and natural products of possible medicinal value, the development of dosage and the safety testing of products. This table also includes information on courses in Pharmaceutical Science (which should not be confused with Pharmacy) which is a multidisciplinary subject covering chemistry, biochemistry, pharmacology and medical issues. Pharmaceutical scientists apply their knowledge of science and the biology of disease to the design and delivery of therapeutic agents. Note: All Pharmacy courses leading to MPharm are four years. Only Pharmacy degree courses accredited by the Royal Phamaceutical Society of Great Britain lead to a qualification as a pharmacist. Check prospectuses and websites.

Useful websites www.pharmweb.net; www.scienceyear.com; www.pharmacycareers.org; www.chemistanddruggist.co.uk.

NB The points totals shown to the left of the institutions are for ease of reference only. It must not be assumed that Tariff points are always used by institutions or that they can be substituted for an offer in grades. The level of an offer is not necessarily indicative of the quality of a course.

COURSE OFFERS INFORMATION

Subject requirements/preferences GCSE English, mathematics and science subjects. **AL** Chemistry and one or two other sciences required for most courses.

Your target offers and examples of courses provided by each institution
380 pts London (King's) – AABc (Pharm MPharm) (IB 36 pts HL 6 chem 6 maths/biol/phys)
360 pts London (Sch Pharm) – AAA–AAB (Pharm) (IB 32 pts HL 655)
    UEA – AAA–AAB (Pharm) (IB 31–32 pts)
340 pts Aston – AAB (Pharm MPharm) (IB 34 pts)
    Bath – AAB (Pharm) (IB 36 pts HL 666)
    Cardiff – AAB–ABB (Pharm) (IB 34 pts HL 6 chem +1 sci)
    Durham – AAB (MPharm) (IB 34 pts)
    Leeds – AAB (Cheml Pharml Eng) (IB 36 pts HL 17 pts)
    Manchester – AAB–ABB 320–340 pts (Pharm MPharm) (IB 33–36 pts HL 766)
    Nottingham – AAB (Pharm MPharm) (IB 36 pts)
    Queen's Belfast – AAB/ABBa (Pharm MPharm) (IB 34 pts HL 666)
    Reading – AAB–ABB (Pharm MPharm)
    Strathclyde – AAB (Pharm MPharm)
    Ulster – AAB 340 pts (Pharm)
320 pts Brighton – ABB (Pharm) (IB 34 pts HL 5 chem)
    De Montfort – 320 pts (Pharm)
    Hertfordshire – 320 pts (Pharm)
    Huddersfield – 320 pts (Pharm)
    Keele – ABB (Pharm) (IB 32 pts)
    Kent – ABB (Pharm) (IB 32 pts)

Portsmouth – ABB (Pharm MPharm) (IB 30 pts)
UCLan – ABB 320 pts (Pharm) (IB 32 pts)
UEA – ABB incl chem (Pharml Chem) (IB 32 pts HL 6 chem)
Wolverhampton – 320 pts (Pharm MPharm)
300 pts **Bradford** – 300 pts (Pharm) (IB 30 pts)
　　　　Hull – 280–300 pts (Pharml Sci)
　　　　Kingston – 300 pts (Pharm)
　　　　Leicester – BBB (Pharml Chem)
　　　　LJMU – 300–320 pts (Pharm MPharm) (IB 26 pts)
　　　　Loughborough – 300 pts (Medcnl Pharml Chem BSc) (IB 32 pts)
　　　　Robert Gordon – 300 pts (Pharm)
　　　　Sunderland – 300 pts (Pharm MPharm)
280 pts **Brighton** – BBC 280 pts (Pharml Cheml Sci) (IB 30 pts)
　　　　London (QM) – 280 pts (Pharml Chem) (IB 28 pts)
　　　　Manchester Met – 280 pts (Pharml Chem) (IB 28 pts)
　　　　Northumbria – 280 pts (Pharml Chem) (IB 25 pts)
260 pts **Greenwich** – 260 pts (Pharml Sci)
　　　　Nottingham Trent – 260 pts (Pharma Medl Chem)
240 pts **Arts London** – 240 pts (Cos Sci)
　　　　Bradford – 240 pts (Pharml Mgt)
　　　　Glamorgan – CCC 240 pts (Pharml Sci)
　　　　Hertfordshire – 240 pts (Pharml Sci)
　　　　London Met – 240 pts (Pharml Sci)
220 pts **Westminster** – CCD (Hlth Sci (Herb Med)) (IB 26 pts)
200 pts **Salford** – 200 pts (Pharml Sci)
　　　　Wolverhampton – 200–260 pts (Pharml Sci)
160 pts **Kingston** – 160 pts (Pharml Cheml Sci)

Alternative offers
See **Chapter 7** and **Appendix 1** for grades/UCAS Tariff points information for the International Baccalaureate, Scottish Highers/Advanced Highers, the Welsh Baccalaureate, the Irish Leaving Certificate, the Cambridge Pre-U Diploma, the Advanced Diploma and the Extended Project.

EXAMPLES OF FOUNDATION DEGREES IN THE SUBJECT FIELD
Aston; Birmingham Met (Coll); Kent (Medway Sch Pharm); Kingston; Preston (Coll); Sunderland City (Coll).

CHOOSING YOUR COURSE (SEE ALSO CH.1)
Some course features
Aston One of the largest pharmacy schools which includes hospital-based clinical teaching.
Brighton (Pharm) Studies include microbiology, clinical pharmacology, pharmacy practice and health psychology reflecting the changing role of the pharmacist.
Hertfordshire (Pharml Sci) Students not meeting the normal entry requirements can apply for an Extended degree which leads to Year 1 entry.
Keele Hospital, industrial and community placements take place throughout the course.
UEA (Pharm) Professional placements begin in Year 1.

Universities and colleges teaching quality See www.qaa.ac.uk; http://unistats.direct.gov.uk.

Top research universities and colleges (RAE 2008) Nottingham; Manchester; London UCK (Coll) (Sch Pharm); Bath; Queen's Belfast; UEA; London (King's); Strathclyde; Bradford; Cardiff.

Examples of sandwich degree courses See **Pharmacology**.

ADMISSIONS INFORMATION
Number of applicants per place (approx) Aston 10; Bath 6; Bradford 10; Brighton 24 (apply early); Cardiff 5; De Montfort 14; LJMU (Pharm) 7; London (King's) 15, (Sch Pharm) 6; Nottingham 8; Portsmouth 20; Robert Gordon 11; Strathclyde 10; Sunderland 20.

Numbers of applicants (a UK b EU (non-UK) c non-EU d mature) Aston a1400 b100 c300 d180; Bradford a1200 b1200 c200.

Advice to applicants and planning the UCAS personal statement Work experience and work shadowing with a retail and/or hospital pharmacist is important, and essential for Pharmacy applicants. Read pharmaceutical journals, extend your knowledge of well known drugs and antibiotics. Read up on the history of drugs. Attend Open Days or careers conferences. **Manchester** Students giving preference for Pharmacy are likely to be more successful than those who choose Pharmacy as an alternative to Medicine or Dentistry.

Misconceptions about this course That a degree in Pharmaceutical Science is a qualification leading to a career as a pharmacist. It is not: it is a course which concerns the application of chemical and biomedical science to the design, synthesis and analysis of pharmaceuticals for medicinal purposes. See also **Pharmacology**.

Selection interviews Yes Bath, Bradford, Brighton, Bristol, De Montfort, LJMU, London (Sch Pharm), London UCK (Coll) (Sch Pharm), Manchester (most), Nottingham, Portsmouth, Reading, Robert Gordon, Strathclyde, UEA, Wolverhampton; **Some** Aston, Cardiff.

Interview advice and questions As work experience is essential for Pharmacy applicants, questions are likely to focus on this and what they have discovered. Other relevant questions could include: Why do you want to study Pharmacy? What types of work do pharmacists do? What interests you about the Pharmacy course? What branch of pharmacy do you want to enter? Name a drug – what do you know about it (formula, use etc)? Name a drug from a natural source and its use. Can you think of another way of extracting a drug? Why do fungi destroy bacteria? What is an antibiotic? Can you name one and say how it was discovered? What is insulin? What is its source and function? What is diabetes? What type of insulin is used in its treatment? What is a hormone? What drugs are available over the counter without prescription? What is the formula of aspirin? What is genetic engineering? See also **Chapter 6**. **Bath** Informal and relaxed; 400 approx selected for interview – very few rejected at this stage. **Cardiff** Interviews cover both academic and vocational aspects; candidates must reach a satisfactory level in both areas. **LJMU** What are the products of a reaction between an alcohol and a carboxylic acid? **Manchester** Candidates failing to attend interviews will have their applications withdrawn. The majority of applicants are called for interview.

Reasons for rejection (non-academic) Poor communication skills. Poor knowledge of pharmacy and the work of a pharmacist.

AFTER-RESULTS ADVICE
Offers to applicants repeating A-levels Higher Bradford, Cardiff, De Montfort, LJMU, London UCK (Coll) (Sch Pharm) AAB, Nottingham (offers rarely made), Portsmouth, Queen's Belfast, Strathclyde; **Possibly higher** Aston, Robert Gordon; **Same** Bath, Brighton, Sunderland, UEA, Wolverhampton.

GRADUATE DESTINATIONS AND EMPLOYMENT (2009/10 HESA)
See **Pharmacology**.

Career note The majority of Pharmacy graduates proceed to work in the commercial and retail fields, although opportunities also exist with pharmaceutical companies and in hospital pharmacies. There are also opportunities in agricultural and veterinary pharmacy.

OTHER DEGREE SUBJECTS FOR CONSIDERATION
Biochemistry; Biological Sciences; Biology; Biotechnology; Chemistry; Drug Development; Life Sciences; Medicinal Chemistry; Microbiology; Natural Sciences; Pharmacology; Physiology.

PHILOSOPHY

(see also **Psychology**)

Philosophy is one of the oldest and most fundamental disciplines, which examines the nature of the universe and humanity's place in it. Philosophy seeks to discover the essence of the mind, language and physical reality and discusses the methods used to investigate these topics.

Useful websites www.iep.utm.edu; www.philosophypages.com; www.philosophy.eserver.org; see also **Religious Studies**.

NB The points totals shown to the left of the institutions are for ease of reference only. It must not be assumed that Tariff points are always used by institutions or that they can be substituted for an offer in grades. The level of an offer is not necessarily indicative of the quality of a course.

COURSE OFFERS INFORMATION

Subject requirements/preferences GCSE English and mathematics. A foreign language may be required. **AL** No specific subjects except for joint courses.

Your target offers and examples of courses provided by each institution

440 pts **London (King's)** – A*AAa (Pol Phil Law) (IB 39 pts)

430 pts **Warwick** – A*AAb–AAAb (PPE) (IB 38 pts)

400 pts **London (King's)** – AAAc (Phil courses) (IB 38 pts)
Oxford – A*A*A (Maths Phil) (IB 39 pts)

380 pts **Bristol** – A*AA–AAB 340–380 pts (Psy Phil) (IB 38–35 pts)
Cambridge – A*AA (Phil) (IB 40–42 pts)
Durham – A*AA (Engl Lit Phil) (IB 38 pts)
London (King's) – AABc (Phys Phil) (IB 36 pts HL maths phys)
Nottingham – A*AA–AAA 360–380 pts (Econ Phil) (IB 38–36 pts)
Oxford – A*AA (Phys Phil) (IB 38–40 pts)

360 pts **Bristol** – AAA (Engl Phil) (IB 37 pts HL 6 Engl)
Durham – AAA (Theol Phil; Phil Theol)
Edinburgh – AAA–BBB (Phil) (IB 34 pts HL 555)
Exeter – AAA–ABB (Phil Joint Hons) (IB 36–34 pts)
London (UCL) – AAA–AAB (Phil courses) (IB 36–38 pts)
London LSE – AAA (Pol Phil) (IB 38 pts HL 766)
London NCH – AAA–AAB 340–360 pts (Phil) (IB 37–38 pts HL 77)
Newcastle – AAA (Phil Comb Hons) (IB 32 pts HL 555)
Nottingham – AAA–A*AB (Maths Phil) (IB 37–36 pts)
Oxford – A*AA (Psy Phil) (IB 38–40 pts)
St Andrews – AAA–AAB (Phil courses) (IB 35–38 pts)
Warwick – AAA–AAB (Phil Joint Hons) (IB 38 pts)
York – AAA (Phil Pol Econ) (IB 36 pts)

340 pts **Birmingham** – AAB–ABB 320–340 pts (Phil) (IB 34–36 pts)
Bristol – AAB (Sociol Phil) (IB 35 pts HL 666)
Cardiff – AAB (Phil) (IB 34 pts)
Exeter – AAA–AAB (Phil) (IB 36–34 pts)
Kent – AAB–BBB (Hist Phil Art) (IB 33 pts)
Lancaster – AAB (Hist Phil) (IB 34 pts)
Liverpool – AAB (Phil) (IB 35 pts)
London (Birk) – AAB (Phil)
London (RH) – AAB–ABB (Mus Phil; Phil; Anc Hist Phil; Dr Phil; Langs Phil)
London (UCL) – AAB–ABB (Hist Phil Soc St Sci) (IB 34–36 pts)
Manchester – AAB (PPE) (IB 35 pts)
Nottingham – AAB (Psy Phil) (IB 34 pts)
Queen's Belfast – AAB/ABBa (PPE)
St Andrews – AAB (Phil Soc Anth) (IB 35 pts)

Sheffield – AAB (Phil) (IB 35 pts)
Southampton – AAB (Phil Pol) (IB 34 pts HL 17 pts)
Sussex – AAB (Phil) (IB 34–36 pts)
Swansea – AAB (PPE)
UEA – AAB–ABB (Phil) (IB 32 pts)

320 pts **Birmingham** – AAB–ABB 320–340 pts (Phil Joint Hons) (IB 34–36 pts)
Essex – ABB–BBB 300–320 pts (Phil Law) (IB 29 pts)
Glasgow – ABB (Phil) (IB 36 pts)
Hull – 320 pts (Law Phil) (IB 30 pts)
Kent – ABB (Hist Sci Phil) (IB 33 pts)
Lancaster – ABB (Film St Phil) (IB 32 pts)
Leeds – ABB–BBC (Phil Joint Hons) (IB 32 pts)
Liverpool – AAB–BBB (Phil Joint Hons) (IB 30 pts)
Newcastle – AAB–ABB 320–340 pts (Phil St Knwl Hum Intr) (IB 32 pts)
Nottingham – ABB (Mus Phil) (IB 32 pts)
Reading – 320–340 pts (Phil courses)
Sheffield – ABB (Phil Joint Hons) (IB 33 pts)
UEA – ABB–BBB (Phil Film St) (IB 32–31 pts)

300 pts **Aberdeen** – BBB (Phil) (IB 30 pts HL 15 pts)
Bristol UWE – 300 pts (Phil)
Dundee – BBB–BCC (Phil Ger)
Edinburgh – AAA–BBB 300–360 pts (Phil Ling) (IB 34 pts HL 555)
Essex – 300–320 pts (PPE) (IB 29 pts)
Hertfordshire – 300 pts (Phil)
Keele – 300–320 pts (Phil) (IB 25 pts)
Leeds – BBB (Gk Civ Phil) (IB 32 pts)
London (Hey) – 300–320 pts (Phil) (IB 30 pts)
Queen's Belfast – BBB (Phil courses) (IB 29 pts HL 655)
Roehampton – 300 pts (Phil)

280 pts **Gloucestershire** – 280–300 pts (Relgn Phil Eth)
Hull – 280–300 pts (Phil BSc) (IB 30 pts)
London (Hey) – 280–320 pts (Phil Relgn Eth) (IB 28–32 pts)
Manchester Met – 280 pts (Phil Joint Hons) (IB 28 pts)
Newman (UC) – 280 pts (Phil Relgn Eth; Phil Theol)
Oxford Brookes – BBC–ABB (Phil (Comb))
Stirling – BBC (PPE) (IB 32 pts)

260 pts **Anglia Ruskin** – 220–260 pts (Phil; Phil Engl Lit)
Dundee – BCC (Pharmacol Physiol Sci) (IB 28 pts)
Greenwich – 260 pts (Phil)
Liverpool Hope – 260–320 pts (Phil Eth) (IB 25 pts)
Nottingham Trent – 260 pts (Phil Joint Hons)

240 pts **Manchester Met** – 240–260 pts (Phil) (IB 28 pts)
Staffordshire – 240 pts (Phil Joint Hons)
St Mary's Twickenham (UC) – 240 pts (Phil) (IB 28 pts)

220 pts **Bath Spa** – 220–280 pts (Phil Eth)
Northampton – 220–260 pts (Phil; Phil Joint Hons)
York St John – 200–220 pts (Relgn Phil Eth)

200 pts **UCLan** – 200–240 pts (Phil (Comb); Phil)
Wolverhampton – 200 pts (Pol Phil)

180 pts **Greenwich** – 180 pts (Phil Int St; Phil Law)
Trinity Saint David – individual offers made after interview 180–240 pts (Phil Joint Hons)

160 pts **Bishop Grosseteste (UC)** – 160 pts (Theol Soc)
Wolverhampton – 160–220 pts (Phil Sociol; Relig St Phil; War St Phil)

80 pts **London (Birk)** – p/t for under 21s (over 21s varies) (Hum Phil)

Open University – contact +44 (0)845 300 6090 **or** www.openuniversity.co.uk/you (PPE)

Check **Chapter 4** when choosing your university and **Chapter 7** on how to read the subject tables.

Alternative offers
See **Chapter 7** and **Appendix 1** for grades/UCAS Tariff points information for the International Baccalaureate, Scottish Highers/Advanced Highers, the Welsh Baccalaureate, the Irish Leaving Certificate, the Cambridge Pre-U Diploma, the Advanced Diploma and the Extended Project.

CHOOSING YOUR COURSE (SEE ALSO CH.1)
Some course features
Exeter A large number of Combined Honours courses are offered in Philosophy including options with modern languages in which a year is spent abroad. Other programmes also allow for a year of study in Europe, North America and Australia.
London (Hey) One of the largest faculties. Philosophy can also be studied with Theology, or Religion and Ethics.
Manchester Philosophy is a broad course covering the main subject topics such as the philosophy of modern religion, modern political thought, psychology, law and a language. Philosophy is also offered with Politics or Criminology.
Oxford Brookes Philosophy can be studied as a single subject or with a range of joint subjects including Anthropology, Film Studies, Mathematics, Psychology, Sociology and Religion and Theology.
York A Single Honours and a range of integrated courses can be studied on an 'Equal' basis in which Philosophy is taken with English, French, German, History, Linguistics, Sociology, Mathematics and Physics. A Politics, Philosophy and Economics course is also offered. See also **Combined Courses**.

Universities and colleges teaching quality See www.qaa.ac.uk; http://unistats.direct.gov.uk.

Top research universities and colleges (RAE 2008) London (UCL); St Andrews; London (King's); Sheffield; Reading; Cambridge (Hist Phil Sci); London LSE; Oxford; Stirling; Bristol; Essex; London (Birk); Nottingham; Leeds; Middlesex; Edinburgh.

ADMISSIONS INFORMATION
Number of applicants per place (approx) Birmingham 6; Bradford 7; Bristol 19; Cambridge 6; Cardiff 8; Dundee 6; Durham (all courses) 14; Hull 19; Kent 9; Lancaster 6; Leeds 10; Liverpool 5; London (Hey) 4; London (King's) 6; London LSE 11; London Met 3; Manchester 10; Middlesex 8; Northampton 3; Nottingham 7; Oxford (success rate) 44%, (PPE) 29%; Sheffield 6; Southampton 7; Staffordshire 8; Trinity Saint David 4; UEA 6; Warwick 9; York 6.

Advice to applicants and planning the UCAS personal statement Read Bertrand Russell's *Problems of Philosophy*. Refer to any particular aspects of philosophy which interest you (check that these are offered on the courses for which you are applying). Since Philosophy is not a school subject, selectors will expect applicants to have read around the subject. Explain what you know about the nature of studying philosophy. Say what you have read in philosophy and give an example of a philosophical issue that interests you. Universities do not expect applicants to have a wide knowledge of the subject, but evidence that you know what the subject is about is important. **Bristol** Deferred entry considered.

Misconceptions about this course Applicants are sometimes surprised to find what wide-ranging Philosophy courses are offered.

Selection interviews **Yes** Bristol (mature students), Cambridge, Durham, Essex, Kingston, Lancaster, Leeds, Liverpool, London (Hey), London (UCL), Newcastle, Oxford (Phil Mod Lang) 24%, (PPE) 18%, (Phil Theol) 6%, Southampton, Staffordshire, Trinity Saint David, Warwick; **Some** Cardiff, Hull, London LSE (rare), York; **No** Birmingham, Dundee, Nottingham, Reading, UEA.

Interview advice and questions Philosophy is a very wide subject and initially applicants will be asked for their reasons for their choice and their special interests in the subject. Questions in recent years have included: Is there a difference between being tactless and being insensitive? Can you be tactless and thin-skinned? Define the difference between knowledge and belief. Was the vertical distortion of El Greco's paintings a product of a vision defect? What is the point of studying philosophy? What books on philosophy have you read? Discuss the work of a renowned philosopher. What is a philosophical novel? Who has the right to decide your future – yourself or another? What do you want to do with your life? What is a philosophical question? John is your husband, and if John is your husband then necessarily you must be his wife; if you are necessarily his wife then it is not possible that you could not be his wife; so it was impossible for you not to have married him – you were destined for each other. Discuss. What is the difference between a man's entitlements, his deserts and his attributes? What are morals? A good understanding of philosophy is needed for entry to degree courses, and applicants are expected to demonstrate this if they are called to interview. As one admissions tutor stated, 'If you find Bertrand Russell's *Problems of Philosophy* unreadable – don't apply!' See also **Chapter 6**. **Cambridge** If you were to form a government of philosophers what selection process would you use? Is it moral to hook up a psychopath (whose only pleasure is killing) to a really stimulating machine so that he can believe he is in the real world and kill as much as he likes? **Oxford** If you entered a teletransporter and your body was destroyed and instantly recreated on Mars in exactly the same way with all your memories intact etc, would you be the same person? Tutors are not so much concerned with what you know as how you think about it. Evidence required concerning social and political topics and the ability to discuss them critically. (PPE) Is being hungry the same thing as wanting to eat? Why is there not a global government? What do you think of teleport machines? Should there be an intelligence test to decide who should vote? **York** Do human beings have free will? Do we perceive the world as it really is?

Reasons for rejection (non-academic) Evidence of severe psychological disturbance, criminal activity, drug problems (evidence from referees' reports). Lack of knowledge of philosophy. **Oxford** He was not able to explore his thoughts deeply enough or with sufficient centrality. **York** No evidence of having read any philosophical literature.

AFTER-RESULTS ADVICE
Offers to applicants repeating A-levels Higher Bristol (Phil Econ), Essex, Glasgow, Leeds, Nottingham (in some cases), Warwick; **Same** Birmingham, Bristol, Cardiff, Dundee, Durham, Hull, Liverpool Hope, Newcastle, Newport, Nottingham (in some cases), Nottingham Trent, St Mary's Twickenham (UC), Southampton, Staffordshire, Stirling, UEA, Wolverhampton, York; **No** Cambridge.

GRADUATE DESTINATIONS AND EMPLOYMENT (2009/10 HESA)
Graduates surveyed 2710 **Employed** 955 **In voluntary employment** 70 **In further study** 605 **Assumed unemployed** 195

Career note Graduates have a wide range of transferable skills that can lead to employment in many areas, eg management, public administration, publishing, banking and social services.

OTHER DEGREE SUBJECTS FOR CONSIDERATION
Divinity; History and Philosophy of Science; History of Art; Human Sciences; Psychology; Religious Studies; Science; Theology.

PHOTOGRAPHY
(see also **Art and Design (Fine Art), Film, Radio, Video and TV Studies, Media Studies**)

Photography courses offer a range of specialised studies involving commercial, industrial and still photography, portraiture and film, digital and video work. Increasingly this subject is featuring in Media courses. See also **Appendix 3**.

Useful websites http://hub.the-aop.org; www.rps.org; www.bjp-online.com.

NB The points totals shown to the left of the institutions are for ease of reference only. It must not be assumed that Tariff points are always used by institutions or that they can be substituted for an offer in grades. The level of an offer is not necessarily indicative of the quality of a course.

Check **Chapter 4** when choosing your university and **Chapter 7** on how to read the subject tables.

COURSE OFFERS INFORMATION

Subject requirements/preferences GCSE Art and/or a portfolio usually required. **AL** One or two subjects may be required, including an art/design or creative subject. Most institutions will make offers on the basis of a portfolio of work.

Your target offers and examples of courses provided by each institution

320 pts **Glasgow (SA)** – ABB (Fn Art (Photo)) (IB 30 pts)

300 pts **Edinburgh (CA)** – BBB 300 pts (Photo) (IB 34 pts)
Glamorgan – BBB 300 pts (Photo)
Huddersfield – 300 pts (Photo)
Middlesex – 200–300 pts (Photo)
Northumbria – 300 pts (Contemp Photo Prac)
Portsmouth – 240–300 pts (Photo)
Sheffield Hallam – 300 pts (Photo)

280 pts **Birmingham City** – 280 pts (Media Comm (Media Photo))
Brighton – BBC (Photo)
Gloucestershire – 280–300 pts (Photojrnl Doc Photo)
Great Yarmouth (Coll) – 280 pts (Photo Dig Media)
Lincoln – 280 pts (Contemp Lns Media)
London Met – 280 pts (Fn Art (Photo))
Manchester Met – 280 pts (Photo) (IB 28 pts)
Northampton – 240–280 pts (Photo Prac)
Norwich (UCA) – BBC (Photo) (IB 25 pts)
Nottingham Trent – 280 pts (Photo/Photo Euro)
Roehampton – 280–340 pts (Photo) (IB 25 pts)
Suffolk (Univ Campus) – 280 pts (Photo Dig Media; Photo)

260 pts **Bournemouth Arts (UC)** – BCC (Photo; Commer Photo)
Coventry – 260 pts (Photo) (IB 26 pts)
De Montfort – 260 pts (Photo Vid)
Derby – 260 pts (Commer Photo) (IB 20 pts)
Southampton Solent – 260 pts (Photo)
Sunderland – 260 pts (Photo)

240 pts **Anglia Ruskin** – 200–240 pts (Photo)
Bolton – 240 pts (Photo)
Bournemouth – 240 pts (Photo)
Bradford – 240 pts (Photo Dig Media)
Bristol UWE – 240 pts (Photo)
Canterbury Christ Church – 240 pts (Photo Comb Hons) (IB 24 pts)
Chester – 240–280 pts (Dig Photo) (IB 26 pts)
Cleveland (CAD) – 240 pts (Photo)
Cumbria – 240 pts (Photo) (IB 30 pts)
De Montfort – 240 pts (Graph Des Photo)
Leeds (CAD) – 240 pts (Photo)
London South Bank – 240 pts (Dig Photo)
Newport – 240–260 pts (Doc Photo; Photo Fash Adv; Photo Art)
Plymouth – 240 pts (Photo) (IB 24 pts)
Ravensbourne – AA–CC (Dig Photo) (IB 28 pts)
Staffordshire – 240 pts (Photojrnl; Fn Art (Photo))
Salford – 240 pts (Photo)
UCLan – 240–260 pts (Photo; Photo Jrnl; Photo Fash Brnd Prom)
Ulster – 240 pts (Photo)

220 pts **Bradford (Coll Univ Centre)** – 220 pts (Photo (Edit Adv Fn Art))
Falmouth (UC) – 220 pts (Press Edit Photo; Mar Nat Hist Photo; Photo; Fash Photo)
Sunderland – 220 pts (Photo Vid Dig Imag)

200 pts **Bedfordshire** – 200 pts (Photo Vid Art)

Canterbury Christ Church – 200 pts (Photo) (IB 24 pts)
Creative Arts – 200 pts (Photo) (IB 30 pts)
Hereford (CA) – 200 pts (Photo)
Leeds Met – 200 pts (Photo Journ) (IB 24 pts)
Plymouth (CA) – 200 pts (Photo)
Swansea Met – 200–360 pts (Photojrnl; Photo Arts)
UEL – 200 pts (Photo)
West London – 200 pts (Photo Dig Imag)
Westminster – BB (Photo Arts)
Wolverhampton – 200 pts (Photo)

180 pts **Farnborough (CT)** – 180 pts (Media Prod Photo)
Hertfordshire – 180 pts (Photo Media)

160 pts **Arts London (CFash)** – 160 pts (Fash Photo)
Blackpool and Fylde (Coll) – 160 pts (Photo)
Colchester (Inst) – 160 pts (Photo)
Robert Gordon – 160 pts (Photo Electron Media) (IB 24 pts)
Sir Gâr (Coll) – 160 pts (Photo)
Southampton Solent – 160–200 pts (Fash Photo)
Westminster – CC (Photo Dig Imag) (IB 26 pts)

120 pts **Grimsby (IFHE)** – 120–240 pts (Commer Photo)
Northbrook (Coll) – 120 pts (Contemp Photo Arts (Prac))
St Helens (Coll) – 120 pts (Photo)
Stockport (Coll) – 120 pts (Photo)

100 pts **and below or other selection criteria (Foundation course, interview and portfolio inspection)**
Arts London – 80 pts (Photo)
Bath Spa – 80–160 pts (Photo Dig Media)
East Surrey (Coll) – 80 pts (Dig Photo)
Kingston – contact admissions office (Photo)

Alternative offers
See **Chapter 7** and **Appendix 1** for grades/UCAS Tariff points information for the International Baccalaureate, Scottish Highers/Advanced Highers, the Welsh Baccalaureate, the Irish Leaving Certificate, the Cambridge Pre-U Diploma, the Advanced Diploma and the Extended Project.

EXAMPLES OF FOUNDATION DEGREES IN THE SUBJECT FIELD
Anglia Ruskin; Arts London; Barking (Coll); Bath Spa; Bedfordshire; Blackburn (Coll); Blackpool and Fylde (Coll); Brighton; Bristol UWE; Bucks New; Cleveland (CAD); Cornwall (Coll); Exeter (Coll); Farnborough (CT); Glamorgan; Gloucestershire; Glyndŵr; Greenwich; Hereford (CA); Hertfordshire; Hull (Coll); Kent; Kirklees (Coll); Leeds (CAD); Leicester; London Met; Manchester (Coll); Mid-Cheshire (Coll); Myerscough (Coll); Nescot; NEW (Coll); Newcastle (Coll); Northbrook (Coll); Nottingham New (Coll); Plymouth (CA); St Helens (Coll); Sheffield (Coll); South Nottingham (Coll); Sunderland; Truro (Coll); Wakefield (Coll); Westminster City (Coll).

CHOOSING YOUR COURSE (SEE ALSO CH.1)
Some course features
Falmouth (UC) Specialist courses in Press and Editorial, Fashion and Marine and Natural History Photography are also offered.
Nottingham Trent Courses in Photography are offered focusing on Documentary, Art Practice, Fashion or with a year in Europe.
Westminster (Clin Photo) The only full-time degree in clinical photography in the UK, it combines a study of photography and digital imaging with science, anatomy, physiology, biology and clinical practice. Work-based learning in a clinical setting forms a large part of the course.

Universities and colleges teaching quality See www.qaa.ac.uk; http://unistats.direct.gov.uk.

Examples of sandwich degree courses Birmingham City; Coventry; Wolverhampton.

Check **Chapter 4** when choosing your university and **Chapter 7** on how to read the subject tables.

ADMISSIONS INFORMATION

Number of applicants per place (approx) Arts London 10; Birmingham City 6; Blackpool and Fylde (Coll) 3; Bournemouth Arts (UC) 7; Cleveland (CAD) 2; Derby 20; Edinburgh Napier 33; Falmouth (UC) 3; Newport 2; Nottingham Trent 4; Plymouth 2; Plymouth (CA) 7; Portsmouth 4; Staffordshire 3; Stockport (Coll) 6; Swansea Met 12.

Advice to applicants and planning the UCAS personal statement Discuss your interest in photography and your knowledge of various aspects of the subject, for example, digital, video, landscape, medical, wildlife and portrait photography. Read photographic journals to keep up-to-date on developments, particularly in photographic technology. You will also need first-hand experience of photography and to be competent in basic skills. **Derby** (Non-UK students) Fluency in written and spoken English important. Portfolio of work essential.

Misconceptions about this course Some believe that courses are all practical work with no theory. **Cumbria** They didn't realise the facilities were so good! **Kirklees (Coll)** Some applicants think that it's a traditional photography course. It's as digital as the individual wants it to be.

Selection interviews Most institutions will interview applicants and expect to see a portfolio of work.

Interview advice and questions Questions relate to the applicant's portfolio of work which, for these courses, is of prime importance. Who are your favourite photographers? What is the most recent exhibition you have attended? Have any leading photographers influenced your work? Questions regarding contemporary photography. Written work sometimes required. See **Chapter 6**.

Reasons for rejection (non-academic) Lack of passion for the subject. Lack of exploration and creativity in practical work. Poorly presented portfolio.

AFTER-RESULTS ADVICE

Offers to applicants repeating A-levels Same Birmingham City, Blackpool and Fylde (Coll), Chester, Cumbria, Manchester Met, Nottingham Trent, Staffordshire.

GRADUATE DESTINATIONS AND EMPLOYMENT (2009/10 HESA)

Cinematics and Photography; graduates surveyed 4730 **Employed** 2085 **In voluntary employment** 95 **In further study** 705 **Assumed unemployed** 435

Career note Opportunities for photographers exist in a range of specialisms including advertising and editorial work, fashion, medical, industrial, scientific and technical photography. Some graduates also go into photojournalism and other aspects of the media.

OTHER DEGREE SUBJECTS FOR CONSIDERATION

Art and Design; Digital Animation; Film, Radio, Video and TV Studies; Media Studies; Moving Image; Radiography.

PHYSICAL EDUCATION

(see also **Education Studies, Sports Sciences/Studies**)

Physical Education courses are very popular and unfortunately restricted in number. Ability in gymnastics and involvement in sport are obviously important factors. See also **Appendix 3**.

Useful websites www.afpe.org.uk; www.uksport.gov.uk; see also **Education Studies** and **Teacher Training**.

NB The points totals shown to the left of the institutions are for ease of reference only. It must not be assumed that Tariff points are always used by institutions or that they can be substituted for an offer in grades. The level of an offer is not necessarily indicative of the quality of a course.

COURSE OFFERS INFORMATION

Subject requirements/preferences GCSE English, mathematics and a science. **AL** PE, sports studies and science are preferred subjects and for some courses one of these may be required. **Other** Enhanced Disclosure (criminal record check) before starting the course. Declaration of Health usually required.

Your target offers and examples of courses provided by each institution
360 pts **Trinity Saint David** – 180–360 pts (PE)
340 pts **Brighton** – AAB 340–380 pts (PE S Teach) (IB 36 pts)
320 pts **Birmingham** – ABB (Spo PE Coach Sci) (IB 32–34 pts)
　　　　Northampton – 280–320 pts (P PE)
　　　　Roehampton – 320 pts (P Educ (PE))
　　　　Sheffield Hallam – 320 pts (PE Yth Spo)
　　　　UEA – ABB (PE Spo) (IB 32 pts)
300 pts **Bangor** – 300–260 pts (Spo Sci (PE))
　　　　Cardiff Met – 300 pts (Spo PE)
　　　　Edge Hill – 300 pts (PE Sch Spo)
　　　　Edinburgh – BBB (PE) (IB 34 pts HL 555)
　　　　LJMU – 300 pts (Spo Dev PE)
　　　　Winchester – 260–300pts (P Educ PE)
280 pts **Brunel** – 280–320 pts (Spo Sci (PE Yth Spo)) (IB 30 pts)
　　　　Leeds Met – 280–260 pts (PE courses)
　　　　LJMU – 280 pts (Educ St PE)
　　　　Manchester Met – 280 pts (PE Spo Ped) (IB 28 pts)
　　　　Oxford Brookes – BBC (Spo Coach PE)
　　　　UCP Marjon – 280 pts (Coach PE)
　　　　Wolverhampton – 280 pts (PE P QTS)
　　　　Worcester – 280 pts (PE Spo St)
260 pts **Bangor** – 260–280 pts (PE Joint Hons; Spo Hlth PE)
　　　　Brunel – BBC (S PE BSc)
　　　　Canterbury Christ Church – 260 pts (PE Spo Exer Sci)
　　　　Cardiff Met – 260 pts (Educ St Spo Physl Actvt) (IB 28 pts)
　　　　Chichester – BCC (PE Spo Coach) (IB 30 pts)
　　　　Newman (UC) – 260 pts (Educ Spo St)
　　　　York St John – 260 pts (Phys Ed Spo Coach)
240 pts **Bedfordshire** – 240–320 pts (PE S QTS)
　　　　Cumbria – 240 pts (PE)
　　　　Glyndŵr – 240 pts (Spo Coach)
　　　　Greenwich – 240 pts (Spo Sci Coach; PE Spo)
　　　　Leeds Trinity (UC) – 240 pts (PE P Spo Dev)
　　　　Plymouth – 240 pts (P PE)
　　　　Staffordshire – 240 pts (PE Yth Spo Coach)
220 pts **London Met** – 220 pts (Spo Sci PE)
200 pts **Anglia Ruskin** – 200 pts (Spo Coach PE)
180 pts **Bedfordshire** – 180–220 pts (Spo St)
　　　　Peterborough (Univ Centre) – 180 pts (Spo Coach PE)

Alternative offers
See **Chapter 7** and **Appendix 1** for grades/UCAS Tariff points information for the International Baccalaureate, Scottish Highers/Advanced Highers, the Welsh Baccalaureate, the Irish Leaving Certificate, the Cambridge Pre-U Diploma, the Advanced Diploma and the Extended Project.

CHOOSING YOUR COURSE (SEE ALSO CH.1)
Some course features
Birmingham (Spo PE Coach Sci) A practical and theoretical programme in sport, physical education and leisure with a placement module in education or the leisure industry.

Chichester (PE Coach) The 3 year modular programme focuses on the teaching of physical education and the coaching of sports activities.
LJMU Courses are offered for those wanting to train as PE teachers or with specialist studies in sport development and management.
UCP Marjon (Coach PE) Course covers coach and sport education and also leads to a PGCE in PE teaching.

Universities and colleges teaching quality See www.qaa.ac.uk; http://unistats.direct.gov.uk.

Top research universities and colleges (RAE 2008) See **Sports Sciences/Studies**.

ADMISSIONS INFORMATION
Number of applicants per place (approx) Bangor 19; Birmingham 5; Brunel 10; Chichester 5; Edge Hill 40; Leeds Trinity (UC) 33; LJMU 4; Newman (UC) 5; St Mary's Twickenham (UC) 9; Sheffield Hallam 60; UCP Marjon 18; Worcester 31.

Advice to applicants and planning the UCAS personal statement Ability in gymnastics, athletics and all sports and games is important. Full details of these activities should be given on the UCAS application – for example, teams, dates and awards achieved, assisting in extra-curricular activities. Involvement with local sports clubs, health clubs, summer camps, Gap Year. Relevant experience in coaching, teaching, community and youth work. **LJMU** Commitment to working with children and a good sports background.

Selection interviews Most institutions. In most cases, applicants will take part in physical education practical tests and games/gymnastics, depending on the course. The results of these tests could affect the level of offers. See also **Chapter 6**. **Yes** Stirling.

Interview advice and questions The applicant's interests in physical education will be discussed, with specific questions on, for example, sportsmanship, refereeing, umpiring and coaching. Questions in the past have also included: What qualities should a good netball goal defence possess? How could you encourage a group of children into believing that sport is fun? Do you think that physical education should be compulsory in schools? Why do you think you would make a good teacher? What is the name of the education minister? **LJMU** Questions on what the applicant has gained or learned through experiences with children.

Reasons for rejection (non-academic) Poor communication and presentational skills. Relatively poor sporting background or knowledge. Lack of knowledge about the teaching of physical education and the commitment required. Lack of ability in practicalities, for example, gymnastics, dance when relevant. Poor self-presentation. Poor writing skills.

AFTER-RESULTS ADVICE
Offers to applicants repeating A-levels Same LJMU, Newman (UC), St Mary's Twickenham (UC).

GRADUATE DESTINATIONS AND EMPLOYMENT (2009/10 HESA)
See **Sports Sciences/Studies**.

Career note The majority of graduates go into education although, depending on any special interests, they may also go on into the sport and leisure industry.

OTHER DEGREE SUBJECTS FOR CONSIDERATION
Coach Education; Exercise and Fitness; Exercise Physiology; Human Biology; Leisure and Recreation; Physiotherapy; Sport and Exercise Science; Sport Health and Exercise; Sport Studies/Sciences; Sports Coaching; Sports Development; Sports Engineering; Sports Psychology; Sports Therapy.

PHYSICS

(see also **Astronomy and Astrophysics**)

There is a considerable shortage of applicants for Physics courses. Many courses have flexible arrangements to enable students to follow their own interests and specialisations, for example circuit design, microwave devices, cosmology, medical physics, solid state electronics.

Useful websites www.scienceyear.com; www.scicentral.com; www.ipem.ac.uk; www.iop.org; www. noisemakers.org.uk; www.NewScientistJobs.com; www.physics.org; www.nature.com/physics.

NB The points totals shown to the left of the institutions are for ease of reference only. It must not be assumed that Tariff points are always used by institutions or that they can be substituted for an offer in grades. The level of an offer is not necessarily indicative of the quality of a course.

COURSE OFFERS INFORMATION

Subject requirements/preferences GCSE English, mathematics and science. **AL** Physics and mathematics are required for most courses.

Your target offers and examples of courses provided by each institution

380 pts **Cambridge** – A*AA (Maths Phys) (IB 40–42 pts HL 766–777)
Durham – A*AA (Phys Astron) (IB 38 pts HL 6 maths phys)
Imperial London – A*mathsAA (Phys Theor Phys) (IB 38 pts HL 666)
London (King's) – AABc (Phys Phil) (IB 36 pts HL maths phys)
London (UCL) – AAA–AAB (Phys) (IB 36–38 pts HL 6 maths phys)
Manchester – A*AA (Maths Phys) (IB 38 pts)
Oxford – A*AA (Phys Phil) (IB 38–40 pts)

360 pts **Bath** – AAA (Phys) (IB 34–36 pts HL 5–6 maths phys)
Birmingham – AAA (Phys Prtcl Phys Cosmo) (IB 34–38 pts)
Bristol – AAA–AAB incl chem phys maths (Cheml Phys) (IB 37–35 pts)
Durham – AAA–AAB (Theor Phys) (IB 37 pts HL 6 maths phys)
Edinburgh – AAA–ABB 320–360 pts (Phys) (IB 37–32 pts)
Exeter – AAA–ABB (Phys) (IB 36–32 pts)
Lancaster – AAA (Theor Phys Maths) (IB 36 pts)
Leeds – AAA–AAB (Theor Phys) (IB 36–34 pts HL 6 maths phys)
Leicester – AAA–AAB (Phys Planet Sci)
Liverpool – AAA–ABB (Astro MPhys) (IB 35 pts HL 6 maths phys)
LJMU – 360–320 pts (Astro MPhys)
London (RH) – AAA–ABB 320–360 pts (Phys Ptcl Phys) (IB 36 pts)
London (UCL) – AAA–AAB incl maths+fmaths+phys (Theor Phys) (IB 36–38 pts)
Nottingham – AAA–AAB (Phys Euro Lang; Phys Med Phys; Phys Nanosci; Phys Theor Phys)
St Andrews – AAA (Phys) (IB 38 pts)
Southampton – AAA (Maths Phys) (IB 36 pts HL 18 pts)
Swansea – AAA 360 pts (Phys MPhys; Theor Phys)
Warwick – AAA (Phys) (IB 36 pts)
York – AAA–ABB 320–360 pts (Phys Phil) (IB 36–32 pts)

340 pts **Cardiff** – AAB (Phys MPhys) (IB 32 pts HL 6 maths phys)
Edinburgh – AAA–ABB 340–360 pts (Cheml Phys) (IB 37–32 pts)
Lancaster – AAB 340 pts (Phys Prtcl Phys Cosmo BSc) (IB 34–36 pts)
Liverpool – AAB–BBB (Phys BSc) (IB 33 pts HL 6 maths phys)
London (King's) – AABc (Phys Med Apps) (IB 36 pts)
London (QM) – 320–340 pts (Phys Prtcl Phys) (HL 6 maths phys)
Loughborough – AAB–ABB (Phys) (IB 34 pts)
Queen's Belfast – AAB (Phys MSci; Theor Phys)
Sheffield – AAB incl maths phys (Phys BSc/MPhys) (IB 35 pts)
Southampton – AAB incl maths phys (Phys Spc Sci) (IB 34 pts HL 17 pts)
Surrey – AAB (Phys Sat Tech BSc) (IB 36–34 pts)

myphysicscourse.org

Finding the right degree

The website *myPhysicsCourse* is your indispensable guide to physics degrees. Not only does the site list all IOP-accredited courses but it also allows you compare courses by:

- university;
- subject combination;
- entry grades;
- location.

For everything from physics with mathematics to physics with music, across the UK and Ireland, visit **www.myPhysicsCourse.org**.

IOP Institute of Physics

Check **Chapter 4** when choosing your university and **Chapter 7** on how to read the subject tables.

Sussex – AAB–BBB (Phys Astro)
York – AAA–AAB (Maths courses) (IB 34–32 pts)
320 pts **Aberdeen** – ABB (Phys Complex Sys Mdl)
Aberystwyth – 320 pts (Mathem Theor Phys) (IB 27 pts)
Cardiff – ABB 320 pts (Phys Med Phys) (IB 28 pts)
Edinburgh – AAA–ABB 320–360 pts (Mathem Phys) (IB 37–32 pts)
Glasgow – ABB (Astron) (IB 32 pts)
Kent – ABB (Phys)
Leeds – ABB (Hist Phil Sci (Phys); Chem Phys)
Liverpool – ABB (Phys Ocn Clim St BSc) (IB 33 pts)
London (QM) – ABB incl maths phys (Astro BSc) (IB 32 pts HL 6 maths phys)
Loughborough – AAB–ABB (Phys Mgt) (IB 34 pts)
Nottingham – AAB–ABB 320–340 pts (Chem Mol Phys) (IB 36–34 pts)
Strathclyde – ABB–BBB (Phys) (IB 30–32 pts)
Surrey – ABB (Phys Nucl Astro BSc) (IB 36–34 pts)
Sussex – AAB–BBB incl phys maths (Phys) (IB 32–35 pts)
Swansea – ABB 320 pts (Phys BSc; Phys Nanotech; Phys Spo Sci)
UCLan – 280–320 pts (Phys)
UEA – ABB incl chem maths (Cheml Phys) (IB 32 pts HL 6 chem maths)
York – AAA–ABB 320–360 pts (Phys Astro) (IB 32–36 pts)
300 pts **Dundee** – BBB–CCD (Phys) (IB 28–32 pts)
Heriot-Watt – BBB (Phys courses)
Hull – 280–300 pts (Phys)
Keele – 300–320 pts (Phys)
LJMU – 300–340 pts (Phys Astron) (IB 24–28 pts)
London (QM) – 300 pts (Theor Phys) (IB 30 pts HL 6 phys maths)
Queen's Belfast – BBB (Phys BSc; Phys Med Apps BSc; Phys Med App MSci)
Salford – 300 pts (Phys Acoust MPhys)
280 pts **Aberystwyth** – 280 pts (Phys) (IB 27 pts)
De Montfort – 280 pts (Hlth Med Phys)
Hertfordshire – 280 pts (Phys)
UCLan – 280–320 pts (Astro)
260 pts **Nottingham Trent** – 260 pts (Phys; Phys Astro; Phys Nucl Tech)
Portsmouth – 220–260 pts (App Phys)
Salford – 260 pts (Phys BSc)
240 pts **Aberdeen** – CCC 240 pts (Phys)
Coventry – 240 pts (Ind Phys)
220 pts **Nottingham Trent** – 220 pts (Phys Foren Apps)
200 pts **Glamorgan** – 200–240 pts (Obs Astron)
160 pts **West Scotland** – CC (Phys)
140 pts **West Scotland** – CD (Phys Nucl Tech)

Open University – contact +44 (0)845 300 6090 **or** www.openuniversity.co.uk/you (Phys Sci)

Alternative offers
See **Chapter 7** and **Appendix 1** for grades/UCAS Tariff points information for the International Baccalaureate, Scottish Highers/Advanced Highers, the Welsh Baccalaureate, the Irish Leaving Certificate, the Cambridge Pre-U Diploma, the Advanced Diploma and the Extended Project.

EXAMPLES OF FOUNDATION DEGREES IN THE SUBJECT FIELD
Cardiff; Cumbria; Durham; Hull; Keele; Kent; Leeds; Leicester; Liverpool; London (QM); London (RH); Loughborough; Manchester; Newport; Nottingham; Nottingham Trent; St Andrews; Salford; Southampton; UCLan.

OTHER HIGHER EDUCATION COURSES IN THIS FIELD
St Andrews.

THE UNIVERSITY *of York*

The Department of Physics

- Flexible MPhys (4-year) and BSc (3-year) degree programmes
- Friendly and dedicated staff
- Beautiful campus environment
- Guaranteed University accommodation for 1st year students
- Key teaching and research areas include nuclear astrophysics, fusion and lasers, nanotechnology, computational and theoretical physics

NEW – AstroCampus – a major redevelopment of the observational facilities on campus - co-locating our high-quality observatory, radio and solar telescopes, along with a student working area, computer facilities, etc. in a custom-built comfortable and safe environment.

Graduate Employment – a key area of concern for many – is taken very seriously at York. Currently 80% of our graduates get jobs within 6 months of graduating – the 3rd highest of ANY Physics department (Guardian University Guide 2012).

Equality – we encourage applications from all, regardless of background. We have been awarded Juno Champion status by the Institute of Physics for our achievements with equality for women.

For further information contact:
Email: physics-undergraduate-admissions@york.ac.uk
Web: http://www.york.ac.uk/physics
Phone: (+44) (0)1904 432241

Check **Chapter 4** when choosing your university and **Chapter 7** on how to read the subject tables.

University of Salford

MANCHESTER

SCHOOL OF COMPUTING, SCIENCE & ENGINEERING

Physicsalford
What will you achieve?

At Salford we're taking a different approach to physics, helping you achieve, invent and discover more in life.

By capitalising on the strengths within the University we are able to offer a range of specialised physics degrees that benefit from close links with a wide range of physics employers.

- BSc/MPhys Pure and Applied Physics
- BSc/MPhys Physics
- BSc/MPhys Physics with Acoustics
- MPhys Physics with studies in North America

The University of Salford campus is just a mile and a half from Manchester city centre, giving you the best of both worlds - a friendly, safe environment but just minutes away from all the fun and opportunities of a big city.

For a prospectus contact us:
t: 0161 295 4545
www.cse.salford.ac.uk/physics

Department of Physics

Durham University

B.Sc. and M.Phys/M.Sci. degrees in Physics, Physics & Astronomy, Theoretical Physics, Mathematics & Physics and Chemistry & Physics

Specialised courses include particle physics, cosmology and photonics

Excellent laboratory facilities include 4 modern telescopes

Supportive college system

Learning based on lectures, tutorials, labs and projects

Internationally renowned research department

http://www.dur.ac.uk/physics
Email: physics.admissions@durham.ac.uk
Tel: +44(0)191 334 3726

Ogden Centre for Fundamental Physics

TRINITY COLLEGE DUBLIN
THE UNIVERSITY OF DUBLIN

Ireland's premier university in the heart of Dublin, founded in 1592

The School of Physics has a long and distinguished history of teaching and research. It has an international reputation in areas ranging from nanoscience to astrophysics.

Undergraduate programmes are offered in Physics, Physics & Astrophysics, Theoretical Physics, Nanoscience.

http://www.tcd.ie/physics
e-mail: physics@tcd.ie
tel: 353-(0)1-896 1675
fax: 353-(0)1-671 1759

School of Physics

Check **Chapter 4** when choosing your university and **Chapter 7** on how to read the subject tables.

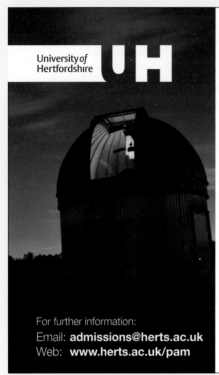

CHOOSING YOUR COURSE (SEE ALSO CH.1)

Some course features

Bath After a first year on the Natural Sciences programme or the Mathematics and Physics course it is possible to transfer to Single Honours Physics in Year 2.

Durham Several courses are offered which include Theoretical Physics and Astronomy. Physics can also be taken jointly with seven other subjects and is also offered as part of the Natural Sciences programme.

Kent The Physics course allows considerable flexibility and enables students to defer their choice between Physics and other degree programmes in the Faculty until the end of the first year. Physics can also be studied with Astrophysics and with a year in the USA.

Loughborough An optional year in paid employment is offered either in the UK or abroad.

Warwick A central core of physics and mathematics is taken by all Physics students, ensuring flexibility and freedom of choice in the courses that follow in the second and third years. Mathematics and Physics, and Physics and Business Studies courses are also available.

Universities and colleges teaching quality See www.qaa.ac.uk; http://unistats.direct.gov.uk.

Top research universities and colleges (RAE 2008) Lancaster; Cambridge; Nottingham; St Andrews; Bath; Edinburgh; Durham; Imperial London; Sheffield; London (UCL); Glasgow; Birmingham; Exeter; Sussex.

Examples of sandwich degree courses Bath; Bristol; Edinburgh; Exeter; Glasgow; Hertfordshire; Imperial London; Loughborough; Nottingham Trent; Surrey; UEA; West Scotland.

ADMISSIONS INFORMATION

Number of applicants per place (approx) Bath 6; Birmingham 6; Bristol 9; Cardiff 4, (Phys Astron) 6; Dundee 5; Durham 6; Edinburgh 9; Exeter 5; Heriot-Watt 5; Hull 7; Imperial London 3; Kent 8;

Check **Chapter 4** when choosing your university and **Chapter 7** on how to read the subject tables.

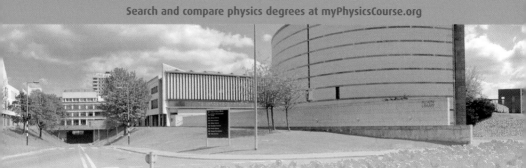

Physics at Lancaster

Physics is a highly influential subject that stretches from the study of the innermost workings of the universe to the development of nanotechnology that will shape the world of tomorrow. Many of the profound discoveries made by physicists have not only captured our imagination and inspired science fiction, but also pervade our modern lives. A student undertaking a physics degree is encouraged to develop skills that provide a sound basis for careers in a broad range of scientific disciplines and a wide variety of other professions. It's wonderful to have the opportunity to study a subject that one is deeply passionate about whilst obtaining a robust qualification respected by employers.

Lancaster University is sited on a purpose-built, self-contained campus populated by over 12,000 students. The rolling hills of the Trough of Bowland dominate the surrounding landscape; the campus is sited approximately 3 miles south of the historic Lancaster city centre on the southern doorstep to the Lake District, which is renowned as having some of the most spectacular scenery in the UK. Physics is one of the oldest departments at Lancaster University; it was established in 1965 and has, over the last half-century, forged a formidable reputation for high quality teaching driven by outstanding research. It topped the UK physics league table in the most recent Research Assessment Exercise (RAE2008) and rated equal with Cambridge, Imperial College London and Oxford in the previous Research Assessment Exercise (RAE2001). This research culture is manifested in the extended project that every fourth-year student undertakes. Moreover, it has the highest staff-to-student ratio of all of the top-ranked research-driven Physics Departments, and scores consistently highly in the National Student Survey. The staff there are, quite rightly, proud of the supportive learning environment that their students enjoy.

Students in the Lancaster University Physics Department are offered the opportunity to choose from a wide range of degree programmes that link with the leading research activities undertaken there. Furthermore, Lancaster has one of the best developed North American exchange programmes of any UK university with numerous co-operating US and Canadian institutions. Students can choose to spend a year of their studies in North America, gaining an international perspective on university life.

Studying physics at Lancaster is a life-enhancing experience which has a lasting impact long after graduation. Many students choose to stay in the Physics Department and undertake postgraduate research degrees; others progress into a wide range of successful careers elsewhere. Whatever path they follow, they take with them a sound framework within which to indulge their natural curiosity in the world around them.

Dr David A Burton
Admissions Tutor

THE UNIVERSITY *of York*

Study Physics at The University of York

The University of York is currently ranked 8th in the UK (The Sunday Times 2011) and 96th in the world (QS World Rankings 2011). We were also the Times Higher Education 'University of the Year 2010'.

Why is it the right place for you to study physics?

We pride ourselves on the quality of the undergraduate experience we offer – as seen in our many satisfied graduates. York has an enviable reputation for having high standards and yet being friendly and welcoming for students from all backgrounds, so anyone has the opportunity to excel.

What can you study?

We have a flexible modular system, offering degrees in Physics, Physics with Astrophysics, Theoretical Physics, Maths and Physics, Physics with Philosophy and Physics with Business Management. All are available as either 3-year BSc and 4-year MPhys, and with an option for a 'year in Europe'. Transfers between degrees are allowed in the 1st year.

How do you study?

We teach via a mix of traditional lectures, small group tutorials, laboratories, workshops and projects. All our students carry out an in-depth research project in their final year – often thought to be the best part of the degree!

How can you find out more?

Why not come along to one of our Open Days, read our undergraduate booklet or visit the website http://www.york.ac.uk/physics ? You can also email any questions to physics-undergraduate-admissions@york.ac.uk .

Be part of a thriving student community in the heart of the UK's fastest growing capital city and the Virgin guide's 'best-kept secret'.

Cardiff School of Physics and Astronomy offers the opportunity to study mainstream Physics or Astrophysics in an internationally renowned, friendly research environment.

- *A range of 3 year (BSc) and 4 year (MPhys) undergraduate degrees, with a core first year to allow for flexibility between schemes.*
- *BSc programmes with a Professional Placement year.*
- *Final year independent projects, working with professional physicists and astrophysicists on real research topics.*
- *An on-site astronomical observatory, laboratories, music studio and clean room facilities for state of the art research.*
- *A refurbished on-site library dedicated to Physics, Computer Science and Engineering with several study areas.*
- *Wi-fi access across the University campus.*
- *An active student society 'Chaos'.*
- *A free standing module system for first years - perhaps learn a new language?*
- *Learn transferable skills allowing excellent employment possibilities.*

For more information please visit our website www.astro.cardiff.ac.uk or email us to physics-ug@cardiff.ac.uk

Lancaster 9; Leeds 7; Leicester 7; Liverpool 4; London (King's) 7; London (QM) 6; London (RH) 9; London (UCL) 6; Loughborough 6; Nottingham 10; Salford 5; Southampton 6; Strathclyde 5; Surrey 5; Swansea 3; Warwick 8; York 5.

Advice to applicants and planning the UCAS personal statement Work experience should be mentioned, together with interests in maths and physics. Admissions tutors look for potential, enthusiasm and interest in the subject. The Institute of Physics can provide information on the work of the physicist. An awareness of the range of careers in which physics is involved should also be mentioned on the UCAS application, together with an explanation of any particular interests and details of books read on physics or mathematics (not science fiction!), and attendance at courses, for example, summer schools or day conferences for physics or engineering. See also **Appendix 3**. **Bristol** Deferred entry accepted.

Selection interviews Yes Aberystwyth, Bath, Cambridge, Durham, Exeter, Heriot-Watt, Hull, Imperial London, Lancaster, Liverpool, London (QM), London (RH), Loughborough, Oxford (Phys) 24%, (Phys Phil) 20%, Sheffield, Strathclyde, Surrey, Swansea, Warwick, York; **Some** Cardiff, Salford, UEA; **No** Birmingham, Dundee, Nottingham.

Interview advice and questions Questions will almost certainly focus on those aspects of the physics A/AS-level course which the student enjoys. See also **Chapter 6**. **Bristol** Why Physics? Questions on mechanics, physics and pure maths. Given paper and calculator and questions asked orally; best to take your own calculator. Tutors seek enthusiastic and highly motivated students and the physicist's ability to apply basic principles to unfamiliar situations.

AFTER-RESULTS ADVICE
Offers to applicants repeating A-levels Higher Bristol, Glasgow, St Andrews, Warwick; **Possibly higher** Aberystwyth, Hull, Leeds, Loughborough, York; **Same** Birmingham, Cardiff, Dundee, Durham, Exeter, Lancaster, Leicester, Liverpool, Salford, Swansea, UEA; **No** Cambridge.

For a quick reference offers calculator, fold out the inside back cover.

Employability –
What can you do to get ahead?

With job markets becoming increasingly competitive, one way you can get ahead is to get some work experience. Not only will you gain some practical experience in a relevant field, a work experience placement will enhance the work-related skills such as team work, communication and leadership, which are so vital when you apply for a job. They will also give you an opportunity to discover your strengths and weaknesses and what sort of work you will most enjoy. You may even get paid!

At Cardiff, we encourage you to make the best use of your vacation time and can help you to find a placement. We also offer two formal degree programmes incorporating a 'professional placement' year. David Gooding has just completed his placement year and you can read more on his story below...

Cardiff undergraduate student David Gooding received a pleasant surprise when he was asked if he wanted to go to Chile as part of his industrial placement. David is on the 'Physics and Astronomy with an Industrial Placement Year' degree scheme. He is currently in his third year of undergraduate studies, and is on placement at the Rutherford Appleton Laboratory in Oxfordshire. He is working as part of a team who are building radio receivers for the ALMA telescope, currently under construction in the Atacama Desert in Chile. The receivers work at a frequency of around 200 GHz, a wavelength of around 1.5 mm.

Members of the team were invited to a meeting in Chile to present details of their progress in building the receivers. David was asked if he would like to go along and help with the presentation. Naturally, he accepted the invitation! So he went to the meeting in Santiago, at which about 50 astronomers and telescope engineers were present. He helped to prepare the presentation, which was actually given by the team leader. After the meeting, some of the delegates took the opportunity to visit the telescope.

The picture above shows David in front of ALMA, which will eventually comprise around 80 high frequency radio antennas joined together. 16 have already been installed on site and have begun observations.

Professor Brian Ellison, David's supervisor at RAL said "This was a unique opportunity for a student, who has worked on this project, to present his work to the wider community, as part of the RAL team."

His supervisor at Cardiff, Professor Derek Ward-Thompson, said "This was very good experience for David, to see a scientific meeting from the inside, and also to visit the telescope. It gave him the chance to see how his part of the project fitted into the overall scheme." David has completed his placement year and commenced the final year of his studies, with experience he could not have gained elsewhere.

Short-term placements can also be valuable and a number of our students go on to undertake placements during their summer vacation. Students have had placements in various sectors including public services, manufacturing and the armed forces. Louisa Hill (left) undertook a placement at Gloucester Royal & Cheltenham General Hospital.

"I was given a week's introductory work. It was unpaid, but it gave me a general idea of what kind of thing I could expect to do as a career in Medical Physics, as well as advice on joining the IPEM and applying for the Master's courses. During the week, I spent each day in a different department - covering Diagnostic radiology, Radiotherapy, Ionising radiation therapy, UVA/UVB and laser therapy and Biophotonics. I received a lot of information about the biophotonic research that PhD students were doing (took about a tonne of notes every day, whoops!) it was very useful for inspiration for my future!"

Louisa is now studying for an MSc in Medical Radiation Physics at Swansea University.

Cardiff's Physics and Astronomy graduates are highly sought after by employers due to their extensive mathematical and analytical skills. Increasingly, graduate employers look to recruit students who have undertaken placements with them.

If you think Cardiff could be the place for you and you want to take advantage of the opportunities we can offer, then consider applying for one of our Professional Placement courses via www.ucas.ac.uk. We look forward to reading your application!

For information, please check out our website - www.astro.cardiff.ac.uk - or send us an email to Admissions@astro.cf.ac.uk

Check **Chapter 4** when choosing your university and **Chapter 7** on how to read the subject tables.

GRADUATE DESTINATIONS AND EMPLOYMENT (2009/10 HESA)
Graduates surveyed 3845 **Employed** 1055 **In voluntary employment** 40 **In further study** 970
Assumed unemployed 245

Career note Many graduates go into scientific and technical work in the manufacturing industries. However, in recent years, financial work, management and marketing have also attracted many seeking alternative careers.

OTHER DEGREE SUBJECTS FOR CONSIDERATION
Astronomy; Astrophysics; Computer Science; Earth Sciences; Engineering subjects; Geophysics; Materials Science and Metallurgy; Mathematics; Meteorology; Natural Sciences; Oceanography; Optometry; Radiography.

PHYSIOLOGY
(see also **Anatomical Science/Anatomy, Animal Sciences, Psychology**)

Physiology is a study of body function. Courses in this wide-ranging subject will cover the central nervous system, special senses and neuro-muscular mechanisms, and body-regulating systems such as exercise, stress and temperature regulation.

Useful websites www.scienceyear.com; www.physoc.org; www.physiology.org; see also **Biological Sciences**.

NB The points totals shown to the left of the institutions are for ease of reference only. It must not be assumed that Tariff points are always used by institutions or that they can be substituted for an offer in grades. The level of an offer is not necessarily indicative of the quality of a course.

COURSE OFFERS INFORMATION
Subject requirements/preferences GCSE Science and mathematics at grade A. **AL** Two science subjects are usually required; chemistry and biology are the preferred subjects.

Oxford (Biomed Sci) Applicants take the BioMedical Admissions Test (BMAT) (see **Chapter 6**).

Your target offers and examples of courses provided by each institution
380 pts Cambridge – A*AA (Nat Sci (Physiol Dev Neuro)) (IB 38–42 pts)
Edinburgh – A*AA (Biol Sci Physiol) (IB 38 pts)
London (King's) – AABc (Physiol) (IB 36 pts)
360 pts Edinburgh – AAA–ABB (Physiol) (IB 37–32 pts)
Leeds – AAA–ABB (Hum Physiol)
Manchester – AAA–AAB 340–360 pts (Pharmacol Physiol (Yr Ind)) (IB 37–33 pts)
340 pts Cardiff – AAB–ABB (Biomed Sci (Physiol)) (IB 34 pts)
Newcastle – AAB (Physiol Sci) (IB 32 pts)
320 pts Aberdeen – ABB (Physiol Ind)
Bristol – AAB–ABB 320–340 pts (Physiol Sci) (IB 35 pts HL 666 incl sci)
Glasgow – ABB (Physiol Spo Sci) (IB 32 pts)
Leeds – ABB (Clin Physiol (Cardio))
Leicester – ABB (Med Physiol) (IB 32–34 pts)
Liverpool – ABB (Physiol) (IB 32 pts HL 6 biol)
Plymouth – 280–320 pts (Hlth Sci Physiol)
300 pts Bristol UWE – (Hlth Sci Physiol)
Swansea – BBB (Clin Physiol)
280 pts Manchester Met – 280 pts (Physiol (Phys Actvt Hlth)) (IB 27 pts)
Ulster – 280 pts (Clin Physiol)
260 pts Dundee – BCC (Physiol Spo Biomed) (IB 28 pts)
Edinburgh Napier – BCC 260 pts (Spo Exer Sci (Exer Physiol))
Sunderland – 260 pts (Physiol Sci)

Wolverhampton – 260–320 pts (Hum Physiol)

240 pts **Aberdeen** – 240 pts (Physiol)
Hertfordshire – 240 pts (Physiol)
Portsmouth – 240 pts (Hum Physiol)
UCLan – 240–260 pts (Physiol Pharmacol)
Westminster – CCC (Physiol Pharmacol)

220 pts **Wolverhampton** – 220–240 pts (Clin Physiol)

200 pts **UEL** – (Med Physiol)

Alternative offers
See **Chapter 7** and **Appendix 1** for grades/UCAS Tariff points information for the International Baccalaureate, Scottish Highers/Advanced Highers, the Welsh Baccalaureate, the Irish Leaving Certificate, the Cambridge Pre-U Diploma, the Advanced Diploma and the Extended Project.

EXAMPLES OF FOUNDATION DEGREES IN THE SUBJECT FIELD
Manchester Met; Westminster.

CHOOSING YOUR COURSE (SEE ALSO CH.1)
Some course features
See also **Biological Sciences**.

Bristol In the first two years Physiology is studied with two other subjects, for example anatomy, pharmacology, psychology, chemistry or biochemistry.
Leeds (Hum Physiol) Course has an optional year in industry or abroad.
Leicester (Med Physiol) Study abroad through the Erasmus scheme is also possible, and a four-year sandwich course is also available.
Newcastle The Biomedical Sciences programme offers seven science subjects, all of which have a common first year. The decision to take Physiology, or any other subject, takes place in Year 2.

Universities and colleges teaching quality See www.qaa.ac.uk; http://unistats.direct.gov.uk.

Top research universities and colleges (RAE 2008) See **Biological Sciences**.

Examples of sandwich degree courses Aberdeen; Cardiff; Leeds; Manchester Met; Ulster; Wolverhampton.

ADMISSIONS INFORMATION
Number of applicants per place (approx) Bristol 6; Cardiff 8; Dundee 5; Leeds 4; Leicester 5; Liverpool 10; London (King's) 5; Newcastle 6.

Advice to applicants and planning the UCAS personal statement See **Anatomical Science/ Anatomy** and **Biological Sciences**.

Selection interviews Yes Cambridge, Leeds, Newcastle, Oxford; **Some** Bristol, Cardiff, Dundee.

Interview advice and questions Past questions include: What made you decide to do a Physiology degree? What experimental work have you done connected with physiology? What future career do you have in mind? What is physiology? Why not choose Medicine instead? What practicals do you do at school? See also **Chapter 6**. **Cardiff** Interviewer expects to see outside interests and ability to mix with people as well as an interest in biological sciences. **Oxford** Over 85% of applicants interviewed. What food (out of choice) was the best to eat before an interview?

AFTER-RESULTS ADVICE
Offers to applicants repeating A-levels Higher Bristol, Glasgow, Leeds, Leicester, Newcastle, St Andrews; **Same** Cardiff, Dundee; **No** Cambridge.

GRADUATE DESTINATIONS AND EMPLOYMENT (2009/10 HESA)
Including Anatomy and Pathology; graduates surveyed 3805 **Employed** 2075 **In voluntary employment** 65 **In further study** 740 **Assumed unemployed** 255

Career note See **Biology**.

Check **Chapter 4** when choosing your university and **Chapter 7** on how to read the subject tables.

OTHER DEGREE SUBJECTS FOR CONSIDERATION

Anatomy; Biochemistry; Biological Sciences; Biotechnology; Dentistry; Genetics; Health Studies; Medicine; Microbiology; Nursing; Optometry; Pharmacology; Radiography; Sports Science.

PHYSIOTHERAPY

(see also Health Sciences/Studies)

Physiotherapists work as part of a multi-disciplinary team with other health professionals and are involved in the treatment and rehabilitation of patients of all ages and with a wide variety of medical problems. On successful completion of the three-year course, graduates are eligible for State Registration and Membership of the Chartered Society of Physiotherapy. See also **Appendix 2**.

Useful websites www.csp.org.uk; www.thephysiotherapysite.co.uk; www.nhscareers.nhs.uk; www. physiotherapy.co.uk.

NB The points totals shown to the left of the institutions are for ease of reference only. It must not be assumed that Tariff points are always used by institutions or that they can be substituted for an offer in grades. The level of an offer is not necessarily indicative of the quality of a course.

COURSE OFFERS INFORMATION

Subject requirements/preferences GCSE English, mathematics and science subjects. Many universities stipulate A/B grades in specific subjects. **AL** One or two science subjects are required. **Other** requirements Occupational health check and Criminal Records Bureau (CRB) clearance.

Your target offers and examples of courses provided by each institution

380 pts **London (King's)** – AABc (Physio) (IB 36 pts)

370 pts **Southampton** – ABBb 370 pts (Physio) (IB 33 pts)

340 pts **Birmingham** – AAB 340 pts (Physio) (IB 34 pts)
Bournemouth – 340 pts (Physio)
Bristol UWE – 340 pts (Physio)
Cardiff – AAB incl biol (Physio) (IB 27 pts)
Edinburgh Queen Margaret – AAB 340 pts (Physio)
Plymouth – 340 pts (Physio)

320 pts **Brunel** – ABB (Physio) (IB 33 pts)
Huddersfield – ABB 320 pts (Physio)
Keele – ABB (Physio) (IB 27 pts)
Kingston – see under London (St George's) 320 pts (Physio)
Liverpool – ABB 320 pts (Physio) (IB 30 pts)
London (St George's) – ABB 320 pts (Physio)
Manchester Met – 320 pts (Physio) (IB 30 pts)
Northumbria – 320 pts (incl 100 pts in Hlth Sci subj) (Physio) (IB 32 pts)
Nottingham – ABB (Physio) (IB 34 pts HL 6 biol)
Oxford Brookes – ABB (Physio)
Sheffield Hallam – 320 pts (Physio)
UCLan – ABB (Physio) (IB 30 pts)
UEA – ABB (Physio) (IB 32 pts HL 6 biol)

300 pts **Brighton** – BBB (Physio) (IB 34 pts)
Coventry – BBB incl A2 biol C **or** above 300 pts (Physio)
Cumbria – 300 pts (Physio)
Glasgow Caledonian – BBB (Physio)
Hertfordshire – 300 pts (Physio)
Leeds Met – 300 pts (Physio) (IB 25 pts)
Leicester – BBB (Physio)
Robert Gordon – BBB 300 pts (Physio) (IB 32 pts)
Salford – BBB 300 pts (Physio) (IB 32 pts)

Teesside – 300 pts (Physio)
Ulster – BBB (Physio)
York St John – 300 pts (Physio)
280 pts **Bradford** – BBC 280 pts (Physio) (IB 32 pts)
UEL – 280 pts (Physio) (IB 26 pts)

Alternative offers
See **Chapter 7** and **Appendix 1** for grades/UCAS Tariff points information for the International Baccalaureate, Scottish Highers/Advanced Highers, the Welsh Baccalaureate, the Irish Leaving Certificate, the Cambridge Pre-U Diploma, the Advanced Diploma and the Extended Project.

EXAMPLES OF FOUNDATION DEGREES IN THE SUBJECT FIELD
Edge Hill; Huddersfield; Keele; Salford.

CHOOSING YOUR COURSE (SEE ALSO CH.1)
Some course features
NHS bursaries are available for all Physiotherapy courses.

Hertfordshire (Physio) One third of the course is spent on practice placements in hospitals and health care units.
Nottingham (Physio) 32 weeks of supervised clinical practice split into eight four-week blocks take place in Years 2 and 3.
Southampton A three-year full-time or four-year part-time course is offered to school leavers.
UEL Physiotherapy is available as full-time, or as full-time situated learning where one-third of the course is practice-based and two-thirds are university-based.

Universities and colleges teaching quality See www.qaa.ac.uk; http://unistats.direct.gov.uk.

ADMISSIONS INFORMATION
Number of applicants per place (approx) Birmingham 9; Bradford 22; Brighton 30, (places for overseas candidates) 6; Bristol UWE 12; Brunel 11; Cardiff 17; Coventry 15; Edinburgh Queen Margaret 11; Glasgow Caledonian 12; Hertfordshire 13; Huddersfield 18; Kingston 9; Liverpool 20; London (King's) 16; Manchester 18; Northumbria 37; Robert Gordon 13; Salford 28; Sheffield Hallam 12; Southampton 15; Teesside 33; UEA 14; UEL 10; Ulster 12.

Advice to applicants and planning the UCAS personal statement Visits to, and work experience in, hospital physiotherapy departments are important although many universities publicly state that this is not necessary. However, with the level of competition for this subject I would regard this as doubtful (see Reasons for rejection). Applicants must demonstrate a clear understanding of the nature of the profession. Give details of voluntary work activities. Take notes of the work done and the different aspects of physiotherapy. Explain your experience fully on the UCAS application. Outside interests and teamwork are considered important. Good communication skills. Observation placement within a physiotherapy department. **Coventry** The University of Leicester part-delivers a BSc Physiotherapy degree. This course is a Coventry University degree that has 30 places based at the Leicester campus. Teaching takes place at Leicester and Coventry. Students are admitted by Coventry but live and mostly study at Leicester. **Manchester Met** We need to know why you want to be a physiotherapist. We also look for work shadowing a physiotherapist or work experience in another caring role. Evidence is also required of good communication skills, ability to care for people and of teamwork and leadership. **Salford** Essential for applicants to seek experience in as wide a range of settings as possible.

Misconceptions about this course Some applicants think that physiotherapy has a sports bias.

Selection interviews Most institutions. **Yes** Birmingham, Bradford, Brighton, Coventry, Huddersfield, London (St George's), Nottingham, Robert Gordon, Salford, Sheffield Hallam, UEA, UEL; **Some** Brunel (mature students), Cardiff (mature students), Edinburgh Queen Margaret, Kingston, Southampton (mature students; who are asked to write about their life experience).

Interview advice and questions Physiotherapy is one of the most popular courses at present and work experience is very important, if not essential. A sound knowledge of the career, types of treatment used in physiotherapy and some understanding of the possible problems experienced by patients will be expected. Past interview questions include: How does physiotherapy fit into the overall health care system? If one patient was a heavy smoker and the other not, would you treat them the same? What was the most emotionally challenging thing you have ever done? Give an example of teamwork in which you have been involved. Why should we make you an offer? What is chiropractic? What is osteopathy? See also **Chapter 6**.

Reasons for rejection (non-academic) Lack of knowledge of the profession. Failure to convince the interviewers of a reasoned basis for following the profession. Failure to have visited a hospital physiotherapy unit. Lack of awareness of the demands of the course. **Birmingham** Poor communication skills. Lack of career insight. **Bristol UWE** Applicants re-sitting A-levels are not normally considered. **Cardiff** Lack of knowledge of physiotherapy; experience of sports injuries only.

AFTER-RESULTS ADVICE
Offers to applicants repeating A-levels Higher Bristol UWE (candidates who fail at interview will not normally be reconsidered), Glasgow Caledonian, Kingston, Teesside, UEA, UEL; **Same** Coventry, Edinburgh Queen Margaret, Salford, Southampton.

GRADUATE DESTINATIONS AND EMPLOYMENT (2009/10 HESA)
See **Health Sciences/Studies**.

Career note The professional qualifications gained on graduation enable physiotherapists to seek posts in the NHS where the majority are employed. A small number work in the community health service, particularly in rural areas, whilst others work in residential homes. In addition to private practice, there are also some opportunities in professional sports clubs.

OTHER DEGREE SUBJECTS FOR CONSIDERATION
Anatomy; Audiology; Biological Sciences; Health Studies; Leisure and Recreation; Nursing; Occupational Therapy; Osteopathy; Physical Education; Psychology; Sport Science/Studies.

PLANT SCIENCES
(including **Botany**; see also **Biological Sciences, Biology, Horticulture**)

Plant Sciences cover such areas as plant biochemistry, plant genetics, plant conservation and plant geography. Botany encompasses all aspects of plant science and also other subject areas including agriculture, forestry and horticulture. Botany is basic to these subjects and others including pharmacology and water management. As with other biological sciences, some universities introduce Plant Sciences by way of a common first year with other subjects.

Useful websites www.kew.org; www.anbg.gov.au; www.scienceyear.com; www.botany.net; www.botany.org.

NB The points totals shown to the left of the institutions are for ease of reference only. It must not be assumed that Tariff points are always used by institutions or that they can be substituted for an offer in grades. The level of an offer is not necessarily indicative of the quality of a course.

COURSE OFFERS INFORMATION
Subject requirements/preferences GCSE Mathematics if not offered at A-level. **AL** One or two science subjects are usually required.

Your target offers and examples of courses provided by each institution
380 pts **Cambridge** – A*AA (Nat Sci (Plnt Sci)) (IB 40–42 pts)
360 pts **Edinburgh** – AAA–ABB 320–360 pts (Plnt Sci) (IB 37–32 pts)
　　　　Manchester – AAA–ABB 320–360 pts (Plnt Sci (Yr Ind)) (IB 37–33 pts)
　　　　Sheffield – AAA incl biol sci (Plnt Sci MBiolSci) (IB 37 pts)

340 pts Birmingham – AAB–BBB (Biol Sci (Plnt Biol)) (IB 32 pts)
           Sheffield – AAB incl biol sci (Plnt Sci BSci) (IB 35 pts)
320 pts Glasgow – ABB (Mol Cell Biol Plnt Sci) (IB 32 pts)
           Nottingham – ABB–BCC (Plnt Sci) (IB 32–26 pts)
           UEA – ABB (Plnt Sci) (IB 32 pts)
280 pts Aberystwyth – 280–320 pts (Plnt Biol) (IB 26 pts)
240 pts Aberdeen – CCC (Plnt Biol) (IB 28 pts)
           Canterbury Christ Church – 240 pts (Plnt Sci)
           Worcester – 240–280 pts (Biol (Plnt Sci))
220 pts Myerscough (Coll) – 220 pts (Arbor)

Alternative offers
See **Chapter 7** and **Appendix 1** for grades/UCAS Tariff points information for the International Baccalaureate, Scottish Highers/Advanced Highers, the Welsh Baccalaureate, the Irish Leaving Certificate, the Cambridge Pre-U Diploma, the Advanced Diploma and the Extended Project.

CHOOSING YOUR COURSE (SEE ALSO CH.1)
Some course features
See also **Biology** and **Horticulture**.

Aberystwyth After a common first year focusing on plant structure, function, physiology and classification, students can tailor their degree scheme through their choice of module options. Field studies in northern Spain and western Ireland are available.
Birmingham Plant Biology is an option in the Biological Sciences programme. Specialisation can take place at the beginning of the course or in Year 2.
UEA It is possible to start on the flexible Biological Sciences programme in which modules are chosen depending on the student's preference.

Universities and colleges teaching quality See www.qaa.ac.uk; http://unistats.direct.gov.uk.

Top research universities and colleges (RAE 2008) See **Biological Sciences**.

ADMISSIONS INFORMATION
Number of applicants per place (approx) Edinburgh 6; Glasgow 4; Nottingham 7; Sheffield 5.

Advice to applicants and planning the UCAS personal statement Visit botanical gardens. See also **Biological Sciences** and **Appendix 4**.

Selection interviews **Yes** Cambridge, Nottingham (depends on application); **No** Dundee.

Interview advice and questions You are likely to be questioned on your biology studies, your reasons for wishing to study Plant Sciences and your ideas about a possible future career. In the past questions have been asked about Darwin's theory of evolution, photosynthesis and DNA and the value of gardening programmes on TV! See also **Chapter 6**.

AFTER-RESULTS ADVICE
Offers to applicants repeating A-levels **Possibly higher** Nottingham; **Same** Birmingham, Sheffield; **No** Cambridge, Imperial London.

GRADUATE DESTINATIONS AND EMPLOYMENT (2009/10 HESA)
Botany; graduates surveyed 100 **Employed** 55 **In voluntary employment** 0 **In further study** 30 **Assumed unemployed** 5

Career note See **Biology** and **Horticulture**.

OTHER DEGREE SUBJECTS FOR CONSIDERATION
Agriculture; Biochemistry; Biological Sciences; Biology; Crop Science (Agronomy); Ecology; Food Science; Forestry; Herbal Medicine; Horticulture; Landscape Architecture; Traditional Chinese Medicine.

PODIATRY (CHIROPODY)

Podiatry is a relatively new term for chiropody and deals with the management of disease and disorders of the ankle and foot. Podiatrists diagnose nail, skin and movement problems, devise treatment plans and carry out treatment for all age groups. Courses lead to state registration and some work shadowing prior to application is preferred by admissions tutors.

Useful websites www.feetforlife.org; www.nhscareers.nhs.uk; www.podiatrynetwork.com; www. podiatrytoday.com; www.podiatrychannel.com.

NB The points totals shown to the left of the institutions are for ease of reference only. It must not be assumed that Tariff points are always used by institutions or that they can be substituted for an offer in grades. The level of an offer is not necessarily indicative of the quality of a course.

COURSE OFFERS INFORMATION

Subject requirements/preferences GCSE Mathematics and science subjects. **AL** Biology usually required or preferred. **Other** requirements Hepatitis B, tuberculosis and tetanus immunisation; Criminal Records Bureau (CRB) clearance (a pre-existing record could prevent a student from participating in the placement component of the course and prevent the student from gaining state registration).

Your target offers and examples of courses provided by each institution

300 pts **Huddersfield** – 300 pts (Pod) (IB 26 pts)
       Southampton – BBB (Pod) (IB 28 pts)
       Ulster – BBB (Pod) (IB 25 pts)
280 pts **Cardiff Met** – 280 pts (Pod)
       Northampton – 260–280 pts (Pod) (IB 24 pts)
260 pts **Brighton** – BCC 260 pts (Pod) (IB 28 pts)
       Plymouth – 240–260 pts (Pod) (IB 27 pts)
240 pts **Edinburgh Queen Margaret** – 240 pts (Pod) (IB 26 pts)
       Salford – 240 pts (Pod) (IB 24 pts)
       UEL – 240 pts (Pod Med) (IB 26 pts)
220 pts **Birmingham Met (Coll)** – 220 pts (Pod)
       Glasgow Caledonian – CCD (Pod)
160 pts **Durham New (Coll)** – 160 pts (Pod)

Alternative offers
See **Chapter 7** and **Appendix 1** for grades/UCAS Tariff points information for the International Baccalaureate, Scottish Highers/Advanced Highers, the Welsh Baccalaureate, the Irish Leaving Certificate, the Cambridge Pre-U Diploma, the Advanced Diploma and the Extended Project.

EXAMPLES OF FOUNDATION DEGREES IN THE SUBJECT FIELD
Huddersfield.

CHOOSING YOUR COURSE (SEE ALSO CH.1)
Some course features
NHS bursaries are available for all Podiatry courses. See also **Health Sciences/Studies**.

Northampton Students manage their own patient cases during the course.
Plymouth Supervised placements in NHS Trusts from Year 1.
Southampton A modular programme with six units studied in each semester, these include orthopaedic triage, surgery and paediatrics.

Universities and colleges teaching quality See www.qaa.ac.uk; http://unistats.direct.gov.uk.

ADMISSIONS INFORMATION
Number of applicants per place (approx) Birmingham Met (Coll) 4; Cardiff Met 8; Huddersfield 2–3; Northampton 2; Salford 3; Southampton 4.

Advice to applicants and planning the UCAS personal statement Visit a podiatrist's clinic to gain work experience/work shadowing experience. Applicants need the ability to communicate with all age ranges, to work independently, to be resourceful and to possess a focussed approach to academic work. Admissions tutors look for evidence of an understanding of podiatry, some work experience, good people skills, and effective communication. Mature applicants must include an academic reference (not an employer reference).

Misconceptions about this course Cardiff Met Prospective students are often not aware of the demanding requirements of the course: 1000 practical clinical hours augmented by a rigorous academic programme. Applicants are often unaware that whilst the elderly are a significant sub-population of patients with a variety of foot problems, increasingly the role of the podiatrist is the diagnosis and management of biomechanical/developmental disorders as well as the management of the diabetic or rheumatoid patient and those who require surgical intervention for nail problems. **Huddersfield** Many people think that podiatry is limited in its scope of practice to treating toe nails, corns and calluses: FALSE. As professionals, we do treat such pathologies but the scope of practice is much wider. It now includes surgery, biomechanics, sports injuries, treating children and high risk patients. Because offers are low it is considered an easier course than, for example, Physiotherapy: FALSE. The course is academically demanding in addition to the compulsory clinical requirement.

Selection interviews Most institutions. **Yes** Huddersfield, Southampton; **Some** Cardiff Met.

Interview advice and questions Past questions include: Have you visited a podiatrist's surgery? What do your friends think about your choice of career? Do you think that being a podiatrist could cause you any physical problems? With which groups of people do podiatrists come into contact? What are your perceptions of the scope of practice of podiatry? What transferable skills do you think you will need? See also **Chapter 6**. **Cardiff Met** What made you consider podiatry as a career? Have you researched your career choice and where did you find the information? What have you discovered and has this altered your original perception of podiatry? What personal characteristics do you think you possess which might be useful for this work? **Southampton** Applicants should show an interest in medical topics. Communication skills are important and an insight into the implications of a career in Podiatry.

Reasons for rejection (non-academic) Unconvincing attitude; poor communication and inter-personal skills; lack of motivation; medical condition or physical disabilities which are incompatible with professional practice; no knowledge of chosen profession; lack of work experience.

AFTER-RESULTS ADVICE
Offers to applicants repeating A-levels Same Cardiff Met, Huddersfield, Salford.

GRADUATE DESTINATIONS AND EMPLOYMENT (2009/10 HESA)
Career note Many state-registered podiatrists are employed by the NHS whilst others work in private practice or commercially run clinics.

OTHER DEGREE SUBJECTS FOR CONSIDERATION
Audiology; Biological Sciences; Health Studies; Nursing; Occupational Therapy; Osteopathy; Physiotherapy.

POLITICS

(including **Government** and **International Politics**; see also **Development Studies, International Relations, Social Sciences/Studies**)

Politics is often described as the study of 'who gets what, where, when and how'. Courses have become increasingly popular in recent years and usually cover the politics and government of the major powers. Because of the variety of degree courses on offer, it is possible to study the politics of almost any country in the world.

Check **Chapter 4** when choosing your university and **Chapter 7** on how to read the subject tables.

Useful websites http://europa.eu; www.fco.gov.uk; www.psa.ac.uk; www.parliament.uk; www.whitehouse.gov; www.amnesty.org; www.direct.gov.uk; www.un.org; www.un.int.

NB The points totals shown to the left of the institutions are for ease of reference only. It must not be assumed that Tariff points are always used by institutions or that they can be substituted for an offer in grades. The level of an offer is not necessarily indicative of the quality of a course.

COURSE OFFERS INFORMATION

Subject requirements/preferences GCSE English, mathematics and a foreign language may be required. **AL** No subjects specified; history useful but an arts or social science subject an advantage.

Your target offers and examples of courses provided by each institution

440 pts **London (King's)** – A*AAa (Pol Phil Law) (IB 39 pts)
Warwick – A*AAa (Econ Pol Int St) (IB 38 pts)

430 pts **Warwick** – A*AAb–AAAb (PPE) (IB 38 pts)

390 pts **Warwick** – AABb (Pol) (IB 36 pts)

380 pts **Cambridge** – A*AA (Pol Psy Sociol (PPS)) (IB 40–42 pts HL 766–777)
Durham – A*AA (PPE) (IB 38 pts)
Exeter – A*AA–AAB 380–340 pts (Econ Pol) (IB 38–34 pts)
London (King's) – A*AA (War St) (IB 39 pts)
London (UCL) – A*AA (Euro Soc Pol St) (IB 39 pts)

360 pts **Bath** – AAA (Pol Econ) (IB 38 pts)
Birmingham – AAA–ABB 320–360 pts (Euro Pol Soty Econ) (IB 34–36 pts)
Bristol – AAA–AAB (Pol Modn Lang) (IB 37–35 pts)
Durham – AAA (Pol) (IB 37 pts HL 17 pts)
Edinburgh – AAA–BBB (Pol Econ Soc Hist) (IB 34–42 pts)
Exeter – AAA–AAB (Ldrshp Pol courses)
Lancaster – AAA (Pol (St Abrd)) (IB 36 pts)
London (QM) – 360 pts (Pol) (IB 32 pts)
London (RH) – AAA–ABB 360–320 pts (Econ Pol Int Rel) (IB 32–35 pts)
London (SOAS) – AAA (Pol) (IB 38 pts HL 766)
London LSE – AAA (Gov Econ) (IB 38 pts HL 766)
Newcastle – AAA–AAB 340–360 pts (Pol Hist) (IB 37 pts)
Nottingham – AAA (Hist Pol) (IB 36 pts)
Oxford – AAA (PPE) (IB 39 pts)
Sheffield – AAA incl hist (Int Hist Int Pol) (IB 37 pts HL 6 hist)
Sussex – AAA–AAB (Law Pol) (IB 35–36 pts)
York – AAA (Phil Pol Econ) (IB 36 pts)

340 pts **Aston** – AAB–ABB 340–320 pts (Pol Int Rel) (IB 34–35 pts)
Birmingham – AAA–AAB 340–360 pts (Pol Econ) (IB 34–38 pts)
Bristol – AAB (Soc Plcy Pol) (IB 35 pts HL 666)
Cardiff – AAB incl hist (Modn Hist Pol)
City – AAB 340 pts (Int Pol) (IB 32 pts)
Essex – AAB–ABB 340–320 pts (Pol) (IB 36 pts)
Exeter – AAB–BBB (Pol Joint Hons) (IB 34–30 pts)
Lancaster – AAb (Pol Int Rel) (IB 34 pts)
Leeds – AAB (Geog Pol)
Liverpool – AAB (Pol Int Bus) (IB 35 pts)
London (Birk) – AAB (Pol Govt; Glob Pol Int Rel)
London (Gold) – AAB (Int St) (IB 28 pts)
London (King's) – AAB (Pol Int Econ) (IB 36 pts HL 665)
London (QM) – 340 pts (Law Pol) (IB 32 pts)
London (RH) – AAB 340 pts (Pol) (IB 34–32 pts)
London (UCL) – AAB (Pol E Euro St) (IB 34–36 pts)
Loughborough – AAB (Econ Pol) (IB 34 pts)
Manchester – AAB (Law Pol) (IB 35 pts)

For a quick reference offers calculator, fold out the inside back cover.

Newcastle – AAB–ABB 320–340 pts (Pol) (IB 34–36 pts)
Nottingham – AAB (Pol courses) (IB 36 pts)
Queen's Belfast – AAB/ABBa (PPE)
Sheffield – AAB (Pol) (IB 35 pts)
Southampton – AAB (Pol Span/Port Lat Am St) (IB 34 pts HL 17 pts)
Sussex – AAB (Pol courses) (IB 35 pts)
Swansea – AAB (PPE)
UEA – AAB (Cult Lit Pol) (IB 32 pts HL 5 Engl)
York – AAB (Pol Int Rel) (IB 36 pts)

320 pts **Aston** – ABB 320 pts (Pol Sociol) (IB 34 pts)
Bath – ABB–BBB (Russ Pol)
Cardiff – ABB–BBB incl Fr (Pol Dip Etud Pol)
Glasgow – ABB (Pol Joint Hons) (IB 36 pts)
Hull – 320 pts (Pol Int Rel) (IB 34–36 pts)
Kent – ABB (Pol Int Rel) (IB 33 pts)
Lancaster – ABB (Pol Sociol) (IB 32 pts)
Leeds – ABB (Euro Pol Fr/Ger/Ital) (IB 34 pts)
Leicester – ABB (Pol)
Liverpool – ABB (Pol Comm St) (IB 33 pts)
Liverpool Hope – 260–320 pts (Pol)
London (RH) – ABB 320 pts (Geog Pol Int Rel) (IB 37 pts HL 666)
London LSE – ABB (Soc Plcy Gov) (IB 37 pts HL 666)
Loughborough – ABB–ABC 300–320 pts (Pol courses) (IB 32–34 pts)
Manchester – ABB (Pol Sociol) (IB 34 pts)
Newcastle – AAB–ABB 320–340 pts (Pol Econ) (IB 34–36 pts)
Nottingham – ABB (Euro Pol) (IB 32 pts)
Strathclyde – ABB (Pol courses) (IB 34 pts)
Sheffield – ABB (Pol Sociol) (IB 33 pts)
Surrey – ABB 320 pts (Pol) (IB 32 pts)
Swansea – ABB–BBB (Pol; Pol Soc Hist; Pol Langs; Pol Comms)
UEA – ABB (Phil Pol) (IB 32 pts)

300 pts **Aberdeen** – BBB (Int Rel)
Aberystwyth – 300 pts (Int Pol Third Wrld)
Birmingham – ABB–BBB (Anth Pol Sci) (IB 32–34 pts)
Brighton – BBB (Pol Sociol) (IB 32 pts)
Bristol UWE – 300 pts (Pol)
Brunel – BBB (Int Pol) (IB 32 pts)
Buckingham – 300 pts (Law Pol)
Edinburgh – AAA–BBB 300–360 pts (Pol) (IB 34 pts HL 555)
Essex – 300–320 pts (PPE) (IB 29 pts)
Hertfordshire – 300 pts (Govt Pol)
Huddersfield – 300 pts (Pol; Pol Contemp Hist; Pol Media)
Keele – 300 pts (Pol)
Newcastle – ABB–BBB 300–320 pts (Pol Sociol) (IB 32 pts)
Northumbria – 300 pts (Pol) (IB 26 pts)
Portsmouth – 240–300 pts (Pol; Pol Sociol)
Queen's Belfast – BBB/BBCb (Pol Joint Hons) (IB 29 pts HL 655)
Reading – 300–320 pts (Pol Int Rel; War Pce Int Rel)
Surrey – BBB 300 pts (Int Pol) (IB 32 pts)
Swansea – BBB 300 pts (Span Pol)
Westminster – BBB (Pol) (IB 28 pts)

280 pts **Aberystwyth** – 280–300 pts (Int Pol) (IB 28 pts)
Bradford – BBC 280 pts (Pol; Pol Pce St; Pol Law)
Brighton – BBC 280 pts (Pol Soc Plcy) (IB 30 pts)
De Montfort – 280 pts (Pol Gov; Pol Sociol)

Check **Chapter 4** when choosing your university and **Chapter 7** on how to read the subject tables.

Lincoln – 280 pts (Hist Pol; Engl Pol)
Manchester Met – 280 pts (Int Pol Phil) (IB 28 pts)
Northampton – 260–280 pts (Pol; Pol Joint Hons)
Nottingham Trent – 280 pts (Pol)
Oxford Brookes – BBC (Int Rel Pol) (IB 31 pts)
Stirling – BBC (Pol) (IB 32 pts)
Salford – 280 pts (Int Rel Pol) (IB 31 pts)

260 pts **Brunel** – 260–300 pts (Pol) (IB 31 pts)
Coventry – BCC 260 pts (Pol Hist)
De Montfort – 260 pts (Int Rel Pol)
Dundee – BCC (Pol) (HL 555)
Greenwich – 260 pts (Pol)
Nottingham Trent – 260 pts (Pol Int Rel)
Oxford Brookes – BCC (Econ Pol Int Rel) (IB 29 pts)
Sheffield Hallam – 260 pts (Pol)
Sunderland – 260 pts (Pol (Comb))
UCLan – 260–300 pts (Pol courses)
Ulster – 260 pts (Soc Plcy Pol)

240 pts **Bangor** – 240–260 pts (Pol Soc Sci)
Buckingham – 240 pts (Pol)
Canterbury Christ Church – 240 pts (Pol Gov; Pol Glob Gov; Pol)
Chester – 240–280 pts (Pol) (IB 26 pts)
London Met – 240 pts (Pol; Pol Bank; Pol Pce Cnflct St)
Manchester Met – 240 pts (Pol) (IB 28 pts)
Plymouth – 240 pts (Pol Int Rel)
Salford – 180–280 pts (Pol) (IB 29 pts)
Ulster – CCC 240–280 pts (Pol Crimin) (IB 24 pts)
Westminster – CCC–BCC (Pol (Comb)) (IB 28 pts)
Worcester – 240–280 pts (Pol Ppl Pwr)

220 pts **Kingston** – 220–360 pts (Pol Jrnl; Pol App Econ)
Winchester – 260–300 pts (Pol Glob St courses) (IB 24 pts)

200 pts **Blackburn (Coll)** – 200 pts (Pol)
Leeds Met – 200 pts (Pol) (IB 24 pts)
Lincoln – 200–260 pts (Pol; Crimin Pol; Int Rel Pol)
Middlesex – 200–300 pts (Int Pol)
UEL – 200 pts (Int Pol)
Wolverhampton – 200 pts (Pol Phil)

160 pts **UHI** – CC–AA (Hist Pol)
Wolverhampton – 160–220 pts (War St)

140 pts **West Scotland** – CD (Pol)

Open University - contact +44 (0)845 300 6090 **or** www.openuniversity.co.uk/you (PPE)

Alternative offers

See **Chapter 7** and **Appendix 1** for grades/UCAS Tariff points information for the International Baccalaureate, Scottish Highers/Advanced Highers, the Welsh Baccalaureate, the Irish Leaving Certificate, the Cambridge Pre-U Diploma, the Advanced Diploma and the Extended Project.

CHOOSING YOUR COURSE (SEE ALSO CH.1)

Some course features

Bangor Political and Social Sciences is offered as a three-year course, which includes modules in psychology, economic and social issues, crime and US history and politics.

Chester The International Development Studies course focuses on socio-economic, political, cultural and environmental aspects, exploring the Third World and comparisons between rich and poor, urban and rural and contemporary and historical. Politics is also offered as a single or combined honours course and covers subjects such as British Government, Political Thinkers and Social Policy.

Essex The Department of Government offers a wide range of courses in two main degrees, Politics and International Relations and Politics. A range of specialist options are available covering world politics, democracy and human rights. Twelve other joint courses are also available.

Kent The Department offers two main programmes: Politics and Politics and International Relations, also with French, German and Italian and an optional year in countries including Finland, Japan or the Czech Republic. Other courses include Social Policy, Economics and Politics, Conflict, Peace and Security and Politics and Social Anthropology.

Universities and colleges teaching quality See www.qaa.ac.uk; http://unistats.direct.gov.uk.

Top research universities and colleges (RAE 2008) (Politics and International Studies) Essex; Sheffield; Aberystwyth; Oxford; London LSE; London (UCL); London (SOAS); Sussex (Int Rel); Warwick; Exeter; Nottingham; Manchester; Cambridge.

Examples of sandwich degree courses Aston; Bath; Brunel; Coventry; De Montfort; Lancaster; Leeds Met; Loughborough; Oxford Brookes; Plymouth; Surrey; UCLan.

ADMISSIONS INFORMATION

Number of applicants per place (approx) Aberystwyth 4; Aston 4; Bath 2; Birmingham 6; Bradford 10; Bristol 14; Brunel 5; Buckingham 2; Cardiff 14; Cardiff Met 3; De Montfort 6; Dundee 6; Durham (all courses) 11; Exeter 8; Hull 11, (PPE) 20; Kent 14; Lancaster 14; Leeds 18; Leicester 11; Liverpool 9; LJMU 6; London (QM) 10; London (SOAS) 5; London LSE (Gov) 17, (Gov Econ) 10, (Gov Hist) 17; London Met 5; Loughborough 4; Newcastle 9; Northampton 4; Nottingham 5; Nottingham Trent 3; Oxford (PPE) 7; Oxford Brookes 12; Portsmouth 6; Salford 7; Southampton 6; Staffordshire 10; Stirling 9; Swansea 3; UEA 15; Warwick 10; York 8.

Advice to applicants and planning the UCAS personal statement Study the workings of government in the UK, Europe and other areas of the world, such as the Middle East, the Far East, America and Russia. Describe visits to the Houses of Commons and Lords and the debates taking place. Attend council meetings – county, town, district, village halls. Describe these visits and agendas. Read current affairs avidly. Be aware of political developments in the major countries and regions of the world including the Middle East, South America, the UK, Europe, USA, China, Korea and Russia. Keep abreast of developments in theatres of war, for example, Afghanistan. Explain your interests in detail. **Aberystwyth** We look for degree candidates with a strong interest in political and social issues and who want to inquire into the way in which the world is organised politically, socially and economically. **Bristol** Deferred entry accepted. **De Montfort** Demonstration of active interest in current affairs and some understanding of how politics affects our daily lives.

Misconceptions about this course Aberystwyth Many students believe that they need to study politics at A-level for Politics courses – this is not the case. **Cardiff Met** Some consider that Politics is a narrow subject, only relevant to those who want a political career. **De Montfort** Some applicants believe that a Politics course only covers the mechanics of government and parliament.

Selection interviews Yes Bath (mature students), Cambridge, Durham, Exeter, Huddersfield, Hull, Leeds (Pol Parl St), Leicester, Liverpool, London (Gold), London (SOAS), London Met, London South Bank, Oxford, Portsmouth, Sheffield, Sussex, Swansea, Ulster, Warwick; **Some** Aberystwyth, Bristol, Cardiff Met, De Montfort, Dundee, LJMU, London LSE, Loughborough, Salford, Staffordshire, York; **No** Birmingham, Essex, Nottingham, Reading, UEA.

Interview advice and questions Questions may stem from A/AS-level studies but applicants will also be expected to be up-to-date in their knowledge and opinions of current events. Questions in recent years have included: What constitutes a 'great power'? What is happening at present in the Labour Party? Define capitalism. What is a political decision? How do opinion polls detract from democracy? Is the European Union a good idea? Why? What are the views of the present government on the European Union? What is a 'spin doctor'? Are politicians hypocrites? See also **Chapter 6**.

Check **Chapter 4** when choosing your university and **Chapter 7** on how to read the subject tables.

De Montfort Why Politics? What political issues motivate your interests, for example environmentalism, human rights?

AFTER-RESULTS ADVICE

Offers to applicants repeating A-levels **Higher** Essex, Glasgow, Leeds, Newcastle, Nottingham, Warwick, York; **Possibly higher** Hull, Lancaster, Oxford Brookes, Swansea; **Same** Aberystwyth, Birmingham, Bristol, Buckingham, Cardiff Met, De Montfort, Dundee, Durham, Lincoln, Liverpool Hope, LJMU, London (SOAS), London Met, London South Bank, Loughborough, Nottingham Trent, Portsmouth, Salford, Staffordshire, Stirling, Sussex, UEA, Wolverhampton; **No** Cambridge.

GRADUATE DESTINATIONS AND EMPLOYMENT (2009/10 HESA)

Graduates surveyed 6750 **Employed** 2765 **In voluntary employment** 225 **In further study** 1315 **Assumed unemployed** 470

Career note The transferable skills gained in this degree open up a wide range of career opportunities. Graduates seek positions in management, public services and administration and in some cases in political activities.

OTHER DEGREE SUBJECTS FOR CONSIDERATION

Development Studies; Economics; Government; History; International Relations; Public Policy and Administration; Social Policy and Administration; Sociology.

PSYCHOLOGY

(including **Behavioural Science, Cognitive Sciences, Counselling** and **Neuroscience**; see also **Animal Sciences, Biological Sciences, Philosophy, Physiology, Social Sciences/Studies**)

Psychology is a very popular subject, with the number of applications rising by 40,000 in the last 10 years. The study attracts three times more women than men. It covers studies in development, behaviour, perception, memory, language, learning, personality as well as social relationships and abnormal psychology. Psychology is a science and you will be involved in experimentation and statistical analysis. The degree is usually offered as a BSc or a BA course and there are many similarities between them. The differences are in the elective subjects which can be taken in the second and third years. It is not a training to enable you to psycho-analyse your friends – psychology is not the same as psychiatry!

To qualify as a chartered psychologist (for which a postgraduate qualification is required) it is necessary to obtain a first degree (or equivalent) qualification which gives eligibility for both Graduate Membership (GM) and the Graduate Basis for Registration (GBR) of the British Psychological Society (BPS). A full list of courses accredited by the British Psychological Society is available on the Society's website www.bps.org.uk. The website also provides careers information and information about all the qualifications needed for careers in the wide-ranging field of psychology. (See **Appendix 3**.)

Behavioural Science covers the study of animal and human behaviour and offers an overlap between Zoology, Sociology, Psychology and Biological Sciences. Psychology, however, also crosses over into Education, Management Sciences, Human Resource Management, Counselling, Public Relations, Advertising, Artificial Intelligence, Marketing, Retail and Social Studies.

Useful websites www.psychology.org; www.bps.org.uk; www.socialpsychology.org; www.psychcentral.com.

NB The points totals shown to the left of the institutions are for ease of reference only. It must not be assumed that Tariff points are always used by institutions or that they can be substituted for an offer in grades. The level of an offer is not necessarily indicative of the quality of a course.

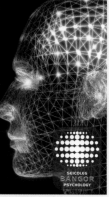
COURSE OFFERS INFORMATION

Subject requirements/preferences GCSE English, mathematics and a science. **AL** A science subject is usually required.

Your target offers and examples of courses provided by each institution

380 pts   **Bath** – A*AA (Psy) (IB 38 pts HL 766)
        Bristol – A*AA–AAB 340–380 pts (Psy Phil) (IB 38–35 pts)
        Cambridge – A*AA (Nat Sci (Psy/Neuro)) (IB 40–42 pts HL 766–777)
        London (UCL) – A*AA–AAA (Psy Lang Sci) (IB 38–39 pts)

360 pts   **Birmingham** – AAA–AAB 340–360 pts (Psy) (IB 34–36 pts)
        Bristol UWE – 360 pts (Psy courses)
        Cardiff – AAA (Psy)
        City – AAA 360 pts (Psy) (IB 34 pts)
        Durham – AAA (Psy) (IB 37 pts)
        Edinburgh – AAA–BBB 300–360 pts (Psy) (IB 34–42 pts)
        Exeter – AAA–AAB (Psy Spo Exer Sci) (IB 36–34 pts)
        Kent – AAA–AAB (App Psy Clin Psy) (IB 33 pts)
        Manchester – AAA–ABB 320–360 pts (Cog Neuro Psy) (IB 37–33 pts)
        Newcastle – AAA–ABB 320–360 pts (Psy) (IB 34 pts)
        Oxford – A*AA (Psy Phil) (IB 38–40 pts)
        Reading – AAA–AAB (Psy Chld Age; Psy Mntl Physl Hlth)
        St Andrews – AAA (Psy) (IB 36 pts)
        Surrey – AAA–AAB (Psy) (IB 34 pts)
        Warwick – AAA (Psy) (IB 38 pts)
        York – AAA–AAB (Psy) (IB 35–36 pts)

Check **Chapter 4** when choosing your university and **Chapter 7** on how to read the subject tables.

340 pts **Aston** – AAB–ABB 320–340 pts (Psy Bus) (IB 33 pts)
Bristol UWE – 340 pts (Crimin Psy)
Cardiff – AAB–ABB (Biomed Sci (Neuro))
Exeter – AAB–AAA 340–360 pts (App Psy) (IB 36–35 pts)
Kent – AAB (Psy) (IB 33 pts)
Lancaster – AAB (Psy Educ) (IB 34 pts)
Leicester – AAB (Neuro Psy)
Liverpool – AAB (Psy) (IB 34 pts)
London (RH) – AAB (Maths Psy)
Loughborough – AAB–ABB (Psy; Soc Psy) (IB 34 pts)
Manchester – AAB (Psy) (IB 36–33 pts)
Newcastle – AAB (Biol Psy) (IB 32 pts)
Nottingham – AAB (Psy Phil) (IB 34 pts)
Reading – AAB–ABBb (Psy Biol)
Sheffield – AAB (Psy BA/BSc) (IB 35 pts)
Southampton – AAB (Educ St Psy) (IB 34 pts HL 17 pts)
Sussex – AAB (Psy Neuro) (IB 35 pts)
Swansea – AAB (Psy)
UEA – AAB (Econ Econ Psy) (IB 34–33 pts)

320 pts **Aston** – ABB–AAB 320–340 pts (Psy Engl Lang) (IB 33 pts)
Bangor – 320–280 pts (Psy Neuropsy; Psy Chld Lang Dev)
Bournemouth – 320 pts (Spo Psy Coach Sci; Psy)
City – ABB 320 pts (Jrnl Psy)
Durham – ABB (App Psy) (IB 34 pts)
Glasgow – ABB (Psy) (IB 36 pts)
Glasgow Caledonian – ABB 320 pts (Psy)
Greenwich – 320 pts (Psy)
Hertfordshire – 320 pts (Psy)
Keele – 300–320 pts (App Psy)
Kent – ABB (Phil Soc Psy) (IB 31–35 pts)
Leicester – ABB (Psy Sociol)
Liverpool Hope – 260–320 pts (Psy; Psy Comb Hons)
LJMU – 320–280 pts (App Spo Psy)
London (Birk) – ABB (Psy)
London (Gold) – ABB (Psy) (IB 30 pts)
London (QM) – ABB (Psy)
London (RH) – 300–320 pts (Psy)
Northampton – 280–320 pts (Psy courses)
Northumbria – 320 pts (Psy)
Nottingham – ABB (Psy Cog Neuro) (IB 32 pts)
Nottingham Trent – 320 pts (Psy)
Oxford Brookes – offers vary depending on 2nd subj ABB (Psy (Comb)) (IB 33 pts)
Portsmouth – 320 pts (Psy) (IB 30 pts)
Queen's Belfast – ABB/BBBb (Psy)
Strathclyde – ABB (Econ Psy; Psy)
UEA – ABB (Psy) (IB 32 pts)

300 pts **Aberdeen** – CCC–BBB 240–300 pts (Neuro Psy; Psy)
Bangor – 260–300 pts (Spo Sci Psy)
BPP (UC) – 300 pts (Law Psy)
Brighton – BBB (App Psy Crimin) (IB 32 pts)
Brunel – BBB 300 pts (Psy courses) (IB 33 pts)
Chichester – 300 pts (Psy) (IB 32 pts)
Coventry – BBB 300 pts (Psy; Spo Psy)
Derby – 300–260 pts (Psy)
Edinburgh – BBB (Cog Sci (Hum)) (IB 34 pts)

Essex – 300–320 pts (Psy) (IB 29 pts)
Glamorgan – 300 pts (Spo Psy)
Heriot-Watt – BBB (Psy courses)
Huddersfield – 300 pts (Psy; Psy Crimin; Psy Cnslg)
Keele – 300–320 pts (Neuro Psy)
Lincoln – 300 pts (Psy; Engl Psy; Psy Chld St; Psy Mark; Psy Soc Plcy)
LJMU – 300 pts (Foren Psy Crim Just)
London (Hey) – 300–320 pts (Phil) (IB 30 pts)
London (QM) – 300 pts incl biol (Biol Psy) (IB 32 pts HL 6 biol)
London Met – 300 pts (Psy)
Manchester Met – BBB (Psy) (IB 30 pts)
Middlesex – 300 pts (Psy Comb courses)
Oxford Brookes – BBB 300 pts (Mus Psy)
Roehampton – 300 pts (Psy Cnslg; Psy Hlth)
Sheffield Hallam – 300 pts (Psy)
UCLan – 260–300 pts (Neuropsy)
Westminster – BBB–AB (Psy) (IB 32 pts)
York – BBB (Sociol Soc Psy)

280 pts **Aberystwyth** – 280 pts (Psy) (IB 27 pts)
Birmingham City – 280 pts (Psy)
Buckingham – 280 pts (Psy)
Cardiff Met – 280 pts (Psy; Educ St Psy)
De Montfort – 260–280 pts (Psy; Psy App Crimin; Educ St Psy)
Derby – 280 pts (Crea Expr Thera (Dance/Dr/Mus/Art))
Edge Hill – 280 pts (Psy)
Gloucestershire – 280–300 pts (Anim Bhv Psy; Educ St Psy; Engl Lit Psy)
Hull – BBC 280 pts (Psy; Psy Phil; Psy Crimin; Psy Spo Sci)
Leeds Trinity (UC) – 280 pts (Foren Psy; Spo Exer Psy; Psy)
LJMU – 280 pts (Crimin Psych) (IB 29 pts)
London (Hey) – 280–300 pts (Phil Theol)
Loughborough – 280–300 pts (Ergon) (IB 30–32 pts)
Manchester Met – 280 pts (Abuse St) (IB 28 pts)
Newman (UC) – 280 pts (Psy)
Nottingham Trent – 280 pts (Ely Yrs Psy Educ; Law Psy; Psy Spec Incl Educ;
   Psy Educ Dev)
Oxford Brookes – BBC (Ely Chld St) (IB 30 pts)
Portsmouth – 280–300 pts (Mark Psy)
Roehampton – 280–340 pts (Psy)
Staffordshire – 280 pts (Psy Crimin)
Stirling – BBC (Psy) (IB 32 pts)
Salford – 280 pts (Psy) (IB 27 pts)
Sheffield Hallam – 280 pts (Crimin Psy; Psy Sociol)
Suffolk (Univ Campus) – 240–280 pts (Psy Sociol; Psy Bus Mgt; Psy Yth St)
Ulster – BBC (Mus Psy)
Worcester – 280 pts (Psy)

260 pts **Aberystwyth** – 260 pts (Psy Engl Lit) (IB 28 pts)
Bolton – 260 pts (Psy; Cnslg Psy; Crimin Foren Psy)
BPP (UC) – 260 pts (Bus Psy; Psy)
Bradford – 260 pts (Psy; Psy Crimin)
Chester – 260–300 pts (Psy courses) (IB 28 pts)
Coventry – BCC 260 pts (Sociol Psy)
Derby – 260–280 pts (Spo Psy Joint Hons)
Dundee – BCC (Psy) (IB 29 pts)
Edinburgh Queen Margaret – 260 pts (Psy; Hlth Psy)
Glyndŵr – 260 pts (Psy)

Check **Chapter 4** when choosing your university and **Chapter 7** on how to read the subject tables.

Greenwich – 260 pts (Crimin Crim Psy)
Kingston – 260 pts (Psy) (IB 30 pts)
Leeds Met – 260 pts (Psy courses) (IB 24 pts HL 6 sci)
London South Bank – 260 pts (Psy Clin Psy; Psy; Psy Chld Dev)
Northampton – 260–280 pts (Mark Psy)
Salford – 260 pts (Psy St Cnslg St) (IB 27 pts)
Sheffield Hallam – 260 pts (Educ St Psy Cnslg)
Sunderland – 260 pts (Psy; Psy Cnslg; Psy (Comb))
Teesside – 260 pts (Psy; Foren Psy; Psy Cnslg; Psy Crimin)
UCLan – 260–300 pts (Spo Psy)
Ulster – 260 pts (Dr Psy)
Winchester – 260–300 pts (Jrnl Psy; Media St Psy; Psy Bus Mgt)
York St John – 260 pts (Psy; Psy Bus Mgt)

240 pts **Aberdeen** – 240 pts (Genet Psy)
Anglia Ruskin – 240 pts (Psy)
Bedfordshire – 240 pts (Psy; App Psy; Hlth Psy; Psy (Crim Bhv); Psy St)
Bradford – 240–280 pts (Econ Psy)
Buckingham – 240–300 pts (Psy Span)
Canterbury Christ Church – CCC 240 pts (Psy)
Chester – 240–280 pts (Cnslg Sk) (IB 26 pts)
Farnborough (CT) – 240 pts (Psy Mark; Psy Crimin)
Glasgow Caledonian – CCC (Psy Interact Enter)
Leeds Met – 240 pts (Psy Soc) (IB 24 pts)
Newport – 240–260 pts (Psy Cnslg St)
Portsmouth – 240–300 pts (Sociol Psy)
St Mary's Twickenham (UC) – 240 pts (Psy) (IB 28 pts)
Southampton Solent – 240 pts (Psy; Hlth Psy; Psy (Cnslg); Psy (Crim Bhv))
UCLan – 240–300 pts (Hlth Psy) (IB 25–28 pts)
West Scotland – CCC (App Biosci Psy)

230 pts **Edinburgh Napier** – 230 pts (Psy; Psy Sociol)

220 pts **Anglia Ruskin** – 220 pts (Psy Crimin)
Bath Spa – 220–300 pts (Psy; Psy Comb Hons)
Bradford – 180-220 pts (Psy Sociol)
Edinburgh Queen Margaret – 220 pts (Psy Sociol)
Peterborough (Univ Centre) – 220–260 pts (Psysoc St)
Plymouth – 220–300 pts (App Psy; Psy; Psy Sociol)
Wolverhampton – 220–240 pts (Psy; Cnslg Psy)

200 pts **Blackburn (Coll)** – 200 pts (App Psy (Cnslg Hlth))
Bradford (Coll Univ Centre) – 200 pts (Cnslg Psy Commun Set)
Bucks New – 200–280 pts (Psy; Crimin Psy)
Cumbria – 200 pts (App Psy)
Glyndŵr – 200 pts (Foren Sci Crim Just)
Middlesex – 200–300 pts (Psy HR Mgt)
Newman (UC) – 200–240 pts (Psy Media Comm) (IB 24 pts)
Staffordshire – 200–280 pts (Psy; Foren Psy)
UEL – 200 pts (Psy; Dev Psy; Foren Psy)
West London – 200–240 pts (Psy Crimin/Cnslg Theor; Psy)

180 pts **Abertay Dundee** – 180 pts (Psy Cnslg)
Bradford – 180–220 pts (Psy Mgt)
Swansea Met – 180 pts (Educ St Psy; Cnslg Psy; Cnslg Educ St; Cnslg Dr; Dr Psy)
Trinity Saint David – 180–360 pts (Psy)
UHI – BC (Psy)

160 pts **Abertay Dundee** – CC (Foren Psychobiol)
Norwich City (Coll) – contact College 160 pts (Psy Sociol)
West Scotland – CC-CD (Psy)

120 pts   **Colchester (Inst)** – 120 pts (Cnslg St)
        Grimsby (IFHE) – 120 pts (Psy St)
 80 pts   **West Anglia (Coll)** – 80 pts (Psysoc)

        Open University – contact +44 (0)845 300 6090 **or** www.openuniversity.co.uk/you
        (Psy; Soc Sci Psy St)

Alternative offers
See **Chapter 7** and **Appendix 1** for grades/UCAS Tariff points information for the International Baccalaureate, Scottish Highers/Advanced Highers, the Welsh Baccalaureate, the Irish Leaving Certificate, the Cambridge Pre-U Diploma, the Advanced Diploma and the Extended Project.

EXAMPLES OF FOUNDATION DEGREES IN THE SUBJECT FIELD
Bedfordshire; Glyndŵr; Middlesex; Petroc; St Mary's Twickenham (UC); Truro (Coll); UEL.

CHOOSING YOUR COURSE (SEE ALSO CH.1)
Some course features
Bangor A leading Psychology department with courses which include clinical and health psychology, neuropsychology and child and language development.
Kent Psychology, Social Psychology, and Applied Psychology courses provide a broad base from which to specialise. Clinical psychology features largely in some programmes. Psychology can be taken with Law, Anthropology and Sociology.
Kingston Psychology is offered as part of the modular course with a choice of some 10 other subjects including languages (French or Spanish), Criminology, Journalism and Creative Writing.
Liverpool Hope The BSc Psychology Single Honours degree confers eligibility for registration with the British Psychological Society. There is also a Sport Psychology degree. Combined courses are also offered.
Loughborough (Ergon) This practical course centres on providing solutions to improve the ways in which people interact with their technical and social environment, for example by finding out how aircraft can be made more safe, by designing workplaces to be more efficient. Students acquire a broad understanding of human stucture, function and behaviour and spend the third year on a relevant industrial placement.

Universities and colleges teaching quality See www.qaa.ac.uk; http://unistats.direct.gov.uk.

Top research universities and colleges (RAE 2008) Cambridge; Oxford; Birmingham; London (UCL); London (Birk); Cardiff; St Andrews; London (RH); York; Glasgow; Bangor.

Examples of sandwich degree courses Aston; Bath; Bristol UWE; Cardiff; Hertfordshire; Huddersfield; Kent; Lancaster; Loughborough; Middlesex; Newcastle; Nottingham Trent; Surrey; Swansea Met; Ulster; Wolverhampton.

ADMISSIONS INFORMATION
Number of applicants per place (approx) Abertay Dundee 5; Aston 6; Bangor 5; Bath 10; Birmingham 9; Bolton 5; Bournemouth 4; Bradford 2; Bristol 17; Bristol UWE 12; Brunel 20; Buckingham 1; Cardiff 10; Cardiff Met 5; Chester 20; City 6; Coventry 7; De Montfort 10; Derby 6; Dundee 6; Durham 20; Edinburgh Napier 6; Exeter 14; Glamorgan 6; Glasgow Caledonian 15; Gloucestershire 50; Greenwich 8; Hertfordshire 22; Huddersfield 3; Hull 14; Kent 15; Lancaster 20; Leeds 12; Leeds Trinity (UC) 13; Leicester 6; Liverpool 21; LJMU 8; London (RH) 10; London (UCL) 18; London LSE 14; London South Bank 7; Loughborough 8; Manchester Met 27, (Psy p/t) 2; Middlesex 10; Newcastle 20; Newman (UC) 3; Northampton 4; Northumbria 2; Nottingham 9; Nottingham Trent 3; Oxford Brookes 29; Plymouth 5; Portsmouth 10; Roehampton 7; Salford 4; Sheffield 12; Sheffield Hallam 10; Southampton 10; Staffordshire 6; Stirling 9; Surrey 10; Sussex 5; Swansea 7; Teesside 10; UCLan 13; UEA (Psysoc St) 6; Warwick 13; Westminster 6; Worcester 9; York 9; York St John 3.

Numbers of applicants (a UK **b** EU (non-UK) **c** non-EU **d** mature) Aston **a**800 **b**100 **c**70 **d**90; Bristol **a**1421 **b**1421 **c**91 **d**156; Derby **a**407 **b**152 **c**5; Leeds **a**1758 **b**36 **c**37 **d**165; London (UCL) **a**1500 **c**250; Manchester Met **a**14 **b**14 **c**14 **d**14; Swansea Met **a**800 **b**800 **c**50.

Check **Chapter 4** when choosing your university and **Chapter 7** on how to read the subject tables.

Advice to applicants and planning the UCAS personal statement Psychology is heavily over-subscribed so prepare well in advance by choosing suitable AS and A-level subjects. Contact the Education and Social Services departments in your local authority office to arrange meetings with psychologists to gain a knowledge of the work. Make notes during those meetings and of any work experience gained and describe these fully on the UCAS application. Reference to introductory reading in psychology is important (many students have a distorted image of it). Demonstrate your interest in psychology through, for example, voluntary or other work experience. **Bristol** General scientific interests are important. Only consider this course if you have some aptitude and liking for scientific study (either in biological or physical sciences). Deferred entry accepted. **Leeds** One A-level subject must be taken from psychology, geography, maths, chemistry, physics or biology.

Misconceptions about this course Some believe a Psychology course will train them as therapists or counsellors – it will not. **Bath** They think that they are going to learn about themselves. **Birmingham** Some applicants underestimate the scientific nature of the course. **Exeter** It's scientific! **Lincoln** Applicants should be aware that this is a science-based course. Academic psychology is an empirical science requiring research methodologies and statistical analysis. **Reading** Not all applicants are aware that it is a science-based course and are surprised at the high science and statistics content. **Sussex** Applicants should note that the BSc course is not harder than the BA course. Many students mistakenly believe that psychology consists of counselling and that there is no maths. Psychology is a science. **York** Some students think psychology means Freud which it hasn't done for 50 years or more. They do not realise that psychology is a science in the same vein as biology, chemistry or physics. Only 20% of Psychology graduates become professional psychologists. This involves taking a postgraduate degree in a specialist area of psychology.

Selection interviews Yes Birmingham, Bolton, Brunel, Buckingham, Cambridge, Durham, Exeter, Glamorgan, Glasgow Caledonian, Glyndŵr, Leeds Trinity (UC), London (UCL) (300 out of 1500 applicants), London Met, London South Bank, Middlesex, Newcastle, Northampton, Norwich City (Coll), Oxford (Exp Psy) 24%, (Psy Phil) 20%, Oxford Brookes, Plymouth, Reading, Swansea; **Some** Anglia Ruskin, Aston, Bangor, Bristol, Cardiff, Derby (non-standard applications), Huddersfield (mature students), Keele, Leeds (mature students), LJMU, Nottingham Trent (for non-standard applications), Roehampton, Salford, Sunderland, UEA; **No** Chichester, Dundee, Essex, Essex, Nottingham.

Interview advice and questions Although some applicants will have studied the subject at A-level and will have a broad understanding of its coverage, it is still essential to have gained some work experience or to have discussed the career with a professional psychologist. Questions will focus on this and in previous years they have included: What have you read about psychology? What do you expect to gain by studying psychology? What are your parents' and teachers' views on your choice of subject? Are you interested in any particular branch of the subject? Is psychology an art or a science? Do you think you are well suited to this course? Why? Do you think it is possible that if we learn enough about the functioning of the brain we can create a computer that is functionally the same? What is counselling? Is it necessary? Know the differences between the various branches of psychology and discuss any specific interests, for example, in clinical, occupational, educational, criminal psychology and cognitive, neuro-, social or physiological psychology. What influences young children's food choices? What stereotypes do we have of people with mental illness? See also **Chapter 6**. **Bangor** Each application is treated individually and considered on its own merits. **Oxford** Ability to evaluate evidence and to have the capacity for logical and creative thinking.

Reasons for rejection (non-academic) Lack of background reading and lack of awareness of psychology; poor communication skills; misunderstanding of what is involved in a degree course. Poor personal statement. Poor grades, especially in GCSE maths. **Exeter** Competition for places – we can select those with exceptional grades. **Surrey** Inarticulate. **Warwick** (BSc) Lack of science background.

AFTER-RESULTS ADVICE
Offers to applicants repeating A-levels Higher Birmingham, City, Loughborough, Newcastle, Portsmouth, Southampton, Swansea, Warwick, York; **Possibly higher** Aston, Northampton; **Same**

Aston (Comb Hons), Bangor, Bolton, Brunel, Cardiff, Cardiff Met, Chester, Derby, Dundee, Durham, Huddersfield, Hull, Lincoln, Liverpool Hope, LJMU, London (RH), London South Bank, Manchester Met, Newman (UC), Nottingham, Nottingham Trent, Oxford Brookes, Roehampton, Salford, Sheffield Hallam, Staffordshire, Stirling, Suffolk (Univ Campus), Sunderland, Surrey, UEA, Ulster, West London, Wolverhampton, York St John; **No** Cambridge.

GRADUATE DESTINATIONS AND EMPLOYMENT (2009/10 HESA)

Graduates surveyed 12,285 **Employed** 7765 **In voluntary employment** 325 **In further study** 3085 **Assumed unemployed** 935

Career note Clinical, educational and occupational psychology are the three main specialist careers for graduate psychologists, all involving further study. Ergonomics, human–computer interaction, marketing, public relations, human resource management, advertising, the social services, the prison and rehabilitation services also provide alternative career routes.

OTHER DEGREE SUBJECTS FOR CONSIDERATION

Anthropology; Behavioural Science; Cognitive Sciences; Education; Health Studies; Neuroscience; Sociology

RADIOGRAPHY

(including **Medical Imaging** and **Radiotherapy**; see also **Health Sciences/Studies**)

Many institutions offer both Diagnostic and Therapeutic Radiography but applicants should check this, and course entry requirements, before applying. Information on courses is also available from the Society of Radiographers (see **Appendix 3**). Diagnostic Radiography is the demonstration on film (or other imaging materials) of the position and structure of the body's organs using radiation or other imaging media. Therapeutic Radiography is the planning and administration of treatment for patients suffering from malignant and non-malignant disease using different forms of radiation. Courses lead to state registration.

Useful websites www.sor.org; www.radiographycareers.co.uk; www.nhscareers.nhs.uk.

NB The points totals shown to the left of the institutions are for ease of reference only. It must not be assumed that Tariff points are always used by institutions or that they can be substituted for an offer in grades. The level of an offer is not necessarily indicative of the quality of a course.

COURSE OFFERS INFORMATION

Subject requirements/preferences GCSE Five subjects including English, mathematics and a science subject (usually at one sitting). **AL** One or two sciences required; mathematics may be acceptable. (Radiothera) One science subject required for some courses. Psychology may not be considered a science subject at some institutions. **Other** requirements Applicants required to have an occupational health check and a Criminal Records Bureau (CRB) clearance. Visit to, or work experience in, a hospital imaging department often required/expected.

Your target offers and examples of courses provided by each institution

320 pts **Exeter** – ABB–BBC (Med Imag (Diag Radiog)) (IB 32–28 pts)
Sheffield Hallam – 320 pts (Diag Radiog)

300 pts **Bradford** – 300 pts (Diag Radiog)
Canterbury Christ Church – 300 pts (Diag Radiog)
Cardiff – BBB (Radiog Diag Radiog Imag)
City – 300 pts (Radiog (Radiothera Onc); Radiog (Diag Imag))
Derby – 300 pts (Diag Radiog)
London (St George's) – BBB (Diag Radiog; Ther Radiog)
Portsmouth – 300 pts (Diag Radiog; Ther Radiog)
Ulster – BBB (Radiog (Diag/Ther)) (IB 25 pts)

Check **Chapter 4** when choosing your university and **Chapter 7** on how to read the subject tables.

280 pts **Birmingham City** – 280 pts (Radiothera; Diag Radiog)
Bristol UWE – 280 pts (Radiothera Onc) (IB 26 pts)
Cardiff – BBC 280 pts (Radiother Onc)
Cumbria – 280 pts (Radiog (Diag))
Leeds – BBC (Radiog (Diag))
Salford – 280 pts (Diag Radiog) (IB 30 pts)
Sheffield Hallam – 280 pts (Radiothera Onc)
Suffolk (Univ Campus) – 280 pts (Diag Radiog; Radiothera Onc)
260 pts **Glasgow Caledonian** – BCC (Rdtn Onc Sci; Diag Imag Sci)
Hertfordshire – 260 pts (Radiothera Onc)
Liverpool – BCC (Radiothera) (IB 28 pts)
Teesside – 260–300 pts (Diag Radiog)
240 pts **Bangor** – 240–260 pts (Diag Radiog Imag)
London South Bank – 200–240 pts (Diag Radiog; Thera Radiog)
Robert Gordon – CCC 240 pts (Diag Radiog) (IB 26 pts)
200 pts **Edinburgh Queen Margaret** – 200 pts (Diag Radiog; Ther Radiog)

Alternative offers
See **Chapter 7** and **Appendix 1** for grades/UCAS Tariff points information for the International Baccalaureate, Scottish Highers/Advanced Highers, the Welsh Baccalaureate, the Irish Leaving Certificate, the Cambridge Pre-U Diploma, the Advanced Diploma and the Extended Project.

CHOOSING YOUR COURSE (SEE ALSO CH.1)
Some course features
Cardiff The year is divided into seven academic and seven clinical blocks. Placements are in radiography departments throughout south Wales.
City Radiography and Oncology and Radiography (Diagnostic Imaging) are offered.
Cumbria Fifty-four weeks of clinical placements in the three-year course are spent in hospitals in northern England. Students' preferences are taken into account.
Exeter (Med Imag (Diag Radiog)) This is a specialist course leading to a career as a diagnostic radiographer.
Portsmouth There is a seven-week exchange programme working in hospitals in Hong Kong.

Universities and colleges teaching quality See www.qaa.ac.uk; http://unistats.direct.gov.uk.

ADMISSIONS INFORMATION
Number of applicants per place (approx) Birmingham City (Radiothera) 8; Bradford 8; Cardiff 3; Derby 6; Glasgow Caledonian 7; Hertfordshire (Diag Radiog Imag) 8; Leeds 10; Liverpool 13; London (St George's) 7; London South Bank 9; Portsmouth 10; Robert Gordon 5; Salford 10; Sheffield Hallam 8, (Radiothera Onc) 3; Southampton 5; Suffolk (Univ Campus) 3; Teesside 10.

Advice to applicants and planning the UCAS personal statement Contacts with radiographers and visits to the radiography departments of hospitals should be discussed in full on the UCAS application. See also **Appendix 3**. **Birmingham City** Evidence needed of a visit to at least one imaging department or oncology (radiotherapy) department before completing the UCAS application. Evidence of good research into the career. **Liverpool** Choice between therapeutic and diagnostic pathways should be made before applying. **Salford** Selectors look for evidence of communication skills, teamwork, work experience in public areas.

Misconceptions about this course There is often confusion between radiotherapy and diagnostic imaging and between diagnostic and therapeutic radiography.

Selection interviews **Yes** Bangor, Birmingham City, Canterbury Christ Church, Cardiff, City, Derby, Edinburgh Queen Margaret, Exeter, Hertfordshire, London (St George's), London South Bank, Portsmouth, Salford, Sheffield Hallam.

Interview advice and questions All applicants should have discussed this career with a radiographer and visited a hospital radiography department. Questions follow from these contacts. Where does radiography fit into the overall health care system? See also **Chapter 6**.

Reasons for rejection (non-academic) Lack of interest in people. Poor communication skills. Occasionally students may be unsuitable for the clinical environment, for example, they express a fear of blood and needles; poor grasp of radiography as a career. Unable to meet criteria for employment in the NHS, for example, health factors, criminal convictions, severe disabilities.

AFTER-RESULTS ADVICE
Offers to applicants repeating A-levels **Higher** London (St George's); **Same** Derby, Salford.

GRADUATE DESTINATIONS AND EMPLOYMENT (2009/10 HESA)
See **Health Science/Studies**.

Career note Most radiographers work in the NHS in hospital radiography departments undertaking diagnostic or therapeutic treatment. Others work in private healthcare.

OTHER DEGREE SUBJECTS FOR CONSIDERATION
Audiology; Forensic Engineering; Health Studies; Medical Physics; Nursing; Occupational Therapy; Physics; Podiatry; Speech Sciences.

RELIGIOUS STUDIES

(including **Biblical Studies, Divinity, Islamic Studies, Jewish Studies** and **Theology**)

The subject content of these courses varies and students should check prospectuses carefully. They are not intended as training courses for ministry; an adherence to a particular religious denomination is not a necessary qualification for entry.

Useful websites www.guardian.co.uk/religion; www.cwmission.org; www.miraclestudies.net; www.academicinfo.net/religindex.html; www.theologywebsite.com; www.jewishstudies.org; www.jewishstudies.virtualave.net; www.jewfaq.org; www.virtualreligion.net; www.jis.oxfordjournals.org.

NB The points totals shown to the left of the institutions are for ease of reference only. It must not be assumed that Tariff points are always used by institutions or that they can be substituted for an offer in grades. The level of an offer is not necessarily indicative of the quality of a course.

COURSE OFFERS INFORMATION
Subject requirements/preferences **GCSE** English and mathematics. For teacher training, English and mathematics and science. **AL** Religious studies or theology may be required or preferred for some courses.

Your target offers and examples of courses provided by each institution

380 pts **Cambridge** – A*AA (Educ Relig St; Theol Relig St) (IB 40–42 pts)
London (King's) – AABc (Relgn Phil Eth) (IB 36 pts)

360 pts **Durham** – AAA (Theol Phil; Phil Theol)
Oxford – AAA (Theol Orntl St) (IB 38–40 pts)
St Andrews – AAA–AAB (Theol)

340 pts **Bristol** – AAB (Theol Sociol) (IB 35 pts HL 666)
Cardiff – AAB (Maths Relig St)
Durham – AAB (Theol; Theol (Euro St))
Exeter – AAB–BBB (Theol courses) (IB 34–29 pts)
Lancaster – AAB 340 pts (Pol Relig St) (IB 30 pts)
London (SOAS) – AAB (Islam St) (IB 36 pts HL 666)
Manchester – AAB–BBB 300–340 pts (Compar Relgn Soc Anth) (IB 36–31 pts)
Nottingham – AAB (Engl St Theol) (IB 34 pts)
St Andrews – AAA (Theol St) (IB 30 pts)
Sheffield – AAB (Bib Lit Engl) (IB 35 pts)

320 pts **Birmingham** – ABB (Theol Relgn) (IB 32 pts)
Glasgow – ABB (Theol Relig St) (IB 36 pts)
Lancaster – ABB (Relig St Sociol) (IB 32 pts)
Leeds – ABB (Theol Relig St)
London (SOAS) – ABB (St Relgns) (IB 34 pts HL 555)
London (UCL) – ABBc (Hist Jew St) (IB 34 pts)
Manchester – AAB–BBB 300–320 pts (St Relgn Theol) (IB 36–31 pts)
Stranmillis (UC) – ABB (Relig St Educ)
Sheffield – ABB (Relgn Theol Bib Ling) (IB 33 pts)

300 pts **Aberdeen** – BBB (Theol, Div, Relig St) (IB 30 pts)
Cardiff – BBB (Relig Theol St; Relig St Span/Ital; Sociol Relig St)
Edinburgh – BBB (Div Class) (IB 34 pts)
Hull – 280–300 pts (Phil Relgn)
Kent – BBB (Relig St)
Leeds – lower access offer ABC/BBB (Islam St) (IB 32 pts HL 15 pts)
Queen's Belfast – BBB/BBCb (Theol) (IB 29 pts)
Roehampton – 300 pts (Theol Rel St) (25 pts)
Trinity Saint David – individual offers made after interview 220–300 pts (Islam St)
Winchester – 260–300 pts (Theol Relig St; Relig St Arch; Relig St Bus Mgt)

280 pts **Gloucestershire** – 280–300 pts (Relgn Phil Eth)
Huddersfield – 280 pts (Relgn Educ)
Leeds – BBC (Russ Civ Theol Relig St) (IB 32 pts)
London (Hey) – 280–320 pts (Ab Relgn; St Relgn; Div; Theol; Phil Relgn Eth)
Newman (UC) – 280 pts (Phil Relgn Eth)
Oxford Brookes – BBC (Relgn Theol)
Stirling – BBC (Relgn) (IB 32 pts)

260 pts **Edge Hill** – 260 pts (Relig Educ QTS)
Hull – 260–300 pts (Hisp St Relgn)
Liverpool Hope – 260 pts (Theol Relig St)
Newman (UC) – 260 pts (Theol)
Newport – 260 pts (Relig St)

240 pts **Canterbury Christ Church** – 240 pts (Theol; Relig St)
Chester – 240–280 pts (Theol Relig St)
Chichester – CCC (Theol Relgn) (IB 30 pts)
Islamic Advanced St (Coll) – 240 pts (Mslm Cult Civ)
Leeds Trinity (UC) – 240 pts (Relig St; Theol)
St Mary's Twickenham (UC) – 240 pts (Theol Relig St) (IB 28 pts)

220 pts **Bath Spa** – 220–280 pts (St Relig)
York St John – 200–220 pts (Theol Relig St)

200 pts **Cumbria** – 200 pts (Relig St)
Middlesex – 200–300 pts (Educ Relig St)
UCLan – 200–300 pts (Islam St (Comb); Relgn Cult Soty (Comb))
Wolverhampton – 160–200 pts (Relig St courses)

160 pts **Bishop Grosseteste (UC)** – 160 pts (Theol Soc)
UHI – CC–AA (Theol St)
Wolverhampton – 160–220 pts (Relig St Sociol; Relig St Phil)

140 pts **Islamic Advanced St (Coll)** – 140–220 pts (Islam St)

Alternative offers

See **Chapter 7** and **Appendix 1** for grades/UCAS Tariff points information for the International Baccalaureate, Scottish Highers/Advanced Highers, the Welsh Baccalaureate, the Irish Leaving Certificate, the Cambridge Pre-U Diploma, the Advanced Diploma and the Extended Project.

EXAMPLES OF FOUNDATION DEGREES IN THE SUBJECT FIELD
Newman (UC); York St John.

CHOOSING YOUR COURSE (SEE ALSO CH.1)

Some course features
Birmingham (Theol) The course covers Christianity, Islam, Judaism, Sikhism, Hinduism and other contemporary spiritualities.
Durham (Theol) The course combines aspects of philosophy, history and social sciences and includes a detailed study of the Old and New Testaments.
Edinburgh MA and Honours and BA General degrees are offered in Religious Studies and Divinity. There is also a Bachelor of Divinity course equipping students for the ordained ministry.
Lancaster (Relig St) A distinguished course offering core and optional modules approaching religion from theological, sociological, anthropological, psychological and philosophical perspectives. The main studies include Judaism, Christianity, Islam, Hinduism, Buddhism and philosophy.
Sheffield (Bib Lit Eng) The only course in England looking at the development of the Bible and its place in contemporary society, politics, art, film, literature and music.

Universities and colleges teaching quality See www.qaa.ac.uk; http://unistats.direct.gov.uk.

Top research universities and colleges (RAE 2008) (Theology, Divinity and Religious Studies) Durham; Aberdeen; Cambridge; Oxford; London (UCL); Manchester; Sheffield; Edinburgh; Nottingham.

ADMISSIONS INFORMATION

Number of applicants per place (approx) Bangor 5; Birmingham 4; Bristol 9; Cambridge 2; Chichester 6; Cumbria 12; Durham 6; Edinburgh 3; Exeter 7; Glasgow 4; Hull 10; Kent 13; Lancaster 6; Leeds 4; Leeds Trinity (UC) 4; Liverpool Hope 6; London (Hey) 4; London (King's) 6; Middlesex 4; Newman (UC) 2; Nottingham 10; Sheffield 7; Trinity Saint David 7; Winchester 6; York St John 2.

Advice to applicants and planning the UCAS personal statement An awareness of the differences between the main religions is important as is any special research you have done to help you decide on your preferred courses. Interests in the religious art and architecture of various periods and styles should be noted. Applicants should have an open-minded approach to studying a diverse range of religious traditions. **Bristol** Deferred entry accepted.

Misconceptions about this course Some students think that you must be religious to study Theology – in fact, people of all faiths and none study the subject. A study of religions is not Christian theology. **Leeds** Some applicants are not aware of the breadth of the subject. We offer modules covering New Testament, Christian theology, Islamic studies, Hinduism, Buddhism, Sikhism, Christian ethics, sociology of religion.

Selection interviews Yes Cambridge, Chester, Durham, Edinburgh, Glasgow, Hull, Lancaster, Leeds, Leeds Trinity (UC), London (Hey), London (SOAS), Oxford (Theol) 38%, Oxford Brookes, Sheffield, Trinity Saint David, Winchester; **Some** Bristol, Cardiff, Southampton; **No** Birmingham, Chichester, Dundee.

Interview advice and questions Past questions have included: Why do you want to study Theology/ Biblical Studies/Religious Studies? What do you hope to do after obtaining your degree? Questions relating to the A-level syllabus. Questions on current theological topics. Do you have any strong religious convictions? Do you think that your religious beliefs will be changed at the end of the course? Why did you choose Religious Studies rather than Biblical Studies? How would you explain the miracles to a 10-year-old? (BEd course). Do you agree with the National Lottery? How do you think you can apply theology to your career? See also **Chapter 6**. **Cambridge** There is a Christian priest who regularly visits India and converted to a Hindu priest. When he is in England he still practises as a Christian priest. What problems might this pose? Do you believe we should eradicate Christmas on the basis that it offends other religious groups? **Oxford** The ability to defend one's opinions and willingness to engage in a lively dialogue are both important.

Reasons for rejection (non-academic) Students not attending Open Days may be rejected. Too religiously conservative. Failure to interact. Lack of motivation to study a subject which goes beyond A-level. **Cardiff** Insufficiently open to an academic study of religion.

Check **Chapter 4** when choosing your university and **Chapter 7** on how to read the subject tables.

AFTER-RESULTS ADVICE

Offers to applicants repeating A-levels Higher Hull, Manchester, St Andrews; **Possibly higher** Cambridge (Hom); **Same** Bangor, Birmingham, Cardiff, Chester, Durham, Glasgow, Greenwich, Lancaster, Leeds, Liverpool Hope, London (SOAS), Nottingham, St Mary's Twickenham (UC), Sheffield, Stirling, Trinity Saint David, Winchester, Wolverhampton, York St John; **No** Cambridge.

GRADUATE DESTINATIONS AND EMPLOYMENT (2009/10 HESA)

Theology and Religious Studies; graduates surveyed 2235 **Employed** 920 **In voluntary employment** 125 **In further study** 695 **Assumed unemployed** 120

Career note Although a small number of graduates may regard these courses as a preparation for entry to religious orders, the great majority enter other careers, with teaching particularly popular.

OTHER DEGREE SUBJECTS FOR CONSIDERATION

Community Studies; Education; History; Philosophy; Psychology; Social Policy and Administration; Social Work.

RETAIL MANAGEMENT

(see also **Business and Management Courses, Business and Management Courses (International and European), Business and Management Courses (Specialised), Marketing**)

This subject attracts a large number of applicants each year and it is necessary to have work experience before applying. The work itself varies depending on the type of retail outlet. After completing their courses graduates in a large department store will be involved in different aspects of the business, for example supervising shop assistants, warehouse and packing staff. They could also receive special training in the sales of particular goods, for example food and drink, clothing, furniture. Subsequently there may be opportunities to become buyers. In more specialised shops, for example shoes, fashion and food, graduates are likely to work only with these products, with opportunities to reach senior management.

Useful websites www.brc.org.uk; www.retailweek.com; www.theretailbulletin.com; www.retailcareers.co.uk; www.retailchoice.com; www.nrf.com.

NB The points totals shown to the left of the institutions are for ease of reference only. It must not be assumed that Tariff points are always used by institutions or that they can be substituted for an offer in grades. The level of an offer is not necessarily indicative of the quality of a course.

COURSE OFFERS INFORMATION

Subject requirements/preferences GCSE English and mathematics at grade C or above. **AL** No subjects specified.

Your target offers and examples of courses provided by each institution

340 pts **Loughborough** – AAB (Rtl Mark Mgt) (IB 36 pts)
      Manchester – AAB (Fash Tex Rtl) (IB 36–35 pts)
      Surrey – AAB (Bus Rtl Mgt) (IB 36 pts)
320 pts **Roehampton** – 320 pts (Bus Mgt (Rtl Mgt Mark))
300 pts **Bournemouth** – 300 pts (Rtl Mgt)
      Cardiff Met – 300 pts (Mark Mgt)
      Heriot-Watt – BBB (Fash Mark Rtl)
      Huddersfield – 300 pts (Rtl Mark Mgt)
      Westminster – BBB (Fash Buy)
280 pts **Birmingham City** – 280 pts (Fash Rtl Mgt) (IB 28 pts)
      Brighton – BBC (Rtl Mark) (IB 28 pts)
      Manchester Met – 280 pts (Rtl Mark Mgt) (IB 28 pts)

Stirling – BBC (Rtl Mark) (IB 32 pts)
UCLan – 240–280 pts (Rtl Mgt (Buy/Fash/Mark))
260 pts **De Montfort** – 260 pts (Rtl Mgt; Rtl Buy (Fash) (Tex))
240 pts **Canterbury Christ Church** – 240 pts (Bus Mgt (Rtl))
Glasgow Caledonian – CCC (Int Rtl Mark)
Southampton Solent – 240 pts (Fash Mark)
UCLan – 240–280 pts (Rtl Mgt (E-Commer/Entre)) (IB 28 pts)
Ulster – 240 pts (Bus Rtl St; Comp Rtl St)

Alternative offers
See **Chapter 7** and **Appendix 1** for grades/UCAS Tariff points information for the International Baccalaureate, Scottish Highers/Advanced Highers, the Welsh Baccalaureate, the Irish Leaving Certificate, the Cambridge Pre-U Diploma, the Advanced Diploma and the Extended Project.

EXAMPLES OF FOUNDATION DEGREES IN THE SUBJECT FIELD
Arts London; Blackburn (Coll); Blackpool and Fylde (Coll); Grimsby (IFHE); Hull (Coll); Llandrillo Cymru (Coll); Manchester Met; UEL; Wolverhampton; Worcester.

CHOOSING YOUR COURSE (SEE ALSO CH.1)
Some course features
Birmingham City (Fash Rtl Mgt) The course focuses on the global fashion industry and design management. It includes fabric sourcing, pattern cutting and manufacturing, and fashion forecasting.
Bournemouth (Rtl Mgt) The course has paid industrial placements and overseas opportunities.
Loughborough (Rtl Mark Mgt) This four-year sandwich course includes a placement year leading to a Diploma in Professional Studies. Retailers are closely involved throughout and provide lectures, case studies, skills workshops and company visits.
Surrey (Rtl Mgt) A long-established course with an optional placement year.

Universities and colleges teaching quality See www.qaa.ac.uk; http://unistats.direct.gov.uk.

Examples of sandwich degree courses Bournemouth; Bradford; Brighton; De Montfort; Gloucestershire; Huddersfield; Leeds Met; Manchester Met; Southampton Solent; Surrey; UCLan; Westminster.

ADMISSIONS INFORMATION
Number of applicants per place (approx) See also **Business and Management Courses**. Bournemouth 8; Manchester Met 10.

Advice to applicants and planning the UCAS personal statement See also **Business and Management Courses**. **Manchester Met** (Rtl Mark Mgt) Evidence of working with people or voluntary work experience (department unable to assist with sponsorships).

Misconceptions about this course See **Business and Management Courses**.

Selection interviews Yes Birmingham City.

Interview advice and questions See **Business and Management Courses**.

Reasons for rejection (non-academic) See **Business and Management Courses**.

AFTER-RESULTS ADVICE
Offers to applicants repeating A-levels No See **Business and Management Courses**.

GRADUATE DESTINATIONS AND EMPLOYMENT (2009/10 HESA)
See **Business and Management Courses**.

Career note Majority of graduates work in business involved in marketing and retail work. Employment options include brand design, product management, advertising, PR, sales and account management.

Check **Chapter 4** when choosing your university and **Chapter 7** on how to read the subject tables.

OTHER DEGREE SUBJECTS FOR CONSIDERATION

Business Studies; Consumer Sciences/Studies; E-Commerce; Human Resource Management; Psychology; Supply Chain Management.

RUSSIAN and EAST EUROPEAN STUDIES

(including **Bulgarian, Croatian, Czech, Finnish, Georgian, Hungarian, Polish, Romanian, Russian** and **Serbian**; see also **European Studies, Languages**)

East European Studies cover a wide range of the less popular language courses and should be considered by anyone with a love of and gift for languages. Many natural linguists often devote themselves to one of the popular European languages studied up to A-level, when their language skills could be extended to the more unusual languages, thereby increasing their future career opportunities.

Useful websites www.basees.org.uk; www.iol.org.uk; www.bbc.co.uk/languages; http://languageadvantage.com; www.languagematters.co.uk; www.reed.co.uk/multilingual; www.cilt.org.uk.

NB The points totals shown to the left of the institutions are for ease of reference only. It must not be assumed that Tariff points are always used by institutions or that they can be substituted for an offer in grades. The level of an offer is not necessarily indicative of the quality of a course.

COURSE OFFERS INFORMATION

Subject requirements/preferences GCSE A foreign language. **AL** One or two modern languages may be stipulated.

Your target offers and examples of courses provided by each institution
380 pts **Cambridge** – A*AA (Asia Mid E St (Russ)) (IB 38–42 pts HL 776–777)
360 pts **Birmingham** – AAA (Econ Russ St) (IB 36–38 pts)
Bristol – AAA–A*AB (Phil Modn Lang) (IB 37–35 pts HL 666)
Manchester – AAA (Russ Chin MML) (IB 37 pts)
Oxford – AAA (Russ) (IB 38–40 pts)
St Andrews – AAA–AAB (Russ courses) (IB 35–38 pts)
340 pts **Exeter** – AAB–ABB 340 pts (Russ) (IB 29 pts)
Manchester – AAB–BBB 300–340 pts (Russ Jap BA) (IB 31–36 pts)
Sheffield – AAB–BBC (Russ St Joint Hons) (IB 35–30 pts)
320 pts **Bath** – ABB–BBB (Russ Pol)
Birmingham – ABB 320 pts (Russ St Cnt E Euro St) (IB 32–34 pts)
Bristol – ABB–BBC (Russ Modn Lang) (IB 33–30 pts)
Glasgow – ABB (Cnt E Euro St) (IB 36 pts)
London (UCL) – ABB incl hist (Russ Hist) (IB 34 pts)
Nottingham – ABB (Hist Russ) (IB 32 pts)
300 pts **Edinburgh** – AAA–BBB 300–360 pts (Russ St) (IB 34–42 pts)
Euro Bus Sch London – check with Bus Sch 240–300 pts (Int Bus (Russ))
Leeds – ABC–BBB (Russ Advnc/Bgn) (IB 32 pts)
London (QM) – 300–340 pts (Russ) (IB 32 pts)
Manchester – AAB–BBB 300–340 pts (Russ St) (IB 31–36 pts)
Nottingham – ABC–BBB (Serb/Cro St)
Sheffield – BBB–BBC (Russ St) (IB 32–30 pts)
280 pts **Leeds** – BBC (Russ Civ Theol Relig St) (IB 32 pts)

Alternative offers
See **Chapter 7** and **Appendix 1** for grades/UCAS Tariff points information for the International Baccalaureate, Scottish Highers/Advanced Highers, the Welsh Baccalaureate, the Irish Leaving Certificate, the Cambridge Pre-U Diploma, the Advanced Diploma and the Extended Project.

CHOOSING YOUR COURSE (SEE ALSO CH.1)

Some course features
See also **Languages**.

Durham Russian is only offered as one of two or three other subjects in the Combined Honours course.
Glasgow At all levels language tuition is given by Russian native language speakers.
London LSE Full degrees in languages are not offered by LSE, but Russian Language and Society can be taken as a degree option on most undergraduate courses.
Nottingham Beginners' courses are offered in Russian which can also be combined with another subject taken from the very wide range available, from Serbo-Croat to Contemporary Chinese Studies.

Universities and colleges teaching quality See www.qaa.ac.uk; http://unistats.direct.gov.uk.

Top research universities and colleges (RAE 2008) (Russian, Slavonic and East European languages) Manchester; Oxford; Sheffield; Cambridge; Bristol; Nottingham; Exeter.

ADMISSIONS INFORMATION

Number of applicants per place (approx) Birmingham 3; Bristol 7; Durham 7; Leeds 3; London (UCL) (E Euro St Bulg) 1; Nottingham 5.

Advice to applicants and planning the UCAS personal statement Visits to Eastern Europe should be mentioned, supported by your special reasons for wishing to study the language. A knowledge of the cultural, economic and political scene could be important. Fluent English important for non-UK students. Evidence of wide reading, travel and residence abroad. See also **Appendix 3** under Languages.

Selection interviews **Yes** Cambridge, Durham, Exeter, London (UCL), Oxford; **No** Nottingham.

Interview advice and questions Since many applicants will not have taken Russian at A-level, questions often focus on their reasons for choosing a Russian degree, and their knowledge of, and interest in, Russia. Those taking A-level Russian are likely to be questioned on the course and on any reading done outside A-level work. East European Studies applicants will need to show some knowledge of their chosen country/countries and any specific reasons why they wish to follow the course. See also **Chapter 6**. **Leeds** See **Languages**.

Reasons for rejection (non-academic) Lack of perceived commitment for a demanding ab initio subject.

AFTER-RESULTS ADVICE

Offers to applicants repeating A-levels **Higher** Bristol, Glasgow, Leeds, St Andrews; **Same** Durham; **No** Cambridge.

GRADUATE DESTINATIONS AND EMPLOYMENT (2009/10 HESA)

Graduates surveyed 220 **Employed** 90 **In voluntary employment** 0 **In further study** 50 **Assumed unemployed** 20

Career note See **Languages**.

OTHER DEGREE SUBJECTS FOR CONSIDERATION

Economics; European Studies; International Relations; Linguistics; Politics; other languages.

SCANDINAVIAN STUDIES

(see also **Languages**)

Scandinavian Studies provides students who enjoy languages with the opportunity to extend their language expertise to learn a modern Scandinavian language – Danish, Norwegian or Swedish – from beginner's level to Honours level in four years, including a year in Scandinavia. The three languages are very similar to each other and a knowledge of one makes it possible to access easily the literature and cultures of the other two. Viking Studies includes Old Norse, runology and archaeology.

Useful websites www.cilt.org.uk; www.iol.org.uk; www.bbc.co.uk/languages; http://languageadvantage.com; www.languagematters.co.uk; www.reed.co.uk/multilingual; www.scandinaviahouse.org; www.scandinavianstudy.org; www.nordicstudies.com.

NB The points totals shown to the left of the institutions are for ease of reference only. It must not be assumed that Tariff points are always used by institutions or that they can be substituted for an offer in grades. The level of an offer is not necessarily indicative of the quality of a course.

COURSE OFFERS INFORMATION
Subject requirements/preferences GCSE Foreign language preferred for all courses. **AL** A modern language may be required.

Your target offers and examples of courses provided by each institution
380 pts   **Cambridge** – A*AA (A-Sxn Nrs Celt) (IB 40–42 pts)
340 pts   **London (UCL)** – AAB–ABB incl hist (Scand St Hist) (IB 34–36 pts)
320 pts   **Nottingham** – ABB (Vkg St) (Ib 32 pts HL 5 Engl)
300 pts   **Edinburgh** – AAA–BBB 300–360 pts (Scand St) (IB 34–42 pts HL 555)

Alternative offers
See **Chapter 7** and **Appendix 1** for grades/UCAS Tariff points information for the International Baccalaureate, Scottish Highers/Advanced Highers, the Welsh Baccalaureate, the Irish Leaving Certificate, the Cambridge Pre-U Diploma, the Advanced Diploma and the Extended Project.

CHOOSING YOUR COURSE (SEE ALSO CH.1)
Some course features
See also **Languages**.

Cambridge (A-Sxn Nrs Celt) Old Norse is offered as part of this degree.
Edinburgh Beginners are provided with a concentrated course in the spoken and written language of their choice from Danish, Norwegian or Swedish. Year 3 is spent in a university or working in one of the Scandinavian countries.
London (UCL) Danish, Norwegian and Swedish are taught from scratch on the Scandinavian Studies courses. Icelandic and one other Scandinavian language are taught on the Icelandic course. No prior knowledge of the languages is required.
Nottingham (Vkg St) Course covers languages, literature, history and archaeology.

Universities and colleges teaching quality See www.qaa.ac.uk; http://unistats.direct.gov.uk.

Top research universities and colleges (RAE 2008) See **German**.

ADMISSIONS INFORMATION
Number of applicants per place (approx) London (UCL) 3.

Advice to applicants and planning the UCAS personal statement Visits to Scandinavian countries could be the source of an interest in studying these languages. You should also be aware of cultural, political, geographical and economic aspects of Scandinavian countries. Knowledge of these should be shown in your statement.

Selection interviews Yes Cambridge.

Interview advice and questions Applicants in the past have been questioned on why they have chosen this subject area, on their visits to Scandinavia and on their knowledge of the country/countries and their people. Future career plans are likely to be discussed. See also **Chapter 6**.

Reasons for rejection (non-academic) One applicant didn't know the difference between a noun and a verb.

AFTER-RESULTS ADVICE
Offers to applicants repeating A-levels No Cambridge.

GRADUATE DESTINATIONS AND EMPLOYMENT (2009/10 HESA)
Career note See **Languages**.

OTHER DEGREE SUBJECTS FOR CONSIDERATION
Archaeology; European History/Studies; History; other modern languages, including, for example, Russian and East European languages.

SOCIAL and PUBLIC POLICY and ADMINISTRATION

(see also **Community Studies/Development, Social Work, Sociology**)

Social Policy is a multidisciplinary degree that combines elements from sociology, political science, social and economic history, economics, cultural studies and philosophy. It is a study of the needs of society and how best to provide such services as education, housing, health and welfare services.

Useful websites www.lga.gov.uk; www.ippr.org.uk; www.swap.ac.uk.

NB The points totals shown to the left of the institutions are for ease of reference only. It must not be assumed that Tariff points are always used by institutions or that they can be substituted for an offer in grades. The level of an offer is not necessarily indicative of the quality of a course.

COURSE OFFERS INFORMATION
Subject requirements/preferences GCSE English and mathematics normally required. **AL** No subjects specified.

Your target offers and examples of courses provided by each institution

360 pts **Edinburgh** – AAA–BBB 300–360 pts (Soc Plcy) (IB 34–42 pts)

350 pts **Queen's Belfast** – BBBb/BBCb (Soc Plcy courses)

340 pts **Bath** – AAB–BBB (Soc Plcy) (IB 32–35 pts)
Bristol – AAB (Soc Plcy Pol) (IB 35 pts HL 666)
London (Gold) – AAB (Econ Pol Pblc Plcy)
Loughborough – AAB (Econ Soc Pol) (IB 34 pts)
Nottingham – AAB–ABB 320–340 pts (Soc Plcy) (IB 34 pts)
Southampton – AAB (Sociol Soc Plcy) (IB 34 pts HL 17 pts)

320 pts **Aston** – ABB 320 pts (Pblc Plcy Mgt courses) (IB 33 pts)
Bath – ABB–BBC (Sociol Soc Plcy) (IB 34 pts)
Birmingham – ABB (Soc Plcy) (IB 32–34 pts)
Edinburgh – AAA–ABB 320–360 pts (Geog Soc Plcy) (IB 37–32 pts)
Glasgow – ABB (Pblc Plcy) (IB 36 pts)
Kent – ABB (Soc Plcy) (IB 33 pts)
Leeds – ABB–BBB (Soc Plcy courses) (IB 32 pts HL 15 pts)
Liverpool Hope – 260–320 pts (Soc Plcy)
London LSE – ABB (Soc Plcy) (IB 36–37 pts)
Sheffield – ABB (Soc Plcy Crimin) (IB 33 pts)

300 pts **Bournemouth** – (Sociol Soc Plcy)
Cardiff – BBB (Soc Plcy Sociol)
Lincoln – 300 pts (Psy Soc Plcy; Crimin Soc Plcy)
Liverpool – BBB (Sociol Soc Plcy) (IB 30 pts)
Loughborough – 300–320pts (Crimin Soc Plcy) (IB 32 pts)
Nottingham – BBB (Soc Wk Soc Plcy) (IB 32 pts)
Sheffield – BBB (Soc Plcy Sociol) (IB 32 pts)

        Swansea – BBB (Soc Plcy Crimin) (IB 30 pts)

        York – BBB (Soc Plcy) (IB 30 pts)

280 pts **Bangor** – 280 pts (Law Soc Plcy)

        Brighton – BBC 280 pts (Pol Soc Plcy) (IB 30 pts)

        Leeds – BBC (Soc Pol Sociol) (IB 30 pts HL 14 pts)

        London Met – 280 pts (Sociol Soc Plcy)

        Manchester Met – 280 pts (PR Dig Comms Mgt) (IB 28 pts)

        Stirling – BBC (Sociol Soc Plcy) (IB 32 pts)

260 pts **Ulster** – 260 pts (Soc Plcy; Soc Plcy Pol; Soc Plcy Econ)

240 pts **Lincoln** – 240 pts (Soc Plcy)

        Llandrillo Cymru (Coll) – 240 pts (Pblc Soc Plcy)

        London South Bank – 240 pts (Soc Plcy; Euro Plcy St; Int Soc Plcy)

        UCLan – 240 pts (Soc Plcy (Comb))

        West Scotland – CCC (Occ Safe Hlth)

220 pts **Bangor** – 220–260 pts (Soc Plcy Joint Hons)

        Bradford – 220 pts (Soc Plcy Sociol) (IB 24 pts)

200 pts **Glyndŵr** – 200 pts (Pblc Soc Plcy)

180 pts **Salford** – 180–240 pts (Soc Plcy) (IB 24 pts)

160 pts **Wolverhampton** – 160–220 pts (Soc Plcy courses)

140 pts **Anglia Ruskin** – 140 pts (Soc Plcy)

        West Scotland – CD (Soc Plcy)

        Open University – contact +44 (0)845 300 6090 **or** www.openuniversity.co.uk/you (Soc Plcy Sociol)

Alternative offers

See **Chapter 7** and **Appendix 1** for grades/UCAS Tariff points information for the International Baccalaureate, Scottish Highers/Advanced Highers, the Welsh Baccalaureate, the Irish Leaving Certificate, the Cambridge Pre-U Diploma, the Advanced Diploma and the Extended Project.

EXAMPLES OF FOUNDATION DEGREES IN THE SUBJECT FIELD

Anglia Ruskin; Blackburn (Coll); Bournemouth; City; Colchester (Inst); Cornwall (Coll); Coventry; Craven (Coll); Cumbria; De Montfort; Grimsby (IFHE); Hull (Coll); Llandrillo Cymru (Coll); Northampton; Northumberland (Coll); St Helens (Coll); Sheffield (Coll); Truro (Coll); UCLan; Wolverhampton.

CHOOSING YOUR COURSE (SEE ALSO CH.1)

Some course features

Anglia Ruskin (Soc Plcy courses) In addition to an optional semester abroad in Year 2 there is also an internship module in which students can gain vocational experience with an organisation.

Kent (Soc Plcy Pblc Sctr Mgt) Course has an option to study a language and many other subjects in Year 1.

London LSE (Soc Plcy) An outside option of special interest to the student is taken in each year of the course. A module in Social Psychology is offered for students taking courses in Social Policy and Criminology.

Sheffield (Soc Plcy Crimin) There is a Year Abroad scheme in the USA and Australia.

Universities and colleges teaching quality See www.qaa.ac.uk; http://unistats.direct.gov.uk.

Top research universities and colleges (RAE 2008) See **Social Work**.

Examples of sandwich degree courses Aston; Bath; Middlesex; Northampton; Surrey.

ADMISSIONS INFORMATION

Number of applicants per place (approx) Aston 8; Bangor 6; Bath 6; Birmingham 5; Bristol 3; Cardiff 4; De Montfort 5; Kent 5; Leeds 10; London LSE (Soc Plcy) 4, (Soc Plcy Sociol) 8, (Soc Plcy Econ) 7, (Soc Plcy Gov) 14; Loughborough 5; Manchester Met 4; Middlesex 12; Nottingham 3; Southampton 6; Stirling 11; Swansea 6; UCLan 6; York 3.

Advice to applicants and planning the UCAS personal statement Careers in public and social administration are covered by this subject; consequently a good knowledge of these occupations and contacts with the social services should be discussed fully on your UCAS application. Gain work experience if possible. (See **Appendix 3** for contact details of some relevant organisations.) **Aston** The course is specially tailored for students aiming for careers in NHS management, the civil service and local government. **Bangor** Ability to communicate and work in a group. **Bristol** Deferred entry accepted. **York** Work experience, including voluntary work relevant to social policy.

Misconceptions about this course York Some applicants imagine that the course is vocational and leads directly to social work – it does not. Graduates in this field are well placed for a wide range of careers.

Selection interviews Yes London LSE, Swansea; **Some** Anglia Ruskin, Bangor, Bath (mature applicants), Cardiff, Kent, Leeds (mature students), Loughborough, Salford, Southampton, York; **No** Birmingham, Nottingham.

Interview advice and questions Past questions have included: What relevance has history to social administration? What do you understand by 'public policy'? What advantage do you think studying social science gives when working in policy fields? How could the image of public management of services be improved? Applicants should be fully aware of the content and the differences between all the courses on offer, why they want to study Social Policy and their career objectives. See also **Chapter 6**.

Reasons for rejection (non-academic) Some universities require attendance when they invite applicants to Open Days (check). Lack of awareness of current social issues. See also **Social Work**. **Bath** Applicant really wanted Business Studies: evidence that teacher, careers adviser or parents are pushing the applicant into the subject or higher education.

AFTER-RESULTS ADVICE
Offers to applicants repeating A-levels Higher Glasgow, Leeds; **Same** Anglia Ruskin, Bangor, Bath, Birmingham, Brighton, Cardiff, Loughborough, Salford, Southampton, York.

GRADUATE DESTINATIONS AND EMPLOYMENT (2009/10 HESA)
Social Policy; graduates surveyed 2525 **Employed** 1910 **In voluntary employment** 60 **In further study** 455 **Assumed unemployed** 140

Career note See **Social Sciences/Studies**.

OTHER DEGREE SUBJECTS FOR CONSIDERATION
Behavioural Science; Community Studies; Criminology; Economic and Social History; Economics; Education; Government; Health Studies; Human Resource Management; Law; Politics; Psychology; Social Work; Sociology; Women's Studies.

SOCIAL SCIENCES/STUDIES

(including **Combined Social Sciences, Criminology, Criminal Justice, Human Rights** and **Police Studies**; see also **Education Studies, Health Sciences/Studies, Law, Politics, Psychology, Teacher Training**)

Most Social Sciences/Studies courses take a broad view of aspects of society, for example, economics, politics, history, social psychology and urban studies. Applied Social Studies usually focuses on practical and theoretical preparation for a career in social work. These courses are particularly popular with mature students and some universities and colleges offer shortened degree courses for those with relevant work experience.

Useful websites www.csv.org.uk; www.intute.ac.uk.

Check **Chapter 4** when choosing your university and **Chapter 7** on how to read the subject tables.

NB The points totals shown to the left of the institutions are for ease of reference only. It must not be assumed that Tariff points are always used by institutions or that they can be substituted for an offer in grades. The level of an offer is not necessarily indicative of the quality of a course.

COURSE OFFERS INFORMATION

Subject requirements/preferences GCSE Usually English and mathematics; a science may be required. **AL** No subjects specified. **Other** requirements A Criminal Records Bureau (CRB) check and relevant work experience required for some courses.

Your target offers and examples of courses provided by each institution

380 pts **Durham** – offers listed are average offers; specific offers will vary depending on the popularity of the subjects in combination A*AA (Comb Soc Sci) (IB 38 pts)

360 pts **Edinburgh** – AAA–BBB (Ling Soc Anth) (IB 34–42 pts HL 555)
London (SOAS) – AAA (Dev St) (IB 38 pts HL 766)
Manchester – AAA (Law Crimin) (IB 37 pts)

340 pts **Aberystwyth** – 340 pts (Hum Rts) (28 pts)
Bath – AAB–BBB (Soc Sci) (IB 32–35 pts)
Bristol UWE – 340 pts (Crimin Joint Hons; Crimin Psy)
Cardiff – AAB (Crimin) (IB 32–34 pts)
Durham – AAB (Crimin) (IB 36 pts)
Essex – 340–300 pts (Sociol Hum Rts) (IB 34–32 pts)
Kent – AAB (Soc Anth) (IB 33 pts)
Lancaster – AAA–AAB 340–360 pts (Socioling) (IB 34–36 pts)
London (UCL) – AAB–ABB (Sci Soc) (IB 34–36 pts)
Southampton – AAB incl geog (Popn Geog) (IB 34 pts HL 17 pts)
Surrey – AAB (Law Crimin) (IB 35 pts)

320 pts **Cardiff** – ABB (Crimin Sociol) (IB 32–34 pts)
City – AAB 320 pts (Crimin) (IB 30 pts)
Essex – ABB–BBB 340–300 pts (Crimin) (IB 34–32 pts)
Kent – ABB (Cult St) (IB 33 pts)
Lancaster – ABB (Crimin) (IB 32 pts)
Leeds – ABB (Crim Just Crimin) (IB 34 pts)
Leicester – ABB (Crimin)
London (QM) – 320–340 pts (Cits Econy Soc Chng) (IB 32 pts)
London LSE – ABB (Soc Plcy Crimin) (IB 36–37 pts)
Manchester – ABB (Crimin) (IB 33 pts)
Queen's Belfast – ABB/BBBb (Crimin)
Sheffield – ABB (Soc Plcy Crimin) (IB 33 pts)
Surrey – ABB (Crimin Sociol) (IB 34 pts)
Sussex – ABB–BBB (Wkg Chld Yng Ppl) (IB 34–32 pts)

300 pts **Aberystwyth** – 300 pts (Crimin) (IB 28 pts)
Brighton – BBB 300 pts (Soc Sci) (IB 32 pts)
Cardiff – BBB (Crimin Educ) (IB 32–34 pts)
De Montfort – 300 pts (Law Hum Rts Soc Just)
Huddersfield – 300 pts (Psy Crimin)
Keele – 300–320 pts (Crimin) (IB 32 pts)
Kent – BBB 280–300 pts (Crimin Joint Hons) (IB 33–31 pts)
Lincoln – 300 pts (Crimin Soc Plcy)
LJMU – 300 pts (Foren Psy Crim Just; Law Crim Just)
London (RH) – BBB (Crimin Sociol)
Loughborough – 300–320pts (Crimin Soc Plcy) (IB 32 pts)
Stranmillis (UC) – BBB (Ely Chld St)
Ulster – 300 pts (Crimin Crim Just)
Warwick – BBB (Chld Educ Soc) (IB 34 pts)
York – BBB (App Soc Sci) (IB 31 pts)

280 pts **Birmingham City** – 280 pts (Crimin Sociol; Crim Invstg; Crimin Scrty St; Crimin Plc)
Brighton – BBC 280 pts (Crimin Sociol) (IB 30 pts)
Bristol UWE – 280–320 pts (Crimin; Crimin Jrnl)
Derby – 280 pts (Foren Sci Crimin)
Edge Hill – 280 pts (Crimin Crim Just)
Glamorgan – BBC (Plcg Sci)
Gloucestershire – 280–300 pts (Crimin)
Huddersfield – 280 pts (Crimin)
Hull – BBC 280 pts (Psy Crimin)
LJMU – 280 pts (Crimin; Crimin Psych) (IB 29 pts)
London Met – 280 pts (Crimin)
Manchester Met – 280 pts (Ely Yrs Comb Hons) (IB 28 pts)
Northumbria – 280 pts (Crimin Foren Sci) (IB 25 pts)
Nottingham Trent – 280 pts (Law Crimin; Crimin)
Roehampton – 280 pts (Crimin)
Staffordshire – 200-280 pts (Plcg Crim Invstg)
Stirling – BBC (Int Mgt St Intercult St) (IB 32 pts)
Salford – 280–240 pts (Crimin; Crimin Cult St)
Sheffield Hallam – 280 pts (Crimin; Crimin Sociol; Crimin Psy; Spo Dev Coach)
Suffolk (Univ Campus) – 280 pts (Sociol Crimin)
Teesside – 280–300 pts (Crm Scn Sci)
UCLan – 280–320 pts (Plcy Crim Invstg)
Westminster – BBC (Crim Just)
260 pts **Bangor** – 260–300 pts (Crim Psy)
Bolton – 260 pts (Crimin Foren Psy)
Bradford – 260 pts (Psy Crimin)
Chester – 260–300 pts (Law Jrnl/Crimin) (IB 28 pts)
Coventry – 260 pts (Crimin)
De Montfort – 260 pts (App Crimin; App Crimin Foren Sci)
Derby – 260 pts (App Crimin)
Edinburgh Napier – BCC 260 pts (Soc Sci)
Greenwich – 260 pts (Foren Sci Crim; Crimin Crim Psy)
Hull – 260–300 pts (Crimin)
Kingston – 260 pts (Crimin Joint Hons; Hum Rts)
Lincoln – 260 pts (Crimin Hist)
Liverpool Hope – 260–320 pts (Crimin)
LJMU – 260 pts (Crimin Sociol) (IB 28 pts)
London (Birk) – BCC (Soc Sci)
Manchester Met – 260 pts (Crimin) (IB 28 pts)
Middlesex – 260 pts (Plcg)
Northampton – 260–280 pts (Crimin)
Plymouth – 260–300 pts (Crimin Crim Just St)
Sheffield Hallam – 260 pts (App Soc Sci)
Sunderland – 260 pts (Crimin)
Teesside – 260 pts (Psy Crimin)
UCLan – 260–300 pts (Crimin Joint Hons)
West London – 260 pys (Crimin)
Westminster – BCC/BB (Soc Sci) (IB 28 pts)
Winchester – 260–300 pts (Crimin)
245 pts **Glasgow Caledonian** – CCC 245 pts (Soc Sci (Crimin); Soc Sci)
240 pts **Abertay Dundee** – CCC (Plcg Scrty)
Bangor – 240–260 pts (Crimin Crim Just) (IB 28 pts)
Bradford – 240 pts (App Crim Just St)
Bucks New – 240–280 pts (Crimin)
Canterbury Christ Church – 240 pts (Police St)

Check **Chapter 4** when choosing your university and **Chapter 7** on how to read the subject tables.

Chester – 240–280 pts (Yth Wrk) (IB 26 pts)
Derby – 240 pts (Chld Yth St)
Farnborough (CT) – 240 pts (Psy Crimin)
Glyndŵr – 240 pts (Crim Just)
Greenwich – 240 pts (Crimin)
Leeds Met – 240 pts (Psy Soc) (IB 24 pts)
Lincoln – 240 pts (Soc Sci; Crimin)
London South Bank – CCC 240 pts (Crimin)
Newport – 240 pts (Crimin Crim Just; Soc St Cnslg St)
Portsmouth – 240–300 pts (Crimin Crim Just)
Robert Gordon – CCC (App Soc Sci)
Sheffield Hallam – 240 pts (Chld St; Chld Play; Ely Chld St)
Southampton Solent – 240 pts (Crimin; Crim Invstg Psy)
Teesside – 240 pts (Crimin courses; Crm Invstg)
UEL – 240 pts (Crimin Crim Just)
Ulster – CCC 240–280 pts (Pol Crimin) (IB 24 pts)

230 pts **Edinburgh Napier** – 230 pts (Crimin)
220 pts **Anglia Ruskin** – 220–260 pts (Crimin courses) (IB 30 pts)
Bishop Grosseteste (UC) – 220 pts (Erly Chld St courses)
Peterborough (Univ Centre) – 220 pts (Crimin)
210 pts **Abertay Dundee** – CC (Crimin St)
200 pts **Bedfordshire** – 200 pts (Crimin; App Soc St)
Blackburn (Coll) – 200 pts (Soc Sci)
Cumbria – 200 pts (Plcg Invstg Crimin)
Doncaster (Coll Univ Centre) – 200 pts (Crim Just; App Soc Sci)
Huddersfield – 200 pts (Soc Sci)
Lincoln – 200–260 pts (Crimin Pol)
Middlesex – 200–280 pts (Yth Just; Crimin)
UCLan – 200 pts (Crimin Crim Just; Hum Rts)
West London – 200–240 pts (Psy Crimin/Cnslg Theor)
Wolverhampton – 200 pts (Plcg; Crimin Crim Just; Crimin)
180 pts **Bedfordshire** – 180–220 pts (Crimin Sociol)
Swansea Met – 180 pts (Pblc Serv)
160 pts **Abertay Dundee** – CC 160 pts (Soc Sci)
Accrington and Rossendale (Coll) – 160 pts (Hlth App Soc St)
London (Gold) – CC (App Soc Sci Commun Dev Yth Wk)
Norwich City (Coll) – 160 pts (Engl Psy Soc)
South Essex (Coll) – 160 pts (Soc St)
UHI – CC–AA (Chld Yth St)
140 pts **West Scotland** – CD (Soc Sci)
80 pts **Cornwall (Coll)** – 80–120 pts (Comb Soc Sci)
UHI – C–A (Soc Sci)

Open University – contact +44 (0)845 300 6090 **or** www.openuniversity.co.uk/you (Crimin Psy St; Soc Sci Econ; Soc Sci Geog; Soc Sci Media St; Soc Sci Pol; Soc Sci Psy St)

Alternative offers
See **Chapter 7** and **Appendix 1** for grades/UCAS Tariff points information for the International Baccalaureate, Scottish Highers/Advanced Highers, the Welsh Baccalaureate, the Irish Leaving Certificate, the Cambridge Pre-U Diploma, the Advanced Diploma and the Extended Project.

EXAMPLES OF FOUNDATION DEGREES IN THE SUBJECT FIELD
See also **Social and Public Policy and Administration**. Bath; Blackpool and Fylde (Coll); Bradford; Bristol UWE; Cumbria; De Montfort; Derby; Duchy (Coll); Grimsby (IFHE); Hull (Coll); Llandrillo Cymru (Coll); Northampton; Peterborough (Univ Centre); St Helens (Coll); Sheffield (Coll); Sunderland City

(Coll); Sussex Downs (Coll); Teesside; Truro (Coll); UEL; Warrington (Coll); West Anglia (Coll); Winchester; Wolverhampton; Worcester; York St John; Yorkshire Coast (Coll).

CHOOSING YOUR COURSE (SEE ALSO CH.1)
Some course features
Canterbury Christ Church Courses are offered in Social Work and Police Studies, the latter offered in conjunction with the Kent Police. There are also courses in Childhood Studies and in Applied Criminology.
Huddersfield There are courses in Criminology, Health and Community Studies and Youth and Community Work. A three-year course is also offered leading to a degree and a Diploma in Social Work.
UCLan Degree courses in Criminology, Deaf Studies and joint British Sign Language, Human Rights and Social Policy are offered on the Combined Honours and joint programmes. The University offers a unit degree scheme that includes courses from economics, psychology and sociology.

Universities and colleges teaching quality See www.qaa.ac.uk; http://unistats.direct.gov.uk.

Top research universities and colleges (RAE 2008) See **Social Work**.

Examples of sandwich degree courses Coventry; De Montfort; Middlesex; Portsmouth; Surrey; Teesside.

ADMISSIONS INFORMATION
Number of applicants per place (approx) Abertay Dundee 1; Bangor 2; Bath 6; Bradford 15; Cornwall (Coll) 2; Coventry 7; Cumbria 4; De Montfort 1; Durham 3; Edge Hill 5; Edinburgh 12; Glasgow Caledonian 9; Hull 5; Kingston 5; Leicester (Crimin) 9; Liverpool 13; London (King's) 5; London LSE (all progs) 14; London South Bank 3; Manchester Met 10; Middlesex 26; Northampton 5; Nottingham Trent 2; Portsmouth 3; Roehampton 6; Salford 12; Sheffield Hallam 7; Southampton 6; Staffordshire 2; Sunderland 11; Swansea 8; UEL 10; West Scotland 5; Westminster 14; Winchester 3; York 5.

Advice to applicants and planning the UCAS personal statement The Social Sciences/Studies subject area covers several topics. Focus on these (or some of these) and state your main areas of interest, outlining your work experience, personal goals and motivation to follow the course. Show your interest in current affairs and especially in social issues and government policies.

Misconceptions about this course Cornwall (Coll) That students transfer to Plymouth at the end of Year 1: this is a three-year course in Cornwall.

Selection interviews Yes Anglia Ruskin, Bangor, Birmingham, Birmingham City, Brunel, Coventry, Cumbria, Doncaster (Coll Univ Centre), Durham, Edge Hill, Essex, Glasgow Caledonian, Hull, Kingston, London South Bank, Newcastle, Newport, Nottingham Trent, Oxford, Roehampton, Salford, Sunderland, UEL, West London, West Scotland, Westminster; **Some** Abertay Dundee, Bath (mature students), Bristol, Cornwall (Coll), Robert Gordon, Staffordshire, UEA, Winchester, York.

Interview advice and questions Past questions have included: Define democracy. What is the role of the Church in nationalistic aspirations? Does today's government listen to its people? Questions on current affairs. How would you change the running of your school? What are the faults of the Labour Party/Conservative Party? Do you agree with the National Lottery? Is money from the National Lottery well spent? Give examples of how the social services have failed. What is your understanding of the social origins of problems? See also **Chapter 6**.

Reasons for rejection (non-academic) Stated preference for other institutions. Incompetence in answering questions.

AFTER-RESULTS ADVICE
Offers to applicants repeating A-levels Higher Essex, Glasgow, Salford (possibly), Swansea; **Same** Abertay Dundee, Anglia Ruskin, Bangor, Bradford, Chester, Cornwall (Coll), Coventry, Cumbria, Durham, Gloucestershire, Leeds, Liverpool, London Met, London South Bank, Manchester Met, Newport, Nottingham Trent, Roehampton, Sheffield Hallam, Staffordshire, Stirling, UEA, Winchester, Wolverhampton.

Check **Chapter 4** when choosing your university and **Chapter 7** on how to read the subject tables.

GRADUATE DESTINATIONS AND EMPLOYMENT (2009/10 HESA)
See **Law**, **Politics** and **Psychology**

Career note Graduates find careers in all aspects of social provision, for example health services, welfare agencies such as housing departments, the probation service, police forces, the prison service, personnel work and residential care and other careers not necessarily linked with their degree subjects.

OTHER DEGREE SUBJECTS FOR CONSIDERATION
Business Studies; Community Studies; Economics; Education; Geography; Government; Health Studies; Law; Politics; Psychology; Public Administration; Social Policy; Social Work; Sociology; Urban Studies.

SOCIAL WORK
(see also **Community Studies/Development, Social and Public Policy and Administration**)

Social Work courses (which lead to careers in social work) have similarities to those in Applied Social Studies, Social Policy and Administration, Community Studies and Health Studies. If you are offered a place on a Social Work course which leads to registration as a social worker, you must undergo the Criminal Records Bureau (CRB) disclosure check. You will also have to provide health information and certification. Check for full details of training and careers in social work with the General Social Care Council (see **Appendix 3**). Students from England receive full payment of fees and student bursaries from the General Social Care Council.

Useful websites www.gscc.org.uk; www.swap.ac.uk; www.ageconcern.org.uk; www.samaritans.org; www.ccwales.org.uk; www.sssc.uk.com; www.niscc.info; www.socialworkandcare.co.uk.

NB The points totals shown to the left of the institutions are for ease of reference only. It must not be assumed that Tariff points are always used by institutions or that they can be substituted for an offer in grades. The level of an offer is not necessarily indicative of the quality of a course.

COURSE OFFERS INFORMATION
Subject requirements/preferences GCSE English and mathematics usually required. **AL** No subjects specified. **Other** An Enhanced Criminal Records Bureau check and an occupational health check required. Check also with universities for applicant minimum age requirements.

Your target offers and examples of courses provided by each institution
320 pts **Birmingham** – ABB (Soc Wk) (IB 32–34 pts)
  Queen's Belfast – ABB (Soc Wk)
  Sussex – ABB–BBB (Soc Wk) (IB 34 pts)
300 pts **Bournemouth** – 300 pts (Soc Wk) (IB 30 pts)
  Brighton – BBB 300 pts (Soc Wk)
  Coventry – BBB 300 pts (Soc Wk)
  De Montfort – 300 pts (Soc Wk)
  Edinburgh – AAA–BBB 300–360 pts (Soc Wk) (IB 34–42 pts)
  Huddersfield – 300 pts (Soc Wk)
  Lancaster – BBB 300 pts (Soc Wk) (IB 30 pts)
  Leeds – BBB (Soc Wk)
  Liverpool Hope – 260–300 pts (Soc Wk)
  Middlesex – 200–300 pts (Soc Wk)
  Nottingham – BBB (Soc Wk Soc Plcy) (IB 32 pts)
  Portsmouth – 300 pts (Soc Wk)
  Strathclyde – BBB (Soc Wk) (IB 28 pts)
  UEA – BBB (Soc Wk) (IB 31 pts)
  Ulster – BBB 300 pts (Soc Wk)
  York – BBB (Soc Wk) (IB 30 pts)

280 pts **Bath** – BBC (Soc Wk App Soc St) (IB 32 pts)
Brunel – BBC 280 pts (Soc Wk) (IB 32 pts)
Bucks New – 240–280 pts (Soc Wk)
Edge Hill – 280 pts (Soc Wk)
Gloucestershire – 280–300 pts (Soc Wk)
Hull – 280 pts (Soc Wk)
Keele – 280 pts (Soc Wk) (IB 26–28 pts)
Kent – BBC (Soc Wk) (IB 33 pts)
LJMU – 280 pts (Soc Wk) (IB 25 pts)
London (Gold) – BBC (Soc Wk) (IB 30 pts)
London Met – 280 pts (Soc Wk)
Manchester Met – 280 pts (Soc Cr) (IB 29 pts)
Northampton – 260–280 pts (Soc Wk)
Northumbria – 280 pts (Soc Wk)
Oxford Brookes – BBC (Soc Wk)
Stirling – BBC (Soc Wk) (IB 32 pts)
Salford – 280 pts (Soc Wk St)
Suffolk (Univ Campus) – 280 pts (Soc Wk)

260 pts **Birmingham City** – 260 pts (Soc Wk)
Bradford – 260 pts (Soc Wk)
Derby – 260 pts (Soc Wrk (App))
Glamorgan – BCC (Soc Wk)
Glyndŵr – 260 pts (Soc Wk)
Greenwich – 260 pts (Soc Wk)
Lincoln – 260 pts (Soc Wk)
LJMU – 260 pts (Hlth Soc Cr Fmly Indiv Comm)
Newman (UC) – (Wk Chld Yng Ppl Fmly)
Nottingham Trent – 260 pts (Soc Wk)
Stockport (Coll) – 260 pts (Soc Wk)
Sunderland – 260 pts (Soc Wk)
Swansea – BCC (Soc Wk)
Wiltshire (Coll) – 260 pts (Soc Wk)
Winchester – 260–300 pts (Soc Cr St courses)

240 pts **Anglia Ruskin** – 240 pts (Soc Wk)
Bedfordshire – 240 pts (Soc Wk; Hlth Soc Cr)
Bristol UWE – 240 pts (Soc Wk)
Canterbury Christ Church – 240 pts (Soc Wk) (IB 24 pts)
Cardiff Met – 240 pts (Soc Wk; Hlth Soc Cr)
Chester – 240–280 pts (Soc Wk) (IB 26 pts)
Chichester – 240 pts (Soc Wk) (IB 30 pts)
Dundee – AB–CCC (Soc Wk)
Hertfordshire – 240 pts (Soc Wk)
Kingston – 240 pts (Soc Wk)
Leeds Met – 240 pts (Soc Wk) (IB 24 pts)
Leeds Trinity (UC) – 240 pts (Wkg Chld Yng Ppl Fmly)
London South Bank – 200–240 pts (Soc Wk)
NEW (Coll) – 240 pts (Soc Wk)
Newport – 240 pts (Soc Wk)
Norwich City (Coll) – 240 pts (App Soc Wk)
Robert Gordon – CCC 240 pts (Soc Wk)
Salford – 240 pts (Prof St Nurs Soc Wk) (IB 26 pts)
Sheffield Hallam – 240 pts (Soc Wk)
Southampton Solent – 240 pts (Soc Wk)
Teesside – 240 pts (Soc Wk)
UCLan – 240 pts (Soc Wk)

Check **Chapter 4** when choosing your university and **Chapter 7** on how to read the subject tables.

230 pts **Plymouth** – 230 pts (Soc Wk)
220 pts **Northampton** – 220–300 pts (Soc Cr Joint Hons)
Nottingham Trent – 220 pts (Yth St)
UCP Marjon – 220 pts (Hlth Soc Wlf)
200 pts **Bradford (Coll Univ Centre)** – 200 pts (Soc Wk)
Cumbria – 200 pts (Soc Wk; Wkg Chld Fam)
Derby – 200 pts (App Commun Yth Wk)
Doncaster (Coll Univ Centre) – 200 pts (Erly Chld St)
West London – 200 pts (Soc Wk)
West Scotland – CCD (Soc Wk)
180 pts **Liverpool (CmC)** – 180 pts (Soc Wk)
Staffordshire – 180–240 pts (Soc Wk)
UCP Marjon – 180 pts (Wrkg Chld Yng Ppl; Ely Chld Educ; Chld Welf Soty; Chld Yng Ppl;
Commun Dev; Yth Commun Wk)
160 pts **Bradford (Coll Univ Centre)** – 160 pts (Erly Yrs Prac)
Colchester (Inst) – 160 pts (Erly Yrs; Hlth Soc Cr)
Durham New (Coll) – 160 pts (Soc Wk)
Glasgow Caledonian – CC (Soc Wk)
London (Gold) – CC (App Soc Sci Commun Dev Yth Wk)
Roehampton – 160–200 pts (Hlth Soc Cr)
South Essex (Coll) – 160 pts (Soc Wk)
Wolverhampton – 160–220 pts (Soc Wk)
100 pts **and below**
 80 pts **Havering (Coll)** – 80 pts (Soc Wk)
Norwich City (Coll) – (Erly Chld St)
UEL – 100 pts (Soc Wk)

Open University – contact +44 (0)845 300 6090 **or** www.openuniversity.co.uk/you
(Soc Wk)

Alternative offers
See **Chapter 7** and **Appendix 1** for grades/UCAS Tariff points information for the International
Baccalaureate, Scottish Highers/Advanced Highers, the Welsh Baccalaureate, the Irish Leaving
Certificate, the Cambridge Pre-U Diploma, the Advanced Diploma and the Extended Project.

EXAMPLES OF FOUNDATION DEGREES IN THE SUBJECT FIELD
See **Social and Public Policy and Administration**.

CHOOSING YOUR COURSE (SEE ALSO CH.1)
Some course features
Brunel Placements are in Years 1, 2 and 3. Students undertake 30 days placement in the first year,
70 in the second year and 100 in the final year.
Coventry The course covers law, human growth and development, communication skills and
partnership working.
UEA (Soc Wk) 200 days spent on placements with social work agencies.

Universities and colleges teaching quality See www.qaa.ac.uk; http://unistats.direct.gov.uk.

Top research universities and colleges (RAE 2008) (Social Work and Social Policy and
Administration) London LSE; Bath; Leeds; Kent; Edinburgh; York; City; Oxford; Sheffield; Lancaster;
Keele; Birmingham; London South Bank; Nottingham Trent; Sussex.

ADMISSIONS INFORMATION
Number of applicants per place (approx) Bangor 8; Bath 8; Birmingham 13; Bradford 10; Coventry
22; Dundee 6; London Met 27; Northampton 7; Nottingham Trent 6; Sheffield Hallam 4; Southampton
10; Staffordshire 3.

Advice to applicants and planning the UCAS personal statement The statement should show motivation for social work, relevant work experience, awareness of the demands of social work and give relevant personal information, for example disabilities. Awareness of the origins of personal and family difficulties, commitment to anti-discriminatory practice. Most applicants for these courses will have significant experience of a statutory care agency or voluntary/private organisation providing a social work or social care service. See also **Social and Public Policy and Administration** and **Appendix 4**.

Selection interviews Yes Anglia Ruskin, Bangor, Birmingham, Birmingham City, Bradford, Brunel, Canterbury Christ Church, Chichester, Coventry, Edinburgh, Glyndŵr, Hull, Liverpool Hope, LJMU, Nottingham, Nottingham Trent, Portsmouth, Robert Gordon, Salford, Sheffield Hallam, Staffordshire, UEA, West London, West Scotland, Winchester, Wolverhampton, York; **Some** Cardiff Met, Dundee.

Interview advice and questions What qualities are needed to be a social worker? What use do you think you will be to society as a social worker? Why should money be spent on prison offenders? Your younger brother is playing truant and mixing with bad company. Your parents don't know. What would you do? See also **Social and Public Policy and Administration** and **Chapter 6**.

Reasons for rejection (non-academic) Criminal convictions.

AFTER-RESULTS ADVICE
Offers to applicants repeating A-levels Same Bangor, Lincoln, Liverpool Hope, Salford City (Coll), Staffordshire, Suffolk (Univ Campus), Wolverhampton.

GRADUATE DESTINATIONS AND EMPLOYMENT (2009/10 HESA)
Graduates surveyed 9590 **Employed** 6945 **In voluntary employment** 85 **In further study** 2335 **Assumed unemployed** 650

Career note See **Social Sciences/Studies**.

OTHER DEGREE SUBJECTS FOR CONSIDERATION
Community Studies; Conductive Education; Criminology; Economics; Education; Health Studies; Law; Psychology; Public Sector Management and Administration; Social Policy; Sociology; Youth Studies.

SOCIOLOGY
(see also Anthropology, Social and Public Policy and Administration)

Sociology is the study of social organisation, social structures, systems, institutions and practices. Courses are likely to include the meaning and structure of, for example, race, ethnicity and gender, industrial behaviour, crime and deviance, health and illness. **NB** Sociology is not a training course for social workers, although some graduates take additional qualifications to qualify in social work.

Useful websites www.britsoc.co.uk; www.asanet.org; www.sociology.org.uk; www.sociology.org.

NB The points totals shown to the left of the institutions are for ease of reference only. It must not be assumed that Tariff points are always used by institutions or that they can be substituted for an offer in grades. The level of an offer is not necessarily indicative of the quality of a course.

COURSE OFFERS INFORMATION
Subject requirements/preferences GCSE English and mathematics usually required. **AL** No subjects specified.

Your target offers and examples of courses provided by each institution
380 pts Cambridge – A*AA (Pol Psy Sociol (PPS)) (IB 40–42 pts HL 766–777)
　　　Warwick – AABc (Law Sociol) (IB 36 pts)
360 pts Edinburgh – AAA–BBB 300–360 pts (Sociol) (IB 34–42 pts)

340 pts **Bath** – AAB–BBB (Sociol) (IB 34 pts)
Birmingham – AAB–ABB 320–340 pts (Sociol Pol Sci) (IB 32–36 pts)
Bristol – AAB (Soc Plcy Sociol) (IB 35 pts HL 666)
City – AAB 340 pts (Sociol) (IB 30 pts)
Durham – AAB (Sociol)
Essex – 340–300 pts (Sociol Hum Rts) (IB 34–32 pts)
Manchester – AAB (Bus St Sociol) (IB 35 pts)
Nottingham – AAB–ABB (Sociol Soc Pol) (IB 32 pts)
Southampton – AAB (Phil Sociol) (IB 34 pts HL 17 pts)
Sussex – AAB (Psy Sociol) (IB 35 pts)
Warwick – AAB (Sociol) (IB 36 pts)
320 pts **Aston** – ABB–AAB 320–340 pts (Psy Sociol) (IB 33 pts)
Bath – ABB–BBC (Sociol Soc Plcy) (IB 34 pts)
Birmingham – ABB (Sociol) (IB 32–34 pts)
Cardiff – ABB (Sociol) (IB 32 pts)
Durham – ABB (Sociol Law)
Essex – 320–300 pts (Sociol Mgt) (IB 30–32 pts)
Exeter – ABB–BBB (Sociol Joint Hons) (IB 32–30 pts)
Glasgow – ABB (Sociol) (IB 36 pts)
Kent – ABB (Sociol) (IB 33 pts)
Lancaster – ABB (Crim Sociol; Relig St Sociol) (IB 32 pts)
Leeds – ABB (Sociol) (IB 33 pts HL 15 pts)
Leicester – ABB (Psy Sociol)
London (Gold) – ABB–BBB (Hist Sociol)
London LSE – ABB (Sociol) (IB 37 pts)
Manchester – ABB (Pol Sociol) (IB 34 pts)
Nottingham – AAB–ABB 320–340 pts (Cult Sociol) (IB 32 pts)
Strathclyde – ABB–ABC (Sociol)
Sheffield – ABB (Sociol Bus Mgt) (IB 33 pts)
Surrey – ABB (Crimin Sociol; Sociol Cult Media) (IB 34 pts)
Sussex – ABB–BBB (Sociol Int Dev) (IB 32 pts)
UEA – ABB–BBB (Pol Sociol) (IB 35 pts)
300 pts **Aberdeen** – BBB (Sociol)
Aston – BBB 300 pts (Sociol courses) (IB 33 pts)
Bournemouth – BBB (Sociol)
Brighton – BBB (Pol Sociol) (IB 32 pts)
Bristol UWE – 300 pts (Hist Sociol) (IB 28 pts)
Brunel – BBB (Anth Sociol) (IB 32 pts)
Cardiff – BBB (Educ Sociol; Sociol Relig St; Sociol Welsh)
City – BBB 300 pts (Sociol Psy) (IB 32 pts)
Essex – 300–280 pts (Hlth St Sociol) (IB 32–30 pts)
Leicester – BBB (Media Sociol)
Liverpool – BBB (Sociol Soc Plcy) (IB 30 pts)
Loughborough – (Sociol) (IB 32 pts)
Manchester – BBB (Sociol) (IB 32 pts)
Manchester Met – BBB (Psy Sociol) (IB 30 pts)
Newcastle – ABB–BBB 300–320 pts (Pol Sociol) (IB 32 pts)
Northumbria – 300 pts (Sociol)
Portsmouth – 240–300 pts (Pol Sociol)
Queen's Belfast – BBB/BBCb (Sociol courses)
Sheffield – BBB (Sociol) (IB 32 pts)
York – BBB (Sociol; Sociol Soc Psy; Sociol Educ)
280 pts **Brighton** – BBC (Sociol) (IB 28 pts)
De Montfort – 280 pts (Pol Sociol)
Edge Hill – 280 pts (Sociol; Engl Sociol; Hist Sociol)

For a quick reference offers calculator, fold out the inside back cover.

Glamorgan – BBC 280 pts (Sociol Educ; Sociol Hist)
Gloucestershire – 280–300 pts (Sociol; Engl Lit Sociol)
Huddersfield – 280 pts (Sociol; Sociol Educ)
Kent – BBC (Sociol (Yr Abrd)) (IB 31–33 pts)
Leeds – BBC (Russ Advnc/Bgn Sociol) (IB 32 pts)
London Met – 280 pts (Sociol)
Nottingham Trent – 280 pts (Sociol)
Oxford Brookes – BBC (Sociol (Comb)) (IB 31 pts)
Roehampton – 280 pts (Sociol)
Stirling – BBC (Sociol Soc Plcy) (IB 32 pts)
Salford – 280–240 pts (Sociol Jrnl) (IB 29 pts)
Sheffield Hallam – 280 pts (Psy Sociol; Sociol)
Suffolk (Univ Campus) – 280 pts (Sociol Yth St; Sociol Crimin)
Westminster – BBC (Sociol) (IB 28 pts)

260 pts **Birmingham City** – 260 pts (Sociol; Sociol Crimin; Sociol Psy)
Brighton – BCC (Sociol Commun Hist) (IB 28 pts)
Brunel – 260–300 pts (Sociol; Sociol Media St) (IB 31–32 pts)
Coventry – BCC 260 pts (Sociol; Sociol Psy; Sociol Crimin)
Derby – 260–300 pts (Sociol Joint Hons)
Hull – 260–300 pts (Sociol Anth)
Keele – 260–320 pts (Sociol) (IB 30 pts)
LJMU – 260 pts (Sociol) (IB 28 pts)
Manchester Met – 260 pts (Sociol) (IB 28 pts)
Nottingham Trent – 260 pts (Sociol Pol)
Plymouth – 260–300 pts (Sociol)
Sunderland – 260 pts (Sociol)
Ulster – 260 pts (Sociol; Sociol Ir Hist; Sociol Commun Dev)
Winchester – (Sociol)

240 pts **Bath Spa** – 240–280 pts (Sociol)
Brighton – CCC 240 pts (Med St Sociol/Educ)
Bristol UWE – 240–300 pts (Sociol) (IB 28 pts)
Canterbury Christ Church – (Sociol Soc Sci)
Chester – 240–280 pts (Sociol) (IB 26 pts)
Greenwich – 240 pts (Sociol)
Kingston – 240 pts (Sociol)
Leeds Met – 240 pts (Crimin Sociol) (IB 24 pts)
London South Bank – 240 pts (Sociol)
Newport – 240 pts (Sociol; Sociol Yth Just; Sociol Soc Welf; Sociol Crim)
Northampton – 240–280 pts (Sociol)
Portsmouth – 240–300 pts (Sociol; Sociol Media St; Sociol Psy)
Staffordshire – 240–200 pts (Sociol)
St Mary's Twickenham (UC) – 240 pts (Sociol)
Salford – 240 pts (Sociol) (IB 29 pts)

230 pts **Edinburgh Napier** – 230 pts (Psy Sociol)

220 pts **Anglia Ruskin** – 220–260 pts (Sociol; Sociol Engl; Sociol Media St)
Bangor – 220–260 pts (Sociol Joint Hons) (IB 24 pts)
Bath Spa – 220–260 pts (Sociol Comb courses)
Bradford – 220 pts (Soc Plcy Sociol) (IB 24 pts)
Edinburgh Queen Margaret – 220 pts (Psy Sociol)
Plymouth – 220–300 pts (Psy Sociol)
Teesside – 220 pts (Sociol)
Worcester – 220–260 pts (Sociol)

200 pts **Blackburn (Coll)** – 200 pts (Sociol)
Middlesex – 200–280 pts (Sociol)
Peterborough (Univ Centre) – 200 pts (Sociol)

Check **Chapter 4** when choosing your university and **Chapter 7** on how to read the subject tables.

UCLan – 200 pts (Sociol)
UEL – 200 pts (Sociol)
180 pts **Bedfordshire** – 180–220 pts (Crimin Sociol)
Bradford – 180–220 pts (Sociol)
Leeds Met – 180 pts (Sociol) (IB 24 pts)
160 pts **Abertay Dundee** – CC 160 pts (Sociol)
Wolverhampton – 160–220 pts (Phil Sociol; Sociol Pol; Relig St Sociol; Sociol)
140 pts **West Scotland** – CD (Sociol)
120 pts **West Anglia (Coll)** – 120 pts (Sociol Engl Lit; Sociol Hist)
 80 pts **West Anglia (Coll)** – 80 pts (Psysoc)

Alternative offers
See **Chapter 7** and **Appendix 1** for grades/UCAS Tariff points information for the International Baccalaureate, Scottish Highers/Advanced Highers, the Welsh Baccalaureate, the Irish Leaving Certificate, the Cambridge Pre-U Diploma, the Advanced Diploma and the Extended Project.

EXAMPLES OF FOUNDATION DEGREES IN THE SUBJECT FIELD
Plymouth; Truro (Coll); Winchester.

CHOOSING YOUR COURSE (SEE ALSO CH.1)
Some course features
Bristol In the first year of the Sociology course students choose two additional subjects from the Faculties of Social Sciences and the Arts. There are joint programmes combining with Philosophy, Social Policy and Theology. Sociology can also be taken with study abroad.
Edinburgh Sociology, the discipline which examines the relationship between individuals and society, is offered as a Single Honours course or with Social Anthropology, Politics, South Asian Studies or Economic History.
Kent A Single Honours course is offered. In Part II, core courses are taken, including social analysis and research practices in sociology, as well as optional third-year courses such as the sociology of politics, education, food, work, gender and the family.
Leeds In the first year of the Sociology degree social, intellectual and cultural trends in contemporary society are studied together with study and research skills. Central problems in sociology and social policy form the core subjects in Year 2, and in Year 3 options are taken from a wide range of topics from which students are asked to choose three for further research.
London LSE A module in social psychology is offered for students taking courses in Sociology.

Universities and colleges teaching quality See www.qaa.ac.uk; http://unistats.direct.gov.uk.

Top research universities and colleges (RAE 2008) Manchester; Essex; London (Gold); York; Lancaster; Surrey; Edinburgh; Warwick; Cardiff; Exeter; Oxford; Cambridge.

Examples of sandwich degree courses Aston; Bath; Brunel; Middlesex; Surrey.

ADMISSIONS INFORMATION
Number of applicants per place (approx) Aston 8; Bangor 1; Bath 7; Birmingham 8; Birmingham City 12; Bristol 8; Brunel 24; Cardiff 5; Cardiff Met 4; City 11; Durham 13; Exeter 5; Gloucestershire 8; Greenwich 5; Hull 11; Kent 10; Kingston 9; Lancaster 12; Leeds 14; Leicester 4; Liverpool 9; LJMU 10; London (Gold) 5; London LSE 10; London Met 3; Loughborough 10; Northampton 3; Northumbria 18; Nottingham 7; Plymouth 9; Portsmouth 12; Roehampton 4; Sheffield Hallam 7; Southampton 4; Staffordshire 10; Sunderland 5; Surrey 6; UEA 15; UEL 8; Warwick 20; Worcester 5; York 5.

Advice to applicants and planning the UCAS personal statement Show your ability to communicate and work as part of a group and your curiosity about issues such as social conflict and social change between social groups. Discuss your interests in sociology on the personal statement. Demonstrate an intellectual curiosity about sociology and social problems. See also **Social Sciences/ Studies**. **Bristol** Deferred entry accepted.

Misconceptions about this course Some applicants believe that all sociologists want to become social workers. **Birmingham** Students with an interest in crime and deviance may be disappointed that we do not offer modules in this area. **London Met** That it is the stamping ground of student activists and has no relevance to the real world.

Selection interviews Yes Aston, Birmingham City, Brunel, Cambridge, City, Derby, Durham, Exeter, Hull, Lancaster, Leeds, Leicester, Liverpool, London (Gold), Loughborough, Newcastle, Portsmouth, St Mary's Twickenham (UC), Surrey, UEL, Warwick; **Some** Anglia Ruskin, Bath (mature applicants), Bath Spa, Bristol, Cardiff, Kent, LJMU, London Met, Nottingham Trent, Salford, Sheffield Hallam, Southampton, Staffordshire; **No** Birmingham, Essex, Nottingham.

Interview advice and questions Past questions have included: Why do you want to study Sociology? What books have you read on the subject? How do you see the role of women changing in the next 20 years? See also **Chapter 6. London Met** Questions will focus on existing level of interest in the subject and the applicant's expectations about studying.

Reasons for rejection (non-academic) Evidence of difficulty with written work. Non-attendance at Open Days (find out from your universities if your attendance will affect their offers). 'In the middle of an interview for Sociology a student asked us if we could interview him for Sports Studies instead!' See also **Social and Public Policy and Administration. Durham** No evidence of awareness of what the course involves. **London Met** References which indicated that the individual would not be able to work effectively within a diverse student group; concern that the applicant had not put any serious thought into the choice of subject for study.

AFTER-RESULTS ADVICE
Offers to applicants repeating A-levels Higher Brunel, Essex, Glasgow, Hull, Newcastle, Nottingham Trent, UEL, Warwick, York; **Possibly higher** Leeds, Liverpool, Portsmouth; **Same** Aston, Bangor, Bath, Birmingham, Birmingham City, Bristol, Cardiff, Coventry, Derby, Durham, Gloucestershire, Kingston, Lancaster, LJMU, London Met, Loughborough, Northumbria, Roehampton, St Mary's Twickenham (UC), Salford, Sheffield Hallam, Southampton, Staffordshire; **No** Cambridge.

GRADUATE DESTINATIONS AND EMPLOYMENT (2009/10 HESA)
Graduates surveyed 6345 **Employed** 3510 **In voluntary employment** 160 **In further study** 1240 **Assumed unemployed** 500

Career note See **Social Sciences/Studies**.

OTHER DEGREE SUBJECTS FOR CONSIDERATION
Anthropology; Economic and Social History; Economics; Education; Geography; Government; Health Studies; History; Law; Politics; Psychology; Social Policy; Social Work.

SPANISH
(including **Hispanic Studies** and **Portuguese**; see also **Languages, Latin American Studies**)

Spanish can be studied by focusing on the language and literature of Spain. Broader courses in Hispanic Studies (see also **Latin American Studies**) are available which also include Portuguese and Latin American studies. See also **Appendix 3** under Languages.

Useful websites www.donquijote.co.uk; http://europa.eu; www.cilt.org.uk; www.iol.org.uk; www.bbc.co.uk/languages; http://languageadvantage.com; www.languagematters.co.uk; www.reed.co.uk/multilingual; www.studyspanish.com; www.spanishlanguageguide.com; see also **Latin American Studies**.

NB The points totals shown to the left of the institutions are for ease of reference only. It must not be assumed that Tariff points are always used by institutions or that they can be substituted for an offer in grades. The level of an offer is not necessarily indicative of the quality of a course.

COURSE OFFERS INFORMATION

Subject requirements/preferences GCSE English, mathematics or science and a foreign language. **AL** Spanish required for most courses.

Your target offers and examples of courses provided by each institution

380 pts **Cambridge** – A*AA (Modn Mediev Langs (Span/Port)) (IB 40–42 pts HL 766–777)
London (King's) – AABc (Hisp St) (IB 36 pts HL 6 Span)
Warwick – AABc (Hist Lit Cult Am) (IB 36 pts)

360 pts **Bath** – AAA (Int Mgt Span) (IB 34 pts)
Bristol – AAA–AAB (Hist Art Modn Lang) (IB 37–35 pts)
Edinburgh – AAA–BBB 300–360 pts (Span) (IB 34–42 pts)
London (RH) – AAA–AAB (Econ Fr/Ger/Ital/Span) (IB 33–35 pts)
London (UCL) – AAA–AAB incl Span (Hisp St) (IB 36–38 pts)
Manchester – AAA (Span courses) (IB 37 pts)
Nottingham – AAA (Law Fr Fr Law/Ger Ger Law/Span Span Law) (IB 38 pts HL 7)
Oxford – AAA (Span courses) (IB 38–40 pts)
St Andrews – AAB (Span) (IB 35 pts)
Southampton – AAA (Maths Fr/Ger/Span) (IB 36 pts HL 18 pts)
Sussex – AAA–AAB (Law Fr/Ital/Span (Yr Abrd)) (IB 35–36 pts)

340 pts **Bath** – AAB (Int Bus Span) (IB 34–36 pts)
Bristol – AAB–BBB (Span Modn Lang) (IB 35–32 pts)
Cardiff – AAB–ABB (Span) (IB 30 pts)
Exeter – AAB–ABB (Span) (IB 32–29 pts)
London (RH) – AAB (Mgt Fr/Ger/Ital/Span) (IB 35 pts)
Newcastle – AAB–ABB 320–340 pts (Span Port Lat Am St) (IB 32 pts HL 6 Span)
Nottingham – AAB (Span Contemp Chin St) (IB 34 pts)
St Andrews – AAA–AAB (Span courses) (IB 35–38 pts)
Sheffield – AAB (Law Ger/Fr/Span) (IB 35 pts)
Southampton – AAB (Span courses) (IB 34 pts HL 17 pts)
Surrey – AAB–ABB (Span courses)
Sussex – AAB–ABB (Dr St Span) (IB 34–36 pts)
UEA – AAB–ABB (Transl Med Fr/Span 3 yrs) (IB 32–33 pts)
York – AAB (Span) (IB 32 pts)

320 pts **Aston** – ABB 320 pts (Span Comb Hons) (IB 33–34 pts)
Bath – ABB (Modn Langs Euro St (Span and Fr/Ger/Ital/Russ)) (IB 34 pts HL 6 Span)
Birmingham – ABB (Span Thea St) (IB 32 pts)
Glasgow – ABB (Hisp St) (IB 36 pts)
Lancaster – ABB 320 pts (Span St) (IB 32 pts)
Leeds – ABB–AAB (Span Wrld Cnma) (IB 34 pts HL 16 pts)
Liverpool – ABB–BBB (Span)
London (RH) – ABB–BBB (Euro St Fr/Ger/Ital/Span; Span Mus; Span Fr/Ger/Ital; Span)
Nottingham – ABB (Hisp St) (IB 32 pts)
Strathclyde – ABB (Span courses)
Southampton – AAB–ABB 320–340 pts (Span Lat Am St) (IB 32 pts)
Sussex – ABB (Span courses) (IB 34–36 pts)
UEA – ABB–BBB (Int Dev St Fr/Span/Jap) (IB 32–31 pts)

300 pts **Aberdeen** – BBB (Span)
Bristol UWE – 300 pts (Int Bus St Span)
Cardiff – BBB (Relig St Span/Ital)
Coventry – 300 pts (Law Fr/Span)
Dundee – BBB–BCC (Law Fr/Ger/Span)
Edinburgh – AAA–BBB 300–360 pts (Bus St Fr/Ger/Span)
Essex – 300 pts (Span St Modn Langs) (IB 30 pts)
Heriot-Watt – BBB (Langs (Interp Transl)) (Fr/Ger) (Ger/Span)) (IB 28 pts)
Hertfordshire – 300 pts (Mark Span; Tour Span)

Hull – 300 pts (Hist Fr/Ger/Ital/Span)
Liverpool – BBB (Hisp St) (IB 30 pts)
Queen's Belfast – BBB/BBCb (Span St; Span Port St)
Salford – 300 pts (Modn Lang Transl Interp St (Fr/Ger/Ital/Port/Span))
Swansea – BBB 300 pts (Span Pol; Span Comp Sci)
UEA – BBB–BBC (Span Int Dev St)

280 pts   **Aberystwyth** – 280 pts (Span courses) (IB 28 pts)
Hull – 280–300 pts (Span)
Leeds – BBC (Russ Advnc/Bgn Span) (IB 32 pts)
Oxford Brookes – BBC (Span (Comb)) (IB 30 pts)
Plymouth – 280 pts (Span courses)
Roehampton – 280–320 pts (Span)
Stirling – BBC (Span Lat Am St) (IB 32 pts)

260 pts   **Coventry** – BCC 260 pts (Span)
Dundee – BCC (Span courses)
Greenwich – 260 pts (Span)
London Met – 260 pts (Span Lat Am St)
Manchester Met – 260 pts (Span St) (IB 28 pts)
Nottingham Trent – 260 pts (Span Joint Hons) (IB 24 pts)
Sunderland – 260 pts (Span (Comb))
UCLan – 260–300 pts (Span (Comb))
Westminster – BCC (Span courses) (IB 28 pts)

240 pts   **Bangor** – 240–280 pts (Span courses)
Buckingham – 240–300 pts (Psy Span; Span Mark)
Chester – 240–280 pts (Span courses) (IB 26 pts)
Coventry – 240–260 pts (Span Bus; Span Int Rel)
Kingston – 240–320 pts (Span courses) (IB 25–27 pts)
Ulster – 240 pts (Bus St Fr/Ger/Span) (IB 24 pts)

220 pts   **Leeds Met** – 220 pts (Span) (IB 24 pts)
Ulster – 220–240 pts (Span)

200 pts   **Glamorgan** – 200–260 pts (Bus Span; Engl Span; Law Span)
Middlesex – 200–280 pts (Span Int Bus)
Portsmouth – 200–280 pts (Span Lat Am St; Span St)

160 pts   **Euro Bus Sch London** – CC (Int Bus Span)

80 pts   **London (Birk)** – p/t for under 21s (over 21s varies) (Span Lat Am St; Span Port; Fr Span)

Alternative offers

See **Chapter 7** and **Appendix 1** for grades/UCAS Tariff points information for the International Baccalaureate, Scottish Highers/Advanced Highers, the Welsh Baccalaureate, the Irish Leaving Certificate, the Cambridge Pre-U Diploma, the Advanced Diploma and the Extended Project.

CHOOSING YOUR COURSE (SEE ALSO CH.1)

Some course features

Heriot-Watt Spanish can be taken with Interpreting and Translating, International Management and Teaching English to Speakers of Other Languages.

London (King's) The University offers a very wide range of courses covering Hispanic, Portuguese and Brazilian Studies.

London Met There is an Open Language programme offered to students to continue a study of a preferred language irrespective of their chosen degree course (see also **Languages**).

UEA For particularly able students, Spanish courses are offered over three years, not the usual four-year course.

Warwick (Hist Lit Cult Ams) A four-year interdisciplinary course, with the third year spent at a university in the Americas. Spanish language is taught throughout, with beginners following an introductory course in Year 1, and students with A-level Spanish taking one more advanced course. There are opportunities to study Spanish American literature as poetry.

Check **Chapter 4** when choosing your university and **Chapter 7** on how to read the subject tables.

Universities and colleges teaching quality See www.qaa.ac.uk; http://unistats.direct.gov.uk.

Top research universities and colleges (RAE 2008) (Iberian and Latin American languages) Nottingham; Cambridge; London (King's) (Port); London (Birk); Durham; London (QM); Leeds; St Andrews; Newcastle; Queen's Belfast.

ADMISSIONS INFORMATION
Number of applicants per place (approx) Birmingham 9; Bristol 7; Cardiff 3; Exeter 5; Hull 14; Leeds 10; Liverpool 3; London (King's) 6; London (QM) 5; London (UCL) 6; Middlesex 2; Newcastle 12; Nottingham 7; Portsmouth 4; Salford 5.

Advice to applicants and planning the UCAS personal statement Visits to Spanish-speaking countries should be discussed. Study the geography, culture, literature and politics of Spain (or Portugal) and discuss your interests in full. Further information could be obtained from embassies in London. See also **Appendix 3** under Languages.

Selection interviews **Yes** Cambridge, Hull, London (RH), London (UCL), Oxford; **Some** Cardiff, Leeds, Roehampton, Swansea; **No** Nottingham.

Interview advice and questions Candidates offering A-level Spanish are likely to be questioned on their A-level work, their reasons for wanting to take the subject and on their knowledge of Spain and its people. Interest in Spain important for all applicants. Student comment: 'Mostly questions about the literature I had read and I was given a poem and asked questions on it.' Questions were asked in the target language. 'There were two interviewers for the Spanish interview; they did their best to trip me up and to make me think under pressure by asking aggressive questions.' See **Chapter 6**.

AFTER-RESULTS ADVICE
Offers to applicants repeating A-levels **Higher** Glasgow, Leeds; **Same** Cardiff, Chester, Hull, Liverpool, London (RH), Newcastle, Nottingham, Roehampton, Swansea; **No** Cambridge.

GRADUATE DESTINATIONS AND EMPLOYMENT (2009/10 HESA)
Graduates surveyed 1100 **Employed** 485 **In voluntary employment** 25 **In further study** 250 **Assumed unemployed** 65

Career note See **Languages**.

OTHER DEGREE SUBJECTS FOR CONSIDERATION
International Business Studies; Latin American Studies; Linguistics; see other language tables.

SPEECH PATHOLOGY/SCIENCES/THERAPY
(including **Deaf Studies** and **Phonetics**; see also **Communication Studies/Communication, Health Sciences/Studies**)

Speech Pathology/Sciences/Therapy is the study of speech defects caused by accident, disease or psychological trauma. These can include failure to develop communication at the usual age, voice disorders, physical and learning disabilities and stammering. Courses lead to qualification as a speech therapist. This is one of many medical courses. See also **Medicine** and **Appendix 3**.

Useful websites www.rcslt.org; www.speechteach.co.uk; www.asha.org.

NB The points totals shown to the left of the institutions are for ease of reference only. It must not be assumed that Tariff points are always used by institutions or that they can be substituted for an offer in grades. The level of an offer is not necessarily indicative of the quality of a course.

COURSE OFFERS INFORMATION
Subject requirements/preferences **GCSE** English language, modern foreign language and biology/dual award science at grade B or above. **AL** At least one science subject; biology may be stipulated,

psychology and English language may be preferred. **Other** requirements Criminal Records Bureau (CRB) and occupational health checks essential for speech sciences/speech therapy applicants.

Your target offers and examples of courses provided by each institution

380 pts **City** – A*AA (Sp Lang Thera) (IB 32 pts HL 555)

340 pts **Edinburgh Queen Margaret** – 340 pts (Sp Lang Thera) (IB 32 pts)
Leeds – AAB–ABB (Ling Phon)
Manchester – AAB (Sp Lang Thera) (IB 35 pts)
Newcastle – AAB (Sp Lang Sci) (IB 34 pts)

320 pts **Leeds Met** – ABB (Clin Lang Sci (Sp Lang Thera)) (IB 32 pts HL 555)
Reading – 320 pts (Sp Lang Thera)
Strathclyde – ABB (Sp Lang Path) (IB 32 pts)
Sheffield – ABB incl sci (Sp Sci) (IB 33 pts)
UEA – ABB (Sp Lang Thera) (IB 32 pts HL 666)

300 pts **Cardiff Met** – BBB 300 pts (Sp Lang Thera) (IB 25 pts)
De Montfort – (Hum Comm (Sp Lang Thera)) (IB 28 pts)
Manchester Met – BBB (Psy Sp Path) (IB 28 pts)
UCP Marjon – BBB (Sp Lang Thera)
Ulster – BBB (Sp Lang Thera)

280 pts **Birmingham City** – 280 pts (Sp Lang Thera) (IB 36 pts)

260 pts **UCP Marjon** – 260 pts (Sp Sci)

200 pts **UCLan** – 200 pts (Df St courses) (IB 28 pts)

Alternative offers

See **Chapter 7** and **Appendix 1** for grades/UCAS Tariff points information for the International Baccalaureate, Scottish Highers/Advanced Highers, the Welsh Baccalaureate, the Irish Leaving Certificate, the Cambridge Pre-U Diploma, the Advanced Diploma and the Extended Project.

EXAMPLES OF FOUNDATION DEGREES IN THE SUBJECT FIELD
Portsmouth.

CHOOSING YOUR COURSE (SEE ALSO CH.1)
Some course features
Cardiff Met Course includes a module in bi-lingual studies which focuses on the needs of multicultural and multilingual groups.
Manchester Met Placements are once weekly or in an eight-week block and may be anywhere in the Manchester region, so temporary accommodation may be needed.
Reading (Sp Lang Thera) Clinics are run on campus in collaboration with the local authority. The course involves the use of computer-assisted analyses of language.
Sheffield (Sp Sci) Course leads to qualification as a speech therapist. (Hum Comm Sci) Focuses on the use of speech and language and how the process fails, for example in autism and dyslexia, but is not a professional qualification in speech therapy.

Universities and colleges teaching quality See www.qaa.ac.uk; http://unistats.direct.gov.uk.

Top research universities and colleges (RAE 2008) (Language and Communication Science) City.

ADMISSIONS INFORMATION
Number of applicants per place (approx) Birmingham City 28; Cardiff Met 10; City 16; De Montfort 5; Edinburgh Queen Margaret 12; London (UCL) 9; Manchester 13; Manchester Met 21; Newcastle 23.

Advice to applicants and planning the UCAS personal statement Contact with speech therapists and visits to their clinics are an essential part of the preparation for this career. Discuss your contacts in full, giving details of any work experience or work shadowing you have done and your interest in helping people to communicate, showing evidence of good 'people skills'. See also **Appendix 3** and **Chapter 6**. **Manchester** Selectors look for some practical experience with individuals who have communication or swallowing difficulties. (International students) Good English required because of placement periods.

Check **Chapter 4** when choosing your university and **Chapter 7** on how to read the subject tables.

Misconceptions about this course Some students fail to differentiate between speech therapy, occupational therapy and physiotherapy. They do not realise that to study speech and language therapy there are academic demands, including the study of linguistics, psychology, medical sciences and clinical dynamics, so the course is intensive. **Cardiff Met** Some are under the impression that good grades are not necessary, that it is an easy option and one has to speak with a standard pronunciation.

Selection interviews Yes Birmingham City, De Montfort, Edinburgh Queen Margaret, London (UCL), Manchester Met, Sheffield, UCP Marjon, UEA.

Interview advice and questions Have you visited a speech and language therapy clinic? What did you see there? What made you want to become a speech therapist? What type of speech problems are there? What type of person would make a good speech therapist? Interviews often include an ear test (test of listening ability). See also **Chapter 6**. **Cardiff Met** Interviewees must demonstrate an insight into communication problems and explain how one speech sound is produced.

Reasons for rejection (non-academic) Insufficient knowledge of speech and language therapy. Lack of maturity. Poor communication skills. Written language problems.

AFTER-RESULTS ADVICE
Offers to applicants repeating A-levels Higher Birmingham City, Cardiff Met; **Possibly higher** Manchester Met; **Same** City, De Montfort, Newcastle.

GRADUATE DESTINATIONS AND EMPLOYMENT (2009/10 HESA)
Career note Speech therapists work mainly in NHS clinics, some work in hospitals and others in special schools or units for the mentally or physically handicapped. The demand for speech therapists is high.

OTHER DEGREE SUBJECTS FOR CONSIDERATION
Audiology; Communication Studies; Deaf Studies; Education; Health Studies; Linguistics; Psychology.

SPORTS SCIENCES/STUDIES
(see also **Leisure and Recreation Management/Studies, Physical Education**)

In addition to the theory and practice of many different sporting activities, Sports Sciences/Studies courses also cover the psychological aspects of sports and of sports business administration. The geography, economics and sociology of recreation may also be included. The England and Wales Cricket Board has introduced the Universities Centres of Cricketing Excellence scheme (UCCE). Details can be obtained from the following centres of excellence: Cambridge Centre www.mccuniversities. org/cambridge; Cardiff/Glamorgan Centre www.mccuniversities.org/cardiff-glamorgan; Durham Centre www.mccuniversities.org/durham; Leeds/Bradford Centre www.mccuniversities.org/leeds-bradford; Loughborough Centre www.mccuniversities.org/loughborough; Oxford Centre www.mccuniversities. org/oxford. See also **Appendix 3**.

Useful websites www.uksport.gov.uk; www.laureus.com; www.wsf.org.uk; www.sta.co.uk; www. olympic.org; www.sportscotland.org.uk; www.baha.org.uk; www.planet-science.com; www. london2012.com.

NB The points totals shown to the left of the institutions are for ease of reference only. It must not be assumed that Tariff points are always used by institutions or that they can be substituted for an offer in grades. The level of an offer is not necessarily indicative of the quality of a course.

COURSE OFFERS INFORMATION
Subject requirements/preferences GCSE English, mathematics and, often, a science subject. **AL** Science required for Sport Science courses. PE required for some Sport Studies courses. **Other** requirements Enhanced Criminal Records Bureau (CRB) disclosure required for many courses. Evidence of commitment to sport.

Your target offers and examples of courses provided by each institution

380 pts **Bath** – A*AA (Mech Manuf Eng Mgt) (IB 36 pts HL 6 maths phys)

360 pts **Birmingham** – AAA–AAB 360–340 pts (Spo Exer Sci) (IB 36 pts)

Exeter – AAA–AAB (Psy Spo Exer Sci) (IB 36–34 pts)

Loughborough – AAA–AAB (Maths Spo Sci) (IB 36 pts)

340 pts **Bath** – AAB (Coach Educ Spo Dev) (IB 35 pts)

Birmingham – AAB (App Glf Mgt St) (IB 34–36 pts)

Durham – AAB (Spo) (IB 32–30 pts)

Exeter – AAB–ABB (Exer Spo Sci) (IB 34–29 pts)

Loughborough – AAB (Spo Sci Mgt) (IB 34 pts)

Nottingham Trent – 340 pts (Spo Exer Sci) (IB 28 pts)

320 pts **Birmingham** – ABB (Spo Sci Mat Sci) (IB 32–34 pts)

Bournemouth – 320 pts (Spo Dev Coach Sci; Spo Mgt)

Brighton – ABB (Spo Coach; Spo Exer Sci) (IB 32 pts)

Cardiff Met – 320 pts (Spo Exer Sci) (IB 25 pts)

Glasgow – ABB (Physiol Spo Sci) (IB 32 pts)

Kent – ABB (Spo Sci) (IB 33 pts)

Lancaster – ABB (Crim Sociol) (IB 32 pts)

Leeds – ABB–BBB (Spo Exer Sci) (IB 32–34 HL 16–15 pts)

Loughborough – ABB (Spo Mgt; Spo Tech) (IB 33 pts)

Sheffield Hallam – 320 pts (Physl Actvt Hlth Exer Sci; Spo Sci Perf Coach)

Swansea – ABB 320 pts (Phys Spo Sci)

UCLan – ABB–BBB (Spo Jrnl) (IB 32 pts)

Ulster – ABB (Spo Exer Sci; Spo Sci)

300 pts **Bangor** – 260–300 pts (Spo Hlth Exer Sci; Spo Sci; Spo Sci Psy)

Brighton – BBB (Spo St)

Cardiff Met – 300 pts (Spo PE; Spo Condit Rehab Msg)

Coventry – BBB 300 pts (Spo Psy)

Dundee – BBB (Spo Biomed)

Essex – 300–340 pts (Spo Sci Biol) (IB 30–28 pts)

Glamorgan – 300 pts (Spo Psy)

Gloucestershire – 300 pts (Spo Dev)

Hertfordshire – 300 pts (Spo Thera; Spo Exer Sci; Spo St)

Kent – BBB (Spo Exer Hlth; Spo Exer Mgt) (IB 33 pts)

Leeds Met – 300 pts (Spo Coach) (IB 26 pts)

Manchester Met – 300 pts (Spo Exer Sci) (IB 28 pts)

Nottingham Trent – 300 pts (Coach Spo Sci) (IB 28 pts)

Salford – 300 pts (Spo Rehab) (IB 29 pts)

Swansea – BBB 300 pts (Spo Sci)

280 pts **Aberystwyth** – 280 pts (Spo Exer Sci) (IB 24 pts)

Bristol UWE – 280 pts (Eqn Spo Sci; Spo Bus Mgt; Spo Thera Rehab)

Brunel – 280–300 pts (Mgt Spo Dev) (IB 32 pts)

Cardiff Met – 280 pts (Spo Dev)

Derby – 280 pts (Spo Exer Sci)

Edge Hill – 280 pts (Spo Dev; Spo Exer Sci; Spo Thera)

Edinburgh – BBC (App Spo Sci) (IB 33 pts)

Glamorgan – BBC (Spo Sci Rgby; Spo Exer Sci; Spo St)

Gloucestershire – 280–300 pts (Spo Educ; Spo Sci; Spo Thera)

Huddersfield – 280 pts (Spo Jrnl; Spo Mark PR; Spo Prom Mark)

Hull – 280 pts (Geog Spo Sci)

Leeds Met – 280 pts (Spo Exer Sci; Spo Recr Dev) (IB 26 pts)

Leeds Trinity (UC) – 280 pts (Spo Dev PE; Spo Exer Psy; Spo Jrnl)

LJMU – 280 pts (Coach Dev)

Manchester Met – 280 pts (Coach St; Spo Mark Mgt) (IB 28 pts)

Check **Chapter 4** when choosing your university and **Chapter 7** on how to read the subject tables.

Northumbria – 280–300 pts (Spo Exer Nutr) (IB 28 pts)
Nottingham Trent – 280 pts (Spo Leis; Spo Sci Maths)
Oxford Brookes – BBC (Spo Exer Sci) (IB 30 pts)
Portsmouth – 280 pts (Spo Dev; Spo Exer Sci)
Salford – 280–300 pts (Leis Tour Mgt) (IB 26 pts)
Sheffield Hallam – 280 pts (Spo Coach)
Stirling – BBC (Spo Exer Sci) (IB 32 pts)
Strathclyde – BBC (Spo Physl Actvt)
Teesside – 280 pts (Spo Thera)
UCLan – 280 pts (Spo Thera)
Worcester – 280 pts (Spo Thera; Spo St; Spo Bus Mgt)

260 pts **Bangor** – 260–280 pts (Spo Hlth PE)
Bristol UWE – 260–300 pts (Spo Biomed) (IB 26–28 pts)
Chester – 260–300 pts (Spo Jrnl) (IB 28 pts)
Coventry – BCC 260 pts (Spo Mark; Spo Mgt; Spo Thera)
Derby – 260–280 pts (Spo Coach Joint Hons; Spo Dev Joint Hons; Spo Msg Exer Thera Joint Hons; Spo Psy Joint Hons)
Dundee – BCC (Physiol Spo Biomed) (IB 28 pts)
Edinburgh – BCC (Spo Recr Mgt) (IB 32 pts)
Edinburgh Napier – BCC 260 pts (Spo Exer Sci (Exer Physiol))
Leeds Met – 260 pts (Spo Exer Thera) (IB 24 pts)
Liverpool Hope – 260 pts (Spo Psy; Spo St)
Newman (UC) – 260–280 pts (Spo St)
Sunderland – 260 pts (Spo Exer Dev; Spo Exer Sci; Spo St; Spo (Comb); Spo Mgt; Spo Coach)
Teesside – 260 pts (Spo Dev; Spo Exer (App Exer Sci); Spo Exer (App Spo Sci); Spo Exer (Coach Sci); Spo Exer (Spo St))
UCLan – 260–300 pts (Spo Psy; Spo Sci; Spo Tech)
Ulster – 260 pts (Spo Tech) (IB 24 pts)

240 pts **Aberdeen** – CCC (Spo Exer Sci; Spo St (Exer Hlth); App Spo Sci Educ)
Bolton – 240 pts (Spo Rehab; Spo Dev)
Canterbury Christ Church – 240 pts (Spo Exer Sci)
Cardiff Met – 240 pts (Spo Biomed Nutr)
Chichester – CCC 240–300 pts (Spo Coach Sci) (IB 28 pts)
Cumbria – 240 pts (Spo Exer Sci; Coach Spo Dev; Spo Exer Thera; Spo St (Spo Physl Actvt Dev))
Edinburgh Napier – 240–260 pts (Spo Exer Sci courses; Spo Tech)
Glamorgan – 240–280 pts (Spo Dev)
Glyndŵr – 240 pts (Spo Exer Sci)
Greenwich – 240 pts (Spo Sci; Spo Sci Coach)
Hull – 240–280 pts (Spo Coach Perf; Spo Exer Sci; Spo Rehab)
Leeds Met – 240 pts (Spo Bus Mgt; Spo Leis Cult) (IB 26 pts)
Lincoln – 240–280 pts (Glf Sci Dev; Spo Exer Sci)
Newport – 240 pts (Spo St)
Nottingham Trent – 240 pts (Eqn Spo Sci; Eqn Psy Spo Sci)
Robert Gordon – 240 pts (Spo Exer Sci)
Roehampton – 240–280 pts (Spo Sci; Spo Exer Sci)
Salford – 240–260 pts (App Spo Sci courses)
Sheffield Hallam – 240 pts (Spo Bus Mgt; Spo Tech; Spo Commun Dev; Spo Cult Soc)
St Mary's Twickenham (UC) – 240 pts (Spo Sci; Strg Condit Sci)
Staffordshire – 240 pts (Spo St; Spo Exer Sci)
UCLan – 240–280 pts (Spo Evnt Mgt; Advntr Spo Sci)
UCP Marjon – 240 pts (Spo Thera; App Spo Sci Coach)
Winchester – 240–280 pts (Spo Coach Dev; Spo Mgt)

WHY STUDY SPORT SCIENCE AT BANGOR?
One of the leading Sport Science Schools in the UK.

The School of Sport, Health and Exercise Sciences is one of the
oldest established and very best academic departments in
sport and exercise science related studies in the UK.

• 80% of research either world leading or at an international level, all staff
  submitted (RAE 2008);
• Awarded an 'Exemplary' (the highest possible) rating for the quality of teaching
  and student support;
• Excellent teaching and research facilities and BASES accredited staff;
• One of the prime university locations for pursuing sport and outdoor activities.

BSc Courses
- Sport Science
- Sport, Health and Exercise Sciences
- Sport, Health and Physical Education
- Sport Science (Physical Education)
- Sport Science (Outdoor Activities)
- Sport Science with Psychology

For more information contact
Admissions, School of Sport, Health and Exercise Sciences,
Bangor University, LL57 2PZ • Tel: 01248 388256
E-mail: shes.admissions@bangor.ac.uk

PRIFYSGOL
BANGOR
UNIVERSITY

220 pts **Birmingham (UC)** – 220 pts (Spo Thera)
Bishop Grosseteste (UC) – 220 pts (Spo Maths)
Kingston – 220–280 pts (Spo Sci; Spo Analys Coach)
Lincoln – 220–280 pts (Spo Mark)
Middlesex – 220–280 pts (Spo Biomed)
Myerscough (Coll) – 220 pts (Spotrf Sci Mgt)
Northampton – 220–260 pts (Spo Exer Sci; Spo Dev; Spo Mark)
St Mary's Twickenham (UC) – 220 pts (Clin Exer Sci) (IB 28 pts)
Southampton Solent – 220 pts (Spo St Bus; Wtrspo St Mgt)
UCP Marjon – 220 pts (Spo Dev; Out Advntr Educ)
Warwickshire (Coll) – 220 pts (Eqn Hum Spo Sci)
York St John – 220–260 pts (Spo Soty Dev; Spo Sci Perf Condit; Spo Sci Injry Mgt)
200 pts **Anglia Ruskin** – 200 pts (Spo Sci) (IB 24 pts)
Bishop Burton (Coll) – 200 pts (Spo Coach Dev Fit)
Bucks New – 200–240 pts (Spo Mgt Coach St; Spo Mgt Ftbl St)
Chester – 200–240 pts (Spo Dev)
Farnborough (CT) – 200 pts (Spo Sci (Exer Hlth Mgt))
Kingston – 200–280 pts (Nutr Spo Sci)
London Met – 200–240 pts (Spo Sci; Spo Dance Thera)
Middlesex – 200–220 pts (Spo Rehab)
Plymouth – 200 pts (Surf Sci Tech; App Mar Spo Sci)
Suffolk (Univ Campus) – 200–240 pts (Spo Exer Sci)
UEL – 200 pts (Spo Dev)
180 pts **Abertay Dundee** – DDD/CC (Spo Psy) (IB 26 pts)
Bedfordshire – 180–220 pts (Ftbl St; Spo Jrnl; Spo St)

Check **Chapter 4** when choosing your university and **Chapter 7** on how to read the subject tables.

      Glamorgan – 180–240 pts (Spo Mgt)
      Trinity Saint David – 180–360 pts (Hlth Exer Spo Sci)
      Wolverhampton – 180–200 pts (Spo Mgt)
160 pts **London South Bank** – CC 160 pts (Spo Exer Sci)
      South Essex (Coll) – 160 pts (Spo St)
      Swansea Met – 160 pts (Spo Mgt)
      West Scotland – CC (Spo Exer Sci)
140 pts **West Scotland** – CD (App Spo Exer Sci)
      Writtle (Coll) – 140–240 pts (Spo Exer Perf courses)
120 pts **Colchester (Inst)** – 120 pts (Mgt Spo)

Alternative offers
See **Chapter 7** and **Appendix 1** for grades/UCAS Tariff points information for the International Baccalaureate, Scottish Highers/Advanced Highers, the Welsh Baccalaureate, the Irish Leaving Certificate, the Cambridge Pre-U Diploma, the Advanced Diploma and the Extended Project.

EXAMPLES OF FOUNDATION DEGREES IN THE SUBJECT FIELD
Accrington and Rossendale (Coll); Anglia Ruskin; Arts London (CComm); Bath; Birmingham (UC); Bishop Burton (Coll); Blackburn (Coll); Blackpool and Fylde (Coll); Bournemouth; Bradford; Brighton; Bristol UWE; Bucks New; Chester; Chichester; Colchester (Inst); Cornwall (Coll); Cumbria; Dearne Valley (Coll); Doncaster (Coll Univ Centre); Duchy (Coll); East Durham (Coll); East Riding (Coll); Easton (Coll); Exeter (Coll); Farnborough (CT); Glamorgan; Gloucestershire; Greenwich; Grimsby (IFHE); Hopwood Hall (Coll); Hull (Coll); Leeds City (Coll); Leeds Met; Llandrillo Cymru (Coll); London Met; Manchester (Coll); Mid-Cheshire (Coll); Middlesex; Myerscough (Coll); Nescot; Newcastle (Coll); Newport; North Lindsey (Coll); Northampton; Norwich City (Coll); Pembrokeshire (Coll); Petroc; Plymouth; Roehampton; St Mary's Twickenham (UC); Sheffield (Coll); South Cheshire (Coll); South Nottingham (Coll); Suffolk (Univ Campus); Tameside (Coll); Teesside; Truro (Coll); UCLan; UCP Marjon; Wakefield (Coll); Warwickshire (Coll); West London; Wigan and Leigh (Coll); Wolverhampton; Worcester (CT); York (Coll).

CHOOSING YOUR COURSE (SEE ALSO CH.1)
Some course features
Birmingham (Spo Mat Sci) This course focuses on the design and materials used in the manufacture of sports equipment. Research placements are offered during summer vacations.
Brighton (Spo Jrnl) A placement project takes place in the final year. The course is accredited by the National Council for the Training of Journalists.
Brunel After a common first year students select their preferred specialisation in administration, coaching, exercise and fitness, physical education or a multi-disciplinary route.
Exeter (Hum Biosci) The course combines molecular biology and biochemistry with exercise and sports science, including biomechanics and human exercise physiology.
Loughborough The University has a national and international reputation in sport, leisure management and physical education.
UCLan A wide range of sport and related courses are provided, some specialising in Adventure Sports and Motor Sport.

Universities and colleges teaching quality See www.qaa.ac.uk; http://unistats.direct.gov.uk.

Top research universities and colleges (RAE 2008) (Sports-related studies) Birmingham; Loughborough; Bristol; LJMU; Stirling; Bath; Leeds Met; Brunel; Bangor; Exeter; Leeds.

Examples of sandwich degree courses Bath; Bournemouth; Brighton; Bristol UWE; Brunel; Cardiff Met; Coventry; Glamorgan; Gloucestershire; Hertfordshire; Huddersfield; Kingston; Leeds Met; London Met; Loughborough; Manchester Met; Nottingham Trent; Salford; Sheffield Hallam; Swansea Met; UCLan; Ulster.

ADMISSIONS INFORMATION

Number of applicants per place (approx) Aberystwyth 5; Bangor 15; Bath (Coach Educ Spo Dev) 8; Birmingham 7; Brunel 6; Canterbury Christ Church 30; Cardiff Met 10; Chichester 4; Cumbria 14, (Spo St) 6; Durham 6; Edinburgh 11; Exeter 23; Gloucestershire 8; Kingston 13; Leeds 25; Leeds Trinity (UC) 35; LJMU 4; Loughborough 20; Manchester Met 16; Northampton 4; Northumbria 30; Nottingham Trent 8; Portsmouth 12; Roehampton 8; St Mary's Twickenham (UC) 4; Salford 30; Sheffield Hallam 7; South Essex (Coll) 1; Southampton 8; Staffordshire 12; Stirling 10; Strathclyde 28; Sunderland 2; Swansea 6; Teesside 15; Winchester 5; Wolverhampton 4; Worcester 10; York St John 4.

Advice to applicants and planning the UCAS personal statement See also **Physical Education** and **Appendix 4**. **Cardiff Met** A strong personal statement required which clearly identifies current performance profile and indicates a balanced lifestyle. **Salford** Previous experience in a sporting environment will be noted. Previous study is preferred in biology/human biology, physics, chemistry, physical education/sports studies. Psychology is preferred. (Coach Sci) For these courses applicants must have proven coaching skills to gain a place. (Spo Sci) These are lab-based courses examining the physical stress of sport on the human body. A sound scientific aptitude is required. Although professional sporting qualifications and high level practical experience cannot take the place of scientific entry qualifications, they will be considered in any borderline applicants holding a conditional offer. Comment on any coaching or competitive experience.

Misconceptions about this course Bath (Spo Exer Sci) This is not a sports course with a high component of practical sport: it is a science programme with minimal practical sport. (Coach Educ Spo Dev) This is not necessarily a course for elite athletes. **Birmingham** (App Glf Mgt St) Applicants do not appreciate the academic depth required across key areas (it is, in a sense, a multiple Honours course – business management, sports science, coaching theory, materials science). **Sheffield Hallam** (Spo Tech) Some applicants expect an engineering course! **Swansea** (Spo Sci) Applicants underestimate the quantity of maths on the course. Many applicants are uncertain about the differences between Sports Studies and Sports Science.

Selection interviews Yes Bath, Cumbria, Durham, Edinburgh, Leeds, Leeds Trinity (UC), Nottingham Trent, Sheffield Hallam, Stirling, West Scotland; **Some** Anglia Ruskin, Cardiff Met, Chichester, Derby, LJMU, Roehampton, St Mary's Twickenham (UC), Salford, Sheffield Hallam, Staffordshire, Wolverhampton; **No** Birmingham, UEA.

Interview advice and questions Applicants' interests in sport and their sporting activities are likely to be discussed at length. Past questions include: How do you strike a balance between sport and academic work? How many, and which, sports do you coach? For how long? Have you devised your own coaching programme? What age-range do you coach? Do you coach unsupervised? See also **Chapter 6**. **Loughborough** A high level of sporting achievement is expected.

Reasons for rejection (non-academic) Not genuinely interested in outdoor activities. Poor sporting background or knowledge. Personal appearance. Inability to apply their science to their specialist sport. Illiteracy. Using the course as a second option to physiotherapy. Arrogance. Expectation that they will be playing sport all day. When the course is explained to them some applicants realise that a more arts-based course would be more appropriate.

AFTER-RESULTS ADVICE

Offers to applicants repeating A-levels Higher Swansea; **Same** Cardiff Met, Chichester, Derby, Dundee, Lincoln, LJMU, Loughborough, Plymouth, Roehampton, St Mary's Twickenham (UC), Salford, Sheffield Hallam, Staffordshire, Stirling, Sunderland, Winchester, Wolverhampton, York St John.

GRADUATE DESTINATIONS AND EMPLOYMENT (2009/10 HESA)

Graduates surveyed 11530 **Employed** 4635 **In voluntary employment** 125 **In further study** 2160 **Assumed unemployed** 455

Career note Career options include sport development, coaching, teaching, outdoor centres, sports equipment development, sales, recreation management and professional sport.

OTHER DEGREE SUBJECTS FOR CONSIDERATION

Anatomy; Biology; Human Movement Studies; Leisure and Recreation Management; Nutrition; Physical Education; Physiology; Physiotherapy; Sports Equipment Product Design.

STATISTICS

(see also **Economics, Mathematics**)

Statistics has mathematical underpinnings but is primarily concerned with the collection, interpretation and analysis of data. Statistics are used to analyse and solve problems in a wide range of areas, particularly in the scientific, business, government and public services.

Useful websites www.rss.org.uk; www.statistics.gov.uk.

NB The points totals shown to the left of the institutions are for ease of reference only. It must not be assumed that Tariff points are always used by institutions or that they can be substituted for an offer in grades. The level of an offer is not necessarily indicative of the quality of a course.

COURSE OFFERS INFORMATION

Subject requirements/preferences GCSE English and mathematics. **AL** Mathematics required for all courses.

Your target offers and examples of courses provided by each institution

440 pts **Warwick** – A*AA–AAB (Maths OR Stats Econ (MORSE)) (IB 39 pts HL 6 maths)

400 pts **Imperial London** – A*A*A (Maths Optim Stats) (IB 39 pts HL 7 maths)
London (UCL) – A*AA–AAA (Stats Econ Fin/Lang) (IB 39–36 pts)
Oxford – A*A*A (Maths Stats) (IB 39 pts)

380 pts **Bath** – A*AA (Stats) (IB 39 pts HL 6 maths)
Bristol – A*AA–AAA 360–380 pts (Maths Stats) (IB 37–38 pts HL 666)
London (UCL) – A*AA–AAA incl maths (Econ Stats) (IB 38–39 pts)

360 pts **Birmingham** – AAA (Mathem Econ Stats) (IB 36–38 pts)
City – AAA 360 pts (Mathem Sci Stats) (IB 32 pts)
Edinburgh – AAA–ABB 320–360 pts (Maths Stats) (IB 37–32 pts)
Glasgow – AAA (Stats (Faster Route)) (IB 38 pts)
Glasgow – AAA–A*AB (Fin Stats) (IB 36 pts)
London (QM) – 360 pts (Maths Stats MSci) (IB 34 pts HL 6 maths)
London LSE – AAA (Stats Fin) (IB 38 pts HL 17 pts)
Manchester – A*AB–AAB (Maths Stats) (IB 36 pts)
Southampton – AAA–AAB (Maths OR Stats Econ) (IB 36 pts HL 18 pts)
York – AAA–AAB (Maths Stats)

340 pts **Lancaster** – AAB (Maths Stats) (IB 34 pts HL 6 maths)
Leeds – AAB (Stats; Maths Stats)
London (QM) – 340 pts (Maths Stats) (IB 34 pts HL 6 maths)
Newcastle – AAB (Stats; Stats Mgt) (IB 34–36 pts HL 6 maths)
Queen's Belfast – AAB (Maths Stats OR MSci)
Strathclyde – AAB (Maths Stats) (IB 32 pts)
Surrey – AAB 340 pts (Maths Stats) (IB 30–32 pts)

320 pts **Aberystwyth** – 320 pts (PMaths Stats) (IB 27 pts)
Edinburgh – ABB–ABC (Econ Stats) (IB 34–42 pts)
Glasgow – ABB (Stats) (IB 32 pts)
Heriot-Watt – ABB (Stats Modl)
Kent – ABB (Maths Stats) (IB 33 pts)
Leeds – ABB–AAB (Biol Stats; Fr/Ger Stats)
Liverpool – ABB (Maths Stats) (IB 33 pts HL 6 maths)

London (QM) – 320 pts (Maths Stats Fin Econ) (IB 34 pts HL 6 maths)
London (RH) – ABB (Maths Stats) (IB 33 pts HL 6 maths)
Queen's Belfast – ABB (Maths Stats OR BSc)
Reading – 320 pts (Stats) (IB 36 pts)
Strathclyde – ABB (Econ Maths Stats)
UEA – AAB incl AL maths A (Bus Stats) (IB 32 pts HL 6 maths)

300 pts **Aberystwyth** – 300 pts (Educ Stats) (IB 28 pts)
Bristol UWE – 300 pts (Stats) (IB 26–28 pts)
Brunel – BBB (Maths Stats Mgt)
Heriot-Watt – BBB (Maths Stats)
Plymouth – 300 pts (App Stats) (IB 29 pts)
Reading – 300 pts (App Stats) (IB 36 pts)

280 pts **Kingston** – 280 pts (Act Maths Stats) (IB 26–28 pts)
Staffordshire – 220–280 pts (Maths App Stats) (IB 26 pts)

260 pts **Greenwich** – 260 pts (Stats Comp)
Oxford Brookes – BCC (Stats) (IB 30 pts)
Portsmouth – 260–300 pts (Maths Stats)

200 pts **Kingston** – 200–260 pts (Med Stats) (IB 26–28 pts)
London Met – 200 pts (Maths Stats)

80 pts **London (Birk)** – p/t for under 21s (over 21s varies) (Stats Econ; Stats Mgt; Maths Stats)

Alternative offers
See **Chapter 7** and **Appendix 1** for grades/UCAS Tariff points information for the International Baccalaureate, Scottish Highers/Advanced Highers, the Welsh Baccalaureate, the Irish Leaving Certificate, the Cambridge Pre-U Diploma, the Advanced Diploma and the Extended Project.

CHOOSING YOUR COURSE (SEE ALSO CH.1)
Some course features
Kingston (Med Stats courses) An optional professional placement year is offered to students.
Warwick (MORSE) Course has a statistics specialisation in Years 3 and 4 of the BSc and MMORSE courses.

Universities and colleges teaching quality See www.qaa.ac.uk; http://unistats.direct.gov.uk.

Top research universities and colleges (RAE 2008) (Statistics and Operational Research) Oxford; Imperial London; Bristol; Warwick; Nottingham; Leeds; Kent; Southampton; Lancaster.

Examples of sandwich degree courses Bath; Bristol UWE; Brunel; Cardiff; Coventry; Glamorgan; Kent; Kingston; Middlesex; Northumbria; Portsmouth; Reading; Staffordshire; Surrey.

ADMISSIONS INFORMATION
Number of applicants per place (approx) Bath 10; Coventry 3; Heriot-Watt 6; Lancaster 11; LJMU 6; London (UCL) 9; London LSE 9; Newcastle 5; Southampton 10; UEL 3; York 5.

Advice to applicants and planning the UCAS personal statement Love mathematics, don't expect an easy life. See also **Mathematics**.

Selection interviews Yes Bath, Birmingham, Liverpool, LJMU, London (UCL), Newcastle, Sheffield; **Some** Greenwich; **No** Reading, UEA.

Interview advice and questions Questions could be asked on your A-level syllabus (particularly in mathematics). Applicants' knowledge of statistics and their interest in the subject are likely to be tested, together with their awareness of the application of statistics in commerce and industry. See also **Chapter 6**.

AFTER-RESULTS ADVICE
Offers to applicants repeating A-levels Higher Kent, Leeds, Liverpool, LJMU, Newcastle, Swansea; **Same** Birmingham.

GRADUATE DESTINATIONS AND EMPLOYMENT (2009/10 HESA)
Graduates surveyed 525 **Employed** 265 **In voluntary employment** 5 **In further study** 150
Assumed unemployed 25

Career note See **Mathematics**.

OTHER DEGREE SUBJECTS FOR CONSIDERATION
Accountancy; Actuarial Sciences; Business Information Technology; Business Studies; Computer Science; Economics; Financial Services; Mathematical Studies; Mathematics.

SURVEYING

(including **Building** and **Quantity Surveying** and **Property Management/Development. For Finiancial Investment in Property see under Finance.**; see also **Agricultural Sciences/Agriculture, Building and Construction, Housing**)

Surveying covers a very diverse range of careers and courses and following a Royal Institution of Chartered Surveyors (RICS) accredited course is the accepted way to become a Chartered Surveyor. There are three main specialisms which involve the Built Environment (Building Surveying, Project Management and Quantity Surveying); Land Surveying (Rural, Planning, Environmental, Minerals and Waste Management); Property Surveying (Commercial and Residential Property and Valuation, Facilities Management, Arts and Antiques). Student membership of the RICS is possible. Not all the courses listed below receive RICS accreditation; check with the university or college prior to applying.

Useful websites www.rics.org/careers; www.brookes.ac.uk/schools/be/about/estates/index.

NB The points totals shown to the left of the institutions are for ease of reference only. It must not be assumed that Tariff points are always used by institutions or that they can be substituted for an offer in grades. The level of an offer is not necessarily indicative of the quality of a course.

COURSE OFFERS INFORMATION
Subject requirements/preferences GCSE English and mathematics grade A–C. **AL** No subjects specified; mathematics useful.

Your target offers and examples of courses provided by each institution
380 pts **Cambridge** – A*AA (Lnd Econ) (IB 40–42 pts HL 766–777)
340 pts **Bristol UWE** – 340 pts (Bld Surv) (IB 24–28 pts)
    Reading – 340 pts (Rl Est)
320 pts **Oxford Brookes** – ABB (Rl Est Mgt) (IB 33 pts)
    Ulster – 320 pts (Quant Surv)
300 pts **Aberdeen** – BBB (Rl Est Mgt)
    Brighton – BBB 300 pts (Bld Surv) (IB 28 pts)
    Bristol UWE – 300 pts (Prop Inv Mgt)
    Glasgow Caledonian – BBB 300 pts (Int Rl Est)
    Heriot-Watt – BBB 300 pts (Plan Prop Dev)
    Kingston – 300 pts (Quant Surv Cnsltncy) (IB 32 pts)
    Loughborough – 300 pts (Commer Mgt Quant Surv) (IB 32 pts)
    Northumbria – 300 pts (Est Mgt) (IB 30 pts)
    Reading – 300–320 pts (Quant Surv; Bld Surv)
    Royal (CAg) – 300 pts (Prop Agncy Mgt)
    Ulster – 300 pts (Bld Surv) (IB 25–32 pts)
285 pts **Glasgow Caledonian** – 285 pts (Bld Surv)
280 pts **Birmingham City** – 280 pts (Bld Surv) (IB 30 pts)
    Bristol UWE – 280 pts (Rl Est)

City – 280–320 pts (Civ Eng Surv) (IB 30–32 pts)
Heriot-Watt – BBC (Quant Surv) (IB 29–31 pts)
Northumbria – 280 pts (Bld Surv) (IB 25 pts)
Nottingham Trent – 280 pts (Bld Surv; Quant Surv Constr Commer Mgt)
Oxford Brookes – BBC–BCC (Plan Prop Dev) (IB 30–31 pts)
Salford – 280 pts (Bld Surv; Quant Surv)
Sheffield Hallam – BBC 280 pts (Quant Surv; Bld Surv)
Westminster – BBC 280 pts (Urb Est Mgt) (IB 26 pts)

270 pts **Anglia Ruskin** – 270 pts (Bld Surv; Quant Surv; Rl Est Mgt)
Glasgow Caledonian – 270 pts (Quant Surv)
LJMU – 270 pts (Rl Est Mgt courses)
Portsmouth – 270–300 pts (Prop Dev)

260 pts **Derby** – 260–300 pts (Prop Dev Joint Hons)
Glamorgan – 260 pts (Rl Est Apprsl Mgt)

240 pts **Bolton** – 240 pts (Bld Surv)
Coventry – 240 pts (Bld Surv)
Edinburgh Napier – 240–280 pts (Quant Surv)
Glyndŵr – CCC 240 pts (Est Agncy)
Greenwich – 240 pts (Constr Surv Mgt) (IB 24 pts)
Harper Adams (UC) – CCC–BCC 240–260 pts (Rur Prop Mgt)
Huddersfield – 240 pts (Prop Dev)
Leeds Met – 240 pts (Quant Surv) (IB 24 pts)
Nottingham Trent – 240 pts (Quant Surv) (IB 28 pts)
Wolverhampton – CCC 240 pts (Quant Surv)

230 pts **CEM** – d/l 230 pts (Bld Serv Quant Surv; Quant Surv; Bld Surv)
Coventry – 230 pts (Quant Surv Commer Mgt)
Robert Gordon – CCC–BBB 230–300 pts (Surv (Quant Surv))
UCLan – 230 pts (Commer Mgt Quant Surv; Bld Surv)
Wolverhampton – 230 pts (Rl Est)

220 pts **Glamorgan** – 220–260 pts (Quant Surv)
London South Bank – 220 pts (Commer Mgt (Quant Surv); Bld Surv)

200 pts **UEL** – CDD 200 pts (Surv Map Sci)

180 pts **Greenwich** – 180 pts (Quant Surv)
Plymouth – 180 pts (Env Constr Surv) (IB 24 pts)

150 pts **West London** – 150 pts (Blt Env (Quant Surv))

Alternative offers

See **Chapter 7** and **Appendix 1** for grades/UCAS Tariff points information for the International Baccalaureate, Scottish Highers/Advanced Highers, the Welsh Baccalaureate, the Irish Leaving Certificate, the Cambridge Pre-U Diploma, the Advanced Diploma and the Extended Project.

EXAMPLES OF FOUNDATION DEGREES IN THE SUBJECT FIELD

Anglia Ruskin (Bld Surv); Glamorgan (Quant Surv), (Prop); Greenwich; Wigan and Leigh (Coll) (Bld Surv).

CHOOSING YOUR COURSE (SEE ALSO CH.1)

Some course features

Anglia Ruskin (Quant Surv) The course shares many common themes with the Building Surveying course but also focuses on management practice, project management and procurement.
Kingston (Prop Plan Dev) The course involves the study of economics, law and business.
Loughborough (Commer Mgt Quant Surv) Accredited by the RICS. Sponsorship is a condition of entry to the course. All suitable applicants are interviewed by the sponsors.
Northumbria (Bld Surv) The course focuses on buildings in use, looking at maintenance, alteration, repair, refurbishment and restoration of existing buildings and also new buildings.

Check **Chapter 4** when choosing your university and **Chapter 7** on how to read the subject tables.

Robert Gordon Common first years for Building and Quantity Surveying students who make a final choice of subject at the beginning of Year 2. This is a feature of other universities eg Edinburgh Napier.

Universities and colleges teaching quality See www.qaa.ac.uk; http://unistats.direct.gov.uk. Check on RICS accreditation.

Examples of sandwich degree courses London South Bank (Quant Surv); Northampton (Quant Surv); Northumbria; Nottingham Trent (Quant Surv); Oxford Brookes (Quant Surv); Robert Gordon (industrial placements may be possible).

ADMISSIONS INFORMATION

Number of applicants per place (approx) Anglia Ruskin 2; Birmingham City (Quant Surv) 4; Cambridge 3; Edinburgh Napier (Quant Surv, all three courses) 12; Glamorgan (Quant Surv) 4, (Prop) 6; Glasgow Caledonian (Quant Surv) 3; Glyndŵr (Prop) 3; Greenwich (Quant Surv) 8; Harper Adams (UC) (Prop) 4; Kingston (Quant Surv) 1, (Prop) 22; LJMU (Quant Surv) 10, (Prop) 15; London South Bank 2; Loughborough (Quant Surv) 9; Northumbria (Quant Surv) 17, (Prop) 17; Nottingham Trent (Quant Surv) 10, (Prop) 3; Oxford Brookes (Quant Surv) 4, (Prop) 5; Portsmouth (Prop) 5; Robert Gordon (Quant Surv) 5; Royal (CAg) (Prop) 3; Salford (Quant Surv) 6, (Prop) 3; Sheffield Hallam (Quant Surv) 7, (Prop) 5; Westminster (Prop) 10; Wolverhampton (Quant Surv) 6.

Admissions tutors' advice Nottingham Trent Candidates should demonstrate that they have researched the employment opportunities in the property and construction sectors.

Advice to applicants and planning the UCAS personal statement Surveyors work with architects and builders as well as in their own consultancies dealing with commercial and residential property. Work experience with various firms is strongly recommended depending on the type of surveying speciality preferred. Read surveying magazines. **Cambridge** Statements should be customised to the overall interests of students, not to the Land Economy Tripos specifically. **Oxford Brookes** Applicants should be reflective. We are looking for at least 50-60% of the personal statement to cover issues surrounding why they want to do the course, what motivates them about the subject, how they have developed their interest, how their A-levels have helped them and what they have gained from any work experience. Extra-curricular activities are useful but should not dominate the statement.

Misconceptions about this course Students underestimate the need for numerical competence.

Selection interviews Yes Birmingham City (Quant Surv), Cambridge (Prop), Glamorgan (Quant Surv), (Prop), Glasgow Caledonian (Quant Surv), Harper Adams (UC) (Prop), Heriot-Watt (Quant Surv), (Prop), Kingston (Quantity Surv), LJMU (Quant Surv), Loughborough (Quant Surv), Nottingham Trent (Quant Surv), Royal (CAg) (Prop), Ulster (Quant Surv); **Some** Abertay Dundee, Anglia Ruskin (Quant Surv), (Prop), Nottingham Trent (Prop), Robert Gordon (Quant Surv), Salford, UEL (Prop); **No** Edinburgh Napier.

Interview advice and questions What types of work are undertaken by surveyors? How do you qualify? What did you learn on your work experience? See also **Chapter 6**. **Cambridge** (Land Econ) Questions on subsidies and the euro and economics. Who owns London? How important is the modern day church in town planning? How important are natural resources to a country? Is it more important to focus on poverty at home or abroad? Is the environment a bigger crisis than poverty? Do you think that getting involved with poverty abroad is interfering with others 'freedoms'? (The questions were based on information given in the personal statement.) Students sit a thinking test and a written exam. **Oxford Brookes** Interviews for applicants who are likely to be offered a place. Telephone interviews for those who cannot attend. Group exercise at interview. No offers without an interview.

Reasons for rejection (non-academic) Inability to communicate. Lack of motivation. Indecisiveness about reasons for choosing the course. **Loughborough** Applicants more suited to a practical type of course rather than an academic one. **Nottingham Trent** Incoherent and badly written application forms.

For a quick reference offers calculator, fold out the inside back cover.

AFTER-RESULTS ADVICE

Offers to applicants repeating A-levels **Higher** Bolton, Nottingham Trent; **Possibly higher** Glamorgan, LJMU; **Same** Abertay Dundee, Coventry, Edinburgh Napier, Oxford Brookes, Portsmouth, Robert Gordon, Salford.

GRADUATE DESTINATIONS AND EMPLOYMENT (2009/10 HESA)

Career note See **Building and Construction**.

OTHER DEGREE SUBJECTS FOR CONSIDERATION

Architecture; Building and Construction; Civil Engineering; Estate Management; Town Planning; Urban Studies.

TEACHER TRAINING

(see also **Education Studies, Social Sciences/Studies**)

Teacher training courses are offered in the following subject areas: Art and Design (P); Biology (P S); Business Studies (S); Chemistry (P S); Childhood (P); Computer Education (P); Creative and Performing Arts (P); Dance (P S); Design and Technology (P S); Drama (P S); English (P S); Environmental Science (P S); Environmental Studies (P); French (P S); General Primary; Geography (P S); History (P S); Maths (P S); Music (P S); Physical Education/Movement Studies (P S); Religious Studies (P); Science (P S); Sociology (P); Textile Design (P); Welsh (P).

For further information on teaching as a career see websites below and **Appendix 3** for contact details. Over 50 taster courses are offered each year to those considering teaching as a career. Early Childhood Studies has been introduced in recent years by a number of universities. The courses focus on child development, from birth to eight years of age, and the provision of education for children and their families. It is a multidisciplinary subject and can cover social problems and legal and psychological issues. Note that many institutions listed below also offer one-year Postgraduate Certificate in Education (PGCE) courses which qualify graduates to teach other subjects.

Useful websites www.tda.gov.uk; www.gtcs.org.uk; www.gttr.ac.uk; http://educationcymru.org; www.education.gov.uk.

NB The points totals shown to the left of the institutions are for ease of reference only. It must not be assumed that Tariff points are always used by institutions or that they can be substituted for an offer in grades. The level of an offer is not necessarily indicative of the quality of a course.

COURSE OFFERS INFORMATION

Subject requirements/preferences See **Education Studies**.

Your target offers and examples of courses provided by each institution
Abbreviations used in this table: ITE – Initial Teacher Education; ITT – Initial Teacher Training; P – Primary Teaching; QTS – Qualified Teacher Status; S – Secondary Teaching; STQ – Scottish Teaching Qualification.

380 pts **Cambridge** – A*AA (Educ (Biol Sci/Geog/Hist/Mdn Langs/Mus/Physl Sci)) (IB 40–42 pts HL 776–777)

360 pts **Loughborough** – AAA (Maths Maths Educ) (IB 36 pts)

340 pts **Brighton** – AAB 340–380 pts (PE S Teach) (IB 36 pts)
Huddersfield – 340 pts (Educ P BA QTS)
Stranmillis (UC) – AAB (P Educ)

320 pts **Northampton** – 280–320 pts (P PE)
Roehampton – 320 pts (P Educ (PE); P Educ (Geog))

Check **Chapter 4** when choosing your university and **Chapter 7** on how to read the subject tables.

Stranmillis (UC) – ABB (Relig St Educ)
Sussex – ABB–BBB (ELT) (IB 32–34 pts)
300 pts **Aberdeen** – BBB (Educ P; Educ S)
Edinburgh – BBB (P Educ) (IB 34 pts)
Glasgow – BBB (Educ P QTS) (IB 32 pts)
Liverpool Hope – 300 pts (P Educ BA QTS)
LJMU – 300 pts (P Educ)
Newman (UC) – 300 pts (P Educ; P S Teach BA QTS)
Roehampton – 300–360 pts (P Educ BA/BSc QTS; P Educ (Maths); P Educ (Mus))
Sheffield Hallam – 300 pts (P Educ)
Winchester – 260–300pts (P Educ PE)
280 pts **Bedfordshire** – BBC 280 pts (P Educ BEd QTS)
Brighton – BBC (S Educ courses)
Chichester – BBC (P Educ Teach) (IB 30 pts)
Cumbria – 280 pts (Ely Yrs Educ QTS; P Educ BA QTS)
Gloucestershire – 280 pts (P Teach BEd QTS)
Leeds Trinity (UC) – BBC (P Educ (7-11) BA)
Manchester Met – 280 pts (P Ed) (IB 28 pts)
Newman (UC) – 280–300 pts (P Educ Arts QTS)
Northampton – 280–320 pts (P Ed Maths)
Northumbria – 280 pts (P Teach; Educ P)
Nottingham Trent – BBC (P Educ BA)
Oxford Brookes – BBC (P Teach Educ) (IB 30 pts)
Stranmillis (UC) – BBC (Bus Ent Educ)
Strathclyde – BBC (Chem Teach) (IB 28 pts)
Wolverhampton – 280 pts (PE P QTS)
260 pts **Bangor** – 260–280 pts (P Educ BA QTS)
Brunel – BBC (S PE BSc)
Canterbury Christ Church – 260 pts (Maths S Educ BSc QTS)
Chichester – BBC (Maths Teach KS 2+3) (IB 28 pts)
Hull – 260 pts (Educ P)
Leeds Met – 260 pts (Ely Yrs Educ QTS) (IB 24 pts)
Stranmillis (UC) – BCC (Tech Des Educ; Maths Sci Educ)
Sunderland – 260 pts (Educ)
West Scotland – BCC/CDDD (P Educ)
Winchester – 260–300 pts (Fr P Teach; P Educ Geog)
York St John – 260 pts (Educ P)
240 pts **Anglia Ruskin** – 240 pts (P Educ Ely Yrs BA; P Educ ITT BA)
Bedfordshire – 240–320 pts (PE S QTS)
Chester – 240–280 pts (P Ely Yrs QTS) (IB 26 pts)
Edge Hill – 240–280 pts (P/S Educ courses)
Greenwich – 240–280 pts (Des Tech QTS; Educ P BA QTS)
Hertfordshire – 240–300 pts (Educ P BEd QTS)
Leeds Trinity (UC) – 240 pts (PE P Spo Dev)
Nottingham Trent – 240 pts (S Des Tech Educ)
Plymouth – 240 pts (P PE; P Teach BEd)
RConsvS – offered jointly with University of Glasgow 240 pts (Mus BEd)
Stirling – CCD–BCC (Educ (P); Educ (S))
St Mary's Twickenham (UC) – 240 pts (P Educ) (IB 28 pts)
Sheffield Hallam – 200–240 pts (S Educ)
Trinity Saint David – 240–360 pts (P Educ)
Winchester – 240–280 pts (Maths P Educ)
220 pts **Anglia Ruskin** – 220–260 pts (Engl Lang Engl Lang Teach)
Bishop Grosseteste (UC) – 220 pts (P Educ BA QTS)
Dundee – AB–CCC (P Educ)

Newport – 220 pts (P Teach St BA QTS; S Teach Des Tech; Educ P)
Nottingham Trent – 220 pts (S Physl Sci Educ)
200 pts   **Kingston** – 200 pts (P BA QTS)
Middlesex – 200–300 pts (P Educ)
UCLan – 200 pts (Brit Sign Lang)
Wolverhampton – 200–260 pts (P BEd; Educ P)
180 pts   **Bradford (Coll Univ Centre)** – 180 pts (P Educ BA QTS)
UCP Marjon – 180 pts (Spec Educ Nds)
160 pts   **UHI** – CC–AA (Educ P)
Wolverhampton – 160–220 pts (Brit Sign Lang)

Alternative offers
See **Chapter 7** and **Appendix 1** for grades/UCAS Tariff points information for the International Baccalaureate, Scottish Highers/Advanced Highers, the Welsh Baccalaureate, the Irish Leaving Certificate, the Cambridge Pre-U Diploma, the Advanced Diploma and the Extended Project.

EXAMPLES OF FOUNDATION DEGREES IN THE SUBJECT FIELD
See **Education Studies**.

CHOOSING YOUR COURSE (SEE ALSO CH.1)
Some course features
Chester Early years and primary teaching degrees.
Chichester Primary teacher training, and postgraduate courses in Primary and Secondary Education.
Cumbria In addition to Primary and Secondary Education courses with specialist options ICT, English, Maths and RE, there are also several options covering outdoor education and leadership.
Durham A three-year teaching course is offered at Queen's campus.
Edge Hill Primary and secondary teaching courses.
Hull BA Primary Teaching covers Sciences, English, and Mathematics; there are also courses in Education with Early Childhood Studies, Social Inclusion and Special Needs, or in Education and Society.
Liverpool Hope Education Studies plus the option to take primary teaching courses with specialisation in a range of subjects.
LJMU Early Years and Primary Education courses are offered and also Outdoor Education, Education Studies and Sport Development and Physical Education.
Middlesex Education Studies can be taken with a National Curriculum subject as a route to a PGCE in Primary or Secondary Education.

Universities and colleges teaching quality See www.qaa.ac.uk; http://unistats.direct.gov.uk.

Top research universities and colleges (RAE 2008) See www.tda.gov.uk (England); www.shefc.ac.uk (Scotland); www.elwa.org.uk (Wales); www.unistats.com. London (Inst Ed); Oxford; Cambridge; London (King's); Bristol; Leeds; Exeter; Manchester Met; Warwick; York; Durham; Sussex; Stirling.

ADMISSIONS INFORMATION
Number of applicants per place (approx) Aberystwyth 6; Anglia Ruskin 1; Bangor 5; Bath 17; Bath Spa 5; Birmingham 8; Bishop Grosseteste (UC) 12; Bristol UWE 20; Brunel (PE) 5; Cambridge 2.5; Canterbury Christ Church 15; Cardiff (Educ) 8; Cardiff Met 3; Chester 25; Cumbria 5; Derby 13; Dundee 5; Durham 8; Edge Hill 17; Edinburgh (P) 3; Gloucestershire 20; Glyndŵr 15; Greenwich 3; Hull 7; Hull (Coll) 4; Kingston 9; Leeds 4; Liverpool Hope 5; LJMU 3; London (Gold) 5, (Des Tech) 4; Manchester Met 23, (Maths) 4; Middlesex 7; Newman (UC) (S Engl) 3, (Theol) 3, (Ely Yrs) 5, (Biol) 7, (Geog) 3, (PE) 6, (Sci) 1; Northampton 7; Northumbria 8; Nottingham Trent 11; Oxford Brookes 6; Plymouth 14; Roehampton 6; St Mary's Twickenham (UC) 19; Sheffield Hallam 7, (PE) 60; Strathclyde 7; Swansea Met 10; Trinity Saint David 10; UCLan 5; UCP Marjon 5; West Scotland 7; Winchester 4; Wolverhampton 4; Worcester 21, (Engl) 51; York 3.

Advice to applicants and planning the UCAS personal statement Any application for teacher training courses requires candidates to have experience of observation in schools and with children relevant to the choice of age range. Describe what you have learned from this. Any work with young people should be described in detail, indicating any problems which you may have seen which children create for the teacher. Applicants are strongly advised to have had some teaching practice prior to interview and should give evidence of time spent in a primary or secondary school and give an analysis of activity undertaken with children. Give details of music qualifications, if any. Admissions tutors look for precise, succinct, well-reasoned, well-written statements (no mistakes!). All applicants for Initial Teacher Training (ITT) courses in England leading to Qualified Teacher Status must register provisionally with the General Teaching Council for England. Check with www.gtce.org. uk for full details. See also **Chapter 6**.

Misconceptions about this course Newman (UC) That the Theology course only concentrates on the Christian/Catholic religions – all major religions are covered.

Selection interviews Check all institutions. It is a requirement that all candidates for teacher education are interviewed. **Yes** Birmingham City, Bishop Grosseteste (UC), Bristol UWE, Brunel, Cambridge, Cardiff Met, Derby, Dundee, Durham, Kingston, London (Gold), Manchester Met (group interviews), Newman (UC), Nottingham Trent, Oxford Brookes, Plymouth, Stockport (Coll), Worcester, York St John; **Some** Anglia Ruskin, Bangor, Cardiff, Lincoln, LJMU, Roehampton, UCP Marjon, West Scotland, Winchester, York.

Interview advice and questions Questions invariably focus on why you want to teach and your experiences in the classroom. In some cases you may be asked to write an essay on these topics. Questions in the past have included: What do you think are important issues in education at present? Discussion of course work will take place for Art applicants. **Cambridge** The stage is a platform for opinions or just entertainment? **Derby** Applicants are asked about an aspect of education. **LJMU** Discussion regarding any experience the applicant has had with children.

Reasons for rejection (non-academic) Unable to meet the requirements of written standard English. Ungrammatical personal statements. Lack of research about teaching at primary or secondary levels. Lack of experience in schools. Insufficient experience of working with people; tendency to be racist.

AFTER-RESULTS ADVICE
Offers to applicants repeating A-levels Higher Oxford Brookes, Warwick; **Possibly higher** Cumbria; **Same** Anglia Ruskin, Bangor, Bishop Grosseteste (UC), Brighton, Brunel, Cambridge, Canterbury Christ Church, Cardiff, Chester, De Montfort, Derby, Dundee, Durham, Lincoln, Liverpool Hope, LJMU, London (Gold), Manchester Met, Newman (UC), Northumbria, Nottingham Trent, Roehampton, St Mary's Twickenham (UC), Stirling, Sunderland, UCP Marjon, UEA, UHI, Winchester, Wolverhampton, Worcester, York, York St John; **No** Kingston.

GRADUATE DESTINATIONS AND EMPLOYMENT (2009/10 HESA)
Graduates surveyed 20,375 **Employed** 27,795 **In voluntary employment** 100 **In further study** 2905 **Assumed unemployed** 1145

Career note See **Education Studies**.

OTHER DEGREE SUBJECTS FOR CONSIDERATION
Education Studies; Psychology; Social Policy; Social Sciences; Social Work.

TECHNOLOGIES

(see also **Biotechnology, Computer Courses, Engineering (Electrical and Electronic), Engineering/ Engineering Sciences, Music**)

Technology covers a wide range of activities and is commonly associated with the engineering industries although there are also scientific and artistic applications. The courses listed below give an insight into the range of technology courses available (see also individual subject tables).

Useful websites www.techreview.com; www.intute.ac.uk.

NB The points totals shown to the left of the institutions are for ease of reference only. It must not be assumed that Tariff points are always used by institutions or that they can be substituted for an offer in grades. The level of an offer is not necessarily indicative of the quality of a course.

COURSE OFFERS INFORMATION
Subject requirements/preferences GCSE English and mathematics required. **AL** Mathematics and/or a science may be required.

Your target offers and examples of courses provided by each institution
340 pts **Leeds** – AAB (Avn Tech Plt St) (MEng IB 36 pts HL 17 pts)
Newcastle – AAB (Cheml Eng MEng) (IB 36 pts HL 5 maths chem)
York – AAB–ABB (Mus Tech Sys MEng)
320 pts **Bristol UWE** – 320 pts (Archit Tech Des) (IB 24–28 pts)
Kent – ABB–BBB (Mus Tech) (IB 33 pts)
300 pts **Aston** – BBB 300 pts (Tech Ent Mgt) (IB 32 pts)
Birmingham City – 300 pts (TV Tech Prod)
Cardiff Met – 300 pts (Archit Des Tech)
Glasgow – BBB (Technol Educ) (IB 32 pts)
280 pts **Bristol UWE** – 280–300 pts (Crea Mus Tech)
Derby – 280 pts (Snd Lt Lv Evnt Tech; Mus Tech Prod; Pop Mus Mus Tech)
Huddersfield – 280 pts (Eng Tech Mgt)
Manchester Met – 280 pts (Fash Des Tech) (IB 28 pts)
Westminster – 280 pts (Archit Tech)
260 pts **Ulster** – 260 pts (Tech Des)
240 pts **Bangor** – 240–280 pts (Crea Tech)
Bolton – 240 pts (Comp Tech)
Chester – 240–280 pts (Multim Tech) (IB 26 pts)
Hertfordshire – 240 pts (Aerosp Tech Plt St: Multim Tech)
Hull – 240 pts (Crea Mus Tech)
Ravensbourne – AA–CC (Mus Prod Media) (IB 28 pts)
Staffordshire – 240 pts (Aero Tech; Auto Tech)
UCLan – 240–280 pts (Inf Sys Des)
220 pts **Plymouth** – 220 pts (Mar Spo Tech)
Swansea Met – 220 pts (Auto Des)
200 pts **Bradford** – 200–240 pts (Tech Mgt)
Cardiff Met – 200 pts incl CD one in sci subj (Dntl Tech)
Doncaster (Coll Univ Centre) – 200 pts (Crea Mus Tech)
Leeds Met – 200 pts (Crea Media Tech) (IB 24 pts)
180 pts **Liverpool (LIPA)** – 180 pts (Thea Perf Tech)
160 pts **SAC (Scottish CAg)** – CC (Grn Tech)
Sheffield Hallam – 160 pts (Des Tech S Educ)
West Scotland – CC (Bus Tech; Multim Tech)
120 pts **Plymouth** – 120–180 pts (Mar Eng)

Open University – contact +44 (0)845 300 6090 **or** www.openuniversity.co.uk/you (Tech)

Alternative offers
See **Chapter 7** and **Appendix 1** for grades/UCAS Tariff points information for the International Baccalaureate, Scottish Highers/Advanced Highers, the Welsh Baccalaureate, the Irish Leaving Certificate, the Cambridge Pre-U Diploma, the Advanced Diploma and the Extended Project.

EXAMPLES OF FOUNDATION DEGREES IN THE SUBJECT FIELD
Askham Bryan (Coll); Bournemouth and Poole (Coll); Petroc; UCLan; UCMK.

CHOOSING YOUR COURSE (SEE ALSO CH.1)

Some course features

Aston (Tech Ent Mgt) The course covers product design, computing and engineering management.
Bangor (Crea Tech) The course is made up of two-thirds core computer science modules and one-third creative industries modules; scholarship and sponsorship opportunities are avaialble on a competitive basis.
Birmingham (Spo Sci Mat Tech) The course focuses on the design and materials of sports equipment for athletes, essential to peak performance.
Newcastle (Biopharml Tech) A new course focusing on the science and processes of developing and large-scale manufacturing of biopharmaceuticals, with opportunities for an industrial placement.

Universities and colleges teaching quality See www.qaa.ac.uk; http://unistats.direct.gov.uk.

Top research universities and colleges (RAE 2008) See **Engineering/Engineering Sciences** and **Materials Science/Metallurgy**.

Examples of sandwich degree courses Aston; Bradford; De Montfort; Glamorgan; Huddersfield; Sheffield Hallam; Teesside; Ulster.

ADMISSIONS INFORMATION

Number of applicants per place (approx) Aston 6.

Advice to applicants and planning the UCAS personal statement See **Engineering/Engineering Sciences**and **Physics**.

Selection interviews Yes Aston, Glasgow, Staffordshire.

Interview advice and questions See **Engineering/Engineering Sciences** and **Chapter 6**.

AFTER-RESULTS ADVICE

Offers to applicants repeating A-levels Same Aston, Staffordshire.

GRADUATE DESTINATIONS AND EMPLOYMENT (2009/10 HESA)

Career note See **Engineering/Engineering Sciences**.

OTHER DEGREE SUBJECTS FOR CONSIDERATION

Architectural Technology; Biotechnology; Design Technology; Digital Technology; Engineering Sciences; Environmental Materials Technology; Fashion Technology; Food Technology; Information Technology; Internet Technology; Marine Technology; Mechanical Engineering; Motorsport Technology; Multimedia Technology; Music Technology; Nanotechnology; Sound Technology; Space Technology; Sports Technology; Web Technology.

TOURISM and TRAVEL

(see also **Business and Management Courses, Business and Management Courses (International and European), Business and Management Courses (Specialised), Hospitality and Hotel Management, Leisure and Recreation Management/Studies**)

Tourism and Travel courses are popular; some are combined with Hospitality Management which provides students with specialisms in two areas. Courses involve business studies and a detailed study of tourism and travel. Industrial placements are frequently involved and language options are often included. See also **Appendix 3**.

Useful websites www.wttc.org; www.abta.com; www.baha.org.uk.

NB The points totals shown to the left of the institutions are for ease of reference only. It must not be assumed that Tariff points are always used by institutions or that they can be substituted for an offer in grades. The level of an offer is not necessarily indicative of the quality of a course.

COURSE OFFERS INFORMATION
Subject requirements/preferences GCSE English and mathematics required. **AL** No subjects specified.

Your target offers and examples of courses provided by each institution

360 pts **Exeter** – AAA–AAB (Mgt Tour) (IB 36–33 pts)

320 pts **Strathclyde** – ABB (Hspty Tour Mgt)
        Surrey – ABB (Tour Mgt) (IB 34 pts)

300 pts **Bournemouth** – 300 pts (Tour Mgt)
        Hertfordshire – 300 pts (Tour Mgt Tour Langs)
        Kent – BBB (Bus St (Tour) (Yr Ind)) (IB 33 pts HL 14 pts)
        Sheffield Hallam – 300 pts (Evnts Mgt Tour Destin; Int Evnts Mgt Tour Destin)

280 pts **Cardiff Met** – 280 pts (Tour Mgt courses; Int Tour Hspty Mgt)
        Derby – 280 pts (Tour Mgt)
        Gloucestershire – 240–280 pts (Tour Mgt)
        Manchester Met – 280 pts (Tour Mgt Evnts) (IB 28 pts)
        Northumbria – 280 pts (Trav Tour Mgt) (IB 28 pts)
        Plymouth – 280 pts (Geog Tour Mgt)
        Salford – 280 pts (Tour Mgt)
        Sheffield Hallam – 280 pts (Int Htl Mgt; Tour Lang; Tour Mgt (Int); Tour Hspty Bus Mgt (Int))

260 pts **Aberystwyth** – 260 pts (Tour Mgt) (IB 28 pts)
        Bolton – 260 pts (Bus Mgt (Tour); Int Tour Mgt)
        Brighton – BCC (Trav Tour Mark) (IB 28 pts)
        Coventry – 260–280 pts (Tour Fr/Span)
        Derby – 260–280 pts (Tour Joint Hons)
        Greenwich – 260 pts (Tour Mgt)
        Hertfordshire – 260 pts (Int Tour Mgt)
        Liverpool Hope – 260 pts (Tour)
        LJMU – 260 pts (Tour Leis Mgt)
        London Met – 260 pts (Carib St Int Tour Mgt) (IB 28 pts)
        Northampton – 260–280 pts (Herit Mgt)
        Staffordshire – 260 pts (Tour Mgt)
        Sunderland – 260 pts (Tour (Comb); Tour Mgt; Int Tour Hspty Mgt)
        Westminster – 260–280 pts (Tour Plan) (IB 26 pts)

240 pts **Aberystwyth** – 240 pts (Cntry Recr Tour) (IB 28 pts)
        Canterbury Christ Church – 240 pts (Tour Mgt) (IB 24 pts)
        Chester – 240–280 pts (Tour) (IB 26 pts)
        Chichester – CCC 240–280 pts (Tour Mgt) (IB 28 pts)
        Edinburgh Napier – 240 pts (Tour Mgt; Tour Entre Mgt; Tour Mgt HR Mgt)
        Glamorgan – 240–280 pts (Tour Mgt; Tour Mark)
        Lincoln – 240 pts (Int Tour Mgt; Spo Tour Mgt; Tour Mgt; Tour Mark)
        Manchester Met – 240–280 pts (Tour Mgt) (IB 28 pts)
        Plymouth – 240 pts (Cru Mgt)
        Robert Gordon – CCC (Int Tour Mgt) (IB 26 pts)
        Suffolk (Univ Campus) – 240 pts (Tour Mgt)
        UCLan – 240–280 pts (Int Tour Mgt; Tour Mgt)
        Ulster – CCC 240 pts (Int Trav Tour Mgt; Int Trav Tour St Langs)

220 pts **Harper Adams (UC)** – 220–240 pts (Leis)
        Hertfordshire – 220–280 pts (Tour joint hons)
        Hull – 220 pts (Tour Mgt; Int Tour Mgt)
        Leeds Met – 220 pts (Ger Tour Mgt)
        London Met – 220 pts (Int Tour Mgt; Int Tour Mgt Trav Mgt)
        Northampton – 220–260 pts (Tour courses; Trav Tour Mgt courses)
        Portsmouth – 220 pts (Hspty Mgt Tour)

Check **Chapter 4** when choosing your university and **Chapter 7** on how to read the subject tables.

St Mary's Twickenham (UC) – 220 pts (Tour Mgt) (IB 28 pts)
Southampton Solent – 220–240 pts (Cru Ind Mgt)

200 pts **Anglia Ruskin** – 200–240 pts (Tour Mgt)
Bedfordshire – 200 pts (Trav Tour; Int Tour Mgt)
Birmingham (UC) – 200 pts (Tour Bus Mgt; Int Tour Mgt; Advntr Tour Mgt)
Bucks New – 200–240 pts (Tour courses)
Edinburgh Queen Margaret – 200 pts (Hspty Tour Mgt; Tour Mgt)
Middlesex – 200–300 pts (Int Tour Mgt)
UEL – 200–220 pts (Int Tour Mgt)
West London – 200 pts (Trav Tour Mgt)
Wolverhampton – 200 pts (Tour Mgt)
York St John – 200 pts (Tour Mgt; Int Tour Mgt; Tour Mgt Mark)

160 pts **London South Bank** – CC 160 pts (Tour Hspty)
SAC (Scottish CAg) – CC 160 pts (Fd Tour Mgt; Eqn Tour Mgt; Nat Tour Mgt)
Swansea Met – 160 pts (Int Trav Tour Mgt; Tour Mgt)
UHI – CC–AA 160 pts (Advntr Tour Mgt)

140 pts **Blackpool and Fylde (Coll)** – 140 pts (Int Rsrt Tour Mgt)
Trinity Saint David – 140 pts (Tour; Tour Mgt)

120 pts **Llandrillo Cymru (Coll)** – 120 pts (Mgt Trav Tour)
Grimsby (IFHE) – 120–240 pts (Tour Bus Mgt)

60 pts **UHI** – D–A (Tour Hosp Prac)

EXAMPLES OF FOUNDATION DEGREES IN THE SUBJECT FIELD

Arts London (CComm); Bath Spa; Birmingham (UC); Bishop Burton (Coll); Blackpool and Fylde (Coll); Bournemouth; Brighton; Chichester (Coll); Cornwall (Coll); Craven (Coll); Dearne Valley (Coll); Doncaster (Coll Univ Centre); Duchy (Coll); Durham New (Coll); Ealing, Hammersmith and West London (Coll); Edge Hill; Exeter (Coll); Farnborough (CT); Grimsby (IFHE); Guildford (Coll); Hertfordshire; Highbury Portsmouth (Coll); Hull (Coll); Leeds Met; Liverpool (CmC); Loughborough (Coll); Mid-Cheshire (Coll); Mid-Kent (Coll); Newcastle (Coll); Northampton; Northbrook (Coll); Norwich City (Coll); Nottingham New (Coll); Plymouth; Plymouth City (Coll); Sheffield (Coll); South Cheshire (Coll); South Devon (Coll); Sunderland; Teesside; Tyne Met (Coll); UCLan; West London; Westminster Kingsway (Coll); Worcester.

CHOOSING YOUR COURSE (SEE ALSO CH.1)

Some course features

Bristol UWE (Tour Env Mgt) Field courses are UK-based in the first year and overseas in the second. Students contribute to the costs of these. There are options to take a year out on placement.
Plymouth (Cru Mgt) The course focuses on the study of cruise tourism and the management of cruise operations. There is an optional year on a cruise ship.
Southampton Solent Courses are offered in Outdoor Adventure and Watersports.
West London In addition to airline travel the course includes modules in retail travel, attractions management, inclusive tour operations and transport management.

Universities and colleges teaching quality See www.qaa.ac.uk; http://unistats.direct.gov.uk.

Examples of sandwich degree courses Bedfordshire; Birmingham (UC); Bournemouth; Brighton; Bristol UWE; Cardiff Met; Chichester; Coventry; Gloucestershire; Greenwich; Harper Adams (UC); Hertfordshire; Huddersfield; Leeds Met; LJMU; Llandrillo Cymru (Coll); London Met; London South Bank; Manchester Met; Middlesex; Northumbria; Plymouth; Portsmouth; Salford; Sheffield Hallam; South Cheshire (Coll); Staffordshire; Sunderland; Surrey; Swansea Met; UCLan; Ulster; Wolverhampton.

ADMISSIONS INFORMATION

Number of applicants per place (approx) Aberystwyth 3; Bath Spa 5; Birmingham (UC) 10; Bournemouth 16; Derby 4; Glamorgan 8; LJMU 10; Northumbria 6; Sheffield Hallam 12; Sunderland 2.

Advice to applicants and planning the UCAS personal statement Work experience in the travel and tourism industry is important – in agencies, in the airline industry or hotels. This work should be described in detail. Any experience with people in sales work, dealing with the public – their problems and complaints – should also be included. Travel should be outlined, detailing places visited. Genuine interest in travel, diverse cultures and people. Good communication skills required. See also **Appendix 4**.

Misconceptions about this course Bath Spa The course is not purely vocational and operational: it also involves management issues. **Wolverhampton** Some applicants are uncertain whether or not to take a Business Management course instead of Tourism Management. They should be aware that the latter will equip them with a tourism-specific knowledge of business.

Selection interviews Yes Brighton, Derby, Sunderland; **Some** Abertay Dundee, Anglia Ruskin, Lincoln, LJMU, Salford.

Interview advice and questions Past questions have included: What problems have you experienced when travelling? Questions on places visited. Experiences of air, rail and sea travel. What is marketing? What special qualities do you have that will be of use in the travel industry? See also **Chapter 6**.

Reasons for rejection (non-academic) Wolverhampton English language competence.

AFTER-RESULTS ADVICE
Offers to applicants repeating A-levels Same Abertay Dundee, Anglia Ruskin, Birmingham (UC), Chester, Derby, Lincoln, LJMU, Manchester Met, Northumbria, St Mary's Twickenham (UC), Salford, Wolverhampton.

GRADUATE DESTINATIONS AND EMPLOYMENT (2009/10 HESA)
Hospitality, Leisure, Tourism and Transport; graduates surveyed 5475 **Employed** 2810 **In voluntary employment** 40 **In further study** 985 **Assumed unemployed** 350

Career note See **Business and Management Courses**.

OTHER DEGREE SUBJECTS FOR CONSIDERATION
Airline and Airport Management; Business Studies; Events Management; Heritage Management; Hospitality Management; Leisure and Recreation Management; Travel Management.

TOWN and COUNTRY PLANNING

(including **Environmental Planning** and **Urban Studies**; see also **Development Studies, Environmental Sciences/Studies, Housing, Transport Management and Planning**)

Town and Country Planning courses are very similar and some lead to qualification or part of a qualification as a member of the Royal Town Planning Institute (RTPI). Further information from the RTPI (see **Appendix 3**).

Useful websites www.rtpi.org.uk; www.townplanningreview.lupjournals.org.

NB The points totals shown to the left of the institutions are for ease of reference only. It must not be assumed that Tariff points are always used by institutions or that they can be substituted for an offer in grades. The level of an offer is not necessarily indicative of the quality of a course.

COURSE OFFERS INFORMATION
Subject requirements/preferences GCSE English and mathematics required. **AL** Geography may be specified.

Your target offers and examples of courses provided by each institution
360 pts Cardiff – AAA–AAB (Geog (Hum) Plan) (IB 32 pts)
340 pts London (UCL) – AAB (Plan Rl Est) (IB 36 pts)
London LSE – AAB (Env Dev) (IB 37 pts HL 666)
Reading – 340 pts (Rl Est)

320 pts **Birmingham** – ABB (Geog Urb Reg Plan) (IB 32–34 pts)
Birmingham (UC) – ABB (Geog Urb Reg Plan) (IB 32–34 pts)
Cardiff – ABB–BBB (Cty Reg Plan) (IB 32 pts)
Liverpool – ABB (Twn Reg Plan MPlan) (IB 33 pts)
London (UCL) – ABB (Urb Plan Des Mgt) (IB 32 pts)
Newcastle – ABB–BBB 300–320 pts (Geog Plan) (IB 30 pts)
Sheffield – ABB (Geog Plan) (IB 33 pts)

300 pts **Bristol UWE** – 300–360 pts (Archit Plan)
Liverpool – BBB (Urb Regn Plan) (IB 31 pts)
Manchester – BBB (Env Mgt) (IB 33 pts)
Northumbria – 300 pts (Plan Dev Surv) (IB 30 pts)
Queen's Belfast – BBB/BBCb (Env Plan)

280 pts **Birmingham City** – 280 pts (Plan Dev)
Heriot-Watt – BBC (Urb Reg Plan)
Newcastle – ABB–BBC 280–320 pts (Twn Plan) (IB 28 pts)
Oxford Brookes – BBC (City Reg Plan) (IB 31 pts)
Sheffield – BBC (Urb St) (IB 30 pts)
Sheffield Hallam – 280 pts (Rl Est)
Westminster – BBC 280 pts (Prop Urb Dev) (IB 26 pts)

260 pts **Dundee** – BCC (Twn Reg Plan) (HL 555)
Sheffield Hallam – 260 pts (Urb Env Plan)

240 pts **Canterbury Christ Church** – 240 pts (Urb Reg St)
Leeds Met – 240 pts (Hum Geog Plan) (IB 24 pts)
London South Bank – CCC (Urb Env Plan)

160 pts **UHI** – CC–AA (Sust Rur Dev)

Alternative offers
See **Chapter 7** and **Appendix 1** for grades/UCAS Tariff points information for the International Baccalaureate, Scottish Highers/Advanced Highers, the Welsh Baccalaureate, the Irish Leaving Certificate, the Cambridge Pre-U Diploma, the Advanced Diploma and the Extended Project.

EXAMPLES OF FOUNDATION DEGREES IN THE SUBJECT FIELD
Anglia Ruskin; Birmingham City; Blackburn (Coll); Derby; Glyndŵr; Grimsby (IFHE); Middlesex; Northampton; Royal (CAg).

CHOOSING YOUR COURSE (SEE ALSO CH.1)
Some course features
Birmingham Urban and Regional Planning is offered combined with Geography. A joint degree in Planning is offered with Economics or Social Policy and a programme in Spatial Planning and Business Management is also available.
Oxford Brookes Two degrees, Planning and Property Development, and City and Regional Planning, are offered as Single Honours courses. The former is accredited by the RTPI when combined with the postgraduate diploma in Planning and the post-graduation Assessment of Professional Competence.
Sheffield Hallam An Urban and Environmental Planning degree is offered with options to specialise in regeneration, environment and conservation and design. A course in Geography and Planning is also available.

Universities and colleges teaching quality See www.qaa.ac.uk; http://unistats.direct.gov.uk.

Top research universities and colleges (RAE 2008) Sheffield; Cardiff; Newcastle; Leeds; Reading; Manchester; Glasgow; London (UCL).

Examples of sandwich degree courses Bristol UWE; Newcastle; Northumbria; Nottingham Trent; Sheffield Hallam.

ADMISSIONS INFORMATION
Number of applicants per place (approx) Birmingham 2; Birmingham City 6; Bristol UWE 6; Cardiff 6; Dundee 5; London (UCL) 6; London South Bank 3; Newcastle 9; Oxford Brookes 3; Sheffield Hallam 6.

OXFORD BROOKES UNIVERSITY

A CENTRE FOR EXCELLENCE

The UK's first 24/24 HEFCE teaching quality Planning Department

Undergraduate honours degrees

BA (Hons)
City and Regional Planning
RTPI accredited

MPlan (Hons)
City and Regional Planning
RICS / RTPI accredited

BA (Hons)
Planning and Property Development
RICS / RTPI accredited

Our research was ranked 5th in the 2008 RAE research power tables for town and country planning.

We also offer a range of postgraduate courses in areas such as climate change, environmental assessment and technology, historic conservation, spatial planning, tourism, international urban planning and urban design.

For more information:
www.planning.brookes.ac.uk

Telephone **+44 (0) 1865 483450** or email **gbutinawatson@brookes.ac.uk**

Advice to applicants and planning the UCAS personal statement Visit your local planning office and discuss the career with planners. Know plans and proposed developments in your area and any objections to them. Study the history of town planning worldwide and the development of new towns in the United Kingdom during the 20th century, for example Bournville, Milton Keynes, Port Sunlight, Welwyn Garden City, Cumbernauld, and the advantages and disadvantages which became apparent. **Oxford Brookes** See entry under **Surveying**.

Selection interviews Yes Bristol UWE, London (UCL), London South Bank, Newcastle, Oxford Brookes (interviews for promising applicants; no offers to applicants not interviewed); **Some** Abertay Dundee, Anglia Ruskin, Birmingham City, Cardiff, Dundee.

Interview advice and questions Since Town and Country Planning courses are vocational, work experience in a planning office is relevant and questions are likely to be asked on the type of work done and the problems faced by planners. Questions in recent years have included: If you were re-planning your home county for the future, what points would you consider? How are statistics used in urban planning? How do you think the problem of inner cities can be solved? Have you visited your local planning office? See also **Chapter 6**.

Reasons for rejection (non-academic) Lack of commitment to study for a professional qualification in Town Planning.

AFTER-RESULTS ADVICE
Offers to applicants repeating A-levels Higher Bristol UWE, Newcastle; **Same** Abertay Dundee, Birmingham City, Cardiff, Dundee, London South Bank, Oxford Brookes.

GRADUATE DESTINATIONS AND EMPLOYMENT (2009/10 HESA)
Graduates surveyed 2675 **Employed** 1170 **In voluntary employment** 25 **In further study** 500 **Assumed unemployed** 160

Check **Chapter 4** when choosing your university and **Chapter 7** on how to read the subject tables.

NICK THORNE

PGDip Urban Design: award winner of the Urban Design
Group's Francis Tibbalds Student Award in February 2010

OXFORD
BROOKES
UNIVERSITY

Questions and answers:

1. Before you came to Brookes what did you study and where?

I graduated in 2005 at De Montfort University, Leicester with a BA (Hons) in Architecture studied in a part time format. Prior to this I studied at Northampton University for an HNC in Building Studies. During both courses I gained valuable experience working in practices concentrated primarily within the residential sector.

2. What made you choose Brookes as a place to study?

I chose Brookes as a location to study for my Part 2 Diploma after recommendation by work colleagues that had previously studied at the university. I was impressed with their portfolios showing exciting projects with a professional finish. I viewed other student's work in the Architecture Yearbook (downloaded from the university website) and liked the blend of conceptual and grounded projects that could offer me an opportunity to explore alternative methods for designing the built environment which could in turn benefit my work in practice.

3. What do you think of the course now you're here?

As a part time student the course has provided me with a creative freedom to explore new ideas whilst balancing a more traditional approach to design within the office. The lecturers are keen for students to develop concepts and expect projects to be justified in critiques as preparation for presenting to a public audience. The course is

one of the best things I have ever done and has enabled me to pursue areas of conceptual architecture that are often limited within an office environment.

4. What are your plans for when you've completed your course, for work or further study?

In the year between completing my Part 2 and preparing for my Part 3 I hope to further my work experience and am looking forward to completing my professional exams at Brookes. In the long term, I hope to setup my own practice and utilise the knowledge gained during my studying and work experiences.

5. What are the best bits of studying at Brookes?

The most enjoyable part of studying at Brookes has been mixing with other likeminded people passionate about architecture. The university offers a range of useful resources that can assist in creating a rich variety of presentation methods. I particularly enjoyed using the laser cutter in the architecture workshop to build scale models of my proposed designs.

6. What advice do you have for others?

The course is very demanding and requires dedication and self-motivation. Expect to lose your weekends to coursework and look forward to many late nights and early mornings! The Diploma can provide a huge sense of reward when at the end of the course you present a high quality portfolio that includes an interesting and diverse range of material for promoting to prospective employers.

All images are examples of Nick Thorne's award winning work.

Career note Town planning graduates have a choice of career options within local authority planning offices. In addition to working on individual projects on urban development, they will also be involved in advising, co-ordinating and adjudicating in disputes and appeals. Planners also work closely with economists, surveyors and sociologists and their skills open up a wide range of other careers.

OTHER DEGREE SUBJECTS FOR CONSIDERATION

Architecture; Countryside Management; Environmental Studies; Geography; Heritage Management; Housing; Land Economy; Property; Public Administration; Real Estate; Sociology; Surveying; Transport Management.

TRANSPORT MANAGEMENT and PLANNING

(including **Logistics, Transport Design** and **Supply Chain Management**; see also **Engineering/ Engineering Sciences, Town and Country Planning**)

Transport Management and Planning is a specialised branch of business studies with many applications on land, sea and air. It is not as popular as the less specialised Business Studies courses but is just as relevant and will provide the student with an excellent introduction to management and its problems.

Useful websites www.cilt-international.com; www.transportweb.com; www.nats.co.uk; www.ciltuk. org.uk.

COURSE OFFERS INFORMATION

Subject requirements/preferences GCSE English and mathematics required. **AL** No subjects specified.

Birmingham GCSE mathematics grade B required.

Your target offers and examples of courses provided by each institution
360 pts **Leeds** – AAA (Econ Trans St)
340 pts **Cardiff** – AAB (Bus Mgt (Log Ops))
         City – AAB 340 pts (Air Trans Ops Mgt)
         Leeds – AAB (Mgt Trans St) (IB 35 pts HL 17 pts)
320 pts **Aston** – BBB–ABB 300–320 pts (Trans Mgt) (IB 32 pts)
300 pts **Aston** – BBB–ABB 300–320 pts (Log) (IB 32 pts)
         Northumbria – 280–300 pts (Trans Des)
         Ulster – 300 pts incl CC (Trans Plan)
280 pts **Loughborough** – 280 pts (Air Trans Mgt)
         Northumbria – 280–300 pts (Bus Log Sply Chn Mgt)
260 pts **Coventry** – BCC 260 pts (Trans Mgt Log)
         Edinburgh Napier – 260 pts (Civ Trans Eng BEng)
         Huddersfield – 260 pts (Air Trans Log Mgt)
         LJMU – 260 pts (Mgt Trans Log)
240 pts **Bristol UWE** – 240–280 pts (Plan Trans)
         Bucks New – 240–280 pts (Air Trans Plt Trg)
         Coventry – 240 pts (Auto Trans Des)
         Plymouth – 240 pts (Cru Mgt)
220 pts **Southampton Solent** – 220–240 pts (Cru Ind Mgt)
200 pts **Bucks New** – contact University 200–240 pts (Airln Airpt Mgt)
         Plymouth – 200 pts (Mar St (Navig/Ocn Ychtg/Merchnt Ship))
180 pts **Greenwich** – 180–220 pts (Bus Log Trans Mgt)
120 pts **Swansea Met** – 120–160 pts (Log Sply Chn Mgt)

Check **Chapter 4** when choosing your university and **Chapter 7** on how to read the subject tables.

Alternative offers
See **Chapter 7** and **Appendix 1** for grades/UCAS Tariff points information for the International Baccalaureate, Scottish Highers/Advanced Highers, the Welsh Baccalaureate, the Irish Leaving Certificate, the Cambridge Pre-U Diploma, the Advanced Diploma and the Extended Project.

EXAMPLES OF FOUNDATION DEGREES IN THE SUBJECT FIELD
Bradford; Greenwich; Suffolk (Univ Campus).

CHOOSING YOUR COURSE (SEE ALSO CH.1)
Some course features
Aston (Log Mgt) This is a business course focusing on the supply chain and distribution industry. There is a four-year course involving paid professional experience.
Bucks New (Air Trans Plt Trg) Students who fail to achieve any of the pilot training modules have the option to transfer to Transport with Pilot Training or Airline and Airport Management.
LJMU (Mgt Trans Log) The course is accredited by the Chartered Institute of Logistics and Transport; there is an option for a placement/sandwich year in industry.
Loughborough (Trans Bus Mgt; Air Trans Mgt) Courses include a year in industry. French, German and Spanish modules can be selected.

Universities and colleges teaching quality See www.qaa.ac.uk; http://unistats.direct.gov.uk.

Examples of sandwich degree courses Aston; City; Huddersfield; LJMU; Loughborough; Plymouth; Sheffield Hallam.

ADMISSIONS INFORMATION
Number of applicants per place (approx) Aston 5; Coventry 5; Huddersfield 5; Loughborough 11.

Advice to applicants and planning the UCAS personal statement Air, sea, road and rail transport are the main specialist areas. Contacts with those involved and work experience or work shadowing should be described in full. **City** (Air Trans Ops ATPL) Applicants need a Class 1 Medical Certificate from the UK Civil Aviation Authority and preferably to have taken a pilot aptitude test before starting the course. Check with admissions.

Selection interviews **Yes** Huddersfield, Loughborough; **Some** Aston, Bucks New.

Interview advice and questions Some knowledge of the transport industry (land, sea and air) is likely to be important at interview. Reading around the subject is also important, as are any contacts with management staff in the industries. Past questions have included: What developments are taking place to reduce the number of cars on the roads? What transport problems are there in your own locality? How did you travel to your interview? What problems did you encounter? How could they have been overcome? See also **Chapter 6**.

AFTER-RESULTS ADVICE
Offers to applicants repeating A-levels **Same** Aston.

GRADUATE DESTINATIONS AND EMPLOYMENT (2009/10 HESA)
Career note Many graduates will aim for openings linked with specialisms in their degree courses. These could cover air, rail, sea, bus or freight transport in which they will be involved in the management and control of operations as well as marketing and financial operations.

OTHER DEGREE SUBJECTS FOR CONSIDERATION
Air Transport Engineering; Civil Engineering; Environmental Studies; Logistics; Marine Transport; Town and Country Planning; Urban Studies.

VETERINARY SCIENCE/MEDICINE

(including **Bioveterinary Sciences** and **Veterinary Nursing**; see also **Animal Sciences**)

Veterinary Medicine/Science degrees enable students to acquire the professional skills and experience to qualify as veterinary surgeons. Courses follow the same pattern and combine a rigorous scientific training with practical experience. The demand for these courses is considerable (see below) and work experience is essential prior to application. Graduate entry programmes provide a route to qualifying as a vet to graduates with good degrees in specified subjects. See also **Appendix 3**. Veterinary Nursing Honours degree courses combine both the academic learning and the nursing training required by the Royal College of Veterinary Surgeons, and can also include practice management. Foundation degrees in Veterinary Nursing are more widely available. Bioveterinary Sciences are usually three-year full-time BSc degree courses focusing on animal biology, management and disease but do not qualify graduates to work as vets. For places in Veterinary Science/Medicine, applicants may select only four universities. Applicants to the University of Cambridge Veterinary School and the Royal Veterinary College, University of London are required to sit the BioMedical Admissions Test (BMAT) (see **Chapter 6**).

Useful websites www.rcvs.org.uk; www.admissionstests.cambridgeassessment.org.uk; www.bvna.org. uk; www.spvs.org.uk.

NB The points totals shown to the left of the institutions are for ease of reference only. It must not be assumed that Tariff points are always used by institutions or that they can be substituted for an offer in grades. The level of an offer is not necessarily indicative of the quality of a course.

COURSE OFFERS INFORMATION

Subject requirements/preferences GCSE (Vet Sci/Med) Grade B English, mathematics, physics, dual science if not at A-level. **Bristol** (Vet Sci/Med) Grade A in five or six GCSE subjects. **Bristol, Glasgow** Grade A or B in physics. **Glasgow** (Vet Sci/Med) Grade A or B in GCSE physics. **Liverpool** (Vet Sci/ Med) English, mathematics, physics, dual science grade B if not at A-level. (Vet Nurs) Five subjects including English and two science. **AL** (Vet Sci/Med) See offers below. (Vet Nurs) Biology and another science may be required. **Other** Work experience essential for Vet Sci/Med and Vet Nurs courses and preferred for other courses: check requirements. Health checks may be required.

Your target offers and examples of courses provided by each institution
390 pts Liverpool – AABb (Vet Sci) (IB 36 pts HL 666)
380 pts Cambridge – A*AA incl 3 AL sci subjs pref (Vet Med) (IB 40–42 pts)
360 pts Bristol – A*AA–AAA incl chem+biol 360–380 pts (Vet Sci) (IB 38–37 pts HL 666)
        Edinburgh – AAA (incl chem+biol+maths/phys) (Vet Med) (IB 36 pts)
        Glasgow – AAA incl A chem+biol (Vet Med) (IB 36 pts)
        London (RVC) – AAA–AAB incl AL chem+biol +1 other (Vet Med)
340 pts Bristol – AAB (Vet Sci incl Pre-Vet Yr) (IB 35 pts HL 666)
        Nottingham – AAB incl biol/chem (Vet Med + Prelim Yr) (IB 38 pts HL 76)
        Surrey – AAB (Vet Biosci) (IB 35 pts)
320 pts Glasgow – ABB incl chem+biol (Vet Biosci) (IB 32 pts)
300 pts Liverpool – BBB incl biol sci (Biovet Sci) (IB 32 pts HL 6 biol 5 sci)
        London (RVC) – BBB incl chem+maths/phys/biol +1 other (Biovet Sci 3 yrs)
280 pts Bristol – BBC incl biol+chem BB (Vet Nurs Biovet Sci) (IB 30 pts HL 655)
        Bristol UWE – 280 pts incl biol (Biovet Sci) (IB 24 pts)
        Lincoln – 280 pts incl biol (Biovet Sci)
        Middlesex – 200–280 pts (Vet Nurs)
260 pts Harper Adams (UC) – AAA–BBB 260–300 pts (Vet Nurs Prac Mgt)
240 pts Edinburgh Napier – CCC 240 pts (Vet Nurs)
        London (RVC) – CCC incl chem+biol (Vet Gateway prog 1 yr)
220 pts West Anglia (Coll) – 220 pts (Vet Nurs App Anim Bhv)
200 pts Bristol UWE – 200–260 pts (incl biol) (Vet Nurs Sci) (IB 26 pts)
        Myerscough (Coll) – 200 pts (Vet Nurs)

160 pts London (RVC) – CC–AA incl 2 sci pref biol (Vet Nurs)
Warwickshire (Coll) – 160 pts (Vet Nrs)

Alternative offers

See **Chapter 7** and **Appendix 1** for grades/UCAS Tariff points information for the International Baccalaureate, Scottish Highers/Advanced Highers, the Welsh Baccalaureate, the Irish Leaving Certificate, the Cambridge Pre-U Diploma, the Advanced Diploma and the Extended Project.

EXAMPLES OF FOUNDATION DEGREES IN THE SUBJECT FIELD

Askham Bryan (Coll); Bicton (Coll); Bristol UWE; Duchy (Coll); Greenwich; Hadlow (Coll); Harper Adams (UC); Myerscough (Coll); Nottingham Trent; Reaseheath (Coll); Sparsholt (Coll); Warwickshire (Coll).

OTHER HIGHER EDUCATION COURSES IN THIS FIELD

London (RVC).

CHOOSING YOUR COURSE (SEE ALSO CH.1)

Some course features

Author's note Veterinary Science/Medicine is a most intensely competitive subject and, as in the case of Medicine, one or two offers and three rejections are not uncommon. As a result, the Royal College of Veterinary Surgeons has raised a number of points which are relevant to applicants and advisers.

1 Every candidate for a Veterinary Medicine/Science degree course should be advised to spend a suitable period with a veterinarian in practice.
2 A period spent in veterinary work may reveal a hitherto unsuspected allergy or sensitivity following contact with various animals.
3 Potential applicants should be under no illusions about the difficulty of the task they have set themselves... at least five applicants for every available place... with no likelihood of places being increased at the present time.
4 There are so many candidates who can produce the necessary level of scholastic attainment that other considerations have to be taken into account in making the choice. In most cases, the number of GCSE grade As will be crucial. This is current practice. Headteachers' reports and details of applicants' interests, activities and background are very relevant and are taken fully into consideration... applicants are reminded to include details of periods of time spent with veterinary surgeons.
5 Any applicant who has not received an offer but who achieves the grades required for admission ought to get in touch, as soon as the results are known, with the schools and enquire about the prospects of entry at the Clearing stage. All courses cover the same subject topics.

Bristol UWE The degree in Veterinary Nursing Science includes 70 weeks of work placement and leads to the RCVS qualification. This course and that of the Foundation Veterinary Nursing Science take place at Hartpury College, Gloucester.

Edinburgh The curriculum of the Veterinary Medicine course falls into three interrelated main parts. The first (pre-clinical) covers the biology and chemistry of the animal body, and the second (foundation clinical studies) deals with the surgery, diagnostic imaging, anaesthesia and pharmacology.

London (RVC) (Vet Gateway) Course guarantees a place on the five-year Veterinary Medicine programme. Applicants require chemistry and biology and any other subject at A-level (except general studies) and there are other conditions for eligibility (see www.rvc.ac.uk). (BSc Biovet Sci 3 yr) Course does not qualify graduates to practise as veterinary surgeons. There is also a six-year Veterinary Medicine Combined course.

Nottingham The course which involves the Preliminary Year is for students without the required science qualifications but who have high academic achievement in non-science or vocational subjects. Successful completion of the course enables direct entry into Year 1 of the five-year course.

Surrey The degree in Veterinary Biosciences focuses on animal health and disease. There are opportunities for professional placements.

Universities and colleges teaching quality See www.qaa.ac.uk; http://unistats.direct.gov.uk.

Top research universities and colleges (RAE 2008) See **Agricultural Sciences/Agriculture**.

Examples of sandwich degree courses Bristol UWE (Vet Nurs); Harper Adams (UC) (Vet Nurs).

ADMISSIONS INFORMATION

Number of applicants per place (approx) Bristol (Vet Sci) 12, (Vet Nurs Biovet Sci) 6; Cambridge 5; Edinburgh 17; Glasgow 20; Liverpool 12; London (RVC) 5; Nottingham 11.

Numbers of applicants (**a** UK **b** EU (non-UK) **c** non-EU **d** mature) London (RVC) **a**759 **b**71 **c**156 **d**172.

Advice to applicants and planning the UCAS personal statement Applicants for Veterinary Science must limit their choices to four universities and submit their applications by 15 October. They may add one alternative course. Work experience is almost always essential so discuss this in full, giving information about the size and type of practice and the type of work in which you were involved. See also **Appendix 3**. **Bristol** Six weeks of work experience including two weeks in a veterinary practice, one week lambing and one week on a dairy farm. **Cambridge** Work experience expected. **Edinburgh** Competition for places is intense: 72 places are available and only one in seven applicants will receive an offer. The strongest candidates are interviewed and are normally required to take with them an additional reference outlining recent work experience with large and small animals; examples include dairy or lambing experience, kennels or catteries, or an abattoir visit. **Glasgow** A minimum of two weeks in a veterinary practice plus experience of work on a dairy farm, working at a stables, assisting at lambing, work at a cattery or kennels and if possible a visit to an abattoir. Additional experience at a zoo or wildlife park. **Liverpool** The selection process involves three areas: academic ability to cope with the course; knowledge of vocational aspects of veterinary science acquired through work experience in veterinary practice and six further weeks of experience working with animals; personal attributes that demonstrate responsibility and self-motivation. **London (RVC)** Six weeks' hands-on experience needed: two weeks in a veterinary practice, and two weeks in another animal environment, for example riding school, zoo, kennels. **Nottingham** Six weeks (minimum) of work experience required and preferably one day at an abattoir.

Misconceptions about this course Bristol UWE (Vet Nurs Sci) Students think that the degree qualifies them as veterinary nurses but in fact RCVS assessment/training is additional. **Liverpool** (Biovet Sci) Some applicants think that the course allows students to transfer to Veterinary Science: it does not.

Selection interviews (Vet Sci and Vet Nurs) All institutions **Yes** Bristol, London (RVC).

Interview advice and questions Past questions have included: Why do you want to be a vet? Have you visited a veterinary practice? What did you see? Do you think there should be a Vet National Health Service? What are your views on vivisection? What are your views on intensive factory farming? How can you justify thousands of pounds of taxpayers' money being spent on training you to be a vet when it could be used to train a civil engineer? When would you feel it your responsibility to tell battery hen farmers that they were being cruel to their livestock? What are your views on vegetarians? How does aspirin stop pain? Why does it only work for a certain length of time? Do you eat beef? Outline the bovine TB problem. Questions on A-level science syllabus. See also **Chapter 6**. **Glasgow** Applicants complete a questionnaire prior to interview. Questions cover experience with animals, reasons for choice of career, animal welfare, teamwork, work experience, stressful situations.

Reasons for rejection (non-academic) Failure to demonstrate motivation. Lack of basic knowledge or understanding of ethical and animal issues.

AFTER-RESULTS ADVICE

Offers to applicants repeating A-levels Higher London (RVC); **Same** Bristol UWE (Vet Nurs Sci), Liverpool (candidates achieving the necessary grades are welcome to reapply); **No** Cambridge, Edinburgh, Glasgow.

Check **Chapter 4** when choosing your university and **Chapter 7** on how to read the subject tables.

GRADUATE DESTINATIONS AND EMPLOYMENT (2009/10 HESA)
Graduates surveyed 660 **Employed** 520 **In voluntary employment** 15 **In further study** 40
Assumed unemployed 35

Career note Over 80% of veterinary surgeons work in private practice with the remainder involved in research in universities, government-financed research departments and in firms linked with farming, foodstuff manufacturers and pharmaceutical companies.

OTHER DEGREE SUBJECTS FOR CONSIDERATION
Agricultural Science; Agriculture; Animal Sciences; Biological Sciences; Biology; Dentistry; Equine Dental Science; Equine Management; Equine Studies; Medicine; Zoology.

ZOOLOGY

(including **Animal Biology**; see also **Agricultural Sciences/Agriculture, Animal Sciences, Biological Sciences, Biology**)

Zoology courses have a biological science foundation and could cover animal ecology, marine and fisheries biology, animal population, development and behaviour and, on some courses, wildlife management and fisheries.

Useful websites www.scienceyear.com; www.zsl.org/ioz; www.zsl.org; www.academicinfo.net/zoo.html.

NB The points totals shown to the left of the institutions are for ease of reference only. It must not be assumed that Tariff points are always used by institutions or that they can be substituted for an offer in grades. The level of an offer is not necessarily indicative of the quality of a course.

COURSE OFFERS INFORMATION
Subject requirements/preferences **GCSE** English and science/mathematics required or preferred. **AL** One or two sciences will be required.

Your target offers and examples of courses provided by each institution
380 pts **Bristol** – A*AA–AAB 340–380 pts (Zool) (IB 38–35 pts HL 666)
Cambridge – A*AA (Nat Sci (Zool)) (IB 40–42 pts)
360 pts **Imperial London** – AAA (Zool) (IB 38 pts HL 66)
Manchester – AAA–ABB 320–360 pts (Zool (Yr Ind)) (IB 37–33 pts)
Sheffield – AAA incl biol sci (Zool MBiol) (IB 37 pts)
Southampton – AAA–ABB 360–320 pts (Zool) (IB 36–32 pts HL 18–16 pts)
340 pts **Birmingham** – AAB–ABB 320–340 pts (Biol Sci (Zool)) (IB 32–34 pts)
Cardiff – AAB–ABB (Zool) (IB 34 pts HL 5 biol chem)
Exeter – AAB–BBB (Zool courses) (IB 34 pts)
Leeds – AAB–BBB 300–340 pts (Zool) (IB 36–32 pts HL 16–15 pts)
Nottingham – AAB–ABB (Zool) (IB 32–34 pts)
St Andrews – AAb (Zool) (IB 32 pts)
Sheffield – AAB incl biol sci (Zool BSc) (IB 35 pts)
320 pts **Durham** – ABB (Zool) (IB 34 pts HL 55)
Edinburgh – AAA–ABB 320–360 pts (Zool) (IB 37–32 pts)
Glasgow – ABB (Zool) (IB 32 pts)
Leicester – ABB (Biol Sci (Zool)) (IB 32 pts)
Liverpool – ABB (Zool) (IB 33 pts HL 6 biol)
Newcastle – AAB–ABB 320–340 pts (Zool) (IB 32 pts)
Reading – 320 pts (Zool)
Roehampton – 320 pts (Zool)
Swansea – ABB (Zool) (IB 33 pts)
300 pts **Aberdeen** – BBB (Zool) (IB 28 pts)
Glamorgan – BBB (Int Wldlf Biol)

London (QM) – BBB (Zool Aqua Biol) (IB 30 pts)
London (RH) – 300–320 pts (Zool) (IB 34 pts)
Queen's Belfast – BBB (Zool) (IB 28 pts HL 555)
280 pts Aberystwyth – 280–320 pts (Microbiol Zool) (IB 27 pts)
Bangor – 280–340 pts (Zoology MZool)
Derby – 280 pts (Zool) (IB 26 pts)
Hull – 280–300 pts (Aqua Zool; Zool)
Manchester Met – 280 pts (Wldlf Biol) (IB 27 pts)
260 pts Bangor – 260–320 pts (Mar Biol Zool) (IB 28 pts)
LJMU – 260–300 pts (Zool) (IB 25 pts)
Nottingham Trent – 260 pts (Zoo Biol) (IB 26 pts)
240 pts Anglia Ruskin – 240 pts (Zool) (IB 24 pts)
Bangor – 240–280 pts (Zool Anim Ecol) (IB 28 pts)
West Scotland – CCC (App Biosci Zool)
200 pts Salford – 200 pts (Zool; Wldlf Cons Zoo Biol)

Alternative offers
See **Chapter 7** and **Appendix 1** for grades/UCAS Tariff points information for the International Baccalaureate, Scottish Highers/Advanced Highers, the Welsh Baccalaureate, the Irish Leaving Certificate, the Cambridge Pre-U Diploma, the Advanced Diploma and the Extended Project.

EXAMPLES OF FOUNDATION DEGREES IN THE SUBJECT FIELD
See also **Animal Sciences**. Cornwall (Coll); Sparsholt (Coll).

CHOOSING YOUR COURSE (SEE ALSO CH.1)
Some course features
See **Biological Sciences**.

Anglia Ruskin (Zool) Study in the USA is an option for one semester.
Durham All Biological Sciences degrees have a common first year, with transfers possible to other degrees or to Natural Sciences in the second year.
Hull (Aqua Zool) Course focuses on the interface between land and water and expands on the animal biology aspects of marine and freshwater biology.
Stirling (Aqua) Exchange programmes with universities in Sweden and the USA are offered.

Universities and colleges teaching quality See www.qaa.ac.uk; http://unistats.direct.gov.uk.

Examples of sandwich degree courses Cardiff; Leeds; LJMU; Manchester; Nottingham Trent.

ADMISSIONS INFORMATION
Number of applicants per place (approx) Aberystwyth 8; Bangor 3; Bristol 13; Cardiff 8; Durham 11; Leeds 7; LJMU 6; London (RH) 6; Newcastle 15; Nottingham 6; Southampton 7; Swansea 6.

Advice to applicants and planning the UCAS personal statement Interests in animals should be described, together with any first-hand experience gained. Visits to zoos, farms, fish farms etc and field courses attended should be described, together with any special points of interest that you noted.

Selection interviews Yes Durham, Hull, Liverpool, London (RH), Newcastle; **Some** Cardiff, Derby, Roehampton, Swansea; **No** Dundee.

Interview advice and questions Past questions have included: Why do you want to study Zoology? What career do you hope to follow on graduation? Specimens may be given to identify. Questions usually asked on the A-level subjects. See also **Chapter 6**.

AFTER-RESULTS ADVICE
Offers to applicants repeating A-levels Higher Bristol, Hull, Leeds, Swansea; **Same** Aberystwyth, Bangor, Cardiff, Derby, Dundee, Durham, Liverpool, LJMU, London (RH), Roehampton, Swansea.

Check **Chapter 4** when choosing your university and **Chapter 7** on how to read the subject tables.

GRADUATE DESTINATIONS AND EMPLOYMENT (2009/10 HESA)
Graduates surveyed 1025 **Employed** 405 **In voluntary employment** 45 **In further study** 245
Assumed unemployed 75

Career note See **Biology**.

OTHER DEGREE SUBJECTS FOR CONSIDERATION
Animal Ecology; Animal Sciences; Aquaculture; Biological Sciences; Biology; Ecology; Fisheries
Management; Marine Biology; Parasitology; Veterinary Science; Wildlife Management.

The choice of a subject to study (from over 50,000 degree courses) and of a university or college (from more than 300 institutions) is a major task for students living in the United Kingdom (UK). For overseas and European Union (EU) applicants it is even greater, and the decisions that have to be made need much careful planning, preferably beginning two years before the start of the course. **NB** Beware that there are some private institutions offering bogus degrees: check www.ucas.com for your university and college choices.

APPLICATIONS AND THE POINTS-BASED IMMIGRATION SYSTEM

In addition to submitting your application through UCAS (see **Chapter 5**) a new Points-based Immigration System is now in operation for overseas students. The main features of this system include:

- **Visa letters** Students will require a special 'visa letter' from their universities before being admitted. This will be sent to you by the university in time for you to apply for your visa.
- **Maintenance** Students will need to show that they are able to pay for the first year's tuition fees, plus £600 per month for accommodation and living expenses. Additional funds and regulations apply for those bringing dependants into the UK.
- **Proof of qualifications** Your visa letter will list all the qualifications that you submitted to obtain your university place and original proof will be required for these qualifications when submitting your visa application. These documents will be checked by the Home Office. Any fraudulent documents will result in your visa application being rejected and a possible ban from entering the UK for 10 years.
- **Attendance** Once you have started your course, your attendance will be monitored. Non-attending students will be reported to the UK Border Agency.

Full details can be obtained from www.ukcisa.org.uk/student/index.php.

SELECTION, ADMISSION AND FINANCE

The first reason for making early contact with your preferred institution is to check their requirements for your chosen subject and their selection policies for overseas applicants. For example, for all Art and some Architecture courses you will have to present a portfolio of work or slides. For Music courses your application often will have to be accompanied by a recording you have made of your playing or singing and, in many cases, a personal audition will be necessary. Attendance at an interview in this country is compulsory for some universities and for some courses. At other institutions the interview may take place either in the UK or with a university or college representative in your own country.

The ability to speak and write good English is essential and many institutions require evidence of competence, for example scores from the International English Language Testing System (IELTS) or from the Test of English as a Foreign Language (TOEFL) (see www.ielts.org and www.ets.org/toefl). For some institutions you may have to send examples of your written work. Each institution provides information about its English language entry requirements and a summary of this is given for each university listed below. International students should note that the recommended threshold for minimum English language requirements is IELTS 6.5–7.0. Recent research indicates that students with a lower score may have difficulty in dealing with their course.

At the end of this book you will find a directory of universities and colleges in the UK, together with their contact details. Most universities and colleges in the UK have an overseas student adviser who can advise you on these and other points you need to consider, such as passports, visas, entry certificates, evidence of financial support, medical certificates, medical insurance, and the numbers of overseas students in the university from your own country. All these details are very important and need to be considered at the same time as choosing your course and institution.

The subject tables in **Chapter 8** provide a comprehensive picture of courses on offer and of comparative entry levels. However, before making an application, other factors should be considered such as English language entry requirements (see above), the availability of English language teaching, living costs, tuition fees and any scholarships or other awards which might be offered. Detailed information about these can be obtained from the international offices in each university or college, from British higher education fairs throughout the world and from the British Council offices abroad and from websites: see www.britishcouncil.org; www.education.org.

Below is a brief summary of the arrangements made by each university in the UK for students aiming to take a full-time degree programme. The information is presented as follows:

- Institution.
- International student numbers.
- English language entry requirements for degree programmes shown in either IELTS or TOEFL scores. These vary between universities and courses. For the IELTS, scores can range from 5.5 to 7.5, and for the TOEFL computer-based test, scores can range from a minimum of 213; for the written TOEFL the usual minimum entry level is 5.0. For full details contact the university or college.
- Arrangements for English tuition.
- International Foundation courses.
- Annual tuition fees (approximate) for full-time undergraduate degree courses. Tuition fees also usually include fees for examinations and graduation. These figures are approximate and are subject to change each year. EU students pay 'home student' fees, except for those from the Channel Islands and the Isle of Man; students from the British Overseas Territories are now treated as home students for fee purposes at universities and other institutions of higher education.
- Annual living costs. These are also approximate and represent the costs for a single student over the year. The living costs shown cover university accommodation (usually guaranteed for the first year only), food, books, clothing and travel in the UK, but not travel to or from the UK. (Costs are likely to rise year by year in line with the rate of inflation in the UK, currently around 3% per year.) Overseas students are normally permitted to take part-time work for a period of up to 20 hours per week.
- Scholarships and awards for non-EU students (most universities offer awards for EU students).

UNIVERSITY INFORMATION AND FEES FOR UNDERGRADUATE INTERNATIONAL STUDENTS

Discussions are taking place at Government level on an increase in tuition fees from 2012. These could affect the fees charged for courses for non-EU/international students. Intending applicants should therefore check university websites before applying. **The fees published below (unless otherwise stated) are those being charged to students in 2011/12 (check websites for 2013/14 fees).**

Aberdeen Approximately 14% of students come from 120 nationalities. IELTS 6.0; for Medicine 7.0. Four-week English course available in August before the start of the academic year. *Fees:* £10,500–£13,200. Clinical Medicine £24,000. *Living costs:* £6000–£7000. Part-time work available (up to 20 hours a week) through Joblink.

Aberdeen (Coll) *Fees:* Non-advanced courses: £5500.

Abertay Dundee About 10% of the student population are international students. *English language entry requirement (or equivalent):* IELTS 5.5. Pre-sessional English course available, also full-time English course September to May and free English tuition throughout degree course. *Fees:* £9500. *Living costs:* £6000–£7000.

Aberystwyth A large number of international students. *English language entry requirement (or equivalent):* IELTS 6.5. Full-time tuition in English available. *Fees:* Arts subjects £8500, Science subjects £9500. *Living costs:* £6000–£7000. International excellence scholarships £1500 per year. Business studies bursaries £500.

Anglia Ruskin International students 21%. *English language entry requirement (or equivalent):* IELTS 5.5. A one-year International Foundation programme available. *Fees:* Arts subjects £9300, Science subjects £10,300. Teacher education £16,500. *Living costs:* £9800.

Arts London A large number of international students. *English language entry requirement (or equivalent):* IELTS 6.5. Courses in Fashion Promotion, Acting, Directing require IELTS 7.5. Language Centre courses in academic English for 12, 24, 34 or 36 weeks. *Fees:* £12,700. *Living costs:* £10,000–£11,000. Scholarships and bursaries available.

Askham Bryan (Coll) *Fees:* Foundation/Bachelor Degree £5500, FE/vocational course £5000.

Aston Over 1000 international students from over 80 countries, with 15% of the total student population from overseas. International Orientation programme at the beginning of the academic year. *English language entry requirement (or equivalent):* IELTS 6.0–6.5. International Foundation programme offered as a bridge to the degree courses. Pre-sessional English classes also available of five and 10 weeks duration. *Fees:* Non-Science programmes £11,700, Social Science and Computing courses £12,950, Engineering and Science courses £14,700. *Living costs:* £7000–£8000. Scholarships offered, including bursaries for Engineering and Science subjects.

Bangor Ten per cent of the student population is made up of international students from 70 countries. Lower cost of living than many other UK cities. *English language entry requirement (or equivalent):* IELTS 6.0. Pre-study English course starting September, January or April depending on level of English proficiency, leads to International Foundation course. One-month or two-month courses before starting degree course also offered. *Fees:* Arts, Humanities and Social Science courses £9600, Business School £10,500, Science courses £11,800. *Living costs:* £6500. International entrance scholarships available.

Bath Over 1500 international students from around 100 countries. *English language entry requirement (or equivalent):* IELTS 6.0. Pre-degree language courses offered, ranging from one month to one year. *Fees:* £12,300–£15,700. *Living costs:* £8500–£9500. Scholarships and awards available, including residential awards for applicants from the Far East and Kenya.

Bath Spa Students from 40 countries. *English language entry requirement (or equivalent):* IELTS 6.0 for subjects supported by the Undergraduate Course for International Students (UCIS). Foundation courses available for students below this score. Subjects not supported by UCIS, entry level IELTS 6.0. *Fees:* £10,000 (plus studio fees £200–£300 for Art and Design courses). *Living costs:* £8000–£8500.

Bedfordshire Over 3000 EU and international students. *English language entry requirement (or equivalent):* IELTS 6.0. General English programmes are offered, including a summer school. *Fees:* £9600. *Living costs:* £6500–£7500.

Birmingham Over 4000 international students from 152 countries. *English language entry requirement (or equivalent):* IELTS 6.0. Courses in Law, Health Science, Medicine and Dentistry require IELTS 7.0. Six, 10 and 20-week English language programmes available, depending on language proficiency, ranging from IELTS 4.5 to 5.5. *Fees:* Non-laboratory subjects £11,340–£13,000, Laboratory subjects £14,650, Clinical Medicine £26,590. *Living costs:* £8000–£9000. International Foundation programme available. Awards are offered by some subject departments including Bioscience, Computer Science, Earth Sciences, Law, Psychology; there are also Engineering scholarships for students from Malaysia.

Birmingham (UC) *Fees:* £8400. *Living costs:* £7500–£8500.

Birmingham City Large number of international students. *English language entry requirement (or equivalent):* IELTS 6.0. Pre-sessional language courses and in-session language support. Orientation programme for all students. *Fees:* Non science courses £9600, lab-based courses £11,050, Conservatoire/Acting courses £12,600–£14,200. *Living costs:* £6000–£7000. Music bursaries.

Bolton Over 500 international students from 60 countries represented. *English language entry requirement (or equivalent):* IELTS 6.0. Courses start in September, some in January. Pre-sessional and in-session English tuition plus Access and Foundation programmes available in Business Management and Engineering. *Fees:* £7900. *Living costs:* £7000–£8000.

Bournemouth A large number of international students. *English language entry requirement (or equivalent):* IELTS 6.0. Preparatory English programme offered, starting in January, April or July depending on applicant's level of English (entry IELTS 4.5/5.0/5.5). Several language schools in the town (see www.englishuk.com.uk or www.baselt.org.uk). Pre-sessional study skills programme also offered. *Fees:* £9500–£11,500. *Living costs:* £7500–£8500. Some subject awards available.

Bradford Over 100 countries represented (22%). *English language entry requirement (or equivalent):* IELTS 6.0. Some students may be admitted to Year 2, depending on qualifications. *Fees:* Science and Engineering courses £12,350, other courses £9800. *Living costs:* £6000–£8500. Ten scholarships to cover the duration of the course.

Brighton Some 1400 international students from over 100 countries. *English language entry requirement (or equivalent):* IELTS 6.0 (or 5.5 for less linguistically demanding subjects). New four-year degree programme (UK4) includes preparatory year. *Fees:* £10,000–£11,500. Medicine £23,678. *Living costs:* £7000–£8000. Fixed fees possible. Merit scholarships for students from Norway and some countries in the Far East and Africa.

Bristol Approximately 1100 students from over 100 countries. *English language entry requirement (or equivalent):* IELTS 6.5 (possibly lower for some Science and Engineering subjects), 7.5 for Medicine. *Fees:* Arts subjects £11,900, Science subjects £14,950, Medicine £27,600. *Living costs:* £6500–£9000. Some bursaries and scholarships for one year from some subject departments including Law, Medicine, Dentistry and Veterinary Science.

Bristol UWE More than 1750 international students. *English language entry requirement (or equivalent):* IELTS 6.0. English language preparatory and pre-sessional courses offered. English modules can also be taken throughout your degree. *Fees:* £10,000–£10,500. *Living costs:* £6500–£9000. Some partial fee scholarships are available in Computing, Mathematics and Engineering, and Law scholarships for students from the Far East, South Africa, the West Indies and North America.

Brunel More than 2000 international students from over 110 countries. *English language entry requirement (or equivalent):* IELTS 6.0 for science/technology subjects, 7.0 for Law, 6.5 for other subjects. English language tuition offered during and before the course but only to improve existing skills. *Fees:* Non-laboratory subjects £9200, laboratory subjects £11,100. *Living costs:* £9500–£12,500. Twenty bursaries offered.

Buckingham Eighty nationalities represented at this small university. *English language entry requirement (or equivalent):* IELTS 6.0. *Fees:* Year 1 £15,060, Year 2 £15,360. *Living costs:* £8000–£9000. Tuition fee discount for students from the Bahamas, Bulgaria and India. Some scholarships for students from the Far East, Russia and Eastern Europe.

Bucks New Around 7.5% of student population are international students coming from 50 countries. *English language entry requirement (or equivalent):* IELTS 6.0. *Fees:* £8500–£9300. *Living costs:* £6000–£7000.

Cambridge Over 1000 international undergraduate students. *English language entry requirement (or equivalent):* IELTS 7.0 overall, with minimum of 6.0 in each element. TOEFL (written) 600 (minimum) and at least 5.0 in TOEFL test of written English. *Fees:* Arts, Humanities, Language and Social Science, Engineering and Science courses £11,829–£15,480. Clinical subjects £28,632, College fees £4400–£5200. *Living costs:* £8600. Awards available, also scholarships for students from Hong Kong.

Canterbury Christ Church International students from 80 countries. *English language entry requirement (or equivalent):* IELTS 6.0. *Fees:* £8880. *Living costs:* £9000.

Cardiff Over 3500 international students from 100 countries. *English language entry requirement (or equivalent):* IELTS 6.0–7.0. Comprehensive selection of pre-sessional language courses from three weeks to nine months. Induction course for all students. International Foundation courses for Business, Law, Engineering, Computer Science and Health and Life Sciences. *Fees:* Arts courses £10,700, science courses £13,750. *Living costs:* £6000–£8000. Law scholarships offered on the basis of academic merit.

Cardiff Met The University has over 800 international students enrolled from 120 different countries. *English language entry requirement (or equivalent):* IELTS 4.5. *Fees:* £8200–£9400. *Living costs:* £5500–£6500.

Chester *English language entry requirement (or equivalent):* IELTS 6.0. International Foundation year available for Business Studies students. *Fees:* £9750. *Living costs:* £6000–£7000.

Chichester International students from several countries. *English language entry requirement (or equivalent):* IELTS 6.0. *Fees:* £8700–£9990. *Living costs:* £7000–£8000.

City A large international community with students from over 160 countries. *English language entry requirement (or equivalent):* IELTS 6.0 (6.5 for Business, Law and Journalism). August and September pre-sessional English language courses, and in-session English workshops. International Foundation programmes in Law, Business, Engineering and Management. *Fees:* £9000–£12,750. *Living costs:* £10,500–£12,500. Scholarships available for applicants for Actuarial Science, Engineering (Cypriot applicants only) and Law.

Coventry About 2500 international students. *English language entry requirement (or equivalent):* IELTS 6.0. *Fees:* Classroom-based £9060, Lab-based £9380. *Living costs:* £6000–£7000. Scholarships available.

Creative Arts *Fees:* £8100–£10,660. *Living costs:* £7500–£10,000.

Cumbria *English language entry requirement (or equivalent):* IELTS 6.0. *Fees:* £8540. *Living costs:* £5000–£6000.

De Montfort Over 1000 international students from more than 100 countries. *English language entry requirement (or equivalent):* IELTS 6.5 (lower for some faculties). In-session English tuition in some degree courses. One-year International Foundation Certificate courses in Business and Law. Orientation programme in September for all students. *Fees:* £9250. *Living costs:* £8500–£9000. Some scholarships for overseas students.

Derby Students from 70 countries. *English language entry requirement (or equivalent):* IELTS 6.0. Courses offered to those needing tuition in English language. Foundation courses (£5200) and pre-sessional intensive English tuition (£2000) offered, and also language support whilst studying for degree. *Fees:* £9250. *Living costs:* £5000–£6000. International scholarships available for applicants from some countries in the Far East.

Dundee Students from 83 countries. *English language entry requirement (or equivalent):* IELTS 6.0. Foundation courses in English and for Business and Art and Design courses. *Fees:* Classroom-based courses £9200–£10,915, laboratory-based courses £10,500, pre-clinical £10,250, clinical courses £25,500. *Living costs:* £6500–£7500. Some awards for overseas students in Arts and Social Sciences, Law, Accountancy, Science and Engineering and Art and Design.

Durham Some 1600 international students from over 120 countries. *English language entry requirement (or equivalent):* IELTS 6.5. Three-day induction programme before the start of the academic year. Intensive English language course is provided if standard of English does not meet the required level. *Fees:* Classroom-based £11,970, Lab-based £15,300.

Edge Hill There is a small number of international students. *English language entry requirement (or equivalent):* IELTS 6.5. *Fees:* £9900. *Living costs:* £5000–£6000.

Edinburgh Some 4000 international students from 120 countries. *English language entry requirement (or equivalent):* IELTS 6.0–6.5. English language support. *Fees:* £12,050–£15,850, Technical Medicine £19,600, Clinical Medicine £23,500. *Living costs:* £7500–£10,000. Merit-based scholarships available, as well as specific scholarships for students from Africa or the Indian subcontinent.

Edinburgh (CA) *Fees:* £12,650.

Edinburgh Napier Approximately 4000 international students. *English language entry requirement (or equivalent):* IELTS 5.5. English language programmes in September and January; English language support through Foundation programmes. *Fees:* £9310–£10,820. *Living costs:* £7000–£9000.

Edinburgh Queen Margaret Some 400 international students from 50 countries. *English language entry requirement (or equivalent):* IELTS 5.5. *Fees:* £10,170–£11,200. *Living costs:* £7500. Some partial scholarships for self-funding students.

Essex International students from over 125 countries. *English language entry requirement (or equivalent):* IELTS 6.0–6.5. English language courses available before entry to degree course. *Fees:* Non-Science courses £10,750, lab-based courses £12,750. *Living costs:* £4000–£6000. Some funding available for students in need.

Euro Bus Sch London *Fees:* Fees are same as for Home/EU students - £11,300–£14,250.

Exeter Over 1500 international students from 120 countries. *English language entry requirement (or equivalent):* IELTS 6.5–7.0. Full-time Foundation programme in English, with opportunity to specialise in Physical Sciences, Computer Science, Business, Politics, History, Sociology or Law. Also pre-sessional courses in English starting in July, August or September as well as in-session support. *Fees:* Non-Science programmes £12,200, Combined Honours £13,400, Science and Engineering programmes £14,500, Pre-Clinical £14,500, Clinical £22,000. *Living costs:* £6500–£8500. Awards available, including some subject and South East Asian scholarships.

Glamorgan Some 1500 international students from 60 different countries. *English language entry requirement (or equivalent):* IELTS from 5.0. Pre-sessional course offered in English, and also a 10–14-week English language skills programme. An International Foundation programme is also offered. *Fees:* £9800. *Living costs:* £6500–£7500.

Glasgow Over 2000 international students. *English language entry requirement (or equivalent):* IELTS 6.5 (higher for some courses). The English as a Foreign Language Unit offers intensive five-week pre-sessional language courses in a Foundation programme covering English language and study skills. *Fees:* Arts and Social Science £10,750; Engineering, Science, Nursing £14,000; Clinical courses £24,750. *Living costs:* £6000–£7500. Fee-waiver scholarships and automatic Fourth Year scholarships available (not for Dentistry, Medicine or Veterinary Science).

Glasgow Caledonian Students from 70 countries. *English language entry requirement (or equivalent):* IELTS 6.0. English language programmes available. *Fees:* £9700–£14,500. *Living costs:* £8000.

Gloucestershire *English language entry requirement (or equivalent):* IELTS 5.5. English language support and mentor scheme with other international students. *Fees:* £8800. *Living costs:* £6500–£7500.

Glyndŵr This new university welcomes students from Europe and worldwide. *English language entry requirement (or equivalent):* IELTS 6.0. *Fees:* £6950–£7950. *Living costs:* £7500.

Greenwich Over 4500 international students (including those from European countries). *English language entry requirement (or equivalent):* IELTS 6.0. Pre-sessional English courses, Access and International Foundation programmes. *Fees:* £9375. *Living costs:* £9500–£10,500. Scholarships open to applicants from 25 countries.

Heriot-Watt Twenty-three per cent of the student population comes from over 90 countries. *English language entry requirement (or equivalent):* IELTS 6.0. Several English language courses are offered; these range in length depending on students' requirements. *Fees:* £9500–£12,000. *Living costs:* £6000–£7500. Some international scholarships are available worth £1500–£2000 for one year.

Hertfordshire Students from over 90 countries are at present studying at the University. *English language entry requirement (or equivalent):* IELTS 6.0. English language tuition is offered in the one-year International Foundation course, in a course for the Foundation Certificate in English for Academic Purposes, and in a pre-sessional intensive English course held during the summer months. *Fees:* Classroom-based courses £8500, laboratory based courses £9500. *Living costs:* £7000–£8000.

Huddersfield International students from over 80 countries. English language courses available and a one-year International Foundation course in English language with options in Business, Computing, Engineering, Mathematics and Music. Students guaranteed entry to Huddersfield courses on completion. *Fees:* £10,750–£11,750. *Living costs:* £6500–£7500.

Hull Ten per cent of students are from outside the EU. *English language entry requirement (or equivalent):* IELTS 6.0. English summer study programme through the three months before the start of the academic year. In-session study in English also available. Foundation programmes for Business and Management degrees. *Fees:* £9800–£11,900, Medicine £22,000. *Living costs:* £5500–£6500. Hull has one of the best overseas scholarship provisions of any British university. Scholarships and bursaries are dependent on subject and which country the student comes from.

Imperial London Some 5000 international students from over 110 countries. *English language entry requirement (or equivalent):* IELTS 6.5–7.0. *Fees:* Engineering £23,000, Natural Science £22,450, Clinical Medicine £39,150. *Living costs:* £10,530–£14,000 (minimum). Scholarships available.

Keele Large number of overseas students. *English language entry requirement (or equivalent):* IELTS 6.0–6.5, 7.0 for Medicine. English language summer school before the start of degree course. International Foundation year degree programmes (entry IELTS 4.5). *Fees:* Classroom-based subjects £9900, lab-based subjects £10,900, Physiotherapy £11,295, Medicine £19,570–£22,900. *Living costs:* £8000–£9000. Some bursaries valued at £1300 per annum.

Kent About 25% of the student population are from overseas. *English language entry requirement (or equivalent):* IELTS 5.5. Foundation programmes (entry IELTS 5.0) offered to prepare students for Arts, Business, Science, Engineering and Law courses. Non-degree courses also offered for one year or less. *Fees:* £11,230–£13,400. *Living costs:* £7000–£14,000. Limited number of scholarships available and some general scholarships for students from Hong Kong and Singapore.

Kingston More than 2000 international students from over 70 countries. *English language entry requirement (or equivalent):* IELTS 6.5. Foundation level Science and Technology courses. Pre-sessional English language courses and free English support during degree studies. *Fees:* Up to £11,000. *Living costs:* £9500–£14,000.

Lancaster Twenty per cent of student population from over 100 countries. *English language entry requirement (or equivalent):* IELTS 5.5–6.0. Pre-sessional and in-session English language courses cover reading, writing, listening and speaking skills. On-campus accommodation throughout your degree course. *Fees:* £9200–£11,100. *Living costs:* £7000–£8000.

Leeds Approximately 4000 students from outside the UK. *English language entry requirement (or equivalent):* IELTS 6.0. *Fees:* £11,800–£15,600, Clinical Medicine and Dentistry £26,750–£29,750. *Living costs:* £7000–£9000. Partial scholarships offered.

Leeds Met Over 2500 international students from 110 countries. *English language entry requirement (or equivalent):* IELTS 6.0 (IELTS 4.0 or 5.0 for the International Foundation programme, starting September or February). Also general English courses. *Fees:* £10,500–£11,500. *Living costs:* £8000–£9000. Small number of scholarships.

Leicester Fourteen per cent of full-time students are from outside the UK. *English language entry requirement (or equivalent):* IELTS 6.0 (IELTS 6.5 for Law, Medicine, Arts and Social Science programmes, 5.5 for the Foundation year). English language preparatory programmes and on-going support Foundation programme. *Fees:* £10,750–£13,750, Clinical Medicine £24,895. *Living costs:* £8500–£9000. Scholarships and bursaries awarded in a range of subjects, with special awards for students from India and Singapore.

Lincoln Over 2000 students from more than 40 countries. *English language entry requirement (or equivalent):* IELTS 6.0. *Fees:* £10,395–£11,460. *Living costs:* £7800–£9000.

Liverpool Approximately 2600 international students from over 100 countries. *English language entry requirement (or equivalent):* IELTS 6.0–6.5. International Foundation course (IELTS 5.0–5.5), 7.0 for Medicine. *Fees:* £10,500–£13,500, Dentistry and Medicine £20,500, Veterinary Science £21,830. *Living costs:* £7000–£8000. Scholarships available, including special awards for students from Hong Kong and Singapore.

Liverpool Hope Approximately 700 international students. *English language entry requirement (or equivalent):* IELTS 6.0. Language courses available. *Fees:* £7100–£8400. *Living costs:* £7000–£8000.

LJMU A large number of overseas students. *English language entry requirement (or equivalent):* IELTS 6.0. Pre-sessional and in-session English tuition available. *Fees:* £10,050–£13,350. *Living costs:* £7000–£8000. Some awards available.

London (Central Sch SpDr) More than 60 International students from over 40 countries are currently following courses. *English language entry requirement (or equivalent):* IELTS 7.0. *Fees:* From £10,000. *Living costs:* £10,500–£14,000.

London (Court) Approximately 25–30% students are from overseas. *English language entry requirement (or equivalent):* IELTS 7.0. *Fees:* Undergraduate courses £13,500. *Living costs:* £9500–£14,000.

London (Gold) Some 1500 overseas students. *English language entry requirement (or equivalent):* IELTS 6.5; IELTS 5.5 for Extension degrees and IELTS 5.0 for entry to the one-year Foundation course. Certificate course in Language and Contemporary Culture or pre-sessional programmes available. *Fees:* £10,680–£13,500. *Living costs:* £9500–£14,000.

London (Hey) *English language entry requirement (or equivalent):* IELTS 6.0. *Fees:* £5490. *Living costs:* £9500–£14,000.

London (Inst Ed) *Fees:* £11,300.

London (King's) A large number of international students (20%). *English language entry requirement (or equivalent):* IELTS 6.5 for Engineering, Nursing, Science courses, 7.0 for Dentistry, Law, Medicine, Physiotherapy and 7.5 for Humanities, Social Sciences. Pre-sessional summer courses and a one-year Foundation course available. *Fees:* Classroom-based £13,250, lab-based £16,800, clinically based subjects £31,150. *Living costs:* £9500–£14,000. Awards available.

London (QM) Large number of international students (20%). *English language entry requirement (or equivalent):* IELTS 6.5. International Foundation course covering English language tuition and specialist courses in Business, Management, Economics, Mathematics, Spanish, Geography and European Studies. The course guarantees progression to linked degree courses including Law. *Fees:* £9000–£11,500, Medicine Years 1 and 2 £14,600. *Living costs:* £9500–£14,000. Several departments operate scholarship schemes for overseas students.

London (RH) Twenty per cent of students from over 120 countries. *English language entry requirement (or equivalent):* IELTS 4.0–5.5 for English language programmes. Ten-month Foundation course with studies in English language and introduction to specialist studies in a range of degree subjects. *Fees:* £11,855–£13,860. *Living costs:* £9500–£14,000. International student scholarships offered.

London (RVC) About 110 international students. *Fees:* £20,300. *Living costs:* £9500–£14,000.

London (St George's) *Fees:* £13,650–£17,743, MBBS £31,108. *Living costs:* £9500–£14,000.

London (Sch Pharm) Approximately 20% of the student body are international students. *English language entry requirement (or equivalent):* IELTS 6.5. *Fees:* £13,350. *Living costs:* £9500–£14,000.

London (SOAS) Large number of international students (30%). *English language entry requirement (or equivalent):* IELTS 7.0. A one-year foundation programme and English language courses available with an entry requirement of IELTS 4.0. Three-day International Students' Orientation programme. *Fees:* £13,890. *Living costs:* £9500–£14,000.

London (UCL) Some 7000 students (34% of the total student body) are from countries outside the UK. *English language entry requirement (or equivalent):* Science and Engineering IELTS 6.5, Arts courses 7.0, Speech Science and Law 7.5. *Fees:* £12,770–£16,725. Medicine £24,950. *Living costs:* £9,500–£14,000. Scholarships available, including awards for students from Hong Kong and China.

London (UCL/Slade SA) *Fees:* £17,560.

London LSE Approximately 5500 international students represent 150 countries. *English language entry requirement (or equivalent):* TOEFL 627 (paper test). Language Centre courses available. *Fees:* £13,680. *Living costs:* £9500–£14,000.

London Met Over 4000 students from 147 countries. *English language entry requirement (or equivalent):* IELTS 5.5. One-year International Foundation programme (IELTS entry requirement 4.5). Full range of English courses. *Fees:* £10,080, Foundation programme £5500. *Living costs:* £9500–£14,000.

London Mountview (Ac Thea Arts) *Fees:* £10,782–£13,251.

London NCH Students must be fully competent in English and if English is not your first language NCH may require you to take a test in English language such as IELTS or TOEFL. All students must submit a piece of written work to apply. *Fees:* £18,000. *Living costs:* £9500–£10,500.

London South Bank Approximately 2500 international students, including 1300 from the EU. *English language entry requirement (or equivalent):* IELTS 6.0. Pre-study English course and a University Foundation course for overseas students. *Fees:* Classroom-based £9000, lab-based £9250. *Living costs:* £9500–£14,000.

Loughborough Some 800 students from outside the UK. *English language entry requirement (or equivalent):* IELTS 6.5. Special courses offered by the English Language Study Unit. One-week residential course for international students before the start of the academic year. *Fees:* £10,400–£13,500. *Living costs:* £4300–£8800. Eight merit-based scholarships offered.

Manchester A high proportion of international students from over 180 countries. *English language entry requirement (or equivalent):* IELTS 6.0–7.5, depending on the high linguistic demands of courses, for example Law, Management and Medicine. Foundation Year programme in Informatics, Engineering, Science and Biological Sciences. English language courses are also offered. *Fees:* £12,300–£15,400. *Living costs:* £9870. Some scholarships and bursaries are available.

Manchester Met A large number of international students. *English language entry requirement (or equivalent):* IELTS 6.0. English language courses in January, April and July. *Fees:* £9900, Architecture £15,000. *Living costs:* £7800.

Middlesex International students from 30 countries around the world. *English language entry requirement (or equivalent):* IELTS 6.0. Foundation course (IELTS entry requirement 4.5). Extended English language course from September to July. International summer school. *Fees:* £10,400. *Living costs:* £9500–£14,000.

Newcastle Over 2500 students from outside the UK. *English language entry requirement (or equivalent):* IELTS 6.5 (7.0 for English, Law and Medicine). English language support and Foundation programmes in Arts and Social Sciences, Business and Finance, Computing, Science and Engineering. *Fees:* £10,840–£13,905 Medicine £13,905–£25,735. *Living costs:* £7500–£8500. Some awards available.

Newport International students from 50 countries. *English language entry requirement (or equivalent):* IELTS 6.0. *Fees:* £7500–£8500. *Living costs:* £5500–£6500.

Northampton Over 700 students from over 100 countries. *English language entry requirement (or equivalent):* IELTS 6.0. English language courses available. *Fees:* £9100. *Living costs:* £5400–£6400.

Northbrook (Coll) *Fees:* £8000.

Northumbria Approximately 2500 international students from over 80 countries. *English language entry requirement (or equivalent):* IELTS 5.5–6.5. English language and Foundation courses. *Fees:* £9300–£10,300. *Living costs:* £7500–£8500. Country scholarships for students from over 15 countries; some merit-based course scholarships.

Nottingham Students from over 130 countries. *English language entry requirement (or equivalent):* IELTS 6.0–6.5 (7.5 for Medicine). *Fees:* £11,990–£15,720, Medicine £16,570–£25,480. *Living costs:* £7500–£8500. Scholarships for siblings and science applicants.

Nottingham Trent Large number of overseas students. *English language entry requirement (or equivalent):* IELTS 6.5. English language courses (19, 10 and 5 weeks) available. *Fees:* £9100–£10,300. *Living costs:* £7500–£8500. Discounted overseas fees for some applicants for Art and Design courses.

Open University Courses are open to students throughout the world with study online or with educational partners. Tutorial support is by telephone, fax, computer conferencing or email. *Fees:* Non-EU students' fees vary depending on type of course.

Oxford Large proportion of international students. *English language entry requirement (or equivalent):* IELTS 7.5 (minimum), TOEFL 650 (275 in the computer-based TOEFL). *Fees:* £13,500, Clinical Medicine £27,550. *Living costs:* £7500–£8500. University and college scholarships and awards are available.

Oxford Brookes Large number of international students. *English language entry requirement (or equivalent):* IELTS scores for Engineering and Construction 5.5; for Business, Social Sciences, Computing and Humanities 6.0; for Law and Psychology 6.5. Large number of English language support courses from two weeks to two years offered by the Centre for English Language Studies. *Fees:* £10,600. *Living costs:* £9000–£9500. Engineering scholarships and family awards.

Plymouth *English language entry requirement (or equivalent):* IELTS 6.0–6.5. 'English for University' courses available with IELTS entry requirement of 4.5. *Fees:* £10,500. *Living costs:* £6500–£7500. Scholarships for applicants from Malaysia.

Portsmouth Students from over 100 countries. *English language entry requirement (or equivalent):* IELTS 6.0 (5.5 for Foundation-level study). Induction, academic skills and language courses available. *Fees:* £9600–£11,000. *Living costs:* £7500–£8500. Scholarships for first-year students.

Queen's Belfast Over 60 countries represented by 2400 international students. *English language entry requirement (or equivalent):* IELTS 6.0–6.5. Special English language summer schools and pre-university language courses are provided, also weekly language courses. Three-day orientation programme held before the start of the academic year. *Fees:* Classroom based courses £9889, Lab based courses £12,115–£13,395, Clinical £25,270. *Living costs:* £7500–£8500. Awards available.

Reading Over 3000 students from 135 countries. *English language entry requirement (or equivalent):* IELTS 6.5–7.0. International Foundation programme offering English language tuition and specialist studies in a choice of 14 subjects. Other pre-sessional English courses offered. *Fees:* £10,896–£12,996. *Living costs:* £6500–£8500. Some scholarships offered.

Richmond (Am Int Univ) *Fees:* £16,000 (non-EU/non-US residents), £27,000 (US residents).

Robert Gordon Approximately 500 international students from over 50 countries. *English language entry requirement (or equivalent):* IELTS 6.0. Pre-entry English programme requirement IELTS 5.0 or above. *Fees:* £8700–£10,700. *Living costs:* £5000–£6000. Partial scholarship scheme.

Roehampton *English language entry requirement (or equivalent):* IELTS 5.5–6.0. *Fees:* £9900. *Living costs:* £7500–£8500.

St Andrews 26% of students from overseas. *English language entry requirement (or equivalent):* IELTS 6.5. Pre-entry English and study skills programmes and Foundation courses specialising in Arts, Science or Social Science subjects. *Fees:* £13,500, Medicine £20,550. *Living costs:* £7500–£8500. Scholarships available.

St Mary's Twickenham (UC) *Fees:* £8100. *Living costs:* £7500–£8500.

Salford Some 1500 international students. *English language entry requirement (or equivalent):* IELTS 6.0. English study programmes and a very comprehensive International Foundation year. *Fees:* £10,100–£11,700. *Living costs:* £7500–£9000.

Scottish Assn Marine Sci *Fees:* £8580.

Sheffield Over 3700 international students. *English language entry requirement (or equivalent):* IELTS 6.0. Preparatory English courses (one–nine months) and an international summer school with English classes. *Fees:* £11,490–£15,100, Clinical Medicine £27,290. *Living costs:* £7000–£8000. Scholarships available for applicants from Africa and the Far East, for siblings and alumni.

Sheffield Hallam Over 80 countries represented by 3000 international students. *English language entry requirement (or equivalent):* IELTS 6.0. English language tuition available on four, eight and 12 week courses (£810, £1700 and £2200 respectively and IELTS entry requirement 4.5). *Fees:* £10,320–£13,520. *Living costs:* £7000–£8000.

SMO *Fees:* £7200

Southampton Over 2000 international students. *English language entry requirement (or equivalent):* IELTS 6.0–6.5. English courses offered and also an International Foundation course covering Arts, Humanities, Social Sciences and Law. *Fees:* £10,820–£13,840, Clinical Medicine £25,500. *Living costs:* £7500–£8500. Awards available in Computer Science, Electronics, Law, Mathematics and Science.

Southampton Solent Students from over 50 countries. *English language entry requirement (or equivalent):* IELTS 6.0. Induction programme and language tuition available. *Fees:* £9100. *Living costs:* £8000.

Staffordshire Students from over 70 countries. *English language entry requirement (or equivalent):* IELTS 5.5–6.0. English tuition available. *Fees:* £9385. *Living costs:* £7500–£8000.

Stirling Thirteen per cent overseas students from 70 nationalities. *English language entry requirement (or equivalent):* IELTS 6.0. English language tuition available. *Fees:* £10,200–£12,250. *Living costs:* £5000–£6000. Some scholarships for students from South East Asia.

Strathclyde Students from 90 countries. *English language entry requirement (or equivalent):* IELTS 6.5. Pre-entry and pre-sessional English tuition available. *Fees:* £12,980. *Living costs:* £7500–£8500.

Sunderland A large number of international students. *English language entry requirement (or equivalent):* IELTS 5.5–6.0. English language tuition available. *Fees:* £8800. *Living costs:* £7000–£8000

Surrey A large international community with 43% from the Far East. *English language entry requirement (or equivalent):* IELTS 6.0. English language courses and summer courses offered. *Fees:* £11,000–£13,750. *Living costs:* £7000–£8000. Scholarships and bursaries offered, including awards for students on Civil Engineering courses.

Sussex More than 2500 international students. *English language entry requirement (or equivalent):* IELTS 6.5. English language and study skills courses available. International Foundation courses offered, covering English language tuition and a choice from Humanities, Law, Media Studies, Social Sciences and Cultural Studies and Science and Technology. *Fees:* £10,900–£13,900, Medicine £23,678. *Living costs:* £8000–£10,800. Forty international scholarships.

Swansea Students from over 100 countries. *English language entry requirement (or equivalent):* IELTS 6.0. Pre-sessional English language courses available and on-going support during degree courses. *Fees:* £9800–£12,600. *Living costs:* £6000–£7000. Some overseas scholarships and prizes.

Swansea (Coll) *Fees:* £1500–£6495.

Swansea Met *English language entry requirement (or equivalent):* IELTS 6.5. *Fees:* £8500. *Living costs:* £5500–£6500.

Teesside Students from over 75 countries. *English language entry requirement (or equivalent):* IELTS 6.5 for Law, English and Humanities, 5.5 for Engineering, Science, Technology and Computing courses and 6.0 for all other courses. Free English courses available throughout the year while following degree programmes. International summer school available. *Fees:* £9750. *Living costs:* £6500.

Trinity Saint David International students are well-represented at the university. More information can be found on the international student section of the website, www.trinitysaintdavid.ac.uk/en/international/aboutus/ or by contacting the international office: internationalcc@trinitysaintdavid.ac.uk. *English language entry requirement (or equivalent):* IELTS 6.0. International Foundation programme. Accommodation possible for each year at university. *Fees:* £9348. *Living costs:* £6500–£7500.

UCLan Large international student population (2000) from many countries. *English language entry requirement (or equivalent):* IELTS 6.0. Competence in written and spoken English required on application. *Fees:* £9000–£9500. *Living costs:* £6000–£7000.

UEA Over 2000 international students from 120 countries. *English language entry requirement (or equivalent):* IELTS 6.0 (higher for some courses). Four, eight and 12-week pre-sessional courses in English and tuition during degree courses. *Fees:* Classroom-based subjects £11,000–£12,200, lab-based subjects £13,700, Medicine £23,250. *Living costs:* £6500–£7500. Scholarships available including awards, based on academic merit, cover part of the cost of tuition fees.

UEL About 3300 international students from 120 countries. *English language entry requirement (or equivalent):* IELTS 6.0. One-year full-time preparatory English course available. *Fees:* Architecture £11,700, Physiotherapy £13,200, other programmes £9300–£9600. *Living costs:* £9500–£14,000.

UHI *Fees:* £7200–£8580.

Ulster Students from over 40 countries. *English language entry requirement (or equivalent):* IELTS 5.5. *Fees:* £8760. *Living costs:* £6000–£7000.

Warwick Over 3500 international students. *English language entry requirement (or equivalent):* IELTS 6.0 for Science courses, 6.5 for Arts courses, 6.5 for MORSE courses, and 7.0 for Social Studies and Business courses. English support available. *Fees:* £13,800–£17,600. *Living costs:* £6500–£7500. More than 20 awards available for overseas students.

West London A large number of international students. *English language entry requirement (or equivalent):* IELTS 5.0 for the International Foundation programme and 5.5 for undergraduate courses. English language support available and also pre-sessional courses. *Fees:* £7500–£8200. *Living costs:* £12,500.

West Scotland Over 1100 international students. *English language entry requirement (or equivalent):* IELTS 6.0. English language Foundation course available. *Fees:* £10,000–10,500. *Living costs:* £6500–£7000. Some first-year scholarships are available.

Westminster Students from 148 countries (51% Asian). *English language entry requirement (or equivalent):* IELTS 6.0. International Foundation certificate courses available focusing on the Built Environment, Mathematics and Computing or Social Sciences and Literature. *Fees:* £10,785. *Living costs:* £10,500–£12,500.

Winchester Some 150 international students from 30 countries. *English language entry requirement (or equivalent):* IELTS 6.0. Language courses available. *Fees:* £9200. *Living costs:* £7500–£8500.

Wolverhampton A large number (2500) of international students from over 100 countries. *English language entry requirement (or equivalent):* IELTS 6.0. English courses available over one or two months or longer. International student programme. *Fees:* £9200. *Living costs:* £7200. Twenty Scholarships for Excellence offered.

Worcester *English language entry requirement (or equivalent):* IELTS 6.0. *Fees:* £9000. *Living costs:* £6000–£6500.

Writtle (Coll) *Fees:* £9250.

York Fifteen per cent of students from outside the UK. *English language entry requirement (or equivalent):* IELTS 6.0. Six-month and pre-sessional English language courses. Intensive vacation courses. *Fees:* £12,000–£15,600. Medicine £23,268. *Living costs:* £7800. Several scholarships for overseas students.

York St John *English language entry requirement (or equivalent):* IELTS 6.0 (3 year degree course or 4 year course including Foundation year). *Fees:* £8500. *Living costs:* £6500–£7500. £8500 except health-related courses £11,600.

BRITISH OVERSEAS TERRITORIES STUDENTS

Students from British Overseas Territories are now treated as home students for fee purposes at universities and other institutions of higher education in the UK. The territories to which this policy applies are:

British Overseas Territories Anguilla, Bermuda, British Antarctic Territory, British Indian Ocean Territory, British Virgin Islands, Cayman Islands, Falkland Islands, Montserrat, Pitcairn Islands, South Georgia and the South Sandwich Islands, St Helena and its Dependencies, Turks and Caicos Islands.

Overseas Territories of other EU member states Greenland, Faroe Islands (Denmark), Netherlands Antilles (Bonaire, Curacao, Saba, St Eustatius, St Marten), Aruba (Netherlands), New Caledonia, French Polynesia, Wallis and Futura, Mayotte, St Pierre et Miquelon (France).

10 | DIRECTORY OF UNIVERSITIES AND COLLEGES OFFERING HIGHER EDUCATION COURSES

SECTION 1: UNIVERSITIES

Listed below are universities in the United Kingdom that offer degree and diploma courses at higher education level. Applications to these institutions are submitted through UCAS except for part-time courses, private universities and colleges, and further education courses. For current information refer to the websites shown and also to www.ucas.com for a comprehensive list of degree and diploma courses (see **Appendix 4**).

Aberdeen This is a city-centre university on Scotland's east coast. (University of Aberdeen, Students Admissions and School Leavers, University Office, King's College, Aberdeen, Scotland AB24 3FX. Tel 01224 272090; www.abdn.ac.uk)

Abertay Dundee The University has a modern city-centre campus. (University of Abertay Dundee, Student Recruitment Office, Kydd Building, Dundee, Scotland DD1 1HG. Tel 01382 308080; www.abertay. ac.uk)

Aberystwyth This is a coastal university with a striking campus. Aberystwyth University has an extensive and valuable package of bursaries and scholarships. Please see www.aber.ac.uk/en/scholarships. The bursaries, with a few exceptions, are open to students from all parts of the UK and EU. Aberystwyth also runs traditional entrance scholarship examinations of two unseen examinations which can be taken either at school or college or at Aberystwyth. Successful applicants gain a prestigious Aberystwyth University scholarship. (Aberystwyth University, Student Welcome Centre, Penglais Campus, Aberystwyth, Wales SY23 3FB. Tel 01970 622021; www.aber.ac.uk)

Anglia Ruskin The University has main campuses in Cambridge and Chelmsford and partner colleges throughout East Anglia. (Anglia Ruskin University, Contact Centre, Bishop Hall Lane, Chelmsford, England CM1 1SQ. Tel 0845 271 3333; www.anglia.ac.uk)

Arts London Six distinctive and distinguished Colleges make up University of the Arts London: Camberwell College of Arts, Central Saint Martins College of Arts and Design, Chelsea College of Art and Design, London College of Communication, London College of Fashion, Wimbledon College of Art. The Colleges offer the University's 20,000 students a diverse range of courses at all levels from foundation and undergraduate to postgraduate and research. (University of the Arts London, 272 High Holborn, London, England WC1V 7EY. Tel 020 7514 6000; www.arts.ac.uk)

Aston This University has a green campus in the centre of Birmingham with academic, sporting and social activities on site. (Aston University, The Registry (Admissions), Aston Triangle, Birmingham, England B4 7ET. Tel 0121 204 4444; www.aston.ac.uk)

Bangor The University has a central site in Bangor on the Menai Straits with partner institutions (including the Welsh College of Horticulture) throughout North Wales. (Bangor University, The Student Recruitment Unit, Bangor, Wales LL57 2DG. Tel 01248 383944; www.bangor.ac.uk)

Bath The University is on a rural campus one mile from the centre of Bath, with partner colleges in Bath, Swindon and Wiltshire. (University of Bath, Recruitment and Admissions, Bath, England BA2 7AY. Tel 01225 383019; www.bath.ac.uk)

Bath Spa This University was created in 2005 and is located on two campuses near Bath, with partner colleges in Wiltshire. (Bath Spa University, Admissions Office, Newton Park, Newton St Loe, Bath, England BA2 9BN. Tel 01225 875624; www.bathspa.ac.uk)

Bedfordshire The University was formed in August 2006 from the merger of Luton University and the Bedford campus of De Montfort University. The main campus is in the centre of Luton, with two campuses in Bedford, and four partner colleges. (University of Bedfordshire, The Admissions Office, Park Square, Luton, England LU1 3JU. Tel 0844 848 2235; www.beds.ac.uk)

Birmingham This is a 'red-brick' university at Edgbaston to the south of the city, with a second campus at Selly Oak. (University of Birmingham, Edgbaston, Birmingham, England B15 2TT. Tel 0121 415 8900; www.bham.ac.uk)

Birmingham City Part-time evening courses are offered for mature students wishing to read for first and higher degrees. Courses are offered in the Faculties of Arts, Science, Social Science and Continuing Education. (Birmingham City University, City North Campus, Birmingham, England B42 2SU. Tel 0121 331 5595; www.bcu.ac.uk)

Bolton The University was created in 2005 and is based at Deane Campus, close to the town centre. (University of Bolton, Recruitment and Admissions, Deane Road, Bolton, England BL3 5AB. Tel 01204 900600; www.bolton.ac.uk)

Bournemouth The University site is in a large coastal resort, with partner colleges in the region also offering courses. (Bournemouth University, Talbot Campus, Fern Barrow, Poole, England BH12 5BB. Tel 01202 961916; www.bournemouth.ac.uk)

Bradford The University's main campus is close to the city centre, with the School of Management two miles away. (University of Bradford, Course Enquiries Office, Richmond Road, Bradford, England BD7 1DP. Tel 0800 073 1255; www.brad.ac.uk)

Brighton Situated on the south coast, the University has five campuses in Brighton, Eastbourne and Hastings. University-validated courses are offered at several partner colleges. Performance on National Student Survey for 2011 was 95%. (University of Brighton, The Registry (Admissions), Mithras House, Lewes Road, Brighton, England BN2 4AT. Tel 01273 600900; www.brighton.ac.uk)

Brighton and Sussex (MS) The campus is located at Falmer, just outside Brighton. (Brighton and Sussex Medical School, BSMS Admissions, University of Sussex, Brighton, England BN1 9PX. Tel 01273 643528; www.bsms.ac.uk)

Bristol This is a city university with halls of residence in Stoke Bishop and Clifton. (University of Bristol, Senate House, Tyndall Avenue, Bristol, England BS8 1TH. Tel 0117 928 9000; www.bristol.ac.uk)

Bristol UWE The University has four campuses in and around Bristol with an associate Faculty at Hartpury, and regional centres in Bath, Gloucestershire and Swindon. It also has links with the Bristol Old Vic Theatre School and the Royal West of England Academy. (University of the West of England, Bristol, Admissions Office, Frenchay Campus, Coldharbour Lane, Bristol, England BS16 1QY. Tel 0117 965 6261; www.uwe.ac.uk)

Brunel The University has a compact campus to the west of London at Uxbridge. Brunel also validates courses at the London School of Theology. (Brunel University, Admissions Office, Uxbridge, England UB8 3PH. Tel 01895 265265; www.brunel.ac.uk)

Buckingham A small independent university, it has two sites within the town some 40 miles north of London offering two-year (eight-term) degrees. (University of Buckingham, Admissions Office, Hunter Street, Buckingham, England MK18 1EG. Tel 01280 820313; www.buckingham.ac.uk)

Bucks New A new university (2007), it has two campuses in High Wycombe and one at Chalfont St Giles and links with partner colleges. (Buckinghamshire New University, Admissions, Queen Alexandra Road, High Wycombe, England HP11 2JZ. Tel 0800 056 5660; www.bucks.ac.uk)

Cambridge The University has 31 colleges located throughout the city. Colleges: Lucy Cavendish, Murray Edwards (formerly New Hall) and Newnham (women only); the following admit both men and women undergraduates: Christ's, Churchill, Clare, Corpus Christi, Downing, Emmanuel, Fitzwilliam, Girton, Gonville and Caius, Homerton, Hughes Hall, Jesus, King's, Magdalene, Pembroke, Peterhouse, Queens', Robinson, St Catharine's, St Edmund's, St John's, Selwyn, Sidney Sussex, Trinity, Trinity Hall, Wolfson. Clare Hall and Darwin admit only graduates. (University of Cambridge, Cambridge Admissions Office, Fitzwilliam House, 32 Trumpington Street, Cambridge, England CB2 1QY. Tel 01223 333308; www.cam.ac.uk)

Canterbury Christ Church The University was created in 2005 with the main campus located near Canterbury city centre and campuses also at Broadstairs, Medway University Centre and Folkestone.The University is the third highest in England for student employability. (Canterbury Christ Church University, Admissions, North Holmes Road, Canterbury, England CT1 1QU. Tel 01227 782900; www.canterbury.ac.uk)

Cardiff The main (Cathays Park) campus of the University is located in the city centre, with the Heath Park campus a mile to the south. (Cardiff University, Admissions, MacKenzie House, 30–36 Newport Road, Cardiff, Wales CF24 0DE. Tel 029 2087 9999; www.cardiff.ac.uk)

Cardiff Met (formerly known as University of Wales, Cardiff) Cardiff Metropolitan University sits in the heart of of the capital and is made up of five Academic Schools: Cardiff School of Art & Design, Cardiff School of Education (one of the leading providers of teacher training in the UK), Cardiff School of Health Sciences (with the recently opened £4.9million research centre), Cardiff School of Management (which offers the largest on campus MBA in the UK) and Cardiff School of Sport. It specialises in courses that are career orientated and have been designed in conjunction with business and industry. (Cardiff Metropolitan University, Llandaff Campus, Western Avenue, Cardiff, Wales CF5 2YB. Tel General Enquiries 029 2041 6070; Admissions Enquiries 029 2041 6010; www.cardiffmet.ac.uk)

Chester The University was formed in 2005 and is located on a campus in Chester, with a second campus in Warrington and three partner colleges. (University of Chester, Undergraduate Admissions, Parkgate Road, Chester, England CH1 4BJ. Tel 01244 512528; www.chester.ac.uk)

Chichester A small university with campuses at Chichester and Bognor Regis. (University of Chichester, Admissions, Bognor Regis Campus, Upper Bognor Road, Bognor Regis, England PO21 1HR. Tel 01243 816002; www.chiuni.ac.uk)

City The University is situated in central London, with Nursing and Midwifery located at St Bartholomew's Hospital. (City University, Undergraduate Admissions Office, Northampton Square, London, England EC1V 0HB. Tel 020 7040 5060; www.city.ac.uk)

Coventry The University has a 33-acre campus in Coventry and a number of teaching centres throughout the city with courses offered in several partner colleges. (Coventry University, The Student Centre, 1 Gulson Road, Coventry, England CV1 2JH. Tel 024 7615 2525; www.coventry.ac.uk)

Creative Arts The University has five colleges – three in Kent (Canterbury, Maidstone and Rochester) and two in Surrey (Epsom and Farnham). (University for the Creative Arts, Enquiries Service, Falkner Road, Farnham, England GU9 7DS. Tel 01252 892883; www.ucreative.ac.uk/enquiries)

Cumbria This new university (2007) was created by the merger of St Martin's College and Cumbria Institute of the Arts. There are campuses in Ambleside, Carlisle, Lancaster, Penrith and London. (University of Cumbria, Fusehill Street, Carlisle, Cumbria, England CA1 2HH. Tel 01228 616234; www.cumbria.ac.uk)

De Montfort The University has two sites in Leicester and nine associated colleges. (De Montfort University, Students Admissions, The Gateway, Leicester, England LE1 9BH. Tel 0116 255 1551; www.dmu.ac.uk)

Derby The University has two campuses: one close to Derby city centre and the second at Buxton. (University of Derby, Admissions, Kedleston Road, Derby, England DE22 1GB. Tel 01332 591167; www.derby.ac.uk)

Dundee A city-centre campus, with the Medical School and School of Nursing located at Ninewells Hospital to the west of the city. (University of Dundee, Admissions and Student Recruitment, Nethergate, Dundee, Scotland DD1 4HN. Tel 01382 383838; www.dundee.ac.uk)

Durham The University has two sites, the main site in Durham city and the second, at Stockton, with two colleges on the Queen's Campus. Durham University is the third oldest university in England and one of the world's leading centres of scholarship and learning. Undergraduate students have access to teaching by world experts, award-winning study facilities, extensive collections of books and learning resources and a unique collegiate system offering a distinctive student experience. It has the second highest completion rate of any UK university (98% of undergraduates successfully complete their degree), a high level of student satisfaction (90% compared with a sector average of 83%) and is a top 3 UK university in the *Sunday Times University Guide 2012*. (Durham University, Undergraduate Admissions Office, University Office, Old Elvet, Durham, England DH1 3HP. Tel 0191 334 6123; www.dur.ac.uk)

Edge Hill This university (formed in 2005) has its campus in Ormskirk near Liverpool. (Edge Hill University, Academic Registry, Ormskirk, England L39 4QP. Tel 01695 650950; www.edgehill.ac.uk)

Edinburgh The University's Central Area is located on the south side of the city centre. The King's Buildings (the main science and engineering campus), Medical School and Vet School are all to the south of the city centre, within easy travelling distance. (Edinburgh University, Student Recruitment and Admissions, 57 George Square, Edinburgh, Scotland EH8 9JU. Tel 0131 650 4360; www.ed.ac.uk)

Edinburgh Napier The University has seven campuses in the centre of Edinburgh and two to the south-west. (Edinburgh Napier University, Information Office, Craiglockart Campus, Edinburgh, Scotland EH14 1DJ. Tel 08452 606040; www.napier.ac.uk)

Edinburgh Queen Margaret This new university (2007) is located on a new, purpose-built campus on the Firth of Forth east of Edinburgh, with student accommodation on site. (Queen Margaret University, Edinburgh, The Admissions Office, Queen Margaret University Drive, Edinburgh, Scotland EH21 6UU. Tel 0131 474 0000; www.qmu.ac.uk)

Essex The University has a parkland campus two miles from Colchester. The University and the South Essex College Partnership also provide degree schemes at the new Southend campus. (University of Essex, Undergraduate Admissions, Wivenhoe Park, Colchester, England CO4 3SQ. Tel 01206 873778; www.essex.ac.uk)

Exeter The University has two sites in Exeter: the Streatham campus is the largest, and the St Luke's campus is a mile away. A third campus (University of Exeter in Cornwall campus) is situated at Penryn in Cornwall. (University of Exeter, Admissions Office, 8th Floor, Laver Building, North Park Road, Exeter, England EX4 4QE. Tel 01392 723044; www.exeter.ac.uk)

Glamorgan The University has four faculties on two campuses in Pontypridd and a faculty in Cardiff. The main campus is at Glamorgan and the new School of Creative and Cultural Industries is in Cardiff city centre. The University has partnerships with the Royal Welsh College of Music and Drama and several other colleges. (University of Glamorgan, Enquiries and Admissions Unit, Pontypridd, Wales CF37 1DL. Tel 08456 434030; www.glam.ac.uk)

Glasgow The University has three campuses, two on the outskirts of Glasgow and one on the Crichton campus at Dumfries. Glasgow School of Art and the Scottish Agricultural College in Ayr are associated institutions. (University of Glasgow, Recruitment, Admissions and International Service, Fraser Building, 65 Hillhead Street, Glasgow, Scotland G12 8QF. Tel 0141 330 3177; www.gla.ac.uk)

Glasgow Caledonian The University has a city-centre campus. (Glasgow Caledonian University, City Campus, Admissions Office, Cowcaddens Road, Glasgow, Scotland G4 0BA. Tel 0141 331 3334; www.gcal.ac.uk)

Gloucestershire Three campuses in Cheltenham and one in Gloucester form the University. It also has partner colleges in Gloucestershire, Herefordshire, Wiltshire and Worcestershire. Many students are home-based. (University of Gloucestershire, Student Recruitment Office, Hardwick Administration Centre, St Pauls Road, Cheltenham, England GL50 4BS. Tel 0844 801 0001; www.glos.ac.uk)

Glyndŵr This is a new university (2008), formerly North East Wales IHE, and is situated in Wrexham town centre. (Glyndŵr University, Plas Coch, Mold Road, Wrexham, Wales LL11 2AW. Tel 01978 290666; www.glyndwr.ac.uk)

Greenwich The main campus of the University is at Greenwich, a second is at Avery Hill in south London and a third is at Medway at Chatham Maritime. There are also partner colleges in east London and Kent. (University of Greenwich, Enquiry Unit, Greenwich Campus, Old Royal Naval College, Park Row, London, England SE10 9LS. Tel 0800 005 006; www.gre.ac.uk)

Heriot-Watt The University has a large parkland campus seven miles west of Edinburgh and a second campus in the Scottish Borders at Galashiels 35 miles to the south. (Heriot-Watt University, Admissions Unit, Edinburgh Campus, Edinburgh, Scotland EH14 4AS. Tel 0131 449 5111; www.hw.ac.uk)

Hertfordshire The University has two campuses in Hatfield. Courses are also offered through a consortium of four Hertfordshire colleges and the University has links with all Hertfordshire further education colleges. (University of Hertfordshire, University Admissions Service, College Lane, Hatfield, England AL10 9AB. Tel 01707 284800; www.herts.ac.uk)

Huddersfield This is a town-centre university with University Centres at Barnsley and Oldham and links to colleges of further education throughout the north of England. As well as teaching excellence, the University also focuses on high quality research. In the most recent Research Assessment Exercise (RAE), Music, History, English, Education, Social Work, Engineering, Computing, Accountancy and Sociology achieved results that were classified as 'world leading' or 'internationally excellent'. This knowledge feeds into its degree courses to ensure they are relevant, up to date and challenging in their content. As a result the University is one of the top 10 UK universities for student satisfaction. Its degrees are relevant to industry and many of the courses have professional body recognition. 70% of students work with employers as part of their degree and the courses are designed to help them make an immediate impact in the workplace. Students work with over 1000 organisations including the BBC, Microsoft, Apple, BMW, Jaguar, Rolls-Royce, GlaxoSmithKline, Cadbury and the Post Office. It is also one of the UK's top 10 providers of sandwich courses plus it is also in the top 10 for employability: 94% of the students go on to work and/or study within six months of graduating. (University of Huddersfield, Admissions Office, Queensgate, Huddersfield, England HD1 3DH. Tel 01484 473969; www.hud.ac.uk)

Hull The main campus is in Hull, two miles from the city centre, with a smaller campus at Scarborough. The results from the 2011 National Student Survey confirm that the University of Hull has improved its position among the leading universities for student satisfaction: the University is now ranked joint 8th place out of mainstream English higher education institutions. The University's continuing good results in the NSS league table proves that students at the University continue to be among the happiest in the country. (University of Hull, Admissions Service, Cottingham Road, Hull, England HU6 7RX. Tel 01482 466100; www.hull.ac.uk)

Hull York (MS) The Medical School is a partnership between the Universities of Hull and York, with teaching facilities on the main campuses of both universities. (Hull York Medical School, Admissions Office, University of York, Heslington, York, England YO10 5DD. Tel 01904 321762; www.hyms.ac.uk)

Imperial London The College became an independent university, separate from the University of London, in 2007. The central site is in South Kensington. Medicine is based mainly at St Mary's Hospital, Paddington, Charing Cross Hospital and Hammersmith Hospital. (Imperial College London, Registry, Level 3 Sherfield Building, South Kensington Campus, London, England SW7 2AZ. Tel 020 7589 5111; www.imperial.ac.uk)

Keele This is a small university on a green campus five miles from Stoke-on-Trent. (Keele University, Academic Registry, Keele, England ST5 5BG. Tel 01782 734005; www.keele.ac.uk)

Kent The University has a spacious campus near Canterbury, and also campuses at Medway, Chatham and Wye, with two associate colleges (South Kent College, Mid Kent College) and two partner institutions (West Kent College, Canterbury College). (University of Kent, Admissions and Partnership Services, The Registry, Canterbury, England CT2 7NZ. Tel 01227 827272; www.kent.ac.uk)

Kingston With four campuses in and around the town and 10 partner colleges, the University has easy access to London. (Kingston University, River House, 53–57 High Street, Kingston upon Thames, England KT1 1LQ. Tel 0844 855 2177; www.kingston.ac.uk)

Lancaster The University has a parkland site three miles south of Lancaster city centre. It is collegiate with each student being a member of one of the eight colleges. (Lancaster University, Undergraduate Admissions Office, Bailrigg, Lancaster, England LA1 4YW. Tel 01524 594910; www.lancs.ac.uk)

Leeds The University is sited on a campus in the centre of the city. (University of Leeds, Undergraduate Admissions Office, Leeds, England LS2 9JT. Tel 0113 243 1751; www.leeds.ac.uk)

Leeds Met The University has two campuses, one in the city and a second in Headingley on the outskirts of Leeds, and partner colleges throughout the region. (Leeds Metropolitan University, Course Enquiries Office, Civic Quarter, Leeds, England LS1 3HE. Tel 0113 812 3113; www.lmu.ac.uk)

Leicester The compact campus is located on the southern edge of the city. (University of Leicester, Admissions Office, University Road, Leicester, England LE1 7RH. Tel 0116 252 5280; www.le.ac.uk)

Lincoln The Brayford and Cathedral campuses are in the city, with the Riseholme Park campus some five miles away. There is also a campus in Hull and associated colleges in Lincolnshire. (University of Lincoln, Academic Registry, Brayford Pool, Lincoln, England LN6 7TS. Tel 01522 886097; www.lincoln.ac.uk)

Liverpool The University has a large city-centre campus. (University of Liverpool, Student Recruitment and Admissions Office, Foundation Building, Brownlow Hill, Liverpool, England L69 7ZX. Tel 0151 794 5927; www.liv.ac.uk)

Liverpool Hope Liverpool Hope University has two campuses, one three miles from the city centre, the other within a brisk walk of it. Liverpool is a vibrant student city offering plenty of cultural, sporting, musical and social opportunities to the students at Liverpool Hope. (Liverpool Hope University, Admissions Office, Hope Park, Liverpool, England L16 9JD. Tel 0151 291 3295; www.hope.ac.uk)

LJMU Liverpool John Moores University is a thriving, vibrant university located at the heart of Liverpool, consisting of three large campuses. (Liverpool John Moores University, Admissions and Information Officer, Byrom Street, Liverpool, England L3 3AF. Tel 0151 231 2021; www.livjm.ac.uk)

London (Birk) The College is situated in Bloomsbury in the London University precinct and provides part-time and evening higher education courses. (Birkbeck, University of London, Malet Street, London, England WC1E 7HX. Tel 020 7631 6000; www.bbk.ac.uk)

London (Gold) The College is located on a single campus in south-east London. (Goldsmiths, University of London, Admissions Office, Lewisham Way, London, England SE14 6NW. Tel 020 7919 7766; www.gold.ac.uk)

London (Hey) The College is on a site in central London. (Heythrop College, University of London, Registry, Kensington Square, London, England W8 5HN. Tel 020 7795 6600; www.heythrop.ac.uk)

London (Inst Ed) (Institute of Education, University of London, 20 Bedford Way, London, England WC1H 0AL. Tel 020 7612 6000; www.ioe.ac.uk)

London (Inst in Paris) The Institute's Department of French Studies and Comparative Studies is located in central Paris and operates in partnership with Queen Mary and Royal Holloway, University of London. (University of London Institute in Paris, 9–11 rue de Constantine, 75340, Paris, France Cedex 07. Tel +33 (0) 1 44 11 73 83/76; www.ulip.lon.ac.uk)

London (King's) The College has campuses in central and south London (Strand, Waterloo and London Bridge) and includes the School of Medicine, the Dental Institute and the School of Biomedical and Health Sciences. (King's College, University of London, Enquiries, Strand, London, England WC2R 2LS. Tel 020 7836 5454; www.kcl.ac.uk)

London (QM) There is a city campus in the East End of London. (Queen Mary, University of London, Admissions Office, Mile End Road, London, England E1 4NS. Tel 020 7882 5511; www.qmul.ac.uk)

London (RH) There is a large campus with halls of residence situated at Egham, 19 miles west from central London and three miles from Windsor. (Royal Holloway, University of London, Admissions Office, Egham, England TW20 0EX. Tel 01784 434455; www.rhul.ac.uk)

London (RVC) The College has campuses in London and Hertfordshire. (Royal Veterinary College, University of London, Royal College Street, London, England NW1 0TU. Tel 020 7468 5147; www.rvc.ac.uk)

London (St George's) Located on a compact site in south-west London, St George's is a specialist health sciences university, having extensive links with many hospitals and practices, and also with Kingston University and Royal Holloway London. (St George's, University of London, Cranmer Terrace, London, England SW17 0RE. Tel 020 8725 2333; www.sgul.ac.uk)

London (Sch Pharm) The School has a central London site close to the London University precinct. (School of Pharmacy, University of London, 29–39 Brunswick Square, London, England WC1N 1AX. Tel 020 7753 5800; www.pharmacy.ac.uk)

London (SOAS) The School of Oriental and African Studies (SOAS) is a college of the University of London and the only Higher Education institution in the UK specialising in the study of Asia, Africa and the Near and Middle East. (School of Oriental and African Studies, University of London, Thornhaugh Street, Russell Square, London, England WC1H 0XG. Tel 020 7898 4034; www.soas.ac.uk)

London (UCL) The College is located in Bloomsbury in the London University precinct. (University College London, University of London, Gower Street, London, England WC1E 6BT. Tel 020 7679 3000; www.ucl.ac.uk)

London LSE The School is located in the heart of London and specialises in the whole range of social science subjects (from Economics, Politics and Law to Sociology, Accounting and Finance). (London School of Economics and Political Science, Undergraduate Admissions Office, Houghton Street, London, England WC2A 2AE. Tel 020 7955 7170; www.lse.ac.uk)

London Met The University has two campuses, one in north London (with the largest (new) science laboratory in Europe) and one in the City, and several partner colleges. (London Metropolitan University, Admissions Office, 166–220 Holloway Road, London, England N7 8DB. Tel 020 7133 4200; www.londonmet.ac.uk)

London NCH NCH is an independent university college, centrally located in Bloomsbury, which is dedicated to providing high academic experience. (New College of the Humanities, 27 Old Gloucester Street, London, England WC1N 3AX. Tel 020 7637 4550; www.nchum.org)

London South Bank The main campus of the University is in Southwark on the south bank of the Thames in London. Other campuses are at Whipps Cross in east London and at Havering in Essex. (London South Bank University, Admissions Office, 90 London Road, London, England SE1 6LN. Tel 020 7815 6100; www.lsbu.ac.uk)

Loughborough On a large rural single-site campus, the University is a mile from the town centre. (Loughborough University, Undergraduate Admissions Office, Loughborough, England LE11 3TU. Tel 01509 263171; www.lboro.ac.uk)

Manchester The University has a large precinct one mile south of the city centre. The University of Manchester has a long tradition of excellence in Higher Education. 25 Nobel Prize winners have either studied or conducted their work there and in the 2008 Research Assessment Exercise (RAE), Manchester was rated third in the UK to Oxford and Cambridge in terms of 'research power'. The recent Shanghai Jiao Tong Rankings placed Manchester at 44th place in the world and fifth in the UK. (University of Manchester, Student Recruitment and Admissions, Rutherford Building, Oxford Road, Manchester, England M13 9PL. Tel 0161 306 1631; www.manchester.ac.uk)

Manchester Met The University has five sites in Manchester and one in Cheshire, at Alsager and Crewe. (Manchester Metropolitan University, Admissions Office, All Saints Building, All Saints, Manchester, England M15 6BH. Tel 0161 247 2000; www.mmu.ac.uk)

Middlesex This is a multi-campus university in north London with associate colleges in the region. (Middlesex University, Admissions Enquiries, The Burroughs, London, England NW4 4BT. Tel 020 8411 5555; www.mdx.ac.uk)

Newcastle The University has a single campus in the city centre. (Newcastle University, Admissions Office, 6 Kensington Terrace, Newcastle-upon-Tyne, England NE1 7RU. Tel 0191 208 3333; www.ncl.ac.uk)

Newport The University has two campuses, in Newport and Caerleon. (Newport, University of Wales, Admissions Office, Caerleon Campus, Lodge Road, Caerleon, South Wales NP18 3QT. Tel 01633 432030; www.newport.ac.uk)

Northampton The University (created in 2005) has two campuses close to the town centre. (University of Northampton, Admissions Office, Park Campus, Boughton Green Road, Northampton, England NN2 7AL. Tel 0800 358 2232; www.northampton.ac.uk)

Northumbria The University has two campuses in and around Newcastle. (Northumbria University, Ellison Place, Newcastle-upon-Tyne, England NE1 8ST. Tel 0191 243 7420; www.northumbria.ac.uk)

Nottingham This is a large campus university to the west of the city with a second campus two miles from the city centre, and a third at Sutton Bonington for the new School of Veterinary Science and Medicine, 10 miles south of University Park. (University of Nottingham, Admissions Office, University Park, Nottingham, England NG7 2RD. Tel 0115 951 5559; www.nottingham.ac.uk)

Nottingham Trent The University has three campuses: City site, in the centre of Nottingham, Clifton and Brackenhurst. The Clifton campus of the University is four miles from Nottingham city centre and caters for Education, Humanities and Science whilst Brackenhurst, near Southwell, focuses on land-based subjects. (Nottingham Trent University, Registry Admissions, Dryden Centre, Burton Street, Nottingham, England NG1 4BU. Tel 0115 848 4200; www.ntu.ac.uk)

Open University This is the UK's largest university for part-time and distance-learning higher education, providing supported distance learning for undergraduate (and postgraduate) students who must be aged over 18 years. Application and registration is made direct to the OU, and not through UCAS (at present). (Open University, Student Registration and Enquiry Service, PO Box 197, Milton Keynes, England MK7 6BJ. Tel 0845 300 6090; www.open.ac.uk)

Oxford The University has 30 colleges and seven private halls admitting undergraduates throughout the city. Colleges: Balliol, Brasenose, Christ Church, Corpus Christi, Exeter, Harris Manchester (mature students only), Hertford, Jesus, Keble, Lady Margaret Hall, Lincoln, Magdalen, Mansfield, Merton, New, Oriel, Pembroke, St Anne's, St Catherine's, St Edmund Hall, St Hilda's, St Hugh's, St John's, St Peter's, Somerville, Queen's, Trinity, University, Wadham, Worcester. Permanent Private Halls: Blackfriars, Campion Hall (men only), Greyfriars, Regent's Park College, St Benet's Hall, St Stephen's House, Wycliffe. (University of Oxford, Undergraduate Admissions Office, University Offices, Wellington Square, Oxford, England OX1 2JD. Tel 01865 288000; www.ox.ac.uk)

Oxford Brookes The University has three main campuses in and around Oxford. (Oxford Brookes University, Admissions Office, Headington Campus, Gipsy Lane, Oxford, England OX3 0BP. Tel 01865 483040; www.brookes.ac.uk)

Peninsula (MS) From 2013 new students will study for University of Exeter or Plymouth University degrees. Please see these institutions for more information. (www.pcmd.ac.uk)

Plymouth The University has two main campuses, one in Plymouth and a second, the Peninsula Allied Health Centre, is four miles north of the main campus. Courses are also offered at eight partner colleges. (University of Plymouth, Central Admissions, Drake Circus, Plymouth, England PL4 8AA. Tel 01752 585 858; www.plymouth.ac.uk)

Portsmouth The main campus of the University is close to the town centre; courses are also taught at colleges in Hampshire and Surrey. A leading, modern university with a strong reputation for teaching and research – many academics are international leaders in their fields and their teaching record received the highest possible rating in the recent Quality Assurance Agency audit. The 2011 National Students Survey places Portsmouth within the top 30 Universities with 85% of students being satisfied or very satisfied with their course. It is a research-active university with a wide range of activities across many subjects – ranging from the Institute of Cosmology and Gravitation to the Centre for European and International Research. Their Faculty of Creative and Cultural Industries have a strong reputation, meeting the need for talented graduates of the fast-growing creative and cultural sector of the economy. (University of Portsmouth, Academic Registry, University House, Winston Churchill Avenue, Portsmouth, England PO1 2UP. Tel 023 9284 8484; www.port.ac.uk)

Queen's Belfast The University has a large campus in the south of the city. (Queen's University Belfast, Admissions Service, University Road, Belfast, Northern Ireland BT7 1NN. Tel 028 9097 2727; www.qub.ac.uk)

Reading Situated on 320 acres of landscaped parkland, the campus won the Green Flag Award in 2011 as the highest-rated University campus in the Scheme's national People's Choice Awards. There are three campuses in the University, with the main (Whiteknights) on a rural campus at the edge of the city, and two others within walking distance. Foundation degrees are taught at two partner colleges.

(University of Reading, Student Recruitment Office, PO Box 217, Reading, England RG6 6AH. Tel 0118 378 8619; www.rdg.ac.uk)

Richmond (Am Int Univ) Richmond, The American International University in London is an independent, not-for-profit, international, liberal arts and professional studies university established in 1972. It educates a multi-cultural student body in the American liberal arts tradition, and provides its students with the intellectual and personal skills that will enable them to exercise influence and succeed in an increasingly interdependent and evolving world. (Richmond, The American International University in London, Queen's Road, Richmond-upon-Thames, England TW10 6JP. Tel 020 8332 8200; www.richmond.ac.uk)

Robert Gordon The University has two campuses in and near Aberdeen city centre. (Robert Gordon University, Admissions Office, Administration Building, Schoolhill, Aberdeen, Scotland AB10 1FR. Tel 01224 262728; www.rgu.ac.uk)

Roehampton Roehampton, London's only campus university, is located in south-west London, close to Richmond Park, and has four colleges: Digby Stuart, Froebel, Southlands and Whitelands. (Roehampton University, Enquiries Office, Erasmus House, Roehampton Lane, London, England SW15 5PU. Tel 020 8392 3232; www.roehampton.ac.uk)

St Andrews Founded in 1413, and the third oldest university in the English-speaking world, this is a town-centre university on the east coast of Scotland. St. Andrews is one of the UK's leading universities and also within the top 25 in the world for Arts and Humanities with the university, as a whole, in the top 100 worldwide. (University of St Andrews, Admissions Application Centre, St Katherine's West, 16 The Scores, St Andrews, Scotland KY16 9AX. Tel 01334 462150; www.st-andrews.ac.uk)

Salford This is a city-centre campus university. All courses are taught in the central campus, except for Midwifery which is taught at Bury and Nursing which is at Eccles. (University of Salford, Admissions Officer, The Crescent, Salford, England M5 4WT. Tel 0161 295 4545; www.salford.ac.uk)

Sheffield The University campus is close to Sheffield's city centre. (University of Sheffield, Admissions Services, Student Services Department, 9 Northumberland Road, Sheffield, England S10 2TT. Tel 0114 222 8030; www.shef.ac.uk)

Sheffield Hallam The University has two campuses, one in the city centre, and the second two miles away. (Sheffield Hallam University, Admissions Office, City Campus, Howard Street, Sheffield, England S1 1WB. Tel 0114 225 5555; www.shu.ac.uk)

Southampton The University has five main campuses in Southampton and Winchester. (University of Southampton, University Road, Southampton, England SO17 1BJ. Tel 023 8059 5000; www.soton.ac.uk)

Southampton Solent Southampton Solent University first became a university in 2005 but has a well-established background in higher education which can be traced back to 1989 and 1856. Situated close to Southampton city centre, the university has two partner colleges. (Southampton Solent University, Student Recruitment, East Park Terrace, Southampton, England SO14 0YN. Tel 023 8031 9000; www.solent.ac.uk)

Staffordshire The University has campuses at Stafford, Stoke, Lichfield, Shrewsbury and several regional colleges. (Staffordshire University, Admissions, College Road, Stoke on Trent, England ST4 2DE. Tel 01782 292753; www.staffs.ac.uk)

Stirling The University is situated on a large rural campus. (University of Stirling, UG Admissions Office, Stirling, Scotland FK9 4LA. Tel 01786 467044; www.stir.ac.uk)

Strathclyde The University's main campus is in Glasgow city centre, with the Jordanhill campus to the west of the city. (University of Strathclyde, 16 Richmond Street, Glasgow, Scotland G1 1XQ. Tel 0141 552 4400; www.strath.ac.uk)

Sunderland The main campus of the University is in Sunderland city centre, with the Sir Tom Cowie campus across the river accommodating the Business School and Informatics Centre. (University of Sunderland, Student Recruitment, Chester Road, Sunderland, England SR1 3SD. Tel 0191 515 2000; www.sunderland.ac.uk)

Surrey The University has a modern campus a mile from Guildford city centre. Some foundation-year teaching takes place in local colleges. (University of Surrey, Undergraduate Admissions Office, Stag Hill, Guildford, England GU2 7XH. Tel 01483 689906; www.surrey.ac.uk)

Sussex The University has a single site campus four miles from Brighton. (University of Sussex, Undergraduate Admissions, Sussex House, Falmer, Brighton, England BN1 9RH. Tel 01273 678416; www.sussex.ac.uk)

Swansea The University is situated in a parkland campus outside Swansea. (Swansea University, Admissions, Singleton Park, Swansea, Wales SA2 8PP. Tel 01792 205678; www.swan.ac.uk)

Swansea Met This new (2008) university (formerly Swansea Institute) is situated in the centre of Swansea. (Swansea Metropolitan University, Admissions Office, Mount Pleasant Campus, Swansea, Wales SA1 6ED. Tel 01792 481000; www.smu.ac.uk)

Teesside This is a city-centre university, with its campus in Middlesbrough. It has links with colleges in the region. (Teesside University, Admissions Office, Middlesbrough, England TS1 3BA. Tel 01642 384228; www.tees.ac.uk)

Trinity Saint David This is a new university (2010) created by the merger of the University of Wales, Lampeter, and Trinity University College Carmarthen with courses run in both Carmarthen and Lampeter. (Trinity Saint David, University of Wales, Academic Registry, Lampeter, Wales SA48 7ED. Tel Carmarthen 01267 676767; Lampeter 01570 422351; www.trinitysaintdavid.ac.uk)

UCLan The University is located on a small campus in the city centre with partner colleges throughout Lancashire. (University of Central Lancashire, Admissions Office, Preston, England PR1 2HE. Tel 01772 201201; www.uclan.ac.uk)

UEA The University is set in parkland close to Norwich. (University of East Anglia, Admissions Office, Norwich Research Park, Norwich, England NR4 7TJ. Tel 01603 591515; www.uea.ac.uk)

UEL The University has campuses in London at Stratford and Docklands. Courses are also offered at several colleges in Greater London. (University of East London, Docklands Campus, 4–6 University Way, London, England E16 2RB. Tel 020 8223 3333; www.uel.ac.uk)

UHI The UHI is based on a partnership of colleges and research centres, each with its own distinctive character. Full-time undergraduate courses are provided by partner colleges (for addresses see Section 3). (University of the Highlands and Islands, Course Information Unit, Executive Office, Ness Walk, Inverness, Scotland IV3 5SQ. Tel 01463 279000; www.uhi.ac.uk)

Ulster The University has four campuses: Belfast, Coleraine, Jordanstown, and Magee in Londonderry. (University of Ulster, Belfast Campus, York Street, Belfast, Northern Ireland BT15 1ED. Tel 028 701 23456; www.ulster.ac.uk)

Warwick The University has a single-site campus situated three miles outside Coventry. (University of Warwick, Student Admissions Office, Coventry, England CV4 7AL. Tel 024 7652 3723; www.warwick.ac.uk)

West London (formerly Thames Valley University) The University has campuses at Ealing, Reading, Slough and Brentford, and links with four sites in west London and associated colleges. (University of West London, Learning Advice Centre, St Mary's Road, London, England W5 5RF. Tel 0800 036 8888; www.uwl.ac.uk)

West Scotland This new university (2007) was formed from the merger of the University of Paisley and Bell College. There are four campuses: Paisley, Ayr, Hamilton and Dumfries. UWS continually invests in its facilities and services as it recognises that good facilities, both academic and social, are needed to support the student learning experience at university. (University of the West of Scotland, Admissions Office, High Street, Paisley, Scotland PA1 2BE. Tel 0141 8483727; www.uws.ac.uk)

Westminster The University has four campuses (Cavendish, Marylebone and Regent in central London and Harrow) and associated colleges including the British Academy of New Music. (University of Westminster, Central Admissions, 35 Marylebone Road, London, England NW1 5LS. Tel 020 7911 5020; www.westminster.ac.uk)

Winchester This is a new university (2005) close to the centre of Winchester with additional sites in Basingstoke and Bournemouth. (University of Winchester, Course Enquiries, West Hill, Winchester, England SO22 4NR. Tel 01962 827234; www.winchester.ac.uk)

Wolverhampton The University has two campuses in Wolverhampton and others in Walsall and Telford. (University of Wolverhampton, Admissions Unit, MX, City Campus North, Camp Street, Wolverhampton, England WV1 1AD. Tel 01902 321000; www.wlv.ac.uk)

Worcester This small new university (2005) is located on a campus a short distance from Worcester city centre. (University of Worcester, Admissions Office, Henwick Grove, Worcester, England WR2 6AJ. Tel 01905 855111; www.worcester.ac.uk)

York The University has a parkland campus on the outskirts of York and a second campus in the city centre. The University is committed to excellence in admissions and aims to provide a professional and fair service for applicants. The University aims not only to select students who have the ability and motivation to benefit from the programmes which they intend to follow and who will make a contribution to university life, but also to ensure that no prospective or existing student is treated less favourably on the grounds of age, race, colour, nationality, ethnic origin, faith, disability, HIV status, sexual orientation, gender, marital or parental status, political belief or social or economic class. There are many reasons why applicants choose York:

- a very high-quality academic experience
- strong financial support package
- a commitment to enhancing employability
- a welcoming and supportive college system
- a chance to develop enterprise skills
- a strong reputation for student support
- affordable and plentiful accommodation
- a lively and stimulating environment
- a beautiful location in one of Europe's finest cities.

(University of York, Admissions and School Liaison, Heslington, York, England YO10 5DD. Tel 01904 433533; www.york.ac.uk)

York St John The University is based on an award-winning campus in the centre of York with almost 6,000 students studying on a wide range of subjects. It has a wide network of regional, national and international partnerships with a highly recognised reputation for its teaching and learning. (York St John University, Lord Mayor's Walk, York, England YO31 7EX. Tel 01904 624624; www.yorksj.ac.uk)

SECTION 2: UNIVERSITY COLLEGES, INSTITUTES, AND SPECIALIST COLLEGES OF AGRICULTURE AND HORTICULTURE, ART, DANCE, DRAMA, MUSIC, OSTEOPATHY AND SPEECH

University Colleges and Institutes provide undergraduate and postgraduate courses in a wide range of subjects and are university-sector institutions. While many universities and university colleges offer courses in art, design, music, drama, agriculture, horticulture and courses connected to the land-based industries, the specialist colleges listed below provide courses at many levels, often part-time, in these separate fields.

It is important that you read prospectuses and check websites carefully and go to Open Days to find out as much as you can about these colleges and about their courses which interest you. Applications for full-time courses at the institutions listed below are through UCAS.

Abbreviations used below A = Art and Design; **Ag** = Agriculture, Animals and Land-related courses; **C** = Communication; **D** = Drama, Performing and Theatre Arts; **Da** = Dance; **F** = Fashion; **H** = Horticulture and Landscape-related courses; **M** = Music.

Academy of Live and Recorded Arts (ALRA) Studio 24, Royal Victoria Patriotic Building, John Archer Way, London, England SW18 3SX. Tel 020 8870 6475; www.alra.co.uk [**D**]

Anglo-European College of Chiropractic 13–15 Parkwood Road, Bournemouth, England BH5 2DF. Tel 01202 436200; www.aecc.ac.uk

Anniesland College Hatfield Campus, 19 Hatfield Drive, Glasgow, Scotland G12 0YE. Tel 0141 357 3969; www.anniesland.ac.uk

Architectural Association School of Architecture 36 Bedford Square, London, England WC1B 3ES. Tel 020 7887 4000; www.aaschool.ac.uk

Arts Educational Schools London Cone Ripman House, 14 Bath Road, London, England W4 1LY. Tel 020 8987 6666; www.artsed.co.uk [**A**]

Arts University College at Bournemouth Wallisdown, Poole, England BH12 5HH. Tel 01202 533011; www.aucb.ac.uk [**A**]

Askham Bryan College Askham Bryan, York, England YO23 3FR. Tel 01904 772277; www.askham-bryan. ac.uk [**Ag**]

Berkshire College of Agriculture Hall Place, Burchetts Green, Maidenhead, England SL6 6QR. Tel 01628 824444; www.bca.ac.uk [**Ag**]

Bishop Burton College Learner Services, York Road, Bishop Burton, England HU17 8QG. Tel 01964 553000; www.bishopburton.ac.uk [**Ag**]

Bishop Grosseteste University College Academic Registry, Newport, Lincoln, England LN1 3DY. Tel 01522 583658; www.bishopg.ac.uk

Bristol Old Vic Theatre School Bristol Old Vic Theatre School is an affiliate of the Conservatoire for Dance and Drama and is an Associate School of the University of the West of England. 2 Downside Road, Clifton, Bristol, England BS8 2XF. Tel 0117 973 3535; www.oldvic.ac.uk [**D**]

British College of Osteopathic Medicine Lief House, 120–122 Finchley Road, London, England NW3 5HR. Tel 020 7435 6464; www.bcom.ac.uk

British School of Osteopathy 275 Borough High Street, London, England SE1 1JE. Tel 020 7407 0222; Student Admissions; 020 7089 5316; www.bso.ac.uk

Camberwell College of Art, University of the Arts London Peckham Road, London, England SE5 8UF. Tel 020 7514 6302; www.camberwell.arts.ac.uk [**A**]

Capel Manor College Administrative Office, Bullsmore Lane, Enfield, England EN1 4RQ. Tel 08456 122122; www.capel.ac.uk [**H**]

Cavendish College London 35–37 Alfred Place, London, England WC1E 7DP. Tel 020 7580 4074; www. cavendish.ac.uk

Central Saint Martins College of Art and Design, University of the Arts London Southampton Row, London, England WC1B 4AP. Tel 020 7514 7022; www.csm.arts.ac.uk [**A**]

Central School of Speech and Drama, University of London The School's main campus is at the Embassy Theatre, 15 minutes by Underground from Central London. Central School of Speech and Drama. Academic Registry, Embassy Theatre, 64 Eton Avenue, London, England NW3 3HY. Tel 020 7722 8183; www.cssd. ac.uk [**D**]

Chelsea College of Art and Design, University of the Arts London 16 John Islip Street, London, England SW1P 4JU. Tel 020 7514 7751; www.chelsea.arts.ac.uk [**A**]

City and Guilds of London Art School 124 Kennington Park Road, London, England SE11 4DJ. Tel 020 7735 2306; www.cityandguildsartschool.ac.uk [**A**]

Cleveland College of Art and Design This is the only specialist art and design college in the north of England, with a campus in the heart of Hartlepool. The College offers excellent facilities and a wide range of industry contacts which are utilised to increase employability. Green Lane, Linthorpe, Middlesbrough, England TS5 7RJ. Tel 01642 288000; www.ccad.ac.uk [**A**]

Colchester Institute Course Enquiries, Sheepen Road, Colchester, England CO3 3LL. Tel 01206 712777; www.colchester.ac.uk

College of Agriculture Food and Rural Enterprise (CAFRE) Greenmount Campus, 22 Greenmount Road, Antrim, Northern Ireland BT41 4PU. Tel 0800 028 4291; www.cafre.ac.uk [**Ag**]

College of Estate Management Whiteknights, Reading, England RG6 6AW. Tel 0800 019 9697; www.cem.ac.uk

Courtauld Institute of Art, University of London The Courtauld Institute of Art is one of the world's leading centres for the study of the history and conservation of art and architecture, and its gallery houses one of Britain's best-loved collections. Based at Somerset House, The Courtauld is an independent college of the University of London. Somerset House, London, England WC2R 0RN. Tel 020 7848 2635; www.courtauld.ac.uk [**A**]

Drama Centre London (part of Central St Martin's, University of the Arts London). Saffron House, 10 Back Hill, London, England EC1R 5LQ. Tel 020 7514 8778; www.csm.arts.ac.uk/drama [**D**]

East 15 Acting School Hatfields, Rectory Lane, Loughton, England IG10 3RY. Tel 020 8508 5983; www.east15.ac.uk [**D**]

Edinburgh College of Art Academic Registry, Lauriston Place, Edinburgh, Scotland EH3 9DF. Tel 0131 221 6027; www.eca.ac.uk [**A**]

European School of Osteopathy Boxley House, The Street, Boxley, Maidstone, England ME14 3DZ. Tel 01622 671558; www.eso.ac.uk

Falmouth University College (including Dartington College of Arts) Admissions Office, Woodlane, Falmouth, England TR11 4RH. Tel 01326 211077; www.falmouth.ac.uk

Glasgow School of Art 167 Renfrew Street, Glasgow, Scotland G3 6RQ. Tel 0141 353 4500; www.gsa.ac.uk [**A**]

Gray's School of Art, Robert Gordon University Garthdee Road, Aberdeen, Scotland AB10 7QD. Tel 01224 263600; www.rgu.ac.uk [**A**]

Guildford School of Acting, GSA Conservatoire Stag Hill Campus, Guildford, England GU2 7XH. Tel 01483 560701; www.conservatoire.org [**D**]

Guildhall School of Music and Drama Silk Street, Barbican, London, England EC2Y 8DT. Tel 020 7628 2571; www.gsmd.ac.uk [**M**]

Harper Adams University College Harper Adams' attractive rural location provides the best of town and country. The University College has been voted Best University College in the *2012 Sunday Times University Guide* for the 5th consecutive year. Admissions Office, Newport, England TF10 8NB. Tel 01952 815000; www.harper-adams.ac.uk [**Ag**]

Hartpury College Hartpury House, Hartpury, England GL19 3BE. Tel 01452 702345; www.hartpury.ac.uk [**Ag**]

Heatherley School of Fine Art 75 Lots Road, London, England SW10 0RN. Tel 020 7351 4190; www.heatherleys.org [**A**]

Hereford College of Arts Hereford College of Arts is one of only five specialist arts colleges in the UK. As a smaller college it can offer personal attention to each student. Access to tutors, workshops and technical demonstrators are readily available and individual workspaces on a number of courses are on offer. Folly Lane, Hereford, England HR1 1LT. Tel 01432 273359; www.hca.ac.uk [**A**]

Leeds College of Art and Design Blenheim Walk, Leeds, England LS2 9AQ. Tel 0113 202 8039; www.leeds-art.ac.uk [**A**]

Leeds College of Music 3 Quarry Hill, Leeds, England LS2 7PD. Tel 0113 222 3416; www.lcm.ac.uk [**M**]

Leeds Trinity University College Student Enquiries Office, Brownberrie Lane, Horsforth, Leeds, England LS18 5HD. Tel 0113 283 7100; www.leedstrinity.ac.uk

Liverpool Institute for Performing Arts Mount Street, Liverpool, England L1 9HF. Tel 0151 330 3009; www.lipa.ac.uk [**D**]

London Academy of Music and Dramatic Art 155 Talgarth Road, London, England W14 9DA. Tel 020 8834 0500; www.lamda.org.uk [**M**]

London College of Communication, University of the Arts London Elephant and Castle, London, England SE1 6SB. Tel 020 7514 6569; www.lcc.arts.ac.uk [**C**]

London College of Fashion, University of the Arts London 20 John Princes Street, London, England W1G 0BJ. Tel 0207 514 7400; www.fashion.arts.ac.uk [**F**]

Marjon, University College Plymouth St Mark and St John Admissions Office, Derriford Road, Plymouth, England PL6 8BH. Tel 01752 636890; www.marjon.ac.uk

Mountview Academy of Theatre Arts Mountview is situated in Wood Green, in the Borough of Haringey, North London, home of Alexandra Palace. It is well placed for easy access to West End theatres, fringe theatres and London nightlife.

Founded in 1945, Mountview offers extensive and stimulating training for those interested in pursuing a Performance, Directing or Technical Theatre career. Clarendon Road, London, England N22 6XF. Tel 020 8881 2201; www.mountview.org.uk [**D**]

Myerscough College Six miles north of Preston, Myerscough College is a Higher and Further Education college dating back to the 19th century. It specialises in education and training for the land-based and sports industries, offering more than 20 different subjects. Myerscough Hall, St Michael's Road, Bilsborrow, Preston, England PR3 0RY. Tel 01995 642222; www.myerscough.ac.uk [**Ag**]

Newman University College Admissions Registrar, Genners Lane, Bartley Green, Birmingham, England B32 3NT. Tel 01214761181; www.newman.ac.uk

Northern School of Contemporary Dance 98 Chapeltown Road, Leeds, England LS7 4BH. Tel 0113 219 3000; www.nscd.ac.uk [**Da**]

Northop College (part of Deeside College, formerly the Welsh College of Horticulture) Holywell Road, Northop, Wales CH7 6AA. Tel 01352 841000; www.deeside.ac.uk/northop [**H**]

Norwich University College of the Arts Admissions, Francis House, 3–7 Redwell Street, Norwich, England NR2 4SN. Tel 01603 610561; www.nuca.ac.uk [**A**]

Plymouth College of Art Tavistock Place, Plymouth, England PL4 8AT. Tel 01752 203434; www.plymouthart.ac.uk [**A**]

Ravensbourne 6 Penrose Way, London, England SE10 0EW. Tel 020 3040 3500; www.rave.ac.uk [**C**]

Reaseheath College Reaseheath, Nantwich, England CW5 6DF. Tel General Enquiries 01270 625131; HE Enquiries 01270 613284; www.reaseheath.ac.uk [**Ag**]

Rose Bruford College Lamorbey Park Campus, Burnt Oak Lane, Sidcup, England DA15 9DF. Tel 020 8308 2600; www.bruford.ac.uk [**D**]

Royal Academy of Dance 36 Battersea Square, London, England SW11 3RA. Tel 020 7326 8000; www.rad.org.uk [**Da**]

Royal Academy of Dramatic Art (RADA) 62–64 Gower Street, London, England WC1E 6ED. Tel 020 7636 7076; www.rada.org [**D**]

Royal Academy of Music, University of London This is Britain's senior conservatoire, founded in 1822. Marylebone Road, London, England NW1 5HT. Tel 020 7873 7373; www.ram.ac.uk [**M**]

Royal Agricultural College Stroud Road, Cirencester, England GL7 6JS. Tel 01285 652531; www.rac.ac.uk [**Ag**]

Royal Ballet School 46 Floral Street, Covent Garden, London, England WC2E 9DA. Tel 020 7836 8899; www.royal-ballet-school.org.uk [**Da**]

Royal College of Music Prince Consort Road, London, England SW7 2BS. Tel 020 7589 3643; www.rcm.ac.uk [**M**]

Royal Conservatoire of Scotland (formerly Royal Scottish Academy of Music and Drama) 100 Renfrew Street, Glasgow, Scotland G2 3DB. Tel 0141 332 4101; www.rcs.ac.uk [**M**]

Royal Northern College of Music 124 Oxford Road, Manchester, England M13 9RD. Tel 0161 907 5200; www.rncm.ac.uk [**M**]

Royal Welsh College of Music and Drama Castle Grounds, Cathays Park, Cardiff, Wales CF10 3ER. Tel 029 2039 1361; www.rwcmd.ac.uk [**M**]

Ruskin School of Drawing and Fine Art 74 High Street, Oxford, England OX1 4BG. Tel 01865 276940; www.ruskin-sch.ox.ac.uk [**A**]

St Mary's University College Twickenham St Mary's is a modern university college offering the best of both worlds - with just under 4,000 students it's easy to feel at home but it's big enough to offer students all the challenges and excitement of a full and rewarding student life. It is located in a pleasant part of South West London with all the advantages of the busy towns of Kingston and Richmond close by, and central London only 30 minutes by train. Registry, Waldegrave Road, Strawberry Hill, Twickenham, England TW1 4SX. Tel 020 8240 4000; www.smuc.ac.uk

Scottish Agricultural College Student Recruitment and Admissions Office, SAC Ayr Campus, Auchincruive Estate, Ayr, Scotland KA6 5HW. Tel 0800 269453; www.sac.ac.uk [**Ag**]

Slade School of Fine Art, University College London As part of UCL, The Slade School of Fine Art is concerned with contemporary art and the practice, history and theories that inform it. It approaches the study and practice of art in an enquiring, investigative, experimental and research-minded way. Gower Street, London, England WC1E 6BT. Tel 020 7679 2313; www.ucl.ac.uk/slade [**A**]

Sparsholt College Hampshire Westley Lane, Sparsholt, Winchester, England SO21 2NF. Tel 01962 776441; www.sparsholt.ac.uk [**H**]

Stranmillis University College Academic Registry, Stranmillis Road, Belfast, Northern Ireland BT9 5DY. Tel 028 9038 4263; www.stran.ac.uk

Trinity Laban Conservatoire of Music and Dance Creekside, London, England SE8 3DZ. Tel 020 8691 8600; www.trinitylaban.ac.uk [**M**]

University Campus Suffolk Admissions Office, Waterfront Building, Neptune Quay, Ipswich, England IP4 1QJ. Tel 01473 338833; www.ucs.ac.uk

University College Birmingham Summer Row, Birmingham, England B15 2TT. Tel 0121 604 1000; www.ucb.ac.uk

Wimbledon College of Art, University of the Arts London Merton Hall Road, London, England SW19 3QA. Tel 020 7514 9641; www.wimbledon.arts.ac.uk [**A**]

Winchester School of Art, University of Southampton Park Avenue, Winchester, England SO23 8DL. Tel 023 8059 7141; www.wsa.soton.ac.uk [**A**]

Writtle College Lordship Road, Chelmsford, England CM1 3RR. Tel 01245 424200; www.writtle.ac.uk [**H**]

SECTION 3: UNIVERSITY CENTRES, FURTHER EDUCATION AND OTHER COLLEGES OFFERING HIGHER EDUCATION COURSES

Changes are taking place fast in this sector, with the merger of colleges and the introduction in 2009 of University Centres. These are linked to further education colleges and to one or more universities, and provide Foundation and Honours degree courses (often part-time) and sometimes postgraduate qualifications.

The following colleges appear under various subject headings in the tables in **Chapter 8** and are in UCAS for some of their courses. See prospectuses and websites for application details.

University Centres

Barnsley University Centre Church Street, Barnsley, England S70 2AN. Tel 01226 606262; www.barnsley.hud.ac.uk

Blackburn College Feilden Street, Blackburn, England BB2 1LH. Tel 01254 55144; Student Hotline 01254 292929; www.blackburn.ac.uk

Bradford College University Centre Admissions Office, Great Horton Road, Bradford, England BD7 1AY. Tel 01274 433333; www.bradfordcollege.ac.uk

College of West Anglia King's Lynn Centre, Tennyson Avenue, King's Lynn, Norfolk, England PE30 2QW. Tel 01553 761144; www.col-westanglia.ac.uk

Doncaster College and University Centre High Melton, Doncaster, England DN5 7SZ. Tel 01302 553773; www.don.ac.uk

Oldham College University Centre Cromwell Street, Oldham, England OL1 1BB. Tel 0800 085 0374; www.hud.ac.uk/oldham

University Centre Folkestone Mill Bay, Folkestone, England CT20 1JG. Tel 0800 804 8500; www.ucf.ac.uk

University Centre Milton Keynes 200 Silbury Boulevard, Milton Keynes, England MK9 1LT. Tel 01908 684444; www.ucmk.ac.uk

University Centre Yeovil 91 Preston Road, Yeovil, England BA20 2DN. Tel 01935 845454; www.ucy.ac.uk

Other Further Education Colleges

Aberdeen College Gallowgate Centre, Gallowgate, Aberdeen, Scotland AB25 1BN. Tel 01224 612000; Information and Booking Centre 01224 612330; www.abcol.ac.uk

Abingdon and Witney College Abingdon Campus, Wootton Road, Abingdon, England OX14 1GG. Tel 01235 555585; www.abingdon-witney.ac.uk

Accrington and Rossendale College Broad Oak Road, Accrington, England BB5 2AW. Tel 01254 389933; Information and Care 01254 354354; www.accross.ac.uk

Adam Smith College St Brycedale Campus, St Brycedale Avenue, Kirkcaldy, Scotland KY1 1EX. Tel 01592 223400; Course Hotline 0800 413280; www.adamsmithcollege.ac.uk

Andover College Andover College, Charlton Road, Andover, England SP10 1EJ. Tel 01264 360000; www.andover.ac.uk

Angus College Keptie Road, Arbroath, Scotland DD11 3EA. Tel 01241 432600; www.angus.ac.uk

Argyll College (UHI partner college – see Section 1) West Bay, Dunoon, Scotland PA23 7HP. Tel 08452 309969; www.argyllcollege.com

Aylesbury College Oxford Road, Aylesbury, England HP21 8PD. Tel 01296 588588; www.aylesbury.ac.uk

Ayr College Dam Park, Ayr, Scotland KA8 0EU. Tel 01292 265184; Admissions 0800 199798; www.ayrcoll.ac.uk

Banff and Buchan College Main Campus, Henderson Road, Fraserburgh, Scotland AB43 9GA. Tel 01346 586100; www.banff-buchan.ac.uk

Barking and Dagenham College Dagenham Road, Romford, England RM7 0XU. Tel 020 8090 3020; www.barkingdagenhamcollege.ac.uk

Barnet College Graseby House, Wood Street, Barnet, England EN5 5UJ. Tel 020 8200 8300; Enrolment/Course Information 020 8266 4000; www.barnet.ac.uk

Barnfield College New Bedford Road Campus, New Bedford Road, Luton, England LU2 7BF. Tel 01582 569500; www.barnfield.ac.uk

Barony College Parkgate, Dumfries, Scotland DG1 3NE. Tel 01387 860251; www.barony.ac.uk

Basingstoke College of Technology Worting Road, Basingstoke, England RG21 8TN. Tel 01256 354141; www.bcot.ac.uk

Bedford College Cauldwell Street, Bedford, England MK42 9AH. Tel 01234 291000; www.bedford.ac.uk

Bexley College Tower Road, Belvedere, England DA17 6JA. Tel 01322 404000; www.bexley.ac.uk

Bicton College East Budleigh, Budleigh Salterton, England EX9 7BY. Tel 01395 562400; www.bicton. ac.uk

Birmingham Metropolitan College (incorporating Matthew Boulton College of Further and Higher Education and Sutton Coldfield College) Jennens Road, Birmingham, England B4 7PS. Tel 0845 155 0101; www.bmetc.ac.uk

Bishop Auckland College Woodhouse Lane, Bishop Auckland, England DL14 6JZ. Tel 01388 443000; Course Enquiries 0800 092 6506; www.bacoll.ac.uk

Blackpool and the Fylde College Ashfield Road, Bispham, Blackpool, England FY2 0HB. Tel 01253 504343; www.blackpool.ac.uk

Borders College Head Office, Scottish Borders Campus, Nether Road, Galashiels, Scotland TD1 3HE. Tel 0870 050 5152; www.borderscollege.ac.uk

Boston College Skirbeck Road, Boston, England PE21 6JF. Tel 01205 365701; Course Information 01205 313218; www.boston.ac.uk

Bournemouth and Poole College Customer Enquiry Centre, North Road, Poole, England BH14 0LS. Tel 01202 205205; www.thecollege.co.uk

Bournville College Bristol Road South, Northfield, Birmingham, England B31 2AJ. Tel 0121 483 1000; Course Enquiries 0121 483 1111; www.bournville.ac.uk

BPP University College of Professional Studies Ltd 68 Red Lion Square, London, England WC1R 4NY. Tel 0845 678 6868; www.bpp.com

Bracknell and Wokingham College College Information Centre, Church Road, Bracknell, England RG12 1DJ. Tel 0845 330 3343; www.bracknell.ac.uk

Braintree College Church Lane, Braintree, England CM7 5SN. Tel 01376 321711; Course Enquiries 01376 557020; www.braintree.ac.uk

Bridgend College Cowbridge Road, Bridgend, Wales CF31 3DF. Tel 01656 302302; www.bridgend.ac.uk

Bridgwater College Bath Road, Bridgwater, England TA6 4PZ. Tel 01278 455464; Course Enquiries 01278 441234; www.bridgwater.ac.uk

Brockenhurst College Lyndhurst Road, Brockenhurst, England SO42 7ZE. Tel 01590 625555; www.brock. ac.uk

Bromley College of Further and Higher Education Rookery Lane, Bromley, England BR2 8HE. Tel 020 8295 7000; Course Enquiries 020 8295 7001; www.bromley.ac.uk

Brooklands College Weybridge Campus, Heath Road, Weybridge, England KT13 8TT. Tel 01932 797797; www.brooklands.ac.uk

Brooksby Melton College Melton Mowbray Campus, Ashfordby Road, Melton Mowbray, England LE13 0HJ. Tel 01664 850850; Course Enquiries 01664 855444; www.brooksbymelton.ac.uk

Burnley College Princess Way, Burnley, England BB12 0AN. Tel 01282 733373; Student Services 01282 733333; www.burnley.ac.uk

Burton College Student Services, Lichfield Street, Burton on Trent, England DE14 3RL. Tel 01283 494400; www.burton-college.ac.uk

Bury College Woodbury Centre, Market Street, Bury, England BL9 0BG. Tel 0161 280 8280; www. burycollege.ac.uk

Calderdale College Francis Street, Halifax, England HX1 3UZ. Tel Course Information 01422 399399; www.calderdale.ac.uk

Cambridge Regional College Kings Hedges Road, Cambridge, England CB4 2QT. Tel 01223 418200; www.camre.ac.uk

Canterbury College New Dover Road, Canterbury, England CT1 3AJ. Tel 01227 811111; Learning Advice/ Courses 01227 811188; www.cant-col.ac.uk

Cardonald College Mosspark Drive, Glasgow, Scotland G52 3AY. Tel 0141 272 3333; www.cardonald. ac.uk

Carlisle College Information Unit, Victoria Place, Carlisle, England CA1 1HS. Tel 01228 822703; www. carlisle.ac.uk

Carmel College Prescot Road, St Helens, England WA10 3AG. Tel 01744 452200; www.carmel.ac.uk

Carnegie College (formerly Lauder College) Pittsburgh Road, Halbeath, Dunfermline, Scotland KY11 8DY. Tel 0844 248 0155; www.carnegiecollege.ac.uk

Carshalton College Nightingale Road, Carshalton, England SM5 2EJ. Tel 020 8544 4444; www.carshalton. ac.uk

CECOS London College 59 Crompton Road, London, England N1 2YT. Tel 020 7359 3316; www.cecos. co.uk

Central Bedfordshire College (formerly Dunstable College) Kingsway, Dunstable, England LU5 4HG. Tel 0845 355 2525; www.centralbeds.ac.uk

Central College of Commerce Cathedral Street, Glasgow, Scotland G1 2TA. Tel Information Unit 0141 552 3941; www.centralcollege.ac.uk

Chelmsford College 102 Moulsham Street, Chelmsford, England CM2 0JQ. Tel 01245 265611; www. chelmsford-college.ac.uk

Chesterfield College Infirmary Road, Chesterfield, England S41 7NG. Tel 01246 500500; www.chesterfield. ac.uk

Chichester College Westgate Fields, Chichester, England PO19 1SB. Tel 01243 786321; www.chichester. ac.uk

City and Islington College The Marlborough Building, 383 Holloway Road, London, England N7 0RN. Tel 020 7700 9200; www.candi.ac.uk

City College Birmingham Fordrough Campus, 300 Bordesley Green, Birmingham, England B9 5NA. Tel 0121 204 0000; www.citycol.ac.uk

City College Brighton and Hove Pelham Street, Brighton, England BN1 4FA. Tel 01273 667788; Course Advisers 01273 667759; www.ccb.ac.uk

City College Coventry Swanswell Centre, 50 Swanswell Street, Coventry, England CV1 5DG. Tel 0800 616202; www.covcollege.ac.uk

City College Plymouth (formerly Plymouth College of Further Education) King's Road, Devonport, Plymouth, England PL1 5QG. Tel 01752 305300; www.cityplym.ac.uk

City of Bath College Student Advice Centre, Avon St, Bath, England BA1 1UP. Tel 01225 312191; www. citybathcoll.ac.uk

City of Bristol College Ashley Down Road, Bristol, England BS7 9BU. Tel 0117 312 5000; www.cityofbristol. ac.uk

City of Sunderland College Bede Centre, Durham Road, Sunderland, England SR3 4AH. Tel 0191 511 6000; HE Admissions 0191 511 6260; www.citysun.ac.uk

City of Westminster College Paddington Green Campus, Paddington Green, London, England W2 1NB. Tel 020 7723 8826; www.cwc.ac.uk

City of Wolverhampton College Paget Road Campus, Paget Road, Wolverhampton, England WV6 0DU. Tel 01902 836000; www.wolverhamptoncollege.ac.uk

Cliff College Calver, Hope Valley, Derbyshire, England S32 3XG. Tel 01246 584202; www.cliffcollege.ac.uk

Clydebank College College Square, Queens' Quay, Clydebank, Scotland G81 1BF. Tel 0141 951 7400; www.clydebank.ac.uk

Coatbridge College Kildonan Street, Coatbridge, Scotland ML5 3LS. Tel 01236 422316; Admissions 01236 436000; www.coatbridge.ac.uk

Coleg Llandrillo Cymru Llandudno Road, Rhos-on-Sea, Wales LL28 4HZ. Tel 01492 546666; www.llandrillo.ac.uk

Coleg Menai Ffriddoedd Road, Bangor, Gwynedd, Wales LL57 2TP. Tel 01248 370125; www.menai.ac.uk

Coleg Sir Gâr Graig Campus, Sandy Road, Pwll, Wales SA15 4DN. Tel 01554 748000; www.colegsirgar.ac.uk

College of Haringey, Enfield and North East London (formed in 2009 from a merger between Enfield College and the College of North East London) Enfield Centre, Hertford Road, Enfield, England EN3 5HA. Tel 020 8442 3055; www.conel.ac.uk

College of North West London Willesden Centre, Dudden Hill Lane, London, England NW10 2XD. Tel 020 8208 5000; Course Information 020 8208 5050; www.cnwl.ac.uk

College Ystrad Mynach Twyn Road, Ystrad Mynach, Hengoed, Wales CF82 7XR. Tel 01443 816888; www.ystrad-mynach.ac.uk

Cornwall College Camborne Campus, Trevenson Road, Pool, Redruth, England TR15 3RD. Tel 01209 616161; www.cornwall.ac.uk

Craven College High Street, Skipton, England BD23 1JY. Tel 01756 791411; www.craven-college.ac.uk

Croydon College College Road, Croydon, England CR9 1DX. Tel Course Information 020 8760 5914; www.croydon.ac.uk

Cumbernauld College Town Centre, Cumbernauld, Glasgow, Scotland G67 1HU. Tel 01236 731811; www.cumbernauld.ac.uk

Darlington College Central Park, Haughton Road, Darlington, England DL1 1DR. Tel 01325 503050; www.darlington.ac.uk

Dearne Valley College Manvers Park, Wath upon Dearne, Rotherham, England S63 7EW. Tel 01709 513333; www.dearne-coll.ac.uk

Derby College Prince Charles Avenue, Mackworth, Derby, England DE22 4LR. Tel 01332 520200; Course Enquiries 0800 028 0289; www.derby-college.ac.uk

Derwentside College Consett Campus, Front Street, Consett, England DH8 5EE. Tel 01207 585900; www.derwentside.ac.uk

Duchy College Rosewarne Campus, Camborne, England TR14 0AB. Tel 01209 722100; www.cornwall.ac.uk/duchy

Dudley College The Broadway, Dudley, England DY1 4AS. Tel 01384 363000; Course Enquiries 01384 363363; www.dudleycol.ac.uk

Dumfries and Galloway College College Gate, Bankend Road, Dumfries, Scotland DG1 4FD. Tel 01387 7340001; www.dumgal.ac.uk

Dundee College Kingsway Campus, Old Glamis Road, Dundee, Scotland DD3 8LE. Tel 01382 834834; Student Services 01382 834844; www.dundeecollege.ac.uk

Ealing, Hammersmith and West London College Gliddon Road, London, England W14 9BL. Tel 020 8741 1688; www.wlc.ac.uk

East Berkshire College Langley Campus, Station Road, Langley, England SL3 8BY. Tel 0845 373 2500; www.eastberks.ac.uk

East Durham College Houghall Campus, Houghall, England DH1 3SG. Tel 0191 375 4700; www.eastdurham.ac.uk

East Riding College Beverley Campus, Gallows Lane, Beverley, England HU17 7DT. Tel 0845 120 0037; www.eastridingcollege.ac.uk

East Surrey College Gatton Point, London Road, Redhill, England RH1 2JT. Tel 01737 788444; www.esc.ac.uk

Eastleigh College Chestnut Avenue, Eastleigh, England SO50 5FS. Tel 023 8091 1299; www.eastleigh.ac.uk

Easton College Easton, Norwich, England NR9 5DX. Tel 01603 731200; www.easton-college.ac.uk

Edinburgh's Telford College 350 West Granton Road, Edinburgh, Scotland EH5 1QE. Tel 0131 559 4000; www.ed-coll.ac.uk

European Business School Inner Circle, Regent's Park, London, England NW1 4NS. Tel 020 7487 7505; www.ebslondon.ac.uk

Exeter College Hele Road, Exeter, England EX4 4JS. Tel 0845 111 6000; www.exe-coll.ac.uk

Fareham College Bishopsfield Road, Fareham, England PO14 1NH. Tel 01329 815200; www.fareham.ac.uk

Farnborough College of Technology Boundary Road, Farnborough, England GU14 6SB. Tel 01252 407040; www.farn-ct.ac.uk

Filton College Filton Avenue, Filton, England BS34 7AT. Tel 0117 909 2297; www.filton.ac.uk

Forth Valley College Falkirk Campus, Grangemouth Road, Falkirk, Scotland FK2 9AD. Tel 01324 403000; www.forthvalley.ac.uk

Furness College Channelside, Barrow-in-Furness, England LA14 2PJ. Tel 01229 825017; www.furness.ac.uk

Gateshead College Baltic Campus, Baltic Business Quarter, Quarryfield Road, Gateshead, England NE8 3BE. Tel 0191 490 2246; www.gateshead.ac.uk

Glasgow College of Nautical Studies 21 Thistle Street, Glasgow, Scotland G5 9XB. Tel 0141 565 2500; www.glasgow-nautical.ac.uk

Glasgow Metropolitan College 60 North Hanover Street, Glasgow, Scotland G1 2BP. Tel 0141 566 6222; www.glasgowmet.ac.uk

Gloucestershire College (The Royal Forest of Dean College and Gloucester College have now merged) Gloucester Campus, Llanthony Road, Gloucester, England GL2 5JQ. Tel 0845 155 2020; www.gloscol.ac.uk

Grantham College Stonebridge Road, Grantham, England NG31 9AP. Tel 01476 400200; Course Information 01476 400200; www.grantham.ac.uk

Great Yarmouth College Suffolk Road, Southtown, Great Yarmouth, England NR31 0ED. Tel 01493 655261; www.gyc.ac.uk

Greenwich School of Management Meridian House, Royal Hill, London, England SE10 8RD. Tel 020 8516 7800; www.greenwich-college.ac.uk

Grimsby Institute of Further and Higher Education Nuns Corner, Laceby Road, Grimsby, England DN34 5BQ. Tel 0800 315002; www.grimsby.ac.uk

Guildford College Stoke Park Campus, Stoke Road, Guildford, England GU1 1EZ. Tel 01483 448500; www. guildford.ac.uk

Hackney Community College Shoreditch Campus, Falkirk Street, London, England N1 6HQ. Tel 020 7613 9123; www.tcch.ac.uk

Hadlow College Hadlow, Tonbridge, England TN11 0AL. Tel 0500 551 434; www.hadlow.ac.uk

Halesowen College Whittingham Road, Halesowen, England B63 3NA. Tel 0121 602 7777; www. halesowen.ac.uk

Harlow College Valizy Avenue, Harlow, England CM20 3LH. Tel 01279 868000; www.harlow-college. ac.uk

Harrow College Harrow on the Hill Campus, Lowlands Road, Harrow, England HA1 3AQ. Tel 020 8909 6000; www.harrow.ac.uk

Hartlepool College of Further Education Stockton Street, Hartlepool, England TS24 7NT. Tel 01429 295000; www.hartlepoolfe.ac.uk

Havering College Ardleigh Green Road, Hornchurch, England RM11 2LL. Tel 01708 455011; Course Information 01708 462 801; www.havering-college.ac.uk

Henley College Coventry Henley Road, Bell Green, Coventry, England CV2 1ED. Tel 024 7662 6300; www.henley-cov.ac.uk

Hereford College of Technology Folly Lane, Hereford, England HR1 1LS. Tel 0800 032 1986; www.hct. ac.uk

Hertford Regional College Ware Centre, Scotts Road, Ware, England SG12 9JF. Tel 01992 411 400; www. hrc.ac.uk

Highbury College Portsmouth Dovercourt Road, Cosham, Portsmouth, England PO6 2SA. Tel 023 9238 3131; www.highbury.ac.uk

Highland Theological College (UHI partner college – see Section 1) High Street, Dingwall, Scotland IV15 9HA. Tel 01349 780000; www.htc.uhi.ac.uk

Hillcroft College South Bank, Surbiton, England KT6 6DF. Tel 020 8399 2688; www.hillcroft.ac.uk

Holborn College Woolwich Road, London, England SE7 8LN. Tel 020 7403 8080; www.holborncollege. ac.uk

Hopwood Hall College Rochdale Campus, St Mary's Gate, Rochdale, England OL12 6RY. Tel 01706 345346; www.hopwood.ac.uk

Hugh Baird College Balliol Road, Bootle, England L20 7EW. Tel 0151 353 4444; www.hughbaird.ac.uk

Hull College The Queen's Gardens Centre, Wilberforce Drive, Hull, England HU1 3DG. Tel 01482 598 744; www.hull-college.ac.uk

Huntingdonshire Regional College California Road, Huntingdon, England PE29 1BL. Tel 01480 379100; www.huntingdon.ac.uk

ifs (School of Finance) The **ifs (School of Finance)** is a registered charity, incorporated by Royal Charter and has a remit to provide the financial services industry with a skilled and competent workforce while also promoting a better understanding of finance amongst consumers. The **ifs (School of Finance)** has a heritage in the provision of financial education spanning 130 years. 8th Floor, Peninsular House, 36 Monument Street, London, England EC3R 8LJ. Tel 01227 829499; www.ifslearning.ac.uk

Islamic College for Advanced Studies 133 High Road, London, England NW10 2SW. Tel 020 8451 9993; www.islamic-college.ac.uk

Isle of Wight College Medina Way, Newport, Isle of Wight, England PO30 5TA. Tel 01983 526631; www. iwcollege.ac.uk

James Watt College Finnart Street, Greenock, Scotland PA16 8HF. Tel 01475 724433; www.jameswatt.ac.uk

Jewel and Esk College Edinburgh Campus, 24 Milton Road East, Edinburgh, Scotland EH15 2PP. Tel 0131 334 7000; Information Services 0131 334 7163; www.jec.ac.uk

K College Brook Street, Tonbridge, England TN9 2PW. Tel 0845 207 8220; www.kcollege.ac.uk

Kendal College Milnthorpe Road, Kendal, England LA9 5AY. Tel 01539 814700; www.kendal.ac.uk

Kensington College of Business Wesley House, 4 Wild Court, London, England WC2B 4AU. Tel 020 7404 6330; www.kensingtoncoll.ac.uk

Kidderminster College Market Street, Kidderminster, England DY10 1LX. Tel 01562 820811; www.kidderminster.ac.uk

Kilmarnock College Holehouse Road, Kilmarnock, Scotland KA3 7AT. Tel 01563 523501; www.kilmarnock.ac.uk

Kingston College Kingston Hall Road, Kingston upon Thames, England KT1 2AQ. Tel 020 8546 2151; www.kingston-college.ac.uk

Kingston Maurward College Kingston Maurward, Dorchester, England DT2 8PY. Tel 01305 215000; Course Enquiries 01305 215032/215025; www.kmc.ac.uk

Kirklees College (formerly Dewsbury College) New North Road, Huddersfield, England HD1 5NN. Tel 01484 437000; www.kirkleescollege.ac.uk

Knowsley Community College Kirkby Campus, Cherryfield Drive, Kirkby, England L32 8SF. Tel 08451 551055; www.knowsleycollege.ac.uk

Lakes College, West Cumbria Hallwood Road, Lillyhall Business Park, Workington, England CA14 4JN. Tel 01946 839300; www.lcwc.ac.uk

Lambeth College 45 Clapham Common South Side, London, England SW4 9BL. Tel 020 7501 5010; Course Information 020 7501 5000; www.lambethcollege.ac.uk

Lancaster and Morecambe College Morecambe Road, Lancaster, England LA1 2TY. Tel 01524 66215; www.lmc.ac.uk

Langside College 50 Prospecthill Road, Glasgow, Scotland G42 9LB. Tel 0141 272 3600; www.langside.ac.uk

Lansdowne College 40–44 Bark Place, London, England W2 4AT. Tel 020 7616 4400; www.lansdownecollege.com

Leeds City College Thomas Danby Campus, Roundhay Road, Leeds, England LS7 3BG. Tel 0113 249 4912; www.leedscitycollege.ac.uk

Leeds College of Building North Street, Leeds, England LS2 7QT. Tel 0113 222 6000; Student Services 0113 222 6000; www.lcb.ac.uk

Leek College Stockwell Street, Leek, England ST13 6DP. Tel 01538 398866; www.leek.ac.uk

Leicester College Freemen's Park Campus, Aylestone Road, Leicester, England LE2 7LW. Tel 0116 224 2240; www.leicestercollege.ac.uk

Leo Baeck College The Sternberg Centre, 80 East End Road, London, England N3 2SY. Tel 020 8349 5600; www.lbc.ac.uk

Lewisham College Lewisham Way, London, England SE4 1UT. Tel General Enquiries 020 8692 0353; Course Enquiries 0800 834545; www.lewisham.ac.uk

Lews Castle College (UHI partner college – see Section 1) Castle Grounds, Stornoway, Isle of Lewis, Scotland HS2 0XR. Tel 01851 770000; www.lews.uhi.ac.uk

Lincoln College Monks Road, Lincoln, England LN2 5HQ. Tel 01522 876000; www.lincolncollege.ac.uk

Liverpool Community College Bankfield Road, Liverpool, England L13 0BQ. Tel 0151 252 1515; www. liv-coll.ac.uk

London College of Business and Computing Millennium Place, 206 Cambridge Heath Road, London, England E2 9NQ. Tel 020 8983 4193; www.lcbc.com

London School of Commerce Chaucer House, White Hart Yard, London, England SE1 1NX. Tel 020 7357 0077; www.lsclondon.co.uk

Loughborough College Radmoor Road, Loughborough, England LE11 3BT. Tel 0845 166 2950; www. loucoll.ac.uk

Macclesfield College Park Lane, Macclesfield, England SK11 8LF. Tel 01625 410000; Information/ Enrolment 01625 410001; www.macclesfield.ac.uk

Mid-Cheshire College Hartford Campus, Chester Road, Northwich, England CW8 1LJ. Tel 01606 74444; www.midchesh.ac.uk

Middlesbrough College Dock Street, Middlesbrough, England TS2 1AD. Tel 01642 333333; Course Information 01642 296600; www.mbro.ac.uk

Mid-Kent College Chatham Maritime Campus, Medway Building, Horsted Centre, Chatham, England ME4 4AG. Tel 01634 888800; www.midkent.ac.uk

Milton Keynes College Wroughton Campus, Chaffron Way Campus, Leadenhall, Milton Keynes, England MK6 5LP. Tel 01908 684444; www.mkcollege.ac.uk

Moray College (UHI partner college – see Section 1) Moray Street, Elgin, Scotland IV30 1JJ. Tel 01343 576216; www.moray.ac.uk

Moulton College West Street, Moulton, England NN3 7RR. Tel 01604 491131; www.moulton.ac.uk

Nazarene Theological College Dene Road, Didsbury, Manchester, England M20 2GU. Tel 0161 445 3063; www.nazarene.ac.uk

Neath Port Talbot College Dwr-y-Felin Road, Neath, Wales SA10 7RF. Tel 01639 648000; www.nptc. ac.uk

Nelson and Colne College Reedyford Site, Scotland Road, Nelson, England BB9 7YT. Tel 01282 440200; www.nelson.ac.uk

Nescot, North East Surrey College of Technology Reigate Road, Ewell, Epsom, England KT17 3DS. Tel 020 8394 3038; www.nescot.ac.uk

New College Durham Framwellgate Moor Campus, Durham, England DH1 5ES. Tel 0191 375 4000; www. newcollegedurham.ac.uk

New College Nottingham The Adams Building, Stoney Street, Nottingham, England NG1 1NG. Tel 01159 100100; www.ncn.ac.uk

New College Stamford Drift Road, Stamford, England PE9 1XA. Tel 01780 484300; www.stamford.ac.uk

New College Swindon New College Drive, Swindon, England SN3 1AH. Tel 01793 611 470; www. newcollege.ac.uk

New College Telford King Street, Wellington, Telford, England TF1 1NY. Tel 01952 641892; www. newcollegetelford.ac.uk

Newbury College Monks Lane, Newbury, England RG14 7TD. Tel 01635 845000; www.newbury-college. ac.uk

Newcastle College Rye Hill Campus, Scotswood Road, Newcastle-upon-Tyne, England NE4 7SA. Tel 0191 200 4000; www.ncl-coll.ac.uk

Newcastle-under-Lyme College Knutton Lane, Newcastle-under-Lyme, England ST5 2GB. Tel 01782 715 111; www.nulc.ac.uk

Newham College of Further Education East Ham Campus, High Street South, London, England E6 6ER. Tel 020 8257 4000; www.newham.ac.uk

North Atlantic Fisheries College (UHI partner college – see Section 1) NAFC Marine Centre, Port Arthur, Scalloway, Scotland ZE1 0UN. Tel 01595 772000; www.nafc.ac.uk

North East Worcestershire College Redditch Campus, Peakman Street, Redditch, England B98 8DW. Tel 01527 570020; www.ne-worcs.ac.uk

North Glasgow College 123 Flemington Street, Springburn, Glasgow, Scotland G21 4TD. Tel 0141 630 5000; www.northglasgowcollege.ac.uk

North Hertfordshire College Monkswood Way, Stevenage, England SG1 1LA. Tel 01462 424242; Courses 01462 424242; www.nhc.ac.uk

North Highland College (UHI partner college – see Section 1) Ormlie Road, Thurso, Scotland KW14 7EE. Tel 01847 889000; www.northhighland.ac.uk

North Lindsey College Kingsway, Scunthorpe, England DN17 1AJ. Tel 01724 281111; www.northlindsey. ac.uk

North Nottinghamshire College Carlton Road, Worksop, England S81 7HP. Tel 01909 504504; Student Services 01909 504500; www.nnotts-col.ac.uk

North Warwickshire and Hinckley College Nuneaton Campus, Hinckley Road, Nuneaton, England CV11 6BH. Tel 024 7624 3000; www.nwhc.ac.uk

North West Kent College Oakfield Lane, Dartford, England DA1 2JT. Tel 01322 629400; www.nwkcollege. ac.uk

Northampton College Booth Lane, Northampton, England NN3 3RF. Tel 01604 734567; www. northamptoncollege.ac.uk

Northbrook College, Sussex West Durrington Campus, Littlehampton Road, Worthing, England BN12 6NU. Tel 08451 556060; www.northbrook.ac.uk

Northern Regional College (formerly North East Institute of Further and Higher Education) Ballymena Campus, Trostan Avenue Building, Ballymena, Northern Ireland BT43 7BN. Tel 028 2563 6221; www. nrc.ac.uk

Northumberland College College Road, Ashington, England NE63 9RG. Tel 01670 841200; www. northumberland.ac.uk

Norton Radstock College South Hill Park, Radstock, England BA3 3RW. Tel 01761 433161; www.nortcoll. ac.uk

Norwich City College Ipswich Road, Norwich, England NR2 2LJ. Tel 01603 773311; www.ccn.ac.uk

Nottingham College International Beeston Centre, Nottingham College International, High Road, Chilwell, Nottingham, England NG9 4AH. Tel 0115 884 2218; Admissions 0115 884 2804; www.snc. ac.uk/international

Oaklands College, St Albans Smallford Campus, Hatfield Road, St Albans, England AL4 0JA. Tel 01727 737080; www.oaklands.ac.uk

Oatridge College Ecclesmachan, Broxburn, Scotland EH52 6NH. Tel 01506 864800; www.oatridge. ac.uk

Orkney College (UHI partner college – see Section 1) East Road, Kirkwall, Scotland KW15 1LX. Tel 01856 569000; www.orkney.uhi.ac.uk

Otley College Otley, Ipswich, England IP6 9EY. Tel 01473 785543; www.otleycollege.ac.uk

Oxford and Cherwell Valley College Banbury Campus, Broughton Road, Banbury, Oxford, England OX16 9QA. Tel 01865 550550; www.ocvc.ac.uk

Pembrokeshire College (Coleg Sir Benfro) Merlins Bridge, Haverfordwest, Wales SA61 1SZ. Tel Main Switchboard 01437 753000; Freephone 0800 716236; www.pembrokeshire.ac.uk

Perth College (UHI partner college – see Section 1) Crieff Road, Perth, Scotland PH1 2NX. Tel 08452 701177; www.perth.ac.uk

Peterborough University Centre Park Crescent, Peterborough, England PE1 4DZ. Tel 0845 872 8722; www.peterborough.ac.uk

Petroc (created through the merger of North Devon College and East Devon College in 2008) Old Sticklepath Hill, Sticklepath, Barnstaple, England EX31 2BQ. Tel 01271 345 291; www.petroc.ac.uk

Plumpton College Ditchling Road, Near Lewes, England BN7 3AE. Tel 01273 890454; www.plumpton. ac.uk

Portsmouth College Tangier Road, Copnor, Portsmouth, England PO3 6PZ. Tel 023 9266 7521; www. portsmouth-college.ac.uk

Preston College Fulwood Campus, St Vincent's Road, Preston, England PR1 6AS. Tel 01772 225000; www.preston.ac.uk

Redbridge College Little Heath, Barley Lane, Romford, England RM6 4XT. Tel 020 8548 7400; www. redbridge-college.ac.uk

Redcar and Cleveland College Corporation Road, Redcar, England TS10 1EZ. Tel 01642 473132; www. cleveland.ac.uk

Regents Business School, London Inner Circle, Regent's Park, London, England NW1 4NS. Tel 020 7487 7505; www.rbslondon.ac.uk

Reid Kerr College Admission Unit, Renfrew Road, Paisley, Scotland PA3 4DR. Tel Main Reception 0141 581 2222; Course Enquiries 0800 527343; www.reidkerr.net

Richmond-upon-Thames College Egerton Road, Twickenham, England TW2 7SJ. Tel General Enquiries 020 8607 8000; Course Enquiries 020 8607 8305/8314; www.richmond-utcoll.ac.uk

Riverside College Halton Kingsway Campus, Kingsway, Widnes, England WA8 7QQ. Tel 0151 257 2020; www.riversidecollege.ac.uk

Rotherham College of Arts and Technology Town Centre Campus, Eastwood Lane, Rotherham, England S65 1EG. Tel 08080 722777; www.rotherham.ac.uk

Royal National College for the Blind College Road, Hereford, England HR1 1EB. Tel 01432 265725; www.rncb.ac.uk

Runshaw College Adult College, Euxton Lane, Chorley, England PR7 6AD. Tel 01772 642040; www. runshaw.ac.uk

Ruskin College Oxford Student Enquiry Office, Walton Street, Oxford, England OX1 2HE. Tel 01865 554331; www.ruskin.ac.uk

Sabhal Mòr Ostaig Founded in 1973, Sabhal Mòr Ostaig is a modern, innovative college which has become internationally recognised as a National Centre for the Gaelic language and culture. The College is an academic partner within UHI and provides high quality education and research opportunities through the medium of Scottish Gaelic. ACC, Sleat, Scotland IV44 8RQ. Tel 01471 888 304; www.smo.uhi.ac.uk

St Helens College Water Street, St Helens, England WA10 1PP. Tel 01744 733766; www.sthelens.ac.uk

Salford College Worsley Campus, Walkden Road, Worsley, England M28 7QD. Tel 0161 631 5000; www. salford-col.ac.uk

Sandwell College Central Enquiries, Oldbury Campus, Pound Road, Oldbury, England B68 8NA. Tel 0800 622006; www.sandwell.ac.uk

School of Audio Engineering Institute SAE Institute Oxford opened in 2008 as the world headquarters of SAE Institute, a global franchise of audio education colleges. The current UK SAE campuses are in

Oxford, London, Liverpool and Glasgow. SAE Institute Head Office, Littlemore Park, Armstrong Road, Oxford, England OX4 4FY. Tel 01865 787150; www.sae.edu

Scottish Association for Marine Science (UHI partner college – see Section 1) Dunstaffnage Marine Laboratory, Oban, Argyll, Scotland PA37 1QA. Tel 01631 559000; www.sams.ac.uk

Selby College Abbot's Road, Selby, England YO8 8AT. Tel 01757 211000; www.selby.ac.uk

Sheffield College PO Box 345, Sheffield, England S2 2YY. Tel 0114 260 2600; www.sheffcol.ac.uk

Shetland College (UHI partner college – see Section 1) Gremista, Lerwick, Scotland ZE1 0PX. Tel 01595 771000; www.shetland.uhi.ac.uk

Shrewsbury College of Arts and Technology London Road, Shrewsbury, England SY2 6PR. Tel 01743 342342; www.shrewsbury.ac.uk

Shuttleworth College Old Warden Park, Biggleswade, England SG18 9DX. Tel 01767 626222; www.shuttleworth.ac.uk

Skelmersdale and Ormskirk Colleges Westbank Campus, Yewdale, Skelmersdale, England WN8 6JA. Tel 01695 52300; www.skelmersdale.ac.uk

Solihull College Blossomfield Road, Solihull, England B91 1SB. Tel 0121 678 7000; www.solihull.ac.uk

Somerset College of Arts and Technology Wellington Road, Taunton, England TA1 5AX. Tel 01823 366366; www.somerset.ac.uk

South Birmingham College Digbeth Campus, High Street, Deritend, Digbeth, Birmingham, England B5 5SU. Tel 0121 694 5000; www.sbirmc.ac.uk

South Cheshire College Dane Bank Avenue, Crewe, England CW2 8AB. Tel 01270 654654; www.s-cheshire.ac.uk

South Devon College Vantage Point, Long Road, Paignton, England TQ2 7EJ. Tel 01803 540505; www.southdevon.ac.uk

South Downs College College Road, Waterlooville, England PO7 8AA. Tel 023 9279 7979; www.southdowns.ac.uk

South Essex College (formerly South East Essex College; merged Jan 2010 with Thurrock and Basildon College) Luker Road, Southend-on-Sea, England SS1 1ND. Tel 01702 220400; www.southessex.ac.uk

South Kent College (formerly South Kent College and West Kent College) Brook Street, Tonbridge, England TN9 2WP. Tel 0845 207 8220; www.kcollege.ac.uk

South Lanarkshire College College Way, East Kilbride, Scotland G75 0NE. Tel Student Admissions 01355 807780; www.south-lanarkshire-college.ac.uk

South Leicestershire College Station Road, Wigston, England LE18 2DW. Tel 0116 264 3555; www.slcollege.ac.uk

South Nottingham College West Bridgford Centre, Greythorne Drive, West Bridgford, Nottingham, England NG2 7GA. Tel 0115 914 6400; www.snc.ac.uk

South Staffordshire College Cannock Campus, The Green, Cannock, England WS11 1UE. Tel 0300 456 2424; www.southstaffs.ac.uk

South Thames College Wandsworth High Street, London, England SW18 2PP. Tel Course Enquiries 020 8918 7777; www.south-thames.ac.uk

South Tyneside College St George's Avenue, South Shields, England NE34 6ET. Tel 0191 427 3500; www.stc.ac.uk

Southampton City College St Mary Street, Southampton, England SO14 1AR. Tel 023 8048 4848; www.southampton-city.ac.uk

Southern Regional College (formerly Upper Bann Institute) Portadown Campus, 36 Lurgan Road, Portadown, Northern Ireland BT63 5BL. Tel 028 3839 7777; www.src.ac.uk

Southgate College High Street, London, England N14 6BS. Tel 020 8982 5050; www.southgate.ac.uk

Southport College Mornington Road, Southport, England PR9 0TT. Tel 01704 392704; www.southport.ac.uk

Southwark College Waterloo Centre, The Cut, London, England SE1 8LE. Tel 020 7815 1500; www.southwark.ac.uk

Stafford College Earl Street, Stafford, England ST16 2QR. Tel 01785 223 800; www.staffordcoll.ac.uk

Staffordshire University Regional Federation SURF was established in May 2000 to deliver higher education courses through further education colleges. This partnership comprises all the FE colleges in Staffordshire and two colleges in Shropshire with Staffordshire University as the lead institution. It supports the development of higher education provision that is accessible and socially inclusive, based on demand - together providing high quality support for students so as to promote high student recruitment, retention, achievement and progression. Partnerships Office, BL166, Blackheath Lane, Stafford, England ST18 0AD. Tel 01782 294000; www.staffs.ac.uk

Stephenson College Thornborough Road, Coalville, England LE67 3TN. Tel 01530 836136; www.stephensoncoll.ac.uk

Stevenson College Edinburgh Bankhead Avenue, Edinburgh, Scotland EH11 4DE. Tel Switchboard 0131 535 4600; Course Enquiries 0131 535 4700; www.stevenson.ac.uk

Stockport College Town Centre Campus, Wellington Road South, Stockport, England SK1 3UQ. Tel 0161 958 3100; www.stockport.ac.uk

Stockton Riverside College Harvard Avenue, Stockton-on-Tees, England TS17 6FB. Tel 01642 865400; www.stockton.ac.uk

Stoke on Trent College Cauldon Campus, Stoke Road, Shelton, Stoke on Trent, England ST4 2DG. Tel 01782 208208; www.stokecoll.ac.uk

Stourbridge College Hagley Road Centre, Hagley Road, Stourbridge, England DY8 1QU. Tel 01384 344344; www.stourbridge.ac.uk

Stow College 43 Shamrock Street, Glasgow, Scotland G4 9LD. Tel 0844 249 8585; www.stow.ac.uk

Stratford-upon-Avon College The Willows North, Alcester Road, Stratford-upon-Avon, England CV37 9QR. Tel 01789 266245; www.stratford.ac.uk

Strode College Church Road, Street, England BA16 0AB. Tel 01458 844400; www.strode-college.ac.uk

Strode's College High Street, Egham, England TW20 9DR. Tel 01784 437506; www.strodes.ac.uk

Stroud College Stratford Road, Stroud, England GL5 4AH. Tel 01453 763424; www.stroud.ac.uk

Sussex Coast College Hastings (formerly Hastings College of Art and Technology) Station Plaza Campus, Station Approach, Hastings, England TN34 1BA. Tel 01424 442222; www.sussexcoast.ac.uk

Sussex Downs College Cross Levels Way, Eastbourne, England BN21 2UF. Tel 01323 637637; www.sussexdowns.ac.uk

Sutton Coldfield College (now part of Birmingham Metropolitan College) Lichfield Road, Sutton Coldfield, England B74 2NW. Tel 0121 355 5671; www.sutcol.ac.uk

Swansea College (Coleg Abertawe) Swansea College, Tycoch, Swansea, Wales SA2 9EB. Tel 01792 284000; www.swancoll.ac.uk

Swindon College North Star Campus, North Star Avenue, Swindon, England SN2 1DY. Tel 0800 731 2250; www.swindon-college.ac.uk

Tameside College Beaufort Road, Ashton-under-Lyne, England OL6 6NX. Tel 0161 908 6789; www.tameside.ac.uk

Telford College of Arts and Technology Haybridge Road, Wellington, Telford, England TF1 2NP. Tel College Reception 01952 642200; Student Services 01952 642237; www.tcat.ac.uk

Thanet College Ramsgate Road, Broadstairs, England CT10 1PN. Tel General Enquiries 01843 605040; Admissions 01843 605049; www.thanet.ac.uk

The London College UCK Kensington Campus, Victoria Gardens, London, England W11 3PE. Tel 020 7243 4000; www.lcuck.ac.uk

The Manchester College (formerly Manchester College of Art and Technology and City College Manchester) Whitworth Street, Manchester, England M11 2WH. Tel 0800 068 8585; www.themanchestercollege.ac.uk

The Oldham College Rochdale Road, Oldham, England OL9 6AA. Tel 0161 785 4000; www.oldham.ac.uk

Totton College Calmore Road, Totton, England SO40 3ZX. Tel 023 8087 4874; www.totton.ac.uk

Trafford College Talbot Road, Stretford, England M32 0XH. Tel 0161 886 7000; www.trafford.ac.uk

Tresham College of Further and Higher Education Kettering Campus, Windmill Avenue, Kettering, England NN15 6ER. Tel 0845 658 8990; www.tresham.ac.uk

Truro College College Road, Truro, England TR1 3XX. Tel General Enquiries 01872 267000; www.trurocollege.ac.uk

Tyne Metropolitan College Embleton Avenue, Wallsend, England NE28 9NJ. Tel 0191 229 5000; www.tynemet.ac.uk

Uxbridge College Park Road, Uxbridge, England UB8 1NQ. Tel 01895 853333; www.uxbridge.ac.uk

Wakefield College Margaret Street, Wakefield, England WF1 2DH. Tel 01924 789111; www.wakefield.ac.uk

Walford and North Shropshire College Oswestry Campus, Shrewsbury Road, Oswestry, England SY11 4QB. Tel 01691 688000; www.wnsc.ac.uk

Walsall College Wisemore Campus, Littleton Street West, Walsall, England WS2 8ES. Tel 01922 657000; www.walsallcollege.ac.uk

Waltham Forest College 707 Forest Road, London, England E17 4JB. Tel 020 8501 8501; www.waltham.ac.uk

Warrington Collegiate Winwick Road, Warrington, England WA2 8QA. Tel 01925 494494; www.warrington.ac.uk

Warwickshire College Leamington Centre, Warwick New Road, Leamington Spa, England CV32 5JE. Tel 01926 318000; www.warkscol.ac.uk

West Cheshire College Chester Campus, Eaton Road, Handbridge, Chester, England CH4 7ER. Tel 0151 356 7800; www.west-cheshire.ac.uk

West Herts College Watford Campus, Hempstead Road, Watford, England WD17 3EZ. Tel 01923 812000; www.westherts.ac.uk

West Highland College (formed from a merger between Lochaber and Skye and Wester Ross College; UHI partner college – see Section 1) An Aird, Fort William, Scotland PH33 6AN. Tel 01379 874000; www.lochaber.uhi.ac.uk

West Lothian College Almondvale Crescent, Livingston, Scotland EH54 7EP. Tel 01506 418181; www.west-lothian.ac.uk

West Nottinghamshire College Derby Road, Mansfield, England NG18 5BH. Tel 0800 100 626; www.wnc.ac.uk

West Suffolk College Out Risbygate, Bury St Edmunds, England IP33 3RL. Tel 01284 701301; www.westsuffolk.ac.uk

West Thames College London Road, Isleworth, England TW7 4HS. Tel 020 8326 2000; www.west-thames.ac.uk

Westminster Kingsway College St James's Park Centre, Castle Lane, London, England SW1E 6DR. Tel Information 0870 060 9800; www.westking.ac.uk

Weston College Knightstone Campus, Weston College, Knightstone Road, Weston-super-Mare, England BS23 2AL. Tel 01934 411411; www.weston.ac.uk

Weymouth College Cranford Avenue, Weymouth, England DT4 7LQ. Tel Reception 01305 761100; Course Applications 0870 060 9800/1; www.weymouth.ac.uk

Wigan and Leigh College Parsons Walk, Wigan, England WN1 1RU. Tel 01942 761111; www.wigan-leigh.ac.uk

Wiltshire College Chippenham Campus, Cocklebury Road, Chippenham, England SN15 3QD. Tel 01249 464644; www.wiltshire.ac.uk

Wirral Metropolitan College Conway Park Campus, Europa Boulevard, Conway Park, Birkenhead, England CH41 4NT. Tel 0151 551 7777; www.wmc.ac.uk

Worcester College of Technology Deansway, Worcester, England WR1 2JF. Tel 01905 725555; www.wortech.ac.uk

Yeovil College Mudford Road, Yeovil, England BA21 4DR. Tel 01935 423921; www.yeovil.ac.uk

York College Sim Balk Lane, York, England YO23 2BB. Tel 01904 770400; www.yorkcollege.ac.uk

Yorkshire Coast College Lady Edith's Drive, Scarborough, England YO12 5RN. Tel 01723 372105; www.yorkshirecoastcollege.ac.uk

APPENDIX 1 UCAS 2013 ENTRY TARIFF POINTS TABLES

GCE A/AS-LEVELS • SCOTTISH HIGHERS/ADVANCED HIGHERS • WELSH BACCALAUREATE • IRISH LEAVING CERTIFICATE • INTERNATIONAL BACCALAUREATE DIPLOMA • CAMBRIDGE PRE-U • PROGRESSION AND ADVANCED DIPLOMA • EXTENDED PROJECT • MUSIC EXAMINATIONS

GCE A/AS-LEVELS

Grade					Tariff Points
GCE & AVCE Double Award	A-level with additional AS (9 units)	GCE A-level and AVCE	GCE AS Double Award	GCE AS and AS VCE	
A*A*					280
A*A					260
AA					240
AB					220
BB	A*A				200
BC	AA				180
	AB				170
CC					160
	BB				150
CD	BC	A*			140
DD	CC	A	AA		120
	CD		AB		110
DE		B	BB		100
	DD		BC		90
EE	DE	C	CC		80
			CD		70
	EE	D	DD	A	60
			DE	B	50
		E	EE	C	40
				D	30
				E	20

Scottish Highers/Advanced Highers

Grade	Higher	Advanced Higher
A	80	130
B	65	110
C	50	90
D	36	72

Welsh Baccalaureate Core

Grade	Tariff points
Pass	120

NB Core points awarded only to candidates obtaining the Welsh Baccalaureate Advanced Diploma

Irish Leaving Certificate

Grade		Tariff points
Higher	Ordinary	
A1		90
A2		77
B1		71
B2		64
B3		58
C1		52
C2		45
C3	A1	39
D1		33
D2	A2	26
D3	B1	20
	B2	14
	B3	7

IB Diploma

IB Diploma points	UCAS Tariff points
45	720
44	698
43	676
42	654
41	632
40	611
39	589
38	567
37	545
36	523
35	501
34	479
33	457
32	435
31	413
30	392
29	370
28	348
27	326
26	304
25	282
24	260

Cambridge Pre-U

Grade	Principal subject	Global perspectives and research	Short course
D1	To be confirmed	To be confirmed	To be confirmed
D2	145	140	To be confirmed
D3	130	126	60
M1	115	112	53
M2	101	98	46
M3	87	84	39
P1	73	70	32
P2	59	56	26
P3	46	42	20

Progression Diploma

Grade	Tariff points
A*	350
A	300
B	250
C	200
D	150
E	100

NB The Advanced Diploma = Progression Diploma plus Additional and Specialist Learning (ASL)

Extended Project – Stand alone

Grade	Tariff points
A*	70
A	60
B	50
C	40
D	30
E	20

Points cannot be counted if taken as part of Advanced Diploma.

NB Full acknowledgement is made to UCAS for this information. For further details of all qualifications awarded UCAS Tariff points see www.ucas.com/students/ucas_Tariff/Tarifftables. Note that the Tariff is constantly updated and new qualifications are introduced each year.

Music examinations

Practical			Theory			Tariff points
Grade 8	Grade 7	Grade 6	Grade 8	Grade 7	Grade 6	
D						75
M						70
	D					60
P	M					55
		D				45
	P	M				40
			D			30
		P	M			25
			P	D		20
				M	D	15
				P	M	10
					P	5

Additional points will be awarded for music examinations from the Associated Board of the Royal Schools of Music (ABRSM), the Guildhall School of Music and Drama, the London College of Music Examinations (LCMM) and Trinity College of Music (music examinations at grades 6, 7, 8 (D=Distinction; M=Merit; P=Pass))

APPENDIX 2
INTERNATIONAL QUALIFICATIONS

Universities in the UK accept a range of international qualifications and those which normally satisfy the minimum general entrance requirements are listed below. However, the specific levels of achievement or grades required for entry to degree courses with international qualifications will vary, depending on the popularity of the university or college and the chosen degree programme. The subject tables in **Chapter 8** provide a guide to the levels of entry to courses although direct comparisons between A-level grades and international qualifications are not always possible except for the three European examinations listed at the end of this Appendix. Students not holding the required qualifications should consider taking an International Foundation course.

International students whose mother tongue is not English and/or who have not studied for their secondary education in English will be required to pass an English test such as IELTS (International English Language Testing System) or TOEFL (the Test of English as a Foreign Language). Entry requirements vary between universities and courses. For the IELTS, scores can range from 5.5 to 7.5, for the TOEFL computer-based test scores can range from a minimum of 213, and for the TOEFL written test the minimum entry score is 5.0 (see www.ielts.org and www.ets.org/toefl).

Algeria Baccalaureate de l'Enseignement Secondaire
Argentina Completion of Year One of Licenciado/Professional Title
Australia Completion of Year 12 certificates
Austria Reifazeugnis/Maturazeugnis
Bahrain Two-year diploma or associate degree
Bangladesh Bachelor of Arts, Science and Commerce
Belgium Certificat d'Enseignement Secondaire Superieur
Bermuda Diploma of Arts and Science
Bosnia-Herzegovina Secondary School Leaving Diploma
Brazil Completion of Ensino Medio and a good pass in the Vestibular
Brunei Brunei GCE A-level
Bulgaria Diploma za Zavarshino Sredno Obrazovanie (Diploma of Completed Secondary Education)
Canada Completion of Grade 12 secondary/high school certificate or equivalent
Chile Completion of secondary education and a good pass in the Prueba de Seleccion Universitaria (formally Prueba de Conocimientos Especificos)
China Completion of one year of a Bachelor degree from a recognised university with good grades
Croatia Matura (Secondary school leaving diploma)
Cyprus Apolytirion/Lise Bitirme Diploma with good grades
Czech Republic Vysvedceni o Maturitni Zkousce/Maturita
Denmark Studentereksamen (HF), (HHX), (HTX)
Egypt Completion of year one of a Bachelor degree or two-year Diploma
Finland Ylioppilastutkinoto/Studentexamen (Matriculation certificate)
France French Baccalaureate
Gambia West African Senior Secondary Certificate Exam (WASSCE) Advanced Level
Georgia Successful completion of Year One of a Bachelor degree
Germany Abitur
Ghana West African Senior Secondary Certificate Exam (WASSCE)/A-levels
Greece Apolytirion of Eniaio Lykeio (previously Apolytirion of Lykeio)
Hong Kong A-levels/ HKALE
Hungary Erettsegi/Matura
Iceland Studentsprof

India High grades from Standard XII School Leaving examinations from certain examination boards
Ireland Irish Leaving Certificate Higher Level
Israel Bagrut
Italy Diploma Conseguito con l'Esame di Stato (formerly the Diploma di Matura) with good grades
Japan Upper Secondary School leaving diploma/Kotogakko Sotsugyo Shomeisho plus foundation year
Kenya Cambridge Overseas Higher School Certificate
Lebanon Lebanese Baccalaureate plus foundation year
Malaysia Sijil Tinggi Persekolahan Malaysia (STPM, Malaysia Higher School Certificate)
Mauritius Cambridge Overseas Higher School Certificate or A-levels
Mexico Bachillerato plus foundation year
Netherlands Voorbereidend Wetenschappelijk Onderwijs (VWO)
Nigeria Successful completion of year one of a Bachelor degree
Norway Diploma of a completed 3-year course of upper secondary education
Pakistan Bachelor degree
Poland Matura/Swiadectwo Dojrzalosci
Portugal Diploma de Ensino Secundario
Russian Federation Diploma of completed Specialised Secondary Education or successful completion of first year of Bakalav
Saudi Arabia Successful completion of first year of a Bachelor degree
Serbia and Montenegro Matura
Singapore Polytechnic Diploma or A-levels
South Korea Junior College Diploma
Spain Curso de Orientacion Universitaria (COU) with good grades
Sri Lanka A-levels
Sweden Fullstandigt Slutbetyg fran Gymnasieskolan
Taiwan Senior High school Diploma
Thailand Successful completion of year one of a Bachelor degree
Turkey Devlet Lise Diplomasi (State High School Diploma) with good grades
Uganda Uganda Advanced Certificate of Education (UACE) or East African Advanced Certificate of Education
Ukraine Successful completion of year one of Bakakavre
USA Good grades from the High School Graduation Diploma with SAT and/or APT

COMPARISONS BETWEEN A-LEVEL GRADES AND THE FOLLOWING EUROPEAN EXAMINATIONS

A-level grades	AAA	AAB	ABB	BBB	BBC	BCC
European Baccalaureate	85%	80%	75%	70%	65%	60%
French Baccalaureate	16 Bien	15 Bien	14 Bien	13 Assez Bien	12 Assez Bien	11 Assez Bien
German Abitur	1.0–1.2	1.3–1.4	1.5–1.8	1.9–2.1	2.2–2.4	2.5–2.7

APPENDIX 3
PROFESSIONAL ASSOCIATIONS

Professional associations vary in size and function and many offer examinations to provide members with vocational qualifications. However, many of the larger bodies do not conduct examinations but accept evidence provided by the satisfactory completion of appropriate degree and diploma courses. When applying for courses in vocational subjects, therefore, it is important to check whether your chosen course is accredited by a professional association, since membership of such bodies is usually necessary for progression in your chosen career after graduation.

Information about careers, which you can use as background information for your UCAS application, can be obtained from the organisations below listed under the subject table headings used in **Chapter 8**. Full details of professional associations, their examinations and the degree courses accredited by them are published in *British Qualifications* (see **Appendix 4**).

Some additional organisations that can provide useful careers-related information are listed below under the subject table headings and other sources of relevant information are indicated in the subject tables of **Chapter 8** and in **Appendix 4**.

Accountancy/Accounting
Association of Accounting Technicians www.aat.org.uk
Association of International Accountants www.aiaworldwide.com
Chartered Institute of Management Accountants www.cimaglobal.com
Chartered Institute of Public Finance and Accountancy www.cipfa.org.uk
Chartered Institute of Taxation www.tax.org.uk
Institute of Accounting Technicians in Ireland www.accountingtechniciansireland.ie
Institute of Chartered Accountants in England and Wales www.icaew.com
Institute of Chartered Accountants in Ireland www.charteredaccountants.ie
Institute of Chartered Accountants of Scotland www.icas.org.uk
Institute of Financial Accountants www.ifa.org.uk
Institute of Internal Auditors www.iia.org.uk
The Global Body for Professional Accountants www.accaglobal.com

Actuarial Science/Studies
Institute and Faculty of Actuaries www.actuaries.org.uk

Agricultural Sciences/Agriculture
Royal Agricultural Society of England www.rase.org.uk

Animal Sciences
British Horse Society www.bhs.org.uk
British Society of Animal Science www.bsas.org.uk

Anthropology
Association of Social Anthropologists of the UK and Commonwealth www.theasa.org
Royal Anthropological Institute www.therai.org.uk

Archaeology
Council for British Archaeology www.britarch.ac.uk
Institute for Archaeologists www.archaeologists.net

Architecture
Chartered Institute of Architectural Technologists www.ciat.org.uk
Royal Incorporation of Architects in Scotland www.rias.org.uk
Royal Institute of British Architects www.architecture.com

Art and Design
Arts Council England www.arts.org.uk
Association of Illustrators www.theaoi.com
Association of Photographers www.the-aop.org
British Association of Art Therapists www.baat.org
British Association of Paintings Conservator-Restorers www.bapcr.org.uk
British Institute of Professional Photography www.bipp.com
Chartered Society of Designers www.csd.org.uk
Craft Council www.craftscouncil.org.uk
Design Council www.designcouncil.org.uk
Institute of Professional Goldsmiths www.ipgold.org.uk
National Society for Education in Art and Design www.nsead.org
Institue of Conservation www.icon.org.uk
Royal British Society of Sculptors www.rbs.org.uk
Scottish Arts Council www.creativescotland.com
Textile Institute www.texi.org

Astronomy/Astrophysics
Royal Astronomical Society www.ras.org.uk

Biochemistry (see also Chemistry)
Association of Clinical Biochemistry www.acb.org.uk
Biochemical Society www.biochemistry.org
British Society for Immunology http://bsi.immunology.org

Biological Sciences/Biology
British Society for Human Genetics www.bshg.org.uk
Genetics Society www.genetics.org.uk
Institute of Biomedical Science www.ibms.org
Society of Biology www.societyofbiology.org

Building
Chartered Institute of Building www.ciob.org.uk
Chartered Institution of Building Services Engineers www.cibse.org
Construction Industry Training Board (CITB) www.cskills.org

Business Courses
Chartered Institute of Personnel and Development www.cipd.co.uk
Chartered Institute of Public Relations www.cipr.co.uk
Chartered Management Institute www.managers.org.uk
Communication, Advertising and Marketing Education Foundation (CAM Foundation)
    www.camfoundation.com
Council for Administration www.cfa.uk.com
Department for Business, Innovation, and Skills www.bis.gov.uk
Institute of Administrative Management www.instam.org
Institute of Chartered Secretaries and Administrators www.icsa.org.uk
Institute of Consulting www.iconsulting.org.uk
Institute of Export www.export.org.uk
Institute of Practitioners in Advertising www.ipa.co.uk
Institute of Sales and Marketing Management www.ismm.co.uk

Chemistry
Institute of Nanotechnology www.nano.org.uk
Royal Society of Chemistry www.rsc.org

Computer Courses
BCS The Chartered Institute for IT www.bcs.org
Institute for the Management of Information Systems www.imis.org.uk
Institution of Analysts and Programmers www.iap.org.uk
Learning and Performance Institute www.learningandperformanceinstitute.com

Consumer Studies/Sciences
Trading Standards Institute www.tradingstandards.gov.uk

Dance
Council for Dance Education and Training www.cdet.org.uk

Dentistry
British Association of Dental Nurses www.badn.org.uk
British Association of Dental Therapists www.badt.org.uk
British Dental Association www.bda.org
British Dental Hygienists' Association www.bsdht.org.uk
Dental Laboratories Association www.dla.org.uk
Dental Technologists Association www.dta-uk.org
General Dental Council www.gdc-uk.org

Dietetics
British Dietetic Association www.bda.uk.com

Drama
Equity www.equity.org.uk
National Council for Drama Training www.ncdt.co.uk
Society of British Theatre Designers www.theatredesign.org.uk

Economics
Royal Economic Society www.res.org.uk

Education and Teacher Training
Department for Education www.education.gov.uk
General Teaching Council for England www.gtce.org.uk
General Teaching Council for Northern Ireland www.gtcni.org.uk
General Teaching Council for Scotland www.gtcs.org.uk
General Teaching Council for Wales www.gtcw.org.uk
Training and Development Agency for Schools www.tda.gov.uk

Engineering/Engineering Sciences
Energy Institute www.energyinst.org.uk
Engineering Council UK www.engc.org.uk
Institute for Manufacturing www.ifm.eng.cam.ac.uk
Institute of Acoustics www.ioa.org.uk
Institute of Marine Engineering, Science and Technology www.imarest.org
Institution of Agricultural Engineers www.iagre.org
Institution of Civil Engineers www.ice.org.uk
Institution of Engineering Designers www.ied.org.uk
Institution of Engineering and Technology www.theiet.org
Institution of Mechanical Engineers www.imeche.org

Nuclear Institute www.nuclearinst.com
Royal Aeronautical Society www.raes.org.uk

Environmental Science/Studies
Chartered Institute of Environmental Health www.cieh.org
Chartered Institution of Wastes Management www.ciwm.co.uk
Chartered Institution of Water and Environmental Management www.ciwem.org
Environment Agency www.environment-agency.gov.uk
Institute of Ecology and Environmental Management www.ieem.net
Institution of Environmental Sciences www.ies-uk.org.uk
Institution of Occupational Safety and Health www.iosh.co.uk
Royal Environmental Health Institute of Scotland www.rehis.org
Society for the Environment www.socenv.org.uk

Film, Radio, Video and TV Studies
British Film Institute www.bfi.org.uk
Skillset (National Training Organisation for broadcast, film, video and multimedia) www.skillset.org

Finance (including Banking and Insurance)
Chartered Institute of Bankers in Scotland www.charteredbanker.com
Chartered Institute of Loss Adjusters www.cila.co.uk
Chartered Insurance Institute www.cii.co.uk
Financial Services Skills Council www.fssc.org.uk
Institute of Financial Services www.ifslearning.ac.uk
Personal Finance Society www.thepfs.org
Securities and Investment Institute www.sii.co.uk

Food Science/Studies and Technology
Institute of Food Science and Technology www.ifst.org
Society of Food Hygiene and Technology www.sofht.co.uk

Forensic Science
Forensic Science Society www.forensic-science-society.org

Forestry
Institute of Chartered Foresters www.charteredforesters.org
Wood Technology Society www.iwsc.org.uk
Royal Forestry Society www.rfs.org.uk

Geography
British Cartographic Society www.cartography.org.uk
Royal Geographical Society www.rgs.org
Royal Meteorological Society www.rmets.org

Geology/Geological Sciences
Geological Society www.geolsoc.org.uk

Health Sciences/Studies
British Academy of Audiology www.baaudiology.org
British and Irish Orthoptic Society www.orthoptics.org.uk
British Association of Prosthetists and Orthotists www.bapo.com
British Chiropractic Association www.chiropractic-uk.co.uk
British Occupational Hygiene Society www.bohs.org
British Osteopathic Association and General Osteopathic Council www.osteopathy.org.uk
Institute for Complementary and Natural Medicine www.i-c-m.org.uk

Institution of Occupational Safety and Health www.iosh.co.uk
Society of Homeopaths www.homeopathy-soh.org

History
Royal Historical Society www.royalhistoricalsociety.org

Horticulture
Institute of Horticulture www.horticulture.org.uk

Hospitality and Hotel Management
Institute of Hospitality www.instituteofhospitality.org.
People 1st www.people1st.co.uk

Housing
Chartered Institute of Housing www.cih.org

Human Resource Management
Chartered Institute of Personnel and Development www.cipd.co.uk

Information Management
Association for Information Management www.aslib.co.uk
Chartered Institute of Library and Information Professionals www.cilip.org.uk

Landscape Architecture
Landscape Institute www.landscapeinstitute.org.uk

Languages
Chartered Institute of Linguists www.iol.org.uk
Institute of Translation and Interpreting www.iti.org.uk

Law
Bar Council www.barcouncil.org.uk
Faculty of Advocates www.advocates.org.uk
Institute of Legal Executives www.ilex.org.uk
Law Society www.lawsociety.org.uk
Law Society of Northern Ireland www.lawsoc-ni.org
Law Society of Scotland www.lawscot.org.uk

Leisure and Recreation Management/Studies
Institute for Sport, Parks and Leisure www.ispal.org.uk

Linguistics
British Association for Applied Linguistics www.baal.org.uk
Royal College of Speech and Language Therapists www.rcslt.org

Marine/Maritime Studies
Nautical Institute www.nautinst.org

Marketing
Chartered Institute of Marketing www.cim.co.uk
Institute of Sales and Marketing Management www.ismm.co.uk

Materials Science/Metallurgy
Institute of Materials, Minerals and Mining www.iom3.org

Mathematics
Council for Mathematical Sciences www.cms.ac.uk
Institute of Mathematics and its Applications www.ima.org.uk
London Mathematical Society www.lms.ac.uk
Mathematical Association www.m-a.org.uk

Media Studies
British Broadcasting Corporation www.bbc.co.uk/jobs
National Council for the Training of Journalists www.nctj.com
Skillset (National training organisation for broadcast, film, video and multimedia) www.skillset.org
Society for Editors and Proofreaders www.sfep.org.uk
Society of Authors www.societyofauthors.org

Medicine
British Medical Association www.bma.org.uk
General Medical Council www.gmc-uk.org
Institute for Complementary and Natural Medicine www.i-c-m.org.uk

Microbiology (see also Biological Sciences/Biology)
Society for General Microbiology www.sgm.ac.uk

Music
Incorporated Society of Musicians www.ism.org
Institute of Musical Instrument Technology www.imit.org.uk

Naval Architecture
Royal Institution of Naval Architects www.rina.org.uk

Nursing and Midwifery
Community Practitioners' and Health Visitors' Association www.unite-cphva.org
Health and Social Care in Northern Ireland www.n-i.nhs.uk
Nursing and Midwifery Council www.nmc-uk.org
Royal College of Midwives www.rcm.org.uk
Royal College of Nursing www.rcn.org.uk

Nutrition (see Dietetics)

Occupational Therapy
British Association/College of Occupational Therapists www.cot.co.uk

Optometry
Association of British Dispensing Opticians www.abdo.org.uk
British and Irish Orthoptic Society www.orthoptics.org.uk
College of Optometrists www.college-optometrists.org
General Optical Council www.optical.org

Pharmacology
British Toxicology Society www.thebts.org
Royal Pharmaceutical Society of Great Britain www.rpharms.com

Pharmacy
Royal Pharmaceutical Society of Great Britain www.rpharms.com

Photography
Association of Photographers http://hub.the-aop.org
British Institute of Professional Photography www.bipp.com
Royal Photographic Society www.rps.org

Physical Education (see Education and Teacher Training and Sports Sciences/Studies)

Physics
Institute of Physics www.iop.org
Institute of Physics and Engineering in Medicine www.ipem.ac.uk

Physiotherapy
Association of Chartered Physiotherapists in Animal Therapy www.acpat.org
Chartered Society of Physiotherapy www.csp.org.uk

Plant Sciences (see Biological Sciences/Biology)

Podiatry
Society of Chiropodists and Podiatrists www.feetforlife.org

Property Management/Development
Chartered Institute of Building www.ciob.org.uk
Chartered Surveyors Training Trust www.cstt.org.uk
National Association of Estate Agents www.naea.co.uk
Royal Institution of Chartered Surveyors www.rics.org

Psychology
British Psychological Society www.bps.org.uk

Public Relations
Chartered Institute of Public Relations www.cipr.co.uk

Quantity Surveying
Chartered Institute of Building www.ciob.org.uk
Royal Institution of Chartered Surveyors www.rics.org

Radiography
Society and College of Radiographers www.sor.org

Social Work
Care Council for Wales www.ccwales.org.uk
General Social Care Council www.gscc.org.uk
Northern Ireland Social Care Council www.niscc.info
Scottish Social Services Council www.sssc.uk.com

Sociology
British Sociological Association www.britsoc.co.uk

Speech Pathology/Sciences/Therapy
Royal College of Speech and Language Therapists www.rcslt.org

Sports Sciences/Studies
British Association of Sport and Exercise Sciences www.bases.org.uk
English Institute of Sport www.eis2win.co.uk

Scottish Institute of Sport www.sisport.com
Society of Sports Therapists www.society-of-sports-therapists.org
Sport England www.sportengland.org
Sport Scotland www.sportscotland.org.uk
Sport Wales www.sportwales.org.uk
Sports Institute Northern Ireland www.sini.co.uk
The Institute for the Management of Sport and Physical Activity www.imspa.co.uk
UK Sport www.uksport.gov.uk

Statistics
Royal Statistical Society www.rss.org.uk

Tourism and Travel
Institute of Travel and Tourism www.itt.co.uk

Town and Country Planning
Royal Town Planning Institute www.rtpi.org.uk

Transport Management and Planning
Chartered Institute of Logistics and Transport www.ciltuk.org.uk

Veterinary Science/Medicine/Nursing
Association of Chartered Physiotherapists in Animal Therapy www.acpat.org
British Veterinary Nursing Association www.bvna.org.uk
Royal College of Veterinary Surgeons www.rcvs.org.uk
Royal Veterinary College www.rvc.ac.uk

Zoology
Royal Entomological Society www.royensoc.co.uk
Zoological Society of London www.zsl.org

Unless otherwise stated, the publications in this list are all available from Trotman Publishing (www.trotman.co.uk / 0870 900 2665).

STANDARD REFERENCE BOOKS

British Qualifications, 42nd edition, Kogan Page Ltd
British Vocational Qualifications, 13th edition, Kogan Page Ltd

OTHER BOOKS AND RESOURCES

Choosing Your Degree Course & University, 13th edition, Brian Heap, Trotman Publishing
Cut the Cost of Uni, Trotman Publishing
Destinations of Leavers from Higher Education 2009/10, Higher Education Statistics Agency Services (available from HESA)
Getting Into course guides: US & Canadian Universities, Art & Design Courses, Business & Economics Courses, Dental School, Engineering Courses, Law, Medical School, Oxford & Cambridge, Physiotherapy Courses, Psychology Courses, Veterinary School, Trotman Publishing
A Guide to Student Life, Lucy Tobin, Trotman Publishing
How to Complete Your UCAS Application: 2013 Entry, Trotman Publishing
Insiders' Guide to Applying to University, 2nd edition, Karla Fitzhugh, Trotman Publishing
Into Higher Education 2009: The Higher Education Guide for People with Disabilities, Skill – The National Bureau for Students with Disabilities
Study in Europe – UK Socrates-Erasmus Student Guide, UK Socrates-Erasmus Council
Studying Abroad, Cerys Evans, Trotman Publishing
Studying and Learning at University, Alan Pritchard, Sage Study Skills Series
Studying in the UK, Cerys Evans, Trotman Publishing
The Times Good University Guide 2013, John O'Leary, Times Books
University Scholarships, Awards and Bursaries, 8th edition, Brian Heap, Trotman Publishing
The Virgin 2013 Guide to British Universities, Piers Dudgeon, Virgin Publishing
Which Uni? Find the Best University for You, Karla Fitzhugh, Trotman Publishing
Working in Accountancy, Sherridan Hughes, Trotman Publishing
Working in Law, Charlie Phillips, Trotman Publishing
Your Gap Year, 7th edition, Susan Griffith, Crimson Publishing

USEFUL WEBSITES

Education, course and applications information
www.direct.gov.uk/en/EducationAndLearning
www.coursediscover.co.uk
www.britishcouncil.org/erasmus
www.hesa.ac.uk
www.opendays.com (information on university and college open days)
http://unistats.direct.gov.uk (official information from UK universities and colleges for comparing courses)
www.ucas.com

Careers information
www.armyjobs.mod.uk
www.careerseurope.co.uk
www.connexions-direct.com
www.tomorrowsengineers.org.uk

www.insidecareers.co.uk
www.isco.org.uk
www.milkround.com
www.nhscareers.nhs.uk
www.prospects.ac.uk
www.socialworkandcarejobs.co.uk
www.tda.gov.uk
www.trotman.co.uk
www.ucreative.ac.uk

Gap Years
www.gapyear.com
www.gap-year.com
www.yini.org.uk (Year in Industry)

Study overseas
www.acu.ac.uk
www.fulbright.co.uk
www.allaboutcollege.com

COURSE INDEX

3D Computer Animation *see* ART and DESIGN (3D Design) 156

3D Computer Generated Imagery *see* ART and DESIGN (3D Design) 156

3D Contemporary Crafts and Products *see* ART and DESIGN (3D Design) 156

3D Design *see* ART and DESIGN (3D Design) 156

3D Design (Ceramics, Glass or Jewellery) *see* ART and DESIGN (3D Design) 156

3D Design (Design Maker/Furniture Interior Design) *see* ART and DESIGN (3D Design) 156, ART and DESIGN (Product and Industrial Design) 152

Abrahamic Religions *see* RELIGIOUS STUDIES 521

Abuse Studies *see* PSYCHOLOGY 512

ACCOUNTANCY/ACCOUNTING 109
   see also FINANCE

Accountancy and Finance *see* ACCOUNTANCY/ACCOUNTING 109, FINANCE 315

Accountancy and Law *see* ACCOUNTANCY/ACCOUNTING 109, LAW 393

Accountancy with Finance *see* ACCOUNTANCY/ACCOUNTING 109, FINANCE 315

Accounting and Banking *see* ACCOUNTANCY/ACCOUNTING 109

Accounting and Business *see* ACCOUNTANCY/ACCOUNTING 109

Accounting and Economics *see* ACCOUNTANCY/ACCOUNTING 109, ECONOMICS 251

Accounting and Finance *see* ACCOUNTANCY/ACCOUNTING 109, FINANCE 315

Accounting and Finance for Contemporary China *see* ACCOUNTANCY/ACCOUNTING 109, FINANCE 315

Accounting and Financial Management *see* ACCOUNTANCY/ACCOUNTING 109, FINANCE 315

Accounting and Financial Studies *see* ACCOUNTANCY/ACCOUNTING 109, FINANCE 315

Accounting and International Business *see* ACCOUNTANCY/ACCOUNTING 109, BUSINESS AND MANAGEMENT COURSES (INTERNATIONAL AND EUROPEAN) 188

Accounting and Law *see* ACCOUNTANCY/ACCOUNTING 109, LAW 393

Accounting and Logistics *see* ACCOUNTANCY/ACCOUNTING 109

Accounting and Management *see* ACCOUNTANCY/ACCOUNTING 109, BUSINESS AND MANAGEMENT COURSES 179

Accounting and Mathematics *see* ACCOUNTANCY/ACCOUNTING 109, MATHEMATICS 422

Accounting and Mathematics/Applied Mathematics/Pure Mathematics *see* ACCOUNTANCY/ACCOUNTING 109, MATHEMATICS 422

Accounting Finance *see* ACCOUNTANCY/ACCOUNTING 109, FINANCE 315

Accounting for Management *see* ACCOUNTANCY/ACCOUNTING 109

Accounting with a European Language *see* ACCOUNTANCY/ACCOUNTING 109, LANGUAGES 386

Accounting with a Modern Language (French/German/Spanish) *see* ACCOUNTANCY/ACCOUNTING 109

Accounting with Economics *see* ACCOUNTANCY/ACCOUNTING 109, ECONOMICS 251

Accounting with Languages *see* ACCOUNTANCY/ACCOUNTING 109, LANGUAGES 386

Accounting with Law *see* ACCOUNTANCY/ACCOUNTING 109, LAW 393

Accounting with Leadership *see* ACCOUNTANCY/ACCOUNTING 109

Accounting, Business Finance and Management *see* ACCOUNTANCY/ACCOUNTING 109, FINANCE 315

Accounting, Finance, and Computer Science *see* ACCOUNTANCY/ACCOUNTING 109, COMPUTER COURSES 219, FINANCE 315

Accounting, Finance, and Mathematics *see* ACCOUNTANCY/ACCOUNTING 109, FINANCE 315, MATHEMATICS 422

Acoustical Engineering *see* ENGINEERING (ACOUSTICS and SOUND) 264

Acoustics *see* ENGINEERING (ACOUSTICS and SOUND) 264

Acoustics and Music *see* ENGINEERING (ACOUSTICS and SOUND) 264, MUSIC 449

Acting *see* DRAMA 239

Acting (Musical Theatre) *see* DRAMA 239

Acting and Collaborative Theatre *see* DRAMA 239

Acting and Contemporary Theatre *see* DRAMA 239

Acting and Media *see* DRAMA 239, MEDIA STUDIES 427

Acting and Musical Theatre *see* DRAMA 239, MUSIC 449

Acting for Film and Television *see* DRAMA 239

Activity and Community Health *see* HEALTH SCIENCES/STUDIES 341

Actor Musicianship *see* DRAMA 239, MUSIC 449

Actuarial Mathematics *see* ACTUARIAL SCIENCE/ STUDIES 114, MATHEMATICS 422

Actuarial Mathematics and Statistics *see* ACTUARIAL SCIENCE/STUDIES 114, MATHEMATICS 422, STATISTICS 554

Actuarial Science and Mathematics *see* ACTUARIAL SCIENCE/STUDIES 114, MATHEMATICS 422

Actuarial Science and Risk Management *see* ACTUARIAL SCIENCE/STUDIES 114

Actuarial Science Combined Studies *see* ACTUARIAL SCIENCE/STUDIES 114, COMBINED COURSES 212

ACTUARIAL SCIENCE/STUDIES 114

Acupuncture *see* HEALTH SCIENCES/STUDIES 341, OCCUPATIONAL THERAPY 468

Acupuncture Studies *see* HEALTH SCIENCES/ STUDIES 341

Administration and Management *see* BUSINESS AND MANAGEMENT COURSES 179

Adult Nursing *see* NURSING and MIDWIFERY 461

Adventure Education *see* EDUCATION STUDIES 256

Adventure Media *see* LEISURE and RECREATION MANAGEMENT/STUDIES 405

Adventure Sports Sciences *see* SPORTS SCIENCES/ STUDIES 548

Adventure Tourism Management *see* LEISURE and RECREATION MANAGEMENT/STUDIES 405, TOURISM and TRAVEL 564

Advertising *see* ART and DESIGN (Graphic Design) 148, BUSINESS AND MANAGEMENT COURSES (SPECIALISED) 193, MARKETING 415

Advertising and Brand Communication *see* MARKETING 415

Advertising and Brand Management *see* BUSINESS AND MANAGEMENT COURSES (SPECIALISED) 193

Advertising and Business *see* BUSINESS AND MANAGEMENT COURSES (SPECIALISED) 193

Advertising and Campaign Management *see* ART and DESIGN (Graphic Design) 148, BUSINESS AND MANAGEMENT COURSES (SPECIALISED) 193

Advertising and Design *see* ART and DESIGN (Graphic Design) 148, MARKETING 415

Advertising and Human Resource Management *see* HUMAN RESOURCE MANAGEMENT 371, MARKETING 415

Advertising and Marketing *see* BUSINESS AND MANAGEMENT COURSES (SPECIALISED) 193, MARKETING 415

Advertising and Marketing Communications *see* BUSINESS AND MANAGEMENT COURSES (SPECIALISED) 193, MARKETING 415

Advertising and Media *see* BUSINESS AND MANAGEMENT COURSES (SPECIALISED) 193

Advertising and Media Relations *see* MEDIA STUDIES 427

Advertising Design *see* ART and DESIGN (Graphic Design) 148, BUSINESS AND MANAGEMENT COURSES (SPECIALISED) 193

Advertising Management *see* BUSINESS AND MANAGEMENT COURSES (SPECIALISED) 193, MARKETING 415

Advertising Management and Brand Management *see* BUSINESS AND MANAGEMENT COURSES (SPECIALISED) 193

Advertising with Marketing Communications *see* MARKETING 415

Advertising, Public Relations and Media *see* BUSINESS AND MANAGEMENT COURSES (SPECIALISED) 193, MARKETING 415

Aero-Mechanical Engineering *see* ENGINEERING (AERONAUTICAL and AEROSPACE) 266

Aeronautical and Aerospace Engineering *see* ENGINEERING (AERONAUTICAL and AEROSPACE) 266

Aeronautical and Electronic Engineering *see* ENGINEERING (AERONAUTICAL and AEROSPACE) 266, ENGINEERING (ELECTRICAL and ELECTRONIC) 283

Aeronautical and Mechanical Engineering *see* ENGINEERING (AERONAUTICAL and AEROSPACE) 266, ENGINEERING (MECHANICAL) 290

Aeronautical Engineering *see* ENGINEERING (AERONAUTICAL and AEROSPACE) 266, PHYSICS 488

Aeronautics *see* ENGINEERING (AERONAUTICAL and AEROSPACE) 266

Aeronautics and Astronautics *see* ENGINEERING (AERONAUTICAL and AEROSPACE) 266

Aeronautics and Astronautics (Advanced Materials) *see* ENGINEERING (AERONAUTICAL and AEROSPACE) 266

Aeronautics and Astronautics (Aerodynamics) *see* ENGINEERING (AERONAUTICAL and AEROSPACE) 266

Aeronautics and Astronautics (Airvehicle Systems Design) *see* ENGINEERING (AERONAUTICAL and AEROSPACE) 266

Aeronautics and Astronautics (Engineering Management) *see* ENGINEERING (AERONAUTICAL and AEROSPACE) 266

Aeronautics and Astronautics (European Studies) *see* ENGINEERING (AERONAUTICAL and AEROSPACE) 266, EUROPEAN STUDIES 307

Aeronautics and Astronautics (Spacecraft Engineering) *see* ENGINEERING (AERONAUTICAL and AEROSPACE) 266

Aeronautics and Astronautics (Structural Design) *see* ENGINEERING (AERONAUTICAL and AEROSPACE) 266

Aerospace and Aerothermal Engineering *see* ENGINEERING (AERONAUTICAL and AEROSPACE) 266

Aerospace Design Engineering *see* ENGINEERING (AERONAUTICAL and AEROSPACE) 266

Aerospace Engineering *see* ENGINEERING (AERONAUTICAL and AEROSPACE) 266, ENGINEERING (MECHANICAL) 290

Aerospace Engineering (Private Pilot Instruction) *see* ENGINEERING (AERONAUTICAL and AEROSPACE) 266

Aerospace Engineering with Management *see* ENGINEERING (AERONAUTICAL and AEROSPACE) 266

Aerospace Engineering with Pilot Studies *see* ENGINEERING (AERONAUTICAL and AEROSPACE) 266

Aerospace Engineering with Propulsion *see* ENGINEERING (AERONAUTICAL and AEROSPACE) 266

Aerospace Engineering, Astronautics and Space Technology *see* ENGINEERING (AERONAUTICAL and AEROSPACE) 266

Aerospace Manufacturing Engineering *see* ENGINEERING (AERONAUTICAL and AEROSPACE) 266, ENGINEERING (MANUFACTURING) 288

Aerospace Materials *see* ENGINEERING (AERONAUTICAL and AEROSPACE) 266, MATERIALS SCIENCE/METALLURGY 419

Aerospace Systems *see* ENGINEERING (AERONAUTICAL and AEROSPACE) 266

Aerospace Systems Engineering *see* ENGINEERING (AERONAUTICAL and AEROSPACE) 266

Aerospace Systems Engineering with Pilot Studies *see* ENGINEERING (AERONAUTICAL and AEROSPACE) 266

Aerospace Technology *see* ENGINEERING (AERONAUTICAL and AEROSPACE) 266, TECHNOLOGIES 562

Aerospace Technology with Management *see* ENGINEERING (AERONAUTICAL and AEROSPACE) 266

Aerospace Technology with Pilot Studies: Multimedia Technology *see* ENGINEERING (AERONAUTICAL and AEROSPACE) 266, TECHNOLOGIES 562

AFRICAN and CARIBBEAN STUDIES 115
see also LANGUAGES

African Language and Culture *see* AFRICAN AND CARIBBEAN STUDIES 115

African Studies with Anthropology *see* AFRICAN AND CARIBBEAN STUDIES 115, ANTHROPOLOGY 127

African Studies with Development *see* AFRICAN AND CARIBBEAN STUDIES 115, DEVELOPMENT STUDIES 235

Agri-Business *see* AGRICULTURAL SCIENCES/AGRICULTURE 117, BUSINESS AND MANAGEMENT COURSES 179

Agri-Business Management *see* AGRICULTURAL SCIENCES/AGRICULTURE 117, BUSINESS AND MANAGEMENT COURSES (SPECIALISED) 193

Agricultural and Crop Science *see* AGRICULTURAL SCIENCES/AGRICULTURE 117

Agricultural and Environmental Science *see* AGRICULTURAL SCIENCES/AGRICULTURE 117, ENVIRONMENTAL SCIENCES/STUDIES 303

Agricultural and Livestock Science *see* AGRICULTURAL SCIENCES/AGRICULTURE 117

Agricultural Business Management *see* AGRICULTURAL SCIENCES/AGRICULTURE 117

Agricultural Engineering *see* ENGINEERING (MECHANICAL) 290

Agricultural Engineering with Marketing and Management *see* ENGINEERING (MECHANICAL) 290

AGRICULTURAL SCIENCES/AGRICULTURE 117
see also ANIMAL SCIENCE
see also FOOD SCIENCES/STUDIES and TECHNOLOGY
see also FORESTRY
see also HORTICULTURE
see also LANDSCAPE ARCHITECTURE

see also SURVEYING

see also ZOOLOGY

Agricultural Technology see AGRICULTURAL SCIENCES/ AGRICULTURE 117

Agriculture (Countryside Management) see AGRICULTURAL SCIENCES/AGRICULTURE 117

Agriculture (Crops) see AGRICULTURAL SCIENCES/ AGRICULTURE 117

Agriculture (Farm Management) see AGRICULTURAL SCIENCES/AGRICULTURE 117

Agriculture (Farm Mechanisation Management) see AGRICULTURAL SCIENCES/AGRICULTURE 117, BUSINESS AND MANAGEMENT COURSES (SPECIALISED) 193

Agriculture (Livestock) see ANIMAL SCIENCES 124

Agriculture (Sustainable Soil Management) see AGRICULTURAL SCIENCES/AGRICULTURE 117

Agriculture and Environment Management see AGRICULTURAL SCIENCES/AGRICULTURE 117, ENVIRONMENTAL SCIENCES/STUDIES 303

Agriculture with Farm Business Management see BUSINESS AND MANAGEMENT COURSES (SPECIALISED) 193

Agriculture with Land Management see AGRICULTURAL SCIENCES/AGRICULTURE 117

Agriculture with Marketing see AGRICULTURAL SCIENCES/AGRICULTURE 117, MARKETING 415

Agriculture, Conservation and Environment see AGRICULTURAL SCIENCES/AGRICULTURE 117, ENVIRONMENTAL SCIENCES/STUDIES 303

Agri-Food Marketing with Business Studies see FOOD SCIENCE/STUDIES and TECHNOLOGY 321, MARKETING 415

Agronomy see AGRICULTURAL SCIENCES/ AGRICULTURE 117

Air Transport and Logistics Management see BUSINESS AND MANAGEMENT COURSES (SPECIALISED) 193, TRANSPORT MANAGEMENT and PLANNING 571

Air Transport Engineering see ENGINEERING (AERONAUTICAL and AEROSPACE) 266

Air Transport Management see BUSINESS AND MANAGEMENT COURSES 179, BUSINESS AND MANAGEMENT COURSES (SPECIALISED) 193, TRANSPORT MANAGEMENT and PLANNING 571

Air Transport Operations see BUSINESS AND MANAGEMENT COURSES (SPECIALISED) 193

Air Transport Operations and Management see ENGINEERING (AERONAUTICAL and AEROSPACE) 266, TRANSPORT MANAGEMENT and PLANNING 571

Air Transport with Pilot Training see TRANSPORT MANAGEMENT and PLANNING 571

Aircraft Engineering see ENGINEERING (AERONAUTICAL and AEROSPACE) 266

Aircraft Engineering with Pilot Studies see ENGINEERING (AERONAUTICAL and AEROSPACE) 266

Aircraft Maintenance Engineering see ENGINEERING (AERONAUTICAL and AEROSPACE) 266

Airline and Airport Management see BUSINESS AND MANAGEMENT COURSES (SPECIALISED) 193, TRANSPORT MANAGEMENT and PLANNING 571

Airline Management see BUSINESS AND MANAGEMENT COURSES (SPECIALISED) 193

Airport Management see BUSINESS AND MANAGEMENT COURSES (SPECIALISED) 193

American (United States) Studies see AMERICAN STUDIES 120

American and Canadian Literature, History and Culture see AMERICAN STUDIES 120, HISTORY 355, LITERATURE 409

American and Canadian Studies see AMERICAN STUDIES 120

American and English Literature see AMERICAN STUDIES 120, ENGLISH 296, LITERATURE 409

American and English Studies see AMERICAN STUDIES 120, ENGLISH 296

American History see AMERICAN STUDIES 120, HISTORY 355

American History with Politics see AMERICAN STUDIES 120, POLITICS 507

American Literature see AMERICAN STUDIES 120, LITERATURE 409

American Literature with Creative Writing see AMERICAN STUDIES 120, LITERATURE 409

AMERICAN STUDIES 120

see also LATIN AMERICAN STUDIES

American Studies (History) see AMERICAN STUDIES 120, HISTORY 355

American Studies and Drama see AMERICAN STUDIES 120, DRAMA 239

American Studies and English see AMERICAN STUDIES 120, ENGLISH 296

American Studies and History see AMERICAN STUDIES 120, HISTORY 355

American Studies and Latin American Studies see AMERICAN STUDIES 120, LATIN AMERICAN STUDIES 391

American Studies and Media Studies see AMERICAN STUDIES 120, MEDIA STUDIES 427

American Studies with English History *see* AMERICAN
   STUDIES 120, HISTORY 355
American Theatre Arts *see* DRAMA 239
Analytical Chemistry *see* CHEMISTRY 199
ANATOMICAL SCIENCE/ANATOMY 122
   see also BIOLOGICAL SCIENCES
   see also PHYSIOLOGY
Anatomical Science and a Modern Language
   see ANATOMICAL SCIENCE/ANATOMY 122,
   LANGUAGES 386
Anatomical Sciences *see* ANATOMICAL SCIENCE/
   ANATOMY 122
Anatomy *see* ANATOMICAL SCIENCE/ANATOMY 122
Anatomy and Human Biology *see* ANATOMICAL
   SCIENCE/ANATOMY 122
Anatomy, Developmental and Human Biology *see*
   BIOLOGICAL SCIENCES 165
Ancient and Medieval History *see* HISTORY
   (ANCIENT) 360
Ancient and Modern History *see* HISTORY 355,
   HISTORY (ANCIENT) 360
Ancient History *see* COMBINED COURSES 212,
   HISTORY (ANCIENT) 360
Ancient History and Archaeology *see*
   ARCHAEOLOGY 131, HISTORY (ANCIENT) 360
Ancient History and Classical Archaeology *see*
   ARCHAEOLOGY 131, HISTORY (ANCIENT) 360
Ancient History and Egyptology *see* HISTORY
   (ANCIENT) 360
Ancient History and Film Studies *see* FILM,
   RADIO, VIDEO and TV STUDIES 310, HISTORY
   (ANCIENT) 360
Ancient History and Greek *see* GREEK 340, HISTORY
   (ANCIENT) 360
Ancient History and History *see* HISTORY 355, HISTORY
   (ANCIENT) 360
Ancient History and Latin *see* HISTORY (ANCIENT) 360,
   LATIN 389
Ancient History and Philosophy *see* HISTORY
   (ANCIENT) 360, PHILOSOPHY 478
Ancient History with Economics *see* ECONOMICS 251,
   HISTORY (ANCIENT) 360
Ancient History with Mathematics *see* HISTORY
   (ANCIENT) 360, MATHEMATICS 422
Ancient Mediterranean Civilisations *see* CLASSICAL
   STUDIES/CLASSICAL CIVILISATION 208, HISTORY
   (ANCIENT) 360
Ancient Near Eastern Studies *see* ARABIC AND
   ANCIENT NEAR AND MIDDLE EASTERN
   STUDIES 129
Ancient World *see* HISTORY (ANCIENT) 360

Anglo-Saxon, Norse and Celtic *see* CELTIC, IRISH,
   SCOTTISH AND WELSH STUDIES 197, ENGLISH 296,
   SCANDINAVIAN STUDIES 527
Animal Behaviour *see* ANIMAL SCIENCES 124
Animal Behaviour and Welfare *see* ANIMAL
   SCIENCES 124
Animal Behavioural Psychology *see* ANIMAL SCIENCES
   124, PSYCHOLOGY 512
Animal Biology *see* ANIMAL SCIENCES 124,
   BIOLOGY 170
Animal Biology and Conservation *see* ANIMAL
   SCIENCES 124
Animal Conservation and Biodiversity *see* ANIMAL
   SCIENCES 124
Animal Conservation Science *see* ANIMAL
   SCIENCES 124
Animal Management *see* ANIMAL SCIENCES 124
Animal Management and Science *see* ANIMAL
   SCIENCES 124
Animal Management and Welfare *see* ANIMAL
   SCIENCES 124
Animal Production Science *see* ANIMAL
   SCIENCES 124
ANIMAL SCIENCES 124
   see also AGRICULTURAL SCIENCES/AGRICULTURE
   see also BIOLOGICAL SCIENCES
   see also BIOLOGY
   see also PSYCHOLOGY
   see also VETERINARY SCIENCE/MEDICINE
   see also ZOOLOGY
Animal Science and Health *see* ANIMAL
   SCIENCES 124
Animation *see* ART and DESIGN (Graphic Design) 148
Animation and Design *see* ART and DESIGN (Graphic
   Design) 148
Animation and Illustration *see* ART and DESIGN
   (Graphic Design) 148
Animation and Motion Graphics *see* ART and DESIGN
   (Graphic Design) 148
Animation and Visual Effects *see* ART and DESIGN
   (Graphic Design) 148
Animation Design *see* ART and DESIGN (Graphic
   Design) 148
Animation Production *see* ART and DESIGN
   (Graphic Design) 148, FILM, RADIO, VIDEO and
   TV STUDIES 310
ANTHROPOLOGY 127
   see also ARCHAEOLOGY
   see also SOCIOLOGY
Anthropology and Archaeology *see*
   ANTHROPOLOGY 127, ARCHAEOLOGY 131

Anthropology and Classical Literature and Civilisation see CLASSICAL STUDIES/CLASSICAL CIVILISATION 208

Anthropology and Law see ANTHROPOLOGY 127, LAW 393

Anthropology and Media see ANTHROPOLOGY 127

Anthropology and Political Science see ANTHROPOLOGY 127, POLITICS 507

Anthropology and Sociology see ANTHROPOLOGY 127, SOCIOLOGY 539

Anthropology with Native American Studies see AMERICAN STUDIES 120, ANTHROPOLOGY 127

Applied Animal Behaviour and Training see ANIMAL SCIENCES 124

Applied Animal Science see ANIMAL SCIENCES 124

Applied Animal Studies see ANIMAL SCIENCES 124

Applied Arts see ART and DESIGN (3D Design) 156

Applied Behavioural Science and Welfare see ANIMAL SCIENCES 124

Applied Biochemistry see BIOCHEMISTRY 162

Applied Biological Science see BIOLOGICAL SCIENCES 165

Applied Biology see BIOLOGY 170

Applied Biomedical Science see BIOLOGICAL SCIENCES 165, BIOLOGY 170

Applied Bioscience see BIOLOGICAL SCIENCES 165

Applied Bioscience and Psychology see BIOLOGICAL SCIENCES 165, PSYCHOLOGY 512

Applied Bioscience and Zoology see BIOLOGICAL SCIENCES 165, ZOOLOGY 576

Applied Biotechnology see BIOTECHNOLOGY 174

Applied Business Computing see COMPUTER COURSES 219

Applied Business Management see BUSINESS AND MANAGEMENT COURSES 179

Applied Chemical and Pharmaceutical Sciences see CHEMISTRY 199

Applied Chemistry see CHEMISTRY 199

Applied Chemistry and Chemical Engineering see ENGINEERING (CHEMICAL) 269

Applied Community and Social Studies see COMMUNITY STUDIES/DEVELOPMENT 217

Applied Community and Youth Work see SOCIAL WORK 536

Applied Community and Youth Work Studies see COMMUNITY STUDIES/DEVELOPMENT 217, SOCIAL SCIENCES/STUDIES 531

Applied Community Studies see COMMUNITY STUDIES/DEVELOPMENT 217

Applied Computing see COMPUTER COURSES 219

Applied Computing Science see COMPUTER COURSES 219

Applied Conservation Biology see BIOLOGICAL SCIENCES 165, BIOLOGY 170, ENVIRONMENTAL SCIENCES/STUDIES 303

Applied Criminal Justice Studies see SOCIAL SCIENCES/STUDIES 531

Applied Criminology see LAW 393, SOCIAL SCIENCES/STUDIES 531

Applied Criminology and Forensic Sciences see LAW 393, SOCIAL SCIENCES/STUDIES 531

Applied Drama see DRAMA 239

Applied Drama and Music see DRAMA 239, MUSIC 449

Applied Drama and Visual Arts see DRAMA 239

Applied Ecology and Conservation see ENVIRONMENTAL SCIENCES/STUDIES 303

Applied Economics see ECONOMICS 251

Applied Environmental Geology see ENVIRONMENTAL SCIENCES/STUDIES 303, GEOLOGY/GEOLOGICAL SCIENCES 335

Applied Environmental Science see ENVIRONMENTAL SCIENCES/STUDIES 303

Applied Equine Studies see ANIMAL SCIENCES 124

Applied Geography see GEOGRAPHY 330

Applied Geology see GEOLOGY/GEOLOGICAL SCIENCES 335

Applied Golf Management Studies see SPORTS SCIENCES/STUDIES 548

Applied Information Technology see INFORMATION MANAGEMENT and LIBRARIANSHIP 375

Applied Language with German see GERMAN 337, LANGUAGES 386

Applied Languages see LANGUAGES 386

Applied Languages and Translating (French/German) see FRENCH 325, LANGUAGES 386

Applied Languages and Translation see LANGUAGES 386

Applied Languages and Translation (French and Spanish) (German and Spanish) see SPANISH 543

Applied Management see BUSINESS AND MANAGEMENT COURSES 179

Applied Marine Biology see BIOLOGY 170, MARINE/MARITIME STUDIES 412

Applied Marine Sport Science see MARINE/MARITIME STUDIES 412, SPORTS SCIENCES/STUDIES 548

Applied Mathematics see MATHEMATICS 422

Applied Mathematics and Physics see MATHEMATICS 422

Applied Microbiology *see* BIOLOGY 170,
MICROBIOLOGY 447
Applied Music *see* MUSIC 449
Applied Pharmacology *see* PHARMACOLOGY 472
Applied Physics *see* PHYSICS 488
Applied Psychology *see* PSYCHOLOGY 512
Applied Psychology (Counselling and Health) *see*
PSYCHOLOGY 512
Applied Psychology and Criminology *see*
PSYCHOLOGY 512, SOCIAL SCIENCES/STUDIES 531
Applied Psychology and Sociology *see*
PSYCHOLOGY 512, SOCIOLOGY 539
Applied Psychology with Clinical Psychology *see*
PSYCHOLOGY 512
Applied Science *see* BIOLOGY 170
Applied Social Science *see* SOCIAL SCIENCES/
STUDIES 531
Applied Social Science, Community Development
and Youth Work *see* COMMUNITY STUDIES/
DEVELOPMENT 217, SOCIAL SCIENCES/STUDIES
531, SOCIAL WORK 536
Applied Social Sciences *see* SOCIAL SCIENCES/
STUDIES 531
Applied Social Sciences (Anthropology) *see*
ANTHROPOLOGY 127, SOCIAL
SCIENCES/STUDIES 531
Applied Social Sciences (Children and Young
People/Crime) *see* SOCIAL SCIENCES/
STUDIES 531
Applied Social Sciences (Criminology) *see* SOCIAL
SCIENCES/STUDIES 531
Applied Social Sciences (Criminology and Psychology
Studies) *see* PSYCHOLOGY 512, SOCIAL SCIENCES/
STUDIES 548
Applied Social Studies *see* SOCIAL SCIENCES/
STUDIES 548
Applied Social Work *see* SOCIAL WORK 536
Applied Sound Engineering *see* ENGINEERING
(ACOUSTICS and SOUND) 264
Applied Sport and Exercise Science *see* SPORTS
SCIENCES/STUDIES 548
Applied Sport Psychology *see* PSYCHOLOGY 512
Applied Sport Science *see* SPORTS SCIENCES/
STUDIES 548
Applied Sport Science and Coaching *see* SPORTS
SCIENCES/STUDIES 548
Applied Sport Sciences and Education *see* SPORTS
SCIENCES/STUDIES 548
Applied Sports Science *see* SPORTS SCIENCES/
STUDIES 548
Applied Statistics *see* STATISTICS 554

Applied Terrestrial and Marine Ecology *see* BIOLOGY
170, ENVIRONMENTAL SCIENCES/STUDIES 303,
MARINE/MARITIME STUDIES 412
Applied Translation *see* LANGUAGES 386
Aquaculture *see* ANIMAL SCIENCES 124
Aquaculture and Fishery Management *see*
AGRICULTURAL SCIENCES/AGRICULTURE 117,
BUSINESS AND MANAGEMENT COURSES
(SPECIALISED) 193
Aquatic Zoology *see* MARINE/MARITIME STUDIES 412,
ZOOLOGY 576
Arabic *see* ARABIC AND ANCIENT NEAR AND MIDDLE
EASTERN STUDIES 129
**ARABIC AND ANCIENT NEAR AND MIDDLE EASTERN
STUDIES 129**
Arabic and Classical Literature *see* ARABIC AND
ANCIENT NEAR AND MIDDLE EASTERN
STUDIES 129
Arabic and Economics *see* ARABIC AND ANCIENT
NEAR AND MIDDLE EASTERN STUDIES 129,
ECONOMICS 251
Arabic and English *see* ARABIC AND ANCIENT
NEAR AND MIDDLE EASTERN STUDIES 129,
ENGLISH 296
Arabic and Islamic Studies *see* ARABIC AND ANCIENT
NEAR AND MIDDLE EASTERN STUDIES 129
Arabic and Mathematics *see* ARABIC AND ANCIENT
NEAR AND MIDDLE EASTERN STUDIES 129,
MATHEMATICS 422
Arabic and Middle East Studies *see* ARABIC AND
ANCIENT NEAR AND MIDDLE EASTERN STUDIES 129
Arabic and Middle Eastern Studies *see* ARABIC
AND ANCIENT NEAR AND MIDDLE EASTERN
STUDIES 129
Arabic and Persian *see* ARABIC AND ANCIENT NEAR
AND MIDDLE EASTERN STUDIES 129
Arabic Cultural Studies *see* ARABIC AND ANCIENT
NEAR AND MIDDLE EASTERN STUDIES 129
Arabic Studies *see* ARABIC AND ANCIENT NEAR AND
MIDDLE EASTERN STUDIES 129
Arabic/English Translation and Interpreting *see*
ARABIC AND ANCIENT NEAR AND MIDDLE
EASTERN STUDIES 129
Arboriculture *see* PLANT SCIENCES 504
Archaeological and Anthropological Sciences *see*
ANTHROPOLOGY 127, ARCHAEOLOGY 131
Archaeological Practice *see* ARCHAEOLOGY 131
Archaeological Science *see* ARCHAEOLOGY 131
ARCHAEOLOGY 131
see also ANTHROPOLOGY
see also CLASSICAL STUDIES/CIVILISATION

see also GEOLOGY/GEOLOGICAL SCIENCES
see also HISTORY (ANCIENT)
Archaeology (Practice/Environmental) see
  ARCHAEOLOGY 131
Archaeology and Ancient History see
  ARCHAEOLOGY 131, HISTORY (ANCIENT) 360
Archaeology and Anthropology see ANTHROPOLOGY
  127, ARCHAEOLOGY 131
Archaeology and Art History see ARCHAEOLOGY 131,
  HISTORY OF ART 363
Archaeology and Classical Civilisation see
  ARCHAEOLOGY 131, CLASSICAL STUDIES/
  CLASSICAL CIVILISATION 208
Archaeology and Environmental Studies see
  ARCHAEOLOGY 131, ENVIRONMENTAL SCIENCES/
  STUDIES 303
Archaeology and Geography see ARCHAEOLOGY 131,
  GEOGRAPHY 330
Archaeology and Heritage Studies see
  ARCHAEOLOGY 131
Archaeology and History see ARCHAEOLOGY 131,
  HISTORY 355
Archaeology and Landscape History see
  ARCHAEOLOGY 131
Archaeology of Ancient Civilisations see
  ARCHAEOLOGY 131, HISTORY (ANCIENT) 360
Archaeology with Anthropology see
  ANTHROPOLOGY 127, ARCHAEOLOGY 131
Archaeology with Palaeoecology and Geography see
  ARCHAEOLOGY 131, GEOGRAPHY 330
Archaeology with Social Anthropology see
  ANTHROPOLOGY 127, ARCHAEOLOGY 131
Archaeology, Anthropology and Art History see
  ANTHROPOLOGY 127, ARCHAEOLOGY 131,
  HISTORY OF ART 363
Archaeology, Anthropology with Art History see
  ANTHROPOLOGY 127, ARCHAEOLOGY 131,
  HISTORY OF ART 363
Architectural Design see ARCHITECTURE 134
Architectural Design and Technology see
  ARCHITECTURE 134, TECHNOLOGIES 562
Architectural Design Technology see
  ARCHITECTURE 134
Architectural Engineering see ARCHITECTURE 134,
  ENGINEERING (CIVIL) 274, ENGINEERING/
  ENGINEERING SCIENCES 260
Architectural Engineering Design see ARCHITECTURE
  134, ENGINEERING/ENGINEERING SCIENCES 260
Architectural Environment Engineering see
  ARCHITECTURE 134, ENGINEERING/ENGINEERING
  SCIENCES 260

Architectural History see ARCHITECTURE 134
Architectural History and Archaeology see
  ARCHITECTURE 134, HISTORY 355
Architectural Planning see ARCHITECTURE 134,
  TOWN and COUNTRY PLANNING 567
Architectural Studies see ARCHITECTURE 134
Architectural Technology see ARCHITECTURE 134,
  TECHNOLOGIES 562
Architectural Technology and Design see
  ARCHITECTURE 134, TECHNOLOGIES 562
Architectural Technology and Environment see
  ARCHITECTURE 134, ENVIRONMENTAL SCIENCES/
  STUDIES 303
Architectural Technology and Management see
  ARCHITECTURE 134
Architectural Technology and Practice see
  ARCHITECTURE 134
Architectural Venue Design see ARCHITECTURE 134
ARCHITECTURE 134
  see also BUILDING and CONSTRUCTION
Architecture (International) see
  ARCHITECTURE 134
Architecture (Space Objects) see
  ARCHITECTURE 134
Architecture and Environmental Design see
  ARCHITECTURE 134, ENVIRONMENTAL
  SCIENCES/STUDIES 303
Architecture and Environmental Engineering
  see ARCHITECTURE 134, ENGINEERING
  (CIVIL) 274
Architecture and Landscape see LANDSCAPE
  ARCHITECTURE 384
Architecture and Planning see ARCHITECTURE 134
Architecture in Creative and Cultural Environments
  see ARCHITECTURE 134
ART and DESIGN (3D Design) 156
  see also ART and DESIGN (Product and Industrial
  Design)
Art and Design (3D Design and Craft) see ART and
  DESIGN (3D Design) 156
ART and DESIGN (Fashion and Textiles) 140
ART and DESIGN (Fine Art) 144
ART and DESIGN (Graphic Design) 148
  see also ART and DESIGN (Fine Art)
  see also FILM, RADIO, VIDEO and TV STUDIES
Art and Design (Graphic Media) see ART and DESIGN
  (Graphic Design) 148
Art and Design (Interdisciplinary) see ART and
  DESIGN (Graphic Design) 148
Art and Design (Multidisciplinary) see ART and
  DESIGN (Graphic Design) 148

ART and DESIGN (Product and Industrial Design) 152

see also ART and DESIGN (3D Design)

Art and Film see FILM, RADIO, VIDEO and TV STUDIES 310

Art and Film and Theatre see FILM, RADIO, VIDEO and TV STUDIES 310

Art and Philosophy see PHILOSOPHY 478

Art Events and Performance see DRAMA 239

Art History see HISTORY OF ART 363

Art History and a Language see HISTORY OF ART 363, LANGUAGES 386

Art History and Archaeology see ARCHAEOLOGY 131, HISTORY OF ART 363

Art History and Classical Studies see CLASSICAL STUDIES/CLASSICAL CIVILISATION 208, HISTORY OF ART 363

Art History and Cultural Studies see HISTORY OF ART 363

Art History and English Studies see ENGLISH 296, HISTORY OF ART 363

Art History and Fine Art see ART and DESIGN (Fine Art) 144, HISTORY OF ART 363

Art History with a Language see HISTORY OF ART 363, LANGUAGES 386

Art History with Medieval History see HISTORY OF ART 363

Art History with Middle East Studies see ARABIC AND ANCIENT NEAR AND MIDDLE EASTERN STUDIES 129, HISTORY OF ART 363

Art History with Psychology see HISTORY OF ART 363, PSYCHOLOGY 512

Art Practice see ART and DESIGN (Fine Art) 144

Art, Philosophy, Contemporary Practices see COMBINED COURSES 212

Artificial Intelligence see COMPUTER COURSES 219

Artist Blacksmithing see ART and DESIGN (3D Design) 156

Arts and Animation see ART and DESIGN (Graphic Design) 148

Arts and Media Informatics see MEDIA STUDIES 427

Arts and Sciences see COMBINED COURSES 212

Arts and Social Sciences see COMBINED COURSES 212

Arts Event Management see BUSINESS AND MANAGEMENT COURSES (SPECIALISED) 193

Arts Festival Management see HOSPITALITY and HOTEL MANAGEMENT 367

Arts Management see BUSINESS AND MANAGEMENT COURSES (SPECIALISED) 193

Arts Management and Choreography and Dance see BUSINESS AND MANAGEMENT COURSES (SPECIALISED) 193, DANCE/DANCE STUDIES 227

Arts Management and Drama see BUSINESS AND MANAGEMENT COURSES (SPECIALISED) 193, DRAMA 239

Arts Management and Events Management see BUSINESS AND MANAGEMENT COURSES (SPECIALISED) 193

Arts Management and Performing Arts see COMBINED COURSES 212

Arts Management and Theatre Studies see BUSINESS AND MANAGEMENT COURSES (SPECIALISED) 193, DRAMA 239

Arts Marketing see MARKETING 415

Arts Media see MEDIA STUDIES 427

ASIA-PACIFIC STUDIES 158

see also CHINESE

see also JAPANESE

see also LANGUAGES

Asia Pacific Studies and Chinese see ASIA-PACIFIC STUDIES 158, CHINESE 206

Asia Pacific Studies and Economics see ASIA-PACIFIC STUDIES 158, ECONOMICS 251

Asia Pacific Studies and International Relations see ASIA-PACIFIC STUDIES 158, INTERNATIONAL RELATIONS 378

Asian and Middle Eastern Studies see ARABIC AND ANCIENT NEAR AND MIDDLE EASTERN STUDIES 129, ASIA-PACIFIC STUDIES 158

Asian and Middle Eastern Studies (Arabic) see ARABIC AND ANCIENT NEAR AND MIDDLE EASTERN STUDIES 129, ASIA-PACIFIC STUDIES 158

Asian and Middle Eastern Studies (Chinese Studies) see ASIA-PACIFIC STUDIES 158, CHINESE 206

Asian and Middle Eastern Studies (Japanese) see ARABIC AND ANCIENT NEAR AND MIDDLE EASTERN STUDIES 129, ASIA-PACIFIC STUDIES 158, JAPANESE 383

Asian and Middle Eastern Studies (Persian) see ARABIC AND ANCIENT NEAR AND MIDDLE EASTERN STUDIES 129, ASIA-PACIFIC STUDIES 158

Asian and Middle Eastern Studies (Russian) see ASIA-PACIFIC STUDIES 158, RUSSIAN and EAST EUROPEAN STUDIES 526

ASTRONOMY and ASTROPHYSICS 159

see also GEOLOGY/GEOLOGICAL SCIENCES

see also PHYSICS

Astronomy, Space Science and Astrophysics see ASTRONOMY and ASTROPHYSICS 159

Astrophysics see ASTRONOMY and ASTROPHYSICS 159, PHYSICS 488

Astudiaethau Plentyndod *see* EDUCATION STUDIES 256

Audio and Media Engineering *see* ENGINEERING (ACOUSTICS and SOUND) 264, MEDIA STUDIES 427

Audio and Music Production *see* ENGINEERING (ACOUSTICS and SOUND) 264

Audio and Music Technology *see* MUSIC 449

Audio and Recording Technology *see* ENGINEERING (ACOUSTICS and SOUND) 264, FILM, RADIO, VIDEO and TV STUDIES 310

Audio and Video Engineering *see* ENGINEERING (ACOUSTICS and SOUND) 264

Audio Engineering *see* ENGINEERING (ACOUSTICS and SOUND) 264

Audio Music Production *see* MUSIC 449

Audio Systems Engineering *see* ENGINEERING (ACOUSTICS and SOUND) 264

Audio Technology *see* ENGINEERING (ACOUSTICS and SOUND) 264, MUSIC 449

Audiology *see* HEALTH SCIENCES/STUDIES 341

Automatic Control and Systems Engineering *see* ENGINEERING (COMPUTER, CONTROL, SOFTWARE and SYSTEMS) 280

Automation and Control *see* ENGINEERING/ ENGINEERING SCIENCES 260

Automotive and Motorsport Engineering *see* ENGINEERING (MECHANICAL) 290

Automotive Design *see* TECHNOLOGIES 562

Automotive Design Technology *see* ENGINEERING (MECHANICAL) 290

Automotive Engineering *see* ENGINEERING (MECHANICAL) 290, ENGINEERING/ENGINEERING SCIENCES 260

Automotive Engineering with Motorsport *see* ENGINEERING (MECHANICAL) 290

Automotive Materials *see* MATERIALS SCIENCE/ METALLURGY 419

Automotive Production and Development *see* ENGINEERING (MANUFACTURING) 288

Automotive Technology *see* TECHNOLOGIES 562

Automotive Transport Design *see* TRANSPORT MANAGEMENT and PLANNING 571

Aviation and Aerospace Management *see* BUSINESS AND MANAGEMENT COURSES (SPECIALISED) 193, ENGINEERING (AERONAUTICAL and AEROSPACE) 266

Aviation Engineering *see* ENGINEERING (AERONAUTICAL and AEROSPACE) 266

Aviation Engineering with Pilot Studies *see* ENGINEERING (AERONAUTICAL and AEROSPACE) 266

Aviation Management *see* ENGINEERING (AERONAUTICAL and AEROSPACE) 266

Aviation Technology and Management *see* ENGINEERING (AERONAUTICAL and AEROSPACE) 266, TECHNOLOGIES 562

Aviation Technology with Pilot Studies *see* ENGINEERING (AERONAUTICAL and AEROSPACE) 266, TECHNOLOGIES 562

Avionic Systems *see* ENGINEERING (AERONAUTICAL and AEROSPACE) 266

Avionic Systems with Pilot Studies *see* ENGINEERING (AERONAUTICAL and AEROSPACE) 266

Avionics *see* ENGINEERING (AERONAUTICAL and AEROSPACE) 266

Ballet Education *see* DANCE/DANCE STUDIES 227

Banking *see* FINANCE 315

Banking and Finance *see* FINANCE 315

Banking and Finance Management *see* FINANCE 315, MATHEMATICS 422

Banking and Finance with a European Language *see* FINANCE 315

Banking and International Finance *see* FINANCE 315

Banking Practice and Management *see* ACCOUNTANCY/ACCOUNTING 109, FINANCE 315

Bengali *see* LANGUAGES 386

Bespoke Tailoring *see* ART and DESIGN (Fashion and Textiles) 140

Biblical Literature and English *see* RELIGIOUS STUDIES 521

Biblical Studies *see* RELIGIOUS STUDIES 521

Biblical Studies with Economics *see* ECONOMICS 251, RELIGIOUS STUDIES 521

Biblical Studies with English *see* RELIGIOUS STUDIES 521

Bioarchaeology *see* ARCHAEOLOGY 131

Biochemical Engineering *see* BIOCHEMISTRY 162, ENGINEERING (CHEMICAL) 269

Biochemical Engineering with Bioprocess Management *see* ENGINEERING (CHEMICAL) 269

Biochemical with Chemical Engineering *see* ENGINEERING (CHEMICAL) 269

Biochemicals *see* BIOCHEMISTRY 162

BIOCHEMISTRY 162
 see also BIOLOGICAL SCIENCES
 see also CHEMISTRY
 see also COMBINED COURSES

Biochemistry (Molecular and Cellular) *see* BIOCHEMISTRY 162

Biochemistry and Biological Chemistry *see* BIOCHEMISTRY 162, CHEMISTRY 199

Biochemistry and Genetics *see* BIOCHEMISTRY 162, GENETICS 328

Biochemistry and Genome Science *see* BIOCHEMISTRY 162

Biochemistry and Microbiology *see* BIOCHEMISTRY 162, MICROBIOLOGY 447

Biochemistry and Molecular Biology *see* BIOCHEMISTRY 162

Biochemistry and Molecular Medicine *see* BIOCHEMISTRY 162

Biochemistry and Nutrition *see* BIOCHEMISTRY 162, NUTRITION 466

Biochemistry with Biomedicine/Genetics *see* BIOCHEMISTRY 162

Biochemistry with Biotechnology *see* BIOCHEMISTRY 162

Biochemistry with Medical Biochemistry *see* BIOCHEMISTRY 162

Biochemistry with Molecular Biology and Biotechnology *see* BIOCHEMISTRY 162, BIOTECHNOLOGY 174

Biochemistry with Studies in the USA *see* BIOCHEMISTRY 162

Bioengineering *see* ENGINEERING (MEDICAL) 295

Biological and Forensic Sciences *see* BIOLOGICAL SCIENCES 165

Biological and Medical Sciences *see* BIOLOGICAL SCIENCES 165

Biological and Medicinal Chemistry *see* BIOLOGICAL SCIENCES 165, CHEMISTRY 199

Biological Anthropology *see* ANTHROPOLOGY 127, BIOLOGICAL SCIENCES 165

Biological Chemistry *see* BIOCHEMISTRY 162, BIOLOGICAL SCIENCES 165, CHEMISTRY 199

Biological Chemistry and Drug Discovery *see* CHEMISTRY 199

Biological Science (Food Science) *see* FOOD SCIENCE/ STUDIES and TECHNOLOGY 321

Biological Science with Genetics *see* BIOLOGICAL SCIENCES 165, GENETICS 328

Biological Science with Pharmacology *see* BIOLOGICAL SCIENCES 165, PHARMACOLOGY 472

BIOLOGICAL SCIENCES 165
see also ANATOMICAL SCIENCE/ANATOMY
see also BIOCHEMISTRY
see also BIOLOGY
see also BIOTECHNOLOGY

see also ENVIRONMENTAL SCIENCES/STUDIES
see also GENETICS
see also HUMAN SCIENCES
see also MICROBIOLOGY
see also PLANT SCIENCES
see also ZOOLOGY

Biological Sciences (Biochemistry) *see* BIOCHEMISTRY 162, BIOLOGICAL SCIENCES 165

Biological Sciences (Biotechnology/Environmental Biology/Genetics) *see* BIOLOGICAL SCIENCES 165

Biological Sciences (Environmental Biology/Plant Biology) *see* BIOLOGY 170, ENVIRONMENTAL SCIENCES/STUDIES 303

Biological Sciences (Genetics) *see* BIOLOGICAL SCIENCES 165, GENETICS 328

Biological Sciences (Microbiology) *see* BIOLOGICAL SCIENCES 165, MICROBIOLOGY 447

Biological Sciences (Physiology with Pharmacology) *see* BIOLOGICAL SCIENCES 165, PHARMACOLOGY 472

Biological Sciences (Plant Biology) *see* PLANT SCIENCES 504

Biological Sciences (Zoology) *see* ZOOLOGY 576

Biological Sciences and Physiology *see* BIOLOGICAL SCIENCES 165, PHYSIOLOGY 500

Biological Sciences with Biomedicine *see* BIOLOGICAL SCIENCES 165

Biological Sciences with Management *see* BIOLOGICAL SCIENCES 165

BIOLOGY 170
see also BIOLOGICAL SCIENCES
see also BIOTECHNOLOGY
see also MICROBIOLOGY
see also ZOOLOGY

Biology (Cellular and Molecular Biology) *see* BIOLOGICAL SCIENCES 165

Biology (Ecology and Environmental Biology) *see* BIOLOGY 170

Biology (Molecular and Cellular) *see* BIOLOGY 170, MICROBIOLOGY 447

Biology (Plant Science) *see* PLANT SCIENCES 504

Biology and Animal Behaviour *see* BIOLOGY 170

Biology and Bioinformatics *see* BIOLOGY 170

Biology and History and Philosophy of Science *see* BIOLOGY 170, HISTORY 355, PHILOSOPHY 478

Biology and Management *see* BIOLOGY 170

Biology and Psychology *see* BIOLOGICAL SCIENCES 165, PSYCHOLOGY 512

Biology and Statistics *see* BIOLOGY 170, STATISTICS 554

Biology with a Modern Language *see* BIOLOGY 170, LANGUAGES 386

Biology with Conservation and Biodiversity *see* BIOLOGY 170, ENVIRONMENTAL SCIENCES/ STUDIES 303

Biology with Forensic Biology *see* BIOLOGY 170

Biology with Microbiology *see* BIOLOGY 170, MICROBIOLOGY 447

Biology with Psychology *see* BIOLOGY 170, PSYCHOLOGY 512

Biology with Science and Society *see* BIOLOGY 170, SOCIAL SCIENCES/STUDIES 531

Biology with Science Communication *see* BIOLOGY 170, COMMUNICATION STUDIES/ COMMUNICATION 214

Biomaterial Science and Tissue Engineering *see* MATERIALS SCIENCE/METALLURGY 419

Biomaterials and Tissue Engineering *see* BIOTECHNOLOGY 174, ENGINEERING (MEDICAL) 295, MATERIALS SCIENCE/METALLURGY 419

Biomedical Chemistry *see* BIOCHEMISTRY 162, CHEMISTRY 199

Biomedical Engineering *see* ENGINEERING (MEDICAL) 295

Biomedical Genetics *see* BIOLOGICAL SCIENCES 162, GENETICS 328

Biomedical Material Science and Tissue Engineering *see* MATERIALS SCIENCE/ METALLURGY 419

Biomedical Materials Chemistry *see* CHEMISTRY 199, MATERIALS SCIENCE/METALLURGY 419

Biomedical Materials Science *see* BIOTECHNOLOGY 174, MATERIALS SCIENCE/ METALLURGY 419

Biomedical Science *see* BIOCHEMISTRY 162, BIOLOGICAL SCIENCES 165, BIOLOGY 170, ENGINEERING (MEDICAL) 295, HUMAN SCIENCES/HUMAN BIOSCIENCES 374, MEDICINE 433

Biomedical Science (Pharmacology) *see* PHARMACOLOGY 472

Biomedical Science and Medical Microbiology *see* MICROBIOLOGY 447

Biomedical Sciences *see* BIOLOGICAL SCIENCES 165, BIOLOGY 170

Biomedical Sciences (Anatomy) *see* ANATOMICAL SCIENCE/ANATOMY 122, BIOLOGICAL SCIENCES 165

Biomedical Sciences (Biochemistry) *see* BIOCHEMISTRY 162, HEALTH SCIENCES/ STUDIES 341

Biomedical Sciences (Forensic) *see* BIOLOGICAL SCIENCES 165

Biomedical Sciences (Genetics) *see* GENETICS 328, HEALTH SCIENCES/STUDIES 341

Biomedical Sciences (Human Health) *see* HEALTH SCIENCES/STUDIES 341

Biomedical Sciences (Neuroscience) *see* BIOLOGICAL SCIENCES 165, PSYCHOLOGY 512

Biomedical Sciences (Physiology) *see* BIOLOGICAL SCIENCES 165, PHYSIOLOGY 500

Biomedical Studies *see* BIOLOGICAL SCIENCES 165

Biomedicine *see* BIOLOGICAL SCIENCES 165

Bioprocess Engineering *see* BIOTECHNOLOGY 174, ENGINEERING (CHEMICAL) 269

Bioprocessing of New Medicines (Business and Management) *see* BIOLOGICAL SCIENCES 165, MEDICINE 433

Bioprocessing of New Medicines (Science and Engineering) *see* BIOLOGICAL SCIENCES 165, MEDICINE 433

Biosciences *see* BIOLOGICAL SCIENCES 165

Biosciences (Human Biology) *see* BIOLOGY 170

Biosciences (Microbiology) *see* MICROBIOLOGY 447

BIOTECHNOLOGY 174

   see also BIOLOGICAL SCIENCES

   see also ENGINEERING (MEDICAL)

   see also TECHNOLOGY

Biotechnology and Microbiology *see* BIOTECHNOLOGY 174, MICROBIOLOGY 447

Biotechnology with a Certificate in European Studies *see* BIOTECHNOLOGY 174

Bioveterinary Science *see* ANIMAL SCIENCES 124, VETERINARY SCIENCE/MEDICINE 573

Brewing and Distilling *see* BIOCHEMISTRY 162, BIOLOGICAL SCIENCES 165, BIOLOGY 170, ENGINEERING (CHEMICAL) 269, FOOD SCIENCE/ STUDIES and TECHNOLOGY 321

British Sign Language *see* TEACHER TRAINING 559

Broadcast and Media Production *see* MEDIA STUDIES 427

Broadcast Audio Technology *see* ENGINEERING (ACOUSTICS and SOUND) 264

Broadcast Information Technology *see* ENGINEERING (ACOUSTICS and SOUND) 264

Broadcast Journalism *see* MEDIA STUDIES 427

Broadcast Media Production *see* MEDIA STUDIES 427

Broadcast Media Technologies *see* MEDIA STUDIES 427

Broadcast Production *see* FILM, RADIO, VIDEO and TV STUDIES 310

Broadcast Technology *see* ENGINEERING (ACOUSTICS and SOUND) 264

Broadcasting *see* MEDIA STUDIES 427

Broadcasting Journalism and Media Communications *see* MEDIA STUDIES 427

Broadcasting, Journalism and Screen Studies *see* MEDIA STUDIES 427

BUILDING and CONSTRUCTION 176
> *see also* ARCHITECTURE
> *see also* HOUSING
> *see also* SURVEYING

Building Construction and Management *see* BUILDING and CONSTRUCTION 176

Building Design Management *see* BUILDING and CONSTRUCTION 176

Building Engineering and Materials *see* BUILDING and CONSTRUCTION 176, MATERIALS SCIENCE/ METALLURGY 419

Building Materials *see* MATERIALS SCIENCE/ METALLURGY 419

Building Project Management *see* BUILDING and CONSTRUCTION 176

Building Services and Sustainable Engineering *see* BUILDING and CONSTRUCTION 176

Building Services Engineering *see* BUILDING and CONSTRUCTION 176, ENGINEERING (CIVIL) 274

Building Services Engineering Project Management *see* ENGINEERING (CIVIL) 274

Building Services Quantity Surveying *see* BUILDING and CONSTRUCTION 176, SURVEYING 556

Building Studies *see* BUILDING and CONSTRUCTION 176

Building Studies (Construction/Maintenance Management) *see* BUILDING and CONSTRUCTION 176

Building Surveying *see* BUILDING and CONSTRUCTION 176, SURVEYING 556

Building Surveying and Engineering *see* BUILDING and CONSTRUCTION 176

Building Surveying and the Environment *see* BUILDING and CONSTRUCTION 176, ENVIRONMENTAL SCIENCES/STUDIES 303

Built Environment *see* DEVELOPMENT STUDIES 235

Built Environment (Architectural Technology) *see* ARCHITECTURE 134, BUILDING and CONSTRUCTION 176

Built Environment (Construction Management) *see* BUILDING and CONSTRUCTION 176

Built Environment (Quantity Surveying) *see* BUILDING and CONSTRUCTION 176, SURVEYING 556

Bulgarian *see* LANGUAGES 386

Burmese (Myanmar) *see* LANGUAGES 386

Business *see* BUSINESS AND MANAGEMENT COURSES 179

Business (Human Resource Management) *see* HUMAN RESOURCE MANAGEMENT 371

Business Accounting *see* ACCOUNTANCY/ ACCOUNTING 109

Business Accounting and Finance *see* ACCOUNTANCY/ ACCOUNTING 109

Business Administration *see* BUSINESS AND MANAGEMENT COURSES 179

Business Administration (Marketing) *see* MARKETING 415

Business and Advertising *see* BUSINESS AND MANAGEMENT COURSES (SPECIALISED) 193

Business and Advertising Management *see* BUSINESS AND MANAGEMENT COURSES (SPECIALISED) 193

Business and Economics *see* ECONOMICS 251

Business and Economy of Contemporary China *see* BUSINESS AND MANAGEMENT COURSES 179

Business and Educational Development *see* BUSINESS AND MANAGEMENT COURSES 179, EDUCATION STUDIES 256

Business and Enterprise Education *see* BUSINESS AND MANAGEMENT COURSES 179, TEACHER TRAINING 559

Business and Enterprise Management *see* BUSINESS AND MANAGEMENT COURSES 179

Business and Finance *see* BUSINESS AND MANAGEMENT COURSES 179, FINANCE 315

Business and Financial Management *see* BUSINESS AND MANAGEMENT COURSES 179, FINANCE 315

Business and Financial Services *see* FINANCE 315

Business and Human Resource Management *see* BUSINESS AND MANAGEMENT COURSES 179, HUMAN RESOURCE MANAGEMENT 371

Business and Human Resources *see* BUSINESS AND MANAGEMENT COURSES 179, HUMAN RESOURCE MANAGEMENT 371

Business and Information Technology *see* INFORMATION MANAGEMENT and LIBRARIANSHIP 375

Business and Law *see* BUSINESS AND MANAGEMENT COURSES 179, BUSINESS AND MANAGEMENT COURSES (SPECIALISED) 193, LAW 393

BUSINESS and MANAGEMENT COURSES 179
> *see also* BUSINESS and MANAGEMENT COURSES (INTERNATIONAL and EUROPEAN)
> *see also* BUSINESS and MANAGEMENT COURSES (SPECIALISED)

see also HOSPITALITY and HOTEL MANAGEMENT
see also HUMAN RESOURCE MANAGEMENT
see also LEISURE and RECREATION MANAGEMENT/
  STUDIES
see also MARKETING
see also RETAIL MANAGEMENT
see also TOURISM and TRAVEL
Business and Management (Accounting/
  Marketing) *see* BUSINESS AND MANAGEMENT
  COURSES 179
**BUSINESS and MANAGEMENT COURSES
  (INTERNATIONAL and EUROPEAN) 188**
see also BUSINESS and MANAGEMENT COURSES
see also BUSINESS and MANAGEMENT COURSES
  (SPECIALISED)
see also HOSPITALITY and HOTEL MANAGEMENT
see also HUMAN RESOURCE MANAGEMENT
see also LEISURE and RECREATION MANAGEMENT/
  STUDIES
see also MARKETING
see also RETAIL MANAGEMENT
see also TOURISM and TRAVEL
**BUSINESS and MANAGEMENT COURSES
  (SPECIALISED) 193**
see also BUSINESS and MANAGEMENT COURSES
see also BUSINESS and MANAGEMENT COURSES
  (INTERNATIONAL and EUROPEAN)
see also HOSPITALITY and HOTEL MANAGEMENT
see also HUMAN RESOURCE MANAGEMENT
see also LEISURE and RECREATION MANAGEMENT/
  STUDIES
see also MARKETING
see also RETAIL MANAGEMENT
see also TOURISM and TRAVEL
Business and Management Studies *see* BUSINESS
  AND MANAGEMENT COURSES 179
Business and Management Studies with Law *see*
  BUSINESS AND MANAGEMENT COURSES 179,
  LAW 393
Business and Marketing *see* BUSINESS AND
  MANAGEMENT COURSES 179
Business and Marketing Management *see*
  BUSINESS AND MANAGEMENT COURSES 179,
  MARKETING 415
Business and Property *see* SURVEYING 556
Business and Public Relations *see* BUSINESS AND
  MANAGEMENT COURSES (SPECIALISED) 193,
  MARKETING 415
Business and Spanish *see* BUSINESS AND
  MANAGEMENT COURSES 179, SPANISH 543
Business and Tourism *see* TOURISM and TRAVEL 564

Business Communications *see* BUSINESS AND
  MANAGEMENT COURSES 179, COMMUNICATION
  STUDIES/COMMUNICATION 214
Business Computer Systems *see* COMPUTER
  COURSES 219
Business Computing *see* BUSINESS AND
  MANAGEMENT COURSES 179, COMPUTER
  COURSES 219
Business Computing and IT *see* COMPUTER
  COURSES 219
Business Computing Solutions *see* BUSINESS
  AND MANAGEMENT COURSES 179, COMPUTER
  COURSES 219
Business Computing Systems *see* BUSINESS
  AND MANAGEMENT COURSES 179
Business Economics *see* BUSINESS AND MANAGEMENT
  COURSES 179, ECONOMICS 251
Business Economics (International) *see*
  BUSINESS AND MANAGEMENT COURSES
  (INTERNATIONAL AND EUROPEAN) 188,
  ECONOMICS 251
Business Economics and Finance *see*
  ECONOMICS 251, FINANCE 315
Business Economics and International Business *see*
  BUSINESS AND MANAGEMENT COURSES 179
Business Economics with a European Language *see*
  ECONOMICS 251
Business Economics with European Study *see*
  ECONOMICS 251, EUROPEAN STUDIES 307
Business Economics with Marketing *see*
  ECONOMICS 251, MARKETING 415
Business Enterprise *see* BUSINESS AND MANAGEMENT
  COURSES 179, BUSINESS AND MANAGEMENT
  COURSES (SPECIALISED) 193
Business Enterprise and Human Resource
  Management *see* BUSINESS AND MANAGEMENT
  COURSES 179
Business Enterprise and Marketing *see*
  BUSINESS AND MANAGEMENT COURSES
  (SPECIALISED) 193
Business Enterprise Development *see* BUSINESS AND
  MANAGEMENT COURSES 179, BUSINESS AND
  MANAGEMENT COURSES (SPECIALISED) 193
Business Enterprise Management *see* BUSINESS AND
  MANAGEMENT COURSES 179
Business Enterprise Systems *see* BUSINESS AND
  MANAGEMENT COURSES (SPECIALISED) 193
Business Entrepreneurship *see* BUSINESS
  AND MANAGEMENT COURSES 179,
  BUSINESS AND MANAGEMENT COURSES
  (SPECIALISED) 193

Business Entrepreneurship and Innovation
see BUSINESS AND MANAGEMENT
COURSES 179

Business Finance see BUSINESS AND MANAGEMENT
COURSES 179, FINANCE 315

Business Finance and Economics see ECONOMICS 251,
FINANCE 315

Business Finance Management see BUSINESS AND
MANAGEMENT COURSES 179, FINANCE 315

Business Information Systems see BUSINESS
AND MANAGEMENT COURSES 179,
BUSINESS AND MANAGEMENT COURSES
(SPECIALISED) 193, COMPUTER COURSES 219,
INFORMATION MANAGEMENT and
LIBRARIANSHIP 375

Business Information Technology see BUSINESS
AND MANAGEMENT COURSES 179, BUSINESS
AND MANAGEMENT COURSES (SPECIALISED) 193,
COMPUTER COURSES 219

Business Law see BUSINESS AND MANAGEMENT
COURSES 179, LAW 393

Business Logistics and Transport Management
see TRANSPORT MANAGEMENT and
PLANNING 571

Business Management see BUSINESS AND
MANAGEMENT COURSES 179,
COMBINED COURSES 212

Business Management (Combined) see BUSINESS
AND MANAGEMENT COURSES 179

Business Management (Finance) see FINANCE 315

Business Management (Finance and Accounting) see
ACCOUNTANCY/ACCOUNTING 109, BUSINESS AND
MANAGEMENT COURSES 179

Business Management (Human Resource
Management) see HUMAN RESOURCE
MANAGEMENT 371

Business Management (Human Resources) see
HUMAN RESOURCE MANAGEMENT 371

Business Management (International) see BUSINESS
AND MANAGEMENT COURSES (INTERNATIONAL
AND EUROPEAN) 188

Business Management (International Business)
see BUSINESS AND MANAGEMENT COURSES
(INTERNATIONAL AND EUROPEAN) 188

Business Management (International Management)
see BUSINESS AND MANAGEMENT COURSES
(INTERNATIONAL AND EUROPEAN) 188

Business Management (Leisure and Tourism)
see BUSINESS AND MANAGEMENT COURSES 179,
LEISURE and RECREATION MANAGEMENT/
STUDIES 405

Business Management (Logistics Operations)
see TRANSPORT MANAGEMENT and
PLANNING 571

Business Management (Marketing) see BUSINESS
AND MANAGEMENT COURSES 179,
MARKETING 415

Business Management (Retail) see RETAIL
MANAGEMENT 524

Business Management (Retail Management and
Marketing) see RETAIL MANAGEMENT 524

Business Management (Supply Chain Management)
see BUSINESS AND MANAGEMENT COURSES
(SPECIALISED) 193

Business Management (Tourism) see TOURISM and
TRAVEL 564

Business Management (Travel and Tourism)
see BUSINESS AND MANAGEMENT COURSES
(SPECIALISED) 193

Business Management and Accountancy see
ACCOUNTANCY/ACCOUNTING 109, BUSINESS
AND MANAGEMENT COURSES 179

Business Management and Economics see
BUSINESS AND MANAGEMENT COURSES 179,
ECONOMICS 251

Business Management and English for International
Communications see BUSINESS AND
MANAGEMENT COURSES 179, LANGUAGES 386

Business Management and Entrepreneurship see
BUSINESS AND MANAGEMENT COURSES 179

Business Management and Finance see BUSINESS
AND MANAGEMENT COURSES 179, FINANCE 315

Business Management and Financial Economics see
BUSINESS AND MANAGEMENT COURSES 179,
ECONOMICS 251, FINANCE 315

Business Management and French/German/
Spanish see BUSINESS AND MANAGEMENT
COURSES (INTERNATIONAL AND EUROPEAN) 188,
LANGUAGES 386

Business Management and Human Resource
Management see BUSINESS AND
MANAGEMENT COURSES 179, HUMAN
RESOURCE MANAGEMENT 371

Business Management and Human Resources see
BUSINESS AND MANAGEMENT COURSES 179,
HUMAN RESOURCE MANAGEMENT 371

Business Management and Information Technology
see BUSINESS AND MANAGEMENT COURSES 179,
COMPUTER COURSES 219

Business Management and Marketing see
BUSINESS AND MANAGEMENT COURSES 179,
MARKETING 415

Business Management in China *see* BUSINESS AND MANAGEMENT COURSES 179, CHINESE 206

Business Management Studies *see* BUSINESS AND MANAGEMENT COURSES 179

Business Management Studies and Human Resource Management *see* BUSINESS AND MANAGEMENT COURSES 179, HUMAN RESOURCE MANAGEMENT 371

Business Management with Finance *see* BUSINESS AND MANAGEMENT COURSES 179

Business Management with a European Language *see* BUSINESS AND MANAGEMENT COURSES (INTERNATIONAL AND EUROPEAN) 188

Business Management with a Modern Language *see* BUSINESS AND MANAGEMENT COURSES (INTERNATIONAL AND EUROPEAN) 188, LANGUAGES 386

Business Management with Finance *see* BUSINESS AND MANAGEMENT COURSES 179, FINANCE 315

Business Management with German *see* BUSINESS AND MANAGEMENT COURSES 179, BUSINESS AND MANAGEMENT COURSES (INTERNATIONAL AND EUROPEAN) 188, GERMAN 337

Business Management with Human Resource Management *see* BUSINESS AND MANAGEMENT COURSES 179, HUMAN RESOURCE MANAGEMENT 371

Business Management with Industrial Experience *see* BUSINESS AND MANAGEMENT COURSES 179

Business Management with Languages *see* BUSINESS AND MANAGEMENT COURSES 179, CHINESE 206, LANGUAGES 386

Business Management with Marketing *see* BUSINESS AND MANAGEMENT COURSES 179, MARKETING 415

Business Marketing *see* MARKETING 415

Business Mathematics and Statistics *see* BUSINESS AND MANAGEMENT COURSES 179, MATHEMATICS 422, STATISTICS 554

Business Operations Management *see* BUSINESS AND MANAGEMENT COURSES 179

Business Purchasing and Supply Chain Management *see* BUSINESS AND MANAGEMENT COURSES 179

Business Retail Management *see* RETAIL MANAGEMENT 524

Business Retail Studies *see* RETAIL MANAGEMENT 524

Business School (International Business (Russian)) *see* RUSSIAN and EAST EUROPEAN STUDIES 526

Business Statistics *see* STATISTICS 554

Business Statistics and Marketing *see* MARKETING 415, STATISTICS 554

Business Studies *see* BUSINESS AND MANAGEMENT COURSES 179, BUSINESS AND MANAGEMENT COURSES (INTERNATIONAL AND EUROPEAN) 188

Business Studies (Finance) *see* FINANCE 415

Business Studies (Human Resource Management) *see* HUMAN RESOURCE MANAGEMENT 371

Business Studies (Marketing) *see* MARKETING 415

Business Studies (Tourism) *see* TOURISM and TRAVEL 564

Business Studies and Accounting *see* ACCOUNTANCY/ ACCOUNTING 109, BUSINESS AND MANAGEMENT COURSES 179

Business Studies and Economics *see* BUSINESS AND MANAGEMENT COURSES 179, ECONOMICS 251

Business Studies and Human Resource Management *see* BUSINESS AND MANAGEMENT COURSES 179, HUMAN RESOURCE MANAGEMENT 371

Business Studies and Japanese *see* BUSINESS AND MANAGEMENT COURSES 179, JAPANESE 383

Business Studies and Law *see* LAW 393

Business Studies and Politics *see* BUSINESS AND MANAGEMENT COURSES 179, POLITICS 507

Business Studies and Retail *see* RETAIL MANAGEMENT 524

Business Studies and Sociology *see* BUSINESS AND MANAGEMENT COURSES 179, SOCIOLOGY 539

Business Studies with a Modern Language *see* BUSINESS AND MANAGEMENT COURSES (INTERNATIONAL AND EUROPEAN) 188, LANGUAGES 386

Business Studies with Economics *see* BUSINESS AND MANAGEMENT COURSES 179, ECONOMICS 251

Business Studies with Environmental Management *see* BUSINESS AND MANAGEMENT COURSES 179, ENVIRONMENTAL SCIENCES/STUDIES 303

Business Studies with Finance *see* BUSINESS AND MANAGEMENT COURSES 179, FINANCE 315

Business Studies with French/German/Italian/ Spanish *see* BUSINESS AND MANAGEMENT COURSES (INTERNATIONAL AND EUROPEAN) 188

Business Studies with French/German/Spanish *see* BUSINESS AND MANAGEMENT COURSES (INTERNATIONAL AND EUROPEAN) 188, FRENCH 325, GERMAN 337, SPANISH 543

Business Studies with French/Spanish *see* BUSINESS AND MANAGEMENT COURSES (INTERNATIONAL AND EUROPEAN) 188

Business Studies with Human Resource Management *see* BUSINESS AND MANAGEMENT COURSES 179, HUMAN RESOURCE MANAGEMENT 371

Business Studies with International Business Management *see* BUSINESS AND MANAGEMENT COURSES (INTERNATIONAL AND EUROPEAN) 188

Business Studies with Marketing Management *see* BUSINESS AND MANAGEMENT COURSES 179, MARKETING 415

Business Studies, Accounting and Finance *see* ACCOUNTANCY/ACCOUNTING 109, ECONOMICS 251, FINANCE 315

Business Systems Management *see* BUSINESS AND MANAGEMENT COURSES 179

Business Technology *see* TECHNOLOGIES 562

Business with American Studies *see* AMERICAN STUDIES 120, BUSINESS AND MANAGEMENT COURSES (INTERNATIONAL AND EUROPEAN) 188

Business with Economics *see* BUSINESS AND MANAGEMENT COURSES 179, ECONOMICS 251

Business with Finance *see* BUSINESS AND MANAGEMENT COURSES 179, FINANCE 315

Business with French *see* BUSINESS AND MANAGEMENT COURSES (INTERNATIONAL AND EUROPEAN) 188, FRENCH 325

Business with Human Resource Management *see* BUSINESS AND MANAGEMENT COURSES 179, HUMAN RESOURCE MANAGEMENT 371

Business with Human Resources *see* HUMAN RESOURCE MANAGEMENT 371

Business with Law *see* BUSINESS AND MANAGEMENT COURSES 179, LAW 393

Business with Logistics and Supply Chain Management *see* BUSINESS AND MANAGEMENT COURSES 179, TRANSPORT MANAGEMENT and PLANNING 571

Business with Mandarin Chinese/European Languages *see* BUSINESS AND MANAGEMENT COURSES (INTERNATIONAL AND EUROPEAN) 188

Business with Marketing *see* BUSINESS AND MANAGEMENT COURSES 179, MARKETING 415

Business with Psychology *see* BUSINESS AND MANAGEMENT COURSES 179, PSYCHOLOGY 512

Business, Accountancy and Economics *see* ACCOUNTANCY/ACCOUNTING 109, BUSINESS AND MANAGEMENT COURSES 179, ECONOMICS 251

Business, Economics and Advertising *see* ECONOMICS 251, MARKETING 415

Business, Economics and Public Relations *see* ECONOMICS 251

Business, Law and Human Resource Management *see* HUMAN RESOURCE MANAGEMENT 371

Business, Management and Marketing *see* MARKETING 415

Cancer Biology and Immunology *see* BIOLOGICAL SCIENCES 165, MEDICINE 433

Caribbean Studies and International Tourism Management *see* AFRICAN AND CARIBBEAN STUDIES 115, TOURISM and TRAVEL, 564

Cell and Molecular Biology *see* BIOLOGY 170, MICROBIOLOGY 447

Cell Biology *see* BIOLOGICAL SCIENCES 165, BIOLOGY 170, MICROBIOLOGY 447

Cell Biology with a Modern Language *see* BIOLOGY 170, LANGUAGES 386

Cellular and Molecular Medicine *see* BIOLOGICAL SCIENCES 165, MEDICINE 433, MICROBIOLOGY 447

Celtic *see* CELTIC, IRISH, SCOTTISH AND WELSH STUDIES 197

Celtic and Archaeology *see* ARCHAEOLOGY 131, CELTIC, IRISH, SCOTTISH AND WELSH STUDIES 197

Celtic and Linguistics *see* CELTIC, IRISH, SCOTTISH AND WELSH STUDIES 197, LINGUISTICS 407

Celtic and Scottish History *see* CELTIC, IRISH, SCOTTISH AND WELSH STUDIES 197, HISTORY 355

Celtic and Scottish Literature *see* CELTIC, IRISH, SCOTTISH AND WELSH STUDIES 197, LITERATURE 409

Celtic Civilisation *see* CELTIC, IRISH, SCOTTISH AND WELSH STUDIES 197

Celtic Civilisation and English *see* CELTIC, IRISH, SCOTTISH AND WELSH STUDIES 197, ENGLISH 296

Celtic Studies *see* CELTIC, IRISH, SCOTTISH AND WELSH STUDIES 197

CELTIC, IRISH, SCOTTISH AND WELSH STUDIES 197
see also HISTORY
see also LITERATURE

Central and East European Studies *see* EUROPEAN STUDIES 307, RUSSIAN and EAST EUROPEAN STUDIES 526

Ceramics *see* ART and DESIGN (3D Design) 156

Ceramics and Jewellery *see* ART and DESIGN (Fashion and Textiles) 140

Chemical and Bioprocessing Engineering *see* ENGINEERING (CHEMICAL) 269

Chemical and Energy Engineering *see* ENGINEERING (CHEMICAL) 269

Chemical and Materials Engineering *see* ENGINEERING (CHEMICAL) 269, MATERIALS SCIENCE/METALLURGY 419

Chemical and Minerals Engineering *see* MATERIALS SCIENCE/METALLURGY 419

Chemical and Nuclear Engineering *see* ENGINEERING (CHEMICAL) 269

Chemical and Pharmaceutical Engineering *see* ENGINEERING (CHEMICAL) 269, PHARMACY and PHARMACEUTICAL SCIENCES 475

Chemical and Process Engineering *see* ENGINEERING (CHEMICAL) 269

Chemical Biology *see* BIOCHEMISTRY 162

Chemical Engineering *see* ENGINEERING (AERONAUTICAL and AEROSPACE) 266, ENGINEERING (CHEMICAL) 269, TECHNOLOGIES 562

Chemical Engineering (Business Management) *see* ENGINEERING (CHEMICAL) 269

Chemical Engineering (International Study) *see* ENGINEERING (CHEMICAL) 269

Chemical Engineering Combined Studies *see* ENGINEERING (CHEMICAL) 269

Chemical Engineering with Biotechnology *see* BIOTECHNOLOGY 174, ENGINEERING (CHEMICAL) 269

Chemical Engineering with Business Management *see* BUSINESS AND MANAGEMENT COURSES 179, ENGINEERING (CHEMICAL) 269

Chemical Engineering with Energy Engineering *see* ENGINEERING (CHEMICAL) 269

Chemical Engineering with Environmental Engineering *see* CHEMISTRY 199, ENGINEERING (CHEMICAL) 269, ENGINEERING/ENGINEERING SCIENCES 260

Chemical Engineering with Environmental Technology *see* ENGINEERING (CHEMICAL) 269

Chemical Engineering with Management *see* ENGINEERING (CHEMICAL) 269

Chemical Engineering with Oil and Gas Technology *see* ENGINEERING (CHEMICAL) 269

Chemical Engineering with Pharmaceutical Chemistry *see* ENGINEERING (CHEMICAL) 269

Chemical Physics *see* CHEMISTRY 199, PHYSICS 488

Chemical with Biochemical Engineering *see* ENGINEERING (CHEMICAL) 269

Chemical with Nuclear Engineering *see* ENGINEERING (CHEMICAL) 269

CHEMISTRY 199
see also BIOCHEMISTRY
see also ENGINEERING (CHEMICAL)

Chemistry and Forensic Science *see* CHEMISTRY 199, COMBINED COURSES 212

Chemistry and Management Science *see* BUSINESS AND MANAGEMENT COURSES (SPECIALISED) 193, CHEMISTRY 199

Chemistry and Mathematics *see* CHEMISTRY 199, MATHEMATICS 422

Chemistry and Molecular Physics *see* CHEMISTRY 199, PHYSICS 488

Chemistry and Physics *see* CHEMISTRY 199, PHYSICS 488

Chemistry for the Offshore Industry *see* CHEMISTRY 199

Chemistry with Bimolecular Sciences *see* CHEMISTRY 199

Chemistry with Analytical and Forensic Science *see* CHEMISTRY 199

Chemistry with Analytical Chemistry *see* CHEMISTRY 199

Chemistry with Analytical Chemistry and Toxicology *see* CHEMISTRY 199

Chemistry with Analytical Sciences *see* CHEMISTRY 199

Chemistry with Archaeology *see* ARCHAEOLOGY 131, CHEMISTRY 199

Chemistry with Biochemistry *see* BIOCHEMISTRY 162

Chemistry with Biomedical Sciences *see* BIOLOGICAL SCIENCES 165, CHEMISTRY 199

Chemistry with Biomedicine *see* CHEMISTRY 199

Chemistry with Bi-organic Chemistry *see* CHEMISTRY 199

Chemistry with Business *see* BUSINESS AND MANAGEMENT COURSES 179, CHEMISTRY 199

Chemistry with Chemical Engineering *see* ENGINEERING (CHEMICAL) 269

Chemistry with Colour Science *see* CHEMISTRY 199

Chemistry with Education *see* CHEMISTRY 199, EDUCATION STUDIES 256

Chemistry with Environmental and Sustainable Chemistry *see* CHEMISTRY 199, ENVIRONMENTAL SCIENCES/STUDIES 303

Chemistry with European Language *see* CHEMISTRY 199, LANGUAGES 386

Chemistry with Extended Studies in Europe *see* CHEMISTRY 199, EUROPEAN STUDIES 307

Chemistry with Forensic Analysis *see* CHEMISTRY 199

Chemistry with Forensic and Analytical Chemistry *see* CHEMISTRY 199

Chemistry with Forensic Chemistry *see* CHEMISTRY 199

Chemistry with Forensic Investigation *see* CHEMISTRY 199

Chemistry with Forensic Science *see* BIOLOGICAL SCIENCES 165, CHEMISTRY 199

Chemistry with French/German/Spanish for Science *see* CHEMISTRY 199, LANGUAGES 386

Chemistry with Management *see* BUSINESS AND MANAGEMENT COURSES 179, CHEMISTRY 199

Chemistry with Materials *see* CHEMISTRY 199, MATERIALS SCIENCE/METALLURGY 419

Chemistry with Materials Chemistry *see* CHEMISTRY 199, MATERIALS SCIENCE/METALLURGY 419

Chemistry with Mathematics *see* CHEMISTRY 199, MATHEMATICS 422

Chemistry with Medicinal Chemistry *see* CHEMISTRY 199

Chemistry with Medicinal Science *see* CHEMISTRY 199

Chemistry with Modern Languages *see* CHEMISTRY 199, LANGUAGES 386

Chemistry with Molecular Physics *see* CHEMISTRY 199

Chemistry with Nanotechnology *see* CHEMISTRY 199

Chemistry with Oceanography *see* CHEMISTRY 199

Chemistry with Pharmacology *see* CHEMISTRY 199, PHARMACOLOGY 472

Chemistry with Teaching *see* CHEMISTRY 199, TEACHER TRAINING 559

Chemistry, Biological and Medicinal Chemistry *see* BIOCHEMISTRY 162, CHEMISTRY 199

Chemistry, Management and Industry *see* CHEMISTRY 199

Chemistry, Resources and the Environment *see* CHEMISTRY 199, ENVIRONMENTAL SCIENCES/STUDIES 303

Child and Youth Community Studies *see* COMMUNITY STUDIES/DEVELOPMENT 217

Child and Youth Studies *see* EDUCATION STUDIES 256, SOCIAL SCIENCES/STUDIES 531

Childhood and Youth *see* EDUCATION STUDIES 256

Childhood and Youth Studies *see* EDUCATION STUDIES 256, SOCIAL WORK 536

Childhood Education and Society *see* EDUCATION STUDIES 256, SOCIAL SCIENCES/STUDIES 531

Childhood Studies *see* EDUCATION STUDIES 256, SOCIAL SCIENCES/STUDIES 531

Childhood, Culture and Education *see* EDUCATION STUDIES 256

Childhood, Youth and Education Studies *see* EDUCATION STUDIES 256

Children and Playwork *see* SOCIAL SCIENCES/STUDIES 531

Children and Young People *see* SOCIAL WORK 536

Children, Welfare and Society *see* SOCIAL WORK 536

Children's Physical Education *see* SOCIAL WORK 536

CHINESE 206
    see also ASIA-PACIFIC STUDIES
    see also BUSINESS and MANAGEMENT COURSES (INTERNATIONAL and EUROPEAN)
    see also LANGUAGES

Chinese (Mandarin) *see* CHINESE 206, LANGUAGES 386

Chinese (Modern) *see* CHINESE 206

Chinese (Modern and Classical) *see* CHINESE 206

Chinese and English Language *see* CHINESE 206, ENGLISH 296

Chinese and Politics *see* CHINESE 206, POLITICS 507

Chinese Business Studies *see* BUSINESS AND MANAGEMENT COURSES 179, CHINESE 206

Chinese Medicine *see* HEALTH SCIENCES/STUDIES 341

Chinese Medicine: Acupuncture *see* HEALTH SCIENCES/STUDIES 341

Chinese Studies *see* CHINESE 206, COMBINED COURSES 212

Chinese/Japanese and Cultural Studies *see* CHINESE 206, JAPANESE 383

Chiropractic *see* HEALTH SCIENCES/STUDIES 341

Choreography *see* DANCE/DANCE STUDIES 227

Choreography and Dance *see* DANCE/DANCE STUDIES 227

Cities, Economies and Social Change *see* GEOGRAPHY 330, SOCIAL SCIENCES/STUDIES 531

City and Regional Development *see* TOWN and COUNTRY PLANNING 567

City and Regional Planning *see* TOWN and COUNTRY PLANNING 567

Civil and Architectural Engineering *see* ARCHITECTURE 134, ENGINEERING (CIVIL) 274

Civil and Coastal Engineering *see* ENGINEERING (CIVIL) 274

Civil and Construction Engineering *see* ENGINEERING (CIVIL) 274

Civil and Energy Engineering *see* ENGINEERING (CIVIL) 274

Civil and Environmental Engineering *see* ENGINEERING (CHEMICAL) 269, ENGINEERING (CIVIL) 274

Civil and Infrastructure Engineering *see* ENGINEERING (CIVIL) 274

Civil and Structural Engineering *see* ENGINEERING (CIVIL) 274

Civil and Timber Engineering *see* ENGINEERING
(CIVIL) 274
Civil and Transportation Engineering *see*
ENGINEERING (CIVIL) 274, TRANSPORT
MANAGEMENT and PLANNING 571
Civil Engineering *see* ENGINEERING (CIVIL) 274
Civil Engineering (Technologies and Operations) *see*
ENGINEERING (CIVIL) 274
Civil Engineering and Architecture *see*
ARCHITECTURE 134, ENGINEERING (CIVIL) 274
Civil Engineering and Environmental Management
see ENGINEERING (CIVIL) 274
Civil Engineering and Management *see*
ENGINEERING (CIVIL) 274
Civil Engineering and Structural Engineering *see*
ENGINEERING (CIVIL) 274
Civil Engineering Surveying *see* ENGINEERING
(CIVIL) 274, SURVEYING 556
Civil Engineering with a Modern Language *see*
ENGINEERING (CIVIL) 274, LANGUAGES 386
Civil Engineering with Architecture *see*
ARCHITECTURE 134, ENGINEERING (CIVIL) 274
Civil Engineering with Business Management *see*
BUSINESS AND MANAGEMENT COURSES 179,
ENGINEERING (CIVIL) 274
Civil Engineering with Construction Management *see*
BUILDING and CONSTRUCTION 176,
ENGINEERING (CIVIL) 274
Civil Engineering with Disaster Management *see*
ENGINEERING (CIVIL) 274
Civil Engineering with International Studies *see*
ENGINEERING (CIVIL) 274
Civil Engineering with Project Management *see*
ENGINEERING (CIVIL) 274
Civil Engineering with Surveying *see* ENGINEERING
(CIVIL) 274, SURVEYING 556
Civil Engineering with Sustainability *see* ENGINEERING
(CIVIL) 274
Civil Engineering with Water and Environmental
Management *see* ENGINEERING (CIVIL) 274,
ENVIRONMENTAL SCIENCES/STUDIES 303
Classical and Archaeological Studies *see*
ARCHAEOLOGY 131, CLASSICAL STUDIES/CLASSICAL
CIVILISATION 208
Classical and Historical Archaeology *see*
ARCHAEOLOGY 131, CLASSICAL STUDIES/
CLASSICAL CIVILISATION 208
Classical and Medieval Studies *see* CLASSICAL
STUDIES/CLASSICAL CIVILISATION 208
Classical and Middle East Studies *see* CLASSICAL
STUDIES/CLASSICAL CIVILISATION 208

Classical Archaeology *see* ARCHAEOLOGY 131
Classical Archaeology and Ancient History *see*
ARCHAEOLOGY 131, HISTORY 355
Classical Archaeology and Classical Civilisation
see ARCHAEOLOGY 131, CLASSICAL STUDIES/
CLASSICAL CIVILISATION 208
Classical Archaeology and Greek *see* ARCHAEOLOGY
131, CLASSICAL STUDIES/CLASSICAL CIVILISATION
208, GREEK 340
Classical Ballet and Dance Performance *see* DANCE/
DANCE STUDIES 227
Classical Civilisation *see* CLASSICAL STUDIES/
CLASSICAL CIVILISATION 208
Classical Civilisation and Art History *see* CLASSICAL
STUDIES/CLASSICAL CIVILISATION 208, HISTORY
OF ART 363
Classical Civilisation and English Studies *see*
CLASSICAL STUDIES/CLASSICAL CIVILISATION 208,
ENGLISH 296
Classical Civilisation and French/German *see*
CLASSICAL STUDIES/CLASSICAL CIVILISATION 208,
FRENCH 325, GERMAN 337
Classical Civilisation and Latin *see* CLASSICAL
STUDIES/CLASSICAL CIVILISATION 208, LATIN 389
Classical Civilisation and Philosophy *see* CLASSICAL
STUDIES/CLASSICAL CIVILISATION 208,
PHILOSOPHY 478
Classical Civilisation with Philosophy *see* CLASSICAL
STUDIES/CLASSICAL CIVILISATION 208,
PHILOSOPHY 478
Classical Civilisation with Study in Europe *see*
CLASSICAL STUDIES/CLASSICAL
CIVILISATION 208
Classical Literature *see* CLASSICAL STUDIES/CLASSICAL
CIVILISATION 208, CLASSICS 210, LITERATURE 409
Classical Literature and Civilisation *see* CLASSICAL
STUDIES/CLASSICAL CIVILISATION 208,
CLASSICS 210
Classical Past *see* CLASSICS 210
Classical Studies *see* CLASSICAL STUDIES/CLASSICAL
CIVILISATION 208
Classical Studies and a Modern Language *see*
CLASSICAL STUDIES/CLASSICAL CIVILISATION 208,
LANGUAGES 386
Classical Studies and Byzantine and Modern Greek
Studies *see* CLASSICAL STUDIES/CLASSICAL
CIVILISATION 208, GREEK 340
Classical Studies and English *see* CLASSICAL STUDIES/
CLASSICAL CIVILISATION 208, ENGLISH 296
Classical Studies with English *see* CLASSICAL STUDIES/
CLASSICAL CIVILISATION 208, ENGLISH 296

Classical Studies with Italian *see* CLASSICAL STUDIES/ CLASSICAL CIVILISATION 208, ITALIAN 381

CLASSICAL STUDIES/CLASSICAL CIVILISATION 208

see also ARCHAEOLOGY

see also CLASSICS

see also HISTORY (ANCIENT)

CLASSICS 210

see also CLASSICAL STUDIES/CLASSICAL CIVILISATION

see also GREEK

see also LATIN

Classics and Ancient History *see* CLASSICS 210, HISTORY (ANCIENT) 360

Classics and English *see* CLASSICS 210, ENGLISH 296

Classics and English Language *see* CLASSICS 210, ENGLISH 296

Classics and Linguistics *see* CLASSICS 210, LINGUISTICS 407

Classics and Modern Languages *see* CLASSICS 210, LANGUAGES 386

Classics and Oriental Studies *see* CLASSICS 210

Classics with Latin *see* CLASSICS 210, LATIN 389

Classics: Greek and Latin *see* CLASSICS 210, GREEK 340, LATIN 389

Climate Change *see* ENVIRONMENTAL SCIENCES/ STUDIES 303

Climate Change and Sustainability *see* ENVIRONMENTAL SCIENCES/STUDIES 303

Climate Science *see* ENVIRONMENTAL SCIENCES/ STUDIES 303, GEOLOGY/GEOLOGICAL SCIENCES 335

Clinical Exercise Science *see* SPORTS SCIENCES/ STUDIES 548

Clinical Language Sciences (Speech and Language Therapy) *see* SPEECH PATHOLOGY/SCIENCES/ THERAPY 546

Clinical Medical Science *see* HEALTH SCIENCES/ STUDIES 341

Clinical Photography *see* PHOTOGRAPHY 481

Clinical Physiology *see* PHYSIOLOGY 500

Clinical Physiology (Cardiology) *see* PHYSIOLOGY 500

Clinical Science *see* HEALTH SCIENCES/STUDIES 341

Clinical Science and Medicine *see* MEDICINE 433

Clinical Sciences *see* BIOLOGICAL SCIENCES 165, HEALTH SCIENCES/STUDIES 341

Coach and Physical Education *see* PHYSICAL EDUCATION 484

Coach Education and Sports Development *see* EDUCATION STUDIES 256, SPORTS SCIENCES/STUDIES 548

Coaching and Sport Development *see* SPORTS SCIENCES/STUDIES 548

Coaching and Sports Science *see* SPORTS SCIENCES/ STUDIES 548

Coaching Development *see* SPORTS SCIENCES/ STUDIES 548

Coaching Studies *see* SPORTS SCIENCES/ STUDIES 548

Coaching Studies and Sports Development *see* PHYSICAL EDUCATION 484, SPORTS SCIENCES/ STUDIES 548

Coastal Geography *see* GEOGRAPHY 330, MARINE/ MARITIME STUDIES 412

Coastal Marine Biology *see* BIOLOGY 170, MARINE/ MARITIME STUDIES 412

Cognitive Neuroscience *see* ANATOMICAL SCIENCE/ ANATOMY 122, BIOLOGICAL SCIENCES 165

Cognitive Neuroscience and Psychology *see* BIOLOGICAL SCIENCES 165, PSYCHOLOGY 512

Cognitive Science *see* PSYCHOLOGY 512

Cognitive Science (Humanities) *see* PSYCHOLOGY 512

COMBINED COURSES 212

Combined Honours in Arts *see* COMBINED COURSES 212

Combined Honours in Social Sciences *see* COMBINED COURSES 212, SOCIAL SCIENCES/STUDIES 531

Combined Honours Literature *see* LITERATURE 409

Combined Studies *see* COMBINED COURSES 212

Combined Studies and Drama *see* COMBINED COURSES 212, DRAMA 239

Commercial and Quantity Surveying *see* SURVEYING 556

Commercial Law *see* LAW 393

Commercial Management (Quantity Surveying) *see* SURVEYING 556

Commercial Management and Quantity Surveying *see* BUILDING and CONSTRUCTION 176, SURVEYING 556

Commercial Music *see* MUSIC 449

Commercial Music Production *see* MUSIC 449

Commercial Photography *see* PHOTOGRAPHY 481

Communication *see* COMMUNICATION STUDIES/ COMMUNICATION 214

Communication and Business Studies *see* COMMUNICATION STUDIES/COMMUNICATION 214

Communication and Media *see* COMMUNICATION STUDIES/COMMUNICATION 214, MEDIA STUDIES 427

Communication and Media Studies *see* COMMUNICATION STUDIES/COMMUNICATION 214, MEDIA STUDIES 427

Communication and Society *see* COMMUNICATION STUDIES/COMMUNICATION 214

Communication Design *see* ART and DESIGN (Graphic Design) 148

Communication Networks Engineering *see* ENGINEERING (COMMUNICATIONS) 278

Communication Studies and Italian *see* COMMUNICATION STUDIES/COMMUNICATION 214, ITALIAN 381

Communication Studies and Popular Culture *see* COMMUNICATION STUDIES/COMMUNICATION 214

COMMUNICATION STUDIES/COMMUNICATION 214
see also BUSINESS and MANAGEMENT COURSES (SPECIALISED)
see also COMBINED COURSES
see also COMMUNITY STUDIES/DEVELOPMENT
see also COMPUTER COURSES
see also ENGINEERING (COMMUNICATIONS)
see also FILM, RADIO, VIDEO and TV STUDIES
see also MEDIA STUDIES
see also SPEECH PATHOLOGY/SCIENCES/THERAPY

Communication Systems *see* ENGINEERING (COMMUNICATIONS) 278

Communication Systems and Electronics *see* ENGINEERING (COMMUNICATIONS) 278

Communication, Advertising and Public Relations *see* BUSINESS AND MANAGEMENT COURSES (SPECIALISED) 193, COMMUNICATION STUDIES/ COMMUNICATION 214

Communication, Culture and Media *see* COMMUNICATION STUDIES/COMMUNICATION 214, MEDIA STUDIES 427

Communication, Media and Culture *see* COMMUNICATION STUDIES/COMMUNICATION 214, MEDIA STUDIES 427

Communication, Media and Journalism *see* COMMUNICATION STUDIES/COMMUNICATION 214, MEDIA STUDIES 427

Communication, Media and Popular Music *see* COMMUNICATION STUDIES/COMMUNICATION 214, MEDIA STUDIES 427

Communications *see* COMMUNICATION STUDIES/ COMMUNICATION 214

Communications and Electronic Engineering *see* ENGINEERING (COMMUNICATIONS) 278, ENGINEERING (ELECTRICAL and ELECTRONIC) 283

Communications Engineering *see* ENGINEERING (COMMUNICATIONS) 278

Communications Systems and Software Engineering *see* ENGINEERING (COMMUNICATIONS) 278, ENGINEERING (COMPUTER, CONTROL, SOFTWARE and SYSTEMS) 280

Communications with Public Relations *see* BUSINESS AND MANAGEMENT COURSES (SPECIALISED) 193, COMMUNICATION STUDIES/ COMMUNICATION 214

Communications, Advertising and Marketing *see* BUSINESS AND MANAGEMENT COURSES (SPECIALISED) 193, COMMUNICATION STUDIES/COMMUNICATION 214, MARKETING 415

Communications, Media and Society *see* COMMUNICATION STUDIES/COMMUNICATION 214, MEDIA STUDIES 427

Community and Applied Dance Theatre *see* DANCE/ DANCE STUDIES 227

Community and Applied Theatre *see* COMMUNITY STUDIES/DEVELOPMENT 217, DRAMA 239

Community and Public Health *see* COMMUNITY STUDIES/DEVELOPMENT 217, HEALTH SCIENCES/ STUDIES 341

Community and Society *see* COMMUNITY STUDIES/ DEVELOPMENT 217

Community and Youth Studies *see* COMMUNITY STUDIES/DEVELOPMENT 217

Community and Youth Work Studies *see* COMMUNITY STUDIES/DEVELOPMENT 217

Community Development *see* COMMUNITY STUDIES/ DEVELOPMENT 217, SOCIAL WORK 536

Community Drama *see* DRAMA 239

Community Health and Rehabilitation *see* HEALTH SCIENCES/STUDIES 341

Community Health and Well-being *see* COMMUNITY STUDIES/DEVELOPMENT 217, HEALTH SCIENCES/ STUDIES 341

Community Leadership *see* COMMUNITY STUDIES/ DEVELOPMENT 217

Community Learning and Participation *see* COMMUNITY STUDIES/DEVELOPMENT 217

Community Learning Development *see* COMMUNITY STUDIES/DEVELOPMENT 217

Community Music *see* COMMUNITY STUDIES/ DEVELOPMENT 217, MUSIC 449

Community Sector Management *see* COMMUNITY STUDIES/DEVELOPMENT 217

Community Services and Enterprise *see* COMMUNITY STUDIES/DEVELOPMENT 217

COMMUNITY STUDIES/DEVELOPMENT 217
see also EDUCATION STUDIES
see also HEALTH SCIENCES/STUDIES
see also NURSING and MIDWIFERY

see also SOCIAL and PUBLIC POLICY and
ADMINISTRATION

see also SOCIAL WORK

Community Youth Work *see* COMMUNITY STUDIES/
DEVELOPMENT 217

Comparative American Studies *see* AMERICAN
STUDIES 120

Comparative Italian and European Studies *see*
EUROPEAN STUDIES 307, ITALIAN 381

Comparative Literature *see* LITERATURE 409

Comparative Literature and Culture *see*
LITERATURE 409

Comparative Literature Studies *see* LITERATURE 409

Comparative Literature with Film Studies *see*
FILM, RADIO, VIDEO and TV STUDIES 310,
LITERATURE 409

Comparative Religion and Social Anthropology *see*
ANTHROPOLOGY 127, RELIGIOUS STUDIES 521

Complementary Health Sciences *see* HEALTH
SCIENCES/STUDIES 341

Complementary Medicine Practice *see* HEALTH
SCIENCES/STUDIES 341

Complementary Therapies *see* HEALTH SCIENCES/
STUDIES 341

Computational Mathematics *see* MATHEMATICS 422

Computational Physics *see* PHYSICS 488

Computer *see* COMPUTER COURSES 219

Computer Accounting and Finance *see*
ACCOUNTANCY/ACCOUNTING 109,
FINANCE 315

Computer Aided Design *see* COMPUTER
COURSES 219

Computer Aided Engineering *see* ENGINEERING
(COMPUTER, CONTROL, SOFTWARE and
SYSTEMS) 280

Computer Aided Mechanical Engineering *see*
ENGINEERING (COMPUTER, CONTROL, SOFTWARE
and SYSTEMS) 280

Computer and Business Studies *see* BUSINESS
AND MANAGEMENT COURSES 179, COMPUTER
COURSES 219

Computer and Communication Engineering *see*
COMPUTER COURSES 219, ENGINEERING
(COMMUNICATIONS) 278

Computer and Digital Forensics *see* COMPUTER
COURSES 219

Computer and Electronic Systems *see* ENGINEERING
(COMPUTER, CONTROL, SOFTWARE and
SYSTEMS) 280

Computer and Information Security *see* COMPUTER
COURSES 219

Computer and Management Sciences *see* COMPUTER
COURSES 219

Computer and Network Engineering *see*
ENGINEERING (COMPUTER, CONTROL, SOFTWARE
and SYSTEMS) 280

Computer and Network Technology *see* COMPUTER
COURSES 219, ENGINEERING (COMPUTER,
CONTROL, SOFTWARE and SYSTEMS) 280

Computer Animation *see* ART and DESIGN (Graphic
Design) 148

Computer Animation and Special Effects *see* ART and
DESIGN (Graphic Design) 148

Computer Animation and Visualisation *see* COMPUTER
COURSES 219

Computer Animation Arts *see* ART and DESIGN
(Graphic Design)148

Computer Arts *see* COMPUTER COURSES 219

Computer Character Animation *see* COMPUTER
COURSES 219

Computer Control Systems *see* ENGINEERING
(COMPUTER, CONTROL, SOFTWARE and
SYSTEMS) 280

COMPUTER COURSES 219

see also ENGINEERING (COMPUTER, CONTROL,
SOFTWARE and SYSTEMS)

see also TECHNOLOGIES

Computer Engineering *see* ENGINEERING (COMPUTER,
CONTROL, SOFTWARE and SYSTEMS) 280

Computer Forensic Investigation *see* COMPUTER
COURSES 219

Computer Forensics *see* COMPUTER COURSES 219

Computer Forensics and Security *see* COMPUTER
COURSES 219

Computer Games *see* COMPUTER COURSES 219

Computer Games and Animation *see* COMPUTER
COURSES 219

Computer Games Animation *see* COMPUTER
COURSES 219

Computer Games Art *see* COMPUTER
COURSES 219

Computer Games Design *see* COMPUTER
COURSES 219

Computer Games Design and Development *see*
COMPUTER COURSES 219

Computer Games Design and Production *see*
COMPUTER COURSES 219

Computer Games Development *see* COMPUTER
COURSES 219

Computer Games Modelling and Animation *see*
ART and DESIGN (Graphic Design) 148,
COMPUTER COURSES 219

Computer Games Production *see* COMPUTER COURSES 219

Computer Games Programming *see* COMPUTER COURSES 219

Computer Games Technology *see* COMPUTER COURSES 219

Computer Gaming *see* COMPUTER COURSES 219

Computer Graphics *see* COMPUTER COURSES 219

Computer Graphics, Vision and Games *see* COMPUTER COURSES 219

Computer Hardware and Software Engineering *see* ENGINEERING (COMPUTER, CONTROL, SOFTWARE and SYSTEMS) 280

Computer Information Systems *see* COMPUTER COURSES 219

Computer Network Management *see* COMPUTER COURSES 219

Computer Network Management and Design *see* ENGINEERING (COMPUTER, CONTROL, SOFTWARE and SYSTEMS) 280

Computer Network Management and Security *see* COMPUTER COURSES 219

Computer Networking *see* COMPUTER COURSES 219

Computer Networking with Server Administration *see* COMPUTER COURSES 219

Computer Networks *see* COMPUTER COURSES 219, ENGINEERING (COMPUTER, CONTROL, SOFTWARE and SYSTEMS) 280

Computer Networks and Security *see* COMPUTER COURSES 219

Computer Science *see* COMPUTER COURSES 219, ENGINEERING (COMPUTER, CONTROL, SOFTWARE and SYSTEMS) 280

Computer Science (Artificial Intelligence) *see* COMPUTER COURSES 219

Computer Science (Bio-Computing) *see* COMPUTER COURSES 219

Computer Science (Digital Media and Games) *see* COMPUTER COURSES 219

Computer Science (Embedded Computing/Intelligent Systems/Mobile Computing/Robotics) *see* COMPUTER COURSES 219

Computer Science (Games) *see* COMPUTER COURSES 219

Computer Science (Games and Virtual Environments) *see* COMPUTER COURSES 219

Computer Science (Games Development) *see* COMPUTER COURSES 219

Computer Science (Network Computing) *see* COMPUTER COURSES 219

Computer Science (Software Engineering) *see* ENGINEERING (COMPUTER, CONTROL, SOFTWARE and SYSTEMS) 280

Computer Science and Artificial Intelligence *see* COMPUTER COURSES 219

Computer Science and Cybernetics *see* ENGINEERING (COMPUTER, CONTROL, SOFTWARE and SYSTEMS) 280

Computer Science and Electronic Engineering *see* ENGINEERING (COMPUTER, CONTROL, SOFTWARE and SYSTEMS) 280

Computer Science and Electronics *see* COMPUTER COURSES 219

Computer Science and Mathematics *see* COMPUTER COURSES 219, MATHEMATICS 422

Computer Science and Software Engineering *see* COMPUTER COURSES 219, ENGINEERING (COMPUTER, CONTROL, SOFTWARE and SYSTEMS) 280

Compzuter Science for Business *see* COMPUTER COURSES 219

Computer Science for Games *see* COMPUTER COURSES 219

Computer Science with Artificial Intelligence *see* COMPUTER COURSES 219, ENGINEERING (COMPUTER, CONTROL, SOFTWARE and SYSTEMS) 280

Computer Science with Business and Management *see* BUSINESS AND MANAGEMENT COURSES 179, COMPUTER COURSES 219

Computer Science with Business Informatics *see* BUSINESS AND MANAGEMENT COURSES 179, COMPUTER COURSES 219

Computer Science with Distributed Systems and Networks *see* COMPUTER COURSES 219

Computer Science with Embedded Systems *see* ENGINEERING (COMPUTER, CONTROL, SOFTWARE and SYSTEMS) 280

Computer Science with Games Technology *see* COMPUTER COURSES 219

Computer Science with High Performance Computing *see* COMPUTER COURSES 219

Computer Science with Image and Multimedia Systems *see* COMPUTER COURSES 219

Computer Science with Intelligent Systems *see* COMPUTER COURSES 219

Computer Science with Management *see* COMPUTER COURSES 219

Computer Science with Mathematics *see* COMPUTER COURSES 219, MATHEMATICS 422

Computer Science with Mobile and Secure Systems *see* COMPUTER COURSES 219

Computer Science with Physics *see* COMPUTER COURSES 219, PHYSICS 488

Computer Science with Psychology *see* COMPUTER COURSES 219, PSYCHOLOGY 512

Computer Science with Robotics *see* COMPUTER COURSES 219

Computer Science with Security and Forensics *see* COMPUTER COURSES 219

Computer Science with Visual Computing *see* COMPUTER COURSES 219

Computer Security with Forensics *see* COMPUTER COURSES 219

Computer Studies *see* COMPUTER COURSES 219

Computer Systems (Forensic/Networks) *see* COMPUTER COURSES 219

Computer Systems and Engineering *see* ENGINEERING (COMPUTER, CONTROL, SOFTWARE and SYSTEMS) 280

Computer Systems and Networks *see* ENGINEERING (COMPUTER, CONTROL, SOFTWARE and SYSTEMS) 280

Computer Systems and Software Engineering *see* ENGINEERING (COMPUTER, CONTROL, SOFTWARE and SYSTEMS) 280

Computer Systems Engineering *see* ENGINEERING (COMMUNICATIONS) 278, ENGINEERING (COMPUTER, CONTROL, SOFTWARE and SYSTEMS) 280

Computer Systems Engineering with Business Management *see* BUSINESS AND MANAGEMENT COURSES 179, COMPUTER COURSES 219, ENGINEERING (COMPUTER, CONTROL, SOFTWARE and SYSTEMS) 280

Computer Systems Integration *see* ENGINEERING (COMPUTER, CONTROL, SOFTWARE and SYSTEMS) 280

Computer Technology *see* COMPUTER COURSES 219

Computer-aided Design Technology *see* ART and DESIGN (Graphic Design) 148, COMPUTER COURSES 219

Computers and Electronics *see* ENGINEERING (COMPUTER, CONTROL, SOFTWARE and SYSTEMS) 280, ENGINEERING (ELECTRICAL and ELECTRONIC) 283

Computers, Networking and Communications *see* COMMUNICATION STUDIES/COMMUNICATION 214, COMPUTER COURSES 219

Computers, Networks and Communication *see* COMMUNICATION STUDIES/COMMUNICATION 214, COMPUTER COURSES 219

Computing *see* COMPUTER COURSES 219

Computing (Artificial Intelligence) *see* COMPUTER COURSES 219

Computing (Computation in Biology and Medicine) *see* COMPUTER COURSES 219

Computing (Computer Systems Engineering) *see* ENGINEERING (COMPUTER, CONTROL, SOFTWARE and SYSTEMS) 280

Computing (European Studies) *see* COMPUTER COURSES 219

Computing (Games, Vision and Interaction) *see* COMPUTER COURSES 219

Computing (Software Engineering) *see* COMPUTER COURSES 219, ENGINEERING (COMPUTER, CONTROL, SOFTWARE and SYSTEMS), 280

Computing and Digital Sound *see* ENGINEERING (ACOUSTICS and SOUND) 264

Computing and Electronics *see* ENGINEERING (COMPUTER, CONTROL, SOFTWARE and SYSTEMS) 280

Computing and Games *see* COMPUTER COURSES 219

Computing and Games Development *see* COMPUTER COURSES 219

Computing and ICT *see* COMPUTER COURSES 219

Computing and ICT with Business Management *see* BUSINESS AND MANAGEMENT COURSES 179, COMPUTER COURSES 219

Computing and Information Systems *see* COMPUTER COURSES 219

Computing and Information Technology *see* COMPUTER COURSES 219

Computing and Mathematics *see* COMPUTER COURSES 219, MATHEMATICS 422

Computing for Business *see* COMPUTER COURSES 219

Computing for Business and Management *see* BUSINESS AND MANAGEMENT COURSES 179, COMPUTER COURSES 219

Computing for Digital Media *see* COMPUTER COURSES 219

Computing Science *see* COMPUTER COURSES 219

Computing Science (Bioinformatics) *see* COMPUTER COURSES 219

Computing Science (Networked Systems and Internet Technologies) *see* COMPUTER COURSES 219

Computing Science (Software Engineering) *see* ENGINEERING (COMPUTER, CONTROL, SOFTWARE and SYSTEMS) 280

Computing Science with Mathematics *see* COMPUTER COURSES 219, MATHEMATICS 422

Computing Science, Imaging and Multimedia *see* COMPUTER COURSES 219

Computing Solutions (Internet) *see* COMPUTER COURSES 219

Computing Solutions (Networks) *see* COMPUTER COURSES 219

Computing Systems *see* COMPUTER COURSES 219, ENGINEERING (COMPUTER, CONTROL, SOFTWARE and SYSTEMS) 280

Computing Technology *see* TECHNOLOGIES 562

Computing with Business/Design/Mathematics/ Psychology/Statistics *see* COMPUTER COURSES 219

Computing with Games Development *see* COMPUTER COURSES 219

Computing with Gaming *see* COMPUTER COURSES 219

Computing with Gaming Design *see* COMPUTER COURSES 219

Computing with Management *see* BUSINESS AND MANAGEMENT COURSES 179, COMPUTER COURSES 219

Computing with Networking *see* COMPUTER COURSES 219

Computing with Retail Studies *see* RETAIL MANAGEMENT 524

Computing/Multimedia with Mobile Development *see* COMPUTER COURSES 219

Conductive Education *see* EDUCATION STUDIES 256

Conflict Resolution *see* INTERNATIONAL RELATIONS 378, POLITICS 507

Conservation and Ecology *see* ENVIRONMENTAL SCIENCES/STUDIES 303

Conservation and Forest Ecosystems *see* FORESTRY 324

Conservation and Restoration *see* ENVIRONMENTAL SCIENCES/STUDIES 303, HISTORY OF ART 363

Conservation and Wildlife Management *see* ENVIRONMENTAL SCIENCES/STUDIES 303

Conservation Biology *see* BIOLOGY, ENVIRONMENTAL SCIENCES/STUDIES 303

Conservation Biology and Ecology *see* BIOLOGY 170, ENVIRONMENTAL SCIENCES/ STUDIES 303

Conservation Biology and Geography *see* GEOGRAPHY 330

Conservation Biology and Management *see* AGRICULTURAL SCIENCES/AGRICULTURE 117, ENVIRONMENTAL SCIENCES/STUDIES 303

Conservation of Objects in Museums and Archaeology *see* ARCHAEOLOGY 131

Construction *see* BUILDING and CONSTRUCTION 176

Construction and Project Management *see* BUILDING and CONSTRUCTION 176

Construction Engineering and Management *see* BUILDING and CONSTRUCTION 176

Construction Engineering Management *see* BUILDING and CONSTRUCTION 176

Construction Management *see* BUILDING and CONSTRUCTION 176, BUSINESS AND MANAGEMENT COURSES (SPECIALISED) 193

Construction Management (Commercial Management) *see* BUILDING and CONSTRUCTION 176

Construction Management (Site Management) *see* BUILDING and CONSTRUCTION 176, BUSINESS AND MANAGEMENT COURSES (SPECIALISED) 193

Construction Management and the Environment *see* BUILDING and CONSTRUCTION 176

Construction Project Management *see* BUILDING and CONSTRUCTION 176, SURVEYING 556

Construction Surveying Management *see* BUILDING and CONSTRUCTION 176, SURVEYING 556

Consumer Behaviour and Marketing *see* CONSUMER STUDIES/SCIENCES 226, MARKETING 415

Consumer Electronics *see* CONSUMER STUDIES/ SCIENCES 226

CONSUMER STUDIES/SCIENCES 226
see also FOOD SCIENCE/STUDIES and TECHNOLOGY
see also HOSPITALITY and HOTEL MANAGEMENT

Contemporary Applied Arts *see* ART and DESIGN (3D Design) 156

Contemporary Arabic Studies *see* ARABIC AND ANCIENT NEAR AND MIDDLE EASTERN STUDIES 129

Contemporary Art History *see* HISTORY OF ART 363

Contemporary Chinese Studies *see* CHINESE 206

Contemporary Craft and Design *see* ART and DESIGN (3D Design) 156

Contemporary Crafts *see* ART and DESIGN (Fashion and Textiles) 140

Contemporary Dance *see* DANCE/DANCE STUDIES 227

Contemporary Fine Art Practice *see* ART and DESIGN (Fine Art) 144

Contemporary History *see* HISTORY 355

Contemporary Jewellery *see* ART and DESIGN (Fashion and Textiles) 140

Contemporary Lens Media *see* ART and DESIGN (Graphic Design) 148, PHOTOGRAPHY 481

Contemporary Military and International History *see* HISTORY 355

Contemporary Music Technology *see* MUSIC 449

Contemporary Performance Practice *see* DRAMA 239

Contemporary Photographic Arts (Practice) *see* PHOTOGRAPHY 481

Contemporary Photographic Practice *see*
PHOTOGRAPHY 481
Contemporary Surface Design and Textiles *see* ART
and DESIGN (Fashion and Textiles) 140
Contemporary Textiles *see* ART and DESIGN (Fashion
and Textiles) 140
Contemporary Theatre and Performance *see*
DRAMA 239
Contemporary Visual Arts (History and Theory) *see*
HISTORY OF ART 363
Contemporary World Jazz *see* MUSIC 449
Cordwainers Fashion Accessories: Product Design
and Development *see* ART and DESIGN (Fashion
and Textiles) 140
Cordwainers Footwear; Product Design and
Development *see* ART and DESIGN (Fashion and
Textiles) 140
Corporate Events and Conference Management *see*
HOSPITALITY and HOTEL MANAGEMENT 367
Cosmetic Science *see* BIOLOGICAL SCIENCES 165,
CHEMISTRY 199, HEALTH SCIENCES/STUDIES 341,
PHARMACY and PHARMACEUTICAL
SCIENCES, 475
Costume Construction for Screen and Stage *see* ART
and DESIGN (Fashion and Textiles) 140
Costume Design *see* ART and DESIGN (Fashion and
Textiles) 140
Costume Design and Making *see* ART and DESIGN
(Fashion and Textiles) 140
Costume for Performance *see* ART and DESIGN
(Fashion and Textiles) 140
Costume Production *see* DRAMA 239
Costume with Performance Design *see* ART and
DESIGN (Fashion and Textiles) 140
Counselling and Drama *see* DRAMA 239,
PSYCHOLOGY 512
Counselling and Educational Studies *see* EDUCATION
STUDIES 256, PSYCHOLOGY 512
Counselling and Psychology *see* PSYCHOLOGY 512
Counselling and Psychology in Community Settings
see PSYCHOLOGY 512
Counselling Skills *see* PSYCHOLOGY 512
Counselling Studies *see* PSYCHOLOGY 512
Countryside Conservation *see* AGRICULTURAL
SCIENCES/AGRICULTURE 117
Countryside Management *see* AGRICULTURAL
SCIENCES/AGRICULTURE 117, BUSINESS AND
MANAGEMENT COURSES (SPECIALISED) 193,
ENVIRONMENTAL SCIENCES/STUDIES 303
Countryside Recreation and Tourism *see*
AGRICULTURAL SCIENCES/AGRICULTURE 117,

LEISURE and RECREATION MANAGEMENT/
STUDIES 405, TOURISM and TRAVEL 564
Creative Advertising *see* ART and DESIGN
(Graphic Design) 148, MARKETING 415
Creative and Media Writing *see* MEDIA
STUDIES 427
Creative and Performing Arts *see* DRAMA 239
Creative and Professional Writing *see*
ENGLISH 296
Creative and Therapeutic Education *see* EDUCATION
STUDIES 256
Creative Art Practice *see* ART and DESIGN
(Fine Art) 144
Creative Arts *see* ART and DESIGN (Fine Art) 144
Creative Computer Games Design *see* ART
and DESIGN (Graphic Design) 148, COMPUTER
COURSES 219
Creative Computing *see* COMPUTER COURSES 219
Creative Design and Marketing *see*
MARKETING 415
Creative Digital Media *see* COMPUTER COURSES 219,
MEDIA STUDIES 427
Creative Direction for Fashion *see* ART and DESIGN
(Fashion and Textiles) 140
Creative Events Management *see* BUSINESS AND
MANAGEMENT COURSES (SPECIALISED) 193
Creative Expressive Therapies (Dance/Drama/Music/
Art) *see* PSYCHOLOGY 512
Creative Media Technology *see* MEDIA STUDIES 427,
TECHNOLOGIES 562
Creative Multimedia *see* ART and DESIGN
(Graphic Design) 148
Creative Music *see* MUSIC 449
Creative Music Production *see* MUSIC 449
Creative Music Technology *see* MUSIC 449,
TECHNOLOGIES 562
Creative Performance *see* DRAMA 239
Creative Product Design *see* ART and DESIGN
(Product and Industrial Design) 152
Creative Technology *see* TECHNOLOGIES 562
Creative Writing *see* ENGLISH 296
Creative Writing and Drama Studies *see*
DRAMA 239
Creative Writing and Film Studies *see* ENGLISH 296,
FILM, RADIO, VIDEO and TV STUDIES 310
Creative Writing and Media *see* MEDIA
STUDIES 427
Creative Writing with English Literature *see*
ENGLISH 296, LITERATURE 409
Crime and Investigation *see* SOCIAL SCIENCES/
STUDIES 531

Crime and Society see SOCIAL SCIENCES/STUDIES 531

Crime Scene Science see SOCIAL SCIENCES/ STUDIES 531

Crime Studies see COMBINED COURSES 212

Criminal Investigation see SOCIAL SCIENCES/ STUDIES 531

Criminal Investigation with Psychology see SOCIAL SCIENCES/STUDIES 531

Criminal Justice see SOCIAL SCIENCES/STUDIES 531

Criminal Justice and Criminology see SOCIAL SCIENCES/STUDIES 531

Criminal Justice Studies see SOCIAL SCIENCES/ STUDIES 531

Criminal Law see LAW 393

Criminal Psychology see SOCIAL SCIENCES/ STUDIES 531

Criminological Studies see SOCIAL SCIENCES/ STUDIES 531

Criminology see COMBINED COURSES 212, LAW 393, SOCIAL SCIENCES/STUDIES 531

Criminology and Criminal Justice see LAW 393, SOCIAL SCIENCES/STUDIES 531

Criminology and Criminal Justice Studies see SOCIAL SCIENCES/STUDIES 531

Criminology and Criminal Psychology see PSYCHOLOGY 512, SOCIAL SCIENCES/ STUDIES 531

Criminology and Cultural Studies see SOCIAL SCIENCES/STUDIES 531

Criminology and Education see SOCIAL SCIENCES/ STUDIES 531

Criminology and Forensic Psychology see PSYCHOLOGY 512, SOCIAL SCIENCES/STUDIES 531

Criminology and Forensic Sciences see SOCIAL SCIENCES/STUDIES 531

Criminology and History see HISTORY 355, SOCIAL SCIENCES/STUDIES 531

Criminology and Journalism see MEDIA STUDIES 427, SOCIAL SCIENCES/STUDIES 531

Criminology and Law see LAW 393, SOCIAL SCIENCES/ STUDIES 531

Criminology and Policing see SOCIAL SCIENCES/ STUDIES 531

Criminology and Politics see POLITICS 507, SOCIAL SCIENCES/STUDIES 531

Criminology and Psychological Studies see SOCIAL SCIENCES/STUDIES 531

Criminology and Psychology see LAW 393, PSYCHOLOGY 512, SOCIAL SCIENCES/STUDIES 531

Criminology and Security Studies see SOCIAL SCIENCES/STUDIES 531

Criminology and Social Policy see SOCIAL and PUBLIC POLICY and ADMINISTRATION 529, SOCIAL SCIENCES/STUDIES 531

Criminology and Sociology see SOCIAL SCIENCES/STUDIES 531, SOCIOLOGY 539, SPORTS SCIENCES/STUDIES 548

Criminology and Youth Studies see SOCIAL SCIENCES/ STUDIES 531

Criminology with Psychology see PSYCHOLOGY 512, SOCIAL SCIENCES/STUDIES 531

Critical Fine Art Practice see ART and DESIGN (Fine Art) 144

Cross-Cultural Communication with Business Management see BUSINESS AND MANAGEMENT COURSES 179, COMMUNICATION STUDIES/ COMMUNICATION 214

Cross-Cultural Psychology see PSYCHOLOGY 512

Cruise Industry Management see BUSINESS AND MANAGEMENT COURSES (SPECIALISED) 193, TOURISM and TRAVEL 564, TRANSPORT MANAGEMENT and PLANNING 571

Cruise Management see BUSINESS AND MANAGEMENT COURSES (SPECIALISED) 193, HOSPITALITY and HOTEL MANAGEMENT 367, MARINE/MARITIME STUDIES 412, TOURISM and TRAVEL 564, TRANSPORT MANAGEMENT and PLANNING 571

Culinary Arts see FOOD SCIENCE/STUDIES and TECHNOLOGY 321

Culinary Arts Management see BUSINESS AND MANAGEMENT COURSES (SPECIALISED) 193, FOOD SCIENCE/STUDIES and TECHNOLOGY 321, HOSPITALITY and HOTEL MANAGEMENT 367

Cultural History with Literature see HISTORY 355, LITERATURE 409

Cultural Production see MEDIA STUDIES 427

Cultural Sociology see SOCIOLOGY 539

Cultural Studies see COMBINED COURSES 212, SOCIAL SCIENCES/STUDIES 531

Culture, Literature and Politics see LITERATURE 409, POLITICS 507

Cultures, Histories, Literatures see HISTORY 355, LITERATURE 409

Cyber Security see COMPUTER COURSES 219

Cybernetics see COMPUTER COURSES 219, ENGINEERING (COMPUTER, CONTROL, SOFTWARE and SYSTEMS) 280

Czech see LANGUAGES 386

Czech and a Modern Language see LANGUAGES 386

Dance see COMBINED COURSES 212, DANCE/DANCE STUDIES 227

Dance and Culture see DANCE/DANCE STUDIES 227

Dance and Drama see DANCE/DANCE STUDIES 227, DRAMA 239

Dance and Movement Studies see DANCE/DANCE STUDIES 227

Dance and Performance see DANCE/DANCE STUDIES 227

Dance and Professional Practice see DANCE/DANCE STUDIES 227

Dance and Theatre Performance see DANCE/DANCE STUDIES 227

Dance Education see DANCE/DANCE STUDIES 227

Dance Performance with Drama Performance see DANCE/DANCE STUDIES 227

Dance Performance with Musical Theatre Performance see DANCE/DANCE STUDIES 227

Dance Practice see DANCE/DANCE STUDIES 227

Dance Practices see DANCE/DANCE STUDIES 227

Dance Studies see DANCE/DANCE STUDIES 227

Dance Theatre see DANCE/DANCE STUDIES 227, DRAMA 239

Dance with Drama see DANCE/DANCE STUDIES 227, DRAMA 239

Dance with Irish see CELTIC, IRISH, SCOTTISH AND WELSH STUDIES 197, DANCE/DANCE STUDIES 227

Dance with Music see DANCE/DANCE STUDIES 227, MUSIC 449

Dance, Performance and Teaching see DANCE/DANCE STUDIES 227

Dance, Theatre and Professional Practice see DANCE/DANCE STUDIES 227

Dance: Urban Practice see DANCE/DANCE STUDIES 227

DANCE/DANCE STUDIES 227
  see also DRAMA

Deaf Studies see EDUCATION STUDIES 256, HEALTH SCIENCES/STUDIES 341, SOCIAL SCIENCES/STUDIES 531, SPEECH PATHOLOGY/SCIENCES/THERAPY 546, TEACHER TRAINING 559

Decorative Arts see ART and DESIGN (Fashion and Textiles) 140

Dental Hygiene and Dental Therapy see DENTISTRY 231

Dental Hygiene and Therapy see DENTISTRY 231

Dental Materials see DENTISTRY 231, MATERIALS SCIENCE/METALLURGY 419

Dental Surgery see DENTISTRY 231

Dental Technology see DENTISTRY 231, TECHNOLOGIES 562

Dental Therapy and Hygiene see DENTISTRY 231

DENTISTRY 231

Design see ART and DESIGN (3D Design) 156, ART and DESIGN (Graphic Design) 148

Design (Interior Design) see ART and DESIGN (Product and Industrial Design) 152

Design (Applied Textiles) see ART and DESIGN (Fashion and Textiles) 140

Design (Digital) see ART and DESIGN (Graphic Design) 148

Design (Graphic Communication) see ART and DESIGN (Graphic Design) 148

Design (Illustration and Animation) see ART and DESIGN (Graphic Design) 148

Design (Moving Image) see ART and DESIGN (Graphic Design) 148

Design (New Media) see ART and DESIGN (Graphic Design) 148

Design (Play) see ART and DESIGN (Graphic Design) 148

Design (Product) see ART and DESIGN (Product and Industrial Design) 152

Design (Silversmithing and Jewellery) see ART and DESIGN (3D Design) 156

Design and Construction Management see BUILDING and CONSTRUCTION 176

Design and Craft for Stage and Screen see DRAMA 239

Design and Innovation see ENGINEERING (MECHANICAL) 290

Design and Operations Engineering see ENGINEERING (MANUFACTURING) 288

Design and Technology see ART and DESIGN (Product and Industrial Design) 152

Design and Technology Education see ART and DESIGN (Product and Industrial Design) 152

Design and Technology Management see ART and DESIGN (Product and Industrial Design) 152, ENGINEERING/ENGINEERING SCIENCES 260

Design and Visual Arts (Graphic Design) see ART and DESIGN (Graphic Design) 148

Design and Visual Arts (Illustration) see ART and DESIGN (Graphic Design) 148

Design and Visual Arts (Surface Design) see ART and DESIGN (Fashion and Textiles) 140

Design Business Management see BUSINESS AND MANAGEMENT COURSES (SPECIALISED) 193

Design Crafts see ART and DESIGN (3D Design) 156

Design Engineering see ENGINEERING/ENGINEERING SCIENCES 260

Design Ergonomics *see* ENGINEERING
(MECHANICAL) 290
Design for Advertising *see* MARKETING 415
Design for Decorative Arts *see* ART and DESIGN
(3D Design) 156
Design for Digital Media *see* ART and
DESIGN (Graphic Design) 148, MEDIA
STUDIES 427
Design for Exhibition and Museum *see*
INFORMATION MANAGEMENT and
LIBRARIANSHIP 375
Design for Film and Television *see* FILM,
RADIO, VIDEO and TV STUDIES 310
Design for Games *see* ART and DESIGN (Graphic
Design) 148
Design for Visual Communication *see*
ART and DESIGN (Graphic Design) 148
Design Futures *see* ART and DESIGN (Graphic
Design) 148
Design Interactions *see* ART and DESIGN (Graphic
Design) 148
Design Management and Fashion Retail *see* RETAIL
MANAGEMENT 524
Design Products *see* ART and DESIGN (Product and
Industrial Design) 152
Design Studies *see* ART and DESIGN (Product and
Industrial Design) 152
Design Technology *see* ART and DESIGN
(Product and Industrial Design) 152,
TEACHER TRAINING 559
Design Technology in Secondary Education *see*
TECHNOLOGIES 562
Design with Engineering Materials *see* MATERIALS
SCIENCE/METALLURGY 419
Design: Multimedia and Graphics *see* ART and DESIGN
(Graphic Design) 148
Development and Peace Studies *see*
DEVELOPMENT STUDIES 235, INTERNATIONAL
RELATIONS 378
Development Economics *see* ECONOMICS 251
DEVELOPMENT STUDIES 235
see also SOCIAL SCIENCES
Development Studies and Economics *see*
DEVELOPMENT STUDIES 235, ECONOMICS 251
Development Studies and Politics *see* DEVELOPMENT
STUDIES 235, POLITICS 507
Development Studies and Sociology *see*
DEVELOPMENT STUDIES 235, SOCIOLOGY 539
Development Studies with International Relations
see DEVELOPMENT STUDIES 235, INTERNATIONAL
RELATIONS 378

Developmental and Cell Biology *see* BIOLOGICAL
SCIENCES 165, MICROBIOLOGY 447
Developmental Biology *see* BIOLOGY 170
Developmental Psychology *see* PSYCHOLOGY 512
Diagnostic Imaging *see* RADIOGRAPHY 519
Diagnostic Imaging and Science *see*
RADIOGRAPHY 519
Diagnostic Radiography *see* RADIOGRAPHY 519
Diagnostic Radiography and Imaging *see*
RADIOGRAPHY 519
Diet and Health *see* DIETETICS 237, HEALTH
SCIENCES/STUDIES 341
Diet, Nutrition and Health *see* NUTRITION 466
DIETETICS 237
see also FOOD SCIENCE/STUDIES and TECHNOLOGY
see also NUTRITION
Dietetics and Nutrition *see* DIETETICS 237,
NUTRITION 466
Digital Advertising and Design *see* ART and DESIGN
(Graphic Design) 148
Digital Animation *see* ART and DESIGN (Graphic
Design) 148
Digital Art and Technology *see* ART and DESIGN
(Graphic Design) 148
Digital Arts *see* ART and DESIGN (Graphic
Design) 148
Digital Broadcast Technology *see* ENGINEERING
(ACOUSTICS and SOUND) 264
Digital Communication Systems *see* COMMUNICATION
STUDIES/COMMUNICATION 214
Digital Communications *see* ENGINEERING
(COMMUNICATIONS) 278
Digital Communications and Electronics *see*
ENGINEERING (COMMUNICATIONS) 278
Digital Design for Fashion *see* ART and DESIGN
(Fashion and Textiles) 140
Digital Electronics *see* ENGINEERING (ELECTRICAL and
ELECTRONIC) 283
Digital Film and 3D Animation Technology *see* ART
and DESIGN (3D Design) 156
Digital Film and Television *see* FILM, RADIO, VIDEO
and TV STUDIES 310
Digital Film and Video *see* FILM, RADIO, VIDEO and
TV STUDIES 310
Digital Film and Visual Effects Production *see* FILM,
RADIO, VIDEO and TV STUDIES 310
Digital Film Production *see* FILM, RADIO, VIDEO and
TV STUDIES 310
Digital Film, Games and Animation *see* ART and
DESIGN (Graphic Design) 148
Digital Forensics *see* COMPUTER COURSES 219

Digital Illustration *see* ART and DESIGN
   (Graphic Design) 148
Digital Media *see* COMPUTER COURSES 219,
   MEDIA STUDIES 427
Digital Media and Communications *see*
   COMMUNICATION STUDIES/COMMUNICATION 214,
   MEDIA STUDIES 427
Digital Media and Marketing *see* MARKETING 415,
   MEDIA STUDIES 427
Digital Media Engineering *see* COMPUTER
   COURSES 219, ENGINEERING (ACOUSTICS and
   SOUND) 264
Digital Media Production *see* ART and
   DESIGN (Graphic Design) 148, MEDIA
   STUDIES 427
Digital Media Technology *see* FILM, RADIO, VIDEO
   and TV STUDIES 310
Digital Music and Sound Arts *see* MUSIC 449
Digital Photography *see* PHOTOGRAPHY 481
Digital Signal and Image Processing *see* ENGINEERING
   (COMMUNICATIONS) 278
Directing *see* DRAMA 239
Disability Studies *see* COMMUNITY STUDIES/
   DEVELOPMENT 217, EDUCATION STUDIES 256,
   HEALTH SCIENCES/STUDIES 341
Disaster Management *see* BUSINESS AND
   MANAGEMENT COURSES (SPECIALISED) 193,
   GEOGRAPHY 330
Disaster Management and Emergency Planning
   see BUSINESS AND MANAGEMENT COURSES
   (SPECIALISED) 193, GEOGRAPHY 330
Disaster Reconstruction and Development *see*
   BUSINESS AND MANAGEMENT COURSES
   (SPECIALISED) 193
Disaster Reconstruction Management *see*
   GEOGRAPHY 330
Discrete Mathematics *see* MATHEMATICS 422
Divinity *see* RELIGIOUS STUDIES 521
Divinity and Classics *see* CLASSICS 210,
   RELIGIOUS STUDIES 521
Documentary Film and Television *see* FILM, RADIO,
   VIDEO and TV STUDIES 310
Documentary Photography *see* PHOTOGRAPHY 481
Documentary Video *see* FILM, RADIO, VIDEO and TV
   STUDIES 310
DRAMA 239
Drama and Applied Theatre *see* DRAMA 239
Drama and Creative Writing *see* DRAMA 239
Drama and Educational Studies *see* DRAMA 239,
   EDUCATION STUDIES 256
Drama and English *see* DRAMA 239, ENGLISH 296

Drama and English Literature *see* DRAMA 239,
   LITERATURE 409
Drama and Film Studies *see* DRAMA 239, FILM,
   RADIO, VIDEO and TV STUDIES 310
Drama and French/German/Italian *see* DRAMA 239,
   FRENCH 325, GERMAN 337, ITALIAN 381
Drama and History *see* DRAMA 239, HISTORY 355
Drama and Literature *see* DRAMA 239,
   LITERATURE 409
Drama and Music *see* DRAMA 239, MUSIC 449
Drama and Performance *see* DRAMA 239
Drama and Performance Studies *see* DRAMA 239
Drama and Philosophy *see* DRAMA 239,
   PHILOSOPHY 478
Drama and Psychology *see* DRAMA 239,
   PSYCHOLOGY 512
Drama and Theatre Arts *see* DRAMA 239
Drama and Theatre Practice *see* DRAMA 239
Drama and Theatre Studies *see* DRAMA 239
Drama in the Community *see* COMMUNITY STUDIES/
   DEVELOPMENT 217, DRAMA 239
Drama Performance *see* DRAMA 239
Drama Performance and Theatre Arts *see* DRAMA 239
Drama Studies *see* DRAMA 239
Drama Studies and Film Studies *see* DRAMA 239,
   FILM, RADIO, VIDEO and TV STUDIES 310
Drama Studies and Spanish *see* DRAMA 239,
   SPANISH 543
Drama with a Modern Language *see* DRAMA 239,
   LANGUAGES 386
Drama with Dance *see* DANCE/DANCE STUDIES 227,
   DRAMA 239
Drama with English/Screen Studies/Music *see*
   DRAMA 239
Drama with Irish *see* CELTIC, IRISH, SCOTTISH AND
   WELSH STUDIES 197, DRAMA 239
Drama with Marketing *see* DRAMA 239,
   MARKETING 415
Drama with Psychology *see* DRAMA 239,
   PSYCHOLOGY 512
Drama, Applied Theatre and Education *see*
   DRAMA 239
Drama, Theatre and Performance Studies *see*
   DRAMA 239
Drawing *see* ART and DESIGN (Fine Art) 144
Dutch *see* LANGUAGES 386

Early Childhood Education *see* SOCIAL WORK 536
Early Childhood Studies *see* EDUCATION STUDIES 256,
   PSYCHOLOGY 512, SOCIAL SCIENCES/STUDIES 531,
   SOCIAL WORK 536

Early Childhood Studies and Linguistics *see* LINGUISTICS 407

Early Years *see* EDUCATION STUDIES 256, SOCIAL SCIENCES/STUDIES 531, SOCIAL WORK 536

Early Years and Education Studies *see* EDUCATION STUDIES 256

Early Years and Educational Development *see* EDUCATION STUDIES 256

Early Years and Special and Inclusive Education *see* EDUCATION STUDIES 256

Early Years Education *see* EDUCATION STUDIES 256, TEACHER TRAINING 559

Early Years Practice *see* SOCIAL WORK 536

Early Years Teaching *see* EDUCATION STUDIES 256

Early Years, Business and Education *see* BUSINESS AND MANAGEMENT COURSES 179, EDUCATION STUDIES 256

Early Years, Psychology and Education *see* EDUCATION STUDIES 256, PSYCHOLOGY 512

Earth and Environmental Science *see* ENVIRONMENTAL SCIENCES/STUDIES 303, GEOLOGY/GEOLOGICAL SCIENCES 335

Earth and Ocean Science *see* GEOLOGY/GEOLOGICAL SCIENCES 335, MARINE/MARITIME STUDIES 412

Earth Science *see* ENVIRONMENTAL SCIENCES/STUDIES 303, GEOLOGY/GEOLOGICAL SCIENCES 335

Earth Science (International) *see* GEOLOGY/GEOLOGICAL SCIENCES 335

Earth Science with Geography *see* ENVIRONMENTAL SCIENCES/STUDIES 303, GEOGRAPHY 330

Earth System Science *see* GEOLOGY/GEOLOGICAL SCIENCES 335

East Asian Studies *see* ASIA-PACIFIC STUDIES 158

East European Studies *see* EUROPEAN STUDIES 307

Eastern Fashion Design *see* ART and DESIGN (Fashion and Textiles) 140

Ecological and Environmental Science *see* ENVIRONMENTAL SCIENCES/STUDIES 303

Ecological and Environmental Sciences with Management *see* ENVIRONMENTAL SCIENCES/STUDIES 303

Ecology *see* BIOLOGICAL SCIENCES 165, ENVIRONMENTAL SCIENCES/STUDIES 303

Ecology and Biogeography *see* ENVIRONMENTAL SCIENCES/STUDIES 303, GEOGRAPHY 330

Ecology and Conservation *see* BIOLOGICAL SCIENCES 165, ENVIRONMENTAL SCIENCES/STUDIES 303

Ecology and Environment *see* ENVIRONMENTAL SCIENCES/STUDIES 303

Ecology and Environmental Biology *see* BIOLOGY 170, ENVIRONMENTAL SCIENCES/STUDIES 303

Ecology and Wildlife Conservation *see* ENVIRONMENTAL SCIENCES/STUDIES 303

Ecology with Environmental Science *see* ENVIRONMENTAL SCIENCES/STUDIES 303

Econometrics and Mathematical Economics *see* ECONOMICS 251, MATHEMATICS 422

Economic and Social History *see* HISTORY (ECONOMIC and SOCIAL) 362

Economic Development Studies *see* DEVELOPMENT STUDIES 235

Economic History *see* ECONOMICS 251, HISTORY (ECONOMIC and SOCIAL) 362

Economic History and Business Studies *see* BUSINESS AND MANAGEMENT COURSES 179, ECONOMICS 251, HISTORY 355

ECONOMICS 251

Economics *see* COMBINED COURSES 212, ECONOMICS 251, FINANCE 315

Economics (International) *see* ECONOMICS 251

Economics and Accountancy *see* ACCOUNTANCY/ACCOUNTING 109, ECONOMICS 251

Economics and Accounting *see* ACCOUNTANCY/ACCOUNTING 109, ECONOMICS 251

Economics and Actuarial Science *see* ACTUARIAL SCIENCE/STUDIES 114, ECONOMICS 251

Economics and Business Finance *see* ECONOMICS 251, FINANCE 315

Economics and Business Management *see* ECONOMICS 251

Economics and Business with East European Studies *see* BUSINESS AND MANAGEMENT COURSES (INTERNATIONAL AND EUROPEAN) 188, ECONOMICS 251

Economics and Econometrics *see* ECONOMICS 251

Economics and Economic History *see* ECONOMICS 251, HISTORY (ECONOMIC and SOCIAL) 362

Economics and Economic Psychology *see* ECONOMICS 251, PSYCHOLOGY 512

Economics and Finance *see* ECONOMICS 251, FINANCE 315

Economics and Finance with International Business *see* ECONOMICS 251, FINANCE 315

Economics and Geography *see* ECONOMICS 251, GEOGRAPHY 330

Economics and Geography/International Relations/Mathematics/Politics *see* ECONOMICS 251

Economics and Industrial Organisation *see* ECONOMICS 251

Economics and International Development *see* DEVELOPMENT STUDIES 235, ECONOMICS 251, INTERNATIONAL RELATIONS 378

Economics and International Economics see
ECONOMICS 251, INTERNATIONAL RELATIONS 378
Economics and International Relations see
ECONOMICS 251, INTERNATIONAL RELATIONS 378
Economics and Law see ECONOMICS 251, LAW 393
Economics and Logistics see ECONOMICS 251
Economics and Management see BUSINESS
AND MANAGEMENT COURSES 179,
ECONOMICS 251
Economics and Management Sciences see
BUSINESS AND MANAGEMENT COURSES 179,
ECONOMICS 251
Economics and Management Studies see
BUSINESS AND MANAGEMENT COURSES 179,
ECONOMICS 251
Economics and Mathematical Sciences see
ECONOMICS 251
Economics and Mathematics see ECONOMICS 251,
MATHEMATICS 422
Economics and Philosophy see ECONOMICS 251,
PHILOSOPHY 478
Economics and Politics see ECONOMICS 251,
POLITICS 507
Economics and Psychology see ECONOMICS 251,
PSYCHOLOGY 512
Economics and Social Policy see ECONOMICS 251
Economics and Sociology see ECONOMICS 251,
SOCIOLOGY 539
Economics and Statistics see ECONOMICS 251,
STATISTICS 554
Economics and Transport Studies see
ECONOMICS 251, TRANSPORT MANAGEMENT
and PLANNING 571
Economics for Business see ECONOMICS 251
Economics Studies see ECONOMICS 251
Economics with a Language see ECONOMICS 251,
LANGUAGES 386
Economics with Accountancy see ACCOUNTANCY/
ACCOUNTING 109, ECONOMICS 251
Economics with Accounting see ACCOUNTANCY/
ACCOUNTING 109, ECONOMICS 251
Economics with Banking see ECONOMICS 251,
FINANCE 315
Economics with Central and East European Studies
see ECONOMICS 251, EUROPEAN STUDIES 307
Economics with Chinese see CHINESE 206,
ECONOMICS 251
Economics with Chinese Studies see CHINESE 206,
ECONOMICS 251
Economics with Computing see COMPUTER
COURSES 219, ECONOMICS 251

Economics with Econometrics see ECONOMICS 251
Economics with Finance see ECONOMICS 251,
FINANCE 315
Economics with French see ECONOMICS 251,
FRENCH 325
Economics with French/German/Italian/Spanish
see ECONOMICS 251, FRENCH 325, GERMAN 337,
ITALIAN 381, SPANISH 543
Economics with French/German/Russian see
ECONOMICS 251, FRENCH 325, GERMAN 337
Economics with Hispanic Studies see ECONOMICS 251,
LATIN AMERICAN STUDIES 391
Economics with Languages see ECONOMICS 251,
LANGUAGES 386
Economics with Management see BUSINESS
AND MANAGEMENT COURSES (SPECIALISED) 193,
ECONOMICS 251
Economics with Marketing see ECONOMICS 251,
MARKETING 415
Economics with Philosophy see ECONOMICS 251
Economics with Political Studies see ECONOMICS 251,
POLITICS 507
Economics with Politics see ECONOMICS 251,
POLITICS 507
Economics with Psychology see ECONOMICS 251,
PSYCHOLOGY 512
Economics with Russian Studies see
ECONOMICS 251, RUSSIAN and EAST
EUROPEAN STUDIES 526
Economics with Social Policy see ECONOMICS 251,
SOCIAL and PUBLIC POLICY and
ADMINISTRATION 529
Economics, Econometrics and Finance see
ECONOMICS 251, FINANCE 315
Economics, Finance and Banking see ECONOMICS 251,
FINANCE 315
Economics, Finance and Management see
ECONOMICS 251
Economics, Mathematics and Statistics see
ECONOMICS 251, MATHEMATICS 422,
STATISTICS 554
Economics, Politics and International Relations see
ECONOMICS 251, INTERNATIONAL RELATIONS 378,
POLITICS 507
Economics, Politics and International Studies see
ECONOMICS 251, INTERNATIONAL RELATIONS 378,
POLITICS 507
Economics, Politics and Public Policy see SOCIAL and
PUBLIC POLICY and ADMINISTRATION 529
Economics/Economic History see ECONOMICS 251,
HISTORY (ECONOMIC and SOCIAL) 362

Economics/Mathematics *see* ECONOMICS 251, MATHEMATICS 422

Economy in Russia *see* RUSSIAN and EAST EUROPEAN STUDIES 526

Editing and Post Production *see* MEDIA STUDIES 427

Education *see* EDUCATION STUDIES 256, TEACHER TRAINING 559

Education (Primary) *see* EDUCATION STUDIES 256, TEACHER TRAINING 559

Education (Secondary) *see* EDUCATION STUDIES 256, TEACHER TRAINING 559

Education and Community Development *see* EDUCATION STUDIES 256

Education and Disability Studies *see* EDUCATION STUDIES 256

Education and Religious Studies *see* EDUCATION STUDIES 256, RELIGIOUS STUDIES 521

Education and Social Policy *see* SOCIAL and PUBLIC POLICY and ADMINISTRATION 529

Education and Social Science *see* EDUCATION STUDIES 256

Education and Sociology *see* EDUCATION STUDIES 256, SOCIOLOGY 539

Education and Sports Studies *see* PHYSICAL EDUCATION 484

Education and Statistics *see* EDUCATION STUDIES 256, STATISTICS 554

Education and Welsh *see* CELTIC, IRISH, SCOTTISH AND WELSH STUDIES 197, EDUCATION STUDIES 256

Education Primary *see* EDUCATION STUDIES 256, TEACHER TRAINING 559

EDUCATION STUDIES 256
  see also TEACHER TRAINING

Education Studies (Primary) *see* EDUCATION STUDIES 256

Education Studies (Primary) with Art *see* EDUCATION STUDIES 256

Education Studies (Primary) with English *see* EDUCATION STUDIES 256, ENGLISH 296

Education Studies (Primary) with Music *see* EDUCATION STUDIES 256, MUSIC 449

Education Studies and Early Childhood Studies *see* EDUCATION STUDIES 256

Education Studies and Early Years *see* EDUCATION STUDIES 256

Education Studies and English *see* EDUCATION STUDIES 256, ENGLISH 296

Education Studies and Modern History *see* EDUCATION STUDIES 256, HISTORY 355

Education Studies and Psychology *see* EDUCATION STUDIES 256, PSYCHOLOGY 512

Education Studies and Sport and Physical Activity *see* EDUCATION STUDIES 256, PHYSICAL EDUCATION 484

Education Studies and Welsh *see* CELTIC, IRISH, SCOTTISH AND WELSH STUDIES 197, EDUCATION STUDIES 256

Education Studies with Physical Education *see* EDUCATION STUDIES 256, PHYSICAL EDUCATION 484

Education Studies with Psychology *see* EDUCATION STUDIES 256, PSYCHOLOGY 512

Education Studies with Psychology and Counselling *see* EDUCATION STUDIES 256, PSYCHOLOGY 512

Education Studies with Special and Inclusive Needs *see* EDUCATION STUDIES 256

Education with Classics *see* CLASSICS 210, EDUCATION STUDIES 256

Education with English *see* EDUCATION STUDIES 256, ENGLISH 296

Education with English and Drama *see* DRAMA 239, EDUCATION STUDIES 256, ENGLISH 296

Education with Mathematics *see* EDUCATION STUDIES 256, MATHEMATICS 422

Education, Culture and Childhood *see* EDUCATION STUDIES 256

Education, Culture and Society *see* EDUCATION STUDIES 256

Education: Primary *see* EDUCATION STUDIES 256, TEACHER TRAINING 559

Education: Primary Psychology *see* EDUCATION STUDIES 256

Education: Secondary *see* EDUCATION STUDIES 256, TEACHER TRAINING 559

Educational Studies *see* EDUCATION STUDIES 256

Educational Studies and Psychology *see* EDUCATION STUDIES 256, PSYCHOLOGY 512

e-Finance *see* FINANCE 315

Egyptian Archaeology *see* ARCHAEOLOGY 131

Egyptology *see* CLASSICAL STUDIES/CLASSICAL CIVILISATION 208

Egyptology and Ancient History *see* HISTORY (ANCIENT) 360

Electrical and Electronic Engineering *see* ENGINEERING (ELECTRICAL and ELECTRONIC) 283

Electrical and Electronic Engineering (Communications) *see* ENGINEERING (COMMUNICATIONS) 278, ENGINEERING (ELECTRICAL and ELECTRONIC), 283

Electrical and Electronic Engineering (Control/Power/ Communications) see ENGINEERING (ELECTRICAL and ELECTRONIC) 283

Electrical and Electronic Engineering with Management see ENGINEERING (ELECTRICAL and ELECTRONIC) 283

Electrical and Electronic Engineering with Management Studies see BUSINESS AND MANAGEMENT COURSES 179, ENGINEERING (ELECTRICAL and ELECTRONIC) 283

Electrical and Electronic Engineering with Mathematics see ENGINEERING (ELECTRICAL and ELECTRONIC) 283, MATHEMATICS 422

Electrical and Energy Engineering see ENGINEERING (ELECTRICAL and ELECTRONIC) 283

Electrical and Mechanical Engineering see ENGINEERING (ELECTRICAL and ELECTRONIC) 283, ENGINEERING (MECHANICAL) 290

Electrical Engineering see ENGINEERING (ELECTRICAL and ELECTRONIC) 283

Electrical Engineering and Electronics see ENGINEERING (ELECTRICAL and ELECTRONIC) 283

Electrical Engineering and Renewable Energy Systems see ENGINEERING (ELECTRICAL and ELECTRONIC) 283

Electrical Engineering with Renewable Energy see ENGINEERING (ELECTRICAL and ELECTRONIC) 283

Electrical Engineering with Renewable Energy Systems see ENGINEERING (ELECTRICAL and ELECTRONIC) 283

Electrical Power Engineering see ENGINEERING (ELECTRICAL and ELECTRONIC) 283

Electrical/Electronic Engineering see ENGINEERING (ELECTRICAL and ELECTRONIC) 283

Electromechanical Engineering see ENGINEERING (ELECTRICAL and ELECTRONIC) 283, ENGINEERING (MECHANICAL) 290

Electronic and Communication Engineering see ENGINEERING (COMMUNICATIONS) 278, ENGINEERING (ELECTRICAL and ELECTRONIC) 283

Electronic and Communications Engineering see ENGINEERING (COMMUNICATIONS) 278, ENGINEERING (COMPUTER, CONTROL, SOFTWARE and SYSTEMS) 280, ENGINEERING (ELECTRICAL and ELECTRONIC) 283

Electronic and Computer Engineering see ENGINEERING (COMPUTER, CONTROL, SOFTWARE and SYSTEMS) 280, ENGINEERING (ELECTRICAL and ELECTRONIC) 283

Electronic and Computer Systems Engineering see ENGINEERING (COMPUTER, CONTROL, SOFTWARE and SYSTEMS) 280, ENGINEERING (ELECTRICAL and ELECTRONIC) 283

Electronic and Digital Systems see ENGINEERING (ELECTRICAL and ELECTRONIC) 283

Electronic and Electrical Engineering see ENGINEERING (COMMUNICATIONS) 278, ENGINEERING (ELECTRICAL and ELECTRONIC) 283

Electronic and Electrical Engineering with Business Studies see BUSINESS AND MANAGEMENT COURSES 179, ENGINEERING (ELECTRICAL and ELECTRONIC) 283

Electronic and Software Engineering see ENGINEERING (COMPUTER, CONTROL, SOFTWARE and SYSTEMS) 280

Electronic Commerce Computing see COMPUTER COURSES 219

Electronic Communications see ENGINEERING (COMMUNICATIONS) 278, ENGINEERING (ELECTRICAL and ELECTRONIC) 283

Electronic Design see ENGINEERING (ELECTRICAL and ELECTRONIC) 283

Electronic Engineering see ENGINEERING (COMMUNICATIONS) 278, ENGINEERING (ELECTRICAL and ELECTRONIC) 283

Electronic Engineering (Telecommunications) (Broadcast Systems) see ENGINEERING (COMMUNICATIONS) 278, ENGINEERING (ELECTRICAL and ELECTRONIC) 283

Electronic Engineering and Communications see ENGINEERING (COMMUNICATIONS) 278

Electronic Engineering and Computer Science see COMPUTER COURSES 219, ENGINEERING (ELECTRICAL and ELECTRONIC) 283

Electronic Engineering and Cybernetics see ENGINEERING (ELECTRICAL and ELECTRONIC) 283

Electronic Engineering and Physics see ENGINEERING (ELECTRICAL and ELECTRONIC) 283

Electronic Engineering and Telecommunications see ENGINEERING (COMMUNICATIONS) 278

Electronic Engineering with a Modern Language see ENGINEERING (ELECTRICAL and ELECTRONIC) 283, LANGUAGES 386

Electronic Engineering with Artificial Intelligence see ENGINEERING (ELECTRICAL and ELECTRONIC) 283

Electronic Engineering with Business Management see BUSINESS AND MANAGEMENT COURSES, 179 ENGINEERING (ELECTRICAL and ELECTRONIC) 283

Electronic Engineering with Communications see ENGINEERING (COMMUNICATIONS) 278, ENGINEERING (ELECTRICAL and ELECTRONIC) 283

Electronic Engineering with Communications Engineering *see* ENGINEERING (COMMUNICATIONS) 278, ENGINEERING (ELECTRICAL and ELECTRONIC) 283

Electronic Engineering with Computer Science *see* ENGINEERING (ELECTRICAL and ELECTRONIC) 283

Electronic Engineering with Computer Systems *see* COMPUTER COURSES 219, ENGINEERING (ELECTRICAL and ELECTRONIC) 283

Electronic Engineering with Management *see* ENGINEERING (ELECTRICAL and ELECTRONIC) 283

Electronic Engineering with Mobile and Secure Systems *see* ENGINEERING (ELECTRICAL and ELECTRONIC) 283

Electronic Engineering with Nanotechnology *see* ENGINEERING (ELECTRICAL and ELECTRONIC) 283

Electronic Engineering with Optical Communications *see* ENGINEERING (COMMUNICATIONS), 278 ENGINEERING (ELECTRICAL and ELECTRONIC) 283

Electronic Engineering with Power Systems *see* ENGINEERING (ELECTRICAL and ELECTRONIC) 283

Electronic Engineering with Space Science Technology *see* ASTRONOMY and ASTROPHYSICS 159, ENGINEERING (ELECTRICAL and ELECTRONIC) 283

Electronic Engineering with Wireless Communications *see* ENGINEERING (COMMUNICATIONS) 278, ENGINEERING (ELECTRICAL and ELECTRONIC) 283

Electronic, Electrical and Systems Engineering *see* ENGINEERING (ELECTRICAL and ELECTRONIC) 283

Electronic, Telecommunications and Internet Engineering *see* ENGINEERING (COMMUNICATIONS) 278, ENGINEERING (COMPUTER, CONTROL, SOFTWARE and SYSTEMS) 280, ENGINEERING (ELECTRICAL and ELECTRONIC) 283

Electronics *see* ENGINEERING (ELECTRICAL and ELECTRONIC) 283

Electronics and Communication Engineering *see* ENGINEERING (ELECTRICAL and ELECTRONIC) 283

Electronics and Communications Engineering *see* ENGINEERING (COMMUNICATIONS) 278

Electronics and Computer Engineering *see* ENGINEERING (COMPUTER, CONTROL, SOFTWARE and SYSTEMS) 280, ENGINEERING (ELECTRICAL and ELECTRONIC) 283

Electronics and Computer Science *see* ENGINEERING (COMPUTER, CONTROL, SOFTWARE and SYSTEMS) 280

Electronics and Computer Systems *see* ENGINEERING (ELECTRICAL and ELECTRONIC) 283

Electronics and Electrical Engineering (Communications) *see* COMMUNICATION STUDIES/COMMUNICATION 214, ENGINEERING (ELECTRICAL and ELECTRONIC) 283

Electronics and Music Technology *see* ENGINEERING (ACOUSTICS and SOUND) 264, ENGINEERING (ELECTRICAL and ELECTRONIC) 283

Electronics and Nanotechnology *see* ENGINEERING (ELECTRICAL and ELECTRONIC) 283

Electronics and Software Engineering *see* ENGINEERING (COMPUTER, CONTROL, SOFTWARE and SYSTEMS) 280, ENGINEERING (ELECTRICAL and ELECTRONIC) 283

Electronics Engineering *see* ENGINEERING (ELECTRICAL and ELECTRONIC) 283

Electronics with Bioelectronics *see* ENGINEERING (ELECTRICAL and ELECTRONIC) 283

Electronics with Satellite Engineering *see* ENGINEERING (COMMUNICATIONS) 278, ENGINEERING (ELECTRICAL and ELECTRONIC) 283

Embedded Computer Systems *see* ENGINEERING (COMPUTER, CONTROL, SOFTWARE and SYSTEMS) 280

Energy Engineering *see* ENGINEERING/ENGINEERING SCIENCES 260

Engineering *see* ENGINEERING/ENGINEERING SCIENCES 260

ENGINEERING (ACOUSTICS and SOUND) 264
see also FILM, RADIO, VIDEO and TV STUDIES
see also MEDIA STUDIES

ENGINEERING (AERONAUTICAL and AEROSPACE) 266

Engineering (Business Management) *see* ENGINEERING/ENGINEERING SCIENCES 260

ENGINEERING (CHEMICAL) 269

ENGINEERING (CIVIL) 274
see also BUILDING and CONSTRUCTION

ENGINEERING (COMMUNICATIONS) 278
see also ENGINEERING (COMPUTER, CONTROL, SOFTWARE and SYSTEMS)
see also ENGINEERING (ELECTRICAL and ELECTRONIC)

ENGINEERING (COMPUTER, CONTROL, SOFTWARE and SYSTEMS) 280
see also COMPUTER COURSES
see also ENGINEERING (ELECTRICAL and ELECTRONIC)

ENGINEERING (ELECTRICAL and ELECTRONIC) 283
see also ENGINEERING (ACOUSTICS and SOUND)

see also ENGINEERING (AERONAUTICAL and AEROSPACE)

see also ENGINEERING (COMMUNICATIONS)

see also ENGINEERING (COMPUTER, CONTROL, SOFTWARE and SYSTEMS)

see also TECHNOLOGIES

Engineering (Electrical and Information Sciences/Electrical and Electronic Engineering) see ENGINEERING (ELECTRICAL and ELECTRONIC) 283

Engineering (Information and Computer Engineering) see ENGINEERING (COMPUTER, CONTROL, SOFTWARE and SYSTEMS) 280

ENGINEERING (MANUFACTURING) 288

see also ART and DESIGN (Industrial and Product Design)

see also ENGINEERING/ENGINEERING SCIENCES

Engineering (Manufacturing Engineering) see ENGINEERING (MANUFACTURING) 288

ENGINEERING (MECHANICAL) 290

Engineering (Mechanical Engineering) see ENGINEERING (MECHANICAL) 290

Engineering (Mechanical with Oil and Gas Studies) see ENGINEERING (MECHANICAL) 290

ENGINEERING (MEDICAL) 295

Engineering (Part II Civil Engineering) see ENGINEERING (CIVIL) 274

Engineering and Business Enterprise see ENGINEERING/ENGINEERING SCIENCES 260

Engineering and Business Studies see BUSINESS AND MANAGEMENT COURSES 179, ENGINEERING/ ENGINEERING SCIENCES 260

Engineering and Design see ENGINEERING/ ENGINEERING SCIENCES 260

Engineering and Management see ENGINEERING/ ENGINEERING SCIENCES 260

Engineering Business Management see ENGINEERING/ENGINEERING SCIENCES 260

Engineering Design see ENGINEERING/ENGINEERING SCIENCES 260

Engineering Design Management see ENGINEERING/ ENGINEERING SCIENCES 260

Engineering for Sustainable Energy see ENGINEERING/ENGINEERING SCIENCES 260

Engineering Geology and Geotechnics see GEOLOGY/ GEOLOGICAL SCIENCES 335

Engineering including a Foundation Year see ENGINEERING/ENGINEERING SCIENCES 260

Engineering Management see BUSINESS AND MANAGEMENT COURSES (SPECIALISED) 193, ENGINEERING/ENGINEERING SCIENCES 260

Engineering Mathematics see ENGINEERING/ ENGINEERING SCIENCES 260, MATHEMATICS 422

Engineering Physics see PHYSICS 488

Engineering Product Design see ENGINEERING/ ENGINEERING SCIENCES 260

Engineering Science see ENGINEERING/ENGINEERING SCIENCES 260

Engineering Sciences see ENGINEERING/ENGINEERING SCIENCES 260

Engineering Technology and Management see TECHNOLOGIES 562

Engineering Technology Management see ENGINEERING/ENGINEERING SCIENCES 260

Engineering with Business see ENGINEERING/ ENGINEERING SCIENCES 260

Engineering with Business Finance see ENGINEERING/ ENGINEERING SCIENCES 260, FINANCE 315

Engineering with Business Management see BUSINESS AND MANAGEMENT COURSES 179, ENGINEERING/ENGINEERING SCIENCES 315

Engineering with Product Design see ART and DESIGN (Product and Industrial Design) 152, ENGINEERING/ENGINEERING SCIENCES 260

Engineering, Economics and Management see ECONOMICS 251, ENGINEERING/ENGINEERING SCIENCES 260

Engineering, Geology, and Geotechnics see GEOLOGY/GEOLOGICAL SCIENCES 335

ENGINEERING/ENGINEERING SCIENCES 260

see also ART and DESIGN (Industrial and Product Design)

see also TECHNOLOGIES

English and American Literature see AMERICAN STUDIES 120, ENGLISH 296, LANGUAGES 386, LITERATURE 409

English and American Studies see AMERICAN STUDIES 120, ENGLISH 296

English and Chinese Studies see CHINESE 206, ENGLISH 296

English and Classical Studies see CLASSICAL STUDIES/ CLASSICAL CIVILISATION 208, ENGLISH 296

English and Contemporary Media see ENGLISH 296, MEDIA STUDIES 427

English and Creative Writing see ENGLISH 296

English and Drama see DRAMA 239, ENGLISH 296

English and Education Studies see EDUCATION STUDIES 256, ENGLISH 296

English and Film see ENGLISH 296, FILM, RADIO, VIDEO and TV STUDIES 310

English and Film and Television Studies see ENGLISH 296, FILM, RADIO, VIDEO and TV STUDIES 310

English and Film Studies *see* ENGLISH 296, FILM, RADIO, VIDEO and TV STUDIES 310

English and French *see* ENGLISH 296, FRENCH 325

English and French Law *see* ENGLISH 296, FRENCH 325, LAW 393

English and French Law/German Law/Italian Law/Spanish Law *see* LANGUAGES 386, LAW 393

English and French/German/Spanish *see* ENGLISH 296, FRENCH 325, GERMAN 337, SPANISH 543

English and German Literature *see* ENGLISH 296, GERMAN 337, LITERATURE 409

English and Greek Civilisation *see* ENGLISH 296, GREEK 340

English and History *see* ENGLISH 296, HISTORY 355

English and History of Art *see* ENGLISH 296, HISTORY OF ART 363

English and Italian Literature *see* ENGLISH 296, ITALIAN 381, LITERATURE 409

English and Journalism *see* ENGLISH 296, MEDIA STUDIES 427

English and Journalism Studies *see* ENGLISH 296

English and Latin Literature *see* ENGLISH 296, LATIN 389, LITERATURE 409

English and Linguistics *see* ENGLISH 296

English and Media *see* ENGLISH 296, MEDIA STUDIES 427

English and Modern Languages *see* ENGLISH 296, LANGUAGES 386

English and Music *see* ENGLISH 296, MUSIC 449

English and Philosophy *see* ENGLISH 296, PHILOSOPHY 478

English and Politics *see* ENGLISH 296, POLITICS 507

English and Psychology *see* ENGLISH 296, PSYCHOLOGY 512

English and Psychology in Society *see* ENGLISH 296, PSYCHOLOGY 512, SOCIAL SCIENCES/ STUDIES 531

English and Scottish Literature *see* CELTIC, IRISH, SCOTTISH AND WELSH STUDIES 197, ENGLISH 296, LITERATURE 409

English and Sociology *see* ENGLISH 296, SOCIOLOGY 539

English and Spanish *see* ENGLISH 296, SPANISH 543

English and Sports Science *see* ENGLISH 296, SPORTS SCIENCES/STUDIES 548

English and Theatre Studies *see* DRAMA 239

English and World Literature *see* LITERATURE 409

English and Writing *see* ENGLISH 296

English Language *see* ENGLISH 296

English Language and Communication *see* COMMUNICATION STUDIES/COMMUNICATION 214, ENGLISH 296

English Language and Communication with Film *see* FILM, RADIO, VIDEO and TV STUDIES 310

English Language and English Language Teaching *see* ENGLISH 296, LANGUAGES 386, TEACHER TRAINING 559

English Language and French/German *see* ENGLISH 296

English Language and Journalism *see* MEDIA STUDIES 427

English Language and Linguistics *see* ENGLISH 296, LANGUAGES 386, LINGUISTICS 407

English Language and Literary Studies *see* ENGLISH 296

English Language and Literature *see* ENGLISH 296, LANGUAGES 386, LITERATURE 409

English Language and Literature with Education *see* EDUCATION STUDIES 256, ENGLISH 296, LITERATURE 409

English Language and Sociology *see* ENGLISH 296, SOCIOLOGY 539

English Language Studies *see* ENGLISH 296

English Language Teaching *see* ENGLISH 296, TEACHER TRAINING 559

English Language with Creative Writing *see* ENGLISH 296

English Language with English Literature *see* ENGLISH 296, LITERATURE, 409

English Language with Literature *see* ENGLISH 296, LITERATURE 409

English Language, Literature and Writing *see* ENGLISH 296, LITERATURE 409

English Language/Literature *see* ENGLISH 296, LITERATURE 409

English Law and French Law/German Law/Hong Kong Law *see* LAW 393

English Literary Studies *see* ENGLISH 296, LITERATURE 409

English Literature *see* COMBINED COURSES 212, ENGLISH 296, LITERATURE 409

English Literature and Community History *see* HISTORY 355, LITERATURE 409

English Literature and Creative Writing *see* ENGLISH 296, LITERATURE 409

English Literature and Culture *see* LITERATURE 409

English Literature and European Literature and Culture *see* EUROPEAN STUDIES 307, LITERATURE 409

English Literature and Film and Theatre Arts *see* FILM, RADIO, VIDEO and TV STUDIES 310, LITERATURE 409

English Literature and French/Spanish *see* FRENCH 325, LITERATURE 409, SPANISH 543

English Literature and History *see* HISTORY 355, LITERATURE 409

English Literature and Language Studies *see* ENGLISH 296, LITERATURE 409

English Literature and Linguistics *see* ENGLISH 296, LINGUISTICS 407, LITERATURE 409

English Literature and Music *see* ENGLISH 296, MUSIC 449

English Literature and Philosophy *see* LITERATURE 409, PHILOSOPHY 478

English Literature and Psychology *see* LITERATURE 409, PSYCHOLOGY 512

English Literature and Sociology *see* LITERATURE 409, SOCIOLOGY 539

English Literature with Creative Writing *see* ENGLISH 296, LITERATURE 409

English Literature with English Language *see* ENGLISH 296, LITERATURE 409

English Literature with Film and Television Studies *see* ENGLISH 296, FILM, RADIO, VIDEO and TV STUDIES 310, LITERATURE 409

English Literature with History *see* HISTORY 355, LITERATURE 409

English Literature with Publishing *see* ENGLISH 296, LITERATURE 409

English Studies *see* ENGLISH 296, LITERATURE 409

English Studies and History *see* ENGLISH 296, HISTORY 355

English Studies and Latin *see* ENGLISH 296, LATIN 389

English Studies and Philosophy *see* ENGLISH 296, PHILOSOPHY 478

English Studies and Russian *see* ENGLISH 296, RUSSIAN and EAST EUROPEAN STUDIES 526

English Studies and Russian and East European Civilisations *see* ENGLISH 296, RUSSIAN and EAST EUROPEAN STUDIES 526

English Studies and Serbian/Croatian *see* ENGLISH 296, RUSSIAN and EAST EUROPEAN STUDIES 526

English Studies and Theology *see* ENGLISH 296, RELIGIOUS STUDIES 521

English Studies with Creative Writing *see* ENGLISH 296

English with Creative Writing *see* ENGLISH 296

English with Cultural Studies *see* ENGLISH 296

English with Drama *see* DRAMA 239

English with Drama and Performance *see* DRAMA 239, ENGLISH 296

English with Film Studies *see* ENGLISH 296, FILM, RADIO, VIDEO and TV STUDIES 310

English with History *see* ENGLISH 296, HISTORY 355

English with Theatre Studies *see* DRAMA 239, ENGLISH 296

English, American and Postcolonial Literature *see* AMERICAN STUDIES 120, ENGLISH 296, LITERATURE 409

Enterprise and Management *see* BUSINESS AND MANAGEMENT COURSES (SPECIALISED) 193

Enterprise Computing: Information Technology Management for Business *see* COMPUTER COURSES 219

Entertainment Design Crafts *see* ART and DESIGN (3D Design) 156

Entertainment Law *see* LAW 393

Entertainment Management *see* LEISURE and RECREATION MANAGEMENT/STUDIES 405

Entrepreneurship *see* BUSINESS AND MANAGEMENT COURSES (SPECIALISED) 193

Environment and Business *see* ENVIRONMENTAL SCIENCES/STUDIES 303

Environment and Conservation *see* ENVIRONMENTAL SCIENCES/STUDIES 303, GEOLOGY/GEOLOGICAL SCIENCES 335

Environment and Development *see* ENVIRONMENTAL SCIENCES/STUDIES 303, TOWN and COUNTRY PLANNING 567

Environment and Enterprise *see* ENVIRONMENTAL SCIENCES/STUDIES 303

Environment and Geophysics *see* ENVIRONMENTAL SCIENCES/STUDIES 303

Environment and Planning *see* ENVIRONMENTAL SCIENCES/STUDIES 303, TOWN and COUNTRY PLANNING 567

Environment and Resource Geology *see* ENVIRONMENTAL SCIENCES/STUDIES 303, GEOLOGY/GEOLOGICAL SCIENCES 335

Environment and Sustainability *see* ENVIRONMENTAL SCIENCES/STUDIES 303

Environmental and Civil Engineering *see* ENGINEERING (CIVIL) 274

Environmental and Countryside Management *see* ENVIRONMENTAL SCIENCES/STUDIES 303

Environmental and Media Studies *see* ENVIRONMENTAL SCIENCES/STUDIES 303, MEDIA STUDIES 427

Environmental and Public Health *see* ENVIRONMENTAL SCIENCES/STUDIES 303

Environmental and Sustainability Studies *see* ENVIRONMENTAL SCIENCES/STUDIES 303

Environmental Archaeology *see* ARCHAEOLOGY 131, ENVIRONMENTAL SCIENCES/STUDIES 303

Environmental Biology *see* BIOLOGY 170, ENVIRONMENTAL SCIENCES/STUDIES 303

Environmental Biology and Geography *see* ENVIRONMENTAL SCIENCES/STUDIES 303, GEOGRAPHY 330

Environmental Chemistry *see* CHEMISTRY 199, ENVIRONMENTAL SCIENCES/STUDIES 303

Environmental Civil Engineering *see* ENGINEERING (CIVIL) 274

Environmental Conservation *see* ENVIRONMENTAL SCIENCES/STUDIES 303

Environmental Construction Surveying *see* BUILDING and CONSTRUCTION 176, ENVIRONMENTAL SCIENCES/STUDIES 303 SURVEYING 556

Environmental Design and Engineering *see* ENGINEERING/ENGINEERING SCIENCES 260, ENVIRONMENTAL SCIENCES/STUDIES 303

Environmental Development *see* TOWN and COUNTRY PLANNING 567

Environmental Earth Science *see* ENVIRONMENTAL SCIENCES/STUDIES 303, GEOLOGY/GEOLOGICAL SCIENCES 335

Environmental Earth Sciences *see* ENVIRONMENTAL SCIENCES/STUDIES 303, GEOLOGY/GEOLOGICAL SCIENCES 335

Environmental Economics and Environmental Management *see* ENVIRONMENTAL SCIENCES/STUDIES 303

Environmental Engineering *see* ENGINEERING/ENGINEERING SCIENCES 260, ENVIRONMENTAL SCIENCES/STUDIES 303

Environmental Geography *see* ENVIRONMENTAL SCIENCES/STUDIES 303, GEOGRAPHY 330

Environmental Geography and Climate Change *see* ENVIRONMENTAL SCIENCES/STUDIES 303, GEOGRAPHY 330

Environmental Geography and International Development *see* ENVIRONMENTAL SCIENCES/STUDIES 303, GEOGRAPHY 330

Environmental Geophysics *see* GEOLOGY/GEOLOGICAL SCIENCES 335

Environmental Geoscience *see* ENVIRONMENTAL SCIENCES/STUDIES 303, GEOLOGY/GEOLOGICAL SCIENCES 335

Environmental Geoscience (International) *see* GEOLOGY/GEOLOGICAL SCIENCES 335

Environmental Hazards *see* ENVIRONMENTAL SCIENCES/STUDIES 303

Environmental Hazards: Science, Policy and Management *see* ENVIRONMENTAL SCIENCES/STUDIES 303

Environmental Health *see* ENVIRONMENTAL SCIENCES/STUDIES 303, HEALTH SCIENCES/STUDIES 341

Environmental Management *see* ENVIRONMENTAL SCIENCES/STUDIES 303, TOWN and COUNTRY PLANNING 567

Environmental Management and Planning *see* ENVIRONMENTAL SCIENCES/STUDIES 303

Environmental Management and Sustainability *see* ENVIRONMENTAL SCIENCES/STUDIES 303

Environmental Mathematics *see* ENVIRONMENTAL SCIENCES/STUDIES 303

Environmental Planning *see* TOWN and COUNTRY PLANNING 567

Environmental Policy with Economics *see* ECONOMICS 251, ENVIRONMENTAL SCIENCES/STUDIES 303

Environmental Science *see* ENVIRONMENTAL SCIENCES/STUDIES 303, GEOGRAPHY 330

Environmental Science (Maritime Conservation) *see* MARINE/MARITIME STUDIES 412

Environmental Science and Geography *see* ENVIRONMENTAL SCIENCES/STUDIES 303

Environmental Science and Outdoor Education *see* ENVIRONMENTAL SCIENCES/STUDIES 303, LEISURE and RECREATION MANAGEMENT/STUDIES 405

Environmental Science with Ecology *see* ENVIRONMENTAL SCIENCES/STUDIES 303

ENVIRONMENTAL SCIENCES/STUDIES 303
see also BIOLOGICAL SCIENCES
see also BIOLOGY
see also ENGINEERING (CIVIL)
see also GEOGRAPHY
see also GEOLOGY/GEOLOGICAL SCIENCES
see also TOWN and COUNTRY PLANNING

Environmental Stewardship *see* ENVIRONMENTAL SCIENCES/STUDIES 303

Environmental Studies *see* ENVIRONMENTAL SCIENCES/STUDIES 303

Environmental Sustainability *see* ENVIRONMENTAL SCIENCES/STUDIES 303

Equestrian Psychology and Sports Science *see* ANIMAL SCIENCES 124, SPORTS SCIENCES/STUDIES 548

Equestrian Sport Science *see* ANIMAL SCIENCES 124, SPORTS SCIENCES/STUDIES 548

Equestrian Sports Science *see* ANIMAL SCIENCES 124

Equestrian Sports Science (Equestrian Psychology) *see* ANIMAL SCIENCES 124

Equine and Human Sports Science *see* ANIMAL SCIENCES 124, SPORTS SCIENCES/STUDIES 548

Equine Business Management *see* ANIMAL SCIENCES 124, BUSINESS AND MANAGEMENT COURSES (SPECIALISED) 193

Equine Dental Science *see* ANIMAL SCIENCES 124, DENTISTRY 231

Equine Management *see* ANIMAL SCIENCES 124

Equine Management (Physiology) *see* ANIMAL SCIENCES 124

Equine Science *see* ANIMAL SCIENCES 124

Equine Science (Behaviour and Welfare) *see* ANIMAL SCIENCES 124

Equine Science and Management (Behaviour and Welfare) *see* ANIMAL SCIENCES 124

Equine Science and Thoroughbred Management *see* ANIMAL SCIENCES 124

Equine Sport Science *see* ANIMAL SCIENCES 124, SPORTS SCIENCES/STUDIES 548

Equine Sports Coaching *see* ANIMAL SCIENCES 124

Equine Sports Performance *see* ANIMAL SCIENCES 124

Equine Sports Science *see* SPORTS SCIENCES/STUDIES 548

Equine Sports Therapy *see* ANIMAL SCIENCES 124

Equine Studies *see* ANIMAL SCIENCES 124

Equine Therapy and Rehabilitation *see* ANIMAL SCIENCES 124

Equine Tourism Management *see* TOURISM and TRAVEL 564

Equitation Coaching Sports Science *see* ANIMAL SCIENCES 124

Ergonomics *see* HUMAN SCIENCES/HUMAN BIOSCIENCES 374, PSYCHOLOGY 512

Estate Agency *see* SURVEYING 556

Estate Management *see* BUSINESS AND MANAGEMENT COURSES 179, BUSINESS AND MANAGEMENT COURSES (SPECIALISED) 193, SURVEYING 556

Ethical Hacking for Computer Security *see* COMPUTER COURSES 219

Ethnomusicology *see* MUSIC 449

European and Middle Eastern Languages (Czech/Russian) *see* LANGUAGES 386, RUSSIAN and EAST EUROPEAN STUDIES 526

European Business *see* BUSINESS AND MANAGEMENT COURSES (INTERNATIONAL AND EUROPEAN) 188

European Business (UK and Germany) *see* BUSINESS AND MANAGEMENT COURSES (INTERNATIONAL AND EUROPEAN) 188

European Economics *see* ECONOMICS 251, EUROPEAN STUDIES 307

European Film and Media *see* EUROPEAN STUDIES 307, MEDIA STUDIES 427

European History *see* EUROPEAN STUDIES 307, HISTORY 355

European Language *see* LANGUAGES 386

European Languages and Film Studies *see* FILM, RADIO, VIDEO and TV STUDIES 310, LANGUAGES 386

European Languages and Management Studies *see* LANGUAGES 386

European Law *see* LAW 393

European Legal Studies *see* LAW 393

European Philosophy *see* PHILOSOPHY 478

European Policy Studies *see* SOCIAL and PUBLIC POLICY and ADMINISTRATION 529

European Politics *see* EUROPEAN STUDIES 307, POLITICS 507

European Politics and International Relations *see* EUROPEAN STUDIES 307, INTERNATIONAL RELATIONS 378, POLITICS 507

European Politics French/German/Italian *see* POLITICS 507

European Politics, Society and Economics *see* EUROPEAN STUDIES 307, POLITICS 507

European Social and Political Studies *see* EUROPEAN STUDIES 307, POLITICS 507

EUROPEAN STUDIES 307

European Studies (French/German/Italian/Spanish) *see* EUROPEAN STUDIES 307, FRENCH 325, GERMAN 337, ITALIAN 381, SPANISH 543

European Studies (French/German/Spanish) *see* EUROPEAN STUDIES 307

European Studies (Humanities) *see* EUROPEAN STUDIES 307

European Studies (Social Sciences) *see* EUROPEAN STUDIES 307

European Studies French/German/Spanish *see* LANGUAGES 386

European Studies with a Modern Language *see* EUROPEAN STUDIES 307, LANGUAGES 386

European Studies with French *see* EUROPEAN STUDIES 307, FRENCH 325

European Studies with French/German/Italian/Spanish *see* EUROPEAN STUDIES 307, LANGUAGES 386

European Studies with Languages *see* EUROPEAN STUDIES 307, LANGUAGES 386

European Theatre Arts *see* DRAMA 239

Event Management *see* BUSINESS AND MANAGEMENT COURSES (SPECIALISED) 193, HOSPITALITY and HOTEL MANAGEMENT 367

Event Management and Hospitality Management *see* HOSPITALITY and HOTEL MANAGEMENT 367

Events and Festival Management *see* HOSPITALITY and HOTEL MANAGEMENT 367

Events and Leisure Management *see* LEISURE and RECREATION MANAGEMENT/STUDIES 405

Events Management *see* BUSINESS AND MANAGEMENT COURSES 179, BUSINESS AND MANAGEMENT COURSES (SPECIALISED) 193, HOSPITALITY and HOTEL MANAGEMENT 367, MARKETING 415

Events Management and Marketing *see* HOSPITALITY and HOTEL MANAGEMENT 367, MARKETING 415

Events Management and Public Relations *see* HOSPITALITY and HOTEL MANAGEMENT 367

Events Management with Arts and Entertainment *see* BUSINESS AND MANAGEMENT COURSES (SPECIALISED) 193, LEISURE and RECREATION MANAGEMENT/STUDIES 405

Events Management with Tourism and Destinations *see* BUSINESS AND MANAGEMENT COURSES (SPECIALISED) 193, TOURISM and TRAVEL 564

Evolutionary Anthropology *see* ANTHROPOLOGY 127

Evolutionary Biology *see* BIOLOGY 170

Exercise and Sport Sciences *see* SPORTS SCIENCES/ STUDIES 548

Exercise Health (Health and Rehabilitation) *see* HEALTH SCIENCES/STUDIES 341

Exercise, Nutrition and Health *see* HEALTH SCIENCES/ STUDIES 341, NUTRITION 466

Exercise, Physical Activity and Health *see* HEALTH SCIENCES/STUDIES 341

Exhibition and Retail Design *see* ART and DESIGN (Product and Industrial Design) 152

Experimental Psychology *see* PSYCHOLOGY 512

Exploration and Resource Geology *see* GEOLOGY/ GEOLOGICAL SCIENCES 335

Exploration and Resource Geology (International) *see* GEOLOGY/GEOLOGICAL SCIENCES 335

Extended Health Biosciences *see* BIOLOGICAL SCIENCES 165

Farm Business Management *see* AGRICULTURAL SCIENCES/AGRICULTURE 117

Fashion *see* ART and DESIGN (Fashion and Textiles) 140

Fashion (Concepts and Communication) *see* ART and DESIGN (Fashion and Textiles) 140

Fashion (Design and Realisation) *see* ART and DESIGN (Fashion and Textiles) 140

Fashion (Footwear and Accessories) *see* ART and DESIGN (Fashion and Textiles) 140

Fashion Accessories *see* ART and DESIGN (Fashion and Textiles)140

Fashion Accessory Design *see* ART and DESIGN (Fashion and Textiles) 140

Fashion and Contour Design *see* ART and DESIGN (Fashion and Textiles) 140

Fashion and Costume for Performance *see* ART and DESIGN (Fashion and Textiles) 140

Fashion and Dress History *see* ART and DESIGN (Fashion and Textiles) 140, HISTORY OF ART 363

Fashion and Textile Buying *see* ART and DESIGN (Fashion and Textiles) 140

Fashion and Textile Design *see* ART and DESIGN (Fashion and Textiles) 140

Fashion and Textile Design with Enterprise *see* ART and DESIGN (Fashion and Textiles) 140

Fashion and Textile Management *see* ART and DESIGN (Fashion and Textiles) 140

Fashion and Textiles *see* ART and DESIGN (Fashion and Textiles) 140

Fashion and Textiles Design *see* ART and DESIGN (Fashion and Textiles) 140

Fashion Atelier *see* ART and DESIGN (Fashion and Textiles) 140

Fashion Brand Management *see* ART and DESIGN (Fashion and Textiles) 140

Fashion Business *see* ART and DESIGN (Fashion and Textiles) 140, BUSINESS AND MANAGEMENT COURSES (SPECIALISED) 193

Fashion Buying *see* RETAIL MANAGEMENT 524

Fashion Buying and Merchandising *see* ART and DESIGN (Fashion and Textiles) 140

Fashion Communication *see* ART and DESIGN (Fashion and Textiles) 140, COMMUNICATION STUDIES/ COMMUNICATION 214

Fashion Communication and Promotion *see* ART and DESIGN (Fashion and Textiles) 140, MARKETING 415, MEDIA STUDIES 427

Fashion Contour *see* ART and DESIGN (Fashion and Textiles) 140

Fashion Design *see* ART and DESIGN (Fashion and Textiles) 140

Fashion Design and Development *see* ART and DESIGN (Fashion and Textiles) 140

Fashion Design and Technology *see* ART and DESIGN (Fashion and Textiles) 140, TECHNOLOGIES 562

Fashion Design Marketing and Production *see* ART and DESIGN (Fashion and Textiles) 140

Fashion Design Realisation *see* ART and DESIGN (Fashion and Textiles) 140

Fashion Design Technology: Menswear *see* ART and DESIGN (Fashion and Textiles) 140

Fashion Design Technology: Womenswear *see* ART and DESIGN (Fashion and Textiles) 140

Fashion Design with Business *see* ART and DESIGN (Fashion and Textiles) 140, BUSINESS AND MANAGEMENT COURSES 179

Fashion Design with Textiles *see* ART and DESIGN (Fashion and Textiles) 140

Fashion Enterprise *see* ART and DESIGN (Fashion and Textiles) 140

Fashion Fabrics and Accessories *see* ART and DESIGN (Fashion and Textiles) 140

Fashion Graphics *see* ART and DESIGN (Fashion and Textiles) 140

Fashion Illustration *see* ART and DESIGN (Fashion and Textiles) 140

Fashion Jewellery *see* ART and DESIGN (Fashion and Textiles) 140

Fashion Journalism *see* ART and DESIGN (Fashion and Textiles) 140, MEDIA STUDIES 427

Fashion Journalism (Print/Broadcast) *see* ART and DESIGN (Fashion and Textiles) 140, MEDIA STUDIES 427

Fashion Knitwear Design and Knitted Textiles *see* ART and DESIGN (Fashion and Textiles) 140

Fashion Lifestyle Products *see* ART and DESIGN (Fashion and Textiles) 140

Fashion Management *see* ART and DESIGN (Fashion and Textiles) 140, BUSINESS AND MANAGEMENT COURSES (SPECIALISED) 193

Fashion Management and Marketing *see* BUSINESS AND MANAGEMENT COURSES (SPECIALISED) 193, MARKETING 415

Fashion Marketing *see* ART and DESIGN (Fashion and Textiles) 140, MARKETING 415, RETAIL MANAGEMENT 524

Fashion Marketing and Branding *see* ART and DESIGN (Fashion and Textiles) 140, MARKETING 415

Fashion Media *see* ART and DESIGN (Fashion and Textiles) 140, MEDIA STUDIES 427

Fashion Media and Promotion *see* ART and DESIGN (Fashion and Textiles) 140

Fashion Menswear *see* ART and DESIGN (Fashion and Textiles) 140

Fashion Merchandise Management *see* ART and DESIGN (Fashion and Textiles) 140

Fashion Photography *see* ART and DESIGN (Fashion and Textiles) 140, PHOTOGRAPHY 481

Fashion Product and Promotion *see* MARKETING 415

Fashion Product Development *see* ART and DESIGN (Fashion and Textiles) 140

Fashion Promotion *see* ART and DESIGN (Fashion and Textiles) 140, MARKETING 415

Fashion Promotion and Imaging *see* ART and DESIGN (Fashion and Textiles) 140, MARKETING 415

Fashion Promotion with Styling *see* ART and DESIGN (Fashion and Textiles) 140

Fashion Public Relations *see* ART and DESIGN (Fashion and Textiles) 140, BUSINESS AND MANAGEMENT COURSES (SPECIALISED) 193

Fashion Retail Management *see* ART and DESIGN (Fashion and Textiles) 140, BUSINESS AND MANAGEMENT COURSES 179, RETAIL MANAGEMENT 524

Fashion Sportswear *see* ART and DESIGN (Fashion and Textiles) 140

Fashion Studies *see* ART and DESIGN (Fashion and Textiles) 140

Fashion Technology *see* ART and DESIGN (Fashion and Textiles) 140, MATERIALS SCIENCE/ METALLURGY 419

Fashion Textiles *see* ART and DESIGN (Fashion and Textiles) 140

Fashion Textiles Retailing *see* ART and DESIGN (Fashion and Textiles) 140, RETAIL MANAGEMENT 524

Fashion with Business Studies *see* ART and DESIGN (Fashion and Textiles) 140, BUSINESS AND MANAGEMENT COURSES 179

Fashion with Photography *see* PHOTOGRAPHY 481

Fashion with Public Relations *see* ART and DESIGN (Fashion and Textiles) 140

Fashion Womenswear *see* ART and DESIGN (Fashion and Textiles) 140

Fashion, Interior Art and Textiles *see* ART and DESIGN (Fashion and Textiles) 140

Fashion, Marketing and Retailing *see* RETAIL MANAGEMENT 524

Fashion: Apparel Design and Construction *see* ART and DESIGN (Fashion and Textiles) 140

Film *see* FILM, RADIO, VIDEO and TV STUDIES 310

Film and Television Studies *see* FILM, RADIO, VIDEO and TV STUDIES 310

Film and American Studies/English Studies/
Television Studies *see* COMBINED COURSES 212,
FILM, RADIO, VIDEO and TV STUDIES 310

Film and English *see* ENGLISH 296, FILM, RADIO,
VIDEO and TV STUDIES 310

Film and French/German/Spanish *see* FILM, RADIO,
VIDEO and TV STUDIES 310, FRENCH 325,
GERMAN 337, SPANISH 543

Film and History *see* FILM, RADIO, VIDEO and TV
STUDIES 310, HISTORY 355

Film and Literature *see* FILM, RADIO, VIDEO and TV
STUDIES 310, LITERATURE 409

Film and Media *see* FILM, RADIO, VIDEO and TV
STUDIES 310, MEDIA STUDIES 427

Film and Media Production *see* FILM, RADIO, VIDEO
and TV STUDIES 310

Film and Media Studies *see* FILM, RADIO, VIDEO and
TV STUDIES 310, MEDIA STUDIES 427

Film and Movie Image Production *see* ART and
DESIGN (Graphic Design) 148, FILM, RADIO,
VIDEO and TV STUDIES 310

Film and Moving Image Production *see* FILM, RADIO,
VIDEO and TV STUDIES 310

Film and Philosophy *see* FILM, RADIO, VIDEO and TV
STUDIES 310, PHILOSOPHY 478

Film and Popular Culture *see* FILM, RADIO, VIDEO and
TV STUDIES 310

Film and Screen Studies *see* FILM, RADIO, VIDEO and
TV STUDIES 310

Film and Screenwriting *see* FILM, RADIO, VIDEO and
TV STUDIES 310

Film and Television *see* FILM, RADIO, VIDEO and TV
STUDIES 310

Film and Television (Fiction/Documentary/
Entertainment) *see* FILM, RADIO, VIDEO and TV
STUDIES 310

Film and Television and Journalism *see* FILM, RADIO,
VIDEO and TV STUDIES 310, MEDIA STUDIES 427

Film and Television Production *see* FILM, RADIO,
VIDEO and TV STUDIES 310

Film and Television Studies *see* FILM, RADIO, VIDEO
and TV STUDIES 310

Film and Television Studies and American Studies *see*
FILM, RADIO, VIDEO and TV STUDIES 310

Film and Television Studies and Cultural Sociology
see FILM, RADIO, VIDEO and TV STUDIES 310,
SOCIOLOGY 539

Film and Television Studies and French *see* FILM,
RADIO, VIDEO and TV STUDIES 310, FRENCH 325

Film and Television Studies and German *see* FILM,
RADIO, VIDEO and TV STUDIES 310, GERMAN 337

Film and Television Studies and Hispanic Studies
see FILM, RADIO, VIDEO and TV STUDIES 310,
SPANISH 543

Film and Television Studies and Music *see*
FILM, RADIO, VIDEO and TV STUDIES 310,
MUSIC 449

Film and Television Studies and Russian *see* FILM,
RADIO, VIDEO and TV STUDIES 310, RUSSIAN and
EAST EUROPEAN STUDIES 526

Film and Television with French/Spanish/Japanese
see FILM, RADIO, VIDEO and TV STUDIES 310,
FRENCH 325, JAPANESE 383, SPANISH 543

Film and Theatre *see* FILM, RADIO, VIDEO and TV
STUDIES 310

Film and TV Production *see* FILM, RADIO, VIDEO and
TV STUDIES 310

Film and TV Screenwriting *see* FILM, RADIO, VIDEO
and TV STUDIES 310

Film and TV Studies *see* FILM, RADIO, VIDEO and TV
STUDIES 310

Film and Video *see* FILM, RADIO, VIDEO and TV
STUDIES 310

Film and Video (Theory and Practice) *see* FILM,
RADIO, VIDEO and TV STUDIES 310

Film and Video Production *see* FILM, RADIO, VIDEO
and TV STUDIES 310

Film and Visual Culture *see* FILM, RADIO, VIDEO and
TV STUDIES 310

Film Animation *see* ART and DESIGN (Graphic
Design) 148

Film Animation and Musical Entertainment *see* FILM,
RADIO, VIDEO and TV STUDIES 310

Film Media *see* FILM, RADIO, VIDEO and TV
STUDIES 310, MEDIA STUDIES 427

Film Media and Culture Studies *see* FILM, RADIO,
VIDEO and TV STUDIES 310

Film Production *see* FILM, RADIO, VIDEO and TV
STUDIES 310

Film Production and Cinematography *see* FILM,
RADIO, VIDEO and TV STUDIES 310

Film Script Studies *see* FILM, RADIO, VIDEO and TV
STUDIES 310

Film Studies *see* FILM, RADIO, VIDEO and TV
STUDIES 310

Film Studies (European) and a Modern Language
see FILM, RADIO, VIDEO and TV STUDIES 310,
LANGUAGES 386

Film Studies and Creative Writing *see* FILM, RADIO,
VIDEO and TV STUDIES 310

Film Studies and English Literature *see* FILM, RADIO,
VIDEO and TV STUDIES 310, LITERATURE 409

Film Studies and Literature *see* FILM, RADIO, VIDEO and TV STUDIES 310, LITERATURE 409

Film Studies and Media Communications *see* FILM, RADIO, VIDEO and TV STUDIES 310, PHOTOGRAPHY 481

Film Studies and Media Writing *see* FILM, RADIO, VIDEO and TV STUDIES 310

Film Studies and Philosophy *see* FILM, RADIO, VIDEO and TV STUDIES 310, PHILOSOPHY 478

Film Studies and Photography and Video *see* FILM, RADIO, VIDEO and TV STUDIES 310

Film Studies and Screen Writing *see* FILM, RADIO, VIDEO and TV STUDIES 310

Film Studies and Sociology *see* FILM, RADIO, VIDEO and TV STUDIES 310, SOCIOLOGY 539

Film Studies and the Visual Arts *see* FILM, RADIO, VIDEO and TV STUDIES 310

Film Studies Combined Honours *see* FILM, RADIO, VIDEO and TV STUDIES 310

Film Studies with English/Media/Script Writing *see* FILM, RADIO, VIDEO and TV STUDIES 310, MEDIA STUDIES 427

Film, Music and Soundtrack Production *see* FILM, RADIO, VIDEO and TV STUDIES 310, MUSIC 449

FILM, RADIO, VIDEO and TV STUDIES 310
  see also COMMUNICATION STUDIES/ COMMUNICATION
  see also MEDIA STUDIES
  see also PHOTOGRAPHY

Film, Television and Cultural Studies *see* FILM, RADIO, VIDEO and TV STUDIES 310

Film, Television and Radio Studies *see* FILM, RADIO, VIDEO and TV STUDIES 310

Filmmaking *see* FILM, RADIO, VIDEO and TV STUDIES 310

Filmmaking and Screenwriting *see* FILM, RADIO, VIDEO and TV STUDIES 310

FINANCE 315
  see also ACCOUNTANCY/ACCOUNTING

Finance and Accountancy for Financial Services *see* ACCOUNTANCY/ACCOUNTING 109, FINANCE 315

Finance and Accounting *see* ACCOUNTANCY/ ACCOUNTING 109, FINANCE 315

Finance and Business *see* BUSINESS AND MANAGEMENT COURSES 179, FINANCE 315

Finance and Economics *see* ECONOMICS 251, FINANCE 315

Finance and Investment *see* FINANCE 315

Finance and Investment Banking *see* FINANCE 315

Finance and Investment Management *see* FINANCE 315

Finance and Management *see* BUSINESS AND MANAGEMENT COURSES 179, FINANCE 315

Finance and Management Studies *see* FINANCE 315

Finance and Statistics *see* FINANCE 315, STATISTICS 554

Finance Management *see* FINANCE 315

Finance with Economics *see* ECONOMICS 251, FINANCE 315

Finance with Mathematics *see* FINANCE 315, MATHEMATICS 422

Finance, Accounting and Management *see* ACCOUNTANCY/ACCOUNTING 109, FINANCE 315

Finance, Investment and Risk *see* FINANCE 315

Finance, Money and Banking *see* FINANCE 315

Financial Analysis and Risk *see* ACCOUNTANCY/ ACCOUNTING 109, FINANCE 315

Financial and Business Economics *see* BUSINESS AND MANAGEMENT COURSES 179, ECONOMICS 251, FINANCE 315

Financial Economics *see* ECONOMICS 251, FINANCE 315

Financial Investment *see* FINANCE 315

Financial Management *see* FINANCE 315

Financial Mathematics *see* FINANCE 315, MATHEMATICS 422

Financial Mathematics and Management *see* FINANCE 315, MATHEMATICS 422

Financial Planning *see* FINANCE 315

Financial Service Management *see* FINANCE 315

Financial Services *see* FINANCE 315

Financial Services, Planning and Management *see* FINANCE 315

Fine and Applied Arts *see* ART and DESIGN (Fine Art) 144

Fine Applied Arts *see* ART and DESIGN (Fine Art) 144

Fine Art *see* ART and DESIGN (Fine Art) 144, FILM, RADIO, VIDEO and TV STUDIES 310

Fine Art (3D and Sculptural Practice) *see* ART and DESIGN (3D Design) 156

Fine Art (Combined Media) *see* ART and DESIGN (Fine Art) 144

Fine Art (Contemporary Practice) *see* ART and DESIGN (Fine Art) 144

Fine Art (Integrated Media) *see* ART and DESIGN (Fine Art) 144

Fine Art (Painting and Drawing) *see* ART and DESIGN (Fine Art) 144

Fine Art (Painting, Drawing and Printmaking) *see* ART and DESIGN (Fine Art) 144

Fine Art (Painting/Printmaking) *see* ART and DESIGN (Fine Art) 144

Fine Art (Photography) see ART and DESIGN
(Fine Art) 144, PHOTOGRAPHY 481
Fine Art (Post Foundation) see ART and DESIGN
(Fine Art) 144
Fine Art (Sculpture and Environmental Art) see ART
and DESIGN (Fine Art) 144
Fine Art and Art History see ART and DESIGN
(Fine Art) 144, HISTORY OF ART 363
Fine Art and Crafts see ART and DESIGN (Fine Art) 144
Fine Art and Professional Practice see ART and
DESIGN (Fine Art) 144
Fine Art Painting see ART and DESIGN (Fine Art) 144
Fine Art Painting and Drawing see ART and DESIGN
(Fine Art) 144
Fine Art Photography see ART and DESIGN
(Fine Art) 144, PHOTOGRAPHY 481
Fine Art Practice see ART and DESIGN
(Fine Art) 144
Fine Art Sculpting see ART and DESIGN
(Fine Art) 144
Fine Art Sculpture see ART and DESIGN
(3D Design) 156, ART and DESIGN (Fine Art) 144
Fine Art Textiles see ART and DESIGN (Fashion
and Textiles) 140, ART and DESIGN
(Fine Art) 144
Fine Arts see ART and DESIGN (Fine Art) 144
Finnish see LANGUAGES 386
Fire Safety and Risk Management see BUILDING
and CONSTRUCTION 176, BUSINESS AND
MANAGEMENT COURSES (SPECIALISED) 193,
ENGINEERING (CHEMICAL) 269
Fire Safety Engineering see ENGINEERING
(CHEMICAL) 269
Fitness and Health see HEALTH SCIENCES/STUDIES 341
Folk and Traditional Music see MUSIC 449
Food and Consumer Management see BUSINESS
AND MANAGEMENT COURSES (SPECIALISED)
193, CONSUMER STUDIES/SCIENCES 226, FOOD
SCIENCE/STUDIES and TECHNOLOGY 321
Food and Consumer Science see CONSUMER STUDIES/
SCIENCES 226, FOOD SCIENCE/STUDIES and
TECHNOLOGY 321
Food and Consumer Studies see CONSUMER STUDIES/
SCIENCES 226
Food and Human Nutrition see NUTRITION 466
Food and Media and Communication Management
see BUSINESS AND MANAGEMENT COURSES
(SPECIALISED) 193, FOOD SCIENCE/STUDIES and
TECHNOLOGY 321
Food and Nutrition see FOOD SCIENCE/STUDIES and
TECHNOLOGY 321, NUTRITION 466

Food and Product Design see ART and DESIGN
(Product and Industrial Design) 152, FOOD
SCIENCE/STUDIES and TECHNOLOGY 321
Food and Tourism Management see FOOD SCIENCE/
STUDIES and TECHNOLOGY 321, TOURISM and
TRAVEL 564
Food Bioscience see FOOD SCIENCE/STUDIES and
TECHNOLOGY 321
Food Consumer and Retail Management see FOOD
SCIENCE/STUDIES and TECHNOLOGY 321
Food Management and Marketing see FOOD
SCIENCE/STUDIES and TECHNOLOGY 321
Food Management and Promotion see BUSINESS AND
MANAGEMENT COURSES (SPECIALISED) 193
Food Marketing and Business Economics see
ECONOMICS 251, FOOD SCIENCE/STUDIES and
TECHNOLOGY 321
Food Marketing and Management see FOOD
SCIENCE/STUDIES and TECHNOLOGY 321
Food Marketing and Nutrition see FOOD SCIENCE/
STUDIES and TECHNOLOGY 321, NUTRITION 466
Food Marketing Management see FOOD SCIENCE/
STUDIES and TECHNOLOGY 321
Food Microbiology see FOOD SCIENCE/STUDIES and
TECHNOLOGY 321
Food Nutrition and Health see FOOD SCIENCE/STUDIES
and TECHNOLOGY 321, NUTRITION 466
Food Product and Supply Management see FOOD
SCIENCE/STUDIES and TECHNOLOGY 321
Food Quality, Safety and Nutrition see FOOD
SCIENCE/STUDIES and TECHNOLOGY 321,
NUTRITION 466
Food Science see FOOD SCIENCE/STUDIES and
TECHNOLOGY 321, NUTRITION 466
Food Science and Business see FOOD SCIENCE/
STUDIES and TECHNOLOGY 321
Food Science and Microbiology see FOOD SCIENCE/
STUDIES and TECHNOLOGY 321,
MICROBIOLOGY 447
Food Science and Nutrition see FOOD SCIENCE/
STUDIES and TECHNOLOGY 321, NUTRITION 466
Food Science and Technology see FOOD SCIENCE/
STUDIES and TECHNOLOGY 321
Food Science Technology see FOOD SCIENCE/STUDIES
and TECHNOLOGY 321
FOOD SCIENCE/STUDIES and TECHNOLOGY 321
see also AGRICULTURAL SCIENCES/AGRICULTURE
see also BIOCHEMISTRY
see also CONSUMER STUDIES/SCIENCES
see also DIETETICS
see also NUTRITION

Food Studies and Nutrition *see* NUTRITION 466

Food Technology *see* FOOD SCIENCE/STUDIES and TECHNOLOGY 321

Food with Nutrition *see* FOOD SCIENCE/STUDIES and TECHNOLOGY 321, NUTRITION 466

Food, Design and Nutrition *see* FOOD SCIENCE/STUDIES and TECHNOLOGY 321, NUTRITION 466

Food, Nutrition and Health *see* FOOD SCIENCE/STUDIES and TECHNOLOGY 321, NUTRITION 466

Food, Nutrition and Health Science *see* FOOD SCIENCE/STUDIES and TECHNOLOGY 321, HEALTH SCIENCES/STUDIES 341, NUTRITION 466

Food, Nutrition and Wellbeing *see* NUTRITION 466

Football Studies *see* SPORTS SCIENCES/STUDIES 548

Football, Business and Finance *see* FINANCE 315

Footwear Design *see* ART and DESIGN (Product and Industrial Design) 152

Forensic Accounting *see* ACCOUNTANCY/ ACCOUNTING 109

Forensic and Analytical Science *see* BIOLOGICAL SCIENCES 165

Forensic and Investigative Chemistry *see* CHEMISTRY 199

Forensic and Medical Sciences *see* BIOLOGICAL SCIENCES 165

Forensic Anthropology *see* ANTHROPOLOGY 127, BIOLOGICAL SCIENCES 165

Forensic Biology *see* BIOLOGICAL SCIENCES 165, BIOLOGY 170

Forensic Chemistry *see* CHEMISTRY 199

Forensic Engineering *see* ENGINEERING/ENGINEERING SCIENCES 260

Forensic Investigation *see* BIOLOGY 170

Forensic Molecular Biology *see* BIOLOGICAL SCIENCES 165

Forensic Psychobiology *see* BIOLOGICAL SCIENCES 165, PSYCHOLOGY 512

Forensic Psychology *see* PSYCHOLOGY 512

Forensic Psychology and Criminal Justice *see* PSYCHOLOGY 512, SOCIAL SCIENCES/STUDIES 531

Forensic Science *see* BIOLOGICAL SCIENCES 165, BIOLOGY 170, HUMAN SCIENCES/HUMAN BIOSCIENCES 374, MEDICINE 433

Forensic Science (Physical) *see* BIOLOGICAL SCIENCES 165

Forensic Science with Anthropology *see* ANTHROPOLOGY 127

Forensic Science with Criminal Justice *see* BIOLOGY 170, PSYCHOLOGY 512

Forensic Science with Criminology *see* BIOLOGICAL SCIENCES 165, SOCIAL SCIENCES/STUDIES 531

Forensic Science/Psychology *see* BIOLOGICAL SCIENCES 165, PSYCHOLOGY 512

Forensic Sciences *see* BIOLOGICAL SCIENCES 165

Forest and Woodland Management *see* FORESTRY 324

Forest Sciences *see* FORESTRY 324

FORESTRY 324

    see also AGRICULTURAL SCIENCES/AGRICULTURE

Forestry and Woodland Conservation *see* FORESTRY 324

FRENCH 325

    see also EUROPEAN STUDIES

    see also LANGUAGES

French (Licence de Lettres) *see* FRENCH 325

French and a Modern Language *see* FRENCH 325, LANGUAGES 386

French and German *see* FRENCH 325, GERMAN 337

French and History *see* FRENCH 325

French and Latin *see* FRENCH 325, LATIN 389

French and Management *see* FRENCH 325

French and Primary Teaching *see* EDUCATION STUDIES 256, FRENCH 325, TEACHER TRAINING 559

French and Spanish *see* FRENCH 325, SPANISH 543

French Studies *see* COMBINED COURSES 212, FRENCH 325

French Studies and Modern Languages *see* FRENCH 325, LANGUAGES 386

French Studies with German/Italian *see* FRENCH 325, GERMAN 337, ITALIAN 381

French with Business *see* BUSINESS AND MANAGEMENT COURSES 179, FRENCH 325

French/German with Statistics *see* FRENCH 325, GERMAN 337, STATISTICS 554

French/German/Hispanic Studies and Philosophy *see* FRENCH 325

French/German/Russian and Drama *see* DRAMA 239, LANGUAGES 386

French/German/Spanish Linguistics *see* LINGUISTICS 407

Furniture and Product Design *see* ART and DESIGN (Product and Industrial Design) 152

Furniture Design *see* ART and DESIGN (Product and Industrial Design) 152

Furniture Product Design *see* ART and DESIGN (Product and Industrial Design) 152

Gaelic *see* CELTIC, IRISH, SCOTTISH AND WELSH STUDIES 197

Gaelic and Development *see* CELTIC, IRISH, SCOTTISH AND WELSH STUDIES 197, DEVELOPMENT STUDIES 235

Gaelic and Media Studies *see* CELTIC, IRISH, SCOTTISH AND WELSH STUDIES 197, MEDIA STUDIES 427

Gaelic and Traditional Music *see* CELTIC, IRISH, SCOTTISH AND WELSH STUDIES 197, MUSIC 449

Gaelic Language and Culture *see* CELTIC, IRISH, SCOTTISH AND WELSH STUDIES 197

Gaelic Studies *see* CELTIC, IRISH, SCOTTISH AND WELSH STUDIES 197

Games and Multimedia Environments *see* COMPUTER COURSES 219

Games Art and Design *see* COMPUTER COURSES 219

Games Design *see* COMPUTER COURSES 219

Games Design and Development *see* COMPUTER COURSES 219

Games Design and English *see* ENGINEERING (COMPUTER, CONTROL, SOFTWARE and SYSTEMS) 280, ENGLISH 296

Games Design and Film and Television Studies *see* ENGINEERING (COMPUTER, CONTROL, SOFTWARE and SYSTEMS) 280, FILM, RADIO, VIDEO and TV STUDIES 310

Games Design and Sonic Arts *see* ENGINEERING (ACOUSTICS and SOUND) 264, ENGINEERING (COMPUTER, CONTROL, SOFTWARE and SYSTEMS) 280

Games Development *see* COMPUTER COURSES 219

Games Software Development *see* ENGINEERING (COMPUTER, CONTROL, SOFTWARE and SYSTEMS) 280

Games Technology *see* COMPUTER COURSES 219

Garden Art and Design *see* LANDSCAPE ARCHITECTURE 384

Garden Design *see* HORTICULTURE 365, LANDSCAPE ARCHITECTURE 384

Garden Design, Restoration and Management *see* LANDSCAPE ARCHITECTURE 384

General Arts and Science *see* COMBINED COURSES 212

General Engineering *see* ENGINEERING/ENGINEERING SCIENCES 260

General Illustration *see* ART and DESIGN (Graphic Design) 148

GENETICS 328

see also BIOLOGICAL SCIENCES

Genetics (Immunology) *see* GENETICS 328

Genetics and Biochemistry *see* BIOCHEMISTRY 162, GENETICS 328

Genetics and Human Health *see* GENETICS 328, HUMAN SCIENCES/HUMAN BIOSCIENCES 374

Genetics and Microbiology *see* GENETICS 328, MICROBIOLOGY 447

Genetics and Molecular Biology *see* BIOLOGY 170, GENETICS 328

Genetics and Psychology *see* GENETICS 328, PSYCHOLOGY 512

Genetics with a Modern Language *see* GENETICS 328, LANGUAGES 386

Genetics with Molecular Cell Biology *see* GENETICS 328, MICROBIOLOGY 447

Geochemistry *see* GEOLOGY/GEOLOGICAL SCIENCES 335

Geographic Information Systems *see* GEOGRAPHY 330

Geographical Information Systems *see* GEOGRAPHY 330

GEOGRAPHY 330

see also BUSINESS and MANAGEMENT COURSES (SPECIALISED)

Geography (Arts/Science) *see* GEOGRAPHY 330

Geography (Combined) *see* GEOGRAPHY 330

Geography (Human) *see* GEOGRAPHY 330

Geography (Human) and Planning *see* GEOGRAPHY 330, TOWN and COUNTRY PLANNING 567

Geography (Physical) *see* GEOGRAPHY 330

Geography and a Language *see* GEOGRAPHY 330, LANGUAGES 386

Geography and Anthropology *see* ANTHROPOLOGY 127, GEOGRAPHY 330

Geography and Archaeology *see* ARCHAEOLOGY 131, GEOGRAPHY 330

Geography and Development Studies *see* DEVELOPMENT STUDIES 235, GEOGRAPHY 330

Geography and Economics *see* ECONOMICS 251, GEOGRAPHY 330

Geography and Economics (Regional Science) *see* ECONOMICS 251, GEOGRAPHY 330

Geography and Environment Management *see* ENVIRONMENTAL SCIENCES/STUDIES 303, GEOGRAPHY 330

Geography and Environmental Management *see* ENVIRONMENTAL SCIENCES/STUDIES 303, GEOGRAPHY 330

Geography and Environmental Science *see* ENVIRONMENTAL SCIENCES/STUDIES 303, GEOGRAPHY 330

Geography and Geoinformatics *see* GEOGRAPHY 330

Geography and Geology *see* GEOGRAPHY 330, GEOLOGY/GEOLOGICAL SCIENCES 335

Geography and International Development *see* DEVELOPMENT STUDIES 235, GEOGRAPHY 330

Geography and International Relations *see* GEOGRAPHY 330, INTERNATIONAL RELATIONS 378

Geography and Media Arts *see* GEOGRAPHY 330, MEDIA STUDIES 427

Geography and Planning *see* GEOGRAPHY 330, TOWN and COUNTRY PLANNING 567

Geography and Politics *see* GEOGRAPHY 330, POLITICS 507

Geography and Social Policy *see* GEOGRAPHY 330, SOCIAL and PUBLIC POLICY and ADMINISTRATION 529

Geography and Sport Management *see* GEOGRAPHY 330

Geography and Sport Science *see* GEOGRAPHY 330, SPORTS SCIENCES/STUDIES 548

Geography and Tourism Management *see* GEOGRAPHY 330, TOURISM and TRAVEL 564

Geography and Transport Planning *see* TRANSPORT MANAGEMENT and PLANNING 571

Geography and Urban and Regional Planning *see* GEOGRAPHY 330, TOWN and COUNTRY PLANNING 567

Geography and Urban and Regional Planning (Joint Honours) *see* TOWN and COUNTRY PLANNING 567

Geography with a Language *see* GEOGRAPHY 330, LANGUAGES 386

Geography with Business *see* BUSINESS AND MANAGEMENT COURSES 179, GEOGRAPHY 330

Geography with Chinese Studies *see* CHINESE 206, GEOGRAPHY 330

Geography with Earth Science *see* ENVIRONMENTAL SCIENCES/STUDIES 303, GEOGRAPHY 330

Geography with English *see* GEOGRAPHY 330

Geography with Environmental Studies *see* ENVIRONMENTAL SCIENCES/STUDIES 303, GEOGRAPHY 330

Geography with European Management *see* GEOGRAPHY 330

Geography with European Studies *see* EUROPEAN STUDIES 307, GEOGRAPHY 330

Geography with Geology *see* GEOGRAPHY 330, GEOLOGY/GEOLOGICAL SCIENCES 335

Geography with International Studies *see* GEOGRAPHY 330

Geography with Marine Studies *see* GEOGRAPHY 330, MARINE/MARITIME STUDIES 412

Geography with Mountain Leadership *see* GEOGRAPHY 330

Geography with Oceanography *see* GEOGRAPHY 330, MARINE/MARITIME STUDIES 412

Geography with Politics and International Relations *see* GEOGRAPHY 330, INTERNATIONAL RELATIONS 378, POLITICS 507

Geography with Psychology *see* GEOGRAPHY 330, PSYCHOLOGY 512

Geography with Scottish History *see* CELTIC, IRISH, SCOTTISH AND WELSH STUDIES 197, GEOGRAPHY 330

Geography with Sports Science *see* GEOGRAPHY 330, SPORTS SCIENCES/STUDIES 548

Geological Hazards *see* GEOLOGY/GEOLOGICAL SCIENCES 335

Geological Oceanography *see* GEOLOGY/GEOLOGICAL SCIENCES 335, MARINE/MARITIME STUDIES 412

Geological Science *see* GEOLOGY/GEOLOGICAL SCIENCES 335

Geological Science (International) *see* GEOLOGY/GEOLOGICAL SCIENCES 335

GEOLOGY/GEOLOGICAL SCIENCES 335
   see also ENVIRONMENTAL SCIENCES/STUDIES
   see also GEOGRAPHY

Geology (International) *see* GEOLOGY/GEOLOGICAL SCIENCES 335

Geology and Archaeology *see* ARCHAEOLOGY 131, GEOLOGY/GEOLOGICAL SCIENCES 335

Geology and Biology *see* BIOTECHNOLOGY 174, GEOLOGY/GEOLOGICAL SCIENCES 335

Geology and Geography *see* GEOGRAPHY 330, GEOLOGY/GEOLOGICAL SCIENCES 335

Geology and Geophysics *see* GEOLOGY/GEOLOGICAL SCIENCES 335

Geology and Ocean Science *see* GEOLOGY/GEOLOGICAL SCIENCES 335

Geology and Palaeontology *see* GEOLOGY/GEOLOGICAL SCIENCES 335

Geology and Physical Geography *see* GEOGRAPHY 330, GEOLOGY/GEOLOGICAL SCIENCES 335

Geology and Planetary Science *see* ASTRONOMY and ASTROPHYSICS 159, GEOLOGY/GEOLOGICAL SCIENCES 335

Geology Studies *see* GEOLOGY/GEOLOGICAL SCIENCES 335

Geology with Marine Biology *see* GEOLOGY/GEOLOGICAL SCIENCES 335, MARINE/MARITIME STUDIES 412

Geology with Physical Geography *see* GEOGRAPHY 330, GEOLOGY/GEOLOGICAL SCIENCES 335

Geophysical Science *see* GEOLOGY/GEOLOGICAL SCIENCES 335

Geophysical Science (International) *see* GEOLOGY/GEOLOGICAL SCIENCES 335

Geophysical Sciences *see* GEOLOGY/GEOLOGICAL SCIENCES 335

Geophysics *see* GEOLOGY/GEOLOGICAL SCIENCES 335, PHYSICS 488

Geophysics (Geology/Physics) *see* PHYSICS 488

Geophysics and Geology *see* GEOLOGY/GEOLOGICAL SCIENCES 335

Geophysics and Meteorology *see* GEOGRAPHY 330, GEOLOGY/GEOLOGICAL SCIENCES 335, PHYSICS 488

Geopolitics *see* GEOGRAPHY 330, POLITICS 507

Geoscience *see* GEOLOGY/GEOLOGICAL SCIENCES 335

GERMAN 337

   see also EUROPEAN STUDIES

   see also LANGUAGES

German and a Modern Language *see* GERMAN 337, LANGUAGES 386

German and Arabic *see* GERMAN 337

German and Business *see* BUSINESS AND MANAGEMENT COURSES 179, GERMAN 337

German and Business German *see* GERMAN 337

German and Comparative Literature *see* GERMAN 337, LITERATURE 409

German and International Relations *see* GERMAN 337, INTERNATIONAL RELATIONS 378

German and Latin *see* LATIN 389

German and Linguistics *see* GERMAN 337, LINGUISTICS 407

German and Marketing *see* GERMAN 337, MARKETING 415

German and Music *see* MUSIC 449

German and Tourism Management *see* GERMAN 337, TOURISM and TRAVEL 564

German and Translation Studies *see* GERMAN 337

German Studies *see* COMBINED COURSES 212, GERMAN 337

German Studies and Italian *see* GERMAN 337, ITALIAN 381

German Studies and Modern Languages *see* GERMAN 337, LANGUAGES 386

Glass *see* ART and DESIGN (3D Design) 156

Glass and Ceramics *see* ART and DESIGN (3D Design) 156

Global Business and Design Management *see* BUSINESS AND MANAGEMENT COURSES (INTERNATIONAL AND EUROPEAN) 188

Global Business and Sustainability Management *see* BUSINESS AND MANAGEMENT COURSES (INTERNATIONAL AND EUROPEAN) 188

Global Business Management *see* BUSINESS AND MANAGEMENT COURSES (INTERNATIONAL AND EUROPEAN) 188

Global Change: Environment, Economy and Development *see* ECONOMICS 251, ENVIRONMENTAL SCIENCES/STUDIES 303

Global Cinema and Culture *see* FILM, RADIO, VIDEO and TV STUDIES 310

Global Development and International Relations *see* DEVELOPMENT STUDIES 235, INTERNATIONAL RELATIONS 378

Global Development and Peace Studies *see* DEVELOPMENT STUDIES 235

Global Financial Management *see* FINANCE 315

Global Health and Humanitarian Relief *see* HEALTH SCIENCES/STUDIES 341

Global Health with Human Rights *see* HEALTH SCIENCES/STUDIES 341

Global Issues and Contemporary Chinese Studies *see* CHINESE 206, ENVIRONMENTAL SCIENCES/STUDIES 303

Global Marketing Management *see* MARKETING 415

Global Politics and International Relations *see* INTERNATIONAL RELATIONS 378, POLITICS 507

Global Studies *see* INTERNATIONAL RELATIONS 378

Golf Management *see* BUSINESS AND MANAGEMENT COURSES (SPECIALISED) 193

Golf Operation Management *see* LEISURE and RECREATION MANAGEMENT/STUDIES 405

Golf Science and Development *see* SPORTS SCIENCES/STUDIES 548

Government *see* POLITICS 507

Government and Economics *see* ECONOMICS 251, POLITICS 507

Government and European Union Studies *see* EUROPEAN STUDIES 307, POLITICS 507

Government and History *see* HISTORY 355, POLITICS 507

Government and Politics *see* POLITICS 507

Graphic and Communication Design *see* ART and DESIGN (Graphic Design) 148, COMMUNICATION STUDIES/COMMUNICATION 214

Graphic and Digital Design *see* ART and DESIGN (Graphic Design) 148

Graphic and Media Design *see* ART and DESIGN (Graphic Design) 148

Graphic Arts *see* ART and DESIGN (Graphic Design) 148

Graphic Arts and Design *see* ART and DESIGN (Graphic Design) 148

Graphic Communication *see* ART and DESIGN (Graphic Design) 148, COMMUNICATION STUDIES/COMMUNICATION 214

Graphic Communication and Illustration *see* ART and DESIGN (Graphic Design) 148

Graphic Communication with Typography *see* ART and DESIGN (Graphic Design) 148

Graphic Communications see ART and DESIGN (Graphic Design) 148

Graphic Design see ART and DESIGN (Graphic Design) 148

Graphic Design (Graphic Illustration) see ART and DESIGN (Graphic Design) 148

Graphic Design (Motion Graphics) see ART and DESIGN (Graphic Design) 148

Graphic Design and Contemporary Lens Media see ART and DESIGN (Graphic Design) 148

Graphic Design and Illustration see ART and DESIGN (Graphic Design) 148

Graphic Design and Interactive Media see ART and DESIGN (Graphic Design) 148, MEDIA STUDIES 427

Graphic Design and Photography see ART and DESIGN (Graphic Design) 148, PHOTOGRAPHY 481

Graphic Design, Illustration and Digital Media see ART and DESIGN (Graphic Design) 148

Graphic Information Design see ART and DESIGN (Graphic Design) 148

GREEK 340
   see also CLASSICAL STUDIES/CLASSICAL CIVILISATION
   see also CLASSICS

Greek (Ancient) see GREEK 340

Greek and Arabic Studies see GREEK 340

Greek Civilisation see CLASSICAL STUDIES/CLASSICAL CIVILISATION 208

Greek Civilisation and Philosophy see GREEK 340, PHILOSOPHY 478

Greek Studies see GREEK 340

Greek with English see ENGLISH 296, GREEK 340

Greek with Latin see GREEK 340, LATIN 389

Green Technology see TECHNOLOGIES 562

Hausa see LANGUAGES 386

Health and Exercise see HEALTH SCIENCES/ STUDIES 341

Health and Human Science see HEALTH SCIENCES/ STUDIES 341

Health and Human Sciences see HEALTH SCIENCES/ STUDIES 341, HUMAN SCIENCES/HUMAN BIOSCIENCES 374

Health and Leisure Studies see LEISURE and RECREATION MANAGEMENT/STUDIES 405

Health and Medical Physics see PHYSICS 488

Health and Nutrition see NUTRITION 466

Health and Psychology see HEALTH SCIENCES/ STUDIES 341, PSYCHOLOGY 512

Health and Social Care see HEALTH SCIENCES/ STUDIES 341, SOCIAL WORK 536

Health and Social Care for Families, Individuals and Communities see HEALTH SCIENCES/STUDIES 341, SOCIAL WORK 536

Health and Social Care Policy see HEALTH SCIENCES/ STUDIES 341

Health and Social Care Studies see HEALTH SCIENCES/ STUDIES 341

Health and Social Policy see HEALTH SCIENCES/ STUDIES 341, SOCIAL and PUBLIC POLICY and ADMINISTRATION 529

Health and Social Studies see HEALTH SCIENCES/ STUDIES 341

Health and Social Welfare see HEALTH SCIENCES/ STUDIES 341, SOCIAL WORK 536

Health and Social Wellbeing see HEALTH SCIENCES/ STUDIES 341

Health and Wellbeing see HEALTH SCIENCES/ STUDIES 341

Health and Well-being see HEALTH SCIENCES/ STUDIES 341

Health and Well-Being see HEALTH SCIENCES/ STUDIES 341

Health Application and Social Studies see HEALTH SCIENCES/STUDIES 341, SOCIAL SCIENCES/ STUDIES 531

Health Care Practice see HEALTH SCIENCES/ STUDIES 341

Health in Contemporary Society see ENVIRONMENTAL SCIENCES/STUDIES 303, HEALTH SCIENCES/ STUDIES 341

Health in Contemporary Society and Guidance and Counselling see HEALTH SCIENCES/ STUDIES 341

Health Promotion see HEALTH SCIENCES/STUDIES 341

Health Promotion and Fitness see HEALTH SCIENCES/ STUDIES 341

Health Psychology see HEALTH SCIENCES/STUDIES 341, PSYCHOLOGY 512

Health Science (Complementary Medicine) see HEALTH SCIENCES/STUDIES 341

Health Science (Herbal Medicine) see HEALTH SCIENCES/STUDIES 341, PHARMACY and PHARMACEUTICAL SCIENCES 475

Health Science and Physiology see HEALTH SCIENCES/ STUDIES 341, PHYSIOLOGY 500

Health Sciences and Physiology see HEALTH SCIENCES/STUDIES 341, PHYSIOLOGY 500

HEALTH SCIENCES/STUDIES 341
  see also COMMUNITY STUDIES
  see also ENVIRONMENTAL SCIENCE/STUDIES
  see also NURSING and MIDWIFERY
  see also OPTOMETRY
  see also PHYSIOTHERAPY
  see also PODIATRY
  see also RADIOGRAPHY
  see also SOCIAL WORK
  see also SPEECH PATHOLOGY/SCIENCES/THERAPY
  see also SPORTS SCIENCE/STUDIES
Health Studies and Social Care *see* HEALTH SCIENCES/
  STUDIES 341
Health Studies and Sociology *see* HEALTH SCIENCES/
  STUDIES 341, SOCIOLOGY 539
Health Studies with Rural Health/Health and Welfare
  see HEALTH SCIENCES/STUDIES 341
Health, Community and Social Care *see* COMMUNITY
  STUDIES/DEVELOPMENT 217, HEALTH SCIENCES/
  STUDIES 341
Health, Exercise and Physical Activities *see* HEALTH
  SCIENCES/STUDIES 341
Health, Exercise and Physical Activity *see* HEALTH
  SCIENCES/STUDIES 341
Health, Exercise and Sport Science *see* SPORTS
  SCIENCES/STUDIES 548
Health, Nutrition and Fitness *see* HEALTH SCIENCES/
  STUDIES 341
Health, Nutrition and Lifestyle *see* HEALTH SCIENCES/
  STUDIES 341, NUTRITION 466
Healthcare Science *see* HEALTH SCIENCES/
  STUDIES 341
Healthcare Science (Cardiovascular/Respiratory and
  Sleep Science) *see* HEALTH SCIENCES/
  STUDIES 341
Healthcare Science (Physiological Science/Life Science/
  Audiology) *see* HEALTH SCIENCES/STUDIES 341
Healthcare Science (Physiological Sciences) *see*
  HEALTH SCIENCES/STUDIES 341
Hebrew *see* ARABIC AND ANCIENT NEAR AND
  MIDDLE EASTERN STUDIES 129, LANGUAGES 386,
  RELIGIOUS STUDIES 521
Hebrew and Israeli Studies *see* ARABIC AND ANCIENT
  NEAR AND MIDDLE EASTERN STUDIES 129
Hebrew and Jewish Studies *see* ARABIC AND ANCIENT
  NEAR AND MIDDLE EASTERN STUDIES 129
Herbal Medicine *see* PHARMACOLOGY 472
Heritage Management *see* TOURISM and TRAVEL 564
Heritage Studies *see* HISTORY 355
Heritage, Archaeology and History *see*
  ARCHAEOLOGY 131, HISTORY 355

Hispanic and Latin American Studies *see* LATIN
  AMERICAN STUDIES 391, SPANISH 543
Hispanic Studies *see* COMBINED COURSES 212, LATIN
  AMERICAN STUDIES 391, SPANISH 543
Hispanic Studies (Latin America/Spain) *see* LATIN
  AMERICAN STUDIES 391
Hispanic Studies and History *see* HISTORY 355, LATIN
  AMERICAN STUDIES 391
Hispanic Studies and Religion *see* LATIN AMERICAN
  STUDIES 391, RELIGIOUS STUDIES 521
Hispanic Studies and Russian *see* LATIN AMERICAN
  STUDIES 391, RUSSIAN and EAST EUROPEAN
  STUDIES 526
Historical Archaeology *see* ARCHAEOLOGY 131
HISTORY 355
  see also HISTORY (ANCIENT)
  see also HISTORY (ECONOMIC and SOCIAL)
  see also HISTORY OF ART
HISTORY (ANCIENT) 360
  see also ARCHAEOLOGY
  see also HISTORY
HISTORY (ECONOMIC and SOCIAL) 362
  see also HISTORY
History (Renaissance/Modern and Modern) *see*
  HISTORY 355
History (Social and Economic) *see* HISTORY
  (ECONOMIC and SOCIAL) 362
History and American Studies *see* AMERICAN
  STUDIES 120, HISTORY 355
History and Archaeology *see* ARCHAEOLOGY 131,
  HISTORY 355
History and Archival Studies *see* HISTORY 355,
  INFORMATION MANAGEMENT and
  LIBRARIANSHIP 375
History and Art History *see* HISTORY 355,
  HISTORY OF ART 363
History and Business Economics with Marketing
  see ECONOMICS 251, HISTORY 355,
  MARKETING 415
History and Comparative Literature *see* HISTORY 355,
  LITERATURE 409
History and Economics *see* ECONOMICS 251,
  HISTORY 355
History and English *see* ENGLISH 296, HISTORY 355
History and English Literature *see* ENGLISH 296,
  HISTORY 355, LITERATURE 409
History and European Languages *see* HISTORY 355,
  LANGUAGES 386
History and French/German/Italian/Spanish *see*
  FRENCH 325, HISTORY 355, ITALIAN 381,
  SPANISH 543

History and Geography *see* GEOGRAPHY 330, HISTORY 355

History and History of Art *see* HISTORY 355, HISTORY OF ART 363

History and History of Ideas *see* HISTORY 355

History and International Relations *see* HISTORY 355, INTERNATIONAL RELATIONS 378

History and Jewish Studies *see* HISTORY 355, RELIGIOUS STUDIES 521

History and Media *see* HISTORY 355, MEDIA STUDIES 427

History and Modern Languages *see* HISTORY 355, LANGUAGES 386

History and Music *see* HISTORY 355, MUSIC 449

History and Philosophy *see* HISTORY 355, PHILOSOPHY 478

History and Philosophy of Art *see* HISTORY OF ART 363, PHILOSOPHY 478

History and Philosophy of Science *see* HISTORY 355, PHILOSOPHY 478

History and Philosophy of Science (Physics) *see* HISTORY 355, PHILOSOPHY 478, PHYSICS 488

History and Politics *see* HISTORY 355, POLITICS 507

History and Russian *see* HISTORY 355, RUSSIAN and EAST EUROPEAN STUDIES 526

History and Sociology *see* HISTORY 355, SOCIOLOGY 539

History and the Medieval World *see* HISTORY 355

History and Welsh History *see* CELTIC, IRISH, SCOTTISH AND WELSH STUDIES 197, HISTORY 355

HISTORY OF ART 363

History of Art (Asia, Africa and Europe) *see* HISTORY OF ART 363

History of Art (Combined) *see* HISTORY OF ART 363

History of Art and a Modern Language *see* HISTORY OF ART 363, SPANISH 543

History of Art and Archaeology *see* ARCHAEOLOGY 131, HISTORY OF ART 363

History of Art and English Literature *see* ENGLISH 296, HISTORY OF ART 363, LITERATURE 409

History of Art and History *see* HISTORY 355, HISTORY OF ART 363

History of Art and Literature *see* HISTORY OF ART 363, LITERATURE 409

History of Art Combined Honours *see* HISTORY OF ART 363

History of Art with Gallery and Museum Studies *see* HISTORY OF ART 363

History of Art with Museum Studies *see* HISTORY OF ART 363

History of Art, Design and Film *see* HISTORY OF ART 363

History of Decorative Arts and Crafts *see* HISTORY OF ART 363

History of Science and Philosophy *see* HISTORY (ECONOMIC and SOCIAL) 362, PHILOSOPHY 478

History with Archaeology *see* HISTORY 355

History with Contemporary Chinese Studies *see* CHINESE 206, HISTORY 355

History with Landscape Archaeology *see* ARCHAEOLOGY 131, HISTORY 355

History, Ancient and Medieval *see* HISTORY (ANCIENT) 360

History, Literature, and Cultures of the Americas *see* AMERICAN STUDIES 120, HISTORY 355, SPANISH 543

History, Museums and Heritage *see* HISTORY 355

History, Philosophy and Social Studies of Science *see* HISTORY 355, PHILOSOPHY 478, SOCIAL SCIENCES/STUDIES 531

Home Economics (Food Design and Technology) *see* FOOD SCIENCE/STUDIES and TECHNOLOGY 321

HORTICULTURE 365
  see also AGRICULTURAL SCIENCES/AGRICULTURE
  see also LANDSCAPE ARCHITECTURE
  see also PLANT SCIENCES

Horticulture (Plantsmanship/Tree Management/ Global Crop Protection) *see* HORTICULTURE 365

Horticulture and Business Management *see* BUSINESS AND MANAGEMENT COURSES 179, HORTICULTURE 365

Horticulture and Plantsmanship *see* HORTICULTURE 365

Hospitality and Food Management *see* HOSPITALITY and HOTEL MANAGEMENT 367

HOSPITALITY and HOTEL MANAGEMENT 367
  see also BUSINESS and MANAGEMENT COURSES
  see also CONSUMER STUDIES/SCIENCES
  see also FOOD SCIENCE/STUDIES and TECHNOLOGY
  see also LEISURE and RECREATION MANAGEMENT/ STUDIES
  see also TOURISM and TRAVEL

Hospitality and Leadership Management *see* HOSPITALITY and HOTEL MANAGEMENT 367

Hospitality and Licensed Retail Management *see* RETAIL MANAGEMENT 524

Hospitality and Marketing Management *see* HOSPITALITY and HOTEL MANAGEMENT 367

Hospitality and Tourism Management *see* HOSPITALITY and HOTEL MANAGEMENT 367, TOURISM and TRAVEL 564

Hospitality Business Management *see* BUSINESS AND MANAGEMENT COURSES (SPECIALISED) 193, HOSPITALITY and HOTEL MANAGEMENT 367

Hospitality Management *see* HOSPITALITY and HOTEL MANAGEMENT 367

Hospitality Management with Culinary Arts *see* HOSPITALITY and HOTEL MANAGEMENT 367

Hospitality Management with Tourism *see* HOSPITALITY and HOTEL MANAGEMENT 367, TOURISM and TRAVEL 564

Hospitality with Events Management *see* HOSPITALITY and HOTEL MANAGEMENT 367

HOUSING 370
 see also BUILDING and CONSTRUCTION
 see also COMMUNITY STUDIES
 see also SURVEYING
 see also TOWN and COUNTRY PLANNING

Housing (Supported Housing/Housing Policy and Practice) *see* HOUSING 370

Housing Management *see* HOUSING 370

Housing Studies *see* HOUSING 370

Human and Physical Geography *see* GEOGRAPHY 330

Human Biology *see* BIOLOGY 170, HUMAN SCIENCES/HUMAN BIOSCIENCES 374

Human Biology and Education *see* BIOLOGY 170, EDUCATION STUDIES 256

Human Biology and Nutrition *see* NUTRITION 466

Human Biology with Sociology and Psychology *see* BIOLOGY 170

Human Bioscience *see* HEALTH SCIENCES/STUDIES 341, HUMAN SCIENCES/HUMAN BIOSCIENCES 374

Human Bioscience (Combined) *see* BIOLOGICAL SCIENCES 165

Human Biosciences *see* BIOLOGICAL SCIENCES 165, BIOLOGY 170, HUMAN SCIENCES/HUMAN BIOSCIENCES 374

Human Communication *see* COMMUNICATION STUDIES/COMMUNICATION 214

Human Communication (Speech and Language Therapy) *see* SPEECH PATHOLOGY/SCIENCES/THERAPY 546

Human Communication Sciences *see* COMMUNICATION STUDIES/COMMUNICATION 214

Human Genetics *see* GENETICS 328

Human Geography *see* GEOGRAPHY 330, HUMAN SCIENCES/HUMAN BIOSCIENCES 374

Human Geography and Planning *see* GEOGRAPHY 330, TOWN and COUNTRY PLANNING 567

Human Medical Science *see* MEDICINE 433

Human Nutrition *see* HUMAN SCIENCES/HUMAN BIOSCIENCES 374, NUTRITION 466

Human Nutrition and Dietetics *see* DIETETICS 237, NUTRITION 466

Human Physiology *see* PHYSIOLOGY 500

HUMAN RESOURCE MANAGEMENT 371
 see also BUSINESS and MANAGEMENT COURSES

Human Resource Management *see* HUMAN RESOURCE MANAGEMENT 371

Human Resource Management and Marketing *see* HUMAN RESOURCE MANAGEMENT 371, MARKETING 415

Human Resource Management with Business *see* HUMAN RESOURCE MANAGEMENT 371

Human Resource Management with Information Systems *see* COMPUTER COURSES 219, HUMAN RESOURCE MANAGEMENT 371

Human Resource Management with Marketing *see* HUMAN RESOURCE MANAGEMENT 371

Human Resource Management with Psychology *see* HUMAN RESOURCE MANAGEMENT 371, PSYCHOLOGY 512

Human Resources with Mandarin *see* HUMAN RESOURCE MANAGEMENT 371, LANGUAGES 386

Human Rights *see* SOCIAL SCIENCES/STUDIES 531

Human Science *see* BIOLOGICAL SCIENCES 165

HUMAN SCIENCES/HUMAN BIOSCIENCES 374

Human Sciences (Pre-Med option) *see* MEDICINE 433

Humanities *see* COMBINED COURSES 212

Humanities and English/French/German *see* COMBINED COURSES 212, LANGUAGES 386

Humanities and Hispanic Studies *see* COMBINED COURSES 212

Humanities and History *see* COMBINED COURSES 212, HISTORY 355

Humanities and History of Art *see* COMBINED COURSES 212, HISTORY OF ART 363

Humanities and Media Studies *see* COMBINED COURSES 212, MEDIA STUDIES 427

Humanities and Philosophy *see* COMBINED COURSES 212, PHILOSOPHY 478

Humanities with English/French/German/Spanish *see* COMBINED COURSES 212

Humanities: War, Conflict and Modernity *see* INTERNATIONAL RELATIONS 378

Hungarian *see* LANGUAGES 386

Icelandic *see* SCANDINAVIAN STUDIES 527

ICT *see* COMPUTER COURSES 219

Illustration *see* ART and DESIGN (Fine Art) 144, ART and DESIGN (Graphic Design) 148

Illustration and Animation *see* ART and DESIGN (Graphic Design) 148

Illustration and Design *see* ART and DESIGN
(Graphic Design) 148
Illustration and Graphics *see* ART and DESIGN
(Graphic Design) 148
Illustration with Animation *see* ART and DESIGN
(Graphic Design) 148
Immunology *see* BIOLOGICAL SCIENCES 165
Immunology and Microbiology *see*
MICROBIOLOGY 447
Immunology and Pharmacology *see*
PHARMACOLOGY 472
Inclusive Education *see* EDUCATION
STUDIES 256
Indonesian *see* LANGUAGES 386
Industrial Product Design *see* ART and DESIGN
(Product and Industrial Design) 152
Industrial Design *see* ART and DESIGN (Product and
Industrial Design) 152
Industrial Economics *see* ECONOMICS 251
Industrial Economics with Insurance *see*
ECONOMICS 251, FINANCE 315
Industrial Physics *see* PHYSICS 488
Industrial Product Design *see* ART and DESIGN
(Product and Industrial Design) 152,
ENGINEERING (MANUFACTURING) 288
Infection and Immunity *see* BIOLOGY 170,
MICROBIOLOGY 447
Infection Biology *see* BIOLOGY 170
Infectious Diseases *see* BIOLOGICAL SCIENCES 165
Informatics *see* COMPUTER COURSES 219,
INFORMATION MANAGEMENT and
LIBRARIANSHIP 375
Information and Communication Technology
see COMPUTER COURSES 219, ENGINEERING
(COMMUNICATIONS) 278, INFORMATION
MANAGEMENT and LIBRARIANSHIP 375
Information and Communications *see*
COMMUNICATION STUDIES/COMMUNICATION
214, INFORMATION MANAGEMENT and
LIBRARIANSHIP 375
Information and Communications Technology
see INFORMATION MANAGEMENT and
LIBRARIANSHIP 375
Information and Communications Technology and
International Development *see* INFORMATION
MANAGEMENT and LIBRARIANSHIP 375
Information and Library Management *see*
INFORMATION MANAGEMENT and
LIBRARIANSHIP 375
Information and Library Studies *see* COMMUNICATION
STUDIES/COMMUNICATION 214

Information and Library Studies and English
Literature *see* INFORMATION MANAGEMENT and
LIBRARIANSHIP 375, LITERATURE 409
Information Communication Technology *see*
COMMUNICATION STUDIES/COMMUNICATION
214, COMPUTER COURSES 219, INFORMATION
MANAGEMENT and LIBRARIANSHIP 375
Information Engineering *see* ENGINEERING
(COMPUTER, CONTROL, SOFTWARE and
SYSTEMS) 280
Information Management and Business Studies
see BUSINESS AND MANAGEMENT COURSES
(SPECIALISED) 193, INFORMATION MANAGEMENT
and LIBRARIANSHIP 375
**INFORMATION MANAGEMENT and
LIBRARIANSHIP 375**
see also COMPUTER COURSES
see also MEDIA STUDIES
Information Management and Web Development *see*
COMPUTER COURSES 219
Information Management for Business *see*
INFORMATION MANAGEMENT and
LIBRARIANSHIP 375
Information Security *see* INFORMATION MANAGEMENT
and LIBRARIANSHIP 375
Information Security Systems *see*
INFORMATION MANAGEMENT and
LIBRARIANSHIP 375
Information Systems *see* COMPUTER COURSES 219,
INFORMATION MANAGEMENT and
LIBRARIANSHIP 375
Information Systems and Management *see*
INFORMATION MANAGEMENT and
LIBRARIANSHIP 375
Information Systems Design *see* TECHNOLOGIES 562
Information Systems Engineering *see* ENGINEERING
(COMPUTER, CONTROL, SOFTWARE and
SYSTEMS) 280, ENGINEERING (ELECTRICAL and
ELECTRONIC) 283
Information Systems for Business *see* COMPUTER
COURSES 219
Information Technology *see* COMPUTER COURSES
219, INFORMATION MANAGEMENT and
LIBRARIANSHIP 375
Information Technology and Multimedia Computing
see COMPUTER COURSES 219
Information Technology and Security *see* INFORMATION
MANAGEMENT and LIBRARIANSHIP 375
Information Technology in Organisations *see*
INFORMATION MANAGEMENT and
LIBRARIANSHIP 375

Information Technology Management see
   BUSINESS AND MANAGEMENT COURSES
   (SPECIALISED) 193, INFORMATION MANAGEMENT
   and LIBRARIANSHIP 375
Information Technology Management and Business
   see INFORMATION MANAGEMENT and
   LIBRARIANSHIP 375
Information Technology Management for Business
   see INFORMATION MANAGEMENT and
   LIBRARIANSHIP 375
Information Technology Management in Business
   see INFORMATION MANAGEMENT and
   LIBRARIANSHIP 375
Information Technology Security see COMPUTER
   COURSES 219
Information Technology, Management and
   Business see INFORMATION MANAGEMENT and
   LIBRARIANSHIP 375
Innovative Manufacturing Engineering see
   ENGINEERING (MANUFACTURING) 288
Instrumentation and Control Engineering see
   ENGINEERING (COMPUTER, CONTROL, SOFTWARE
   and SYSTEMS) 280
Integrated Engineering see ENGINEERING/
   ENGINEERING SCIENCES 260
Integrated Mechanical and Electrical Engineering see
   ENGINEERING (MECHANICAL) 290
Interaction Design see COMPUTER COURSES 219
Interactive Arts see ART and DESIGN (Graphic
   Design) 148
Interactive Digital Media see MEDIA STUDIES 427
Interactive Media see MEDIA STUDIES 427
Interactive Media with Animation see ART
   and DESIGN (Graphic Design) 148, MEDIA
   STUDIES 427
Interdisciplinary Art Design and Media see ART
   and DESIGN (Graphic Design) 148, MEDIA
   STUDIES 427
Interdisciplinary Human Studies see HUMAN
   SCIENCES/HUMAN BIOSCIENCES 374
Interdisciplinary Science see NATURAL SCIENCES 457
Interior Architecture see ARCHITECTURE 134, ART and
   DESIGN (Product and Industrial Design) 152
Interior Architecture and Design see ART and DESIGN
   (Product and Industrial Design) 152
Interior Architecture and Property Development see
   ARCHITECTURE 134
Interior Design see ART and DESIGN (Product and
   Industrial Design) 152
Interior Design (Decoration) see ART and DESIGN
   (Product and Industrial Design) 152

Interior Design Environment Architectures see ART
   and DESIGN (Product and Industrial Design) 152
Intermedia Art see ART and DESIGN (Graphic
   Design) 148
International Accounting see ACCOUNTANCY/
   ACCOUNTING 109
International and Political Studies see POLITICS 507
International Business see BUSINESS AND
   MANAGEMENT COURSES 179, BUSINESS AND
   MANAGEMENT COURSES (INTERNATIONAL
   AND EUROPEAN) 188, INTERNATIONAL
   RELATIONS 378
International Business (Arabic/Chinese/French/
   Russian/Spanish) see BUSINESS AND
   MANAGEMENT COURSES (INTERNATIONAL AND
   EUROPEAN) 188
International Business (Mandarin/Russian/Spanish)
   see BUSINESS AND MANAGEMENT COURSES
   (INTERNATIONAL AND EUROPEAN) 188
International Business (Russian) see RUSSIAN and
   EAST EUROPEAN STUDIES 526
International Business and Environmental
   Sustainability see BUSINESS AND MANAGEMENT
   COURSES (INTERNATIONAL AND EUROPEAN) 188,
   ENVIRONMENTAL SCIENCES/STUDIES 303
International Business and Finance see BUSINESS
   AND MANAGEMENT COURSES (INTERNATIONAL
   AND EUROPEAN) 188, FINANCE 315
International Business and French see BUSINESS AND
   MANAGEMENT COURSES (INTERNATIONAL AND
   EUROPEAN) 188, FRENCH 325
International Business and French/German/Spanish
   see BUSINESS AND MANAGEMENT COURSES
   (INTERNATIONAL AND EUROPEAN) 188
International Business and German see BUSINESS
   AND MANAGEMENT COURSES (INTERNATIONAL
   AND EUROPEAN) 188, GERMAN 337
International Business and Globalisation see
   BUSINESS AND MANAGEMENT COURSES
   (INTERNATIONAL AND EUROPEAN) 188
International Business and Italian see ITALIAN 381
International Business and Languages see BUSINESS
   AND MANAGEMENT COURSES (INTERNATIONAL
   AND EUROPEAN) 188, LANGUAGES 386
International Business and Languages (French/
   German/Italian/Spanish) see BUSINESS AND
   MANAGEMENT COURSES (INTERNATIONAL AND
   EUROPEAN) 188
International Business and Marketing see BUSINESS
   AND MANAGEMENT COURSES (INTERNATIONAL
   AND EUROPEAN) 188, MARKETING 415

International Business and Spanish *see* BUSINESS AND MANAGEMENT COURSES (INTERNATIONAL AND EUROPEAN) 188, SPANISH 543

International Business Finance *see* FINANCE 315

International Business Management *see* BUSINESS AND MANAGEMENT COURSES (INTERNATIONAL AND EUROPEAN) 188

International Business Management and French/German/Spanish *see* BUSINESS AND MANAGEMENT COURSES (INTERNATIONAL AND EUROPEAN) 188

International Business Management and German *see* GERMAN 337

International Business Management with French *see* FRENCH 325

International Business Strategy *see* BUSINESS AND MANAGEMENT COURSES (INTERNATIONAL AND EUROPEAN) 188

International Business Studies *see* BUSINESS AND MANAGEMENT COURSES (INTERNATIONAL AND EUROPEAN) 188

International Business Studies with Language *see* BUSINESS AND MANAGEMENT COURSES (INTERNATIONAL AND EUROPEAN) 188

International Business Studies with Spanish *see* BUSINESS AND MANAGEMENT COURSES (INTERNATIONAL AND EUROPEAN) 188, SPANISH 543

International Business with Arabic *see* ARABIC AND ANCIENT NEAR AND MIDDLE EASTERN STUDIES 129, BUSINESS AND MANAGEMENT COURSES (INTERNATIONAL AND EUROPEAN) 188

International Business with Finance and Language *see* BUSINESS AND MANAGEMENT COURSES (INTERNATIONAL AND EUROPEAN) 188, FINANCE 315, LANGUAGES 386

International Business with French/German *see* BUSINESS AND MANAGEMENT COURSES (INTERNATIONAL AND EUROPEAN) 188

International Business with French/German/Spanish *see* BUSINESS AND MANAGEMENT COURSES (INTERNATIONAL AND EUROPEAN) 188, LANGUAGES 386

International Business with French/Spanish *see* BUSINESS AND MANAGEMENT COURSES (INTERNATIONAL AND EUROPEAN) 188

International Business with German *see* BUSINESS AND MANAGEMENT COURSES (INTERNATIONAL AND EUROPEAN) 188, GERMAN 337

International Business with Human Resource Management and 2 Languages *see* BUSINESS AND MANAGEMENT COURSES (INTERNATIONAL AND EUROPEAN) 188, HUMAN RESOURCE MANAGEMENT 371

International Business with Italian *see* BUSINESS AND MANAGEMENT COURSES (INTERNATIONAL AND EUROPEAN) 188, ITALIAN 381

International Business with Language *see* BUSINESS AND MANAGEMENT COURSES (INTERNATIONAL AND EUROPEAN) 188, LANGUAGES 386

International Business with Marketing and Languages *see* BUSINESS AND MANAGEMENT COURSES (INTERNATIONAL AND EUROPEAN) 188, MARKETING 415

International Business, Finance and Economics *see* BUSINESS AND MANAGEMENT COURSES (INTERNATIONAL AND EUROPEAN) 188, ECONOMICS 251, FINANCE 315

International Development *see* DEVELOPMENT STUDIES 235, POLITICS 507

International Development and International Relations *see* DEVELOPMENT STUDIES 235, INTERNATIONAL RELATIONS 378

International Development Studies *see* DEVELOPMENT STUDIES 235, INTERNATIONAL RELATIONS 378

International Development Studies with French/Spanish/Japanese *see* FRENCH 325, INTERNATIONAL RELATIONS 378, JAPANESE 383, SPANISH 543

International Development with Social Anthropology and Politics *see* DEVELOPMENT STUDIES 235

International Development: Third World with NGO Management *see* DEVELOPMENT STUDIES 235

International Economics *see* ECONOMICS 251

International Economics and Finance *see* ECONOMICS 251, FINANCE 315

International Economics and Trade *see* ECONOMICS 251

International Economy Management *see* BUSINESS AND MANAGEMENT COURSES (INTERNATIONAL AND EUROPEAN) 188, ECONOMICS 251

International Education *see* EDUCATION STUDIES 256

International Equine and Agricultural Business Management *see* ANIMAL SCIENCES 124, BUSINESS AND MANAGEMENT COURSES (SPECIALISED) 193

International Events Management with Tourism and Destinations *see* BUSINESS AND MANAGEMENT

COURSES (SPECIALISED) 193, INTERNATIONAL RELATIONS 378, TOURISM and TRAVEL 564

International Fashion Marketing see ART and DESIGN (Fashion and Textiles) 140, MARKETING 415

International Finance see FINANCE 315, INTERNATIONAL RELATIONS 378

International Finance and Trade see FINANCE 315

International Football Business Management see BUSINESS AND MANAGEMENT COURSES 179

International History and International Politics see HISTORY 355, INTERNATIONAL RELATIONS 378, POLITICS 507

International Hospitality and Tourism Management see TOURISM and TRAVEL 564

International Hospitality Management see HOSPITALITY and HOTEL MANAGEMENT 367

International Hotel and Tourism Management see HOSPITALITY and HOTEL MANAGEMENT 367

International Hotel Management see BUSINESS AND MANAGEMENT COURSES (INTERNATIONAL AND EUROPEAN) 188, TOURISM and TRAVEL 564

International Journalism see MEDIA STUDIES 427

International Law see INTERNATIONAL RELATIONS 378, LAW 393

International Management see BUSINESS AND MANAGEMENT COURSES (INTERNATIONAL AND EUROPEAN) 188

International Management and Spanish see SPANISH 543

International Management and Business Administration with French/German/Italian see BUSINESS AND MANAGEMENT COURSES (INTERNATIONAL AND EUROPEAN) 188

International Management and French see BUSINESS AND MANAGEMENT COURSES (INTERNATIONAL AND EUROPEAN) 188, FRENCH 325

International Management and German see BUSINESS AND MANAGEMENT COURSES (INTERNATIONAL AND EUROPEAN) 188, GERMAN 337

International Management Science see BUSINESS AND MANAGEMENT COURSES (INTERNATIONAL AND EUROPEAN) 188

International Management Science (Language) see BUSINESS AND MANAGEMENT COURSES (INTERNATIONAL AND EUROPEAN) 188

International Management Studies and Intercultural Studies see BUSINESS AND MANAGEMENT COURSES (INTERNATIONAL AND EUROPEAN) 188, SOCIAL SCIENCES/STUDIES 531

International Management Studies with European Languages and Society see BUSINESS AND MANAGEMENT COURSES (INTERNATIONAL AND EUROPEAN) 188, EUROPEAN STUDIES 307, LANGUAGES 386

International Management with American Business Studies see BUSINESS AND MANAGEMENT COURSES (INTERNATIONAL AND EUROPEAN) 188

International Marketing see MARKETING 415

International Marketing and Business see MARKETING 415

International Media and Communication Studies see MEDIA STUDIES 427

International Politics see INTERNATIONAL RELATIONS 378, POLITICS 507

International Politics and Conflict Studies see INTERNATIONAL RELATIONS 378

International Politics and Languages (French/ German/Italian/Spanish) see INTERNATIONAL RELATIONS 378, LANGUAGES 386

International Politics and Philosophy see INTERNATIONAL RELATIONS 378, PHILOSOPHY 478, POLITICS 507

International Politics and Policy see POLITICS 507

International Politics and Security Studies see INTERNATIONAL RELATIONS 378, POLITICS 507

International Politics and Strategic Studies see INTERNATIONAL RELATIONS 378

International Politics Third World see POLITICS 507

International Real Estate see SURVEYING 556

INTERNATIONAL RELATIONS 378
  see also DEVELOPMENT STUDIES
  see also EUROPEAN STUDIES
  see also POLITICS

International Relations and a Modern Language see INTERNATIONAL RELATIONS 378, LANGUAGES 386

International Relations and American Studies see AMERICAN STUDIES 120, INTERNATIONAL RELATIONS 378

International Relations and Business see INTERNATIONAL RELATIONS 378

International Relations and Development Studies see DEVELOPMENT STUDIES 235, INTERNATIONAL RELATIONS 378

International Relations and English Language see ENGLISH 296, INTERNATIONAL RELATIONS 378

International Relations and Finance see FINANCE 315, INTERNATIONAL RELATIONS 378

International Relations and German see GERMAN 337, INTERNATIONAL RELATIONS 378

International Relations and Global Development *see* DEVELOPMENT STUDIES 235, INTERNATIONAL RELATIONS 378

International Relations and Global Issues *see* INTERNATIONAL RELATIONS 378

International Relations and History *see* HISTORY 355, INTERNATIONAL RELATIONS 378

International Relations and Law *see* INTERNATIONAL RELATIONS 378, LAW 393

International Relations and Management Studies *see* INTERNATIONAL RELATIONS 378

International Relations and Peace Studies *see* INTERNATIONAL RELATIONS 378

International Relations and Politics *see* INTERNATIONAL RELATIONS 378, POLITICS 507

International Relations and Security Studies *see* INTERNATIONAL RELATIONS 378

International Relations and Thai and South East Asia Studies *see* ASIA-PACIFIC STUDIES 158, INTERNATIONAL RELATIONS 378

International Relations with French/German/ Italian *see* INTERNATIONAL RELATIONS 378, LANGUAGES 386

International Relations with Law *see* INTERNATIONAL RELATIONS 378, LAW 393

International Relations with Politics *see* INTERNATIONAL RELATIONS 378, POLITICS 507

International Relations with Welsh *see* CELTIC, IRISH, SCOTTISH AND WELSH STUDIES 197, INTERNATIONAL RELATIONS 378

International Resort Tourism Management *see* TOURISM and TRAVEL 564

International Retail Marketing *see* RETAIL MANAGEMENT 524

International Social Policy *see* SOCIAL and PUBLIC POLICY and ADMINISTRATION 529

International Spa Management *see* BUSINESS AND MANAGEMENT COURSES (INTERNATIONAL AND EUROPEAN) 188, BUSINESS AND MANAGEMENT COURSES (SPECIALISED) 193

International Sport and Event Management *see* BUSINESS AND MANAGEMENT COURSES (SPECIALISED) 193

International Studies *see* INTERNATIONAL RELATIONS 378, POLITICS 507

International Studies and Political Science *see* INTERNATIONAL RELATIONS 378, POLITICS 507

International Studies with Economics *see* ECONOMICS 251

International Tourism and Hospitality Management *see* HOSPITALITY and HOTEL MANAGEMENT 367, TOURISM and TRAVEL 564

International Tourism and Management *see* BUSINESS AND MANAGEMENT COURSES 179, TOURISM and TRAVEL 564

International Tourism Management *see* TOURISM and TRAVEL 564

International Tourism Management and Travel Management *see* TOURISM and TRAVEL 564

International Tourist Management *see* TOURISM and TRAVEL 564

International Travel and Tourism Management *see* BUSINESS AND MANAGEMENT COURSES (SPECIALISED) 193, TOURISM and TRAVEL 564

International Travel and Tourism Studies with Languages *see* LANGUAGES 386, TOURISM and TRAVEL 564

International Wildlife Biology *see* ANIMAL SCIENCES 124, BIOLOGY 170, ZOOLOGY 576

Internet Communications Technology *see* COMMUNICATION STUDIES/COMMUNICATION 214, ENGINEERING (COMMUNICATIONS) 278

Internet Computing *see* COMPUTER COURSES 219

Internet Computing and Systems Administration *see* COMPUTER COURSES 219

Internet Engineering *see* ENGINEERING (COMPUTER, CONTROL, SOFTWARE and SYSTEMS) 280

Interpreting (British Sign Language/English) *see* LANGUAGES 386

Investment and Financial Risk Management *see* FINANCE 315

Investment, Finance and Banking *see* FINANCE 315

Irish *see* CELTIC, IRISH, SCOTTISH AND WELSH STUDIES 197

Irish and Celtic Studies *see* CELTIC, IRISH, SCOTTISH AND WELSH STUDIES 197

Irish History *see* CELTIC, IRISH, SCOTTISH AND WELSH STUDIES 197, HISTORY 355

Irish Language and Literature *see* CELTIC, IRISH, SCOTTISH AND WELSH STUDIES 197, LITERATURE 409

Irish Studies *see* CELTIC, IRISH, SCOTTISH AND WELSH STUDIES 197, COMBINED COURSES 212

Islamic Studies *see* ARABIC AND ANCIENT NEAR AND MIDDLE EASTERN STUDIES 129, RELIGIOUS STUDIES 521

IT Management for Business *see* COMPUTER COURSES 219, INFORMATION MANAGEMENT and LIBRARIANSHIP 375

Italian *see* ITALIAN 381, LANGUAGES 386

Italian and a Modern Language *see* ITALIAN 381

Italian and Management *see* ITALIAN 381

Italian and Marketing *see* ITALIAN 381, MARKETING 415

ITALIAN 381

Italian Studies and Modern Languages *see* ITALIAN 381, LANGUAGES 386

Italian Translation Studies *see* ITALIAN 381

Italian with Linguistics *see* ITALIAN 381, LINGUISTICS 407

JAPANESE 383

   see also ASIA-PACIFIC STUDIES

   see also LANGUAGES

Japanese and Linguistics *see* JAPANESE 383, LINGUISTICS 407

Japanese and Screen Studies *see* JAPANESE 383

Japanese Studies *see* ASIA-PACIFIC STUDIES 158, JAPANESE 383

Japanese Studies (Combined) *see* COMBINED COURSES 212, JAPANESE 383

Jazz *see* MUSIC 449

Jazz, Popular and Commercial Music *see* MUSIC 449

Jewellery and Metal Design *see* ART and DESIGN (Product and Industrial Design) 152

Jewellery and Object *see* ART and DESIGN (3D Design) 156

Jewellery and Silversmithing *see* ART and DESIGN (3D Design) 156, ART and DESIGN (Fashion and Textiles) 140

Jewellery Design *see* ART and DESIGN (3D Design) 156, ART and DESIGN (Fashion and Textiles) 140

Jewish History *see* HISTORY 355

Journalism *see* MEDIA STUDIES 427

Journalism and Communications *see* COMMUNICATION STUDIES/COMMUNICATION 214, MEDIA STUDIES 427

Journalism and Creative Writing *see* MEDIA STUDIES 427

Journalism and English Literature *see* LITERATURE 409, MEDIA STUDIES 427

Journalism and Media *see* MEDIA STUDIES 427

Journalism and Media Cultures *see* MEDIA STUDIES 427

Journalism and Media Studies *see* MEDIA STUDIES 427

Journalism and Psychology *see* MEDIA STUDIES 427, PSYCHOLOGY 512

Journalism and the News Industry *see* MEDIA STUDIES 427

Journalism and War Studies *see* INTERNATIONAL RELATIONS 378, MEDIA STUDIES 427

Journalism Media and Sociology *see* MEDIA STUDIES 427, SOCIOLOGY 539

Journalism Studies *see* MEDIA STUDIES 427

Journalism, English and Media *see* ENGLISH 296, MEDIA STUDIES 427

Journalism, Media and Cultural Studies *see* MEDIA STUDIES 427

Journalism, Media and English Literature *see* LITERATURE 409, MEDIA STUDIES 427

Korean *see* CHINESE 206, LANGUAGES 386

Korean Studies *see* ASIA-PACIFIC STUDIES 158

Land Economy *see* ECONOMICS 251, LAW 393, SURVEYING 556

Land Use and Environment Management *see* AGRICULTURAL SCIENCES/AGRICULTURE 117, ENVIRONMENTAL SCIENCES/STUDIES 303

Landscape and Garden Design *see* LANDSCAPE ARCHITECTURE 384

LANDSCAPE ARCHITECTURE 384

   see also ART and DESIGN (Product and Industrial Design)

   see also HORTICULTURE

Landscape Architecture with Ecology *see* ENVIRONMENTAL SCIENCES/STUDIES 303, LANDSCAPE ARCHITECTURE 384

Landscape Architecture with Planning *see* LANDSCAPE ARCHITECTURE 384

Landscape Management *see* LANDSCAPE ARCHITECTURE 384

Language (French/German/Italian/Spanish) and Linguistics *see* FRENCH 325, GERMAN 337, ITALIAN 381, LANGUAGES 386, LINGUISTICS 407, SPANISH 543

Language and Communication *see* COMMUNICATION STUDIES/COMMUNICATION 214, LANGUAGES 386

Language and Culture *see* LANGUAGES 386

Language and Linguistics *see* LANGUAGES 386, LINGUISTICS 407

Language and Literature in Education *see* EDUCATION STUDIES 256, LITERATURE 409

Language and Society *see* LANGUAGES 386, LINGUISTICS 407

Language Learning *see* LANGUAGES 386

Language Studies *see* LANGUAGES 386

Language with TESOL *see* LANGUAGES 386

Language, Literacy and Communication *see* COMMUNICATION STUDIES/COMMUNICATION 214, LINGUISTICS 407

LANGUAGES 386
  see also AFRICAN and CARIBBEAN STUDIES
  see also ARABIC and ANCIENT NEAR and MIDDLE
    EASTERN STUDIES
  see also ASIA-PACIFIC STUDIES
  see also CELTIC, IRISH, SCOTTISH and WELSH
    STUDIES
  see also CHINESE
  see also ENGLISH
  see also FRENCH
  see also GERMAN
  see also GREEK
  see also ITALIAN
  see also JAPANESE
  see also LATIN
  see also LINGUISTICS
  see also RUSSIAN and EAST EUROPEAN STUDIES
  see also SCANDINAVIAN STUDIES
  see also SPANISH
Languages (Interpretation and Translation) *see*
  LANGUAGES 386
Languages (Interpretation and Translation) (French/
  German) (German/Spanish) *see* FRENCH 325,
  GERMAN 337, SPANISH 543
Languages and Contemporary European Studies *see*
  EUROPEAN STUDIES 307, LANGUAGES 386
Languages and Linguistics *see* LANGUAGES 386,
  LINGUISTICS 407
Languages and Literature of Scotland *see* LANGUAGES
  386, LITERATURE 409
Languages and Philosophy *see* LANGUAGES 386,
  PHILOSOPHY 478
Languages Studies *see* LANGUAGES 386
Languages with International Business *see* BUSINESS
  AND MANAGEMENT COURSES (INTERNATIONAL
  AND EUROPEAN) 188
LATIN 389
  see also CLASSICAL STUDIES/CLASSICAL
    CIVILISATION 208
  see also CLASSICS
  see also GREEK
Latin American and Hispanic Studies *see* LATIN
  AMERICAN STUDIES 391
LATIN AMERICAN STUDIES 391
  see also AMERICAN STUDIES
  see also SPANISH
Latin American Studies and Screen Studies *see* LATIN
  AMERICAN STUDIES 391
Latin and Greek *see* GREEK 340, LATIN 389
Latin and Language Studies *see* LANGUAGES 386,
  LATIN 389

Latin and Medieval History *see* LATIN 389
Latin Studies *see* LATIN 389
LAW 393
  see also SOCIAL SCIENCES/STUDIES
Law (Combined) *see* LAW 393
Law (England/Northern Ireland) *see* LAW 393
Law (European) *see* EUROPEAN STUDIES 307,
  LAW 393
Law (European and International) *see* LAW 393
Law (European Legal Studies) *see* LAW 393
Law (Exempting) *see* LAW 393
Law (International) *see* LAW 393
Law (International Legal Studies) *see* LAW 393
Law (Scots) *see* LAW 393
Law (Scots and English) *see* LAW 393
Law and Business *see* BUSINESS AND MANAGEMENT
  COURSES 179, LAW 393
Law and Business Studies *see* BUSINESS AND
  MANAGEMENT COURSES 179, LAW 393
Law and Chinese *see* CHINESE 206, LAW 393
Law and Criminal Justice *see* LAW 393, SOCIAL
  SCIENCES/STUDIES 531
Law and Criminology *see* LAW 393, SOCIAL SCIENCES/
  STUDIES 531
Law and European Studies *see* EUROPEAN STUDIES
  307, LAW 393
Law and Finance *see* FINANCE 315, LAW 393
Law and French *see* LAW 393
Law and German *see* GERMAN 337, LAW 393
Law and German/French/Spanish *see* FRENCH 325,
  GERMAN 337, LAW 393, SPANISH 543
Law and Human Rights *see* LAW 393, SOCIAL
  SCIENCES/STUDIES 531
Law and International Relations *see* INTERNATIONAL
  RELATIONS 378, LAW 393
Law and International Studies *see* LAW 393
Law and Italian *see* ITALIAN 381
Law and Management *see* LAW 393
Law and Philosophy *see* LAW 393, PHILOSOPHY 478
Law and Politics *see* LAW 393, POLITICS 507
Law and Social Policy *see* SOCIAL and PUBLIC POLICY
  and ADMINISTRATION 529
Law and Social Welfare *see* LAW 393
Law and Sociology *see* LAW 393, SOCIOLOGY 539
Law and Spanish *see* LAW 393, SPANISH 543
Law and Taxation *see* LAW 393
Law Human Rights and Social Justice *see* LAW 393,
  SOCIAL SCIENCES/STUDIES 531
Law plus Maitrise en Droit Francais *see* LAW 393
Law with Advanced Studies *see* LAW 393
Law with American Law *see* LAW 393

Law with American Legal Studies see LAW 393
Law with American Studies see AMERICAN
STUDIES 120, LAW 393
Law with Business see BUSINESS AND MANAGEMENT
COURSES 179, LAW 393
Law with Business Finance see FINANCE 315,
LAW 393
Law with Business Law see LAW 393
Law with Criminology see LAW 393, SOCIAL
SCIENCES/STUDIES 531
Law with Economics see ECONOMICS 251, LAW 393
Law with European Law see LAW 393
Law with French see FRENCH 325, LAW 393
Law with French and French Law/German and
German Law/Spanish and Spanish Law see
FRENCH 325, GERMAN 337, LANGUAGES 386,
LAW 393, SPANISH 543
Law with French Law and Language see FRENCH 325,
LAW 393
Law with French Law/German Law/Hispanic Law/
Italian Law see LAW 393
Law with French/German/Spanish see FRENCH 325,
GERMAN 337, LAW 393, SPANISH 543
Law with French/Spanish see FRENCH 325, LAW 337,
SPANISH 543
Law with Human Resources Management see
HUMAN RESOURCE MANAGEMENT 371, LAW 393
Law with Human Rights see LAW 393
Law with International Development see LAW 393
Law with International Relations see INTERNATIONAL
RELATIONS 378, LAW 393
Law with International Studies see INTERNATIONAL
RELATIONS 378, LAW 393
Law with Irish see CELTIC, IRISH, SCOTTISH AND WELSH
STUDIES 197, LAW 393
Law with Journalism/Criminology see LAW 393,
MEDIA STUDIES 427, SOCIAL SCIENCES/
STUDIES 531
Law with Legal Studies in Europe see LAW 393
Law with Literature see LAW 393, LITERATURE 409
Law with Management see BUSINESS AND
MANAGEMENT COURSES 179, LAW 393
Law with Management Studies see BUSINESS AND
MANAGEMENT COURSES 179, LAW 393
Law with Marketing see LAW 393, MARKETING 415
Law with Philosophy see LAW 393,
PHILOSOPHY 478
Law with Politics see LAW 393, POLITICS 507
Law with Proficiency in French/Italian/Spanish
see FRENCH 325, ITALIAN 381, LAW 393,
SPANISH 543

Law with Psychology see LAW 393,
PSYCHOLOGY 512
Leadership and Politics see POLITICS 507
Learning Disability Studies see EDUCATION
STUDIES 256
Legal Studies see LAW 393
Leisure see TOURISM and TRAVEL 564
Leisure and Events Management see HOSPITALITY
and HOTEL MANAGEMENT 367, LEISURE and
RECREATION MANAGEMENT/STUDIES 405
Leisure and Lifestyle Management see LEISURE and
RECREATION MANAGEMENT/STUDIES 405
**LEISURE and RECREATION MANAGEMENT/
STUDIES 405**
see also HOSPITALITY and HOTEL MANAGEMENT
see also SPORTS SCIENCES/STUDIES
see also TOURISM AND TRAVEL
Leisure and Sports Management see LEISURE and
RECREATION MANAGEMENT/STUDIES 405
Leisure and Tourism Management see LEISURE and
RECREATION MANAGEMENT/STUDIES 405, SPORTS
SCIENCES/STUDIES 548
Leisure Management see LEISURE and RECREATION
MANAGEMENT/STUDIES 405
Leisure Marketing see LEISURE and RECREATION
MANAGEMENT/STUDIES 405, MARKETING 415
Liberal Arts see COMBINED COURSES 212
Lighting Design see ART and DESIGN (Product and
Industrial Design) 152
Lighting Design and Technology see ENGINEERING
(ELECTRICAL and ELECTRONIC) 283
Linguistics see COMBINED COURSES 212,
LINGUISTICS 407
Linguistics and Advertising see LINGUISTICS 407,
MARKETING 415
Linguistics and Communications see COMMUNICATION
STUDIES/COMMUNICATION 214, LINGUISTICS 407
Linguistics and English Language see ENGLISH 296,
LINGUISTICS 407
Linguistics and English Literature see LINGUISTICS
407, LITERATURE 409
Linguistics and Language see LANGUAGES 386,
LINGUISTICS 407
Linguistics and Philosophy see LINGUISTICS 407,
PHILOSOPHY 478
Linguistics and Phonetics see LINGUISTICS 407,
SPEECH PATHOLOGY/SCIENCES/THERAPY 546
Linguistics and Psychology see LINGUISTICS 407,
PSYCHOLOGY 512
Linguistics and Social Anthropology see
LINGUISTICS 407, SOCIAL SCIENCES/STUDIES 531

Linguistics with Chinese/Japanese see CHINESE 206, LINGUISTICS 407

Linguistics with French see FRENCH 325, LINGUISTICS 407

LITERATURE 409
 see also ENGLISH

Literature and History see HISTORY 325, LITERATURE 409

Literature and History of Art see HISTORY OF ART 363, LITERATURE 409

Literature and Myth see ENGLISH 296, LITERATURE 409

Literature and World Context see LITERATURE 409

Literature Combined Honours see LITERATURE 409

Live and Studio Sound see ENGINEERING (ACOUSTICS and SOUND) 264

Live Music see MUSIC 449

Logistics see TRANSPORT MANAGEMENT and PLANNING 571

Logistics and Supply Chain Management see TRANSPORT MANAGEMENT and PLANNING 571

Magazine Journalism see MEDIA STUDIES 427

Magazine Publishing see ENGLISH 296, MEDIA STUDIES 427

Maîtrise in English and French Law see LAW 393

Make-Up and Prosthetics for Performance see ART and DESIGN (Fashion and Textiles) 140

Make-Up for Media and Performance see ART and DESIGN (Fashion and Textiles) 140

Management see BUSINESS AND MANAGEMENT COURSES 179

Management (Combined) see BUSINESS AND MANAGEMENT COURSES 179

Management Accounting see ACCOUNTANCY/ ACCOUNTING 109, BUSINESS AND MANAGEMENT COURSES 179

Management and Business see BUSINESS AND MANAGEMENT COURSES 179

Management and Human Resource Management see HUMAN RESOURCE MANAGEMENT 371

Management and Leadership see BUSINESS AND MANAGEMENT COURSES, 179

Management and Marketing see MARKETING 415

Management and Marketing of Fashion Textiles see MARKETING 415

Management and Media Studies see MEDIA STUDIES 427

Management and Organisation see BUSINESS AND MANAGEMENT COURSES 179

Management and Organisation (Human Resource Management) see HUMAN RESOURCE MANAGEMENT 371

Management and Spanish see BUSINESS AND MANAGEMENT COURSES 179, SPANISH 543

Management and Sport Development see SPORTS SCIENCES/STUDIES 548

Management Economics see ECONOMICS 251

Management of Hospitality see HOSPITALITY and HOTEL MANAGEMENT 367

Management of Manufacturing Systems see ENGINEERING (MANUFACTURING) 288

Management of Sport see SPORTS SCIENCES/ STUDIES 548

Management of Travel and Tourism see TOURISM and TRAVEL 564

Management Science see BUSINESS AND MANAGEMENT COURSES 179

Management Science (Accounting) see ACCOUNTANCY/ACCOUNTING 109

Management Sciences see BUSINESS AND MANAGEMENT COURSES 179

Management Sciences and Accounting see ACCOUNTANCY/ACCOUNTING 109, BUSINESS AND MANAGEMENT COURSES 179

Management Sciences and French/German/ Spanish see BUSINESS AND MANAGEMENT COURSES (INTERNATIONAL AND EUROPEAN) 188, LANGUAGES 383

Management Studies see BUSINESS AND MANAGEMENT COURSES 179

Management Studies with French and Spanish see BUSINESS AND MANAGEMENT COURSES 179, FRENCH 325, SPANISH 543

Management Studies with French/German/Spanish see BUSINESS AND MANAGEMENT COURSES (INTERNATIONAL AND EUROPEAN) 188, FRENCH 325, GERMAN 337, SPANISH 543

Management Studies with French/Spanish/ Japanese see BUSINESS AND MANAGEMENT COURSES 179, FRENCH 325, JAPANESE 383, SPANISH 543

Management with Accounting see ACCOUNTANCY/ ACCOUNTING 109, BUSINESS AND MANAGEMENT COURSES 179

Management with Asian/Chinese Studies see ASIA-PACIFIC STUDIES 158, BUSINESS AND MANAGEMENT COURSES (INTERNATIONAL AND EUROPEAN) 188

Management with Banking and Finance see FINANCE 315

Management with Entrepreneurship see BUSINESS AND MANAGEMENT COURSES (SPECIALISED) 193

Management with French/German/Italian/Spanish see BUSINESS AND MANAGEMENT COURSES (INTERNATIONAL AND EUROPEAN) 188, FRENCH 325, GERMAN 337, ITALIAN 381, SPANISH 543

Management with Human Resource Management see BUSINESS AND MANAGEMENT COURSES 179, HUMAN RESOURCE MANAGEMENT 371

Management with Human Resources see HUMAN RESOURCE MANAGEMENT 371

Management with International Business see BUSINESS AND MANAGEMENT COURSES (INTERNATIONAL AND EUROPEAN) 188

Management with Leadership see BUSINESS AND MANAGEMENT COURSES 179

Management with Marketing see BUSINESS AND MANAGEMENT COURSES 179, MARKETING 415

Management with Tourism see TOURISM and TRAVEL 564

Management with Transport Studies see TRANSPORT MANAGEMENT and PLANNING 571

Management, Transport and Logistics see BUSINESS AND MANAGEMENT COURSES (SPECIALISED) 193, TRANSPORT MANAGEMENT and PLANNING 571

Manufacturing and Mechanical Engineering see ENGINEERING (MANUFACTURING) 288, ENGINEERING (MECHANICAL) 290

Manufacturing Engineering see ART and DESIGN (Product and Industrial Design) 152, ENGINEERING (MANUFACTURING) 288

Manufacturing Engineering and Management see ENGINEERING (MANUFACTURING) 288

Manufacturing Systems Engineering see ENGINEERING (MANUFACTURING) 288

Marine and Composites Technology see MARINE/MARITIME STUDIES 412, MATERIALS SCIENCE/METALLURGY 419

Marine and Freshwater Biology see BIOLOGY 170, MARINE/MARITIME STUDIES 412

Marine and Natural History Photography see MARINE/MARITIME STUDIES 412, PHOTOGRAPHY 481

Marine Biology see BIOLOGY 170, MARINE/MARITIME STUDIES 412

Marine Biology and Coastal Ecology see ENVIRONMENTAL SCIENCES/STUDIES 303, MARINE/MARITIME STUDIES 412

Marine Biology and Conservation see MARINE/MARITIME STUDIES 412

Marine Biology and Oceanography see BIOLOGY 170, MARINE/MARITIME STUDIES 412

Marine Biology and Zoology see BIOLOGY 170, MARINE/MARITIME STUDIES 412, ZOOLOGY 576

Marine Biology with Oceanography see BIOLOGY 170, MARINE/MARITIME STUDIES 412

Marine Chemistry see CHEMISTRY 199, MARINE/MARITIME STUDIES 412

Marine Coastal Resource Management with Marine Biology see MARINE/MARITIME STUDIES 412

Marine Ecology and Conservation see ENVIRONMENTAL SCIENCES/STUDIES 303, MARINE/MARITIME STUDIES 412

Marine Engineering see MARINE/MARITIME STUDIES 412, MATERIALS SCIENCE/METALLURGY 419, NAVAL ARCHITECTURE 459, TECHNOLOGIES 562

Marine Engineering and Technology see MARINE/MARITIME STUDIES 412

Marine Environmental Science see ENVIRONMENTAL SCIENCES/STUDIES 303, MARINE/MARITIME STUDIES 412

Marine Environmental Studies see ENVIRONMENTAL SCIENCES/STUDIES 303, MARINE/MARITIME STUDIES 412

Marine Geography see GEOGRAPHY 330, MARINE/MARITIME STUDIES 412

Marine Geoscience see MARINE/MARITIME STUDIES 412

Marine Geoscience (International) see MARINE/MARITIME STUDIES 412

Marine Operations see MARINE/MARITIME STUDIES 412

Marine Science see MARINE/MARITIME STUDIES 412

Marine Sports Technology see ENGINEERING (MECHANICAL) 290, MARINE/MARITIME STUDIES 412, TECHNOLOGIES 562

Marine Studies (Navigation/Ocean Yachting/Merchant Shipping) see MARINE/MARITIME STUDIES 412, TRANSPORT MANAGEMENT and PLANNING 571

Marine Technology see NAVAL ARCHITECTURE 459

Marine Technology with Mechanical Engineering see ENGINEERING (MECHANICAL) 290, MARINE/MARITIME STUDIES 412

Marine Vertebrate Zoology see MARINE/MARITIME STUDIES 412, ZOOLOGY 576

MARINE/MARITIME STUDIES 412
see also BIOLOGY
see also ENVIRONMENTAL SCIENCES/STUDIES
see also NAVAL ARCHITECTURE

Maritime Business *see* BUSINESS AND MANAGEMENT COURSES 179

Maritime Business and Management *see* BUSINESS AND MANAGEMENT COURSES (SPECIALISED) 193, MARINE/MARITIME STUDIES 412

Maritime Business and Maritime Law *see* LAW 393, MARINE/MARITIME STUDIES 412

Maritime Business with French/German/Spanish *see* BUSINESS AND MANAGEMENT COURSES (INTERNATIONAL AND EUROPEAN) 188, LANGUAGES 386

Maritime History *see* HISTORY 325, MARINE/MARITIME STUDIES 412

Maritime Law *see* LAW 393, MARINE/MARITIME STUDIES 412

Maritime Studies *see* MARINE/MARITIME STUDIES 412

Maritime Studies (Ocean Yachting) *see* NAVAL ARCHITECTURE 459

MARKETING 415

see also BUSINESS and MANAGEMENT COURSES

Marketing (Combined) *see* MARKETING 415

Marketing Advertising and Public Relations *see* MARKETING 415

Marketing and Advertising *see* MARKETING 415

Marketing and Advertising Management *see* MARKETING 415

Marketing and Brand Management *see* BUSINESS AND MANAGEMENT COURSES (SPECIALISED) 193, MARKETING 415

Marketing and Business *see* BUSINESS AND MANAGEMENT COURSES 179, MARKETING 415

Marketing and Design *see* MARKETING 415

Marketing and Finance *see* FINANCE 315, MARKETING 415

Marketing and Human Resource Management *see* HUMAN RESOURCE MANAGEMENT 371, MARKETING 415

Marketing and Innovation *see* MARKETING 415

Marketing and Language *see* LANGUAGES 386, MARKETING 415

Marketing and Law *see* LAW 393

Marketing and Management *see* BUSINESS AND MANAGEMENT COURSES 179, MARKETING 415

Marketing and Media Practice *see* MARKETING 415

Marketing and Multimedia *see* MARKETING 415

Marketing and Psychology *see* MARKETING 415, PSYCHOLOGY 512

Marketing and Public Relations *see* MARKETING 415

Marketing and Retail *see* MARKETING 415

Marketing and Sales *see* MARKETING 415

Marketing and Spanish *see* MARKETING 415, SPANISH 543

Marketing Communications *see* COMMUNICATION STUDIES/COMMUNICATION 214, MARKETING 415

Marketing Management *see* BUSINESS AND MANAGEMENT COURSES (SPECIALISED) 193, MARKETING 415, RETAIL MANAGEMENT 524

Marketing Management and Branding *see* MARKETING 415

Marketing Management with Consumer Studies *see* CONSUMER STUDIES/SCIENCES 226, MARKETING 415

Marketing Management with Fashion *see* MARKETING 415

Marketing Psychology *see* MARKETING 415, PSYCHOLOGY 512

Marketing with Advertising Management *see* MARKETING 415

Marketing with Digital Media *see* MARKETING 415

Marketing with Event Management *see* MARKETING 415

Marketing with Events Management *see* MARKETING 415

Marketing with Media Communications *see* COMMUNICATION STUDIES/COMMUNICATION 214, MARKETING 415

Marketing with Psychology *see* MARKETING 415, PSYCHOLOGY 512

Marketing with Public Relations *see* MARKETING 415

Marketing, Advertising and Communications *see* MARKETING 415

Marketing, Advertising and Public Relations *see* BUSINESS AND MANAGEMENT COURSES (SPECIALISED) 193, MARKETING 415

Marketing, Communications and Advertising *see* COMMUNICATION STUDIES/COMMUNICATION 214, MARKETING 415

Marketing, Design and Communication *see* MARKETING 415

Mass Communication *see* COMMUNICATION STUDIES/COMMUNICATION 214

Mass Communications *see* MEDIA STUDIES 427

Material Science and Technology *see* MATERIALS SCIENCE/METALLURGY 419

Materials *see* MATERIALS SCIENCE/METALLURGY 419

Materials and Design *see* MATERIALS SCIENCE/METALLURGY 419

Materials Engineering *see* MATERIALS SCIENCE/
METALLURGY 419

Materials Science *see* MATERIALS SCIENCE/
METALLURGY 419

Materials Science and Energy Engineering *see*
ENGINEERING/ENGINEERING SCIENCES 260,
MATERIALS SCIENCE/METALLURGY 419

Materials Science and Engineering *see* ART and
DESIGN (Fashion and Textiles) 140, MATERIALS
SCIENCE/METALLURGY 419

Materials Science and Engineering (Biomaterials) *see*
MATERIALS SCIENCE/METALLURGY 419

Materials Science and Engineering (Industrial
Management) *see* MATERIALS SCIENCE/
METALLURGY 419

Materials Science and Engineering (Modern
Language) *see* LANGUAGES 386, MATERIALS
SCIENCE/METALLURGY 419

Materials Science and Engineering with
Business Management *see* BUSINESS AND
MANAGEMENT COURSES 179, MATERIALS
SCIENCE/METALLURGY 419

Materials Science with Nuclear Engineering *see*
MATERIALS SCIENCE/METALLURGY 419

MATERIALS SCIENCE/METALLURGY 419

Materials with Management *see* MATERIALS SCIENCE/
METALLURGY 419

Materials with Nuclear Engineering *see* MATERIALS
SCIENCE/METALLURGY 419

Materials, Economics and Management *see*
ECONOMICS 251, MATERIALS SCIENCE/
METALLURGY 419

Mathematical and Management Studies *see*
MATHEMATICS 422

Mathematical and Theoretical Physics *see*
MATHEMATICS 422, PHYSICS 488

Mathematical Biology *see* BIOLOGY 170,
MATHEMATICS 422

Mathematical Computation *see* COMPUTER COURSES
219, MATHEMATICS 422

Mathematical Economics and Statistics *see* ECONOMICS
251, MATHEMATICS 422, STATISTICS 554

Mathematical Engineering *see* MATHEMATICS 422

Mathematical Physics *see* MATHEMATICS 422,
PHYSICS 488

Mathematical Science *see* MATHEMATICS 422

Mathematical Science with Statistics *see*
MATHEMATICS 422, STATISTICS 554

Mathematical Sciences *see* MATHEMATICS 422

Mathematical Sciences with a European Language
see LANGUAGES 386, MATHEMATICS 422

Mathematical Studies *see* MATHEMATICS 422

MATHEMATICS 422

 see also PHYSICS

Mathematics (European Studies) *see* EUROPEAN
STUDIES 307, MATHEMATICS 422

Mathematics (Pure) *see* MATHEMATICS 422

Mathematics and Applied Statistics *see* MATHEMATICS
422, STATISTICS 554

Mathematics and Biology *see* BIOLOGY 170,
MATHEMATICS 422

Mathematics and Business *see* BUSINESS AND
MANAGEMENT COURSES 179, MATHEMATICS 422

Mathematics and Business Management *see*
BUSINESS AND MANAGEMENT COURSES 179,
MATHEMATICS 422

Mathematics and Computer Science *see* COMPUTER
COURSES 219, MATHEMATICS 422

Mathematics and Computing *see* COMPUTER
COURSES 219, MATHEMATICS 422

Mathematics and Economics *see* ECONOMICS 251,
MATHEMATICS 422

Mathematics and Finance *see* FINANCE 315,
MATHEMATICS 422

Mathematics and Financial Management *see*
FINANCE 315, MATHEMATICS 422

Mathematics and Humanities *see*
MATHEMATICS 422

Mathematics and its Applications *see*
MATHEMATICS 422

Mathematics and Management *see* BUSINESS
AND MANAGEMENT COURSES 179,
MATHEMATICS 422

Mathematics and Management Studies *see*
MATHEMATICS 422

Mathematics and Meteorology *see* MATHEMATICS 422

Mathematics and Music *see* MATHEMATICS 422,
MUSIC 449

Mathematics and Philosophy *see* MATHEMATICS 422,
PHILOSOPHY, 478

Mathematics and Physics *see* MATHEMATICS 422,
PHYSICS 488

Mathematics and Psychology *see* MATHEMATICS 422,
PSYCHOLOGY 512

Mathematics and Religious Studies *see* MATHEMATICS
422, RELIGIOUS STUDIES 521

Mathematics and Science Education *see*
MATHEMATICS 422, TEACHER TRAINING 559

Mathematics and Sports Science *see* MATHEMATICS
422, SPORTS SCIENCES/STUDIES 548

Mathematics and Statistics *see* MATHEMATICS 422,
STATISTICS 554

Mathematics and Statistics and Operational Research *see* MATHEMATICS 422, STATISTICS 554

Mathematics and Statistics with Computational Mathematics *see* MATHEMATICS 422, STATISTICS 554

Mathematics and Statistics with Management *see* MATHEMATICS 422, STATISTICS 554

Mathematics and Welsh *see* CELTIC, IRISH, SCOTTISH AND WELSH STUDIES 197, MATHEMATICS 422

Mathematics Secondary Education *see* TEACHER TRAINING 559

Mathematics Teaching Key Stage 2+3 *see* TEACHER TRAINING 559

Mathematics with Accounting *see* ACCOUNTANCY/ ACCOUNTING 109, MATHEMATICS 422

Mathematics with Actuarial Science *see* ACTUARIAL SCIENCE/STUDIES 114, MATHEMATICS 422

Mathematics with Astronomy *see* ASTRONOMY and ASTROPHYSICS 159, MATHEMATICS 422

Mathematics with Biology *see* BIOLOGY 170, MATHEMATICS 422

Mathematics with Business Studies *see* BUSINESS AND MANAGEMENT COURSES 179, MATHEMATICS 422

Mathematics with Computer Science *see* COMPUTER COURSES 219, MATHEMATICS 422

Mathematics with Computing *see* MATHEMATICS 422

Mathematics with Economics *see* ECONOMICS 251, MATHEMATICS 422

Mathematics with Education *see* EDUCATION STUDIES 256, MATHEMATICS 422

Mathematics with Engineering *see* ENGINEERING/ ENGINEERING SCIENCES 260, MATHEMATICS 422

Mathematics with Finance *see* FINANCE 315, MATHEMATICS 422

Mathematics with Finance and Accounting *see* ACCOUNTANCY/ACCOUNTING 109, FINANCE 315

Mathematics with Financial Mathematics *see* FINANCE 315, MATHEMATICS 422

Mathematics with French/German/Spanish *see* FRENCH 325, GERMAN 337, MATHEMATICS 422, SPANISH 543

Mathematics with Languages *see* LANGUAGES 386, MATHEMATICS 422

Mathematics with Management *see* BUSINESS AND MANAGEMENT COURSES 179, MATHEMATICS 422

Mathematics with Management and Finance *see* MATHEMATICS 422

Mathematics with Mathematical Computation *see* COMPUTER COURSES 219, MATHEMATICS 422

Mathematics with Mathematics Education *see* MATHEMATICS 422, TEACHER TRAINING 559

Mathematics with Music *see* MATHEMATICS 422, MUSIC 449

Mathematics with Physics *see* MATHEMATICS 422, PHYSICS 488

Mathematics with Spanish *see* MATHEMATICS 422, SPANISH 543

Mathematics with Statistics *see* MATHEMATICS 422, STATISTICS 554

Mathematics, Operational Research and Statistics *see* MATHEMATICS 422

Mathematics, Operational Research, Statistics and Economics *see* ACTUARIAL SCIENCE/STUDIES 114, ECONOMICS 251, MATHEMATICS 422, STATISTICS 554

Mathematics, Optimisation and Statistics *see* MATHEMATICS 422, STATISTICS 554

Mathematics, Statistics and Computing *see* COMPUTER COURSES 219, STATISTICS 554

Mathematics, Statistics and Financial Economics *see* FINANCE 315, MATHEMATICS 422, STATISTICS 554

Mathematics/Applied Mathematics/Pure Mathematics *see* MATHEMATICS 422

Mathematics: Primary Education *see* EDUCATION STUDIES 256, MATHEMATICS 422, TEACHER TRAINING 559

Mechanical and Automotive Engineering *see* ENGINEERING (MECHANICAL) 290

Mechanical and Electrical Engineering *see* ENGINEERING (MECHANICAL) 290

Mechanical and Low Carbon Transport Engineering *see* ENGINEERING (MECHANICAL) 290

Mechanical and Manufacturing Engineering *see* ENGINEERING (MANUFACTURING) 288, ENGINEERING (MECHANICAL) 290

Mechanical and Marine Engineering *see* ENGINEERING (MECHANICAL) 290, NAVAL ARCHITECTURE 459

Mechanical and Materials Engineering *see* ENGINEERING (MECHANICAL) 290, MATERIALS SCIENCE/METALLURGY 419

Mechanical and Medical Engineering *see* ENGINEERING (MECHANICAL) 290

Mechanical and Offshore Engineering *see* ENGINEERING (MECHANICAL) 290

Mechanical and Vehicle Technology *see* ENGINEERING (MECHANICAL) 290

Mechanical Design *see* ART and DESIGN (Product and Industrial Design) 152

Mechanical Design and Manufacture *see* ENGINEERING (MANUFACTURING) 288, ENGINEERING (MECHANICAL) 290

Mechanical Design and Manufacturing Engineering *see* ENGINEERING (MANUFACTURING) 288, ENGINEERING (MECHANICAL) 290

Mechanical Design and Technology *see* ENGINEERING (MECHANICAL) 290

Mechanical Design Engineering *see* ENGINEERING (MECHANICAL) 290

Mechanical Electronic Systems Engineering *see* ENGINEERING (MECHANICAL) 290

Mechanical Engineering *see* ENGINEERING (MANUFACTURING) 288, ENGINEERING (MECHANICAL) 290

Mechanical Engineering (Advanced Materials) *see* ENGINEERING (MECHANICAL) 290, MATERIALS SCIENCE/METALLURGY 419

Mechanical Engineering (Aerospace) *see* ENGINEERING (AERONAUTICAL and AEROSPACE) 266, ENGINEERING (MECHANICAL) 290

Mechanical Engineering (Automotive) *see* ENGINEERING (MECHANICAL) 290

Mechanical Engineering (Automotive/Biomedical) *see* ENGINEERING (MECHANICAL) 290

Mechanical Engineering (Bioengineering) *see* ENGINEERING (MECHANICAL) 290

Mechanical Engineering (Engineering Management) *see* ENGINEERING (MECHANICAL) 290

Mechanical Engineering (Industrial Management) *see* ENGINEERING (MECHANICAL) 290

Mechanical Engineering (Mechatronics) *see* ENGINEERING (MECHANICAL) 290

Mechanical Engineering (Naval Engineering) *see* ENGINEERING (MECHANICAL) 290

Mechanical Engineering (Sustainable Energy Systems) *see* ENGINEERING (MECHANICAL) 290

Mechanical Engineering and Computer Aided Design *see* COMPUTER COURSES 219, ENGINEERING (MECHANICAL) 290

Mechanical Engineering and Energy Engineering *see* ENGINEERING (MECHANICAL) 290

Mechanical Engineering with Aeronautics *see* ENGINEERING (AERONAUTICAL and AEROSPACE) 266, ENGINEERING (MECHANICAL) 290, ENGINEERING/ENGINEERING SCIENCES 260

Mechanical Engineering with Automotive Design *see* ENGINEERING (MECHANICAL) 290

Mechanical Engineering with Bioengineering *see* ENGINEERING (MECHANICAL) 290

Mechanical Engineering with Building Services *see* BUILDING and CONSTRUCTION 176, ENGINEERING (CIVIL) 274, ENGINEERING (MECHANICAL) 290

Mechanical Engineering with Business *see* BUSINESS AND MANAGEMENT COURSES 179, ENGINEERING (MANUFACTURING) 288, ENGINEERING (MECHANICAL) 290

Mechanical Engineering with Composites *see* ENGINEERING (MECHANICAL) 290

Mechanical Engineering with Control *see* ENGINEERING (MECHANICAL) 290

Mechanical Engineering with European Studies *see* ENGINEERING (MECHANICAL) 290, EUROPEAN STUDIES 307

Mechanical Engineering with Financial Management *see* ENGINEERING (MECHANICAL) 290, FINANCE 315

Mechanical Engineering with French/German/Italian *see* ENGINEERING (MECHANICAL) 290, LANGUAGES 386

Mechanical Engineering with Management *see* ENGINEERING (MECHANICAL) 290

Mechanical Engineering with Materials *see* ENGINEERING (MECHANICAL) 290, MATERIALS SCIENCE/METALLURGY 419

Mechanical Engineering with Materials Engineering *see* ENGINEERING (MECHANICAL) 290, MATERIALS SCIENCE/METALLURGY 419

Mechanical Engineering with Microsystems *see* ENGINEERING (MECHANICAL) 290

Mechanical Engineering with Renewable Energy *see* ENGINEERING (MECHANICAL) 290

Mechanical Manufacturing and Engineering Management *see* ENGINEERING (MANUFACTURING) 288, SPORTS SCIENCES/STUDIES 548

Mechatronic and Robotic Engineering *see* ENGINEERING (COMPUTER, CONTROL, SOFTWARE and SYSTEMS) 280

Mechatronic Engineering *see* ENGINEERING (ELECTRICAL and ELECTRONIC) 283, ENGINEERING (MECHANICAL) 290

Mechatronics *see* ENGINEERING (MECHANICAL) 290

Mechatronics and Robotic Systems *see* ENGINEERING (MECHANICAL) 290

Mechatronics, Robotics and Mechanical Engineering *see* ENGINEERING (MECHANICAL) 290

Media *see* MEDIA STUDIES 427

Media (Applied Linguistics) *see* LINGUISTICS 407

Media (Film) Production see FILM, RADIO, VIDEO and
TV STUDIES 310
Media (Music) see MEDIA STUDIES 427,
MUSIC 449
Media and Communication see COMMUNICATION
STUDIES/COMMUNICATION 214,
MEDIA STUDIES 427
Media and Communication Studies see
COMMUNICATION STUDIES/COMMUNICATION 214,
MEDIA STUDIES 427
Media and Communications see COMMUNICATION
STUDIES/COMMUNICATION 214,
MEDIA STUDIES 427
Media and Communications (Media Photography)
see PHOTOGRAPHY 481
Media and Creative Industries see MEDIA
STUDIES 427
Media and Cultural Studies see MEDIA
STUDIES 427
Media and Culture see MEDIA STUDIES 427
Media and English Literature see LITERATURE 409,
MEDIA STUDIES 427
Media and Journalism see MEDIA STUDIES 427
Media and Marketing see MARKETING 415
Media and Pop Culture see MEDIA STUDIES 427
Media and Sociology see MEDIA STUDIES 427,
SOCIOLOGY 539
Media Arts see MEDIA STUDIES 427
Media Communication see COMMUNICATION STUDIES/
COMMUNICATION 214
Media Communications see COMMUNICATION
STUDIES/COMMUNICATION 214, MEDIA
STUDIES 427
Media Communications and Culture see
COMMUNICATION STUDIES/COMMUNICATION 214,
MEDIA STUDIES 427
Media Industries and Literature see LITERATURE 409
Media Practice see MEDIA STUDIES 427
Media Practices (Mass Communications)
see COMMUNICATION STUDIES/
COMMUNICATION 214
Media Production see FILM, RADIO, VIDEO and TV
STUDIES 310, MEDIA STUDIES 427
Media Production (Television and Radio) see FILM,
RADIO, VIDEO and TV STUDIES 310, MEDIA
STUDIES 427
Media Production (Video and New Media) see
FILM, RADIO, VIDEO and TV STUDIES 310, MEDIA
STUDIES 427
Media Production and Music see MEDIA STUDIES 427,
MUSIC 449

Media Production and Photography see
PHOTOGRAPHY 481
Media Production and Technology see MEDIA
STUDIES 427
Media Professional Studies see MEDIA STUDIES 427
MEDIA STUDIES 427
see also COMMUNICATION STUDIES/
COMMUNICATION
see also COMPUTER COURSES
see also ENGINEERING (ACOUSTICS and SOUND)
see also FILM, RADIO, VIDEO and TV STUDIES
Media Studies and Psychology see MEDIA STUDIES
427, PSYCHOLOGY 512
Media Studies with Sociology see COMMUNICATION
STUDIES/COMMUNICATION 214, MEDIA
STUDIES 427
Media Studies with Sociology/Education see MEDIA
STUDIES 427, SOCIOLOGY 539
Media Technology see MEDIA STUDIES 427
Media Writing see MEDIA STUDIES 427
Media, Communication and Cultural Studies see
COMMUNICATION STUDIES/COMMUNICATION 214,
MEDIA STUDIES 427
Media, Communication and Cultures see
COMMUNICATION STUDIES/COMMUNICATION 214,
MEDIA STUDIES 427
Media, Communications and Culture see
COMMUNICATION STUDIES/COMMUNICATION 214,
MEDIA STUDIES 427
Media, Culture and Communication see MEDIA
STUDIES 427
Media, Culture and Society see MEDIA STUDIES 427
Media, Film and Television see FILM, RADIO, VIDEO
and TV STUDIES 310
Media, Music and Sound see MUSIC 449
Medical and Pharmacological Sciences see
PHARMACOLOGY 472
Medical Anthropology see ANTHROPOLOGY 127
Medical Biochemistry see BIOCHEMISTRY 162,
BIOLOGICAL SCIENCES 165
Medical Biology see BIOLOGY 170
Medical Biotechnology see BIOTECHNOLOGY 174
Medical Cell Biology see BIOLOGY 170, MEDICINE 433,
MICROBIOLOGY 447
Medical Electronics and Instrumentation
see ENGINEERING (ELECTRICAL and
ELECTRONIC) 283
Medical Engineering see ENGINEERING (ELECTRICAL
and ELECTRONIC) 283, ENGINEERING
(MECHANICAL) 290, ENGINEERING (MEDICAL)
295, MATERIALS SCIENCE/METALLURGY 419

Medical Genetics see BIOLOGICAL SCIENCES 165, GENETICS 328

Medical Imaging (Diagnostic Radiography) see RADIOGRAPHY 519

Medical Materials Science see MATERIALS SCIENCE/METALLURGY 419

Medical Microbiology see MICROBIOLOGY 447

Medical Microbiology and Virology see MICROBIOLOGY 447

Medical Neuroscience see ANATOMICAL SCIENCE/ANATOMY 122

Medical Pharmacology see PHARMACOLOGY 472

Medical Physics see ENGINEERING (MEDICAL) 295, PHYSICS 488

Medical Physiology see PHYSIOLOGY 500

Medical Product Design see ART and DESIGN (Product and Industrial Design) 152, ENGINEERING/ENGINEERING SCIENCES 260

Medical Science see BIOLOGICAL SCIENCES 165, HEALTH SCIENCES/STUDIES 341

Medical Sciences see BIOLOGICAL SCIENCES 165

Medical Sciences and Humanities see HUMAN SCIENCES/HUMAN BIOSCIENCES 374

Medical Statistics see STATISTICS 554

Medicinal and Biological Chemistry see BIOCHEMISTRY 162, BIOLOGICAL SCIENCES 165, CHEMISTRY 199, MEDICINE 433

Medicinal and Pharmaceutical Chemistry see CHEMISTRY 199, PHARMACY and PHARMACEUTICAL SCIENCES 475

Medicinal Chemistry see CHEMISTRY 199, MEDICINE 433

Medicinal Horticulture see HORTICULTURE 365

MEDICINE 433
   see also BIOLOGICAL SCIENCES

Medicine and Surgery see MEDICINE 433

Medicine Extended Programme see MEDICINE 433

Medicine with a Foundation Year see MEDICINE 433

Medicine with Genetics see GENETICS 328

Medicine with Pre-Med Year see MEDICINE 433

Medieval and Early Modern History see HISTORY 355

Medieval and Modern History see HISTORY 355

Medieval and Renaissance Studies see ENGLISH 296, HISTORY 355

Medieval History see HISTORY 355

Medieval History and Archaeology see ARCHAEOLOGY 131, HISTORY 355

Medieval Studies see HISTORY 355

Medieval Studies and Latin see LATIN 389

Mental Health Nursing see NURSING and MIDWIFERY 461

Mental Health Nursing and Social Work see NURSING and MIDWIFERY 461

Metallurgy see MATERIALS SCIENCE/METALLURGY 419

Metallurgy and Materials Engineering see MATERIALS SCIENCE/METALLURGY 419

Metalwork and Jewellery see ART and DESIGN (3D Design) 156

Meteorology see ENVIRONMENTAL SCIENCES/STUDIES 303, GEOGRAPHY 330

Meteorology and Climate see ENVIRONMENTAL SCIENCES/STUDIES 303, GEOGRAPHY 330

Meteorology and Climate Science (International) see GEOGRAPHY 330

Meteorology and Oceanography see ENVIRONMENTAL SCIENCES/STUDIES 303, GEOGRAPHY 330, GEOLOGY/GEOLOGICAL SCIENCES 335, MARINE/MARITIME STUDIES 412

Microbial Biotechnology see BIOTECHNOLOGY 174, MICROBIOLOGY 447

Microbial Genetics see GENETICS 328, MICROBIOLOGY 447

MICROBIOLOGY 447
   see also BIOLOGICAL SCIENCES
   see also BIOLOGY
   see also BIOTECHNOLOGY
   see also GENETICS

Microbiology (Medicine) see MICROBIOLOGY 447

Microbiology and Biotechnology see BIOTECHNOLOGY 174, MICROBIOLOGY 447

Microbiology and Immunology see MICROBIOLOGY 447

Microbiology and Modern Languages see LANGUAGES 386, MICROBIOLOGY 447

Microbiology and Molecular Biology see MICROBIOLOGY 447

Microbiology and Virology see MICROBIOLOGY 447

Microbiology and Zoology see MICROBIOLOGY 447, ZOOLOGY 576

Microcomputer Systems Engineering see ENGINEERING (COMPUTER, CONTROL, SOFTWARE and SYSTEMS) 280

Microelectronics see ENGINEERING (ELECTRICAL and ELECTRONIC) 283

Middle Eastern Studies see ARABIC AND ANCIENT NEAR AND MIDDLE EASTERN STUDIES 129

Middle Eastern Studies and Screen Studies see ARABIC AND ANCIENT NEAR AND MIDDLE EASTERN STUDIES 129

Midwifery see NURSING and MIDWIFERY 461

Midwifery Practice *see* NURSING and MIDWIFERY 461

Midwifery Studies *see* NURSING and MIDWIFERY 461

Midwifery Studies with Registration *see* NURSING and MIDWIFERY 461

Mining Engineering *see* ENGINEERING (MECHANICAL) 290, MATERIALS SCIENCE/METALLURGY 419

Mobile Telecommunications *see* ENGINEERING (COMMUNICATIONS) 278

Modelmaking *see* ART and DESIGN (3D Design) 156

Modern and Contemporary History *see* HISTORY 355

Modern and Medieval Languages *see* LANGUAGES 386

Modern and Medieval Languages (Classical Greek) *see* GREEK 340

Modern and Medieval Languages (Classical Latin) *see* LATIN 389

Modern and Medieval Languages (French) *see* FRENCH 325

Modern and Medieval Languages (German) *see* GERMAN 327

Modern and Medieval Languages (Italian) *see* ITALIAN 381

Modern and Medieval Languages (Linguistics) *see* LANGUAGES 386, LINGUISTICS 407

Modern and Medieval Languages (Spanish/ Portuguese) *see* SPANISH 543

Modern Ballet *see* DANCE/DANCE STUDIES 227

Modern European History *see* HISTORY 355

Modern European Languages *see* LANGUAGES 386

Modern European Languages and History *see* HISTORY 355, LANGUAGES 386

Modern European Studies *see* EUROPEAN STUDIES 307, LANGUAGES 386

Modern Greek *see* GREEK 340

Modern History *see* HISTORY 355

Modern History and Politics *see* HISTORY 355, POLITICS 507

Modern History in Russia *see* RUSSIAN and EAST EUROPEAN STUDIES 526

Modern Language *see* LANGUAGES 386

Modern Language and Business Management *see* LANGUAGES 386

Modern Language and Linguistics *see* LANGUAGES 386, LINGUISTICS 407

Modern Language and Linguistics (Russian) *see* LANGUAGES 386, LINGUISTICS 407, RUSSIAN and EAST EUROPEAN STUDIES 526

Modern Language Studies *see* LANGUAGES 386

Modern Language Studies (Italian) *see* ITALIAN 381, LANGUAGES 386

Modern Language Studies French/German/Italian/ Spanish *see* LANGUAGES 386

Modern Languages *see* LANGUAGES 386

Modern Languages (Russian +2nd Language) *see* RUSSIAN and EAST EUROPEAN STUDIES 526

Modern Languages and Business Studies *see* LANGUAGES 386

Modern Languages and European Studies *see* EUROPEAN STUDIES 307, LANGUAGES 386

Modern Languages and European Studies (French and Spanish/Italian/Russian/German) *see* FRENCH 325, LANGUAGES 386

Modern Languages and European Studies (German and French/Italian/Russian/Spanish) *see* GERMAN 337, LANGUAGES 386

Modern Languages and European Studies (Spanish and French/German/Italian/Russian) *see* LANGUAGES 386, SPANISH 543

Modern Languages and Linguistics *see* LANGUAGES 386, LINGUISTICS 407

Modern Languages and Translation and Interpretation *see* LANGUAGES 386

Modern Languages and Translation and Interpreting Studies (French/German/Italian/Portugese/ Spanish) *see* FRENCH 325, GERMAN 337, ITALIAN 381, LANGUAGES 386, SPANISH 543

Modern Languages Double Honours *see* LANGUAGES 386

Modern Languages French *see* FRENCH 325

Modern Languages Japanese *see* JAPANESE 383

Modern Languages Spanish *see* SPANISH 543

Modern Languages with Business *see* BUSINESS AND MANAGEMENT COURSES 179, LANGUAGES 386

Modern Languages with Film Studies *see* FILM, RADIO, VIDEO and TV STUDIES 310, LANGUAGES 386

Modern Middle Eastern History *see* ARABIC AND ANCIENT NEAR AND MIDDLE EASTERN STUDIES 129, HISTORY 355

Modern World History *see* HISTORY 355

Molecular and Cellular Biology *see* BIOLOGY 170

Molecular and Cellular Biology with Plant Science *see* PLANT SCIENCES 504

Molecular Biology *see* BIOLOGICAL SCIENCES 165, BIOLOGY 170, MICROBIOLOGY 447

Molecular Biology and Genetics *see* BIOLOGY 170, GENETICS 328, MICROBIOLOGY 447

Molecular Biosciences (Biochemistry) *see* BIOCHEMISTRY 162

Molecular Cell Biology *see* BIOLOGY 170

Molecular Genetics *see* BIOLOGICAL SCIENCES 165, GENETICS 328

Money, Banking and Finance *see* FINANCE 315

Money, Banking and Finance with Languages *see* FINANCE 315, LANGUAGES 386

Motion Graphics *see* ART and DESIGN (Graphic Design) 148

Motorcycle Engineering *see* ENGINEERING (MECHANICAL) 290

Motoring Journalism *see* MEDIA STUDIES 427

Motorsport *see* ENGINEERING (MECHANICAL) 290

Motorsport Design and Management *see* ART and DESIGN (Product and Industrial Design) 152, ENGINEERING (MECHANICAL) 290

Motorsport Design Engineering *see* ENGINEERING (MECHANICAL) 290

Motorsport Engineering *see* ENGINEERING (MECHANICAL) 290

Motorsport Engineering and Design *see* ENGINEERING (MECHANICAL) 290

Motorsport Management *see* BUSINESS AND MANAGEMENT COURSES (SPECIALISED) 193

Motorsport Technology *see* ENGINEERING (MECHANICAL) 290

Motorsports Engineering *see* ENGINEERING (MECHANICAL) 290

Motorsports Technology *see* ENGINEERING (MECHANICAL) 290

Moving Image Production *see* FILM, RADIO, VIDEO and TV STUDIES 310

Multilingual Studies with International Relations *see* INTERNATIONAL RELATIONS 378, LANGUAGES 386

Multimedia *see* MEDIA STUDIES 427

Multimedia and Internet Systems Engineering *see* ENGINEERING (COMMUNICATIONS) 278

Multimedia and Web Computing *see* COMPUTER COURSES 219

Multimedia and Web Design *see* MEDIA STUDIES 427

Multimedia Business and Entrepreneurship *see* MEDIA STUDIES 427

Multimedia Journalism *see* MEDIA STUDIES 427

Multimedia Journalism Professional Practice *see* MEDIA STUDIES 427

Multimedia Technologies *see* TECHNOLOGIES 562

Multimedia Technology *see* COMPUTER COURSES 219, TECHNOLOGIES 562

Museum and Gallery Studies *see* ART and DESIGN (Fine Art) 144, HISTORY OF ART 363, INFORMATION MANAGEMENT and LIBRARIANSHIP 375

Museum and Heritage Studies *see* HISTORY OF ART 363, INFORMATION MANAGEMENT and LIBRARIANSHIP 375

MUSIC 449

see also COMBINED COURSES

see also ENGINEERING (ACOUSTICS and SOUND)

see also TEACHER TRAINING

Music (Classical Music) *see* MUSIC 449

Music (Combined) *see* MUSIC 449

Music (Jazz) *see* MUSIC 449

Music (Performance) *see* MUSIC 449

Music (Popular Music) *see* MUSIC 449

Music (Production) *see* MUSIC 449

Music and Arts Management *see* BUSINESS AND MANAGEMENT COURSES (SPECIALISED) 193, MUSIC 449

Music and Audio Technology *see* MUSIC 449

Music and Creative Industries Business *see* MUSIC 449

Music and Creative Writing *see* ENGLISH 296, MUSIC 449

Music and Drama *see* DRAMA 239, MUSIC 449

Music and Film Studies *see* FILM, RADIO, VIDEO and TV STUDIES 310, MUSIC 449

Music and French/German/Italian/Spanish *see* LANGUAGES 386, MUSIC 449

Music and Management Sciences *see* BUSINESS AND MANAGEMENT COURSES 179, MUSIC 449

Music and Media *see* MEDIA STUDIES 427, MUSIC 449

Music and Media Management *see* MUSIC 449

Music and Philosophy *see* MUSIC 449, PHILOSOPHY 478

Music and Popular Music *see* MUSIC 449

Music and Psychology *see* MUSIC 449, PSYCHOLOGY 512

Music and Sound Recording (Tonmeister) *see* ENGINEERING (ACOUSTICS and SOUND) 264, MUSIC 449

Music and Sound Technology *see* ENGINEERING (ACOUSTICS and SOUND) 264, MUSIC 449

Music and Sound with Drama *see* DRAMA 239, MUSIC 449

Music Arts Management *see* MUSIC 449

Music BEd *see* TEACHER TRAINING 559

Music Business *see* BUSINESS AND MANAGEMENT COURSES (SPECIALISED) 193

Music Composition *see* MUSIC 449

Music Composition and Professional Practice *see* MUSIC 449

Music Composition and Technology *see* MUSIC 449

Music Culture (Theory and Production) *see* MUSIC 449

Music Informatics *see* MUSIC 449

Music Journalism *see* MEDIA STUDIES 427, MUSIC 449

Music Management Artist Development *see* MUSIC 449

Music Performance *see* MUSIC 449

Music Performance and Professional Practice *see* MUSIC 449

Music Practice *see* MUSIC 449

Music Production *see* MUSIC 449

Music Production Arts *see* MUSIC 449

Music Production for Media *see* MUSIC 449, TECHNOLOGIES 562

Music Promotion *see* MUSIC 449

Music Studio Technology *see* ENGINEERING (ACOUSTICS and SOUND) 264

Music Technology *see* MUSIC 449, TECHNOLOGIES 562

Music Technology (Audio Systems/Sound for Media) *see* ENGINEERING (ACOUSTICS and SOUND) 264

Music Technology and Electronics *see* ENGINEERING (ELECTRICAL and ELECTRONIC) 283, MUSIC 449

Music Technology and Innovation *see* MUSIC 449

Music Technology and Performance *see* MUSIC 449

Music Technology and Production *see* MUSIC 449, TECHNOLOGIES 562

Music Technology and Sonic Arts *see* MUSIC 449

Music Technology Production *see* MUSIC 449

Music Technology Systems *see* ENGINEERING (ACOUSTICS and SOUND) 264, TECHNOLOGIES 562

Music Theatre *see* DRAMA 239, MUSIC 449

Music with a Modern Language *see* LANGUAGES 386, MUSIC 449

Music with Dance *see* DANCE/DANCE STUDIES 227, MUSIC 449

Music with Drama *see* DRAMA 239, MUSIC 449

Music with Irish *see* CELTIC, IRISH, SCOTTISH AND WELSH STUDIES 197, MUSIC 449

Music with Political Studies *see* MUSIC 449, POLITICS 507

Music with Psychology *see* MUSIC 449, PSYCHOLOGY 512

Music, Theatre and Entertainment Management *see* BUSINESS AND MANAGEMENT COURSES (SPECIALISED) 193, COMBINED COURSES 212

Music/Popular Music *see* MUSIC 449

Musical Composition *see* MUSIC 449

Musical Instrument *see* MUSIC 449

Musical Performance *see* MUSIC 449

Musical Theatre *see* DRAMA 239, MUSIC 449

Musical Theatre Performance *see* DRAMA 239, MUSIC 449

Muslim Cultures and Civilisation *see* ARABIC AND ANCIENT NEAR AND MIDDLE EASTERN STUDIES 129, RELIGIOUS STUDIES 521

Nanoelectronics *see* ENGINEERING (ELECTRICAL and ELECTRONIC) 283

Natural and Environmental Science *see* ENVIRONMENTAL SCIENCES/STUDIES 303, NATURAL SCIENCES 457

Natural Hazard Management *see* ENVIRONMENTAL SCIENCES/STUDIES 303

Natural History *see* ANIMAL SCIENCES 124

NATURAL SCIENCES 457
 see also BIOLOGICAL SCIENCES
 see also CHEMISTRY

Natural Sciences (Astrophysics) *see* ASTRONOMY and ASTROPHYSICS 159

Natural Sciences (Biochemistry) *see* BIOCHEMISTRY 162

Natural Sciences (Biological and Biomedical Science) *see* BIOLOGICAL SCIENCES 165

Natural Sciences (Chemistry) *see* CHEMISTRY 199, NATURAL SCIENCES 457

Natural Sciences (Earth Science) *see* GEOLOGY/GEOLOGICAL SCIENCES 335

Natural Sciences (Genetics) *see* GENETICS 328

Natural Sciences (Materials Science) *see* MATERIALS SCIENCE/METALLURGY 419

Natural Sciences (Neuroscience) *see* ANATOMICAL SCIENCE/ANATOMY 122, BIOLOGICAL SCIENCES 165

Natural Sciences (Pathology/Microbial Sciences) *see* BIOLOGICAL SCIENCES 165

Natural Sciences (Pharmacology) *see* PHARMACOLOGY 472

Natural Sciences (Physics/Physical Science/Astrophysics) *see* PHYSICS 488

Natural Sciences (Physiology, Development and Neuroscience) *see* PHYSIOLOGY 500

Natural Sciences (Plant Science) *see* PLANT SCIENCES 504

Natural Sciences (Psychology/Neurology) *see* PSYCHOLOGY 512

Natural Sciences (Zoology) *see* ZOOLOGY 576

Natural Sciences with Study in Europe *see* EUROPEAN STUDIES 307, NATURAL SCIENCES 457

Nature Tourism Management *see* TOURISM and TRAVEL 564

Naturopathy *see* HEALTH SCIENCES/STUDIES 341

Nautical Science *see* NAVAL ARCHITECTURE 459

NAVAL ARCHITECTURE 459
 see also MARINE/MARITIME STUDIES
Naval Architecture and Marine Engineering *see*
 NAVAL ARCHITECTURE 459
Naval Architecture Ocean Engineering *see* NAVAL
 ARCHITECTURE 459
Naval Architecture Small Craft Engineering *see* NAVAL
 ARCHITECTURE 459
Naval Architecture with Ocean Engineering *see*
 MARINE/MARITIME STUDIES 412, NAVAL
 ARCHITECTURE 459
Naval Architecture with Small Craft Engineering *see*
 NAVAL ARCHITECTURE 459
Network and Mobile Computing *see* COMPUTER
 COURSES 219
Network Computing *see* COMPUTER COURSES 219
Network Management and Design *see* COMPUTER
 COURSES 219
Network Technology *see* ENGINEERING (COMPUTER,
 CONTROL, SOFTWARE and SYSTEMS) 280
Networks and Security *see* COMPUTER
 COURSES 219
Neuropsychology *see* PSYCHOLOGY 512
Neuroscience *see* ANATOMICAL SCIENCE/
 ANATOMY 122, BIOLOGICAL SCIENCES 165
Neuroscience and Psychology *see* ANATOMICAL
 SCIENCE/ANATOMY 122, PSYCHOLOGY 512
Neuroscience with Biochemistry *see* ANATOMICAL
 SCIENCE/ANATOMY 122, BIOLOGICAL SCIENCES
 165, CHEMISTRY 199
Neuroscience with Cognitive Science *see*
 ANATOMICAL SCIENCE/ANATOMY 122,
 PSYCHOLOGY 512
Neuroscience with Pharmacology *see*
 PHARMACOLOGY 472
News Journalism *see* MEDIA STUDIES 427
Nuclear Engineering *see* ENGINEERING
 (CHEMICAL) 269
Nursing *see* NURSING and MIDWIFERY 461
Nursing (Adult) *see* NURSING and MIDWIFERY 461
Nursing (Adult/Children's/Learning Disabilities/
 Mental Health) *see* NURSING and
 MIDWIFERY 461
Nursing (Learning Disability and Social Work) *see*
 NURSING and MIDWIFERY 461
Nursing (Mental Health) *see* NURSING and
 MIDWIFERY 461
NURSING and MIDWIFERY 461
 see also BIOLOGICAL SCIENCES
 see also COMMUNITY STUDIES/DEVELOPMENT
 see also HEALTH SCIENCES/STUDIES

Nursing Practice *see* NURSING and MIDWIFERY 461
Nursing Pre-Registration *see* NURSING and
 MIDWIFERY 461
Nursing Science *see* NURSING and MIDWIFERY 461
Nursing Studies *see* NURSING and MIDWIFERY 461
NUTRITION 466
 see also DIETETICS
 see also FOOD SCIENCE/STUDIES and
 TECHNOLOGY
Nutrition (Dietetics) *see* DIETETICS 237,
 NUTRITION 466
Nutrition and Dietetics *see* DIETETICS 237,
 NUTRITION 466
Nutrition and Exercise Sciences *see* NUTRITION 466
Nutrition and Food *see* FOOD SCIENCE/STUDIES and
 TECHNOLOGY 321, NUTRITION 466
Nutrition and Food Science *see* FOOD SCIENCE/
 STUDIES and TECHNOLOGY 321, NUTRITION 466
Nutrition and Health *see* HEALTH SCIENCES/
 STUDIES 341, NUTRITION 466
Nutrition and Health Promotion *see* NUTRITION 466
Nutrition and Human Health *see* NUTRITION 466
Nutrition and Psychology *see* NUTRITION 466,
 PSYCHOLOGY 512
Nutrition and Public Health *see* HEALTH SCIENCES/
 STUDIES 341, NUTRITION 466
Nutrition and Sport Science *see* NUTRITION 466,
 SPORTS SCIENCES/STUDIES 548
Nutrition with Food Consumer Sciences *see* FOOD
 SCIENCE/STUDIES and TECHNOLOGY 321,
 NUTRITION 466
Nutrition, Exercise and Science *see* NUTRITION 466
Nutrition, Health and Lifestyle *see* NUTRITION 466
Nutrition, Physical Activity and Community Health
 see NUTRITION 466
Nutritional Biochemistry *see* BIOCHEMISTRY 162,
 NUTRITION 466
Nutritional Science *see* NUTRITION 466

Observational Astronomy *see* ASTRONOMY and
 ASTROPHYSICS 159, PHYSICS 488
Occupational Safety and Health *see* SOCIAL and
 PUBLIC POLICY and ADMINISTRATION 529
OCCUPATIONAL THERAPY 468
 see also HEALTH SCIENCES/STUDIES
Ocean Chemistry *see* CHEMISTRY 199, MARINE/
 MARITIME STUDIES 412
Ocean Exploration *see* MARINE/MARITIME
 STUDIES 412
Ocean Science *see* MARINE/MARITIME STUDIES 412
Ocean Sciences *see* MARINE/MARITIME STUDIES 412

Ocean, Earth and Climate Science see GEOLOGY/
GEOLOGICAL SCIENCES 335
Oceanography see MARINE/MARITIME STUDIES 412
Oceanography and Computing see MARINE/
MARITIME STUDIES 412
Oceanography with French see FRENCH 325,
MARINE/MARITIME STUDIES 412
Oceanography with Physical Geography see
GEOGRAPHY 330, MARINE/MARITIME STUDIES
412
Oceans, Climate and Physical Geography see
GEOGRAPHY 330, MARINE/MARITIME STUDIES 412
Off-Road Vehicle Design see ENGINEERING
(MECHANICAL) 290
Off-Road Vehicle Design with Marketing and
Management see ENGINEERING
(MECHANICAL) 290
Offshore Engineering see ENGINEERING (CIVIL)
274, ENGINEERING/ENGINEERING SCIENCES
260, MARINE/MARITIME STUDIES 412, NAVAL
ARCHITECTURE 459
Oil and Gas Management see BUSINESS AND
MANAGEMENT COURSES (SPECIALISED) 193
Operations Management see BUSINESS AND
MANAGEMENT COURSES 179, BUSINESS AND
MANAGEMENT COURSES (SPECIALISED) 193
Ophthalmic Dispensing see OPTOMETRY (OPHTHALMIC
OPTICS) 471
Ophthalmic Dispensing with Management see
OPTOMETRY (OPHTHALMIC OPTICS) 471
OPTOMETRY (OPHTHALMIC OPTICS) 471
Oral Health Science see DENTISTRY 231, HEALTH
SCIENCES/STUDIES 341
Oral Health Sciences see DENTISTRY 231, HEALTH
SCIENCES/STUDIES 341
Oriental Studies (Arabic/Arabic and Islamic Studies/
Arabic Language) see ARABIC AND ANCIENT
NEAR AND MIDDLE EASTERN STUDIES 129
Orthoptics see HEALTH SCIENCES/STUDIES 341,
OPTOMETRY (OPHTHALMIC OPTICS) 471
Osteopathic Medicine see HEALTH SCIENCES/
STUDIES 341
Osteopathy see HEALTH SCIENCES/STUDIES 341
Outdoor Activity Leadership and Coaching see
LEISURE and RECREATION MANAGEMENT/
STUDIES 405
Outdoor Adventure Education see SPORTS SCIENCES/
STUDIES 548
Outdoor Adventure Leadership and Management
see LEISURE and RECREATION MANAGEMENT/
STUDIES 405

Outdoor Adventure Management see LEISURE and
RECREATION MANAGEMENT/STUDIES 405,
TOURISM and TRAVEL 564
Outdoor Education see EDUCATION STUDIES 256
Outdoor Leadership see LEISURE and RECREATION
MANAGEMENT/STUDIES 405
Outdoor Recreation see LEISURE and RECREATION
MANAGEMENT/STUDIES 405
Outdoor Studies see LEISURE and RECREATION
MANAGEMENT/STUDIES 405
Outdoor Studies (Environment) see LEISURE and
RECREATION MANAGEMENT/STUDIES 405
Outside Broadcast Technology see ENGINEERING
(ACOUSTICS and SOUND) 264

Painting see ART and DESIGN (Fine Art) 144
Palaeobiology and Evolution see ARCHAEOLOGY 131,
GEOLOGY/GEOLOGICAL SCIENCES 335
Palaeobiology and Palaeoenvironments see
ENVIRONMENTAL SCIENCES/STUDIES 303
Palaeontology and Evolution see BIOLOGICAL
SCIENCES 165
Paramedic Practice see NURSING and MIDWIFERY 461
Paramedic Practitioner see NURSING and
MIDWIFERY 461
Paramedic Science see HEALTH SCIENCES/
STUDIES 341, NURSING and MIDWIFERY 461
Pathology and Microbiology see MICROBIOLOGY 447
Peace Studies see INTERNATIONAL RELATIONS 378
Performance see DRAMA 239, MUSIC 449
Performance (Dance) see DANCE/DANCE STUDIES 227
Performance (Drama) see DRAMA 239
Performance and Acting see DRAMA 239
Performance and Media see DRAMA 239, MEDIA
STUDIES 427
Performance and Production see MUSIC 449
Performance and Visual Arts (Dance) see DANCE/
DANCE STUDIES 227
Performance and Visual Arts (Theatre) see
DRAMA 239
Performance Arts see DANCE/DANCE STUDIES 227,
DRAMA 239
Performance Costume see ART and DESIGN (Fashion
and Textiles) 140
Performance Design and Practice see DRAMA 239
Performance for Live and Recorded Media see
DRAMA 239, MEDIA STUDIES 427
Performance for Stage and Screen see DRAMA 239
Performance Musical Theatre see DRAMA 239
Performance Sound see ENGINEERING (ACOUSTICS and
SOUND) 264

Performance Sportswear *see* ART and DESIGN (Fashion and Textiles) 140

Performance Studies *see* DRAMA 239, MUSIC 449

Performing Arts *see* DRAMA 239

Performing Arts (Dance) *see* DANCE/DANCE STUDIES 227

Performing Arts (Drama) *see* DRAMA 239

Performing Arts (Theatre Performance) *see* DRAMA 239

Persian *see* ARABIC AND ANCIENT NEAR AND MIDDLE EASTERN STUDIES 129, LANGUAGES 386

Persian and Linguistics *see* ARABIC AND ANCIENT NEAR AND MIDDLE EASTERN STUDIES 129, LINGUISTICS 407

Persian and Social Anthropology *see* ANTHROPOLOGY 127, ARABIC AND ANCIENT NEAR AND MIDDLE EASTERN STUDIES 129

Persian Politics *see* ARABIC AND ANCIENT NEAR AND MIDDLE EASTERN STUDIES 129, POLITICS 507

Persian with Islamic Art and Architecture *see* ARABIC AND ANCIENT NEAR AND MIDDLE EASTERN STUDIES 129

Persian with Islamic Studies/History *see* ARABIC AND ANCIENT NEAR AND MIDDLE EASTERN STUDIES 129, HISTORY 355

Petroleum Engineering *see* ENGINEERING (CHEMICAL) 269

Petroleum Geosciences *see* GEOLOGY/GEOLOGICAL SCIENCES 335

Pharmaceutical and Chemical Sciences *see* CHEMISTRY 199, PHARMACY and PHARMACEUTICAL SCIENCES 475

Pharmaceutical and Medicinal Chemistry *see* CHEMISTRY 199, PHARMACY and PHARMACEUTICAL SCIENCES 475

Pharmaceutical Chemistry *see* CHEMISTRY 199, PHARMACY and PHARMACEUTICAL SCIENCES 475

Pharmaceutical Management *see* PHARMACY and PHARMACEUTICAL SCIENCES 475

Pharmaceutical Science *see* PHARMACY and PHARMACEUTICAL SCIENCES 475

Pharmaceutical Sciences *see* PHARMACY and PHARMACEUTICAL SCIENCES 475

PHARMACOLOGY 472
   see also BIOLOGICAL SCIENCES
   see also HEALTH SCIENCES/STUDIES
   see also PHARMACY
Pharmacology and Business *see* PHARMACOLOGY 472

Pharmacology and Physiological Sciences *see* PHARMACOLOGY 472, PHILOSOPHY 478

Pharmacology and Physiology *see* PHARMACOLOGY 472, PHYSIOLOGY 500

Pharmacology with Molecular Genetics *see* GENETICS 328, PHARMACOLOGY 472

PHARMACY and PHARMACEUTICAL SCIENCES 475
   see also BIOCHEMISTRY
   see also CHEMISTRY
   see also HEALTH SCIENCES/STUDIES
Philosophical Studies *see* PHILOSOPHY 478

PHILOSOPHY 478
   see also PSYCHOLOGY
Philosophy (Combined) *see* COMBINED COURSES 212, PHILOSOPHY 478

Philosophy and a Modern Language *see* FRENCH 325, PHILOSOPHY 478, RUSSIAN and EAST EUROPEAN STUDIES 526, SPANISH 543

Philosophy and Art History *see* HISTORY OF ART 363, PHILOSOPHY 478

Philosophy and Economics *see* ECONOMICS 251, PHILOSOPHY 478

Philosophy and English *see* ENGLISH 296, PHILOSOPHY 478

Philosophy and English Literature *see* LITERATURE 409, PHILOSOPHY 478

Philosophy and Ethics *see* PHILOSOPHY 478

Philosophy and Film *see* FILM, RADIO, VIDEO and TV STUDIES 310, PHILOSOPHY 478

Philosophy and Film Studies *see* FILM, RADIO, VIDEO and TV STUDIES 310, PHILOSOPHY 478

Philosophy and German *see* GERMAN 337, PHILOSOPHY 478

Philosophy and History *see* HISTORY 355, PHILOSOPHY 478

Philosophy and Languages *see* LANGUAGES 386, PHILOSOPHY 478

Philosophy and Law *see* LAW 393, PHILOSOPHY 478

Philosophy and Linguistics *see* LINGUISTICS 407, PHILOSOPHY 478

Philosophy and Mathematics *see* MATHEMATICS 422, PHILOSOPHY 478

Philosophy and Modern Languages *see* LANGUAGES 386, PHILOSOPHY 478

Philosophy and Music *see* MUSIC 449, PHILOSOPHY 478

Philosophy and Politics *see* PHILOSOPHY 478, POLITICS 507

Philosophy and Psychology *see* PHILOSOPHY 478, PSYCHOLOGY 512

Philosophy and Religion *see* RELIGIOUS STUDIES 521

Philosophy and Religious Studies *see* PHILOSOPHY 478, RELIGIOUS STUDIES 521

Philosophy and Social Psychology *see* PHILOSOPHY 478, PSYCHOLOGY 512

Philosophy and Sociology *see* PHILOSOPHY 478, SOCIOLOGY 539

Philosophy and Theology *see* PHILOSOPHY 478, PSYCHOLOGY 512, RELIGIOUS STUDIES 521

Philosophy Combined Honours *see* PHILOSOPHY 478

Philosophy with International Studies *see* PHILOSOPHY 478

Philosophy with Law *see* LAW 393, PHILOSOPHY 478

Philosophy with Scottish History *see* CELTIC, IRISH, SCOTTISH AND WELSH STUDIES 197, PHILOSOPHY 478

Philosophy with Social Anthropology *see* ANTHROPOLOGY 127, PHILOSOPHY 478

Philosophy, Logic and Scientific Method *see* PHILOSOPHY 478

Philosophy, Politics and Economics *see* ECONOMICS 251, PHILOSOPHY 478, POLITICS 507

Philosophy, Religion and Ethics *see* PHILOSOPHY 478, RELIGIOUS STUDIES 521

Photo Journalism *see* MEDIA STUDIES 427, PHOTOGRAPHY 481

Photographic and Digital Media *see* PHOTOGRAPHY 481

Photographic and Electronic Media *see* PHOTOGRAPHY 481

Photographic Art *see* PHOTOGRAPHY 481

Photographic Arts *see* PHOTOGRAPHY 481

Photographic Journalism *see* MEDIA STUDIES 427, PHOTOGRAPHY 481

Photographic Practice *see* PHOTOGRAPHY 481

PHOTOGRAPHY 481
   see also ART and DESIGN (Fine Art)
   see also FILM, RADIO, VIDEO and TV STUDIES
   see also MEDIA STUDIES

Photography (Combined) *see* PHOTOGRAPHY 481

Photography (Editorial, Advertising and Fine Art) *see* PHOTOGRAPHY 481

Photography and Digital Imaging *see* PHOTOGRAPHY 481

Photography and Digital Media *see* PHOTOGRAPHY 481

Photography and Fashion and Brand Promotion *see* ART and DESIGN (Product and Industrial Design) 152, PHOTOGRAPHY 481

Photography and Media *see* PHOTOGRAPHY 481

Photography and Video *see* PHOTOGRAPHY 481

Photography and Video Art *see* PHOTOGRAPHY 481

Photography for Digital Media *see* PHOTOGRAPHY 481

Photography for Fashion and Advertising *see* PHOTOGRAPHY 481

Photography in the Arts *see* PHOTOGRAPHY 481

Photography, Video and Digital Imaging *see* FILM, RADIO, VIDEO and TV STUDIES 310, PHOTOGRAPHY 481

Photography/Photography in Europe *see* PHOTOGRAPHY 481

Photojournalism *see* MEDIA STUDIES 427, PHOTOGRAPHY 481

Photojournalism and Documentary Photography *see* PHOTOGRAPHY 481

Physical Activity, Health and Exercise Science *see* SPORTS SCIENCES/STUDIES 548

Physical and Environmental Geography *see* GEOGRAPHY 330

Physical Earth Science *see* GEOLOGY/GEOLOGICAL SCIENCES 335

PHYSICAL EDUCATION 484
   see also SPORTS SCIENCES/STUDIES

Physical Education (Primary) and Sport Development *see* PHYSICAL EDUCATION 484, TEACHER TRAINING 559

Physical Education and School Sport *see* PHYSICAL EDUCATION 484

Physical Education and Sport *see* PHYSICAL EDUCATION 484

Physical Education and Sport and Coaching *see* PHYSICAL EDUCATION 484

Physical Education and Sport and Exercise Science *see* PHYSICAL EDUCATION 484

Physical Education and Sport Pedagogy *see* PHYSICAL EDUCATION 484

Physical Education and Sports Coaching *see* PHYSICAL EDUCATION 484

Physical Education and Sports Studies *see* PHYSICAL EDUCATION 484

Physical Education and Youth Sport *see* PHYSICAL EDUCATION 484

Physical Education and Youth Sport Coaching *see* PHYSICAL EDUCATION 484

Physical Education Primary *see* PHYSICAL EDUCATION 484, TEACHER TRAINING 559

Physical Education Secondary Teaching *see* PHYSICAL EDUCATION 484, TEACHER TRAINING 559

Physical Education with Outdoor Education *see* PHYSICAL EDUCATION 484

Physical Geography see ENVIRONMENTAL SCIENCES/
STUDIES 303, GEOGRAPHY 330
Physical Geography and Geology see GEOGRAPHY
330, GEOLOGY/GEOLOGICAL SCIENCES 335
Physical Geography with Geology see GEOGRAPHY
330, GEOLOGY/GEOLOGICAL SCIENCES 335
Physical Science see PHYSICS 488

PHYSICS 488
see also ASTRONOMY/ASTROPHYSICS
Physics and Astronomy see ASTRONOMY and
ASTROPHYSICS 159, PHYSICS 488
Physics and Astrophysics see ASTRONOMY and
ASTROPHYSICS 159, PHYSICS 488
Physics and Business Studies see BUSINESS AND
MANAGEMENT COURSES 179, PHYSICS 488
Physics and Complex Systems Modelling see
PHYSICS 488
Physics and Cosmology see ASTRONOMY and
ASTROPHYSICS 159
Physics and Management see BUSINESS AND
MANAGEMENT COURSES 179, PHYSICS 488
Physics and Mathematics see MATHEMATICS 422,
PHYSICS 488
Physics and Music see MUSIC 449, PHYSICS 488
Physics and Philosophy see PHILOSOPHY 478,
PHYSICS 488
Physics and Pilot Studies see PHYSICS 488
Physics with a European Language see LANGUAGES
386, PHYSICS 488
Physics with a Language see LANGUAGES 386,
PHYSICS 488
Physics with Acoustics see ENGINEERING (ACOUSTICS
and SOUND) 264, PHYSICS 488
Physics with Astronomy see ASTRONOMY and
ASTROPHYSICS 159, PHYSICS 488
Physics with Astrophysics see ASTRONOMY and
ASTROPHYSICS 159, PHYSICS 488
Physics with Business Management see
BUSINESS AND MANAGEMENT COURSES 179,
PHYSICS 488
Physics with Forensic Applications see PHYSICS 488
Physics with Mathematics see MATHEMATICS 422,
PHYSICS 488
Physics with Medical Applications see ENGINEERING
(MEDICAL) 295, PHYSICS 488
Physics with Medical Physics see PHYSICS 488
Physics with Meteorology see GEOGRAPHY 330,
PHYSICS 488
Physics with Nanoscience see ANATOMICAL SCIENCE/
ANATOMY 122, PHYSICS 488
Physics with Nanotechnology see PHYSICS 488

Physics with Nuclear Astrophysics see ASTRONOMY
and ASTROPHYSICS 159, PHYSICS 488
Physics with Nuclear Science see ENGINEERING
(CHEMICAL) 269, PHYSICS 488
Physics with Nuclear Technology see PHYSICS 488
Physics with Ocean and Climate Studies see MARINE/
MARITIME STUDIES 412, PHYSICS 488
Physics with Particle Physics see PHYSICS 488
Physics with Particle Physics and Cosmology see
ASTRONOMY and ASTROPHYSICS 159,
PHYSICS 488
Physics with Philosophy see PHILOSOPHY 478,
PHYSICS 488
Physics with Photonics see PHYSICS 488
Physics with Planetary Science see ASTRONOMY and
ASTROPHYSICS 159, PHYSICS 488
Physics with Satellite Technology see
PHYSICS 488
Physics with Space Science see PHYSICS 488
Physics with Space Science and Technology see
ASTRONOMY and ASTROPHYSICS 159,
PHYSICS 488
Physics with Sports Science see PHYSICS 488,
SPORTS SCIENCES/STUDIES 548
Physics with Studies in Musical Performance see
MUSIC 449, PHYSICS 488
Physics with Theoretical Astrophysics see
ASTRONOMY and ASTROPHYSICS 159
Physics with Theoretical Physics see PHYSICS 488
Physics, Astrophysics and Cosmology see
ASTRONOMY and ASTROPHYSICS 159,
PHYSICS 488
Physics, Astrophysics and Space Science see
ASTRONOMY and ASTROPHYSICS 159,
PHYSICS 488
Physiological Science see PHYSIOLOGY 500
Physiological Sciences see PHYSIOLOGY 500

PHYSIOLOGY 500
see also ANIMAL SCIENCES
see also PHILOSOPHY
see also PSYCHOLOGY
Physiology (Physical Activity and Health) see
PHYSIOLOGY 500
Physiology and Pharmacology see PHARMACOLOGY
472, PHYSIOLOGY 500
Physiology and Sports Biomedicine see PHYSIOLOGY
500, SPORTS SCIENCES/STUDIES 548
Physiology and Sports Science see PHYSIOLOGY 500,
SPORTS SCIENCES/STUDIES 548
Physiology, Sport Science and Nutrition see
NUTRITION 466, PHYSIOLOGY 500

PHYSIOTHERAPY 502

Planetary Science with Astronomy *see* ASTRONOMY and ASTROPHYSICS 159

Planning and Development *see* TOWN and COUNTRY PLANNING 567

Planning and Development Surveying *see* SURVEYING 556, TOWN and COUNTRY PLANNING 567

Planning and Economics *see* DEVELOPMENT STUDIES 235, TOWN and COUNTRY PLANNING 567

Planning and Property Development *see* SURVEYING 556

Planning and Real Estate *see* TOWN and COUNTRY PLANNING 567

Planning and Social Policy *see* SOCIAL and PUBLIC POLICY and ADMINISTRATION 529, TOWN and COUNTRY PLANNING 567

Planning and Transport *see* TRANSPORT MANAGEMENT and PLANNING 571

Planning Development *see* SURVEYING 556

Plant and Soil Science *see* PLANT SCIENCES 504

Plant Biology *see* BIOLOGY, PLANT SCIENCES 504

Plant Science with a Modern Language *see* LANGUAGES 386, PLANT SCIENCES 504

PLANT SCIENCES 504

   see also BIOLOGICAL SCIENCES

   see also BIOLOGY

   see also HORTICULTURE

Podiatric Medicine *see* PODIATRY (CHIROPODY) 506

PODIATRY (CHIROPODY) 506

Police and Criminal Investigation *see* SOCIAL SCIENCES/STUDIES 531

Police Sciences *see* SOCIAL SCIENCES/STUDIES 531

Police Studies *see* SOCIAL SCIENCES/STUDIES 531

Policing *see* SOCIAL SCIENCES/STUDIES 531

Policing and Criminal Investigation *see* LAW 393, SOCIAL SCIENCES/STUDIES 531

Policing and Security *see* SOCIAL SCIENCES/STUDIES 531

Policing, Investigation and Criminology *see* SOCIAL SCIENCES/STUDIES 531

Polish *see* LANGUAGES 386

Political and International Relations *see* INTERNATIONAL RELATIONS 378, POLITICS 507

Political Economy *see* ECONOMICS 251, POLITICS 507

Political History *see* HISTORY 355

Political Science *see* POLITICS 507

POLITICS 507

   see also DEVELOPMENT STUDIES

   see also INTERNATIONAL RELATIONS

Politics (International Politics) *see* INTERNATIONAL RELATIONS 378, POLITICS 507

Politics and a Modern Language *see* LANGUAGES 386, POLITICS 507

Politics and Applied Economics *see* POLITICS 507

Politics and Banking *see* POLITICS 507

Politics and Business *see* BUSINESS AND MANAGEMENT COURSES 179, POLITICS 507

Politics and Communication Studies *see* COMMUNICATION STUDIES/COMMUNICATION 214, POLITICS 507

Politics and Communications *see* COMMUNICATION STUDIES/COMMUNICATION 214, POLITICS 507

Politics and Contemporary History *see* HISTORY 355, POLITICS 507

Politics and Criminology *see* POLITICS 507, SOCIAL SCIENCES/STUDIES 531

Politics and East European Studies *see* EUROPEAN STUDIES 307, POLITICS 507

Politics and Economic and Social History *see* HISTORY (ECONOMIC and SOCIAL) 362, POLITICS 507

Politics and Economics *see* ECONOMICS 251, POLITICS 507

Politics and Education *see* EDUCATION STUDIES 256, POLITICS 507

Politics and English Language *see* ENGLISH 296, POLITICS 507

Politics and Finance *see* FINANCE 315, POLITICS 507

Politics and Global Government *see* POLITICS 507

Politics and Global Studies *see* INTERNATIONAL RELATIONS 378, POLITICS 507

Politics and Government *see* POLITICS 507

Politics and History *see* HISTORY 355, POLITICS 507

Politics and History of Art *see* HISTORY OF ART 363, POLITICS 507

Politics and International Business *see* POLITICS 507

Politics and International Relations *see* INTERNATIONAL RELATIONS 378, POLITICS 507

Politics and Journalism *see* MEDIA STUDIES 427, POLITICS 507

Politics and Languages *see* LANGUAGES 386, POLITICS 507

Politics and Law *see* LAW 393, POLITICS 507

Politics and Media *see* MEDIA STUDIES 427, POLITICS 507

Politics and Modern History *see* HISTORY 355, POLITICS 507

Politics and Parliamentary Studies *see* POLITICS 507

Politics and Peace and Conflict Studies *see* POLITICS 507

Politics and Peace Studies *see* INTERNATIONAL RELATIONS 378, POLITICS 507

Politics and Philosophy *see* PHILOSOPHY 478, POLITICS 507

Politics and Policy *see* POLITICS 507, SOCIAL and PUBLIC POLICY and ADMINISTRATION 529

Politics and Portuguese/Russian/Spanish *see* LANGUAGES 386, POLITICS 507

Politics and Religious Studies *see* POLITICS 507, RELIGIOUS STUDIES 521

Politics and Science *see* POLITICS 507

Politics and Social Anthropology *see* ANTHROPOLOGY 127, POLITICS 507

Politics and Social History *see* POLITICS 507

Politics and Social Policy *see* POLITICS 507, SOCIAL and PUBLIC POLICY and ADMINISTRATION 529

Politics and Social Science *see* POLITICS 507

Politics and Sociology *see* POLITICS 507, SOCIOLOGY 539

Politics and Spanish/Portuguese and Latin American Studies *see* LATIN AMERICAN STUDIES 391, POLITICS 507, SPANISH 543

Politics of the International Economy *see* INTERNATIONAL RELATIONS 378, POLITICS 507

Politics Studies *see* POLITICS 507

Politics with French/German *see* FRENCH 325, GERMAN 337, POLITICS 507

Politics with International Relations *see* INTERNATIONAL RELATIONS 378, POLITICS 507

Politics with Media *see* MEDIA STUDIES 427, POLITICS 507

Politics, Diploma in Etudes Politiques *see* POLITICS 507

Politics, Philosophy and Economics *see* ECONOMICS 251, PHILOSOPHY 478, POLITICS 507

Politics, Philosophy and Law *see* LAW 393, PHILOSOPHY 478, POLITICS 507

Politics, Psychology and Sociology (PPS) *see* POLITICS 507, PSYCHOLOGY 512, SOCIOLOGY 539

Politics: People and Power *see* POLITICS 507

Polymer Engineering *see* MATERIALS SCIENCE/ METALLURGY 419

Popular Music *see* MUSIC 449

Popular Music and Performance *see* DRAMA 239, MUSIC 449

Popular Music Performance *see* MUSIC 449

Popular Music Production *see* MUSIC 449

Popular Music Studies *see* MUSIC 449

Popular Music Technology *see* MUSIC 449

Popular Music with Music Technology *see* MUSIC 449, TECHNOLOGIES 562

Population and Geography *see* GEOGRAPHY 330, SOCIAL SCIENCES/STUDIES 531

Port and Maritime Management *see* MARINE/ MARITIME STUDIES 412

Portuguese *see* LANGUAGES 386, SPANISH 543

Portuguese and Brazilian Studies *see* LANGUAGES 386, LATIN AMERICAN STUDIES 391

Portuguese and Money, Banking and Finance *see* FINANCE 315, LANGUAGES 386

Portuguese and Spanish *see* SPANISH 543

Portuguese Studies and Modern Languages *see* LANGUAGES 386

Press and Editorial Photography *see* PHOTOGRAPHY 481

Primary and Early Years *see* TEACHER TRAINING 559

Primary and Secondary Teaching *see* TEACHER TRAINING 559

Primary Education *see* EDUCATION STUDIES 256, TEACHER TRAINING 559

Primary Education (Mathematics) *see* EDUCATION STUDIES 256, MATHEMATICS 422, TEACHER TRAINING 559

Primary Education (Music) *see* EDUCATION STUDIES 256, MUSIC 449, TEACHER TRAINING 559

Primary Education (Physical Education) *see* PHYSICAL EDUCATION 484, TEACHER TRAINING 559

Primary Education and Geography *see* GEOGRAPHY 330, TEACHER TRAINING 559

Primary Education and Modern Languages *see* EDUCATION STUDIES 256, LANGUAGES 386

Primary Education and Teaching *see* TEACHER TRAINING 559

Primary Education Arts *see* EDUCATION STUDIES 256, TEACHER TRAINING 559

Primary Education with Early Years *see* TEACHER TRAINING 559

Primary Education with Geography *see* EDUCATION STUDIES 256, GEOGRAPHY 330, TEACHER TRAINING 559

Primary Education with Maths *see* MATHEMATICS 422, TEACHER TRAINING 559

Primary Education with Modern Languages *see* EDUCATION STUDIES 256, LANGUAGES 386

Primary Education with Physical Education *see* PHYSICAL EDUCATION 484, TEACHER TRAINING 559

Primary Physical Education *see* PHYSICAL EDUCATION 484, TEACHER TRAINING 559

Primary Teacher Education *see* TEACHER TRAINING 559

Primary Teaching see TEACHER TRAINING 559

Primary Teaching and Education see TEACHER TRAINING 559

Primary Teaching Music see EDUCATION STUDIES 256, MUSIC 449

Primary Teaching Studies see TEACHER TRAINING 559

Primary/Secondary Education see EDUCATION STUDIES 256, TEACHER TRAINING 559

Print and Online Journalism see MEDIA STUDIES 427

Print Journalism see MEDIA STUDIES 427

Printed Textiles and Surface Pattern Design see ART and DESIGN (Fashion and Textiles) 140

Printing see ART and DESIGN (Fine Art) 144

Process Control see ENGINEERING (CHEMICAL) 269

Product and Furniture Design see ART and DESIGN (Product and Industrial Design) 152

Product and Industrial Design see ENGINEERING (MANUFACTURING) 288, ENGINEERING/ ENGINEERING SCIENCES 260

Product design see ART and DESIGN (Product and Industrial Design) 152

Product Design see ART and DESIGN (Product and Industrial Design) 152, ENGINEERING/ ENGINEERING SCIENCES 260

Product Design (3D Animation) see ART and DESIGN (Product and Industrial Design) 152

Product Design (Children's Products and Toys/ Sustainable Design) see ART and DESIGN (Product and Industrial Design) 152

Product Design and Manufacturing see ART and DESIGN (Product and Industrial Design) 152, ENGINEERING (MANUFACTURING) 288

Product Design and Development see ART and DESIGN (Product and Industrial Design) 152, ENGINEERING/ENGINEERING SCIENCES 260

Product Design and Innovation see ART and DESIGN (Product and Industrial Design) 152, ENGINEERING/ENGINEERING SCIENCES 260

Product Design and Management see ENGINEERING (MANUFACTURING) 288

Product Design and Manufacturing see ART and DESIGN (Product and Industrial Design) 152, ENGINEERING (MANUFACTURING) 288

Product Design and Modern Materials see ART and DESIGN (Product and Industrial Design) 152

Product Design and Technology see ART and DESIGN (Product and Industrial Design) 152, ENGINEERING/ENGINEERING SCIENCES 260

Product Design Engineering see ART and DESIGN (Product and Industrial Design) 152,
ENGINEERING (MANUFACTURING) 288, ENGINEERING (MECHANICAL) 290, ENGINEERING/ ENGINEERING SCIENCES 260

Product Design Futures see ART and DESIGN (Product and Industrial Design) 152

Product Design Sustainable Futures see ART and DESIGN (Product and Industrial Design) 152

Product Design Technology see ART and DESIGN (Product and Industrial Design) 152, ENGINEERING/ENGINEERING SCIENCES 260

Product Design: Consumer see ART and DESIGN (Product and Industrial Design) 152

Product Design: Jewellery and Fashion see ART and DESIGN (Fashion and Textiles) 140

Product Design: Sports see ART and DESIGN (Product and Industrial Design) 152

Product Design: Toy see ART and DESIGN (Product and Industrial Design) 152

Product Innovation see ENGINEERING/ENGINEERING SCIENCES 260

Product Innovation and Development see ENGINEERING/ENGINEERING SCIENCES 260

Product Innovation Design and Development see ART and DESIGN (Product and Industrial Design) 152

Production Design see ENGINEERING/ENGINEERING SCIENCES 260

Production Engineering and Management see ART and DESIGN (Product and Industrial Design) 152, ENGINEERING/ENGINEERING SCIENCES 260

Professional Accounting see ACCOUNTANCY/ ACCOUNTING 109

Professional Acting see DRAMA 239

Professional Dance and Musical Theatre see DANCE/ DANCE STUDIES 227

Professional Stage Management see DRAMA 239

Professional Studies in Nursing and Social Work see NURSING and MIDWIFERY 461, SOCIAL WORK 536

Professional Writing see ENGLISH 296

Project and Construction Management see BUILDING and CONSTRUCTION 176

Project Management (Construction) see BUILDING and CONSTRUCTION 176

Project Management for Construction see BUILDING and CONSTRUCTION 176

Property Agency and Management see MARKETING 415, SURVEYING 556

Property and Urban Development see SURVEYING 556, TOWN and COUNTRY PLANNING 567

Property Development see SURVEYING 556

Property Development and Valuation *see* SURVEYING 556

Property Finance and Investment *see* BUILDING and CONSTRUCTION 176

Property Investment and Management *see* SURVEYING 556

Property Management *see* BUSINESS AND MANAGEMENT COURSES (SPECIALISED) 193

Property Management (Building Surveying) *see* BUILDING and CONSTRUCTION 176

Property Planning and Development *see* SURVEYING 556

Prosthetics and Orthotics *see* BIOTECHNOLOGY 174, ENGINEERING/ENGINEERING SCIENCES 260, HEALTH SCIENCES/STUDIES 341

PSYCHOLOGY 512

see also BIOLOGICAL SCIENCES

see also PHILOSOPHY

see also PHYSIOLOGY

Psychology (Combined) *see* COMBINED COURSES 212, PSYCHOLOGY 512

Psychology (Consumer Studies) *see* CONSUMER STUDIES/SCIENCES 226

Psychology (Counselling) *see* PSYCHOLOGY 512

Psychology (Criminal Behaviour) *see* PSYCHOLOGY 512

Psychology and Biology *see* BIOLOGY 170, PSYCHOLOGY 512

Psychology and Business *see* BUSINESS AND MANAGEMENT COURSES 179, PSYCHOLOGY 512

Psychology and Business Management *see* BUSINESS AND MANAGEMENT COURSES 179, PSYCHOLOGY 512

Psychology and Cognitive Neuroscience *see* PSYCHOLOGY 512

Psychology and Counselling *see* PSYCHOLOGY 512

Psychology and Criminology *see* PSYCHOLOGY 512, SOCIAL SCIENCES/STUDIES 531

Psychology and Educational Development *see* PSYCHOLOGY 512

Psychology and English Language *see* ENGLISH 296, PSYCHOLOGY 512

Psychology and English Literature *see* LITERATURE 409, PSYCHOLOGY 512

Psychology and Health *see* PSYCHOLOGY 512

Psychology and Human Resource Management *see* HUMAN RESOURCE MANAGEMENT 371, PSYCHOLOGY 512

Psychology and Language Sciences *see* LANGUAGES 386, PSYCHOLOGY 512

Psychology and Management *see* BUSINESS AND MANAGEMENT COURSES 179, PSYCHOLOGY 512

Psychology and Marketing *see* MARKETING 415, PSYCHOLOGY 512

Psychology and Philosophy *see* PHILOSOPHY 478, PSYCHOLOGY 512

Psychology and Social Policy *see* PSYCHOLOGY 512, SOCIAL and PUBLIC POLICY and ADMINISTRATION 529

Psychology and Society *see* PSYCHOLOGY 512, SOCIAL SCIENCES/STUDIES 548

Psychology and Sociology *see* PSYCHOLOGY 512, SOCIOLOGY 539

Psychology and Spanish *see* PSYCHOLOGY 512, SPANISH 543

Psychology and Special and Inclusive Education *see* EDUCATION STUDIES 256, PSYCHOLOGY 512

Psychology and Speech Pathology *see* PSYCHOLOGY 512, SPEECH PATHOLOGY/SCIENCES/THERAPY 546

Psychology and Statistics *see* PSYCHOLOGY 512, STATISTICS 554

Psychology and Youth Studies *see* PSYCHOLOGY 512

Psychology in Education *see* EDUCATION STUDIES 256, PSYCHOLOGY 512

Psychology of Sport and Exercise *see* PSYCHOLOGY 512, SPORTS SCIENCES/STUDIES 548

Psychology Studies *see* PSYCHOLOGY 512

Psychology Studies and Counselling Studies *see* PSYCHOLOGY 512

Psychology with American Studies *see* AMERICAN STUDIES 120, PSYCHOLOGY 512

Psychology with Applied Criminology *see* PSYCHOLOGY 512

Psychology with Child and Language Development *see* PSYCHOLOGY 512

Psychology with Child Development *see* PSYCHOLOGY 512

Psychology with Child Studies *see* PSYCHOLOGY 512

Psychology with Clinical and Health Psychology *see* PSYCHOLOGY 512

Psychology with Clinical Psychology *see* PSYCHOLOGY 512

Psychology with Cognitive Neuroscience *see* ANATOMICAL SCIENCE/ANATOMY 122, PSYCHOLOGY 512

Psychology with Cognitive Science *see* HUMAN SCIENCES/HUMAN BIOSCIENCES 374, PSYCHOLOGY 512

Psychology with Counselling *see* PSYCHOLOGY 512

Psychology with Counselling Studies *see* PSYCHOLOGY 512

Psychology with Criminology see PSYCHOLOGY 512, SOCIAL SCIENCES/STUDIES 531

Psychology with Criminology/Counselling Theory see PSYCHOLOGY 512, SOCIAL SCIENCES/STUDIES 531

Psychology with Interactive Entertainment see PSYCHOLOGY 512

Psychology with Media and Communications see COMMUNICATION STUDIES/COMMUNICATION 214, MEDIA STUDIES 427, PSYCHOLOGY 512

Psychology with Neuropsychology see PSYCHOLOGY 512

Psychology with Neuroscience see HUMAN SCIENCES/HUMAN BIOSCIENCES 374, PSYCHOLOGY 512

Psychology with Philosophy see PHILOSOPHY 478, PSYCHOLOGY 512

Psychology with Sociology see PSYCHOLOGY 512, SOCIOLOGY 539

Psychology with Sport and Exercise Science see PSYCHOLOGY 512, SPORTS SCIENCES/STUDIES 548

Psychology with Sport Science see PSYCHOLOGY 512, SPORTS SCIENCES/STUDIES 548

Psychology with Studies in Europe see EUROPEAN STUDIES 307, PSYCHOLOGY 512

Psychology, Childhood and Ageing see PSYCHOLOGY 512

Psychology, Mental and Physical Health see PSYCHOLOGY 512

Psychosocial Studies see PSYCHOLOGY 512, SOCIOLOGY 539

Public and Social Policy see SOCIAL and PUBLIC POLICY and ADMINISTRATION 529

Public Health see HEALTH SCIENCES/STUDIES 341

Public Health (Environmental Health) see ENVIRONMENTAL SCIENCES/STUDIES 303

Public Health (Nutrition) see HEALTH SCIENCES/STUDIES 341, NUTRITION 466

Public Health and Nutrition see HEALTH SCIENCES/STUDIES 341, NUTRITION 466

Public Policy see SOCIAL and PUBLIC POLICY and ADMINISTRATION 529

Public Policy and Management see SOCIAL and PUBLIC POLICY and ADMINISTRATION 529

Public Relations see BUSINESS AND MANAGEMENT COURSES 179, BUSINESS AND MANAGEMENT COURSES (SPECIALISED) 193, MARKETING 415, MEDIA STUDIES 427

Public Relations and Communication see MARKETING 415

Public Relations and Digital Communications Management see BUSINESS AND MANAGEMENT COURSES 179, SOCIAL and PUBLIC POLICY and ADMINISTRATION 529

Public Relations and Human Resource Management see HUMAN RESOURCE MANAGEMENT 371

Public Relations and Marketing see BUSINESS AND MANAGEMENT COURSES (SPECIALISED) 193

Public Relations and Marketing Communications see BUSINESS AND MANAGEMENT COURSES (SPECIALISED) 193, MARKETING 415

Public Relations and Media see BUSINESS AND MANAGEMENT COURSES (SPECIALISED) 193, COMMUNICATION STUDIES/COMMUNICATION 214, MEDIA STUDIES 427

Public Relations with Marketing see MARKETING 415

Public Services see SOCIAL and PUBLIC POLICY and ADMINISTRATION 529, SOCIAL SCIENCES/STUDIES 531

Publishing and English see ENGLISH 296, MEDIA STUDIES 427

Publishing Media see BUSINESS AND MANAGEMENT COURSES (SPECIALISED) 193

Publishing, Journalism and Media see MEDIA STUDIES 427

Publishing, Media and Cultural Studies see MEDIA STUDIES 427

Pure and Applied Physics see PHYSICS 484

Pure Mathematics see MATHEMATICS 422

Pure Mathematics and Statistics see MATHEMATICS 422, STATISTICS 554

Quantity Surveying see BUILDING and CONSTRUCTION 176, SURVEYING 556

Quantity Surveying and Commercial Management see BUILDING and CONSTRUCTION 176, SURVEYING 556

Quantity Surveying and Construction and Commercial Management see SURVEYING 556

Quantity Surveying Consultancy see BUILDING and CONSTRUCTION 176, SURVEYING 556

Radiation, Oncology and Science see RADIOGRAPHY 519

Radio see FILM, RADIO, VIDEO and TV STUDIES 310

Radio Production see FILM, RADIO, VIDEO and TV STUDIES 310

RADIOGRAPHY 519
    see also HEALTH SCIENCES/STUDIES

Radiography (Diagnostic) see RADIOGRAPHY 519

Radiography (Diagnostic Imaging) see RADIOGRAPHY 519

Radiography (Diagnostic/Therapeutic) *see* RADIOGRAPHY 519

Radiography (Radiotherapy and Oncology) *see* RADIOGRAPHY 519

Radiography: Diagnostic Radiography and Imaging *see* RADIOGRAPHY 519

Radiotherapy *see* RADIOGRAPHY 519

Radiotherapy and Oncology *see* RADIOGRAPHY 519

Real Estate *see* SURVEYING 556, TOWN and COUNTRY PLANNING 567

Real Estate and Appraisal Management *see* SURVEYING 556

Real Estate Management *see* SURVEYING 556

Real Estate with Planning Development *see* TOWN and COUNTRY PLANNING 567

Recreation and the Environment *see* LEISURE and RECREATION MANAGEMENT/STUDIES 405

Religion *see* RELIGIOUS STUDIES 521

Religion and Education *see* EDUCATION STUDIES 256, RELIGIOUS STUDIES 521

Religion and the Contemporary World *see* RELIGIOUS STUDIES 521

Religion and Theology *see* RELIGIOUS STUDIES 521

Religion, Culture and Society *see* RELIGIOUS STUDIES 521

Religion, Philosophy and Ethics *see* PHILOSOPHY 478, RELIGIOUS STUDIES 521

Religion, Theology and the Bible *see* RELIGIOUS STUDIES 521

Religion, Theology, the Bible and Linguistics *see* RELIGIOUS STUDIES 521

Religious and Theological Studies *see* RELIGIOUS STUDIES 521

Religious Education *see* RELIGIOUS STUDIES 521

Religious Studies *see* RELIGIOUS STUDIES 521

Religious Studies and Archaeology *see* ARCHAEOLOGY 131, RELIGIOUS STUDIES 521

Religious Studies and Business Management *see* BUSINESS AND MANAGEMENT COURSES 179, RELIGIOUS STUDIES 521

Religious Studies and Philosophy *see* PHILOSOPHY 478, RELIGIOUS STUDIES 521

Religious Studies and Sociology *see* RELIGIOUS STUDIES 521, SOCIOLOGY 539

Religious Studies and Spanish/Italian *see* ITALIAN 381, RELIGIOUS STUDIES 521, SPANISH 543

Religious Studies Education *see* RELIGIOUS STUDIES 521, TEACHER TRAINING 559

Renewable Energy *see* ENVIRONMENTAL SCIENCES/STUDIES 303

Renewable Energy Engineering *see* ENGINEERING/ENGINEERING SCIENCES 260

Reproductive Biology *see* BIOLOGY 170

Retail Buying (Fashion) (Textiles) *see* ART and DESIGN (Fashion and Textiles) 140, RETAIL MANAGEMENT 524

Retail Leisure Management *see* BUSINESS AND MANAGEMENT COURSES 179, LEISURE and RECREATION MANAGEMENT/STUDIES 405

RETAIL MANAGEMENT 524
see also MARKETING

Retail Management (Buying/Fashion/Marketing) *see* RETAIL MANAGEMENT 524

Retail Management (E-Commerce/Entrepreneur) *see* RETAIL MANAGEMENT 524

Retail Marketing *see* MARKETING 415, RETAIL MANAGEMENT 524

Retail Marketing Management *see* MARKETING 415, RETAIL MANAGEMENT 521

Retail, Marketing and Management *see* RETAIL MANAGEMENT 524

Retailing, Marketing and Management *see* MARKETING 415, RETAIL MANAGEMENT 524

Robotic and Intelligent Systems Engineering *see* ENGINEERING (COMPUTER, CONTROL, SOFTWARE and SYSTEMS) 280

Robotics *see* ENGINEERING/ENGINEERING SCIENCES 260

Robotics and Intelligent Systems *see* ENGINEERING/ENGINEERING SCIENCES 260

Roman Civilisation and Russian Civilisation *see* CLASSICAL STUDIES/CLASSICAL CIVILISATION 208

Romance Languages *see* LANGUAGES 386

Romanian *see* LANGUAGES 386

Rural Business Management *see* BUSINESS AND MANAGEMENT COURSES 179

Rural Business Management (Food) *see* FOOD SCIENCE/STUDIES and TECHNOLOGY 321

Rural Land Management *see* AGRICULTURAL SCIENCES/AGRICULTURE 117, BUSINESS AND MANAGEMENT COURSES (SPECIALISED) 193

Rural Property Management *see* SURVEYING 556

Rural Resources Management *see* AGRICULTURAL SCIENCES/AGRICULTURE 117

RUSSIAN and EAST EUROPEAN STUDIES 526
see also EUROPEAN STUDIES
see also LANGUAGES

Russian and Spanish *see* RUSSIAN and EAST EUROPEAN STUDIES 526, SPANISH 543

Russian and a Modern Language *see* LANGUAGES 386, RUSSIAN and EAST EUROPEAN STUDIES 526

Russian and Chinese *see* CHINESE 206, RUSSIAN and EAST EUROPEAN STUDIES 526

Russian and Geography *see* GEOGRAPHY 330, RUSSIAN and EAST EUROPEAN STUDIES 526

Russian and History *see* HISTORY 355, RUSSIAN and EAST EUROPEAN STUDIES 526

Russian and Japanese *see* JAPANESE 383, RUSSIAN and EAST EUROPEAN STUDIES 526

Russian and Politics *see* POLITICS 507, RUSSIAN and EAST EUROPEAN STUDIES 526

Russian and Sociology *see* RUSSIAN and EAST EUROPEAN STUDIES 526, SOCIOLOGY 539

Russian Civilisation, Theology and Religious Studies *see* RELIGIOUS STUDIES 521, RUSSIAN and EAST EUROPEAN STUDIES 526

Russian Studies *see* COMBINED COURSES 212, RUSSIAN and EAST EUROPEAN STUDIES 526

Russian Studies with Central and East European Studies *see* RUSSIAN and EAST EUROPEAN STUDIES 526

Russian with Business Management *see* BUSINESS AND MANAGEMENT COURSES (INTERNATIONAL AND EUROPEAN) 188, RUSSIAN and EAST EUROPEAN STUDIES 526

Sanskrit *see* ASIA-PACIFIC STUDIES 158

SCANDINAVIAN STUDIES 527

Scandinavian Studies and History *see* HISTORY 355, SCANDINAVIAN STUDIES 527

Scenography and Theatre Design *see* FILM, RADIO, VIDEO and TV STUDIES 310

Science and Football *see* SPORTS SCIENCES/ STUDIES 548

Science and Society *see* SOCIAL SCIENCES/ STUDIES 531

Science Foundation *see* BIOLOGY 170

Sciences (Combined) *see* BIOLOGICAL SCIENCES 165

Scots Law *see* CELTIC, IRISH, SCOTTISH AND WELSH STUDIES 197, LAW 393

Scottish Archaeology *see* ARCHAEOLOGY 131

Scottish Cultural Studies *see* CELTIC, IRISH, SCOTTISH AND WELSH STUDIES 197

Scottish Ethnology *see* CELTIC, IRISH, SCOTTISH AND WELSH STUDIES 197

Scottish Historical Studies *see* HISTORY 355

Scottish History *see* CELTIC, IRISH, SCOTTISH AND WELSH STUDIES 197, HISTORY 355

Scottish History and Archaeology *see* ARCHAEOLOGY 131, CELTIC, IRISH, SCOTTISH AND WELSH STUDIES 197, HISTORY 355

Scottish Literature *see* CELTIC, IRISH, SCOTTISH AND WELSH STUDIES 197, LITERATURE 409

Scottish Music *see* MUSIC 449

Scottish Studies *see* CELTIC, IRISH, SCOTTISH AND WELSH STUDIES 197

Screen Cultures and Media Practice *see* MEDIA STUDIES 427

Screenwriting *see* FILM, RADIO, VIDEO and TV STUDIES 310

Scriptwriting *see* ENGLISH 296

Scriptwriting (Film, Television and Radio) *see* ENGLISH 296, FILM, RADIO, VIDEO and TV STUDIES 310

Scriptwriting and Performance *see* DRAMA 239, ENGLISH 296

Sculptural Metals *see* ART and DESIGN (Product and Industrial Design) 152

Sculpture *see* ART and DESIGN (3D Design) 156, ART and DESIGN (Fine Art) 144

Secondary Design Technology Education *see* TEACHER TRAINING 559

Secondary Education *see* EDUCATION STUDIES 256, TEACHER TRAINING 559

Secondary Physical Education *see* EDUCATION STUDIES 256, PHYSICAL EDUCATION 484, TEACHER TRAINING 559

Secondary Physical Science Education *see* TEACHER TRAINING 559

Secondary Teaching Design Technology *see* TEACHER TRAINING 559

Serbian/Croatian Studies *see* RUSSIAN and EAST EUROPEAN STUDIES 526

Set Design for Stage and Screen *see* DRAMA 239

Sexual Health Studies *see* HEALTH SCIENCES/ STUDIES 341

Ship and Port Management *see* MARINE/MARITIME STUDIES 412

Ship Science *see* MARINE/MARITIME STUDIES 412, NAVAL ARCHITECTURE 459

Ship Science (Advanced Materials) *see* MATERIALS SCIENCE/METALLURGY 419, NAVAL ARCHITECTURE 459

Ship Science (Engineering Management) *see* NAVAL ARCHITECTURE 459

Ship Science (Naval Architecture) *see* NAVAL ARCHITECTURE 459

Ship Science (Naval Engineering) *see* NAVAL ARCHITECTURE 459

Ship Science (Yacht and Small Craft) *see* NAVAL ARCHITECTURE 459

Slavonic Studies *see* RUSSIAN and EAST EUROPEAN STUDIES 526

Small Craft Technology see MARINE/MARITIME STUDIES 412, NAVAL ARCHITECTURE 459

Social and Architectural History see ARCHITECTURE 134, HISTORY (ECONOMIC and SOCIAL) 362

Social and Cultural History see HISTORY (ECONOMIC and SOCIAL) 362

Social and Political Sciences see POLITICS 507

SOCIAL and PUBLIC POLICY and ADMINISTRATION 529

  see also COMMUNTY STUDIES/DEVELOPMENT

  see also SOCIAL WORK

Social Anthropology see ANTHROPOLOGY 127, SOCIAL SCIENCES/STUDIES 531

Social Anthropology and Criminology see ANTHROPOLOGY 127, SOCIAL SCIENCES/ STUDIES 531

Social Anthropology and Sociology see ANTHROPOLOGY 127

Social Care see SOCIAL WORK 536

Social Care Studies see SOCIAL WORK 536

Social History see HISTORY (ECONOMIC and SOCIAL) 362

Social Policy see SOCIAL and PUBLIC POLICY and ADMINISTRATION 529, SOCIOLOGY 539

Social Policy and Criminology see SOCIAL and PUBLIC POLICY and ADMINISTRATION 529, SOCIAL SCIENCES/STUDIES 531

Social Policy and Economics see ECONOMICS 251, SOCIAL and PUBLIC POLICY and ADMINISTRATION 529

Social Policy and Politics see POLITICS 507, SOCIAL and PUBLIC POLICY and ADMINISTRATION 529

Social Policy and Sociology see SOCIAL and PUBLIC POLICY and ADMINISTRATION 529, SOCIOLOGY 539

Social Policy with Economics see ECONOMICS 251, SOCIAL and PUBLIC POLICY and ADMINISTRATION 529

Social Policy with Government see POLITICS 507, SOCIAL and PUBLIC POLICY and ADMINISTRATION 529

Social Policy with Politics see POLITICS 507, SOCIAL and PUBLIC POLICY and ADMINISTRATION 529

Social Psychology see PSYCHOLOGY 512

Social Science (Criminology) see LAW 393, SOCIAL SCIENCES/STUDIES 531

Social Science and Criminology see SOCIAL SCIENCES/ STUDIES 531

Social Sciences (Combined) see SOCIAL SCIENCES/ STUDIES 531

Social Sciences and Economics see ECONOMICS 251, SOCIAL SCIENCES/STUDIES 531

Social Sciences and Geography see GEOGRAPHY 330, SOCIAL SCIENCES/STUDIES 531

Social Sciences and Media Studies see SOCIAL SCIENCES/STUDIES 531

Social Sciences and Politics see SOCIAL SCIENCES/ STUDIES 531

Social Sciences and Psychological Studies see PSYCHOLOGY 512, SOCIAL SCIENCES/STUDIES 531

SOCIAL SCIENCES/STUDIES 531

  see also ANTHROPOLOGY

  see also COMMUNITY STUDIES/DEVELOPMENT

  see also HEALTH SCIENCES/STUDIES

  see also LAW

  see also POLITICS

  see also PSYCHOLOGY

  see also SOCIAL and PUBLIC POLICY and ADMINISTRATION

  see also SOCIOLOGY

Social Studies see SOCIAL SCIENCES/STUDIES 531

Social Studies and Counselling Studies see SOCIAL SCIENCES/STUDIES 531

SOCIAL WORK 536

  see also COMMUNITY STUDIES/DEVELOPMENT

  see also SOCIAL and PUBLIC POLICY and ADMINISTRATION

Social Work (Applied) see SOCIAL WORK 536

Social Work and Applied Social Studies see SOCIAL WORK 536

Social Work and Social Policy see SOCIAL and PUBLIC POLICY and ADMINISTRATION 529, SOCIAL WORK 536

Social Work Studies see SOCIAL WORK 536

Society, Culture and Media see MEDIA STUDIES 427

Sociolinguistics see LINGUISTICS 407, SOCIAL SCIENCES/STUDIES 531

SOCIOLOGY 539

  see also ANTHROPOLOGY

  see also SOCIAL and PUBLIC POLICY and ADMINISTRATION

  see also SOCIAL SCIENCES/STUDIE

Sociology (Combined) see COMBINED COURSES 212, SOCIOLOGY 539

Sociology (Social Science/Humanities) see SOCIOLOGY 539

Sociology and Anthropology see ANTHROPOLOGY 127, SOCIOLOGY 539

Sociology and Business Management see BUSINESS AND MANAGEMENT COURSES 179, SOCIOLOGY 539

Sociology and Community Development *see* SOCIOLOGY 539

Sociology and Community History *see* SOCIOLOGY 539

Sociology and Crime *see* SOCIOLOGY 539

Sociology and Criminology *see* LAW 393, SOCIAL SCIENCES/STUDIES 531, SOCIOLOGY 539

Sociology and Education *see* EDUCATION STUDIES 256, SOCIOLOGY 539

Sociology and English *see* ENGLISH 296, SOCIOLOGY 539

Sociology and English Literature *see* LITERATURE 409, SOCIOLOGY 539

Sociology and Film Studies *see* FILM, RADIO, VIDEO and TV STUDIES 310, SOCIOLOGY 539

Sociology and History *see* HISTORY 355, SOCIOLOGY 539

Sociology and International Development *see* DEVELOPMENT STUDIES 235, SOCIOLOGY 539

Sociology and Irish History *see* CELTIC, IRISH, SCOTTISH AND WELSH STUDIES 197, SOCIOLOGY 539

Sociology and Journalism *see* MEDIA STUDIES 427, SOCIOLOGY 539

Sociology and Management *see* SOCIOLOGY 539

Sociology and Media Studies *see* MEDIA STUDIES 427, SOCIOLOGY 539

Sociology and Philosophy *see* PHILOSOPHY 478, SOCIOLOGY 539

Sociology and Political Sciences *see* POLITICS 507, SOCIOLOGY 539

Sociology and Politics *see* POLITICS 507, SOCIOLOGY 539

Sociology and Psychology *see* PSYCHOLOGY 512, SOCIOLOGY 539

Sociology and Religious Studies *see* RELIGIOUS STUDIES 521, SOCIOLOGY 539

Sociology and Social Policy *see* SOCIAL and PUBLIC POLICY and ADMINISTRATION 529, SOCIOLOGY 539

Sociology and Social Psychology *see* PSYCHOLOGY 512, SOCIOLOGY 539

Sociology and Social Science *see* SOCIOLOGY 539

Sociology and Social Welfare *see* SOCIOLOGY 539

Sociology and Welsh *see* CELTIC, IRISH, SCOTTISH AND WELSH STUDIES 197, SOCIOLOGY 539

Sociology and Youth Justice *see* SOCIOLOGY 539

Sociology and Youth Studies *see* SOCIOLOGY 539

Sociology with Human Rights *see* SOCIAL SCIENCES/STUDIES 531, SOCIOLOGY 539

Sociology with Law *see* LAW 393, SOCIOLOGY 539

Sociology with Psychology *see* SOCIOLOGY 539

Sociology, Culture and Media *see* MEDIA STUDIES 427, SOCIOLOGY 539

Software and Electronic Engineering *see* ENGINEERING (COMPUTER, CONTROL, SOFTWARE and SYSTEMS) 280

Software Applications Development *see* COMPUTER COURSES 219

Software Development *see* ENGINEERING (COMPUTER, CONTROL, SOFTWARE and SYSTEMS) 280

Software Engineering *see* ENGINEERING (COMPUTER, CONTROL, SOFTWARE and SYSTEMS) 280

Software Engineering and Management *see* BUSINESS AND MANAGEMENT COURSES 179, ENGINEERING (COMPUTER, CONTROL, SOFTWARE and SYSTEMS) 280

Software Engineering Management *see* ENGINEERING (COMPUTER, CONTROL, SOFTWARE and SYSTEMS) 280

Software Product Design *see* ART and DESIGN (Product and Industrial Design) 152, ENGINEERING (COMPUTER, CONTROL, SOFTWARE and SYSTEMS) 280

Sonic Arts *see* MUSIC 449

Sound and Multimedia Technology *see* ENGINEERING (ACOUSTICS and SOUND) 264

Sound Arts and Resources *see* ENGINEERING (ACOUSTICS and SOUND) 264

Sound Design *see* ENGINEERING (ACOUSTICS and SOUND) 264

Sound Design and Technology *see* ENGINEERING (ACOUSTICS and SOUND) 264

Sound Engineering *see* ENGINEERING (ACOUSTICS and SOUND) 264

Sound Engineering and Design *see* ENGINEERING (ACOUSTICS and SOUND) 264

Sound Engineering and Production *see* ENGINEERING (ACOUSTICS and SOUND) 264

Sound Recording *see* ENGINEERING (ACOUSTICS and SOUND) 264

Sound Technology *see* ENGINEERING (ACOUSTICS and SOUND) 264, MUSIC 449

Sound Technology and Digital Music *see* ENGINEERING (ACOUSTICS and SOUND) 264, MUSIC 449

Sound, Light and Live Event Technology *see* TECHNOLOGIES 562

Sound/Broadcast Engineering *see* ENGINEERING (ACOUSTICS and SOUND) 264

South Asian Studies *see* ASIA-PACIFIC STUDIES 158

South East Asian Studies *see* ASIA-PACIFIC STUDIES 158

Spa Management *see* HOSPITALITY and HOTEL MANAGEMENT 367

Space Science and Robotics *see* ASTRONOMY and ASTROPHYSICS 159, ENGINEERING (COMPUTER, CONTROL, SOFTWARE and SYSTEMS) 280, PHYSICS 488

Space Systems Engineering *see* ENGINEERING (AERONAUTICAL and AEROSPACE) 266

SPANISH 543
   see also LANGUAGES
   see also LATIN AMERICAN STUDIES

Spanish (Combined) *see* SPANISH 543

Spanish and a Modern Language *see* LANGUAGES 386, SPANISH 543

Spanish and Business *see* BUSINESS AND MANAGEMENT COURSES 179, SPANISH 543

Spanish and Contemporary Chinese Studies *see* CHINESE 206, SPANISH 543

Spanish and French/German/Italian *see* SPANISH 543

Spanish and International Business *see* BUSINESS AND MANAGEMENT COURSES (INTERNATIONAL AND EUROPEAN) 188, SPANISH 543

Spanish and International Media Communications Studies *see* COMMUNICATION STUDIES/ COMMUNICATION 214, MEDIA STUDIES 427, SPANISH 543

Spanish and International Relations *see* INTERNATIONAL RELATIONS 378, SPANISH 543

Spanish and Latin American Studies *see* LATIN AMERICAN STUDIES 391, SPANISH 543

Spanish and Legal Studies *see* SPANISH 543

Spanish and Marketing *see* MARKETING 415, SPANISH 543

Spanish and Music *see* MUSIC 449, SPANISH 543

Spanish and Politics *see* POLITICS 507, SPANISH 543

Spanish and Portuguese *see* SPANISH 543

Spanish and Portuguese Studies *see* SPANISH 543

Spanish and World Cinema *see* FILM, RADIO, VIDEO and TV STUDIES 310, SPANISH 543

Spanish Language with International Development Studies *see* SPANISH 543

Spanish Studies *see* SPANISH 543

Spanish Studies and Geography *see* GEOGRAPHY 330, SPANISH 543

Spanish Studies and Modern Languages *see* LANGUAGES 386, SPANISH 543

Spanish with Computer Science *see* SPANISH 543

Spanish with English Literature *see* LITERATURE 409, SPANISH 543

Spanish with French/German/Italian/Russian *see* LANGUAGES 386, SPANISH 543

Spanish with History of Art *see* HISTORY OF ART 363, SPANISH 543

Spanish with Theatre Studies *see* DRAMA 239, SPANISH 543

Spanish, Portuguese and Latin American Studies *see* LATIN AMERICAN STUDIES 391, SPANISH 543

Spatial Design *see* ART and DESIGN (Product and Industrial Design) 152

Spatial Economics and Development *see* DEVELOPMENT STUDIES 235, ECONOMICS 251

Special and Inclusive Education and Educational Development *see* EDUCATION STUDIES 256

Special Education Needs *see* EDUCATION STUDIES 256, TEACHER TRAINING 559

Special Educational Needs *see* EDUCATION STUDIES 256

Special Educational Needs and Inclusion *see* EDUCATION STUDIES 256

Speech and Language Pathology *see* SPEECH PATHOLOGY/SCIENCES/THERAPY 546

Speech and Language Sciences *see* SPEECH PATHOLOGY/SCIENCES/THERAPY 546

Speech and Language Therapy *see* SPEECH PATHOLOGY/SCIENCES/THERAPY 546

Speech Pathology and Therapy *see* SPEECH PATHOLOGY/SCIENCES/THERAPY 546

SPEECH PATHOLOGY/SCIENCES/THERAPY 546
   see also COMMUNICATION STUDIES/ COMMUNICATION

Speech Science *see* SPEECH PATHOLOGY/SCIENCES/ THERAPY 546

Speech Sciences *see* SPEECH PATHOLOGY/SCIENCES/ THERAPY 546

Sport *see* SPORTS SCIENCES/STUDIES 548

Sport Analysis and Coaching *see* SPORTS SCIENCES/ STUDIES 548

Sport and Biomedicine *see* SPORTS SCIENCES/ STUDIES 548

Sport and Business Management *see* SPORTS SCIENCES/STUDIES 548

Sport and Coaching *see* PHYSICAL EDUCATION 484

Sport and Coaching Development *see* SPORTS SCIENCES/STUDIES 548

Sport and Community Development *see* COMMUNITY STUDIES/DEVELOPMENT 217, SPORTS SCIENCES/ STUDIES 548

Sport and Dance Therapy *see* SPORTS SCIENCES/ STUDIES 548

Sport and Exercise *see* SPORTS SCIENCES/STUDIES 548

Sport and Exercise (Applied Exercise Science) *see* SPORTS SCIENCES/STUDIES 548

Sport and Exercise (Applied Sport Science) *see* SPORTS SCIENCES/STUDIES 548

Sport and Exercise (Coaching Science) see SPORTS SCIENCES/STUDIES 548

Sport and Exercise (Sport Studies) see SPORTS SCIENCES/STUDIES 548

Sport and Exercise Development see SPORTS SCIENCES/STUDIES 548

Sport and Exercise for Health see SPORTS SCIENCES/STUDIES 548

Sport and Exercise Management see SPORTS SCIENCES/STUDIES 548

Sport and Exercise Performance see SPORTS SCIENCES/STUDIES 548

Sport and Exercise Science see SPORTS SCIENCES/STUDIES 548

Sport and Exercise Science (Exercise Physiology) see PHYSIOLOGY 500, SPORTS SCIENCES/STUDIES 548

Sport and Exercise Sciences see SPORTS SCIENCES/STUDIES 548

Sport and Exercise Studies see SPORTS SCIENCES/STUDIES 548

Sport and Exercise Therapy see SPORTS SCIENCES/STUDIES 548

Sport and Exercise with Psychology see PSYCHOLOGY 512, SPORTS SCIENCES/STUDIES 548

Sport and Leisure see LEISURE and RECREATION MANAGEMENT/STUDIES 405, SPORTS SCIENCES/STUDIES 548

Sport and Leisure Management see LEISURE and RECREATION MANAGEMENT/STUDIES 405

Sport and Marketing see MARKETING 415, SPORTS SCIENCES/STUDIES 548

Sport and Mathematics see MATHEMATICS 422, SPORTS SCIENCES/STUDIES 548

Sport and Physical Activity see SPORTS SCIENCES/STUDIES 548

Sport and Physical Education see PHYSICAL EDUCATION 484, SPORTS SCIENCES/STUDIES 548

Sport and Recreation Management see LEISURE and RECREATION MANAGEMENT/STUDIES 405, SPORTS SCIENCES/STUDIES 548

Sport and Tourism Management see TOURISM and TRAVEL 564

Sport Biomedicine see SPORTS SCIENCES/STUDIES 548

Sport Business Management see SPORTS SCIENCES/STUDIES 548

Sport Coaching see SPORTS SCIENCES/STUDIES 548

Sport Coaching and Physical Education see PHYSICAL EDUCATION 484

Sport Coaching Science see SPORTS SCIENCES/STUDIES 548

Sport Coaching, Development and Fitness see SPORTS SCIENCES/STUDIES 548

Sport Conditioning, Rehabilitation and Massage see SPORTS SCIENCES/STUDIES 548

Sport Development see SPORTS SCIENCES/STUDIES 548

Sport Development and Coaching Science see SPORTS SCIENCES/STUDIES 548

Sport Development with Coaching see SOCIAL SCIENCES/STUDIES 531

Sport Development with Physical Education see PHYSICAL EDUCATION 484

Sport Journalism see MEDIA STUDIES 427, SPORTS SCIENCES/STUDIES 548

Sport Management see BUSINESS AND MANAGEMENT COURSES 179, SPORTS SCIENCES/STUDIES 548

Sport Management and Coaching Studies see SPORTS SCIENCES/STUDIES 548

Sport Management and Football Studies see SPORTS SCIENCES/STUDIES 548

Sport Marketing see MARKETING 415, SPORTS SCIENCES/STUDIES 548

Sport Massage and Exercise Therapies see OCCUPATIONAL THERAPY 468, SPORTS SCIENCES/STUDIES 548

Sport Psychology see PSYCHOLOGY 512, SPORTS SCIENCES/STUDIES 548

Sport Psychology and Coaching Science see PSYCHOLOGY 512

Sport Rehabilitation see SPORTS SCIENCES/STUDIES 548

Sport Science see SPORTS SCIENCES/STUDIES 548

Sport Science (Exercise and Health Management) see SPORTS SCIENCES/STUDIES 548

Sport Science (Human Performance) see SPORTS SCIENCES/STUDIES 548

Sport Science (Outdoor Activities) see SPORTS SCIENCES/STUDIES 548

Sport Science (Physical Education) see PHYSICAL EDUCATION 484, SPORTS SCIENCES/STUDIES 548

Sport Science (Physical Education and Youth Sport) see PHYSICAL EDUCATION 484

Sport Science and Coaching see PHYSICAL EDUCATION 484, SPORTS SCIENCES/STUDIES 548

Sport Science and Material Science see MATERIALS SCIENCE/METALLURGY 419, SPORTS SCIENCES/STUDIES 548

Sport Science and Mathematics see MATHEMATICS 422, SPORTS SCIENCES/STUDIES 548

Sport Science and Physical Education see PHYSICAL EDUCATION 484

Sport Science for Performance and Conditioning *see* SPORTS SCIENCES/STUDIES 548

Sport Science with Psychology *see* PSYCHOLOGY 512, SPORTS SCIENCES/STUDIES 548

Sport Science, Performance and Coaching *see* SPORTS SCIENCES/STUDIES 548

Sport Sciences *see* SPORTS SCIENCES/STUDIES 548

Sport Sciences and Biology *see* BIOLOGY 170, SPORTS SCIENCES/STUDIES 548

Sport Sciences and Management *see* SPORTS SCIENCES/STUDIES 548

Sport Studies *see* PHYSICAL EDUCATION 484, SPORTS SCIENCES/STUDIES 548

Sport Studies (Exercise and Health) *see* SPORTS SCIENCES/STUDIES 548

Sport Studies (Sport and Physical Activity Development) *see* SPORTS SCIENCES/STUDIES 548

Sport Studies and Business *see* SPORTS SCIENCES/STUDIES 548

Sport Technology *see* SPORTS SCIENCES/STUDIES 548

Sport Therapy *see* SPORTS SCIENCES/STUDIES 548

Sport Therapy and Rehabilitation *see* SPORTS SCIENCES/STUDIES 548

Sport, Culture and Society *see* SPORTS SCIENCES/STUDIES 548

Sport, Exercise and Nutrition *see* NUTRITION 466, SPORTS SCIENCES/STUDIES 548

Sport, Health and Exercise Science *see* SPORTS SCIENCES/STUDIES 548

Sport, Health and Physical Education *see* PHYSICAL EDUCATION 484, SPORTS SCIENCES/STUDIES 548

Sport, Health, Exercise and Nutrition *see* NUTRITION 466

Sport, Leisure and Culture *see* SPORTS SCIENCES/STUDIES 548

Sport, Physical Activity and Health *see* SPORTS SCIENCES/STUDIES 548

Sport, Physical Education and Coaching Science *see* PHYSICAL EDUCATION 484

Sport, Recreation and Development *see* SPORTS SCIENCES/STUDIES 548

Sport, Society and Development *see* SPORTS SCIENCES/STUDIES 548

Sports and Exercise Science *see* SPORTS SCIENCES/STUDIES 548

Sports and Exercise Therapy *see* SPORTS SCIENCES/STUDIES 548

Sports and Marketing and Public Relations *see* MARKETING 415, SPORTS SCIENCES/STUDIES 548

Sports Biomedicine *see* SPORTS SCIENCES/STUDIES 548

Sports Biomedicine and Nutrition *see* NUTRITION 466, SPORTS SCIENCES/STUDIES 548

Sports Business Management *see* BUSINESS AND MANAGEMENT COURSES 179, SPORTS SCIENCES/STUDIES 548

Sports Coaching *see* SPORTS SCIENCES/STUDIES 548

Sports Coaching and Performance *see* SPORTS SCIENCES/STUDIES 548

Sports Coaching and Physical Education *see* PHYSICAL EDUCATION 484

Sports Coaching Studies *see* SPORTS SCIENCES/STUDIES 548

Sports Development *see* SPORTS SCIENCES/STUDIES 548

Sports Development and Physical Education *see* SPORTS SCIENCES/STUDIES 548

Sports Education *see* EDUCATION STUDIES 256, SPORTS SCIENCES/STUDIES 548

Sports Event Management *see* BUSINESS AND MANAGEMENT COURSES (SPECIALISED) 193, SPORTS SCIENCES/STUDIES 548

Sports Journalism *see* MEDIA STUDIES 427, SPORTS SCIENCES/STUDIES 548

Sports Leisure Management *see* LEISURE and RECREATION MANAGEMENT/STUDIES 405

Sports Management *see* BUSINESS AND MANAGEMENT COURSES (SPECIALISED) 193, LEISURE and RECREATION MANAGEMENT/STUDIES 405, SPORTS SCIENCES/STUDIES 548

Sports Marketing *see* MARKETING 415, SPORTS SCIENCES/STUDIES 548

Sports Marketing Management *see* BUSINESS AND MANAGEMENT COURSES 179, MARKETING 415, SPORTS SCIENCES/STUDIES 548

Sports Materials *see* MATERIALS SCIENCE/METALLURGY 419

Sports Media *see* MEDIA STUDIES 427

Sports Medicine *see* HEALTH SCIENCES/STUDIES 341, SPORTS SCIENCES/STUDIES 548

Sports Product Design *see* ART and DESIGN (Product and Industrial Design) 152

Sports Promotion and Marketing *see* MARKETING 415, SPORTS SCIENCES/STUDIES 548

Sports Psychology *see* PSYCHOLOGY 512, SPORTS SCIENCES/STUDIES 548

Sports Science *see* SPORTS SCIENCES/STUDIES 548

Sports Science and Injury Management *see* SPORTS SCIENCES/STUDIES 548

Sports Science and Rugby *see* SPORTS SCIENCES/STUDIES 548

Sports Science with Management *see* SPORTS SCIENCES/STUDIES 548

Sports Sciences *see* SPORTS SCIENCES/STUDIES 548

Sports Studies *see* SPORTS SCIENCES/STUDIES 548

Sports Technology *see* SPORTS SCIENCES/STUDIES 548

Sports Therapy *see* SPORTS SCIENCES/STUDIES 548

Sportsturf Science and Management *see* SPORTS SCIENCES/STUDIES 548

Stage Management *see* DRAMA 239

Stage Management and Technical Theatre *see* DRAMA 239

Statistical Modelling *see* STATISTICS 554

Statistical Science *see* STATISTICS 554

STATISTICS 554

see also BUSINESS COURSES

see also MATHEMATICS

Statistics and Business Management *see* STATISTICS 554

Statistics and Computing *see* COMPUTER COURSES 219, STATISTICS 554

Statistics and Economics *see* STATISTICS 554

Statistics and Management *see* STATISTICS 554

Statistics and Management for Business *see* STATISTICS 554

Statistics with Finance *see* FINANCE 315, STATISTICS 554

Statistics with Management *see* STATISTICS 554

Statistics, Economics and Finance/Language *see* STATISTICS 554

Street Arts *see* DRAMA 239

Strength and Conditioning Science *see* SPORTS SCIENCES/STUDIES 548

Structural and Fire Safety Engineering *see* ENGINEERING (CHEMICAL) 269

Structural Engineering and Architecture *see* ARCHITECTURE 134, ENGINEERING (CIVIL) 274

Structural Engineering with Architecture *see* ARCHITECTURE 134, ENGINEERING (CIVIL) 274

Studies in Film *see* FILM, RADIO, VIDEO and TV STUDIES 310

Studio Recording and Performance Technology *see* ENGINEERING (ACOUSTICS and SOUND) 264

Study of Religion *see* RELIGIOUS STUDIES 521

Study of Religion and Theology *see* RELIGIOUS STUDIES 521

Study of Religions *see* RELIGIOUS STUDIES 521

Surf Science and Technology *see* MARINE/MARITIME STUDIES 412, SPORTS SCIENCES/STUDIES 548

Surface Design and Printed Textiles *see* ART and DESIGN (Fashion and Textiles) 140

Surface Pattern Design *see* ART and DESIGN (Fashion and Textiles) 140

Surface Pattern Design (Contemporary Applied Arts Practice) *see* ART and DESIGN (Fashion and Textiles) 140

Surface Pattern Design (Textiles for Fashion) *see* ART and DESIGN (Fashion and Textiles) 140

Surface Pattern Design (Textiles for Interiors) *see* ART and DESIGN (Fashion and Textiles) 140

SURVEYING 556

see also BUILDING and CONSTRUCTION

Surveying (Quantity Surveying) *see* SURVEYING 556

Surveying and Mapping Science *see* BUILDING and CONSTRUCTION 176, GEOGRAPHY 330

Surveying and Mapping Sciences *see* SURVEYING 556

Sustainable Built Environment *see* BUILDING and CONSTRUCTION 176

Sustainable Communities *see* HOUSING 370

Sustainable Development *see* ENVIRONMENTAL SCIENCES/STUDIES 303

Sustainable Energy Engineering *see* ENGINEERING (CIVIL) 274

Sustainable Energy Technology *see* ENVIRONMENTAL SCIENCES/STUDIES 303

Sustainable Engineering *see* ENGINEERING/ENGINEERING SCIENCES 260, ENVIRONMENTAL SCIENCES/STUDIES 303

Sustainable Forest Management *see* FORESTRY 324

Sustainable Land Management *see* AGRICULTURAL SCIENCES/AGRICULTURE 117

Sustainable Rural Development *see* DEVELOPMENT STUDIES 235, TOWN and COUNTRY PLANNING 567

Swahili *see* LANGUAGES 386

System and Computer Engineering *see* ENGINEERING (COMPUTER, CONTROL, SOFTWARE and SYSTEMS) 280, ENGINEERING (ELECTRICAL and ELECTRONIC) 283

Systems and Control Engineering *see* ENGINEERING (COMPUTER, CONTROL, SOFTWARE and SYSTEMS) 280

Systems and Control Engineering (Engineering Management) *see* ENGINEERING (COMPUTER, CONTROL, SOFTWARE and SYSTEMS) 280

Systems Engineering *see* ENGINEERING (COMPUTER, CONTROL, SOFTWARE and SYSTEMS) 280

TEACHER TRAINING 559

see also EDUCATION STUDIES

Technical and Production Arts *see* DRAMA 239

Technical Effects for Performance *see* ART and DESIGN (Fashion and Textiles) 140, FILM, RADIO, VIDEO and TV STUDIES 310

Technical Theatre *see* DRAMA 239

Technical Theatre and Stage Management *see* DRAMA 239

Technological Education *see* EDUCATION STUDIES 256, TECHNOLOGIES 562

TECHNOLOGIES 562

Technology and Design Education *see* ART and DESIGN (3D Design) 156, TEACHER TRAINING 559

Technology and Enterprise Management *see* BUSINESS AND MANAGEMENT COURSES (SPECIALISED) 193, TECHNOLOGIES 562

Technology Management *see* TECHNOLOGIES 562

Technology with Design *see* ART and DESIGN (Product and Industrial Design) 152, TECHNOLOGIES 562

Telecommunication and Network Engineering *see* ENGINEERING (COMMUNICATIONS) 278

Telecommunication Engineering *see* ENGINEERING (COMMUNICATIONS) 278

Telecommunication Systems *see* ENGINEERING (COMMUNICATIONS) 278

Telecommunications *see* ENGINEERING (COMMUNICATIONS) 278

Telecommunications and Computer Networks Engineering *see* ENGINEERING (COMMUNICATIONS) 278

Telecommunications and Network Engineering *see* ENGINEERING (COMMUNICATIONS) 278

Telecommunications Engineering *see* ENGINEERING (COMMUNICATIONS) 278

Telecommunications System Engineering *see* ENGINEERING (COMMUNICATIONS) 278

Television *see* FILM, RADIO, VIDEO and TV STUDIES 310

Television and Film Design *see* FILM, RADIO, VIDEO and TV STUDIES 310

Television and Film Production *see* FILM, RADIO, VIDEO and TV STUDIES 310

Television and Video Production *see* FILM, RADIO, VIDEO and TV STUDIES 310

Television Production *see* FILM, RADIO, VIDEO and TV STUDIES 310

Television Studio Production *see* FILM, RADIO, VIDEO and TV STUDIES 310

Television Technology Production *see* FILM, RADIO, VIDEO and TV STUDIES 310, TECHNOLOGIES 562

Textile Design *see* ART and DESIGN (Fashion and Textiles) 140

Textile Design and Design Management *see* ART and DESIGN (Fashion and Textiles) 140

Textile Surfaces *see* ART and DESIGN (Fashion and Textiles) 140

Textile Technology (Business Management) *see* ART and DESIGN (Fashion and Textiles) 140

Textile/Surface Design *see* ART and DESIGN (Fashion and Textiles) 140

Textiles *see* ART and DESIGN (Fashion and Textiles) 140

Textiles and Fashion Design *see* ART and DESIGN (Fashion and Textiles) 140

Textiles and Surface Design *see* ART and DESIGN (Fashion and Textiles) 140

Textiles for Fashion *see* ART and DESIGN (Fashion and Textiles) 140

Textiles for Fashion Interiors *see* ART and DESIGN (Fashion and Textiles) 140

Textiles in Practice *see* ART and DESIGN (Fashion and Textiles) 140

Textiles: Innovation and Design *see* ART and DESIGN (Fashion and Textiles) 140

Thai *see* LANGUAGES 386

Theatre *see* DRAMA 239

Theatre and Drama *see* DRAMA 239

Theatre and Drama Studies *see* DRAMA 239

Theatre and Performance *see* DANCE/DANCE STUDIES 227, DRAMA 239

Theatre and Performance Design *see* ART and DESIGN (Product and Industrial Design) 152, DRAMA 239

Theatre and Performance Studies *see* DRAMA 239

Theatre and Performance Technology *see* DRAMA 239, TECHNOLOGIES 562

Theatre and Professional Practice *see* DRAMA 239

Theatre Arts *see* DRAMA 239

Theatre Arts (Performance) *see* DRAMA 239

Theatre Design *see* ART and DESIGN (Product and Industrial Design) 152, DRAMA 239

Theatre Design and Performance *see* DRAMA 239

Theatre Practice with Costume Construction *see* ART and DESIGN (Fashion and Textiles) 140, DRAMA 239

Theatre Practice with Lighting Design *see* ART and DESIGN (Product and Industrial Design) 152, DRAMA 239

Theatre Practice with Performance Arts *see* DRAMA 239

Theatre Practice with Production Lighting *see* ART and DESIGN (Product and Industrial Design) 152, DRAMA 239

Theatre Practice with Prop Making see ART and DESIGN (Product and Industrial Design) 152, DRAMA 239

Theatre Practice with Puppetry see DRAMA 239

Theatre Practice with Scenic Art see ART and DESIGN (Fine Art) 144, DRAMA 239

Theatre Practice with Scenic Construction see BUILDING and CONSTRUCTION 176, DRAMA 239

Theatre Practice with Stage Design see ART and DESIGN (Product and Industrial Design) 152, DRAMA 239

Theatre Practice with Stage Management see BUSINESS AND MANAGEMENT COURSES (SPECIALISED) 193, DRAMA 239

Theatre Practice with Technical and Production Management see BUSINESS AND MANAGEMENT COURSES (SPECIALISED) 193, DRAMA 239

Theatre Practice with Theatre Sound see DRAMA 239, ENGINEERING (ACOUSTICS and SOUND) 264

Theatre Practice: Creative Producing see DRAMA 239

Theatre Studies see DRAMA 239

Theatre Studies and Technical Stage Production see DRAMA 239

Theatre Studies with English Literature see DRAMA 239, LITERATURE 409

Theatre, Performance and Event Design see DRAMA 239

Theatre, Television and Performance see DRAMA 239

Theological Studies see RELIGIOUS STUDIES 521

Theology see RELIGIOUS STUDIES 521

Theology (European Studies) see RELIGIOUS STUDIES 521

Theology and Music see MUSIC 449, PHILOSOPHY 478

Theology and Oriental Studies see RELIGIOUS STUDIES 521

Theology and Philosophy see PHILOSOPHY 478, RELIGIOUS STUDIES 521

Theology and Religion see RELIGIOUS STUDIES 521

Theology and Religious Studies see RELIGIOUS STUDIES 521

Theology and Society see PHILOSOPHY 478, RELIGIOUS STUDIES 521

Theology and Sociology see RELIGIOUS STUDIES 521, SOCIOLOGY 539

Theology, Divinity and Religious Studies see RELIGIOUS STUDIES 521

Theoretical and Computational Physics see PHYSICS 488

Theoretical Physics see PHYSICS 488

Theoretical Physics with Mathematics see MATHEMATICS 422, PHYSICS 488

Therapeutic Radiography see RADIOGRAPHY 519

Third World Development see DEVELOPMENT STUDIES 235, INTERNATIONAL RELATIONS 378

Tibetan see LANGUAGES 386

Tourism and Business see TOURISM and TRAVEL 564

Tourism and Business Management see TOURISM and TRAVEL 564

Tourism and Hospitality see TOURISM and TRAVEL 564

Tourism and Hospitality Practice see HOSPITALITY and HOTEL MANAGEMENT 367, TOURISM and TRAVEL 564

Tourism and Language see LANGUAGES 386, TOURISM and TRAVEL 564

Tourism and Leisure Management see TOURISM and TRAVEL 564

Tourism and Leisure Studies see LEISURE and RECREATION MANAGEMENT/STUDIES 405, TOURISM and TRAVEL 564

Tourism and Marketing see MARKETING 415, TOURISM and TRAVEL 564

TOURISM and TRAVEL 564
   see also BUSINESS and MANAGEMENT COURSES
   see also HOSPITALITY and EVENT MANAGEMENT
   see also LEISURE and RECREATION MANAGEMENT/ STUDIES

Tourism Business Management see TOURISM and TRAVEL 564

Tourism France/Spain see TOURISM and TRAVEL 564

Tourism Management see BUSINESS AND MANAGEMENT COURSES (SPECIALISED) 193, TOURISM and TRAVEL 564

Tourism Management (International) see BUSINESS AND MANAGEMENT COURSES (INTERNATIONAL AND EUROPEAN) 188, BUSINESS AND MANAGEMENT COURSES (SPECIALISED) 193, TOURISM and TRAVEL 564

Tourism Management and Human Resources Management see TOURISM and TRAVEL 564

Tourism Management and Marketing see MARKETING 415, TOURISM and TRAVEL 564

Tourism Management and Tourism with Languages see TOURISM and TRAVEL 564

Tourism Planning see TOURISM and TRAVEL 564

Tourism with Spanish see SPANISH 543, TOURISM and TRAVEL 564

Tourism, Entrepreneurship and Management see TOURISM and TRAVEL 564

Tourism, Hospitality and Business Management (International) see BUSINESS AND MANAGEMENT COURSES (INTERNATIONAL AND EUROPEAN) 188, TOURISM and TRAVEL 564

Tourism, Management with Events see TOURISM and TRAVEL 564

TOWN and COUNTRY PLANNING 567

    see also DEVELOPMENT STUDIES

    see also ENVIRONMENTAL SCIENCE/STUDIES

    see also HOUSING

    see also SURVEYING

    see also TRANSPORT MANAGEMENT and PLANNING

Town and Regional Planning see TOWN and COUNTRY PLANNING 567

Town Planning see GEOGRAPHY 330, TOWN and COUNTRY PLANNING 567

Traditional Chinese Acupuncture see CHINESE 206, HEALTH SCIENCES/STUDIES 341

Translating and Interpreting with Language see LANGUAGES 386

Translation see LANGUAGES 386

Translation Studies see LANGUAGES 386

Translation Studies (French) see LANGUAGES 386

Translation Studies (Spanish) see LANGUAGES 386

Translation Studies French/German/Spanish see LANGUAGES 386

Translation, Media and French/Spanish see FRENCH 325, MEDIA STUDIES 427, SPANISH 543

Translation, Media and French/Spanish/Japanese see FRENCH 325, JAPANESE 383, MEDIA STUDIES 427, SPANISH 543

Transport and Business Management see BUSINESS AND MANAGEMENT COURSES 179, TRANSPORT MANAGEMENT and PLANNING 571

Transport Design see ART and DESIGN (Product and Industrial Design) 152

Transport Management see BUSINESS AND MANAGEMENT COURSES (SPECIALISED) 193, TRANSPORT MANAGEMENT and PLANNING 571

Transport Management and Logistics see TRANSPORT MANAGEMENT and PLANNING 571

TRANSPORT MANAGEMENT and PLANNING 571

    see also ENGINEERING/ENGINEERING SCIENCES

    see also TOWN and COUNTRY PLANNING

Transport Planning see TRANSPORT MANAGEMENT and PLANNING 571

Transport Product Design see ART and DESIGN (Product and Industrial Design) 152, ENGINEERING/ENGINEERING SCIENCES 260

Transportation Design see TRANSPORT MANAGEMENT and PLANNING 571

Travel and Tourism see TOURISM and TRAVEL 564

Travel and Tourism Management see TOURISM and TRAVEL 564

Travel Tourism Management see TOURISM and TRAVEL 564

Travel, Tourism and Marketing see MARKETING 415, TOURISM and TRAVEL 564

Tropical Disease Biology see BIOLOGY 170

Turkish see LANGUAGES 386

Turkish and Modern Greek Studies see ARABIC AND ANCIENT NEAR AND MIDDLE EASTERN STUDIES 129, GREEK 340

TV Production see FILM, RADIO, VIDEO and TV STUDIES 310

Urban and Environmental Planning see TOWN and COUNTRY PLANNING 567

Urban and Regional Planning see TOWN and COUNTRY PLANNING 567

Urban and Regional Studies see TOWN and COUNTRY PLANNING 567

Urban Environment Planning see TOWN and COUNTRY PLANNING 567

Urban Estate Management see SURVEYING 556

Urban Planning, Design and Management see TOWN and COUNTRY PLANNING 567

Urban Regeneration and Planning see TOWN and COUNTRY PLANNING 567

Urban Studies see TOWN and COUNTRY PLANNING 567

Urban Studies and Planning see TOWN and COUNTRY PLANNING 567

Veterinary Biosciences see VETERINARY SCIENCE/MEDICINE 573

Veterinary Gateway programme see VETERINARY SCIENCE/MEDICINE 573

Veterinary Medicine see VETERINARY SCIENCE/MEDICINE 573

Veterinary Medicine and Surgery see VETERINARY SCIENCE/MEDICINE 573

Veterinary Medicine with Preliminary Year see VETERINARY SCIENCE/MEDICINE 573

Veterinary Nursing see VETERINARY SCIENCE/MEDICINE 573

Veterinary Nursing and Applied Animal Behaviour see VETERINARY SCIENCE/MEDICINE 573

Veterinary Nursing and Bioveterinary Science see VETERINARY SCIENCE/MEDICINE 573

Veterinary Nursing and Practice Management *see* VETERINARY SCIENCE/MEDICINE 573

Veterinary Nursing Science *see* VETERINARY SCIENCE/MEDICINE 573

Veterinary Science with Pre-Veterinary Year *see* VETERINARY SCIENCE/MEDICINE 573

VETERINARY SCIENCE/MEDICINE 573

Video *see* FILM, RADIO, VIDEO and TV STUDIES 310

Video Arts *see* FILM, RADIO, VIDEO and TV STUDIES 310

Vietnamese *see* ASIA-PACIFIC STUDIES 158

Viking Studies *see* SCANDINAVIAN STUDIES 527

Virology and Immunology *see* BIOLOGICAL SCIENCES 165

Virtual Engineering *see* ENGINEERING (COMPUTER, CONTROL, SOFTWARE and SYSTEMS) 280

Visual and Performing Arts *see* DRAMA 239

Visual Arts *see* DRAMA, FILM, RADIO, VIDEO and TV STUDIES 310

Visual Arts and History *see* FILM, RADIO, VIDEO and TV STUDIES 310, HISTORY 355

Visual Communication *see* ART and DESIGN (Graphic Design) 148

Visual Communications *see* ART and DESIGN (Graphic Design) 148

Viticulture and Oenology *see* FOOD SCIENCE/STUDIES and TECHNOLOGY 321

War and Society *see* INTERNATIONAL RELATIONS 378, POLITICS 507

War Studies *see* HISTORY 355, HISTORY (ECONOMIC and SOCIAL) 362, INTERNATIONAL RELATIONS 378, POLITICS 507

War Studies and History *see* HISTORY 355, INTERNATIONAL RELATIONS 378

War Studies and Philosophy *see* HISTORY 355, INTERNATIONAL RELATIONS 378, PHILOSOPHY 478, POLITICS 507

War, Peace and International Relations *see* INTERNATIONAL RELATIONS 378, POLITICS 507

Watersports Studies and Management *see* LEISURE and RECREATION MANAGEMENT/STUDIES 405, MARINE/MARITIME STUDIES 412, SPORTS SCIENCES/STUDIES 548

Web and Mobile Application Development *see* COMPUTER COURSES 219

Web and Multimedia *see* COMPUTER COURSES 219

Web and Multimedia Design *see* COMPUTER COURSES 219

Web Computing *see* COMPUTER COURSES 219

Web Design *see* COMPUTER COURSES 219

Web Design and Development *see* COMPUTER COURSES 219

Web Design and Technology *see* COMPUTER COURSES 219

Web Development *see* COMPUTER COURSES 219

Web Media *see* COMPUTER COURSES 219

Web Systems Design *see* COMPUTER COURSES 219

Web Technologies *see* COMPUTER COURSES 219

Web Technology *see* COMPUTER COURSES 219

Website Development *see* COMPUTER COURSES 219

Welsh *see* CELTIC, IRISH, SCOTTISH AND WELSH STUDIES 197, COMBINED COURSES 212

Welsh History *see* CELTIC, IRISH, SCOTTISH AND WELSH STUDIES 197, HISTORY 355

Welsh History and Archaeology *see* ARCHAEOLOGY 131, HISTORY 355

Welsh with Education *see* CELTIC, IRISH, SCOTTISH AND WELSH STUDIES 197, EDUCATION STUDIES 256

Wildlife and Media *see* ANIMAL SCIENCES 124

Wildlife Biology *see* ZOOLOGY 576

Wildlife Conservation *see* ANIMAL SCIENCES 124

Wildlife Conservation and Ecology *see* ANIMAL SCIENCES 124, BIOLOGICAL SCIENCES 165

Wildlife Conservation and Zoo Biology *see* ANIMAL SCIENCES 124, ZOOLOGY 576

Wildlife Management *see* ANIMAL SCIENCES 124

Wireless Mobile Communications Systems Engineering *see* ENGINEERING (COMMUNICATIONS) 278

Working with Children and Families *see* SOCIAL WORK 536

Working with Children and Young People *see* COMMUNITY STUDIES/DEVELOPMENT 217, SOCIAL SCIENCES/STUDIES 531, SOCIAL WORK 536

Working with Children, Young People and Families *see* SOCIAL WORK 536

World Cinema *see* FILM, RADIO, VIDEO and TV STUDIES 310

Writing and English Literature *see* ENGLISH 296, LITERATURE 409

Writing and Film Studies *see* ENGLISH 296, FILM, RADIO, VIDEO and TV STUDIES 310

Writing Fashion and Culture *see* ART and DESIGN (Fashion and Textiles) 140

Yacht and Powercraft Design *see* MARINE/MARITIME STUDIES 412, NAVAL ARCHITECTURE 459

Yacht Production and Surveying *see* MARINE/MARITIME STUDIES 412, NAVAL ARCHITECTURE 459

Youth and Community Development *see* COMMUNITY STUDIES/DEVELOPMENT 217
Youth and Community Education *see* COMMUNITY STUDIES/DEVELOPMENT 217, EDUCATION STUDIES 256
Youth and Community Work *see* COMMUNITY STUDIES/DEVELOPMENT 217, SOCIAL WORK 536
Youth Community Development *see* COMMUNITY STUDIES/DEVELOPMENT 217
Youth Community Work *see* COMMUNITY STUDIES/DEVELOPMENT 217
Youth Justice *see* SOCIAL SCIENCES/STUDIES 531
Youth Studies *see* SOCIAL WORK 536
Youth Work *see* SOCIAL SCIENCES/STUDIES 531
Youth Work and Community Development *see* COMMUNITY STUDIES/DEVELOPMENT 217

Youth, Community Work and Applied Theology *see* COMMUNITY STUDIES/DEVELOPMENT 217

Zoo Biology *see* ANIMAL SCIENCES 124, BIOLOGY 170, ZOOLOGY 576
ZOOLOGY 576
see also AGRICULTURAL SCIENCES/AGRICULTURE
see also ANIMAL SCIENCES
see also BIOLOGY
Zoology and Aquatic Biology *see* ZOOLOGY 576
Zoology and Conservation *see* ZOOLOGY 576
Zoology with a Modern Language *see* LANGUAGES 386, ZOOLOGY 576
Zoology with Animal Ecology *see* ZOOLOGY 576
Zoology with Marine Zoology *see* ZOOLOGY 576

INDEX OF ADVERTISERS

Anglo-European College of Chiropractic	342–3
Bangor University	513, 551
Bath Academy	x–xi
Bath Spa University	3
BPP University College	xxii–xxiii, 113, 185, 403
British College of Osteopathic Medicine	347–9
Bristol Old Vic Theatre School	245, 246
Brunel University	iv, 223, 244, 299, 313, 350, 423, 429, 455
Cardiff University	498, 499
CIFE (Council for Independent Education)	vi–vii
The City Law School	ix, 393–405
The College of Law	395, 396–7
University Centre Doncaster	iv, 5
Duff Miller	233, 443
Durham University	493
Gabbitas Educational	7
University of Greenwich	28–9
Guildford School of Acting	248, 249
University of Hertfordshire	494
Hull College	ix, 150, 187, 229, 244, 263, 350
ifs School of Finance	xiv, 315–21
Institute of Physics	487–500
Institution of Chemical Engineers	269–74
Lancaster University	495, 496
Leicester College	v
Liverpool John Moores University (LJMU)	viii
Maastricht University	66–8
Mander Portman Woodward	Outside back cover, iii, 142, 181, 434
Mountview Academy of Theatre Arts	240, 242–3
Myerscough College	Inside back cover, 118, 125
Oxford Brookes University	569, 570
Oxford International College	56–8
Oxford Tutorial College	xiii
Regent's College London	191
Royal Society of Chemistry	199–206
St Mary's University College, Twickenham	402
University of Salford	492
University of Southampton	344, 462, 470
University of Surrey	204–5, 351–3
Trinity College Dublin	493
Trinity Saint David, University of Wales	xii, 38–9
University College London,	272, 439
University of York	491, 497